Nalini de Sielvie

Thistles *in the* Wind

An Autobiography

authorHOUSE®

AuthorHouse™ UK
1663 Liberty Drive
Bloomington, IN 47403 USA
www.authorhouse.co.uk
Phone: 0800.197.4150

Published by AuthorHouse 11/12/2018

ISBN: 978-1-5462-9756-7 (sc)
ISBN: 978-1-7283-8039-1 (e)

30131 05663957 5

by the same author

Dark Shores - Return to Serendib
Wild Poppies - Stories and Verse
An Eternal Summer
Is this your Caruso? Biography of Tenor Luigi Campeotto
Catsville
Edge of Nowhere
Serendib - Isle of Dreams
Return to Enchantment

Contents

About the Author

Nalini de Sielvie has published eight books to date (fiction, short stories and poems).

Nalini came to Australia with her husband in 1972, and has two sons. She holds diplomas in journalism, scriptwriting, commercial art and pianoforte, and worked for the Commonwealth Government from 1986 to 2005 before changing direction. Currently she teaches piano at a local primary school besides painting and writing.

Writers World Queensland, and other publications have published Nalini's award-winning short stories, articles and poems in several anthologies. She also contributes articles, poems, and stories to various magazines and local newspapers. Her stories and poems appeared in a recently published anthology, "Wild Poppies" and in the Society of Women Writers Victoria anthology, "Climb the Mountain."

In 1995, Nalini was included in "Who's Who of Australian Writers" and is a current member of the Society of Women Writers, Writers Victoria, Australian Writers Guild, Peninsula Arts Society, and was president of Authors Australia Inc. (independent publishers).

website: www.nalinidesielvie.com

Introduction

Until we are fully grown
We seldom think of childhood,
like thistles in the wind has blown.
All that's dear swept away for good.
Nor all regrets, our tears and pain,
Make the thistle whole again.

This is exactly how I think of my childhood when we were like one, whole thistle nestled in the comfort of our family home, until the inexorable rushing winds of life scattered us far and wide, like thistles in the wind. I have delved into the deepest recesses of my mind to gather myriads of memories that stand out like sign posts along the road of life I travelled with my loved ones.

I started writing down my recollections sometime in 1987, because I wanted to record events as accurately as possible before the onslaught of time and age dimmed or distorted my memories. In writing a memoir, although one has to be as objective as possible, my perceptions of a situation and events may differ from another's point of view. And in adhering strictly to factual events, it is not my intention to confess another's sins, offend or disparage any person living or dead. But I dislike sugar-coated memoirs, when truth is caramelised, and dipped in the treacle of imaginary bliss, recalling non-existent happy times.

Like most people who write their story, I want to set the record straight, and review my life accordingly. Writing an honest account of my life, and sharing my experiences, has given me a sense of liberation, and proves that the human spirit sometimes *can* and *will* overcome any adversity.

Although this autobiography was written particularly with my two sons and my family in mind, it is also a nostalgic attempt to retrace steps along a path that can only be travelled in memory now. It is a record of yesteryears with all its joys, sorrows, disappointments, and triumphs. Some events shine like stars in the velvet night, illuminate my mind, and bring a smile or a tear as I remember my dear ones to whom I dedicate this work. Memories sustain us in our autumn years, lighting up the road ahead, and easing the burden of life's arduous journey. So I begin my travels down memory lane to when it all started.

PART 1

Lotus Isle

Chapter 1

My parents seldom spoke about their past, but when I was old enough, I coaxed my father to tell me how he met my mother. And usually, after a couple of drinks of arrack, he was quite obliging. But my mother was a reticent person who did not like to dwell on their early days, no matter how much I tried to glean information.

Even today, my father's slurred words echo in my mind. "Granny was frothing mad when they brought us back home, and she yelled at your poor mother, trembling in fear, 'You will have to get married immediately! No doubt about that! God only knows what you have been up to!' Carmen, you were such a pretty young girl, and I loved you very much, so I was prepared to marry you even though you were only fourteen and I was nineteen."

I heard the rest of their story from my mother's sister, Aunty Rita, who was one year younger than her. She told me how Granny had stood threateningly over the young lovers and demolished them with her dreaded tongue-lashings. My parents hardly dared to say anything in their defence. My father just stood there looking sheepish and red-faced with embarrassment, while my mother wept copious tears. So their married life began full of old-fashioned drama and passion in true Shakespearean style.

My father was slender, of average height, and with ruddy-face. He was a very handsome young man. And my mother was petite and slim with long, wavy, brown hair, eyes to match, and full lips. They were a good-looking couple in their youth and for as long as I can remember. We called our father Thathie and our mother Ammie.

He was a popular young man, and all his friends and colleagues called him Raja. Thathie, whose full name was Jayasena Bandara Bowathage Rajapakse, was born to Bowatha Rajapakse Mudiyanselage Punchi Bandara and Sapugolla Ratnayake Mudiyanselage Anulawathi Kumarihamy, on 21 August 1926.

We called our grandfather Mutha and our grandmother Athamma. Mutha's father's name was Bowatte Rajapakse, and Mutha's mother was Seela Udurawalla. Nothing more was known about Mutha's parents except their names and that they had three boys and two girls.

Athamma's father was R.M. Apuhamy (I do not know what the initials stood for), and her mother's name was Leela Ratnayake. Athamma was the eighth child in a family of six girls and four boys. Her father was a registrar of births, deaths, and marriages and spoke four languages: Sinhalese, English, Sanskrit and Pali. He was well-versed in Ayurvedic medicine too. When the first sub-post office opened in their home town, R.M. Apuhamy applied for the post and was successful in obtaining a job.

When Thathie reached his nineteenth year, Mutha encouraged him to join the Ceylon Government Railway. At that time, it was every Ceylonese parent's ambition to get his or her sons into public service so they could retire with a good pension in their old age, and this ambition is still alive in some parents to this day. Mutha and Athamma had cherished fond hopes of their son contracting a brilliant marriage with a respectable Sinhalese girl who would bring a huge dowry and replenish their empty coffers.

Thathie was a well-educated and highly intelligent young man who had been educated in one of the best Catholic colleges in Ceylon. He was well-versed in Latin and English literature, and once he was accepted as a junior officer in the railway on 22 December 1943, he was deemed a most eligible bachelor.

Thathie journeyed to Nuwara Eliya, a quaint, picturesque town known as Little England because of several English-style cottages and mansions that European settlers had built there. And its cool, misty climate was reminiscent of the British Isles. The town was a popular holiday resort. Visitors stayed in the sprawling colonial-style Grand Hotel with its lush, green, and manicured lawns and gardens.

A fairly large race course attracted punters from all over the island; social clubs, botanical gardens close by, and a large natural lake for fishing on the outskirts of town were some of the main attractions. Thathie commenced his first job away from his home and soon made friends with another railway employee, Robert Daniels, who soon invited him to lodge at his house.

Grandpa Robert was in his mid-thirties or so and married to Granny, whose name was Primrose Abigail (nee Webster). Her family called her Bubsy. Granny's father, Walter Walker Webster was a Scotsman. He and his brothers had sailed over from Britain to help build the infrastructure of the island. He had also worked for the Ceylon Government Railway as a design technician. Her mother, Mina Ruston, was of Portuguese descent and came from Goa in India.

Granny was born in 1913, as fourth in a family of twelve siblings. Grandpa and she had met in Kadugannawa quite by chance when she was sixteen. He had courted her without delay (so Granny told me), and they were soon married at Christ Church, Kadugannawa. They had five children over the next few years. The eldest, Abigail Beda Carmen, was born on 9 February 1930, and then came Yolanda (we called her Rita), Anthony, Malcolm, and Marie.

Grandpa was a field patrol linesman responsible for checking rail tracks. He spent most of his time shunting along the tracks in a little wagon together with a couple of assistant linesmen. My mother, Carmen, was barely fourteen when Thathie first appeared on her doorstep as a boarder. And it was inevitable that a handsome young man and a very pretty young girl, who were thrown in each other's company constantly, should end up falling desperately in love with each other, even though they were keenly aware of overwhelming social barriers that existed between them because of their different backgrounds.

Thathie hailed from a Buddhist Kandyan Sinhalese family, and Ammie was a Catholic Burgher whose mother was as strict as one of the puritanical pilgrims who had embarked on the Mayflower and sailed to America centuries ago. Granny ruled the roost with an iron will (and hand) right from the beginning of her married life. She was as fair-complexioned as a European with light-brown eyes and wavy hair, and she had a wide mouth and broad nose. She stood less than five feet tall, and with age, she grew plump and stumpy.

I suppose she must have been an attractive girl, but all I can remember is a bad-tempered, nagging old woman who actually frothed at the mouth whenever she was angry. Granny was a formidable character who was not to be thwarted in any way by anyone at any time, but as she grew older, she mellowed somewhat and became as harmless as a toothless tigress. No one took her tantrums seriously then, but in her heyday, no man, woman, child, or servant escaped this virago's temper.

If she was in one of her tempestuous moods, everyone stayed out of her way as much as possible, especially Grandpa, who bore the brunt of her bad temper with philosophical indifference and stoicism. Granny did not show much warmth or fondness for us when we were young, but she mellowed and thawed a little in later years and we basked in her tepid affection.

She valued education above all things in her life, except perhaps a passion for gold jewellery, and ensured that all her children were well-educated in private Catholic schools. She loved music and singing too and even played the harmonica; she had invested in a piano very early in their marriage.

A fervent, almost fanatical Catholic, she endeavoured to instill the fear of God into all her children from their young age. Granny mispronounced some words, which we found quite amusing when we were older. Like, "mortiage" for mortgage, "charaty" for charity, and once she told me that, *"Conscience is the universe of the heart."* I tried to interpret that saying for a long time, but it still does not make any sense to me.

Grandpa was of average height, lanky and loose-limbed. He was not too particular about his appearance; from the time I remember, he was carelessly dressed in a crumpled shirt and baggy trousers. He had a few teeth left but never wore dentures so his speech was a bit thick and sloppy and he chewed food with gums. Mild-mannered and peace-loving, he lived in fear of his overbearing wife whose tongue damaged a person's ego more effectively than any physical pain a cat-o'-nine-tails whip could have incurred.

Going back to my parents' romance, before long, Carmen and Raja were so deeply in love that they decided to elope and get married, because to marry with their parents' consent and blessing was just wishful thinking. So they escaped Granny's strict supervision for a few days and indulged in a romantic interlude. But unfortunately for the young couple, Granny and Grandpa were hot on their heels and dragged them home in utter disgrace. Then they faced a dilemma.

Thathie was not their choice of a husband for Carmen, but they could not allow him to "disgrace" their daughter by taking advantage of her and getting away without facing consequences. They were truly in a predicament. To relieve her anger, Granny beat Ammie unmercifully, reproaching her twelve hours a day for bringing shame and scandal to the family besides "ruining" herself irrevocably.

Thathie did not escape lightly either, as Grandpa chastised him soundly with many a physical blow. As my grandparents conceded that they faced a hopeless situation, all parties finally agreed to a marriage between the young couple. Granny's one concern was that Carmen would have a baby out of wedlock and disgrace them further.

Both my grandfathers were docile, gentle-mannered men who lived in complete awe of their termagant wives, while my grandmothers were very strict, sharp-tongued, and haughty women. When my parents' marriage took place, Thathie told me that his parents sent him a bottle of poison and a black flag with a message. "From this day onwards, you are dead to us, and it would have been better if you took this poison and killed yourself." So deep was their animosity. And on the day of their marriage on 15 May 1945, Thathie said it had been more like a funeral than a wedding house.

And so, Ammie and Thathie began married life in the most unpleasant atmosphere imaginable as they were compelled to live with Granny and Grandpa because they had no where else to go. Granny constantly nagged Ammie about the terrible evil she had brought on them all, and that she had thrown away her young life by giving up school and music. Granny's invariable complaint was, "I bought you a piano as well, and see how ungrateful you are to throw away all that!" It was an endless litany of accusations and the young couple had no choice but to put up with this misery and nagging until they could afford a place of their own.

Fortunately, a few months after their marriage a railway bungalow fell vacant (it was a large three-bedroom house but was referred to as a bungalow in the Colonial manner). Thathie and Ammie moved into this house speedily, which was not very far from Granny's place. It was a hard grind at the beginning but they survived. Ammie gave birth to their first daughter, Nilanthi, on 18 August 1946.

Coincidentally, Granny had given birth to her youngest daughter, Rosemarie, on 5 July 1946. This closeness in birth dates influenced Nilanthi and us very much, as Rosemarie was more like a sister than an aunt.

My parents rarely spoke about how they survived those first years, but Ammie mentioned that after Nilanthi's birth, Mutha and Athamma gradually reconciled. Ammie knew however that Athamma never fully accepted her and always referred to her as "Lansiya" (Burgher).

Before Nilanthi's birth Thathie had travelled to his parents' home carrying an olive branch and had not returned home for weeks. Ammie was desperate, wondering if his parents had used a charm on him. This was something most people believed in then and still do. Some Ceylonese used all sorts of so-called magic charms to get what they wanted.

Many tales abound of hapless victims falling ill, getting killed, or falling in and out of love, as the case may be - all attributed to evil charms. Ammie lived in fear, until one day Thathie breezed along as if nothing had happened. He gave no explanations either.

To comprehend the bitter opposition to their marriage one must have a general idea of what Ceylon, or Sri Lanka as it is called today, was like in the early twentieth century.

Ceylon is a tiny island shaped like a teardrop at the southernmost tip of India but is independent of its large neighbour. Three different nations colonised the island from 1505 onwards. First, the Portuguese, then Dutch, and finally under British rule at the time Thathie was born. Several races inhabit Ceylon, including Muslims, Tamils, Europeans, Malays, Indians and people from various other parts of the world.

As Ceylon had been under three different foreign powers, it was inevitable that another race of Europeans descended from mixed marriages should emerge, namely the Burghers. Any person with a smidgeon of European blood was referred to as a Burgher.

Most of the Burghers were mainly of Portuguese, Dutch or British origins, and they were happy-go-lucky amiable sort of people who loved to enjoy life to the fullest. All races lived comfortably and amicably except that in the early part of the twentieth century, mixed marriages were seldom or never tolerated between Sinhalese and Burghers, Tamils and Sinhalese or Muslims with any other race besides their own.

It was acceptable for a Muslim to marry three wives, but most non-Muslim women did not find this situation tolerable, to say the least. A few unions took place though when lovers from different races married in the teeth of parental opposition. Family and friends however ostracized them for the rest of their lives.

Socially, the Burghers were the most extroverted people and led a merry life, dancing and partying without a care in the world. Sinhalese people looked askance at their way of life and in good-natured ridicule conned an apt phrase. "Burgher buggers became beggars by buying brandy bottles."

The Burghers had a reputation for being very fond of alcoholic beverages, in direct contrast to Sinhalese, Muslims and Tamils who were mostly ascetic teetotallers according to individual religious precepts.

The Burghers retorted in kind by ridiculing Sinhalese peoples' fondness for oil cakes (kavun). "Sinhalaya modaya, kavun kanda, yodhaya." Much of its punch is lost in translation, but the gist of it is that a Sinhalese is a fool, but has a gigantic appetite for oil cakes. Mutual banter and good-natured ridicule without malice was quite common among different races then.

After several years of negotiation, without bloodshed or civil war, Ceylon finally gained independence from Britain on 4 February 1948. D.S Senanayake became the first Prime Minister of independent Ceylon.

It was the worst turn of events when racial hatred and bloodshed resulted during the early 1980s. The tense political situation between the Government and Tamil Tigers who demanded a separate homeland in the north of the Island, ended in civil war.

Sinhalese and Tamils had lived harmoniously for centuries with intermittent spurts of war between India and Ceylon in ancient times. But the enormity of the racial tension and civil war that lasted more than twenty five years till early 2005 or so, was one of the saddest periods in the history of that resplendent island.

This brief outline of existing conditions indicates the social background at the time of my parents' marriage. In a nutshell, it was acceptable to socialise with Sinhalese, Tamils and Burghers, but when it came to inter-marrying, that was definitely taboo. Thathie's parents ranked high in the social structure. Proud, aristocratic people, who claimed to be noble and had royal blood in their lineage. They belonged to the best Kandyan families and were proud of their heritage. Although caste structure still exists among some Sinhalese, today's generation is not as class-conscious, and barriers within the social structure are not as insurmountable.

Mutha was born in December 1888, and Athamma on 7 February 1904. Daisy was Thathie's elder sister, and he had three younger brothers, Wije, Wimala, and Chanda. Mutha lived on a tea-estate up-country. All the villagers loved him as he was a placid old gentleman with a dry sense of humour. When I was a child, he still wore calf-length breeches, and floral-patterned satin waistcoats. He had a light-olive complexion, large, dark, eyes, aquiline nose, thin lips and shoulder-length silver-grey hair. He was slim, of medium height, with strong noble features, and was a very kind, gentle-natured man.

Mutha always chewed contemplatively on a smelly, black cigar even when it was not lit up. Athamma was a tall, fair-complexioned woman of dignified bearing. She had a long narrow nose, thin lips, high cheekbones and small dark eyes. Her features were sharp, but her tongue was even sharper, and lashed out scathingly whenever she was displeased. Her family and menials shuddered before the full onslaught of her temper.

Athamma was kind and loving towards us children and was never harsh. She was a bitterly-disillusioned woman though. When I was older, I found out she had every reason to be so because of what she had endured during the early years of her marriage. She married Mutha at a very young age, and although she belonged to a wealthy, ancient, and highly-respected Kandyan family, Athamma was not very educated. She had attended junior school only, and could read and write Sinhalese but not English. Mutha on the other hand was an educated man who had studied under the Colonial system, and was a medical dispenser.

A marriage-broker arranged their union as was customary. Athamma was considered to be a very good matrimonial catch, as she had an enormous dowry, consisting of paddy fields, land, small tea-estates, money, and jewellery. The innocent young bride was unaware of how her husband handled her affairs and her dowry until it dwindled away. It was too late then to salvage anything.

Mutha had a secret passion for gambling. I still find it hard to believe when I remember his kind, gentle mien and wise eyes. He did not drink or indulge in any other vices (as far as the family knew), except gambling. He had persuaded Athamma to sign over her dowry gradually. They lost everything except the house in which they lived in and a few surrounding acres. When she was older and wiser and understood the enormity of Mutha's gambling debts, she shut herself up like a clam. She seethed in icy rage and embarked on a bitter feud with Mutha that lasted to the end.

Their lives lacked sweetness and forgiveness and they lived like strangers, only speaking to each other when absolutely necessary. Athamma did not even pretend to be slightly polite, as she was caustic and venomous whenever she addressed Mutha. She referred to him as "Naki Hora" (old thief). He ignored her insults and angry silences completely, never retorting in kind and kept his peace, always a gentleman, even in disgrace and ruin.

They had five children. Daisy, the eldest, was duly married off to a postmaster who lived in the cool, hilly town of Haputale. Her husband, Ulwita, was from a respected and rich Kandyan family too, and it was hoped she would be tolerably happy with him. I gazed with fascination at a photograph taken on their wedding day. He wore ceremonial costume of a Kandyan chieftain and a tri-cornered, be-jewelled head-dress.

She was draped in a traditional Kandyan 'osaria' style of sari, and adorned with heirloom jewellery, delicate silver head-dress, heavy gold bracelets, chains, and bangles. To my awed childish eyes, Ulwita and Daisy looked very impressive.

Daisy was of medium height, very slim, with large, dark eyes, narrow nose, small mouth, and long black hair to her waist. She was a pretty, gentle-mannered girl; quiet, well-spoken and well-educated in a Catholic school. She resembled Thathie closely and was just as fair-complexioned. Everyone in our family called her Daisy Akka (sister), as Thathie and her younger brothers addressed her.

During this time domestic help was very cheap, so Ammie employed a servant girl to help with the baby. Ammie had to learn house-keeping very quickly at her age. I think she did an extremely good job, because she always maintained a well-organized, tidy home. Thathie, as was obligatory for all good railwaymen, was very fond of arrack (an alcoholic drink brewed from coconut flowers). He had a rollicking time with his many friends, partying the days away and some long nights too while on duty.

It was his inherent nature to be generous, hospitable, and very kind to all. Gradually, Grandpa reconciled to their marriage and became one of Thathie's drinking buddies. Thathie was a popular young man with the railway families.

Ammie had five children over the next decade. Nihal was born on 15 May 1948, Shirani on 8 June 1950, and I arrived on 23 February 1952. A few years later, Nelune was born on 25 February.

A cherished memory and one of my earliest recollections is that of Mutha's and Athamma's house in the village of Paranagama, close to Welimada. It was a large, rambling, blue-stone house, with a delightful garden full of multi-coloured gerbera, bountiful fruit trees and shrubberies.

As children, it was the greatest adventure to climb up a narrow, creaking staircase to a gloomy little attic and rummage around where Athamma stored pumpkins, grains, rice, melons, and other edibles. Down below on the ground floor, Mutha converted one bedroom into a medical dispensary. An iron-framed, single bed stood in a corner, as they slept in separate rooms. In this room were over-laden shelves with large, glass bottles full of rainbow-coloured fluids that fascinated me. I gazed at swirling, luminous, red, green, amber, and blue liquids shining like sparkling jewels.

Mutha, with a grave, solicitous expression on his benign face, placed a stethoscope on the chest of an anxious patient, and then prescribed a dose or two of the colourful liquids. No matter what their ailment was, he administered a dose of his colourful decoctions. He was by no means a quack. In fact, all the people regarded him very highly, because he cured their aches, pains, and all their ailments very quickly (and no one died under his care), he joked.

In later years, when we were young adults, Mutha, with a glint of amusement shining in his eyes, admitted that some of his medicines contained only crushed aspirin, with which he treated some hypochondriacal patients. Mutha's grateful patients always brought him gifts of betel leaves, rice, a bottle of arrack, and other tokens of gratitude. Mutha had retired a couple of years ago, and only kept his dispensary open to while away time and prevent the onslaught of boredom.

We spent some of our school holidays with Athamma and Mutha, and they were unfailingly kind, because they thought their eldest son's children were very special. On such occasions Athamma ambled down to the bottom of the sloping garden while we trailed behind her. She picked large mushrooms and cooked them so deliciously that they tasted just like curried eggs.

They abstained from meat as Buddhists, and I relished the way Athamma prepared vegetables in varied delicious recipes. The old kitchen was quaint and cosy with an open fireplace, and a large, blackened, iron kettle that was always on the boil. The waist-high hatch door leading to the compound was just right for passers-by to lean on and pass the time of day with Athamma while she cooked or grumbled at some clumsy menial who happened to help her then.

She puffed and huffed into the smoky fireplace, or blew through a black, tubular iron rod called a bataliya, muttering dark curses and oaths if the green wood did not catch immediately. We sat on rickety wooden stools and watched her prepare the meal. This was the warmest place in the entire sparsely furnished, cold house.

Whenever I became moody or threw a tantrum as a child, Thathie said, "On the night you were born, on our way to hospital, the car stalled and stopped near the dark, brooding lake. Although we made it to the hospital, you arrived on a stormy tempestuous night. That's why you are like the stormy weather." When I was in my teens and withdrew into my own private sphere, he said, "You are inscrutable like the sphinx." I did not agree, but I admit I was always quite reserved.

Ammie told us Thathie was intoxicated even while she was in labour in hospital, and he hardly knew when the babies were born, as he was too busy flirting with the pretty nurses. She was quite jealous of Thathie, because women found him attractive, and he too delighted in their flirtatious attentions. Thathie, however, was the best of fathers and loved us deeply. He would do anything to please us.

Ammie upbraided him in chagrin sometimes, "*I* am the *mother,* but you act as if *you* had the children all by yourself and I had nothing to do with it because you always say, '*My children*' when you refer to them." Thathie showed how much he loved and cared for us by his never-failing support, and was inordinately proud of our achievements.

Ammie took good care of us as children although she was such a young mother. She fed us wholesome meals, clothed us beautifully, and rigorously maintained our good health, as she dosed us with the most bitter and disgusting worm treatments. I marvel at the fact that being such an innocent girl emotionally, she took on the role of mother and wife with such ease and success.

A dreaded memory was when Ammie insisted that she wormed us with a dose of nauseating stuff called Antipa and castor oil. Starved of solid foods for a whole day, we sat around like wilted, rag dolls, white-lipped and lethargic until we were fed rice porridge at lunch-time and then starved again till dinner-time.

This was a three-monthly ritual, and we dreaded this treatment more than any other punishment Ammie could have meted out. Perhaps it would be a good idea to introduce this childhood ordeal today, seeing that nothing daunts the modern child anymore. I am positive that a good dose of Antipa and castor oil would subdue the most incorrigible child.

Thathie was transferred to Bandarawela in 1954, where Nelune was born later. When Nilanthi was a few months old, Ammie engaged Menika, who was about seven or eight years old at the time, to help around the house and mind the babies. Menika came from a village close to Ragalla, and Athamma had found her for Ammie. Menika means gem in Sinhalese, and that is what she proved to be over the next twenty years or so that she lived with us as a beloved member of our family.

My first recollections are of that house in Bandarawela; a large, weather-board house painted white, with an over-grown, sprawling, garden surrounding it. The house had four large bedrooms, spacious living and dining areas. A long, open passage and flight of steps connected the main house to the kitchen, bathroom, store-room and pantry. Shrubberies sprouted on both sides of this open corridor covered with a corrugated tin roof. When it poured down heavily, the rain whipped furiously as we ran up and down this narrow passageway.

The bathroom was a large, cemented area outside where Menika filled bath tubs to bathe us in, as it was convenient to boil kettles of water in the near-by kitchen. We did not have running hot water, and as the climate in Bandarawela was quite temperate, we had hot water baths only when the weather was icy. Usually we bathed in cold water drawn from the cement tank.

A high wall enclosed one side of the house and gave us complete privacy. The front faced a side street, and it was a constant source of amusement to watch pedestrians trail along. A very high retaining wall rose at the back of the house where railway lines ran overhead. The whole house vibrated each time a train shunted and chugged away.

Railway authorities feared the house was built in a most unsuitable place. Earth tremors, which occurred regularly during the wet season, could weaken the retaining wall and bury our house underneath. I was vaguely aware of adult conversation about such fears. These concerns however, had no power to throw me into dejection, or affect my enjoyment of life. It was enough that my parents worried about such details, while I lived in a wonderland. Nothing much bothered or hindered me in the pursuit of childish pleasures.

Ammie kept an immaculately clean, comfortable home, and fed us amply. I still marvel that Ammie adjusted so well, and was such an excellent house-keeper, wife and mother. She cut her long, curly, brown hair short and wore a sari instead of dresses.

She was very attractive, with a good sense of fashion and colour co-ordination, and dressed beautifully whenever she went out. At home, she wore a housecoat, which was a long gown buttoned at the front. Ammie sewed these housecoats in bright, floral patterns, and was always dressed neatly. She was a perfect hostess too when her many friends visited.

Menika was a teenager when I was about six, and was just like a second mother or older sister. Sadly however, when Ammie and Thathie left Nuwara Eliya, they lost touch with her parents. She was virtually an orphan now, as none of her family visited. One of my most poignant memories is of Menika crying her eyes out almost every evening, as she sat in the kitchen and lamented loudly. "Oh *where* is my mother? I want to see my parents! I want to go home to my family!"

She was inconsolable for some time while I looked on wide-eyed and helpless at her anguish. Then just as suddenly, like a ray of sunshine bursting through after a sudden shower, she dried her tears and got on with the business of cooking dinner, determined to brush aside her grief and desolation. How she had such fortitude to bear her sorrow and concentrate on the work at hand is beyond me, as she was just a naive, uneducated young girl.

Although Ammie promised to make enquiries, she was unable to trace Menika's family. When I was older, I wondered if Ammie feared that if Menika left us, she would not return. Menika had become indispensable to Ammie and to the whole family. She was Ammie's second-in-command, an efficient cook and housemaid too. It would be impossible for her to manage our household without Menika's capable assistance.

Menika was a short, sturdy, and pleasant-faced woman, with long, black hair tied in a konde (bun). Her small, dark eyes sparkled intelligently, and her round face, with a snub nose and wide, friendly mouth was never morose or unpleasant. She was clean as freshly washed linen, and always wore a sarong with a floral blouse.

Village women wore cloth and jacket, and domestic help in some houses then were not allowed to wear sandals inside the house. It was a sign of respect, as it was deemed the poor servants were socially inferior to their employers. These attitudes and behaviour now are well and truly out the door. I am pleased that they are treated equally and with respect today.

Menika showered us with warmth and love, and being deprived of her own family she took us to her heart. We woke up to the sound of her gentle tap on the bedroom door, as she brought in steaming cups of tea, and always served with a bright smile. She often said she would be quite happy and content to live with us always, if only she could visit her family now and then. It was such a little thing to ask, but cruel fate did not grant Menika's dearest wish for many years to come.

Her love was evident in so many little ways, and she was an excellent cook. She could turn out culinary delights that had to be tasted to be believed. Such imagination and improvisation was truly amazing in a simple, young servant girl. Menika turned a plain dish of mashed potato and boiled cabbage into something special; the mash was shaped like chicks, with black peppercorns for eyes and tips of red peppers for beaks. The large cabbage arranged around the torso of a doll, represented a Victorian lady in a layered gown. I was always rapt with her marvellous creations. Even as a child, I thought she was a marvellous cook. In retrospect, I am convinced she was the best cook I have known, next to Ammie of course, because she trained Menika.

If I just close my eyes now, I can almost savour Menika's culinary delicacies redolent in the large, cosy kitchen. She was clever not only in the kitchen but in the garden as well, as she had a green thumb. The kitchen garden flourished under her care and bore some excellent vegetables and greens of many varieties.

She could sew neatly, and impressed us when she turned out her own version of a home-made brassiere that she called a bodice. Menika kept the house spotless as well. These talents will indicate what a priceless young woman Menika was, and how important she was in our household. Although she was illiterate, she composed little songs and verses, or stories to amuse us during long, lazy afternoons when Ammie had forty winks, and we children trailed behind Menika, begging to be amused.

She had an endless store of droll stories and songs (heaven knows where she got the inspiration), and as she cuddled one of us on her lap, she kept us riveted with anecdotes until it was time for afternoon tea. The fireplace was cleaned out and new wood kindled to boil water in the soot-blackened iron kettle. The huge iron kettle was one of Athamma's wedding presents to Ammie and Thathie, and was an heirloom. That kettle remained in their possession for as long as I can remember.

While the water boiled, Menika asked what sweetmeat we would like on that particular day, as afternoon tea was always special, with various sweetmeats, cakes or biscuits, served with a cup of tea. As we all clamoured for our favourite sweetmeat, she chose one (which I am sure she had decided on beforehand), and started pounding flour, sesame seeds and jaggery, to make some delectable thallagulli (sesame seed balls).

She laughed and joked as she got tea ready, and by that time we were so famished we really did not care what she had prepared. Ammie woke up just in time to partake of the tea Menika laid out on the table. We rushed around Ammie to get her attention, as we prattled on about our childish concerns and adventures.

Nelune, the new baby, was everyone's little darling. Menika cuddled her on her lap and sang lullabies. I tagged along behind her to the large expanse of garden where she grew cabbages, tomatoes, beans and leafy greens. We played hide-and-seek, and had several adventures in the vegetable patch, slashing and destroying tomatoes and cabbages, as children are wont to do when they are chasing imaginary villains.

Nilanthi and Nihal were the liveliest pair imaginable, and embroiled in many scrapes. One day, when they were about ten and twelve years old, they perched too close to the fireplace. In the midst of a heated argument, Nilanthi pushed Nihal so hard that he fell right into the burning fire. He was badly burned right down his thighs and legs. Nilanthi was properly chastised, as Ammie and Thathie were frantic with worry because Nihal had narrowly escaped death.

Nilanthi was blossoming into a pretty young girl. She was of medium height, slender, and had a very fair complexion, dark brown eyes and dark hair cascading almost to her knees. She wore her hair in long braids, which came in very handy for Nihal to grab hold of whenever he chased her around the house and garden, threatening to cut off her hair with a large pair of scissors. We laughed hysterically at their pranks and thought Nihal was the funniest boy alive.

He was the greatest tease I have ever known. Although it was never malicious, he delighted in tormenting and teasing Nilanthi more than any of us. He was a robust, handsome, fair-complexioned boy, and looked more Anglo-Saxon, with ruddy face, curly, brown hair and brown eyes. Shirani was a quiet little girl, with an indomitable spirit and determined nature, with olive-skin, black hair and eyes. I too am olive-skinned with dark brown eyes and hair.

As a child, I was so skinny and weak that Ammie massaged me with olive oil and kept me on a mat in the sun. I am not sure what this daily oil bath was supposed to do, but they believed it would make my bones strong and healthy. Nilanthi teased Shirani mercilessly because she rose to the bait easily. She called her disparaging names and made Shirani cry often. Nilanthi called me a skeleton, ghost, and stick. Nelune was a cute, rosy-complexioned baby, with dark brown eyes and brown hair, and none of us ever teased her.

I did not have to endure as much as Shirani, who resented all the name-calling. But as I was growing up, Nilanthi and Nihal baited me unmercifully, and very often I burst into angry tears in sheer frustration. In spite of all the teasing and sibling squabbles, five of us shared a special bond and loved each other dearly.

The garden abounded with trees, shrubs and flowers, with profuse areas of Lady Lace (Queen Anne Lace), red carnations, and multi-coloured geraniums in hanging baskets. The red carnations bring to mind a family ghost story that I must relate by and by. One particular tree that we called the Nikka tree (Menika's name for it), had a long, low branch that was our pretend horse.

We indulged in many hours of fun, swinging high and low on that over-burdened branch (all of us on it at times). But one day, the sorely tried branch came crashing down with a mighty groan, and we tumbled down one on top of the other. Thathie was very angry of course for damaging the tree. I am unsure though if he was concerned about the tree, or more frightened that one of us could have sustained a nasty injury. We soon picked ourselves up, laughing in spite of our bruises. We were very much alive and well, with hardly a scratch. But that was the end of our rides, and we never had another mount as sturdy and faithful as that Nikka branch.

Those early days were full of never-ending fun, laugher and games. It seems to me like all I ever did was play all day, eat and sleep, get up early and play again until night time. Perhaps that is what most children do before beginning the rigours of school life. Many friends, relatives and acquaintances dropped in regularly. Some of them stayed for very long periods, because in Ceylon, a guest was treated like a God. And cynical witticisms such as, "guests and fish smell after three days" never applied to any of our guests. Oh no, on the contrary, it was a pleasure and a privilege to entertain, and accommodate them even at the expense of one's own family.

To ensure the guests were comfortable, well-fed and happy, they were served the best food. No matter how much food there was in the pantry, Ammie said. "Keep those patties and cutlets for the visitors." Mind you, I thought this was grossly unfair, and I disliked the thought of all the very best food being kept for visitors. This goes to show how well Ammie and Thathie treated our guests. So they stayed on and on, and nobody even asked them when they were leaving.

It is amazing when I think about it now, that some of those people were never employed in their lives and spent whole months at our place or another relative's house. And then in twelve months it was time for another visit again. Still, it was such good fun when the house was full of visitors, and we laughed and played more enthusiastically than ever.

In the evenings, Thathie had a merry time with his friends, while Ammie and Menika prepared hot, spicy, fried beef or porkies, a piquant pork sausage, and other nibbles to keep the men from getting too drunk on an empty stomach. They referred to these nibbles as bites, and they sang, danced and drank a great deal of arrack. It was their entertainment for the day, and many of the gutsy old songs I recall are Thathie's renditions of "Pistol Packing Mama" and "She'll Be Coming Round The Mountain" (each verse getting more bawdy and riotous), until we children were sent packing to bed, while the adults carried on their revelries.

Our table was always laden with superb dishes of spicy meats, curried vegetables, and ghee or yellow rice. I can almost savour the curried pathola (gourd), stuffed with minced meat, that nobody cooked just the way Menika did. She rose at dawn to prepare an elaborate breakfast of string hoppers or hoppers (rice flour pancakes), milk rice, curries and sambals. No wonder our guests lingered, as Menika's cooking was well worth their sojourn.

My parents were so hospitable and generous, that our house was open not only to friends and relatives but to practically anyone who needed a place to stay, no matter from what walk of life they came. Once, a tall, thin, quietly spoken, middle-aged man arrived. He respectfully asked Thathie if he could have a room to store vegetables in, which he sold at the market daily.

He was a farmer from Thathie's village, and Mutha had sent him, knowing he would be treated well. We had a large, empty store-room that Thathie allowed him to use. He stacked loads of fresh vegetables there and set out to market daily to sell his produce. We called him Elolu Karaya (vegetable man). I think he lasted a few months and then returned to his village, as he did not make as much money as he had anticipated.

I vividly recall a strange character, Weerappu, a wrinkled, old, Tamil woman. She was slightly deranged, so everyone said, and she sought asylum in our house whenever the town people chased her away. She was harmless enough, but had a terrible temper when roused, and gave vent to a stream of curses and abuse. I feared this dreadful apparition of a dark-skinned, skeletal old hag, draped in a smelly, tattered sari that hardly covered bony limbs and her bare, wrinkled breasts.

Weerappu's lips were cracked and stained red with constant betel-chewing, and her dirty, straggly, matted grey hair really stank. She lit a fire in our garden on chilly days and stood over it, and rasped hoarsely in a cackling voice, "I'm warming my backside." I do not recall when she disappeared from our lives, but cruel adults and children sometimes threw stones at the mad woman. She ran screaming in fear, as she sought refuge in our house. Menika told us some nasty people must have been driven her away as we never saw her again.

Our house was situated beside the road that led to the town. We sat on the fence sometimes to watch one of the many processions go by. Some days it was a funeral, a wedding, or a religious procession, which afforded us plenty of amusement and unholy merriment (there was no television then).

One day, as we watched a wedding procession, the various expressions of some people threw us into a fit of giggles. Nihal roared with laughter, and I followed suit. Unfortunately, one of the party took exception to our rude behaviour and banged on our front door to complain. Nihal and I, fearing we were in trouble, dreaded Thathie's anger. We ran and hid behind the kitchen door. But he soon found us and smacked Nihal. "You started this mischief!" And then a clout on my head. "That's for following his bad example!" We were properly chastised, and our high spirits quickly subdued. It was seldom Thathie smacked us, or lost his temper, but when he did, we dreaded the consequences.

One chilly evening, when I was about six years or so, Menika was bathing me in a tub of warm water. She emptied the suds and poured a kettle of boiling water into the tub. Before she added cold water, she suddenly ran off on an errand because she had remembered something. There I stood on the cold, cement floor, naked and shivering, teeth chattering. The steaming hot water looked very inviting. I dipped my right foot into the scalding water, and next minute, my agonised screams rent the air. Menika ran back to find me hopping around in pain, as I had quickly removed my foot from the tub. She was very upset and remorseful as I wailed and moaned.

Ammie scolded her severely for her carelessness, which upset Menika even more, and very soon she was in tears too. Malcolm, Ammie's younger brother, who was staying with us, as he was on school holidays, rushed to the local shop to get some ointment.

Malcolm was a tall, lanky, pleasant-faced young man, with slightly protruding front teeth. He had an endless supply of jokes, and was always good-humoured and kind. He was very close, and spent most of his holidays with our family. While he went off on his errand, Ammie and Menika applied home remedies, such as cold, tea leaves, and butter to ease my scalded foot, but nothing relieved my pain that night, and I still shudder to think of it.

I tried to sleep until I was taken to hospital in the morning, and vividly recall painful days that followed. I hobbled around on one foot, with the other heavily bandaged. That was lesson number one; never ever put my foot in boiling water; literally never, but figuratively, yes, many times.

Thathie was generous with our weekly pocket money. As soon as Shirani, Nelune and I had twenty five cents each, we ran up to the little shop down the road, where they sold sweets, soft drinks, and various other items of dubious origins. These little shops were called boutiques. The term was loosely applied to any precarious structure, whether it was four posts covered with a thatched roof of coconut palms, or something more elaborate, like a mud-hut, or brick and timber construction. It all depended on how affluent the mudalalie (shop-keeper), happened to be.

It was a great deal of money for us in the late 1950s, and we eagerly bought three bottles of ginger beer, then ran home quickly to empty the contents down our thirsty throats. Whenever he asked what we purchased, Thathie could never understand why all three of us spent our pocket money on ginger beer, instead of buying various goodies and sharing them. But we liked ginger beer so well, that we preferred to enjoy a whole bottle each, even though we had no more pocket money left till the following week.

Another dubious-looking character, who was called Bookie, visited regularly. He was always equipped with a racing guide, so Thathie could indulge in a flutter now and then. I think Thathie was more astonished than anyone else, when one fine day, he actually won a substantial amount of money. Surprisingly (for Thathie that is), he decided to invest his winnings on an old Ford motor car.

He could not drive at all, and that was why we were so surprised. It was a shiny, black, second-hand Ford, and caused a great deal of excitement when it was driven up the driveway to our house. The car cost about a thousand rupees, and Thathie was inordinately proud of it. He announced that he would take the whole family to Kataragama (a holy place of worship), to fulfil a vow.

Chapter 3

Christmas was always the best holiday season. Ammie and Thathie asked us months ahead if there was any particular toy that we liked. I asked for the same item as far back as I can remember. A toy piano, as Thathie could not afford a real one. Invariably, each year I found a toy piano that was sometimes pink, white, blue or black. Ammie somehow included an extra toy, like a doll, or a tea set.

Those toy pianos lasted less than twelve months, because the notes would go dumb after a few frantic thumping sessions. I first learned to play Elvis Presley's famous song, "Wooden Heart" on my toy piano when I was about six or seven years old. My parents were quite impressed with my musical aptitude at such an early age.

We accompanied Ammie to the big stores in Bandarawela, Cargill's and Millers, who had wonderful window displays during Christmas. Magical winter or nativity scenes were colourfully displayed in the large windows. On one such occasion, I was especially entranced by a cheeky-looking mechanical monkey playing a drum, and a large, furry bear resplendent in Highland costume, clashing cymbals when its key was wound up. Such wonderful toys, but well beyond our budget, I knew. Ammie looked at me sternly and said. "Put those toys back on the shelf Dolly, you know you can't have them." My family called me Dolly since I was born, and the pet name stuck.

No amount of coaxing made Ammie include such fancy toys in her Christmas list however, and I had to be content with my modest gifts. I soon forgot those unattainable toys as we continued window-shopping and walked along busy, brightly decorated streets. We greeted happy, smiling people along the way, full of Christmas spirit and bubbling with good cheer.

I wonder if it was because I was a child then, but the "Joie de vivre" of those yesteryears can never be recaptured. Ammie's shopping expedition at an end, we returned home laden with parcels and goodies, but not the Christmas presents, which were to be delivered later on. I never knew when they actually arrived, but Nilanthi would somehow find out where Ammie hid them, and whispered. "Come, I'll show you where the presents are hidden."

We trailed behind her cautiously, while she rummaged in closets and cupboards, and poked around any interesting-looking objects concealed in recesses. When she happened to discover the hidden treasures, she was triumphant. Excitement reaching fever pitch and frantically curious, I touched them excitedly, trying to guess what was inside each fascinating parcel. Ammie soon found out what Nilanthi was up to and scolded her for being so naughty.

Days before Christmas, cooking and baking aromas filled the house as Ammie and Menika chopped, sliced, and diced fruits and nuts for the delicious rich cake that was full of every single preserved fruit imaginable. It is an old Ceylonese recipe that I still use. We all helped with the stirring of this marvellous cake, not to mention licking spoons and bowls clean once Ammie poured the thick, fruity mixture into two or three large baking trays lined with layers of newspapers. Aluminium foil and baking paper were unheard of in our household then.

A large, portable oven was placed on top of the kerosene oil stove, and it took over three hours to bake the cakes. The corners were invariably burnt slightly, and we eagerly ate the crusts that Ammie trimmed. When the cake cooled, it was cut into generous squares and wrapped individually in red cellophane, then trimmed with gold or green ribbons around the little parcels. Our visitors were served these daintily decorated cakes. Ammie and Menika also cooked hundreds of patties, cutlets, coconut rock and milk toffees, besides several other traditional sweetmeats.

Thathie ensured we had a ten foot cypress tree that he requested someone to procure from a forest in Nanu Oya. A porter delivered the massive tree, trussed up with string to keep branches in place. Fragrant cypress perfumed the house for several days, and we always decorated the tree on Christmas Eve before we attended midnight Mass.

This ritualistic, midnight Mass was a sore trial. Although nights were cold, she would not let us wear coats or jumpers inside church. Ammie took great pains to sew beautiful frocks for us, and she did not want us to hide our pretty dresses under coats.

We removed our coats inside the church and handed them over to Menika. She requisitioned them until the time was right to wear them and be comfortable once more. We could cry and grumble as much as we wanted to, but Ammie's word was law. Until all her friends admired and complimented her on her tailoring, we had to endure the chilly interior of the church.

Shirani, Nelune and I always had identical frocks, but Nilanthi's were different as she was a teenager. Ammie bought bolts of material from a travelling Chinaman, as it was cheaper to buy in bulk. He carried his wares on a bicycle, and pedalled his way through streets and homes of every budget-conscious housewife, so we always had new clothes for Christmas and New Year.

The service finally ended after a couple of hours (those were the days of Latin Masses and three half-hour sermons in English, Sinhalese and Tamil), all delivered by the same priest. He felt obligated (I thought), to astound the congregation with his proficiency in all three languages.

Warmly rugged up afterwards once we were duly admired, and Ammie was paid several compliments on her dress-making skills, we ran around with our friends and engaged in endless prattle. Although Menika professed to be a Buddhist, she joined us for midnight Mass every year. After the service, she too participated in our Christmas celebrations.

Finally, when Ammie and her friends had finished exchanging all the latest news, we walked home briskly in the chilly December dawn. My eyes were wide open, and not a trace of weariness in my steps as I anticipated the joy of things to come on Christmas morn, and I do not mean just the birth of our Saviour.

As every child knows, and still believes, Christmas means presents galore, loads of food glorious food, and revelry for twelve mad, merry days, but festivities always exceeded twelve days. Christmas went on for weeks, and even into late February. People would still be celebrating, as they grinned and murmured sheepishly. "After all, it's *still* the Christmas Season, so have some rich cake and a little wine." Yes, they were splendid days of fun and joy indeed. When presents were handed out at last, I shouted in delight and surprise, as I had something extra in my parcel, even though I knew before-hand what I asked.

Thathie was usually in the background during these festive occasions. In retrospect, I think that although he wanted with all his heart to make us happy during Christmas, his feelings regarding Ammie's religion and our preference for Catholicism, hurt and angered him. I was blissfully unaware of any troubled, underlying currents then and enjoyed myself thoroughly.

Menika too received a little gift; a few metres of fabric for a jacket or sarong. Thathie surprised Ammie with an expensive silk sari, or jewellery, and she looked shocked at his extravagance, while he enjoyed the excitement and our surprised looks. Then we played till five or six o'clock in the morning until we were ready to drop with exhaustion. Finally, half asleep, we went to bed. I dreamed of new toys, food and festivities still to come on Christmas day.

By the time we woke up and dressed in our best frocks, the kitchen was a hive of activity, with spicy, fragrant cooking aromas tantalising my taste buds. The traditional festive meal was, yellow-rice cooked in ghee, chicken curry, curried potatoes, fried egg-plant, pappadams, home-made chilli vinegar sauce, beef or pork smoore (spicy Dutch roast), cutlets (spicy meatballs), besides salads, boiled eggs coloured in pastel shades, chutney and several other side dishes.

Dessert was usually tropical fruits, or caramel pudding made with jaggery and coconut milk. It was truly a feast, and I devoured everything voraciously. Then it was time to play again and look forward to dinner, which was sometimes left-overs, but at other times, steamed vegetables with roast beef, or something light after such an enormous lunch.

I have a vivid recollection of Ammie's glamorous saris, especially one that she used to wear on some Christmas days for midnight Mass. It was her favourite; a midnight-blue georgette sari, with a matching blouse elaborately embroidered with sequins and opaque plastic petals that shone iridescently, like the inside of an oyster or abalone shell. She wore lantern-shaped amethyst earrings and looked very beautiful. I still have those earrings that she gave me when I was older.

Ammie said I always liked to watch her dress up and told everyone. "My mother looks like a queen in all her splendour." She owned a small vial of an expensive French perfume, 'Evening In Paris.' It nestled seductively in a pretty box lined with royal-blue satin, exuding luxury and sophistication. It still has the power to evoke a powerful memory of those early days. If I close my eyes, I can almost smell the heavy, exotic perfume that Ammie used so sparingly; just a dab on her wrist, and the fragrance lingered for days.

Many years later, I searched far and wide without success for the same perfume. It was discontinued, and now bottled as "Soir de Paris" but it did not have the same fragrance as the original.

We lived in that old, weather-board bungalow for about eight or ten years. I remember distinctly, as if it was only yesterday, something Thathie said. He became very philosophical and made profound speeches when he was intoxicated (which was on most evenings). We were quite accustomed to seeing him in this state.

On this particular instance, he gathered us around and slurred solemnly. "Children, today is the last day of 1959! It will never come back again!" I can almost smell the stale arrack fumes as he spoke. He looked so sad, but I did not understand then how poignant it was to watch the end of an old year drawing to a close. I tried to arrange my face solemnly, but I do not think any of us really cared whether it was the last day in 1959 or not. Still, it must have made a very deep impression on me because I remember the day so well and Thathie's exact words.

Another Christmas in Bandarawela remains deeply etched in my mind. Torrential monsoon rains continued for weeks, causing floods and mud-slides, and blocked the rail track in some places close by. Our house was declared unsafe, because of its position below the retaining wall. We were forced to evacuate and move in with another railway family, Mr and Mrs Stork, until the danger passed.

He was an engine driver, and a very good friend of Thathie's, and his wife and he were a kindly, middle-aged couple. Their two lively teenagers, Christine and Randolf, were just the sort of companions for Nilanthi and Nihal to get into mischief with, as we soon discovered. The Storks' house was further down the road and was not in any danger. While Ammie and Thathie worried about our abandoned house and furniture that we had been unable to remove, we had a great time playing hide-and-seek in their well-tended garden. Mr Stork cracked walnuts and sang Christmas carols to amuse us and while away the long, rainy days.

Several other railway families lived in the vicinity too, and their children were playmates right through those early years. I led a carefree life, running around rail tracks, climbing trees, hiding under bridges, and generally behaved like an ordinary, happy child.

Once the danger passed and the rain eased, we moved back. It stood solid without being buried under a mud-slide, as authorities had feared, until it was demolished many years later.

Two families closest to our house geographically and socially, were the Rodrigos' and the Raymonds. Mr Rodrigo and Mr Raymond were Thathie's bosom buddies, who were officers-in-charge like him. They whiled away the monotony of railway life by consuming huge quantities of arrack daily. Mr and Mrs Rodrigo had four children, from age two to eight, but Mr and Mrs Raymond were childless; needless to say, we children were always in and out of the Rodrigos' house and vice versa.

The days passed swiftly, with each of us involved in our own little sphere of activity, and all the surrounding area was our play-ground. The rail tracks, bridges, tunnels, hillocks, and grassy banks under bridges, were my favourite places for adventures and privacy from adults. I played childish games and never spared a thought for worries and woes of my parents. In turn, they never discussed financial difficulties, frustrations and struggles.

The only unpleasant fact in my young life, was that Thathie drank more than he should. Ammie, quite rightly, tried to make him see the error of his ways, which always ended in loud arguments. I wondered then why Ammie did not leave him alone and save us all an unpleasant situation. Now I understand how frustrating and unfair her life must have been. Thathie hated to be chided for his drinking habits, and angrily retorted. "If my *mother* couldn't stop me from drinking, how *dare* you try to stop me!"

No matter how drunk Thathie was, he never ill-treated us, which made us believe in his love. It gave us confidence to ask him even the most absurd things, knowing very well he would try his best to give us whatever we wanted. Later, I tried to analyse his extreme kindness, wondering if that was his way of compensating for the unpleasantness he caused us with his heavy drinking. Ammie had to cope with emotional problems too, and it is only now that I understand her attitude and behaviour then.

She had had to deal with many problems as a teenage bride, and now with Thathie's drinking problem, it was an added burden. She had five young children to bring up, and run a home almost on her own. It was admirable that although outwardly quiet, gentle, and submissive, she had a strong, tenacious streak and determination that kept her true to her Catholic faith, in spite of Thathie's incredible opposition. She was also courageous in the way she accepted her marriage and made the most of it.

These problems made her seem detached and quite remote when I was a child. As she was pre-occupied with many difficulties, we found it easier to approach Thathie. She always kept a neat, comfortable home, fed and clothed us, but when it came to warmth and affection, Ammie was not overly demonstrative.

In later years, she said that it was not in her nature to be effusive, but affirmed that she loved us dearly. I believe she really did, in her own way. But I deeply regret I missed out on having a closer relationship with Ammie in my childhood.

I recall her walking up and down the garden, knitting furiously, lips moving silently (in prayer or muttered complaints), I am unsure. Perhaps it was how she coped with stress. She ignored Thathie's boisterous behaviour and pottered in the garden among her well-loved plants.

Between my teachers, nuns, and Ammie, they inculcated in me a strong sense of morality, decency and good manners, for which I am grateful. Ammie taught me many valuable lessons by her example, especially her deep faith. I learnt many practical things too later; good house keeping, thriftiness, sewing, knitting, cooking and gardening. Ammie was good at art, and a proficient pianist as well, and she played the church organ in later years. She was blessed with a good sense of humour, and laughed at some of the annoying things Thathie did. He too possessed a great sense of humour, and love of the ludicrous. In making light of her troubles, she found relief in her stressful marriage. I believe it is easier to understand our parents when we grow older and try to build bridges.

Thathie was demonstratively affectionate, especially after a few drinks. He became sentimental and loving towards his family and slurred affectionately. "Carmen, my dear, I love you very much." At which, Ammie shrugged her shoulders, shook her head, and retorted irritably. "Then you wouldn't drink so much!" And without missing a beat, he replied calmly. "Then Carmen, please go to hell!"

Some afternoons, all five of us climbed into their big double bed, as Thathie had a habit of resting on Sunday afternoons, reading newspapers, comic books, or a novel. He read aloud, and I thoroughly enjoyed the stories and time spent in this manner. If he read comics and chuckled, I pestered him to read out loud, and he replied with a flicker of impatience. "It's impossible to explain comic book humour, unless you read it yourself!" This made me determined to read as quickly as possible. To this day, I have not lost my passion for a good book, and dearly love those early comic books and cartoon characters. They were so much a part of my childhood that they are like dear old friends one does not forget with time.

Thathie quoted Latin sometimes to express his emotions (especially when he was drunk). He had a large collection of good novels and classics, and I am grateful to him for having passed on his love of books. My siblings and I read a great deal right through our childhood and teenage years. I am still an avid reader and habitually read every night.

When Thathie attended senior school, Mutha bought him a set of Encyclopaedia Britannica, consisting of ten impressive, gilt-edged, red volumes. Thathie treasured them, and they still looked new when we were children. He allowed us to read them only after we washed our hands and sat down at the dining table. It was sheer bliss to open one of those great volumes, spread it out, and handle them reverently, as if they were the most sacred objects. Such was the care and love accorded to this wealth of knowledge and beauty that I discovered between their pages.

To me they were priceless, and it is an enduring sadness they were lost through many moves, changes and journeys in our lives. Thathie said they were irretrievably lost when they were stored in someone else's house. It was during a period they were compelled to live elsewhere. I hoped for a long while to find that same edition someday, because I could not reconcile myself to modern day encyclopaedias with endless reference and year books. This was long before the advent of internet, that most astonishing source of information at one's fingertips.

I have moved on with the times, as we all must, and the wealth of knowledge to be found on the internet, is astounding. But I suppose it is nostalgia, and my love for things past, that makes me sigh whenever I think of that amazing set of books. I am glad I had the opportunity to lose myself in a fantastic voyage of learning and discovery when I opened the first volume.

This is yet another debt of gratitude I owe Thathie, and to Mutha, for having had the foresight to make such an excellent purchase. The superb stories I read, and all the information I absorbed, were like rich compost, gathering and maturing in the fertile regions of my imagination, ready to be utilised someday.

Chapter 4

Nilanthi and Rosie shared a special bond from their childhood. In fact we all treated Rosie more like our sister than an aunt. She related to us better, as her siblings were much older. Although Rita, Anthony, Malcolm, and Marie were still at home then, Rosie preferred to spend her school holidays with us.

Rosie was tall for her age; slim, with curly, short black hair and an infectious laugh. She had two slightly crooked front teeth, but she never wore braces. Her black eyes sparkled mischievously, and she could joke and tell stories that made us laugh till our jaws ached. She was the epitome of audacity and mischief, and Granny and Grandpa could hardly restrain her wild, exuberant nature.

Even at thirteen, she was independent, strong-minded and impudent. Sometimes, she travelled with either Marie or Malcolm during school holidays and obstinately refused to return home in spite of Granny's threats and coaxing. Granny was at a total loss, not knowing how to control her incorrigible child. But Rosie was always a welcome guest, as far as our family was concerned. There was never a dull moment when she was around, and her good humour and laughter were contagious wherever she went.

Thathie bought Nihal a large, shiny black tricycle on his twelfth birthday, and warned him not to ride out too far, but to stay in a safe area close to home. Now Rosie, who was staying with us then with Malcolm and Marie, coaxed Nihal to let her ride first. Nilanthi, Nihal, and Rosie vanished for a long time. Thathie and Ammie were very worried by evening.

Thathie sent a porter to find out what had happened to the three of them, but he returned without any news. Around six or seven o'clock that evening, the scruffy trio returned, dragging the damaged and muddied tricycle behind them. Nihal limped badly, as he had injured the calf of his leg severely. Crestfallen and remorseful, Rosie explained that Nihal had gone through a barbed wire fence, and had suffered a nasty gash on his leg, that now exposed nerves and tendons. He was rushed to hospital immediately, and all thought of punishment forgotten. The tricycle was soon mended, but the long red scar on Nihal's leg remained all his life.

When Rosie visited another time, the three of them decided to go on a picnic to the surrounding wooded hills, and our neighbours, Christine and Randolf joined them too. They were gone all morning, but around noon, we heard a great commotion outside as the five of them ran for dear life, with Christine covering her head with her skirt. An angry swarm of bees buzzed around them, and Christine yelled out in pain as they stung her posterior. They shouted out in distress as the bees stung them in various parts of their anatomy.

Rosie had poked a stick into a beehive, causing the bees to take offence at such a rude form of interrogation, and had attacked with a vengeance. It took the adventurers a while to recover from that escapade. As I said, there was never a dull moment whenever Rosie visited. These minor mishaps however were only juvenile rehearsals in preparation for later adventures, when she developed an advanced sense of mischief and dare-devilry.

One evening, when Nihal came home after school and found that afternoon tea was not yet ready, he pulled out Menika's konde and proceeded to pour a basin of water on the kitchen floor. This angered Ammie so much that she belted him soundly until he became feverish and was put to bed. Then Ammie began to worry and panic, as she was afraid Thathie would quarrel with her for belting Nihal so severely. She sponged his legs with warm water, applied liniment, and bathed his brow with eau de cologne so that by the time Thathie arrived home, Nihal's fever had abated slightly. Thathie received a modified version of Nihal's naughty behaviour and subsequent punishment.

In almost every house then, a large wooden box, with separate compartments for various condiments, rice and grains, was a mandatory item. This storage bin was referred to as the rice box, and stood in a convenient corner of the kitchen or store room, where such a bulky, unsightly thing did not hinder local traffic.

We had one of them sitting right at the end of a corridor close to the dining room, where a sturdy old dining table with a storage cupboard underneath it stood. Ammie stored green bananas to ripen inside. The cupboard absorbed the aroma of ripe bananas, spicy sweetmeats, patties and cakes, so that each time the cupboard door was opened, combined aromas wafted deliciously, and that aroma still lingers in my memory. She also kept home-made goodies there, especially at Christmas time. Tins of Kraft Cheddar cheese, cakes, savoury short eats, all stored and ready for visitors during the festive season.

Ammie sometimes asked me to check the cheese or cakes in the cupboard, in case mice discovered them. As I was extremely fond of Cheddar cheese, I took a big bite from one of the half-opened tins. Then poker-faced, I reported to Ammie. "Yes, the mice have definitely got at the cheese!" I wonder *if* and *when* Ammie realized I was the phantom mouse.

To get back to the rice box incident before I digressed, I must mention that Thathie's two nieces, Swarna and Manel (Daisy Akka's daughters), who attended Little Flower convent too, boarded with us. And so did Chanda, Thathie's youngest brother, who was still in his teens. He attended St Joseph's college with Nihal. The two girls were in their mid-teens as well and were quite attractive. They were of average height, very fair-skinned, with dark eyes and knee-length black hair.

They were at that flirtatious age when they were interested in boys, and most of the time they whispered and giggled with Nilanthi about their little affairs. A few years older than Nilanthi, they found her a good confidante. I was curious, and tried to eavesdrop on their conversations, but they always shooed me off and scolded me for being a curious little girl.

The nuns in our convent were strict disciplinarians and strait-laced moralists. So whenever they chased me away I taunted them. "I'll *tell* Mother Concilia about you!" She was our principal, and a direct descendent of a Spanish Inquisitor, I had no doubt. They became really mad whenever I threatened them.

I really have digressed I know, but I do have to mention these people who lived with us then, as the following anecdote involves them. It was customary for the three girls, Swarna, Manel, and Nilanthi to spend their evenings whispering and giggling, as they exchanged mutual secrets. Ammie and Menika meanwhile quibbled about the next meal, and what ingredients were required for meals next day.

On one such evening, a sudden tap on the window pane froze everyone, and we saw a furtive shadow lurking in the dusky night. This frightened the three girls so badly that they all got up and rushed blindly down the corridor. Menika had left the rice box lid open to show Ammie the lack of condiments to cook the next meal. Next moment, all three girls tumbled into the rice box one on top of the other! We younger children yelled with laughter to see the older girls all squashed up in the rice box, as they made such a foolish spectacle of themselves. Menika groaned underneath their combined weight and frantically shoved the girls away.

Nihal was the culprit of course, as he wanted to scare the girls. He succeeded so well that his face turned red as a beetroot as he tried to restrain laughter that threatened to explode when he came in and saw them all piled up in the rice box. I can tell that the girls were not one bit amused as they rearranged their frocks and faces back to normal.

I attended school at the age of five, and was quite a favourite with the teachers, because I learnt to read and write early. I loved history, and any old stories well enough, but did not take to Arithmetic and Geography. School was fun, with many friends and hold good memories.

The strict nuns and teachers were the bane of my school life, but otherwise, it was a happy period in that early carefree, playground of life. The nuns knew Thathie was a Buddhist, and whenever they spoke to Ammie, they whispered conspiratorially. "We'll *pray* for your husband's conversion, Mrs Rajapakse." Ammie always looked teary whenever they said those words. Prayer times in school too went like this. "We pray for the conversion of sinners and *non*-Catholics, and for protection against *Communists*."

The threat of "Cold War" the Soviet Union, and "Iron curtain" loomed large in those days. Communism was a dirty word to the nuns and all Catholics. I grew up thinking it was some kind of deadly plague that threatened to annihilate humanity, and never understood what that word meant until I was much older.

Dorothy, a little girl in my class, whose father was a European planter, lived near-by on a tea estate. She arrived at school every morning in a chauffeur driven car (a shiny black Peugeot). One day, she invited me to her home after school, and we drove in her nice car. When we arrived there and knocked on the front door, no one opened it. Dorothy took me around to the backyard to an outdoor kitchen area.

An ebony-skinned, haggard woman, with stained red lips and gums due to betel leaf chewing, squatted on the kitchen floor. A few other Tamil women who were sitting there chattered away in their language. Dorothy mumbled. "This is my mother." I later discovered that her mother was a labourer on the estate where her father worked as a planter. Dorothy looked so embarrassed that she began to cry. I did not know about her mother's social standing, and felt sorry for her, as I did not know what to say.

As children it did not worry us at all, but the adults whispered it was a scandalous situation about the white planter and Tamil tea plucker, who were living together "in sin" as no one believed they were legally married. One would think such a matter was insignificant in today's society, but it was a major social taboo then.

Menika sometimes boiled chick peas or lentils, which we called gram, and prepared roast beef sandwiches, with mustard paste ground with sugar, vinegar and salt; she made a flask of hot tea, and then took us to the park or esplanade. Sadly, this park was later turned into an artificial lake, but a tennis club stood there at the time. We watched trim, taut, white-clad figures running around energetically as they hit tennis balls.

In this beautiful treed park, swings, see-saws, merry-go-rounds and slides were the main attraction where we all had a turn and played to our hearts content. Finally, when we were near exhaustion and all the food was consumed, we trudged back home around five or six o'clock in the evening. On our way home from such an excursion one day, we spied a crowd gathered behind the railway station, and they all stared up at the summit of the hill beyond.

Someone in the crowd claimed he had spotted a cobra (unheard of in Bandarawela). As far as we knew, no deadly snakes slithered around in that cool climate, only the harmless, black garandiya. Most people gaped at the hill-top where the cobra was supposed to be coiled, with a mixture of scepticism and fear.

We too joined the gaping crowd for a while until Menika hurried us home. On the way she regaled us with this yarn about a cobra jealously guarding a hoard of precious stones on the hill-top. Someone had even spotted a glimmering mass up there. They really believed a treasure trove was up there, if only someone was brave enough to tackle the cobra. I believed every word Menika said, and so did the others.

Thathie treated us to a good movie once in a while. He walked with us halfway, then stopped and said. "Walk ahead, and I'll catch up with you soon." We knew then he wanted to nip in for a quick drink to the hotel or tavern we had just passed. We did not like this at all (through experience). Since he had the money, we had to stand outside and wait for him to buy our tickets.

The Royal Theatre was a fairly good cinema then, and screened English movies frequently, and another one catered mainly to the Sinhalese and Tamil population. That other one was referred to as the "Tent" because that was exactly what it was; an enormous old tent, that I am sure was the property of an erstwhile circus gone broke. It had been converted to a cinema, and one only had to see the crowd for a Sunday matinee, to know just how popular that uncomfortable, draughty old tent was with Sinhalese and Tamil film goers.

Now the "Tent" was strictly out of bounds for respectable, middle-class people, because of the rowdy element that patronized it, as it cost only fifty cents to get in. The very front row was called the gallery, where rough, bawdy men sat and gave free expression to their feelings. They hooted, whistled and made catcalls, or jeered at any scene on the big screen. The love scenes especially made them whistle and shout, as they made lewd remarks to one another. Even in other cinemas, wherever these rowdies were present, they were an annoyance to other patrons.

During the short intermission, the gallery rowdies all turned around and gawked at the people sitting up in the balcony or middle rows. Their rude comments and leers were quite offensive. But no one could stop them, as anyone who paid for a ticket was free to go into any cinema. Management was helpless. I remember sitting through intermissions, cringing and blushing at the behaviour of these unpleasant hooligans. It was a relief when lights were off and the movie started rolling again.

When Rosie visited once, she decided to take Menika for a Sinhalese film to the Tent. Now we all knew it was out of bounds, and so did Menika, but the temptation to do something forbidden was quite exciting. We dressed up for the matinee show and followed Rosie. Ammie and Thathie were unaware of our plans, and we thought it was good fun. But during the show, somehow we began to feel dreadfully uncomfortable, as the rowdies kept jeering and hooting at us. This was their territory, and we were intruders. They sure made us feel we did not belong. We quickly ran out of the Tent long before the film ended.

As I mentioned, Thathie took us to movies. If there was a good movie at the cinema in Diyatalawe, we boarded a train, as it was a few miles from Bandarawela. It was great fun to travel on a train, eat at a Chinese restaurant and get back home late in the night. One such movie I remember vividly was, "The Seven Voyages Of Sinbad The Sailor." Not only the colourful movie, but because of what happened when we came home late that night.

Ammie never joined us on these outings, not even once. She did not enjoy English movies, and preferred Sinhalese or Hindi films, which was what she told us whenever we tried to persuade her to join us for a movie. No matter how much we pleaded, Ammie remained adamant that she would not derive any pleasure at the movies.

Her catch phrase was, "You all go with Thathie, I'll stay at home." We were to hear this phrase right through our childhood. In all that time, I recall Ammie joining us only once when I was a teenager. But the movie, "Escape From Bahrain" proved to be such a boring movie, that Ammie was triumphant. She said that she should never have come to watch such a tedious movie.

On that particular evening, when we went to the movies, Ammie stayed home as usual. When we came home, the place was in darkness, as Ammie and Menika had gone to sleep. Thathie was intoxicated, and talked about "cabbages and kings." We were all very tired and sleepy, and I just flopped into bed. Almost immediately, a loud commotion erupted and banished all thought of sleep.

I jumped out of bed, and so did the others. I can still picture Thathie struggling drunkenly with Ammie, as he tried to extricate something from her hand. They argued fiercely, and Ammie threatened to swallow rat poison. I watched in fear as they struggled and fought, while we cried and snivelled, just like frightened mice. Finally, when they had calmed down somewhat, Thathie threw away the rat poison, and we all settled down to get some sleep. It was very confusing and sad, as I never could understand what all the fighting was about then. Thathie was such a loving father, and I could see no harm in him, and wondered who had started the quarrel first.

It is a sad memory of my parents' continual quarrels, but now I understand what made Ammie so angry and frustrated. When we were older, we cautioned Ammie to keep quiet and not argue with Thathie when he was drunk. But she never ever did listen, and because he was drunk most of the time, their quarrels and arguments never stopped. I have to admit though that Ammie was quite right in not tolerating Thathie's bad behaviour. It took immense courage to constantly stand up for her rights.

Thathie, on the other hand, enjoyed his role vastly as a roaring lion in our household. He expected everyone to cower in fear when he was after a few drinks. When he was sober, he was quiet as a mouse, but after drinks, his self-control and restraint flew out the window.

He too must have been extremely frustrated and angry sometimes because of financial difficulties, and his youthful marriage. An officer in the railway did not earn much money, and I know Ammie was extremely budget-conscious. Thathie was fortunate that she was so careful, and clever in managing the household. He was irresponsible with money though, and that was one of the sore points in their marriage.

Many years later, he joked that he would always be a "schoolboy at heart" and he never wanted to grow up. I think Freud would have found this "Peter Pan syndrome" quite fascinating; frustrated youth burdened with responsibility, finding relief in alcohol, and escaping irresponsibility? Who can analyse the dark labyrinth of the human heart and mind.

(1)Mutha in centre, Athamma with Wimala, Ammie
& Thathie with Nilanthi & Nihal

Chapter 5

While playing hide-and-seek with my friends one day, I became very short of breath, and my heart pounded like an over-worked engine. "I *always* say a Hail Mary when I get this way." I gasped. Thathie happened to be listening near the window, and he looked angry when he heard me. He shouted out with a threatening look on his usually benign face. "Come inside at *once* Dolly!" But I ran away and hid in the garden until (I fervently hoped), he had forgotten my religious comment.

The reason for such fear was that he was very anti-Catholic in his younger days. He barely tolerated Ammie's church going, let alone any of us displaying religious fervour at home. She related some incredible stories of their early days together, when he would hide her clothes and shoes, so she could not attend Sunday Mass.

He had stomped in during Mass once, and taken her home forcibly. These stories of religious intolerance may seem absurd now, but it was no joking matter for Ammie or us then. I think most of their quarrels stemmed from religious and cultural differences, as well as Thathie's excessive drinking habits.

Christmas time was especially busy for Ammie, as she baked several trays of fruit cake for all the shopkeepers, whom she patronized during the year. Sometimes, she asked one of us children to carry a tray of cake or some savoury dish for them. They were so impressed with such a token of goodwill, that they reciprocated with a small gift for our family.

The postman, porters, vegetable vendors, and odd-job people, trailed up to our front door at Christmas time. Ammie served them cakes and short eats, while Thathie had a few bottles of arrack ready for the veteran drinkers. This custom prevailed as long as I can remember, and many Ceylonese still uphold this tradition.

One day, Granny's sister, Pansy, and her husband, Victor, arrived on a holiday. My memory of them is dim, as we did not see them very often. Aunty Pansy, however, is part of our family history, and so, I must include this strange story. Being about eight years old then, I have only a vague recollection of the events that took place. Most of it was discussed in adulthood when I learnt all the facts.

The story goes that on her visit to our home, Aunty Pansy was delighted with Ammie's collection of red carnations. She admired our garden greatly. But not long after this visit, she fell seriously ill, and in a matter of days she lay on her deathbed. I do not know the cause of her death, but just before, she requested Ammie to send a bouquet of red carnations. Whether Ammie was too busy, or it was just an oversight, Aunty Pansy's request was not granted. A telegram arrived shortly afterwards to inform us of her death.

Her sudden death devastated her husband, and their only daughter, Therese. At the end of that traumatic period, they came down for a brief visit, in search of rest and solace. Uncle Victor described the last moments of Aunty Pansy's death, and he was grieved it had been so harrowing. The poor soul had tried her best to cling to the last threads of life, and refused to believe it was the end. Unfortunately, her soul was reluctant to leave her earthly mould and return to its Maker.

She gripped her husband's hand so tight when she breathed her last, that it had been quite an effort to pry her fingers loose. She had fought to the end, biting her pillow and crying out she would not die. Anyway, that night, when Uncle Victor and Therese arrived, odd noises and strange happenings took place. Ammie arranged a bowl of red carnations on the dining table, but next morning, only stems remained, without a single flower. The holy pictures on the little altar that Thathie allowed Ammie to have in our room, were all turned face down.

Therese complained someone had struck her on her upper thigh, and there it was! finger marks clearly outlined in blue. Uncle Victor searched high and low for his spectacles, and someone discovered them out on the driveway.

Now these were somewhat extraordinary events, but Ammie and Thathie were sceptical about any supernatural causes, as our visitors were prone to believe. No one had an explanation though. Ammie scolded Nilanthi that morning, thinking she had picked the red carnations from the bowl out of pure mischief, but Nilanthi vehemently denied this accusation.

Therese and Uncle Victor firmly believed it was Aunty Pansy's spirit. So the adults decided to arrange another bowl of red carnations and see what happened. Imagine our consternation next morning, when the flowers were missing again! This time there seemed to be no doubt Aunty Pansy's restless spirit was responsible for the missing carnations.

My parents immediately sent a large bouquet of red carnations to be placed on her grave, and later that day, a priest blessed and exorcised our home. After these peace offerings and exorcism, her spirit must have been appeased, because no more episodes of missing carnations took place. Strange as it may sound, although I like most flowers and foliage, I dislike red carnations even to this day. I do not grow them in my garden, and neither do I have any red carnations inside the house in vases. The rest of my family share this dislike too, which goes to prove how deeply that incident has affected us. Ammie once told me Therese is psychic, and her mother's spirit follows her wherever she goes.

During those years in Bandarawela, Mutha's memory stands out vividly, as he visited regularly. I still picture him riding up the driveway on his old motorcycle; shoulder-length silver hair flying in the breeze, a kindly smile on his benevolent face. He was such a dignified gentleman. He spoke very few words, and when he did take out his cigar to make an observation, he was full of wisdom and compassion. It was very hard to picture him as the hardened, heartless husband, who had gambled away his wife's fortune.

He invariably carried a packet of Ovaltine or Marie biscuits, and gave it to one of us. Mutha did not talk with us a great deal, or dandle us on his knees, but he usually conversed affectionately with Ammie. Athamma rarely visited, but Mutha and Ammie developed a lasting rapport. Mutha seldom or never touched alcohol, so he did not condone with Thathie's drinking. Ammie had a sympathetic ally in Mutha, as she complained to him of Thathie's excessive drinking habits.

I thought Mrs Loos was the most beautiful woman I had ever seen in my life. She lived next door to Granny in Maharagama, and must have been in her late twenties or so in those early years. Grandpa retired some years ago because of an injury he had suffered when he fell off a railcar and could not work in the railway again. Thathie often wondered (aloud), if Grandpa had been under the influence of alcohol at the time of his accident.

Granny, who was the driving force in that marriage, invested his retirement funds in a large house in Maharagama. She always related how she bought that house for her family's security, and how with great difficulty, she coped with Grandpa's early retirement. Her tenacity and foresight were admirable. She educated her children and looked after them, while Grandpa "retired" to the background in every sense of the word, leaving Granny to manage everything in her capable way.

That house in Maharagama is the only place I recall, as I was too young to remember their other houses in Paranthan and Nuwara Eliya.

To get back to Mrs Loos, whom we called, "Mimi" (just like her children did), she was not only beautiful and kind, but an excellent housekeeper as well. I still remember what a lovely home she kept, with polished, red cement floors sparkling like glass, and not a speck of dust or dirt anywhere.

Mimi kept a fantastic aviary in her garden, with hundreds of coloured birds and budgerigars, who sang and whistled all day long. Some were so tame that they flew over to sit on her shoulder. She had four children then, and whenever we visited, she fussed around and doted on me.

On one occasion, Mimi gave me the most beautiful doll imaginable. This doll had long, thick black eyelashes, and a pouting red mouth that opened to show two small white teeth. I loved that wonderful doll, and could only murmur thanks incoherently. Mimi knew I had a passion for dolls, collecting all sorts and sizes, like some children collected stamps or butterflies.

Mimi resembled Jean Simmons, the movie star. She had the same facial bone structure, light-grey eyes, a nice figure, and dressed beautifully. Once, she looked stunning in a red frock, matching lipstick, with her glowing complexion, like peaches and cream. I thought she looked very beautiful indeed, and I loved her very much. As a child I was finicky with my food, and whenever we had lunch at their place, Mimi fried an egg, or something special, because I did not eat chicken, meat or fish, and she served tinned peaches or pears for dessert.

To get back to the doll, when we returned home from our holiday, Mimi's doll became my current favourite. I carried it around everywhere. It said "Mama" and "Papa" each time I tilted it, and to me, that was its main attraction. It could talk.

One day, at one of my dolls tea parties, I fed this doll a cup of cold water tea, which bungled the mechanism, and it did not talk anymore.

To my childish mind, this sudden muteness on my favourite's part, meant only one thing. It was dead. No doubt about it. Amid a flood of tears and misery that no adult or any of my siblings witnessed, I dressed the doll in her best dress. Then I took her in ceremony (as I had observed at funeral processions), to the farthest end of the garden, dug a hole, and buried her forever.

Just to show how quickly a child forgets the deepest sorrow, within a few days or weeks, I had even forgotten the place where I had buried the doll. It slipped my mind completely until many months later. When I was older, and the rest of the family discovered my silly mistake, they told me dolls cannot die. I tried frantically to rescue the poor doll from her untimely grave, but try as I would, I just could not find the spot where I had buried it, and that was the end of that.

our family in 1960. Shirani, Nelune & me in Front row. Nilanthi & Nihal on right.Ammie & Thathie last rows with granny, grandpa & their children.

Chapter 6

The days flew swiftly between school and home. Every morning, four of us, except Nelune, who was still too young to attend school, dressed, put on straw hats, and carried our books (in my case, a slate and a pencil) and walked through town, passed St Joseph's college, where Nihal took leave of us. Then we continued our long walk up the steep flight of winding steps that led to Little Flower convent on the hill. It must have been a few miles up and down, and I wonder how my sisters and I walked so far.

I did not know then our house was to be demolished soon, and we had to move. One of the privileges railway officers enjoyed, was a rent-free house. They were referred to as bungalows, but it was a misnomer, because these bungalows were really large, spacious buildings that afforded ample accommodation for big families. The window frames and doors were invariably painted grey (standard railway colour). Porters and gardeners maintained premises, ran errands, and did odd-jobs around the house, and most officers lived comfortably in the Ceylon Government Railway houses.

Ammie and the rest of us were very sad at the forthcoming upheaval, as the old railway bungalow, scene of so many childhood joys and sorrows, was very dear to us. Ammie grew several varieties of colourful geraniums in hanging baskets at the front of the house, and many other plants and shrubs in the garden. She loved her plants, and pottered away happily for hours. It was a bountiful garden, with large avocado and pomegranate trees that bore abundant fruits, and now we had to leave all that behind.

We had cats and dogs as far back as I can remember, but one favourite dog of mine was Rover; a large, mixed breed, with gentle manners and loving nature. Rover followed us all the way to school and having seen us there safely, he wagged his tail and returned home, his duty done for the day.

A dog-catcher the council employed to shoot stray dogs in town, happened to have fallen out with Ammie and Thathie over a trivial matter. And his cowardly act of revenge still angers me. Although he knew Rover belonged to us, he shot him down on his way home from school one day. Poor, gentle, Rover, who never harmed anyone in his life. He lopped his tail off, as proof of the number of dogs culled for the day. A friend who had witnessed the dastardly deed brought dead Rover home.

I still remember my anguish over faithful Rover's untimely death. I broke my heart countless times over the demise of my pets, until a newcomer usurped their treasured memory and made me forget my old faithful friends. One of our many dogs once had a large, assorted litter. Ammie did not want to keep any of them. No one wanted them either, as they were such a mish mash litter, so Ammie's only solution was to drown them.

Down the garden, where earth was excavated to make mud-bricks for a garage, was a deep hole. It had rained for many days, and this hole was full of muddy water, and a broad plank bridged the muddy expanse. I sometimes walked across gingerly, holding my breath, in case I lost my balance and fell into the muddy hole.

One day, when I was standing on this narrow bridge and gazing at the muddy depths, my eyes fell on some floating objects down there. I looked closely, and stared in disbelief and distress. I saw the poor little puppies, bellies swollen like balloons fit to burst, floating grotesquely in their murky grave. I could not believe it. I loved to play with them and cuddle their soft, warm little bodies, with their newborn milky smell, and tiny, wet noses snuffling me affectionately.

I ran up to Ammie, tears blinding me, and demanded to know what had happened to the puppies. Ammie, straight-faced, explained that the dog had carried her pups one by one and dropped them into the muddy hole. Although I could not understand such cruelty, I believed her, and cried my eyes out for those hapless, bloated dead puppies.

Once, when our convent held a fete, Ammie sent four of us, with Nilanthi in charge, as Nelune was still too young for such outings. The fete was starting at 7pm, and this was a very late night indeed, as Ammie had strict notions about us going to bed by eight o'clock every night.

Wide-eyed, I drank in the exciting atmosphere; grand stalls with massive signs that screamed out "Lucky Dips" "Mystery Envelopes" "Spin The Wheel" etc. etc. These amusements cost five or ten cents a go then. One of the nuns looked at me keenly and asked. "How much money do you have tonight dear?" I held up my shining twenty five cent coin proudly, and the two nuns tittered and burst out laughing. One said to the other. *"Only* twenty five cents! Just imagine that Sister, that's all she's got to spend tonight!" Their laughter followed me, as I burnt with shame and indignation.

It was a great sum of money to me, and Ammie, who was always a thrifty housewife, must have found it difficult to give four of us extra pocket money. As a child, I never questioned Ammie or Thathie why I could not have things beyond our means. I just accepted whatever I received with a grateful heart. Anything extra must have cost them a great deal of hardship, and I appreciated whatever I had very much. That nun's callous remarks made me feel humiliated, and she spoilt my enjoyment that night.

We were fortunate, that unlike today's children living in a consumer-driven society, and constantly bombarded with television commercials and other media promoting superficial values, we only had radio and cinema to influence and entertain us. But they hardly made an impact on our way of life, or our beliefs, the way media brainwashes the modern generation. And we were satisfied with very little entertainment. It was a more innocent era I suppose, and we were unaware of drug addiction, and all the criminal activity associated with drug abuse. The scourge of illegal drugs such as "Ice" was not rampant like today.

One night, just as Ammie and Thathie dressed to go out for a dinner party, Nilanthi, who did not want to be left at home, instigated Shirani to cry and fuss so they would not be able to go. Shirani cried and yelled and threw such a tantrum, that although Ammie chastised her, she would not stop crying. Ammie cancelled her dinner party, thanks to Nilanthi's mischief.

Rita's wedding was a grand occasion, and there is an old photograph of me as a flower girl, dressed in pink organza, white socks and shoes, following Rita down the aisle. She was a very beautiful bride, and we thought Roland was lucky to have married such a lovely lady, as she had always been our favourite aunt.

Roland was of average height, swarthy and thickset, with heavy features and large black eyes. He was reserved, and in my childish mind, quite unattractive, so it was difficult for me to understand why someone as pretty as Rita married him. Whispers and hints of why she married Roland was sometimes discussed in our family, but I did not know anything about that matter until I was much older.

The actual ceremony and reception has slipped my mind, but I do recall travelling to Colombo and boarding a double decker bus to Maharagama. Those trips to Colombo remain deeply etched in my mind, as they had a magical quality, like visiting Wonderland.

Getting off the train at the huge Fort Station, with its colourful kiosks well-stocked with apples wrapped in green tissue paper, and exuding a delicious fragrance, magazines and books stacked on shelves, porters bustling around, trains arriving and departing every few minutes from various platforms, was the most exciting moment. A deep, muffled, rumbling voice over loudspeakers, announcing times and platform numbers of departing and arriving trains, set my mind in a whirl. I drank in so many new sights and sounds, that I just loved this exciting journey to Colombo.

The towering overhead pedestrian bridges that had to be crossed, as they were the only exits from the station, were especially terrifying, because I suffered from vertigo and still do. Just looking up at the tall, imposing wooden structures made me dizzy. It was a great trial to cross those bridges, and such a huge relief to run outside into the warm, balmy air and feel my feet on terra firma once again.

The bus-stand stood just outside Fort Station. As we boarded a red, double-decker bus (cast-offs from Britain to the colonies), I invariably ran up to the second level and sat by a window, so I could drink in the exciting hustle and bustle of the big city. Living in a quiet, peaceful town like Bandarawela all year round, these occasional trips to Colombo were twice as enjoyable.

After Rita's wedding and reception, we returned home to our everyday routine. But a few weeks later, Rita and Roland, who had spent their honeymoon in Ella, a lovely, scenic spot up-country, paid a surprise visit on their way back to Colombo, and stayed a few days with us. Full of fun and laughter, Rita was delightful company, and we loved having her with us, but all too soon it was time for them to leave.

That first December after Rita's marriage, she coaxed Ammie and Thathie to let us spend Christmas with her, and the five of us were delighted when our parents reluctantly agreed. It was the first time we were going to be away from home, and especially at Christmas. All through our childhood and adolescence, they never allowed us to stay anywhere without them, so this was indeed a great concession on their part. I could hardly contain my excitement.

Rita entertained us very well, and on Christmas Eve, she sent us off to another room and told us to wait there until she called. Some time later, when Rita led us to the darkened room, she switched on the lights, and we beheld the most delightful nativity scene, and a huge, Christmas tree sparkling and glittering with tinsel and lights, all decorated and ready for us.

It was a brilliant sight, and I never forgot that magical scene.

Later on, we went to the police grounds and listened to Christmas carols until midnight. The sight of thousands of flickering candle flames in the warm, velvety night was breathtaking indeed. Then all too soon our Christmas holidays came to an end and we returned home, full of great memories, presents, and thankful hearts to our beautiful Aunty Rita, who had gone out of her way to entertain us.

Chapter 7

A telegram arrived one day about a year later. Rita was in a serious condition in hospital. Ammie said Rita knocked over a kerosene lamp while she was in the bathroom, and accidentally burnt herself. As the door was locked, it took Roland some time to break it down. They suffered severe burns, and although Roland underwent many operations, he lost the use of his fingers.

Rita was in hospital for over ten months, and doctors gave up all hope of her survival. They told Granny to resign herself to her daughter's death. But Granny said she never lost hope. She prayed and watched over Rita through days and nights, while Rita underwent umpteen skin-grafts and operations.

It was a nightmarish period, and we mourned the loss of Rita's beauty. She was severely scarred, and could not stretch out one arm. Her face was still attractive though, as some scars healed in time, and only a few deep ones remained. Roland was completely dependent on Rita, to dress, feed, and bathe him, as he could not use his hands at all.

He learnt how to hold a pen between his finger stumps, and worked as a clerk in the railways until he retired. Rita too returned to work as a stenographer at Walkers, because her fingers remained intact. In years to come, they had two children, Lucille and Adrian, who were Rita's main source of joy and comfort.

Who is to say why this beautiful young girl and her husband endured such a tragic accident. Rita coped bravely, and never lost her sense of humour, or her merry laughter right through the years. She made their marriage work, which lasted till they died. But that tragedy made Roland very bitter, angry, and chronically morose.

When I was older, I heard whispers of scandal that wafted in our family circle. Roland was insanely jealous and possessive of Rita. So he employed a detective to follow her everywhere. He drove Rita to the brink with his irrational suspicion. We never knew whether in a moment of desperation, she decided to end it all.

Before she met Roland, Rita was in love with a very rich, handsome, young man, but Granny opposed that affair, as he was not a Catholic Burgher. They arranged Rita's marriage to Roland, but I do not know why she agreed. When her first love heard about her accident, he sent a big bouquet of red roses, and almost immediately after, he suffered a fatal heart attack. Rita was unaware he was in the same hospital, while she lay in a coma. That was her tragic tale, as I heard from my parents.

Wimala, Thathie's younger brother, was a very slack student at school, and consequently, he was uneducated and unemployed, unlike his siblings, who were well-educated, and held good jobs. He was of average height, scrawny, swarthy, and with a sly, hangdog look. Wimala was extremely fond of arrack, and was an alcoholic. His parents tolerated him in their home, as he had nowhere else to go, but he was a sore trial to them.

Thathie, and his brother, Wije, helped him financially. Wimala tried several odd jobs, but never held one. He even ran a small grocery shop situated in their garden, that we found interesting. However, he did not make any profit, and spent weeks with us instead. He helped Ammie around the house and garden. Thathie lent him the Ford car to run a taxi business, but he never succeeded at anything.

Wimala's only source of consolation was arrack, and that was a common bond between Thathie and him. Athamma and Mutha despaired of ever seeing Wimala holding onto a job, or succeeding at anything, and accepted the fact he was a never-do-well.

His troubled parents then had the strangest notion that marriage would help him settle down. Accordingly, the Kapuwa (matchmaker), brought a proposal. The prospective bride was an orphan, without a big dowry, but was well-brought up, and attractive. She would suit Wimala very well (so the matchmaker said). Her foster parents were relieved to be rid of her. Poor unsuspecting bride.

Wimala was not a big, matrimonial prize either, so both parties agreed to the marriage. He and his wife hoped to live with his parents, as he was totally dependent on them for food, lodging and pocket money.

After a few drinks though, Wimala suffered from delusions of grandeur, and was an insufferable braggart. When we visited sometimes, he boasted how wealthy his parents had once been, and pointed out distant, paddy fields, swaying gently in light breezes, that Athamma had once owned. Now, thanks to his father's gambling, not one of those fertile fields belonged to them. He was very bitter, and after a few drinks, he made scathing remarks about Mutha.

In his muddled logic, Wimala blamed his parents for his adverse situation in life. He was convinced that had he inherited land, he would have been well off. All they owned now were the house and surrounding area, and this property too was divided equally between Daisy, Thathie, and his brothers. It was a delightful property, with a small tea estate, an abundance of fruit trees, vegetables, and many varieties of flowers, trees, and shrubs.

The land sloped gently, with narrow, uneven steps cut into the earth that meandered down to a little well. It was a fair distance to carry fresh water up to the house, but when Mutha was prosperous, there was never a shortage of servants to do his bidding. Women from near-by villages helped Athamma with chores; pounded paddy, and packed rice into Hessian bags, and did several tasks in the big old house. Everyone who helped was fed, and went away happy, with a full stomach, and gifts of rice and vegetables.

A vivid picture emerges of green vegetables, creeping marrows and melon vines entwined in the ground, swaying trees surrounding the boundary, and misty, blue hills in the distance. I loved that place dearly, as it held many good memories. It was a happy place, because Athamma and Mutha loved us dearly, and made us feel very special whenever we visited. A charming picture still remains in my memory, of a sandy, gravel driveway leading up to the grand old blue-stone house, surrounded by beds of colourful gerbera.

To get back to Wimala's marriage, the prospective bride was Sunethra. And on the morning of their wedding, Anthony, Ammie's brother, accompanied us to Paranagama too.

Anthony was tall, slim, and good-looking, with a habitual, good-humoured smile. He had wavy black hair, and delighted in the funny side of life. Ammie's siblings were blessed with a great sense of humour, all except Marie. Deeply religious, she took life very seriously, even as a teenager, and was always interested in arts and music. Marie was dark-skinned, slim, attractive, of average height, and with long, wavy black hair.

We dressed up in our best clothes, and Ammie looked very glamorous in an expensive silk sari, and matching earrings. Thathie sported a bow tie, and looked very dashing too. The black and white photograph of us taken in front of the Ford car, still evokes a happy memory, just as if it was yesterday.

We arrived in Paranagama, where we found everyone astir in frantic preparation for a traditional Kandyan Sinhalese wedding ceremony. My first impression was of tons of food everywhere. One of the large rooms was converted into a pantry, and great bunches of plantains (bananas), hung on meat hooks from the ceiling.

Long tables covered with snow-white linen cloths, groaned under mountains of traditional sweetmeats, too numerous to describe. Great platters of kavun, kokis, halape, lavaria, dodol, and mung kavun, just to name a few of the popular Sinhalese sweetmeats, adorned the tables. It was an enormous banquet that went on forever. In my childish mind, I doubted that the guests could possibly consume such a gargantuan quantity of food. Throughout the day though, I watched in disbelief as the food slowly diminished. And guests continued to gorge, with a positive lack of consideration for waistlines or calories.

The ceremonial wedding bower, Poruwa, was elaborately decorated with garlands of highly perfumed flowers. Under this structure, Wimala and his hapless bride stood. She, with downcast eyes, and in a most self-conscious, modest manner. The celebrant tied their fingers together in a symbolic knot (the bond of marriage), and children dressed in white cloths and jackets, sang the traditional Jaya Mangala (wedding song). Gold rings were exchanged, and then the bridal couple sat in the living room, while people shuffled past them for hours on end (I thought), offering good wishes and advice.

All that time the bridal couple sat there, seemed an eternity to me. Finally, towards late evening, when every guest had eaten and drunk as much as they could hold, the couple were finally escorted to a gaily festooned car. Amid cheers, farewells, fire crackers, and mandatory ribald comments from some drunken wits, they finally drove away in a cloud of dust to honeymoon in a nearby guest house. After our goodbyes, we drove home, but I was already asleep before we reached Bandarawela.

Thathie decided to take the family to Kataragama to fulfil a vow. I just cannot imagine how our family of seven, besides Menika, Athamma, Sunethra, and a servant boy, fitted inside the old Ford. Wimala drove, because Thathie admitted he was an erratic and nervous driver. Each time he was meant to drive forward, he reversed (especially after drinks). And the car jerked and hopped about in all directions, doing a kangaroo hop, as Thathie frantically changed gears. For the safety of all concerned, Thathie never sat at the wheel again.

We squeezed into that car, packed tight like a box of matches, but we had a fantastic trip to Kataragama. When we passed through dense jungles, we saw plenty of wildlife in national parks and sanctuaries. Hordes of wild monkeys chattered cheekily high up in the trees, or wandered close to the road; gentle-eyed, spotted deer leapt and vanished into dark undergrowth at the sound of our car, and herds of roaming elephants trumpeted wildly in the jungles.

It was better than any safari, and we children loved every moment of it. When we entered a cocoa estate, we stopped and tasted the sweet, luscious cocoa kernels someone offered. Wide, deep rivers, and sparkling streams that wound around green countryside entranced me, and finally, we sighted the vast, beautiful Mahaveli River gleaming in the dusk. We arrived in the holy city, where hundreds of pilgrims and penitents gathered annually, to worship and chastise themselves.

We bathed in shallow parts of the river, where I could see glistening, white sand below. It was very warm and humid, and the river was a hive of activity, because almost every person there was bathing or washing. All the children had a whale of a time, as we revelled in the sheer pleasure of freedom, and pervading holiday atmosphere. I did not heed the holy people, or solemn faces of penitents, who trailed around the streets, because to me, it was just a great holiday, and I was determined to enjoy myself to the fullest.

We stayed in a rest house there, and in the evening, we walked around crowded streets of the town, peeping through windows of holy shrines and temples. Although unbaptized, I considered myself a Catholic, and felt uncomfortable going into Buddhist and Hindu temples. The nuns and clergy inculcated in me that it was against our religion to visit such places of worship, and the fifties' were still times of religious intolerance and prejudice.

Thathie, and the others, who were Buddhists, went inside the temples with floral offerings, to worship and meditate. Ammie, and the five of us stayed outside, only peeping in out of sheer curiosity, and a delicious sense of surreal uneasiness. The nuns sternly rebuked us if we even mentioned Buddhist activities, and it was unthinkable to visit temples and shrines. I glimpsed marvellous frescoes, and monumental statues of Lord Buddha inside some of those temples. But as a child, I was just as prejudiced, and full of religious hang-ups.

Processions of devotees and penitents marched through the narrow streets carrying lighted torches, flames flickering on solemn fanatical faces. They stuck hooks into some penitents backs, and dragged them along with cords attached to them. These masochists danced and leapt in the air in wild religious ecstasy, chanting and swaying to rhythm of drums, and shrill singing of priests and participants.

Those bizarre scenes are branded in my mind. I watched fire-walkers in open-eyed wonder, and did not comprehend how they emerged unscathed and jubilant at the other end of burning coals. Some devotees, with beatific smiles, lay on beds of nails, and looked as comfortable as if lying on a spring mattress. Such extreme forms of self-torture horrified me, and I had nightmares, just thinking about such self-inflicted pain. I still do not understand how or why they accomplished such feats.

After a few more days of sightseeing, we returned home, tired, but impressed with all the new sights and experiences during our journey. We drove via Hambantota, a sea-side fishing village. My recollections of this town, are of large, buzzing, hungry flies swarming all over, as we tried to eat a meal at the guest house, that left much to be desired. We did not delay at Hambantota, and soon headed towards the salubrious climate in Bandarawela.

As for Wimala, marriage did not in any way steady his unstable character. He became worse in fact, as he drank more heavily, abused and beat his young wife, continued being unemployed, and a failure at everything he tried. Sunethra bore children with predictable regularity almost every other year, until she had four boys and one girl. She lost her looks, her figure, and any hopes she may have cherished of a satisfactory marriage, and was reduced to a sad, overworked drudge.

On a visit to Welimada, many years later, I was deeply distressed to see Sunethra struggle down almost half a mile to the well. She then lugged two buckets of water up the steep incline, just to wash pans, and for cooking purposes. Wimala did not even help her with such heavy work.

She told me that on some days, she stood under the Jak trees until a ripe fruit fell down, so she could collect the seeds and boil them to feed her family. When I questioned about her life, her dejected reply was, "I live from sorrow to sorrow daily." Those heart-rending words still ring in my ears, as I picture her careworn face and hands, as she struggled up the pathway with heavy buckets. Wimala somehow contrived to lay hands on enough money to buy arrack daily, but never gave Sunethra any money to buy food for the family. To make matters worse, he flew into a rage when she could not serve a decent meal for lunch or dinner, so he smashed up all the earthenware pots.

She posed this question to me passionately. "How on earth can I afford to buy new pots every time he smashes them, when we don't have enough money to buy food?" Yes, it was a very sad situation for Sunethra and her family. But no one could find a solution to help Wimala, short of getting him to join Alcoholics Anonymous, which was unheard of in Ceylon then. Most women erroneously accepted anti-social behaviour of drunken husbands, and domestic violence, as their karma (destiny).

His parents now had the added burden of supporting Wimala's growing family. My parents helped with whatever money they could spare, and Ammie sent Wimala boxes of peaches and avocados from our garden, so he could sell them. He visited often, and after a few drinks with Thathie, he still boasted about his parents' past wealth, and how rich he could have been, if not for Mutha's folly.

Wimala deteriorated rapidly, and grew gaunt through years of alcoholic abuse. Thathie, Wimala, and Chanda turned to alcohol from their early days, but Wije was a steady, hard-working man, who held a responsible job in the state archives. He married Anulawathie, a quiet, unassuming lady, and they had one daughter, Dolly, and two sons.

Wije resembled Thathie slightly, but he had an olive-complexion, and was not as lean as Thathie. Chanda was tall, slender, and good-looking, with classical features, and curly black hair. Not only was Chanda very fond of arrack, but he was inordinately attracted to women, and they were drawn to him too, so his life was one long carousel.

Chapter 8

Some of our frequent visitors in Bandarawela, were Granny, Grandpa, and their children. Whenever one of them happened to be on holidays, or when the temperatures soared in Colombo, they came over promptly. I loved my uncles and aunts, and we had some of the best times with them during those visits. Anthony took us hiking everywhere, especially to a waterfall under the great bridge on the rail track, where a deep, dark pool gleamed below.

We tumbled down the steep incline to this cool, green pool, and spent hours swimming around. Then we splashed under the sparkling waterfall that glistened in the sunshine, and cascaded down like sheets of diamonds. Anthony carried us on his shoulders one by one, as he waded into the deep end of the pool. I shrieked in fear, as the thunderous resonance of the waterfall roared in my ears. Nilanthi sat on a rock and watched us frolic, but she was too nervous to bathe in the dark pool.

After a couple of hours in the cool water, we walked back on the rail track, until we found a secluded place in the woods, or a gurgling little stream, and we stopped to have a delicious picnic. We watched people washing clothes, or bathing under sparkling water spouts, and sometimes joined in their fun. These pleasant interludes spent with our uncles and aunts forged strong bonds between us in our early years.

I can still picture our empty house, bereft of all furniture, the day before we moved out, and only ghostly silence in our once happy home. One of my school friends, Dulcie, and her family, visited us late that evening to wish us farewell, even though we were just moving to another house near by. It was customary for neighbours and friends to drop in, just to see that everything was alright. With only a naked bulb dangling forlornly from the ceiling in our bedroom, we decided to play a game of "Four Corners" there, and our shrill laughter echoed eerily through the bare house.

We referred to the house we moved into as, Raymond's house, for obvious reasons, because Mr Raymond was our landlord. I do not know if the railway reimbursed my parents for renting a house, perhaps they did. Our old house was demolished later. In due time, we took a great liking to Raymond's house, as it was modern, and more convenient than the old railway bungalow.

It was a large, spacious house; semi-circular in front, with casement windows all around. The only major drawback was the lavatory, which was situated right on top of a steep incline at the back of the house, with rough, uneven steps cut into the red earth. It was an effort going to the toilet at nights, especially when it rained, and the red earth ran in muddy rivulets down the incline. I tried to control bladder and bowels till morning (without much success though).

The lavatory stood right below the property boundary of Mrs Stephens, a hostile, shrewish, middle-aged Tamil lady, who had a grown-up daughter, and a son, Robert. He was about twenty, and quite a Casanova. Robert was sturdy, dark-skinned, and with a conceited look on his coarse features. He believed a girl should count herself lucky to rouse his interest. This is what I heard adults say, and so I was prejudiced against the young man.

As our house stood between two properties belonging to Mrs Stephens, it caused many problems all round. She particularly disliked anyone using the short cut that ran through her property, which took us directly to Poonagala main road.

Mrs Jayamane, another tyrannical, old Sinhalese lady, owned the adjoining property at the rear end, and if we so much as stepped into her garden, she screamed at us like a demented Banshee. She seemed to have eyes everywhere, because no matter what time of day, or how quietly we sneaked past her garden, she spotted us with her telescopic vision.

Just a few tall trees divided these properties. Many arguments, conflicts, and complaints ensued as a result of our "trespassing" because we just could not help ourselves when we played hide-and-seek, or took a short cut through the forbidden garden. No matter how smart we thought we were in outwitting these old women, they somehow caught us in prohibited territory, and stormed in to complain to Ammie.

The land sloped from Poonagala road right down to the railway track below, and the houses stood in the following order. In the first house, just below the main road, lived Mr Muller, and his young grandson, Barry. Mr Muller was a hunch-backed, short, fierce-looking old gentleman. He had bushy, white eyebrows, keen blue eyes, and an acerbic tongue. To me, he seemed very old then, but may have been only in his sixties or so. His rambling cottage was a potpourri of various architectural styles, East and West blended in hotch-potch style.

It was an endless source of delight to visit his cottage, and watch him cook a meal over a rackety kerosene oil stove, or clean up the place, with a grubby apron tied around his ample waist. A length of cord or string held up his tatty old trousers. Mr Muller spoke a mixture of English and Sinhalese, and although his tone was gruff, he did not fool us, because underlying kindness rippled beneath his rough exterior.

His garden was quainter than his cottage, full of interesting nooks overflowing with flowers and shrubs of every species. In one corner of the garden, Barry built a model rail track, meandering through a village amid scenic countryside. It was a marvellous model town, complete with winding rail track, toy trains, roads, hills and valleys, miniature people and trees; hills dotted with tiny living plants and shrubs, rivers, bridges, tea estates and factories, lakes and tiny houses.

I hope Barry knew then what immense pleasure I derived playing with his model village in that marvellous garden. I was fascinated to watch him adding, planting, and creating more beauty in his wonderland whenever we visited. It was Barry's one great passion, and he put his heart and soul into its creation.

Inside the cottage, I gazed spellbound at a large, black and white photograph that hung in the parlour. It was that of a beautiful, bare-shouldered, young girl, with a mass of curly hair framing an angelic countenance. This young beauty we discovered, was Mr Muller's only daughter, and Barry's mother. Ammie discussed these old scandals with her friends whenever she thought I was not listening.

That lovely young girl had left Barry and her husband, and eloped with another man. Mr Muller was left holding the baby, as her ex-husband abandoned the child after his wife left him. Barry was in his early teens when we first met him; a tall, lanky youth with an acne problem. He was as mischievous as a monkey, and totally devoid of his mother's beauty.

Below Mr Muller's house, lived the afore-mentioned Mrs Stephens, a widow with her two children, then Raymond's house, and right down our garden, a large, treed property, abundant with olive and guava trees that also belonged to the dragon lady, Mrs Stephens. Mrs Jayamana's house stood beyond that where a gravel road below was considered common property.

A winding, footpath from Poonagala road ran through the middle of this sloping land, dividing the houses I have mentioned. On the left hand side, was a huge block of land, as large as all these three properties combined, with a magnificent house right in the centre, and the treed property sloped down to the common road. It was a very large block, and belonged to Mr Muller too. He built that stunning house for his only daughter, but it was unoccupied now, shuttered and barred. An embodiment of the old man's broken dreams, and sadness. He did not talk about it at all, but it was plain to see he still cherished hopes of his daughter returning to that house, or perhaps he intended Barry to live in it someday.

Ammie soon cast longing eyes at that large, attractive house, with casement windows, and splendid gardens surrounding it. It became her dream house. It had five or six bedrooms, with attached bathrooms to a couple of them, which was a luxury in some houses then, and my parents seriously considered buying that dream house.

Thathie was transferred to Fort Station in Colombo then. He left us behind with Ammie, while he lodged with Granny and Grandpa in Maharagama. We missed him dearly, and I looked forward to weekends when he came home for two days, but I was very upset when he left us again on Sunday night. Ammie looked after us admirably, and I still wonder how she coped raising five children all by herself, as Thathie was away much of the time.

One night, as we sat down to dinner, we heard a soft tap on the window. And next moment, we started yelling our heads off when Count Dracula's eerie, leering face peered through the windowpane. Ammie sent Nihal to investigate, and of course it was Barry. He succeeded in frightening us children completely.

Dracula, the movie, was showing then, and was the current rage. Barry, who was a very clever boy, made up a mask with bloody fangs and bushy, black eyebrows, just like in the movies with Christopher Lee. He draped a black cloak over his shoulders, and with his tall, lanky build, he looked quite the part. He grinned cheekily when he saw how well his prank had succeeded. Ammie did not know whether to laugh or to scold him, so she did both, as she saw how frightened we were. Ammie threatened to tell Mr Muller, if he did not leave immediately, and stop playing practical jokes on us.

Barry left, a crestfallen Count Dracula, but irrepressible as always. We knew he would think of something else to amuse or frighten us, according to his whims. We enjoyed many good times, plenty of laughs, and bad times as well in that house.

Ammie loved dogs, and so did I, and I picked up stray mongrels whenever I saw one on the road. However, Ammie gave them away as quickly as I brought them home, even though I cried my eyes out each time my strays were taken away from me.

Nilanthi had many friends who visited us regularly; two sisters, Lorna and Chrissie, and Charmaine, were her closest friends. They loved to dress up in saris, and pose for photographs, that Chanda obligingly removed, and they still remain in the family album.

Chanda, who boarded with us, along with Swarna and Manel, flirted outrageously with all the young girls. He was very popular, especially with Lorna. Chrissie and Lorna had contracted polio as children, and in their teens now, Lorna's mouth twisted grotesquely to one side, and Chrissie's leg was lame. They were otherwise quite pretty, except for these slight, physical defects. Chanda, however, found Lorna very attractive, and formed a strong attachment.

Nilanthi was fifteen now, and a very pretty teenager, with long, dark brown hair, which was her pride and crowning glory. But whenever Nihal quarrelled with her, he still pulled her long braids, or threatened to cut them off, and chased her around, brandishing a pair of large scissors.

Every day, we walked a long way to Little Flower convent and back, and Nilanthi said, "This is a long, long journey that we are going on for the next few years, and we have to keep on walking and walking." It was a great distance to walk then. But as no buses or cars went our way, we just accepted it as part of our daily lives without complaining or moaning about it.

Many years later, I understood Nilanthi's words about our journey through school life, and it was not just the physical journey she referred to.

One day, while walking home from school, a schoolboy from St Joseph's college followed us closely, and pestered Nilanthi to give him a ring she wore on her finger. By the time we neared home, her resistance was worn down, or she was willing to oblige the boy; whatever the reason, she gave her ring to the delighted schoolboy. He hurried away, casting meaningful glances at Nilanthi, while she blushed in confusion.

Now all three of us, who stared with unashamed curiosity, chorused aloud, "we'll tell Ammie what you did!" Nilanthi burst into tears, and cried out, "If you tell Ammie, I'm going to hit a stone on my stomach and kill myself!"

We looked at her in fear, in case she carried out her alarming threat. When we reached home however, it did not prevent us brats from sneaking to Ammie about Nilanthi's awful deed. Ammie was a disciplinarian when it came to such matters.

She ensured we kept in line, without displaying any weakness on her part, so we were well-disciplined, kept regular hours where meals, homework, and bed-time were concerned. Nilanthi was absolutely forbidden to have boyfriends, even as pen pals. But she could not help attracting them, as she was such a pretty young girl, and she was not to blame if boys fell in love with her or vice versa.

That episode of the ring ended with Nilanthi getting a sound beating and scolding from Ammie, with dire threats thrown in for good measure, that she would inform Thathie, and Mother Superior about her brazen behaviour with strange boys etc. etc. Nilanthi cried and pleaded desperately, and Ammie relented slightly.

Ammie was a very good organiser too, and ran our household like clockwork, with Menika as her second-in-command. We did at least one hour of homework daily, dinner was sharp at seven o'clock, and after a bit of fun and games, bedtime was at nine o'clock.

Every night, she packed Thathie's meal of rice and curry, and wrapped it up in a banana leaf. Then the five of us, Menika and Ammie, walked along the rail track to the station at eight o'clock, in time for the night mail to Colombo. The guard promised to deliver Thathie's meal personally.

I am still full of admiration for Ammie's wifely devotion and concern for Thathie, as she did not want him to miss out on a delicious, home-cooked meal for lunch. On one such nocturnal walk, I stumbled in the dark, and hit my shin bone on one of the metal posts at the side of the track. I still bear that scar.

Whenever Thathie was home for the weekend, he was just like Santa Claus visiting us, with his bags full of delicious sweets and goodies, comic books, toys, and sometimes, clothes or shoes. We sent him drawings of our feet sizes outlined on a sheet of paper, and using them as a guide, he purchased shoes for us. He was a caring father.

Before he returned to Colombo on Sunday nights, Ammie embraced him and cried heartily. I blinked hard, fighting back tears, and stared at pictures on the walls, because I did not want anyone to see me cry.

My parents appreciated the funny side of life, and I believe that helped them weather many storms and troubles in their young lives. Thathie said he was an eternal schoolboy, a perennial Peter Pan. This trait caused him to forget his sense of responsibility sometimes, and led him to strife.

Whenever five of us were together, we had fun, and a sense of the ridiculous made us forget our cares, as we laughed and joked about ludicrous situations and people. On-lookers may have thought we had nothing but sunshine and laughter in our lives, but our laughter concealed any sadness or trouble we faced as children. Ammie and Thathie loved those family get togethers, when we laughed and joked as if there was no tomorrow.

One day, Mrs Stephens stormed in angrily. And Ammie was furious to learn that her son, Robert, and Nilanthi had been exchanging love letters. The old woman said she had "accidentally" come across their letters, but personally, I believe she must have snooped around her son's room.

"I saw them talking over the fence!" she screeched accusingly. Talking to boys, and exchanging love letters, were deemed a serious crime in the eyes of puritanical parents such as Mrs Stephens, and to a lesser degree, my parents.

Such a commotion exploded that day, and Ammie, who had only Nihal as the man in the house, sent for Mr Muller in her hour of need. Now, what this doddering old man was expected to do, was beyond me. In the full force of her anger, Ammie wanted a "token" father figure present while she meted out suitable punishment.

Mr Muller stammered and stuttered, totally bewildered, and at a loss to know what he was expected to do. After some hesitant advice to Nilanthi, he stumbled out of the house hastily. Banda, a teenage boy, who had just come into service, was invaluable to Ammie now. He delighted in the role of spy, and reported any chance conversation the young lovers had.

I watched wide-eyed as Ammie beat Nilanthi soundly to the accompaniment of tongue lashing and fearsome threats. She bundled up Nilanthi's uniforms and threw them into the disused well at the bottom of the garden, saying she was not going to attend school anymore. It was such a drama that day, and the scene remains fresh in my mind. Nilanthi, meanwhile, cried buckets of tears, till she finally went to bed.

What made matters worse was that Ammie and Mrs Stephens disliked each other immensely, and were openly hostile. She gloated now, and blamed Nilanthi for leading her precious son astray. And Ammie made Nilanthi's life quite miserable with relentless scolding. But it did not prevent Robert from carrying on behind his mother's back. He continued to exchange letters, and stole brief moments with Nilanthi over the fence.

In spite of her threats, Ammie did not stop Nilanthi's schooling. Instead, she wrote to the principal, Mother Concilia, whose notion of proper upbringing coincided closely with that of the Spanish Inquisition. Banda sneaked to Ammie if he so much as glimpsed Robert around the garden, or just smiled at Nilanthi.

Banda was very clever, and carved toys out of wood. He had a sense of fun too, as he loved to browse through our picture books and comics. I walked up to the library in Bandarawela town, just to read comics, as dozens of shiny new ones came in every week. Banda came to accompany me home when it got too late, but sometimes he sat in the library and went through comics, chuckling and giggling aloud.

Several diversions filled my days, and sometimes, when Swarna and Manel went home for holidays to Haputale, where their father was post master, five of us joined them to spend a few days.

Chapter 9

That house in Haputale where Daisy Akka and Ulwita lived alone, was cold, large, and cheerless, and reminded me of Charles Dickens's story, "Bleak House." I noticed too that Daisy Akka and Ulwita hardly spoke to each other. And it seemed a strange sort of marriage, as they lived like strangers. Family gossip, and a breath of scandal wafted around them, but the skeleton in the closet remained hidden behind lock and key.

I did find out later they had separated for some time, and had reconciled for the sake of the children. But I never discovered the inexplicable reason behind Ulwita's frosty, unforgiving attitude towards Daisy Akka. Perhaps she committed an indiscretion a long time ago, and he nursed a deep resentment? Who knows, but it was obvious Ulwita neglected her as a wife for the rest of their married lives. I often wondered why Daisy Akka walked around with head bowed low, and an air of crushed defeat.

I remember her as a frail, sad person most of her life. But she was very kind, pleasant, and soft-spoken, and never raised her voice to the children, or to anyone else for that matter. Ulwita sometimes took us on his motorcycle around town, and in the evenings he amused us with his magic tricks, especially cards.

Manel and Swarna were not very close to each other then. And later in life, their relationship deteriorated further when Ulwita made an unfair property settlement, leaving most of his assets to Manel, who was his favourite even then. But as a child, I had no idea of all these underlying emotions and intrigues. I spent those holidays playing in their garden most of the time, as it was abundant with pear trees burdened with luscious fruits.

It was always good to return home, and away from such a cold, depressing house, and back to our warm, happy environment.

Ulwita died when he was in his sixties, and Daisy Akka continued to live with her daughter, Manel, and her family until the end of her days.

I corresponded with her regularly through the years; her gentle letters were affectionate, and her fine handwriting impressed me. Her world revolved around her grandchildren, and great grandchildren, who were fortunate to have her for a long time. She lived to be well over ninety five or more, although she suffered from dementia and blindness at the end.

In the months that followed, Chanda's romance with Lorna blossomed, as they were very much in love. Ammie gave her seal of approval, as she was fond of Lorna and Chanda, so she visited often with her sister.

Marie and Elmo visited once, as they were dating. Elmo was tall, well-built, and good-looking, with black hair and eyes. He was Aunty Pansy's son. But he married someone else a couple of years later, as their teenage romance lasted only as long as their brief holiday. Elmo brought his tame pet squirrel, and it climbed everywhere. It ran around the garden, and scampered in when Elmo whistled. I loved holding the soft, furry little animal whenever Elmo was busy entertaining Marie, and was sad when he took that cheeky little squirrel back.

After about one year in Raymond's house, it was a great moment when Mr Muller agreed to sell his vacant house for about twenty thousand rupees, which was a small fortune then. And in preparation for the sale, Mr Muller cleaned up rubbish stored in the house, and aired it.

He unearthed some rare treasures (to my childish mind), soft furs and stoles, some still intact, with beady-eyed fox heads, furry tails, and paws (an animal activist's nightmare); several old books, odd bits of furniture, pictures, and many forgotten items too numerous to mention. It was as if the old man had unlocked a past era, as we watched the pile grow bigger and bigger in the garden.

Sometimes, he held some object in his hand, as if a memory awakened, gazed wistfully, and then shoved it away, as if ashamed of his weakness. He spoke gruffly, and cut short my questions, as though memories he stirred were too painful. I often wondered about his wife, and whether he was widowed or divorced, but no one ever mentioned anything about his past, so I never knew Mr Muller's history.

He told us to keep anything we wanted from the jumble he had thrown in the garden, and waved his arms around airily, as if to denote he could not care less if we took the whole lot. The overgrown garden, neglected now, would have been a fantastic place once.

A dozen or more peach trees heavily laden with large, juicy fruits grew around the front. Pomegranate, Cherimoire, Avocado, Guava, Mango trees, and many other attractive ornamentals grew profusely as well. Ammie already planned what she would plant at the bottom of the garden, as it sloped down to the road below. She thought red cannas bordering the side of the stone steps would look effective, and proved a colourful feature when they bloomed.

Ammie also planted every variety and colour of gladioli she could find, and in time the garden looked spectacular. As it was going to take another month or so for us to move in to the dream house, our life continued as normal at Raymond's house; going to school, playing till late evening, and in my case, accumulating dogs and cats whenever I saw a stray.

I owned a few story books with enchanting pictures, most of which were nursery rhymes and fairy tales. As books were very expensive, and a luxury, it was a great privilege to possess those few books. I had one special book that I loved very much, as it had the most beautiful illustrations I had ever seen. One day, when I came home from school, I ran to get my favourite book and read for a while. Imagine my horror and anger when I discovered all the pictures were neatly cut out, and Ammie happily pasting them on flower pots to decorate them! Only a book lover would understand my anguish.

I bawled my eyes out, "It was my favourite book, why did you cut out the pictures?" Ammie must have felt guilty and remorseful, but she never let on or apologised to me (unheard of for a parent to apologise to a child in those days). All she said was, "*Stop* acting like a *baby!* That was an *old* book anyway!" She did not pacify me with the promise of another or a better book. No, she just ignored me, and went on pasting those beautiful pictures on her flower pots. In time, I forgave her, and forgot all about the book, once I accumulated a few more.

Banda took us children to visit his parents one day. We walked along the rail track away from the station, where houses stood on either side of the track. Then we climbed a steep road, and arrived at his home, which was a clean mud-brick dwelling with a thatched roof. The garden and mud floor of the house were swept clean, and as we sat on chairs and benches, Banda proudly showed off his little domain.

His parents were kind, humble old people, who said they were honoured that we visited, and treated us hospitably. We had tea, and I ate biscuits hungrily. Later, I watched with great interest a game called "Booruwa" (donkey), that they played with small sea shells.

Banda, his father, Nihal, and a few other male companions, were the main players. One of them picked up five or six shells in his hand, and with a little twist of the wrist tossed them up, just like throwing dice, and dropped the shells on the ground. Excited yells greeted this, as players strained to see which way the shells had fallen. An innocent pastime (I thought), until I found out that it was a form of small time gambling for rather modest stakes.

After that interesting visit to his home, we returned late with an excitable Banda. He could not stop talking about future plans he had discussed with his parents. He was very clever and intelligent, and knew he did not want to be a servant boy for the rest of his days. Now he hoped to work on a sugar plantation in remote jungles in the north, as the money they offered was very tempting. He enthused wildly, "They even give us *boots*! I get to wear *boots*!" He seemed to think free boots alone was a great incentive to work in the plantations.

Mrs Herath was a splendid teacher at Little Flower convent, whom I remember well. She was about six feet tall, slim and graceful; an attractive, rosy-complexioned lady, with long, black hair, twisted and braided around her head, and held with a net. She was married to a Sinhalese gentleman, a highly-respected government agent in Bandarawela, and although she was a Burgher, she always wore a Kandyan sari.

My love of history and English literature grew deeper because of her exceptional ability to make history come alive. She organised many plays for end of term concerts, and no matter how small a part it was, I would invariably act in the plays, and so would Nilanthi and Shirani. Those were exciting and grand experiences, walking on stage self-consciously, knowing that all our friends, parents, and teachers were in the audience. My parents attended these concerts sometimes, if they could.

School life was good and enjoyable in Little Flower convent. Ammie was quite friendly with all our teachers, especially Mrs Herath, who lived in a large, impressive house on the outskirts of Bandarawela town. Many fruit and guava trees of every variety grew in their huge garden that extended to a few acres.

Her teenage daughter, Loren, attended Good Shepherd convent in Kandy, an exclusive, private school. She was a fun-loving girl, who entertained us with all sorts of droll stories about her classmates and teachers. Whenever we visited them, we quickly headed off to the garden, and ate guavas until I felt sick. Ammie and Mrs Herath compared notes about us, I am sure.

Loren taught us how to concoct a mouth-watering snack. She scooped out seeds from green mangoes, filled them with pepper and salt, and using a guava stick as a pestle, she pounded pepper and salt in the hollow of the mango. We cut them into thin wedges and devoured the fruit greedily. It was yummy, and Loren mumbled with her mouth full, "Isn't this simply scrumptious?"

Nilanthi and I went with Ammie on these visits, and returned home loaded with bags of guavas for the rest of the family. Mrs Herath sometimes lent her slide viewer, View Master (before the advent of videos and DVD's), together with numerous slides of Biblical stories, cartoons and fairytales. I spent hours of pure bliss viewing those magical, three-dimensional slides that seemed so real. One vivid scene I particularly recall is the story of St John the Baptist and Salome, when Salome presents his head on a golden platter to her mother, Herodias. It was gruesomely detailed in technicolour, and its realism repulsed yet fascinated me.

Our geography teacher, Miss Violet, was a great friend of Mrs Herath's, and some days, they wore identical saris and jackets, which I thought was quite amusing. Miss Violet was not very tall, dark-skinned, with curly, black hair that she wore in a bun at the nape of her neck. She was gap-toothed, and her front teeth were noticeably apart. When she laughed aloud, her gravely voice grated harshly on my ears. She was pleasant, but I found her classes utterly boring compared to Mrs Herath's.

Another teacher, Miss Vinasathambi, had the longest hair I ever saw. Her black braids cascaded to her ankles, and when she walked fast, it was mesmeric to watch the braids swing from side to side. She was of average height, slender as a sapling, fair-skinned and attractive. I forget what subject she taught us, but to me her long hair was a constant source of interest. Ammie visited June and Lorna sometimes, two pretty Burgher girls in their mid-twenties. Their father was an engine driver in the railway, and he carved two elegant lamp stands out of guava branches for Ammie. I have the smaller one that my parents gave me. It still sits on my desk, and brings back tender memories of those halcyon days.

My friend, Coreen, was a year older, and she told me droll stories about her family and friends. At nine years of age, she was more mature, and the bizarre things she said did not make much sense, but I understood only later. She was cute and precocious, and a favourite with the teachers, and her older sister, Rita, was in Nilanthi's class.

One day, while playing "catch" during lunch break, Coreen and I ran along concrete paths that surrounded the convent blocks. We rushed in from opposite directions, when wham! The lights went out! We collided into each other so hard that I felt my head spinning around dizzily. Coreen's head bumped into my eye, and it was swelling up fast.

Sobbing and badly shaken, I stood before Mrs Herath. She immediately bathed my eye with iced water, and sent me home with Nilanthi. It was a long walk home, and Ammie was very upset to see my bruised eye now turning black. I had a few days off from school, and plenty of fussing at home, which assuaged my pain somewhat.

One evening, soon after that, I chased butterflies, and imprisoned them in an old biscuit tin that I decorated with moss and flowers. Menika said it was the Siripada season (pilgrimage to Adam's Peak), and all these beautiful, blue butterflies flew up to the Peak, and dashed themselves against rocks in homage to Buddha. Deeply distressed at such meaningless mass suicide, I was determined to save as many as possible.

I chased them (without a net), and suddenly slipped down a precipice near a Jak tree, where the soft, treacherous bank was covered with gravel and broken glass. Badly bruised, I required immediate medical attention. A few fragments of glass, and some gravel embedded in my side had to be removed, which was quite painful.

Some days later, we waited at the railway station one night, hoping to catch a glimpse of Prime Minister, Mr Bandaranaike. He alighted from the train shortly, and spoke briefly to the staff. I vaguely remember the Prime Minister's toothy smile, and a few handshakes all around. As his train disappeared into the misty night, I climbed down to the tracks under another stationary train to save my pet dog embroiled with a stray. Next moment, the other dog bit my arm viciously. The Prime Minister's brief stopover was definitely forgotten in the panic that followed, and the rest of the night remained a blur of pain. I still have that scar on my arm.

My parents said they had nightmares, because I was always getting into some scrape or another, and sometimes was badly injured. Thathie once told me, "I still wake up in a sweat, when I think of what could have happened, if that train had pulled out of the station!"

Elmo and Doreen visited one day while still on their honeymoon. Doreen was a very pretty lady. She had a great time teasing Elmo as she flipped through our family album and came across photographs of Marie and him together. Elmo's ears and face turned red as a capsicum at her good-humoured banter. Menika giggled and whispered to Nilanthi that Doreen was scantily clad in a sheer negligee when she took their morning tea. But I failed to see anything amusing in that piece of information, and told Menika so. But she giggled helplessly.

We spent a few days or weeks at Granny's place when we were on school holidays. The train journeys there were exciting, and the compartment was crowded with boxes full of provisions to last us during our stay. Sometimes, as we stepped in at Granny's, she started an argument with Ammie, which dragged on. Anthony intervened, and yelled, "For God's sake Mummy, stop arguing! Carmen and Raja have just arrived with the children, and they have brought enough provisions to last a month!"

I never understood the reason for Granny's displeasure, but in a few minutes, Rosie, Malcolm, and Anthony joined us as we ran out to the paddy fields or shrub land near-by. Rosie smoked as a very young girl, so it was an excuse to get out of the house for some time, while she lit up cigarette after cigarette, and joked away the hours. Malcolm and Anthony turned a blind eye as they could not stop her bad habit.

Granny employed an emaciated, young Tamil girl, Rasamani, a good worker, but she was never good enough for Granny. I hated to hear the girl screaming in pain whenever Granny beat her for a slight misdemeanour. Rosie too defended the girl whenever she got into trouble, which made Granny angrier. But in spite of the rough treatment, Rasamani lived with Granny for a very long time until she was an old woman.

Chapter 10

One afternoon, while Shirani and I were playing in the garden, we spied some ripe guavas, and shiny big olives that had fallen from Mrs Stephen's trees on to our side of the garden. Naturally, we picked up the delicious fruits, and enjoyed every delectable bite. But the sharp-eyed dragon spotted us, and ran up in a huff to complain angrily that we had stolen her fruits.

Ammie chastised us, but we were unrepentant, as we stubbornly maintained we were entitled to eat fruits that fell on *our* side of the property. Such incidents in the meandering road of my childhood, impacted on me strongly. Although I was too young to ponder about the meaning of life, morality, ethics, and principles, the nuns and teachers, together with Ammie, helped weave my moral fibre with a deeply-rooted conviction of right and wrong. An intrinsic conscientiousness was firmly instilled in my young mind, together with an inevitable guilt complex, as a result of a strict Catholic upbringing.

The guilt started with little omissions, and "venial sins" that had to be confessed to the nuns and to our parents. All childish mischief and misdemeanours took on gargantuan proportions of sinfulness. And as I was constantly told, "God is watching you all the time," it tended to throw a damper on my childish enjoyment and pleasures sometimes. But in spite of strict disciplinarians around, I took childish pleasure in indulging in all sorts of adventures and escapades, no matter what the consequences were. I lived my childhood days to the fullest.

The nuns related stories about the lives of saints, and I did try hard to emulate their exemplary behaviour (but not with much success I am afraid). Reading good literature at an early age too, filled my mind with lofty aspirations. I was determined to uphold noble principles, and go through life as courageously as the heroes and heroines who lived in my story books.

I never stopped to question actions of other family members, as we were all growing up in our own little private worlds. We loved each other dearly, and stood by each other whenever one of us got into a scrape. We were, and are strong individualists, every single one of us. We followed our own dreams, but right through childhood and adulthood, a special bond of love, devotion, and loyalty bound us together closely.

Nilanthi was the beauty in the family; Nihal, a great tease, and a practical joker, I was impulsive and a dreamer, who loved books and music, Shirani was strong-willed, intelligent and quiet, and Nelune was just beginning to show signs of being a good mimic (like Nihal). We all possessed a keen sense of humour, and derived great amusement when people around us exposed their idiosyncrasies. The slightest hint of absurdity or stupidity was enough to send us into fits of giggles and laughter.

The great day came when we finally moved to 'Our House' as we called it. We went to school as usual, and when we returned home that afternoon, Ammie arranged everything with the help of Menika and Banda, so we just slipped comfortably into the same routine in our new home. We girls shared a large bedroom at the front of the house, with an attached bathroom. I am at a loss to know where to start to describe that wonderful house, and my first impressions of it. But to me, and the rest of the family, it was just perfect in every sense of the word.

Our bedroom window looked out to a garden full of multi-coloured gladioli and peach trees. Nihal had his own room, and my parents occupied the middle bedroom. Ammie planned to rent out the fourth largest bedroom to a few boarders, so she could subsidise mortgage repayments. The rest of the house was airy and spacious, and Ammie made every room attractive and cosy. She was in her element now, planning the garden, and re-decorating the house exactly as she pleased. Thathie never bothered about domestic details, and left all that to Ammie. The rear of the house contained a separate dining room, pantry and kitchen, besides a large storage-room. Ammie soon turned overgrown patches into a delightful garden, and instructed Banda to cut steps down the slope of the front garden to the common pathway at the bottom. On either side of these steps, Ammie planted red cannas that blossomed most of the year, creating superb colour and interest in the garden.

Banda was a good carpenter too, and built a hot house on the side of the main house. He made mud bricks in the garden, and built a shed. Ammie kept all sorts of flowering plants inside, and hanging baskets full of trailing plants and geraniums. I played doll house inside that shed, and had a great time there. One day, Banda decided to build us a tree house on one of the spreading mango trees at the bottom of the garden.

The tree house was quite an impressive structure when it was completed, as it had two levels, and a rope hanging from the centre (just like in the Tarzan movies). It would take numerous pages to describe the many games we played, and the hours of unalloyed pleasure in that tree house, as we pretended to be hunters, and raided all the fruit trees.

Menika too joined in the fun, and allowed us to devour sweet tamarillos from her kitchen garden, but in the heat of our hunting raids, we sometimes snatched more fruit and vegetables than was allowed. At such times, we were in Menika's bad books, and she scolded us for being so naughty and destructive.

The days passed happily as we flitted between school and home. Thathie still worked at Fort Station, and came home only on weekends. I set out my nursery table and chairs, with about ten dolls seated around it, and waited impatiently for Thathie to come home on Saturday mornings with plenty of goodies. Then I feasted on all the food, and pretended the dolls had eaten it all.

School was interesting too, because I liked learning, and at eight years, I once memorized all the verses of the "Village Blacksmith" by Oliver Goldsmith. And I recited it in such a sing-song fashion that I wonder how my teacher, Sr Lourdina, ever kept a straight face. She took us outdoors in warm weather for English lessons, and as we sat under the shade of a giant old Eucalyptus tree, I listened attentively to her remarkable stories.

Sr Lourdina was another excellent teacher, and I gazed at her in awe, as in stirring tones she recited all the best-loved, great poetry, instilling and awakening in me a passionate love for this form of writing, that she described as the "Purest form of expression." As Shirani and I were together during most of our lessons, because our two classes shared the same room, a friendly rivalry rose between us sometimes. And we were quick to carry tales to Ammie, if one of us got into trouble.

Right through childhood, and up to our early teens, Shirani and I quarrelled incessantly over the most trivial matters, but later on, we bonded well, and grew very attached. It was an amazing transition from childhood to adulthood, and five of us remained best of friends through the years. No one ever quarrelled with Nelune though, because she was the baby in the family, and everyone's pet. Nilanthi was a proper little spitfire, who quarrelled with the rest of us, called us nicknames, and made us cry.

Although we bawled and yelled and complained to Ammie, it did not stop Nilanthi from teasing us or Nihal mostly, and vice versa. I was quite hot-tempered as a child, and my temper reached boiling point when Nilanthi and Nihal teased me endlessly. They cheated shamelessly at "Snakes and Ladders" and "Ludo" just to annoy me, and when I was reduced to tears, they laughed and teased me all the more. It was a real trial then to control my temper, and hold my tongue in the face of such blatant cheating. And it was only years later that I learnt to bite back retorts, control my temper, and laugh off trivial matters.

Even at a very young age, I had a highly-developed sense of fairness, and a passion to speak out my mind truthfully, no matter what the consequences, and a keen sense of duty and justice. My family noticed these traits, because I was never afraid to voice my opinion, and could not bear to see a servant being ill-treated, and eagerly protected helpless animals. I assumed the role of champion of the underdog, no matter at what cost.

One day, when Barry was painting a garden wall in bright red, and Nihal, face upturned, stood under the ladder holding it steady, Barry, in a spirit of pure mischief, swished the loaded paint brush right across Nihal's face! Imagine Nihal's expression, and his outrage as he promptly slapped Barry so hard that the latter's face turned just as red as Nihal's. Nihal's temper was much more volatile and alarming than mine, and on many occasions his temper exploded under the slightest provocation.

Barry seriously under-estimated Nihal's tolerance levels that time. He jumped down from the ladder, looked at Nihal like a stunned mullet, and ran inside before he burst into tears. Nihal was furious, as he spent hours rubbing and cleaning his face with turpentine and soap, until he had cleaned most of the red paint off his face.

Ammie took in four young schoolboys as boarders, and co-incidentally, one of the boys happened to be the besotted teenager, who had pestered Nilanthi for her ring. Whether Ammie was aware of it or not, I do not know, but that romance too died a natural death, just like all teenage infatuations.

These young boys, being away from their own families, readily adopted us, and became our extended family, and on some evenings they joined in our "sing-along" or games, and we had happy times. On one such occasion, one of the boys annoyed Nihal with a silly comment, and Nihal lost his temper. He gave the boy such a scolding that the poor fellow just melted into his room with a hang dog look. The others hastily put aside their mouth organs and silver spoons, with which they had been making music, and vanished just as silently into their room. Nihal, I suppose, had assumed the role of "Head of the family" while Thathie was away, and he frowned upon anyone who tried to be too familiar with us.

Elsie, a spindly, unattractive spinster, who taught at our school, boarded with us for some time too. She had large, uneven teeth, straggly hair, and spittle flew out when she lisped. We called her "Elsie teacher" and she brought a large, tin trunk with her. She padlocked it every morning before going out. One day, she cried and yelled angrily that someone had opened her trunk and pilfered some items. She would not be pacified, and shouted out, "I know how I lock the trunk, and which way the padlock stays! Someone has broken into my trunk! I'm leaving here!" So she left almost immediately, and I did not see her again.

Once, we all got together and started teasing Banda over something or another, and to our utter dismay, he vengefully pulled down our tree house board by board! Only the forlorn rope dangled before my incredulous eyes. How *could* he have done such a thing! I cried remorsefully now, as we had not intended to make him that angry. I took one small board, and set it across the branches, where I sat sadly and watched Menika potter about in her vegetable garden.

She smiled cheerfully, and held out some fruit to pacify me, so I sat there slightly mollified, as I munched on the delicious fruit. I had spent many happy hours there, and had so much of fun, especially when I wanted to hide from people, like the time some of Nilanthi's sophisticated friends from Colombo visited.

They sat on the bench under the tree, discussing a movie they had seen, "Adam and Eve." One of the girls giggled, and whispered to Nilanthi. "And they had *no* clothes on!" Nilanthi was agog, and all ears. My curiosity was roused. I moved closer, but they saw me snooping in the tree house and chased me away.

Nihal went to the movies alone sometimes, but if I asked him to take me with him, he obliged, if he was in a good mood. One movie I saw with Nihal was, "G.I BLUES" starring Elvis Presley, who was well on his way to the pinnacle of popularity and stardom. I was so excited after the movie, that I could not stop talking about it, especially the "Punch and Judy" scene, where Elvis sings "Wooden Heart."

Mutha, who happened to be visiting us, smiled kindly at my non-stop chatter, while the rest of the family kindly asked me to "put a lid on it." On another occasion, Nihal took Nelune and me to see a horror movie, "The Mummy" which was an Adults Only movie. The cinema manager pointed this out to Nihal, who replied airily, "I can't send the children back home alone, and anyway, I'm sure they won't be scared of such stuff, and if they do get scared, they will just shut their eyes and go to sleep!" Nihal persuaded the manager to let us in to the cinema with him, and he finally gave in, as he knew Nihal and our family quite well.

However, the frightful scene of the "Mummy" rising from a misty, murky swamp, and hobbling off with the terrified heroine, and the scary scenes that followed right through the movie, were branded in my memory for years, and caused many nightmares. I wonder how it affected Nelune. Perhaps she was too young to be scared. We walked back home subdued, but I did not want to show Nihal how scared I was of the "Mummy" because then he would refuse to take me to the movies again.

Chapter 11

A fluffy, white dog that we named Tony, came into our lives around this time. His black eyes shone through furry brows, and I had a great deal of fun dressing him up in striped pyjamas. He had such a droll expression on his face that I laughed merrily when I got him to sit up on his hind legs. One evening, during dinner time (I had finished mine earlier), I was playing with Tony under the dining table. Deeply engrossed in a marrow bone, he ignored me completely, which made me angry, so I yanked his tail very hard. Next moment he snapped back and sank his sharp teeth into my hand.

I yelled out in pain. Ammie scolded, and shouted angrily when she saw the wound was deep, and my hand bled profusely. *"Don't* you know better than that to tease Tony when he's chewing a bone?" I kept on crying and snivelling while she washed the wound with disinfectant.

I was in pain all night, as my hand throbbed and ached. One of the boarders took me to the clinic next morning where a nurse cleaned and dressed the wound. Fortunately, Tony was immunised against rabies, so I did not need twenty one injections, which was mandatory then for a dog bite. One would think after this experience I would leave dogs well alone. But no, just a few weeks later, when we were seeing Thathie off at the station one night, Tony got into a fight with a stray dog.

The dogs snarled, bit, spat and rolled onto the track under two trains stopped at the platform. I slipped under one of the trains without anyone noticing, and tried to pull Tony away, and suffered another gash on my upper arm. Thathie spotted me and yelled angrily, as he pulled me from under the train. He was very annoyed, but only because he was frightened of what could have happened if the trains had pulled out. The family regarded me as a mischievous, foolhardy child.

A rich couple with an only daughter, Primrose, who was about my age, lived down the road. She was a "poor little rich girl" because although her parents doted on her, and gave her everything money could buy, she always complained about how lonely she was without any brothers and sisters to play with. She ran up the steep steps to spend every spare moment she could, as our home was always full of noisy laughter and enjoyment. We played tricks on each other or quarrelled over some trivial matter, which Primrose loved. She watched our antics delightedly, while hugging the most beautiful doll I had ever seen. That doll was a real beauty, with golden curls, and blue eyes fringed with thick black lashes. I secretly coveted that doll, and wished with all my heart I could have it or one just like it.

One afternoon, while playing "tea party" with our dolls, a servant girl ran up to call Primrose home. "Come home now, because your aunt and uncle arrived from Colombo." Primrose was so excited, she promptly left her beautiful doll behind, saying, "You can have her! I don't want a doll, now that my aunt and uncle are here!" She scampered off, and there I was, holding the much-longed for doll. The joy of acquisition was great indeed.

I just finished re-seating my doll family, with the newcomer taking precedence, when the servant girl ran up again. "Nona is very angry with Primrose missy for giving her doll to you, and she wants me to bring it back immediately!" Talk about fleeting joys. What a pang it caused me to hand over that doll.

Further down the road, four girls and their mother lived in a large house. Nilanthi made friends with them, and they visited often, and vice versa. In the last house down that road, lived an old widowed lady, who was reputed to be very cruel to her servant girl. We heard awful stories about her brutality to the young woman, and Menika said, "I'm so thankful I don't get beaten up and treated as badly as that poor girl."

One day, we heard the shocking news, that in desperation, the poor servant girl jumped in front of an express train. She escaped death narrowly, but was badly injured. We saw her once after a long time, with shaven head and deep scars. I often wondered what became of her, as she had no family, and was compelled to live with the old tyrant.

Nihal enjoyed dressing up as a soldier, and he posed for photographs whenever he was in uniform. They still bring back happy memories of those days. He attended the cadet camp in Diyatalawa, and when he returned home, he was full of amusing anecdotes. Nihal was extremely proud of his achievements there, and wanted to be a soldier.

The four of us studied in English, as Little Flower convent was still a private school. But Nihal studied in Sinhalese, as St Joseph's college phased out English classes. This led to a hotch potch of languages at home, as we conversed fluently in English and Sinhalese. My parents always spoke to each other in English, but they sometimes spoke to us in Sinhalese. In later years, it was only English. It was an advantage knowing both languages then. I also understood a smidgen of Tamil, because we had many friends and neighbours, who spoke Tamil. Nilanthi spoke all three languages fluently.

I was not too keen on learning Sinhalese grammar, because it seemed very difficult then. I skipped Sinhalese classes quite happily, even though it was only a half hour lesson. So I never did master Sinhalese grammar, although I spoke it fluently.

Our religious practices too were mixed, because Thathie did not consent to our baptism. Although we attended Sunday school after Mass, and went to Catholic schools, the nuns told us we did not really "belong" to the Catholic church because we were not baptised.

This state of religious limbo was brought home forcibly one day. A nun asked all the Catholic children to raise their hands. My hand was up instantly, but she reprimanded me sternly. "Put down your hand at once, you are a *non*-Catholic!" I was flabbergasted. I thought of myself as a Catholic, especially because of Ammie's daily example, and her deep, religious beliefs that she instilled from my early days.

I heard titters and stifled giggles in the class room, and being very sensitive, I resented the nun's words. Whenever we asked Ammie, "Why aren't we baptised?" she replied solemnly, "Thathie won't give permission." Although Nihal attended a Catholic college, he was loyal to Thathie. He thought that as the only son, he was duty-bound. Nihal declared he was a Buddhist, but he never went to a temple, or followed any of Buddha's precepts and philosophy. He just wanted Thathie to know he was on his side.

This sort of religious division in our family though never affected us. But stress and friction arose whenever it came to questions of schooling, education, and our baptism.

I was enthusiastic about Catholicism all my life. And I am grateful to Ammie for bringing me up as a Catholic, as I faithfully observed all the doctrines and rituals of the Catholic church from my young days. Those were the days when one had to abstain from food and water three hours before receiving Holy Communion. Fasting and abstinence were obligatory on certain days, especially Good Friday.

Ammie set a good example, as she attended Sunday Mass faithfully, observed holy days of obligation, did penance by fasting and abstinence. Her faith was almost child-like faith, which I found admirable, because that was exactly what Jesus Christ asks of us, to have faith in him, like children. I loved to hear Biblical stories, and remembered religious knowledge lessons well, which proved to be useful when we finally received the Sacraments one day.

Ammie taught me how to be reverent in church, modesty and decency in speech and attire, especially in church, or when we visited friends. I did not understand exactly what modesty meant then, as it was just an interesting word. But when I was older, I appreciated Ammie's efforts to instil good values, and for teaching me the importance of self-respect.

Bold, loud colours were definitely taboo during Lent and Good Friday, and we wore short, white lace veils in church. Ammie was a good example of a devout, convinced Catholic, who did not give up her religion when she married an intolerant Buddhist. She continued to uphold her beliefs, and even in the teeth of violent opposition she brought us up as Catholics too. I never fail to esteem her for such courage.

A few railway families employed Edwin, an odd-job man, to deliver lunch packets to school children. Some mothers sent hot rice and curry neatly served on a plate, and tied up with a large tea cloth. Edwin brought these delicious meals stored inside a large, wooden box he carried on his head.

He was a stumpy, bow-legged man, with a thick lower lip jutting over his upper lip, and concealed uneven gold-capped teeth. He wore baggy, knee-length khaki shorts. All the children made up a ditty, and sang it loud whenever Edwin came. It was not very polite, and went like this in Sinhalese, "Edwin padda, Colombota ahuna." It loses its punch in translation, but meant, "Edwin farted, and was heard in Colombo!" We just roared with laughter, as the children sang this ditty non-stop, much to the old man's annoyance.

It was rather unkind, considering that he brought our daily meals. The food always tasted absolutely delicious, and I was ravenous by lunch time. Long tables and benches stood under cover in a corridor, where we sat and ate our meals. Sometimes, as I sat enjoying my hot, delicious meal, teachers stopped and exclaimed. "My, that smells delicious!" I reddened with embarrassment, as I stood in awe of my teachers, and was not on such familiar terms with them.

Compulsory bun and milk rations were issued to all school children, irrespective of social and financial standing. Some charitable organisations in Western countries, supplied powdered milk, and flour for the buns. With due respect to those well-meaning organisations, I must say, that *never* in my life have I tasted such awful milk, and it was torture to swallow that smelly, gooey fluid. I was so nauseated every time I had to drink it, that finally I persuaded Ammie to write a letter to the nuns, saying the milk made me ill. The sickly smell of it seeps into my memory and nauseates me still just thinking about it. Honestly, it was that bad.

Every morning, the milk powder was dissolved in a huge, stainless steel cauldron, and a nun (like one of the witches in Macbeth), stood over it with a ladle. Children queued up and held tin mugs, reminiscent of orphans in the story, Oliver Twist, but unlike starving little Oliver, they never ever asked for more. It was compulsory to eat a rock-hard bun, and swallow that awful concoction daily. If anyone made a fuss or refused such unpalatable nourishment, the nuns read a lecture on "sinful pride" and "waste." But to my great relief, I was finally exempted from this bun and milk ritual.

Sundays were very special days, as the church was full of Ammie's and our friends. And to me, the best part of going to church, was the social inter-action after Mass. We played, while Ammie chatted, and it was always more than an hour or so later when we returned home.

During Lent and on Good Fridays, we wore black, grey or white, and on Easter Sunday, it was always red and white (symbolic colours of the risen Christ). She never failed to observe these rituals. Imagine Ammie's chagrin one Good Friday, as we knelt devoutly in church, when Nilanthi breezed in a little later, wearing a white dress with a bright red collar and belt. Ammie flushed with annoyance and embarrassment. She tried to catch Nilanthi's eye so she could order her to go home at once, and change into something more appropriate. Nilanthi did not notice or pretended not to, until Mass was over.

Once home, Ammie berated Nilanthi. She said all the people had stared at Nilanthi, and she was mortified because her eldest daughter made such a spectacle of herself. Nilanthi however, did not show much concern about what the congregation thought.

During religious knowledge class one day, Mother Concilia requested all those who had boyfriends, to come forward and own up, as she would be very pleased if they confided in her. Nilanthi was first to confess her teenage romances. What followed was such a revelation, that Nilanthi must have felt as if a bulldozer ran her over.

Mother Concilia's attitude changed abruptly, and all the other nuns and she ostracised Nilanthi. They even advised her friends to stay away from Nilanthi, and she led a very unhappy life for sometime. When Thathie heard about it, he said, "Nilanthi, you are the most naive person I have ever seen!" And this characteristic led to most of her troubles in later life.

The feast day of St Therese, Little Flower of Jesus, was a great day of celebration at school. A life-sized statue of the saint stood in a niche at the entrance to the chapel, which was always decorated with pink roses. On these feast days, the nuns were especially nice to us, and after an impressive concert that the staff organised, they gave us bags of lollies, and whistling lollipops.

Most of us took part in the plays, musical performances, recitations, and singing, and we memorized our parts months before the concert. We stayed back after school, during lunch breaks, and every available moment of the day for daily rehearsals. I took this business of acting very seriously.

If it was the nativity scene at Christmas, I was sure to get the part of a petrified angel (due to my ability to stand absolutely still without blinking, I suppose, rather than any claim to angelic looks or behaviour). The plays were sometimes based on historical events, or romantic stories, and comedies. Nilanthi acted as "Pied Piper of Hamelin" once, and wore a red and yellow costume, while we had forgettable parts of children following the Pied Piper across the stage, never more to be seen again (in the story or the play).

In the dressing rooms below stage, excitement mounted to fever pitch, as we waited impatiently for our cues to prance on stage. Nuns, teachers, and parents, sewed our beautiful costumes. I am amazed at the hours of cutting and sewing involved in making such elaborate costumes, and getting them ready on time.

Although our parents and teachers were in the audience, I soon forgot my self-consciousness and stage fright, once I warmed up to my role. These school productions, though not on a grand scale, instilled in me a love of theatre and drama. I had a retentive memory, and this helped me obtain various roles later on in school life too. Sr Lourdina coached and helped overcome my "sing-song" recitation of poetry, and sometimes, I even managed to recite with some feeling, even at such a young age.

The convent and surrounding grounds were a constant source of enjoyment.

Thick, old, cypress trees trimmed low, bordered the entrance to the convent, and we hid under them when we played hide-and-seek, or sat on the thick branches, just chatting away during recess. The broad, sweeping staircases were also favourite hiding places, but I especially loved visiting the chapel, as it was serene and beautiful.

Sometimes at lunch break, I went in for a quick visit to the chapel, and gazed out of large casement windows at the blue sky. The sun shone, trees stirred in gentle breezes, and happy laughter and voices drifted up to the windows. The fragrance of roses mingled with incense and candle wax, filled the air, and polished, brass candelabra shone brightly in the warm sunshine. The kaleidoscope of colours streaming in through stained glass windows was just magical. It was such a very special feeling to know all was well everywhere, and I did not have a care in the world.

As Pippa so aptly noted, "God's in his Heaven, all's right with the world." I was becoming spiritual and profound imperceptibly then, and was drawn towards the mysticism of Catholism. It was like waiting in the antechamber of a mysterious institution, breathless with anticipation of what was in store, once I became a "proper, baptised" Catholic.

The nuns constantly reiterated, "*Only* baptised souls can enter heaven." I yearned for that day to be baptised, and experience the grace and privilege of belonging to the Catholic church. It may have been my "soul's awakening" to the grandeur and spirituality inherent in all human beings. But it was also the beginning of a deep yearning to find tranquil, beautiful retreats to fill my soul with gladness.

Not that I was always in the chapel mind you, but a few times during the week, I found I could not resist the attraction of that marvellous sanctuary. I was not saintly by any means, in fact quite the opposite, as I was a mischievous, high-spirited little girl, always in some scrape at home, and in school. My Spirituality, and childish mischief co-existed somewhat uncomfortably.

Chapter 12

It was a great shock when Thathie told us that Prime Minister, Mr Bandaranaike, was assassinated. Newspapers and radio were full of the tragic story, and the country mourned his untimely death. His widow, Mrs Sirimavo Bandaranaike, won elections just after, and was then the first woman Prime Minister in the world.

She was quite popular with some people, but spent the next few years taking over tea estates, foreign companies, hospitals, and even private schools. Her government nationalised everything. Soon, most of the foreign investors left, together with European tea planters, and nuns, who worked in hospitals and schools. The long arm of the Government stretched out insidiously to take over anything and everything they could in a fervent outbreak of nationalism.

It was no surprise then, when the government announced that all Catholic and private schools were to be nationalised. Mrs Bandaranaike's Sri Lanka Freedom Party, made this decision. Eventually, even the name of the island was changed to "Sri Lanka." The nuns and teachers were absolutely devastated, but I did not have the remotest idea of what the implications meant. Our school was like a desolate mourning house, as parents and teachers whispered about the unstable future.

Many English and Irish nuns returned to their native countries, once the government took over. Most private hospitals that were run by dedicated missionary nuns, were soon nationalised too. Parents supported nuns and teachers, as they demonstrated angrily outside school, and we had a few days off until the matter was resolved.

I did not understand anything then, and it was just an unexpected holiday, as far as I was concerned. The nuns told us we could not attend Little Flower convent until further notice. Our parents sent us to a nearby government school until then, because they did not want us to miss school.

I vaguely remember walking along the rail track to a remote, noisy school, where a motley collection of rude, hostile village children mockingly called us "convent children" and teased us at every turn. English classes were unavailable, and it was very confusing and uncomfortable in that crowded school. Most of our friends stayed home, as only some parents sent their children to the local government school, not knowing how long it would take to resolve the issue.

The nuns failed in their attempt to hold onto their beloved convent, and the government closed in with sweeping changes. Little Flower convent was re-named "Mahavidyala" (high school), and this wave of fierce nationalism swept the country. Most of the foreign nuns and priests left soon after. English classes were phased out over the next few years, and the whole education system changed to Sinhalese, with English and Tamil taught as secondary languages. Tamil students' primary language remained Tamil, and Sinhalese students' was Sinhalese. This left minority nationalities like Burghers and Muslims in a quandary, as they had to choose which language they wanted to be educated in.

Fortunately, we still continued studying in English, due to a sunset clause for English classes to be phased out in a few years time. It was a very sad period in Ceylon's history, as many dedicated professionals left the country, and it also forced many Burghers to immigrate, because of such short-sighted, drastic changes.

When we returned to the convent a few weeks later, the nuns were very angry with us for having attended a government school, and accused us of "disloyalty" to the convent. I was utterly confused, and I still do not fully understand the intrigues that went on then. Before too long, the once exclusive Catholic convent was opened to non-Catholic children as well, and it was rumoured some children attended school just to get free milk and buns. This was the government's introduction to subsidised "free education" in all schools.

I believe it is a basic human right for any individual seeking education to have ready access to receive one. Free education in theory, is commendable, but the aftermath of this socialistic move, proved detrimental in some ways. Every village child, who received a basic education, was now left disgruntled with his or her lot. Not for them the trade and industry of their parents, who tilled the soil and kept dairy farms.

Anyone with a modicum of education, now flooded the main towns of Colombo or Kandy, seeking white collar jobs. Thousands of educated, unemployed, totally dissatisfied youth hankered after jobs they were not qualified for, but were too proud to return to agriculture or trade in their villages. It was the beginning of the end of a golden era in that beautiful island. And it was inevitable that restless, unemployed youth should rebel against the government.

We lived in our house for about a year, when another thunder-bolt disrupted our lives. Thathie announced he was transferred to Polonnaruwa, which in railway terms, was an "uncongenial" station. It was mandatory for all railway officers to serve at least one year in one of those awful, lonely stations. Polonnaruwa, situated in the heart of Ceylon, was a remote place in 1960. I have never visited the place since then, but I hear it is quite different today, with an increased population, and tourism.

Thathie did not want to spend a whole year in Polonnaruwa without his family this time. He could not visit on weekends, because it was a very long distance from Bandarawela. My parents decided to move. Decisions were quickly made, and our house was rented out.

We had a railway bungalow in Polonnaruwa. At first, I was sad and bewildered to leave my friends, and the beautiful house and garden behind. But not for long, as the prospect of a new place, new surroundings, and school, was quite exciting.

It did not matter what we children thought about the whole matter anyway, because, once our parents decided we were moving, that was it. The nuns and teachers, especially Sr Lourdina, made it worse. "You are leaving this beautiful, cool, climate, and going to live in that hot, wild place! I do hope you children and your parents will be alright!" A sense of adventure and excitement overcame me at the prospect of living in an entirely different environment. But, we had lived in Bandarawela as far back as I could remember, and it was sad to leave the old, familiar places behind.

Anyway, a change of scene would be welcome, I thought, and I only dwelt on the novelty of the situation, little realising how very different life would be in Polonnaruwa. Ammie, Menika, and another little servant boy, also called Banda, took over the main packing. The former Banda left us some time ago, seeking better employment in a sugar cane plantation. His parting words, with his face split in a wide grin, was, "They even provide *boots* on the plantation!" This was an added inducement, as most of the servants went barefoot then.

My mind is a blur regarding those last few days in Bandarawela, but Ammie and Nilanthi were red-eyed and sad, each thinking of the numerous friends they left behind. We younger ones amused ourselves as we always did aboard trains, namely, running up and down corridors, closing and opening shutters, and generally having a great time, with Nihal chasing us around, and teasing as usual.

Nilanthi must have missed her friends already, because she cried a great deal till the train was well past Bandarawela. We slept on bunk beds in the sleeping cars, washed our faces in tiny, stainless steel basins that closed up in a recess when not in use.

It was an adventure travelling in the sleepy train for hours on end, and staying wide-awake listening to the rhythmic sound of wheels rattling on the track. Or the sound of a lonely whistle blowing and fading away in the distance, as we passed little country stations. Red and green signal lights loomed out of inky darkness, bringing the train to a grinding halt, or slowing down, as another train whizzed past in a blur of amber lights. These images remain to this day.

I had a phobia about sleeping on bunk beds then, fearing the top bunk would crash down on the person sleeping in the lower one, which was usually Ammie or Menika. This frightful thought kept me awake for hours, until my eyes closed in sheer exhaustion. Towards morning, after we finished our ablutions, we ate a substantial breakfast in the restaurant car, then changed trains at Polgahawela. The train chugged slowly, and a few hours later, we were ready to start our new life.

My first impression of Kaduruwela, the little station where we got off, about two miles from the main town of Polonnaruwa, was its utter remoteness, barren surroundings, and blazing hot sun. Rampant swarms of flies and insects welcomed us to our dwelling place.

The main road ran in front of our house, and alongside the road, stood a few shops, and a hotel. Four or five railway bungalows sprawled some distance away opposite the railway station. Our house, like the rest of the railway bungalows, was situated at the bottom of a spacious garden, and we ran along a narrow, stony path into the house.

Numerous trees and thick undergrowth, overgrown and neglected, sprouted everywhere. The house was quite large and airy. Tall, spreading trees stood like sentinels in the backyard, overshadowing the house, and made it cooler, and less stark than the surrounding areas.

Although we had running water, it was not fit to drink or for cooking, only for washing clothes and bathing, and soon, we discovered another novelty. Our drinking water arrived daily in large, wooden barrels, transported by train all the way from Batticoloa. One of the porters rolled the barrel down the road, or wheeled it on a trolley to our house, and this drinking water usually lasted all day.

When we arrived in Polonnaruwa then, it was teeming with wild life, ancient ruins. and colossal stone carvings of Buddha, and some ancient Kings. It had once been a capital city of kings in previous centuries, but only ruins, and vestiges of past glory and grandeur remained of the marvellous city. Though these ancient ruins and carvings still remain, the area is now highly-populated, and wild life can be seen only in sanctuaries.

One of my greatest delights, was discovering a broad, winding river, flowing right behind our backyard. We spent every single hot afternoon splashing around or swimming in that river. It abounded with various species of tropical fish and eels, and I squealed in fright each time I felt one of the slimy things swish close to me, or I accidentally stepped on one. Still, it did not deter me from swimming in the river every day, no matter what the weather was like. It was mostly dry, hot, humid and sunny, with rare spells of bad weather or rain to relieve the dusty aridity.

I watched some men from a near-by hotel once, catching eels in a bucket, and taking them to their kitchens. I never ate fish in that hotel again. I was convinced they cooked eels, and passed them off as fish, because some people relish eel, and call it a variety of fish anyway. Not for me though, as my childish impressions are of slimy, black, slithering reptiles that I always considered to be water snakes.

Never have I seen such a profusion of crawling, flying, buzzing insects, like those that plagued our lives in Polonnaruwa. Indoors or out, they bothered us with constant droning, whining or stinging, but worst of all, the tiny pests sometimes crawled inside my ears or up my nose. It was a nasty experience dealing with these horrid insects, and it was not at all the kind of place I had anticipated. The huge, red ants had to be seen to be believed, and the memory of their sting brings a tear to my eye even now, as it was such a painful sensation.

Red ants crawled all over my legs and back, whenever I sat out on the grass or on a tree stump, and my agonised howls meant one thing, bee stings or ant bites. If the equally deadly mosquitoes bit us, it took ages to heal, and sometimes turned into septic sores that ached and itched for months. I still bear traces of such a scar on my ankle that did not heal for a long time.

Thathie in front row second from left in Bandarawela station.
Menika with Nilanthi, Chanda & baby Shirani. Four of us on our
way to school. Frolics in the river with Anthony & friends.

Chapter 13

Once we settled down a few days later, we went on a memorable excursion to Polonnaruwa., I was fortunate to see ancient ruins, gigantic stone statues of Buddha, and King Parakramabahu (one of the ancient kings of Ceylon), just on the outskirts of town. I stood on stone carvings, and ran around quite unrestrained, but now these ancient monuments are well-protected, with barricades around to avoid vandalism. I could never forget the astounding spectacle of those colossal stone statues, crumbling palaces, temples and monuments, silent witnesses to the grandeur and glory of a past era and kingdom.

On the banks of Topawewa, an artificial lake, which dated to the time of King Parakramabahu, stood a large rest house. The timber structure that protruded halfway into the water, was cool and comfortable inside, and we stopped there for refreshments.

Malcolm took me to this lake whenever he visited, and taught me how to swim, and stay afloat in water. I am grateful for his never-failing kindness, patience, and perseverance. The tip of a small island emerged in the middle of the lake, but in the height of drought, when the lake dried up considerably, a large area of the little Island was visible. Malcolm urged me to swim from the shore right up to that island and back again, and thanks to him I was quite a strong swimmer then.

The question of schooling was foremost now, once Ammie achieved a semblance of routine, and organisation at home. It was decided that we girls attend a government co-ed school, called "Thopawewa Maha Vidyala" (grand-sounding title for a high school), situated in the main town. Nihal, however, was to board at St Anthony's college, Kandy, as Thathie and Ammie wanted him to be educated in a private Catholic college. St Anthony's was a prestigious, and exclusive school, with priests and brothers in charge still, and escaped the wave of nationalism so far.

The only drawback was, the college's strict rule of enrolling baptised Catholics only. This forced Thathie to change his mind, and after all these years, he finally gave "permission" to baptise us. Ammie was triumphant, and so was I, that at last, I was going to be part of the Catholic church.

This did not prove to be such a simple task though. The parish priest, Fr Carlo Perera, insisted we receive further instructions in religious knowledge at Sunday school classes first. Nihal was due to start school in the first term, which did not leave much time, but we were keen, and attended Sunday school classes faithfully. Fr Carlo drove around in a battered, white van, gathering his fold every Sunday, and we spent almost two hours after Mass, learning catechism and prayers.

My parents enrolled four of us at the government school, after an interview with the poker-faced principal, Mr Direkze. He was a stern, middle-aged, portly man, with hair plastered down with Brylcreem. He looked as if he did not find much to be amused at, because he seldom or never smiled. We commenced school almost immediately, and once we started attending that remote, village school, I had an idea why Mr Direkze looked so severe and sour-faced, as if he was sucking lemons. I found much to be amused at however, as the village children from farming and rural communities, proved to be earthy and droll.

Their crude sense of humour sometimes made me laugh, but at other times irritated me. Not many middle-class families inhabited the area, and four of us, spruced up in starched, white uniforms, white socks, and white canvas shoes, were something of an oddity, as most children ran around barefooted, and wore any old clothes. They found us amusing, and called us derogatory names, referring especially to our convent background. They ridiculed our fluency in English, as they knew only Sinhalese. Translations of their taunts and jeers do not sound as witty, but they were very clever, and sounded quite funny when they shouted out, "Ingrese badayanawa" (we suffered from English diarrhoea).

Gradually, some of the children started wearing Bata slippers to school, and smartened up their appearance. The little boys behaved like hooligans, and I dreaded them, because they resorted to physical violence sometimes, when teachers were not around to protect me. Talk about playground bullies! They were the worst in that school.

My class teacher, Mrs Neelawathie, took a great liking to me, as she was childless. Whenever she upbraided the others, she asked me to stand up in front of the classroom, and said, "Look at this child, this is the way *convent* children dress, and behave! Not like you hooligans! Why can't you lot take an example?" This in turn, enraged the boys so much, that one big boy chased me all around the school compound threatening to hit me with a ruler. He shouted rude names, and called me "teachers pet" but I somehow eluded him, and ran back to the classroom. Once under the teacher's watchful eye, I felt safe until next recess.

Another disadvantage was switching over to Sinhalese classes. I learnt all subjects in Sinhalese now, which was confusing, as I was not good in Sinhalese. Still, I managed alright, because at the end of term examinations, I came third in a class of thirty, which pleased my teachers.

Mrs Neelawathie was from a typical rural background; loud and crude, with an earthy sense of humour in her treatment of naughty children, especially the boys. She was very nice and kind to me though, and even visited our home a few times to let my parents know how I was progressing. I did not take to her though, because I found her physically unattractive, with large buck teeth, some missing on both sides of her jaw, coarse features, and a raucous laugh.

She asked me to accompany her on shopping expeditions, because she took such a fancy to me. And Ammie, who felt sorry for her, urged me to join Mrs Neelawathie. But I did not accept her invitations, and found many excuses to evade her each time.

She curled up on the chair, with feet tucked under during classes, and sometimes nibbled on green mangoes. Some girls whispered mischievously, "Teacher has doladuk" (pregnancy cravings).

Our religious knowledge classes progressed well, as I was very good in catechism, thanks to the nuns at Little Flower convent, and Fr Carlo Perera was quite impressed with my ready answers. He knew we had a good Catholic background, in spite of our father being a Buddhist. So he decided to baptise all five of us, along with fifty other children, when the Bishop visited soon.

We were to be baptised on day one, receive First Holy Communion the following day, and Confirmation on the third day. This was because the Bishop's visits were rare in this part of the country. Now, in a fervent grip of evangelism, I related stories of Jesus Christ's birth, life, and ultimate sacrifice on the cross to redeem all people, to the children in my classroom, who were predominantly Buddhists.

At the end of my narrative, one little girl shed bitter tears, and cried out, "*Your* God has done so much for the world, what did *our* Lord Buddha do for us?" And she was inconsolable. I had not meant to upset her with the story of the crucifixion, but I loved repeating what I learnt at catechism classes.

I wonder if other children ever had a similar experience of receiving three of the most sacred sacraments in the Catholic church, over three consecutive days. It was absolutely frantic with many preparations, but Ammie kept it simple, as we wore our Sunday best, and not white satin, lace and flowers.

Nihal, who was quite tall for his age, dressed neatly in a white shirt, pair of white shorts, and a dark tie. A photograph taken with Ammie in a studio after our baptism, still evokes pleasant memories of that special day.

It was a great feast day when the Bishop arrived, and the small, mud-brick church was decorated with many beautiful flowers, and garlands made out of coconut flowers and palms. A platform was constructed outside the church for the Bishop to celebrate Mass outdoors, as the church was too small to accommodate the people who crowded in to hear the Bishop.

One amusing incident stands out, because with all the rush and excitement of that day, Ammie and Fr Carlo forgot to procure Godparents. Just before the ceremony started, Fr Carlo ran down the road, urgently calling after a young man, who was pedalling away furiously, and enlisted him to stand as our Godfather. A pious-looking, old lady, who was reciting the rosary in church, graciously acquiesced to Fr Carlo's request to be our Godmother.

So, two complete strangers stood as our Godparents, and to this day, I do not know who they were, or what became of them. It was a great and amazing moment in my life though when I finally received the Sacrament of baptism.

All through my young days the nuns had drilled into me the importance of being a *baptised* Catholic, and of "belonging" to God, and the Catholic church. Now, I truly felt I was a real Catholic at last, and I celebrated my baptism in awe. It was one of the greatest gifts Ammie gave me. All the parishioners prepared a banquet fit for royalty that day. We sat down with fifty other children at long tables, covered in snow-white linen tablecloths, and gorged ourselves on loads of traditional sweetmeats, fruits, milk rice, and soft drinks, until we could eat no more.

We received First Holy Communion next day, and Confirmation on the third day. It was like a "shotgun conversion" for us.

Nihal was soon packed off to boarding school at St Anthony's. I missed him badly, as it was the first time he was away from home for such a long period.

He came home on weekends though, and we lit a huge bonfire in the garden, and waited impatiently. He arrived with a broad grin on his ruddy, handsome face, and a whole heap of jokes and stories to keep us in stitches. Nihal was very tall and strong now, and looked older than his age. Thathie remarked that he was becoming more mature too. He was very kind and loving, as he missed us greatly too when he went back to college on Sunday nights.

We made friends with some of the railway people in other bungalows, and they too joined us in our vigil for Nihal. A few of them were lonely young bachelors, who appreciated our family gatherings, with all the noise, music, and jokes that abounded whenever we were together. An added attraction no doubt, was Nilanthi, who was a pretty teenager.

Nihal boarded a bus in Kandy on Friday afternoons, and arrived around nine o'clock, always grinning, no matter how arduous the trip was. We ran up to him, and greeted him fondly, like a long lost brother. Nelune was his special pet, and sometimes, he brought us little gifts with his pocket money. With every visit, Nihal was becoming more sophisticated, and Thathie observed that he was "acquiring polish."

Nihal allowed us to join in a game of cricket, or rugger whenever he played with Banda. But come to think of it, I do not remember much batting or bowling, as Banda and Nihal made us girls field for them, until we rebelled, and demanded a turn at the wicket too. We did not mind really, as it was great fun to be allowed to play cricket with Nihal.

We did not join in their rough game of rugger though. When Nihal tried to teach Banda how to "tackle" Banda learnt so quickly, and so well, that before Nihal knew what hit him, Banda lunged at him and brought him crashing down to earth, severely injuring Nihal's knees and shins. Nihal grinned through his pain at frightened Banda, "*Well done*! That was *very good*!" And he limped off painfully to dress his wounds.

Chapter 14

Our garden in Polonnaruwa was a veritable jungle of about half an acre. It was almost impossible to clear up the dense growth, even with the help of a few porters from the station, and casual labour. As we were leaving in a year's time, it did not justify cleaning up the huge block, because it was a Herculean task.

I sat in that tangled growth for hours, and watched all sorts of creepy, crawly things, and shuddered when snakes, lizards, iguanas, and other reptilian-like creatures slithered around. Hunting boldly, or busily building, they stopped and looked at me askance, as if this was *their* domain, and *I* was the intruder. I did not blame them either, as they had lived there for so long without being evicted from their habitat.

The iguanas crept out of sand dunes, and sun-bathed nonchalantly, and from their free and easy manners, behaved as if they were lords of all they surveyed. The Buddhists did not harm them, or chase them away, because they believed in reincarnation. What looked like an ugly, withered old lizard or goanna, could well turn out to be ancient Aunt Lizzie, or Uncle Godfrey in their new form of life.

Firmly convinced of rebirth, Buddhists did not wilfully harm rodents, insects, animals or reptiles. I think it is a pity though that they do not extend the same reverence to human lives as well, because in times of civil wars and terrorism, they unmercifully slaughtered each other.

We spotted cobras slithering in the undergrowth many times, and Menika warned us that if anyone killed a cobra, its mate would somehow find the killer, and strike the victim dead with its venomous bite. Most people believed this superstition, and no matter how deadly and dangerous, they seldom killed a cobra.

I became a vegetarian during this time, as I could not bear to eat meat, fish or chicken. I went off fish after I saw wriggling eels in the river taken to a hotel one day.

When Ammie kept a few chickens in Bandarawela, I witnessed Menika's gory executions of my pet chickens; headless animals running around, or some with twisted necks, still squirming and wriggling painfully.

Menika never learnt the art of killing the poor chickens painlessly, and I could not bring myself to eat those unfortunate chickens, whom I named personally. No way would I eat Milly, the speckled hen, or fat, brown Patty. So while the rest of the family enjoyed a delicious chicken curry, I sat and wailed, "You are eating *my pet* hens!"

I was off meat, because one day, while sitting on the fence, and watching the world go by, a bullock cart rolled along drunkenly. When it passed me by, my stomach turned when I saw the contents inside. A huge, decapitated head of a bull or a cow, with glazed eyes wide open, and a reproachful stare death had stamped permanently. I was horrified at the sight, and if *that* was how meat came to the table, I certainly did not want to eat it. But I mixed chicken or Oxo cubes in vegetable soups, and that made me a semi-vegetarian, I suppose, as they were made from beef and chicken extracts (my siblings pointed out gleefully).

The much-longed for rains failed to sluice the parched land for many months now, and I almost fainted with constant heat and dust. This part of Ceylon was the driest, and a very hot area, especially with lack of seasonal rains. The bus journey back home from school was agony, as it was the hottest time of the day around two o'clock. It was sweltering inside the crowded bus, as it soared to about forty degrees Celsius. My throat ached, and I was parched, as we did not carry water bottles.

A small, variety shop stood behind the bus stand, and sometimes we sheltered in its cool interior until the bus arrived. The manager objected to this however, and shooed us off, as he did not want all the school children wandering inside his shop, which was understandable, from his point of view.

One night, after a trip to Polonnaruwa town, we were returning home in a hired car with Ammie and Thathie, when we saw the manager of that variety shop trudging along wearily. I asked Thathie to stop the car, and offered him a lift home.

After this little favour, the man was so grateful, that he told us we could stay inside his shop as long as we liked until the bus arrived after school. But I cheekily stipulated that we also get a drink of water while we waited. He laughed as he readily agreed to this condition.

Herath Bandara, one of Thathie's distant relatives from Paranagama, managed a grocery shop, situated in the heart of town. He soon made our acquaintance, and became a daily visitor, as he had no other friends, or family in Polonnaruwa. He was very fond of us children, and gave many gifts and toys, and took us sight-seeing in hired cars, and was generally good to our family.

We called him "Herath Marma" (Uncle). He was a young man in his late twenties or so; tall, and quite good-looking. Herath always wore a snow-white sarong and tunic, called an Ariya suit, a traditional form of male attire, and sported a large, expensive, gold wrist watch.

All was well, until he fell in love with one of Nilanthi's classmates, Padma, a very pretty, fair-complexioned, tall and slender girl, with long, black hair. She visited sometimes, and when Herath saw her, he became infatuated with Padma, even though she had a boyfriend, and did not want to know Herath. Padma's boyfriend was very jealous of her, and somehow learnt that Herath was dangling after her, so he threatened to beat him up, if he did not leave his girlfriend alone.

Nilanthi and Herath spent many hours engaged in whispered conversations about this affair. Eager to play Cupid, Nilanthi invited Padma over whenever Herath was present. And before long, the young girl succumbed to Herath's wooing, as he was quite handsome, and had charming manners. He was very generous too, a real big spender, fond of giving presents, not only to us children, but his girlfriend as well.

Herath drove us around everywhere in hired cars, and Padma joined us on these trips sometimes. No doubt she was impressed with all this entertainment and attention, that must have been very attractive to a young and innocent schoolgirl. After a few months of this passionate affair, Herath, for some unknown reason, suddenly jilted the girl, and she lost both her boyfriends. She was quite upset (to say the least), but I hope she recovered in time. Nilanthi's friendship was strained after Herath's inexplicable behaviour, and Padma did not visit us again after that affair ended.

I started to collect a menagerie here too, as there were so many different species of animals. On one occasion, someone gave me a baby monkey, which was the funniest little creature I had ever possessed. I restrained it on a strong, metal chain all day, and let it out only when I came home from school, and had time to play with it.

It sat on my shoulder and chattered away incessantly, and made the most grotesque faces imaginable. I took it down to the river for a swim sometimes, and I had a great time watching my monkey's antics, and trying to make sense of his crazy chattering. He screeched madly, and clung to my neck when anything or anyone scared him. I really loved that funny little monkey, so imagine how I felt when I came home from school one day, and Menika looked me straight in the eye and told me the monkey escaped.

I could not believe my ears, and told Menika so, because I had the strongest suspicion she had set it free when I was not around. I ran to the garden calling its name, and was thoroughly disappointed when it did not jump on my shoulder as it usually did whenever I called him. Then I spotted him sitting high up on the tallest tree, looking down at me, like a wise, wrinkled old philosopher, but he remained deaf to all my pleading and cajoling.

I guessed Menika's chasing him away had deeply offended his sensibility, and he had lost faith in human beings. That was the end of that, and I was left crying with chagrin. Menika showed little sympathy, as she abhorred keeping animals in captivity, which was against her religious beliefs.

I continued missing and bemoaning my absconding monkey, so one of Thathie's friends gave me a fully grown monkey, who was not at all lovable or easy to tame. On several occasions, when I least expected it, he attacked viciously, grabbing hold and sinking his sharp teeth into my arms or legs. I kept him chained most of the time, as he was waiting for a chance to escape its fetters. He was unaware that an active, and passionate animal liberationist lived in the heart of my family, and only bided her time to get rid of this pest (not pet, as Menika complained).

The monkey broke loose from its chain one day. Ammie found him sitting on the dining table, with the butter dish wide open, solemnly stirring the soft butter, and licking his fingers thoughtfully, just like a connoisseur of dairy products. He looked comical, with butter all over his face and fingers, but Ammie and Menika were not amused at all, and they issued an ultimatum, "The monkey must go." When I returned home from school a few days after the butter episode, Menika grinned cheekily and exclaimed, "Dolly Baby, wandura giya!" (the monkey has gone).

It was too bad, because I knew she had set it free, but I cannot honestly say I was heartbroken, as he was a very naughty monkey. Menika believed it was a sin to hold any animal in captivity, and as a Buddhist, she too believed in reincarnation. She was convinced that animals were somehow distantly related to her, and could well be her great-grandfather, grand uncle or aunt. I did not hold it against Menika, but as a child, I was extremely angry with her, because I was helpless to prevent her from liberating my pets. She released them with the same zealous crusading spirit in which I collected them, in the belief I was giving them a good home.

I discovered a giant tortoise plodding ponderously in the garden one day. And undaunted with Menika's animal liberation activity, I immediately built a rough fence around it, and claimed it as my very own pet. It was enormous, and had an intricate, black and yellow, diamond-patterned shell. I stood on its shell, and watched it withdraw its huge ugly legs and head reproachfully, as it grimly observed my childish pranks from the dim recess of its rock-hard shell.

I enjoyed this new pet for a few days only, before Menika released it on compassionate grounds. She upbraided me sternly, "Dolly Baby, harima narakai, may ibba thiyaganna may punchi kooduwe!" (It is very wrong to enclose such a huge tortoise in a small pen). Menika's story was that the giant tortoise escaped, but I knew better. It was always the same old tale, whenever I returned home from school. *How* she got rid of the evidence, and lumbered that huge, heavy tortoise, with its ponderous gait, was a mystery to me. But my pet tortoise well and truly disappeared.

Chapter 15

Thathie's railway friends in Batticoloa sometimes sent a box of live, king crabs, and as Menika refused to kill them, Mrs Subramaniam, the lady next door, expertly massacred the crawling crustaceans. I never saw such enormous crabs, and it was horrifying to watch them being killed. But when the pot of curried crabs simmered, I forgot my revulsion, and enjoyed the succulent, exquisite taste of crabmeat.

We enjoyed many delicious meals, as people provided us with various delicacies, and some meats we had not tasted before; like dried venison soaked in spices, and fried with chillies, a delectable dish fit for a king. Although I did not eat meat or chicken, I was coaxed into trying venison, which I nibbled on gingerly, and quite liked it.

I did not realise it then, but it was truly a gourmet's delight, as we feasted on king crabs, prawns, fruits and vegetables, that grew only in this hot region. In retrospect, I enjoyed one long, hot, adventurous holiday, interspersed with school days.

On one trip to Polonnaruwa town, I persuaded Ammie to give me one rupee to purchase an exquisite doll (a sort of early version of a Barbie doll made in Japan). I was delighted when Ammie agreed, and spent a great deal of time cutting out fabrics, making clothes, and dressing up this doll, which I still have.

While playing hide-and-seek one night, I tripped over a fallen branch in the garden, and sprained my ankle badly. Malcolm, who was holidaying with us, said, "Fiery Jack is a *most* efficacious balm, and will soothe your sprained ankle in no time!" We had a tin of this balm at home, so Menika soon applied it on my ankle. She did not know however, that it had to be applied *lightly,* and massaged my ankle so thoroughly, that it nearly burnt off my skin.

After a few minutes, instead of soothing relief, my skin was badly inflamed due to Menika's rigorous massage. I was in severe pain, as nothing eased the burning. I cried helplessly, so Malcolm ran to the nearest hotel, and got some ice. It helped a little, but I endured a restless night, due to Menika's over-enthusiastic application of aptly named "Fiery Jack" balm.

We socialised with few people, mostly railway families in the area, and a farm manager and his family, who lived in a large, modern house on a huge farm on the outskirts of Polonnaruwa town. We visited those nice, friendly people sometimes, and vice versa. The farm manager's wife was a large, attractive lady, and they had two equally large children (the result of good living on the farm, consuming gallons of fresh milk and produce I suppose).

On our visits to the farm, I watched in fascination all the complicated machinery whirring and buzzing away, especially milking devices, and the wonder of milk pasteurized and bottled before my very eyes. The manager offered us large tumblers of warm milk (straight from the cow), and it was absolutely delicious.

Whenever they dined with us, Thathie drank a great deal of arrack with the manager, until they were both quite intoxicated. Then everyone danced the "Baila" (a Ceylonese dance), and Thathie's improvised version had to be seen to be believed. He executed the most intricate steps and manoeuvres I have ever seen, and it never failed to send us into peals of laughter to watch him dancing. Such dexterity of feet and movement in one as drunk as Thathie, was simply incredible. I laughed till my sides ached. It was even funnier to hear him singing "Pistol-Packing Mama" in boisterous tones, with much gusto, appropriate gestures and actions. The very house reverberated with the sound of his raucous singing, and our laughter.

Thathie had a storehouse of jokes and anecdotes too, that he regaled for our entertainment. His favourite one was that of a Ceylonese politician visiting abroad. The story goes that while touring Waterloo, his British guide declared, "And here's where Napoleon fell," at which, the politician rubbed his shoes on the ground gingerly and replied, "yes, yes, rather slippery, isn't it?"

After a few drinks, Thathie insisted on repeating tongue-twisters, to show he was not intoxicated. With much giggling and slurring he recited. "She sells sea shells on the sea shore," while we waited hopefully for the slightest slip of his tongue. He knew several spoonerisms too, "You have hissed the mystery lectures." (missed the history lectures).

We had great, fun-filled times, and on such occasions, Menika's cooking was even more superb. The memory of those delicious meals still lingers, long after events have passed. She served pastel-coloured string hoppers with her unique beef curry, seeni sambal (sweet and spicy onions), and other culinary delights to please our palates.

One day, another family, who lived some distance, invited us for lunch. That occasion is branded in my memory for a very amusing reason. Ten of us arrived punctually at about eleven thirty, a polite time to arrive, as most people ate at twelve noon, or thereabouts. First, they served mandatory cool drinks, tea and coffee for those who preferred hot beverages, and sweet biscuits for the children.

I was absolutely ravenous, as we children had worked up great appetites, when shortly after our arrival, the men started making preparations to go deer hunting. Honestly, this was no joke. I still remember how hungry, and angry I was when the hunting party stepped out at twelve thirty to hunt deer for our lunch. I could have cried with exasperation, and the desperation of a starving child. We sat around staring listlessly at each other.

We had little or no inclination to pursue childish amusements, like hide-and-seek, or indulge in conversation either, because by then, we all suffered from extreme hunger and short tempers. The clock ticked away each second leadenly, and our hostess did nothing to alleviate the pangs of hunger, in the way of serving snacks or refreshments till lunchtime. Ammie engaged our hostess in desultory conversation, while Menika tried to amuse us languid children.

The next part of this episode is even more incredible and hilarious. We heard the weary hunters making quite a racket outside around three o'clock or so. They returned without any bounty. Obviously, they had no luck shooting deer. And the hostess, perhaps quite used to this manner of haphazard entertaining with her luckless hunter of a husband, now announced without any embarrassment whatsoever, that deer was off the menu, and we had to settle for chicken instead. More tears of chagrin and hunger fell down my cheeks at this news.

I glumly observed one of the servants, hatchet in hand, chasing a reluctant rooster, and coaxed the bird. "Here, chook, chook, chick, chick," to which cajoling, the indignant rooster paid not the slightest heed. He quite rightly objected to being our belated lunch, which was served around five o'clock or later.

I never ate chicken then, another reason for my vexation, so I ended up with a boiled egg, curried vegetables and rice. And so, the tardiest lunch party we had ever attended, and day of the great deer hunt (that never was), finally ended on a subdued note. Years later, I appreciated the funny side of it, but I was definitely not amused then.

During school holidays and weekends, we went on several trips to the magnificent beaches at Kalkudah and Parsikudah, where miles of pristine, white sand glistened, and lofty, coconut palms swayed gently in warm, ocean breezes. The calm sea was an expanse of deep blue sapphire, reflecting the azure sky in its depths. It was a magnificent sight, and still evokes beautiful, happy memories of carefree days and joyous laughter of youth, as I frolicked in the sunshine.

While we picnicked, played on the beach, and devoured all the goodies Ammie and Menika prepared, Thathie enjoyed drinking Palmyra palm toddy that locals brewed, and sold in nearby fishermen's' huts. We usually had company, as Thathie's friends joined us on these outings. But if he had no one, then porters, train drivers, or railway guards were quite happy to join him for a drink, as the railway station was near by.

From curious, excited chattering of on-lookers who followed us around, I think it was quite a phenomenon in that remote outstation, to see a group of high-spirited children, and their parents, enjoying a day out on the beach. Unfortunately, those remote beaches are full of tourists and hotels today, and we were very lucky to have enjoyed those vast empty beaches, and spectacular locations when not a single tourist was in sight.

Whenever we had time away from our many activities and school work, Shirani, Nelune and I tried building a shed out of mud bricks we found in our garden. It was to be our club house, and we laid out bricks in single rows, and kept adding more bricks one on top of the other, bonding each layer with thick mud.

When our edifice reached a foot or so, much to our dismay and frustration, down crashed the whole structure! We kept trying several times, never knowing that the foundation required a broader row of bricks across, and a wall could not be built on a base with only one row of bricks.

We were ambitious architects though, and even constructed a window and a door in our building. Then we watched with bated breath, in case our mere breathing should bring down the entire structure, like the famous walls of Jericho, that required a great deal of trumpet blowing before the walls came crashing down. Our "Walls of Kaduruwela" swayed drunkenly before crumbling down invariably.

Tempers flew, as we angrily accused each other of poor workmanship, and sudden movements that brought the wall down; nevertheless, we did not give up. We just kept right on building on the same unstable foundation, made wild accusations, quarrelled, and insulted. Then doggedly built row by row of bricks, in direct opposition, and defiance of gravity, and laws that governed architecture.

Sad to say though, we never did complete the mud brick walls, and the project was finally abandoned. When one of my friends visited soon after, I pointed out the crumbling brick work. "There lie the famous ruins of our club house" (Polonnaruwa being famous for its ancient ruins), my friend appreciated the jest, and we had a good laugh about it.

Chapter 16

Malcolm and I went swimming in the Parakrama Samudra sometimes, and we spent hours just splashing around the lake, once swimming lessons were over. One evening, after our usual frolics in the water, we heard a commotion emitting from a van parked near the lake. A man announced over a loud speaker. "We're holding an amateur singing competition, and everyone is welcome to participate." Malcolm, and the rest of the family, urged me to sing a song. As I was quite audacious, I did not hesitate to walk up to the microphone and burst into song, which went like this.

"Come little robin and sing me a song,
Here by the brooklyn that murmurs along.
Pray tell me who cares for you all the long day?
Is it the Father to whom we all pray?
Where is your mother and where is your home,
Aren't you afraid to be out all alone?
Oh no little children, for God cares for me,
And I am as happy as happy can be."

My family, and the crowd greeted my musical effort enthusiastically, even though most of them did not understand the words I sang in English. The compere asked, "Aren't you the little girl I saw swimming far out in the Samudra Lake?" Another round of loud applause, before he presented a small souvenir as a prize. I was quite pleased when I stepped down from the platform.

On another one of our outings to Kalkudah beach, Daisy Akka, and Ulwita, joined us, together with their daughter, Manel, husband, Sugath, and baby daughter, Kumudini. When she was about eighteen, Manel was married to a man her parents chose, and the whole family visited sometimes.

We hired a motor boat, and the owner took us far out to sea that day, and we enjoyed ourselves immensely. Thathie, Ulwita, and Sugath had an equally rollicking time, drinking arrack and local toddy.

It was a glorious day, with deep blue skies, calm water, and warm, balmy breezes. Even as a child, I loved the sea, lakes, rivers and streams, and was told that my star sign, Pisces, is the reason for my passion. Who knows, but I am happiest, if I can spend hours in the sea, pool, or in a bath.

Ulwita, who was full of arrack and toddy, was quite drunk. Suddenly, without warning, he picked me up and threw me overboard, as he slurred, "You are a good swimmer, now try swimming back to the shore!" After my initial shock, I felt I was sinking right down to the very bottom, and could even see the glistening sea bed below. My natural instinct to survive forced me to struggle up to the surface, and I inhaled a lungful of fresh air.

Salt water was in my eyes, up my nose, and throat. I swallowed a great deal too, and my sore eyes and nose irritated me very much. I was furious with drunken Ulwita, grinning foolishly. I wanted to punch his face for throwing me in the water without warning. Then slowly, but surely, I swam back to the shore, until I felt my feet touch the sandy ground, and then I collapsed on the beach, exhausted and extremely angry.

It was a long swim for me, more than a mile or so. My parents watched anxiously, in case I could not swim that far. Thathie sobered up pretty quickly after this incident, and repeated, "*What* would have happened, if you got caught in the propeller!" Ulwita laughed drunkenly, and it made me madder. My whole day was spoilt, as salt water stung my eyes, and I sneezed and spluttered for the rest of the day.

Another friend of Thathie invited us on a safari one day, to deep, remote areas of Polonnaruwa, where herds of wild elephants roamed in the heart of dense jungles. He told us we could watch wild animals prowling around, and drinking at waterholes, while we stayed safely in a little hunting lodge he owned. This was a very exciting, adventurous prospect, and we eagerly prepared for the journey.

We drove in a Land Rover through the remote interior into the very heart of the jungle. There we beheld herds of elephants, deer, and hundreds of grey monkeys, who jumped wildly from tree-tops, chattering hysterically, threatening us intruders trespassing in their domain. Above the noise of gibbering monkeys, we heard wild cats and leopards roar, and eerie death screams of some animal caught in a predator's jaw, as it unsuspectingly drank at the water hole. It was frightening, and yet exciting, as we had never before experienced the wild jungle at such close quarters.

The lodge was small, with minimum comforts, and as the sun set over the edge of the jungle, Thathie's friend bundled us into his Land Rover once again, and drove to a spot where we observed wild animals at waterholes. It was indeed worth the drive and discomfort, as it was truly an unforgettable sight, watching majestic animals in their natural habitat. We stayed at a safe distance from them anyway, so we were not in any sort of danger.

That night, elephants trumpeted stridently, as they stalked the grounds, but it was not frightening, as I felt safe within the four walls of the lodge. The awesome majesty of those magnificent wild animals, roaming freely in their habitat, was an amazing and exhilarating experience. On our return journey, we stopped at various places, and even ventured on a suspension bridge that spanned the Maha Veli river.

I still tremble with fear when I think of that fragile, swaying rope bridge we crossed that day, as I suffered from vertigo even as a child, and still cannot bear heights. After much eating, singing, and drinking (on Thathie's and his friend's part), we finally arrived home after our exciting safari in the jungle.

One day, we travelled in a railcar with engine driver, Rusten, one of Thathie's numerous railway friends. He allowed us to travel in the engine cabin, where we looked out of the wide, front windows. I spent my time inspecting interesting devices and gadgets, and occasionally, looked out at endless tracts of wilderness, and vast, desolate plains, typical of the landscape in that region. The only excitement in this monotonous landscape was the sight of a wild elephant or buffalo on the track.

Sometimes, the railcar smashed into a buffalo with such force and loud thud, that the whole railcar vibrated with the shock of the impact, as the unfortunate animal catapulted far out into the scrub. On this particular occasion, a bright, sunny day, like most days in this arid region, we were happily on our way to Kalkudah, to picnic on the beach. We saw a young man walking along casually on the rail track. No one gave the man a second glance, as it was a familiar sight to see a villager walking along the track, after shopping, visiting or working.

Instead of moving away and jumping aside, as most people did when a railcar approached, the man suddenly threw himself under the speeding railcar, and laid his head on the track. I will never forget the sickening thud, as the railcar hit the man and smashed him to pieces. I did not get off when we stopped, but driver Rusten, and some ghoulish passengers wanted to have a look. I am certain it must have been a gory sight, because of driver Rusten's graphic description of the scene, although nothing much was left of the poor man.

We turned back, and headed off to the previous station, for driver Rusten to make a statement regarding the suicide. They found a letter inside the man's pocket stating his reasons. He was unemployed, and could not support his wife and baby, and so it was "goodbye cruel world." I could not forget that tragic incident for days to come, and the whole family was subdued too.

Twelve months in the "uncongenial" town of Polonnaruwa flew by quickly, interspersed with several memorable trips to scenic places like Batticoloa, Parsikudah, Kalkudah, and Trincomalee beach resorts.

Another exciting trip was to see the famous frescoes on the walls of the rock fortress in Sigiriya, and then onto the dagobas at Dambulla. Those places we visited, left indelible impressions on my mind, some pleasant, others not so pleasant.

The awesome grandeur of Sigiriya, rock fortress of the ancient king Kasyapa, and frescoes painted on the rock face of the fortress, were remarkable, and Dambulla too, has to be seen to be believed. The magnificent rock paintings, statues, and carvings that has stood the test of time, are a tribute to our ingenious ancestors.

The only drawback at Sigiriya was, I had to be carried "piggy back" up the steep steps carved out of the rock, until we reached the summit. I just could not bear to climb up the narrow stairway, with nothing but a fragile railing on the side to prevent an accident. Menika carried me up most of the way, and after we spent several hours wandering around the rock fortress, marvelling at ruins of black granite swimming pools, gigantic lions at the entrance, and throne, all carved out of rock, we finally returned home.

Anthony left for England around this time, and our family travelled up to bid him farewell at the harbour in Colombo. It was a frightening experience to board a small boat that ferried us across, and then clamber up to the huge passenger liner. Anthony studied mechanical engineering, and so did Malcolm. Granny had a great respect for education, as she attended junior school only. She insisted that her children followed worthwhile careers, and told us how much she sacrificed to educate Malcolm and Anthony.

Rosie attended St Bridget's convent in Colombo, and Marie studied at a good private school as well. Before Anthony sailed away, our whole family sat for a photograph at a studio, which I still have in my album. As Anthony sobbed and said goodbye, one of the sailors remarked, "Smart boy, crying eh? Don't worry, you'll be fine!" So the first one in the family spread his wings, and we watched his ship sail away from the harbour.

Our twelve months in Polonnaruwa was almost at an end before we knew. And looking back, it seems we travelled a great deal, and spent almost every weekend at some interesting spot or another.

We made a special trip to Colombo around this time, to watch the superb film, "Ben-Hur" starring Charlton Heston. It was greatly publicised, and everyone who saw it, insisted we should see it too, so there we were on our way. It was truly one of the greatest movies I had seen then. My only regret was, that while the grand chariot race thundered across the silver screen, there I sat, feeling miserable and sick; my jaws and throat ached so much, I could hardly bear the pain.

Thathie bought icy chocs (my favourite), vanilla ice cream coated with crispy chocolate. But I could hardly eat it, because of the incredible ache in my jaw, so I dumped it under the seat. The long movie finally ended, and we returned to Granny's place, where we usually stayed on our trips to Colombo. My aching cheeks swelled up drastically, as if I had stuffed cotton inside my mouth. The diagnosis, mumps! We returned to Polonnaruwa a day later, and then followed a very painful week or so. I was delirious, and ran a high temperature, with Ammie and Menika forcing me to drink fluids, while the fever ran its normal course and subsided. At last, I was on the mend, and my temperature returned to normal, but I do not recall any of my siblings contracting mumps at the same time.

Besides mumps, horrid insects, and mosquitoes, whose severe stings took months to heal, plagued me. I suffered an ear infection that caused constant pain, and discharge from my ears. It healed eventually, once the doctor syringed both ears, and gave me a dose of antibiotics. The rest of the family and I had had just about enough of Polonnaruwa by then. So we were delighted when Thathie announced he was transferred to Hatton, a small, up-country town, situated in the cool, hilly regions of the island.

Thathie was also promoted to assistant station master, a great achievement, as he was quite young then. He said that the on-going joke in the railway was, that every officer diligently perused obituary notices in newspapers, eager to find out which of the old station masters had died, because no one got promoted until then. Thathie's ambition was to become a station master long before he turned sixty, as most of the other station masters were over sixty or more.

Before we knew it, the days flew by, and there we were, all packed up and ready for our next move to Hatton. Our furniture was loaded into one wagon, and the livestock, including my cat, dogs, and chickens in another. Rosie was with us, and as usual, much laughing and hilarity went on. She told us she bought cigarettes on credit from one of the shops down the street, and promised to pay the shopkeeper soon.

As the shopkeeper knew Rosie was related to Thathie, he had no qualms in obliging her. Now, as they all stood watching the train pull out of the station, the shopkeeper's mouth opened wide in disbelief, when he saw Rosie board the train and wave cheekily at him. She laughed her head off at the flabbergasted expression on his face, as she did not pay him, and considered it a huge joke.

We left Polonnaruwa at the end of 1961, and I have no recollections of Christmas celebrations that year. Another unanswered question was, what had happened to our house in Bandarawela? My parents did not discuss their financial affairs with us, but eventually, I learnt that the people who rented the place, defaulted. The mortgage repayments went into arrears, and my parents lost their house. That was it, and they never mentioned the matter again.

Top left Rita. On our way to Welimada. Ammie and Thathie. Rita's wedding and on honeymoon. Malcolm and Rosie. Nihal in cadet uniform

Chapter 17

The train pulled in slowly at Polgahawela station, where we changed trains to travel on to Hatton. One can only imagine the confusion as we transferred our luggage, and animals onto the next train. The wagon with our furniture, was soon hitched on to the next train without delay, but our pets and personal belongings we carted around, were extremely cumbersome, to say the least. I lugged my pet cat in a rusty old bird cage, as I had nothing else to transport her in.

Rosie, Nilanthi, and Nihal thought it hilarious to see the poor nervous cat trembling inside a birdcage. Next moment, when my attention was elsewhere, they released it, and that was the last I saw of my poor cat. The three of them chased it down the track on the pretext of catching it, but I saw them throwing stones at the unfortunate, confused feline, who was scared stiff, as it ran for dear life. I wonder if that cat ever found a good home, or went completely berserk and neurotic at this sudden misfortune.

I cried a great deal, and was very angry with the three of them, until we reached Hatton. To make matters worse, the poor dogs were ailing. Many years later, Rosie recalled this cat incident, and apologised profusely. "I'm *so sorry* for that mean trick we played on you, chasing your pet cat away. Please forgive me." I told her it was so long ago, that I forgave and forgot such childhood pranks.

My first impression of Hatton, was a misty, cold, sleepy, up-country town, with an air of tranquillity. We climbed a steep road to reach our new house, which was second in a row of six or seven railway bungalows. It was a charming, spacious house, with a nice garden, and the backyard sloped down to a sheer drop overlooking the rail track below. Strange, how safety issues were never considered then, as it was very dangerous for children, and even adults, if you happened to walk down at night, or in wet weather, and missed your step.

The railway authorities did not go to the expense of fencing off the edge, and I marvel at the total inadequacy of safety issues then. A narrow, footpath, beaten through tall grass, wound around both sides of that slope down to the rail track. I ran down this winding footpath to the rail track below sometimes. Then walked along the track, until I reached lovely, secluded, shady places, with little streams and brooks gurgling through leafy woods.

I loved the place, and our garden too, as it was full of adventurous places to hide in. The house was large, with four bedrooms, and two small store-rooms, or pantries on either side of the dining room. I wanted one of the pantries for my own bedroom, as they were large enough to hold a single bed, and a small table. I immediately went about converting this store-room into a liveable bedroom. A fairly wide window overlooked a section of garden on one side of the house, and whenever I played in the garden, I crept in through this window (just for the fun of it).

I risked broken limbs many times, jumping out of that window onto the garden below, so I could snatch some raw peas when Menika was not looking. It was quite a high window, and I am surprised that except for a few grazes, I did not injure myself seriously. My passion for books was rampant now, and I devoured endless adventure stories, classic novels, and especially those written by Enid Blyton, queen of childrens' fiction.

Her superb stories enthralled me, and I yearned to be in the thick of such daring exploits, and excitement in everyday life, and was always on the lookout for anything that bore the remotest semblance to an adventure. My imagination constantly fired up, I was totally lost in a magical world of my own, as I sat on the broad ledge of the window, and gazed at the stars and moon. Then as I grew older, I indulged in all sorts of romantic dreams, and sat on that window sill for hours.

We settled down comfortably in our bedrooms. My parents occupied the adjoining room next to Nilanthi, Shirani and Nelune. Nihal had his own room right at the end of the house next to a lage store-room and the kitchen. The house had a parlour, large sitting room, family area, and dining room. It was a large, comfortable house, but what I liked most of all was the huge, guava tree that grew right outside the kitchen window. Its spreading branches overhanging the roof made it an easy climb to the roof top.

This was a most convenient way to escape trouble, and some people whom I did not want to meet. The first few days were chaotic, as we set about getting things in order, and the saddest memory of those early days was losing our lovable dog, Tony. I was devastated when he succumbed to distemper, and was inconsolable for some time.

Ammie was upset too, as she loved dogs, especially cute little Tony. He had been with us since Bandarawela, and it was heart-breaking when we buried him at the bottom of the garden. And it would take a long time for another canine to replace Tony in my heart. In time though, Ammie purchased an Alsatian dog (German shepherd), as she intended to breed them.

When we first arrived in Hatton, I noticed hundreds of squirrels scampering around in our garden, and occasionally managed to seize one of them. But sometimes, I was left holding a bushy tail in my hand, as the petrified little squirrel broke off and whizzed up a tree. Their needle-sharp teeth punctured my fingers several times, but that did not stop me from trying to capture one. And whenever I caught one, I imprisoned it in a little cage, fed it plantains, and left plenty of water too.

Squirrels could be tamed, and were great pets, but I could not keep one alive long enough to domesticate it. I put them into a little box at nights, and kept them near my bed, but come morning, much to my sorrow, they lay motionless, with little paws upended, mouths open, and displaying long, sharp teeth. Invariably, they all died on me, and I deeply mourned the demise of those furry little squirrels. These apt words rang in my ears.

"Oh ever thus from childhood's hour; I never loved a tree or flower, it was sure to die; I never nursed a dear gazelle, to gladden me with its soft black eye; and when it came to know and love me, it was sure to die!"

After only one year at St Anthony's college, Nihal was now enrolled at St John Bosco's college, which stood right in front of the railway bungalows. Every evening we watched the Christian Brothers pacing up and down their balcony or front yard, as they meditated or recited the rosary. One of them, Bro. Alphonso, was a frequent visitor, and he organised plays in the college, as he was very fond of drama and music. Bro. Alphonso was a stocky, well-built man, with black hair, a bushy black beard, and wore square, black-framed spectacles. The principal was a grumpy, middle-aged man, and Nihal promptly dubbed him "Brother Pilo." Nihal said he was so grouchy, because he must have "piles" (haemorrhoids).

St Anne's church stood a little distance away from the college, and St Gabriel's convent was on a hilltop, just a stone's throw from our house, so the convent buildings were visible from our front porch. In other words, we lived conveniently, in the immediate vicinity of schools and church. Although we were close to these amenities, the railway station was about half a mile or so away, and the main town was further than the station. We usually walked to town or to the station, and Thathie walked to and fro from the station daily, as we did not have transport.

The main unpacking over, we went with Thathie to meet the principal of St Gabriel's convent, a tall, middle-aged, and dignified English nun. In spite of her imposing exterior, and firm, thin-lipped mouth, I glimpsed a humorous sparkle in her pale-blue eyes. We were enrolled at St Gabriel's convent, and started school the following week.

On our way home from the interview, Thathie upbraided Nilanthi for speaking to Mother Superior with both hands in her pockets, which to him was a sign of disrespect. Nilanthi let this criticism go over her head.

After spending a few more days with us, Rosie returned to Maharagama. But Malcolm, who arrived a day after we moved, decided to stay on a few more weeks. Ammie placed two long, planter boxes on either side of the parlour, and as Malcolm was a very good artist, she asked him to paint some scenery on them.

He loved trains, and that was what he painted on the planter boxes. One was of a Canadian diesel engine that he admired very much, winding through hills and dales, and the other, was a brick red engine in a similar setting. Everyone admired his work, and he was very proud of his art. Malcolm was an avid collector of model trains too, and owned a large collection of engines and trains of every description. He set them out on tracks whenever we visited, and kept us amused for hours.

We settled down to a new way of life in Hatton, surrounded by Catholic schools and church, which factor, impacted on me profoundly over the following years.

My first day at the convent, was a great change from "Thopawawe Mahavidyala." All the children were polite, well-behaved, and neatly dressed, and as it was not a co-ed school, hooligans and ruffians, like the little boys in Polonnaruwa, did not plague me.

One of the girls, with an exotic name, Scheherazade, introduced herself shyly, and after general assembly, I walked with her to our classroom. It was a small classroom with fifteen students.

The school buildings sprawled out on three separate levels. And long, winding steps connected them with classrooms and compounds on each level for sports, and play time. The main sports ground was at the very top level where children played net ball; on the second level, was a badminton court, and also a special building for "Home Science" with a well-equipped kitchen, bedroom, several dolls, sewing machines, and a first aid room.

The girls were taught how to be good mothers, and housewives, according to prevailing notions then of what "good domestic skills" meant. We practiced first aid, cooking, sewing, and all other tasks that were considered mandatory to run a smooth household. The nuns had very strict notions of what every good wife and mother should know, and were determined to mould exemplary mothers and wives at St Gabriel's convent. It did not seem to matter, if some girls preferred to be single and career-oriented, because the nuns firmly believed that all girls should be well prepared in every aspect of "Home Science."

On the topmost level, stood a large library, and senior classrooms. Our classroom was on the last level, and faced the main road, church, boarding house, and orphanage. Most of the teachers were Irish and English nuns, but some were local nuns, with a few Sinhalese and Tamil female teachers. Male teachers were not employed in the convent then, but only one male teacher taught there many years later.

Two grades shared one classroom, due to lack of space, and small number of English students, as English classes were phased out of most schools then. Sinhalese was now the primary language in most schools, while English and Tamil were considered secondary languages. I was in the last group of students who completed senior school in English, with Sinhalese as my second language.

Only seven girls were in grade five, and eight in grade six. A few were Muslims, Burghers, and of mixed race like us, whose father or mother was either Sinhalese or Tamil, and married to a Burgher. I became good friends with Gnei Fawzia, Loretta, Scheherazade, and some other girls. Shirani and I once again shared the same classroom, which led to hilarious and sometimes awkward moments for us. If one of us got into a scrape, we were very quick to tell tales about the other.

Naturally, we had our own set of friends, resulting in competition and friendly rivalry between our two groups, whether sports, essay competitions, debates, and so on. As we settled in at St Gabriel's, we amused ourselves playing pranks on each other, but mostly on unpopular teachers (of which we had a few). One of them in particular, was our Sinhalese teacher, with the ludicrous name of Miss Queenie.

Oh, but she was the crankiest character of them all, and to our huge amusement, she wore ornate butterfly-shaped spectacles. A large, black mole marked her cheek, which according to daily fancy, she outlined in various shapes with an eyebrow pencil; one day it looked like a Bo-leaf, next, a perfect circle or oblong etc. Her sparse black hair was pulled back severely, and knotted in a tight bun on top of her head. She sneeringly referred to us as the "Burgher Class" and lashed out at us with such heavy sarcasm that we trembled under her Spartan treatment.

Miss Queenie was never pleasant or kind to anyone, but always hostile. She screeched out in a high-pitched tone, like a wicked old witch. We in turn, mimicked her waddling gait, with her large, protruding posterior, and made fun of her prim, pedantic ways. Before class commenced sometimes, she bundled us outside to weed her garden plot, where she tried to grow sugar cane, hot chillies, red onions, and other vegetables.

The Prime Minister, Mr Dudley Senanayake, had initiated this move, with a vision of making the country self-sufficient. Schools were encouraged to grow vegetables (with student labour), cultivate crops, and do all the hard work. When Miss Queenie was particularly nasty to us, and we wanted to get our own back, we weeded the plots indiscriminately, pulling out tender young plants and seedlings along with weeds. It was a rare and rewarding sight then, and made up for many insults, canings, and sarcasm, just to see her turn red with fury. She shrieked, screamed, and spat high-flown Sinhalese epithets that we did not understand.

Then some naughty girl pulled out sugar cane plants, and started beating it on a rock. And when Miss Queenie, bursting with fury, questioned her about it, the girl innocently replied, "I'm only trying to break a piece of sugar cane for me to eat." Miss Queenie shook with anger and suppressed fury, as she burst out in Sinhalese (because as a rule she never ever spoke to us in English). "You stupid, stupid child, you have to *cut* sugar cane, not dash it on a rock to break off a piece!"

She waddled off in a huff to get a knife, and then spent the next few minutes cutting pieces of the damaged sugar cane, which she distributed among us. It was difficult to maintain a dignified silence, and eat sugar cane at the same time, but amid smothered giggling and sniggering, we ate up all the sugar cane. These extra activities expended a large portion of the forty five minute Sinhalese lesson, but we did not care or complain.

One afternoon, we sat around laughing and chatting as usual before Miss Queenie entered the room. But as I had my back turned towards the door, I did not hear her silent entrance, so she could catch us talking, and punish us for unruly behaviour. We stood up immediately when she entered, but as my foot was entangled around the desk leg, I could not stand up straight. I tried my best to turn around although it was very awkward.

Her eagle eye flitted around the classroom, and immediately spied all was not well, as my posture was extremely sloppy. She waddled towards me ominously, her posterior bulging out more prominently as it was wont to do whenever she was displeased or angry.

She screeched in her high-pitched voice. "*Why* aren't you standing up straight?" I stood there bright red with embarrassment, my foot still twisted. Suddenly, she prodded me with her umbrella and caught me off guard. Next moment, I lost my balance completely, and much to my classmates amusement and merriment, I toppled down in a heap.

Miss Queenie's surprise exceeded mine. She looked at me, sarcasm oozing out of every pore, and barked out, "Moka? Jabara kalantha the?" (what? You got a fainting fit?). Mere words cannot convey her sarcasm and tone.

My face, red as a chilli pepper, I stood up with as much decorum as I could muster under the circumstances. I prayed fervently for the lesson to end soon, as suppressed giggles of my companions only made it harder for me to look serious. She forbade us to speak English in her class, but one of the girls now stood up innocently, and questioned her in English, which sparked another spasm of anger. I was spared further chastisement.

Miss Direkze, another fire-breathing dragon, was a bane in my life too. She was not related to the previous principal in Polonnaruwa, whose name she shared though. She wreaked terror in my heart, and in the hearts of every other timid school girl whom she intimidated. A fair-complexioned, Burgher, she was a spinster in her late forties, with large, prominent dark eyes. She wore square, black-framed spectacles (a schoolgirl caricaturist's delight), and she was always dignified and proper, with a slow, ponderous gait.

One of the many rules she inculcated into our young minds was, "A lady must *never ever* walk fast or run, even if there is a fire!" So, we walked sedately (in a ladylike manner), whenever she was around. One would think these were extreme restrictions for energetic, young girls, but there it was.

Those were her rules, and such was my fear of Miss Direkze, that if I was capering about, or running in a "hoity toity" fashion (her very own phrase), I immediately slowed down to a "lady-like" walk the minute she passed by. She was a stickler for proper behaviour at all times, and also demanded absolute dog-like devotion and respect.

She lived in a large room in the convent, with another spinster teacher, Miss Chelliah, and it was amusing to hear them address each other as, "Chelliah" and "Direkze." Sometimes, when I ran errands for one of them, I peeked in curiously, and glimpsed a spotless room, with everything in place, and a screen dividing their beds.

Miss Direkze was a cranky old lady no doubt, but when I grew older and more mature, my respect increased, and I grudgingly admired her values and ethics. As an adult, I appreciated her more than ever for the principles and ideals she instilled when I was an impressionable schoolgirl. Still, I cannot deny that she was most certainly a bane in my school life then, because her eagle eye never missed a thing.

She sneered, and her voice dripped with sarcasm when she called out *"Scheherazade"* as she picked on her for some misdemeanour. Miss Direkze thought her name was too exotic, and each time she called her over, she made it a point to stress every syllable in her unusual name, stating that such a moniker belonged to the "Arabian nights."

We could not do anything wrong without her noticing it, and bringing it to our attention, or worse still, complain to our parents and Mother Superior. Miss Queenie and Miss Direkze marred my otherwise happy, carefree school days. I was reputed to be a mischievous but "bright" student, and as long as my homework was up to date, I was alright. I made it a point to be ahead of my school work, so there were no complaints to my parents. I was usually the leader in any mischief, because

I was daring, and thought nothing of taking risks that less intrepid girls would take (a result of reading too many adventure stories).

If I suggested anything particularly adventurous, my friends followed, as long as they did not face consequences. Like the time we ventured to forbidden territory, where numerous fruit trees grew all around the convent property. While running around at recess, we happened to see luscious cherry or "Chinese" guavas, glistening temptingly high up in the trees. My friends dared me to climb and get some. I clambered up without even stopping to remove my bright red jumper that I wore over a navy blue pinafore and white blouse.

I gobbled down a heap of delicious guavas, as first pickings were rightfully mine I declared, before throwing small branches of heavily laden fruit to my hungry friends below. Suddenly, a loud banging on the window pane in one of the nearby classrooms, arrested my determined ravaging. An angry teacher shouted out, "*Red jersey*, get down from that tree at once!" Obviously, she spotted my bright jumper that I did not have the foresight to remove. I certainly did not have the makings of a fruit plunderer.

I could not escape, because she knew exactly who I was, and prepared to march me straight up to Mother Superior's office. I pleaded and cajoled so earnestly that she relented, and let me off with a severe warning. How true the saying, "Forbidden fruit tastes sweeter" because never in my life have I tasted such delicious guavas!

Chapter 18

Sr Josephine Agnes was no doubt my favourite teacher; she looked like a petite, porcelain doll, with a creamy-white complexion, beautiful, dark eyes set in an exquisite, heart-shaped face. Her voice and manner had a quiet, underlying irony. She could be sarcastic, and mete out nasty remarks when displeased. But I was one of her "diligent" students (she said), so I always tried to remain in her good books.

History, which Sr Josephine taught admirably, was my favourite subject, next to English literature. I enjoyed both subjects very much, and excelled in them, and had no problems coping with homework. She did not pick on me as much as she did on "lazy students" as she addressed them. History came alive when she described stirring events leading up to the French Revolution, or uttered subtle insinuations when describing King Louis XV's mistress, Madame de Pompadour.

She embellished history with her own cynical remarks and observations, and I pictured people, places, and events that she described so well. I cannot deny though, that whenever I looked at a picture of Napoleon's strong, handsome face, I had a soft spot for him, even though he was a power hungry megalomaniac. And those he wreaked war against dubbed him "the enemy of mankind."

Sr Josephine was indeed a remarkable teacher. I am grateful to her for awakening a love of ancient and medieval history. Her favourite expression was, "*Try* to see everything in your *mind's eye,*" and to this day, I follow her advice. We soon discovered that Sr Josephine and Miss Direkze were antagonists.

They derided each other's teaching methods and behaviour, and made no secret of the fact that they held each other in contempt. Now, as I liked one, and feared the other, it was no mean task to keep them both happy, and to stay in their good books *all* the time. If one of them suspected that I spent too much time on a subject with the other, she showed marked disapproval.

Miss Direkze taught geography (which I did not like), and English grammar. Although I tried my best, I sometimes failed to please either of them. Once, Sr Josephine observed in her quiet, ironical manner. "Some children are very *diplomatic,* because they try to get on with two opposite people at the same time!" I knew she referred to me. One day, I was well and truly in a scrape, and remained in Sr Josephine's black books for a long time.

We had three different school "Houses" with their own colours. Red for Caritas (Charity), blue for Veritas (Truth), and green for Felicitas (Joy). Miss Direkze was head of Veritas House, Miss Chelliah, of Caritas, and Sr Josephine, that of Felicitas. When we were allotted Houses, we did not have a choice, and that seemed unfair to me.

Most of my good friends were in Veritas, and all the unpopular girls (as I thought), belonged to Felicitas, who never seemed to win any events at the Annual Sports Meet. Veritas and Caritas excelled in every sport, and I longed to be part of Veritas. I watched them wistfully, enjoying a rollicking good time inside their bright blue tent.

Even Miss Direkze thawed visibly on such occasions, and she laughed in a way that made her large, flabby stomach wobble like a jelly. I made a momentous decision, and renounced my allegiance to Felicitas. Ripping off the green ribbon from my shoulder, I donned a blue one instead, and crossed over to the enemy. Miss Direkze welcomed me gleefully, as it was a trump card against her rival, Sr Josephine, to enlist a defecting member.

My joy was short-lived though when on the following day I had to face her in the classroom. I sat down apprehensively after the usual morning salutation. Sr Josephine set her books down on the desk in a pensive manner, then looked up sorrowfully, just like a wounded Madonna. She cast a melancholy glance around the classroom, and still avoiding my eye, emitted a deep sigh from the very depths of her soul.

"I'm sorry to say there is a little *traitor* in this classroom who has left Felicitas House and joined Veritas. This is not *allowed,* and that person must return to Felicitas *immediately*!" I blushed with embarrassment, but was determined not to return to Felicitas if I could help it, and remained in Veritas "illegally" until the day I left St Gabriel's Convent. In due time Sr Josephine Agnes forgave my "treachery" as she termed it.

Shirani, and all my other friends joined Girl Guides except me. I already manifested a determined reluctance to follow the crowd. I wanted to be totally different to everyone else even at that early age, and never felt any peer pressure to be "one of the crowd" and revelled in my individualism. I read that my name "Nalini" means "free spirit" and I was perfectly happy doing only what I *chose* to do, and if others wanted to follow me, I had no objection.

I never aped anyone, just to belong to a set. It was the other way around, as my friends followed me. It is very sad that modern children are so afraid to be themselves, and unable to say "no" to peer pressure. Psychologists tell us that children dislike being different to their peers. So they dress alike, look alike, take drugs, smoke cigarettes, and indulge in sexual exploits, just because they are too afraid to stand up and be themselves.

It was a different era then, obviously. But if children could only grow up without being pressured into situations that they really do not want to get into, many teenage problems would lessen. I was never afraid to turn back on anything I did not really like, or wanted to do.

In a spirit of mischief, I taunted the new Girl Guides, and Shirani especially, when they paraded in the universal green uniform, brown belts, and badges. When they recited their mottos, I sang out the very opposites of them, such as, "Guides are dumb, Guides are slow, Guides are helpless wherever they go, and not *always* prepared" as one of their mottos, was to "Always be prepared." Until they complained in exasperation to Miss Eva, the Guide Leader.

Miss Eva listened to their complaints solemnly, as they repeated the ditties I sang out. When they finished, she turned and told me off roundly. "And *you* are all of those things rolled into one!" The delighted Girl Guides greeted this sally with shouts of laughter. I was temporarily chastened, and did not tease them for some time.

The days vanished, with many incidents, glad and sad. Life was crowded, with many events, and memorable parties on every occasion. My parents invited huge crowds, and sometimes, our school friends, and their parents attended these parties, where much singing, dancing, eating, and drinking took place. We acquired a reputation for throwing lavish parties.

My love of books increased with the years. I literally devoured many classics and children's books eagerly. And I had such a voracious appetite, that it astonished my family and teachers, especially Miss Direkze, who was school librarian as well. One day, burning with fever at school, I was told to go home immediately. But I borrowed a few books from the library before I left. Miss Direkze touched my fevered brow, and said almost kindly, "Go home straight to bed, and don't read too much."

This avid reading however, broadened my horizons, and enriched my imagination with so much adventure, fun and laughter in my otherwise well-organised, mundane routine. I remember the saying, "Those who read, live a thousand lives," because we cannot possibly experience everything life has to offer. So when we read, we are enriched with life experiences of thousands.

After I recovered, I pretended I was a brave adventurer. I went off on daring safaris through narrow paths in tea estates, grazing arms and legs on jagged, newly pruned branches, but not caring at all. I always seemed to have cuts and grazes all over, and my family laughed and teased me, as they found my adventurous behaviour quite amusing.

Many sparkling streams, and miniature waterfalls, abounded in Hatton, not to mention a large, river near by where I fished. My lonely treks along the railway track and down foot paths where few people walked, took me to fantastic, enchanted places, and I still see them in my "Mind's eye." It was peaceful, safe, and lovely in woods and glades, under tall trees besides murmuring streams.

Only the sound of gurgling brooks, or the sudden intrusion of a bird's cry disturbed my reveries in the green mantle of silence and tranquillity. I sat and fished for hours, gazing at ripples in the water, and ever-changing patterns, fashioned with sun and clouds reflected in crystal clear waters flowing by. As I sat there alone, filled with joy, the beauty and wonders of nature around intoxicated me.

It was the perfect setting for my embryonic creativity, growing steadily, nourished and nurtured with the richness and varied accumulation of those early sensations. My mind, like a sponge, absorbed and retained every beautiful scene and impression. And the glorious response within my being overwhelmed me, until I felt I was about to explode with teeming thoughts demanding expression. My feelings cried out for utterance, and my childish mind yearned to create words to express these emerging emotions.

Everything we experience and see in our impressionable age, is gathered like rich nutrients and leaf mould, enriching the soil of our imagination. These early images that seeped through my consciousness, were vital ingredients that left a lasting impact on my imagination and creativity.

It was with a sense of exhilaration that I returned home after these solitary wanderings. Now, it is unthinkable, to allow a young child or an adult to wander off alone in such places, as times have changed drastically, even in Ceylon, and in the whole world, where no one is safe anymore. Sadly, we live in a violent, depraved society, with no regard for human life anymore. When I was a child, I did not have the slightest suspicion that I could be in any danger at all. I never heard of all the frightful things that could happen to a child or an adult, if some deranged person followed and attacked.

Sometimes, if I was lucky, I caught a few silvery sprats, and imprisoned them in a large, "Horlicks" bottle, with a string tied around it, and walked home proudly with my "catch." Then I emptied the tiny fish into a small tank under the guava tree, which was just a shallow, muddy hole I dug up and filled with water. I covered it with a wire mesh to deter marauding felines, and afterwards ran indoors happily to pursue some other juvenile game or play with my sisters.

It never failed to shock me the following morning, when I saw the unfortunate fish either dead, or dying, and the murky water all dried up to a thick crust of mud. The cats had a feast, after getting through the loosely covered mesh, and angled the luckless fish with dainty paws. But it did not occur to me why the hole kept drying up! No one told me I had to cement the floor of the tank, or lay a plastic sheet inside to hold the water. I learnt from experience that water evaporated quickly in the muddy hole, no matter how much I filled it up.

During this stage of my life, at eleven years, I suffered a very serious bout of religious mania. The outward manifestation of my mental state was evident when I plastered holy pictures on my bedroom walls from top to bottom. I also fixed an old soup ladle painted pale pink, at the entrance to my room. It contained holy water, and everyone had to dip their fingers, and bless themselves before they entered my room.

Religious paraphernalia adorned my room; rosary beads, statues, pictures, and prayer books. I also sculptured some good (in my opinion), clay busts of Jesus Christ, and Our Lady, and spread them on the window sill to dry. Nihal, and other members of the family however, belonged to a different school of thought and opinion regarding my sculptures. They waited until the coast was clear, and then used my sculptures as missiles to throw at stray cats and dogs in the neighbourhood.

Nihal found my religious zeal hilarious, and promptly dubbed me, "Sister Josephine Agnes." I ignored jokes and jibes in a martyr-like fashion, and went about with undiminished fervour. The religious bug had bitten me badly, and I did not care about the ridicule I suffered. Ammie boasted to the nuns, Christian Brothers, and priests about my devotion. "Dolly attends *daily* Mass in the morning, and novenas, rosary, and benediction whenever there is a service in the evenings."

The Brothers at St John Bosco's looked upon me as a little saint. I did not want to draw such attention, but Ammie could not help boasting about my religious fervour. Then one day, along came Bro. Jude into our lives. And being the most ludicrous religious fanatic I had ever met, he cured me of religious fanaticism once and for all, when I saw what it had done to him. Ammie had talked to him about my devotion and piety, and he *insisted* on seeing my room with all the holy pictures.

He was so impressed, and much to my amusement and chagrin, he called me, "Queen Philomena" (my baptism name), and addressed me as, "Sister Philomena." He was mentally unstable, I believe, because his behaviour was rather eccentric. If he happened to see a female, he quickly hid his hands behind his back, and never permitted himself to shake hands with a member of the opposite sex.

Bro. Jude preached about chastity and purity, till I could stand it no longer, because I was unaware of what he was talking. He was stout, of medium height, and wore thick spectacles with square black frames. He had a hoarse intense voice, stilted speech, and a nervous twitch in his eyes.

He visited our home daily, whenever he came down from his college in Negombo. And he invariably singled me out, almost pushed me into my room where he started preaching about chastity (his favourite subject), and told me I should *never* allow any boy to touch me, or come near me.

He presented me with a large album, full of beautiful, holy pictures, with an inscription, to "My Queen Sister." This was nauseating, especially when he admonished me, "*Don't* let anybody touch your lips, because you must be a bride of Christ etc etc." I was only a child, and could hardly comprehend what he rambled on about, but was old enough to figure out that he was a raving lunatic. I just loathed his silly behaviour. In any case, I had enough of the whole religious phase by now, and contemplated re-decorating my room.

One morning, when I was sitting up on the guava tree, I saw Bro. Jude plodding up to our house, and quickly decided I was never ever going to listen to his mad ramblings again. Only one thing to do, I decided. I climbed right up to the top of the guava tree, and jumped onto the roof, balancing precariously, while I crouched and crawled to escape being noticed. I lay flat on the roof where I could hear him without being seen.

I heard Ammie and Menika calling me, then Bro. Jude joined them under the guava tree. And I almost giggled when I heard him say in his pompous manner, "*Where* is Sister Philomena Mrs Rajapakse? Call the police, I think she is missing!" I nearly choked with laughter, but there was no way I intended going down and be subjected to any more of his pious lectures. So there I stayed, and did not move a muscle, and hoped Bro. Jude would soon go away.

After much more calling and searching, I watched him return to the college, and I climbed down wearily, and felt sore, after staying in an awkward position for so long. Then I bolted down the backyard towards the rail track. Unfortunately or fortunately, Bro. Jude's keen eye spotted my retreating figure, and he finally got the message. Later that day, he told Ammie in a sorrowful voice, "I saw Sister running and hiding from me, pray for her Mrs Rajapakse, she will be a nun someday I know!"

Whether Bro. Jude was partly or solely to blame for my complete changeover from religious fanaticism to other teenage interests, I do not know. But soon after this incident, we heard he suffered a nervous breakdown. I am positive it was all due to his inhibitions, paranoid behaviour, suppressed emotions, and all sorts of hang-ups that I analysed when I was older.

We thought it was all a big joke then, and Ammie whispered to her friends, and others, who happened to mention Bro. Jude's condition. I took down all the holy pictures one by one, and as most of them were damaged with globs of paste, into the bin they went. Out came the ladle with holy water, and all the rest of the religious paraphernalia that crowded my room. I think this religious phase was due to the nuns constantly bombarding us about "vocations" and how God "called" certain people to follow him. It was a natural response to a spiritual awakening in me, and died a natural death.

I was keen on sewing, and building dolls furniture, with rather restricted materials. I cut worn-out blankets, and made teddy bears out of them, and when my friends saw them, they immediately requested me to make some for them too. I enjoyed creative work, and took great pride in these little projects. Now that my religious phase was over, I was happily engaged in various other childish amusements, a healthier alternative no doubt.

Chapter 19

The walls in my room looked bare and untidy, with paste marks, and several holes I had made to hang pictures, and also due to my inept carpentry efforts. The heavy shelving I fixed, supported by very small nails, could not bear overloaded shelves, and were prone to crash down on me in the middle of the night, while I slept. No matter how many times I nailed the shelves in place, my favourite books fell on my head at the most inopportune moments. When Marie, who was very artistic, visited one day, I enlisted her to decorate my room.

We pasted large sheets of butchers paper on the walls, as we could not afford wallpaper. Then painted strawberries, leaves, and tendrils in watercolours. With my aid (or hindrance), Marie did a very good job of painting our improvised wallpaper, and I was very proud of our efforts. We also re-enforced the shelves with stronger nails, and they were in place, with my books intact.

Ammie's collection of "Woman and Home" magazines, inspired me to decorate my bed with a pretty frill around it, and a coverlet, like in the pictures in those magazines. A single bed did not fit into my closet-sized bedroom, so I used two wooden boxes, and a foam mattress for a bed, and the end result was quite pretty, I thought.

The small window in my room looked out to the Weerakoon's garden. And beneath my window, Menika had dug a vegetable patch, where I sat and ate raw peas. Mrs Weerakoon frowned on my unladylike exploits, and I did not like her, because she spied on me. I was susceptible to physical appearances of people as a child, and exaggerated their defects, if they were nasty. Mrs Weerakoon had large, protruding teeth, so we promptly nicknamed her "coconut-scraper mouth." Her husband had an identical set of teeth, and when they stood side by side and smiled, they were a perfect match.

On the other side of our garden, lived Mr and Mrs Samarakoon, and their only daughter. The wife was short and stout, with a homely face, but kind-hearted. She was very possessive of her unattractive husband, who always struck me as sly and unattractive, but these were childhood impressions of our neighbours.

Mr Samarakoon had a large, black mole at the tip of his hooked nose, and never met anyone's eye directly whenever he slinked in and out of his house. My first impressions were confirmed, when neighbours gossiped about the couple, and it was whispered that he was a philanderer. The jealous wife was very suspicious, and sometimes we heard loud voices, as they argued and threw things around.

When I was a child, I believed all beautiful people were good and kind, just like in fairy tales, and the physically unappealing, were wicked and evil. I am certain most children think the same even to this day. But now I know that that supposition is a fallacy. Because sometimes, the truth is quite the opposite. And I agree with Shakespeare's keen observation in "Twelfth night" "that beauteous wall doth oft close in pollution."

Anything and everything was a never-ending source of amusement though, even peculiar, or unattractive people, provoked our sense of humour. Their oddities and peculiarities supplied Nihal with plenty of material to keep us amused. His talent for mimicking mannerisms and voices was incomparable. And he kept us in stitches with his impersonations of all our acquaintances and teachers. When we had nothing better to do on some afternoons, the five of us sat around for hours, just talking, laughing, joking, and amusing ourselves with various anecdotes, and of course, Nihal's impersonations. Later on, when Nelune was older, she too could imitate mannerisms and tone of voice perfectly, but in a more dry-humoured fashion, and was never as riotous as Nihal.

A childless couple lived in the house opposite, and the wife was a simple soul (as Ammie said), while the husband was reputed to be a Casanova. They employed a buxom young servant woman, and Menika always giggled when she alluded to her, because it was common gossip that the husband was sexually active with the servant woman. The wife, of course, was the last one to know, and had no inkling of what the neighbours knew, and gossiped about her husband.

Although I was only a child, even *I* could not help noticing the servant woman growing bigger and bigger, especially around her stomach. She started wearing large, maternity blouses to hide her growing concern. And still the wife did not see, or *refused* to see what was becoming painfully obvious to the rest of the world.

Once, when Ammie remarked that the servant woman was gaining weight rapidly, the innocent wife replied, "She eats a lot of rice for lunch *and* dinner, and that's why she's getting so fat by over-eating!" Talk about naiveté. The neighbourhood ladies indulged in an orgy of gossip, and derided the wife's stupidity.

A few weeks later, while I was playing outside, I heard an awful, heart-rending scream from their house. Menika, and some of us ran up to see what was the matter. The servant woman writhed on the floor, howling her lungs out as she gripped her bloodied leg in agony. I glimpsed a deep gash down the calf of her leg, and she screamed. "I cut my leg on a piece of glass in the garden!" Now I realise it was quite an *impossible* accident, and the truth of the matter was, she inflicted it herself.

The distraught wife did not know what to do, as the servant woman yelled and demanded to be taken to a hospital immediately. People were running around everywhere, and soon a hiring car arrived at the scene. The hysterical woman was bundled into it, and rushed off to the nearby hospital. That evening, we heard she gave birth to a baby, and the truth was out now. When she started going into labour, she slashed her leg deliberately with the kitchen knife, so she would be taken to hospital immediately under the pretext of an accident. The utter guts of that woman to have inflicted such a severe injury on herself amazed me then, and still does.

Tongues wagged incessantly, as the local gossips whispered that the husband was responsible for the woman's pregnancy. When she returned from hospital, she and her baby were sent packing to her own home in some remote village, and the scandalous affair faded away. As I said, it was all rumour. I sometimes wondered what the real story was, because the servant woman could very well have had a secret lover, who had fathered her child, and perhaps the husband was blameless.

Mr and Mrs Fernandopillai lived in one of the bungalows close to us. She was a Sinhalese lady, married to a Tamil man from Jaffna, and they had three little girls, and one small boy. Mrs Fernandopillai was expecting her fifth child, when due to some trivial incident, Ammie and she had an altercation that lasted for as long as we lived there. She was however, quite pleasant and friendly whenever we went over to play with her children.

At the very end of the row, lived Mr and Mrs Joseph, with their ten children. She was a buxom, cheerful lady from Jaffna, who liked to bake cakes, and iced them in the most gaudy colours imaginable. When she finished feeding her large brood, she brought some left-over cakes for us, that I was reluctant to eat, as they looked so unappetizing. Her strident laugh rang out merrily, as she told Ammie. "I used to be a *beauty queen* in my young days!" I gazed at her homely, moon-like face, and wondered if she was pulling Ammie's leg. The station master goods, lived next to the Josephs house; he was a middle-aged gentleman, with three promiscuous young daughters, notorious for their frivolous and flighty behaviour. All three overweight daughters were unattractive (so I thought then), and because their father was never sober at home, the girls ran amok. They had no mother, and I do not know if he was divorced or a widower.

I watched the station master goods totter home drunkenly after work, and his daughters complained he went straight off to bed. As our house was second from the beginning of the row, all the neighbours had to pass by our house to reach their homes. So, we knew when the three daughters entertained all sorts of sleazy characters. We were not allowed to visit their home, especially Nilanthi, who was inclined to befriend the three girls, as they were of similar age.

The girls however, came over often to talk with Nilanthi, and discussed their love affairs with her. Thathie was not as bad as that station master goods, when it came to drinking at work, as Thathie came home quite sober sometimes. If he had been working a late shift however, he staggered home late at night or early dawn, and tried his best not to be too conspicuous, as he had to pass the college on his way to and from work. He did not want the Brothers to know he was drunk.

Everyone though, soon knew Thathie had a drinking problem. The parish priest, Brothers, and nuns, allied themselves with Ammie, in the hope they could implore heavenly intervention, for him to abstain from liquor, and be converted. The constant phrase on their lips was, "Pray for your father's conversion." Ironically, Thathie, who was quite anti-Catholic, especially in the early days of his marriage, was now surrounded by a Catholic college, church and convent.

Our house became a focal point for all religious meetings, and social events that any of them organized. Nuns, Brothers, and priests, seemed to be in our lives and home constantly, as they inundated us with daily visits. Ammie always treated them as honoured guests, and even Thathie extended his hospitality, and looked sheepish whenever they visited.

Ammie became involved in numerous church activities, and was organist too, which led to many meetings in our house, as they dropped in to discuss various musical aspects of church services. My greatest source of delight then was a battered old piano that the good Brothers loaned us temporarily, as they had no use for it when they purchased a new piano.

It was out of tune, and had a few "dumb" notes, but this did not prevent me from learning, and playing many tunes by ear. I derived many hours of musical delight from that old piano, as long as we had it. I thumped away patiently for long periods (much to the amusement and annoyance of my family no doubt).

Besides Ammie's involvement in the church, Nilanthi too was chosen as leader of many groups at school. She was especially talented in singing, and dancing, and always played a major role in annual school concerts. Nihal learnt to play steel and Spanish guitars, and formed his own band, "The Blue Boys" of which Nihal was lead singer and guitarist.

Five boys played in that band, and practiced their repertoire diligently after school at our house, on some weekends, and every spare moment they had away from their other activities. Felix Stephen, and his brother, Phil, were part of the band, and Nihal's good friends.

Thathie bought a new tape recorder for us, which cost him about eight hundred rupees, a small fortune in 1964. We appreciated Thathie's generosity greatly, especially Nilanthi and Nihal, who used it mostly, as we younger children were not allowed to operate it.

Nihal needed the tape recorder for band practice, and Nilanthi for her singing and dancing. They taped their favourite songs during "Sunday Choice" and other popular radio program. Shirani, Nelune, and I, were merely on-lookers, and had no rights to the treasured tape recorder.

It soon became a bone of contention, as they wanted to use it at the same time, and they were at constant loggerheads. Technically, it was Nihal's birthday present. And he said it was very big-hearted of him to allow Nilanthi to operate the highly valued tape recorder.

Many arguments and quarrels erupted during radio programs, because each wanted to record their favourite songs. Nihal, strongly objected to this infringement of his rights. He sometimes resorted to extreme measures, and stopped Nilanthi from taping her favourite songs. She retaliated likewise, so this constant haggling continued.

One particular incident occurred during a concert at St Gabriel's. Nilanthi taped music on one of those large spools for her dance routine. But Nihal, who was in a tetchy mood, refused to let her take the tape, or do any more recording, because he was using it.

They bickered and quarrelled. Nilanthi cried and complained. Meanwhile, urgent messages came from the school. The dance routine was about to commence, could Nilanthi bring the taped music immediately. Nihal, who was very-hot tempered then, grabbed the tape off Nilanthi, as she pestered him to let her have the tape recorder. Next moment, he dashed the spool on the ground. There it lay, like a pile of tangled brown spaghetti. I stared wide-eyed at Nilanthi, who looked stricken.

Once the initial shock passed, Nilanthi realized the awful predicament she was in, and bawled out broken-heartedly, as she tried to untangle the mess. Nihal stormed out to his room (remorsefully, I am certain). Nilanthi could do nothing. She sent a message that she was unable to provide the music, as the tape was ruined.

One can imagine the confusion, and utter disappointment, as the hapless dancers barely had time to rehearse, and improvised with some other music. That dreadful situation still strikes me as one of the tragedies in Nilanthi's life then. She became very unpopular with teachers, nuns, and her friends for a very long time.

Nihal's moods were mercurial, and transient as ripples on the calm surface of a lily pond. One moment he was exuberant, and clowned around, as he mimicked someone in a high-pitched voice, like the comedian, Jerry Lewis. Or he talked like a baby, which made me laugh so much that tears ran down my cheeks. Next moment, he flared up like Vesuvius, and was a raging tornado, as he lost his temper over some untimely comment.

It was to our advantage to gauge his mood swings, and woe betide if we failed to do so, as we felt the full brunt of his temper. Like the time I sat with nose buried in a book, but quietly observed Nihal trying to patch a broken tape. Perspiration dripped down his large palms, and he turned red, as he clumsily tried to execute the intricate patch up job. I found it amusing, as he looked very funny, turning redder and redder, with the sheer effort of concentrating, and holding the tape in his sweaty palms.

I burst out laughing, and teased, "*Carrot* fingers, *carrot* fingers, can't patch the tape!" I never knew what struck me. In two or three long strides, he loomed over me, and two resounding slaps choked the taunts in my throat. My cheeks turned as red as his. I learnt never to taunt him again, or annoy him when he was in the middle of a difficult task, and in a bad temper.

Herath Marma, arrived one day, to board his twelve-year old brother with us, as he wanted him to be educated at St John Bosco's college. He was a spindly village boy, with large ears, and big bulging eyes. He had a very long name, so Nihal promptly christened him "Boniface."

Why Nihal picked that moniker I have no idea, but never was Boniface more apt, and we were delighted at such an appropriate alias for our new-found relative. The name stuck to him for as long as he stayed with us. I think Nihal's mischievous sense of humour prompted him to choose that name, because our parish priest, Fr Boniface, was a replica of Friar Tuck. He was fat and round, with an enormous belly that wobbled when he laughed. He had a long, grey beard, and prominent blood-shot eyes, due to over-drinking. Fr Boniface was a direct contrast to the tall lanky youth, who bore his name now.

Whenever I visited the church, which was habitual, I met Fr Boniface walking, or rather waddling around the church gardens in the evenings. He had a raucous jolly laugh, and exclaimed cheerfully, "I'm *exercising*, so I can eat more when I go out for dinner tonight." And he mentioned one of the local planter's or some important person's name. His life was one hectic social whirl, wining and dining with some snobbish planters, as he depended on their goodwill for donations, so he often socialised with them.

Chapter 20

St Anne's fete, was a great day, not only for us school children and parishioners, but for most of the people as well. It was one of the high lights of the year, where people from every walk of life socialised, and enjoyed the occasion. All the students of St Gabriel's and St John Bosco's participated in the fete, irrespective of religious beliefs. Exciting stalls, raffles, games, and various science and art exhibitions, were some of the main attractions. The fete was always a profitable success, and the parish depended heavily on this event. Ammie told Fr Boniface that I owned a large collection of dolls, and would not mind donating a couple of them as prizes for one of the many raffles.

I had about fifteen dolls of every size and shape, and I loved them all equally, although I was growing too old to play with dolls. One evening, just before the fete, I met Fr Boniface outside church, and was surprised when he said with a big smile splitting his round face, "I had a *vision* that you have many dolls, and you can make a great sacrifice if you donate a couple of them for a raffle!" Imagine my surprise at such a request.

Being rather naive, I immediately agreed to donate my best twins dolls, with golden locks and cute faces. I sewed pretty dresses, packed them in a cardboard box padded with cotton wool, and gave them away with a pang.

Nihal, and his band, "The Blue Boys" entertained the crowd, while Nilanthi, Shirani, Nelune, and I, helped out in the numerous stalls, and attended to little tasks. They were splendid, happy days, and we spent all day, and most of the evening, involved in the fete, and watched hordes of people swarming in the parish grounds.

The planters and their friends condescended to support the fete, and usually bought a few knick knacks from some stalls, and many raffle tickets. Once, Nihal and I sang, "The Lightning Express" a popular song by the Everley Brothers. Nihal accompanied on the guitar, while our friends cheered us. Yes, they were fun-filled, happy days alright, when nothing seemed to matter except enjoying every moment. And "Sorrowing songs, were yet unsung," as I wrote in later years.

It was even more interesting spying on older girls during these occasions, and to catch them flirting with college boys. I carried tales to Ammie, as little children often do, until they know better.

We took part in all the concerts that Bro. Alfonso and the nuns organised. They were held in the convent, and sometimes in the college hall. Miss Direkze produced and directed some of the plays. I once had the minor role of dormouse, in "Alice In Wonderland." My only lines were "Treacle" that I drawled out sleepily now and then, to the amusement of the audience.

Rosemarie played Alice, and being very tall and big-made at sixteen, Thathie commented wryly when he reviewed the play. "She is a very *large* Alice, isn't she?" He and Ammie were in the audience, and we all agreed that Rosemarie was too big, and could not understand why she was cast in the role.

Nelune and I played minor roles as slave girls in the Biblical story, "Joseph The Dreamer." Another time, I was "Liza" and a boy called Patrick, was "Henry" in that amusing song, "There's A Hole In The Bucket." Those old photographs still bring a smile, and many good memories.

Bro. Alfonso hired a van with a trailer at Christmas, and we enacted the nativity scene on the back of it. I was cast as Virgin Mary once, and it was tough work kneeling on the hard floor of the trailer, as we bumped along narrow roads, singing carols to entertain poor children on tea estates.

Our school held several speech contests too, and my friends and I became friendly rivals, vying for first prize. I memorized long passages, and poetry easily, and sometimes came first. Miss Direkze spent several hours after school and during recess, coaching and encouraging us to deliver our lines with feeling.

Mother Superior was one of the judges, and reiterated. "*Don't* recite poetry in sing song fashion! Try to recite your lines with feeling!" Though I must say, that at my age, I could hardly be expected to have any depth of feeling when delivering my lines.

The church was built in the shape of a large cross, with a long, central aisle, and two wings; one side was reserved for the rich people and planters, and the other for nuns, teachers, and clergy. We always sat in the main section of the church among people from every walk of life, including beggars, mad men and women, (as we thought), because they sat mumbling, and stared dazedly at the rituals going on at the altar.

The orphans of St Gabriel's convent, occupied one whole side of the main section. Some of these orphans were unwanted, or illegitimate children of poor people. But others were illegitimate children that some planters or business people fathered. The women dumped their unwanted babies on the convent doorsteps. The cruellest aspect of their existence was that they were made to feel, look, behave, and acknowledge the fact they were worthless orphans. And to me, they were reminiscent of hapless waifs in Victorian times that Charles Dickens wrote about in his novels.

The orphans were constantly reminded of their sinful parents, who conceived them shamefully, and the nuns so charitably fostered now. If Christian charity it was to dress them in the most ill-fitting clothes, over-sized shoes, without laces, frumpy skirts, and crushed dresses, with hems let down. A more pathetic-looking bunch of children I had never seen, as they were herded into church on Sundays. They were painfully reminded of their ignominious situation, and to pay for the sins of their parents.

I always felt sad to see the wild, hungry expressions in the eyes of those orphans, deprived of warmth and love. The nuns meant well, no doubt, but in their practical manner, they made the orphans know, and feel they depended on the goodwill of the church and convent for their very existence. The children were dressed shabbily, so as to eradicate all traces of vanity, worldliness, and attractiveness, that could lead them down the road to hell, like their sinful parents.

The meek children shuffled in two by two, row after row, took their allocated places humbly, and only their eyes spoke of the utter desolation of their lives. A few nuns knelt in the very last row behind them, so they could keep an eye on them, and admonish any child, if they showed even a hint of frivolous or inappropriate behaviour inside God's house.

Marie Clare was a light-complexioned girl of Anglo-Ceylonese parentage, who was one of the orphans in my class, and I sympathised with her especially. She was so naughty, and incorrigible most of the time, that the nuns constantly punished and restrained her wild behaviour. Miss Direkze was her deadly antagonist. She nagged her continually, and made her life a misery, with cruel references to her obscure parentage.

When Miss Direkze humiliated her in many ways, the poor girl blushed shamefully, but her eyes glittered with a hard, stubborn look that spoke volumes defiantly, that she was never ever going to change her ways, or even try to behave better. How blind and foolish those disciplinarians were.

Another "trouble maker" as the school referred to those girls, who did not conform to hard and fast rules of the convent and orphanage, was a big, strong, Tamil girl. She had such an aggressive temperament, that once, in sheer rebellion and retaliation, she set fire to her dormitory. One can only imagine the punishment the nuns meted out.

As I mentioned, church-going was something of a social event in our week. Every Sunday, being very fashion-conscious now, I spent a long time deciding what to wear, and how to look different. I succeeded pretty well, as Ammie sewed beautiful clothes, and knitted some very unusual caps, and jumpers to match some of the outfits. Invariably, on the following Sundays, we were amused to see that some girls copied our styles and fashions faithfully. Ammie usually sewed the identical pattern for the three of us with the same fabric. But Nilanthi had different dresses made out of beautiful fabrics, as she was older, and more sophisticated.

Before one Easter, Ammie knitted away frantically for many months, to complete some exquisite Fair Isle jumpers in red and white, with matching caps. Three of us wore deep red, pleated skirts, red and white Fair Isle jumpers, with matching caps, white socks and shoes. Ammie's friends exclaimed at the beautiful jumpers and caps, and then we set a trend for wearing caps to church instead of lace veils.

Midnight Mass on Christmas Eve, was a great celebration too. We all sang in the church choir, with Ammie accompanying on the organ. After Mass however, was just about the best part of celebrations, as we laughed, talked and greeted mutual friends and strangers, who always had a smile for each other. The echo of our carefree laughter rings out through the years, and leaves me feeling incredibly nostalgic, as I yearn for those joyous, fun-filled days again.

Countless friends gathered around, as we admired each other's beautiful new Christmas clothes. We then waited in mounting excitement to get home and open presents and compare our gifts. The only sad memory that marred these happy occasions, was Thathie's drunken behaviour. He waited till we came home to start an argument with Ammie, thus throwing a damper on our goodwill and cheer.

After we consumed large slices of Christmas cake, small glasses of home-made wine, or sherry, and opened presents, we listened apprehensively to the commotion that erupted from our parents room. It was very difficult then to understand why Thathie was so aggressive and quarrelsome, especially on these festive days.

In retrospect, I believe he felt left out, because he did not join us for Mass, or any other religious celebration. Then again, Thathie had a drinking problem, and never stopped drinking all his life. He always made various excuses for his destructive habit. In making Ammie miserable, he little realized how scared and unhappy he made us too.

Thathie never abused or beat us when he was drunk, but the noise and aggression frightened me deeply, as I did not know if he was physically violent towards Ammie or not. Their fights were always in their bedroom, and we did not witness violence, except loud noises, and raised voices. None of us knew the exact reason for their interminable arguments and quarrels. But the major contributing factors must have been his heavy drinking, and different religious and cultural backgrounds; that is solely my perception.

Most childhood memories of these festive occasions are flawed, because of Thathie's behaviour. After all the fun and laughter with our friends, and brief moments of enjoyment at home, I invariably crept into bed silently, eyes wet with unshed tears for my parents, and mingled with self-pity.

I hasten to add though, that with the resilience of children, I was happy as a clown next day. Thathie's behaviour did not shatter my daily childish joys. In spite of the belief that children growing up in an environment of domestic violence, suffered deep, psychological scars, I am grateful I survived unscathed, and I am positive my siblings did too. We were secure in the knowledge our parents loved us deeply, and I never resented Thathie for the unhappiness he caused us through our childhood.

Thathie was quite jolly after a few drinks, but one too many, and he invariably succumbed to the different stages of drunkenness (as Shakespeare so aptly noted). In the first stage of intoxication, he was witty, and entertained us with his innumerable store of anecdotes and jokes. From jollity, he slipped into deep despondency that leapt into aggression almost immediately, before he stumbled into oblivious slumber. Nihal vowed he would never touch alcohol or cigarettes, seeing the consequences of alcoholism.

On the eve of Corpus Christi, a great feast day in the church, the whole congregation walked in procession from the church to the convent grounds. Then passed the college, and ended at the grounds there, with a celebration of Mass. We witnessed another unpleasant scene at home.

The road was brightly festooned with palm leaves, garlands of crepe paper and flowers on the previous day. As the procession had to pass our driveway, the Brothers requested permission to decorate that area of our garden as well. Ammie agreed, but she overlooked Thathie's perversity.

That afternoon, he was quite drunk, and shouted angrily, threatening to pull down the decorations, saying he did not want them in our garden. Grumbling and muttering loudly, he finally went to bed, and we waited anxiously for the procession to pass by our house. Fortunately, he fell asleep, and we breathed a sigh of relief when the priest and congregation carrying the blessed statue, passed by without any incident. Thathie was exhausted after his uproar and banging things around, and now slept soundly.

That same evening, after Mass and celebrations were over, we hardly dared to speak aloud, or move around when we returned home, as we were afraid Thathie would wake up and start quarrelling with Ammie again. Our lives were constantly marred with the fear he would get drunk, and then start a fight. His drinking problem seemed to grow worse each year, and evenings and nights became intolerable. It came to a stage when I was actually relieved when he was on night duty.

It was more difficult to remain silent as I grew older, and watch them abuse each other and hurl insults, and sometimes resort to physical violence. Nihal declared he would not stand by and watch them come to blows. I worried that someday Nihal would lose his temper and confront Thathie.

A deeply etched memory remains, of one cold morning when Nihal returned after early Mass where he served as altar boy. He found the front door locked because Thathie was angry with him for spending too much time in church. It tugs at my heart still when I remember Nihal, with bowed head, and a patient look of humility, walking round the house to the kitchen door, and Menika quickly letting him in. He was on the brink of deciding whether to become a priest or not (as a result of the strong religious influence around us), and Thathie was very angry over this.

Wilfred, one of the college school masters, boarded with us too. He shared a room with Nihal and Boniface, until Boniface returned to his village a couple of years later. We called him Wilfred Sir. He was a good-looking, quiet, pleasant-mannered young man, of average height, and scrupulously neat. His clothes were spotless, and his hair combed back and greased with Brylcreem. Wilfred Sir was in his early thirties or so, and the Brothers recommended him, as his home-town was somewhere in Matale, a long distance from Hatton.

He played the steel guitar very well, and tutored Nihal in guitar lessons. He also sang melodiously, especially an old song called, "O Sugar Moon," which he taught Nihal to sing and play. I teased Nihal, because I thought it very funny the way he swayed his head from side to side each time he changed chords. Wilfred Sir was very kind to us children, and was almost like an elder brother. He became close to our family, and within a few months, he shared all our family secrets, troubles, as well as our simple joys.

During Sri Pada season, Thathie was stationed at Maskeliya, a few hours journey from Hatton. And sometimes, the whole family visited him there and made a picnic of it. The scenery was absolutely breathtaking, and Thathie enjoyed being station master at Maskeliya, where hordes of pilgrims headed off to the sacred peak in an ever flowing stream of humanity.

On one of our visits, we bathed in one of the wide, sparkling rivers that ran through the countryside, and a near-tragedy occurred that day. Swirling undercurrents coursed through some deep parts of the river, and without thinking about it, someone waded in too deep.

I was the only one in the group who could swim fairly well. Suddenly, we heard a cry for help. And who should venture to rescue the drowning person, but Menika, who could not even stay afloat, let alone save a drowning person.

To make matters worse, Ammie followed, then Lorna (Chanda's girlfriend). They splashed and floundered, shouting and clinging to each other for dear life.

Chanda sat on the rocks laughing his head off, as he thought it was very funny, never dreaming they were mortally afraid, and in danger of drowning.

I understood their fear, and swam out, dragging one by one. And when Chanda and Wilfred Sir saw them crying in distress, they too jumped in and helped me drag them to safety. A classic case of blind leading the blind, as none of them could swim at all, but went to the rescue without a second thought. Dear courageous, but foolhardy souls.

Chapter 21

Later that year, we journeyed to Kandy and watched the spectacular Perahera (procession), one of the great traditions through the ages. This great Perahera of magnificently decorated elephants, was how chieftains and loyal subjects paid tribute to the ancient Kings of Kandy.

We stayed at a friend's house, and in the evening, crowded on to the balcony to watch the grand spectacle. The extravagantly bedecked elephants, with jewelled purdahs on their backs, paraded majestically down the main road.

The sacred relic of Lord Buddha's tooth was enshrined in a jewelled casket, and the Perahera ended at the Dalada Maligawa (Temple of the Tooth relic). The Buddhists firmly believed (and still do), that this was indeed a true relic of the Lord Buddha, and venerated it accordingly.

The agile female and male dancers, brilliantly clad, and adorned with splendid, towering headgear, danced with primitive abandon to the pulsating rhythm of pounding drums. To watch dancers leap high in the air, and gyrate acrobatically, as they danced down the street to the beat of booming drums, was an awesome spectacle. This grand sight made a deep impression on me, and I still picture sights and sounds of that Perahera, as if it was yesterday.

The best part of that trip (in my opinion), was when Ammie bought me a large, beautiful doll for fifteen rupees. It was the biggest doll in my collection. But not long after that trip, when I returned home from school one day, that treasured doll disappeared from my collection. Ammie presented it to one of the little children in the neighbourhood on her birthday.

I still accumulated pets and dolls at an alarming rate; budgerigars, squirrels, cats, two dogs (stray mongrels), and miscellaneous fauna in my menagerie. One such pet, was a cross-bred Alsatian, Sheba. She was a gentle, intelligent animal, with dreamy-brown eyes. After a few drinks, Thathie observed that Sheba and Nilanthi wore similar expressions. I laughed at his droll comments, but Nilanthi was not amused.

Another one of my pets, was a cute, lovable Dachshund. I named her Gina, because Gina Lollobrigida, "La Lollo" was then one of my favourite movie stars. Gina, the Dachshund, was so devoted to me, that she stuck like glue wherever I went.

She even followed me to school half way down the road, and then ran off home only when I chased her away.

She curled up with me while I read in the evenings. And if anyone so much as touched me (just to tease her), Gina growled menacingly, and snarled viciously at the offender. I smuggled her into my bedroom at nights, and tried to keep her quiet under the blankets. Her heavy breathing and loud snores however, soon alerted Menika and Ammie, who reprimanded me severely, and put her out immediately. She was such a loyal dog though, and was my favourite pet then. One day, I found a woolly, black, stray pup that looked like a cross between a poodle and several obscure breeds. I promptly took it under my protection.

The streets were always full of unwanted stray dogs and cats, and no one cared if anyone took them home. The council did what it could to destroy these poor unwanted animals, but it was a losing battle. Many maimed, blind cats and dogs roamed the roads and countryside, because people injured them badly, when they caught the animals stealing food from houses and shops.

It was one of my childhood passions to build a home for stray animals, especially when I saw sad-looking, starved animals limping or running away in fear from vicious attackers. I still have not lost that ambition, or zeal to rid poor nations of unwanted strays.

To get back to the cross poodle, I named it Ebony, for obvious reasons. I nursed this playful, fluffy pup for a few weeks only, when it vanished one day. My tears of anger and sorrow never moved Ammie and Menika; poker-faced they told me it had probably run away. The cats and dogs were so miserably thin, and starved that they ate anything that was thrown their way, as they did not have luxuries like pet food to tempt fussy appetites.

I fed my pets left-over rice and curries, and though mixed with pepper or hot chilli sometimes, the animals just ate up everything, and wanted more. So, I could not understand why Ammie did not want me to keep so many cats and dogs, because we never spent extra money buying special food for them anyway.

Shortly after Ebony went missing, I visited one of my friends, who lived near the bus terminal, when I happened to see this black, woolly dog lazing around in front of a shop. I stopped and called out, "Ebony, Ebony" and to my great delight mixed with sorrow, the dog wagged its curly tail and ran up to me.

The shop-keeper said it was given to him, and I knew exactly who had given my pet away. I could not ask it back, as it seemed happy enough, so I left it at that. When I mentioned that I saw Ebony at a shop, Ammie responded vaguely. So, we had the same problem repeatedly, with me acquiring pets and dolls, and Ammie giving them away just as resolutely as I collected them.

I visited my friend, Gnei Fawzia often, as she lived in Dickoya, which was about fifteen minutes by bus, and another of my classmates, Yvonne, who was the only daughter of Mr and Mrs Fernandez. Her father was a "Tea Maker" at Wanaraja Estate in Dickoya, but his designation was rather misleading. He did not spend all his time brewing tea, but was in charge of the tea-making process in the factory.

The first time I visited Yvonne, I wondered what was wrong with her brother, Clim, because he made all sorts of odd noises, and guttural sounds in very loud tones.

It was with great reluctance and embarrassment that Yvonne told me her brother was deaf, and had a speech impediment. Clim was a short, stocky, young boy, with strong features, and his efforts to join in a conversation were painful to watch. He made signs, which his family understood, but we outsiders found hard to follow. Mrs Fernandez contracted German Measles during pregnancy, and consequently, her son was born deaf, and vocally disadvantaged. They had Yvonne and Clim only, and it must have been sad.

Yvonne too was short, stocky, and muscular. Her shoulder-length hair was tightly curled, and she had small, narrow eyes, thin lips, sharp features, and a shrewish expression. She wore butterfly-shaped spectacles, and was always very neat, and quite the opposite of me in every way. One day, when she wore a tight, mini skirt, and Roman sandals (tied-up with lacing round her ankles), Nihal remarked that she looked like a Roman soldier, because of her strong, muscle-bound legs, and sturdy figure. Although it was naughty of him, when I looked at her again, it was an apt description.

Even at the age of twelve, Yvonne was a very strong character, and her parents, and brother stood in awe of her. Her word was law in the household, and how this came about I do not know, but to her family, Yvonne was, "*She* who must be obeyed." Yvonne was mature beyond her years, and held rather worldly views, and liked to boss everyone around, including me. But I did not like anyone to do that, especially Yvonne.

The greatest incentive to visit her, was a beautiful new piano that her parents bought her. She studied music, because her parents wanted her to, but could not play any tunes by ear, and had no inclination, or ear for music, so she found it a chore.

Whenever I visited her, I wanted to sit at the piano for hours, and make beautiful music on that exquisite instrument, but Yvonne hardly let me sit there for a few minutes, before she exclaimed, "Come along now, that's enough, let's go outside and play."

We were friendly rivals from the moment we met in school. Being an only daughter, she was thoroughly spoilt, and indulged in every way, and materially, she could afford to out-do me ten times over.

If I bought anything, she immediately bought the same thing the very next day. I was a voracious reader, and collector of books, especially "Schoolgirls Picture Library" series that were so popular in the sixties. I just had to have the four publications every month. They cost one rupee each, which was a considerable sum of money for me. And so I saved, scrimped, begged, and borrowed from my family.

It was easy for Yvonne to quickly purchase every single copy published in the last few years. And she could afford the four monthly issues without any effort either. She flaunted her collection gloatingly, and I could not help longing for such good fortune.

But Rosie was so generous, that she collected the four issues and posted them sometimes, whenever I could not afford it. The hardest part to bear was that I loved music passionately, and longed to own a piano, but I could not even dream of such a luxury. These were sore childhood trials

Yvonne, on the other hand, who really did not care much about music, owned the most beautiful instrument I had ever seen. These were difficult lessons to understand in the school of life, but we still remained friendly rivals, and visited each other frequently.

One day, I built a rackety doll house, with old boxes, and bits and pieces, when I saw a picture of a superb doll's house in a magazine. It could hardly compare with the beautiful one in the magazine, but I was quite elated, and proud of my handiwork. When Yvonne visited, I showed her my attempt at carpentry. She immediately demanded that Clim build her one, as he was very good at woodwork. And it did not take him long to construct the most ostentatious, and magnificent, miniature mansion one could possibly imagine.

While admiring it wholeheartedly, I could not help thinking how little use she would make of that splendid doll's house. She stopped playing with dolls long ago, but that was how competitive she was in everything. Sure enough, it was just for display, and being a tomboy, she did not waste time playing with dolls. Whenever I visited Yvonne however, I had a great deal of fun playing in the river below their garden, where she said she once found precious stones (pulling my leg no doubt), but her parents confirmed it. I searched the river bed for hours, hoping to find precious stones, but never did I pick up anything that even vaguely resembled a gemstone.

Her parents were very kind and hospitable, and cooked some tasty dishes for my enjoyment. Their excellent cook was great at baking scones, and the memory still lingers of pleasant afternoons that I spent, devouring delicious scones, with plenty of butter, jam, and whipped cream.

Fruit trees grew abundantly, and I returned home laden with baskets of fruits and flowers. It was a delight to wander in their well-kept, profuse garden in beautiful surroundings, and everything money could buy. And to me it was a fairy-tale sort of a place.

Chapter 22

Mr Fernandez took us on a guided tour of the tea factory sometimes. And we played hide-and-seek in those mysterious, aromatic passages, with machinery that hummed and whirred incessantly, churning tons of fragrant tea leaves for domestic use and exportation. The tea was then packed in small chests, and distributed to many parts of the world. Ceylon tea was famous then, as it is now. I was not particularly interested in tea making technicalities, but the intricate machinery, and marvellous fragrance of tea leaves in the huge, airy factory delighted me.

My parents started visiting them gradually and vice versa, which led to many parties at our houses. When the latest dance craze, the "Twist" gained popularity in mid 1960, we were amused and impressed to watch Clim join in whenever we started Twisting. He kept up the pace and rhythm that he must have felt, although he could not hear the music. Our parents held countless dinner parties for our friends, and life could not have been happier than this period in my existence.

We listened to "Sunday Choice" on the radio eagerly, as this was the musical playground where our favourite pop stars made it to the "Hit Parade." We considered it a personal triumph, if one of our favourite singers, such as Elvis Presley, Jim Reeves, Cliff Richards, Ricky Nelson, and the Beatles, just to name a few of the famous singers then, made it to the top ten that week. And it all depended on how many of their songs the DJ's played on the program as well. What a lot of fun this past time was for most teenagers then.

If one of my favourites was the winner, I spent the rest of the afternoon gloating over the sore losers, and was generally a pain in the neck. Nihal was an Elvis fan, with Jim Reeves, his second favourite; Nilanthi preferred Jim Reeves only. Shirani too was an Elvis fan, but I liked Jim Reeves, and his "sickly sentimental" songs (his program was called Strictly Sentimental). I enjoyed listening to other singers too, but to a lesser degree. Nelune did not have any strong preferences, as she was still too young.

Nihal and Nilanthi, as usual, were fierce competitors, and argued often over their musical preferences. As a result of violent musical disputes, Nihal chased Nilanthi around the house, and they sometimes came to blows. The funny side of their incessant quarrels was that Nihal had not outgrown his habit of grabbing her long hair. And he still threatened to cut off her braids with a pair of big blunt scissors he found somewhere.

The rest of us looked on, giggling uncontrollably, and were reduced to gales of laughter. Nilanthi was mortally afraid that in a moment of madness, Nihal would carry out his terrible threat, and really snip off her beautiful long hair. So the days passed, with each of us growing up in our own little private world.

One thing that was evident to our parents, and everyone else, was the strong bond that existed between the five of us. In spite of Nihal and Nilanthi's frequent altercations, they loved each other very much, and eventually stopped quarrelling altogether in their late teens. Although we were developing strong, and unique personalities, no one influenced, curbed, or over-shadowed each other's development in any way.

Nilanthi was greatly admired, and many young boys at St John Bosco's college were smitten. Thathie's young, bachelor friends, hung around our place most evenings, as they came on the pretext of visiting Thathie, but we knew the real attraction was Nilanthi. One of these admirers, Ryan, was a tall, lanky young man, with pale-blue eyes, who was quite drunk most evenings, as he always had bloodshot eyes, and a red face.

Ryan's friend, Melville, was also attracted to Nilanthi, but no one knew how serious their intentions were, because they did not declare their love or propose to her. Nilanthi was about seventeen or eighteen then, and perhaps they thought she was too young for marriage.

Melville was slender, of average height, and a pleasant-looking young man, who was fond of reading. He always came around with the excuse to borrow a book from Thathie's ample library. We had fun whenever they came, as they sang, told jokes, and made merry with Thathie till late evening, till finally, we younger children were sent off to our rooms to finish our homework or to bed.

Wimal, another young man, played the piano beautifully. And one evening, as he played the old piano, and sang a heart-rending version of "He'll Have To Go" by Jim Reeves, the door banged loudly. Nihal burst into the room, his face red as a beetroot. He thundered, "*How* can I do my homework, when you make such a damned *racket* here?" And Nihal slammed down the piano lid.

Wimal's face puckered with embarrassment, as he mumbled his apologies and rushed out of the house. We understood Nihal's rude and abrupt behaviour though, because he thought the fellow had a crush on Shirani, who was only fifteen then. Nihal could not stand the sight of any Casanova (as he called them), making up to his sisters.

Shirani was a very attractive teenager; slender and long-legged, with large, intelligent eyes, a great sense of humour, and an infectious laugh. She was fun-loving, and very popular with some of the boys and young men in our circle, who took an interest in her. But Shirani was very studious, and in spite of several admirers, preferred to concentrate on her studies, as her ambition was to become a doctor.

Nelune was Nihal's favourite little sister. He was always very protective of her, and never hurt or teased her like the rest of us. He did not actually quarrel with us, but he was an incorrigible practical joker. I was often reduced to tears after one of his teasing bouts. But Nilanthi was the constant butt end of his practical jokes and witticisms, whenever he was in one of his bantering moods.

Girls and boys from our schools were in and out of our house, as some of their parents asked Ammie if their children could come over during lunch break. This was due to lack of drinkable water at the schools, and washing up facilities. Ammie invited these children to have their lunch in our home, and generously provided lunches for a couple of other girls, whose parents were quite poor. They were our friends, and lunched at our place for as long as we were in Hatton.

Mr and Mrs Rodrigo, whom we knew when they were in Bandarawela, lived in Talawakale then, which was a few stations from Hatton. They boarded their children, Rozanne and Derry with us, as they found it difficult to travel to Hatton daily on very early morning trains. Rozanne was a precocious little girl of about ten, and her brother, Derry, was about seven or eight.

Ammie added another bed in the large bedroom, but this did not affect me, as I still had a little room all to myself. We treated Rozanne and Derry just like our own brother and sister, and they soon became part of our extended family. We had great times with them, especially after school, and late into the nights, until Ammie or Thathie called out that it was past bedtime.

It was one long, session of pranks, and pillow fights, with us girls always choosing Derry to play the villain. Sometimes, we bullied him into playing any other role in our games that we did not feel inclined to play. We covered him up with a blanket, and then played hide-and-seek, shouting out to Derry that he was an evil "Black Ant" on the prowl. He could not see where he was going, and that was half the fun, as he blundered around trying to find us, and we shrieked and screamed if he got anywhere close. We jumped on top of tables, and wardrobes, in a frenzied effort to escape the clutches of that rather strange specimen of the ant world.

We dragged home big bundles of firewood, sometimes, heavily pruned branches of tea bushes. Then we stacked them in the back garden as high as we could, and lit a grand, blazing bonfire. Later, we tried very hard to put up a tent with some old sheets. Unfortunately, none of us possessed the technical skill required for this operation. We usually ended up hot, bothered, and angry, after many frustrated attempts to make the old sheets stand up in the semblance of a tent. But, no matter how doggedly we hitched them up, the sheets obstinately collapsed on us.

Undaunted, we sat down on the sheets, and proceeded to snack on boiled peas, and whatever goodies we coaxed out of our dependable Menika, who quite enjoyed all our fun and games. She just watched and giggled at our futile attempts, and in her own way, comforted us with food. After eating ravenously, not inside a tent, but outdoors anyway, with mosquitoes and ants to provide background music with a sting, we abandoned our plan to sleep out in a tent. We trailed indoors to make up another exciting game until bedtime.

Menika usually assisted us in most games and pranks that she thought were funny and adventurous, like we did, as in the case of the "tea pot" episode. Rozanne, Derry, Shirani, and I formed a Club, which cost members twenty five cents a week for providing privileges and entertainment, especially in the way of lollies and other goodies. We planned all sorts of ways to amuse ourselves, and ventured out into the countryside on picnics.

Nelune absolutely refused to join our little Club, because she declared the membership fees were exorbitant, and did not join in our fun and games. So we did not include her in our activities, because it was for members only. She was not unduly concerned, and we attributed this indifference to her extreme youth, and did not hold it against her.

One day, the Club members decided it was time for a tea party somewhere in a picturesque setting over the tea-clad hills of Hatton. We asked Menika to make us some roast beef sandwiches, with a hint of home-made mustard paste. We also pilfered tea leaves, sugar, and some mugs. Rozanne had the tricky business of smuggling the tea pot, which was a big, aluminium pot with many a dent and scratch.

Still, this was the one Menika used daily to brew tea for the family, and she refused to let us have it, because she needed it for afternoon tea, she said. In a few minutes though, Rozanne jumped out of the kitchen window, waving the tea pot triumphantly, much as a great warrior exhibited his trophy after some dangerous exploit. We shouted our approval, and soon set off on our expedition over the hills.

It was close to two or three o'clock in the afternoon when we set off through thorny patches, and muddy paths that wound up hill and down dale. But just like the jaded old knight of yore, who searched high and low, "Nowhere could we find a spot of ground, that looked like Eldorado!"

The sun was sinking fast, and long, shadows began to creep in, along with thick mist that Hatton was renowned for, so we were ready to have our picnic just about anywhere. Thorns and mud that we encountered so far, definitely quenched our thirst for adventure. Finally, in desperation, and hunger, we picked a most horrid, damp, muddy field (it had rained for days before). And everywhere we looked, the earth was soggy and quite unsuitable to sit upon.

To make matters worse, we could not find any dry bits of wood or twigs that we in youthful optimism, forgot to bring when we set out. Still, we did try to get one going, as we collected likely bits of twigs and leaves to start a fire. I arranged three small rocks in a circle, and started building a fire inside, an improvised outdoor stove to place the teapot. We blew and blew, and huffed and puffed, until we coaxed a grey, wisp of smelly smoke from our pathetic little fire. What joy, what an achievement, when we finally glimpsed a tiny, red glow trembling hesitantly, afraid of its own brilliance, as it emerged bashfully from damp wood.

We encouraged the heroic little red spark with more huffing and puffing, until a wavering flame burned half-heartedly. Quick to make use of this timid spark, we placed the tea pot on the three rocks, and waited anxiously for the water to boil. After what seemed like *hours,* the water was hardly lukewarm; all the sandwiches devoured by now, nothing remained, but to brew tea with luke-warm water, and head off home before it got too dark.

One can only imagine the unpalatable tea we brewed that day! Smoky, smelly, tepid, and bad as dish water, but we gulped down the bitter brew, like true Spartans, because none of us wanted to acknowledge that the tea party had been an enormous failure right from the start.

With the indomitable spirit of children, we hurried back, laughing and joking about our mishap all the way home. In the meantime, when it was time for tea, Ammie searched for the tea pot. But Menika, knowing we must have taken it, stubbornly denied any knowledge of its whereabouts. We had delayed the family tea indeed, and wondered if Ammie was really mad at us. When we reached home, Rozanne sneaked the tea pot back on the shelf. Ammie could never figure out how the tea pot went missing, and later turned up just like that.

Menika did scold us a little, but she never told tales, so we left it at that. I am sure Ammie guessed we children were behind this little mystery. A few days later, I mentioned our disastrous tea party, and Ammie found it too funny to scold us anyway.

Then we tried our hand at jam making, to raise funds for our Club. The many luckless tales of jams that would never set, or set too hard, are too sticky to mention. However, we did try our best, and although most of our endeavours were dismal failures, we had a lot of fun. We carried out our ideas and schemes enthusiastically, which was the important thing, I suppose.

Miss Padma was a young teacher, who taught Sinhalese at the convent. She walked past our house daily, on her way to and from school. She was tall and slender, flat as a plank, with long-lashed, smiling-brown eyes set in a pleasant, round face. Ammie asked her to tutor me, as I was not very good in Sinhalese. Miss Padma became very close to our family, and in due course, she too boarded with us, as she travelled a long way from her village by bus and train.

I dreaded those extra Sinhalese lessons after school, and ran down to the bottom of the garden, where I hid in a ditch whenever she came around. I heard Menika calling me for tuition one evening, and retorted, "I'm *not* afraid of Miss Padma or her mother!" And ran off quickly.

I did not know she heard me. She laughed and giggled, as she said, "So, you are not afraid of me or my mother eh?" I blushed, but did not reply, as I was too embarrassed. She was a very nice, kind, young lady, and soon, Wilfred Sir started to dangle after her, but she did not encourage him at all. They chatted to each other after dinner, while she blushed and looked coy. Wilfred Sir proposed to her some time later, but she refused him, for reasons best known to her. And soon after, she moved out of our lives, just like Wilfred Sir, and I wonder what became of them, as they did not visit or keep in touch.

top right - Nihal in front of our house in Hatton. Thathie (left).
Our family with Wilfred in Maskeliya. Nihal, Nelune &
me in Watagoda with Adam's Peak in the distance.

Chapter 23

Some evenings, Rozanne, who was a jolly, mad-cap girl, dressed up in Thathie's baggy trousers, coat and hat. She then proceeded to give such a rollicking imitation of a drunken gentleman, that we held our sides and laughed till tears rolled down our cheeks. Derry was her side-kick and stooge, and together they kept us in stitches with their antics. We also staged many plays and concerts with a limited cast, each one playing umpteen roles, with very little change in scenes and costumes.

It was good for our developing personalities; children, being brutally honest critics, we all endured scathing, and unflattering reviews from one another. I strived to memorize lines and give my best performance. Sometimes, we invited Ammie and Thathie, and other family members, who were highly diverted at our innocent pranks and amateur productions.

Nihal was very fond of Derry, and Derry thought Nihal was a paragon. When we sat around discussing what we wanted to be when we grew up, much to our amusement, Derry promptly exclaimed, "I want to be *just* like Nihal someday!"

Thathie was still stationed in Maskeliya due to the pilgrim season, and he was quite happy to be there as he liked the small outstation. Most of the Buddhists made a pilgrimage to the beautiful mountain, "Adam's Peak" or "Sripada" in Sinhalese. The Lord Buddha was supposed to have left his foot print on the summit of the mountain. And the faithful paid homage at the site of the huge, footprint set in concrete now.

We visited Thathie on weekends, and had a great time. One weekend, our entire family decided to climb Adam's Peak. Though it was an unforgettable experience, it was also a most harrowing climb for anyone, especially young children. I dare say an experienced mountaineer, who has scaled the Alps or the Himalayas, would deem Adam's Peak mere child's play. But to a young child, it was almost a superhuman effort.

What started as a fun climb turned out to be a nightmare. I kept ascending step after steep step hewn on the mountain side. I thought I would never reach the summit, because it looked so lofty and inaccessible, no matter how high I climbed. In the dark, misty evening, the atmosphere was mysterious; the torches pilgrims carried, as they travelled slowly round the mountain, looked like a string of fairy lights, and cast a magical spell on the whole scene.

We started out at sunset, and soon it was late night. Hundreds of pilgrims kept climbing till dawn, depending on how energetic they were. We stopped often for refreshments at all the little tea shops on the way. But the worst part was, that whenever I stopped climbing even for a little while, my legs trembled like an aspen tree. My aching muscles rebelled at this unwonted exercise.

The gruelling climb finally ended in the wee hours of morning, and we settled down in a suitable area to rest our weary limbs. Thathie visited the temple to pay homage, and knelt at the giant imprint of Lord Buddha's foot. A throng huddled on the summit to witness the spectacular sunrise. And to watch the great shadow of the Peak falling on surrounding plains and valleys below.

The grandeur of that awesome sight is beyond description. No one can imagine its splendour, unless they actually witness that majestic sunrise. As the first rays of the sun gleamed in the rosy sky, a murmur arose from worshippers. The murmur grew into a tumultuous crescendo, which resounded through the peaceful dawn. Their cries of adoration, "Sadhu, Sadhu" filled the air. It was a very uplifting experience. I witnessed the most magnificent sunrise I ever saw, and watched the enchanted, glowing dawn tint distant valleys and vistas below.

The lame and elderly devoutly joined their hands, praising the Lord Buddha for the miracle of this sunrise. Some cynics said that the enormous foot print does not belong to a human being, least of all to Lord Buddha. And others say that it is Adam's footprint, as he stood on the summit after he was banished from the Garden of Eden. The fact remains though, that a huge footprint is visible there, and no one knows how it originated.

One day, soon after that ascent, we heard the stunning news that our favourite pop singer, Jim Reeves, was killed, when the small aircraft he was piloting crashed during a thunderstorm near Nashville, Tennessee. His business partner and manager, Dean Manuel (who was also pianist in Reeves' backing group), was killed as well.

We mourned his death as if he was a member of our family. The radio stations played his hit songs constantly. A few days later, we read about the tragedy in the newspapers as follows:

"On July 31, 1964, Reeves and Manuel had left Batesville, Arkansas, en route to Nashville..........While flying over Brentwood, they encountered a violent thunderstorm...... The plane faded from the radar screens at around 17.02 and all radio contact with the craft was lost. One of the major causes of the crash was deemed to have been that the small airplane had become caught in the centre of the thunderstorm, and that Reeves had become disoriented by "Pilot's vertigo", which would have resulted in him not realizing in which direction the plane was travelling, be it up, down, left or right.

Both Reeves and Randy Hughes, the pilot of Patsy Cline's ill-fated plane, were trained by the same instructor. It is now understood that Reeves was, in fact, flying the plane upside down, and he assumed he was raising the craft some distance in an attempt to clear the path of the storm. Of course, this disastrously (and fatally) resulted in him taking the airplane downward and straight to the ground.

This would have explained why, when the wreckage was eventually found some 42 hours later, the engine and nose of the plane were buried deep in the ground........

On the morning of August 2, 1964, after an agonizing and intense search (aided by such people as Chet Atkins, Eddy Arnold, Stonewall Jackson and Ernest Tubb) the bodies of Jim Reeves and Dean Manuel were found amongst the wreckage of the shattered plane. At 13:00 that afternoon, radio stations across the United States announced to their shocked and stunned audiences that Jim Reeves had been killed in a plane crash. In what can only be described as sad coincidence, riding high in the UK singles chart at the time was "I Won't Forget You" (written by Harlan Howard). The song later became a top ten hit in the United States.

Many thousands of people turned out to pay their last respects to Jim Reeves at his funeral, which took place on August 4, 1964."

Needless to say what a tragedy this was to all his devoted fans, and I never forgot the velvet-voiced singer for a long time.

I had a great party on my thirteenth birthday, and invited about ten or twelve friends. Some of the guests were just six and seven years old, as they were my friends' younger sisters, but the little ones tagging along did not worry us. All four Muller girls, aged between twelve and six came too, as they lived nearby. Mrs Muller was a fair-complexioned, slender Burgher lady, with faded looks, but always had a smile for us children. She had a large family, and was constantly busy and over-whelmed with the demands of her children.

They lived in one of the flats in a block of apartments, and although it had a second storey, it was a tiny, confined place. It is beyond me to figure out how this large family, which included Mrs Muller's brother and sister, lived in that closet-sized flat. Ammie and Mrs Muller were good friends, and she visited us often, but her husband, a taciturn man, seldom socialised with us.

To get back to my birthday party, I wore a beautiful new dress. It had red and white panels, with red daisies embroidered on the white panels, and white daisies on the red.

Nilanthi, who was very clever at sewing, completed all the embroidery, once Ammie finished sewing the dress. Ammie persuaded her to finish the embroidery for days, as Nilanthi found it a chore, and said she had better things to do with her time.

I had matching red shoes, and a red bow to tie back my long hair. I pranced around, quite pleased with my beautiful clothes. We played many games, and hide-and-seek all over the place; in our garden, the convent, church, and college grounds. The children had a great time chasing each other, and did not mind getting their shoes and clothes quite dirty.

Then at six o'clock, we switched on the radio to hear a special program for children. It was very popular, as parents sent greetings to their children, and requested their favourite songs. Nihal sent my name in. The announcer greeted me, and played a song especially for me. I clapped my hands delightedly.

Everyone sang "Happy Birthday" when I cut my cake, and then it was off to play again. The adults, Melville, Wimal, Ryan, (Thathie's boozing buddy), Mrs Joseph, and her dozen children, Mr and Mrs Fernandez, Mrs De Bruin, and her daughters, Loretta and Rosemary, besides many other railway families, continued drinking, and making merry till late at night.

The only major damper was, Ammie invited Miss Direkze. And she sat in a corner all evening, primly eating string hoppers with a fork and knife. Ammie and Thathie always entertained lavishly. So the party went on till very late, until all the food and drinks were consumed.

I kept asking Ammie afterwards, "*Why* did you invite Miss Direkze anyway? Now she will have enough to say about our 'boisterous behaviour' when I go back to school." It was too late now to worry about her, and I was glad we enjoyed ourselves very much, in spite of her formidable presence.

I jotted some childish doggerel in class one day, and Miss Direkze pounced before I could hide them. So I was in her bad books, because I wanted to write some witty lines about her.

At this stage, I wanted to be an author some day, inspired by Enid Blyton, queen of children's literature, and the perennial classics. I even scribbled a childrens story, "Green Gilpin Lost" (in the style of my favourite author). It was about a house that disappeared from sight, and how some adventurous children tried to locate the place.

I even illustrated the story with some sketches, and was pleased as punch with my efforts, and though I asked Rita to type it up, she never did. I also dabbled in water colours, and the family good-humouredly acknowledged my talents in that direction. But I did not like my art teacher, or the constraint of painting classes. Being a "Free spirit" I preferred to paint the way I felt, and not some boring objects and subjects that the teacher wanted me to emulate.

Chapter 24

Nilanthi finished her senior school exam, and waited for results, before she decided on a career. She liked nursing or teaching, and toyed with the idea of following one of those professions. The nuns persuaded her to teach prep class for a negligible salary. Nilanthi was happy, and proud to earn a living, no matter even if it was a pittance.

She loved her work, and enjoyed teaching the little children to sing. She also painted some beautiful posters and murals for the classroom. Nilanthi even played little tunes on the piano (with one finger), as she laughingly admitted. But the little ones cherished her, and enjoyed all she did.

Lakshman Silva, a local tea planter, entered our lives about this time. He was the son of one of Thathie's railway acquaintances, nicknamed "Dadi Bidi Silva" (because of his initials D.B). He asked Thathie to contact Lakshman, on Mayfield Estate, Kotagala, which was close by. Thathie agreed to socialise with him, if he wanted to. His father confided that Lakshman lived quite an isolated life.

Life on a tea estate could be very lonely, especially for a bachelor, as his nearest neighbour was the superintendent of the estate. And most of the time, the assistant superintendent did not spend much time socialising with his boss. They could visit clubs daily, if they were so inclined, but the clubs were situated quite a distance from the estates. Occasionally, they attended dinner dances, or rugger matches at the clubs. Small dinner parties held at various planters bungalows, interrupted an otherwise monotonous routine. Generally speaking, it was an isolated, and tedious existence on a tea plantation.

Thathie, no doubt, felt that the least he could do for his old friend, was to contact Lakshman and see how he fared. A few weeks later, Lakshman invited our whole family for lunch on the following Sunday. We dressed up for the occasion with a sense of curiosity and excitement. As the hired car wound through hilly roads and undulating scenery, I was very impressed when I glimpsed a large, blue-stone mansion.

The sharp descent from the main road dipped past the tea factory, and the picturesque house nestled beneath tea-clad hills. A long, white gravel driveway curved around manicured lawns. In the surrounding formal gardens, roses, azaleas, and hydrangeas bloomed profusely. It was a modest replica of an English-style country manor. The '"appu" who was butler cum valet, was an elderly, pleasant man. He was dressed in a white shirt and sarong, and opened the door.

We trailed in quietly, subdued at the somewhat austere, but impressive interior. The large, living room was neatly furnished, and had an open fireplace. But one immediately noticed the definite lack of a feminine touch. It was certainly a bachelor's residence; practical and masculine. No flowers, cushions, or ornaments anywhere, unlike our cosy home.

We sat down, whispering and giggling, as we looked around our surroundings, and waited for our host to appear. I sank into a great armchair upholstered in dark, green fabric that stood beside an open casement window. And I inhaled the delightful fragrance of gardenias that wafted gently inside. I still associate the scent of gardenias with that first visit to Mayfield Estate. Amid our frivolous comments, muttered in under-tones, Lakshman made an entrance. He was about six feet tall, powerfully-built, swarthy, and with large, protuberant black eyes.

He was all smiles and politeness, but I was surprised, and intimidated to see such a huge man, as I was a petite child. He greeted us civilly enough, but conversed mostly with Thathie, while I took stock of him. He was dressed in khaki shorts, checked shirt, and knee-length beige stockings (complete planter gear, for our benefit no doubt).

Shortly afterwards, lunch was announced. We were served fruit juices only, while Thathie and Lakshman drained a few glasses of arrack. Ammie, who never drank alcohol, sipped a fruit juice as well. Whenever Thathie persuaded her to have a tot when she was unwell, she grimaced, and swallowed the arrack as if it was poison. She never smoked either, as she could not stand the smell of tobacco.

The pleasant, but timid appu, Anjun, bustled around serving us. Lakshman yelled orders at the poor, dazed man, who kept running around nodding, "Yes Sah, no Sah," as he hopped and jumped as fast as his tired old limbs allowed him. Dessert was a delicious, caramel pudding that Anjun made (his signature dish, as we discovered), and the resident cook made the rest of the meal.

It was not a very enjoyable or relaxed meal though, because Lakshman was not an easy-going, conversational type, who could amuse us and keep us riveted to our seats. Thathie addressed him as "Lucky" after a few drinks, and the name stuck. But none of us ever called him "Lucky" not even Nilanthi. He told Thathie all about the tea manufacturing process; how many bushels the factory churned out annually, what the crop had been like, how many workers they employed, and no change of topic relieved us until we left.

Once we were shown around the gardens and spacious house, and after a polite interval between dessert and coffee, we returned home, much to my relief. I found the afternoon pretty heavy-going and boring, and none of us were impressed with Lakshman. Thathie slurred, "So children, what do you think of Lucky?" I replied bluntly. "I didn't like the way he made that poor old appu run around. No, I wasn't impressed with Lakshman at all." "But he is quite polite." Thathie replied. The others did not comment, least of all Ammie, who did not take to him either.

About a week or so after that visit, to our great surprise, a motorcycle roared up the road and braked at our house. The Brothers and students at St John Bosco's college stared incredulously at the astonishing spectacle. Lakshman was perched precariously on a motorcycle that was much too small for a man of his girth. He came on the slender pretext of seeing Thathie on some business, but his bulging eyes searched for Nilanthi. When she finally appeared, he was quite content to sit and gaze at her, without making a move to attend to whatever business he had with Thathie.

Nilanthi, aware of his obvious admiration, was quite flattered. And perhaps Thathie was already convinced that it would be a good match. Because on our way home that day, he enumerated the social advantages, and luxurious lifestyle a planter's wife enjoyed. The material advantages certainly appealed to Nilanthi no doubt. And although she was not in love with him, she developed a lukewarm attachment, that she thought was sufficient for marriage.

He was twelve years older, and when he stood next to Nilanthi, they looked like "Beauty and the Beast." Nilanthi was slender and pretty, and he towered over her. After this visit, he did not hesitate to call on Nilanthi almost daily, and invited us for dinners and lunches a few more times during this period. Obviously, Lakshman was in love with Nilanthi (or so we thought), and courted her with Thathie's silent blessing.

Ammie did not comment, or show any favour towards this attachment, as she did not find Lakshman particularly pleasing as a prospective son-in-law. Perhaps she stood in awe of him, as he seemed to look down on everyone from his imposing height (literally and figuratively). He suffered a "Gulliver" complex, and thought he could intimidate us, like the "Lilliputians." Our relatives soon knew about his courting, and were quite pleased at this advantageous matrimonial "catch."

It was socially beneficial to marry a tea planter, because of their elevated status and social life, as some of them aped and hob-nobbed with European planters at their exclusive clubs and homes. All these bright prospects must have dazzled Nilanthi, so she did not repulse Lakshman's advances. I doubt though that she was ever in love with him then or later. Nihal's friends nicknamed Lakshman, the "Gorilla."

They teased him about the "Gorilla" courting his sister, but it was not malicious, and all in good fun. Nihal and I did not take to Lakshman at all, but I do not know how strongly Shirani and Nelune felt. The consensus was, we did not like him, because he was condescending. I suppose I resented him to a certain extent, as it meant he would marry Nilanthi, and break up our family unit. I was very young then, and I suffered from a delusion that we would always live together in our happy home.

I could not help noticing that he hardly deigned to speak to Ammie, or any of us except Nilanthi, but his indifference did not affect me at all. He boasted about his privileges, and told Nilanthi he had a great deal to offer, in the way of material advantages.

We knew his father was an engine driver in the railway, and Lakshman was from a middle-class family. But he did not take the trouble to speak to anyone in our circle of friends, as he turned up his nose whenever the nuns or Brothers visited. He had no claim to wealth, and did not belong to a so-called "higher caste" but his superior attitude was infuriating, to say the least. Lakshman did not advance in my esteem, or improve with further acquaintance either.

He antagonized me with his sarcastic comments about my religious zeal, as he was a Buddhist. One day, when Lakshman was visiting, Nihal and I were on our way to church for evening service, as was habitual. He commented sarcastically to Nilanthi, "Why don't they become a priest and a nun?" This made us very angry, and we hardly spoke to him after that.

Malcolm followed Anthony to England, once he too qualified as a mechanical engineer, as he wanted to further his prospects. He wrote to us regularly, and hoped to visit soon. I missed Anthony and Malcolm very much, and now Rosie spoke of going overseas, once she completed her final exams, as trainee nurses were in demand.

During the course of Nilanthi's strange courtship, Rosie arrived suddenly one day. And in her usual, zany manner, she bragged that she boarded the night mail express train, without Granny's knowledge or permission. We considered it a great joke, and told her it was very adventurous, until, Granny zoomed in on the horizon like a vengeful battleship later that day. She declared full scale war on all and sundry, especially her mischievous daughter.

Granny was furious. And I learnt what "frothing mad" and "foaming at the mouth" really meant. Because in her fury, Granny manifested these symptoms to the utmost. She worked herself to a great passion, as she spent a sleepless night waiting for Rosie to come back home, she said. Then boarded the next train to Hatton, suspecting Rosie's obvious destination. When Rosie spied Granny charging in wrathfully through the front door, out through the back door she ran, and crept inside one of the classrooms in the convent buildings and hid there.

She was loath to face Granny's wrath, and refused to be taken home, like a naughty child. Nilanthi and Nihal joined her too in solidarity. The three of them hid in the school buildings, and instructed us younger ones to bring them food and drink. They planned to stay away until Granny calmed down, and the fierce tempest of her fury subsided.

Granny stirred up a huge commotion, and her loud lamentations filled our house that day. She berated everyone in sight, and demanded that Rosie be found and severely punished, for all the trouble she was causing her poor mother. Alas, we could not oblige Granny, because the culprit was in hiding, and at her age, Granny was reluctant to play hide-and-seek with her impish daughter. She spent the next few days locked in this impasse, until Rosie finally relented. Rosie sent word that she would return home, but on her own terms, and not with Granny either.

Granny received this dispatch with more scolding, and threats to thrash Rosie soundly, if she did not come back immediately, and return home with her. Rosie ignored all these frantic messages that we amused children carried back and forth. We found the whole situation hilarious, not knowing what Granny endured with her obstinate daughter.

Nilanthi and Nihal returned home after the first day, but Rosie, in her role of fugitive, took refuge in our empty classroom. She told me later that she urinated there, because there was no toilet. We children cleaned up the mess when we went to school next day. And the teacher was just as puzzled as we were, not knowing who broke in to urinate there.

Finally, Granny left with ominous grumbling. Rosie agreed to return home on her own. But after a few drinks, Thathie was in such a raging temper because he and Ammie bore the brunt of Granny's anger, that as soon as he saw Rosie, he grabbed hold of her and beat her soundly.

Rosie did not utter a sound, as I watched Thathie chastising her. Her lips tightened, and her face was grim. She was undaunted and unrepentant. Thathie bundled her on the next train, back to long-suffering Granny.

Five of us with Ammie on our First Communion day. Nilanthi & Nihal In Polonnaruwa. Me on the tricycle. Nelune and me in Hatton. Group in front of our house in Hatton and St John Bosco's College in background

Chapter 25

News that Nilanthi was "carrying on" with a Buddhist planter, spread like a raging bushfire. And the nuns, without much ado promptly dismissed her from her teaching post, saying, "We cannot keep you, now that you are engaged to a *Buddhist!*" Nilanthi was shattered, and cried her eyes out, especially when all the beautiful paintings and murals she executed with so much love, were retained. The nuns passed them on to her successor, Gertrude, one of Nilanthi's previous classmates.

More was to follow, as we faced another incident at evening service one day. Fr Augustine, assistant parish priest, who had once been a frequent visitor, and was on very good terms with our family, walked up to Nilanthi, and hissed vindictively, "Unless you *leave* the church *immediately*, I will not continue with the service!"

Nihal was so angered at such blatant intolerance, that he marched us out of church. We all left, except Ammie, who tearfully pleaded with the priest to let Nilanthi stay on for service, but Fr Augustine remained adamant.

He was a short, stocky man, always neat, and dressed in snow-white vestments. His hair was cut short and plastered down with Brylcreem, and he wore square, gold-rimmed spectacles. Fr Augustine was the epitome of a pedantic priest, and a stickler for obeying church rules to the letter. He said because Nilanthi was engaged to a Buddhist, she was forbidden to attend church in future.

I think he over-exerted his priestly power, and appeared to be very narrow-minded then. Nilanthi stopped attending church from that day onwards, and we were disgusted, and disillusioned with the priest's attitude. It was a difficult situation to accept, as we were a devout, church-going family. Lakshman gloated, and ridiculed the church and the priests for their bigotry. Nihal was very angry and upset at what he termed, "The callousness of some Catholic priests."

Lakshman played for time. It became obvious he was not in a hurry to get married, confident that a beautiful young girl was waiting whenever he was ready. But he told Nilanthi that he dreaded breaking the news to his parents, who would be seriously displeased with him, if he married a Catholic girl, who was half-Burgher, and without a dowry. His parents believed his social standing would attract an eligible bride with a rich dowry, so he kept his courtship a secret. However, religion and nationality would not have weighed as much with his parents, as the absence of a substantial dowry (I believed).

I understood these matters when I was older, and when the family discussed the affair. Lakshman mentioned the existence of an obscure stipulation in his contract with the tea company; that he could not get married for a certain period of time, but only he knew the veracity of the matter. Whatever his reasons, much to Nilanthi's chagrin, Lakshman kept stalling, and hesitated to set a date whenever she mentioned wedding plans.

One day, when I came home after school, Ammie told me that my pet Gina, was at the vet's. She was very sick after she had a litter of six puppies. A few days ago, she started acting very strangely. I was the only one who could touch her, as she growled and snarled at every one else when they came near.

I tried to rescue three or four mangled puppies that she had bitten viciously, in a moment of pain. Ammie was concerned that she had contracted rabies, and told me not to go near her. But I fed and petted her, as it was heart-wrenching to watch her in so much pain. Her belly was still swollen, and she could hardly walk. When she tried to stagger around, Nilanthi and the others screamed and jumped on top of tables. So that day, when Ammie told me she was at the vet's, I was happy for a while, until I saw Nilanthi making signs, and silently mouthing something to Lakshman, who just walked in. I immediately suspected something was amiss, and when I burst into tears, Nilanthi told me Gina was dead. The vet wanted to perform an autopsy to find out what was wrong with her.

Later, the vet informed us that he found a dead puppy in her uterus still, and that was the reason for her pain and strange behaviour. Poor Gina! How much I missed her, and I moaned her loss for a long time.

As Lakshman's strange courtship continued, several funny moments amused the rest of us. Like the time when Nilanthi wanted to show how accomplished she was in needlework and knitting. She was expert at sewing, but knitting was another matter, as she did not know the difference between knit and purl. After a triumphant moment, when she sewed an enormous dressing gown, patterned in brown and white squares, she rashly agreed to knit him a jumper as well, when he requested her to knit one.

What a predicament Nilanthi was in. That little white lie led to a hilarious situation. Ammie, who was a skilled knitter, worked at the jumper during the day. When Lakshman visited in the evenings, Nilanthi sat with the half-completed jumper on her lap. To his enquiries as to why she did not knit while he was there, she replied, "I'm *tired* of knitting all day!" This situation caused much mirth among us, and we teased her unrelentingly.

Whenever Lakshman came, they sat in the front parlour, while we children usually hung around in the main living room, where we listened to music or just talked and joked with Nihal. At such times, a puckish spirit entered Nihal. He grabbed a blackened clay pot (chatty), and hid behind the door that separated the parlour and living room.

As soon as he saw Nilanthi looking his way, he masked his face with the pot and pranced around, which made it very difficult for Nilanthi to keep a straight face.

As Lakshman sat opposite her, he could not see what Nihal was doing. Sometimes, after a heroic effort, and much biting of lips and screwing up of her face, she excused herself, rushed to the living room, and just burst out laughing.

Nihal did this to tease Nilanthi about Lakshman's swarthy, "moon" face, but he was not malicious in any way, only very mischievous, when he played practical jokes. I laughed till my jaws ached, so did the others. But Lakshman never knew what caused so much hilarity in the adjoining room, and remained ignorant.

He usually stayed till about ten or eleven o'clock in the night, and Nihal had ample time to play more practical jokes on Nilanthi. He removed a few slats from her bed, and left about two at the ends, just to support the mattress. Then he turned off the bedroom lights and hid somewhere until she came in.

We pretended to be fast asleep, as she came in quietly, and got ready for bed, and then, crash! Bang! The peaceful silence was shattered.

Nilanthi fell in a heap, as the mattress doubled up under her. Her screams brought Ammie and Thathie to the room, but instead of scolding Nihal, they stood there looking at him amusedly, red-faced and merry at the success of his practical joke. Menika, and the servant boy too joined in these revelries and laughed their heads off, though it was rough on Nilanthi, the butt end of Nihal's practical jokes.

We thought it was very funny then, as Nilanthi checked her bed every night after that, but Nihal was still clever enough to catch her off guard. And when she least expected it, the occasional sound of Nilanthi crashing through her bed was still heard.

After some months, Lakshman did not turn up for days, and this continued for a couple of weeks. Nilanthi was in a sad state, as she did not know what to think, and she cried a lot. She was under pressure to get married, and she did not want to displease Thathie. I felt sorry for her, as she was in a quandary. No messages, letters or phone calls from Lakshman at all, as he used to phone Thathie at the station whenever he could not visit. Nilanthi wrote and asked him what was going on, but he ignored her letters.

About three weeks later, he strutted in, grinning broadly, and looking smug, as if nothing was wrong. He confessed to Nilanthi that he was having second thoughts about getting married so soon, as he was afraid of repercussions he would face, from his parents and his company.

Nilanthi was very upset over his fickle behaviour, and after a tearful reunion, he agreed to fix a date. Thathie too was very annoyed, and reprimanded Lakshman. "I do not want my daughter compromised. It is a shocking scandal that you visited her almost *daily* for many months, and totally unacceptable for you to get cold feet at this late date!" So amid tears, promises, and reproaches, they made arrangements for their wedding.

Chapter 26

Ammie was pregnant in 1965, and the baby was due in May. Although I was too young to realise the implications, Ammie gained considerable weight, and grew even larger towards the end of her pregnancy. I heard whispers that Ammie was overdue, but she did not do anything about it. And I do not recall Ammie going for regular check-ups either, perhaps she did.

She went about with great difficulty, and was very uncomfortable. Ammie was in her mid-thirties, and should have taken more care.

Nihal teased Ammie. "If it cries too much in the night, I'll chuck it down the hill!" Ammie scolded him, and told him not to be silly. Her knitting needles click clacked away, as she knitted beautiful baby clothes. I wonder if we felt a little threatened. A baby in our lives, to take up all the love and attention of our parents.

One evening, soon after, Ammie's contractions began. Thathie promptly admitted her to the nursing home in Hatton. And he suggested, "Why don't five of you go to a movie, as I don't want you moping at home worrying about Ammie." He paid for our tickets as usual, but did not join us. We watched a forgettable movie; a teeny bopper sixties film, "Some People" about teenagers rebelling against authority, and out to have a good time.

A great deal of singing, dancing, and pop music filled most of it, which was the reason why we went to see it I suppose. We sang the catchy lines all the way back. "S--o--m--e people think that kids today have gone astray...." and so forth.

When we returned at about ten o'clock, Thathie came to tell us that Ammie was still in labour. He looked haggard, so we hurried to the nursing home with him to stay with Ammie, until the baby was born. But after midnight, doctor said it was no use waiting any longer. He did not know when the baby would arrive, and told us it would be better for us to go home. Thathie stayed on, and promised to let us know as soon as the baby was born.

We returned home, and tried to sleep, as we had school next day. Thathie stumbled home towards dawn, looking anguished, grey and fatigued. I was scared when I saw him. I feared the worst that he brought terrible news. Without saying another word, he burst into tears and sobbed brokenly. "The baby is dead!" We were shattered, to say the least.

I felt such an awful coldness creeping over me, and my throat constricted, as I whispered, "How is Ammie?" Thathie wept and mumbled with difficulty. "The only way to save Ammie was to sacrifice the baby." Such primitive methods seemed incredible. This was supposed to be a fairly modern nursing home, with good doctors, and medical attention. Why they did not perform a Caesarean operation, is something I never knew. If only some doctor had the common sense to help Ammie when she was in labour for so long, the baby would have lived.

Ammie was unaware she had gestational diabetes, and suffered from diabetes for the rest of her life. She was subject to severe migraine headaches from then onwards. She carried an enormous amount of excess fluid, and the baby weighed sixteen pounds. The gory details of how the doctor dislocated the baby's shoulders to remove it, as Ammie laboured in vain, and the many complications that set in, are too vivid, and painful to record. Thathie blurted out details, and he was a broken man that day.

Our family was devastated when this tragedy touched our lives so suddenly. Athamma, and some other relatives, visited soon. We went to school next day, but we were allowed to visit Ammie during lunch interval. I vividly recall the face of the beautiful, infant girl, deprived of life so cruelly.

She had curly black hair, and a rosy complexion, and looked as if she was six months old. This is what the adults said, and their words are imprinted in my mind. But the image of that baby's face is still vivid. It was not red, and puckered, like most new-born infants. Instead, she had a lovely serene look, just like an angel, who was fast asleep.

Although worn-out, and heart-broken after her gruelling ordeal, Ammie spoke, as we stood around her. She asked if we saw the baby, as she refused to see the dead infant, saying it was unbearable. But I think it was unfortunate that Ammie never knew what an angelic baby she gave birth to, and had only our inadequate descriptions to remember her all through life.

The funeral was arranged without much ado. And in a couple of days before Ammie was discharged, our infant sister was buried in the nearby cemetery. A few friends, and close relatives attended the burial. Gradually, the poignant memory dimmed, but left our family subdued. Our usual high spirits, and mischievous sense of fun, were quenched during this period of sadness and mourning. This was the first time that dark clouds of grief descended on our lives, and none of us remained untouched.

Ammie did not say much when she returned home from hospital. But she quickly gave away all the knitted baby clothes to friends, and the orphans in the convent.

A few weeks after this heart-breaking incident, Lakshman, Nilanthi, and some of the family decided to climb Adam's Peak. Ammie, Nelune, and I stayed home with Menika and the servant boy. We were not inclined to experience the tortuous climb again, and decided to give this expedition a miss.

I was playing as usual, and wandering around the house and garden, when sometime around noon, Nelune started to get excruciating stomach pains, and rolled around in agony. We assumed she ate too many lollies, and had an upset stomach. So, we did not take much notice of her complaints. But when Ammie dosed her with milk of magnesia, she retched violently, and looked worse. Ammie began to worry, and decided to take her to the nursing home immediately.

None of our neighbours were around to ask for help (as it usually happens in an emergency), as everyone was out. Finally, with the greatest difficulty, our servant boy got a hiring car, and we rushed Nelune to the nursing home. It took over an hour to get a hiring car, and by the time doctor saw Nelune, he diagnosed acute appendicitis. She needed an immediate operation, and Ammie was distressed. But she had no choice except to agree.

That night, when the family returned from their expedition, they were very upset, especially Thathie, who was overwhelmed. Nelune was the baby, and everyone, especially Ammie and Thathie, doted on her. The operation was performed without any complications, but Nelune was not discharged for a few days. Granny visited, and stayed with Nelune.

When Nelune returned home, Granny fussed over her constantly, and did not allow her to carry anything heavy, even a small, bowl of water. Much to Nelune's chagrin, Granny kept a very stern eye on her, to see that she followed doctor's orders precisely. Regardless of how minor the procedure was then, the word "Operation" connoted all sorts of fears and misgivings, and the patient was unashamedly molly-coddled. Today, it is just the opposite, as patients are discharged as soon as the anaesthetic wears off, and they can stand up. Nelune recovered well, inundated with tender love and care, and did not have any complications.

A couple of months after my thirteenth birthday, when I went to the toilet at school one day, to my utter disgust and consternation, I discovered signs of my first menstruation. I was very shy, and embarrassed about this most natural occurrence, so I decided to keep it a secret from Ammie. This was because, years back in Bandarawela, they made a great fuss at Nilanthi's "Attending age" as Ceylonese referred to this event.

Nilanthi was confined to her room, with strict orders not to leave it, or face any male member of the family, and threatened with eternal bad luck, or some such flim flam superstition, if she did not observe rules. At the end of seven days, at an auspicious time, she was bathed in a tub, full of fragrant flowers. To crown it all, our parents held a huge party, to announce the occurrence. I cringed at the mere thought of such a spectacle. Shirani too endured similar treatment in Hatton, when her day came. And so, I decided that no way would I meekly tolerate such embarrassing nonsense. With characteristic reticence, and bravado, I kept my secret from Ammie, and the family.

When I went home that evening, I bathed in cold water, and suffered much discomfort, and cramps in silence, but kept my secret. I thought I was very clever in concealing my periods for three months. And I took great care not to betray any outward signs, until one day, Granny found me out. She was staying with us for a few weeks during Nelune's convalescence, when her eagle eye spotted a stain on my bed sheets. She immediately informed Ammie. I was brought forth before the investigation tribunal, consisting of Ammie, Granny, and Menika. Dates, times, exact month, everything, was verified, and mulled over carefully, before Granny was satisfied.

I replied cheekily, "This is *not* the first time that it happened!" This caused many moans, and groans, as they shook their heads in annoyance. Stern disapproval, and disbelief, rumbled ominously when I ended my account of the matter. What *irretrievable* damage, and misfortune had I brought on myself, by facing males during my first menstruation. I could not for the world understand this superstition, and where it originated from, that even your own father, and brother, could not see you during the first seven days, until you were bathed and "cleansed." I was immediately isolated in my room, until the tribunal debated, and deliberated about my assertions.

Then I said that I noted the event in my diary three months ago, and that I would not be confined to my room for even one day, let alone seven days. They scolded me severely, saying how wrong it was to conceal such an important incident for three months. Granny was utterly scandalised, and could not get over such a thing. She kept repeating, "Never before have any of my girls done such a thing! You are very naughty, and should not be allowed out of your room!"

The long and short of it was, I won the day. And I congratulated myself on escaping a most distasteful custom. I was quite impervious to the stern, disapproving looks Granny cast my way.

Chapter 27

Nilanthi went ahead with her wedding plans without much fuss. Ammie firmly declared none of us would attend a civil ceremony at a registrar's office. She wanted Nilanthi to get married in church, according to Catholic rites. It was a very sad decision, and upset Nilanthi greatly, but we were too young to have a say in the matter. Lakshman arranged everything in such a clandestine manner, so that no report of the wedding would reach his parents, or his company. Athamma, Mutha, and Daisy Akka, visited a few days before.

It was quite distressing for our relatives, and grandparents too, because they wanted a wedding worthy of their eldest grand-daughter, according to Kandyan Sinhalese tradition. They were not at all happy with such furtive preparations, when it should have been a joyous occasion for the bride and her family.

Athamma and Daisy Akka brought their jewellery for Nilanthi to wear with a Kandyan-style sari. But Nilanthi obstinately refused to wear ostentatious jewellery, or bedeck herself according to their tradition. She disliked ornate, old-fashioned jewellery, and wanted to wear a plain white sari, with no other adornment, except a dainty gold chain, matching earrings, and a single white rose in her hair. Athamma's disappointment, and chagrin were obvious, but Nilanthi was obstinate.

I prepared to go to school, and the wedding party, consisting of Thathie, Mutha, Athamma, Daisy Akka, and Nilanthi, who carried a small bouquet of white roses, headed off in a hired car to the registry. It was very melancholy, to think of our eldest sister getting married in this quiet manner, without any fuss and joy.

No grand wedding breakfast, no happy toasts, laughter, or excitement, that usually precedes such an important event. And everything was just as mundane as ever. Ammie was unyielding too, and upheld her decision to boycott the wedding, unless it was held in a Catholic church.

I missed Nilanthi very much from the moment she left home, and felt sad that she began her new life in such a secretive manner. They did not even go away on a honeymoon. Lakshman insisted on being at Mayfield Estate straight after the wedding. So her married life on the pleasant, but lonely tea plantation, began immediately after the ceremony. He hoped his parents and the company directors reconciled to his marriage in time.

A few days later, Nilanthi visited unexpectedly, and she cried a great deal, because she missed her home and family dearly. She pleaded with Ammie to send Nihal, or one of us to keep her company for a few days, until she got used to her solitary new life. I did not accompany Nilanthi, because I disliked Lakshman immensely. But Nihal agreed to spend some time, because he too missed her very much, and was upset to see her weep inconsolably.

A subtle change overcame me after Nilanthi's marriage, as I missed her so much. I soon forgot all her teasing, quarrelsome ways, and bemoaned the loss of my dear sister, now that she was no longer a part of our happy family. We grew even more attached to her, and to each other than ever before. I matured a little, as I realised the importance, value, and joy of true family affection.

Whatever the reason for this metamorphosis, our mutual love, and family ties bonded indestructibly. I now looked on Nilanthi as a paragon, and she in turn liked to play "Lady bountiful." Nothing was too good, or too much for Nihal, and her little sisters. Whenever she visited, Nilanthi brought plentiful supplies of fresh fruit, and vegetables from her garden, and gave us pocket money, and pretty clothes.

The first few months were good, and Nilanthi was happy, and contented to a certain degree, as she liked to help the family in any way she could. Nihal sat for his senior school certificate, and spent a great deal of time visiting Mayfield, to keep Nilanthi company. And he also toyed with the idea of becoming a tea planter.

He was impressed with the life-style on an estate. And Lakshman, who was still in a honeymoon phase, made vague promises to, "Put in a word" to his superiors, so he could start as a "Creeper" (a trainee planter). In anticipation, Nihal splashed out on some proper "Planter gear," knee-length khaki shorts, checked shirt, long socks, and work boots.

Of course, I could not resist making fun of Nihal, and we had a good laugh whenever he was rigged out, but he did not mind the teasing, and hoped he would soon get a break. As time went on, and nothing happened, I knew Lakshman did not bother to even lift his little finger to help Nihal get a job on an estate.

From certain remarks he made to Nilanthi, it was obvious he was very envious of Nihal's good looks, and friendly personality, as Nihal cut a handsome, dashing figure, when he dressed as a planter. Whenever he returned from one of his visits to Mayfield, he kept us in stitches with droll imitations, and stories about Lakshman's snobbery. Although Nilanthi made friends with other planters' wives in months to come, she said they could not take our place.

Nilanthi was the soul of generosity whenever we visited her, and insisted we accompanied her to movies, or to the planters Club at Darawela. She was greatly changed from her spitfire days, and I was amazed at how marriage mellowed her overnight.

On such occasions, when we visited the exclusive club, Nilanthi dressed up in a new sari, or evening dress, and looked stunning. Lakshman strutted around her like a proud peacock, as if examining an objet d'art. He liked to show off his beautiful, young wife to other planters, in the belief they envied him, so he was usually in a good mood when we visited the club. We enjoyed ourselves greatly too, as we sipped beer shandies, lemonade, or Guinness stout, and indulged in luxuries that only the privileged classes in Ceylon could afford. I liked some aspects of Nilanthi's lifestyle, but not the pomposity that existed among some of the planters.

The club had an old piano in the hall, and Nihal sometimes dared me to play that instrument, when we were a little light-headed after our shandies. Never one to turn down a challenge, I thumped out some favourite pop songs, while Nihal stood by humming, singing, or teasing, according to his whimsical moods.

Those were good days at the beginning of their marriage, when Lakshman was keen to impress, and show how important, and affluent he was. He treated us generously at the club, where he chalked up a huge bill for drinks (on credit). I was unaware then that Lakshman, like most of the other planters, lived solely on credit, and settled at the end of each month, as they were paid monthly.

Back at Mayfield, Lakshman reverted to an indifferent, and ungracious host, while Nilanthi did most of the talking and entertaining. It was very uncomfortable whenever he was around. Meal times were especially diverting, because having lived alone for a long time, Lakshman's table manners were appalling. He never passed the dishes around, but always served himself first, kept all the dishes in close proximity around him, and began to eat heartily, without a second thought or concern for his guests. This embarrassed Nilanthi very much, as we looked on in silent mirth while the charade commenced. It was very challenging for her to be a good wife, and a good sister at the same time.

She served Lakshman all the curries first, and then hoped he would pass the dishes around. But as he concentrated solely on his meal, Nilanthi's silent, meaningful glances did not pierce his thick skin, until finally, she exclaimed in chagrin. "Lakshman, *please* pass the dishes to the others will you? Can't you see they haven't been served as yet?"

Mildly surprised at Nilanthi's exasperated tone, he looked up, piled some more food onto his plate, before reluctantly passing the dishes around very slowly. He looked quite alarmed, in case he missed out on his third, or fourth helping, although the ample food was enough to feed another dozen or so guests.

His behaviour caused us much laughter, when he went on "Muster" and was not around. When he returned late afternoon, he napped, before final muster in the evening before dinner. Nilanthi was happy, and cheerful, talking and laughing, just like old times, when he was away. And we too felt restrained in his company, because the only topic he was interested in, was the business of tea making; how much tea his factory made in a year, the crop, the tea pluckers problems. Anything and everything related to his work, but not general topics that were of any interest to us.

We became very bored at the end of his tedious conversation, and avoided him at all costs. Anjun was a delightful old appu, and to our great amusement, he answered Nilanthi's summons with, "Yes Lardie," and "No Lardie," as he could not say, 'lady' properly. He was a kind, fatherly man, who was very fond of Nilanthi. In her lonely, hours, she talked and joked with Anjun, and the other servants while she helped in the kitchen.

All these free and easy manners with the servants, went much against his grain, because he tried to emulate European planters. He treated the servants with utter contempt, like dirt beneath his feet. Lakshman upbraided Nilanthi often, stating that it was not proper to be in the kitchen, or converse with servants. But she blithely ignored him, and continued to pass her long, solitary hours talking and laughing with the domestics.

She was used to treating servants kindly, because of the relationship we enjoyed with Menika, who was like a family member. Nilanthi's easy, unsophisticated manners, endeared her to all the servants. But she made him very angry, as she was too immature to play the role of an arrogant, tea planter's wife.

The senior superintendent's wife, Devika, was an imposing woman of Amazon proportions. But she soon became Nilanthi's confidant, and mentor, as she coached her in her new role. Devika proved to be invaluable, and instructed Nilanthi how to cater for, and entertain large parties; what sort of duties were expected of her on the plantation, and overall, she was a good friend.

Devika was not beautiful, but she had pleasant features, and a graceful figure. Sometimes she invited us to her magnificent mansion, where I looked around in awe at such grandeur. She had good taste, and the house was elegantly furnished. With money, servants, and social standing, she indulged lavishly in her expensive tastes. On an early morning visit once, she ordered her appu to serve us corn-on-the-cob outdoors. We sat and enjoyed the delicious corn, amid vast expanses of rolling, immaculate lawns, formal gardens, masses of flower beds, graceful trees, and foliage, while Devika chatted away in a relaxed, charming manner.

It was a setting fit for a princess. I almost envied her this splendid mansion, and exquisite gardens, not knowing, or understanding then that all these splendours were dearly bought. A dark, poignant element coursed through the lives of some of these solitary wives, who were like tiny, desert islands in their magnificent settings. Still, I suppose, most of the young wives did not do too badly. Their indulgent husbands bestowed money, jewellery, and clothes, besides occasionally mingling in European planters society (which some of them aspired to).

The beautiful mansions, and gardens alone, were enough to make anyone happy (so I thought then). Life on a plantation would have been bearable, if only the wives had some sort of occupation, to prevent neurosis, and tedium creeping in like cancer. Unfortunately, most of them did not have fulfilling lives to ward off boredom, and so they became discontented, and unhappy. Most of Nilanthi's friends suffered from the same complaint; loneliness, and ennui.

Nilanthi asked me to paint some water colour studies. I painted some bright azaleas in a dark vase, which she told me was quite good. I asked Marie for some oil paints, and attempted a large portrait of Audrey Hepburn, dressed in a black and white costume, as she appeared in the film "'My Fair Lady." Nilanthi hung that in her living room.

I enjoyed painting, and writing short verses even then, although I was usually the butt end of Nihal's jokes and teasing. I ignored the "critics" and dabbled in writing and painting, releasing the creative stimulus dawning within. I wonder what became of those early paintings.

Thathie bought a shiny, new bicycle for Nelune that Christmas. The very next day, Shirani and Nelune dared me to ride over to Mayfield, and surprise Nilanthi. Now, I never rode a bicycle before, but boldly accepted their challenge. Around ten o'clock next morning, without Ammie's or Thathie's permission, I got on the bicycle, and wobbled along the main road to Mayfield.

I gained confidence every minute, and congratulated myself on my progress, until I came to a few, sharp descents, applied the brakes suddenly, and somersaulted right into tea bushes and a ditch. Badly bruised, and completely surprised at the bicycle's strange behaviour, I promptly mounted, repeated the same mistake, and landed in some shrubbery below. I fell about three or four times, until I finally reached the last, steep, descent to the estate, and then fell right over the side of the road. I hurt my arm badly, not to mention the new bicycle, that now looked battered, and muddy, with a bent pedal.

I was aghast. How could I return home? Some tea pluckers, and labourers immediately came to my assistance, and helped me wobble up to the bungalow, while another dragged the bicycle behind. Nilanthi laughed merrily when I related my mishaps. But she soon patched me up, tied a sling round my arm, and fed me, as I was ravenous. The bicycle was sent to a mechanic for repairs. She phoned Thathie in the evening, and told him I was alright, and would come home in a couple of days time. She did not mention about the bicycle, or that I hurt my arm.

I rested a few days until my arm healed, then Lakshman drove me home with the repaired bicycle secured in the boot of the car. No one was wiser, until I told the family how many times I fell into ditches, and tea bushes. They laughed heartily, so did I. At least I learnt how to ride a bicycle properly after that episode.

Chapter 28

During school holidays that same year, we travelled to Maharagama with Ammie and Thathie. Shirani was suffering with sinusitis, and Granny asked her to stay in Maharagama for a few weeks. She said the warm climate, and Ayurvedic medicines would cure her.

Shirani wore a bandage around her forehead, and inhaled foul smelling concoctions, to relieve her headaches. She wore black, square-framed glasses then. We teased her, and called her Nana Muscouri, (the Greek pop singer who wore similar glasses).

That holiday was especially memorable, with much fun and laughter with Rosie, who amused us endlessly, with her jokes and pranks. She treated us to movies, walks on Galle Face Green, and visits to glorious beaches. We enjoyed ourselves very much, whenever Rosie was around, as she extracted the best out of any situation, no matter how mundane.

Annabelle (Anjo), our friend next door, joined us on our bicycle expeditions sometimes. But as we had only three bicycles, we were somewhat restricted, and ended with us younger ones riding on the pillion with Rosie, Anjo, or Nihal.

It was a great shock when Anjo's parents, Mimi and Sam, divorced, and he re-married. He soon brought his new wife home to be their step-mother. The scandal rocked the small community in Maharagama. But as we lived hundred miles away, we only heard fragments of the story. Granny, who lived next door to them, knew all the sordid details, and it shocked her puritanical values to the core. Sam was rumoured to have had an affair with the other woman (his secretary), for some time.

When Granny heard of this, and Sam re-married, she absolutely forbade us to have anything to do with them. I thought this was very unfair, as we were long-time friends, and every holiday, Anjo and Barbara (Barlo), her elder sister, always joined in our fun and games. They were Rosie's good friends too, and she did not care about Granny's rules, because we included them in all our outings and games.

Anjo and Barlo had three brothers; Barlo was the eldest, then Herman, (Sonna), Anjo, Peter, and Maurice. They were lovely children, and I was very fond of them, and Mimi. We could not cut off our ties, just because of Granny.

The idea they now had a "wicked stepmother" endeared them to me more than ever. Anjo was full of fun, and she immediately joined in any crazy scheme Rosie suggested. We rode around town, perched precariously on the bicycle pillions, squealing and giggling, as the bicycles lurched dangerously over bumpy roads, full of pot holes. Rosie headed off to the paddy fields, and dismounted, then sat in dry canal beds below, and smoked cigarettes to her heart's content, without fear of Granny interrupting to chastise her.

We played hide-and-seek, or just sat around, while Rosie enjoyed her smokes. Most of our expeditions were a ruse, just to get away from Granny's eagle-eyed surveillance, so Rosie could smoke and joke unrestrainedly. I never knew anyone else who loved life, and laughed so much as our Rosie. Everything in life was one big joke, and I do not think I ever saw her looking serious, glum, or ill-tempered. She had a happy, optimistic nature, and most people loved her, as much as we did.

As children, we looked up to Rosie, and considered it great fun to help her outsmart Granny, who was a bane in our childhood, because she was so very strict with everyone. And whenever we visited, we had to be well-behaved, to avoid her displeasure. She caught Rosie red-handed a few times, when she occupied the outside lavatory for a very long time. Smelling a rat (or rather a cigarette), Granny walked around the premises, and spied wispy, blue smoke curling through cracks in the old door.

What a commotion ensued that day, as she chastised Rosie severely. We were terrified of Granny, because she flew into such a grand passion. And not even mild-mannered Grandpa could calm her down. He wisely kept out of her way until the storm abated. No one escaped her lashing tongue, and cane, until the full force of her anger died down eventually.

In spite of many beatings, scoldings, threats, and warnings, Rosie did not give up smoking. And whether in direct opposition to Granny, or because she was addicted, she remained a smoker for many years. She passed a cigarette around, and I tried to smoke. But my siblings and I did not acquire that distasteful habit.

It was during this unforgettable holiday in 1965, that I first experienced a teenage "crush" at thirteen. It was not exactly a romance as such, but to me, it was the dawning awareness of young love. The object of my passion was the boy next door. It happened under such mundane circumstances, that before I knew what struck me, cupid's arrow had well and truly lodged deep within. Since I was a very young child, my family teased me about Clifford, the boy who lived next door to Granny's house.

They only had to say "Clifford" and I bawled out angrily, because I hated their teasing, and did not know what it was all about when I was a little girl. The family story goes, that when I was about five years old, and Clifford, three years older, he was seen kissing me on my cheek, while playing under a coconut tree. Everyone witnessed this innocent kiss, and were thoroughly amused.

From then onwards, all they had to do to make me mad and cry, was to sing out, "coconut tree." I ran and told Ammie to make them stop teasing me. So, when it happened, I was completely surprised. One day, as I was walking down the narrow lane that divided Granny's property from her neighbours, I saw a young boy seated on a bench. He was languidly observing builders constructing a new house.

I did not recall seeing Clifford over the last ten years or so. In my mind, he was still the detestable little boy, who had kissed me, and was the cause of all the teasing I endured. I was pleasantly surprised now to see a good-looking boy glance my way briefly. I flushed with embarrassment, and whispered to Rosie, "*Who* is that boy over there?" Rosie went off into peals of laughter. "Why, that's *Clifford*!" I was incredulous!

What happened during the next few hours, and days, are best described as a hazy dream world, as I was swept along in a maelstrom of emotions. I fell "in love" suddenly, and felt this strange new feeling awakening inside. Besotted, was more like it. I could hardly wait to ask Rosie more details about him.

Rosie soon told Anjo, and before long, everyone knew I had a "crush" on him, including Clifford. I was discomfited, and very shy, but Rosie thought it was a huge joke. She had no qualms in broadcasting my feelings to everyone, as nothing was sacred to her.

In a matter of days, she smuggled notes hidden inside a newspaper (so Granny and Marie would not know). And she arranged a rendezvous in a nearby parkland, that locals referred to as, "thung kale" (purple woods). We called it "Blueberry Hill," because of the inedible, purple berries that festooned the bushes. I met Clifford only once, when Rosie, Nihal, and the others lurked behind shrubbery and spied on us. We were so shy, and tongue-tied, that we only said, "Hello," and that was the end of the matter, as far as everyone was concerned.

We left Maharagama next day, and I never had a chance to see him alone, or wish him goodbye before I left. Marie and Granny watched me constantly, and Granny forbade me to even speak to Clifford. And they succeeded very well in keeping us away from each other.

My parents, and Granny, considered it a mortal sin to have a boyfriend. And such normal, teenage behaviour was frowned upon, and absolutely forbidden. They treated young love as something unnatural, and shameful. When I went back to school, it was painfully obvious to my friends, and teachers, that something was the matter with me, as I changed noticeably.

My school work did not suffer though. And I took great pains to improve my writing, which was an illegible scrawl before, to a more acceptable scrawl now. I took great care of my appearance too, spending hours in front of the mirror doing up my hair, or just day dreaming. Such affectations did not escape eagle-eyed Miss Direkze, or the other teachers.

I spent my leisure time writing notes and letters to Clifford, and asked one of my friends to post them for me. I did not receive any response to my letters, and it was a sad, heartbreaking time. I did not know what to do, as I experienced pangs of unrequited love, and felt miserable. I wrote to Anjo, and Rosie for news, but they had no answers. It seemed as if my young love (or infatuation), was blighted and doomed before it even began.

Clifford was sixteen then, and I was only thirteen. But being very romantic, sentimental, and sensitive, I suffered the usual pain and heartbreak that followed a hopeless love, even though we hardly spoke to each other, and were total strangers. I doubt anyone realized the intensity of my feelings then, least of all Clifford. Several factors contributed to fuel the spark of love into an all-consuming blaze.

My love was unrequited, forbidden, and being hundred miles apart, distance certainly lent enchantment to the view. It was inevitable that I should imbue all kinds of heroic, and noble attributes to my teenage idol. My emotions engulfed me completely. I found great relief in pouring out my feelings in ten page letters. I believe that my early attempts at creative writing, emerged around this period.

If Granny was more sensible about the whole affair, it would have run its natural course, and faded in time. She did not know that the moment she forbade me to have anything to do with him, the more determined I was to disobey. I pictured myself as a star-crossed heroine, like Shakespeare's Juliet, and believed "love would conquer, and triumph" against all opposition.

I treasured the two brief notes, which he sent at the beginning of our correspondence. And I left them in my desk at school, as I was afraid my parents would find them. They were unaware of my infatuation as yet, and I did not want them to find out anyway, as Thathie would have chastised me immediately.

One morning, to my utter consternation, the two little notes vanished from my desk. I could not imagine what had happened. And I wondered, if in a scatter-brained manner (as I sometimes did), I dropped them somewhere. I wandered around the school compound, looking for them. They were the only notes I ever had, and I moaned my loss.

In the days that followed, Miss Direkze picked on me for various small misdemeanours. She threw veiled hints about young girls carrying on with boys, all of which went right over my head. I did not have the slightest notion her verbal missiles were directed at me. Her voice dripped with sarcasm, whenever she addressed me. Because I was none too popular since the day she pounced on me for having scribbled some childish doggerel. She had sneered, "So, we have a budding *poet* here!"

She called me over to her desk when I was alone in the classroom one day. And smiled nastily, with a sly, "I know all about you," sort of look. She then severed the sword of Damocles that was suspended by a thread over me. I reeled under the shock, when she crowed. "I *know* you have a boyfriend, Clifford, and I'm going to talk to you about this matter very seriously." I could not deny this statement. I blushed furiously, as I often did under pressure, and perspired profusely.

One had to understand what sort of puritanical old maids our teachers were then, to even comprehend the fear they instilled. Their stern gaze, or threats to take up the matter with the principal and our parents, terrified me. And they succeeded only too well in inculcating my tender mind the horrors of mortal sin, Hell, and punishment.

I woke up anxiously every day, filled with apprehension. And I wondered if this was the day of judgement, when Miss Direkze told my parents about my correspondence with (Heaven forbid), a teenage boy. How ridiculous it seems, that I lived in such great fear over such a trivial matter.

I wrote dozens of drafts, before I finally sent off a letter to Clifford. And in my abstracted manner, I rolled up these drafts, and threw them out of my window, where they landed in the middle of Mr Weerakoon's backyard. Mr "Snoopy" Weerakoon picked up my discarded love letters, and promptly sent them to Thathie.

One evening, when Thathie came home, I knew at a glance I was in trouble. He was after a couple of drinks, and called me up before him. I stood trembling, when he told me in no uncertain terms that I must stop my foolish behaviour immediately. He vowed to beat me soundly, if he ever caught me exchanging letters with Clifford again. This was the first time Thathie threatened me with physical punishment, as the worst he had meted out before, was a thundering slap.

I could not believe how foolishly I had betrayed my secret, and it now became a family joke. Nihal teased me endlessly about my teenage infatuation (as they called it). Each time he saw me, he laughed merrily, and quoted a few lines from my discarded letters. I blushed furiously, and seethed, but endured his good-humoured teasing as nonchalantly as possible.

A few months later, when the parish priest held a youth convention at St Anthony's college in Kandy, twenty girls and boys from St Gabriel's, and St John Bosco's, travelled with a few nuns, and Fr Augustine to participate in the event. We boarded a train at Hatton, and I wore a candy-striped, full skirt, white blouse, and flat-heeled shoes to match. I really liked the candy-striped shoes that had belonged to Nilanthi, but they were so worn-out now, that the sole gaped open like a crocodile's jaws. But I was determined to wear them, and spent that whole day dragging my feet slowly, in case the sole fell off.

It was a long day, and I can barely recall what the discussions were about, but it finished late afternoon, and we were quite exhausted. As I sat in the train, with my long hair flowing free, Fr Augustine smiled and said, "Your hair is like a waterfall, so long, and wavy!" I did not reply, as I did not know how to react, and thought it was an inappropriate comment anyway. Also, I did not forget how he asked Nilanthi to leave the church. And he was not getting into my good books again.

Chapter 29

Nilanthi was pregnant towards the end of that year, and she asked me to accompany her to Colombo. We travelled by train, and stayed with one of Lakshman's aunt's in Nugegoda. She was very pleasant and kind, and her daughter, Padma, was a friendly young girl too. She said she would like to visit me one day. Nilanthi was a sympathetic listener, and I confided in her about my secret love, and how heartbroken I was at Clifford's continued silence.

She mentioned it to Padma's brother, who offered to contact him on my behalf. I was grateful to the young boy. Because I wanted to give Clifford a framed picture of pop singer, Cliff Richards, with the caption underneath, "The Boy Who's Always There." I cut out the picture from a magazine, and framed secretly. And I waited for an opportunity to present it, but Clifford did not meet the boy, and that was that.

Nilanthi was very kind, and tried to console me. "There's nothing much you can do when someone does not love you in return." And the words of a popular song came to mind forcibly. "Love is an ocean of emotion, so don't get caught in the tide, till there's an ocean of emotion, coming from the other side." That song could very well have been written just for me. And it became my daily mantra, along with every other sentimental song, as I wallowed in melancholy.

When I returned home after that brief stay in Nugegoda, it was almost Christmas time. I joined the others, and decorated the house, and Christmas tree excitedly. In the midst of our gaiety and laughter, Thathie came home late that evening, looking dejected and sober for once. He summoned us, and unfolded his story. "Last night when I was sleeping for a short while, the porter on duty gave the wrong signal to two midnight trains, which resulted in a near collision! I may be *interdicted* for this terrible mistake, as I was the officer-in-charge when this happened."

Thathie was just appointed station master, Watagoda, and was due to take up his new position in January 1966. At the age of forty or so, he was the youngest station master to be appointed, and was very proud and excited at the prospect. Now his future was uncertain, and he did not know how to cope. He nodded solemnly, "Light some candles for me too, when you go to church tonight, and say a special prayer that all will go well."

That Christmas day, we were a subdued family indeed, as we waited for the outcome of this situation. Just after 1 January, 1966, Thathie received orders from the general manager, to proceed to Watagoda, and occupy the station master's house there. The penalty for Thathie's mistake that night, was demotion, to station master goods, at Talawakale, one station before Watagoda.

Thathie was severely disappointed, and upset, but as it was for twelve months only, he bore it up as best as he could. The transfer to Watagoda was exciting, and we prepared for the move, after more than four years in Hatton. As usual, Ammie and Menika organised, packed, and attended to all the numerous details. Thathie sent porters to help them, and soon, all our furniture was packed into a couple of wagons in a goods train and transported to Watagoda.

We travelled in a steam engine train, through picturesque countryside, and soon arrived at Watagoda, with its spectacular scenery. The misty mountain, Adam's Peak, was clearly visible from our garden. And just behind our house, a lovely lake gleamed, like a sheet of silver satin, embossed with purple and white lotus blossoms.

As I stood in our backyard, I glimpsed the Great Western mountain ranges, looming majestically, in deep shades of misty blue and grey. I was delighted with the panorama, and the bluestone house was very attractive too, with large, spacious bedrooms, and a veranda at the entrance. Ammie soon set about arranging pots and plants, indoors and outdoors. She high-lighted the shape of the asymmetrical blue stones by outlining them with white paint. I helped one of the servant boys with the painting, and it looked quite effective when we finished, as the house looked quaint and attractive.

Thathie travelled to Talawakale daily, and we soon settled into a routine. The only disadvantage was, getting up at five o'clock, to catch the early morning train to Hatton, as Shirani, Nelune, and I still attended St Gabriel's convent.

Miss Direkze taught shorthand and typing, and about ten of us studied these two subjects under her strict guidance. It was a good decision to learn those skills, and I was happy I did. My friends teased me and called me, "Miss Dictionary," as my nose was always buried in one, improving my vocabulary, whenever I had free time in class,.

Nilanthi gave birth to a baby girl, Tamara Kumari, on 7 April 1966. She was a cute little thing, and her parents doted on her. Nilanthi sewed lovely baby clothes, and dressed her up like a doll. They employed Nawamani, a young girl from the tea estate, as Tamara's Nanny. She was efficient, and a quiet, well-mannered, Tamil girl in her late teens, and cared for the baby devotedly. Nilanthi was relieved of all the mundane tasks involved in looking after an infant.

Nihal tried his best to find a job on one of the tea plantations, and attended several other job interviews as well. He kept busy at home with various projects, and even planted corn in the garden, and was so proud of his first crop. Menika, although she went about working steadily, and efficiently, as always, still pined for her home and family. And it was about this time when an extraordinary incident took place.

One morning, Menika told Shirani excitedly that she dreamed of her village, and remembered the address of her house there. It was uncanny (I thought), but she implored Shirani to send a letter to this address. A few weeks later, a young man in his teens, and an old woman, turned up, claiming to be Menika's brother and mother. Talk about miracles! Ammie was astounded, and could not believe what had happened. Shirani and Menika did not confide in her, or any of us, until the family arrived.

Menika prostrated and worshipped her mother, crying out loudly, "Are you *really* my mother? Appoi Amma, *why* did you forget me for so many years?" It was pitiful to hear her, and she was inconsolable for some time, while her mother tried to comfort her with kind words and embraces.

We left them alone, and after some time, her mother told Menika that her father was senile, and suffered from dementia. Menika had three sisters, and this was her youngest brother. Soon, Menika decided to return to her village with them. Ammie was very upset, and disappointed to lose Menika, whose face was now wreathed in smiles. She promised to return after she visited her family. We waved goodbye, and I watched with sadness, as she left after more than twenty years with us.

A few weeks later, I was absolutely overjoyed when Menika returned. And on seeing us again, she burst into tears, and uttered brokenly, "I was born under an *unlucky* star!" After her tears subsided, she told us that her relatives treated her just as if she was *their* servant, and made her do all their chores. She cried bitter tears over her father's inability to recognise her. After this emotional outburst, she settled down into a routine, and said she would only visit her mother sometimes.

Sometime in March that year, Rosie visited briefly, and wished us goodbye. She decided to enrol as a trainee nurse in England, and soon boarded a plane to join Anthony and Malcolm, who were living in London then. I cried when Rosie left, as it would never be the same again, without her exuberant presence in our lives.

On Nihal's 18th birthday that same year, my parents organised a grand party, and invited over than fifty guests. Menika, who was with us then, made hundreds of pastel-coloured string hoppers, buriyani rice, numerous curries, sambals etc.

Many people whizzed through our home that night, so their faces remain a blur. Girls and boys from our schools, Ammie's and Thathie's close friends, relatives, and of course, Nilanthi, Lakshman, and Tamara. It was a wonderful night; full of fun, music, games, and loads of food.

Surfeited with food, and soft drinks, about twenty of us teenagers, my parents, and some older guests, decided to walk to the lake at midnight. An enormous full moon shone down benignly. We sang, laughed, and joked incessantly, until inhabitants of that quiet little town, straggled out one by one, to see what the noise was all about.

We laughed to see sleepy-eyed people peeping through windows and doors, thinking the station master's family had gone berserk. Our friends did not stop talking about that night for a long time. Dawn and Yvonne came too, and our main purpose was to give Nihal and Dawn some time alone. So we surrounded them as we walked along, and hid them from Ammie's and Thathie's view.

A few months ago, Nihal developed a crush on Dawn, Yvonne's cousin. We did our best to give them some privacy now, because no one else knew about his preference except Shirani, Yvonne, and I. The ruse worked, and they spent a few moments together, without our parents discovering their secret.

Dawn was of average height, dark-skinned, and slender, with pleasant, though not very pretty features. We found it difficult to understand what Nihal saw in her. Moreover, she was painfully shy, and had the personality of a nervous mouse. She hardly said a word when they were together, and was not very talkative with her girl-friends either.

Nihal boarded the train to Hatton at times, and returned with us after school. We carried their love letters to each other, and sometimes, out of sheer mischief, Shirani and I opened Dawn's letters. And we laughed at all her spelling mistakes, which was unkind, but we were not malicious. Then we teased Nihal about the contents of the letters, until he lost his temper, and threatened to beat us, if we did not stop our nonsense.

We visited Yvonne, and when we went out walking, Dawn and Nihal chatted, and got to know each other a little better. But he said that she was so shy and reserved, that he did not know if she really loved him or not.

Nihal did not like long hair, and said he preferred short, hair-styles (like Dawn's), and he told me my hair was very messy. So, one day, he cut my long hair, and styled it into a very short bob. Ammie was annoyed with him, but I did not mind, although I did look strange, with short hair framing my round face. Anyway, I knew it would grow back very fast.

When the weather was warm, Nihal, and the three of us swam in the murky lake, over-grown with lotus flowers that were attached to enormous tubular roots, floating beneath the exotic flowers. We made sure we swam in shallow areas only, and avoided going out to the middle of the lake. But one day, I swam out too far, and soon found myself in deep waters, literally, as I tried to disentangle my legs from slimy roots, gripping like tentacles.

I was exhausted, and shouted out to Nihal. He swam quickly towards me, and we struggled for a while, as he tried to untangle the roots. When we swam back to shore, I let go of his shoulders, once my legs were free. And he dragged me out of the tangled roots and back to shallow waters again. That was a scary experience, and never more did I venture out that far again.

Those six months or so in Watagoda were filled with various outings and events; one of them being the famous car rally in Nuwara Eliya, held in April each year. Nihal, Shirani, and I, together with Clim, and some other friends, spent an exciting day at the rally, and then picnicked in the botanical gardens in Hakgala. I was delighted with all the exotic blooms there, and we finally returned home late in the evening.

We spent most evenings watching the last trains pull out of the platform, as we sat on our front porch and waved to all the passengers. Then we went for long walks along the rail track or round the lake; listened to the radio, and went to bed early, as we were up at five o'clock every morning. I hated those early mornings, as my pet hate was waking up before sunrise, and half asleep, I boarded the slow train to Hatton. Early rising does not worry me as much, because I need less sleep now

Once on board the train however, I had fun with the other children. One of the most brilliant sights I have ever seen, was the sunrise over Adam's Peak, as the train wound its way past St Clare's waterfall. The skies turned misty pink and grey, before the fiery cartwheel ascended majestically. No words could ever describe the grandeur of that scene, or the awe that filled my whole being whenever I witnessed that spectacular sight each morning.

School was stimulating, as Mother Directress sometimes read out Jane Austen's works, including "Pride and Prejudice," Shakespeare's "Twelfth night" George Elliot's "Mill on the floss" and Oliver Goldsmith's plays. They consisted part of our English literature syllabus, besides poetry by Lord Byron, Percy Bysshe Shelley, and John Keats. I waited impatiently for those wonderful moments, when I was transported into another world, with such beguiling characters. I read those books over and over again, and never tired of them.

Malcolm visited Ceylon often, as he was courting Indrani, whom he knew since they were children. And Percy, her brother, was his best friend. Indrani and her family were staunch Buddhists, and frowned on their courtship. Malcolm despaired, as he was anxious to marry her soon.

Whenever he visited, we hiked to Mayfield Estate through tea estates, and along winding, narrow roads. He was melancholy at times, but still laughed and joked, as he related anecdotes about life in London. Antipathy towards migrants was still rampant in the sixties. And he told us that signs like, "Dogs and Indians not allowed" were posted in front of some pubs and hostels.

I was aghast at such racial discrimination, and thought Malcolm was exaggerating. But obviously he was not, as he underwent many negative experiences during his first years in London. He hated the cold, miserable winters too, and spent as much time as he could in Ceylon, when it was height of winter there. Malcolm said the freezing, foggy winters were very depressing, and he could never get used to them.

Lakshman's young relative, Padma, visited one day, as she had promised, and we had a great time walking up the hills of Watagoda, and exploring dense woodlands, and valleys that we had not seen before. Padma was good company, but after she left a week or so later, we never heard from her again.

Chapter 30

Sometime in mid 1966, Thathie received orders to vacate the house in Watagoda, as the newly-appointed station master was due to arrive soon. We were in a quandary, as Thathie did not know where to move. The station master in Hatton, a friend of Thathie's, lived alone in a large, two-storey house in Hatton. He suggested that we move upstairs, as he had a room and living areas downstairs.

His wife and family were in Batticaloa, and he said that he did not need such a big house. In due course, we shifted to that spacious house, situated close to the station. It was a fine-looking place, and we quickly organized our rooms.

We occupied four bed-rooms, and a large living area, which was ample. And Ammie arranged outdoor furniture, and potted plants on the broad balconies at the front and back of the house upstairs. We discovered an old fire-place in the living room that was closed up. Nihal opened the flue and cleaned the chimney. But when he lit a fire, to our dismay, black smoke billowed down and engulfed the whole house.

We laughed, coughed, and spluttered and ran out of the house. It took hours to get rid of the smoke, as the chimney was blocked with nests. The infuriated birds squawked and fluttered around angrily when Nihal smoked them out. It was the last time we lit that fire.

Nihal wanted to study agriculture, so Thathie enrolled him at Aquinas College in Colombo, where he boarded at the campus for a few months. He came home every few weeks or so, looking quite unhappy. And he said most of the boys were wealthy show-offs, who threw money around, and drove sporty cars to college.

He spent about three months there. Like most teenage boys, he was keen to try out various jobs, until he found his niche. After that stint, he tried motor mechanics. One of Thathie's relatives owned a garage in Bandarawela, and he arranged an apprenticeship for Nihal.

Nilanthi invited Nihal, Shirani, and me to a dance at the Darawala club one day. It was our first dance, and we were very excited. But although we knew how to "twist" and "shake" none of us knew ballroom dancing. We did not care though, as we happily prepared for the event.

Rita gave Nilanthi one of her beautiful evening dresses, and Nilanthi altered it to fit me. The fabric was a gorgeous, dark-blue, taffeta, embossed with tiny, black velvet stars. Rita had very good taste. It was an exquisite dress, with a close-fitting bodice, full skirt, and black lace trimming.

Soon, it was sewn up to fit me, and I felt like a princess. On the evening before the dance, Ammie suggested that Mrs Muller's sister, and brother, should demonstrate some basic steps, as they were good dancers. All dressed up in our new clothes, we hurried over to their small apartment, and watched them dance a "quick step." Then we each took a turn with them, and thought that was enough to get by.

After that evening, Aloysius, (Mrs Muller's brother), wrote long love letters, declaring his undying love for me, and dispatched them through his little nieces. I was annoyed, as I thought he was very unattractive. I showed his letters to Nihal, and the others, who laughed in amusement. He was very dark-skinned, prone to acute acne, and sleazy-looking, with a pencil-thin moustache. All of five feet, nothing, with shoulder-length hair, oiled and sculptured high, he strutted around in tight jeans, and cowboy boots. And was firmly convinced that he was irresistible to the opposite sex, as he leered at every female. When I did not respond to his letters, he became quite nasty. He fumed past our house several times a day, just so he could scowl darkly if he happened to see me.

To get back to that first dance, the club was decorated with huge garlands of flowers, and exotic blooms everywhere. I was dazzled with the sights and sounds that evening, and enjoyed my first dance very much. At first, Shirani and I danced only with Nihal, as he too was very bashful, and did not like to ask any girl to dance, in case they refused. We sat on chairs placed along the edge of the dance floor, and several young men looked our way. Finally, a good-looking young man, who introduced himself as Christopher, asked me to dance.

I was petrified, as I did not know how to dance well, but we seemed to get by alright, and he thanked me for the dance. Lakshman came over just then and grinned. "That young man is a planter from one of the near by estates, and I'm happy you danced with him." He kept a strict eye on us all night, as he did not want us to dance with any other young men, unless they were planters. I was overcome with smoke and alcoholic fumes though, as all the young men drank copiously through the night.

When the music started again, Christopher asked me for another dance, and I did not refuse. Shirani had many partners too, and Nihal finally worked up enough courage to ask one of the girls to dance. He grinned, as we swept past each other across the floor.

We returned home at day break, and stopped to eat some "godamba rotis" for breakfast at a wayside café. And later, we slept till noon, but I enjoyed myself thoroughly that night.

On our way back, Lakshman said, "I will find you a nice planter, when you are old enough. Christopher has a reputation for drinking too much, so forget about him. And that other bugger you were dancing with, is not a planter, so don't encourage him!" I ignored him, as he was very rude to a young man who danced with me once. I knew him slightly, as he was distantly related to Aloysius, and we met at Mrs Muller's place a few times. He was quite pleasant, and not as repulsive as Aloysius.

A number of young men worked on the "Maskeliya project" then, as a huge dam was under construction. This young man, Terence, drove bulldozers. A few days later, I received love letters from him, declaring his eternal love. But I was not interested, as Clifford was still the one.

We attended several house parties, and at one of them, I met another young man, Aubrey, who also worked in Maskeliya with Terence. When we were introduced, he exclaimed, "So, you are the girl Terence keeps talking about!" We danced a few times, and then he told me that he found me very attractive, and could he write to me. Although he was good-looking, with light-grey eyes, and pleasant manners, I did not want to correspond with him either. He would not take no for an answer though, and I received a few letters from him, which I did not acknowledge.

A few months later, I was shocked to hear that Aubrey was killed in an accident, while driving a bulldozer. He was about twenty five then, and I was very upset that such a vibrant young man died so tragically. A few other interesting boys appeared in my limited sphere from time to time. But I never lost my heart to any of them, as the flame still burned bright for my first love.

The nuns and priests organized a youth convention, which included girls and boys from Kandy diocese, and students from our convent and college. The events took place at St Gabriel's convent, and St John Bosco's college over a period of five days. We had heaps of fun getting to know some of the girls and boys from Kandy. One of those girls, Rosemarie Thomas, was a very pretty and smart young girl, who led all the debates and discussions.

I admired her very much, as she was sophisticated and clever. Many years later, when I saw her at a dance, and introduced myself, she did not remember who I was. She looked at me vaguely and said, "Your face is familiar, but I can't remember where we met." It was ironic that she made such a deep impression on me, but she hardly remembered who I was.

All through that convention, an impertinent young boy from Kandy, followed me around boldly. And whenever Fr Cuthbert asked for a volunteer, this boy (whose name eludes me), immediately called out, "Nalini!" He was slender, with pleasant features, and was of average height. But his foolish grin, and inane giggle irritated me.

Fr Cuthbert was amused. And one evening he said, "Nalini, is the *only* name I keep hearing from my friend here! Is there *anyone* else who wants to volunteer." I blushed with embarrassment, as everyone looked at me. That boy was a pest. He did not leave me alone, even though I told him very politely, to get lost.

On the last day of the convention, we walked from Hatton to Dickoya, to Wanarajah Estate, where Mr Fernandez organized afternoon tea. What a load of fun and laughter we enjoyed all the way there and back! The boys teased the girls playfully, and many formed romantic attachments.

It was a time when nuns and priests were thawing out rigid rules that their predecessors had set. And were enlightened enough to allow girls and boys to socialise more freely. They hoped to encourage youth, and strengthen their faith. That was the topic under discussion most of the time, as the church was deeply concerned about the sexual liberation in the sixties. I was a little too young to understand the in-depth discussions. But it was a step in the right direction, when I recalled the strict disciplinarians in our previous convent.

We held many parties, and enjoyed happy days, and entertainment for about six months there until the end of December 1966. Thathie was appointed station master, Gampola, in the New Year, and we rejoiced that Christmas. About fifty guests came for a farewell dinner (one of many such dinners), and we travelled to Maharagama a few days later as Malcolm was expected.

One evening, all dressed up in a close-fitting "shift" dress, in muted shades of mauve and purple, and my hair worn in a beehive (sixties style), I sat in the porch, chatting with Malcolm, and the others. By and by, I noticed Clifford walking up and down the lane. It was late evening, and I did not see him clearly in the dusk. But he obviously saw me, because when we returned home a few days later, I had a marvellous surprise.

It was just before Christmas, and I received a beautiful Christmas card from him. It was so unexpected, that I walked around in a daze, my feet hardly touching the ground. He mentioned I was changed indeed, and looked quite grown-up now. He just wanted to know how I was, and apologized for his long silence.

It was more than twelve months since our last communication. I ran out to the shops immediately, and spent ages rummaging through dozens of cards, just to find the right one. It was the happiest time that Christmas, and in response, I wrote him a long, ardent letter. He replied almost immediately, and so our correspondence resumed unexpectedly.

Nilanthi invited us once again. This time to the New Year's ball at Radalla Club. It was quite a distance away, but the three of us accompanied them and had a great time. Nihal danced with us whenever we were free, and he asked a few other girls to dance too. We heard Damian, a planter, sing on stage, and we thought he was very talented, as he imitated Elvis Presley. Damian was tall, sturdy, and good-looking, with a pleasant, friendly manner. He was engaged to a girl called Barbara, with whom he danced all night. She stood about five feet tall, but was slim and attractive.

I did not notice her family members particularly. We only knew about Damian's engagement through a mutual friend. It was early dawn when we finally reached home, and I fell into an exhausted sleep till midday. So, I greeted the first day of 1967 rather sleepily. But we enjoyed further entertainment that evening when all our friends turned up to wish us farewell (again).

Rodney, a pleasant-faced, young man, started visiting daily a few months ago, because he liked Shirani very much. Thathie invited him to one of our parties earlier on, and since that day, he was very friendly with us. Rodney was in his late twenties, and was very tall, with a light-complexion, and grey eyes. He was quite good-looking, and Shirani liked him too. Rodney was seeing her regularly now (with Thathie's taciturn approval).

He delighted in teasing me, because I rose to the bait unfailingly. He was another "friendly" critic, who appraised my artistic efforts honestly. And he encouraged me too." You have talent, and you must keep working at it." We liked Rodney, because he was full of fun, and had a great sense of humour. He spent the last day with us, and decided to travel to Gampola.

On the day we left, a huge crowd came to see us off at the station. And according to railway tradition, they set off ear-splitting fire crackers under the train, as it slowly pulled out of the station. It was a great journey, and I loved every part of the changing scenery, as we approached the warmer climate in Gampola.

The railway bungalow, situated just above the rail track, was not too far from the station. It was a spacious, rambling old house, and I loved it immediately. And the massive, revolving platform that turned engines around, was right in front of our garden. The powerful engine lights beamed into our bedroom window at nights. A long corridor, with timber trellis on one side, was very spacious. Shirani, Nelune, and I converted this area into our bedroom. Although the house consisted of five bedrooms, a large dining area, living room, and a front porch, we preferred that corridor, as it was cool and airy.

The garden abounded with fruit trees; jumbu, mangoes, and several other tropical fruits that thrived in this balmy climate. A narrow pathway wound through our front garden, connecting the main road to the rail track. We soon found out that it was a public thoroughfare. People took a short cut down this path, but it did not bother us. It was good to see people walking along the track, smiling and waving if they happened to see us in the garden.

Soon, everyone in Gampola knew us. The post master, businessmen, and their families, and a solicitor called Lucien, who befriended Thathie, and visited often. Thathie enrolled me at Zahira college, as it was the only school where I could complete my final year in English. Shirani and Nelune attended a Catholic convent there, and changed over to Sinhalese classes.

At Zahira college, a Muslim school, I stuck out like a sore thumb, because I was the only girl who wore a knee-length, white uniform. All the other girls wore white "Punjabi" costumes (ankle-length, baggy pants), with knee-length, uniforms over them, and covered their heads with white shawls. My parents wrote to the principal, requesting a dress-code exemption. I was a Catholic, not a Muslim, and it was for one year only. The principal, a middle-aged man, was quite reasonable, and did not press the point. But some unruly boys teased and booed at me. They were outraged that I did not wear traditional Muslim clothes to school.

I dared not go out during recess, for fear of being teased, so I sat in the classroom or library, and devoured book after book. My English teacher, highly impressed with my essays, read them aloud in class. Once, I even forgot sports, and when the physical education teacher found me, she caned me on both hands (for reading in the library and not turning up for sports).

The classroom teacher called me up one day, and said, "You have to trim your hair, or tie it back in a pony tail because your long, thick hair is too wild and unruly!" I tied my hair back next day. She was pleased, and said, "Ah, that's much better and neater now!" They were so particular then.

Our neighbours were friendly, pleasant people, and visited us often. Their daughters, Geetha and Yasodha, two shy, pretty teenagers soon became our good friends. They dropped in whenever they had time in the evenings, and we bonded well, and their parents socialised often too. An enormous mango tree spread out in their garden, and when the tree was loaded, we had a feast. The jumbu tree in our garden too yielded plenty of luscious fruits, that we shared with our neighbours.

Nihal was now lodging with one of Thathie's relative's in Bandarawela, and was apprenticed as a motor mechanic on a very small wage. Sometimes, he came home for a few days, carrying modest gifts for each one of us. It was always great fun on these occasions, and we laughed and joked whenever he spent time with us.

After working as an apprentice for a few months though, Nihal contracted a severe bout of wanderlust, and was determined to travel abroad. Rosie, who left in 1966, wrote happy, glowing letters, about how great England was, and encouraged Nihal to come over.

Student nurses globally, enlisted then, and received training in some of the best hospitals in England. Nihal was sorely tempted to travel overseas. He said that once the nursing training period was over, he could always follow a course in motor mechanics, or another line of work.

Now that his heart was set on this new venture, he could think of nothing else. He was quite frustrated, due to lack of funds required for his trip. He mooned around the house, thinking of a way to raise money.

Thathie was aware of Nihal's determination to travel overseas, and promised to help him somehow. But Nihal was reluctant to worry Thathie, as he knew it was a substantial amount of money. Airfare to London was about three thousand rupees, a small fortune then.

When Nihal was home some evenings, Thathie treated us at the local club. And we spent memorable times, with music, laughter, dancing, and pleasant company. Everyone respected Thathie immensely, as a station master's job was a prestigious position. People from everywhere visited to ask him favours.

He was extremely generous, and never refused to help anyone if he could, so they liked him very much. Our house was full of people, almost every evening, and lavish parties every few weeks. We received free cinema tickets regularly to all the cinemas in Gampola. But Ammie never allowed us to go alone, unless we had a chaperone. She reprimanded us sternly. "Where on *earth* did you hear of young girls going out on their *own* to see movies? You won't set foot outside this house, unless Thathie or Nihal accompanies you!" We could argue, and cajole till we were blue in the face, but all to no avail. We grumbled and moaned about how *unfair* it was to waste free tickets, but Ammie never relented. We had to be content until someone was around to chaperone us.

Some time after we left Hatton, we heard that the station master, who shared his house so generously, was found dead in his room one night. The rumours were, that he died of alcoholic poisoning, as he was a very heavy drinker. It was very upsetting, but we never knew the truth behind his solitary, untimely death.

Chapter 31

Nilanthi travelled with Tamara to Gampola quite often. And she arrived in a car loaded with vegetables, fruits, and flowers from her garden. We welcomed her gladly, because of her unfailing good-humour, and infectious laughter. I confided in her, as she lent a sympathetic ear, and laughed or advised as she thought best.

My latest *fiasco* (I absolutely refuse to call it a party), sent her into helpless gales of laughter. But time gradually softened the initial pangs of misery, and acute embarrassment I suffered on my fifteenth birthday. Shirani and I sent out invitations to some sophisticated friends in Colombo. They arrived around eight o'clock, but my party started at four thirty, and all the children left by eight. So, when four teenage boys, immaculately dressed in evening suits, stood on our doorstep, the party was well and truly over.

Thathie slumbered uneasily in a drunken stupor, and roared aggressively when he heard the boys laughing and talking. Shirani and I tried our best to drown out the racket. But it was painfully obvious our guests were aware of what was going on, and they left within the hour. It was indeed the most embarrassing evening I endured.

When Lakshman was unable to join, Nilanthi and Tamara came with their driver. We had a great time driving around Kandy and Gampola, eating at Chinese restaurants, shopping to our heart's content, and we joined Thathie at the club some evenings.

Nihal accompanied us on those merry days, if he was visiting. It was the height of enjoyment to listen to old and new favourites on an old juke box at one of the Chinese restaurants. We had many friends in Kandy then, but most of them migrated to various parts of the world over the next few years. It was a wonderful time for me, with nothing but music, laughter, and enjoyment, and no major world issues, or domestic politics marred my blissful world.

The sixties heralded many new cults, music, and fashions. The Beatles, Tom Jones, and Elvis, to name a few stars, were at the height of their fame. We young ones imitated our idols, in the way we dressed, our attitudes, beliefs, and our music. Statements like, "Make Love, Not War" and "Give Peace A Chance" made a lot of sense. And everywhere I went, I delighted in repeating those phrases, like mantras.

Dances, movies, carnivals, fetes, house parties, social calls, all this, and more, absorbed a great deal of my time, but I progressed well at school, in spite of these social distractions. We participated in them with our parents, and that says something for the good relationship that existed between us.

Now when I look back, 1967 was one of the happiest years of my life at home. So much happened then, and so many different friends and people entered and exited our lives. The twelve months in Gampola vanished swiftly. The only cloud that constantly hovered over those halcyon days, was Thathie's daily drinking bouts. It made me unhappy, because my parents ended up in heated arguments almost every evening.

Sometimes, Nilanthi invited me to Mayfield, and I went with her. Then I visited all my friends in Hatton, the nuns and teachers at St Gabriel's too. They were amused when I related my experiences in Zahira college. Yvonne, Dawn, and Mr Fernandez visited regularly. And when they did, we crowded into the back seat of his well-maintained, black, Morris Minor car. And tightly packed, like a box of matches, we headed off on a picnic to Peradeniya Gardens, or on a shopping spree to Kandy.

I am uncertain of the exact month or date when Mrs Fernandez died. But it happened somewhere at the end of 1965, a few months before we left Hatton. Mrs Fernandez, who was quite robust, fell ill suddenly for no apparent reason, and died within a few weeks. She was stricken with an unknown disease, and people whispered that she was charmed. This was a commonly held superstition, if anyone fell ill suddenly and died.

Mr Fernandez and Clim were devastated, and endured a sad time. But Yvonne quickly recovered, and grasped the household reins firmly. When we visited before the funeral, the corpse was laid out in the parlour. All the mourners shuffled along in single file around the coffin, and placed a kiss on her cold brow. I was scared stiff even to look at the corpse. But as my parents, Mr Fernandez, and his family looked at me expectantly, I kissed that dead face.

I think it was the bravest thing I did then, when I shut my eyes tight and quickly brushed my lips on that frozen cheek. I still feel a revulsion to kiss corpses, no matter if they are family or friends, and I believe it is an unhygienic, repulsive practise. If I possibly can, I even avoid looking at corpses at funerals.

Yvonne did not change much in the last few months, and it was difficult for Mr Fernandez to keep her in line. She was brazenly flirtatious, and unafraid of him. He toyed with the idea of marrying her off as quickly as possible, to escape responsibility. He confided in Ammie that he was looking around for a suitable partner. And a distant relative in India, was a likely candidate. He was about fifteen years older than Yvonne, but to Mr Fernandez, age was not a major drawback.

Nazeema, a very pretty Muslim girl at school, was a close and dear friend. She led such a cloistered and restricted life, compared to the freedom I enjoyed, that I was extremely sorry, and visited her often. She was allowed to visit me now and then, provided her elder brother or sister chaperoned her.

Although she was only a few months older than me, she looked about eighteen, because she was tall, and well-built. I was petite at just five feet, with no hopes of growing any taller. She told me she was in love with a Tamil boy, who lived close to her home, but worked in Kandy. He had attended Zahira college too, and that was how they met. Nazeema and I hit upon a clever strategy to help them communicate, without rousing her eagle-eyed father's suspicion.

I walked to the local post office in the evenings, and telephoned Nazeema. Her father answered, and I asked for Nazeema in dulcet tones. When her vigilant father was satisfied that it was only a school friend on the phone, he handed the receiver to his demure daughter. In the meantime, her boyfriend, who was present (by prior arrangement), took the receiver from me, and talked to his sweetheart for as long as he wished. Nazeema told me that she said, "Yes Dolly," "No Dolly," and her boyfriend thought she called him "Darling."

Such was our devious method to deceive her stern parents, who were strictly medieval (so I thought then). I visited her almost every other evening, because I passed her house, on my way to the convent. Mother Superior instructed me in religious knowledge, in readiness for my senior school exam.

She offered to help me, as they did not employ Catholic teachers at Zahira college. The lessons were at five thirty every evening. The convent chapel, adjoining the church and surroundings, was mystical, and serene. As I sat with the devout nun instructing me, I was filled with a great sense of peace and joy. In my youthful ardour and idealism, I seriously toyed with the idea of spending my days in this beautiful haven of peace.

Mother Superior permitted me to play the piano in the quiet parlour after classes. It was just amazing to play that instrument, even though I knew to play melodies only "by ear." When I say "play," it was with minimal expertise, as I mostly improvised. But I was passionate about the piano, and love of music flowed in my veins constantly. I kept badgering Thathie to buy me a piano accordion at least, as it was better than not having an instrument at all.

Poor Thathie! He would have given us anything we asked for, if *only* he could have afforded. I now realize how difficult it was for him to raise money for extra things we wanted, and which he longed to give. Thathie was the soul of generosity, when it came to us. He always said, "Money is for spending, and not for putting aside." With such an easy-going philosophy, we would have been in deep waters, if Ammie was not thrifty.

To get back to my spiritual awakening, and religious vocation, I sometimes stopped at Nazeema's house after these inspiring visits to the convent. And I waited for our servant girl to accompany me home, as it became quite dark by six o'clock. Even I was not foolhardy enough to walk home alone.

Their house, a long, narrow, building, stood on the side of the main road. At any given time, Nazeema, or her elder sister, Fawzia, sat by the window. Their bodies covered and hidden from view, with only black, kohl-lined eyes peeping over chintz curtains of the window. To me, there was something tragi-comic in this spectacle of two young girls watching life go by, and unable to flow along with the tide.

A staunch Muslim, their taciturn old father, passed the time away, lounging on an armchair, legs up on a stool, with his ever watchful eyes on his two timid daughters. They in turn, commented on all the passers-by for his entertainment. I usually found Nazeema's mother, modestly draped, and smothered under layers of clothes, in Muslim fashion, invariably cooking a meal. She offered refreshments whenever I dropped in.

Her parents did not speak English, so they addressed me in Sinhalese, which they spoke fluently. Adjoining their house, was a modest-sized grinding mill, where Fouz, the eldest son, operated the family business. He sat at a small desk at the entrance of the mill, talking to customers all day long.

I helped Nazeema and her boyfriend keep up a steady communication via telephone, and letters sent to my address, for which small favour, the young lovers expressed eternal gratitude. They did not hold any hope of getting married in the near future, or any day at all, due to different social and religious backgrounds. And that, in my romantic mind, was a tragedy.

Nazeema's elder sister, Fawzia, was a tall, scrawny, unattractive girl, with a receding chin, but she was quite pleasant and friendly. As she sat around day after day, her only ambition was to get a decent marriage proposal, and escape her present tedious existence.

It seemed to me though, that it was a case of, "Jumping from the frying pan into the fire." Her husband would most certainly curtail her freedom, exactly as her father did; only a different cage, in a different setting. I pondered on the unfairness of such social inequalities. To tell the truth though, Nazeema and her sister were not overly concerned about their restricted freedom. Their customs were instilled from childhood, and they faithfully abided by them.

Nazeema's eldest sister, Faridah, was married recently. I happened to be visiting at the time of her "'Home Coming." She was a very attractive girl in her early twenties. She walked in, beautifully dressed in a colourful costume, and bejewelled with gold ornaments from head to toe. As she blushed prettily and sat in the parlour talking to her family, the bridegroom entered.

I was aghast. Talk about "Beauty And The Beast." He was a short, fat, swarthy man, with beady eyes, and sported a Groucho Marx moustache. To my hyper-sensitive mind, it was totally unacceptable, that such a lovely, young girl was "sacrificed" to this unattractive man. It irked my romantic nature, and I walked home, musing on the incomprehensible situations in life.

On my next visit to Nazeema's, I told her half seriously, half jestingly that I was toying with the idea of becoming a nun. Her reaction was vehement, to put it mildly. She exclaimed in horror. "But Dolly, how *could* you even bear to think of hiding inside a convent, and never get married!" I was amused, yet partly vexed with her. But I knew I was just going through a melancholy period in my life, because all correspondence from Clifford stopped once again, and I felt ill-used.

Everything looked fine outwardly, and I was constantly busy with many friends, school, and amusements. But I had melancholy, despondent moments too. I painted, and wrote during my free time, and found great solace and satisfaction in these pursuits. I could not afford oil paints and canvases, so I made do with ordinary house paints, which were fairly cheap, and I diluted them with turpentine. Hard board primed with white paint, were not the best supports either. But I painted landscapes, still-life studies, and attempted portraiture sometimes, copying pictures from magazines and photographs.

I also loved relating stories, whether my own, or reading out loud from a book. When visitors saw my paintings, they encouraged me, and told Thathie. "You must see that she continues painting, as she is quite talented for her age." None of my family though, took my artistic pursuits seriously, and were always ready to offer their unsolicited criticism. Like the time I attempted a picture of Jesus (an ambitious project). Nihal grinned and commented, "The sleeve of Jesus' robe looks like the mouth of a vase!" I am glad I followed my heart, and continued painting, without taking much notice of my critics. I only knew that the desire to paint, write, and play music, was rampant within me.

Thathie surprised me completely one night. He did not come home till about ten o'clock, and we were worried about him. A hiring car stopped outside, and soon, we heard his footsteps scrunching up the gravel driveway. He staggered slightly, as he walked in with a very large package that he carried with difficulty. He smiled sheepishly, as he gave me a beautiful red and gold accordion player.

I hugged him gratefully, and thanked him for his generosity. From then on, I played that instrument whenever I had a free moment. A few months ago, I purchased a toy wind instrument, called a "clarinova" for thirty rupees, which had very restricted notes and sounds. Much to Thathie's delight, I played several melodies on that little toy instrument. So he bought me an accordion, for about seven hundred rupees. I treasured that superb gift with love and gratitude.

Shortly afterwards, Nelune and I boarded a train to Kandy, and auditioned for the "Maliban Talent Quest," a popular, weekly radio show. Nelune accompanied on drums, and I played "Blue Berry Hill" on the accordion. The judges were members of a well-known band, "The Jetliners" and their lead singer was Mignon Ratnam. We were not selected to appear on the show, but it was a good experience. It was enormous fun watching hopeful singers, and musicians perform nervously or confidently.

Chapter 32

On Nihal's nineteenth birthday, on 15 May 1967, which was our parents wedding anniversary too, they organised a lavish party for over fifty people. Thathie hired two chefs, who cooked outdoors, and turned out steaming hoppers, while Ammie served dozens of delicious curries, and sambals. The garden was ablaze with bright lights strung up from trees and posts, and the music continued till long past midnight.

We had a superb time. But later, I complained to Nihal that Lucien, a forty-five year old divorced man, was a pain in the neck, with his repugnant, unwanted attentions. Nihal replied, straight-faced, but with a mischievous twinkle. "You must get used to these old men paying you compliments, and taking an interest in you, because you're growing up now, and that's the way it is in the real world." I thought he was joking as usual, and was peeved at his lack of sympathy for my outraged feelings. Lucien, a solicitor, lived in a stunning house, with only his servants to care for him, as his wife deserted him one year ago.

Thathie befriended him out of pity, and he soon became a regular visitor, though quite unwelcome (to me). He was tall, bald, solidly built, with an aquiline nose, and fleshy, slobbering lips. I found him repulsive, especially when I realised he was actually trying to *flirt* with me, a *fifteen-year* old school girl. It offended every particle of my romantic idealism.

Lucien was a nervous, dithering man, and Thathie said, "He's a little bit off his mind, since his wife left him." I thought he was a big joke, but a bigger nuisance, as he was very impertinent. I ran and hid in my room whenever I saw him striding jauntily up to our house, spruced up and saturated with strong, after-shave lotion. He invariably carried a box of chocolates, or a little trinket for me, which I refused to accept. The whole family thought it was quite funny, and laughed at his infatuation (as they called it).

Shortly after this party, Nihal made a momentous decision, and accepted a position as a trainee nurse in England. It was a good opportunity for young people to travel abroad. And since Nihal contracted a serious bout of wanderlust, he could not rest until he fulfilled his latest dream.

Visions of making it good in another job overseas, inspired Nihal to venture out as soon as he could get the money for his ticket. But he was aware of Thathie's financial situation. Angry, frustrated, and as grumpy as a sore bear, he sat around all day listening to the radio, or strumming his guitar endlessly. I fully understood the extent of Nihal's frustration, as he was unable to raise money to buy a ticket, because job opportunities in small country towns were rare.

Thathie, however, understood Nihal's hopes and frustrations only too well, and promised he would somehow raise the money. Nihal was elated, and the next few weeks were a whirlwind of activity, as the whole family became involved in getting Nihal equipped for his overseas trip. It was still a remarkable event, and a great adventure in 1967, for anyone to travel overseas. And people were not as blasé' about flying in a plane, as they are today.

I was so excited for Nihal, and so were the others, although I could not imagine life without his presence at home. But as teenagers, we had happy visions of future treats in store for us, in the way of imported clothes, shoes, perfumes etc. Malcolm, who was holidaying then, tried his best to discourage Nihal from travelling to England, as he thought nursing was not the right job for Nihal. But Nihal was adamant, as he said he would find a better job as soon as his two year contract was over.

So, the preparations continued. A tailor-made, dark-blue suit, shirts, pants, and a few pairs of new shoes completed the list. Ammie and Thathie bought him everything a young man required to travel overseas. Time sped by, and before I knew, we stood at Katunayake Airport in Colombo, tearfully wishing my beloved brother adieu.

Nihal was very tall now, and he looked so handsome and elegant in his new clothes, that I felt a pang as walked up smartly to the plane. Thathie raised his hands in a blessing, and a prayer, as it took off, and soon disappeared beyond the hazy, blue horizon. I have a strong recollection of Thathie sobbing brokenly on the train, all the way back. I watched helplessly, unable to comfort him. Thathie was grieving for his only son, who left the nest so soon, I mused, unaware of the full extent of his heartache.

Ammie did not come to the airport, as she avoided the painful parting. We were a sad little family now, with only three of us, and our parents. I missed Nihal at every turn, and waited to hear from him impatiently. Life could never be the same, without his teasing, laughter, and music to entertain us.

Nilanthi was ill with severe kidney infection, and was admitted to Kandy hospital. Lakshman said it was better for her to be near us.

He left the car behind with the driver, so we could visit Nilanthi daily. As we were at school, and Ammie was busy with household chores, we did not have time to visit. When we finally visited, she was angry, and cried bitterly. She complained that she was lonely, and did not want to stay in hospital any longer. Nilanthi was discharged after a week. She was much better, and left soon after. Lakshman was annoyed when he heard that we did not visit her daily. But we could not do much about it.

A few weeks later, we journeyed to Maharagama, as Malcolm, who was holidaying, was leaving next day. I did not want to go to the airport with the rest of the family, and preferred to stay back, with Uncle Barlow to keep me company.

He was Granny's youngest brother; tall, skinny, with a guttural voice. A bachelor in his forties or so, he boarded with Granny, and worked as a cashier in a night club.

Uncle Barlow was partially deaf, due to an accident in the army, when he stood too close to an explosive. His thin, weather-beaten face was deeply lined, and his thick, black, eloquent eyebrows spoke volumes, as they moved up and down, or met in a frown. He dyed his hair black, and Rosie joked that he used boot polish. Because, black streaks trickled down his forehead and face when he perspired.

He was very kind and sympathetic, when I confided in him about my love for Clifford. And was always ready to outsmart Granny if he could, as she treated him like a wayward child. I asked him to organise a rendezvous with Clifford, when Granny was out of the way.

When Uncle Barlow heard me out, he replied solemnly. "Put an onion under your armpit, and run around the house several times, and you will get a high fever, then Granny will leave you at home to rest." Hearing these words from a veteran soldier like Uncle Barlow, I believed implicitly that it was an efficacious method to raise my temperature.

Shortly afterwards, I smuggled the required onion from the kitchen when no one was looking, and ran around the house as discreetly as possible, so as not to rouse Granny's suspicions. However, all my running around with a smelly onion stuck under my armpit, did not raise my temperature even one iota. I concluded that Uncle Barlow, who had a strange sense of humour, was just pulling my leg. It must have been an amusing sight to see me labour in vain, with an onion snuggled in my armpit. Talk about love's labour lost!

In desperation, I feigned a stomach ache at the eleventh hour, and said I could not move, and it would be best for me to rest at home. But sharp-witted, suspicious Granny was not so easily taken in. She insisted that I accompanied them, and rest at Rita's place with the two servant girls, if I did not want to come to the airport. Seeing that my little scheme was thoroughly foiled, I gave in with a good grace. I said I would rather go to the airport (even with a bad stomach ache), than stay at Rita's with only the servant girls to keep me company.

The best thing that happened towards the end of the year was, Menika's brother wrote, saying that she wanted to come back into service again. She came back once when we were in Watagoda, and left for the second time, a few weeks after we moved to the station master's house in Hatton.

It was quite a while now, and how much I missed her, and longed to see her again. She arrived by train, wreathed in smiles and greetings, as she walked down the rail track, dressed in a white sari and sandals. She never wore sandals or slippers at our house. We embraced and kissed, as she tearfully greeted each one of us.

Her poignant tale unfolded gradually. She said that her sisters made her slave for them endlessly, which made her think she would be better off serving our family. Menika resumed her former duties, but whenever Ammie nagged her for some minor misdemeanour, she was dejected, and tried to cope with her misfortunes.

She told me that she was born under a sad, "unlucky star." And according to Buddhist philosophy, she thought she was a sinful person in a previous birth. Hence the reason why, that she suffered in atonement. She bemoaned desolately, because she had no love or joy in any place. Ammie soon dismissed the two cheeky, servant girls, who served us extremely badly, and reluctantly. They came from a tea estate in Hatton, and Ammie soon sent the impertinent teenagers packing to their parents.

Someone gave me a Dachshund puppy, that I named Ricky, and Ammie acquired a pedigreed, Alsatian dog, as she bred them now. I doted on my pets, though Ricky was not as possessive as Gina was, but I liked him well enough.

One day, I urged my English teacher to organise a trip to Colombo, to watch the timeless movie classic, "My Fair Lady." It drew thousands of people then. I saw it once, and raved about Rex Harrison, and Audrey Hepburn so much, that my teacher laughingly agreed to make it an "educational excursion."

When we were in Hatton the previous year, we travelled to Colombo and watched 'The Sound Of Music' at the Liberty Cinema too. I liked to see both these exceptional movies on the wide screen again, but that was too much to ask my teacher. She wanted to include some other places of interest. So it did not seem as if we went for the sole purpose of watching a movie, no matter how highly acclaimed it was (so she said).

The day of the excursion arrived, and we boarded a bus in Gampola around 4am. Surprisingly, Nazeema was allowed to join, as her parents were usually so very strict with her. They knew the teacher and me well, so they probably thought she could not come to much harm with a group of girls.

Thathie gave me twenty five rupees to spend, but I made sandwiches, and only bought a couple of soft drinks to quench my thirst. I did not like to spend all that money. Our parents were not wealthy, and to me, it was a great deal of money that Thathie could ill afford.

It was a memorable trip though, as we toured the museum, zoo, and Bata shoe factory, before ending up at Liberty Cinema for the matinee. Our trip was justified, as we soaked in a few cultural experiences for the day. It was a fitting finale to watch the unforgettable movie, "My Fair Lady" and still remains one of my all-time favourites. Yes, it was a lovely experience seeing that splendid movie a second time. And I do not hesitate to say that I watched it umpteen times since then, and it still transports me into a splendid, musical world.

After snacking on sandwiches, and a cup of coffee, we boarded the rackety old bus, and rumbled back to Gampola. Needless to say, we had only one topic of conversation for the rest of the week, our exciting trip to Colombo, and the excellent movie.

Chapter 33

Nihal wrote often, and sent gifts of perfume, hair spray, latest fashion magazines, taped music, clothes, and whatever else he could afford with his modest wages. He wrote that he was settled in well, and sent many photographs of him with friends, living it up in London and Europe. He kept in regular touch with Rosie, and her friends too, although they worked in different hospitals. Nihal seemed to enjoy life very much.

Malcolm and Anthony kept their distance, and did not socialise much with Nihal. Anthony was married to Barbara, a German lady, and they had two little boys, Kevin and Kristian. Their daughter, Tania, was born some years later. We were very pleased and proud of Nihal. He was doing an apprenticeship in motor mechanics, and studying nursing.

My parents were happy too. It seemed that Nihal made the right choice to follow his dreams. Reading his letters, and the marvellous places he visited, theatres, galleries, Shakespeare country, all the places I yearned to see, I longed to be in England too, after my senior school examination.

At the end of December, Thathie announced he was transferred again. This time he had a choice, Watagoda or Wattawala, two up-country stations, close to Hatton. We all voted for Watagoda, as we had happy memories of that dear place, and we knew the people and area. Wattawala was a dreary sort of place then. We passed that station several times to and from Colombo, and it looked more isolated than Watagoda.

Thathie tried desperately to stay on at least another year in Gampola. He did not explain why, but obviously the thought of transferring out seemed to prey heavily on his mind. This drove him to drown his sorrows in arrack more than ever. Sometimes, porters in the station bundled him into a hiring car, and sent him home after work, as he was unfit to walk even half a mile back home.

Our lives continued in much the same way, except for an occasional dance or social event to lighten up the days. I suffered severe pain, symptomatic of kidney infection, and was admitted to Kandy hospital. It was an unpleasant experience in that strange hospital, and I was overjoyed when Ammie and Thathie took me home after a few days. I was advised to take care for a few weeks, and was on medication. But I soon recuperated, and was back on my feet.

Lucien sometimes invited us for dinner to his elegant mansion, and his cook turned out some delicious meals, especially succulent, roast spare-ribs, served with vegetables, and several other dishes. I usually wandered around the living room, admiring the general surroundings, and some exquisite paintings on the walls. His ex-wife showed very good taste in furnishing that charming house.

French windows opened out to well-tended gardens, and swimming pool. He provided everything money could buy to make his erstwhile wife happy, but she left him for another man. He had a large collection of records too, and played them on his stereo-system, as he liked dancing.

A few months later, Lucien gave up his repulsive fixation with me, because I rebuffed him often, and vehemently. He returned from Colombo one day with a plump, plain-looking wife. After he finished introductions, he commented sardonically. "It's better to have a *plain* wife, than a beauty with no heart!" His first wife was a beauty queen. She married him for his wealth, and position, as she came from a very large, impoverished family (so the local gossips whispered).

Finally, his strange, unwelcome infatuation that caused me so much embarrassment and annoyance, ended with his second marriage. About five or six years later, we heard that he died suddenly of a heart attack.

One night, as we dressed for a dance at the local club where "Sam The Man" a popular Ceylonese singer, and saxophone player, was performing, Thathie arrived home early, quite drunk and aggressive. Ammie and he were accompanying us, and we were dressed up to the nines. He started an argument abruptly with Ammie over some trivial matter. And as tempers started flying, objects followed suit. Thathie picked up an elegant, dining-room chair that Ammie recently purchased, and smashed it angrily against the wall.

Needless to say, this scene dampened my anticipation, but with the resilience of youth, I was determined to go out and enjoy myself, in spite of this domestic violence (a word I did not know existed then). I accepted our family life philosophically. Deep down inside me though, I wondered what made Thathie behave in such a meaningless, destructive manner. I vowed in my heart, that I would never follow their example, *if* and *when* I married. And I told myself that I would never ever marry a man who drank alcohol.

The dance was great, and the music excellent. I requested Sam to play "Stranger On The Shore," which he did, magically. That night, Rodney, Shirani, Lucien, and his new wife, Nelune and Ammie were there. But Thathie stumbled into bed to sleep off his ill-humour and intoxication.

I was busy, and studied hard for my final examinations, but I still kept up a sporadic correspondence with Clifford. Our "on again, off again" long distance romance progressed slowly. As we were a little older now, we grew to know each other slightly better through our lengthy letters. We described our likes and dislikes, music and movies that we enjoyed, and found many mutual interests.

I did not know what kind of career I wanted to pursue after my examination, which I hoped to pass with nothing less than credits and distinctions, because I studied diligently. I dreamed of many things I would like to be though, as I dabbled in painting, writing and music. My ambition then was to excel in one, or *all* of these fields.

At the age of eleven or twelve, I declared I was going to be an author someday. But seriously, I could not pursue a career as a writer, unless I became a journalist first. I did not stop dreaming of becoming a famous musician, author, or artist some day.

The years somehow corroded and whittled away all those ambitious ideals, born in the first flush of youthful optimism, and enthusiasm. And I wonder what happened to that idealist of long ago. All childish dreams, and ideals die a natural death, unless fate and fortune are kind enough to intervene. The reality then was, that most of my contemporaries ended up as nurses, stenographers (shorthand typists), and teachers, while only a very few went on to become doctors, lawyers and engineers.

My friends in Hatton, and Miss Direkze, who was friendlier now, corresponded regularly. I visited Rosemarie and Loretta, Fawzia, Yvonne and Dawn sometimes. And I spent a few days at Mayfield, whenever I was on holidays. Tamara, who was fascinated with the piano accordion, and called it a "La La" followed me around whenever I played it. I fled down the garden path to a secluded corner, and played the piano accordion to my heart's content, without Tamara hanging around, and demanding to play the "La, La" too.

Nilanthi helped me with some beading on a white, shift dress that I was sewing for a gala dance in Kandy. Influenced by the "Punjabi" costume, I wanted to wear the shift over white, satin pants, and drape a white, chiffon shawl. Devika came over, and admired the bead work and design. Lakshman and Nilanthi attended the gala dance, and so did Ammie and Thathie. It was a memorable night, and we had heaps of fun till the early hours of dawn.

Shirani and I accompanied our parents to Maharagama for a few days before Christmas that year. Rodney was allowed to take Shirani for a movie (with me as chaperone). Clifford joined us at the cinema, on our very first real date. But we were incredibly shy, and did not know what to say to each other, as we held hands timidly for the first time. Rodney teased me all the way home.

Clifford and I hardly spoke to each other before, so I was elated to share even a brief conversation with him. The movie, "It's Never Too Late" remains a blur in my memory, as we shared a few tender kisses for the first time. I was dazed for hours afterwards, so I hardly know how I walked home.

Nazeema's romance ended suddenly, and her boyfriend inexplicably broke off all communication. She was heartbroken, as he gave no explanation. But personally, I think he realized the futility of their love, and came to his senses before they became too serious. She was still very young, and being a Muslim, she would abide by her parents wishes when it came to marriage.

I sympathised heartily with her, as I knew how much I suffered when Clifford withdrew into total silence after that momentous holiday. I kept her company through the first few weeks of that broken love affair. As it was her first love affair too, she ran the full gamut of all the emotions; angst, and misery associated with a broken heart. Some influential people sent petitions to the local Member of Parliament, requesting Thathie's stay in Gampola to be extended. But the petition was unsuccessful, and we started packing up to leave in early January 1968.

That Christmas Eve, was a depressing, dreary affair, with only Shirani, Nelune, and me at home with Ammie, Thathie, and Menika. Thathie was quite drunk early in the day. The parish priest visited that evening, as he accompanied Nelune and me home, after we participated in the nativity play at the convent. We were cast as angels, but I played the role of Virgin Mary as well in the second act.

We arrived home with the priest right into the midst of a fierce domestic row, and hastily hurried out of our parents way. Apparently, peace and goodwill decided to elude our home that Christmas Eve, and no festive meal was forthcoming either. I turned to my piano accordion, as it was my priceless treasure then. And I derived immense joy, expressing my deepest emotions through music.

Shirani, Nelune, and I, hurried outside, and built a bonfire at the far end of the garden. Then we sat around the fire, while I played Christmas carols on the accordion, with Shirani and Nelune singing along. By and by, our music attracted Geetha and Yasodha next door, who soon joined us. The grim humour of it was, that every time our parents voices rose in anger, I played the accordion even louder, hoping to drown out unpleasant sounds and shouting. And so we sang, and I played on till after midnight.

Finally, towards dawn, when all was quiet on the Western front, and the squabble ended with a truce, we crept inside and went to bed. Next day, there appeared to be a lull after the storm, and Ammie organised a delicious lunch for Christmas. And we all went about as if nothing bad or depressing happened the night before. Thathie was subdued, and hardly spoke to anyone, as he slept off his bad humour and hangover.

When the time came to leave in the New Year, we held a grand, farewell party that lasted till dawn. And a few days later, we left Gampola amid thunderous firecrackers, and friends bidding us goodbye. My final examinations were over, and I did my best. The results were due in about three months. It was a period of anxiety, as every final year student knows, wondering what the future held, once results were out. Shirani passed her final exam the year before. But she re-sat, as she wanted to acquire more credit passes, to study medicine. She was very academic, and always studied hard to achieve her goals.

Malcolm accompanied us to Watagoda, as he was back again for a few weeks. He was almost qualified to be accredited in England, and visited Ceylon often. It was a traumatic time for him then, as he was determined to marry Indrani, his childhood sweetheart, but he faced severe opposition from her family. Malcolm tried hard to convince Indrani to marry him, with or without her family's blessing. But Indrani, being a dutiful daughter, did not agree, and this situation threw him into depths of misery.

He confided his woes, but no matter how depressed he was, his good-humour could not be subdued. Malcolm was a very funny and amusing person to be with. He sent us into peals of laughter, with his droll stories about life in London, and related endless anecdotes. So, we were a merry party when we arrived in Watagoda that day.

However, when we entered the place, we found the house was just painted, and the concrete floors were still wet, after much scrubbing and mopping. It was a dismal sight. Ammie and Menika set about bringing some semblance of order. Malcolm and the three of us went sight-seeing around the spectacular lake and hills.

He too loved the splendid scenery in Watagoda, and avidly photographed the views. When we returned, a warm delicious meal awaited us. Then Malcolm told the three of us to pose outside, with Nelune on drums, Shirani holding the clarinova, and me playing the accordion. He called our band the "Blue Berries From Watagoda." That photograph still evokes happy memories.

Nilanthi, Lakshman, and Tamara dropped in later that evening. She was overjoyed, because we were now close to Mayfield Estate, and she could visit us more often and vice versa. Malcolm returned to Colombo after a few more days. I decorated our room with pictures of my favourite movie stars. We had our old bedroom back; all three of us in one room. And the extra one Nihal occupied previously, was now a spare room. But I imagined I could still hear his laughter echo there in the silence of the night.

Chapter 34

Nelune wanted to attend Good Shepherd convent in Kandy, as she was reluctant to return to St Gabriel's again. She made friends with some students from Good Shepherd convent, and was keen to study there. It was a prestigious girls school, run by nuns, and achieved very good examination results. So Thathie enrolled Nelune there. They decided to board her at the Basnayake's, a nice family in Kandy. In late January 1968, we travelled with Nelune to Kandy.

Nelune was pleased to resume her studies in English, as studying in Sinhalese the last year, proved too daunting. How our parents could afford private school *and* boarding fees, was a matter they did not discuss with us. I parted from Nelune sadly, as I would miss her dearly, but since it was for her benefit, I tried to be happy for her sake.

As we settled down in Watagoda once again, I revelled in the glorious scenery all around. And the flickering flame of creativity that burned within me since childhood, now burst into an unquenchable inferno of passionate intensity. The Muses consumed me day and night, as I dabbled in lyrical poetry, painting, and music. The exquisite beauty of the landscape inspired and stimulated my artistic senses more than ever before. I constructed verses in my head before falling asleep sometimes, and could hardly wait to write them down on paper.

Filled with inspiration, as my imagination raged like a forest fire, I even completed the outline of my first romantic novel during that period. I did not own a typewriter, and with more time on my hands, now that I did not have to study for exams, I painstakingly filled page after page with my scrawl.

All sorts of romantic notions, incredible plots, a bit of Romeo and Juliet, and every other blighted romance went into that first novel. But I was proud as Punch when I finally wrote with a flourish, "The End." I tied up my handwritten manuscript of twenty thousand words, with a piece of string, and called it "Changing Tides." and intended to type it one day, and send it off to a publisher.

That first novel did not see light of day for many years, and remained hidden, pending severe editorial amputation. Several pages of superfluous sentimentality must be deleted (I knew), before it went to print. I kept that original manuscript though, as a memento of my romantic, youthful days, when I viewed life through rose-coloured glasses. It is a poignant reminder of great expectations, hopes, and aspirations of youth; wraith-like shadows of forgotten ambitions, and ideals that loom only in distant memories now.

Beautiful Watagoda was so inspiring, that my creativity just seemed to overflow ad infinitum. Shirani and I walked for miles along the rail track, or around the lake and hills, breathing in the beauty of the wild, crocus-covered hillocks, pale mauve orchids, ferns and bracken that covered the wayside and hills profusely. We seldom came home without carrying an enormous bunch of wild flowers to arrange in vases around the house.

I entered an art competition held at school, and painted Watagoda lake, with Adam's Peak in the background. It was a large watercolour painting, and I kept my fingers crossed, but I won only a recommendation. Mother Directress encouraged me to enter a literary competition that was open to all high schools in Ceylon. It could be an essay, short story, or article. I wrote a short story called "Return To Enchantment" a nostalgic story about a young woman revisiting scenes of her childhood.

When Mother Directress read my story, she was very impressed, and asked me, "Are you *sure* this is your own work?" I replied, "It *is* an original story, Mother Directress!" She was very pleased, and told me it should win a commendation at least, but I did not get any feedback from the judges. Thathie read it too, and praised me. But when he was drunk, he muttered sarcastically, "Just because you can write *two* words of philosophy, don't think you know *everything*!"

I awaited my examination results anxiously, and sometimes, I visited my teachers and nuns at St Gabriel's. Mother Directress often advised me, and encouraged me to continue studying, because she said I was a very good student, and could achieve great things academically some day. I did not tell her though, that I toyed with the notion of becoming a secretary, as I thought it was a glamorous job.

I perused the daily newspapers eagerly, looking for a suitable position, but every job required a minimum pass in the senior school certificate, with credit passes in English, shorthand and typing. I just had to be patient until the results were out. The thought of getting a job, and being independent, was like an elixir to me, because it meant I would live somewhere near Colombo.

Uncle Barlow decided to stay with us for some time, as Ammie wanted him to help her around the house. He kept us in stitches with his droll views on life in general, and pithy comments on every aspect of human behaviour. Once, he said seriously, "It doesn't matter how ugly a woman's face is, because when the lights are off, only one thing matters!" This, and other such comments amused us, and we laughed merrily.

He was very kind, and especially helpful to me, as he conveyed my messages and letters to Clifford. He travelled to Maharagama every so often and visited Clifford, so he could bring back letters or news of him. He was very intelligent, and a well-read man. He often observed that Nilanthi was like Tolstoy's tragic heroine, "Anna Karenina." And his only term of endearment was, "You buggers," which was quite funny the way he said it in his guttural voice.

Nelune came home only for holidays, and with each visit, it was evident that her great sense of humour developed rapidly. She was more sophisticated too, and entertained us with all sorts of funny stories. Her favourite past time was to act as a stand-up comedian, and ad lib as she went along. I constructed a simple "wardrobe" on one side of the wall, which I covered with a pretty floral curtain that could be drawn to both sides like a stage curtain. Uncle Barlow fixed shelves and a rod across for hangers.

Nelune usually hid behind this curtain, while we, the audience, waited for her to make a grand entrance. Then followed hours of delightful comedy, as she could mimic, recite, and tell excellent jokes, until tears streamed down our faces. And even Ammie and Thathie enjoyed her comedy shows immensely.

In the days that followed though, Thathie looked more harassed and depressed. He continued the same pattern of behaviour, and heavy drinking, even more so than before, but did not share his problems with Ammie or his friends. His bosom buddies were a couple of co-workers, but only when it came to drinking bouts. Thathie may have inadvertently confided in those co-workers, when he was intoxicated. But be that as it may, the events that followed soon after, shook our family, and our lives to the very foundations.

Meanwhile, life went on in the same uneventful manner, until I celebrated my sixteenth birthday. Mr Fernandez dropped in with a gift of fawn-coloured, silk fabric. And he said that Yvonne wanted me to have it, as her "going-away" outfit was made of the same fabric.

Yvonne was married off to a distant cousin in India, when she turned sixteen, because she required constant vigilance. Mr Fernandez did not want to be responsible for her after the death of his wife. Yvonne often wrote sad letters. She described her married life to a virtual stranger, who was about thirty years then, and with whom she had absolutely nothing in common.

She lamented the loss of her freedom, but was unable to change her situation. I sympathised with her deeply, because I knew her as a fun-loving, exuberant girl, now buried in some remote place in India, and tied down to a total stranger.

She invited Shirani and me to visit her, as she was lonely, without her many friends in Ceylon. We jumped at the idea, and Thathie thought it would be a good experience for us to travel overseas. But Ammie vehemently vetoed the plan, saying that it was outrageous for two girls of our age to go "gallivanting" abroad (as she termed it), without proper chaperonage. So that was that, and we abided by her decision.

It was a very quiet birthday, although Nilanthi dropped in later with a present and flowers. Tamara was a talkative little girl of almost two, and kept us amused. She was a cute, smart little girl, and we doted on her.

A few weeks after my sixteenth birthday, Uncle Barlow agreed to chaperone Shirani and me to the Thomian Fair in Colombo, which was a gala event then. The saddest part though, was that on the eve of our departure to Colombo, Menika, who could not take Ammie's nagging any longer, broke the news that she was leaving for good, and would never return. Ammie still treated Menika like a naughty little servant girl, and not as an adult. Menika did not tolerate being treated as such, and she told me that it was better to take her chances with her own family, and suffer the consequences.

I was very upset and heartbroken, as I realised how much I would miss this dear person, who mothered me, and was with us long before I was born. When we lived in Hatton, and Ammie punished Menika for some minor misdemeanour, she locked her outside. The five of us stood out with Menika in solidarity, until Ammie relented and let us in. That was how close we were to Menika, because she was like an older sister.

Although I was depressed and cried when Menika said goodbye and embraced me, part of me was very excited at the prospect of going to Colombo for the fair. And the full impact of her departure did not hit me until I returned home next day, and found her familiar, affectionate face absent from our family circle once again.

Shirani, Uncle Barlow, and I boarded the "Podi Menike" train at about two thirty in the afternoon, and arrived at Fort Station around 8pm or so. Shirani and I quickly changed into our "mod-gear" in the privacy of the train compartment, and dolled up for the evening.

Rodney and Clifford met us at the railway station, and accompanied us to the fair, where we had an unforgettable time. Uncle Barlow proved to be a good sport, and trailed behind us, so he could be easy in his conscience that he was keeping an eye. Around midnight, we headed back to the station, to catch the first train back to Watagoda at dawn. I simply cannot imagine how I kept up all night, without the least sign of fatigue.

Rodney and Clifford left us at Fort Station, and we sat in the waiting room for a while until our train arrived. Just before the train pulled out of the platform, they returned (after a brief nap), to bid us farewell. Parting was indeed such sweet sorrow. The return journey home was spent re-living every moment spent in the company of our sweethearts, as Shirani and I chatted away drowsily.

Uncle Barlow conversed good-humouredly too, and amused us with his jokes until the train pulled in at Watagoda. It was when we came home that the full impact of Menika's departure hit me. And I was very unhappy about it for a long time.

In the bungalow overlooking the lotus lake, lived a young planter, Damian and his wife, Barbara. Co-incidentally, he was the same young man who sang at the New Year's dance in 1966. He was a pleasant, good-humoured man, and Thathie was quite friendly with him. Damian was at the station often on business matters, or just to socialise sometimes. He married Barbara about a year ago, and they had one child, Jeremy. Barbara was an attractive, friendly person, with a fair-skinned complexion, dark eyes, and long, black hair.

We sometimes saw a group of people alight from one of the trains, who Thathie said were Damian's in-laws. Barbara and Damian visited us occasionally, and we formed a slight acquaintance. Ammie baby-sat their gorgeous baby, who had an angelic face, and light-grey eyes. My parents doted on Jeremy.

A few weeks later, I received my examination results. Although I passed with two credits in history and religious knowledge, two distinctions in English language and literature, passes in Sinhalese and arithmetic, I required one more credit to continue advanced level. English language and literature were considered one subject, in tallying credits and distinctions, which seemed unfair to me. I believed that with my results, I should be eligible. So I persuaded Thathie to enrol me at Holy Family convent in Bambalapitiya. It was a very good school, and I hoped they would accept me.

Once again, Shirani and I were allowed to travel to Colombo alone, but this time, Uncle Barlow was not there to chaperone us, as he returned to Granny's place some days ago. When we arrived at Fort Station, we boarded a bus to Maharagama, and stood happily at Granny's front door.

Granny however, was far from impressed that we travelled alone, and criticized our parents for allowing us too much freedom. But when she knew the purpose of our visit, she was slightly mollified, and agreed to accompany me to Holy Family convent next day.

The interview turned out to be a great disappointment. The principal, a strict nun, *insisted* that I needed one more credit in another subject. I was very dejected, and I argued, and I pleaded. But she was inflexible as stone, and would not bend the rules for anyone.

Granny added, "My grand-daughter is very keen to pursue her studies, can't you please consider Mother Superior?" But all to no avail. With tears of mortification and disappointment, I returned home with Granny, who did not say much.

I spent the rest of the day mooning around, nursing my grievances, and thinking uncharitably of the granite-hearted nun. She well and truly dashed my hopes for the future. By and by, I glimpsed Anjo beckoning me from her garden, as I stood at the kitchen window. I walked over to the fence, and Anjo said, "Why don't you join me for a bath at the well, and drop in for a snack afterwards?" I agreed, as the gloomy atmosphere at Granny's place was stifling. Anjo's brother, Sonna, Clifford, and some other boys, were having a jolly good time at the adjoining well. I soon forgot my melancholy thoughts as we waved to each other.

Anjo invited the boys to come over as well, and it was dusk when we walked down the lane back to Granny's house. Clifford and I lagged behind, stealing tender moments, then I heard Grandpa tottering noisily down the scoria- covered lane. I panicked for a moment, wondering how he would react if he saw me. But much to my surprise, he just shuffled along, oblivious to people around him. He was hazy after drinks, and did not recognise any of us in the dusky twilight. My good fortune though was short-lived, and all hell broke loose when we entered the house.

Anjo's stepmother, Diana, visited Granny during our absence, to inform her of her grand-daughter's "doings" and "carrying on," as Granny termed our innocent rendezvous. She flew into a grand passion, and threatened to write to my parents *immediately* to tell them I was meeting Clifford in secret etc. etc. I listened silently. Shirani was not in so much trouble as I was, but she was deemed guilty by association. Anjo was on Granny's blacklist, and she was not welcome either.

I was the main offender, and a criminal in Granny's eyes. Absolutely overcome with fear now, I trembled like an aspen, as her fierce temper and words struck terror in my heart. I held Granny in complete awe, and the mere thought of my parents finding out about my young love, staggered me completely. They were under the impression that my teenage infatuation died a natural death a long time ago.

Thathie intercepted our letters in Gampola. And sometimes, I found Clifford's letters thrown in the bin, or in the garden. I dared not ask about those letters, as he was under the misconception we stopped communicating.

Grandpa retreated to his dark, lonely room, and was fast asleep on his armchair, and very wisely stayed out of the raging storm. Shirani and I returned home next day, after Granny gave me such a tongue-lashing, and forbade us to set foot out of the house until we boarded the train.

Marie accompanied us, to ensure I had no more chance meetings with Clifford, and we boarded a bus to Fort Station. She was Granny's vigilante, and disapproved of Clifford as much as Granny did. I could not understand their antipathy, especially Marie, whom I expected to be more sympathetic. I was rather crest-fallen about the whole business, and in a couple of days Granny's dreaded missile landed home.

Chapter 35

Granny's threat, like the sword of Damocles, was hanging over my head by a thread. I almost felt a sense of relief now, as the worst would soon be over. It would be very difficult for teenagers today, to even imagine a fraction of the dread our parents and elders instilled in us. Their word was law, and woe unto us if we dared defy them. Many a resounding slap, and hard thumps on my head, did I endure, as punishment for my misdemeanours.

The scolding, accusations, and sermons were unbearable at times. I sulked around the house, feeling absolutely miserable, not knowing what course of action to take. Thathie forbade me to correspond with Clifford in future, and this led to more subterfuge. Anjo, who was always there to aid me, enclosed his letters with hers. And Thathie did not suspect anything amiss, when he saw Anjo's handwriting on the envelopes.

He assumed Anjo was sending me messages or news of Clifford, and we were forced to resort to such excessive lengths. In retrospect, I can hardly believe how scared I was of being found out. To me, we were star-crossed lovers, and I wallowed in sentimentality. Lachrymose and sullen, I withdrew into my own world where I found solace in writing, art and music. I constantly listened to all the Jim Reeves' songs that Nihal and Nilanthi taped. And I played sad songs on the accordion too, hoping my parents would get the message and relent, but they did not.

Shirani stopped seeing Rodney, and Thathie was relieved, because he said she was too young to think of getting engaged. Barbara soon befriended her, and Thathie was pleased that she did not appear to be broken-hearted over Rodney.

Shirani toyed with the idea of starting an English class in Paranagama, for village children, and she hoped to stay with Athamma and Mutha. Thathie was enthusiastic about this idea, and encouraged Shirani to go ahead with it. She was very busy now, travelling to Paranagama often, as she set about organising a classroom.

When I told Mother Directress about my results, she advised me to re-sit the final examination, and achieve one more credit, if I wanted to continue higher studies. This seemed like a good idea. So I woke up at first light to resume the exhausting journey in goods trains to Hatton and back. Thathie set the alarm for five o'clock. When I did not budge out of bed, he left the light on in my room, saying, "Time to get up now, or you'll miss the train."

How I hated those cold, dark mornings. I gulped down breakfast in a mighty hurry, raced to the station in chilly, rainy weather, and boarded the freezing goods train that chugged along sluggishly. The only consolation was the magnificent scenery. and awe-inspiring sunrise over the hills and dales of Watagoda.

One morning, when I got off the train, I walked behind a very short, dark-skinned girl with frizzy hair, who wore such a skimpy, crumpled mini-skirt, that her panties showed. Her broad bum wobbled, as she waddled along on short, fat legs that were bow-legged. A few boys followed her and sniggered in derision, and I was embarrassed for her. I doubt she knew her panties were on display. And I found out much later that she was Barbara's sister, Geraldine.

The train reached Hatton around 7am, so I had plenty of time to sit on a bench in the playground and read a book, or finish my homework. I spent hours reading on the train to and from school, for which I am grateful, as I finished numerous books.

A poignant circumstance was, that none of my old friends were at school any more. English classes were phased out, and I sat at the back of the room with children who studied in Sinhalese. I did my best to follow all subjects in Sinhalese, and translated my notes to English. Everything was changed. And a wave of nostalgia for those good times only a couple of years ago, swept over me. I sighed each time I saw our previous cosy house down below the convent boundary.

Another family occupied it now. It was difficult to believe that house was once the scene of those joyous days. And my ears filled with the sound of happy laughter, and music, like distant echoes of my childhood. In years to come, recurring dreams of us back in that house haunted me.

Miss Eugene, taught music at St Gabriel's. Her parents, Mr and Mrs Lane, ran a modest hotel, the "Crown" on the outskirts of Hatton town, close to the convent. Thathie often patronized the hotel (mostly to drink), but they also served reasonably-priced meals. Ammie knew them well, and she arranged meals for me there, because she insisted I have a nice, hot meal at lunch time. Mrs Lane charged about two or three rupees, for a plate of rice and curry, and always served it with two large pappadams. The meals were cheap, but quite tasty.

I was very keen to study piano, so Ammie asked Miss Eugene to give me lessons after school. She charged about fifteen rupees a lesson. I continued enjoying lunch at the Crown Hotel for as long as I attended St Gabriel's convent. And Miss Eugene gave me piano lessons after school. But after about four or five lessons, I had to stop, due to financial reasons. The added expense of piano lessons was just too much. So, much to my disappointment, I was unable to continue lessons. Miss Eugene was very encouraging, and told me I showed great promise, and it was a shame I had to stop.

It was almost six o'clock when the slow train chugged up to Watagoda, and I was ravenous by then. As soon as I came home, I enjoyed a huge bowl of Ammie's delicious, marrow bone and vegetable soup, which was always simmering. After I finished homework, dinner was around eight o'clock. Shirani was living in Paranagama, with Athamma and Mutha, so I was the only one at home. I missed my siblings very much, and looked forward to their visits.

When I was at Zahira college, I entered a religious knowledge competition, organised by the Kandy Diocese. And on 1 June 1968, I was delighted to win second prize, which was a beautiful, Illustrated New Testament Book. The parish priest and nuns congratulated me. They were impressed that I won second prize in the whole Diocese, even though I was attending a Muslim school then. I was grateful to Mother Superior in Gampola, who instructed me so well that whole year. One of the young priests in Hatton exclaimed, "What a pity you are not a boy! You could have entered the priesthood, and studied theology!"

Whenever Shirani came home, we woke up at six o'clock on Sunday mornings, and caught the early morning train to Talawakale, to attend Mass. The engine driver, who knew Thathie and us well, stopped the train at St Clare's platform, which was an unscheduled stop, as there was no station there for passengers. The narrow platform was mainly for tea estates to load tea chests.

And although we were dressed in our Sunday best, and high heels, we jumped down from the train, and walked more than two miles to church and back. A steep flight of steps from St Clare's platform, ascended to the main road above, and I enjoyed the exhilarating walk in cool, balmy air.

Overlooking St Clare's waterfalls, and sparkling like a white diamond, stood an elegant mansion. I told Shirani that I loved to live in a house like that, set on a hill-top and overlooking such a spectacular view. It was a planter's bungalow, and I could not help longing to live in such a beautiful place. After Mass, if we were fortunate enough, we caught a slow, rumbling bus that passed the church. And we gladly boarded the rickety, overcrowded bus to save a long walk back to Talawakale station.

The bus sometimes went all the way to Watagoda. And that was a bonus, as public transport, especially on a Sunday, hardly catered to people in remote areas. It was almost midday by the time we returned home, as it was such a long, tedious journey. But we did not mind, as we had all the time in the world to spare.

On one Sunday morning, Barbara's younger brother, travelled in the same compartment with us. We giggled mischievously when we caught sight of him intently reading a magazine "True Romances." It tickled our sense of humour, as we thought it was a little too early in the day for that sort of literature. But he was oblivious to our glee, and kept reading and smoking non-stop.

When the train slowed down at St Clare's platform, we found the door jammed. The young man jumped up and yanked it open. I thanked him politely before I alighted. I did not give the matter much thought, or remember him particularly after that day. I only knew that he was Barbara's brother, but I did not know his name.

Our lives meandered along placidly, each one of us wrapped up in our private worlds of joys and sorrows. Whenever I felt melancholy, I found an outlet for my emotions in art, music and literature. And I never failed to play the piano accordion daily, as I found solace in its sweet tones. Shirani and I read avidly, sewed clothes, knitted, or potted around in the garden, and went on long walks every evening, no matter what the weather was like.

We listened to the radio, and taped music often. Nihal wrote regularly, and Nilanthi visited every week or so. Shirani and I drew closer than ever before. Nelune still boarded in Kandy, and came home only during school holidays.

We travelled to Talawakale with Thathie for a movie sometimes, and occasionally we visited Barbara. It was very quiet and serene, compared to the hectic twelve months in Gampola. But I was never bored or unhappy. Spiritually and emotionally, I think it was good, as I had many quiet, pleasant, and meditative times.

Shirani and I discussed our girlish dreams, ambitions, hopes, and ideals on our daily walks. The exquisite scenery kindled an eternal love of beauty in my young soul. Starry-eyed and romantic, I never failed to wish upon the evening star, to make my dreams come true.

As children, Shirani and I quarrelled at the slightest provocation. But now, we depended on each other a great deal for company, understanding, and moral support.

A strong bond, always existed between the five of us. No matter how far away we were, we always maintained this link by letters or phone calls. Although we missed the others dearly, there was no turning back the clock, and time slipped by inexorably.

Nihal settled down very well, and was happy in what he was doing. He was enjoying himself hugely, and I was very happy for him. His letters were always cheerful, optimistic, and full of fun. He never forgot us, as he sent gifts of stockings, fashion magazines, hair sprays, and perfumes.

Shirani and I kept busy, as we sewed all the latest modes from London. And in my spare time, I painted a few large pictures on cardboard with oil pastels, of my favourite characters; Catherine and Heathcliff from "Wuthering Heights" (one of my favourite novels), and some other characters from romantic novels. Those sad-faced, and star-crossed lovers, decorated my bedroom walls. I was pleased with my work, and thought they were quite good (in my youthful vanity). But I truly regret that my early art works were lost forever when we moved house.

One of Thathie's friends left his motorcycle at the station for a few days, and I was determined to learn how to ride it. So, one day, when Nelune came home, we took turns to ride it, and thought it great fun. I whizzed up and down the straight road in front of our house. But on braking suddenly, I fell over on my side. I burnt the calf of my leg badly on the hot metal plate. That dampened my enthusiasm, and I did not venture on the motorcycle again.

Chapter 36

One morning, somewhere in June that year, I woke up to the sound of a great commotion. Ammie sobbed inconsolably, as she held a note, and mumbled incoherently. Officers and porters from the station tried to comfort her, without success. I soon learnt that Thathie disappeared, leaving behind a suicide note, bidding us farewell, just like that. I can hardly bear to think of that day, let alone write about it even now, without suffering intense pangs of agony. I thought of everything Thathie meant to us, and could not foresee a future without him.

He wrote that on the previous day, some auditors checked the account books, and found a discrepancy of three thousand rupees. They bundled the books to Colombo for further investigation. Thathie panicked, because unknown to us, he "borrowed" money from the petty cash fund, to replace funds he took in Gampola station. He required only a few more months to replace the money without being found out.

Ethically, it was wrong. But Thathie always intended to return the money in instalments, as soon as possible. Fate intervened however, and the transfer to Watagoda came at the worst possible time. He was unable to replace the money within that limited time, due to mounting bills. As far as I understood then, Thathie borrowed money in Watagoda, to replace the funds in Gampola.

The authorities frowned upon such "fiddling" of accounts. And dipping into petty cash, was termed "misappropriation" of Government funds. It did not matter, even if he had every intention of repaying the unauthorised "loan" or that it was such an insignificant amount. The enormity of the offence was undiminished, whether it was two or twenty rupees. It was a very serious offence indeed, punishable by dismissal, and loss of all retirement benefits.

Ammie did not know if the sky had fallen on her head that day. And as she was a diabetic, prone to severe migraines, she took to bed with a massive headache, and could hardly get up for the rest of the day.

Shirani and I coped as well as we could, tending to Ammie, and trying to hide our terrible fears and grief over this calamity. The secure, comfortable world I knew for so long, suddenly collapsed without warning. Thathie did not confide in Ammie how he raised funds to purchase Nihal's ticket.

We later discovered that none of this would have happened, and Thathie would have replaced the money soon, had he not divulged his secret to one of his co-workers, when he was drunk one day. That man wanted to get rid of Thathie, as he was next in line for his job. He betrayed Thathie's secret to the auditors. They sprang a surprise on him, before he had had time to replace the money and balance the account books.

Poor Thathie! How my heart ached for him. He was generous to the point of imprudence. He risked his job, and the career he was so proud of, as he always boasted that he was the youngest station master in the railway. And he threw away his whole life for a "'mess of pottage" so to speak.

Someone later told him. "If it had been a *fortune*, then it would not have been so bad, but to lose your job for such a small sum is so unfortunate!" Whether the number of zeroes involved mattered or not, is a moot point however. My recollections of that day are that Shirani and I just sat in a stupor. I was paralysed with fear until we heard some news of Thathie. I just could not believe he would desert us, and take away his own life. But because of his heavy drinking, there was no saying what he would do under the influence of alcohol.

I prayed, cried, hoped, and despaired, running the gamut of a wild, emotional see-saw. On that fateful day, I left behind forever my carefree, girlish world, and experienced the grim realities of the harsh world.

Nelune still had a few years to complete her education, but my last year at St Gabriel's convent did not cost anything. Thathie wrote that he left enough money to pay Nelune's board and school fees. I think the fear of losing Thathie, besides settling all the mundane financial problems and cares, tormented Ammie, as she lay battling with her migraine.

We phoned Nilanthi, and she came over with Lakshman later that day. It is a wonder I can even recall some of the details of that dreadful, traumatic day. But as evening shadows grew longer, and rosy dusk settled into deep violet night, I heard the lonely whistle of the last train pulling out of the station. A few heart-stopping moments later, I heard the sound of footsteps on the gravel drive, but dared not raise my hopes, in case it was only a porter with evil tidings. None could imagine our relief, joy, and wild welcome, as Thathie walked in, red-eyed and intoxicated. His lips twisted in a bitter self-mocking smile. I shouted out "Thathie!"

All my emotions, joy, and relief exploded in that one short word of welcome, as I rushed to embrace him. He enfolded us, including Ammie, who welcomed him tearfully, without reproaches, for having put us through such pain and misery, and for shattering our home and lives so devastatingly.

He slurred tearfully, "I thought that all of you would be ashamed of me, and I couldn't face any of you, but I didn't have the courage to jump in front of a train either! Carmen, I went to the General Manager and pleaded with him to keep me on, as I would replace the money *immediately*, but he would not listen to me, and I am now interdicted (that awful word again), from now on until the full inquiry has finished. He said I can remain in this house until the matter is finalized."

We were slightly relieved that we did not have to pack up and leave immediately. And we clung to him lovingly, saying that we would see this business through, as a family. He committed a grave offence I knew, but for such an unselfish cause. I begged God he would not lose his much-loved job as station master. The bad news spread around like an epidemic, faster if possible.

We endured grave-faced sympathisers, who treated our home like a funeral parlour. Most of them were "Job's comforters," as they came to remind Ammie of everything she would lose when Thathie was dismissed. Such fatalistic statements, and gloating from people, who feigned friendship in good times, was totally revolting.

The nuns and priests waylaid us after Mass, to find out what happened. They shook their heads disapprovingly, as they all knew Thathie drank heavily, and assumed he must have used the funds for selfish reasons. We did not tell them the real reason why he took the money, and as usual, all sorts of vicious rumours floated around. Some said Ammie was extravagant, and encouraged Thathie to take the money, and so on. It was very difficult for me to put on a brave face and go about normally. But that is just what I did, and so did Shirani and Ammie.

All the prestige and perks of being the station master's children, disappeared overnight. And I burned with the humiliation we suffered. People referred to Thathie's disgrace in undertones wherever we went. And the station staff, who were once servile, and ever ready to do anything for Thathie and us, became arrogant and rude. It was very painful for him, to say the least.

Damian and Barbara were good to us, and visited regularly, as they tried to console Ammie. Barbara helped in practical ways too, and sometimes brought a few groceries. Thathie's brother, Wije, offered to lend the money immediately, to replace the missing funds. It was heart-warming to find out the true qualities of people in times of adversity.

Nilanthi and Lakshman visited often too, but she told us that Thathie's situation now was a very sore point with Lakshman. He constantly threw it in her face, and he did not want any of his acquaintances or friends to find out about it.

Granny and Marie descended on us soon. Granny sat with Ammie, consoling her in the following manner. "My *poor, poor* child, to think of all the *comforts* you will have to give up! You have never been used to going without anything from your childhood! Remember, how well I used to look after you, and you had to go and get married so *young*! My *poor* Carmen!"

Ammie burst into a fresh deluge of tears, and remained inconsolable. Although we stayed in that house for a long while after this event, it was very painful for Thathie to be stripped of his authority and self-respect. And to rub salt in his open wound, the newly appointed station master, was none other than the officer who "dobbed" in Thathie.

I still picture Thathie leaning over the parapet wall, gazing at his beloved station, and sobbing brokenly. Ammie too changed overnight. From a happy, generous person, she became a troubled, penny-pinching housewife, as she desperately tried to feed her family, and keep up a semblance of our previous comfortable life-style.

It amazes me even now, that without a regular income, no social benefits, or any assistance whatsoever, how Ammie kept us well-fed regularly, and how Thathie was able to still indulge in cigarettes and drinks. He was not a heavy smoker though, and sometimes liked to smoke cigars or a pipe. We put on brave faces, as we went about our daily business, and outwardly, our lives appeared to be unchanged.

Chapter 37

I wonder how we survived during those dreadful months. And my parents never liked to talk about that harrowing period. Perhaps Thathie's relatives, and Athamma and Mutha may have helped us survive. Thathie disappeared for days, and Ammie said he chopped firewood in Paranagama, to earn some money. Some people, under the pretext of sympathising, appeared only to gloat over our misfortunes. So I thought, in my youthful pride, and bruised self-esteem.

I kept all these miserable tidings to myself, and did not write to Clifford about the matter. But a few months later, he came to know through someone whose father worked in the railway. He wrote a very comforting letter, saying he could hardly believe what had happened to an upright man like Thathie.

The only good memories of those dark days are the "readings" by the "fire-bucket" on most cold evenings. I borrowed books from the library, and one of my favourites then was, Oliver Goldsmith's, "She stoops to conquer." Shirani or I read out loud, to amuse our parents.

The "fire bucket" was just that. A deep, narrow perforated bucket. We filled it with small lumps of coal that engine drivers tossed down, for porters or servant boys to pick. The little boys and girls in the area filled up bags of coal for a small sum, and Ammie bought some from them.

We lit the fire bucket out in the garden. When it stopped smoking, and the hot coals burnt brightly, we carried it into the kitchen. After dinner, we dragged stools or chairs close to the fire bucket, and spent the next few hours listening to fantastic tales, that one of us read aloud.

Thathie and Ammie enjoyed these times just as much we did, and it certainly helped us to forget our troubles for a while. It was the most precious, quality time that we shared in many years. And remains in my memory as a time of "laughter through tears." Thathie tried very hard to abstain from liquor. But he was hopelessly drunk some nights, and then, home was just too miserable for everyone.

Once, Ammie and I stayed at Nilanthi's for a few days, as Shirani was in Paranagama. We needed a change badly, and Thathie stayed back. Late one evening, we received a phone call from one of the porters, saying Thathie was in a very bad way.

I was in tears, as I dressed quickly, and Lakshman drove me to Watagoda. The lights were all switched off. I heard our beautiful, German Shepherd dog, Pepe, whine outside where he was tied up. I released him soon, and gave him some water and food, as the stale food in his plate was putrid.

Thathie lay in a stupor, and mumbled that he tried to electrocute himself by sticking his finger in one of the electric bulb sockets. Fortunately, he was unsuccessful.

Lakshman carried Thathie to the car. I asked him if I could bring the ailing dog too, as he was still a puppy at six months. Thathie sat in the back seat or rather sprawled there, and I sat in the front with Pepe on my lap. He was still whining. I was heart-broken to think of him tied up for a few days, with nothing to eat but rotten food.

Pepe was sick on the way, and vomited all over me, so I could hardly wait to have a bath. When we arrived at Mayfield, I quickly took Pepe to the garden, while Lakshman helped Thathie out of the car. I ran a hot water bath, and waited impatiently to enjoy a long soak. The appu woke up and tended to Pepe, who just lay down in a heap, rolling his gentle, brown eyes at me, as if in mute gratitude. He tried to wag his tail in acknowledgement of his freedom and deliverance from suffering. But the effort was too great, because he was so weak.

It was almost midnight, and I wondered where Thathie was. The appu found him lying in the hot water bath, and quickly helped him out. By then the hot water ran out, and I ended up having a lukewarm bath. Thathie was back to his usual self the following day, and Ammie vowed never to leave him on his own again. It was a wretched business, and to make matters worse, Pepe died the following day. He was ailing for about a week since we left him at home. We buried him in the garden, and then returned to Watagoda with heavy hearts.

Just after this upheaval in our lives, I spent one morning at the convent, drawing up some posters for an art exhibition. The nuns, who were aware of my artistic ability, requested assistance with the posters. I agreed gladly, as it was an excuse to get out for the day. I wrote to Clifford, asking him if he could meet me that day.

He travelled down, in response to my letter. But the only time we spent together, was aboard a crowded train from Hatton to Watagoda. It was not the usual, slow, goods train either, so we had less than one hour together. I felt very guilty, as he boarded the next train back to Colombo. He was under the impression I would spend more time with him. But now, all I could do was just wave goodbye, as the train pulled out of the platform. I watched it chug along slowly on that long journey back.

I cherished even such brief interludes, as it was almost impossible to meet regularly. We grew close, and I was devoted to him. I hoped that one day, we would be together. I loved him with all the intensity of first love, even though I was only sixteen. He was very quiet, and reserved, and never spoke of how he felt. But his ardent letters revealed his deep love. So I was content, as I admired the strong, silent type. And just knowing he travelled hundred miles, to spend one hour with me, was enough proof of his attachment.

I wanted to save my parents money, and my travelling time, by staying with Nilanthi and attending school from Mayfield. She was very happy, because it meant she would have company on the isolated estate.

It was about three or four miles from Mayfield to Hatton. As I was a keen walker, on some days, I walked the whole distance to school and back. My food was kept warm when I returned from school, and Nilanthi mothered me during my stay.

I confided all my troubles in her still, and she listened patiently, showering me with love and kindness. I enjoyed myself, and indulged in luxuries such as daily hot water baths, and delicious food prepared by the appu.

However, I never felt comfortable whenever Lakshman was around. And for that reason I did not like staying too long. I heard him moving around very early every morning. Then he sneaked up suddenly as I breakfasted, wrapped his long, ape-like arms around and tried to grope me. I pushed his arms away, and quickly got up from the table and hurried out.

I was shocked, as I saw him praying before Lord Buddha's picture just before he prowled over to grab me. I was too embarrassed to tell Nilanthi about it, and avoided being alone with him. I went home on weekends, and then it was good being at home again. Nilanthi usually packed loads of things for us, fresh fruits and vegetables from her garden, and a few pretty clothes for me sometimes.

One day, while I was at Mayfield, I summoned up the courage to ask Lakshman, if I could invite Clifford for a supper dance at Darawala club. And if it was possible for him to stay at Mayfield after the dance, as he would return to Colombo on the early morning train. I had little hope of him agreeing, and was astonished when he replied in an unusually, good-humoured manner. "Why not?" When I told Nilanthi, she observed that he sometimes surprised her.

It was uncharacteristic of him, but I was pleased. Then it was a matter of "What shall I wear for this special dance?" Shirani came up with a bright idea, as she was learning how to do "Tatting," a form of lace-making on a wooden frame. She promised to make some lace fabric, which I wanted to line with mauve satin.

With an abundance of goodwill, and soaring ambition, Shirani began her project. After many days, she produced a reasonable length of "lace" that looked like fish net. We set about cutting it, and sewed a full-length, evening dress. The only problem however, was when we cut the lace, it tended to fall apart, and bits of thread came loose at the seams.

Undeterred by such a minor setback, like disintegrating lace, we lined the dress with mauve satin. And it was a marvellous creation (in our eyes). Shirani was immensely proud of her handiwork, and I packed the dress carefully. Shiromani, a good friend of mine from St Gabriel's convent, agreed to come too.

I visited her often, as her younger sister, Darshani, and she, were very musical. They had an old piano, and an accordion, which they played very well. I sat at that piano for hours, and their mother was impressed. She often told me, "You are very talented, and I hope you learn to read music one day."

When I arrived at Mayfield, Nilanthi took one look at our exquisite creation, and shook her head in dismay. She tried hard not to burst out laughing, as she said, "You simply *can't* wear *this* thing to the dance Dolly! *Look* at all the bits of thread hanging out here, there and everywhere! I'm sure it will all fall apart before the end of the dance!" I agreed reluctantly, as I saw what a sorry state the dress was in, even after my careful packing.

The threads just came apart at the slightest touch of the dress and fell everywhere. I panicked! What on earth could I wear? I did not think of bringing another dress, and I had no time to take a train back to Watagoda to get another one. Nilanthi came to my rescue. She suggested that I wear one of her beautiful saris draped like a "lungi" (sarong), and one of her evening blouses.

She pacified me, "You will look nice in it anyway." But I was sorely disappointed. I wanted something very special for the dance, and now with Nilanthi's help, I improvised. When I finally finished dressing, Nilanthi exclaimed that the soft blue silk "lungi" and matching blouse, looked very elegant. I was somewhat mollified. Our "Lace Creation" became a standing joke for many years.

Lakshman offered to pick Clifford from the station at Hatton, on our way to the dance. It was meant to be an evening of disappointments though, because the old steam engine chugged along and ground to a halt, but Clifford was not on that train. Lakshman did not want to delay any longer, so we did not wait for the next train. We picked up Shiromani, and went on to the dance.

I hid my disappointment and chagrin as well as I could, and the rest of the evening did not matter at all, I thought sadly. Shiromani, a shy, pretty girl, who was my good friend for many years, now sat with me at the table, listening to music. She stood up to dance a few times with equally shy, young boys, but I refused to dance with anyone else. I was terribly upset, and in my gloomy mood, I was bad company.

My thoughts were on someone who was not there. I wondered what happened, as we made this date a few weeks ago. Perhaps he was delayed somewhere, and would turn up later in the evening, I hoped. And I thought of him wistfully.

My wishful thinking became reality next moment. He came down the broad staircase from the entrance of the club, that led to the dance floor below. I looked at Shiromani, and exclaimed joyfully, "Isn't he an *angel* to make it somehow!" To which she replied, "Of course he is, and looks like one too!" Clifford looked very handsome. His tall, slim figure stood out in evening clothes. He was everything my romantic heart yearned for.

He came up to me, and smiled. "I missed the train, so I had to take a bus instead." It was such a long journey to Hatton by bus, but he kept his promise that he would be at the dance. I was elated, to put it mildly. I introduced him to Lakshman, who now behaved in a most superior manner, and hardly spoke a word to him.

Clifford looked very tired, but after a drink, and some conversation, we danced away happily until just past midnight. Lakshman growled, "Time to go home!" We dropped Shiromani, and on our way to Mayfield, no one spoke a word at all. It was very uncomfortable for Clifford.

Nilanthi showed him to the guest room. I slept on a spare bed in Nilanthi's and Lakshman's room, as they had only one spare bedroom. We hardly spoke to each other in the morning, as Clifford was anxious to get back. He did not want any breakfast either. When I asked him the reason for his hasty departure, he replied, "Lakshman is very snobbish isn't he?" I knew then he was not at ease in his presence. Lakshman told Nilanthi, "Clifford is a mere *schoolboy,* and I have no time for him."

A little later on in the morning, Lakshman drove him to the station, and that was that. I complained to Nilanthi about Lakshman's behaviour, and she replied, "There's nothing we can do about it, that's the way he is." I left Mayfield that afternoon, as I was quite annoyed with him.

Sometime that year, Clifford and his friends, spent a few days in Nuwara Eliya. It was the popular "season," with dances, car racing, and other events over a few weeks. The sleepy little town came alive, as visitors from everywhere gathered in Nuwara Eliya, to escape the hottest time of year in Colombo.

Nelune came home for holidays, and we spent a great deal of time attending various activities in Nuwara Eliya. Clifford and I walked with our friends around the parks and lakeside, and enjoyed a few brief moments together.

One day, during the "season" I persuaded my parents to let me attend a dance in Nuwara Eliya, with some girls whom they knew. Shirani and I walked up to Barbara's place, to ask her if she could send one of the servants with me, as it was too late in the evening for me to travel alone by train. It was one of Ammie's conditions, that one of the servants should accompany me on the train to Nanuoya. My friends were meeting me, and then travelling to Nuwara Eliya by bus.

Shirani did not want to go for some reason, and I needed a chaperone. It was drizzling slightly, so I wore a black raincoat, and a red, straw hat. When I knocked on the door, Barbara's brother, Conrad, opened the door. When I told Barbara about my errand, she readily agreed to send one of her servants with me.

It was a memorable evening, and we danced till late, then walked back to my friend's house. We stayed up till dawn, just enjoying being together, before we boarded an early morning bus to Nanu Oya, and then took a train.

I was surprised when Bro. Alphonso got into the bus, and sat down in front of us. He recognized me, and asked, "How is Nihal doing in London?" I nodded. "He's happy, and well Brother." He looked inquiringly at Clifford, and I stammered, "This is my cousin." I could not think of anything else to say. Bro. Alponso inclined his head slightly, and we did not talk any more till the bus stopped at Nanu Oya station.

I wondered if he would tell Ammie that he saw me with my cousin, but before long, I got off the train at Watagoda, and Clifford travelled back to Colombo. All I could do was spend the rest of the day in a romantic haze, as I re-lived every minute of that magical night.

Shirani and I visited Barbara and Damian often, as Barbara was very friendly. She joked with us, and helped to while away the time when we needed company. Sometimes, Babs (as we now called her), invited us to spend the evenings there. And knowing how fond I was of hot baths, she invited me to indulge in that luxury.

Another dance was coming up at Talawakale club shortly, and in her usual good-humoured way, Babs said, "Why don't you invite Clifford to that dance? Connie (Conrad), and Jenny (Geraldine), will be there too." This time, she invited Clifford to stay with them. Damian picked him up at Watagoda station on the day of the dance.

My parents were in the dark about my plans, and it was quite nerve-racking, pretending I was going to a dance with Babs, Damian, and her siblings. This time, it was an unforgettable dance. And we were very happy, as Babs and Damian were such good company. During the dance, Geraldine came up to me and said, "Connie has fallen for you!" I looked at her askance, wondering why she told me this, knowing that Clifford and I were "going steady."

Clifford stayed at Bab's after the dance. I visited on the following day, and spent a short time there until it was time for him to take the midnight train. Connie and Geraldine were there too, and during lunch, Geraldine was blatantly flirtatious. She dated a couple of boyfriends, and was currently having an affair with a cousin.

She rolled her eyes, smirked, and asked him boldly, "what made you pick Dolly?" He just smiled, but did not respond. She hardly knew him, and he did not even speak to her, so I could not get over her audacity. When she asked Babs later, "How did *she* get such a nice boy?" Her envy was obvious.

in retrospect, I think she told me that Connie was interested in me, because she was keen on Clifford when she saw him.

That event, somewhere in September 1968, was our last dance together. And the events that occurred soon after, changed my life forever. When he held me, and kissed me goodbye that night, I had the strangest feeling that it was for the last time. I lay awake, listening to the lonely sound of a whistle blowing, as the train pulled out of the station.

Clifford and I met only a few times over the last couple of years, and so did not have much time to get to know each other really well. He was not one to express his feelings. And although his letters were full of loving sentiments, I felt he did not communicate his deepest thoughts and emotions. But that was just the way he was.

Chapter 38

Since that dance, Connie visited regularly, and we too were at Bab's quite often, as he wanted to teach me to waltz and jive. We spent time listening to popular music, and I learned how to waltz and jive with Connie. Babs and Damian teased me endlessly. They said Connie was in love with me, but I did not believe them. He was just an acquaintance, as far as I was concerned.

Connie travelled with me sometimes when I returned home from school. He scribbled notes in my books, and bought plantains for me. I did not take his attentions seriously, and thought he was just teasing me. He told me repeatedly, "All that glitters is not gold, and you can't know your mind at sixteen." He tried his best to convince me that Clifford was not the one for me.

When Shirani and I went for walks, I carved a large heart on hill sides, with the initials "CD" in the middle of it. One day, I noticed it was scratched out. I found out it was Connie, and could not believe he was so impudent.

The weeks slipped by without any other events, until Babs, Damian, Connie, Geraldine, Shirani, and I went for a supper dance at Bogowantalawa club on 18 November 1968.

Clifford could not make it for some reason. And although I was disappointed, I spent that evening laughing and joking at Bab's as we dressed up for the dance. Ammie and Thathie accompanied us to Mr Fernandez's place, where Clim joined us too. Bogowantalawa was not too far from their place. And amid much laughing and talking, we arrived at the club.

I dressed up in a long skirt of gold brocade, with a chiffon blouse, and a flower in my hair, which I wore in a beehive style. And I thought I looked quite grown up for my age. I glimpsed Nihal's erstwhile girlfriend, Dawn, dressed in a long, white, evening dress. She really lived it up that night, as she did the "shake, rattle and roll" with no inhibitions whatsoever.

I could not believe this was the same shrinking violet, who was so shy, that she hardly spoke two words to Nihal when they were together. They stopped corresponding after he left, and she seemed quite frivolous, and happy. We spoke Briefly, but did not mention Nihal.

Connie partnered me, because having taught me how to waltz and jive, he wanted to dance only with me all evening. He never gave anyone else a chance. That was how it all happened. He told me, "I fell in love with you when I first saw you with your long hair, and when you came up in your black coat and red hat, that was it! I was determined to get you!" He wooed me earnestly that night until he wore down my resistance. It may seem surprising that I changed my mind so quickly, and transferred my affections to Connie on such short acquaintance. But being sixteen, and susceptible to flattery, I went along with the tide.

He sat beside me on the train, and held my hand all the way home, much to the amusement of Babs and Damian. They believed this was the beginning of a new romance. But I was all mixed up emotionally, uncertain if this was the right decision. Connie was just the opposite of Clifford.

He stood five feet three inches tall, and was sturdy, with a broad face, strong features, brown eyes, and a very short neck. He dressed neatly, straight black hair combed to a side, and was full of good humour. Connie was garrulous too, and had no trouble expressing his feelings. I noticed though that his thoughts sometimes lagged far behind his tongue, as he blurted out anything that came to his mind. Now he paid extravagant compliments, and flattered me constantly, which was a new experience. It was quite an ego trip, and although I looked on this as a harmless flirtation, I had no idea he was deadly serious about this interlude. I had second thoughts already, and wondered how on earth I could extricate myself from his unwanted attentions. I should never have allowed him to encroach on me like this, I mused sadly.

Ammie was incredulous, and scolded me severely, "How can you give up Clifford for that short Connie? Stop your nonsense and tell Connie not to visit you anymore!" She had a soft spot for Clifford, and thought he was devoted to me. My parents referred to him as, "that short Connie" for a long time.

He was seven years older than me, and a very resolute young man, as he took advantage of an immature teenager. But I dreaded the thought of writing Clifford a "Dear John" letter. Connie persuaded me that we were *meant* for each other. And he had the added advantage of visiting me, without hindrance.

His catch phrase from then onwards was, "*If* you love me, you will write to Clifford immediately, and tell him to return all your letters!" I was to hear that phrase for many years. But I did not ask him to return my letters, as I was still very uncertain of my feelings. All that Connie did during those first few days, was follow me around like a lovesick adolescent, flattering me continuously. Babs told me, "Connie will treat you like a queen, and do everything for you, he's crazy about you, and I will be so happy to have you as a sister-in-law, and not our cousin, Lena." Needless to say, I was very pleased with such blatant adulation, and did not stop to think what I was getting into.

Babs invited Shirani and me for lunch the day after the dance, and we met most of the family. Connie's fifty year old mother, Freda, was of medium height, thickset, with a benevolent expression on her care-worn face. She was light-complexioned, with short, dark hair. Godwin, his father, was a thin, frail-looking gentleman in his late sixties, and a few inches shorter than his wife. He was bald, and light-complexioned too, with large, dark eyes, and a habitual, grumpy expression on his wizened face. He hardly spoke to me when we were introduced,

He worked as a clerk at the Tea Research Institute, in Talawakale, and was recently retired. Geraldine was dark-skinned, about four feet six inches tall, stumpy and bow-legged, with heavy features, and shoulder length, frizzy hair. Twelve year old Cristobel was cheeky, and amused me with her childish talk. She was very short too, with long, black hair, round face, dark eyes, and looked like an Indonesian.

She told me gravely, "Connie is heart-broken, because he was in love with our cousin, and she turned him down, as she already has a boyfriend." When Connie heard this, he was furious, and told his mother, "Mummy, tell that wretch to shut up! She's talking nonsense!"

I learnt later that it was true, as he tried his best to woo his Aunty Ella's eldest daughter, Lena. But she spurned him in favour of her long-time boyfriend. Aunty Ella was his mother's younger sister, and Connie still boarded at this aunt's place in Dehiwela. He was an apprentice draftsman at Thurairajah's, an architectural firm in Colombo.

The youngest member, Paul, was a naughty boy of about five. I did not talk much to the family, but they appeared to be friendly. Connie doted on his family, especially his mother. He told me that his eldest brother, Patrick (whose pet name was Cuckoo), was a Catholic priest, and lived in Berlin. And another brother, Roland (a year older than Connie), was a Christian Brother in Moratuwa (his pet name was Tucko). Geraldine was Jenny, Conrad was Connie, Cristobel, Bella; Barbara, Esme, and Wendy did not have pet names.

Esme, an older sister, was a nun in a convent in Negombo. When she was twenty, she fell in love with a cousin, but was forbidden to marry him. So she joined a nunnery, and remained one for ten years. His eldest sister, Wendy, was married to a planter, Brian, and they had two daughters, Sherone and Valerie. But I did not meet them on that occasion. He spoke in great detail about his siblings, parents, and relatives, so I gathered he was very close to his family.

Connie too was in a seminary for a few years, until he decided it was not for him, when he witnessed some Brothers behaving inappropriately with young boys. He giggled and said, "I couldn't have been a priest or a Brother, because I would have raped all the nuns!" I looked at him askance, but he was serious. And he said, "Daddy's one ambition was to see us all join religious orders. When I left the seminary, he locked the door, and didn't let me in, and Babs took me in through the back door."

I called his mother "Aunty" and his father "Uncle" as we addressed most adults then. Connie and I walked around the gardens and the lake below after lunch. He grabbed me clumsily and kissed me awkwardly. After fumbling around, he grinned, "I didn't hear any bells ring, did you?" And he giggled helplessly. I was embarrassed, and did not know how to respond. I was more determined than ever to end this fiasco. I did not feel any love for him then.

Babs laughingly said, "Daddy was shouting out, '*who* is that woman in a blue dress walking around with my son?' He's after a few drinks, so don't go near him Connie." I soon learnt that Connie's father was just as badly addicted to arrack as Thathie was.

A couple of days later, Connie peremptorily demanded Clifford's love letters, as he wanted to destroy them. I am not sure what made me hand over those treasured letters, but I did. And instead of destroying them, he read every single one of them, just to find out *exactly* what went on between us. When he had the audacity to tell me what he did, I was shocked, and thought it contemptible. It was such an invasion of my privacy, but he did not have any qualms about it.

This was a very confusing time, as I was completely trounced. I hardly had much time or space, to consider the full implication of this new state of affairs. At the beginning of our acquaintance, I thought Connie was quite nice and amusing, and liked him a little, but that was all I felt for him. I never knew he fell in love from the first time we met (as he claimed).

Clifford's letters remained unanswered over the next few weeks, and he wanted to know why I did not reply. But I was too cowardly to let him know what happened. My teenage infatuation was the most innocent affair, as I was very young and naïve. I idolised Clifford, and thought he was perfect in every way, as I was an incurable romantic then. So I imbued him with every noble quality. But doubts assailed me sometimes, whether he loved me as deeply. All teenagers endure the same process of falling in love for the very first time, and then face reality when the dream ends.

I was filled with apprehension when much against my will, Connie spoke to Thathie about his feelings for me. He told me, "I don't want to carry on with you in a clandestine manner, like Clifford. I want to get permission from your father and court you freely." Connie did not like cloak and dagger situations (he said), and was determined to ask Thathie's permission. Although Thathie restrained himself admirably until Connie left the house, he abused me verbally for getting involved with an unemployed man of twenty three.

I felt the earth rock beneath me. He appeared to be very tolerant while Connie was talking to him. But his mood changed abruptly the moment we were alone. He growled angrily, "You must concentrate on your studies, and get through exams, or else I'll put a stop to all this romantic nonsense. I tolerated Connie only because I don't want to offend Damian and Barbara, otherwise I would have told him to get out!" I knew Thathie regarded them kindly, and would not offend them.

Ammie was very annoyed with me for breaking up with Clifford, and scolded me for being heartless and fickle, as his letters arrived faithfully every week. Clifford requested heartbreaking, sentimental songs on late night programs on the radio, that I heard many times. Ammie reproached me even more for breaking up and hurting him.

I wished I could turn back the clock and make things right between us, but Connie was a dominant force that I could not withstand. He clung to me tenaciously, and insisted that I forget Clifford. He presented a smiling, besotted facade to the world, but when we were alone, he threatened me seriously. "I'll *kill* you if you ever leave me!" And being very naive, I believed he would carry out this terrible threat, if I broke off with him.

He frightened me when we were alone, and intimidated me sometimes. But when he realized how apprehensive I was, he quickly smiled and pretended everything was alright. In my quiet moments, I wept bitterly. I did not know what I got myself into, and racked my brain desperately to find a way out of this bewildering situation.

Connie alarmed me, as he practically coerced me into being his girlfriend, even though I was not very sure of myself. From the beginning, I glimpsed flashes of irrational behaviour, and jealousy, especially towards Clifford. What I could not understand was, why he pursued me so relentlessly, knowing I loved another. He pretended that I was in love with him too, and did not give me a chance to change my mind. Connie persisted in his daily visits, and took advantage of every moment.

Once, when we visited his Aunty Florrie in Talawakale, he sat in the back seat of the vehicle. He could not keep his hands off me, as his fingers were like hyperactive, groping tentacles. I was very uncomfortable, and shoved him away. Clifford and I held hands, and shared a few kisses, that was all, but Connie was very bold and forceful.

When we returned home, he withdrew into a cocoon, and refused to talk to me. When I asked, "What's wrong?" he replied, "I shouldn't have got involved with you." I was so surprised, that I told Babs about his perplexing behaviour. She said, "Oh, that's Connie alright. He's very moody, just ignore him."

I went home and shed angry tears, and could not believe he was such a cad. He broke up my affair with Clifford, groped me all evening, and then told me that he should not have got involved with me. Babs, Damian, and Connie came around ten o'clock that night. Connie grinned sheepishly, as he sidled up to me. "I'm sorry Dolla, I was in a bad mood. Won't happen again." Obviously, Babs spoke to him, and made him apologise. I was at a loss to fathom his moods.

Christmas came along before I knew it. Babs visited early one morning and said that Damian was transferred to Kataboola Estate, near Gampola. They left within a few weeks after this, and we spent a quiet Christmas at home. Connie was with his family, who rented a house in Gourawila, near Hatton.

Rosanne and Derry visited one evening, and we decided to sing carols, and distribute lollies to all the little children in the tea estate and surrounding areas. We asked local people for donations, and bought heaps of lollies. We packed them in small bags, and Rosanne dressed up as Santa. She carried a sack full of lollies on her back, and we walked around the neighbourhood. I played carols on the accordion, while the others followed around, singing as loudly as possible.

It was good fun, and we came home, pleased that we made a few children happy with bags of lollies. Later on though, much to their amusement, I was intoxicated, after gulping down a glass of Ammie's home-made beetroot wine. I bawled my eyes out, and lamented bitterly for breaking up with Clifford so foolishly. Thathie heard me, and sternly bid me to stop crying and go to bed.

New Year 1969 dawned quietly, and our lives meandered steadily, without any perceptible changes. My parents never invited him to stay overnight, whenever Connie visited. So, much to his chagrin, he returned to Gourawila very late at nights.

When Lakshman and Nilanthi visited once, Ammie decided to go back with them. Connie, who was visiting, was not invited. And on our way to Mayfield, Lakshman dropped him near Aunty Florrie's place. It was very late at night, and Connie told me he was terrified, as he had to pass a cemetery on his way. He was very upset because my parents treated him indifferently. They did not encourage him in any way, but he continued to visit often.

A few weeks later, when Lakshman and Nilanthi visited us again, she cried broken-heartedly. She told Ammie that Lakshman was constantly abusing her verbally about Thathie's "disgrace" and resorted to physical violence too. Thathie, who was after a couple of drinks, eavesdropped in the adjoining room. He roared like a wounded lion and attacked Lakshman, who utterly astonished, keeled over when Thathie pushed him down angrily.

They came to blows, and Thathie yelled out angrily, "How *dare* you ill-treat my daughter, and abuse her because of my mistakes?" It was a ludicrous but pathetic sight, to see the two men struggling. Thathie, helpless as a tiny sprat, wrestled with Lakshman, who was like a giant octopus, with long, sinewy arms, and trunk-like legs. We soon parted them, and Lakshman shouted out angrily, "Nilanthi, *get* in the car!" and hugging Tamara fearfully, she left.

He was furious with Nilanthi for talking about their marital problems with her parents. But his atrocious behaviour towards her did not change. They did not visit us for some time after that incident. Nilanthi wrote or phoned us at the station. We did not have a phone in the house, so whenever she called, one of the porters ran over with a message, and then we had a long chat.

Once, when I was at Mayfield, Babs invited Nilanthi, Lakshman, and me for lunch to Kataboola, as Connie was there too, so we had a nice time. After lunch, Connie spent a couple of hours showing me his family album, and pointed out every single family member and relative. He thought I found them just as interesting as he did. But halfway through, I did not know who was who. It was a peculiar way for a boyfriend to behave, I thought, as he was more absorbed in his family album than in entertaining me.

It was a beautiful scenic area though, and we walked beside a broad, winding river in the twilight, just as a large, golden moon appeared over the horizon. We returned home after ten o'clock that night.

I contemplated finding a job in Colombo, as I re-sat my exam, and the results were good. And I still toyed with the idea of becoming a stenographer in some firm. I passed shorthand and typing, with two distinctions in English language and literature; credit passes in history, religious knowledge, and passes in three other subjects. But these results were still inadequate to continue higher studies, so I abandoned the idea of re-sitting the exam to get more credits, as I now wanted a job.

Connie visited on 20 July 1969, and we sat glued to the radio for hours, until the announcer finally exclaimed excitedly, "Neil Armstrong has *landed* on the moon!" What an incredible sensation that was! The first man to land on the moon. We could hardly credit our ears, that this great event was realized in our life time. Neil Armstrong's words were played over and over again, "One small step for a man, but a giant leap for mankind!" We were elated, and stayed up till very late that night.

I persisted in sending job applications weekly, only to receive negative responses, due to my lack of experience, and youth. One day however, I was overjoyed when Zeniths, an advertising agency in Colombo, called me for an interview. I was excited, and Thathie was happy too, as he wanted me to do something useful, so he accompanied me to Colombo.

We met Geraldine and Esme on the train. Esme was Connie's older sister, who was just out of the nunnery after ten years. In her thirties, she resembled his mother closely; with similar features, but very short, and plump, like two dumplings joined in the middle. She was quite friendly and conversational though, and said she was happy I was Connie's girlfriend, as she did like him courting their cousin.

I ignored Connie's plea not to apply for a job in Colombo, or anywhere else, because he was dead set against my going to work. I was fast learning that in spite of his jokes, and light-hearted ways, he was very obstinate, and jealous beyond reason.

But being a strong-minded person too, and still not completely under his thumb, I was determined to find employment, whether he liked it or not. It was strange that he still held such old-fashioned notions, that a girl should stay home until she married. His two older sisters, and his cousin, whom he courted, did just that, so he wanted me to follow suit.

Mr Fernando, the manager, told me I was selected out of twenty applicants. And he asked me to start almost immediately. Although I did not have much experience at interviews, I was enthusiastic and bright. Mr Silva, the copywriter at Zeniths, was a pleasant, middle-aged gentleman. He told me later, that when I breezed in through the door, oozing confidence, and with a big smile on my face, all the staff agreed, "*She* is the one who'll get the job."

I started my first job as a stenographer there. Thathie quickly contacted one of his old friends, the station master at Wellawatte, a busy, seaside town. And he arranged for me to board there. They wanted hundred rupees a month, and the wife provided breakfast and dinner. Breakfast was always a thick slab of bread, with butter and jam. I took sandwiches for lunch, but dinner was usually a good meal of rice and curry.

Shirani spent a few days with me, and my first taste of independence was exhilarating, except for the fact that Thathie instructed the station master and his family, not to allow Connie to visit me. The wife was a plump, good-natured woman, with no other interest in her mundane life besides the kitchen, and her husband's welfare.

I thought her husband was a chauvinist, who lounged all evening, while his large, overweight, teenage daughter read newspapers to him, or massaged his temples when he was unwell. She kept him company every evening. I discovered that the daughter slept in his bed, and not his wife, who slept in a separate room.

The son was equally podgy, and short like his mother and sister. He was an obnoxious boy of about thirteen years. And I had to live with these utter strangers, who had stranger habits. As I was at work all day, and stayed in my room minding my own business after dinner, I did not have to socialise with them. I found great solace playing my piano accordion, and once, Nelune and I applied to audition for the "Maliban Talent Quest" on radio.

Thathie and Connie accompanied us to the studio, where we auditioned successfully, and were selected to perform on one of the forthcoming shows. I sang

"The Great Pretender" by the Platters, and accompanied myself on the accordion, while Nelune played drums.

They recorded our performance, to be played a few weeks later. And ever since then, Connie demanded, "*Why* did you sing that *particular* song?" He was not happy at all. But a few months later, he auditioned as well, and sang, 'Visions' by Cliff Richards. They played it on the show a few weeks later. He had a good voice, but he was nervous, and quavered slightly.

Shirani, Bernard (a young man who was seeing Shirani then), Connie, and I were returning after a movie one Saturday afternoon, when the two plump brats spied us walking down the lane. The fat boy chortled gleefully in Sinhalese, "Ah, Baduth ekka, horu!" (caught the thieves with stolen goods). I was very annoyed at his cheek, and knew he would sneak to his father.

My parents decided to leave Watagoda, and rent a house in Kelaniya, so that Nelune and I could travel from home. They were alone in that sad, empty house, and decided it was time to move on. Thathie's case was still not finalised, and he lived in limbo, uncertain of his future. He did not apply for any other job, until he knew the outcome.

Nelune, who was still boarded in Kandy, now wanted to attend Holy Family Convent in Bambalapitiya, where I tried to get in once. She was in year ten, and I was happy when Nelune was accepted, and excelled in her studies.

Most of our furniture, and some items, were soon sold. And in early August 1969, we moved into a comfortable, three bed-room house in Kelaniya.

Connie and I went to the movies straight after work on Saturday afternoons. And coincidentally, Thurairajah's office, was a few blocks from Zeniths. Mr Fernando saw me one day, as I walked back to work with Connie, after my lunch break. Later that day, he called me to his office, and questioned me mockingly. "*How* did you find a boyfriend here so *quickly*?" When I told him I knew Connie already, he was even more surprised, and demanded nastily, "Did you apply for this job for *that* reason?" I did not reply, as I blushed in confusion.

Mr Fernando was a tall, swarthy, intimidating man, with small, black eyes, and a walrus moustache. He was brutal whenever he was crossed. I saw hapless young executives, and artists break down miserably under his barrage of verbal abuse. I knew how to keep out of his way, and spoke only if the boss spoke to me, and I gained experience in the ways of the world. The first few months at Zeniths were good, because, like all work places, I met some nice people, and some who were not so nice.

Being naïve, I did not ingratiate myself to the boss, or his second-in-charge, Mrs Dean, a tall, dark, forceful lady, who made up in boldness what she lacked in looks. She wore a sari way down her midriff, exposing rolls of fat on her hips and non-existent waistline. All the other female employees crawled up to her with fulsome compliments, and hung onto her words. But not me, I *had* to be different, so I soon paid the price.

The male employees too, thought I was young and innocent. They flirted with me, but a few discouraging stares and words kept them at bay. Connie phoned me daily. And Colleen, the receptionist, an inquisitive, sharp-witted girl, listened in to all our conversations, and teased me endlessly.

We engaged in frequent quarrels, because of Connie's extreme jealousy. Whenever we argued, Colleen made sure she heard the whole conversation, so she could repeat every detail. I did not know I made enemies so soon, and provided Mr Fernando with negative feedback about me.

Mr Silva, the copywriter, was a good person. I soon discovered he was a qualified journalist, who founded the Ceylon College of Journalism. I was very keen to take up that course, and soon enrolled to study by correspondence, and kept busy in the evenings. I paid modest instalments out of my wages, which was about two hundred rupees monthly.

It was great to be at home in my own room again, even though Shirani, Nelune, and I shared one large bedroom, and our parents, another room at the front of the house.

Thathie dressed in his white station master's uniform, wore his cap, and pretended to go to work every morning. He wanted the landlord (who lived opposite), to believe he was still employed. We learnt later on, that the landlord was aware of Thathie's situation, but played along with his subterfuge, just to save him embarrassment.

Thathie travelled by bus several times, with a hot, home-cooked meal, and stood outside my office until it was lunchtime. I was very moved when I saw him standing in the scorching sun, with a parcel in his hand. He smiled and told me that Ammie wanted me to have a warm meal at lunch time. My parents did so much to please me. In turn, I tried to be dutiful too. And I contributed whatever I could towards the rent, and so did Shirani, who was employed at a florist's in Colombo.

Chapter 39

Mr Fernando re-located the office premises a couple of months later. And as I was the youngest member in the team, I had the honour of lighting oil lamps and serving milk rice. It was a tradition, whenever a change of residence, or any major event occurred in a family. Although I liked working at Zenith's, I soon discovered about some rorts that went on whenever competitions were held. For instance, some employees actually put their own names in winning envelopes, and did some dishonest things, which appalled me.

Mrs Dean did not like my beehive hair style (I heard), and so, Mr Fernando called me to his office one morning, and growled, "You must let your hair down, as your hairdo is too high!" He summoned me to take dictation sometimes, and then asked, "How do you like it here?" I replied, "It's alright, except I like to practice shorthand more, and there isn't enough typing to keep me busy all day."

To my surprise, he grunted unpleasantly, "That's the exact opposite of what I've heard! I'm told you don't work fast enough!" I looked at him in disbelief, and left his office with angry tears stinging my eyes. Colleen asked me what was wrong, and when I told her, she whispered knowingly. "When some of them don't complete their work, they blame you for not getting the typing done in time, and sneak to Mr Fernando that you are slack." I was lost for words at such despicable behaviour. A few months later, ten of us were made redundant, due to cost cutting, and so ended my first job.

Thathie was forced to take early retirement, and was granted a pension. Ammie somehow managed to feed us well, with Shirani and me contributing towards the rent. But when I stopped work, I could not help financially.

Thathie still drank heavily, and whenever Connie visited, I faced angry scenes after he left, as my parents were not happy that he visited daily.

The constant nagging made me very sad and angry, and I wished I could find another job soon, so I could be independent. Also, Connie's insane jealousy wore me down. He demanded to know how I spent every minute of the day; where I went, whom I saw etc. etc. I felt like a butterfly pinned down, and fluttered my wings desperately to escape the emotional stranglehold.

Shirani was seeing Bernard, whom she met in Welimada a few months ago. He was in his early thirties, quite tall, and wore square, black-framed spectacles. Bernard had a strong, baritone voice, and he sang popular ballads to entertain us. He visited Shirani once at Watagoda, and since then, they were going steady. The four of us went for movies sometimes, and when we returned, Thathie waited for us, drunk and abusive. Connie and Bernard left as quietly as possible on those occasions.

Rosie visited Ceylon, and she soon cut my hair to a shoulder length bob, which made Connie furious, as he always admired my long hair and told me. "I fell for your long hair!" He sulked about it for days, and was really mad at Rosie for cutting my hair. But I liked it very much, as it was easier to manage.

She could not believe I broke off with Clifford, and asked me, "Why did you do it Dolly? He was your first love, and you were so much in love. Connie is very possessive of you, I can see, and he's too old for you anyway." Once when we travelled on a bus, Rosie overheard our conversation, as Connie demanded, "What are you thinking of? Tell me!" And I retorted irritably, "Why, do you want to analyse me?" Rosie thought it was hilarious, and teased me. "Ha, ha, so you don't want Connie to analyse you?" If ever I was pensive, or did not want to talk, he pounced on me and demanded, "Are you thinking of that bugger? What are you thinking about?" Rosie did not believe I was serious about him, and warned me about his extreme jealousy. I told her I had no intention of getting engaged to him, and not to worry about me, as I hoped to extricate myself from this unwholesome affair very soon.

Although I kept applying for several jobs, I was unsuccessful, and I became quite frustrated. So many teenagers were looking for employment, and I was just one among thousands, who had limited work experience.

I now had to contend with a disruptive home life, and a possessive boyfriend, who did not like me going out anywhere without him. He was very pleased I did not work now. Because he had no idea I wanted to find something challenging, and meaningful in my life. Fortunately, I was busy studying journalism, which was a two year course. I sat up till all hours every night, writing short stories, articles, and poems that reflected my youthful experiences and observations.

I still perused job vacancies columns diligently, and continued to apply for various positions. And one day, I was called for an interview at the Ceylon Broadcasting Corporation. It was a secretarial position, and I liked the idea of working in the media. I got ready happily on the day, but Connie insisted that he accompanied me. He was very unhappy and negative about my interview, and nagged me all the way and repeated, "It's not a nice place for a young girl to work in." I tried hard to ignore his unhelpful comments, and concentrate on the forthcoming interview. When the bus stopped in front of the building, I was surprised to see a long line of about fifty hopeful young girls and boys waiting to be interviewed.

I stood in line and waited patiently, but Connie kept hissing in my ear, "*If* you love me, you will *not* go for this interview! *Prove* that you love me!" This was the sort of persuasive talk I listened to for over an hour. My resolve weakened with his constant badgering. I wondered how to get through an interview in such emotional turmoil.

Finally, as the line grew shorter, and I looked at Connie's determined face, I relented, and walked away. He was overjoyed. I did not speak to him all the way home. But he was all smiles, and in a good mood, now that he got his own way. I proved how pliable I was. I do not know why I allowed him to take control, as I should have sent him about his business. He knew he could persuade me to do his bidding from then on. I did not apply for any more jobs after that episode.

Babs and Damian considered immigrating to Australia. Connie too talked about joining them someday. Ammie felt threatened and sad when she heard about this new development. When I was sitting at the dining table one day, writing one of my stories, Ammie, stopped her sweeping, came up to me, and burst into tears. She placed her hands on my shoulders and sobbed, "I always thought that someday when you were grown up, I could live with you and get away from Thathie! Now, I don't even have that hope, if you go to Australia with Connie."

I felt very sad for Ammie, but did not realise how much she meant it, and what she suffered daily. Thathie was a good, kind man, but when he drank, he was impossible to live with, as he became abusive, and insulted all and sundry.

Malcolm visited that Christmas in 1969, and he met Connie at Granny's place. He told me later, "Connie is a nice young man," and took to him kindly. Granny and Marie liked him too, because he was a Catholic Burgher, and were glad I broke up with Clifford.

It was a fairly quiet Christmas, and Connie celebrated the season with his family. Marie and Neville, who were engaged for some time, wanted to get married in mid-January 1970, and great preparations were underway.

The reception was at Sesatha Hotel in Colombo, and they invited every single relative and friend on both sides. I wore a cream brocade "shift" dress, with matching gloves that I borrowed from the lady next door. She lived in England for some time, and had nice clothes, gloves, and accessories. When she saw my dress, she immediately offered me a pair of elegant gloves to complete my outfit.

Connie too was invited, and I thought the wedding ceremony was impressive. Marie looked lovely, and her face glowed. The grand reception was everything they expected. Granny and Grandpa were very proud of Marie, as she glided around gracefully, conversing with guests. Shirani, Connie and I left the reception early, and as we walked to Granny's house, Bernard suddenly strutted down the road.

Shirani broke up with him a few weeks ago, and he said he came to ask his ring back. He was nasty, and glared at us aggressively. We were sorry for him, but we could not help him, as she told us he drank too much, was abusive, and they were incompatible. Shirani returned his ring, and that was the end of that affair.

Babs and Damian planned to leave at the end of January 1970. Connie, who was a devoted brother, told me he would miss Babs and Damian very much, as he was very close to them. He doted on his mother unashamedly, and always spoke lovingly of her, and his family members. But he was not close to his father. None of his siblings were close to him either, as he was a taciturn, grumpy old man, fond of drinking alone every evening, as I discovered later. The children clung to their mother, and depended on her solely for their emotional needs.

The day of their departure arrived swiftly. Connie's family stayed in a hotel in Colombo until they left. We went for a dinner dance the night before, and I met Wendy and Brian for the first time, and his brother Roland. He was Connie's double, except that he was about two inches taller, and rounder than Connie. And he appeared to be quite friendly and polite.

Brian was a planter on Mahacoodagala Estate, close to Nuwara Eliya. He was tall, bulky, and very quiet. He sported a clipped moustache, and wore thick spectacles. He smiled vaguely, but stayed in the background most of the time. Wendy, on the other hand, was very cheerful, and in her mid-thirties, and somewhat over-weight. She was pretty, with delicate features, fair-complexioned, and had wavy brown hair. Their two children, ten year old Sherone, and eight year old Valerie, were quiet little girls.

Wendy was of average height, and taller than the rest of the family. Esme, Geraldine, Mr and Mrs de Sielvie, Cristobel, and Paul, were all present. Connie and I joined them next day, and accompanied them to the airport. It was very sad to see them leave, as they were very close to Babs and Damian. We waited until the plane vanished among the clouds.

Connie wanted to immigrate to Australia now. I did not even consider such an idea, as I did not intend to get married so soon, and leave Ceylon. I was turning eighteen that February, and in my mind, I had many years ahead before I got married.

My parents still not approve of Connie. Ammie nagged me constantly whenever he visited and left in the evenings. She threw a plate of rice at me once, and struck me violently, because I argued with her over some trivial matter. It was uncharacteristic of her to be physically abusive, but I did not realize then how much pressure she was undergoing with Thathie's drinking. But after that incident, I decided I had enough, and wanted to leave home, as my pride was deeply wounded.

Connie turned up regular as sunrise every evening after work, in spite of a frosty reception, and Thathie's verbal abuse, after one too many. One day, I told Nelune I was fed up with all the scolding, and the stressful life at home, and wanted to visit Nilanthi for a brief respite. I wanted to have some time alone, and break off with Connie, as he was too dominant and jealous, for my liking.

For some vague reason, I believed my parents would refuse to let me visit Nilanthi, and so I did not ask them permission. I told Connie instead, and he said he wanted to accompany me to Hatton, and then travel on to visit his parents in Nuwara Eliya, where they now lived in a rented house. Call it youthful pride and rebellion, but I just wanted to get away without my parents knowledge. Had they known Connie was accompanying me, they would immediately stop me travelling with him.

Strangely enough, I did not even call Nilanthi, or drop a line to ask her if she was home that day. A few days after my eighteenth birthday, I packed up some clothes in a small cardboard box, as I did not have a small suitcase. Next morning, around five o'clock, Nelune accompanied me to the bus terminal at Kelaniya. Now just to make me laugh, she carried the small box on her head (coolie style), which did amuse me, and I could not help giggling at her antics.

I boarded a bus to Fort Station, but panicked when I got off, as I did not have a train ticket, and waited anxiously for Connie to turn up. He arrived twenty minutes later. He was never on time for anything, which irked me now. It was a consoling thought that I out-witted my parents, I looked forward to a peaceful sojourn at Mayfield, without Connie's suffocating presence, and my parents nagging. My conscience was lulled, as I told Nelune to inform my parents I had gone to Nilanthi's.

The train was fairly crowded, but after an uneventful journey, we boarded a bus in Hatton, and arrived at Mayfield at about six o'clock in the evening. A grinning servant greeted us with the news that Nilanthi and Lakshman left for Colombo that very same morning. Talk about fickle fate overturning plans of mice and men.

I went into extreme panic mode. I could not return home that night, as it would be dawn when I arrived. And if my parents knew Connie accompanied me, hell would be a cooler place. I could not stay alone at Mayfield, with only a male servant as chaperone either. I was in a quandary, and my thoughts raced wildly. Connie suggested that I travel with him to his parents home, and then decide what to do.

Uncle found employment as a clerk in a tea estate close to Nuwara Eliya, where they rented a house. It was the only practical solution, but one with momentous consequences. I was thrown headlong into a series of unfortunate events that sealed my fate inexorably. And there was no turning back from then onwards.

I trudged back wearily to the bus stop on the main road. I sat in the bus and gazed at the gloomy night through the grimy window. And my pensive reflection mirrored the inner tumult I was going through. Little did I realize I had no control over forthcoming events that shaped my destiny. I questioned fate for the rest of my life. Why did this happen, when all I wanted was to extricate myself from Connie's tenacious hold. It must be some divine jest, and who was I to rail against the Gods.

In the meantime, Nilanthi and Lakshman arrived in Colombo that same night. When Nelune told them I went to Mayfield, they had no idea about my plans to visit. Now they all panicked, and jumped to the conclusion that Connie and I must have eloped. I suppose they cannot be blamed for thinking the worst, as that was how it seemed. Only Connie and I knew it was the last thing on our minds, when we boarded a train on that fateful day.

Connie's parents lived in a rented house called "Lilybourne." It was situated on a hillock, and was a spacious house, with about five bedrooms, a large kitchen and living area. Two lodgers occupied the front room, and a tiny room adjoined the kitchen at the back of the house, which Connie converted into his bedroom. Paul and Cristobel were the only ones living with his parents then.

When we arrived very late that night, his parents were in bed already, and I was thoroughly embarrassed at my predicament. But Aunty was very understanding, when Connie explained what happened, and what a quandary I was in, as my parents would think we eloped. Uncle did not comment at all, and just mumbled under his breath. He was not very pleased.

Aunty accompanied me to the convent adjoining the church next morning, and I agreed to board there for a while until the dust settled down. She explained to Mother Superior about my parents, and if I could stay for some time. The nun was all kindness, and agreed to keep me for a nominal fee. She showed me a closet-sized bedroom furnished with a single bed and one small table.

Connie's parents were good to me, especially his mother, whom I liked very much from the start. Although his father was a quiet man, he too was kind in his own way. When he knew me better, he grew very fond of me, and the feeling was mutual.

Now I looked out and glimpsed the church roof from my window. I composed myself after while, sat at the table, and wrote about these harrowing events in my note book. Then I wrote letters to Ammie, and the rest of the family, explaining exactly what happened. I hoped they would understand, as I did not mean to leave home permanently in such a clandestine manner.

The garden and surroundings of the convent were very peaceful, and after the turmoil at home, I was happy to find peace. A sense of isolation and emotional solitude commenced from then. I did not socialise with the other girls and young women who boarded there, as I was embarrassed to tell anyone the reason why I was here. Because everyone believed I eloped, and was hiding from my parents.

I suppose in the eyes of the world, that was exactly how it looked, but only I knew I did not elope. I felt physically sick, just thinking how I compromised myself, when all I wanted was respite from Connie, and a means of extricating myself out of a complicated situation. I felt very lonely and desperate at times, and cried myself to sleep every night, cut off from family and social contact. Connie returned to Colombo the very next day, and stayed at his Aunt's place, as he was still working in Colombo.

I had a letter from Ammie, in response to mine a week later, as I told her that I was staying in a convent. Ammie wrote to the nuns immediately, saying that all those stories I told them about parental opposition were untrue, and they wanted me to return. After reading Ammie's letter, Mother Superior called me to her office and advised me. "You have only known Conrad for one year, and you should consider going back home, without rushing into anything you will regret later on!" Wise words, but how little youth heeds the voice of experience and reason.

I was very uncomfortable after this discussion, and a few days later, when Connie and Aunty visited, I returned to Lilybourne. He was angry with me for no apparent reason, and scowled as he hissed, "We'll take this *misery* home Mummy." He stopped working at Thurairajah's office, and hoped to find employment in Nuwara Eliya.

I noticed the change in Connie immediately, as he became a total stranger. I did not know what bipolar meant then, but I soon discovered Connie's split personality. I now thought of him as "Doctor Jekyll And Mr Hyde." Although I experienced his bouts of extreme jealousy and anger before, overall he appeared to be a carefree, light-hearted person. Now he was an angry, sullen stranger, which confused and hurt me deeply. I could not believe I was so utterly deceived in his true character that he masked so well all this time.

When he coerced me into being his girlfriend, he was adoring, gentle, and humble in his behaviour towards me, pretending my wish was his command. But now he unmasked, and I witnessed a totally different character.

Whether real or imaginary, he aired all the slights he suffered at my parents' hands. I did not realize how deeply he resented their treatment of him. Every time he argued with me, he shouted, "You are like your *father*! Remember how he treated me when I came to visit you?" I retorted, "But he didn't abuse you or beat you up!

What else did you expect my father to do? He was only protecting his daughter."
So it went on, and he became more possessive, and insanely jealous beyond belief.

Once, when we visited his elderly Aunty Florrie, whose wrinkled face resembled an old chimpanzee, Connie blurted out, "Damn disgrace Dolly, Aunty Florrie looks younger than you!" I asked him later why he said that, and he just giggled inanely. "I wanted to make Aunty Florrie happy." Bewildered, and under enormous pressure at what befell us so unexpectedly, we squabbled constantly. I was a hyper-sensitive teenager, and was easily hurt. But after every stormy episode, he insisted he loved me, and cared for me deeply. I tried to excuse his insane behaviour. Perhaps this unforeseen situation we found ourselves in through no fault or plan of ours, accounted for his anger and frustration.

Aunty, who witnessed our constant quarrels, consoled me, "Connie's behaving like this because he has no job, but once he finds a job and gets married, he will be fine." I wanted to believe her assurances. Meanwhile, Ammie wrote disparaging letters about Connie, and caused us endless trouble. But I replied I did not care what they said, and became more obstinate when they criticized him.

Once again, my parents forced me to do the exact opposite of what they wanted. Finally, they wrote that they wanted to talk to me, before I did anything foolish.

Chapter 40

My parents were absolutely furious and shattered at what happened, but the more they insisted I returned home, the more obstinate I became, and did not want to face the inevitable repercussions. It was a very sad and bitter period, because I was just an angry, rebellious teenager.

I had no one to turn to for guidance, and help to assess my situation with clarity. All I could think of was, the scolding and censure I would be subjected to, if I returned home. And I certainly did not want to go back like a lamb. The alternative was to tolerate Connie's irrational behaviour, and hope he would change in time. It was not a great choice either way.

Connie, who corresponded regularly with Babs, now decided that the only solution was to immigrate to Australia. And his parents too agreed that it would be best to get married, and immigrate as soon as possible. Although I was too young and inexperienced to make such a hasty decision about such a serious step, I did not stop to consider the consequences. I was convinced it was impossible for me to return home, because the world thought the worst of me. We did not live together as a married couple, and slept in separate rooms, but we knew that the world thought otherwise.

I could hardly bear the humiliation of my situation, being a very sensitive, idealistic teenager. And I had to decide which was the lesser of the two evils facing me. So I allowed myself to be swept along in this inexorable tide that sealed my fate. We decided to get married. Connie's parents consulted a lawyer, who was a family friend. He took one look at me, and exclaimed, "This girl looks only about *twelve* years old!" He could not believe I was eighteen. I wore my hair in pig tails, and perhaps that too would have accounted for my youthful appearance.

Connie looked for jobs in any capacity around Nuwara Eliya town, and knocked on every door, but to no avail. He helped his parents with all the odd jobs around the house; carried bags of rice from the market, and did their grocery shopping too. He lugged umpteen kettles of boiling water to fill bathtubs for his father, or for the two lodgers, as they did not have running hot water. He was a very hardworking and determined man in everything he did.

We even designed greeting cards one day. I painted pictures on the front of the cards with coloured texta pens, and composed verses, which Connie wrote out in his neat fist. We sold those cards to some shops, including Cargill's, for about twelve rupees a dozen. It was a great feeling of achievement when we received payment for our combined efforts, and then we spent our earnings on movie tickets. We spent several hours on this enterprise each day, and produced hundreds of cards over the next few months.

Somewhere towards the end of March, Connie bought me an amethyst ring, surrounded with white sapphires. I designed the ring, which was a replica of Ammie's engagement ring, which I always admired. We went to church one day and asked the priest to bless us, and considered ourselves engaged.

Nilanthi visited me once, and tried to convince me to return home, but I was adamant and turned a deaf ear to her pleas. The following months were dreadful and traumatic, to say the least. I was becoming increasingly upset, and concerned over our endless altercations over some trivial matter or another. And I was nonplussed, as I did not provoke him, or ignite the short fuse of his inexplicable bad temper, which was always on the verge of exploding.

After a particularly stormy scene one day, I decided to leave. When my parents visited and pleaded with me to return, while Ammie cried her eyes out, I felt so bad and guilty, that I agreed to go back to Mayfield with them. They did not come inside the house, but stayed out on the road.

I did not tell Connie, or his family that I wanted to visit my parents, because he would have stopped me. I just boarded a bus with them, and breathed a sigh of relief that I was escaping a soul-destroying relationship.

Thathie did not say anything to me when we arrived at Mayfield, but he travelled to Mutha's and Athamma's place, where he stayed for some time. Ammie was very sad and angry. She nagged me constantly for being stubborn, and throwing caution to the winds in my determination to marry Connie. He phoned me daily, cried broken-heartedly, and begged me to come back, and threatened to kill himself if I did not return.

He declared he would never let me go, that he loved me truly, and was sorry for all the times he hurt me, and so on. Just like all lovers do when they kiss and make up. He wanted to get married quickly, and promised that all would be well once we married and immigrated. I replied, "Why don't you go first, settle down, find a job, and then I can join you later on." But he was adamant, and said, "I will never leave without you!"

Granny came over once when Connie visited me at Mayfield, because he wanted to convince me that I should return and get married. When she heard him, she exclaimed, "You can't marry Dolly! She's too young, and she doesn't know how to cook, or sew or do anything!" I was annoyed, and then Connie started an argument, which ended with my tossing his engagement ring back. He was forced to leave alone that day.

I was caught in a tug-of-war between my family and Connie. But I was still very confused, and spinning around in a whirlwind of emotions. He applied enormous pressure to get married and immigrate. When I weighed the positive factors in this situation, I envisaged a better future in a new country, rather than the bleak one I faced at home, or in Nuwara Eliya. I decided it was better to start life in a new country.

I was weary, and my resistance was low with Connie's daily barrage, so one day, I just packed up my clothes and said I was visiting some friends in Hatton. Connie met me at the station, and we returned to his parents home. Aunty was happy to see me, and she constantly assured me that once we were married, and Connie had a regular job, he would be fine. She said we would get along without so many arguments and difficulties. I believed her implicitly, as I was still very naive.

I soon discovered it was just an illusion, like all youthful hopes and dreams. Because no one can change their *essential* character and behaviour. Although they can deceive for a while, their true self will emerge in the end. What I experienced briefly at Mayfield, convinced me that I could not retrace my steps and go back either.

I no longer had a home to go back to, as my parents vacated the house in Kelaniya. And sometime later, they rented a house in Maharagama. The mere thought of facing Thathie's drunken behaviour every evening, was very depressing. I had no one to confide in. And no one understood that the more they tried to bully me, the more obstinate I became, and did just the opposite.

I can only wonder at my resilience even as a teenager, because I did not break down under the mental strain, and instead, continued with my studies in journalism. I wrote short stories, and articles, and completed my assignments in the evenings. Perhaps writing was my salvation then, and helped me retain my equilibrium through that dark period. I gave vent to my emotions through my creativity. At least it relieved the frustrating situation I was hurtled into. I did not have my much loved piano accordion any longer, as I did not carry that with me when I left. So, without musical or artistic outlets now, I only had my writing.

I soon discovered that Uncle, in some ways, was worse than Thathie after drinks. He was as quiet as a mouse all day, and went to work without uttering one word to his wife or children. But every evening, after a few drinks of arrack, all I heard was his constant grumbling, and cursing until he fell asleep.

Aunty had a habit of dithering around in her dressing gown all morning. And when it was time for Uncle to come home for lunch, she invariably rushed around trying to prepare something in a hurry. She quickly served him a plate of rice, and half-cooked curries.

He always came home for lunch, as he worked close by, and even though she knew his routine, lunch was never ready on time. By now I was in the habit of helping her with the preparation of the meal; scraping coconut, washing rice, peeling onions, and garlic, and generally speeding up the cooking process. This daily mismanagement of time, was a sore point with Uncle. And fortified with a few stiff drinks, he got his own back every evening with a string of abuse and complaints.

He complained about food all the time, "Is *this* a bloody meal for a man to eat? Bloody *bitch*! She's drinking all the arrack!" Aunty retorted angrily, "Shut your mouth Sweeta! I only had one drink!" Connie, Cristobel, Paul, and I melted into the background, quiet as mice, until they sorted out their differences.

Uncle rarely joined the family at dinner time, but stayed in his room drinking and cursing. Sometimes he banged on the bedroom door and yelled, "Come and say the rosary you *sinners*! You are living in *sin*!" Aunty rushed forward to my defence. "Leave them alone Sweeta, Dolly is a good girl, they are not doing anything wrong!" How much I hated those times!

One evening, while Connie poured boiling water into a plastic container, and placed it on a shelf, he accidentally spilled some on my head, as I was sitting on a low stool in the kitchen. I yelled out in pain, and he hissed angrily, "Be *quiet*! You want Daddy to hear you and come here to find out what's going on?" I stifled my groans, and Aunty placed cold tea leaves on my scalp to stop blisters forming.

Aunty filled me in with all the family gossip, and I knew everything about everyone. Connie heard her one day, scowled at me and said, "*Don't* tell these bitches and bastards about *our* family Mummy!" That was how he referred to me and his in-laws.

Uncle was well-known in the parish for his devout habit of attending church every Sunday. And he carried a cross to all the sick people and prayed for them, and Aunty joined him in these good works too. But his behaviour at home in the evenings, and the way he treated his wife, were totally opposite to his pious facade. It was something I never understood.

Geraldine visited a friend in Maharagama, and then met Clifford. She chatted him up, and before long they started dating, although she was a few years older than him. And in a matter of months they were engaged, as she hoped to immigrate soon, and sponsor Clifford. Connie's family knew about their affair. But Connie and I were the last ones to know, until they turned up one day, and took us by complete surprise.

This unexpected turn of events hardly met with Connie's approval. He was insanely jealous of me, and especially of Clifford, even though it was just an innocent teenage affair. He did not want me to leave the little bedroom where I spent most of my time, or even speak to Clifford. I could not help wondering why he got involved with Geraldine. And I felt very guilty, and churned up inside when I saw him again. The flickering flame of my first love was not completely extinguished yet. Connie's harsh treatment, did nothing to lessen the hurt I felt for having broken up with Clifford, who always treated me tenderly. Instead of making me forget him, I was forced to compare the vast difference in their characters.

Connie was abusive, and insulting during their stay, and I cried rivers, because he made me so unhappy. When I yelled at him to stop tormenting me, he became violent, and started shoving me around. I cried out for him to stop. He called his mother and shouted, "Slap her Mummy, she's *hysterical!*" Aunty ground her teeth and hissed at me, "Stop crying and shouting, do you want your boyfriend to hear you?" Words cannot describe my humiliation and misery. She did not mean to be unkind, but I wished the earth opened up and swallowed me.

When they sat for a meal one day, Aunty told me not to hide in the room, but to go out and face Clifford. I joined them at the table, and tried to converse as naturally as possible. Connie, who refused to join, hid behind a door and looked furious. He scowled fiercely and gestured for me to leave the table, and mouthed, "You *bitch*! Come here at once!" I ignored him, until I finished eating.

He pounced on me as I came out, shoved me into the bedroom and abused me with a string of vile invective. I slapped him hard and said, "Stop it, you *bastard*!" Next moment, he slapped me even harder. "You *bitch*! Don't you ever call me a bastard or slap me again!" My head spun, and I spent the rest of the day crying in bed. I could not believe that he called me names and slapped me so hard.

I decided to leave him for ever, if I had a chance. He calmed down by evening and shed repentant tears. "I'm so sorry Dolla! Forgive me! I won't ever do that again!" I was willing to believe him once again, and forgave his dreadful behaviour. But it was very difficult to be affectionate to someone like him. Whatever tenderness and affection I had initially, was quickly eroding, as he chipped away at my heart and emotions.

Connie was furious with Geraldine for getting "involved" with Clifford, as he termed it. And I could not believe he fell in love with her just like that. They stayed a few more days before returning to Colombo, and left nothing but bitterness in their wake. I could hardly bear to watch him being unduly effusive, when he was the embodiment of reserve during the few times we spent together. I wondered if such undue display of affection was for my benefit.

A few weeks later, Connie wrote to Geraldine and insisted that Clifford return all my love letters. So she brought them the next time she visited. Connie immediately locked himself in his room, and spent hours reading every single one of my letters. I felt utterly betrayed, as I believed he would destroy them without sending them to Connie. It would have been chivalrous of Connie not to read those innocent, impassioned epistles either.

No doubt Connie wanted to find some incriminating facts about our relationship. But he was greatly disappointed to read only an infatuated teenager's declarations of eternal love. He did not behave like a gentleman, and neither did Clifford, but I was no stranger to disillusion now. I ignored Connie's references to my letters, whenever we quarrelled. He chose to read them. And if he wished to torture himself, that was his business, as I could not change the past, because he knew I loved Clifford, when he intruded into my life.

Connie decided that with or without my parents consent, we would get married on 18 November (the night he declared his love at the dance). Babs said it would be easier to sponsor us, if we were married. She wrote enthusiastically about how wonderful Australia was, and that we would be very happy if we came there.

Aunty took me to a local dressmaker, a wizened old man. He measured me up, and sewed my wedding dress, and a "going away" outfit. Uncle's niece, Terry, was married to Kassi, a Muslim, and he was a senior naval officer. They lived in Trincomalee, so Uncle asked them if we could spend a few days there on our honeymoon, to which they agreed.

Connie's parents spent about five hundred rupees on our wedding. And with the buoyancy of youth, I believed that all would be well in the future. We registered our marriage at the registrar's office in Talawakale, with Aunty and Uncle as witnesses.

Roland and Geraldine arrived that evening to attend our wedding next morning. Connie and I decorated the church with garlands of white roses. And when we left the church late in the evening, one of the Christian Brothers from the local college drove us back in his truck.

Aunty made my bouquet of white roses the night before. Cristobel, who was supposed to help, giggled and laughed, as each flower kept falling off the wire frame. It was finally done though, and Aunty told Connie he was not allowed to see me, or speak to me that night. She said it was bad luck to see the bride before the wedding.

I woke up at 6am, and Uncle took me to church in a hired car. Connie, Roland, Paul, Cristobel, Geraldine, and Aunty left earlier. Robin, a young man, who knew Connie's family, stood as best man.

Everything was done without much fuss, as Connie was paranoid that my parents would stop the wedding, if they knew about it. None of my family members were present, only a few strangers, and his immediate family. It was a very simple ceremony, and we knew the celebrant, Fr Cuthbert well. He was very supportive, and spoke to us at length, because he knew my parents were opposed to our marriage. We were pleased to have him officiate at our wedding.

When we returned, we relaxed a while with the family. They sang hymns and songs for a couple of hours (for our entertainment I gathered). Wendy and Brian visited in the evening, and she carried a huge bouquet of flowers from their garden.

Connie and I visited them a few times on the estate, and she always treated me well. I was very fond of Wendy, and her children too. Unfortunately, Wendy suffered a nervous breakdown a few years back, and she fell into fits of despondency. And at such times she was heavily sedated till she recovered.

On one occasion, when Connie and I saw her with Brian at a movie, she looked white as milk, and appeared to be completely dazed. When Connie saw her in such a state, he lost his temper and yelled at Brian. "If anything happens to my sister, I will see that you and your mother pay for it!"

Brian's mother was not on good terms with Wendy, or her family. When this threat reached her ears, she wrote a poison letter to Connie, disparaging me as that "woman" he brought home. And said she would take legal action because he threatened her life.

Her family spoke of Wendy's "nervous breakdown" in whispers. They all blamed Brian, and his mother for Wendy's problems. And Connie insisted that her mother-in-law was responsible for her breakdown. When I knew Wendy better, I understood that she was dependent on alcohol, to get through her day. And what her family thought were unstable "moods" was just plain intoxication. But with fierce loyalty, and refusal to face facts, none of them accepted that she had an alcoholic problem. She continued to live in a hazy world of escapism, and as her children were boarded in Kandy, they did not witness her erratic behaviour too often.

Wendy was happy and excited that evening though, because we were now married, and she was in an exuberant mood. She coaxed Brian to give us twenty five rupees as a wedding present. After they left, we took a hiring car to the Priory guest house, to spend our honeymoon.

It was a dark, dingy old place, and the hot water ran out before I could finish my bath. Connie drank a bottle of beer, and afterwards, we climbed into an uncomfortable, cold bed. We returned to Lilybourne the next morning, where we spent time with the family.

We did not consummate our marriage the night before. Connie spoke to his mother about it, saying I found it too painful. She told me she was very embarrassed to discuss such a subject with her son, and advised him to take me to a doctor. That was what we did later that day. Connie asked him if there was a blockage to cause me so much pain. After his examination, doctor said, "I can't find any blockages, it's normal for some discomfort, but don't worry."

We boarded a train to Trincomalee the following evening. Terry and Kassi were very hospitable, and treated us well. We went sight-seeing in a boat, and visited lovely sanctuaries, where wild deer roamed freely, and came to be hand-fed. We removed some photographs, but unfortunately, we did not collect them from the studio before we left Nuwara Eliya.

Kassi was a tall, broad-shouldered man, with striking features, black hair and eyes, and bushy eyebrows. Terry was a thin, petite, fair-complexioned woman, with a shrewish expression, and a harassed look in her dark eyes. She was difficult to converse with, as she was touchy and abrupt in her responses. Kassi was more conversational and entertaining though.

Their house stood on a hill over-looking Trincomalee harbour, and commanded a spectacular view. They had two gorgeous boys, aged about three and four. But all was not well between the couple. They constantly bickered and nipped at each other like two crotchety old crabs.

Just as we arrived, Kassi whispered urgently to Connie, "Don't mention I was in Colombo, Terry doesn't know about it." We saw him once when we visited Esme and Geraldine in their rented room in Wellawatte, and that was how we knew something was going on. Terry suspected Kassi of having an affair with Esme (as we found out later), and she was very uptight about it during our visit.

He was very sociable though, and was a very good host too. One night, he demonstrated how to eat crabs using just two fingers, without making too much of a mess. But in the evenings, he sat alone on the porch over-looking beautiful Trincomalee harbour. And he sipped a scotch on the rocks, while listening to sentimental songs by Jim Reeves, with a melancholy expression stamped on his strong features.

Connie's behaviour did not change much after marriage either, because he was insanely jealous, and picked on me over the slightest thing. He did not like me talking too much to Kassi, or anyone for that matter. I spent most of my time crying, and feeling sorry for myself. And I asked him, "What will they think of me not joining them, and spending time crying in bed?" He responded, "They'll think you are strange!" That was it. He laughed and joked with them when I was not around. We did not have much joy together, except for the scenic trips.

When the few days were over, we boarded a train back to Nuwara Eliya. Connie was very unkind, and unpleasant to me right throughout that home- coming journey. He accused me of misdemeanours I was not guilty of, and did not behave like a bridegroom in the remotest way. If someone just happened to look at me, he flew into a rage. That day, some young soldiers travelled in the same compartment with us, and they sat opposite, staring curiously at me now and then.

I closed my eyes, and pretended to sleep all the way, but Connie was seething, as he could not stop them from staring. As we walked home, he banged the suitcase against my legs, causing me much pain. He vented his anger and frustration on me, and shouted, "Those fellows were staring at you all the time!" I replied, "What can I do about that? *Stop* hitting me with that suitcase, you are hurting me!" And that was how I, a young bride of eighteen, returned from my honeymoon.

His insecurity stemmed from the fact that he was very short, and he felt inadequate in the presence of other men. He felt that way all his life, but how I could help him, was beyond me. He was impossible to live with at times, and I was greatly distressed by his constant jealousy, and irrational behaviour.

It was early December, and we planned to spend Christmas in Kandy with Damian's mother, Mrs Rogers. We decided to spend our first Christmas alone, away from Connie's parents and mine.

My parents were not reconciled to our marriage yet, and Ammie wrote regularly, bemoaning my hasty decision, and warning me of dire consequences. We spent a quiet Christmas with Mrs Rogers, who was a gentle, kindly old lady. Diana, her servant woman, cooked some delicious meals for us. Mrs Rogers was in her late seventies or so, with silver-grey hair tied back in a bun at the nape of her neck.

Connie and I walked around Kandy town, and we visited Brian's mother in hospital. It was the first and only time I met her. The poor woman was very ill, and incoherent. She kept muttering, "I've done terrible things in my life! I'm sorry." We heard she died in hospital a few weeks later.

Chapter 41

The days passed by with nothing much happening once we returned to Nuwara Eliya. We stayed in that cramped and claustrophobic room, with just a camp cot to sleep on. But his parents were very kind, and they never made me feel out of place. Aunty reprimanded Connie whenever he quarrelled with me. I helped her in the kitchen daily, and in whatever way I could, as I grew very fond of them. Connie too did chores around the house daily.

I was close to Cristobel and Paul, and they liked to listen to all the stories I read or related. Whenever Connie came into the room, he chased them away. "Get out now, leave us alone!" He did not like them spending time with me listening to fairy tales and other stories. Aunty was very happy with me, as she said I was so respectful towards them. I gave her my time, and listened to her for hours on end.

Uncle drank too much every evening, and we heard him mumble and complain about everything. Food was a constant source of annoyance to him, as he habitually complained and demanded, "Is *this* a meal for a man to eat?" Or that the food was tasteless, to which Aunty retorted angrily, "Sweeta, (they called each other Sweeta even in the midst of their most violent arguments), you will have to eat nothing but rice and water one day, for all your complaints!"

Connie yelled out in pain one morning, just after he finished brushing his teeth. I asked him what was wrong, but he could hardly talk as he bent over. Aunty ran up and asked, "What's wrong Connie?" He groaned, "I've hurt my back Mummy! I was just coughing, and then I got this excruciating pain in my back!" "We'll have to take you to the doctor," she said.

He got dressed with the greatest difficulty, and told his mother," I want you to take me to doctor's Mummy, and I don't want Dolla to come." When they returned a couple of hours later, after a painful trip by bus to Nuwara Eliya town, Connie went straight to bed.

He had a slipped disc, and needed to rest for a few days. But he was not an easy patient, nor very patient, as he screamed in pain at the slightest movement. I did not realize how painful a slipped disc could be, and found his fussing and yelling quite wearying. But I understood how painful it was, when I hurt my back many years later. Connie could not do heavy lifting or take a wrong turn from then onwards, as he ended up with a bad back.

He was also very scared of going to the outside toilet at nights, and told me to stand outside with a torch until he finished. He was also petrified of spiders and dogs. In later years, I killed spiders, and kept dogs away from him. Aunty had filled their minds with superstitions and myths, so Connie was afraid of many things in his life.

A few weeks after we married, we boarded a train to Colombo before Christmas, and stayed in the small, confined room that Esme and Geraldine rented. Clifford visited Geraldine every evening, and after he left, Connie abused me verbally, as he hated the thought of him being near me. Whenever we quarrelled, he was physically violent now. He shoved and pushed me, as he followed me to the bathroom and vented his anger on me.

I felt so desperate at times, that on one occasion I yelled, "I've had enough of your accusations and behaviour! Take me to a convent where I can find peace!" I was so adamant, that he reluctantly agreed. We boarded a bus to a convent in Moratuwa. I cried and told the nuns that I was very unhappy with Connie, as he abused me physically and verbally. They looked solemn, and said, "It's early days in your marriage, try to be patient, and it will turn out alright." They did not want me to stay, so I returned with Connie.

He was subdued on our way back, and kept saying, "Sorry, I love you," but never said, "sorry, I won't do it again." I relented over and over again each time he said, "sorry," as I could not bear to see him shed tears. I did not understand then that he could not control his angry outbursts. When he was back to normal, I wanted to believe he would not hurt me again. But his moods changed like quick silver, and left me uncertain as to what he would do and say next.

When we were in Colombo once, Shirani said she would join us for a movie, with her current boyfriend, Ranjith. Connie and I boarded a bus, then waited at the cinema for a long while, but they did not turn up.

On our way back, we sat in the top deck of a double decker bus, and as I looked out the window, I saw a crowd gathered round a wrecked car. When the bus stopped, we jumped off and rushed to the scene of the accident, as I had a premonition. And it was Ranjith's car! Shirani was thrown out of the windscreen; her face was badly bruised, and her eyes were swollen. A pedestrian was killed, and the police were taking statements. It was a dreadful situation, and Shirani was admitted to hospital. The case was settled outside court, and Ranjith charged with culpable driving.

We did not visit my parents then, as Connie believed they would try to break up our marriage. So he did not want me to see them yet, even though I missed them, and wanted to be with them very much.

I sat for the journalism examination in December 1970. But just before, Connie argued and said some hurtful things to upset me, because he resented my decision to sit for the exam. I tried to put his venomous words out of my mind, and concentrated on the written exam, which I passed easily, and with very good results.

Aunty encouraged me to complete the course, and gave me fifty rupees for the train fare to Colombo, to sit for the exam. Now, I was very pleased I had this diploma, in spite of all the drawbacks during the last couple of years.

We rushed to see a movie one evening, in June 1971. And as we were late, I ran up the steps to the cinema, forgetting I was about two months pregnant. I started bleeding heavily next day, and doctor said I would miscarry that night.

Aunty and Uncle were away visiting relatives, but Geraldine was spending a few days at home then. I passed the embryo around midnight, and it was very painful, so I rested for a few days. The doctor advised me not to get pregnant again before twelve months. We did not use contraceptions, as it was against our Catholic faith. So we tried the "rhythm method" hoping I would not get pregnant again too soon. I tried my best to understand Connie, and to make our marriage work, although we still had stormy days.

We sent Babs all the relevant documents as soon as we were married, and she sponsored us without delay. Now we waited anxiously to hear from the Australian High Commission.

A few months later, we moved to another house, in a tea estate called "Summerhill" a few miles from Nuwara Eliya. Uncle was born in that same old house, and it was a solid house, but thoroughly neglected. We spent a long time cleaning it up.

Connie and I occupied a larger bedroom now, and I soon made it comfortable, although we still slept on a camp cot. The only other furniture that we could fit in, was a small cupboard and dressing table. We had no electricity, so we managed with a few kerosene oil lamps and candles. The evenings turned dark rapidly, and by four thirty, the gloomy old house was not very pleasant. We finished dinner early, and we were in our room by eight o'clock, reading by the light of a kerosene lamp.

It was very scenic around though, and every afternoon, we went for long walks through dense shrubs and tea plantations. Those idyllic walks were like warm, sunny spells during those bleak days. I was still very receptive to beautiful places and things around me.

Our marriage though was fraught with tension, and we constantly teetered on the edge of an emotional volcano. In spite of some good qualities, Connie was insanely jealous of me, and everyone who came near me, especially Clifford. He was extremely possessive, even though I gave him no cause for such behaviour, and his insecurity was his own worst enemy.

Esme left for Australia in August 1971, and Geraldine hoped to leave as soon as she raised money for her ticket. Esme wrote that she worked in a factory, and was staying with Babs and Damian in Brighton, Melbourne. She said everything was wonderful in Australia, and assured Geraldine she would get a job in the same factory too.

Connie and I were interviewed some time ago, and within a few weeks, we heard our application was approved. Now it was a matter of finding money for our tickets. So began another round of visits to various people, whom the travel agent said wanted money transferred to relatives overseas. It was one way to avoid bank fees and taxes I suppose.

The agent told us to contact a tea planter, who lived near Hatton. We visited him a few weeks before Geraldine left, as she too needed money for her ticket. Wendy and she accompanied us to Mayfield, and we stayed with Nilanthi for two days. We met Heron Dias, police inspector of Hatton, for the first time then. He was a tall, stern-looking man, who spent a great deal of time at Mayfield.

He was supposed to be Lakshman's friend, but accompanied Nilanthi whenever she shopped or visited friends in town. One evening, when we joined Heron to the Darawela Club, Connie ended up being very sick, as he had a few mixed drinks. He vowed he would never mix drinks again, as it took him a couple of days to overcome his hangover.

We visited the planter next day. He lived in an elegant mansion set amid rolling green lawns, and brilliant flowers bloomed profusely. We had tea with his family, and soon clinched the deal. He gave us two thousand rupees, and told us to give his relatives thousand rupees, and to repay the balance when we started working. He hoped to immigrate within the year too. We promised to repay his money as soon as possible, vastly relieved that we could buy our tickets now. Geraldine left a few weeks later.

Patrick (Cuckoo), was expected home in December that year. In preparation for his visit, Connie unearthed a can of silver paint lying around, and painted the walls of the dark, damp kitchen silver, and the outside toilet too. The dining room was converted to a spare room, and Connie cut up old newspapers (for toilet paper), and stored them in the outside toilet.

When Cuckoo arrived though, he was far from impressed with all that was done for his benefit. And he told me later, "I sat and cried in the toilet when I saw the square bits of newspaper! And I was so frightened of being alone at night in that gloomy room, that I wanted to knock on your door and ask if I could stay with you and Connie." He did not say anything until a couple of days later.

Everyone called him Cuckoo, and he did not seem to mind it at all. He was far from being "cuckoo" though, as he was a great person, and we became good friends. Cuckoo was of medium height and build, with black hair, and eyes, and sported a trim beard. He was good-looking, and gentle-mannered in the way he spoke and behaved.

Uncle wanted him to celebrate Mass in the house, and invited all the people around, as he was very proud of his son, the "priest." Cuckoo obliged, but he did not tell his parents, or the family that he left the priesthood a couple of years ago, due to problems with his superiors. He was now a freelance journalist/translator, fluent in German, Italian, Sinhalese, Tamil, and English. So he kept up the pretext, and told us later, "Once a priest, always a priest, and I can celebrate Mass if I want to."

He met Thathie in 1966, when we were in Watagoda, and remembered many interesting conversations with him. He told me how much he enjoyed those talks with Thathie, as he was well-read, like him. Cuckoo loved to discuss various topics, from religion to books, and social issues, and his favourite saying was, "Let's talk about cabbages and kings."

When he was not busy with the others, he always had time to talk with me, and he said, "My goodness Dolly, you are like your father, well-read and informed." We walked everywhere with him on the estate, and I enjoyed his amiable company very much.

A day or so after his arrival, Wendy invited us to Mahacoodagala, and we walked through pine forests when we got off the bus on the main road. Cuckoo was much more comfortable there. He said that when he returned to Colombo, he wanted to organize a hotel room for the entire family to stay until he left. But the few days and nights we spent at Wendy's, were very distressing for me. Connie stayed up with Cuckoo till dawn, and I was very scared of sleeping alone in a large, cold bedroom, so I did not sleep until he came to bed. When I told him how I felt, he did not care, and just started an argument. Cuckoo suffered from insomnia, and never slept through the night. So he was happy to stay up with Connie, as they chain-smoked, and discussed family affairs.

Whenever we visited Wendy though, she treated us well, and we spent happy times with them and their two little girls. Cuckoo did not stay long in Summerhill, as he booked into a hotel in Colombo. He asked Aunty, Uncle, Paul, and Cristobel to come up to Colombo and stay with him until he left. He had no intention of visiting Summerhill again.

We finally arrived in Maharagama, after more than one year of my not seeing my parents. We decided to stay with them for a while, as we were immigrating in early 1972. It was a tearful reconciliation, and all was forgiven, as I embraced them fondly. They gradually reconciled to our marriage, and were resigned to my immigrating soon. We still flared-up occasionally, as Ammie still could not forget how I left home, and got married so suddenly.

I was pregnant again in November 1971, but did not tell the family about it, as Connie told me, "We'll keep it to ourselves for the time being." That was a peculiarity I could not understand, because he told me not to discuss anything with anyone, even something as important as my pregnancy.

Nihal was expected that Christmas too, and so were Rosie, Malcolm and Anthony, his wife, Barbara, and two sons, Kevin and Kristian. It was going to be a great family reunion after so long. Marie and Neville were immigrating to the United States soon after Christmas. Marie found a job as a primary school teacher in Michigan, and Neville, a lawyer, hoped to find suitable employment too.

The day we went to the airport, and I saw Nihal walking through the doors, I just burst into tears. It was so long since I saw him and my family. He was more mature, and spoke with a slight accent, otherwise he had not changed too much in his manner or appearance. I hugged him emotionally, and he was just as affectionate as always.

Shirani and Ranjith seemed to be getting along well, and he became quite friendly with Connie. They went out together daily, trying to organise various matters before we left. Every morning Connie woke up early, got dressed and said, "I'm going to meet Ranjith, as he knows someone who wants to send gems over to Australia, and will give me a good commission, so we'll have some money when we get there." I believed his story, and although it was good to spend time with my parents and family all day, without Connie hanging around me, I wondered why he came home so late in the evenings without a single gem stone in sight.

This went on for a few weeks, and sometimes he said, "We had a few beers and lunch, but the gemstone merchant didn't turn up." One evening, Thathie looked at me and said, "Don't worry my dear, Connie loves you very much. He'll be home soon." I never got to the bottom of that story, and why they did not meet the gem merchant eventually. He just clutched at straws, as far as I was concerned.

Nihal was just as amazing a brother as ever. I confided in him how, and why I ended up getting married so soon, as I wrote him a few letters when I was in Nuwara Eliya. I did not tell Nihal though, that on the pretext of posting them, Connie once intercepted my letters, in which, I desperately pleaded for him to intervene, so Connie would let me go home. Such a commotion erupted that day. But I fought on principle, because Connie should not have read my letters. He told Aunty about it, and she upbraided me for asking Nihal to mediate.

Nihal said he liked Connie, as he seemed to be a nice, friendly young man, and he hoped we could make our marriage work. Connie was generous, and kind to my family, and got along well with Nihal, and the others. The facade he presented to the world was that of a cheerful, loving husband. He called me "Angel" "Queen" "Honey" and "Sweetheart." But when we were alone, it was usually "Huns" (short for Honey), which he hissed at me when he was annoyed, or "Dolla." And so, no one knew what his true nature was like.

I never told my parents what my married life was really like, because they would have said, "We told you so! You rushed into this marriage, now you have to lie on the bed you made." My young pride would not allow such humiliation.

Nihal joked, laughed, and carried on just as before, and together with Rosie, they kept us in stitches with all their stories about London, and their life as trainee nurses. My parents rented out a large house close to Granny's place, and one day, much to our surprise, Dawn breezed in. Ammie wrote to Mr Fernandez that Nihal was in Ceylon. But he lost interest in Dawn completely when he left five years ago. And now it was quite the opposite, because Dawn was crazy about Nihal.

She stayed overnight, and when Nihal held her hand once, she asked him coyly, "Will I get pregnant?" He was disgusted at such feigned naiveté, and told her very resolutely that he did not want to see her again. When Dawn finally took the hint, and left a day later, Anjo's older sister, Barlo, befriended Nihal. They had a great time, much to Ammie's annoyance, because she wanted Nihal to make up with Dawn.

Nilanthi travelled up to Maharagama, and stayed on for a few days at a time. So, after a long separation, our family was complete once again, at least for a little while. Nilanthi was about six months pregnant then, and Tamara, who was five, kept us amused with her cheeky ways and chatter.

We noticed a new development was under way. Heron visited Nilanthi regularly in Maharagama, and took her out dancing or to the movies. I did not like him at all, because he was up to no good.

When we visited Nilanthi in Mayfield, Heron was a regular visitor there. He was almost fifty, with five grown up children. His eldest daughter was the same age as Nilanthi, who was twenty five years then.

Nilanthi endured a very troubled marriage with Lakshman right from the start. He was a violent, brutal man, who abused her physically when he was angry. She also discovered that he had liaisons with various women whenever she was away. That was why he sent her off to Gampola often.

Once, he hurled a dish at her, which sliced the calf of her leg. And the doctor, who attended her, insisted that she lodged a complaint against Lakshman. Ironically, Heron was present on that day when Nilanthi visited the police station. That was how they started seeing each other, as he was sympathetic and kind.

Heron was fond of singing, and playing the harmonica, besides dancing too. He was a contrast to Lakshman, and though much older than Nilanthi, she found him amusing and entertaining. Connie and I did not talk to Heron. And he told Nilanthi, "Dolly doesn't like me does she?" It was obvious I disliked him very much then.

Cuckoo visited us often too, and he became very friendly with Nihal, as they shared a lot in common. Such splendid, happy days, with so much fun and laughter! I tried hard to make believe that none of the traumatic events in the past couple of years took place. And I was content to be with my family once again.

Just before Christmas, Cuckoo organised a memorable dinner at a Chinese restaurant. Before dinner, Cuckoo and our entire family watched "The Graduate" starring Dustin Hoffman and Anne Bancroft. It was a great movie, with a marvellous sound track, featuring Simon and Garfunkle's hits. Later, we ended the evening with a delicious, seafood dinner.

Lakshman stormed in late at night a few days later. He looked threatening as a black thunder cloud, and hardly spoke to anyone. He immediately started a row with Nilanthi and shouted out, "I wish I had *never* married you!" She stood at his side silently, looking solemn and unhappy. But when he left next day, she was all smiles, and happily dressed up to go dancing with Heron. If Lakshman was aware of what was going on between Heron and Nilanthi, he did not take any steps to stop their affair.

We attended midnight Mass on Christmas Eve, and I walked with Nihal and the family all the way to church and back. But a sad memory lingers, because Thathie was intoxicated, and went to bed after his drunken babbling and hollering. Nihal looked pensive, and did not say much. But we enjoyed a delicious lunch next day, and a huge dinner party in the night.

On New Year's Eve, Heron invited our entire family to a dance, but Connie and I did not join them, which I regretted later, as it was the last time our family would be together. Connie did not like Heron either, and told me that on principle, he would not go out with him and Nilanthi.

This was another bone of contention, as he told me sanctimoniously, "I can't imagine any of *my* sisters behaving like Nilanthi! I hope *you* won't be like her! Damn disgrace, the way she's carrying on with that bugger!" And on and on he nagged me about something beyond my control. Even Cuckoo was not very impressed when he saw Heron hanging around Nilanthi daily. But he was more tolerant, as he lived in Germany for many years, and was not narrow-minded, or judgemental.

Connie and I went to another dance on New Year's Eve, and arrived home after midnight. I had a great time with my family next day, and we visited Granny after lunch. Nihal and Rosie were leaving in a few weeks time, but I did not mention I was pregnant to Nihal or the others.

One beautiful, sunny morning, our entire family travelled in a mini bus to the glorious beach at Hikkaduwa, and enjoyed a superb time there. A funny incident happened that caused much hilarity among us. Because, the moment we arrived at the beach, Anthony's wife, Barbara, a pleasant, German lady, changed into a tiny bikini, and promptly dropped on the beach and sprawled on the pristine, warm sand. The driver of the mini bus looked at her in amusement and nodded to Anthony. "Suddo Auvva dhakina kotta, yakka nagginawa!" (when white people see the sun, they get the devil into them). Anthony was highly diverted, but did not tell him she was his wife.

When we heard the driver, we laughed a great deal. Ammie and Thathie were happy, and enjoyed the family outing very much. Nilanthi joined us, but Heron could not or did not want to. So it was very enjoyable (to me), without any undercurrents to spoil our family day. Tamara was very troubled now, as she was boarded at Bishop's College in Colombo, and sensed that Nilanthi did not pay her whole-hearted attention as before.

Whenever Heron came to pick Nilanthi to take her for a dance or a movie, Tamara bawled her eyes out and shouted angrily, "I *hate* Uncle Heron, I hate Uncle Heron! Don't take Mama away!" We carried Tamara and pacified her, then took her for a walk until Nilanthi and Heron left. This was very distressing, not only for the little girl, but for us too. We did not know how to make things right between them.

The night that Nihal and Rosie left for London, I stayed behind with Shirani and Nelune, as I was very tired. Connie accompanied the others to the airport. But a few hours later, I heard Nihal's voice, "Dolly, Baba, Shirani, I'm back!" He called Nelune by her pet name "Baba" which she disliked intensely, and never responded to it, so Nihal just teased her.

I jumped out of bed quickly, surprised to see Nihal and Rosie. It was marvellous to see him, as I was upset and cried since he left, not knowing when I would see him again. He told us the flight was cancelled till the following day, so we had a few more hours to spend with him. How happy I was to see my beloved brother again. I missed him deeply when he left in 1967, and I hated this second goodbye. I spent a happy day with the family, before Nihal and Rosie left again that evening. The last few weeks were full of meetings and partings, with many family members flying out to various parts of the world.

Connie and I were leaving for Melbourne on 16 February 1972. Everything was settled, and Roland agreed to drop us off at Katunayake Airport. So, for the last time, we journeyed down to Summerhill to pack up our clothes. Aunty was very happy to see us, as Cuckoo left at the end of January, and she missed him very much. She cried a great deal when we left. We comforted her because they would soon join us, as Babs sponsored the whole family. We returned to Maharagama a few days later.

Roland was very annoyed, because for some reason or another, we delayed on the day of our departure, and were late for the plane. He drove his van in a mad rush to get us in time to the airport. The mobile steps were already disappearing, as we ran across the terminal and boarded the plane at the eleventh hour.

Thathie and Roland were the only ones who stood waving at us from the airport, and we had no time for tears and long farewells. I watched Thathie join his hands in prayer and a blessing, as the plane began to taxi. An overwhelming sense of grief engulfed me as the plane took off and hovered over central Ceylon. I glimpsed green, tea estates down below for the last time. The outline of my beautiful, island home vanished swiftly from view as the plane soared above the clouds.

I was leaving my homeland and family for good; it was a heart-wrenching experience. I wept unashamedly as I sat back with fastened seat belt. Connie did not hold me, or speak any words of consolation, even though he knew how distressed I was to leave my family.

Not a word of comfort did he offer me, as he was too busy chatting to flight attendants, and ordering food and drinks. After so many months of planning, organising, and facing several set-backs, we were finally on our way to Australia. The reality of another major change in my life, struck me forcibly then.

It was less than three hours flight to Singapore, and we arrived at Changi Airport in good time. Singapore was humid, just like Colombo, and when we stepped out of the airport, we boarded a coach that wound its way through busy streets to the hotel, where we stopped for one night. We were due to arrive in Melbourne on 17 February 1972.

We looked around the shopping areas, and enjoyed our first taste of being overseas. As we had limited funds, we did not buy many things, but just walked around Orchard Street shopping centre for a couple of hours. Connie bought some reasonably priced shirts, and a few souvenirs for Babs, and the others, and I bought a pretty dress and matching shoes.

The brief stop-over in Singapore was quite an experience, and the pleasant, spotless city, and vast airport with dazzling shops, impressed me very much. In the evening, we boarded a coach to the airport once again, and soon we were on our way to Melbourne. The sight of Singapore harbour, with myriads of twinkling lights at night, was an unforgettable sight, as the plane hovered slowly before gliding into the night.

Top: Nihal & Nelune with Janice's mum, Vera. Below:
Nihal & Janice on their wedding day

Nihal&Janice

Nihal's early days in London

our engagement & wedding day . Stacy's first x'mas. Christian
with Mewsette our pet cat. Frolics on the beach at Marlo.

Stacy & Christian

PART 2

Southern Stars

Chapter 1

The plane approached Melbourne towards early morning, and a popular song by Olivia Newton-John, "Banks Of The Ohio" drifted over the sound system. Breakfast was served before landing at six o'clock. And as a strong aroma of grilled lamb chops, bacon and eggs on toast, and sausages, wafted down the aisle, I was nauseous.

The new airport at Tullamarine was completed that year. And much to my relief, after the fairly long flight from Singapore, we finally arrived in Melbourne. It was a pleasant flight, but I was anxious to get off the plane and start our new life in Australia as soon as possible. It was strange to see airport officials getting on board and spraying disinfectant around, before passengers disembarked, and the fumes almost choked me.

We hired a taxi after we passed through customs without much hassle, as we had nothing to declare. Everything seemed so big and strange to me, and on our way to East Brighton, where Babs and Damian lived, all I heard on the radio were news bulletins about murders, rapes, and robberies. I must say that I was terribly frightened at the apparent crime rate in Australia.

When we finally arrived in front of a red, brick-veneer house on a quiet street, we sprang a surprise on Babs, as she did not expect us that morning. We laughed and hugged, as we were pleased to see them. Jeremy was about five years old then, and a delightful little boy. He kept gazing at us curiously, but could not remember us at all. Babs said, "Damian is still out, as he works night shift at a local supermarket, and finishes later on in the morning."

After breakfast, Ralston, a friend of theirs, dropped in without ceremony. He was a tall, brawny man, in his thirties or so, with bushy, side-whiskers, and bloodshot eyes. After the introductions, Babs asked him to drive us around local factories and look for work immediately. We just had time for a quick snack and a cup of coffee, before we went off with Ralston. He drove a taxi and knew his way around the streets. In retrospect, I cannot believe we did not even stop to relax that day, and take in some local sights before embarking on job-hunting.

After making several enquiries at various factories, we finally ended up in Chesterville Road, Moorabbin. We looked around for any sort of process work, but did not find any suitable vacancies in the factories. We also stopped at a health benefits office, to get medical insurance. Babs urged us to do so, when I told her I was pregnant. That night, when Esme and Geraldine returned after work, they too were happy to see us.

They worked at Liptons tea factory in Knoxfield, and did late shifts, as they earned more money than on day time shifts. As they were staying with Babs too, the house was quite crowded then.

Over the following days, Connie and I were surprised at the number of visitors every evening. A crowd gathered for dinners and parties, and Babs and Damian attended dances regularly. Babs was caught up in a dizzy, social whirl that she seemed to revel in.

Although Damian was his usual friendly self, we noticed he was much more subdued now. And we felt an underlying sense of something not quite right in their lives. Connie suspected something amiss immediately, and asked Babs, "Why does Ralston visit you all the time when Damian is working?" she replied hastily, "He's just a very good *friend* of ours, and he's married to my school friend Pauline, who lives close by." But Connie told me, "I'm not so sure about Ralston, and I suspect funny business, as I don't trust him. I don't know why Damian tolerates that bugger." It was ironical that Babs was in a similar situation as Nilanthi, but I did not tell him, "Now, what do you think, when you gave me such a hard time over Nilanthi's affair?"

That very first week, I was extremely homesick, and did not feel too well either, due to my pregnancy. I felt strange and "displaced" in this confusing environment, with hordes of strangers in and out of the house at all times of the day and night. I longed for a quiet place of my own.

I went to bed around nine o'clock a few days later, after watching a beauty pageant with the others. I thought Connie would follow me soon, but he was more interested in watching the program, as Damian and he enthusiastically compared "vital statistics" of the contestants. I waited patiently till after midnight. When he finally came to bed, I asked him why he took so long, and this led to a full scale argument.

He started pushing and shoving me around in spite of my condition, and I shouted hoarsely, "I want to leave you! I *hate* it here!" Then I sobbed myself to sleep, thinking how cruel he was. In the morning he asked Babs, "Can she go to a doctor and get an abortion?"

Babs was surprised. She advised us not to be hasty, as things would work out alright, once we found a place of our own, and Connie started working. It was incredible he should ask his sister such a thing. I knew he said many things without stopping to think how hurtful his words were. Later, he pleaded and said, "I'm so sorry. I didn't mean it."

I found it stifling, unsettling, and very confusing, and wanted to move out as soon as possible. And Connie too agreed it was not the best place, due to underlying currents between Babs and Damian. We returned $200 of the money we brought to the person concerned, and were left with about $200 for expenses.

Connie paid Babs $50 for one week's board, and then we went flat hunting. In a day or so, Connie found work as a process worker at Schweppes, and expected a basic wage of about $35 a week, so we thought we could afford to rent a flat.

We finally found a furnished, bed-sitter in Moorabbin, and moved out eagerly, as it was the first time we were on our own since we were married. The rent was $15 a week, and it was great to have a place of our own at last. A pleasant, middle-aged lady showed us around, and told us we had to share the toilet and laundry with another lodger, who lived in a bungalow in the back yard.

Now, the very first day Connie left me alone and went to work at Schweppes, I was simply petrified even to go out to the toilet, because I glimpsed the long-haired lodger, who I thought was a hippie. After hearing news bulletins on radio, and seen reports of all the crimes on television, I was extremely scared, and panicked when I thought of setting foot outside. So I sat indoors all day, and hastily rushed to the toilet and back, before anyone could see me.

When Connie returned home, he took one look at my flushed face and asked, "What's wrong?" He saw that I was very upset. When I explained how I felt, and that I dared not go out, even for a breath of fresh air, he told me that he would ask if I could work at Schweppes too, so I would not be alone. I accompanied him next day, and the foreman employed me. He asked me to unload empty bottles, that Connie tossed in carelessly, onto a conveyor belt. Ten men and women stood on either side of the belt, and all day long we emptied dirty bottles onto the conveyor belt. Whenever I failed to keep the bottles upright, a large woman yelled out in a strong, Aussie accent, "Hai, stind them up, they're brikin!" It took me a while to understand what she was saying.

I found it difficult to stand on my feet too long. And the eagle-eyed foreman, unaware of my condition, watched me whenever I scuttled along to the dingy dark toilet and sat down for a few minutes. Soon, my regular trips aroused suspicion, and the rest of the workers queried, "Why you take so many toilet breaks?"

One foul-smelling, amorous Greek, put his arms around me, and tried to "chat" me up, but I shrugged him off with a frown. The puzzled man questioned, "You no like me?" Connie, who was watching intently in the background, muttered grimly, "*No*, she *no* like that sort of thing!"

I experienced a few amusing moments with multi-cultural workers, and the Australians were very surprised to hear us speak good English. They asked us curiously, "*How* did you learn to speak English so quickly?" It was a revelation when we said we were educated in English in Ceylon.

At lunch time, we sat outside on one of the benches, and ate our sandwiches. And in the evenings, we spent most of our time scanning newspapers, looking for better jobs, especially Connie, as he wanted to find work as a draftsman.

When we got paid on a Thursday, we took taxis to various places next day, as Connie attended many interviews at architectural firms. I did not last long at Schweppes, as the work was too strenuous for me.

We looked around for a one-bedroom flat in Ormond, as the bed-sitter was too cramped, and not very comfortable, with shared toilet and laundry. We rented a flat in Leila Rd, Ormond, for $20 a week. Babs took us to Myers Store at Southland one day, and introduced us to the lure of "hire purchase" plan.

We bought a new fridge, dining table, four chairs, a sewing machine, and some cushions to sit on. I longed for a typewriter, so Connie bought me a Remington portable typewriter on my birthday, which was a great present. Now, I happily typed away most of the day. I had nothing else to do in that small flat, once I finished sewing curtains for the bedroom and lounge, and matching cushion covers.

He acquired the habit of buying a bottle of beer on his way home every evening, and enjoyed it very much as he relaxed. We did not argue too much during those first few weeks in our flat. As we did not own a television set yet, we read in the evenings till late. Every evening, we walked along the streets of Ormond for a couple of hours, and I went for weekly check-ups to Dr Rustomjee in Malvern, whom Babs recommended. We boarded trains to and from Malvern, and walked to his office on Wattletree Road.

Esme and Geraldine visited us regularly after work, as they too found it too hectic at Bab's place. They spent a few hours with us, and left late at night. I was very fond of Babs, Esme, and all his family members, and always maintained an affectionate relationship with them. And I had no one else in this new country except them. And although I was unfailingly kind to Geraldine, and treated her well, she never overcame her jealousy. Just like Connie was jealous of Clifford, she too could not forget that I was Clifford's girlfriend. Whenever she spoke to me, her words had a subtle sting. In later years, she denigrated Clifford to me, and told me how lucky I was to have married Connie, and "escaped" Clifford. I could not help noticing her ever-present antipathy towards me.

One evening, she told us that she sponsored Clifford, and planned to get married as soon as he came over. This news enraged Connie, and his mood changed dramatically when they left.

We were in that flat only a few weeks, when Connie stretched a stomach ligament while lifting heavy boxes. Damian and Babs rushed him to Alfred hospital, but I stayed behind, as I was tired and unable to run around too much. The doctor recommended complete rest for a couple of weeks, and so Connie stopped working at Schweppes.

We did not apply for Social Security benefits, as we were unaware of assistance to new migrants, so after a few days, we went about desperately seeking work. Every morning, we walked up and down Chesterville Road, knocking on every factory door, until finally, "Lockers And Weavers" offered us work.

Connie dragged out massive rolls of wire netting, and I watched a weaving machine, and trimmed wires with a pair of pliers. My hands, unused to such rough work, were scratched and bleeding at the end of the day. Connie could hardly move after such back-breaking work. We did not turn up next day, and did not get paid for one day's work either.

We were on the road again next morning, knocking on every door. After a couple of hours, I stopped in the middle of the road. I was tired and burst into tears and moaned. "Why did we come here to suffer like this!" He tried to pacify me, but I was too upset. One evening, Babs and Damian dropped in to tell Connie that a night shift was available in a milk bar, and he should go for it.

When I heard them persuading him to go for an interview, I was very upset, to say the least, and cried bitterly, because I did not want to stay alone at nights, especially not in my condition. So, on second thoughts, Connie refused to take up that job. I encouraged him to find a job as a draftsman, and I scrutinized vacancy advertisements in all the newspapers.

He sent out resumes that I typed, to various architects. But so far, he was unsuccessful, because he had no experience in Australia. One morning, I packed his sandwiches, and he went out to work in a factory, where the foreman promised him work. Around lunch time, when I looked out from the balcony, I saw him returning.

I had just received a telegram from an architectural firm in Nunawading, and I waved it about excitedly. But I asked, "Why aren't you at work?" He looked dejected and replied, "The foreman wanted a '*bigger*' and '*stronger*' man to do some very heavy lifting, and refused to take me on, because I'm too short and small-made." He took the telegram from me listlessly, but when he opened it, his face split into a happy smile. "They want me to start work next week at Joe Saraty's, an architect in Nunawading!" We were elated, and thanked God for this lucky break at last.

Connie bought a drafting board earlier on, and he prepared a portfolio, as he did not bring any of his drawings with him. He was an excellent draftsman, and his work was impressive. Joe Saraty was more than impressed with Connie's portfolio, when he interviewed him.

We did not own a car then. Connie woke up very early in the morning, when it was still dark, boarded a train to Richmond, a bus to Nunawading, and walked up to Joe's office adjoining his house. Joe, his wife Maria, and their daughter, were very kind people, and eager to offer assistance to a young migrant couple.

Four other draftsmen worked there, and Connie settled in well. When Joe and his wife knew I was pregnant, and also realised how tiring it was for Connie to take trains and buses to work, they suggested that we move to Nunawading. And they started looking for a suitable place for us to rent.

Chapter 2

We accompanied Esme to a house in Oakleigh one day, as she too was looking for a flat. A Yugoslav lady had a room to let, and said she was married to Bronco, but was now divorced. When Esme met him through this lady, he soon became her partner. Geraldine was still staying with Babs until Clifford's arrival.

I spent most days knitting, and sewing baby clothes, besides writing whatever came to my mind. Connie sipped a few glasses of beer in the evenings, and we spent time reading. The one-bedroom flat was very basic, with an attached bathroom, and a separate lounge and kitchen, but it was comfortable, and to us it was luxurious.

We did not buy a lounge suite, and sat on large cushions, but we owned a kitchen table, four chairs, and a large fridge. I did most of my writing and sewing on that kitchen table. No matter what our marital problems were, I was determined to be a good wife and mother, and build a comfortable home. I wanted to excel as a cook too, and be competent in my new role.

We joined Readers Digest book club, so I soon collected books on motherhood, cooking, and household hints. I learnt new recipes, and Connie was happy. He told his family, "Dolly cooks delicious meals every day, and she can cook Chinese, or any other cuisine now."

He praised me to his mother too, as she said, "Connie is always saying how clean and methodical you are in whatever you do. He's so happy you are so tidy, because he likes to keep everything in order." And he often said, "Thank God you are so particular, because I would have got mad if I had a scatterbrain wife, who did everything slip shod in a big hurry."

He was quite content to see me settling down, and taking care of household chores. But as my pregnancy advanced, he helped with the washing and cleaning. At times though, he could be the most infuriating person. But I had no choice, and could not change the course of destiny. And I always hoped we would get along eventually.

He said that when Wendy and Babs were pregnant, they drove their husbands crazy with endless demands, cravings, and morning sickness. Babs was violently sick, if she just smelled a whiff of cigarette smoke. Connie thought I would be the same, and did not see how he could stop smoking around me, as he smoked even in bed.

I was healthy, and hardly sick except for occasional heartburn. And much to his surprise, I never worried him with strange demands and cravings, and went through my pregnancy with hardly any difficulty. He was relieved that he did not have to give up smoking, and said, "This is the easiest pregnancy I have seen!" I liked ripe peaches very much, and relished quite a few daily, and that was about the only craving I had.

The only other change was, he graduated to two bottles of beer daily, instead of one, and by the end of the evening, Connie was drunk. And what I hated most, was his "beer talk." Just meaningless babble about imaginary slights, and sins of omission and commission.

I had not learnt the futility of reasoning with an intoxicated person as yet, so our scenes became worse and more frequent. The term "domestic violence" was not familiar in my vocabulary. But all I knew was, that my husband was drinking and behaving *exactly* like his father and mine.

I purchased an electric Singer sewing machine, which was very useful, as I sewed most of my clothes, and baby clothes. One day, Connie told me about a vacant flat in Nunawading, for $25 a week. He now earned about $75 a week, so we knew we could afford the rent.

We boarded a train and walked to the premises to have a look, which was a two-bedroom flat on the ground floor of a two-storey house. An Italian couple, Luigi and Maria owned Number 7, Luckie Street, and we thought the name was a good omen.

No green lawns or flower beds though, only concreted pathways and cacti all around. "Low maintenance garden" Luigi explained. The backyard however, was full of tomatoes, green chillies, herbs, and vegetables. They had three young boys, Raphael, Sergio and Angelo, and were happy to rent the place to us. It had two bedrooms, a large living area, kitchenette, indoor toilet, and laundry. After we signed a lease, Maria, who was a home-machinist, said, "I very happy if you teach me English." I agreed, and she smiled happily.

They spoke limited English, but we understood them. Luigi was a short, rotund, balding man, ruddy-faced, and with deep blue eyes. Maria was attractive, about forty years, of average height, slim, with short, brown hair and eyes. She was about ten or fifteen years younger than Luigi, and she told me they were married by proxy about fifteen years ago. Luigi planted vegetables in the large back yard, and brewed his own red wine, which he drank daily, as we noticed from his red eyes, and ruddy cheeks.

We rented a small truck, and transported our few pieces of furniture to the flat. Joe and Maria visited and gave us an electric heater and some cooking utensils. Our neighbours, Glenda, and her husband Ron, were very kind and friendly Australians too. She came around often for a long chat, and told me that Ron ate only steaks and chips, or steaks with vegetables, every single evening, but she liked spicy foods.

I sometimes shared a hot curry with her, which she enjoyed very much. She befriended me, and offered me various hints, and good advice about child-rearing, as she had four little boys, and was expecting another. Glenda was a tall, large lady, with a long, flat-tipped nose that was always red and sore, as she had hay fever or an allergy.

Our flat was partly furnished, with a bulky, old lounge-suite, upholstered in a dark brown, faded fabric, and Venetian blinds hung in the lounge and bedrooms. I sewed curtains, and set up the nursery in the second bedroom. We moved to this flat somewhere in mid-June, and the memory of cold, damp, concrete floors, still lingers. Luigi offered to take us to the doctor for my check ups, and sometimes drove us to Forest Hills shopping centre too. Connie and I walked from Luckie Street, to Forest Hills, some evenings, and then came home in a taxi with our groceries. We walked most of the time, even though I was eight months pregnant.

Luigi told us, "Sommatime I can take you to shops, sommatime I can do this for you." I was under the impression he would do all this in summer, and wondered why they had to wait until summer. This was until I learnt to understand their Italian accent.

Babs, Damian, Geraldine, and Esme visited occasionally. Esme's partner, Bronco, a large, brawny Yugoslav, who drank heavily, and laughed very loud, accompanied her, as she lived with him. He was a professional painter, and his broad, weathered face was always flushed (with wine or brandy). He had black hair, blue eyes, and gold-capped teeth, that gleamed when he smiled. Bronco lived in a large house in Oakleigh, with his four teenage sons, and Esme. He spoke limited English, but was full of good-humour, and willing to help us in any way he could.

A few weeks after we moved, we bought a second-hand, black and white television set. And we spent most evenings watching it, while I knitted, and Connie sipped his beer.

The television went berserk sometimes, as it hissed loudly and zigzagged patterns across the screen. Connie waved the aerial around frantically, until wavy lines settled down to a fuzzy picture, and transmission resumed. Those first few months were comparatively peaceful, as he was content when I sat beside him and devoted all my time to him.

He held my hand and told me not to move, because he just wanted me to pet and pamper him. Then I wearied of such restrictions, and wanted to do other things around the place, or just knit for a few hours and relax, which made him irritable.

I kept in touch with my family regularly, and also with Cuckoo, who wanted to know how we fared in this land of opportunities. So far, I was unable to send him good tidings. But now, he was just as elated as we were, to hear that Connie was employed as a draftsman, and did not end up in a factory.

Connie hurt his back at home one day, lifting some heavy boxes, and ended up in bed with a slipped disc. He was annoyed to be restricted, and screamed at me, if I was doing some work somewhere else in the house. "Come here you bitch! Where are you?" He took out all his anger and frustration on me. And when he swore at me for no other reason except that he was in pain, I kept out of his way, and only took his food and drink. It was very trying at times, as I did not understand why he abused me when he was in pain, as if I was to blame.

In spite of my determination to excel in whatever I did, whether it was being a good wife, housekeeper, and mother, words cannot express my homesickness, and sadness during this period of settling down in another country. But I wrote guardedly, as I did not want my parents to know I was so unhappy in this new country, and especially not about my marital woes.

Everything was strange and different; the people, lax moral codes, and ethics as depicted on television. I wondered how on earth I could survive in such an environment. When we asked Babs about churches in Australia, she replied carelessly, "*No one* goes to church here, not like in Ceylon." But when we attended Mass on Sundays, the church was always packed, and many devoted Catholics attended Sunday Mass still. Babs said that just because she stopped attending Mass, and so did Esme and Geraldine. But Connie and I wanted to practise our faith, and attended Sunday Mass regularly.

When I wrote that I was extremely homesick for my family and Ceylon, Granny commented, "Connie and Dolly are unhappy in Australia because they are so short!" It was laughable, as I failed to see how our height had anything to do with settling down in a new country. And anyway, I was the only one who was unhappy, as Connie loved it here right from the start. It was everything he dreamed of, and some of his family were here, while the rest were arriving later that year. His sisters revelled in this lax society too, where "anything goes" was the motto.

They followed the most outrageous fashions, micro-mini skirts, hot pants, and skimpy tank tops (all the rage then). But I adhered to my strict upbringing, in the way I behaved and dressed, and my skirts were just a few inches above my knees. Connie liked me to dress modestly, because he said that the surfeit of legs, thighs, and bosoms everywhere, did not leave anything to the imagination. And he said, "It's a breath of fresh air to see you dressed properly like a lady, without exposing your body for the world to see." Babs was slim, and had the legs and figure for mini-skirts, but Esme, and Geraldine would have been wiser to avoid hot pants and micro-mini skirts, that were very unflattering on them.

Although I wanted to buy nice clothes and things, and also to send some home, money was very scarce, and I could not afford luxuries. I soon discovered "opportunity" or "charity shops" where they sold clothes and items for a few dollars or cents. And these became my favourite places to shop.

Fabrics were very cheap at Spotlight and Bargain Box, so I sewed all my dresses, and baby clothes, for a very reasonable price. I even sewed Connie's shirts, ties, slacks, and pyjamas too; knitted several tank tops, pullovers, and jumpers. I made him a pair of woollen bed-room slippers once, that he found more comfortable than ready-made slippers.

In spite of such thrift, we still had a very large monthly bill to pay towards a hire purchase loan. Initiated to the debt-ridden, consumer society of the western world now, we delighted in buying goods that were way beyond our reach in Ceylon. Everything screamed out, "Own it now, and pay later!"

I shopped for about ten dollars a week then, and still had a couple of dollars left over. Eggs were twenty cents a dozen, bread and milk even cheaper. With the few dollars I saved each week, I had enough to indulge in opportunity-shop clothes and shoes.

Maria invited me over one day, saying, "I have special treat for you Dolly!" She was all smiles, and very pleasant, as she liked to talk in English, so she could speak more fluently. I was happy to oblige, and spent a little time teaching her new words. When I went upstairs with her, she asked me to take a seat, and then brought out a large cake, and cut a generous slice.

It looked like a delicious chocolate cake, so I took a small bite. Although it was quite sweet, it had a different texture and flavour. I inquired, "What kind of cake is this Maria?" To my dismay, she replied, "It's made from pig's blood! Very good eh? Our friends kill pig and we collect all blood to make cake." I stopped myself from retching, and politely told her I could not eat anything as I was feeling sick. Believing it was due to my pregnancy, she did not force me to eat any more.

Maria had a very good voice, and sometimes she burst into song on her way upstairs and down, or as she sewed away. I did not know anything about opera then, but she loved singing arias. She told me her dearest ambition was to sing in opera, but her parents put a stop to her dreams when they shipped her off to get married.

When I had time to spare, I stopped by to chat in their stuffy garage where they sewed. Luigi knew how to over lock, and together they worked away for hours each day. He hurt his back at work, and was on compensation payments. So they told us not to let any strangers come inside the flat, as they could be investigators from Luigi's company.

He worked in the garden, and sewed long hours during the day. But if he saw one of us, he limped painfully, dragged his leg, and held his back, as he climbed up the stairs to their apartment.

When Maria was stressed, and complained about headaches, Luigi nodded at me, and looked at her sceptically, "*Iffa* you gotta bad headache, better you *cutta* offa head and getta *new* one!" Maria glared angrily at him, screwed her mouth tight, and sewed away furiously.

Quite often I heard her scream at Sergio, her second son, who always seemed to be in trouble. I smiled at him as he stood in the garden, red-faced and defiant, but quite unrepentant for whatever misdemeanour he was guilty of, until Maria screamed at him to come home for dinner.

On 22 of August, I started painful contractions all day. And as they kept coming quicker, and more severely as evening fell, I told Connie I had better go in to hospital. Dr Rustomjee booked me in to Margaret Coles Maternity Hospital at Prahran, and Luigi drove us there.

I had baby clothes, flannel nappies I sewed, and my nightwear, all packed up in a suitcase, so I was organized, and did not panic. Over the last few months, I read extensively on how to care for my body, and learnt breathing exercises, and applied olive oil daily, to avoid cracked, and painful nipples when breast-feeding.

I kept breathing in and out deeply, but on the way, the contractions kept coming very quickly. I was in great pain whenever the car rattled and jerked over bumpy roads. I almost forgot how to relax and do breathing exercises when spasms engulfed me. Finally, we reached the hospital about eight or nine o'clock in the night.

The nurse on duty told Connie that as it was my first time, I would not have the baby soon, and could be in labour for a long time. She advised him to go home and get some rest, and she would call him before the baby was born. He gave Luigi's and Maria's phone number, as we did not have a phone. Whenever his family wanted to contact him, they usually left a message with them. He told me he was going home, so he did not leave Bab's number.

As soon as he left, I was wheeled to a very dark, cell-like room, where I had to lie down on a narrow, uncomfortable bed. And each time the contractions assaulted me, I screamed out in pain, as I could hardly bear the excruciating ripples of pain tearing through my body.

I pressed the bell desperately, and a cold, stern-faced nurse in her mid-thirties or so entered the room, and hissed, "Shut up you *stupid* fool! *Stop* acting like a schoolgirl!" I cried out, "But it's paining so much! I can't help shouting!" She glanced at me angrily, turned on her heel, and left without another word.

I shouted out in agony and desperation, and she came into the gloomy room a second time to scold me in the same harsh tones. I passed out after that, as she shoved a mask over my face. The next thing I remember was, Dr Rustomjee's deep voice urging me to, "Push, push, push *harder!*" My legs were strapped up, and strong hands pinned me down.

Much later on the following morning, I woke up crying uncontrollably, as I recalled my nightmarish experience. When Dr Rustomjee came in, I told him how the nurse scolded me and was so rude.

I noticed my bruised arms where the nurse had gripped tight, but he smiled reassuringly and said, "You were given a little gas to knock you out, and it's best not to complain about the nurse to the hospital."

I gave birth to a healthy baby boy around 2am or so, and he weighed six and a half pounds; he was well, but it was a forceps delivery, because the umbilical cord was wrapped around his neck. So his head was pulled to a side where the forceps held him. I had about ten or eleven stitches, which added to my pain and discomfort.

They brought in the baby soon, all washed and wrapped up in a soft blanket. I looked at its tiny, red, wrinkled face, and was instructed to nurse the baby. Connie was still not around, as the nurse said he could not be contacted at the number he had given. When they finally got through, it was long after the birth, as he had stayed the night at Bab's.

He was annoyed with the nurses, although they said they tried to contact him several times. I was too tired to ask him why he did not give Bab's number, if he meant to stay there. Still crying and upset, I told him what I endured. When he spoke to Dr Rustomjee, he was told the same thing, that it was best to keep quiet until I left the hospital.

I could not believe what a rude, uncaring nurse I had had the misfortune to have with me on that night. And wherever she is today, I hope she realized what a dreadful time she gave a frightened, and lonely twenty year old girl. Babs and Damian drove Connie to hospital, and were pleased I had a safe delivery.

When I returned home after a week, Connie had shopped around with Geraldine and Babs, and bought a wardrobe and a chest of draws for the nursery. I would have liked to select furniture myself, but he surprised me. A few weeks earlier, we bought a second-hand cot and painted it cream. I sewed pale blue curtains, and decorated the room in cream and blue, as we did not know the baby's sex.

Damian and Babs drove us home from hospital, and Connie took care of the meals etc. until we settled in to our new routine. And soon, I cared for the baby without anyone's help, as I had no problems. I loved the beautiful little boy dearly, and wanted to do my best for him.

Soon after, in the middle of an altercation, I was upset to learn that Geraldine had criticized my parents because Clifford wrote about a domestic incident involving them. Connie spat at me angrily now, "You are like your *mother!*" She disparaged me too, and said he was a "hen-pecked" husband. I was jolted, because I was fond of his family, and could not believe they could be so insincere.

I was disgusted, because she waited to undermine me when I was in hospital. And I asked him why his family believed he was hen-pecked. He replied, "When Bab's friend visited to sell life insurance, you told her we didn't need any, so that woman told Babs I'm a hen-pecked husband."

I knew it was quite the opposite, so I did not worry about anyone said. But I was distressed, as I was very fond of them, and treated them well whenever they visited.

Connie chose the baby's name, "Stacy" as it meant "rock" according to the book of names. I made other suggestions, but he did not favour any of them. He named the baby, Stacy Conrad. Esme, Bronco, Babs and Damian, stood as Godparents.

The days and nights were bitterly cold in that concrete-floored flat, as the only heating was the radiant heater Maria and Joe gave us. The bedrooms had bare boards without rugs, and an old threadbare piece of carpet covered the lounge floor. The first few months were the worst, as I was up a few times during the night. I woke up shivering to breast feed Stacy. And half- asleep, I heard the faint "clip clop" of a horse-drawn milk cart, doing its early morning rounds.

Stacy was a normal, healthy baby, and soon learned to recognize people and things. He was very fair-complexioned, with beautiful, light-grey eyes, and dark brown hair. I loved him with all my being, as most mothers love their children. Whenever he slept, and I had time to spare, I painted large posters with oil crayons, of Walt Disney cartoon characters, such as Donald Duck, Mickey Mouse, and Goofy, and pasted them on the nursery walls.

I sewed a great deal, and knitted several sweaters for Connie too. Maria over locked the seams, so the clothes looked professional.

A few months later, Wendy, Brian, and their two girls, came with Babs and Damian. After a happy re-union, they wanted to surprise Connie too, and drove to Joe's office. Connie returned with them shortly, and we had a great time, as Wendy was very happy to be with her family.

Aunty, Uncle, Cristobel, and Paul, were expected sometime in October that year, and then the family would be together again, except Roland and Cuckoo.

Wendy was a very loving, sincere person, and she was very fond of me. I too loved her in return, and the two girls as well. All the years I knew Wendy, she was not two-faced. So she was always welcome, because I cared for her very much.

It was a shame that Wendy turned to alcohol, cigarettes, and gambling (bingo and poker machines), more than ever, in order to escape reality. She loved to eat extremely hot curries, and her family called her cooking, "Wendy's revenge" because she added too much chilli and pepper.

Her favourite drink was sweet sherry, as it was cheap, but she enjoyed whisky whenever she could get it. Her family were embarrassed when she drank too much.

Because she ended up making a spectacle of herself at family gatherings. But she was harmless, and drank herself to oblivion without hurting anyone in the process, except herself.

Connie's family arrived a few weeks later, and together with Babs, he organized a two-bedroom flat in Mckinnon. They furnished it completely, so it was comfortable. They visited immediately with Babs and Damian, and were smitten with Stacy, as he was such a gorgeous baby.

We enjoyed a happy re-union, and they said they would visit soon. I was glad to see Aunty again, as I missed her warm, homely presence. Uncle was quiet as usual, and was not overly impressed with Australia, but he told me that he missed his friends and homeland. Cristobel and Paul were excited, and revelled in their new surroundings, especially the novelty of television.

Chapter 3

That same year in November, I was pregnant again, and I was greatly distressed. I cried at the doctor's office, "I just don't know *how* to go through this pregnancy and have *another* baby so soon!" He was a kindly doctor, and looked at me sympathetically "You are young and healthy. It would be a *pity* to terminate this pregnancy. Why don't you have the baby, and you'll find that they'll be good company for each other as well. It's best to have your family when you are young." I was twenty then.

When Connie's parents heard about it, Uncle muttered, "Sweeta, tell these fellows to be careful, they must take precautions for Dolly not to get pregnant so soon!" And this sage counsel from a man who fathered twelve children, because his wife did not take the pill! It was ironical, but at the same time, it was good of him to be concerned about me.

I did not know how to broach the subject of birth control with Connie, as he was so set in his ways about the Catholic church's teachings. He would not even discuss the pill, or any form of contraceptive, which was very frustrating and unfair. I was the one who suffered the consequences. He believed in the "rhythm method" just like his parents, and that was why Aunty was pregnant almost every year, until menopause. I was determined not to follow in her footsteps, and decided to take the contraceptive pill once I had this baby.

When Stacy was three months old, we took him to Forest Hills shopping centre during Christmas. A jolly-faced Santa Clause entertained the children, and we removed a photograph of Stacy sitting on Santa's lap. We spent that Christmas with his family. Stacy slept through the night, and we settled down to a routine now.

I bathed and settled Stacy by five o'clock every evening, so when Connie came home after work, he relaxed, and did not worry about the baby. I washed nappies during the day, and he hung them out for me. Whenever Maria saw him hanging out the washing, she said, "Your husband help you with washing Dolly?" I did not bother to explain, but he did wash the nappies sometimes.

We did not own a dryer, or a washing machine then, so we hung the nappies outside, then dried them in front of the radiant heater. Connie was so insecure, and wanted me to pay him constant attention, so I made sure the baby did not take up all my time when he was home. He was content that I bathed and fed Stacy, and he was in bed, so we could spend the evenings together. I read extensively about new parents, and how important it was for the father to be involved in the child's development, but Connie did not take to fatherhood naturally.

He was clumsy when he held the baby, and said, "Here take him Dolla, I might drop him!" I learnt how to bathe and care for Stacy without any trouble though. Connie was determined not to spoil the baby, and told me, "You mothers spoil children, I know. I will see to it that he is disciplined right from the start. Don't carry and pamper him when he cries, put him in his cot!" And so on with peremptory orders, little realizing, or admitting he was a "Mummy's Boy." I carried and petted Stacy whenever he was not around, because he did not like me to cuddle him even when he cried.

Joe Saraty invited us to a Christmas party at one of the popular restaurants near-by. One of Connie's colleagues, Wally, offered to pick us up in the evening. I sewed a full-length, evening dress, with dark green crepe fabric, and was happy to socialise with outsiders for a change, as I did not have any friends then. I bathed and fed Stacy that evening, and then tucked him in his cot. I knew he would sleep soundly till early morning, but I told Maria we were going out for a few hours, and to keep an eye on Stacy, in case he woke up. It was the first time we left Stacy alone.

Before we left though, Connie warned me, "*Don't* dance with *anyone* else, or accept any drinks if they offer you, and sit beside me all evening, okay?" I nodded.

Wally and his wife picked us up, and we had a pleasant evening at the restaurant. They sat opposite us, and Wally paid compliments in a friendly manner. He was a little intoxicated, and he said, "I love how your dark eyes sparkle in the candlelight!" Connie looked grim with annoyance. Then Wally got up, looked at me keenly, and asked, "Can I have this dance?" I felt embarrassed as I mumbled, "Thank you, but I dance only with my husband." His face turned red, and he sat down awkwardly.

The drive back home was uncomfortable, to say the least, as Wally was obviously offended. But I was ordered not to dance with anyone, and I was the one who had to live with Connie, so I obeyed rules.

I had plenty of spare time in the evenings, once Stacy was in bed, so I made use of those hours either sewing or knitting. When he was about six months old, one of the first soft toys I made for Stacy, was a golliwog, about two feet high, and as tall as him. The day I finished it, I sat it down in a corner of the room, and watched Stacy. His face lit up with the biggest smile, and he crawled towards it. In a matter of minutes he embraced the golliwog, and from that moment, it was his favourite toy and constant companion.

Whenever he was upset or in his cot, he kept the golliwog on top of him and made funny noises, chuckled and smiled at it, as if it was a real person. It was a smart-looking golliwog too; dressed in tartan overalls, with a fine head of curly black wool, a wide red slash of a mouth, and big white buttons for its eyes. Later on, I made two large golden-fleeced teddy bears, as I enjoyed making soft toys.

I also knitted a two-piece suit in emerald green wool for Aunty, and she was very happy. We forged a close bond, ever since I stayed with her, and I treated her like a second mother. She confided in me whenever she was concerned about her family, and I always listened to her, and gave her my time and affection.

Clifford arrived in early 1973, and they were married in mid-January that same year, and moved to a rented a flat in Springvale. We did not receive a wedding invitation, and Connie told me he did not want to attend their wedding either. He was still not reconciled to his sister marrying Clifford. Geraldine told me they sent us an invitation, but I did not see one. I wondered if Connie threw it away, but he always insisted we did not receive one.

Their marriage was a dark shadow in our lives always, and he took out his anger and frustration on me. Connie was convinced that Clifford married his sister, just to get even with him for breaking up our affair, and he told me they would never be welcome in our home.

Wendy and Brian rented a unit in Mckinnon too. Uncle, Aunty, Cristobel Paul, Sherone, Valerie, and Paul, visited often during this period. The girls loved to bathe and dress Stacy, and enjoyed spending time with him. He was a very interesting, delightful baby.

Although Connie was relatively happy at Joe Saraty's, we knew he could earn more money, if he worked for a bigger company. With this in mind, I perused every single paper for possible vacancies. One day, I read an advertisement for an architectural draftsman, at Safeway head office in Mulgrave.

I urged Connie to apply for that job, and we did not lose any time sending in his resume immediately. He was called for an interview, because he now had work experience in Australia. The manager was very impressed with his portfolio, and Joe Saraty gave him an excellent reference, as he was hard-working and reliable. We were elated when he was selected, and Connie left Joe Saraty in July 1973, and joined Safeway, with better prospects and conditions. His wages increased to over $100 a week, and his new boss, Lance Cousins, told him he was happy to employ such a hard-working, excellent draftsman. Lance was an architect, and was very helpful and supportive as well.

Nelune arrived just a few months before Christian was born, as we sponsored her, and Nihal paid for her ticket to Australia. How overjoyed I was to see her again! She arrived in a taxi one morning, although she told us she would contact us when she arrived in Melbourne. But decided to surprise us instead. We still did not have a telephone in our flat, and Maria and Luigi conveyed messages.

Nelune stayed with us for one week only, as Connie was very keen for her to live on her own. He did not want anyone (especially my family members), staying, in case they found out his true character. He insisted she would be better off living on her own. Nelune found employment almost immediately, at National Mutual Building Society in the city.

She boarded with a Ceylonese lady, in Albert Park for a short while, and then moved to Mrs Smith's, in Pascoe Vale. Mrs Smith was a kind old lady, who treated Nelune well. Every Friday evening, Nelune visited us, and stayed over the weekend, which was absolutely wonderful. And she enjoyed spending time with Stacy too. Nelune learnt how to drive, and before the year was out, had her licence, and bought a pale-blue Datsun.

When I started getting contractions towards late evening, on 28 August, I packed up my suitcase without delay. And Luigi drove us to Margaret Coles hospital immediately. I prayed earnestly I would not get that same nasty nurse again. So, I could hardly believe my eyes when I saw her coming out of the maternity ward! It was late evening, and she just finished up, and another nurse came on duty.

This time too, Connie did not go home, but went to Wendy's place, because he said they would help him with Stacy. When I went into labour soon after, the nurse could not contact him at Luigi's till after the birth. It was another little baby boy, weighing almost the same as Stacy, and he was born around 4am. They gave me "gas" this time too, and ended up with the same number of stitches.

This time though, my arms were not bruised. But the words, "Push, push" rang through my foggy consciousness, until I heard the doctor say, "It's a boy!" Connie arrived by the time they washed the baby, and I fell asleep immediately. We named this baby Christian, as I chose it this time, and Connie liked it too.

When I came home after a week, Connie said, "I'm going to Wendy's now, and I'll bring the girls here so they can help you." I did not need any help, and just wanted him to be close, and keep me company. But he was totally oblivious to the fact that I needed emotional closeness, after my harrowing experience. He boarded a train, and was gone for a few hours. And he returned late at night, with Sherone and Valerie, who spent a few days with us.

When Nelune visited every Friday evening, I finished feeding the two babies, put them to sleep, and then did some quick shopping at Forest Hills. And we spent the evening watching episodes of "Columbo" which was a huge hit on television then, as we snacked on kabana and drank 7UP lemonade. They were good times with Nelune.

Christian started spluttering and coughing every few hours in the night until I fed him. Nelune imitated him well, as he had a funny way of making his needs known. I was on my toes constantly, with a new-born baby, and a twelve-month old toddler. I loved them with all my heart, but did not spoil them, and was quite firm when it came to training them to a routine. I found I could cope well with the two babies, once they settled down.

Stacy crawled all over the cold, vinyl-clad, concrete floors, so I spread flannel sheets in the corridor for him to crawl over. The flat was frosty as an ice block, with only a small strip heater in the lounge, so we bought two more small heaters for the bedrooms.

I washed countless nappies, as we could not afford disposable nappies then, and dried them in front of the heater when it rained. Some evenings, Connie fed the babies, and made their meals as they grew older. We never left them with babysitters, or with anyone in his family, as I wanted to care for them all by myself.

Aunty and Uncle visited at the end of that year, and asked Connie, "Can you sponsor Lena? Tucko is interested in her, and they want to come to Australia and get married." This was the first we knew about that affair. Roland left the brotherhood, and worked somewhere in Colombo. We did not know he too was in love with his cousin, and was serious about marrying her.

Connie did not even ask me, but agreed, as he was the only close relative who could sponsor his cousin, because he had a secure job with a regular income. I thought it was odd that they fell for the same cousin. Roland too had boarded at

Aunty Ella's, and where Connie failed, he succeeded in breaking up her long-time affair with her boyfriend. Her father belted him for seducing his daughter, and made him promise to marry her.

Cuckoo wrote that he left the priesthood, and married a German lady, Regina, a nurse. He told us he left a few years ago, but did not want to tell his parents, because he did not want to upset them. Uncle's hopes that all his children would join religious orders, ended in disappointment.

Lena arrived within a few months after she was sponsored, and the family brought her to visit us. I met her a couple of times before in Ceylon, and found her plain, and uninteresting, with the personality of a blackboard. When I tried to converse with her, all she did was grin sheepishly, and answer, "Yes" or "No."

She was about my height and age, swarthy, with crooked, protruding front teeth, light-brown eyes, and sparse black hair. When I first met Connie, he told me that he felt sorry for her, because she suffered hair loss due to a medical condition. And he said, "She's ugly like a witch, but I love her!" Her short hair was permed now, and she looked very plump.

When Connie saw her, he behaved like a Jack-in-the box, all wound up with excitement. He immediately started playing sentimental Jim Reeves records, and asked her in an affected manner, "Do you like Jim Reeves?" And he buzzed around her like a dizzy bee, thinking it bothered me. Bursting with insecurity about Clifford, he laboured under a misapprehension that he could make me jealous by flirting with her. I looked at him in disbelief, as it was quite acceptable for him to be as flirtatious as possible with anyone, and I had to accept his double standards without question.

Connie always felt more at ease among ladies, and he seldom made friends with any males. At any social gathering, he sidled up to the young females, and flirted outrageously, as he was a "Ladies man." When I caught him ogling a scantily-clad woman on the street, I said, "Stop staring." And embarrassed, he retorted, "You have an inferiority complex, because you are a Sinhalese!"

Skin colour was very important to him, because he was fair-skinned. He could not understand why his colleagues called him "coloured" or "black." Aunty was just as bad, because she first commented on whether the person was "black" or "light-skinned" when describing someone she met for the first time.

Lena boarded with Aunty and Uncle for a few months, and waited for Roland to arrive. But Roland stunned the family when he informed them he married another girl, Shiranthi, whom he met at a "Born again" Christian service. He wrote to say he would not be migrating to Australia in the near future. Not only did he leave the Brotherhood, and the Catholic church, but he became a Jehovah's Witness, like Shiranthi, and his letters were full of Biblical references. Every sentence was followed with "Praise the Lord" and "Alleluia."

Lena moved out and rented a flat close to Aunty's. In due time she met another man, with whom she lived for a while. She fell pregnant, and married him when the baby was almost due.

We attended the annual children's party that Safeway held in Christmas 1973. Brian drove us there with his family, as he had bought a roomy, Ford Falcon car.

Connie carried Stacy, while he had a burning cigarette in his mouth. Unfortunately, Stacy grabbed the end of the cigarette.

His screams and cries were very distressing, as he did not know what hurt him. It also happened to be the two fingers he sucked on, and every time he put his fingers in his mouth, he yelled out in pain. That was the first lesson he learnt, not to touch fire, or anything that smoked. But I was more annoyed with Connie, that he had a cigarette in his mouth while carrying a toddler.

Chapter 4

Nelune sponsored Shiranthi Basnayake, her friend from Kandy convent, somewhere in early 1974. When she arrived in Melbourne, Nelune drove down with her, and she was still the same friendly, unassuming girl she had always been, and I was fond of her. It was great because Nelune visited almost every weekend. Connie took driving lessons now as he hoped to buy a car soon.

He still travelled to work by bus, and found it very tedious. Anjo and Barlo surprised us shortly after Shiranthi's arrival, as they too immigrated to Australia. It was just like before, and we enjoyed some good times when they visited on weekends. They all boarded in various inner city suburbs, and Nelune still lived with Mrs Smith.

Somewhere in 1974, about six months after Christian was born, I was pregnant again. My period was about one month late, and this time, I knew I could not go through another pregnancy again. I asked Babs if she knew of a good doctor who would terminate my pregnancy. She recommended a trustworthy doctor in the city, who helped her a few times.

Connie was adamant, that as a good Catholic, I must not take contraceptive pills. But obviously the "rhythm method" did not work for me, and I was very angry I had to endure this trauma.

It was over soon, and I came home feeling drained. It cost about two hundred dollars, and Connie asked Nelune for the money. That same evening, we started our all too familiar arguments over some trivial remark, and he yelled out angrily, "You didn't suffer enough you *bitch*, you should have *bled* to death!" I looked at him in utter disbelief and sadness, wondering how he could utter such words. And although he was remorseful a little while later, the hurt did not go away so easily, just because he said, "Sorry."

Even after this abortion, he still did not agree to my taking contraceptives. I cried desperately, as I wondered how many more times I would have to terminate unwanted pregnancies.

Aunty, Uncle, and Paul arrived one Saturday afternoon, when Nelune, Shiranthi, Anjo, and Barlo were visiting. Aunty and Uncle usually boarded a train on weekends and visited us often without prior notice, as they loved the children dearly, and wanted to spend time with them. Cristobel worked as a checkout girl in a supermarket, and we did not see her very often, but Paul joined them sometimes.

That day, Aunty was very upset, and quite unlike her placid self. She started raging about my family, and shouted at Nelune, "*Your* elder sister left her husband for another man, and your parents are always fighting we hear, so it's not as if *your* family is so perfect!"

I was at a loss to understand why she was so rude, when she burst out crying, "Barbara and Damian are getting a *divorce*! That wretch is running around with Ralston and wants to live with him!" She was in an emotional whirlpool and sobbed uncontrollably.

Uncle and Aunty were very fond of Damian, and could not believe Babs was divorcing him, especially as Jeremy was still a little boy. They were married for about eight years now. Connie pacified Aunty, and told her to calm down, but he too could not understand why she attacked my family.

They spent the night, and we discussed the issue at length. Aunty said she never liked Ralston from the start, and could not accept Babs' decision to divorce. The news shocked them deeply, and Uncle grumbled about the immoral life in Australia, and said he wanted to go back to Ceylon.

Shirani married Ranjith Perera in August 1972, and their son, Roshan, was born on 2 February 1974. She finished training at Maharagama Teachers College, and now wrote to say they wanted to immigrate to Australia, as life was difficult.

I was delighted, and sponsored them without delay, and waited eagerly for their arrival. I still did not have any friends, as I had no transport or a phone to contact anyone. It was a great relief therefore to have my sisters with me, as I did not socialise with anyone else except Connie's family.

Nihal wrote often, and so did everyone else in the family. I kept in constant touch too, as I was very homesick and missed them dearly. I collected used-clothes, food items, and knick knacks, then sent boxes to Nilanthi and my parents every year from then on.

Nilanthi gave birth to a baby boy, Tanesh, on 18 June 1973, and Nelune undertook to be his Godmother. She promised to pay for his education, which she did all through his school life at a private college.

Connie and I stood as Roshan's and Tanesh's Godparents by proxy. Nilanthi lost the baby she was pregnant with in 1972, and though it was a full term baby boy, it survived only a few days, so she was thrilled to have another baby boy soon after.

On 3 February 1975, Shirani, Ranjith and Roshan arrived in Melbourne. Nelune picked them at the airport and drove them down.

Roshan was a beautiful, but very naughty toddler, and demanded constant attention. Nelune, Connie and I, rented a two-bedroom flat in Nunawading for them, and furnished it with bare necessities. It was about twenty minutes walk from where we lived.

Connie organized a job for Ranjith at the ice cream plant at Safeway Mulgrave. Shirani pushed Roshan in a pram, and visited me on some days. When we tried to have a siesta, as we were exhausted running around our toddlers, Roshan just sat up and bawled his eyes out, demanding Shirani to stay up too and play with him.

Shirani was a qualified teacher, so she kept looking for jobs in local schools. She was pleased when the nuns at Killester College, in Springvale, selected her, because of a very good work record in Ceylon. When Shirani started her new job, they moved to a bigger unit in Springvale, which was closer to work for them.

Now we saw each other only on some weekends whenever Nelune drove over. We depended on public transport or taxis, as we still did not own a car. When she got her driver's licence a few months later, Shirani bought a red Mazda, and it was great because we saw each other more often.

I was pregnant again around this time, and we struggled financially. Connie asked Shirani $200 for an abortion, and we drove there one afternoon, but Ranjith was still at work. So Shirani said, "I'll give you the money, but no need to mention it to him." We agreed, and then I went ahead with the abortion.

This time, whether he liked it or not, I *insisted* that I was going on the pill. I told him that I was not going to have another abortion, because that was it. He took me to the doctor reluctantly. And I explained that I had two abortions because my husband did not want me to take the pill. He shook his head in disbelief, but did not comment, and wrote out a prescription. He advised me about possible side effects etc. I was relieved to know I would not get pregnant again.

Connie was irresponsible about financial matters too, and kept getting into deeper waters. He asked Nelune to sign as a guarantor, to get a loan and consolidate debts. But the interest was so high, that we were just sinking into a deep financial muddle. He borrowed money from my sisters many times, and they generously helped us out. I wanted to get part-time work, but he would not hear of it. So I kept looking for any sort of work I could do from home, like sewing, for example.

He thought he would get a windfall to clear our debts, so he started gambling on horse and greyhound racing. He placed small bets only, as he could not afford large amounts, but even twenty dollars a week on gambling, was something beyond our means. He seldom won, but that did not prevent or discourage him from trying.

I was overjoyed when Nelune and Shirani visited on some weekends, as I was very isolated without any friends, phone, or transport. But Connie's behaviour became worse now. Because every time Shirani and Ranjith visited and left, he started an argument over any trivial remark I may have made.

He could not wait to see them drive off before he demanded angrily, "What did you *mean* by saying that? What were you and Shirani *talking* about?" Soon, it was a full scale brawl, and he ended up being verbally and physically abusive.

Once, as we were driving to Shirani's, he started to squabble, and next moment, he struck my face hard. The children were in the back seat, so I did not say anything, but I cried all the way. He barked angrily, "Now don't go telling your sister that I slapped you!" And he glared at me suspiciously. When we arrived there, I just smiled and pretended nothing was wrong, although my cheek was still sore and red.

He was paranoid that I would discuss our marital woes with my sisters, so whenever they visited, he hung around like a bad smell, and did not leave us alone to enjoy a sisterly chat. After a while, he calmed down and said, "*Ever* since your sisters came to Australia, we have been fighting!" I asked him patiently, "In what way are they to blame? We have always been fighting *ever* since we got married! You just imagine the worst always." He did not reply, but he was irrationally afraid that they would find out about his bad behaviour.

He had increased his intake of alcohol too, which made matters worse. From two bottles of beer, it was now six or eight stubbies, and he started drinking as soon as he came home. The first thing he did was, open a bottle of beer, gulp it down eagerly and exclaim, "I *needed* that to relax!"

He was drunk by seven or eight o'clock every night, and then there was no reasoning with him. I was relieved that the children were safely tucked in their cots, and all I had to do was shut my mouth and not retaliate. I was learning to be passive, and avoid confrontation at all costs, so the children would not witness our quarrels.

In the early days, he enjoyed the variety of dishes I prepared, and told his family what a good cook I was. As he relished offal, every week he bought ox tail, liver, or ox tongue for a few cents, as the butcher told him that no one bought offal. He was very fond of hot ox tail or tongue curry, and always enjoyed those dishes.

But now, meal times were especially trying, as he criticized everything, because he was full of beer, and had no appetite. He grumbled about the lack of salt or chilli in the curries. And he reminded me so much of his father, who behaved in exactly the same manner, that I told him angrily, "You are *just* like your father!" He grew angrier still and retorted, "Don't you dare compare me to my father! I'm not like him!" I replied, "Yes, you are," and left him alone. He was fixated with food, and became worse through the years, as he seemed to have lost his taste buds due to smoking and drinking. And nothing tasted as good as Ceylon curries (so he complained).

One evening, just after he came home from work, he was playing with Stacy, when he started screaming suddenly. I ran to see what was the matter, and he shouted, "Take this bugger away from me, he's *annoying* me!" Stacy was distressed and in tears. I stared in disbelief, as Connie tore buttons off his shirt with his teeth, and ripped his shirt to pieces! I cried out, "What *are* you doing in front of Stacy! Why are you so angry?" He could not speak, but kept tearing his shirt, and roared like a madman. I carried Stacy to his room, and hugged him till he settled down.

Later, he mumbled, "Sorry, I was so angry and frustrated at work today. They treat me like a little office boy, and got me to photocopy all the drawings, when I was employed as a draftsman!" I asked, "but *why* did you take it out on Stacy, and behave so violently in front of a little child? Don't you know they learn from the adults?" He did not like to be told anything, so he ignored me. But I became more afraid of his angry outbursts, especially in front of our little boys. I knew he could not control his temper, but did not realize then that he had an anger-management problem.

While the children slept for a couple of hours in the afternoons, I painted a few landscapes and still-life studies in oils on small canvases, or wrote poetry and articles. In between, I sewed and knitted all their clothes and mine, as it was too expensive to buy ready-made clothes.

Connie wanted all his shirts to be taken in, and tapered in the current "body-shirt" trend, which were close-fitting shirts, and pants had to be shortened too, so I had plenty of sewing on my hands. He was quite pleased to wear those shirts that I sewed, and told me his workmates could not believe I had sewn them.

I read about J.R.R Tolkein in a newspaper article one day, and immediately bought a copy of "The Hobbit" and so began my lifetime enthralment with Tolkein's fantasy world. When I finished reading "The Lord Of The Rings" I asked Connie to read those amazing books too. He did finish reading them over a long period of time, and was quite intrigued with the stories as well. Ever since then, I read those books over and over again, and never tired of that marvellous creation.

I loved the afternoons when I spent time with the children, and watched "Play School" or "Sesame Street" and laughed with them. Then as evening drew near, and I prepared them for bed, after their dinner, I dreaded the nights, as I had to endure Connie's bad behaviour. It was very seldom we had a peaceful time now, without him getting into a drunken brawl and hurting me physically and emotionally.

Although I tried to ignore him, it was very difficult to appease him when he behaved so unreasonably, especially after drinks. He insisted that the children were in bed when he came home around five thirty. So, he did not spend much time with them, as he was eager to have his beer and "relax." Usually, I read bedtime stories to the children until he came home. He peeped in to say goodnight, and that was his fatherly duty done for the day. My wifely duty was to sit by his side and fondle him, while he sipped a beer and watched television.

Even if I wanted to do something else, he would not hear of it, because that was his conjugal privilege. He was so drunk sometimes that he forgot what he was saying. And if a pretty woman appeared on some show, he leered drunkenly and muttered, "Must fuck her!" I looked at him and asked, "What did you say?" He giggled inanely and covered his mouth. Or else he strutted around the room mumbling, "I'm just bubbling with lust!" I found his drunken behaviour revolting, but if I objected, it always ended in a full blown argument. It was my daily routine to see that the children were safely tucked up in bed, and did not witness his bad behaviour.

He stayed up late some nights, and I was fast asleep when he tumbled into bed after midnight. Next morning he exclaimed, "I was watching a show with some gorgeous women, and I had a good wank!" It was degrading and hurtful to say the least. And I could not understand why he wanted to tell me what he did, except that he wanted to humiliate me.

It was habitual now for him to stay up late, and he did not come to bed when I turned in. When I woke up some mornings, I found my knitting unravelled and thrown on the floor, or my poster drawings torn in pieces.

When I questioned him about his destructive behaviour, he just grinned sheepishly, but never offered an apology, or explained why he behaved so deplorably. He pretended that he could not remember, and his invariable excuse was, "I had one too many, I don't know why I did that." That was it.

Connie's entire family, except Cuckoo and Roland, were in Australia now. And very often Aunty, Uncle, and Paul travelled by train and stayed with us a few days. Several family parties and get-togethers took place then, but we did not attend them, because Connie did not want me to be in the same room as Clifford. He was extremely possessive, and his jealousy was as irrational as ever.

He complained that work was sometimes very frustrating, as he constantly had to prove his worth to his boss and colleagues. They accepted that he was a very good draftsman, but subjected him to a great deal of good-humoured teasing about his height and accent, as most new Australians endure. He came home angry, and sulked and vented his frustrations on me.

Some time in June 1975, Connie wanted to buy a second-hand car, as travelling was becoming too tiring. And we needed transport to get around with the children as well. He bought a 1972 rouge-red Renault for $2000, and a friend of Damian's stood as guarantor. Now we had a car loan, as well as a hire purchase loan, and monthly repayments gouged a large slice out of Connie's wages. Gradually, we found ourselves in financial strife as monthly bills poured in.

Social Security paid Child Endowment (as Family Allowance was called then), of $2 per child fortnightly; a couple of years later, it increased to about $6 per child fortnightly. I saved these payments in a Christmas Club account, as they were sent in my name. At the end of the year, I had about sixty dollars with negligible interest. And it was very pleasant to buy a few extras and clothes for the children. Sometimes, I bought clothes and shoes at opportunity shops to send home.

I still toyed with the idea of finding part-time work, but Connie remained adamant. He did not like the idea of my working anywhere, as he wanted to be the sole wage-earner, even though a second income would have helped us immensely. It was a struggle though with two children, and living on one modest income with huge bills piling up.

We drove around very often, now that we owned a car, and it was convenient for Connie, as he did not spend long hours waiting for public transport anymore. We soon moved into a two-bedroom, weather-board house in O'Shannessy Street, Nunawading, which cost about $30 a week in rent.

It had a large backyard where the children could play safely, but it was a draughty old house, with threadbare carpet throughout. Connie spent a great deal of time and energy tiling the kitchen walls and laying vinyl on the kitchen floor. The toilet and laundry were outside the house, and it was an eerie place to visit, especially at nights. The children were toilet-trained in the bathroom inside, where I kept a chamber pot and a small toilet seat for them to sit on.

Luigi and Maria were unhappy when we left, and retained our bond of $50. They said the walls were dirty, with marks left behind when I took down the large posters from the nursery room walls. Another one of Connie's quirks got us into their bad books, as he said, "*Don't* tell Maria and Luigi we're moving to a house close-by, just say we're going to Mitcham," which was the next suburb.

I did not know the reason why, but I had to abide by what he told me to do. We refrained from giving them our new address, and Connie kept the spare key after we moved, so he could go back and clean the flat.

Maria misunderstood the reason why he kept the spare key, and was very upset about it. A few days after we moved, she stood on the front step of our house, gesturing angrily. Stacy and Christian stared at her through the window as she shouted out, "Tell your mum to open the door!" When I let her in, she spat out a string of abuse. She accused us of keeping the spare key for some ulterior reason.

All my explanations did not pacify her, and she screamed, "*Why* good girl like you do this thing to me?" Later that evening, Connie, Uncle, and I went to return the key. When she saw us Maria started abusing Connie, "You dirty *Indian* man! Why you not give back my key?" When Connie tried to calm her down, she screamed even louder. Uncle, who watched in disbelief, asked quietly, "Shall I call the police Connie?"

We left her still yelling at us in the distance. That was how I learnt how volatile some Italians could be. Luigi did not get involved, and stayed indoors. It was a sad way to part after three years. But later on, whenever we met them in church, they smiled politely enough, but we did not indulge in mutual visits again. Glenda too, who was a very good neighbour, rarely visited, as she now had another baby boy to look after. She wanted a girl, but had five boys now.

Our immediate neighbours in O'Shannessy Street, were two elderly couples without children or pets living with them. Whenever I was in the garden with the children, they looked over their fences and greeted me or just waved. We invited them for dinner once, and I cooked roast beef with vegetables. We tried to be neighbourly and get acquainted, but they never reciprocated.

Connie took this as a personal affront, and blamed me, saying, "They must have heard you when we fight!" This made me very angry, and I replied, "You are the one who shouts and makes a big noise, so why blame me?" He was afraid the neighbours must have heard us brawling, and he looked sheepish whenever he saw them outside. But I continued to wave and speak to them, if I saw them pottering in their gardens.

Once, when he was in the middle of an argument, he kicked the bedroom wall and made a big hole in it. When Aunty visited us just after that incident, she noticed the hole, and asked Stacy, "Who made that hole in the wall?" and he replied, "Dad kicked the wall." She looked at me seriously, "Is it true Dolly? I never knew Connie was behaving like this."

I did not discuss our problems with Aunty or his family. But she was the only one who knew what was going on in our lives, as she visited often, and stayed over for a few days. She had also witnessed Connie's bad behaviour when we lived with them for two years. Aunty did not say much then, but at least she was aware of what Connie was capable of doing when he was angry.

Another time, when he came home after work, I was in the bathroom, just finishing bathing the children. He wanted my immediate attention, but I said, "I'm busy now, wait till I finish." Next moment, I felt the full force of his violent kick in the calf of my leg. I cried out in pain as I keeled over the bath. He had his boots on, and the pain was so intense that tears streamed down my cheeks.

I managed to dry the children and get them dressed, before limping painfully to the kitchen to feed them dinner. Then I got into bed and cried bitterly. He was in the lounge, watching television and guzzling down his beer. Christian came up to me, his large eyes round with concern, "Did Dad kick you Mum?" he asked softly. I turned over, smiled at him, then hugged them both. Stacy stood by quietly, without saying a word.

I could not get over Connie's behaviour, as I never provoked him. No matter what bad language he used, I never resorted to name-calling or foul- language. I was brought up to be lady-like, and would never sink down to his level. He sometimes abused me in Sinhalese, and when I asked him why, he shouted mockingly, "Have you *forgotten* your language! You are a Sinhalese haliya (loud-mouthed woman)." When I could not hold my tongue any longer, the worst I called him was, "You bastard!" That made him roar angrily as he chased me around the house.

When he got hold of me, he grabbed my waist-length hair, twisted it around his hand, so he could jerk my head and drag me by my hair; or he gripped my throat, deliberately pressed his thumbs on the hollow of my neck, and squeezed hard, until I choked and spluttered and was hoarse for days.

Once, he twisted my right hand so violently that I thought it would break, but ended up with a sprained wrist for weeks. It was a miracle that I survived his physical abuse. Because in his blind rage and drunken fits, he did not know or care how badly he hurt me. And the inevitable refrain was, "Sorry Dolla, I won't do it again! I promise!"

Looking back, had I known that I was a victim of domestic violence, I would have definitely sought help. But unlike now, where there is so much awareness of this terrible problem in society, and men are being educated to respect women, I cannot remember anyone talking about this issue. Although I am sure there must have been support groups somewhere, had I been brave enough to talk about my situation.

I read a leaflet recently, listing behaviours that are regarded as types of abuse, and which most women accept as part of their unhappy lives. That type of abuse, was exactly what I suffered at Connie's hands. The following were *some* of the typical behaviours, and though not in point form here, I endured *all* of these behaviours and worse:

Not giving personal space or privacy; playing mind games, feeling trapped; insanely jealous of *everyone;* not accepting responsibility for his actions; made me feel anxious, isolated me from friends and my family; threatened to harm or kill if I left; shouting often, and had immense anger issues; no access to money of my own; blaming me for his mistakes; *controlling* behaviour; made me feel afraid; checked my mail; wanted to know *where* I was all the time; called me names and put me down; constantly checked my whereabouts; was mean, rude and inappropriate; sabotaged my ability to work or study;

He threatened me, hit, punched, slapped, and once, he even spat on my face when he had a mouthful of cheese. I wept uncontrollably, as I stood under the shower and washed the spittle and cheese from my face and hair. He did not make me feel respected at all when he treated me like that. This was the sort of abuse I endured, and which no one knew about.

My weakness was, that I forgave him every time, like a good Christian. He told me, "You *must* forgive and forget." If I did not, it was pointless my going to church on Sundays and receiving Holy Communion. Religion, to me, means living a good life, not hurting anyone, and being an example in the way I speak and behave; church-going was only to belong to a community, and not the beginning and end of religion.

To Connie though, religion was two separate ways of living, as he was very particular about going to church, and not missing Sunday Mass. But as soon as we came home, his behaviour was totally opposite to what I expected of a good Christian.

He woke up early on Saturday mornings sometimes, and told me, "I'm going to visit Mummy, and I'll take the children for a drive, you can have a break." He returned very late in the evening, and I worried, as the children had a routine, bath and dinner before six o'clock. He never told me what he did all day, and I did not ask.

I spent the day cleaning the house, then painted, or wrote poems and short stories, as it was peaceful. Later, I wondered why *I* could not visit my sisters to have a break, instead of being stuck in the house, while he went visiting his family on his own. But I never questioned him, as he took it for granted that he could do just as he pleased. If I wanted to visit my sisters, he had to accompany me, and so it was over the years.

Chapter 5

On our fifth wedding anniversary, 18 November 1975, we drove to the picturesque town of Bright, and Paul and Aunty accompanied us. The drive was memorable, and I enjoyed the beautiful scenery along the way. Christian was just making sounds and short words, but did not talk in sentences. Stacy was a chatter-box though, and at three years, he spoke quite fluently.

On one of our long drives in Bright, we lost our way on the Omeo Highway in the night, and returned to the holiday unit well after 2am. The children, even with wet underpants, hardly stirred or complained. We were blessed with these two beautiful boys, and they were easy to take around anywhere, as they never fussed or complained.

Connie knocked down two rabbits on our way back, and Aunty skinned, cleaned, and salted them in the early hours. She curried them for Cristobel, who had asthma, as Aunty believed rabbit meat was good for asthma.

We spent an unforgettable time visiting scenic places like Mount Buffalo, Mt Hotham, and the splendid Alpine region around Bright, which was impressive. Soon, it was time to return home, and on our way back, we stopped at All Saints Winery.

A few months ago, we bought a puppy from a Lost Dog's Home, and left it with Shirani when we went to Bright. The puppy was a mongrel, but very cute, until it grew up to be too big, and we had to return it to the home.

Since Connie bought the car, he drove to races at Sandown Park in Springvale, or greyhound races at Olympic Park in the city. I loathed gambling in any form, and especially horse and dog races (as I thought it a cruel sport, being an animal-lover). But when he persuaded me once, the children and I spent a boring afternoon at Sandown Park.

I had to keep the children amused for hours on end, while the races were going on, and they endured what must have been utterly tedious for such young children. Then one night, he wanted me to join him to the races at Olympic Park, and I did go. But afterwards, I was determined not to repeat the venture, as I did not find it worthwhile to spend so many hours, and money on gambling.

On another occasion, when Sherone and Valerie spent a few days with us (as they visited quite often on their own), Connie drove off to the races one night. I went to bed around 10pm, but did not fall sleep, as I waited for him to come home. It was almost one o'clock in the morning when he finally returned, and I was furious. He had not won anything, and I asked him why he was so late, because he told me he would be home before midnight.

Our row erupted into a full scale brawl, and next morning, Sherone told me, "We heard you both arguing last night. Are you okay?" I was embarrassed, but assured them it was alright. When Connie came home in the evening, he wanted to go out again. I said I was too tired, so he scowled and muttered, "You are *always* tired! I'm going out for a drive with the girls." He took Sherone and Valerie home and returned late.

A few days later, he woke up one Saturday morning, after exercising his conjugal rights. I was busy cleaning up the house, when he started abusing me over some trivial issue and spat out, "I can find a *better* woman than you to look after the children!" I stormed up to him and demanded, "What do you mean by that? I will take care of *my* children, remember that!" He knew how fiercely I loved my boys, so he quickly left the house.

Connie's parents, and Paul still visited regularly, as they liked to spend a few days with us, and his parents doted on Stacy and Christian. They said they were very happy, as it was peaceful at our place, without any confusion. Connie usually refrained from drunken behaviour when they were visiting. Aunty said, "How well you have trained the children Dolly, they are so well-behaved and don't worry anyone."

Whenever they came, we rolled out a spare mattress in the lounge room, where the three of them slept till late in the day, especially Uncle, as he liked to stay in bed when it was cold. Aunty found light work in a factory, and Uncle cleaned schools in the evening.

They were ineligible to receive age pensions for ten years, because the family had sponsored them. So they had to support themselves, as Paul was still attending school. Cristobel was working part-time work in a supermarket, and at sixteen, she did exactly as she pleased. Her parents had no say, or control over her, and she started going out with boyfriends from then onwards. She visited sometimes, and I was just as fond of her as I always was, and she enjoyed chatting and sharing her experiences with me.

While we were driving through the Dandenong's with Shirani and family once, I saw two beautiful kittens for sale. Connie agreed to let me take one, and Shirani took the other, because Roshan wanted it. I named mine Mewsette; it was a cute, lovable kitten, and snuggled under my blanket every time I went to bed.

Mewsette was so well-trained that she stayed indoors all day, and once, when she was unable to go out, she did her business in the bath tub. The children too were very fond of Mewsette, as she was a good cat, and did not scratch or bite. Her only fault was that she had an enormous appetite, and ate constantly, so that very soon she became a big, fat cat.

When I was pregnant with Christian, I found a stray female cat at Maria's flat, and kept it outdoors. But it hung onto the fly screen door all night, and caterwauled non-stop, until Maria complained about the noise and we gave it to the RSPCA.

Somewhere in 1976, I read an advertisement in the newspapers for "home-machinists." I told Connie I could sew at home, as I had a good machine, and the extra money would be very useful. Connie agreed, because I did not have to go out to work. We drove to Flinders Lane, in the city, and met the person concerned.

Mr Novakis was in his forties or so; a pleasant-looking, tall, broad-shouldered Latvian. And when he saw us, he smiled kindly, knowing what it was like for new migrants in Australia. I took one of the gowns I sewed for a dance. It was a full-length, white dress made with jersey fabric, and floral chiffon sleeves. It was very neatly sewn, and when Mr Novakis examined it, he complimented me, "You are a very good seamstress, I can see. I will employ you."

The work though, was sewing doona covers. He said the bolts of material had to be cut carefully into required sizes, i.e. single, double, queen, and king. He also showed me how to sew little strips of material to join both sides of the doona. They were marked with pin points, where strips of fabric were sewn on. Then I had to sew piping on one side, before joining the two sides. It was very fiddly work, but Mr Novakis told me that it was the only way to sew doonas, so that there were no "cold spots" once they were filled with eiderdown.

Although it looked a little difficult at the start, I knew I could master it. And the best thing that happened was, Mr Novakis employed me, and gave me a chance that day. I was so elated, even though the earnings were a meagre $1.50 per doona cover for so much of work. And it took over one hour to sew each one. So began my career as a home-machinist. I spread out those heavy bolts of material on the dining or lounge room floor, and measured carefully, until I cut several doona covers. Large pieces were left over at the end of the bolt, which I turned into pillow cases or sheets for us. Mr Novakis never minded that, as long as I cut the required number of doonas out of each bolt.

The cotton fabric came in pastel shades of pink, blue, cream, and apple green. I included some of those sheets and pillow cases in the boxes I sent Ammie and Nilanthi. When Rose, the Avon lady, who visited often over the last few months, saw them, she wanted to buy a few sheet sets too, so I sold them at $7 a set.

She kept asking for more, and eventually I found out that she sold them to her friends at $15 a set. A lady knocked on my door one day, and asked if I still sold sheets at that price, and so I learnt of Rose's little enterprise.

When I asked her about it, she replied, "It's *too* cheap at $7, that's why I charged more." Rose and I became fairly well-acquainted over the last few months, and she told me she was a Burgher from Ceylon. She was a very fair-skinned, attractive lady, who looked more Anglo-Saxon.

I told her that I did not care how much she charged her customers. And after a while, I stopped selling them to her, as I gave them away as presents to the family. The fabric was so durable, that the sheets I sewed and sent home, lasted for decades, and I too had them for years, as they never wore out.

I watched the children, as they played beside me while I sewed. Stacy and Christian cut up bits of cloth, and attempted to join them, but as I did not give them needles, it became frustrating for them to pretend they were sewing. I related stories to amuse them instead, and I usually stopped sewing at three o'clock, so I could watch

Sesame Street, or the Muppet Show with them. They were gentle, peaceful times together, and I loved my two little boys passionately. I was very happy that I could watch them growing up, instead of leaving them in a childcare centre with strangers.

My constant prayer was, that I would always be around to take care of them, until they were old enough. I could not bear the idea of leaving my precious sons alone with Connie and a strange woman, who could never take my place as their mother. I prayed to God fervently to keep me safe and well until my boys were grown up.

They were gorgeous toddlers, and I maintained a wholesome, daily routine. Connie was not in the habit of spending much time with the children, playing or reading to them. So, it was up to me to finish my work, and then read bedtime stories or watch childrens' programs with them.

One afternoon, as I was washing up at the kitchen sink, I watched the children play in the backyard. To my horror, Stacy picked up a large rock and brought it down hard on Christian's head. I rushed outside and tried to stop the bleeding, and also calm down both children, who bawled their eyes out. It was about four in the afternoon, and Connie arrived within half an hour.

We rushed Christian to the doctor's. It was a deep cut, but not too serious, and Dr Rustomjee patched up his wound with a large band aid. He shook his head at Stacy, "You *mustn't* play with rocks and hit your little brother again!" I know Connie chastised Stacy, as we were so scared and worried about this incident, but Stacy was more frightened, when he saw blood gushing down Christian's face.

A few months after our trip to Bright, I noticed that Christian was learning to talk quickly. And very soon, it was natter natter between them all the time. They called each other "Son" and even in the midst of their most heated quarrels, I smiled in amusement when I heard one reprimand the other, "*Son, don't* do that!"

Every Saturday morning, Connie packed up all the doona covers I sewed during the week, and delivered them to Mr Novakis's factory in the city. The children and I joined him sometimes, and Mr Novakis invited us to have a drink at the pub next door, where he ordered his favourite meal. He loved steak, fried eggs, and chips for his lunch *and* dinner, and consumed an enormous meal with gusto.

Whenever Connie was short of funds, he asked Mr Novakis to advance my wages to meet some expense or other, so we were very grateful to him for his kindness. I earned only $50 or $60 a week, but that money helped to buy a few extra things.

Connie drove on his own sometimes, to pick up bolts of material, and to ask my wages in advance. He returned late in the afternoon, lugging a carton of beer he bought with *my* earnings, then spent all evening drinking. And to top it all, he ended up brawling drunkenly. I burned with indignation at such behaviour, as I thought it was the height of injustice that I never got to spend even a dollar of my wages on myself.

When I mentioned how I felt, and that I should spend some of the money on myself, he started abusing me. "You want to be a *women's libber*? It's *our* money, not yours!" And when I shouted out, "Don't *touch* me or hurt me!" He taunted, "*Who* do you think you are? The *Queen*?"

His parents continued to visit us almost every weekend, and stayed with us a few days. Paul seldom joined them now, as he had his own interests and friends. They did not stay with anyone else then, and Uncle disliked visiting Geraldine's place especially, because he told us, "I don't like that fellow's attitude." Geraldine had said Clifford did not want them staying overnight.

I always treated Connie's parents well, as if they were my own, and they felt at ease. They were very fond of me because I respected them. Aunty said they liked visiting Wendy and Brian too, because they were comfortable with them. Babs moved out with Jeremy, and lived with Ralston in a flat, Esme was with Bronco, and Connie and I were the only ones who invited his parents to join us on trips.

Connie had nightmares sometimes. He grabbed hold of me in his sleep and tried to strangle me. I woke up terrified and shook him, "Connie, *wake up*! you are *dreaming*!" When he opened his eyes and slackened his hold, he looked dazed and muttered, "What happened?" I replied angrily, "You were trying to *choke* me! What on earth's the matter with you?" "Sorry Dolla, I had a bad dream that you were leaving me!" After a few minutes of cajoling, and apologising, he drifted off to sleep. But I remained wide-awake, wondering if it was safe for me to go back to sleep.

I bought a record of Tom Jones, as I admired his voice very much, ever since he topped the charts with, "Green Green Grass Of Home" and "Delilah." I could not listen to the radio when Connie was around, because he picked on me if a particular song was playing, and demanded, "*Why* do you like that song? Are you thinking of that bugger?" And so on.

He looked suspiciously at the record I bought and then played it immediately. One of the hits, "Without Love" was my favourite, and I was just enjoying it, when he started to fume and shouted, "I know why you like this record cover because it reminds you of Clifford!" Even a picture of any man with curly black hair, was a threat to Connie. Next moment, he smashed the record to pieces and tore up the cover in a frenzy. I looked at him aghast, and wondered when he would ever stop such maniacal behaviour.

And when we watched a movie, I never knew how the evening would end, because he sipped a beer quietly for a while, then all hell broke loose, if a man with dark, curly hair appeared, or the movie turned out to be a love triangle. He sank into a black mood and muttered angrily, "*Bloody* women! *Always* the ones to make trouble!"

The uncontrollable, green-eyed monster within him could not be restrained. And had I known better then, I would have insisted that he addressed his anger-management issues, and seen a counsellor. But he would have refused, and denied he had a problem. Not only was he unable to control his anger and jealousy, but he had a personality disorder all his life, because I have no other explanation for his irrational behaviour.

When he was in a mellow mood, I was content to bask in his tenderness, and my heart overflowed with affection, as all I wanted was kindness. But he could not sustain these mercurial lulls for long, and reverted to an insanely jealous, foul-mouthed drunkard within minutes. A little love and understanding, was not too much to ask, and we could have been comparatively happy. But his self-destructive behaviour continually drove a wedge between us.

I read an advertisement in the Age one day by the Melbourne Institute of Art, "Diploma in Commercial Art, now available." It was a correspondence course over two years, with monthly payments of thirty dollars. I was keen to take that course, so I told Connie, "I want to follow this course, and use some of my earnings to pay for it." He considered it for a while, but was non-committal. But he eventually agreed, when he knew that I was determined to enrol.

I submitted poems and articles to various magazines in Australia and overseas, as it was something to look forward to, as I hoped they would be published. But after months of waiting, all I got were rejection slips, and I collected a whole heap of them over the years.

A publisher in England replied once, "We will publish your poetry in our next anthology if you send thirty dollars." As I was still naive about some charlatans in the publishing industry then, I promptly sent a money order (with Connie's permission) to an address in London.

I waited and waited, but no response and no anthology. My first lesson, "Beware of wolves preying on innocent would-be writers." I wrote to Nihal about it, and he checked out the address, and confirmed that it was non-existent. Undaunted, I kept submitting my work to more reputable firms, but did not forward any more money orders.

I wanted to pursue an artistic career too, and thought it would be useful to obtain a diploma in commercial art. When the first lesson arrived, I spent a few hours each day completing assignments. The tutor was pleased, and commented, "You have a good eye for drawing, and we need to develop your talent." I was happy.

I still managed to buy weekly groceries within $15 to $20, and saved on other expenses, as I sewed and knitted most of my clothes and the children's clothes too. But I stopped sewing shirts and slacks for Connie, as he could now afford to buy ready-made clothes. And besides, he did not want to wear home-made shirts anymore.

After Babs and Damian divorced, she lived with Ralston, who was her friend, Pauline's, estranged husband. It was a shock to the whole family, and Aunty was very upset. But they did not stay together long, as Ralston reconciled with Pauline after one year or so. Babs moved on, until she met someone else. Ralston died of a heart attack a few years later, and Pauline met with a terrible death about two decades later, when her drug-crazed son bashed her to death.

When Nelune and Nihal visited Ceylon in early 1976, they purchased a block of land close to Granny's place in Maharagama, so that Ammie and Thathie could build a house there. At last, they would have a permanent home, as they were renting all this time.

Towards the end of 1976, I was devastated when Rosie wrote that Nihal had an "incurable disease" that she did not mention. I could not believe it was possible for my beloved brother to suffer anything deadly, and a false sense of security lulled my fears. But when he became seriously ill, we heard that Nihal had leukaemia, and the prognosis was poor.

The chances of surviving the deadly disease were nil, and I wept so bitterly that I could hardly open my eyes. And yet, part of me believed there must be a cure somehow. Nihal wrote remarkably cheerful letters, saying he was getting better all the time, and that he was studying to be a social worker.

Always an optimist, he kept busy and happy, so I really believed he was going to get well someday. Nelune travelled to England a few times to see him, and enjoyed some great times with Nihal and Janice, whom he had married recently.

Janice, an English girl, was a nurse, and even though she knew Nihal was ill, she went ahead and married him. They did not have any children, but were very happy together, as they loved each other dearly. Nelune was very fond of Janice, and she told me what an amazing person she was. Although I had not met her yet, I knew from her letters that she was very loving and caring.

Janice wrote greeting cards on his behalf now, as Nihal's letters were gradually becoming infrequent. Nihal wrote lengthy letters previously, and sent me books, including one that I requested, the "Writer's Year Book," a few novels by Graham Green, and "The Complete Works Of Shakespeare," which I still treasure. I still did not believe anything bad would happen to our Nihal. And I hoped and prayed he would be miraculously cured.

Chapter 6

I sewed for hours on end sometimes, and hardly noticed time passing. Because in-between, I did household chores, cared for the children, cooked for us, and made separate meals for the children. I did not feed them spicy or hot curries as yet, and they enjoyed a variety of wholesome food.

Wendy and Aunty travelled by train one day, and hid in the laundry outside. And when I went outside for fresh air, they sprang a surprise on me. They spent the day with us, and we had a good time, as they loved Stacy and Christian very much.

When Connie returned home, he dropped them off at Mckinnon. Wendy worked at Stegbar then, and was very generous with presents for the two boys. Once, when we lived in Luigi's flat, she spent about $40 on a small red car that Stacy could sit inside and pedal away, but Connie was very annoyed with her for spending so much money on a toy car.

He told me that he was afraid Stacy would fall off the car, the way his baby brother, Ronald, had done. He had died a few days after his fall from a toy car, and the family believed he suffered from concussion. Anyway, Connie gave the car to one of Glenda's sons, who was much older. Wendy was disappointed, but Connie was adamant, and told her not to buy such expensive toys again.

We struggled to make ends meet, and Connie soon found that credit cards were easily obtainable. He had American Express, and another couple of cards that soon reached maximum limits. Just like today, interest rates on credit cards were exorbitant. But we were inexperienced about finances, and before we knew, we were in debt for a few thousand dollars, including the car loan.

It was very frustrating for us, and most of the friction was due to financial reasons, besides other issues, which often ended up in violent scenes and quarrels. I found it increasingly difficult to cope, and always found a sympathetic confidante in Shirani. I tried to protect my children from witnessing any of our altercations, as I had hated my parents' quarrels when I was a child. And if I could help it, I never wanted my children to go through the same sadness and fear I experienced at home.

To avoid confrontation, it was best to be passive, and let Connie vent his frustrations on me. But it was incredibly difficult to bite back retorts, and refrain from justification in the midst of unfair and hurtful accusations. What made me sad and angry was, the utter injustice of being treated so badly when I did nothing to provoke him.

I tried to be a good wife in every way, although I was by no means a paragon. I kept the house tidy and clean, cooked delicious meals every day, dressed neatly, and was never slovenly in my habits, so why was he always so critical and ready to pick on me?

He was frustrated about the way they treated him at work too, because although he was a very good draftsman, whenever it came to promotions, he was overlooked. Subtle discrimination was prevalent in the workplace, even though some of his superiors pretended they were not bigoted. Connie told me that they treated him more like an "office boy" than a professional draftsman. But he was not one to cower down to any unfair treatment, and stuck to his guns, until they recognised his worth and ability eventually.

I never wrote home about our personal troubles, so they were blissfully unaware of our situation, and were under the impression all was well. Connie's one solace after work was to indulge in a few bottles of beer daily. On very rare occasions, I enjoyed a small glass of Guinness Stout, and sometimes, a glass of red or white wine with a meal. Connie favoured beer then, as whisky was too expensive, and besides, he had not yet acquired a taste for it.

When I collected plenty of clothes, food items, and knick knacks, I packed them up in boxes and carried them to the post office. Sea mail was quite reasonable then, and I was able to help Nilanthi, and my parents with a few small items they needed, and luxury food items that they enjoyed. Connie was always generous in such matters, and sometimes helped me to pack the boxes.

He also helped with the childrens' washing and cleaning whenever he could, and sometimes cooked their meals when I was too tired or busy. Everyone said I was very lucky to have such a helpful, and supportive husband, which he was, in some ways. But no one knew about the dark side; the tension and frequent domestic violence that marred our lives, and which I endured silently. I was still isolated, without a phone, car, or any social interaction with friends. My best friends were Shirani and Nelune, for which I was grateful.

We entertained a few of Connie's colleagues sometimes, and invited our neighbours for dinner too. Brian worked with Connie, and lived in Glen Waverly. He and his wife, Janine, were a nice, young couple, and visited a few times, as they liked spicy food, but they reciprocated only once. They had no children, but kept two large sheep dogs, who sprawled all over their sofas. Liz and Peter remembered the Chinese banquet I cooked, and mentioned it decades later, as Liz told me, "I'll never forget the delicious meal you gave us that night."

Connie's family still visited us now and then, and his parents stayed for a few days. Cristobel did not finish her education in high school here, and only completed grade five in Ceylon. She worked in a factory now, and was going out with a Greek man, and we did not see her as often. He was the first of many boyfriends.

Esme lived on her own in a flat in Ormond, as she could not cope with Bronco's teenage sons. They still saw each other, and went out, but Esme said she was happier living alone. Although she had a few partners, none of them were long-lasting relationships.

We visited Esme with the two children sometimes, and she always commented on how well they behaved. They never touched any of her ornaments or books. But sat quietly for a couple of hours and watched television, while they ate McDonalds or Kentucky fried chicken, which they relished, and was an occasional treat.

Geraldine and Clifford moved to New Zealand a few months after they married, and returned to Australia a couple of years later. We attended a few family gatherings then, as Connie was relieved they were not around. They too severed all ties with us since their marriage.

Nihal was not doing too well, and Nelune travelled to England once more to be with him after he started chemotherapy. And they managed to have an enjoyable time, in spite of his illness and aggressive treatment. When he felt better, they even travelled to Scotland and Europe for a few days. Some great photographs of Nihal, Nelune, Janice, and her brother, John, taken on that memorable holiday, evokes happy times.

In January 1977, I was extremely distressed one morning, after a particularly stormy scene the night before. I walked to town and called Shirani from a public telephone booth, as she was at home that day. I told her about the hell I was going through with Connie, and all the physical and mental abuse he inflicted on me constantly, and I begged her to help me move out somewhere.

Then I came home and wrote a brief note, telling Connie that I was leaving him for good. Shirani drove over within the hour, and I packed a couple of plastic bags with the children's clothes and mine, and we rushed out quickly. I left behind my machine, paintings, and tapestries I had sewn.

After I settled down, I spent the day with her, and the children were happy playing with Roshan. We chatted, and I explained what I endured with Connie all these years. She advised me, and we discussed what I should do to find a lasting solution. Around three o'clock, I was terrified when Shirani told me that Connie just pulled up in the driveway and demanded to see me.

Shirani denied I was there, and I held the children close and whispered to them to be very quiet, as we were just playing a game. He had gone home early that day, read my note, and assumed I was at Shirani's.

I heard Connie's raised voice as he argued with Shirani. And after some time, he drove off in a huff, as Shirani accused him of abusing me physically and mentally, and that he even tried to break my wrist. She was very angry with him, as she was under the impression we had a perfect marriage, because of his facade. It was a revelation when I opened the flood gates of domestic violence I was subjected to from the start.

After Connie left, Shirani told me that the best thing was to go to a women's refuge. Ranjith and she were going through a difficult period as well, and were just working out their problems. So, it was not possible for us to stay with them, especially if Connie continued to harass her. Ranjith had not returned from work as yet. Shirani phoned a few places, and then drove me to a women's refuge in St Kilda, where she left me with the children.

I looked out of the small window of a dark room and glimpsed the sea across the street, so I took the children to the beach and enjoyed a brief respite. After I showered and bathed the children, I went into the kitchen and mingled with a few desolate, sad-faced women, huddled together in this unsightly building, all escaping intolerable situations in their homes. I fed the children whatever food was available, a casserole of some kind, bread, butter and vegemite, and I tried to eat something too.

Then I went back to the room and just bawled my eyes out. I was so miserable, and did not know what to do in this situation. I went to pieces emotionally, as this was not what I wanted in my life, to end up in a refuge, with the bruised and battered women in our society. I had no money, not even a few dollars, no job, so how was I going to survive with two toddlers, I pondered.

When I was away from Connie, all our disagreements and troubles did not seem insurmountable. And I thought I should give our marriage another chance, and work things out for the sake of the children. A part of me longed to be loved and treated gently, and I have to admit, that in spite of his despicable behaviour, somewhere deep in my heart, I could still find enough affection for him, because he could be good when he wanted to. Now I was remorseful, and felt sorry for him, as I did not want to hurt him by leaving him permanently. I just wanted him to change his ways and treat me well, and if this was the only way to get through to him, I hoped he would learn a lesson.

It is impossible to explain my mixed emotions then, because I desperately wanted to have a good marriage, and bring up the children in a safe environment. After a little while, I went downstairs, picked up the public phone and called Shirani. When I started crying, and explained how miserable I felt in this refuge, she understood, and said they would come over immediately. It was about seven or eight o'clock that night when Shirani phoned Connie, and he drove over within the hour to pick us up at their place.

He did not say much as he grabbed the plastic bags and threw them violently into the boot of the car. He wanted to stop at his parents flat, and said, "I have to see Mummy because she was very upset when I told her you had left the house." When Aunty saw me, she burst into tears, hugged me tight, then whispered, "Very good that you left him Dolly! That should teach him a lesson to treat you better! But I'm so happy you came back, I would have *died* if you didn't return!" I was very moved when she said this, and just nodded as I returned her embrace.

On the way home, he was angry and sullen, and did not talk to me at all. But once I settled the children in their beds, he stalked into the bedroom, stood over me menacingly and growled, "If you *ever* leave the house again, I will shoot you in front of your sisters!" His ego was badly bruised, now that his family knew I had left him, even for a day. He blamed Shirani totally, and not once did he admit that it was his fault. In fact, his sisters thought it was entirely *my* fault, because he was such a perfect husband.

Our marriage did not improve even after that short break. Connie deeply resented the fact that Shirani helped me, and he did not want to socialize with them now. Visits were restricted, so Shirani and I met whenever he was not at home. Nelune still drove down whenever possible, but I was very stressed when Connie was around. Because he was more suspicious than ever that I would confide in her about his bad behaviour. Although Nelune had a pretty good idea what he was really like, I did not tell her about the physical abuse, as she would have been devastated to know the truth.

One night, he was so drunk when he got into bed, that he continued arguing and abusing me non-stop. Suddenly, he grabbed hold of the fleshy part over my left breast with his teeth, and bit so hard that I cried out in pain. But he would not let go, until I screamed and managed to push him away. The skin tore and his teeth left a swollen blue ellipse; blood dripped everywhere.

He sobered up at once when he saw the wound, and he started sobbing, "*Sorry* Dolla, I'm so *sorry*!" Then he rushed out, brought a bowl of hot water and began to bathe and massage the wound with a towel until the swelling subsided.

I was afraid he meant to rip off my skin with his teeth. And now I was really terrified of this sadistic man, who took out his frustration and anger on me whenever he felt like it. I started making plans to escape his clutches once more. This time, I would plan it better, and find a place of my own, instead of going to one of those awful refuges. I was going to bide my time, but decided this was it.

We enrolled Stacy at a pre-kindergarten school, where he spent half a day, and I walked with him every morning. Sometimes, I stayed a little while longer to help out the staff and keep an eye on him. I told Connie that the children needed to socialise with others of similar age now, as we held only family parties for their birthdays.

At first Stacy was very timid, but gradually, he joined the other children. He was very clever at building things with leggo, and all the children looked on with great interest as he constructed buildings and bridges.

In August 1977, just after Christian's birthday, I knew I had reached the end of the road again. I tried my best, and gave him another chance, but he was just as bad, or worse than before. I pleaded with Shirani once again, to help me move out with the children. This time, she rented a two-bedroom flat in Noble Park, and furnished it with a single bed for the children, and a mattress for me, and gave me kitchen utensils, pots and pans too. One morning, soon after, I left a note for Connie, telling him I was leaving home. Before we drove to Noble Park, I asked Shirani to stop at the post office so I could change my address. As I walked inside, to my utmost surprise and consternation, Connie stood there beside me. "*What* are you doing here?" he demanded suspiciously. "I came to get some stamps, and was just going for a drive with Shirani."

My heart thumped furiously, and I hoped he would not notice how nervous I was. I panicked, in case he followed us and stopped me from going to the flat. "Come with me, and we'll go home now," he insisted. He was particularly nasty the night before, and he had a habit of coming home unexpectedly, to see how I was after his violent behaviour the previous night.

He walked back with me and stood near Shirani's car, and the children chortled happily, "We're going to a holiday home Dad!" That was what I told them, as I packed hurriedly, and told them we were going on a short trip. Connie could not say anything in front of Shirani, so I broke in quickly, "Why don't you go home, and we'll be there soon."

Shirani drove off speedily, before he could follow us. I could not breathe easily until we reached the flat. And then I had to deal with the childrens' questions, "Is Dad coming too?" "When is Dad coming here Mum?" I replied calmly, "Soon Stacy, now settle down."

I felt such a great sense of relief and joy to have escaped at last. But I knew it was only the beginning, as I did not know what he would do when he read my note. I was sad, and felt guilty that poor Shirani would have to face the brunt of his anger again, but she promised that she would not disclose my whereabouts for the present. I could not have asked for a better friend than Shirani, who stood by me through the worst times, and did her best to help me in whatever way she could.

He phoned Shirani a little while later, and demanded to know where I was, but she said, "Dolly doesn't want to be contacted just yet." Then he cried his eyes out, saying he was so sorry for hurting me, and he would change his ways, if *only* I came back home, because he missed us.

Shirani paid the bond and rent for a couple of weeks, and I continued sewing for Mr Novakis, to earn enough to pay next month's rent, and buy groceries. I applied for an allowance from Social Security, as I knew I was entitled to some assistance, and received one fortnightly cheque. Then I consulted Ananda, a lawyer, who was married to Shiranthi, Nelune's friend. I showed him the wound on my chest, and told him about the physical and mental abuse I endured. He contacted Connie, and as a mutual friend, tried to help us reconcile.

When Connie heard I consulted Ananda, he retorted, "*That* was just a *love bite,* and her skin bruises *easily*, I didn't hurt her!" When Ananda repeated this, I was furious, and very upset that he lied so blatantly. He then told Ranjith, "*I'm* not paying any maintenance for the children! If the sisters broke up the marriage, let them look after her!"

Right through our separation, he did not admit for one moment to his family, or to the lawyer that it was his fault. He blamed Shirani, and said, "Dolly wants to go back to Ceylon, that's why she left me." He told his family too that my skin bruised easily, and he never hurt me physically. When I heard all his lies, I knew what a cowardly bully he was; he could not even accept blame for what he did. Shirani and I visited a second-hand dealer, and I bought an old bed and some chairs for the flat.

In the meantime, Connie painted an unfair picture, that I left him for no reason at all, and he acted like the heartbroken, wronged husband. His family believed him, and labelled me a "bitch." I was fond of his family, and treated them well whenever they visited, and never thought they misjudged me. But they only heard what Connie told them, and anyone's heart would melt, the way he cried.

Aunty, though, always said it was Connie's fault, and did not blame me at all for leaving him. When the family disparaged me, Aunty always stood up for me. And she said that whenever she took my side, Geraldine retorted, "You always had a soft spot for Dolly." And she said, "I can't tell anything good about you, Jenny gets upset, because I boast what a good cook you are, and how well you bring up the children. I admire you, because you were so young when you got married Dolly, and see how well you do everything." She was a fair-minded person, and good to me.

After about two weeks, Connie wrote long letters, and sent them through Shirani, begging me to come back, and said that he realised what I had been going through. The children kept asking me, "Where is Dad?" I told them he was away on business, and would come home soon.

I was emotionally drained, and part of me still clung to the illusion and hope of a good marriage with a *changed* person. But I still had not learnt one important lesson in life: *We cannot change anyone else, except ourselves.* And being very inexperienced still, I believed Connie would learn his lesson and change his behaviour completely.

But in spite of being unhappy and financially insecure, I was determined to stay away from him for some time. I should have consulted a counsellor or joined a support group, but had no idea of what was available then. Moreover, I was embarrassed to discuss my problems with any one else except Shirani.

When I look back, I wish with all my heart that I was courageous enough to have severed the emotional bond completely then. I would have been a happier person on my own, and brought up the children in a more stable environment, without witnessing violence.

Shirani and Ranjith drove me to the city to deliver the sewing to Mr Novakis, as I did not own a car or have a licence to drive. When I told Mr Novakis I was now on my own, he was quite sad, and tried to advise me, just like an old uncle.

Connie sold all our furniture, and rented a flat as well. But I had no idea then that his flat was just a few blocks from where I was. It was a very traumatic time for me with the children, as I struggled financially. It was a sparsely furnished two-bedroom flat, without a back yard or any privacy, and about ten flats opposite and around me.

I was afraid to go out anywhere, as the surroundings were unfamiliar. The road outside the flat led to Springvale Road. And I sometimes walked up with the children, and looked at the busy road, uncertain of how to get around in such busy traffic. I did not take public transport or a taxi, so I was stuck in the flat all the time, unless Shirani or Nelune visited and took me out for a drive.

I cried myself to sleep every night, worn-out with the emotional upheaval of leaving the security of my home, and trying to cope with two small children. The future was bleak and uncertain, as I did not have a well-paid job, or any prospect of finding a good job either. In fact, I was just an emotional wreck. Shirani was my only close support, and visited me almost daily. Nelune came on weekends, and tried to cheer me up, offering to help in any way she could. Nilanthi and I corresponded often, but she did not know what was happening in my life then.

Connie kept sending letters through Shirani, as Ranjith was still working at Safeway's, and he said he wanted to meet me to discuss reconciliation.

So, after a few weeks, I agreed to meet him at Shirani's, and when he saw me, he burst into tears, hugged me, and tried to kiss me. I told him we had to discuss many issues, before we made up. He swore he would stop drinking and gambling, if only I came back.

He knew I could never resist such pleading. The outcome of this meeting was that we made up. Because when he told me that he regretted his actions deeply, I was sorry to see him so upset and devastated. I agreed to a reconciliation. I asked him why he lied to Ananda about my wound being a "love bite" and he replied, "I thought you were going to court, and I would have denied *everything,* because I didn't want to be accused of physical abuse, and didn't want to pay anything. That's what my lawyer told me to do."

I was unaware he consulted a lawyer too, but I overlooked that part of his behaviour. We were apart for less than a month. He knew my weakness was a soft, compassionate heart, and I could never fail to be moved when he broke down in tears. Part of me knew I was being foolish to go back, another part desperately wanted to believe him, forgive, and try again. We had several thorny issues to settle, but after that meeting, he immediately moved into the unit I rented, and vacated his.

On the following weekend, when we delivered the sewing to Mr Novakis, he was quite surprised to see Connie again, and declared, "So, you are *friends* again? I'm very happy for you both. Now you must try to work things out." It was then that he told me to purchase an industrial sewing machine, so I could sew a lot faster than on a domestic machine, and make more money sewing larger quantities.

He agreed to buy me a machine, and deduct a modest amount towards it each week. He was the kindest person I came across during that dark period in my life. Connie started working a few hours as a night stacker in Safeway at Frankston. He told me that Aunty went with him every night, as he was so lonely and scared.

His family members were very upset with me, as they did not know the real reasons why I left him. They had no idea at all what our personal problems were or what an abusive, drunkard Connie was. The one who walks out of a marriage, usually gets all the blame, and some of them were ready to believe the worst of me.

The story Connie told them was, that I wanted to go back to Ceylon, and that was why I left, but no one ever knew what my private reasons were. Connie did not want me to discuss anything with his family, and he told me, "Just forget everything, don't say anything to them."

I heard he said many negative things about me, that I left him suddenly, hoping he would get a shock and fall dead. When I confronted him, he said, "Well, what else could I think when you left me like that!" He did not admit for a moment that it was his behaviour that drove me away. Connie was paranoid that I would discuss our problems with his family, and forbade me to talk about why I had left.

After a few days, he mumbled, "You will get to know about it anyway, but one night, when I visited Esme, she told me to drop Lena off at her flat near by. So I did, but nothing happened." She was living on her own then, and Esme thought Connie would find consolation with her.

Aunty understood the situation more than anyone else, as she had witnessed our stormy scenes sometimes, and did not blame me at all. She said she had complete faith in me, and assured me that it was not my fault I left home, but she never said anything to Connie, as she did not want to upset him.

Connie and I started all over again, furnishing the place with second-hand goods. The flat looked quite cosy, once we arranged a few items of furniture, and I filled it with indoor plants, which was quite the trend then. It was not too bad living in that unit for one year, as we travelled a great deal during that time, because we did not like staying in such a cramped place. The industrial sewing machine took a lot of space in the bedroom, and half the room was full of fabric that I cut and sewed. It was dusty and crowded, but we had no choice, as I signed a lease for a year, and we could not move anywhere else.

Babs had moved in with Peter, and was living quite close to us in a unit in Noble Park. She visited often, and advised us, but she had her own problems too. A couple of years later Aaron was born, but she and Peter separated some time after that.

Uncle was very unhappy in Australia, and wanted to go back to Ceylon. When Connie and I visited them one evening, the whole family gathered to discuss the matter, and they made plans to send them back to Ceylon. But a few days later, Aunty absolutely refused to go back, saying, "The whole family is here, and I don't want to return."

We suggested that Uncle should go on a holiday at least, but Aunty cried out in dismay, "No, no! He will go and run me down to his sister and the relations in Ceylon! Don't send him alone!" So that was the end of that, but Uncle never failed to tell me, "I want to be buried in Talawakale! I want to go back home!"

It was sad, because he did not have a single friend of his own age or background. And he spent the whole day watching television, and drinking port that he liked much better than whisky. Aunty found employment in a factory called John Crundells, and was quite happy sewing bits and pieces.

Once, Uncle tried to work as a cleaner in a factory, and Aunty laughed as she explained, "They sent him up a ladder to clean windows, and two men had to go up and bring him down, because he couldn't climb down again." Poor Uncle, he was frail, and in his late seventies then, so it was quite unrealistic to expect him to work. But he did clean a school for a few months until he was too tired to continue. He loved visiting us, as he was very fond of Stacy and Christian, and kept saying, "Bring the two fellows Dolly, I want to see them!"

We travelled around various parts of Victoria then, and we always took Aunty and Uncle, as Paul, who was a teenager now, did not want to join us anymore. We discovered many beautiful areas, but our favourite places were Marlo, Lakes Entrance, and Bairnsdale.

One weekend, while walking by the pier in Bairnsdale, we saw a middle-aged couple tinkering in their boat; they waved, and we started chatting, as we wanted to sail in a hired boat, and asked them directions. None were available, and after a while, Marge called out, "Don and I are going out in our boat for a couple of hours, would you like to join us?" The children were with us, but not Aunty, as she did not join us this time.

We had a lovely trip, as red-headed Marge was a pleasant, vivacious lady, who loved the children immediately. Don was a tall, lanky, retired detective, with grey, tousled hair. They showed the children how to fish, but unfortunately, Stacy did not see the fishing rod Don held, and when Don whipped around, the rod caught Stacy in the eye, and he yelled out in pain.

It took some time to comfort him, but he was happy when he caught a yellow-jacket fish, and though he had a bruised eye, he fished happily for a while. We invited them to our caravan for a drink that evening, and became better acquainted, and exchanged addresses and phone numbers. From then on, we were in regular contact.

A few months later, we visited them, and they treated us well. Marge showed her recent work; she was taking painting classes, and had completed some impressive landscapes. She said she never painted in her life, and in her late sixties now, she discovered a talent for painting.

One Sunday evening, when we returned home after a trip, our pet cat, Mewsette, crawled from behind a bush in the garden. She mewed pitifully, and dragged one of her hind paws behind her before hiding under the bed. I coaxed her out with great difficulty, and found she had a broken paw.

After examining her next morning, the vet told us that someone shot her with a pellet gun used for shooting birds. And he had seen similar injuries in cats and dogs before. It cost $60 to set her broken leg, but she recovered well, and was running around in no time at all.

We found twenty dollars in a car park once, so I asked Connie to buy a dog with that money. And we ended up buying a five-year old basset hound, after I read a local advertisement. He was pedigreed, and looked lovable, but turned out to be the most stubborn, badly trained dog we ever owned.

He sat on all the chairs, and growled at Connie, or anyone else who tried to sit there. And one night, he urinated on our bed post. The flat was highly malodorous with his smell, as we could not put him out anywhere. We walked him daily, but he was an incorrigible dog.

While we were driving home one day, Droopy (as I called him), sat on the back seat with the children. Suddenly, Christian screamed out in pain. His cheek was bleeding, and my heart almost stopped, thinking the dog injured him severely. Connie dragged Droopy from the car, quickly put him in the boot, and we rushed to Dr Rustomjee's clinic. It was late evening, and after he dressed it up, he assured us that it was not a very deep wound.

Christian suffered from shock, and hurt his inner cheek too. His face swelled up and turned red, but he was alright. How fortunate that he escaped with such a minor injury, and I shuddered at the thought of the dog mauling him.

His previous owners sold Droopy, as they were going overseas, and we thought he was good with children (that is what they told us). Now we considered giving him back to the RSPCA, as he was not to be trusted around children.

Chapter 7

Sometimes, his parents, Paul, Wendy, Brian, and their girls, joined us on our weekend trips. They were memorable, as we drove around many places in Victoria. Once, we even drove to Canberra, and returned via popular ski resorts Jindabyne and Thredbo. And on another occasion, Connie decided to drive all the way to Adelaide and back in a couple of days time. Wendy and Aunty joined us, and it took us over ten hours to get there. Adelaide was a very quiet city, full of churches at every corner, but quite serene and picturesque.

On our way back, we stopped at Mt Gambier, and saw the amazing Blue Lake, a volcanic crater. It was an apt name, because the lake was a deep, sapphire-blue that glistened like a jewel in the sun. We returned on the following day, and although it was tiring, we enjoyed the trip.

Bronco rented his house in Rye, on the Mornington Peninsula, to Connie's parents. It was a nice, three-bedroom house, but situated in a very remote area, and away from the main bus route. Paul still lived with them, but he stopped school, and was out fishing with friends, or doing odd jobs most of the time. Cristobel shared a flat with a friend, close to Dandenong, and worked in a factory there.

Uncle was very lonely down there, and whenever he phoned, he always said, "I'm *dreaming* of Stacy and Christian, *please* come soon." So we drove down to Rye often with the children.

We attended a family party there once, and were returning very late at night, when our car skidded and rolled over. Connie drove furiously, as he argued and shouted at me, because Clifford exchanged a few brief words with me. But it was enough to make him see red, and he could hardly wait to get me in the car to start his verbal abuse.

The first few days after we reconciled, he made an effort not to drink too much, and behaved slightly better. But before long, we were back in the same groove. He drank and brawled, and sometimes shoved me around in the middle of a verbal assault.

I cried desperately, and asked him why he came back into my life, if he could not change his ways. He had added reason now, because I left him for a few weeks, and he just could not overlook that. He knew I was capable of leaving him again, but he did not try to control his anger and jealousy.

That night, we escaped with only a few scratches, but I ended up with whiplash. We sat in the car yelling angrily at each other. I was badly frightened, and annoyed with him for picking a fight when I was so tired and sleepy. The windows of near-by houses suddenly lit up, and very soon a police car arrived. The people reported, "A noisy argument and accident." The police drove us back to Rye, and the family were surprised to see us. When they checked our car, all four tyres were slashed, but we never found out who was responsible.

Clifford offered to drive us back home, and Connie had no option but to accept. Geraldine and he dropped us sometime in the early hours of dawn. The children were asleep at home, as we never engaged a baby-sitter. They slept through the night, and I did not worry about leaving them for a couple of hours occasionally. We believed they were much safer asleep in their beds, without a stranger to look after them. So we set out in the evening without any qualms.

The car was badly damaged, and he could not drive it for a few weeks. He arranged transport to work and back, with one of his female colleagues, until the car was repaired.

Mr Novakis paid $500 to purchase an industrial machine, and deducted $20 a week from my wages. A few months later, I was very distressed to hear he suffered a massive stroke and died instantly. Although his partner continued to employ me, she did not give me as much work as before. I worked for a few other factories as well, who gave me similar work.

When the Renault was repaired, Connie traded it in for a bronze, Holden Sunbird. The day we left our old car behind, Christian cried a great deal, because he loved the Renault, in which we travelled to so many places. Our accountant advised Connie to lease a car, as he used it for business, picking up and delivering my sewing. We registered our business under the name of "Dolcon" and the lease cost about $200 a month.

The children were starting primary school soon, and I told Connie I must get a driver's licence, as I had to drop and pick them from school, and he agreed. I had about ten driving lessons with a stern-looking, Scottish lady. And I was elated to get my licence at my very first attempt. It was ten dollars a lesson, but well worth it.

Although Connie promised to stop drinking, gambling, and cut down on smoking, he never did, and soon slipped back to his old habits. He drank too much, and our quarrels were worse than ever, because I left him. He was angry that I confided in Shirani, as she accused him of physical abuse. And told him, "You have injured her so many times, and nearly broke her right hand, so she won't be able to type anymore!" He was furious because I exposed his true nature.

Babs asked us to baby-sit Jeremy whenever she went out, and I was very fond of him. He was a very intelligent, handsome young boy, and he kept us amused for a few hours with his delightful conversation.

We held a few dinner parties in that small flat, and the year flew by quickly. Connie held a surprise party on my birthday, and invited his whole family, including Clifford and Geraldine. All through the night, Connie pretended he was alright. But when the guests left, he ignored me completely, and did not respond to anything I said.

I was puzzled, and asked, "*Why* aren't you talking to me? Why are you so angry?" He scowled, "You were talking to Clifford weren't you? *Why* do you want me to talk to you now?" "I was only being polite to him as a guest! How can I ignore him after you invited him? Why did you ask them in the first place, if you didn't want me to talk to him?"

I was angry and frustrated that he ended my birthday so unpleasantly. He pretended to his family that he did not have a problem with Clifford, but that was just a facade.

A few weeks later, we received $1000 from the insurance company for the Renault, as the car was a write-off. I asked Connie not to spend it, as I wanted to save a deposit for a house, and encouraged Connie to strive towards this goal. He still worked a few extra hours doing a night shift at Frankston Safeway. And we managed our budget reasonably well.

I had a few more assignments to complete for my course, and found time only at nights, once I finished sewing, and the children were asleep. It was a busy time, as I took on extra work from other factories, like Kimptons Doonas, and Danish Eiderdowns. I had plenty of work now, and earned about $100 a week. I eagerly browsed through real estate columns daily, as new houses were advertised for sale, with a minimum deposit of $1000 dollars only.

We drove around looking at prospective houses almost every weekend now. Finally, we saw one that we liked very much, in a new suburb called Rowville, close to Ferntree Gully. It was a three-bedroom, brick-veneer house, and was advertised for $40,000. But we negotiated, and purchased it for $37,500. That was number 13, Barbican Court. A few other houses were under construction in the court then.

We enjoyed spectacular views of the Dandenong Ranges and valley beyond, from the dining room, and to us, this was a dream house. After the dreary old place in O'Shannessy Street, and the cramped, two-bedroom flat in Noble Park, this house was all that we could have hoped for.

The house was situated on a quarter acre block of land, so the children had a large backyard to play in. The master-bedroom came with a semi-ensuite, but no carpets or ducted heating, only a gas heater in the lounge; the kitchen was large and spacious, but without an exhaust fan. In fact, it was just a basic, shell of a house, with nothing included, not even driveways. Two concrete strips led up to the house, and that was it. But after our previous units, and the draughty old house in Nunwading, this place was a mansion indeed.

We moved into the new house on 18 November 1978, and the first thing we did was to install a telephone. What a thrill that was! Finally, I was able to communicate with family, and friends (when I made some).

The night we moved in, all four of us slept on a mattress. And in the night, Stacy suffered a severe bout of gastroenteritis, and vomited all over. Poor Stacy was very sick, and I was distressed to watch him suffer. He recovered in a couple of days though. But it added to the confusion of moving in, as I was deeply concerned about his condition, as he did not eat much or drink anything for twenty four hours.

Mewsette went missing a day later, and all my calling, and whistling did not help. I stood on the driveway every morning and evening for about one week and called out to her. And on the sixth day, I thought I heard a very faint mew. The children and I quickly ran towards the sound of that mewing, and stopped at a house at the bottom of the court. It was still under construction, and when we walked around, we heard the unmistakable sound from beneath the house.

I quickly opened the trap door, and to my great joy and relief, poor Mewsette crawled out. She was thin as a reed, scraggy, and disoriented. I am not sure how she survived her ordeal, as she was obviously locked in under the house when the builders left the site one day. I carried her gently, and soon nursed her back to good health, and her previous weight.

Droopy proved to be an incorrigible hound, as he barked constantly at our neighbours, Geraldine and Jeff, who was a policeman. One day, when our front door was open, another neighbour's pig terrier from the opposite house, dashed inside and attacked Droopy in the lounge. Streaks of blood splattered on the pristine white walls, and the neighbour (another Sri Lankan), rushed in, and had the audacity to complain about Droopy injuring *his* dog!

None of Connie's family knew we moved into our own home, so when we broke the news, they were very surprised. They always discouraged us, especially Babs, who said it was too much of a responsibility to own a house. We held a house-warming party for the whole family sometime in December that year, and Connie brewed a potent punch that almost knocked everyone out.

He wanted to prove that he was no longer jealous of Clifford, so he invited them too. Connie was polite, and kept up appearances during the party, but it was a different story when we were alone. He simply could not control his anger and resentment, but I tried my best to ignore his behaviour.

The backyard was nothing but a soggy mass of clay, so we had it rotary-hoed, and treated with gypsum, before we sowed lawn-grass. We decided to return Droopy to the RSPCA, as we did not have fences around to keep him in. He was one dog I was not sorry to let go.

We worked very hard setting up the garden on a very restricted budget, and we spent every single free day and weekend doing the garden. I helped Connie with the heavy work, while the children did their best weeding and carrying lighter things. Connie was accident-prone, and even if he went out to mow the lawn or prune some shrubs, I soon heard him screaming in pain. He was always in a hurry to get things done, and had no patience, so invariably he cut his finger or bruised some part of his body.

One weekend, when he pruned a shrub with a Stanley-knife, he sliced his palm across. I called a doctor immediately, as he was shivering and moaning in pain. The doctor stitched up the wound, as it was quite deep.

I dreaded when he went out to do anything, because it meant he would soon shout that he hurt himself. He was never gentle or careful when he did anything, as it was always a matter of rushing, shoving, and pulling to get the job done quickly.

This tendency to injure himself while doing even the smallest job, continued without abatement. While washing a drinking glass one day, he scrubbed it so hard that it broke into pieces, and he cut his hand badly. I was always running around with band aids or washing his wounds. Connie hurt his back several times while carrying heavy pots, and was forced to rest a few days then.

I called Nihal only a few times, as overseas rates were exorbitant, and he was very pleased we moved into our own home. And a few months later, when some of his friends visited Melbourne, Janice and Nihal sent us a house-warming gift of an exquisite candelabra. I called and said, "Thank you for the candlestick, Nihal and Janice." And I can still hear his amused guffaw, "*That's a candelabra, not a candlestick!*" I laughed with him, and shared a few more minutes of jokes and laughter, before I called off. He sounded well, and assured me he was getting better, and even talked about going to Ceylon with Janice soon, so my fears for his health were allayed.

Our mortgage repayments were about $400 a month, and interest rates were soaring then. We hoped and prayed we could meet our repayments without difficulty. Connie brought home a great deal of extra work, and drafted till late at night. He stopped the night shift at Safeway, because he was too busy with his full-time job.

The children started primary school at St Jude's, Scoresby, in January 1979. And their first day at school was memorable, and I removed photographs of them dressed up in their smart new uniforms. I dropped Connie at Mulgrave around 8am, the children at school, then came home and sewed till around midday.

Connie called sometimes, and asked me to bring his lunch when he did not take anything from home. I quickly packed up his meal, and stayed for an hour or so until he finished eating in a nearby park. Then back to sewing again, before picking up the children, and Connie, later on in the evening. That was how we managed with one car.

I knitted their school jumpers in royal-blue wool, and sewed their shirts and pants, as we had to scrimp on everything. It was a private school, and uniforms were expensive, besides the added expense of school fees. So we saved a considerable amount of money on their clothes.

One day, quite unexpectedly, the transmission in that new car just went dead. Connie leased a Holden Commodore, as the Sunbird was not worth repairing. It was bronze-coloured too, and drove beautifully. We travelled all over Victoria frequently, as it was a very comfortable car to travel in.

Shirani and Ranjith too bought their own home in Hampton Park in 1978, where Suresh was born on 28th June 1979. He was a cute baby, and we stood as his Godparents. It was a comfortable, three-bedroom house, one in a row of about ten houses, flanking Pound Road, and twenty minutes to Rowville. Nelune rented a flat in Armadale, and we visited her sometimes.

Nihal was seriously ill in early 1979, and Nelune flew over to be with him. My never-ending regret is that because we were in such a tight, financial situation, it was impossible for us to travel, and be with Nihal. Connie was adamant that we all went together, or not at all, and he would not even hear of letting me go on my own.

Just before Nihal became so ill, Nelune, Shirani, and I went for tests to find out if our bone-marrow was compatible, so Nihal could have a transplant. Unfortunately, the three of us were not, and Nilanthi said that Heron absolutely refused to allow her to go for the test.

Whatever his reasons for not permitting Nilanthi to undergo that test, we never knew if her marrow was compatible or not with Nihal's. She divorced Lakshman, and married to Heron now. They lived on a coconut estate in Colombo and she was quite happy with him, and their son Tanesh.

Janice wrote to say they appealed widely for a donor, but were unsuccessful. Marrow transplant held only a slight chance of saving his life, but we all wanted him to have that option somehow.

Nelune was heart-broken when she returned from London, and told us Nihal had shrunk to less than half his size. He was in hospital for a long time, exhausted, and deteriorating, with all sorts of experimental drugs and treatment.

We were told to expect the worst, but with the optimism of youth, I believed a miracle would somehow save my beloved brother. I could not even begin to imagine how life would be without him to brighten my days. His letters continued to be full of buoyancy right up to the very end. And he wrote that he was feeling so much better, that Janice and he planned to be in Ceylon that Christmas. They booked tickets already, as he was keen for Janice to meet his family.

I was thrilled at the prospect of going home too, if only we could afford it. It was now seven years since I last saw my parents, Nilanthi and Nihal. Connie was quite keen to go back too, so he said he would borrow the money for our tickets.

Towards dawn on 19th September, 1979, Janice broke the shattering news that Nihal was dead. Her grief-stricken voice echoed in my ears for a long time, as she sobbed, "I loved him so much!" Nihal was admitted to hospital with an infection, where his organs shut down gradually. I wept inconsolably at the enormity of my loss, and could not believe my beloved brother left us so suddenly.

I dropped the children at school in the morning, and through my blinding tears and anguish, I questioned why fate struck such a cruel blow, to take away my dearest brother at the age of thirty one years.

Those early days were unbearably bitter and sad, and it is very painful to re-live them even now. Janice cried broken-heartedly every time she phoned, as she told me how much she loved Nihal. And, as planned, she intended visiting Ceylon in December.

Janice promptly forwarded the money that Nihal had bequeathed to Ammie and Thathie in his will. My parents utilised the funds to build a modest house on the block of land that Nihal and Nelune purchased for them on Temple Road, Maharagama. They wrote to say that the house would be completed in December that year.

My parents were living in India for six months just before Nihal died, and although they had wanted to travel to London, they were unable to make it. Thathie was appointed manager in one of the Buddhist headquarters in Bombay, and Ammie joined him there.

Later on, Thathie related how Ammie had hung holy pictures on the walls of that Buddhist residence, where he was in charge, and exposed him to religious controversy with his Buddhist colleagues. I could hardly fail to appreciate the lighter side of this situation, as I can only imagine the faces of those Buddhist monks, when they walked in and beheld such evidence of Christian devotion.

Thathie worked as a proof-reader at Lake House Publishers for over ten years. And was always on the lookout for employment of some sort, as he was in his early fifties, and did not relish the idea of total retirement. He worked in smaller publishing companies over the next few years, after he left Lake House Publishers.

Chapter 8

In spite of my heartache, misery, and overwhelming grief for Nihal, the thought of visiting my parents, and Nilanthi, was some consolation. But Nihal would not be there to make me laugh, and entertain in his inimitable fashion.

We did not have any savings. So Connie approached some of his family members for a loan, which he promised to repay as soon as he could. But Geraldine had sneered, "*Why* don't you cut your coat according to your cloth?" And none of them were willing to help out. She was especially nasty. Connie said that when we reconciled, he called her with the news. But she was not happy at all, and had snapped, "Don't let her keep you under *her* thumb!" His family believed Connie was a hen-pecked husband. And he did nothing to disabuse that belief either, until years later when they found out his true colours.

Most of them showed no sympathy at all, although I lost my only brother, and had not seen my family for seven years. But Aunty burst into tears when I told her, and Uncle said, "Sweeta, let's go to see Dolly just to console her." Cuckoo and Wendy too were very sad about Nihal. And Cuckoo comforted me, "Your brother was a very special, wonderful boy! May he be at peace now."

The family did not know that Connie would never let me go without him and the children. Though I would not have left the children behind anyway, so it was a matter of a family trip, or not at all.

We borrowed money from a finance company, and soon organised our trip. It cost us $2500 for tickets, and we had $500 spending money for one month. The factories I worked for, assured me that they would have plenty of work when I returned, as most of them closed till mid-January. We borrowed money on this assurance, as we thought we could afford to repay the loan without too much stress.

That journey took us about eighteen hours, as we went via Bali and Singapore, and spent several hours in transit. The two boys were good as gold, even though they were bored to tears, just hanging around airports. It was the cheapest flight available (on our budget), as the travel agent told us, so we could not complain. Finally, after a gruelling flight, we arrived in Colombo to a memorable homecoming.

Almost every single member of my family came to greet us at the airport, and they all came in Malcolm's car. Heron, Nilanthi, Tanesh, Tamara, and Rani, the servant girl, arrived in his jeep. Granny, Malcolm, Indrani, Ammie, and Thathie, stood there smiling, eyes wet with happy tears. How I rejoiced to be with my family once again!

We laughed and talked all the way home, and we did not sleep a wink, even though it was early morning when we finally arrived in Maharagama. The modest house had just been completed, and the toilet floor was still wet with newly poured concrete.

The children felt a little shy and uncomfortable, as they did not understand why things were not like they were in Australia. A deep well was dug in the backyard, and had no protective fence or rail around it, so I feared for the childrens' safety. Nilanthi suggested that it would be best if we stayed at her place.

Ammie and Thathie understood our concern for the children, and tried not to mind too much when we went to Nilanthi's place next evening. I had little gifts for everyone, and it was great fun distributing them. They cried bitterly whenever we spoke of Nihal. But they looked forward to meeting Janice, who was due to arrive soon. Nelune was expected in a few days time as well.

We had the most fantastic time that Christmas at the coconut estate in Meegoda, as Heron and Nilanthi entertained the whole family there.

Marie and Neville arrived shortly after from the United States, and so did Anthony, Barbara, and finally Rosie, Christine and Janice.

I took to Janice immediately. She was wonderful, and so sincere, and I could not have wished for a better sister-in-law. Janice was a very attractive, tall, slim lady, with light-brown hair, and blue eyes. I was deeply grieved when we picked her up at the airport though, as I kept thinking that Nihal too would have been here, had it not been for cruel fate. After she settled down, and I got to know her better, Janice related all the details about Nihal's illness, and his final days.

When Janice finished, not a dry eye was there around the table. We consoled each other, as she was extremely emotional, and it was obvious that her suffering was unbearable. I loved Janice for being so caring and loving, not only to Nihal, but to his family too, and we all loved her dearly.

Janice wrote the following account of their brief life together when she returned to London:

"I first met Nihal at a hospital dance in 1973. We had both been appointed to work at East Ham Memorial Hospital and this was our first meeting before starting work on the same ward. It was an Orthopaedic Ward called Manor Ward. Nihal was appointed Charge Nurse and I was to be his Staff Nurse. We both got on very well together and found we had a lot in common. My Mum was also working at the hospital and had previously met Nihal. She told me about this very 'charming young man' she had been introduced to, and I too found this to be so.

Before very long we were going out together. We moved from the Nurses Home where we had both been living, to rented accommodation in Ilford. My brother John and his Swedish girlfriend, Tove, also lived there together with several Sri Lankan friends of Nihal. These were very happy, unforgettable times. We were one big happy family and almost every night somebody would cook and by the end of the evening there was a party! Asoka and Raj were two very good friends, but I lost touch with Asoka through the years.

Eventually, we decided to buy our own house and in 1975, around the time my dad was killed in an accident at work, we moved to Sherrard Road in Forest Gate. It was an upsetting time and Nihal was a great support to mum and me. By this time Nihal had left the hospital and had commenced a Degree Course in Politics at the Polytechnic of Central London, which is now a University. I was promoted to his job and became a Ward Sister. We were happy in our new home and continued meeting up with our old friends regularly. Asoka came to stay with us while he was saving for his own place and life went on smoothly.

By the end of 1976 Nihal appeared to be unwell. He was breathless and didn't have energy. I was concerned and tried to persuade him to see a doctor but he refused. He developed a cough and started bleeding from his gums. I asked a Sri Lankan, Dr Pathmanathan, who I worked with to come to see Nihal at home, to persuade him to seek help. The outcome was that he agreed to see the Medical Officer at the Polytechnic. Things moved quickly from there and Nihal was admitted to hospital for tests.

I'll never forget the day when I was summoned to the Doctor's office and he told me that Nihal had Acute Lymphoblastic Leukaemia and his prognosis was not good. I asked him if he was going to die and he said, "yes," I asked how long he had to live and he replied, "maybe 6 months," I then had to walk back to Nihal's bedside as though nothing had happened, although it was the end of my world too. My lip was twitching as I tried to suppress my emotions. Nihal noticed this and asked what was wrong.

I pretended but then he said, "it's not as though I have diabetes, at least I can still have a pint!" he was still trying to make me laugh and keep my spirits up at this desperate time. Nihal underwent vigorous treatment with radiation and chemotherapy and by Christmas we decided to get married. We married on the 12th of Jan 1977 at St Margaret's Church in East London. The hospital chaplain whom we had befriended, Father Patrick, married us.

Just a couple of days after the wedding, all Nihal's hair fell out. I remember him saying, "God, let me keep my hair for the wedding ceremony." For the next two years Nihal had various hospital admissions and treatments. He continued with his studies despite feeling very ill on occasions but he never complained. He was an inspiration to everyone. We tried to continue as normal, even taking camping holidays in France.

We travelled to Lourdes several times. Nelune visited and we made a trip to Scotland and travelled around England. We continued with our social activities as much as we could.

Nihal always had a lot of faith and attended Mass very regularly, taking solace in the Church. In 1978 he completed his course and was awarded a B.A. in Politics. He managed to secure a job at the end of 1978 as a Social Worker for the Royal Borough of Kensington and Chelsea.

He was really enjoying his job and was popular with all his colleagues. However the illness had returned and by June 1979 he was gravely ill. The only hope was a bone marrow transplant, and although many people were tested, a compatible donor was never found. Nihal died on the 19th of September at 7.45pm at the University College Hospital after a courageous battle."

This just about sums up Nihal's indomitable, optimistic, and brave character that could not be dimmed or beaten by the terrible disease that finally destroyed him.

Stacy and Christian soon made friends with Tanesh and the neighbouring children, and they had a great time chasing each other in the surrounding wilderness. The children squealed in fright whenever they caught sight of harmless black snakes (garandiyas). We spent long hours at beautiful beaches, and at nights, Heron organised "hopper" feeds at Green Cabin, or Galle Face Green.

We also visited the fantastic Dehiwela Zoo, and the children were delighted to watch elephant parades, chimpanzees, and apes of all breeds and sizes just "monkeying" and cavorting around. The month just flew by, and it was indeed the most unforgettable time I spent with my family. But sadly, only Shirani and Nihal were absent, as Shirani could not make it.

Uncle Barlow, Granny, and Grandpa, spent the days with us too, as did Malcolm, Indrani, Rosie, and Christine. Nilanthi accidentally injured her hand when cutting up a chicken one day, and was unable to do much until we left; fortunately, Rani was an active, capable young girl, who did most of the cooking and cleaning under Nilanthi's guidance.

Chapter 9

Connie, the children, and I boarded a train to visit our relatives in Bandarawela, Welimada, Talawakale, and Badulla (all up-country), and it proved to be a nerve-wracking experience. To start with, the train was so crowded that we did not get seats for many hours. The children just sat on the grimy floor, as they were worn-out standing so long. It was late and dark when the train finally stopped at Bandarawela, and a taxi drove us slowly to the guest house. And I could not see how much the town had changed since 1960.

We ordered dinner, and thinking that the quickest meal would be toast, bacon and eggs, we waited hungrily for dinner to be served. The children ate a snack, so we left them sleeping in the room. Connie and I sat in the dining room from around 8.30pm till 10.30. The waiter finally brought in a huge dish of about one kilogram of fried bacon and half a dozen eggs with thick, soggy slices of toast.

Connie demanded irritably, "*Why* did it take so long to serve dinner, and why so much of bacon?" The stuttering waiter replied nervously, "We had to go out to the shops to buy bacon sir, as we didn't have any left, and thinking you'd be very hungry, the cook fried the whole lot!" I was too tired and hungry now to eat more than a mouthful.

Next morning, we visited Swarna and her husband, Jine, who were happy to see us. And he exclaimed, "you look just like Nilanthi! you have everything she has!" Connie asked me what he meant, and I shrugged my shoulders because I did not know either. Swarna was just the same friendly person she had always been, and that was the only time I saw her in years to come.

Sugath, Manel's husband, picked us up from there, and we visited Daisy Akka, Manel, and her family, who lived in a modest house on a hill top just outside Bandarawela town. Much to my alarm, Sugath reversed his Mini- Minor car right up the sharp incline without blinking an eye! It was a very uncomfortable house, with a dark toilet outside that the children were afraid to use.

Connie bought a bottle of arrack for the men that night. And it was amusing to watch Sugath pouring bumper drinks for himself first, without so much as offering Connie a tot. Finally, Connie helped himself, seeing that Sugath had no intention of sharing the bottle with anyone else.

The children watched in fascination, as Sugath used a brass "spittoon" during dinner. He chewed betel leaf endlessly, and aimed the red spittle into the brass bowl without any sign of embarrassment, as it was the accepted norm for betel-chewers. Sugath was a short, dark, stumpy man, with a walrus moustache and crude manners.

We spent an uncomfortable night, and the following morning, we packed tightly into the Mini, then headed off to Welimada to visit Athamma, Wimala, and family. As we neared Paranagama, the scenery still appealed to me immensely, just like before when I visited the place with my parents.

I knew they could ill afford to feed such a large crowd, so we stopped in the little village town and bought groceries for lunch. When Sunethra saw us, she could not stop crying. She was a kind, loving person, whom fate had treated with scant regard for her happiness and welfare.

Wimala was soon drunk with the arrack Connie provided, and I ignored his senseless blabbering. Athamma, on hearing we were in Ceylon, quickly boarded a train that morning, and travelled to Maharagama. I was greatly disappointed, and I sincerely hoped she would still be there when we returned. Mutha died a few years ago, and I missed his dear, dignified presence in the old house very much, and was very anxious to see Athamma this time.

Sunethra walked all the way to the well below the sloping garden, and heavily laden with a bucket of water, climbed uphill again. My heart went out to her, when I saw how hard she worked here all by herself. Their children were very young still, and it was sheer joy to watch them relishing the tasty meal that Sunethra cooked.

She told me they hardly ever ate fish or meat, as they simply could not afford to. The main meal was always rice, and jak-seed curry, as she picked up the seeds when the ripe fruits fell off the trees. When I asked her how she was getting on, she replied in Sinhalese, that she lived daily from, "sorrow to sorrow." Wimala beat her up, and broke all the clay pots in the kitchen. And then she had no pots to cook in, reducing them to virtual starvation on some days. I gave her one thousand rupees to help tide her over, and I promised to help out with clothes and money whenever I could.

After this harrowing and depressing visit, we boarded a train to Badulla, to visit Connie's Uncle, Irwin, his wife, Yvonne, and family. Uncle Irwin was Aunty's younger brother, and in his late forties. I met him and Yvonne a few times in Nuwara Eliya just after we were married. He was short and stout, and resembled Aunty closely in features and manners, and was a pleasant, jolly person.

Yvonne was tall, plump, very fair-skinned, with grey eyes, and short brown hair. She would have been pretty, if not for her large, bulging eyes and receding chin, which, in profile, made her look like a haughty frog. She was easy-going though, and liked to read romantic novels, and we got on well. Tania, their daughter, was an attractive teenager, and their two boys were good-looking children of about ten and twelve. One of the boys met us at the station, and we took a taxi to their home. It was a nice, clean house, and we were comfortable there.

Uncle Irwin and Connie went off early next morning to buy king crabs, and Aunty Yvonne cooked them for lunch. We enjoyed the crab curry very much, and spent another day there, before boarding a train to Talawakale.

When we arrived there, my mind went back to those days in Watagoda. How many times I had travelled across the bridge over the wide river, and watched the beautiful St Clare's water falls! I felt such a pang, as a tremor of nostalgia overcame me and I could hardly stop my tears.

It was almost lunch time, and we were reluctant to go straight to Aunty Florrie's place. So we took a taxi to the rest house by the river, and ordered rice and curry for lunch (after our bacon and egg dinner fiasco), we thought it wiser to order local fare.

The meal was delicious, and we enjoyed it very much. We had just finished, when a gentleman, who introduced himself as "Mr Welsh" stood before us smiling in a friendly fashion. He was a swarthy, lean, middle-aged man, whose English name belied his looks. He said he was a friend of Aunty Florrie's and Uncle Gerry's. Someone saw us lunching here, and news spread rapidly that some relatives of the Beckmeyers were in town.

We arrived with Mr Welsh in a hiring car at Aunty Florrie's Lilliputian house that looked like the "House that Jack built." And no matter which way you looked at the structure, it slanted alarmingly at precarious angles. Aunty Florrie was a tiny, wrinkled lady in her eighties, reminiscent of a curious chimpanzee; her dark, beady little eyes almost disappeared in folds of loose skin, and she bustled around excitedly now.

Uncle Gerry too looked like a wizened, mischievous chimp, but they were kind, hospitable people, and did their best to entertain us well in their old-fashioned manner. She was Uncle's younger sister, and she kept asking us constantly, "How is Sonna boy?" (Uncle's pet name).

That evening, I heard Aunty Florrie instructing Sweetie, the dark-skinned, stocky, middle-aged woman, who helped her in the kitchen. And was amused to hear her say, "My nephew and his wife and children have come from *Australia*, so we must give them an *English* dinner! Go and get some vegetables for a stew!" I thought it was good of her to be so concerned about our meals, but was highly amused at what ensued that evening.

Sweetie, after a couple of hours marketing, returned with only two scraggy, shrivelled-up carrots, and nothing else! Aunty Florrie flew into a grand passion, and we heard a loud commotion in the kitchen. Finally, when dinner was served, it turned out to be rice and curry, with various short eats that Mr Welsh hurriedly bought from the market.

The toilet was a strange construction. Because each time I sat on the commode, it swayed gently to one side, and then slowly back again to the other. It caused much discomfort, as I was afraid of toppling over to one side completely. And I held the children on the toilet seat to steady them until they finished. Finally, we went to sleep, overcome by our experiences in this "ginger-bread" house. Connie gave some money to the old couple, Sweetie, and Mr Welsh, and amid tears and good wishes, we left Talawakale next morning.

We got off the train at Watagoda, and walked near the lake with the children. But I could hardly believe this was the same place where Connie and I had met in 1968. Several small huts and dwellings dotted the hill-sides, and the pristine scenery I loved so much, was now spoilt with the onslaught of progress.

An old woman whom we called "Thunder Balls" because of her large, sagging breasts that she barely covered up, as she did not wear a blouse or anything else underneath, now suddenly spotted us. She approached me, her betel-stained mouth split from ear to ear in a broad grin, displaying blackened teeth and discoloured gums. I gave her some money, and she was happy and joined her hands in a blessing.

We spent seven days up-country, visiting all our relatives, and now at last we boarded a train back to Colombo. The children were well-behaved, and endured every single discomfort and new experience with amazing buoyancy. When I related our travel anecdotes to the family, they were amused, but glad to see us back safely.

Athamma, who was still at Ammie's place, looked frail and old, as she was in her early eighties. When she saw me, she embraced and blessed me, saying, "I hope my tired old eyes will see you *once* more before I die." I spent as much time as possible with Athamma, and she left a few days later amid teary farewells.

I gave her some money, and asked her to take care and keep well. I sincerely hoped I would see her again, but that was the last time I saw her. Athamma took a great liking to Janice as well, and we spent some memorable evenings just chatting and getting to know Janice better. I promised to keep in touch when it was time for Janice to leave, and that is what we did all through the years, as we grew very close.

Aunty's younger sister, Maude, invited us, and about twenty five relatives for lunch one day. She was very dark, but with the same broad features like Aunty. Maude wore cloth and jacket, and tied her long, grey hair in a bun, and she looked like a village woman. Connie was very fond of her, as she was his Godmother, and she treated us well. They were very keen to hear about Aunty and Uncle, and how they fared in Australia. That was the main reason for this huge gathering, and Connie too wanted to meet as many of his mother's relatives as possible in this short time.

Aunty's sisters, and eldest brother, Uncle Bertie, and his wife, Mavis, were there. Along with Litta, the oldest sister, toothless and podgy, with about twelve children, and umpteen grandchildren and great grandchildren; Molly and her husband, Edward (who visited us in Nuwara Eliya before we left Ceylon), Dorothy, the youngest, and her son, Brian, besides hordes of cousins, second cousins, nephews and nieces, swarmed in that small house. We spent all day with them, and next day, we visited Roland and his wife, Shiranthi, who lived near Colombo.

When we arrived at their modest home, Shiranthi and the servant girl were in the middle of a massive clean-up, and the place looked liked a tsunami had passed over. Shiranthi was a pleasant-looking, tall, slim lady in her late twenties or so; she was dark-complexioned, with large, black eyes, and a friendly, toothy smile.

She served soft drinks, and told us that Roland was working, but would be home soon, as she sent him a message to come early. Benjamin and Rebecca, their children, were about four and two respectively, and frolicked around like two mischievous monkeys. She could not get them to behave, as they whizzed around like tornadoes. Roland arrived shortly. He worked in a petrol station, and seemed quite happy in his new life. Connie said he would visit them again before we left.

A couple of days before our departure, he started nagging me from early morning to have dinner with Roland and family, saying, "I promised to go tonight." I replied, "Why did you promise without asking me? I want to spend these last few days with my family." But this led to an angry outburst, as he just could not understand my need to spend time with my family. It had been such a brief three weeks, as we spent a whole week visiting his relatives.

No matter how much I tried to explain how I felt, he kept on harassing me, until Heron and Nilanthi noticed our quarrel, and wanted to know what was going on. Connie told them, "Who does she think she is for me to get permission! I have promised to have dinner with my brother tonight, and she won't come!" I replied, "Why don't you go on your own and keep your promise, while I stay with my family?" But that was not good enough, as he wanted me to accompany him. We had a very unpleasant night, but it was not the first time Connie and I fought and argued even while on holiday.

I enjoyed being with my family very much, but he deeply resented my happiness, because I did not give him my undivided attention. That night, he gnashed his teeth and threatened me in bed, "I will *cut* you into little *pieces* like a fish!" But no one even guessed what was going on, as Connie was very friendly and generous to everyone, and I was adept at keeping up appearances. He hated to see me laughing and having fun with my family because he was so possessive.

We spent New Year's Eve on Galle Face Green, and as we watched the fireworks display, a loud cracker burst very close to Nilanthi's feet, and frightened her badly. I happened to meet my dear friend, Shiromani, quite by chance. She too was married, and we had a long chat, and reminisced about our school days.

The day finally arrived when I had to say goodbye again. I cried bitterly as the plane circled over the tiny, green speck of my island home, and was lost in the hazy mist of the ocean, as we left Ceylon further and further behind.

The children were distressed to see me in tears, but I could not help crying. I was heartbroken to leave my family behind, not knowing when I would see them, and whether we would all be together again. I wept when I thought of Nihal, and the last time I had seen him in 1972.

Connie scowled and muttered, "*Something* must be wrong with you to cry so much!" I sobbed, "I miss my family! *When* will I see them again!" But he was totally unsympathetic, and did not even try to console me. We stayed one night in a nice hotel in Singapore. I was emotionally exhausted, so while I rested, Connie took the children to the top of the building to view the city lights.

We ordered a meal for Stacy and Christian in the room, and put them to bed before we dined in the hotel restaurant. They were such good, obedient children, and no matter where we were, they did not fuss about anything, and took everything in their stride.

Chapter 10

A few days after we returned from our brief holiday, it was time to get back to work and settle down. The children resumed school at the end of January 1980, and I drove with Connie to the factories to collect my quota of work. But to my utmost dismay, they told me things were very slow, and they had no work for me at the moment. I panicked as we drove to several other quilt manufacturers to find work, but it was the same story everywhere.

A few months ago, we purchased a new colour television set for about one thousand dollars; we sold that for five hundred dollars, just to meet the monthly mortgage repayment. I had bought an electric organ for hundred dollars, when we were in the flat, but traded it in for a better one, which cost eight hundred dollars. It was a great instrument, and I spent most of my spare time playing it. When Connie suggested we sell that too, I was very reluctant to part with it, and refused to sell it.

Money was very scarce now, and bills were piling up. Connie worked long hours drafting, as his boss gave him extra work to bring home. But we could not see the situation easing, unless I found work soon. Long hours of work and mounting bills were very stressful, and our quarrels became frequent and violent.

Stacy was very ill in Ceylon with tonsillitis, and Dr Rustomjee advised us to have his tonsils taken out. So we admitted him to Dandenong hospital soon after our return. We did not have to pay any hospital bills, as it was a public hospital. Stacy recovered quickly, and when we took him home that night, he was extremely thirsty and kept crying, "Water, water," which made me feel very sorry for him.

In the days that followed, Stacy stayed home with me, and I pampered him more than usual, spending time reading, or talking to him. He dragged his bean bag into the sewing room, and there he sat talking about various topics, as he was a highly intelligent child, with a strong personality. He questioned everything, and always wanted to learn more. Christian was a quiet, placid little boy, and usually gave in to Stacy's demands, just to avoid confrontation. But he stood up for his rights whenever he felt his older brother treated him unjustly.

We found ourselves in serious financial difficulty now, as lease payments for the car were due, besides monthly bills. We borrowed about five thousand dollars for our trip, and to consolidate some of our credit cards. It was a struggle to make ends meet on one wage only. After several weeks of telephoning every single local factory, I finally found work at "Bedmaster" in Bayswater.

Connie dropped the sewing off every morning at about 6am, before heading to work, and I sewed mattress covers all day. Every night he packed them up and dropped them off the following morning. The wages were very poor indeed, at about sixty dollars a week; with all the picking up and delivering, it really was not much, but helped a little. After about six months, Bedmaster ran out of work, and once again we were in a quandary.

Connie was desperate, and spoke to Fr Noel about our financial troubles, and Father lent him $2000, as Connie had written some cheques without sufficient funds in the bank. Father admonished him, "Conrad, don't you know it's an *offence* to do that? I will lend you the money from emergency funds, and if *ever* you are in a position to repay it, I will appreciate it."

It took many years to repay that debt, but Connie paid it back eventually, with something extra, and Father just said, "I *knew* you would repay it someday. Thank you Conrad." He was a very understanding and compassionate priest, and it was then that he advised Connie to consult a financial counsellor at the Catholic Family Welfare Agency in Dandenong, and to go on a strict budget.

Connie contacted them immediately, and that was how we met Carol. It was the best decision we made, as she saved us from bankruptcy and heartbreak. When she interviewed us, and we put down our commitments on paper, she nodded solemnly, "You are in a very *dire* situation, and the best thing is to declare yourselves bankrupt!" Connie and I were flabbergasted! We absolutely refused to take such a step, and asked her how we could get out of our financial morass, which was precipitated when I could not find regular work.

When Carol knew we would not consider bankruptcy and lose our home, but were willing to work even harder, to find extra income to pay off our debts, she immediately contacted all the finance companies. Then she negotiated suspension of payments for a couple of months. Carol explained our predicament to the creditors, and told them we were prepared to honour our debts, if we were given an extension of time.

She arranged to reduce all the repayments substantially over a longer term, so we could manage within our current means, until such time as our income increased. When she finally worked out a very strict budget for us, we had only fifty dollars a week left for groceries, Connie's cigarettes, drinks, and other expenses.

We agreed to abide by this commitment and be debt-free. Connie soon found a cleaner's job at Adams Pies, in Mulgrave, where he worked a couple of hours every evening. I had to manage the grocery bill within thirty or forty dollars, but I made sure we never went without good, wholesome food. I shopped carefully, and bought less expensive brands and cuts of meat.

Fortunately though, after a few months of this Spartan existence, I found work at Vita Pacific in Bayswater, where they manufactured sofas and divans etc. The head machinist, Pam, a thin, faded, middle-aged Scottish woman, dropped in weekly and sewed a sample of whatever they required. I observed her carefully, and then sewed countless numbers of sofa, divan, cushion, and quilt covers. The factory delivered and picked up the finished work weekly, and I earned $100 or so a week, which helped greatly.

It was a long, bitter struggle that year, as we tried to get our finances back to a semblance of stability. The children still attended St Jude's and were not deprived of good food or clothing. And like most little children, hardly understood the pressures we were undergoing then. I protected them from troubled reality, so they could live a normal, happy life.

When Stacy started school, he was six and a half years old, and as he was way ahead of other prep children, they promoted him to grade one after a few weeks in prep. Stacy could read, write, and count up to hundred, as I taught him at home. This promotion was good for Stacy's morale, and he was very happy, as he had been in the same grade with Christian at the start.

Fr Noel came to know us well, and we invited him for dinner a few times. Once, when I prepared a Chinese banquet, and being unfamiliar with the types of Australian fish, and he asked me what kind of fish I served, I could not tell him. So, he started naming every species of available fish, and when I said I still did not know, he gave up and declared, "Oh well, that *mysterious* fish certainly was delicious!"

That night, after Father left, Connie was in a black mood and snapped angrily, "Him being a *priest*, he spent the whole evening conversing *only* with you! See how he turned his chair towards you and chatted away!" I replied, "He was just being polite, as you were rushing around the kitchen, and he had no one else to talk to." So, we had another argument over that. Though we rarely entertained, Connie invariably picked on me over some imaginary slight, or my sins of omission and commission.

Since the previous year, I suffered extremely painful menstrual cycles, and Dr Rustomjee diagnosed endometriosis. He said it was a common problem among women, where bleeding occurs outside the uterus, causing excruciating pain. Every month I was prostrate, and nothing eased my pain, no matter if I sat up, lay down, or stood up. The throbbing was indescribable, as if my insides were being pushed down my rectum. And a constant stabbing pain, like a sharp object twisting in my groin.

I consulted several doctors, and finally, a gynaecologist prescribed Danasol, which had several side-effects, like bloating and weight gain. I was on Danasol for five years, and if I stopped taking it for a month, the excruciating pains returned with a vengeance. It was a very trying and painful time, and doctors said the only solution was to have a hysterectomy, or take Danasol until I reached menopause. I was not yet thirty, so I did not seriously consider a hysterectomy, and continued on the same medication.

We drove down to Rosebud often, where Connie's parents rented a three-bedroom house now. They had moved from Rye, because it was too isolated. But Aunty and Uncle were still lonely down there, and were always keen to have visitors. Sometimes, Uncle phoned me and said, "I'm *dreaming* of Stacy and Christian, can you come tonight?" So when Connie came home, we drove down to Rosebud, had a late dinner, and returned by midnight. They too visited often, and spent time with us. They slept in our bedroom now, as they were older, and Uncle was very frail. We shared a mattress in the sewing room.

Uncle stood in the doorway of the sewing room, conversing with me. He looked at the bundles of fabric reaching up to the ceiling in one corner, and exclaimed "My, what a lot of sewing you have to do Dolly, it must be very tiring." I nodded and replied, "What else can I do Uncle, we need the extra money." Aunty rushed up just then, and shouted, "*Sweeta*! Don't worry Dolly! She has to finish the sewing!" He lost his temper at such times and grumbled, "See how that woman talks to me! Bloody *bitch*!" And he shuffled off irritably, to watch television or get into bed and have a nap.

He loved Stacy and Christian dearly, and always said, "What *nice* children they are! As soon as they come home from school they ask me, 'did you have a good day Grandpa?' Such good children! God bless them!" He was a very lonely man, and missed his friends and colleagues in Ceylon very much. He often told me sadly, "You know where I want to be *buried* Dolly? Next to Ronno's grave in Talawakale!" Ronno was the toddler they had lost, but he never returned, not even on a holiday.

Connie's family visited us frequently, especially Aunty, Uncle, Wendy, and Brian. I always made them feel welcome, as I was very fond of them. Every month or so, we kept aside a weekend to visit his family (except Geraldine and Clifford), whom we seldom or never visited and vice versa). And when it was one of their birthday's or anniversary's, I made it a point to buy cards and gifts for them. Connie was always too busy to bother about such things. He told me that he depended on me to remember, which I did, as I wrote them in my birthday book.

The children were growing up fast, and I usually joined them on their school excursions. One of the most memorable days, was their first trip to the Melbourne Zoo. And I removed some great photographs, as they stood in awe next to the animal cages. I enjoyed being with Stacy and Christian, and sharing these good times with them.

Our debts were gradually reducing now, as we worked extremely hard, and sometimes, the children helped Connie with the colouring-in of his plans. Both were very good at drawing, and exceptionally clever in many things. Stacy loved watching "Dr Who" on television, playing footy, and reading, while Christian liked sports and running. They joined Little Athletes, and on some Saturdays, Connie or I drove down to watch them running or playing footy.

Whenever his parents visited, the children took Aunty for long hikes down to the paddocks, and around Wellington Road, where the old wishing-well once stood on a hillock. One day, Aunty told me that she had to creep under barbed wire fences in the paddocks, to keep up with them. They thought it was great fun to take her on their long hikes, and laughed as they related their adventures with her.

I bought a budgerigar from a pet shop, and very soon, Chirpy, was as tame as could be. It sat on my shoulder, or clawed up the long zips when I sewed them on to cushion covers. When the children came home from school, it followed them around, and usually perched on Stacy's shoulder while he watched television.

I was careful not to leave windows open when it flew around the house, because it would escape. Also, Mewsette sat outside, watching the flying morsel of food hungrily, and just waited for a chance to get her claws into Chirpy. That little feathered-friend, was a delightful companion, while I sat and sewed long hours, listening to its cheerful twittering.

Once, when I was sewing away, the needle pierced right through the fleshy tip of my middle finger. I was alone, so without panicking, I just unscrewed the needle from the machine, and carefully pulled it out of my finger, making sure the point did not snap off. Then I washed it with disinfectant, applied a band aid around it, and continued sewing. When I told Connie, he was surprised that I took the needle out myself. My finger was swollen for a few days, but healed soon.

Babs gave birth to a baby boy in January 1980, and they christened him Aaron. She was living with Peter, and they decided to get married some months later. Esme met Paul Maschio, a salesman at a Myers store, and soon, they moved in to a flat in Malvern. They were married a few years later, and bought a house in Ferntree Gully. We became well acquainted with his mother, Josephine.

Josephine was in her late fifties then; four feet seven, rather plump and top heavy. She had short, wavy, silver-grey hair, aquiline nose, thin lips, and dark eyes. She loved to dress well, and spent a great deal of money on expensive clothes and shoes.

I grew very fond of Josephine, and she told me about her life in Italy; how she met her husband, whom she loved dearly, and how he died of rheumatic fever when he was in his mid-forties. I loved to hear her recall her past, and she found I was a good listener. I never tired of her stories, even if she repeated them a few times over.

Josephine was widowed at forty-five, and never married again. She lived in a flat in Noble Park, after she sold her house in Dandenong, where she lived with her youngest son, Fabio. Josephine and I got on very well, and she loved to visit us, or have us over for a meal. She told me with tears in her eyes, "If only *you* were my daughter-in-law, I will be a millionaire!" The poor thing wanted to be fussed over, and listened to, more than anything else. Sometimes, Esme picked her and brought her to their place. A little later, she left her with us, and she went off to visit her sisters or Aunty.

One day, Josephine complained, "Your sister is very very *strange* Connie! She tells me to come, and then leaves me alone, and goes to see your mother!" Josephine accompanied us on long drives, and we remained on good terms all through her life.

Esme told me she had no patience with her, and was annoyed when she heard that Josephine referred to her as "That *black* bitch!" So she never got on with her, but resented the fact I was close to her mother-in-law, who in turn loved me dearly.

Nelune transferred to Sydney sometime later that year, and worked at AMP Insurance, and liked Sydney very much. I missed her dearly, but she visited us whenever she could, and phoned me often.

Sometime in 1981, Ammie wrote to say that Grandpa had died. He had type two diabetes for many years, and was admitted to hospital, due to a foot injury that did not heal. He lasted only a few weeks in hospital, because he ended with blood poisoning. Grandpa was in his late eighties then.

Chapter 11

At the end of 1982, Cuckoo, his wife, Regina, and children, Krishan, and Clarissa, arrived in Melbourne for a long holiday. It was about ten years since we last saw him, and he had gained a few extra kilograms in that time. He had also suffered a mild stroke, and a heart attack in that time. Regina, a nurse, looked after him well, until he regained the use of his arm, which was better now. But his blood pressure was very high, which she monitored constantly.

Regina was a pleasant, practical, and cheerful person. She had very short brown hair, dark eyes, and was of average height and build. Ten-year old Krishan was a bright spark, with black hair and eyes, and was very fair- complexioned. At eight years, Clarissa was cute as a button, and as fair as her brother; she had wavy, light-brown hair, and grey eyes. They were delightful children, who got on well with Stacy and Christian.

That Christmas was memorable, and incessant parties with Connie's family. Cuckoo was very good, as he was caring, and gentle with everyone, and he understood people well. He was a kindred spirit, and we spent hours discussing several topics, whether it was politics, arts, religion, or social issues. It reminded me of the times in Watagoda, when Thathie was in a mellow mood, and not too drunk, and we discussed every topic we could think of. I missed those rational talks very much. Cuckoo was blessed with a great sense of humour, and he joked about various aspects of life, even though they were serious issues. But he somehow saw the funny side of the situation.

Krishan and Clarissa liked to play with Chirpy, and Mewsette, especially Clarissa. But one day, when they were taking turns to play with Chirpy, they left the cage door open, and did not realise the windows were wide open. After they left, I called Chirpy, but she did not come back. I saw her sitting on top of a gum tree in the garden, preening away busily, and she turned a deaf ear to all my calling, whistling, and cajoling.

I was very upset to think of her flying off into the wild, where she did not have much chance of survival. But I knew that her instinct to be free, was stronger than a gilded cage, no matter how secure and comfortable it was. A few days later, Mewsette too disappeared, and never came back, so I grieved deeply for my two beloved pets.

We drove up to Sydney with Aunty and Paul, as her brother, Uncle Bertie, and his wife, Aunty Mavis, were visiting relatives in Sydney. We stayed with Nelune in Crows Nest, where she shared a luxury apartment with a girlfriend.

One evening, as I chatted and laughed with them, Connie burst into the kitchen and yelled, "*Stop* acting like a *schoolgirl* Dolly!" My cheeks burned. All I did was laugh at some joke Nelune made. A few minutes later, shamefacedly, he apologized to Nelune and her friend, "I'm *sorry*, I know I shouldn't have said that, and she does look like a schoolgirl doesn't she?" He tried to wheedle out of an awkward situation, but I was not appeased, as I was embarrassed to be yelled at like that.

I prepared lunch for Uncle Bertie, and Aunty Mavis, in Nelune's apartment one afternoon. And Uncle Bertie (after a few whiskeys), tearfully mumbled, "How *happy* I am to have met you all here and *thank* you for cooking such a delicious lunch for us Dolly." He resembled Aunty closely, but was dark-complexioned, and quite bulky. Aunty Mavis was a tall, thin lady, with a heavily painted face, who was very fond of bingo (I heard). She too enjoyed a glass or two of whisky, and became quite friendly, and mellow in the afterglow of its influence.

We returned to Melbourne after a few days, then drove with Cuckoo, Regina, Stacy, and Christian, up to Mount Kosciusko, and Jindabyne. Clarissa and Krishan stayed behind with Babs at Noble Park, where Peter and Babs rented a large house. They attended a local school, and Cuckoo did not want them to miss school.

Cuckoo and his family stayed with Babs for most of their holiday, and visited the others daily. They also toured around Victoria, and New South Wales in coaches.

We stayed in a caravan at Jindabyne, and a cabin in Tumut, and had a most enjoyable trip. Cuckoo recalled the times when he met Nihal and Thathie, and said, "You remind me very much of Nihal, he was such a sensitive, wise young man, and I used to enjoy talking with your father too. They were well-read, weren't they? What a shame poor Nihal died so young!" And he was full of sympathy whenever he mentioned Nihal.

Cuckoo and Regina enjoyed themselves very much, and I grew very close to them during that trip, as we shared many hours of profound discussions and laughter. Although Regina did not speak English at all, she understood what was said, and very often, Cuckoo translated. But she could speak a few words of English when she really wanted to.

When it was time to leave next morning, Connie spent a long time sweeping, cleaning, and dusting, while Regina sat outside reading a book, then she said something in German. Cuckoo translated, "Regina says we should be on our way and make use of the weather, without Connie *wasting* time cleaning up here," which was very true.

Although I swept and put things in order, Connie went through the place all over again. This was nothing new to me, as he was obsessive about cleaning, even at home. I told Cuckoo, "As you know, I'm a very clean, tidy person, and my house is always neat and spotless, but he spends a lot of time cleaning after me. He can't help himself."

On our way down a steep, winding road, the car started to stall, and Connie shouted, "Get out of the car Cuckoo, and take Regina and the children with you!

We'll meet you at the bottom of the road, and I'll call roadside assistance." Cuckoo asked, "What about Dolly?" he replied, "S*he'll* stay with me! If we die, we go *together*!" I looked at him and asked, "What about Stacy and Christian, if we *both* die, who's going to look after them?" "*Someone* will take care of them, don't you worry." And without another word, he drove off before I could get out of the car.

I did not say anything more, as I wanted to avoid a scene and confrontation in front of them. After waiting about one hour for roadside assistance to check the car, they could not find anything seriously wrong with it, and said it was safe for us to drive back.

Whenever they visited, she looked at the pile of sewing in the room and said, "Dolly, *mountain* of sewing! *How* you do so much?" She found it hard to believe I could plough through so much of work in a week's time.

A few days after our return to Melbourne, Regina left, as she had to start work, but Cuckoo stayed behind with the children. He visited often with the children. And while we sat up and chatted till late at night, the children usually ran outside, or played in their rooms. Some days, Connie and he talked about family issues till dawn. I went to bed by ten or eleven o'clock the latest, as I had to start sewing early.

One night, he told me, "The family are divided about who's to blame for you both not attending all the gatherings. Mummy says it's Connie's fault, but the sisters all think it's Dolly's fault!" Connie replied immediately, "I have to say that Dolly has never stopped me from visiting, or attending those gatherings. It's because *I* don't want to, as I have my reasons."

Cuckoo looked at me, but did not say anything, as he knew Connie was insanely jealous, especially of Clifford. Connie was also annoyed with Babs for divorcing Damian, and living with Ralston, until she married Peter. He was very fond of Damian still, and had heated arguments with Babs, as he blamed her totally.

Geraldine and Clifford were separated then, because she believed he was having an affair with Christine, his brother's wife. But he met Cuckoo a few times and denied all allegations, saying that they had other problems, as she was extremely jealous of him.

When we met her at Aunty's place once, Geraldine told me, "Clifford is living at Wally's place now, and they are all having a ball!" She was very angry and bitter about the alleged affair, and whenever she met me, she made it a point to disparage him.

One evening, Cuckoo was chatting to us as usual, when Krishan burst in, and exclaimed heatedly in German. And he kept tugging at Cuckoo's sleeve. Suddenly, Cuckoo burst out laughing. Chuckling, he explained, "Krishan wants me to come and kill Stacy, and he says if I don't do it, he'll go and kill Stacy by himself." We laughed, as Stacy had annoyed Krishan for some reason, and he was determined to get revenge. Clarissa tended to hang around with Christian, as they were the younger siblings.

Almost every night when Cuckoo visited us, he asked me jokingly, "Have you got pittu Dolly?" He loved pittu (steamed rice flour with shredded coconut), and beef curry. Krishan called curry "garlic sauce" and when he asked me for some, I served him every sauce I could think of. But he looked crestfallen, and shook his head, "*That's* not *garlic sauce*!" Finally, Cuckoo told me what he meant by garlic sauce.

Some evenings, if other family members were present, we had a sing song, and I played the electric organ, as Cuckoo loved to sing. One of his favourite songs was, "Oh Danny Boy." Then, if the children were playing quietly, he took out his scrap book, and pressed all the wild flowers he had gathered in Australia. Regina and he toured Canberra in a coach, and they saw quite a lot of the coastal areas as well.

When Uncle and Aunty left the house in Rye, we found them a small unit for rent near Branson Avenue, Rosebud. Connie and I packed everything, and helped them move out, but they vacated that place in a few months time, and moved to a three-bedroom, brick-veneer house in Rosebud.

They lived there for a few years, until Cuckoo and Regina persuaded them to leave Rosebud and rent a flat close to Babs, in Noble Park. This was because they felt isolated, and missed the family very much. Paul worked part-time hours in an amusement park in Rosebud, and was hardly at home.

Sometime in mid-April that year, Uncle was very ill with flu. But he came with Cuckoo and Aunty one evening. Cuckoo now drove a car he had borrowed from Jamie, an ex-boyfriend of Cristobel's, who still kept in touch with the family.

Uncle wheezed heavily, and rasped as he entered the house, "I'm going to *throw* away my cigarettes and give up smoking from today!" Then he tottered weakly to the kitchen and smiled at me, "What a nice smell of *curry*! Just like Ceylon!" They had dinner and left late that night.

A few days later, on 20 April, we visited them in their flat in Noble Park, as it was Krishan's birthday next day. Uncle looked very ill, but when it was time to take a photograph with the whole family, he stumbled out of bed, and sat in the lounge for the photograph. When he saw me, he said, "I have no appetite at all." And I replied, "Dandelion tea is good when you don't have an appetite. Do you like to try some?" He looked at me and whispered feebly, "*If* you can Dolly, can you get some of that dandelion tea for me?" I nodded, "I will bring some as soon as possible."

Everyone fussed a great deal whenever Uncle wanted a drink, but over the last few years, he drank only sweet sherry and port. Regina and Cuckoo told Aunty to let him enjoy a couple of drinks, because at his age, what harm could it do now. Connie poured him a generous glass of port, and Uncle was happily sipping it when we left around midnight.

The following morning, Babs called me around 9am, "Dolly, I *think* Daddy is dead!" I asked in disbelief, "What do you *mean*, you *think* he's dead? What's happened?" She replied, "Cuckoo called me and said Mummy is in a bad state as Daddy was lying cold in his bed this morning."

I had the most unpleasant task of phoning Connie at work and breaking the news to him. We drove there as soon as Connie came home, and Uncle was still lying in bed in the same position that Aunty found him that morning. She had tied a coloured scarf around his face, to prevent his jaw dropping down (she told us), and he looked very frail and pathetic.

Tearfully, she explained, "I had just given him his cup of tea this morning, and he dropped it as his hands were lifeless and he couldn't hold the cup." Full of remorse, she sobbed, "I shouted at him when he dropped the cup on the floor."

When she realised he was dying, she quickly gave him a crucifix to hold onto, and he died peacefully.

The next few days were very busy, as I cooked meals for the family, and took them down every evening, as Aunty was grieving, and not in a state to be cooking. Geraldine was living on her own, and had no responsibilities, so she spent most of her time with Aunty.

When it came to funeral arrangements, none of the family had the means to pay for it. Connie and I had some modest savings now, so we paid one thousand dollars for all the funeral expenses. We did so, because Uncle and Aunty looked after us for two years. They also paid five hundred rupees for our wedding, and had been generous in their own small way. I was very fond of Uncle, and grieved that he died in such a sad state. As I said, he was very unhappy in Australia, and spoke constantly of returning to Ceylon one day.

He had written a poignant verse about his "Island home" and we read it with sadness. Connie said, "Dolla, write a poem for Daddy, because you knew him well, I will read it after the service." Cuckoo persuaded me to play Uncle's favourite hymns during rosary, on the evening before his funeral. And although I was apprehensive about playing in public, I resolved to do my best, and played the organ in church.

Cuckoo was very pleased, and said, "You did well Dolly, Daddy would have been very happy." Uncle's coffin was closed up, as the family, for some unknown reason, did not want mourners to gaze upon his corpse. This caused speculation. And people asked if something was wrong with Uncle, whether some disease had disfigured him.

Wally and Christine turned up for the funeral, and so did Clifford. When Christine walked over to Geraldine to condole, she shouted out, "I don't want *your* sympathies!" Cuckoo was shocked, and admonished her later, "You don't *behave* like that in church Jenny, *especially* when someone offers you condolences! You should have acted like a *lady* and been more civilised!"

She was not concerned though, and when we returned to the flat, all she could do was tear Clifford's reputation to pieces. And she blamed him totally for the breakdown of their marriage. We had to listen to her angry outburst for hours on end, as she brought out every single detail of what she had endured with him through the years. And she fumed at me, "You are so *lucky* you escaped him! You would have had a nervous breakdown now, if you had to put up with him!" I knew she had no clue about Connie's behaviour, and what I endured with him.

Once the funeral was over, and Uncle's ashes were placed in a niche at the Necropolis in Springvale, Cuckoo went about finding another place for Aunty. She did not like to stay in that flat where Uncle died, and had been there only two weeks. He found a semi-detached flat before long, and helped Aunty to settle in there. Paul lived by himself in the house in Rosebud, and Aunty paid the rent there with her pension. How she managed to pay rent for the flat too, is beyond me. Paul dated several girls now, and he did not want to move into the flat with Aunty.

Cuckoo visited us almost every evening. And sometimes, Aunty came with him during the day, and we had a great time chatting, while I took a break from sewing. He joked, "My heavens Dolly, you live here like a *nun,* and Connie keeps you hidden here like Clifton Clovers hid his daughter on Wolverton Mountain!" (a popular song then). He laughed and told me that he knew how jealous Connie was, and that Aunty had related all our marital woes to him. He liked visiting with Aunty during the day. Because he knew I was very restrained whenever Connie was around, as he flew off the handle if I said too much.

He bemoaned the fact that he could not be more disciplined with his eating habits, as he tended to gain weight without even trying. This was because he saw how strict I was with my timetable, and eating habits.

He said, "Mummy tells me how *industrious* you are Dolly, you *never* waste a minute of your time! You are such a good example to my sisters. She says you cook so well, and do everything very methodically. Mummy praises you to the sky! I can see now she is right, and Connie is very lucky to have married you. But I know he's very jealous, especially of Clifford. The family knows all about that."

I just nodded and went on sewing the tapestry, which he admired very much, and told me about the Black Forest in Germany. The tapestry was a forest scene, with an old cottage, windmill, and pond, and Cuckoo sang an old German song about the Black Forest. We spent many happy days enjoying his company and never-ending store of tales and anecdotes.

On the last evening before Cuckoo left Melbourne, he visited us. On his way out, he touched all the young trees in the garden and said, "Goodbye wattle, gum, eucalyptus, I'll never see you again!" Connie drove to the airport, but I could not go due to my work load.

And so, Cuckoo left with the children sometime in July 1983, and he never returned to Australia again. I cared for him just like an older brother, as I missed Nihal badly, and it helped to have someone so kind, and understanding. I wished he could have stayed longer, because it was so easy to converse with him about any subject. He was never judgemental, or bigoted, and I was grateful for those memorable times we had shared.

The children learnt to speak fluent English in six months, and Cuckoo was glad they achieved so much. I grew very close to Regina and him, and we corresponded regularly, or else he phoned often. Regina picked up the phone and listened to my messages, and Cuckoo translated for her. Connie wrote to him too, but he left the details to me. Cuckoo was very interested in everything that went on in our lives, and around us, especially my artistic pursuits. He encouraged me to keep writing and painting.

Chapter 12

In December 1983, Sherone and Glen were married. It was a nice ceremony, and they held a grand reception at a restaurant in Clayton, but we left the children at one of their friend's places in Rowville, as only adults were invited. We knew the family well, and I met their mother in school daily, so she said that it was no trouble at all to mind them. We returned late in the night and picked up the children, who were exhausted after a long day of playing.

In spite of taking medication, I still suffered severe pain with endometriosis. After several more consultations, the gynaecologist advised me to have a hysterectomy, if I did not plan to have any more children. The medication was not effective after a few years, and there was no other solution. I thought about it for a long period, and then decided to go ahead.

I was thirty-two years then, but I was certain I did not want to have any more children. After Christian's birth, I was pregnant twice, and as I was only a month overdue both times, I had terminated the pregnancies. The doctor also said that it would be very difficult, or impossible to have any more children because of the endometriosis.

I stopped work sometime in March 1984, to have the operation. As recovery was very slow and painful, I was in hospital almost ten days, and could hardly move around. I weighed fifty kilograms before the operation, but my weight dropped to forty five kilograms when I returned home. I recuperated gradually, and after a month or more, I felt much better. But when it was time for my next cycle, to my utter surprise and dismay, the same excruciating pain engulfed me like before.

When I went back to the gynaecologist who performed the operation, he told me, "There is residual endometriosis too close to the spine that I could not scrape off, so you still have to take medication and the contraceptive pill to ease monthly pains. I did not perform a full hysterectomy, as your ovaries are still intact, which means monthly menstruation cycle will still happen."

I was shocked and angry, to say the least, as a hysterectomy was quite unnecessary, if I had to take medication until menopause. Connie was furious with the gynaecologist, but I could not do anything else, except go on the pill once again. He was a Sri Lankan gynaecologist that Dr Rustomjee recommended.

308

I stopped work as a machinist after the hysterectomy, as it was too strenuous, and wanted a break from sewing, before I looked for some other sort of work. Financially, we were in a better situation, as Connie was earning a good wage at Safeway. He was promoted to a supervisor's position and now had a company car.

Although we were not too badly off now, Connie was still unable to control his insane bouts of jealousy and anger. One night, as I was reading in bed, he started a row, and started punching and pushing me around. Then he grabbed the bedside lamp and jammed it into my eye. I shouted in pain as my eye started to swell up.

He was lying down beside me and smoking, as he continued to smoke inside the house and in our bedroom. Even though Stacy hated the smell of tobacco, Connie did not go outside when he smoked. He threw away his cigarette now and jumped out of bed. My eye was bruised and swollen, so I bathed it with some ice.

Next morning, I made an appointment to see the local doctor. Connie told me, "I'm coming with you, and you must tell the doctor that you bumped into a door handle, do you hear?" When the doctor saw me, he asked, "How did you get that injury?" I looked down and mumbled, "I walked into a door."

He looked at me keenly, and then at Connie. I had a feeling he guessed the truth, but he nodded slightly and said, "Keep putting some ice on it. Fortunately, your eye is not damaged, only some bruising around." I did not talk to Connie for a couple of days. I was too angry.

He never allowed me to visit any doctor on my own, and he had a habit of telling the doctor *my* symptoms even before I opened my mouth. On a few occasions, when I started telling doctor how I felt, he kept butting in, so I could hardly get a word in. This continued for many years, until I was assertive enough to tell him to mind his own business, and let me tell the doctor what my complaint was.

When Rosie visited later that year, I mentioned this incident to her, and she was horrified, "How on earth have you allowed him to treat you like this? You were always so *independent* and *strong*! What has happened to you?" I could not begin to describe even a jot of what my marriage was like.

Connie also had a habit of muttering and cursing, just like Uncle did. I heard him banging things around the house and mumbling, "*Cursed* devils!" I asked him why he was cursing, and with whom he was so angry. He snapped irritably, "I'm *not* cursing, I'm *praying*! It's not you anyway, I'm angry with some other people."

But he did not stop that habit, and whenever he argued, he shouted, "*Curse* the day I met you! Wish I had *never* married you!" I retorted, "I could say the *same,* as I wish *I* had never married you either!" That really enraged him, as he roared and attacked me. It was alright for him to curse and say anything, but I was not allowed to retaliate. This never-ending cycle of hurt and arguments went round and round.

Sometimes, when he was very drunk, and embroiled in a violent argument, he grabbed a kitchen knife and held it to my throat, shouting out, "I'm going to *kill* you!" I struggled and escaped his strong grip, then ran out to the garden, panting for breath.

I truly believe it was divine providence that saved me and the children from his violent, uncontrollable temper. Because when I looked at his intoxicated, juddering face, distorted with so much anger, I feared he could have stabbed me to death in one of his insane rages. But in a minute, his mood changed from murderous rage to remorse. I could not stop him from threatening me with knives, and knowing how much it hurt and frightened me, he took the upper hand.

When Stacy's baby teeth dropped, I noticed that a few extra teeth were growing over his molars. The dentist said he had to take those extra teeth out and wear braces when he was a little older. Braces were expensive, just like today, and cost $2500 then. We paid it in monthly instalments, and he started wearing braces when he was fourteen years. One of us drove him to an orthodontist in Dandenong every month.

Every time Connie lost his temper, and slapped Stacy, his inner cheeks bled, as the braces cut his cheeks. But I could never stop his violence, no matter how much I told him not to hurt the children.

Once, when we visited Esme and Paul for dinner with Rosie, the children were playing in the room with Roshan and Suresh. They made a big noise, and were just fooling around, but Connie rushed in and slapped Stacy so hard that his mouth began to bleed. He was not wearing braces then, but his extra teeth always cut into his cheeks.

Paul was shocked, and told Esme, "Is that how Connie treats his children, to slap them till they bleed?" They were upset when they saw Stacy's bleeding mouth. The children were subdued, but Connie had to prove he was in charge, and he could do as he pleased no matter where we were. I was very upset for Stacy, when he cried angrily at the injustice of being the only one to be punished for no reason. And he felt humiliated to be slapped in front of the other children.

Sometime in August 1984, Roland, Shiranthi, and their two children, arrived in Melbourne. The rest of the family rented out a unit for them in Dandenong. The two children were still naughty and full of mischief, but soon adjusted to their new way of life, as they attended school and made new friends.

But Shiranthi missed her family very much, as she had no one of her own here. I sympathised with her, as I knew exactly what it was like to leave family behind, and start life in a new country. A few months after their arrival, Connie and I visited them one evening. Roland was asleep, and Shiranthi looked very depressed, with swollen, red eyes, as if she had been crying.

She sobbed and blurted out, "Connie, *all* your sisters *ate* me up!" He asked, "What do you mean?" she said, "They all came here and sat around with me in the middle, and said I'm causing a lot of trouble in the family and gave me a hard time. I wish I had never come here! I have no family here and they all made me feel so bad. Tucko never took my side, as he *always* takes his sisters' side. Now he's sleeping after we had a big fight." We stayed a little longer, and I tried to pacify her, as she was crying inconsolably, then as Roland did not get up, we left shortly after.

Whenever we went away on a day trip over the next few years, we invited Shiranthi, Roland, and the children to join us. Shiranthi and I became very close, and I never had any issues with her. But from the time she came here, the ill-feeling between her and Roland's sisters did not ease. She said they interfered in her life constantly, especially Geraldine, but not Babs, who was very fond of her.

Once, when we drove to Lakes Entrance with them, we had a great time looking around, and then stopped for a barbeque by the sea. And on our way back, when

Connie filled up petrol, he was not concentrating, and filled diesel instead. We had a proper drama then, as he had to let out all the diesel, and re-fill with petrol. He shouted at me, "*Why* didn't you tell me it was diesel? Weren't you looking when I was filling up?" I replied, "How can I see what you were doing? I was in the car and didn't know what you were doing." So it was. I was to blame, no matter what went wrong.

Shiranthi and Roland were very involved in their evangelical church, and soon, Cristobel, Babs, Geraldine, and their brother Paul, converted to "Born again' Christianity. Connie was incredulous, and demanded, "*How* can you change your religion when you are *baptized* Catholics? Daddy will be rolling in his grave to think of you lot leaving the church! I was baptized a Catholic, and will die a Catholic!"

He had many arguments with Roland and his siblings over this issue, but I told him it was up to them to follow whatever religion they wanted to, and it was none of our business. They visited often, and Shiranthi confided all her troubles in me, and I listened with empathy.

A few years later, when Shiranthi's brother was killed in an accident, she wanted to visit her family. When I saw her, she was in tears, as she said that she did not have enough money for her trip. I gave her a gold ring, set with precious stones, and told her to sell it in Sri Lanka, if she needed some money. She was very emotional, and said, "No one has ever done this for me! I'll always remember your kindness."

Some time later, she wanted to visit her family again when her mother died, and I gave her $200, as I was very sorry for her, because she did not work, and they were struggling financially. I heard Geraldine saying to Roland, "*She* didn't let you come to see us when Daddy died, so *why* should you let her go to see her family?" I sympathised heartily with Shiranthi.

One of Connie's colleague's asked if he wanted a German Shepherd dog, as his wife just had a baby, and she did not want the dog around. It was about one year old, and knowing I loved dogs, Connie agreed to take it. He was a striking, gentle dog, and I called it Max, but he hardly romped and played. instead, he just lay around, looking at me with soulful eyes.

I was very fond of Max, and looked after it well. Connie bought large marrow bones, but Max just gnawed the ends lethargically. I thought it unusual for a dog to be so disinterested in bones, so I suggested we take it to a vet. Max was with us for a few weeks only.

He took some x-rays because I mentioned that he hardly raised his head to look at me. The diagnosis - cancer in his spine that had spread rapidly, and the vet did not want to operate. He said the kindest thing would be to put him to sleep, as they could not give him anything for his pain or cure him.

When it was done, I broke my heart over Max, and cried for days, as I loved that gentle-natured dog. But it hurt more to think he was in so much pain, and I did not know about it. I suspected that Connie's colleague knew he was a sick dog, and got rid of him. We paid fifty dollars to put him down, and that was the end of Max.

In late October 1984, Shirani, Nelune, and I asked Thathie and Ammie to visit us. But Ammie refused, as she was reluctant to leave the house behind, due to the volatile political situation then. I was sad and disappointed, as I wanted to pamper Ammie, and give her all the food she loved to eat, but it was not meant to be.

Thathie was more than happy though, and it was a great day when he arrived in Melbourne. Connie and I picked him up at the airport, and he stayed with us. He slept in Christian's bedroom, and the boys shared the larger room with the bunk beds. At this stage, we still did not have carpets, but the floor-boards looked alright. I bought an old deerskin rug at an opportunity shop to arrange in Thathie's room.

He was quite comfortable and happy staying with us, and he visited Shirani and Ranjith on weekends. We had unforgettable times together, as Rosie sprang a surprise and arrived in Melbourne in early December. It was great to see her too, and we had splendid times. She stayed with Shirani and Ranjith, but we got together every single day. Christmas was a very happy time, and after Boxing Day, we drove up to Sydney in two cars.

Connie now had a company car, a silver Datsun. We stopped at many places on the way, and sometimes, Rosie and Thathie exchanged places in our car. When I asked Rosie to look around at the scenery, she inquired derisively, "*What* scenery? If you want scenery, you must visit *England!*" She thought the endless scrub and flat bush-land were very dull, and I laughed at her cheeky retort.

We arrived at Strathfield, as we planned to stay with Anjo, who invited us there. She had just moved in to a large, rambling old house, and was busy cleaning it up. The garden was over-grown too, and the place needed a great deal of work, but she opened her home and heart to us, and we had a great time. We enjoyed barbeques with Barlo, her husband, Clifford, Anjo, and Ronald. Anjo now had two little girls, besides her eldest son, Peter, and they were all nice, well-behaved children.

Anjo treated us very well, and just before New Year, Barlo invited us to spend a couple of days at her place in Homebush. It was a pleasant, spacious house, and Barlo and Clifford, were very kind and hospitable too. Rosie joked and laughed away the hours, as Barlo and she reminisced about their childhood pranks.

Barlo made me laugh with her antics to keep us longer. Connie and I planned to get back to Melbourne on the 31st, as we thought it was time to leave. But Barlo locked the front door, and did not let us go, no matter how much we pleaded with her. She was determined that we spend New Year with her. Connie became quite heated, as he did not like to be told what to do, but he finally agreed, on condition that we left on the 2nd of January.

We enjoyed a barbecue on the 1st, and Barlo took us sight-seeing to various places around Homebush. We spent a couple of days at Nelune's place in Mosman just before New Year, and she joined us at Barlo's every day. As Nelune had a one-bedroom apartment, we could not stay with her. Finally, we left Sydney a few days later than we planned.

It was a memorable time in Sydney, and I was sad to leave our good friends behind. Thathie enjoyed himself thoroughly too, and he told us it was great to be with family and friends. But he missed Ammie very much, I could tell. And his constant refrain was, "What a shame Ammie can't enjoy all this delicious food! How much Ammie would have liked to see these beautiful places!"

On some days, I collected all my coins to buy a train ticket for Thathie, as he loved travelling by train, and spending the day in the city. He had a beer at one of the pubs, ate fish and chips, and returned in the evening, immensely pleased with his outing. He was quite independent, once he knew the bus and train timetables.

When he stayed home, I gave him a glass of beer just before lunch, and in the evenings, when Connie was home, he enjoyed a "tot" of whisky with him. After a couple of "tots" Thathie became very talkative as usual, and kept us amused with his anecdotes and jokes. He told us about the time he went to India, as manager of the Buddhist Centre in Madras, and how he was doing well there, until Ammie decided to join him after a few weeks.

And much to his chagrin and amusement, she pasted all her Holy Pictures on the walls of the Buddhist Centre! Thathie told her to take them down immediately, before the monks saw them. And he told her, "*How* can I explain that you are a *Catholic,* when they think I'm such a staunch Buddhist, and that's why I got this job?"

We took Thathie for a barbecue to the Dandenong's once, and he loved Ferntree Gully, where the old steam engine, "Puffing Billy" still chugged along. He came with us to a few family gatherings, and once, to Aunty's flat in Corrigan St, Noble Park, where she now lived.

Connie said that Geraldine told him, "*Don't* go behind Dolly's father, calling him 'Thathie' 'Thathi,' you remember how he *ill-treated* you when you visited Dolly?" Connie had replied, "*That* was so long ago, and now it's all different. I'm really fond of him, and want to treat him well."

I could not believe such vindictive behaviour, and that she wanted to influence Connie in such a negative manner. But from what Aunty told me, I knew she was insincere, and seized any opportunity to disparage me. Aunty was naturally garrulous, but whenever she visited, and drank a few glasses of whisky, her tongue ran amok without a halt, like a derailed train. She enjoyed gossiping, and just babbled on without filtering her conversation. And she liked to talk with me, but was careful not to say too much when Connie was around. So, I was fully aware of what went on in the family. She told me, "Appoi, I can't mention anything good about you, Jenny gets very angry, because she still has that jealousy about you, that you were Clifford's girlfriend, and she is very jealous of him too. I'm careful not to praise you when she's around as she gets very upset. But Wendy and Cuckoo love you very much, and they always say something good about you." I knew that, and it was the reason why they were dear to me.

When we returned from Sydney, I was keen to start work again. Connie asked one of his colleagues at Safeway, who worked in the advertising section, if there was a vacancy. I received a diploma in commercial art in 1981, and now decided to find work in that field. And I still wrote profusely, contributed articles, poems, and stories to local papers regularly.

When I was called for an interview at Safeway, I was elated. The manager was quite impressed with my portfolio, and asked me to design some posters and signs. He read some of my published articles, and poems in newspapers and magazines and asked if he could keep them for a while, saying he would return them, and he promised to contact me soon. Unfortunately, nothing eventuated, and he sent me a cheque for the hours I spent drawing up signs and posters.

When I told Thathie how keen I was to find work in an advertising agency, he joined his hands in benediction, saying he was confident that I would get a job soon. He was always the same, as he encouraged, prayed, and blessed my endeavours with the utmost sincerity.

We took Thathie for long drives to all the interesting tourist spots, and sometimes, Shirani and Ranjith joined us too. We had a great deal of fun and laughter during those few weeks with Thathie and Rosie. Thathie constantly lamented though, "I *wish* Ammie was here to enjoy all this good food, and wonderful places, and your beloved company!"

He enjoyed travelling to Dandenong Market by bus sometimes, and bought little gifts for Ammie and his friends. I could not help him much with pocket money, as I was not working now, and we were still on a very strict budget. But I gave him whatever I could spare for travelling and spending money. He came with me whenever I drove down to pick up the children, who now attended St Simon's primary school in Rowville.

The school opened recently, and a new church was under construction too. Connie and I helped out in the school and church community sometimes, and I spent a couple of hours at school, teaching the little ones to knit and sew. They were amusing times, and I really enjoyed my time there, as Christian and Stacy loved to see me in their school. They participated in school plays as well, and it was fun preparing costumes, and attending their plays and other events.

They enjoyed great times with the children in the court too, and Chris and Tim were their best friends. Tim was a few years younger than Christian, but they were close, while Chris and Stacy, who were about the same age, spent time getting into boyish mischief. The Caribbean Market nearby was out of bounds, unless we accompanied them. But the four boys sneaked in there, and told me all about it a few days later.

They built a raft to take down to the creek, but soon, they were back, sodden to the core, minus the raft that fell apart after a few wobbly minutes in the creek. Stacy cried in frustration, but hammered poles together once again, determined to get the raft afloat, no matter what.

One afternoon, Stacy and Christian told me, "Mum, come with us to the lake, as we want to test the raft." I agreed, and the three of us walked to the lake down the road. We stayed afloat for about twenty minutes, before I told them, "That's long enough, I think we should head back." Stacy said, "Mum, you are brave, because we thought you wouldn't come with us on the raft."

They were full of admiration, as they did not believe I had confidence in their wobbly raft. But as they knew how to swim, I was not too worried if it came apart.

We went for long walks together, as Rowville was unspoilt and rural then. They loved to scramble in the dense bushland in the valley, and I am thankful that we never encountered snakes. But quite often in hot weather, we saw brown snakes slithering across the road.

Stacy and Christian built a tree house in one of the blue gums in our garden. And it was such a good structure, that it was quite water-proof, and they enjoyed sleeping inside their tree house whenever they could.

Thathie accompanied Shirani and Ranjith on long drives, and he was very pleased to see all the interesting places in Melbourne. But all too soon, he was packing up to leave. He was anxious to get back in time for Ammie's birthday on 9 February, and he asked me jokingly, "Is it possible to take some lamb chops for Ammie?"

I bought a few chops and froze them, before packing them in a plastic bag. Rosie and Thathie were flying directly to Ceylon, which took about ten hours, and we hoped the frozen chops would not be spoilt. It was such a luxury item in Ceylon, and I was so pleased when Ammie wrote to say how much she enjoyed the succulent, Australian lamb chops. Thathie too always wrote about how much he enjoyed the "tender, juicy, Australian meat" that he had relished here.

They left Melbourne at the end of January 1986. Rosie's cases were full of things that Barlo and Anjo gave her for their friends and family in Ceylon. She emptied most of the things into her hand luggage at the airport, and her shoulders sagged with the weight. The strap bruised her arms, and she struggled to carry a huge load.

Rosie was very obliging, and did not like to refuse their request, as they were so kind to her, and to our family. It was a sad farewell at the airport, and I still picture Rosie, shoulders bent over with the weight of Barlo's bags, filled with chocolates and goodies.

Once he returned, Thathie wrote to say that he enjoyed himself thoroughly, and wanted to immigrate to Australia soon. But Ammie was adamant, and did not want to leave her home. We sponsored them anyway, and their application was approved, but Ammie still refused to come.

Now I understand what a big step it was for her to leave the security and comfort of her familiar surroundings, her family, and friends. It was not meant to be, and I accepted Ammie's decision philosophically. But Thathie was bitterly disappointed, and drank so heavily, that he ended up in hospital with serious liver problems. He recovered in time, and although he tried to control his drinking, he could not give it up altogether.

I read an advertisement requesting manuscripts on folklore from any country. The publisher was based in Melbourne, so I wrote to him, and he replied immediately, saying that he was most interested in Sri Lankan folklore, and wanted to arrange a meeting. Connie drove me to the city, where I had an interesting interview with the publisher, who was a stout, short gentleman in his late sixties, with sparse grey hair, and a slight limp. He reminded me of Mr Pickwick from a Charles Dickens novel. I signed a contract, and he promised to pay me an advance when I sent him the final manuscript.

I did exhaustive research, and compiled all the Sri Lankan folklore I could find. I enjoyed the project immensely, visiting several local libraries, and reading dozens of tales. I typed enough stories, and submitted a first draft.

The publisher arranged to visit me at home a few days later (when Connie was present), and we had further discussions.

After several months of waiting, and umpteen revisions, I received a letter one day, to say that his business had folded up, and he could not publish my book. It was a great disappointment, but the publisher called me a few times to say how sorry he was, and that I should try another publisher, because he was confident that my book would sell without any problems.

Chapter 13

Sometime later in 1985, I applied for a paste-up artist's job in the city, and was delighted when a small printing press in North Melbourne employed me. Connie was more amenable now regarding my decision to go out to work, as the children were older, and did not need me at home all the time. He asked me to drive his company car, as it was more reliable than the old Commodore that we still had.

My first impression of the printing press was of a small, dingy building, with about twenty people working there. I was shown to a dark, crowded room with a few scattered tables. The manager was quite friendly, and impressed with the art work, and my portfolio. He even wanted to buy one of my small oil paintings of the Snowy River in Orbost.

He had a strange manner of stretching out his lips in a contrived smile, totally at variance with the cold, unfriendly glint in his pale blue eyes, especially when he was displeased. He pretended to smile, but just when I thought he was being nice and friendly, his lips drew back immediately into a scowl.

Just a day or so after I started work there, Connie and the children surprised me during my lunch break, and the four of us had lunch in a small café. The children were on school holidays, and Connie had taken some time off. We did not want them to be on their own, even though Stacy was almost thirteen, and Christian twelve years old then.

One morning, the manager called me up, and turned on his fake smile as he told me, "There just isn't *enough* work to keep you going here, and the best place for you would be an advertising agency." I was quite unprepared for this, and left work that evening with sodden eyes, and wept all the way home. I was very disappointed at this sudden dismissal, without any notice and lasted there only one month.

In the months that followed, I applied for hundreds of jobs as a journalist, paste-up artist, or any other job in an advertising agency or in the media. I was called up for a few interviews, and it was the same story; I did not have any work experience in Australia as a journalist, and so it was difficult to employ me. In the meantime, I read an advertisement in the newspapers that Public Service examinations were to be held soon, and I immediately applied to sit for one.

In August 1985, I was called for an examination, which was to be held on 24 August, a day after Stacy's 13th birthday. We held a party for about thirteen of his friends, and they rioted all evening. Aunty came over to "lend a hand" with the boisterous boys, who nearly killed each other, as they played rough games on the lawn outside. One of his friends, Gary, who gorged on lollies all through the evening, stayed over, and continued their fun and games until late that night.

On our way to the city next morning, Gary was sick in the car. We were supposed to drop him at his house earlier on, but he wanted to come with us to the city. And he kept throwing up in the car all the way there, as we did not have a plastic bucket or paper bags. We stopped soon, and Connie had the unpleasant task of cleaning Gary and the car, while I went into the hall. I could not get over the unpleasant smell of vomit that seemed to linger everywhere, and I felt very queasy.

All the same, I did my best, and when results were released sometime later, I was advised that I passed the examination, but jobs would be allocated according to an order of merit. I was on a waiting list, and had to be patient until I was appointed.

I was busy writing as usual, while waiting to hear about an appointment, and started a novel that year, with the working title of, "Alice, Angel Of Death" and later published as "Edge of Nowhere." It was based on a teenage girl's drug addiction, and aids-related death, which was a huge issue at the time, as the deadly disease had just reared its ugly head, and some famous names succumbed to the scourge.

After almost thirteen years of marriage, Geraldine had a baby boy, Adam, in November that year. After a couple of years separation, they reconciled, and it came as a great surprise when she fell pregnant.

A few weeks later, Geraldine visited with the baby and Esme, while I was washing the car. And she spent the whole day talking about her troubled marriage, her past etc. Esme stood as Adam's Godmother, and doted on him from the day he was born. The whole family fussed over the baby and Geraldine, as no one expected her to become a mother.

I could not resist buying a white rabbit from the pet shop, and called it Snuffles. Since I lost Mewsette and Chirpy, I wanted to have another pet, and I thought a bunny would be easy to look after. Connie built a sturdy hutch that we kept under the shady gum trees in the backyard. Very soon, Snuffles became tame and followed me around like a dog.

He even ventured inside the house, with twitching nose and red eyes gleaming mischievously. Whenever I called him, he had a trick of leaping in the air, then twisting around like a corkscrew, before landing in the grass. It was very amusing to watch him. The children and their friends enjoyed feeding Snuffles fresh celery and carrots, and he was a much-loved pet.

Stacy and Christian, who were now in years six and seven, attended St Joseph's College in Ferntree Gully. I dropped them off in the mornings and picked them up after school, as I did not like them to take the bus, until they were more settled at school.

Financially, we were finding things a little difficult now, with added expenses, so I wanted to work and help with the family budget. I persistently rang all the local factories daily. But I did not want to work as a sewing machinist again, because I had had enough of sewing, and sold the industrial machine a few months ago. Now I just wanted light, process work in any factory.

In response to my phone call, in late January 1986, one of the factories in Bayswater, "High Title Group" said they had a vacancy with an immediate start. They produced woollen under-blankets, and the foreman who interviewed me, was impressed that I spoke good English. He asked me to start work next day. Connie worked in Bayswater then, as Safeway re-located their drawing office from Mulgrave.

I entered the massive, dark, factory, that was cold, and looked dreary even though it was late summer. Several non-English speaking migrants, especially Vietnamese, Indians, and Asians, worked there. The manager, Mr Title, was also impressed when I spoke fluent English. Most of the workers could hardly speak the language, and they all asked me how I learnt to speak English so well, because I was a migrant too. And I had to keep explaining that I was educated in English in Ceylon, which they found hard to believe.

My first task for the day was to watch a dozen large spools being re-wound, and ensure the wool did not snap. All day long I kept an eye on the whirring spools, and tied up broken woollen threads whenever they snapped. I took a book next day, and whenever the foreman was not around, I read a few pages, just to break the monotony of watching those endless spools spinning round and round. About six women worked in another section, where they spun under-blankets on huge looms.

Joy, a middle-aged blonde, and talkative Australian lady, with an enormous hair-do, initiated me into the life of a factory worker. Two Vietnamese women, the older, hatchet-faced and taciturn, and her niece, Van, the younger, sharp-featured and bad-tempered, spoke broken English. They watched me constantly with glittering black eyes.

At lunch time, I was amused, when these two Vietnamese women cleared up piles of blankets, and lit a small gas stove right in the middle of the factory floor to cook their lunch! None of the other workers or the foreman said anything, as they squatted and ate noodles from their bowls.

The canteen was just around the corner, where some of the men and women hung out during lunch break. But these two women always cooked their lunch in this manner. I was surprised they were allowed to do so, due to the fire hazard. Obviously, that factory did not adhere to occupational health and safety issues then.

The two women chatted to me in broken English, and asked in perplexity, "*Why you work in factory when you speak good English?*" I just smiled and replied, "I need any job at present." Soon, management "promoted" me to the looms, as they told me I was a good, and reliable worker. I read a book on most days, while the spools filled up, as it was mind-numbing to watch the clattering, rotating spools all day long.

Pia, a large, Indian woman, made me laugh when she spoke to me about her previous jobs. She told me that once, she was "Plucking puroot" (fruit), in South Australia. Pia made droll comments about some of the "Fast females" who worked there and flirted with the foreman. It was an interesting time in my life, as I met so many different people in that factory.

Mr Title was a haughty, middle-aged gentleman, who seldom made an appearance or spoke to the workers. Whenever he did approach, we watched with foreboding, as we were certain it was bad news for the workers. I worked there till late April, until I received a most welcome letter from the Department of Social Security, offering me a clerical position in the city. I turned it down though, as the travelling was too much. They wrote back, saying I had to wait until something closer to home was available.

Within a few weeks though, I was notified about a vacancy at Knox City. I was elated! Finally, I could work in a better environment than this. When I told the manager about it, he was quite pleased for me, and wished me well.

But Van looked at me with envious, glinting eyes and sneered deprecatingly, "May be you only at *counter* in Social Security eh?" I replied easily, "*That* would be better than this job!"

Chapter 14

In February that year, we visited Longlo Kennels in Croydon, and as I always wanted a Dachshund, we bought a puppy. But we were not allowed to take it home until it was three months old. He reminded me of my old pets, Gina and Ricky, and I called him Dash. We kept him in the laundry when we went out, because just two weeks after we brought Dash home, I started work at Social Security.

Connie went at lunch time to check up on him or give him a bone. Our neighbours, Anita and Peter, told me that Dash barked non-stop all day long, until we came home. It was good that they liked animals though, and did not complain about his barking.

We soon discovered that Dash was a nervous, aggressive, and very temperamental dog, and was only loyal to me. I could scold him or give him a disciplinary smack, and he bore it meekly. But if anyone else so much as raised their voices to him, he bared his teeth and growled menacingly.

Unfortunately, he was a stubborn little dog, although he was a pedigreed, fine-looking specimen, and cost two hundred dollars. I was sorry I got him now, and not when I was home all those years. Then I would have spent more time training him, and he would not have been lonely all day.

When we brought Dash home, he was quite friendly with Snuffles, the bunny, and waddled to the hutch and pilfered celery and carrots. I was amused when Dash gobbled up just about anything; fruits or vegetables, they were all the same to him, as long as it was edible.

But as he grew older, I feared for Snuffles, because Dash was unpredictable. I reluctantly decided to give the rabbit to one of the neighbours, as their children loved it, and promised to take care of it. Stacy and Christian were sad too, but they visited it daily, and gave me a report on how Snuffles was doing. A few months later though, I was very upset to hear that he died of starvation and neglect.

We walked Dash every evening, but only I could take him, as he would not let anyone else hold the lead. When Connie tried to drag him along once, he would not budge, but just sat on the pavement, stubborn as a mule, while Connie dragged and tugged. Then in utter frustration and anger, Connie strung him up on his lead, and kept him dangling a few minutes at the end of the lead.

I told him not to be so cruel, but he did not listen. Two men were parked in a near-by van, and one shouted out, "*That* isn't a nice thing to do! I'll *report* you to the RSPCA for animal cruelty!" Connie was abashed, but stuck his finger at the man and said, "Get *stuffed*! M*ind* your own business!" I walked off with Dash quickly. And the poor dog wagged his tail, as he followed me obediently, because he took orders only from me.

On 15 May 1986, when I turned up at Knox Social Security, the manager, John Carpenter, interviewed me, and said, "Look, this is going to be a very boring job for you because you will initially do only file away and mail duties. You are over-qualified for this job!" (he was referring to my diplomas in journalism and commercial art). But I replied, "I'm very keen to have a go, as I will learn to adapt."

John, whom everyone called "Carps" was in his late forties; of average height, with a craggy face, deeply furrowed brow, and cheeks. He seemed pleasant enough, but avoided eye contact while talking to me, and kept looking out the door. I was feeling a little nervous, but just then, he spotted a young girl walking past, and called out, "Hey Noisy, get me a cup of coffee will ya?" Noisy was a pretty young girl called Katrina, who was in her mid-twenties. John liked her very much, and got her to make his coffee daily (so I gathered). After his coffee, he relaxed slightly, and started asking me relevant questions.

When he finished, he repeated, "You'll find this work very mundane, as I can see you are over-qualified for this job." And once again, I replied fervently, "I'd like to try anyway." And he said, "You will be on probation for six months, and if you 'fit' in, you will be made permanent." I thanked him, and he called out to Katrina again, "Noisy, take Nalini around and introduce her to the rest of the people."

Katrina was a pleasant, attractive young girl, and we soon made friends. She was Officer-In-Charge of the registry division, which included afore-mentioned duties that "Carps" had outlined. To my great relief and joy, I commenced work at Social Security Knox, on 26 May 1986. So, began my career in the Department of Social Security. The office was situated in the Knox Tower building, in Wantirna. And I glimpsed great views of the Dandenong ranges and surrounding areas, from the top floor.

It took a while initially to get accustomed to the routine, but the young girls and boys were friendly, and keen to help me along. I was willing to learn, so I had no problem getting along with any of the staff members. About ten of us sat around a large table every morning, sorting out correspondence, filing away, and helping the clerks. Some of them acted like demi-gods in the public sector hierarchy.

Those clerks looked down on us "clerical assistants" as if we were second-rate citizens. It was an eye-opener to realize how biased, and full of themselves some people were in this department.

The day began with us "clerical assistants" standing at the mail desk, and sorting, stamping, and distributing correspondence. Then we sorted all the "corre" alphabetically, and filed them away, if there was no further action required. The files were stored in pigeon holes, where the clerks put them once they were finished with them. This was a time of paper records, when every single piece of paper went on a client's file. The data entry staff keyed in relevant data taken from paper records, updated addresses, change of bank details etc.

Several nice people worked there at the same clerical assistant level. Katrina, whom we called Tina, was engaged to be married soon, and was full of wedding plans during her free time. Jody, a pregnant young mother with a toddler, was a cheerful person, Margaret, a loud-mouthed, boisterous Italian girl in her late twenties, who still lived with her parents, was good friends with Tina; Vivian, a very pretty girl of Italian and Australian parentage, was quiet-spoken, but friendly.

Some of those people remained life-long friends. One was Mary Hancock, a tall, slender, attractive lady, with light-brown eyes, and a great sense of humour. Her two girls also attended St Jude's Scoresby, and we had met a few times when we picked up our children after school. She was good friends with Tina as well.

Liz, who had an enormous weight problem, was married to Gerry, an American. She too was quite pleasant and friendly, and we remained friends. Several others, like Margaret, Linda, Sheila, (another Ceylonese), Kate, and Vivian visited me sometimes. But some of them have lost touch over the years. I was happy to have so many friends now, after years of isolation.

Nan, an Asian girl, did not get along with most people, as she was outspoken, and did not hesitate to let them know how she felt, if she did not like the way she was treated. She was a union member, and resorted to their advice whenever she had the smallest issue with management. Everyone referred to her as, "Union Nan" behind her back.

When she saw that I got along well with most of the staff, she warned me, "Don't be on good terms with Tina, as she's John's *favourite!*" Liz was Nan's best friend, and they spent lunch breaks together, without socialising with the others.

Sheila treated me better than some other clerks did. We became good friends, and visited each other for meals. The most arrogant clerks were Kate, an Australian, and Margaret, a Scottish woman. They did not even give me or the other assistants the time of day.

The files were stored in a large area with narrow aisles in between, so that at any given time, only two girls could file away, as we sometimes used a step ladder to reach the topmost shelves. I soon became accustomed to see "Carps" sneaking behind us, grab one of the girls and smooch them. As I was new, he did not try this on me yet, but none of the girls were safe from his groping arms and sloppy kisses. He crept up behind the girls when they were at their desks, then started rubbing and massaging their shoulders and necks.

One morning, I walked into the lunch room around 8am. And there he was, helping himself to a large tumbler of red wine from a cask that sat on top of the fridge. I was surprised, to say the least. He did not see me, as he gulped down the wine. I noticed he was a nervous wreck, with shaky hands and trembling lips, until he had his daily "fix" in the mornings. He never looked one straight in the eye, and had a shifty, sly aspect. I did not like him at all, and I soon heard rumours that he was a tippler, and drank heavily right through the day.

He put his arms around me only a couple of times, before he got the message that I was a very reserved person, who did not like his approach. He left me alone, but sometimes paid effusive compliments, and ogled every female in the place. He was a strange, sleazy man, and I found his behaviour offensive. But I had to be polite and professional, for the sake of workplace harmony, without letting him cross boundaries or take liberties with me.

"Carps" had his favourites, and all the young girls were invited to his office for a daily "chat." Tina was on top of the list, and he paid her higher-duties as Officer-In-Charge of registry division. I was not included in those daily get-togethers, for which I was glad. Because I soon learnt that he used his favourites to glean information about office politics. And that was how he ran the office, because he did not know how to mingle professionally, and get to know his staff.

I liked Tina though, and we soon became good friends. Our team got on well with each other, and I invited them for afternoon tea on some weekends. We had loads of fun and laughter then. Connie stopped gardening to come inside and ask me, "*What's* going on? *What's* the big joke?" I could not explain about the funny incidents at work, so I replied, "We're just talking about the clients we come across, that's all."

I did not realize at the start, that just like a "new kid on the block" I was on probation with all the staff. Some of them picked on my work, and reported everything to "Carps." A tinge of racism rippled among some of the clerks and assistants. As they were unaware I was a qualified journalist, and commercial artist, with a good command of the English language, they tried to pick on my work.

When he put them in the picture, a distinct change in attitude was apparent, and they gradually accepted me. Three months later, I was "reviewed" and he told me, "I'm satisfied with your progress so far, and in another three months, you will be made permanent, *if* you continue working in the same manner."

Before long, I quickly moved up in the hierarchy of the department. Although I joined at the lowest level, clerical assistant, grade one, I was soon promoted to grade three, and undertook duties as a "batching officer" which included checking and registering all the data entry the typists submitted.

Each morning, if there were any errors, data was re-entered on the system. It was a long, tedious process in those days, before computers updated data online immediately. I was quick and efficient in my duties, so I earned everybody's respect, as I did my job well, and met daily deadlines. And when the initial probation period of six months ended, much to my relief, I was made permanent.

My wages commenced at $400 gross a fortnight. Ammie and Thathie were very proud and pleased that I now had a secure job in the Commonwealth Government of Australia. Financially, we were comfortable now, but suddenly, disaster struck and destroyed our security. One morning, in mid-October 1986, Connie called me at work to say he was retrenched. No previous warning, nothing. His department closed down in the wake of the merge between Safeway and Woolworths.

I was deeply shocked. Connie's manager, Norm, notified him the department was closing down, and he was out of a job. Just like that. Not even a few weeks notice, nothing. When Connie told me this shattering news, my knees buckled under with disbelief. How ironic that I now had a secure job, and Connie was retrenched. I told him not to worry, that he would find another job easily, with his long years of experience now.

When I went home that evening, it was just dreadful to think that after fifteen years of loyal service, the company treated Connie with such scant consideration. His payout was only about thirty thousand dollars or so. We decided to pay off all outstanding debts, so we would have only the mortgage to worry about. After all the debts were discharged, he had a small amount left over, which he deposited into a savings account, just in case we needed extra to pay bills.

Although it was a crushing experience, we dealt with this blow as well as we could, and Connie immediately looked around for another job. Our security was gone; and we had a mortgage to worry about, school fees, and living expenses. He used American Express frequently, and bought goods on credit. Sometimes, when we dined out, he paid with his card; now he knew he had to stop spending on his credit card until he found another job.

Lance, his immediate boss, gave him an excellent reference, and Norm too was confident that Connie would find another drafting job soon. Connie pleaded with Norm to let him work in another department at Safeway, so he could continue his service, and superannuation contributions. But Norm did not care to help him, and told him that he wanted all his "boys" to find jobs elsewhere.

I spoke to "Carps" about Connie, and he said, "Mary's husband, Peter, works for the Commonwealth Employment Services, why don't you ask your husband to see him?" So, he did try that avenue, and Peter said he would look out for a suitable position, but nothing came out of it. Over the next two or three weeks, he tried several places unsuccessfully.

Shirani and Ranjith were separated then, due to some family problems, and Shirani was going through a very tough time, paying the children's private school fees, and a mortgage as well. When Ranjith found out Connie was retrenched, he phoned one night, and taunted him, "That's it, no more work for you at Safeway! No company car now!" He did not take any notice of Ranjith and hung up. We did not understand Ranjith's behaviour, but put it down to the unhappy state of affairs then.

Lance told Connie that Coles Supermarket in the city, had a vacancy for a draftsman, and he would speak to the manager on his behalf. Before long, he was employed at Coles, and he was out of work less than a month. He had to give up the company car, and once again we managed with one car.

Before I drove to work, I dropped the children at St Joseph's College, in Ferntree Gully, and then Connie at Ferntree Gully station, from where he boarded a train to the city He caught a bus from the station in the evening, as it stopped near Kelletts road, and it was a five-minute walk home.

One of the good outcomes was, that we paid off every single debt to the finance companies, but he held onto the American Express card. The financial counsellor, Carol, was overjoyed when she heard that we paid off all our debts. She asked if she could use our case as an example, as budgeting, and hard work, were crucial when it came to debt-management. We agreed, as we were quite elated we were debt-free at last.

Safeway did not give him a termination package or compensation, so Connie was very bitter about the way he was treated after fifteen years of loyal service to the company. He received only his holiday, and long service leave payments.

After settling our debts, we had about ten thousand dollars left, so we spent it on home-improvements.

We carpeted the house with a luxurious, fawn-coloured carpet, and bought some new furniture too. The house looked very nice and cosy now, and we also installed ducted-heating throughout. Connie painted the whole house in warm beige, and the place looked almost new. I sewed new curtains in a dark shade of peach, to match the cushions of the pine lounge suite. Connie stained the raw pine-wood in a deep mahogany.

Christian and Stacy were very helpful around the house and garden, and very often, Christian helped me to clean and vacuum the house. They weeded the garden too, and tried their best to help us. In return, we gave them extra pocket money some times. They surprised us once, by cooking a delicious meal, and even made a few cutlets! They were good at cooking basic dishes, but later on, Christian became an excellent cook.

He complained a few times that Stacy pulled the sheets, and doona cover from his bed. And I upbraided Stacy, and told him to stop doing that, but he just grinned and said, "I didn't do it!" Christian's bed continued to be rumpled, although he made up his bed every morning, and was always very neat and particular about his room.

I thought Stacy was being naughty, until one evening, I happened to pass by and saw Dash jumping on Christian's bed, and pulling all the sheets and covers onto the floor. I called Christian and showed him who the culprit was, and we apologized to Stacy for suspecting him. He just laughed at the amusing sight of Dash going berserk on the bed.

Just before Christmas 1986, Rosie called me one morning, and said, "Dolly, I'm at Melbourne airport, and I want to surprise Shirani and Connie, so can you please come and pick me up now?" I hesitated, "I've never driven to the airport on my own Rosie, I'm a bit nervous." She laughed as usual and said, "Come on Dolly, you can do it!" So I agreed. I had some misgivings, but looked at the Melways road map, and took a chance. It was over one hour's drive from Rowville, through very busy roads via the city.

I do not know how I managed, because the memory of that drive is hazy, but I somehow arrived at the airport safely, and saw Rosie standing outside. We hugged and kissed happily, and she said, "*Now* we're going to Connie's office and we'll *surprise* him!" This was yet another challenge, to drive through the heart of the city and find a parking space.

I parked as close to Coles as possible, and we walked into the old building. Then I asked someone to let Connie know that his wife was here to see him. When he came out of the lift, his face was a study when he saw Rosie with me. We laughed and chatted, while Rosie kept joking with Connie, because she was pleased to see how surprised he was. When we arrived home, she asked me to call Shirani and invite her for dinner that evening.

When Shirani knocked on the door around five o'clock and Rosie opened it, she could not believe her eyes! So, it was a great Christmas that year, as we enjoyed Rosie's company very much. She stayed with Shirani because she was on her own now. And on some days, Rosie and Shirani cooked dinner and brought it over in the evening, so we all enjoyed a delicious meal together.

Once, Rosie and Shirani visited me at Knox city, and took me out for lunch to Myers cafeteria at the topmost level. Then all too soon her holiday was over, and she left in late January.

Stacy was manifesting signs of teenage rebellion, and had problems at St Joseph's College. We met Fr Julian Fox, the principal, who told us it was quite normal for boys to go through difficult stages with their parents. We suggested a boarding school, but Father said he did not think much of boarding schools, and to be patient with Stacy.

Although he was skinny as a bean pole, Stacy was convinced that he was overweight. He refused to eat any "fatty foods" including meats, eggs, and all proteins, and his diet consisted of only fruits and vegetables. He had constant rows with Christian, and refused to confide in Connie or me about what ailed him. He locked himself in the bathroom, and cried out in anger and frustration. When I asked him what was wrong, he bawled out, "My knees are too *fat*!"

The boys bullied him in school, and he told me they put him inside a garbage bin one day, which wounded his dignity greatly. At that time, teachers and parents were hardly aware of the lasting psychological damage bullying can do to vulnerable young children. It was the accepted "norm" that all boys went through bullying. And you were not supposed to "dob in" bullies, as they would only make life more intolerable for the victim. We were blind to the writing on the wall, and Stacy continued to be difficult, sullen and withdrawn.

Thank goodness there is now so much awareness of the great harm that bullying can do. All schools are vigilant about such behaviour in schools, as so many vulnerable children have been driven to suicide, because of this insidious behaviour in schools.

He did not want me to come near him at all, or even kiss him goodnight, shouting out, "*Don't touch* me!" His behaviour puzzled me, but I failed to find out what the underlying problem was, thinking that it was adolescent blues and rebellion. I regret to this day that we did not consult a counsellor, and seek help.

One day, in desperation, I took him to our family doctor, and asked Stacy to talk about his problems, if he could not confide in his parents. I told the doctor that Stacy was hostile and angry, and did not even let me kiss him goodnight. The doctor said, "A boy's best friend is his mother, Stacy, why are you so angry with her?" Stacy did not respond, as he just could not open up about his problems.

He was a brilliant student, and did well at school all these past years, and still achieved high grades, but it was his behaviour that worried us. I hoped he would outgrow this difficult phase soon.

I was going through a very stressful period at home with Connie and Stacy. Christian was very quiet and patient, enduring Stacy's verbal abuse, and bullying. Stacy and Connie never saw eye to eye in anything, and it was traumatic for the whole family, because of constant arguments, bickering, and physical punishment. Connie firmly believed in the saying, "spare the rod and spoil the child." I was caught up in the middle of all these altercations, because I did not want him to be so strict with Stacy, knowing that he had troubles at school too.

Connie sometimes grabbed him by his pyjama top, tore off the buttons in anger, or dragged him by the scruff of his neck in front of me, and shouted out, "Stacy called me a *bastard* and said he will *kill* me!" I had to calm them both, and save Stacy from a severe beating. I told Connie later that if he continued to use physical violence on Stacy, he would naturally retaliate in anger and frustration, and to stop treating him so harshly. But he was blind to reason.

He constantly nagged him about his clothes, his untidy room, and everything else that Stacy did. If I tried to reason with Connie, it was to no avail, because he said children must be "disciplined" and his idea of discipline was physical punishment.

Christian kept out of trouble, and Connie rarely smacked him. I never resorted to physical punishment, as I did not believe in hitting a child. No matter how much Connie punished Stacy, he was not afraid of standing up to him, and expressing his opinion, which drove Connie mad. He wanted the children and me to agree with everything he said and did. He spat in Stacy's face many times, and I suffered Stacy's humiliation and anger, when I heard him bawling in the bathroom as he washed and showered.

It was the most degrading thing Connie could do, as I knew how it felt to be spat on. When I asked him, "*Why* did you spit on Stacy?" He replied, "I can't help it, that's what I do when I get angry!" I replied, "Why can't you be rational, and reason with him, without getting physically violent?" And he retorted, "So, now, you want a *rational* man?" I looked at him aghast, as I could not understand what he meant; did he accept the fact that he was irrational?

Stacy was a very intelligent child, who did well in school, as I mentioned. And so was Christian, who achieved high grades, completed his projects efficiently, and was generally placid in his outlook and temperament. He tolerated Stacy's troublesome behaviour with equanimity, but sometimes, I saw him crying silently in his room at some cutting remark Stacy made.

Fr Fox visited us a couple of times, as he knew we were concerned about Stacy, and that we even considered sending him to a boarding school. But he dissuaded us, as he believed Stacy was better off at home, than in a boarding school, where bullying was worse.

Stacy's behaviour perplexed me, and I wondered how I could help him overcome his problems at school. But he locked himself in his room every evening, and did not confide in us at all. He came out only in time to watch his favourite program "Doctor Who."

If Connie was smoking in the kitchen, Stacy wrapped his scarf around his nose and mouth, and tried not to inhale smoke. This was another bone of contention between them, as Connie did not stop smoking inside the house. And Stacy kept saying how bad it was to smoke, and he did not want to be a passive-smoker.

Connie did not stop nagging Stacy, and shouted at him over some minor misbehaviour, so it was impossible for him to follow his favourite program. This frustrated Stacy so much, that he dashed the remote control and stomped off to his room. Connie chased after him, and they came to blows. Christian and I endured this constant state of affairs and disharmony in the house as well as we could.

In the meantime, I did not stop writing, in spite of all the domestic turbulence, and full time work etc. And as always, writing was an emotional outlet. I entered several literary competitions that local newspapers and magazines held. One of my first awards, was for a short story called "Charlie wins the lottery." The editor of the newspapers contacted me, and even sent a reporter to Knox office to interview, and take my photograph.

The newspaper published my winning story, and I was elated. The prize was a fifty dollar book voucher, but the important thing was to have won first prize. The next achievement was, when I won first prize again in a competition that another newspaper, "The Heart of Waverley" held. And they published "The Artist's story" featuring my photograph too.

I also compiled all my short stories and poems I wrote from around 1968 till the present, and hoped to publish an anthology soon. I told Thathie about it, and he tried to find a publisher in Ceylon. Lake House was the biggest publisher then, and he negotiated terms with them, so I kept my fingers crossed.

I made several friends at work now, and when they visited on some weekends, we had a great deal of fun and laughter. Most of them were young girls, and once, when we were just chatting away, Connie burst into the room, and started moving chairs around. He stopped near Maria, a pretty young girl, and grinned, "I really didn't *have* to move the chairs, I only wanted to touch your legs!" Maria wore shorts that day, and he thought he was being funny. But she blushed self-consciously, and I did not know what to say either. I ignored Connie, and we continued talking, though I never knew what made him say such things. When I told him he embarrassed Maria, he just laughed it off.

A week before she married, Tina held a "Hen's Night" at Barbarino's restaurant in the city, and Connie dropped me there in the evening. It was the first time I went out on my own to socialise with my friends. But before he left, he admonished me, "Don't have any drinks, in case they are mixed and you will end up drunk." My friends heard him and teased me all evening, "Con is not here, so have a drink Nalini! Go on, you won't get drunk!" But I was happy with a glass of lemonade, as I did not drink alcohol anyway.

Tina married at the end of September 1987, and invited most of her friends at work to her grand wedding. The church ceremony was in the afternoon, and the reception was at night. Connie and I spent a couple of hours in a restaurant near Albert Park Lake, until the reception started. It was a lavish wedding, and Tina was a lovely bride. Mary Hancock was matron of honour, and Margaret, one of the bridesmaids. She knew Leo, the bridegroom, for a couple of years now, and was happy that they were finally married. Tina invited "Carps" too.

They travelled to Phuket for their honeymoon, and she returned to work a few weeks later. She transferred to an office close to Hadfield, where they lived. We visited each other a couple of times, together with Mary and Peter. Leo and Tina had four boys over the years, and we kept in touch for a long time, until her Christmas cards stopped. But Tina suffered many health issues over the years. And a few decades later, she was diagnosed with Motor Neuron Disease, and she deteriorated rapidly.

I just could not believe it could have happened to someone as beautiful and vibrant as Tina.

I received a few text messages from her before she died, and Mary, who remained good friends with her to the end, attended her funeral. She told me how poignant it was to watch that young family, and Leo, grappling to understand the magnitude of their loss.

One Saturday evening, in October 1987, I just finished re-potting some plants, and came inside for a snack. But when I sat down to nibble a piece of cheese, my heart suddenly started to race incredibly fast, and did not slow down for a couple of hours. I felt strange, and light-headed, but did my chores slowly, had a shower, then went to bed, thinking it would pass.

By midnight, I started coughing and choking, and felt sick in the pit of my stomach, as I was nauseous. My heart beat was still very rapid, and when I told Connie I was feeling very sick, he called an ambulance. He was shocked to see me looking so ill. I cried helplessly, because of the severe pain in my chest, and I could hardly breathe. Christian and Stacy woke up in fear, and watched paramedics jabbing needles into my arm. Then they rushed me to Dandenong Hospital, as my blood pressure was very low, and my pulse rate was over 250 beats per minute.

Geraldine and Jeff, peeped over the fence when they heard the ambulance siren. They were upset when Connie told them, as they thought I had suffered a severe heart attack. Christian wanted to accompany Connie to hospital. And I can still picture him in his blue dressing gown, frightened, and with tearful eyes staring wide. Stacy was upset and crying too, but Connie told him to stay home and try to sleep. Poor children, they were so distressed. Connie told me that Christian sat alone in the car until early morning, while he was with me in emergency.

Christian was very close to me, and I knew he felt this trauma deeply, and my heart ached for him. Stacy was very concerned too, in spite of his difficult behaviour. And I knew that he loved me just as much as I loved him.

I was in severe pain, as I could not breathe properly. They kept asking me so many questions, injected morphine, and then took x-rays. My lungs were full of fluid, so they inserted a catheter and drained out the fluid.

Next morning, they told me that I had pulmonary oedema (water in the lungs), due to my rapid heart beat. I was in hospital for a week until they found out the cause for this sudden attack. The first thing Connie said when he saw me awake next morning was, "You have *proved* to the world what a bastard I am! They will all say you had a heart attack because of me!" I did not respond, as I was too ill to argue.

It was not a heart attack, but tachycardia, and from then onwards, I consulted a few heart specialists to find out what caused it. I suffered severe chest pains, and shortness of breath since that first attack, and was off work for a month. I had visitors daily, and Margaret, from work, visited me in hospital with an enormous bouquet of flowers from all my friends.

When I returned to work, personnel contacted me, and said that I was taken off "batching" duties, as there was some pressure in that job. I was advised to do less stressful work. So, I was allocated to indexing, and file away duties only. My progress in the department came to a standstill from then on, until the heart specialist could diagnose my condition.

Aunty Molly had immigrated to Melbourne, somewhere in 1986, as her son, Ian, sponsored her. Ian was in his mid-forties, and still a bachelor, so Aunty Molly lived with him in a rented unit. Before she arrived, Ian visited often, and said he was seeing an Australian girl. But Aunty Molly soon put a stop to that. She wanted him to marry one of his distant cousins in Sri Lanka, and hoped to bring her over soon.

Connie always invited his mother, and Aunty Molly, to join us wherever we travelled, so that they spent a great deal of time with us. They visited on some weekends too, and spent a few days with us, and we took them out for meals or drives. The two old ladies were very amusing, and most of the time they cracked ribald jokes between themselves.

I thought it was a sign of sexual repression, because they always talked about sex. They told me everything about their families, and I heard all the gossip from these two, as they became very garrulous, and uninhibited after a few glasses of whisky. I was very fond of them, and treated them just like my own. They appreciated all I did, and were very affectionate too.

Chapter 15

We travelled to Ceylon that Christmas, after eight years. Although Thathie visited in 1985, I had not seen Ammie and Nilanthi all this time, and was anxious to see them again. Stacy was not keen to join us, but wanted a computer instead, so we bought him one for about $800. He was very clever with computers, and was happy for a while, until he wanted a faster, and better one. Christian wanted to join us, but we decided it was best for them to stay with Shirani for that one month. We thought they would be very bored in Ceylon, now that they were teenagers, and had their own friends and other interests.

In hindsight, it was a mistake to leave them behind, as I missed them very much. I could not be totally happy and relaxed. Christian was very upset, and sad to say goodbye. I consoled him, and said it was only a month, and time would fly quickly.

It was awful to leave the children behind, as it was the first time I was parted from them. But knowing how often Connie and Stacy clashed, I thought it was good to have a break. Unfortunately, Christian had to stay back too. He was resigned in the end, and accepted our decision with characteristic forbearance. He spent most of his time carving out a small branch, and painted a fantastic tree on it, as a gift for me. I was so impressed and moved, and I still have it on my desk.

When we arrived in Colombo, I thought Rosie would join us, but she did not turn up. Ammie and Thathie were very concerned when they learnt I was so unwell, and they too hoped I would recover completely. I took medication now to keep my heart beat normal, until the specialists found out the reason for tachycardia.

I finished compiling the collection of short stories and poems entitled, "Return To Enchantment." And Thathie found a publishing house in Ceylon, who agreed to publish it. But it was subsidised publishing, and cost a thousand dollars for one thousand copies. I sent Thathie the money in instalments, as I wanted him to check each stage of the publishing, before I paid the full amount. He acted on my behalf, and I was confident he would handle it satisfactorily.

I enjoyed a great holiday with the family, but an awful experience marred our stay. A week before our return to Melbourne, Thathie, Connie, and I, boarded a private coach to Slave Island, to check some blinds for their windows, as Ammie told me it was very hot without blinds. Then we took a "three-wheeler" (mini-taxi) to our next destination.

On our return journey, Thathie wanted us to save on taxi fare, and urged us to board a very crowded bus, with standing room only. Connie carried our passports, tickets, camera, cash etc in his shoulder bag. And as he stood among the throng, someone from behind kicked him on the calf of his leg. He bent over to rub it, and thought nothing of it, until we got off the bus and sat in a taxi to take us to another shop.

Connie's face turned sickly pale, like barley water, when he saw the long slit at the bottom of his shoulder bag! I had some money and travellers cheques, so we paid the taxi fare. Shattered and sick at heart, we returned home, as we lost our tickets, passports, Connie's credit cards, driver's licence, and about five hundred dollars in cash in his wallet.

Heron informed his brother, Maurice, who was inspector of police in that region. And next day, we met Maurice in his office. He instructed his driver to take us around anywhere we wanted to; firstly, to the Australian Embassy, and then the airlines office. Our holiday was absolutely spoilt because of the theft, and Connie was furious at every Sri Lankan. He scolded them non-stop, and called them all a pack of thieves.

He did not stop complaining and moaning about everything. Because since his retrenchment, he was very embittered about the way Safeway treated him, and constantly harped about the unfairness of it all. Although he worked at Coles now, he never got over his retrenchment.

He kept saying, "I worked hard for fifteen years, only to get the boot without any consideration!" My family and I listened to him sympathetically, and tried to appease him. But the dark cloud that descended on him, engulfed him constantly, and our last week was completely spoilt.

We removed photographs for new passports, and paid extra to get airline tickets reissued, and we went through an absolute nightmare for one week. When we went to endorse our new passports at the Australian Embassy, the official surprised us, "You are very *lucky* Mr and Mrs de Sielvie! Here are your original passports, and driver's licence! A parcel was thrown over into the compound last evening, containing your passports, driver's licence, and tickets." The rest of our documents, including credit cards, cash, and camera were not returned.

The film roll in the camera was very special, as we held a party there to celebrate Tamara's twenty-first birthday (which was in April that year). And as most of the family were present, we thought it was a good idea. We lost those photographic memories, which could not be replaced.

That was the most harrowing holiday experience, and Connie just could not get over the sickening incident. He was very worried about the credit cards, even though he cancelled them.

It came as another shock when he received a statement from American Express, charging him $500 for purchases made in India! We sent photocopies of our passports, to prove we never travelled to India then. They sorted it out in the end, and we did not have to pay back that money.

As soon as we arrived in Rowville, we picked up Stacy and Christian, and were pleasantly surprised to see Rosie. She wanted to spend New Year with us.

I was overjoyed to see my two boys again, as I missed them very much. They too were very happy to see us and return home, especially Stacy, as he wanted to play games on his new computer. Connie did not allow him to take the computer to Shirani's, which was a pity, as he would have been happy then.

Although Shirani did her best, the children were very homesick, and felt restricted. It was a mistake to leave them, as they were very sad to be away from us, and their familiar surroundings, especially Christian. We boarded Dash at Longlo Kennels, in Croydon, and we picked him up later that day. He was boisterous as ever, and ran around chasing Rosie and the children.

Nelune visited briefly in early January 1988. And one evening, as we all sat around laughing, and talking, I suffered another tachycardia attack, which ended in a quick trip to the emergency unit at Dandenong Hospital. Rosie panicked, and was very worried when she saw me turn very pale. Connie drove me to emergency, because the doctors told me not to wait too long if I had an attack. Rosie, Nelune, and Connie stayed with me until the doctors brought down my heartbeat to normal again, and we came home late that night.

Rosie advised me earnestly, "You *must* see a good heart specialist Dolly, because this is not good for your heart, to go through frequent attacks with such a rapid heart beat as high as 250 to 300 beats per minute!" I promised I would follow her advice and see another specialist soon.

Rosie mentioned she was suffering from severe headaches then. And she was diagnosed with an inoperable, but benign brain tumour, for which she needed to undergo radiation soon. I did not believe it was serious, as Rosie was still the same, jolly person. But sometimes, she suddenly became quiet, and closed her eyes in pain whenever the blinding headaches hit her.

It was difficult to believe anything was seriously wrong with her though, as she hardly ever complained. And it did not prevent Rosie from organising a memorable dinner at the "Theatre Restaurant-Draculas" one night, where we had a great deal of fun and laughter with Shirani and Rosie.

In February 1988, one of Connie's previous colleagues, Peter Jones, offered him a position at Composite Buyers, in Ferntree Gully, at a higher salary, and company car. Peter persuaded Connie to accept this job, as he was in urgent need of a good draftsman. He was just settling down at Coles, and although he did not have a company car, or the same generous wages as before, he knew he would progress there in time. But he was tempted to take up Peter's offer.

Coles moved their office from the city to Toorak now, and Connie dropped me at Knox, and the children at St Joseph's, then drove to work. He considered the current situation, and decided to accept the job. It was closer to home, the wages were attractive, and came with a company car.

When he called Peter, he came home and signed up the deal. Connie asked him, "Peter, can you *assure* me that I will have at least five years with you, as the children have to be educated, and we have a mortgage to pay off." Peter replied confidently,

"Sure, Conrad, there's plenty of work to keep us going for a long time. Don't worry." So, based on this verbal assurance, Connie left Coles, after little more than a year.

After the last tachycardia attack, I applied for part-time hours, which personnel approved, and I returned to work soon. Connie inquired everywhere, regarding the best heart specialist in Melbourne, as the previous specialist I consulted, was very disappointing, to say the least.

Dr Rustomjee, referred me to one of his colleagues, Dr Obeyseykera, who was eminent in Ceylon. But, he was semi-retired now, as he was in his early seventies. When I consulted him, he went through all the reports, and did some tests. He told me that according to the data, I had suffered heart-failure. But his diagnosis was inconclusive, and I did not have much confidence in him.

One of Connie's previous colleagues at Safeway, told him about a very good heart specialist, who had treated him at Monash Medical Centre, and advised me to consult Dr Harper. When I requested a referral from Dr Obeysekera, he was quite offensive, and wrote a nasty letter about us to Dr Rustomjee, as he felt that his professional standing was threatened. I did not care about his attitude anyway, and made an appointment to see Dr Harper. After the initial consultation, Dr Harper advised me to undergo a procedure called a "catheterisation." A tube was to be inserted into the arteries to find out the cause of my complaint.

In early 1988, I was admitted to Monash Hospital for this procedure. It was very painful, and uncomfortable. They did not give a local anaesthetic when they inserted a catheter through my upper chest, and kept injecting fluids for about three hours, inducing tachycardia, and monitoring my heart beats. I was desperate to go to the toilet, but the nurse said I could not move, until the tests were completed. I do not know how I managed to hold on, without emptying my bladder right then and there. It was a very risky procedure then, although I was unaware of the dangers. I signed a consent form, stating that the doctors and hospital would not be held responsible for any mishap. A few years later, I read about a woman who died during this procedure.

While I was recovering in hospital overnight, Dr Harper breezed in, "We have found out the *cause* of your problem! It's a secondary electrical impulse, which sends wrong messages to your heart, and no matter what we did, you had tachycardia attacks! My advice to you is to have an operation soon to fix the problem, but we can't guarantee a *hundred* percent success rate!"

He told me it was open heart surgery, and I just flinched at the thought. I decided I would not undergo that operation; particularly, as there was no guarantee. He prescribed further medication to regulate my heart beat, and I stayed in hospital for three days, before I was discharged.

From then on, whenever I suffered an attack, Connie rushed to see his doctor, or went to emergency for a check up the very next day. And he kept rubbing his chest, and complained of severe chest pains. He may have suffered anxiety and stress too whenever I was in hospital, but Aunty and his sisters asked me why he went to doctor's every time I was unwell.

Nelune put it very amusingly, when she heard about his visits to emergency or the doctor. "I believe Connie has got an *acute* case of good health!" It was also his way of showing everyone how much my attacks affected him, and that he was not to blame for my illness. Aunty always asked me, "*Is* Connie *worrying* you Dolly? Is that the reason you get these attacks?" And although I told her several times that it was a medical condition, she did not really believe me, as she knew how stressful my life was with Connie.

Our neighbours, Geraldine, and her sister, Judy, were very kind and concerned too, and visited me often.

When Rosie visited earlier that year, Geraldine walked into the backyard, looking very distressed. She told us that her only brother, Brian, was diagnosed with bowel cancer. She was very distressed, and crying bitterly. But she came around to tell me she was going to Adelaide to be with him and his family. Brian was my age, and his wife had just given birth to their third child, a girl, only a few days ago.

We met Geraldine's parents, Birdie and George, her sister, Judy, and Brian, some time back. Now, every time they visited Geraldine, they came over to see us too. While she was crying now, and telling us about Brian, Dash came running up. Although I warned her, "*Don't* come any closer Geraldine! Watch the dog!" She was too distraught to heed my warning, and next moment, Dash nipped her ankle. She screamed in pain and surprise.

I was very upset, as it was the last thing she needed at a time like this. I took her inside the house, and bathed her ankle. It was a superficial wound, and the skin had hardly broken, but she was in pain. Rosie joked, "You can *sue* Dolly for this injury!" Geraldine laughed and said, "I'm only worried about my brother, and he's not going to die! I'm going to see him, and just came over to tell you I'll be going tomorrow." I nodded, "Hope Brian recovers soon, and I wish him all the best."

I apologized profusely, but knew it was no use. She was very distressed, and after that incident, she hated Dash with a vengeance. His constant barking too annoyed them, and now it was an added insult to injury. Dash made enemies of almost all the neighbours, especially the children, whom he barked at and nipped indiscriminately.

Brian was on naturopathic medications only, as he refused any invasive treatment, and he died a few days later after Geraldine arrived. He was thirty-six years old; his eldest daughter was twelve, and younger son about ten. The family was devastated, and I was greatly moved, as I was close to Geraldine and her family. We remained good friends with them through the years, especially with her parents.

Geraldine came over with Adam, her toddler, one afternoon, and while I was chatting to her, Adam crept up to the coffee table, and pulled the cup of tea onto the floor. The tea was boiling hot, as I had just poured it, and not added milk as yet. His screams brought us running to the lounge from the kitchen.

The cup of tea was spilt right across our new carpet, leaving an ugly, dark stain. But worse still, Adam scalded his fingers, and bawled his head off. Geraldine had just been telling me that a few weeks earlier, he pulled down a kettle of boiling water from the kitchen bench at Judy's place, and his shoulder was a mass of scarred tissue and red welts across. Poor Adam! He was such a mischievous toddler.

Geraldine rushed back home with Adam, while I tried my best to get the tea stain out of the carpet. But nothing helped, as I sponged, and dried, and shed tears of chagrin. The immaculate carpet was spoilt beyond repair, as the tea was a strong brew, and soaked right through.

Chapter 16

Violence erupted in Sri Lanka between the JVP, the Government, and Tamil Tigers now. And earlier rumblings of a few years ago, were warning signs of impending civil war. The JVP ran riot everywhere, and fought to control the country. Nilanthi and Heron now faced danger on the farm where they lived, as Heron was a security guard, and employed to keep trouble-makers out. They lived in fear of their lives, and fled to Maharagama, where they stayed with Ammie and Thathie for a while.

When terrorists stormed their farm one night, and set fire to several homes, fortunately for them, they were not there. When Nilanthi called to tell me about their situation, she cried desperately. So we quickly organised to bring them over on a holiday, and paid for their tickets. As Connie still had some money left over from his superannuation payout, he spent about $3000 on their tickets.

Tanesh wanted to stay with Heron's brother, Maurice, and his wife, Cynthia. But Nilanthi and Heron arrived at the end of October 1988. Heron was in tears when we met them at the airport, because he was so relieved to get out of that trouble spot, and thanked us profusely. It was great to see Nilanthi again, and she too was overjoyed to be with us.

But a few days later, once the euphoria subsided, Heron was very homesick for Ceylon, and the way of life over there. He cried often, as he was miserable. Nilanthi, though, enjoyed every moment that she spent with us. And when I asked if they would like to stay in Australia permanently, they were agreeable, and decided to apply for residency, including Tanesh.

A couple of weeks later, Nilanthi missed Tanesh very much, and cried constantly when she thought of him. When I told Connie how upset she was, he bought a ticket for him too, which cost about $1500, and soon they were all re-united. We had only one spare room, so we bought a double-bed, and they all slept in one room.

A week or so later, we were very surprised, when Tamara joined them, and now all *four* of them shared one small room, and bed. It was very cramped, and uncomfortable for everyone, but I enjoyed having them. Heron was not too happy to see Tamara, and he told us, "She's *bad* news! Wherever she goes, she creates trouble!"

The constant tension between Stacy and Connie increased a hundredfold, as Connie disciplined him relentlessly whenever he got out of hand. He could not vent his frustrations on anyone else (because of our guests), so Stacy was at the receiving end. He nagged me about every single one of his minor misdemeanours, and would not leave Stacy alone.

Stacy, who was sixteen years old, was only trying to assert himself. But Connie treated him like a little boy whenever he was rebellious, and they came to physical blows several times. Stacy talked long on the phone, and Connie demanded that he cut short his conversations, which angered Stacy greatly. Then Stacy took out his frustration on Christian, so it was a constant state of friction, and arguments in the house, which marred their visit.

Whenever Stacy was rude or refused to obey Connie, he chastised him saying, "I *don't* care even if the *Queen* is here, I will correct you when I have to!" Stacy became more stubborn, and complained bitterly about Connie to Heron, Tanesh, and the neighbourhood children.

One evening, he hit Christian across his head with his guitar, and the way Christian screamed, we thought he burst an ear drum. We rushed him to emergency, but not before Connie grabbed Stacy's guitar, and brought it down on his head just as hard, until it broke.

This was the sort of behaviour I was forced to witness daily, and I could not stop them from being so destructive. Every time Connie chastised Stacy, he dragged him in front of me, tore off his pyjama top or t-shirt, and then struck Stacy in front of me, until I yelled at him, "*Stop* behaving like an animal! For God's sake, try to be reasonable and sort out your problems rationally!" Connie and I invariably argued in the end, and came to blows too, because of his violent behaviour.

When Heron witnessed these scenes, he advised Connie often, "*Don't* hit the children Connie at their age, they are teenagers now, and if they raise their hands to you, what are you going to do then?" But that did not stop him from hitting Stacy at the slightest provocation. He could not take out his frustration on anyone else, except his wife and children. He stopped using physical violence on me, ever since I had that first tachycardia attack. Now, it was only verbal abuse, but he had no qualms about hitting Stacy.

A few months before, one of Stacy's friends at Mater Christi Girls School, asked him to partner her at a Debutante Ball. He agreed, but was quite uneasy, as he told me that he did not know how to dance. I played some popular music records, and showed him how to do a quick step, and a waltz.

And I assured him that they would play disco music most of the time, once the formal dances were over, and he should get through the evening without a problem. We rented a formal suit for the occasion, and he looked very smart. And he told me later that he enjoyed himself very much, and I was happy to hear he had a good night with his friends.

I worked three days a week now, which was good, and not too stressful. When I returned to work after our holiday in Ceylon, we had a new manager, as "Carps" was sacked for sexual harassment. All the female employees finally had enough of his unwanted attentions, and signed a petition to get rid of him.

The current manager hardly left his office, and sat reading a newspaper and drinking coffee all day. He was not sociable at all; whether he was afraid of being too friendly, and of being accused of sexual harassment, I do not know. But he seldom smiled or conversed with anyone. He was stout, middle-aged, grey-haired, and a man of very few words.

Nilanthi brought four hundred copies of my published anthology, "Return To Enchantment" as it was only a very slim volume of poems, and short stories. I received a copy earlier, and was thoroughly disappointed at the artwork, and quality of the cover. The printing was passable, with a few spelling mistakes, but I wished that I had been there to ensure a better quality book.

I engaged a printer in Hawthorn and printed new covers. Then I ripped the shoddy ones, and re-glued each new cover carefully. The black and white cover I designed, looked more professional now. I sold copies to libraries, and people I knew, for six dollars a copy, hoping to recover the cost of printing at least. That was my first experience of "self-publishing" (by proxy), and I learnt a great deal.

One day, Connie drove Nilanthi, Heron, Tanesh, and Tamara, all the way to Sydney via Canberra, dropped them at Nelune's place, and returned home the following day. He was exhausted, but we hoped they would be happy at Nelune's for a while. They stayed a few weeks, and returned by coach, in time for Christmas.

When I was off work, I took Heron and Nilanthi shopping, with very limited funds. I gave them twenty dollars each, to spend at the Reject Shop, which was the most affordable place to shop (as they discovered). When we finished, we had a snack at a café, and as Heron loved ice cream and chocolates, he always asked for some.

It was scorching that Christmas, and the temperature soared above thirty eight degrees. When we attended midnight Mass, we just sweltered inside the crowded church, and could hardly wait to come home. Nelune came over too, and we enjoyed a memorable time.

Our house was packed, but I loved having my family with me, and it was a very special Christmas with my loved ones. I cooked a traditional Ceylonese lunch, and everyone enjoyed the delicious rice and curries. Connie was ready to fly off the handle at a moment's notice though, and Nilanthi watched anxiously, as she knew what he was like.

Our days were spoilt with Connie's constant nagging, and his strict treatment of Stacy especially. Christian managed to keep out of trouble, and avoided Connie's temper. The tension was sometimes unbearable, as I tried to keep peace between Connie and Stacy.

On New Year's Day, we drove up to Westgate Bridge with Nilanthi and Heron, and enjoyed the brilliant city sights. But the children did not accompany us, as they preferred to stay home.

On some evenings, when I tried to write a submission in support of their application for permanent residency, Connie burst into the room angrily. Then started his usual complaints about Stacy's minor wrong-doing.

When I refused to be drawn into an argument, and continued writing, he shouted angrily, "What is more important to you, that *submission,* or this rascal's *behaviour?*" I replied, "He's not doing anything *wrong* Connie, leave him alone, and I have to finish this in time to lodge their application." I tried to shut out this constant onslaught on my nerves, but he was totally impossible to live with most of the time.

It was very generous of him to pay for their tickets, and he treated them well. But he complained to me constantly about the children. And the uncertainty of Nilanthi's and Heron's situation preyed on him, as he was not too happy about them staying with us indefinitely.

He told them often, "If you are approved to stay permanently, you will have to find a flat, and try to get some sort of work Heron." I suppose that was an added problem now. He was afraid that if they stayed with us, we would be financially responsible for them.

I told him not to stress me, as it was not good for my heart, but that did not matter at all. But, he told Nilanthi, "*Don't* cry and be upset, as it's not good for Dolly to get worried." When she told me this, I did not understand how he could behave so badly to me, but warn my family not to stress me.

I lived in the most nerve-racking environment imaginable now, and there seemed to be no solution.

Heron's children did not visit them, except Pam, his eldest daughter, and her husband, Alan. They gave him fifty dollars when they visited, and promised to come again. Money was a problem, as Heron and Nilanthi did not have any funds with them, and I was very sorry to see their plight. I gave them whatever I could afford, and on my days off work, I took them to Waverley Gardens, or Dandenong Market. Heron liked the Reject Shop very much, as things were so cheap.

Now that Nilanthi was determined to stay, I prepared a submission in support of their application. Then I drove with them to Box Hill, and met the immigration officer, who immediately withheld their passports, until such time as their application was processed. The application fee was $300 then. My friend, Sheila, from work, and her husband, Terence, invited us to dinner once, and we had a good time. But Heron criticized Terence all the way back, as he did not like him, even though he was a pleasant and genial host. We took Heron and Nilanthi for many drives as well, but Heron was not impressed at all, and criticized everyone and everything in Australia. He was miserable now, and did not like Nilanthi having a good time with us either.

Esme and Paul invited them for dinner, and when she came to pick them, Nilanthi tried to sit in the front seat, but Esme shouted, "*You* sit in the *back* seat Nilanthi, and let Heron sit in the front." Nilanthi said she was very embarrassed and upset about it. Esme had ignored her all evening, and treated Heron, as if he was an honoured guest.

I explained the reason. "Aunty told me that when Cuckoo was in college, he brought Maurice, once, as they were in school together. Because of that brief visit long ago, Aunty and Esme claim that they are very old friends, and that Maurice was interested in Esme. Don't worry about her behaviour."

Esme made it a point to visit daily, although Heron did not have much to say to her, and she stayed on till very late in the night. She also had a very competitive streak, and wanted everything I had. Whether it was clothes, shoes, or something for the house, she had to have the same thing. But I was fond of her, so this foible did not bother me.

Through the years, she told Christian and Stacy, "When you complete Year 12, I will give you a thousand dollars each." And she did not give them birthday presents, because she said she was saving money to give them later. When Christian passed Year 12, and reminded Esme, she said, "I don't have money." That was a great disappointment, and he did not trust her again, as she broke her promise.

Shirani and Ranjith were working out their problems, and were in the process of reconciling. She asked Nilanthi and Heron to spend a few days with her, to give me some respite. Tamara caught up with some Sri Lankan friends, and socialised with them every evening.

Heron, Nilanthi, and Tanesh, stayed a month with Nelune, and Heron did a few odd jobs for Nelune's neighbours, and Lady Ashton, who lived next door to Nelune. He was happy doing some gardening, and cleaning up, for which he earned a few dollars.

When they returned to Melbourne by coach, Heron told us that he did not want to stay, and insisted on returning to Ceylon as soon as possible. He was very unhappy, and kept saying, "I *hate* Australia! I want to go back to my home and country! Your sister can come back when I die, and get married again!"

Nilanthi was inconsolable, as she longed to be with us, and could not bear the thought of going back. Heron was very jealous and possessive of Nilanthi too, because of their age difference. She told me that he felt threatened here, as she would have to earn a living if they stayed. And he was of the old school, where he believed that a woman's place was at home.

He told me that it was very stressful living in a small, confined room, and unable to go about, or earn any money, as they did not have working visas. He knew Connie was unhappy too, and Heron did not like the constant tension in our house.

His children still did not visit him, except Pam and Alan, who came a couple of times. The others did not want to see him, as they were still very hurt about his separation from their mother. Peter, his son, was away then, but he was very kind to Nilanthi, and was not angry with his father.

Nilanthi pleaded with Heron not to go back, as she loved Australia very much, and wanted to be with us, but he was adamant. So, a few days later, he demanded to go to the immigration office, to get their passports and withdraw their application. I drove them to Box Hill again, and they got their passports back. Nilanthi cried non-stop, but Heron was implacable, and determined to go back, so we bought return tickets for them.

We celebrated our birthdays at a Chinese Restaurant that February, and Heron, Nilanthi, and Tanesh joined us. Connie's family visited often, and he invited Aunty for dinner too. Esme continued to drop in almost every single evening, and stayed for hours, regardless of how tired we were and wanted to be alone. She hung a long face, and sat moping in a corner until about ten thirty in the night, and then dragged herself away. We were puzzled as to why she wanted to be with us every evening, and did not care whether she was welcome or not.

Tamara stayed on in Sydney for some time, and when she returned, she lived with her friends in Melbourne. As she did not keep in touch with us, she was unaware that Nilanthi and the rest were returning to Ceylon. They left amid tearful farewells in April 1989. I cried just as much as Nilanthi, not knowing when we would meet again.

She told me later, that she threw up all the way to Singapore, as she felt emotionally and physically sick. Poor Nilanthi, it was her destiny to go back, although she longed with all her heart to remain in Australia. Before they left, I told Nilanthi that the home situation was too much for me to bear, and I could not see any other solution, except to leave Connie.

Nilanthi witnessed enough of my daily trials with Connie, and understood the enormous pressure of living with a person like him. He had spent so much money on their tickets, but unfortunately, the way he behaved, and the things he said, cancelled all his generosity.

Heron could not bear the tension whenever Connie was around, and had said, "*Why* did Connie spend all that money to bring us down, and then for us to witness his bad behaviour?" Every evening, Heron sat in the garden till late at night, just to avoid being around Connie.

Sometimes, Connie barged into the kitchen, and tried to take over whatever I was doing; he made a loud noise, banged and crashed crockery, until he dropped, broke something, or injured himself. Then Heron looked at him sternly, and told Nilanthi, "*Why* doesn't Connie leave the kitchen to Dolly, and just come here and try to relax with us?"

A few days after they left, Tamara came in a taxi, rushed inside, and demanded, "*Where* is my mother Dolly?" I replied, "They left a few days ago, as Heron didn't want to stay." She started crying and embraced me, then told me that she was returning home in a few days time.

When we received our phone bill later that month, it was over $800, as Tamara had made numerous overseas calls. Connie was very annoyed with her for running up such a huge telephone bill. She stayed with Shirani for a while after visiting me that day, and then disappeared.

Soon after, Shirani told me that a woman phoned and abused her for abandoning Tamara. Shirani was shaken, and denied such accusations. And when she asked to speak to Tamara, she came on the phone and brazenly replied, "why, can't you remember how I lived with you, and you threw me out after destroying my passport and identification!" Shirani was stunned at such blatant lies, and asked her what she was up to, but she hung up.

Tamara never went back to Ceylon. Nilanthi told me that she had let down her friends and employer, who advanced her money for her trip. She stayed permanently, and asked Nelune to find her a job at Optus, which Nelune did. And she worked there for a short while.

We never heard from her for a long time, but one day, Paul Maschio dropped in and asked me, "Do you know where your niece is staying?" I was puzzled as to why he wanted to know, and replied, "I don't know, as she has never contacted me for a long time." Paul said, "Do you know that she owes my boss, Angelo, more than thousand dollars?" I was embarrassed. He said he worked at a chemist's in South Yarra, where Tamara cashed some cheques. After that, every time Paul visited, he asked me the same question as to her whereabouts.

Tamara contacted Nelune some time later to ask money, as she was heavily indebted, but Nelune could not help her with such an enormous sum. I have no idea how she fared after that, as she did not contact any of us for a long time. All I know is that wherever she went, she left behind a trail of debt and deception.

Nilanthi said Tamara went on a holiday to the States, and stayed with Heron's relatives, who lent her money. But when her cheques bounced, they were very angry, and complained bitterly to Heron and Nilanthi. And he said, "One thing, she is a *rotten* egg! Where she has got such terrible habits from, I don't know!"

I could not believe that this was the same person whom I had loved very much all these years. She was a total stranger now, and I did not know who she was any longer.

Although Shirani and Ranjith reconciled after their temporary separation, Connie still had some misgivings, and he did not visit them. But Shirani and I kept in touch, and visited on weekends, as the children were attached to each other.

Rosie wrote to say that her health was not too good, and she could not drive anymore. I was very distressed, and could hardly believe this was happening to our dear Rosie.

Chapter 17

Just after Nilanthi and Heron returned to Ceylon, the situation at home became intolerable, with constant tension and aggression between us. We hardly communicated without getting into an argument, and there was no solution to our problems.

I hated profane language, and swearing, as I was brought up never to use bad language. My parents never swore at each other or at us, and I did not know the "F..." word until I met Connie. He told his family and friends, "Dolly is a lady, because she never swears, no matter how angry she gets." And I have always refrained from swearing, as I detest foul language. But he used the "F..." word in almost every sentence, and knowing how much I hated bad language, he persisted.

His parents too, constantly used swear words, so did his siblings. I taught the children from their early days not to use profane language, but Connie's bad example did not help. He told me, "It's because I associate with all the builders and contractors that I have got used to speaking like them."

I replied that it was bad enough that almost every single person, especially teenagers in public places, or on television, and movies, used bad language, without having to listen to it in my own home.

Connie could be very nice, and behaved affably when he wanted to, but in a matter of moments, his mood changed, and he was completely different. In later years, I often wondered if Connie suffered from bi-polar, and should have been treated for it, as I have never seen a person behaving so irrationally, and contrary-wise.

He was kind and pleasant for a little while only, until some very minor incident irritated him, or a fit of jealousy overcame him. When I asked him one day, "*When* are you going to stop being so jealous, since we have been married so long, and have young sons?" He replied, "I will be jealous of you till I *die!*"

Since my tachycardia attacks, Connie stopped smoking inside the house, and now smoked in the garden. But I hardly had a peaceful evening at home with the children, as Connie vented all his anger on Stacy. When I went to bed at night, he stayed up drinking till late. Then he came barging in through the sliding door into the bedroom, woke me up, shouted about some issue or other, or else started an argument with Stacy. I was awake most of the night, and could hardly get up in the morning to go to work.

One night, in the middle of an argument, he woke up the children, and locked himself in their room for a long time. I do not know what he told them, but he staggered out later and yelled at me, "I'm going to Mummy's now, and when I return, I want you and the children out of this house!" I ignored him, and he drove off in a huff. I do not know where he went to at that time of the night, but he returned a few hours later.

Stacy's behaviour too was causing me grief, and I did not know how to help him, because he did not confide in me. I was going through problems at work, because I could hardly concentrate due to my mental state. The evenings and nights were nightmarish, and some nights, I hardly had slept at all.

In desperation, I confided in a few friends at work about the serious problems at home. And they advised me to see a counsellor, or to leave Connie. I knew he would never agree to see a counsellor, because he believed we did not have any problems. It was all Stacy's or my fault, as he was a "model husband" and blameless.

Mary transferred to the Commonwealth Employment Services, at the end of 1987, but I had one or two close friends at work whom I trusted. I thought about my impossible situation at home, and decided that this time, I would leave him, and go away as far as possible, so he could not contact me, and beg me to come home again.

I thought of a bold plan, as I had reached the point of no return, and knew it was the right time and decision to leave him, as I did not want to end up with a nervous breakdown or fall ill. The children were old enough to cope on their own, I thought, and would survive. I wanted to break the chains completely that bound me to Connie, as cornered and helpless, I suffocated in this emotionally charged environment.

One day Stacy told me sadly, "Mum, you are the meat in the sandwich," because I had to keep intervening each time Connie and Stacy failed to see eye to eye, and then Connie and I ended up quarrelling. Christian kept out of the way, and quietly observed these daily scenes with sorrowful eyes.

I felt an overwhelming need to get away as far as possible from it all. But deeply regret that I did not explain my feelings to Stacy and Christian then. I could not bear to say goodbye, as I was too emotional, and cowardly to face them. The reason I left without telling Connie or the children, was that I really feared for my life, knowing how violent he could be. Partners and husbands have killed so many women when they wanted to leave a relationship. That was always my fear, that Connie would carry out his threats to harm me.

I browsed through vacancy bulletins, and Public Service gazettes, where several vacancies were advertised in Western Australia. I wanted to run away to the furthest place, and leave my troubles and problems behind. In due course, I spoke to the manager about my intention to leave home, due to domestic violence. I asked to be transferred to Geraldton, Western Australia, as soon as possible, as I believed the further I was from Connie, it was better for me.

The manager was surprised at my request, and said, "Geraldton is a very *remote* area. Where would you stay? Do you know anyone there? Any friends?" I shook my head and replied, "I want to go away to the furthest place possible, due to personal problems." After a few more minutes, he rang up personnel, while I was in his office, and said, "we'll get the ball rolling, and try to arrange a transfer out within a couple of weeks. Sure you will be able to manage?" I believed I was strong, and resolute enough to make a new life in a new place, so I nodded, "I'm sure I can manage." So, he organized my transfer without much ado. I thanked him and left his office.

Although I was apprehensive, I was determined to break away. Next, I opened a bank account in my name only, because my wages were going into a joint account. As I was working part-time, my net wage was about $400 a fortnight, and a one-way ticket to Perth cost $200. I whizzed around energetically planning my "great escape."

I confided in Shirani, who was doubtful of my venture, but supported me as she always did, because she knew what the situation was like at home. Shirani never discouraged me, and helped in practical ways. I planned everything without a fuss, and wanted to travel light.

One morning, in early May, I left home, with only a small suitcase full of clothes, and personal items. I booked a room in a motel in Perth for three days, which cost around $250.

The manager gave me a letter of introduction, saying, "Contact the manager in Geraldton DSS as soon as you arrive, and give him this letter." I wondered how I could afford to rent a place on my meagre wages. And intended to find a cheap caravan park close to work, until I found a reasonable flat.

I left without a word of warning to Connie or to my sons, and my heart was leaden with grief. I fervently hoped that Stacy and Christian would understand, and forgive me for the pain I caused them. I just could not tell them I was leaving, in case I broke down and changed my mind when I saw their sad faces.

When Shirani saw me with a small suitcase, she said, "You are taking just *one* small suitcase, and that's all you have to show for all those years of hard work." Her voice was sad. She drove me to the airport, and I cried non-stop, until she dropped me off. I thanked her, as she stood by me in all my decisions, no matter how foolhardy. And after a teary farewell, I tried to calm down.

It was the most painful, and depressing few hours in the plane, and I cried all the way to Perth. I was emotionally vulnerable, because I was already missing my children, and the security of my home. Only a woman who is compelled to leave behind *everything* she worked for, and helped to build over a lifetime, can understand my mixed emotions.

It was the most difficult decision in the world for me to leave. And I felt sick at the thought of leaving home and my children, but it was the only way out to preserve my sanity. Anyone who thinks it was easy to break up, and walk away from the security of my home, is greatly mistaken. I told myself repeatedly that I was acting in my best interests.

The trouble was, that when I was at home, and Connie stifled my very soul, I knew I had to escape or die. But when I was away from him, and had time to reflect, and put everything in perspective, I began to have doubts. Was it my fault that I could not be more patient and tolerant with Connie? Was there a chance to make our marriage work? Then a voice told me sternly, *but how many chances have you given him? And how many more times must you forgive and forget?* My inward conflict raged, and Perth drew closer.

The plane landed shortly, and I noticed how small the airport was, in comparison to Melbourne. I took a taxi to a motel in the city, that nestled beside the wide Swan River. It was a breath-taking scene, but I had no heart to enjoy it. The Swan River was magnificent; shimmering and broad as a band of satin flowing smoothly beside the surrounding city, and glistened like a mirror. I felt strange, elated, nervous, and yet was confident that I could make a fresh start here among strangers.

The motel was a short distance from the city, and proved to be a dark, dingy, two-storey building, with a flight of steps to the second level. I paid off the taxi, and lugged my suitcase up the stairs. The room was dark, smelly, and eerie. Loneliness and fear gripped me, as the enormity of my actions hit me with the full force of a golf ball on my skull. I felt very strange, and uncomfortable being alone here. So I sat down and wept heartily, wondering what on earth could I do here by myself?

That evening, I walked down the road to a telephone box near a milk bar, and phoned Nelune. She told me Connie called her, and he was devastated, and asked me to consider returning home. And he had sounded very upset and desolate, and Christian and Stacy were very distressed too, not knowing where I was. I felt grieved to hear that, and was more confused than ever, as it seemed we could not live together, or live apart. I told her not to let him know where I was just yet, until I decided what to do.

I bought some soup packets and bread at the milk bar, walked back to the motel, and made a cup of soup, and had some bread with it for dinner. More tears, grief, and remorse. I listened to every creaking noise and footstep outside, and my heart was in my mouth, not knowing what sort of people lurked outside. I did not sleep at all, though I could hardly keep my eyes open, and I could not wait till daylight.

After a sleepless night of fear in that small dark room, with its sparse furniture, and mouldy smell, I woke up, determined to make this work. I was soon ready to visit the office in Geraldton early next morning. I boarded a bus, and was amazed to see how very wide the streets were, and how sparsely populated the suburbs were.

I thought of Polonnaruwa, in Sri Lanka; so remote, hot and dry, an alien land that was far from my idyllic mental images of Perth. True, I had wanted to get away as far as possible from Connie, and this was far enough alright. But as I stopped outside the office, I hesitated, and started an internal debate. And after a while, I decided not to go inside the office, and give the letter of introduction. Instead, I walked into a nearby caravan park, and enquired about their rates.

The woman quoted $100 a week, but when I looked around, and saw some of the people living there, I lost my nerve. And I almost ran across the street to board a bus back to the motel. My tears blinded me, and a speeding car almost knocked me down, as I stumbled across the street.

A free bus service operated to the city, so I boarded a bus, and looked around Perth. I walked along St George Terrace, and thought to myself that all cities looked the same, in some ways. Perth had the beautiful Swan River gracefully embracing the city; Melbourne, the Yarra, and the sapphire ocean wrapped around Sydney.

The motel room cost about sixty dollars a night, and I had booked it for three days, until I found a place to rent. I was concerned now that I would be unable to afford this motel room, if I did not find a cheaper place immediately. I had a light snack for lunch, and went back to the motel. Then I wrote long letters to Nelune and Shirani, walked down to the letter box and posted them. I stopped at the phone box and called Nelune again. The calls cost a great deal of money, and my meagre savings were dwindling fast.

I did not know how to pay the motel bill next week. Reality hit me like an avalanche, crippling my bravado and confidence that I could survive on my own. I spoke to Nelune, and told her what the situation was like, and the remoteness of Geraldton. Nelune offered to buy me a ticket to Melbourne, and told me once again that it was not a good idea to be alone in Perth.

Later that evening, I worked up enough courage to phone Connie, and told him I was in Perth. He was relieved to hear from me, but incredulous when he knew where I was. He could not believe it, and asked me, "What are you doing there?" I cried brokenly and said, "I'm so unhappy with our situation at home, and this was my only chance to try and escape." He promised, "I *will* change Dolla! I won't put you through so much stress again! Please come back home. I love you! The boys miss you too!" He was overjoyed when I agreed to give him another chance, and said that I would come back next day. We felt overwhelmed.

When I called Nelune again to tell her what happened, she organized a ticket, and was happy that I was going back home, and trying to work things out with Connie. She consoled me, "I'm sure he has learnt a lesson this time, and things will be better."

I did not sleep at all the second night either, and was up early next day. As soon as I was ready, I took a taxi to the airport, and boarded another flight back to Melbourne. Connie met me at the airport, and we talked, cried, and made up.

The children were glad to see me, and Connie told them I had just gone away on a "retreat" for a couple of days. He told his family too that I was away on a retreat. No one knew I had gone to Perth, except Shirani, Nelune, and Connie. I was full of remorse when I saw the childrens' smiling faces. Next moment, I was taken aback when he told Stacy and Christian to kneel down in front of me, "Now, say you are *sorry* and beg Mum to forgive you both!"

Christian told me later that he said, "Are you happy that you both have driven your mother away from home!" It was so very unfair of Connie to blame them, and I felt terrible, because it was not their fault at all. I told them they should not feel guilty in any way. I did not appreciate the fact that Connie told them I left home because I was upset by their bad behaviour. It was nothing of the sort, as the main reason was our inability to get along peacefully.

This was a sore point once again. Connie *never* accepted that he was in the wrong, and when I left him, it was always someone else's fault. He blamed the children now, and made them feel guilty for something they were not responsible for. I was very angry with Connie. The words choked me when I tried to convince Stacy and Christian that my leaving had nothing to do with their behaviour, and that it was all Connie's fault.

My nightmarish stay in Perth was over, but I awoke in my familiar, dreadful world where nothing ever changed. I still had not learnt from experience that Connie could *never* change his true nature, and only *I* could change my attitude towards him, and not let him hurt me anymore.

He managed to control his temper for a few days, and did not drink as much, but within a week, we were back to square one. Everything was still the same as before. Connie was more sullen and angry, because of my drastic steps to escape him.

I lost face at work too, so I rang personnel to request another transfer to Boronia office. I just could not bear to face my colleagues, and the manager after this last fiasco. I was incredibly sad and crushed, and my confidence was shattered after that traumatic experience in Perth.

On 15th May 1989, I transferred to Boronia Social Security, after staying home for ten days, on special leave. I had wanted a change from Knox, but I soon realised I was among some very difficult, unpleasant people in Boronia, until they knew me better, and were friendlier.

The manager who interviewed me, was a short, broadly built man, in his mid-forties. He had bright blue eyes, and wore a large moustache. His name was John too, but they called him "Horse" for some reason unknown to me. I gave him a brief outline of my history, and the reason why I transferred to Boronia.

He listened attentively, and appeared to be sympathetic, but he said, "I want a full-time worker here for a start. Can you do that?" I agreed at once. I was still a grade one clerical officer, and I was transferred at that level. But I was paid as a level three officer at Knox, and on "higher duties."

John introduced me to Heather, the Family Payments team leader, or "Determining Officer" as they were called. She was a tall, thick-set woman, with the most unpleasant, unhappy face I had seen. Her long nose was narrow, and she had piercing, cold blue eyes, and thin lips that seldom smiled. Her badly cut mop of straggly grey hair hung limply round her face, with its habitual, unfriendly expression.

She grunted in acknowledgement, stole a cursory glance at me, and then continued working as she ignored me completely. I told John I was capable of doing all the duties of a level one officer, except overpayments (as I had not received training in that area). When John told Heather about this, she deliberately set out to prove that I knew nothing at all, and had to be trained in all aspects of Family Payments once again. I was fortunate to be a permanent officer, or else she would have definitely seen to it that I was ousted out of DSS because she was so biased.

The first friendly person I met was Cindy, who started work at Boronia on the same day, and we conversed politely in the lunch room. Cindy was a pleasant-looking girl in her early twenties, and we got on well. Lorraine (Vivian's mother), was a very nice, friendly person too, and we soon became good friends. She was one of the typists; a broad, middle-aged, kindly person, who still retained a vestige of youthful good looks. She suffered from type two diabetes, and seemed tired and ill sometimes.

We remained friends for many years, and when Connie knew her husband, Tony, better, we socialised often, as Tony relished hot curries. We still kept in touch till she turned eighty, then her health deteriorated, with the onset of early dementia. A few years later, she was admitted to a nursing home. But Tony, in his late eighties now, still goes riding his bicycle daily.

Heather was my immediate supervisor, and as I said, she was a disagreeable, grim-faced woman in her late forties. She made my life intolerable during the first six months, until we became better acquainted, and she changed her attitude completely. Heather suffered with severe back problems, and perhaps that accounted for her ill-humour towards most people.

She had a caustic tongue, and seldom smiled or laughed; a divorcee, with two teenage sons, who resembled her physically, she had endured an unhappy marriage. It ended in a vitriolic divorce, which left her harsh and embittered (so they said). She had few friends, and no one liked her, but that did not make my situation any better.

She picked on my work constantly, and tossed the files back on my desk, until I was almost in tears, as she did not approve any of my work. Heather tried my patience to the limit. And I spent my days re-submitting my work, until she finally decided to approve, when she could not nit-pick anymore.

The other workers in that section were taciturn too, and unfriendly at the start. Pam, a Scottish woman in her late twenties, hardly spoke to me at all, and only spoke to the others, if she was spoken to. She was the other Determining Officer in the section, and sometimes, I submitted my work to her, but she was just as finicky as Heather. They seemed to have an agreement between them to make my life as difficult as possible.

Another team member, also called Pam, was a tall, anorexic woman in her late thirties. She had pale-green eyes, and shoulder-length, straggly red hair (dyed with Henna). Geoff, was a bigoted Australian, and was recovering from a car accident, that had impaired not only his hearing, but his personality as well. He was caustic, with a barbed tongue, and temperament, and always made racist comments. He was of average height, about forty-five, with a bushy, black beard, and cold, grey eyes. Day after day, I sat among these unfriendly people, head bent low, working as hard as I could.

Trevor, a young Australian, who had just joined the department, was on probation. The other staff members stood in awe of Heather, and Trevor was so intimidated, that he hardly dared ask anyone for help, and approached only me, if he had any questions. He was nervous as a mouse facing a hungry cat, and very unsure of himself.

I was always ready to answer his questions though, and helped him with work-related issues. Once, he burst out in frustration, "Heather is an *impossible* woman! *Nothing* pleases her!" I could understand his irritation and agreed with him. After that, he worked up courage to tell Heather, "You are *destroying* that poor woman, with your constant picking and negativity!" Soon after that conversation, Heather ambled ponderously towards me one morning.

She had a bad back, and I excused her behaviour on account of that. Now she glared grimly, her pale blue eyes piercing through me, and hissed, "I would *appreciate* it, if you do not discuss me with Trevor!" I looked at her in disbelief and replied, "I'm not feeling too well, as I have a heart problem, and you don't help, with your constant picking, and throwing back work at me!" She turned away without speaking, and lumbered back to her desk.

Some people in other sections were friendly though; Cindy, Lorraine, Jenny, a Malaysian lady about my age, and Barbara, a Polish lady in her forties, who all worked in the Pensions section. I joined them during my breaks, and they sympathised with me because they knew who Heather was, and we had a few good laughs.

Trevor did not make it through probation, and was dismissed after three months, based on Heather's negative reports. She said he was inefficient, and unsuitable to work at DSS. Heather's decision influenced John very much, as he did not know anything about work procedures in any section, and no matter how unfair they were, he believed the supervisors.

Sometime later, a very pleasant Indian lady joined our team, and was on probation too. But Heather, and every single person there were so prejudiced against her, that although she was a graduate with many qualifications, Heather wrote a negative report, and made sure she was not granted a permanent position in the department. They made her life unbearable in the short time she was there, and one staff member asked me then, "How did you slip through the net in such a biased environment, because you are a migrant too?" I replied, "Fortunately, I was made permanent at Knox, otherwise Heather would have made sure I was out the door too."

John was not as bad as "Carps" where female staff were concerned, and fixed his interest mostly on the pretty twins, Wanda, and Felicia. They were two audacious young girls, who swore like drunken sailors. And they could not utter a single sentence, without a dozen four letter words thrown in for good measure. Felicia worked as a temporary officer at Knox, but transferred to Boronia, as her sister, Wanda worked there, and John made her a permanent staff member. That was how things were then, as a manager could employ anyone he liked. He thought the twins were fantastic in every way, and they were his hot favourites.

On my first day there, he tried to be extra nice to me, and was very attentive during an office "Happy Hour." He offered me champagne, and said, "It's great to have you here with us Nalini!" Then he came up to my desk, and perched on the edge, as he engaged me in conversation. I did not encourage his behaviour in anyway, and remained reserved, as I did not care to curry favour with the boss.

Though he was a married man with teenage children, John flirted openly with Wanda. And once, I glimpsed them locked in a close embrace in the filing rack aisle, but I hurried away immediately, as it was none of my business.

As months went by, and Heather continued to harass me, in desperation, I told John about her behaviour. But he replied, "There is nothing I can do about her attitude Nalini. We all know she is a very difficult person, who has worked in the department for over twenty years, and expects everyone to do her bidding. Just be patient, and try not to mind too much."

A few months later, I suffered another severe attack of tachycardia, and was in hospital for a couple of days. Heather thawed slightly by December that year, and did not throw back my work any longer, as she grudgingly accepted me.

I made friends with most of the office staff, and was settling in as well as I could. Pam, the anorexic lady, joined the department about six months ago. And when a vacancy was advertised at grade two level, Heather recommended Pam, instead of me, although I was in the department three years, and had more experience.

I was bitterly disappointed, and spoke to John about it, but he replied, "There's no one to support your claim here, and Heather recommended Pam, there's nothing much I can do about it." That was my first encounter with the slippery business of promotions and selections in the public service. It was all up to managers, who promoted their favourites without much fairness. I swallowed the bitter pill of disillusion in my career, and went on working steadily. Soon, I earned the respect of my colleagues, and Heather's grudging acceptance.

Once, while shopping in Boronia, I saw an elegant lounge-suite in a small furniture shop, Andersons, which closed down long ago. I told Connie I wanted to buy that suite. It was upholstered in an old-fashioned rose-pattern, in pale pinks and greens called, "Oxford Spring" and cost $1200. I paid a deposit, and wanted to collect it in a few weeks time after we sold our old lounge-suite, which was dark-stained pine, with matching glass-topped coffee table, and two side tables.

I sewed cushions for that set in a very pretty fabric; it had a beige background, cream-coloured cherry blossoms, leaves in pale browns, ochre, and a hint of tangerine. And I sewed new curtains in a soft shade of watermelon to match the cushions. But we got only $150 for the whole lot, as second-hand dealers never paid that much.

I purchased that lounge-suite sometime later that year. Most of our furniture was second-hand, and when they delivered the new lounge-suite, I was pleased, as it looked elegant.

Christmas was busy, with the usual parties with Connie's family. Stacy and Christian were growing up fast, and had their own friends and interests now, so they did not accompany us to those family dinners.

Connie and I were no closer, and we came to blows each time we argued, and it was always the same ending. I tried hard to create a semblance of normalcy in our home, but he only had to take a few extra drinks, to ruin any family harmony.

When the children and I sat at dinner, he walked around with a glass of whisky in one hand, and a cigarette in his mouth. And he insisted that we listened to his monologue, although the three of us were trying to hold a conversation. He did not like any of us expressing opinions on any subject, as he thought his opinion was all that mattered.

We just had to listen to him, and agree with everything he said, if we wanted peace, while he droned on and on with his "whisky talk." If Stacy got impatient and retorted, that was it. Slap, bang, crash, and abuse. He waited for the smallest opportunity to come down on Stacy, so he could shout, "Go to your room at *once!*" Christian and I sat quietly, and watched this behaviour almost every day, as we circled on the same merry-go-round.

Meals were such an issue too. Connie wanted "grainy" rice, "red" curries, and extra salt and chilli in everything. The children and I preferred our rice well-cooked, and not too much chilli and salt in the curries. This was a constant source of complaints, as the food was never to his liking. Very rarely did he praise a meal, or say he enjoyed it. But Aunty told me, "Connie always praises your cooking to me, and the family, and he says you make the best curries because you make your own curry powder." But he did not want to give me the satisfaction of receiving his compliments.

Although Connie had many good qualities, he suffered from a personality-disorder. Before drinking whisky, he was usually sullen, uncommunicative, and moody; after a couple of drinks, he was expansive, idiotically jocular, giggly, and sentimental; and after a few too many, he was angry, suspicious, hostile, and violent.

He was generous with money, but never with his time towards me, or the children. He did not know how to communicate with any of us, or to "bond" with his wife and children. He thought that working and earning a steady income, keeping a tidy garden, disciplining the children constantly, was all that was required of a good father, and husband.

He helped me in the house, if I asked him to, but I always cleaned and vacuumed the place because he had enough to do in the garden. Connie was handy around the house, and attended to anything if it needed repairs. No matter how much I tried to keep things tidy, and clean windows too, he frowned and said, "*I* have to wash the windows one day, and vacuum the house to do a really good job!" But he never had time.

He reminded me of Felix Unger in the "Odd Couple" because no matter where we went, he always washed glasses before he used one. Thathie found his compulsive washing and cleaning quite amusing, and so did some of the family. If I washed lettuce, he took it back to the kitchen sink immediately, and washed it all over again. It was infuriating, but that was his fetish.

If I was tired or unwell, he cooked a meal, which was good, and I appreciated his help. But what I could not bear, was the constant nagging, and "barking" at me and the children; the hostility and complaints whenever he was around me. His voice went through my head like red hot hammers. Any given time, I heard his grating voice, "*Huns*! *Where* are you? Come here at *once*!" That word "Huns" was meant to be a term of endearment, and a contraction of "Honey" but he made it sound like an expletive.

My head spun around, just listening to him barking for no reason. When he could not nag the children, he trailed behind, and badgered me about all their misdemeanours, until I retorted, "What do you want me to do about it? Why don't you wait till they're home and talk to them yourself?" He scowled and walked away, muttering curses under his breath when he thought I could not hear him.

Many times I heard him, and when I asked who were the "Cursed devils," he denied it. I said, "You sound just like your father. He muttered and cursed his family every evening after drinks." He got mad at me then, and shouted, "I'm *praying* you *stupid woman*! And don't you *dare* compare me to my father!" I ignored his muttering, and left the room. I heard his curses, and to say he was praying, was pathetic.

Nothing was ever right, or good enough for him. He constantly criticized Stacy, and if he offered to help in the garden, he chased him away, saying, "You can't do a *good* job, let Christian help me." Stacy suffered low self-esteem at this constant barrage of criticism, and his resentment of Christian and us, grew like a cancer within him. We had problems with Stacy then, as he was getting into mischief at school, with his boyish pranks that were not very serious, but he was also losing interest in his studies.

I suffered a few more tachycardia attacks during this period, at home and once in the swimming pool. The office adjoined a swimming pool, so I swam for an hour after work, three times a week. That particular evening, the water was cold, and as I stepped inside the pool, I felt my heart racing, and then very rapid beats. Most of the time, my heart beat returned to normal, after a couple of hours rest. I was on medication now, and it helped, but sometimes if I forgot to take my tablets, invariably I suffered an attack.

I hurt my back once when I tried to lift a heavy pot at home, and was in bed for a week. The x-rays showed a weak spot in my vertebrae, and the doctor advised me to be careful in future, as I would suffer from chronic back pain. Swimming helped, but if I took a wrong turn, I ended up with excruciating pain, and muscle spasms that laid me low for a few days.

It did not help my back either, when I slipped down a narrow ramp in Coles supermarket one evening after work, and ended up flat on my back. I was so embarrassed that I got up as quickly as possible, and returned to my car, even though people around me asked, *"Are* you okay? Do you want to complain to the manager?" I replied, "No, I'm fine," and walked away hastily. Stacy wanted to change schools, as he had problems at St Joseph's, and was playing truant. We enrolled him at another local school, but after a few weeks there, he said it was not the right school for him.

He was in year eleven now, and we hoped he would continue his education, until he completed year twelve. He was going through a very difficult time in his life. In the evenings he asked Connie to drop him off at the station in Dandenong or Ferntree Gully, so he could spend the evenings and nights with friends.

Christian worked steadily at school, and so far, he did not seem to encounter the same problems as Stacy. But he too needed braces to correct his front teeth, and started wearing braces when he was in his early teens. Their teeth were very good, as a result of wearing braces.

One evening, just as I came home from work, Stacy called to ask me for a lift, as he said he had only one shoe on. Astonished, I asked him, "What happened?" He sobbed bitterly, "The boys removed my Doc Martin shoes and threw one shoe out of the window of the bus!" I was tired, and irritated, so I said, "You better get home somehow, as I just got home, and I'm too tired to pick you up now!"

About an hour later, Stacy limped home, with only one shoe on. My heart still aches at that memory. If only I had picked him up that evening, I would not feel so much pain and remorse now. He did not say much, and went straight to his room.

I had training in Box Hill next day, and as I drove along Burwood Highway, early in the morning, I saw a familiar shoe on the roadside. I did not believe it was possible, but I quickly pulled over to the side of the road, and yes, it was a Doc Martin shoe! I was elated, and wanted to turn back home and break the good news to Stacy. He was so sad, because he bought that pair of shoes for $200 with his pocket money, which he saved.

I got through the day somehow, and when I showed Christian the shoe in the evening, he laughed happily. Later on, when he saw Stacy coming down the driveway, Christian placed the shoe on top of his head, and walked out to meet him. Stacy's face broke out in a broad grin, as his eyes fell on his treasured Doc Martin shoe. That evening was a much happier one for Stacy.

News from London was bad. Christine told us Rosie was very ill after radiation, and was now unable to drive around or do much. I grieved for poor Rosie; the indomitable, unsinkable Rosie, now laid low in this terrible manner. The tumour had grown slightly, and the pressure on her brain was causing problems now, as she suffered epileptic fits too, and was on medication to control them. I did not want to believe she was so ill, and was inclined to think that perhaps she exaggerated her symptoms.

Rosie and Christine headed off to spend time with Granny, as doctors were not very optimistic. I was shocked to hear that they gave her only six months to live, and she was heavily dosed with umpteen tablets. Christine nursed her day and night, while Rosie lay zombie-like. It was a very distressing period in my life, to know Rosie was so ill. She did not want to visit Melbourne again, as she said, "Things will never be the same again due to the trouble with Ranjith, now that he is back with Shirani, and he'll never accept me."

In spite of all these upheavals and dramas in my life, I spent most of my spare time writing. And from 1990 onwards, I entered several literary competitions held by Writers World, Queensland, and won many awards. All my winning entries were published in their anthologies. And once, I wrote a poem for Stacy, "Lost Threads Of Communication," which was highly commended and published. I wrote that in my anguish, when I could not get close to Stacy, or understand his behaviour.

I also painted landscapes and still-life. Connie gave me a portable easel many years ago, and I set it up in the bathroom, where I could clean up the paint on the tiled floor. I had no other place in the house, but even in this cramped area, I still managed to finish a number of paintings.

These were some of the creative outlets I indulged in, besides playing the electric organ whenever I could. I liked doing macramé too, and learnt how to make plant holders, and completed a few for hanging baskets in the kitchen, besides making pot pourri lace hats.

When some people saw the pretty straw-hats, decorated with artificial flowers and layers of lace around, they wanted to buy them, and I sold each one for ten dollars. I dried rose petals and lavender, and added essential oils for extra fragrance. Those hats were very much in demand, and I enjoyed making them, besides painting miniatures, pressed flowers in frames, pin cushion dolls, in Victorian dresses, and other craft work. Whenever the school held a fair, and needed craftwork for stalls, I was happy to provide some of my items, which sold easily.

I had few friends in Boronia office, but I confided in them, because I found life increasingly unbearable, and once again, my only means of salvation was escape from this misery at home. Perhaps, I was foolhardy going to Perth, without enough money or friends there. I thought about it daily. Would I succeed in leaving, and staying away from Connie, if I had good friends, money, a secure job, and a place of my own?

Looking back at this period in my life, one would think I was constantly wanting to run away and "escape" my problems at the slightest hint of trouble. But the reality was, that every time I returned, I expected a changed man, a better deal, more understanding, and effort on his part to get on with me. Though each time I left and returned, I compounded the problem, adding coals to the raging fires of doubt and suspicion.

He was most insistent I did not discuss my leaving him with his family, because he wanted to show the world he was a perfect husband. It was all *my* fault, as if something was wrong with me, and not with him, as I ran away from home for no reason, and returned to a forgiving husband. He was so obstinate, and set in his ways, and I now understood that he could never change. And he did not even try to understand what drove me away in such desperation, as it was never easy to walk out.

The only reason I left was because he would never have left home and gone away on his own. He said he loved me, and cried so much when I returned, that I felt sorry for him. I asked, "*If* you love me so much, why don't you treat me better, and be kind and tender? That's all I want from you, to be treated kindly, nothing else. I don't want to be harassed constantly, and nagged at every turn about the children, or the dog or anything."

This was because he said it was my fault that Dash did his business everywhere in the garden, and I had not trained him to use one spot only. He had only negative things to say about everything, and everyone, so it was impossible to stay in his company even for a few minutes, without my head reeling, and an urge to tell him to shut up.

I dropped gentle hints, "*Why* do you have to be so negative about everything? Why don't you try and look on the bright side?" But he was more embittered and angry about his retrenchment, which he never overcame. He carried on a monologue for hours, about the unfair treatment he had suffered, and how badly he had been treated.

I confided in a few friends at work that I was going through enormous personal problems at home, as well as health issues. The social worker was very sympathetic, and encouraged me to move out, and find a nice place and get on alone, rather than live in a destructive environment. I always imagined things would improve at home, once Connie knew I would leave him again if he did not behave. But he was so obstinate, and incorrigible, that he never accepted the fact he was to blame for my leaving.

He never admitted he had a drinking problem either, as he told everyone that he only had a "small tot" in the evenings, whereas in reality, he was drunk every night. He muttered under his breath, "So, you went to Perth eh?" And if I threatened to leave him, he shouted, "*Get out* of here! I *don't* care!" Minutes later, he sobbed and pleaded, "I'm *sorry* Dolla! I didn't mean it, you know I love you!" This was the invariable pattern.

I decided to leave for good next time, and looked around for a flat, as I was back in the same old rut. Connie did not even try to change for the better. I found a suitable unit in early July, and was determined to leave. I even signed up a lease, but this time, I would tell the children, and Connie that I was leaving.

I prepared myself emotionally, to face this upheaval one more time. But a few days before my escape, I hesitated, because I was too weary to go through the trauma of leaving home again. I felt drained, and was at a very low point. I changed my mind, cancelled the lease, and decided to endure whatever happened.

A few weeks later, Rosie asked if I could join her, and I worked up the courage to tell Connie that I wanted to go to Ceylon on my own. I desperately needed to get away from the home situation, or else I did not know what I would do. I told him I would love to see Rosie again, and needed a holiday on my own, as I needed a break, otherwise we would end up separating again. He listened grimly and replied, "So, that's a fine joke now, you have to get away by yourself, what about me?" I told him I needed breathing space.

After some consideration, even though he was not too happy, he reluctantly agreed, when I said it was only for two weeks. But when I booked the ticket, I told him I would stay for a month. By now, he was aware that he had to compromise, or else I would leave him again. But he always said he did not like us going on separate holidays, like some of our friends. I told him it was difficult to leave the children, and our home, if we both went away, even though the boys were old enough to manage on their own.

I concealed my excitement at the prospect of spending one whole month with my family, and looked forward to my trip eagerly. I boarded a plane to Ceylon on 16 June 1990. Connie dropped me at the airport, and I wished the children goodbye at home. As the plane took off, I breathed a sigh of relief, as I desperately wanted a break from the stressful environment at home. It was so crushing, with constant scenes, and aggressive behaviour between Stacy and Connie, and was very depressing to watch the futility of it all. There seemed to be no solution to this on-going clash between father and son.

We had no idea then that Stacy may have been experimenting with mild drugs, which would have accounted for his mood swings, and uncontrollable anger. Connie disciplined him with an iron-fist, but instead of achieving a good outcome, Stacy became more and more isolated and alienated from us. He did not return home for a few days sometimes, and when we questioned him, he replied, "I've been with friends." I tried hard to understand him, but there was no denying that the traumatic situation with Stacy and Connie, added fuel to our already volatile marriage.

The whole family met me at Katunayake Airport in Ceylon, and we were overjoyed to see each other again. I went straight to Ammie's and Thathie's place, where I could hardly go to sleep with such excitement. I talked for hours, but I knew they were very tired, as it was well past midnight when we returned from the airport.

Next morning, Nilanthi arrived bright and early at 7 o'clock, and I teased her, "How come you are here at the *crack* of dawn?" We laughed and talked all day, and Ammie kept saying, "How happy and relaxed you are, without a husband to *annoy* you!" I phoned Connie from Granny's place to say that I arrived safely.

He sounded gloomy, and the children too were sad when I spoke to them, and he told me they missed me very much. But I had come for a month, and was not going to return any earlier, so I replied, "Time will pass quickly before you know."

When I saw Rosie later that day, I was shocked. She was bald, and bloated with steroids, numerous medication, and radiation. Rosie spoke slowly, in a slurred voice, but smiled happily as we hugged each other. She was heavily sedated, and slept most of the day, and Christine nursed her tenderly, like a mother. Granny spent hours kneeling in front of the altar, and recited the rosary constantly for Rosie to get better.

Rosie consulted a very good neurologist in Colombo, who reduced her medication, and also gave her a glimmer of hope, unlike the one in London, who said she had only six months to live.

One evening, about a week later, Rosie felt well enough to dress up, and invited some of her good friends, Nilanthi, and me, for dinner at Mount Lavinia Hotel. We enjoyed a memorable night, and she laughed and joked just like before. She wore a cap to cover her baldness, and a loose kaftan to hide her bulk.

She also organised dinner at the famous "Akasa Kade" at Ceylinco Hotel, where we met Sam the man (band leader), and enjoyed that evening too. Sam came over to our table often, and asked each one of us to dance with him. Rosie joked as she limped to the floor, "I'm the nondi kakula (lame- legged), dancer!" When he danced with me, he said, "I'll be coming to Melbourne soon. Can I phone you about the dances I'm going to play at, as I like you to be there with your friends." I nodded, "Okay. I'll try to be there."

Rosie and Christine left after a couple of weeks, and she looked much better than when I first saw her. Malcolm took her to the specialist the previous day, who assured her that she had improved dramatically. I was very sad when she left, but she hugged me and said, "I'll *never* forget that you came to see me in Ceylon when I was sick." I was glad that I spent at least two weeks with Rosie.

They left because she had to start treatment again, but even after her brief stay, the change was noticeable, as she was already improving, and felt more energetic. The whole family went to the airport once again, and I returned to Ammie's and Thathie's place. Malcolm told me a few days later, "I hope nothing happens to Rosie, because the doctor in London said she won't last another year."

Nilanthi wanted me to spend a few days with her on the farm, and I painted two or three landscapes, as I bought some oil paints, and brushes in Colombo. I felt rejuvenated already, and laughed more often, as I relaxed with my family. It was wonderful to be free, and be the person that I was born to be.

Although I stayed with Nilanthi, we visited Ammie and Thathie every evening, as I did not want to miss out spending time with them either. Granny wanted us to accompany her to St Anthony's church in Kochikade, and we boarded a bus from Maharagama. When we arrived there, she opened a flask of tea that Leela had prepared, along with some egg sandwiches. Granny chuckled happily, "This is a picnic we are having." I enjoyed that time with Granny, and came home quite tired.

Malcolm visited every evening, and we had a great deal of fun, laughing and chatting. Connie called me at Granny's place a few times, to let me know how the children and he were faring. He said he missed me very much, and wanted me to return home soon. But I still had a few more days left to spend with my family. And I did not know when we would meet again, so I would not curtail my visit.

I wanted to give my parents some money towards a ceiling in the lounge room, and a local carpenter gave a reasonable quote. Ammie had waited a long time to get a ceiling in the living area, so I withdrew $300 from my credit card, and asked the carpenter to start work immediately.

The remaining days of my holiday were chaotic, as the man turned up early in the morning, and hammered away all day. It disrupted the peace at home, but all in all, it was a relaxed time. I desperately needed this respite to restore my equilibrium, and decide what to do in the bleak future.

I did not see the completed ceiling, as it took him four weeks to finish the job. But Ammie was delighted when the room finally had a ceiling. Nilanthi and I spent many hours shopping at "Liberty Plaza." And once, we took Granny's servant girl, Leela, to a Chinese restaurant, and I treated her to a nice meal. The poor girl was elated with the new experience of being "waited on" for a change, instead of serving us.

I painted a landscape for Ammie, which impressed Malcolm so much, that he wanted it the moment he saw it. Ammie was happy to give him the painting, as he was always very kind and generous to her. He joked characteristically, "All it needs is a nice train chugging through the trees, and it will look just like up-country!" I protested immediately, "No, no, don't *spoil* my painting Malcolm!" We both laughed, and he replied, "*Only* kidding, you know I won't change your painting."

Ammie asked me to paint a mermaid on the bathroom wall, as she had always wanted me to paint one for her. She was very sentimental, and remembered the time I painted a mermaid in our bathroom at Kelaniya. We had a large water tank in the bathroom there, and I painted a mermaid, with her tail dipping inside the water tank, which was very effective.

When Malcolm saw the one I just finished, he exclaimed, "You have covered all the *interesting* bits!" Granny, who was standing behind him retorted, "What do you mean, *interesting bits*! It's very good Dolly, I like it modest like that!" It was because I painted the mermaid's long hair cascading over her breasts. We had a good laugh.

In spite of the jokes and laughter, we were very upset about Rosie, and Malcolm especially, as he said, "I *hope* poor Rosie lives for a long time!" He was afraid she would die any day now, even though Christine phoned to say that there was a marked improvement in her condition, since their return. We were glad to hear this good news.

Malcolm and Indrani did not have children, although they were married over ten years. So, a few years ago, they adopted a baby girl, Imalie. Granny doted on her, and Malcolm loved her dearly too. Imalie was always sitting on his lap, while Granny and he petted her fondly. But Indrani was not very demonstrative, although she too cared for the little girl very much. Imalie was growing up to be a very pretty young girl, and was always clinging onto Malcolm. I sent her clothes and gifts too, because I was very fond of her, and Malcolm appreciated it very much.

I was very happy, painting, and relaxing with my family for a month. And how very grateful I am for that fantastic month spent with my parents, Nilanthi, Granny, Malcolm, Rita, Rosie, and Christine. Daisy Akka visited often too, and once, she invited us to Manel's place (where she lived), for lunch. She told me, "It's with *my* pension money Dolly, so don't worry about my family, as I want to make a nice lunch for you and the others." I thanked her and said I would definitely be there.

Wimala spent a few days at Ammie's too, and commented that I worked like a "boy" when he saw me in jeans and t-shirt, climbing a ladder to fix some curtains. I sewed matching cushion covers on Ammie's ancient Singer machine, pedalling away furiously, with beads of perspiration pouring down my face in that humid weather. I wanted to do as much as possible to make sure the house was fixed nicely, the way Ammie wanted.

It was unbearably hot in the afternoons, and we had fans whirring all day, so I was able to do all the little tasks for Ammie. One afternoon, Mrs Gunapala, her neighbour, walked in and said, "How *nice* if your daughter lived close by, instead of in Australia! She would be such a help to you!" Ammie smiled and agreed, but her eyes filled, as she knew I would be leaving soon.

When I was at Nilanthi's, Heron took us to a nearby rest house one evening. It was very peaceful, and situated by a river. The cool breezes were very refreshing, as we sat in the veranda and ordered cool drinks. We spent a couple of hours relaxing there, before heading home for dinner.

Tanesh lived in a house in Moratuwa, with its resident caretaker for company, as it was closer for him to travel to school. But Nilanthi and Heron lived in another house on a chicken farm, as Heron was working as a security guard again. The general manager, who owned both houses, was happy for Tanesh to stay in that house, rather than leave it vacant. They lived in Moratuwa a few months, before Heron was employed on the chicken farm.

Whenever Tanesh was at home, he entertained us with his jokes and pranks. He loved playing practical jokes on everyone, especially Ammie, who found his particular brand of humour quite annoying. She told me, "Tanesh emptied a jar of my face creme and filled it with something else that I applied on my face, but I knew something was wrong with it as it did not look the same."

Tanesh thought it was hilarious, but poor Ammie was not amused, as she said, "I was very angry because *anything* could have happened to my face, not knowing what he had put in my make-up!" I asked Tanesh not to play such pranks on Ammie in future. But he just laughed, because he knew he could not resist making Ammie the butt end of his jokes. We thought Nihal's mischievous genes manifested in Tanesh, but Nihal did not hurt anyone, especially Ammie, or go to such extremes like Tanesh.

Ammie also said, that when Heron took them for a drive once, she had inquired, "Where are we going?' Tanesh replied, "Kannatha Cemetery!" And when Ammie asked, "Why?" He retorted, "To *bury* you!" Ammie cried when she told me that she did not understand why he joked at her expense. Tanesh was not one bit sorry about his tomfoolery, as he thought he was being very funny.

Soon, my respite came to an end, and among tears and sadness, I left Ceylon, after a memorable holiday. I felt refreshed, and ready to face whatever the future held. And before long, I was home again after an uneventful flight.

Chapter 18

Connie's Aunty Ella, invited us to Helen's wedding in August that year. She was Lena's youngest sister. When I was in Ceylon, I bought a russet-coloured satin skirt; it was pleated, and gathered up with a black buckle at the front, just like an ancient Egyptian garment. I decided to wear it to the wedding, with a black lace top. It was unusual, and cost about eighty dollars. When Ammie saw it, she exclaimed, "Dolly, you *must* send me a photo of you in that outfit!"

The wedding was a big event, and I wore my special outfit, complete with a black satin hat, black gloves, and shoes. Before we left, I asked Connie to remove a photograph, so I could send it to Ammie, which he did. Everyone noticed my striking skirt, and complimented me on it, asking me where I bought it.

One of the young male guests (after too many drinks), dragged me forcibly to the dance floor, saying, "I like your hat and your beautiful outfit!" I could not refuse to dance, because he held me and swirled me across the floor. Connie was not impressed at all, and sat morosely. I came back to the table, as soon as the music stopped.

Connie kept sidling up to his cousins and aunts all evening, and hung around them, but it did not worry me, as he was happy chatting to all his relatives, especially with Lena. We stayed till long after midnight, until the bride and groom went away. The mother of the bride, howled and wept as if she was at a *funeral* and not a wedding. It was her youngest daughter's wedding, but the way she carried on, it was quite histrionic, and embarrassing to watch.

I wore that outfit once more, when Sam the man played at a dance a few months later. When Sam saw me, much to Connie's chagrin, he rushed over, grabbed me, and waltzed across the floor. And when we came back to the table, Sam exclaimed, "Dolly, your outfit is out of this world!" Connie replied irritably, "It *is* out of this world all right! It's from *Sri Lanka!*" Sam looked discomfited, wished us good night hastily, and returned to the band.

Connie hissed angrily, "How *dare* you dance with him!" I replied, "He's just being friendly, and he dragged me to the floor, what could I do. He's just a nice, old man, what's there to be jealous of him?" He sneered, "Your sister went with an *old* man, didn't she?" A jibe at Nilanthi, as Heron was so much older than her. Sam was about sixty then. I did not dance with Sam after that, as Connie made sure, and danced with me for the rest of the night.

Cristobel came one day soon after, and asked if she could borrow that skirt for some occasion, so I told her, "You can have it for keeps." She was very happy. And another time, when I knitted a lacy-patterned jumper, in hot- pink angora wool, Cristobel wanted that too. Although I just finished knitting it, and had not worn it yet, I gave it to her, because I was very fond of her, and treated her like a sister.

She did not have a steady job then, and could not afford to buy expensive clothes, so I was sorry, and helped whenever I could. I even gave her a pretty ruby ring, that she coveted. I did not mind distributing my clothes or personal items, as long as it made someone happy.

A few days later, our lives were jolted once again, when Composite Buyers retrenched Connie on 17 August 1990. He handed over his company car, and this time too, he was paid only a few months wages, which was about ten or twelve thousand dollars, and included his superannuation contribution. He was totally shattered once again, and left the company car, a silver Falcon, at the office in Ferntree Gully, then walked back home. This was a bitter blow, as he was doing well at Coles, before Peter persuaded him to join Composite Buyers.

Connie went through a dreadful time at this second retrenchment, and life became even more tense now. He was very dejected, as he could not find a suitable job, although he tried several places. We went around in the same circle, like two mice on a treadmill, repeating the same destructive pattern. Although he promised not to over-indulge in whisky, it was his only solace now to cope with this adversity.

A month later, one of his previous colleagues at Woolworths, offered him a few hours casual work, doing general office work, photocopying etc. He had no choice, but to accept this job. This was a sad come-down for him, from building supervisor, with a company car, generous fringe benefits, and freedom, to an office-boy.

While I was at work, he cleaned the house, cooked, tidied the garden, and did all the odd jobs around the place. But, his only relief every evening, was alcohol, as he tried to forget his troubles. This period in our lives was worse than ever, and I escaped to work. I was back on full-time hours to help with the budget, as we did not want to slide back to debt and financial disaster.

Christian, who seemed to have grown up overnight, while we battled on with Stacy, and with each other, started seeing Linda, a lovely fifteen-year old girl, who lived nearby in Rowville Lakes Estate. He brought her over to introduce her one day. But after Linda left, Connie berated Christian, "You *can't* bring any girlfriends home, *unless* you are serious about marrying her! I will *not* tolerate that, do you hear?"

This old-fashioned notion was exacerbated, because of his brother, Paul's way of life from the age of fifteen. He brought a string of girlfriends home, and had not settled down with any of them as yet. His girlfriends tagged along to all the family get-togethers too, and after we got to know them well, he invariably broke up a few months later, and found another.

Connie was furious with Paul, and feared that our sons would follow his bad example. But I knew Stacy and Christian were sensible, and I talked to them about the facts of life, so I was confident they would behave wisely.

Christian was quiet when he went to bed that night, but I told him I really liked Linda, as she seemed to be such a well-mannered girl, and we became good friends from then on. But Linda did not visit often, as Christian may have told her about Connie's archaic notions, and attitude, so he spent all his free time at her place.

In the past few years, Christian had spent his evenings, and weekends at David and Eileen's place, our neighbours, who lived two doors from us. They had young boys, and one girl, who adored Christian, and treated him like their big brother. As Christian was keen on cars, and mechanics, he liked to hang around David, and watch him fixing cars, or go out with them when the young boys went for car races with David.

Now that he had a girlfriend, he did not spend as much time at David's, and the little boy, Michael, ran across often to ask me, "*Where's* Christian? Is he coming to visit us?"

Geraldine, our neighbour, divorced Jeff, and was seeing another man, Alan now. Birdie and George sold their home in Adelaide, where they lived for over thirty years, and moved to Bexsarm Crescent, in Rowville, one street before ours. Birdie said that after their son Brian died, they just wanted to move away, as his wife was now with someone else, and living her own life.

We had many good times with Birdie and George, as I was very fond of them, and enjoyed their company. I bonded with them, because they too lost an only son, so we supported each other. They were sad to hear about Rosie, especially Geraldine, who had taken a great liking to her. She told me that her marriage to Jeff was on the rocks for a long time. And they had hoped Adam's birth would save it, but they grew further apart.

Her parents, however, were glad her marriage was over, because George said, "Jeff is the *laziest* fellow imaginable! Never did anything around the house to help Geraldine. Only worked every night and slept all day." George helped her financially, so she could stay in the same house with Adam. Her new partner, Alan, visited her often, and they planned to get married soon.

Just before Christmas that year, we heard that Malcolm suffered a severe heart attack, and was in hospital. He was working too hard, trying to build his house in Pannipitiya, which was still incomplete, after several years of snail-like progress. I sent him a card wishing him well, and I wrote to Indrani too.

After all the recent trouble with Stacy, we thought it would be a good idea to send him abroad to get away from bad company, and to broaden his horizons. I spoke to Rosie, who was quite happy to have him for a holiday, and Connie asked Cuckoo if Stacy could visit him too. He agreed, and so later that year, we decided to send Stacy to London, and Germany.

Stacy too wanted to get away from Melbourne, due to various reasons, and we drove him to Tullamarine Airport on 9 December 1990. It was sad, and very painful as we said goodbye, to think that my young son was leaving home for the first time. Stacy was apprehensive about his journey. But I reassured him that he would be fine, as Nelune was flying to London too, and would meet him in Colombo. This was a relief, as Stacy was only eighteen years then. Although he acted tough, he was naive in many ways, when it came to worldly matters, and mundane details of travelling overseas.

He looked very handsome, and debonair in a dark suit. Christian and Stacy were of average height, and very good-looking boys. I was concerned about them not growing any taller than Connie and me, when they were younger. But with all their sport and cycling, especially Christian, they grew much taller than their parents.

I hugged Stacy now, and wished him all the best. He had such a charming smile (without braces now), and beautiful, smiling, grey eyes. How much he reminded me of Nihal at that age, when he left for London. I was happy for Stacy, and hoped he could sort himself out, away from the troubled home environment, and negative influence of some friends.

Anthony called me one night just after Stacy left, and was very rude. He told me that it was impossible for him to stay at Rosie's place, because she was very ill then, and we had to arrange another place for Stacy. Then Janice called me next day, and said that Stacy could stay with them, and she was more than happy to have him. I was very grateful for her kindness, as Stacy was very happy to be with Janice and her family. The relatives overseas loved him, and thought he was a delightful person, so I was glad he was getting on.

Stacy impressed everyone with his keen intelligence, ready wit, and pleasant personality, and he had a loving, gentle disposition towards everyone too. He loved animals, and wanted me to get a kitten or a puppy when he was younger. That Christmas was very sad, without Stacy at home, and I missed him dearly. Connie and I went for evening Mass on Christmas Eve.

The next few days were spent visiting some of his family members, and Aunty. Christian spent time with Linda and her family, as they visited her grandmother quite often in Lara, near Geelong. He was still a loving, caring son to me, and we had long chats whenever he was home. I was happy he had a nice girlfriend, and he enjoyed spending time with Linda, and her family.

Connie decided to send Stacy on to Berlin, after Christmas, to spend time with Cuckoo. But once he arrived in Berlin, Cuckoo kept calling us regularly, to give us an update. Something went wrong there, as Stacy associated with people who smoked marijuana, and took other drugs too, (Cuckoo said). Stacy's personality changed overnight, and his mood swings resulted in destructive behaviour sometimes.

Cuckoo called at midnight once, to tell us that Stacy stayed out every night, and he feared for his safety. Stacy wrote sometime later, saying that he wanted to return home. But I replied that it was not the right time, as we intended selling the house in Rowville. In retrospect, I truly regret that we asked him to stay on a few more months, and travel back to London, as Cuckoo and Regina were going away on holiday.

They dropped Stacy off at the station, and he travelled to Frankfurt by train. He boarded a plane to London from there, but had no place to stay, so he ended up staying at Anthony's and Barbara's place. Anthony was fuming, because Stacy was sent off to London without proper arrangements. He called Cuckoo immediately, and berated him for sending him back. Cuckoo was very upset, and said that Anthony was the rudest man he had ever spoken to, and was taken aback by Anthony's heavy-handed manner, and arrogance. Stacy ended up staying a few days with Anthony and Barbara before he returned home.

My career progressed well now, as I established myself, and was respected as a hard-working, honest person. I always put on a bright smile at work, no matter what was going on at home, so most of them did not have the slightest inkling about my problems. The only two people who were aware of my troubles were Heather, who had surprisingly taken me under her wing, and Lesley, a pleasant, single mother in her thirties. Her good-looking son, Sam, was five years then, and she doted on him, as her whole world was wrapped around him.

Heather still intimidated me, although she had thawed, and developed a luke-warm affection for me. When I came to work looking quite distressed on some days, she wheedled the truth out of me. So she knew all about Connie's behaviour, and the violent altercations between him, Stacy, and me. Very soon, she supported, and helped me to progress in the department. When she learnt of my heart problem, she changed her attitude, and treated me quite well.

And she sent me out to the counter, and reception often, saying, "You have great people skills, and you help calm down angry clients." It was amusing though, when a client once said, "Can I speak to the little black Sheila who helped me yesterday? She was very nice, and I want to see her again." When one of the ladies told me this, and asked me to interview the man, I could not help but laugh at this description. From that day onwards, I asked the staff members, "Does anyone want to see the little *black Sheila* today?"

Heather nominated me to attend several courses that the department and Union offered, as she was my direct supervisor. I attended these courses regularly at Box Hill, and other venues, and found them very useful.

One of the courses was on being "assertive'" and I learnt that my problem was, I had never been assertive with Connie right from the start. The trainer said, "Passive people have no choice but resort to *Flight* not *Fight*, when confronted with problems."

I gained a lot of insight through these self-development courses, and in my heart, I was always waiting for the right time to take control of my life. The trouble with me then, was that I was hopelessly confused, and an emotional wreck. I wanted the comfort, security, and all that being married to Connie meant. And to continue living in the beautiful home that I created with so much love, and attention to artistic detail.

On the other hand, I wanted to break the shackles of a dysfunctional, and unhappy marriage, that never seemed to improve. We just tore each other apart every time we tried to reach out to each other. And it made me think of that line from Rudyard Kipling, "Two islands shouting across oceans of misunderstandings."

Connie now wallowed in a morass of self-pity, and misery about his retrenchment. But ever since I knew him, he was always a miserable person, and born under an unhappy, discontented star. Even when he had a good, stable job, and material comforts, he always found something to be angry and miserable about.

I burnt with resentment at every insult and hurtful word he spoke. But he thought when he said "Sorry" everything was fine, and never understood the power of words; that once spoken, they could never ever be taken back, and they take a life of their own, living forever and ever in a person's memory.

I could not help accumulating all the hurtful things, until they became a mountain of resentment and grief. As a good Catholic, I tried to forgive, but I did not *forget*. I was God-fearing, attended Sunday Mass, and holy days of obligation, but Stacy and Christian stopped going to church, when they were in their teens. I told Connie not to force them to join us, because religion was an individual choice. In spite of his grumbling and nagging, they steadfastly refused to go to church, although they had a Catholic education.

In the meantime, Connie found part-time work as a draftsman in a local company, and we managed with one car once again. He kept busy around the house and garden, when he was not working. I suffered a few more tachycardia attacks, which usually ended up with a few days in hospital. It was very trying, and each time I was admitted to emergency, the doctors advised me that I should seriously consider an operation. I kept putting it off though, and was on various kinds of medication, and even tried naturopathic remedies (much to the heart specialist's scorn).

On 14 January 1991, I woke up with a vivid recollection of a dream I had the night before. At first, it was a muddled, hazy sort of a dream, but then things began to happen. Suddenly, there I was, hanging precariously from the window ledge of a tea factory, of all places! Even the place was familiar. It was Wanarajah Estate in Dickoya. The sound of whirring machinery vibrated in my ears, as I desperately tried to climb in through a window. I could even see Mr Fernandez, the Tea Maker, standing on the back steps of his house and waving at me quite nonchalantly.

As I glanced up, all I could see were evil, menacing faces, intent on capturing me, and feeding me to the voracious machines to make "tea chowder" out of me. People everywhere, above and below, all intent on destroying me. My lacerated fingers groped along the window ledge, and next moment, I was clutching wildly at empty space around me. Arms, legs flying through the air, and yet, no thuds, no bumps, no hard landings. Miraculously soft and airy was my descent to the bottom, and as it happens in dreams, no broken limbs or bruises either. I picked myself up, and started running and running in the gathering darkness. Shadows leapt out behind and around me.

Now I felt the parched agony in my mouth, and my breath came out in tortured gasps. My heart pounded like thunder, and yet, I ran and ran. Then I knew I would faint with exhaustion, because my panting breath emanated in such deafening gasps, that it sounded like thunder claps in my ears. Surely, my pursuers must have heard the drum beats of my thudding heart?

Then I glimpsed the hedge at Granny's place in Maharagama, and I dived into the bushes to catch my breath. My pursuers stopped, and vanished into the thicket as well. As I lay almost dying, like a fish in the last throes of its agony, quivering, and swallowing a lungful of oxygen, my heart raced like the Orient Express. And the pulsating beats were so thunderously fierce and rapid, that my head spun around. I knew I must give up my ghost now, as I could not breathe anymore.

Closer, closer now, I see the shadow drawing ever closer, and ready to pounce, attack, and destroy me. I am unable to breathe. Faster, faster, pounding faster, my heart gives way, and I collapse.

When I opened my eyes, I was in bed, but my heart beat was abnormally rapid, and I was bathed in cold perspiration. I tried to remember why I was so frightened, and why I was gasping for breath. As the mists cleared in my foggy memory, I recalled my nightmare, and I wondered, can one really be *frightened* to death in a dream?

My pounding heart warned me that if I had not woken up in time, I would have surely died of fright in my sleep. Sweet dreams tonight (I hoped), and not be scared to death. Perhaps that was how people "died" in their sleep. No one will ever know what night terrors overcame them, and snuffed out their lives. I wondered what that dream meant, but still cannot interpret it.

I always remembered to send birthday cards to Malcolm and Indrani, as their birthdays were one day apart in April. This year was no exception. Malcolm asked me for a model train engine, as he was an avid miniature train collector. I promised I would look for that particular engine, which I did, and made inquiries everywhere, but did not find that model. He had a marvellous collection of trains, and a whole room in his house was set up with train tracks and model towns.

I called him on Easter Sunday to wish him for his birthday. Christine and Rosie were in Ceylon then, as Rosie always went home for Granny's birthday at the end of April. And even now, she was with Granny, no matter how ill she was.

Rosie spoke to me, after I greeted Malcolm. She said that a few days before, Malcolm suffered a second heart attack, and the doctor advised him to take it easy, and not exert himself too much. I was very happy to hear Rosie sounding more like herself, and quite cheerful and exuberant like before.

When Malcolm spoke to me, in answer to my questions about his health, he replied, "This Rosie is *fussing* over me for nothing! I'm quite well, don't worry about me. Thanks for trying to get that engine for me Dolly. If I can only make it to my fiftieth birthday, I'll be just fine! Take care and God bless." I replied, "Goodbye and God bless you too." I had posted their birthday cards the day before.

Rosie called late at night on Wednesday, 3 April. Malcolm suffered a third heart attack at about 3pm Ceylon time. He was forty nine years old, and just one week away from his fiftieth. I remembered his words, "If I could *only* make it to my fiftieth, I'll be fine!" How sad and ironic life was! Malcolm was devastated about Rosie's illness, and feared she would be dead within the year. And there was Rosie, recovering gradually, almost back to her normal self, and Malcolm suffered a third heart attack. He did not survive the last one, and died without regaining consciousness.

His doctor had advised him to take things easy, and to avoid stress. He was building a house in Pannipitiya then, which alone was stressful enough, especially in Ceylon, where "builders from hell" drove one crazy with their constant delays, and snail-like progress.

Rosie told me, that contrary to doctor's orders, Malcolm walked a long distance in scorching heat, to finalise a bank loan, and that evening he was rushed to hospital with severe chest pains. He was a diabetic for many years, and the third heart attack was fatal. So, instead of Rosie, Malcolm left us suddenly.

It was a terrible blow to everyone, as he was a very loving and caring uncle, brother, and son. Anthony and Marie attended his funeral, and Ammie was devastated, as she cried on the phone and told me, "My darling brother is no longer here to help and comfort me. He was such a wonderful brother!"

I was deeply shaken, and I grieved for a kind, gentle, peace-loving uncle, who was more like a big brother to me for as long as I remembered. Tears were of no avail; death strikes randomly and suddenly, and life goes on. Malcolm was buried at Pannipitiya cemetery on 8 April.

Chapter 19

I suffered another severe tachycardia attack while I was at work in early June 1991. The ambulance arrived within minutes, and one of my friends rang Connie, who drove to the hospital behind the ambulance. He stayed with me in emergency, until he knew what the doctors intended doing.

This was his better side, as he was very concerned whenever I was rushed to hospital. But later, he told me, "How many *other* husbands would spend their time by their wife's bedside when they get sick? You consider yourself *lucky* that I care so much about you!" I did not reply, although I wanted to say that there were several husbands, who cared just as much, or more about their wives.

He developed "sympathy pains syndrome" ever since I suffered the first attack. And every time I had one, or any other illness, Connie immediately developed the *exact* symptoms. While I was treated in emergency, he went to casualty, and complained of chest pains, and asked the nurses to do an ECG etc. A doctor checked him, and said he was fine, but he kept on massaging his chest all the time he was at my bedside.

He looked haggard and worried, and moaned, "It's the *anxiety* I go through every time you end up here, I get severe chest pains!" Poor Connie. Perhaps he craved notice and sympathy, as he walked around rubbing his chest constantly, and seeking attention, as if he was the patient.

I tried to be patient and tolerant of his idiosyncrasies, but it was irritating, because I was so unwell, and *he* wanted me to fuss over him. While I recovered in hospital for a couple of days, he visited, looking angry and flustered, as he recited a litany of complaints about everything, including the dog, Christian, and every other issue. He was insensitive, and did not realize I could not face so much anxiety and stress especially after an attack.

I was drained, after morphine and shock treatment. If I tried to hint gently that I was tired and in pain, he retorted angrily, "*No one* knows what *I* have to go through! It's bad enough you getting sick like this, but I have to put up with all these other problems as well!"

When I returned home after a few days in hospital, we argued fiercely over some issue, and he locked himself in Christian's room, and yelled, "Get out, if you are not happy with me!"

I went back to work after a week, and everyone said I looked awful, as I was worn-out and pale. When I confided in Shirani, she was very concerned about me, and decided to move out again. I looked for a flat close to work, and told Shirani that it was definitely the *last* time, as I just could not live with Connie any longer. The family doctor advised me too, "Try and avoid stress and conflict, as it will kill you, if you keep getting these attacks so often." He had no inkling of the daily stress at home.

A few weeks later, Shirani drove me around looking for a place, and I found a one-bedroom flat in Boronia, close to where I worked. I had no car, as Connie dropped me at work every morning, and picked me up in the evenings.

He applied for a drafting position at Safeway head office in Mulgrave, when a vacancy was advertised in early July. I typed up his resume, and he rushed off to post it one evening. A few days later, he was pleased when he got the job, as he was selected from about one hundred and fifty applicants. This eased my mind considerably, and I did not feel too guilty about leaving him, now that he had a permanent job. His self-esteem restored, his mood improved slightly, and he started working full-time. Connie was happy for the time being, as our financial situation eased greatly. But we just did not communicate anymore, as we were caught up in a circle of hurt and anger most of the time. I could hardly stop crying when I went to work some days, because I was up all night, due to an altercation at home.

Some of my good friends were very supportive, especially the social workers there. Heather was a staunch ally, and Lesley too. They grew close to me, and so did Cindy, Lorraine, Lynne, and Yu-lin. Our supervisor, Wayne, was a great boss, and the kindest man I worked with. He was always supportive, and helped me in many ways.

Heather planned my move this time. Her friend volunteered to bring his van and trailer to transport the new lounge-suite I bought, and a single bed. That was all the furniture I was taking. I could not take the much-loved electric organ, and had to sacrifice that, as I could always get another keyboard, I consoled myself. And I thought that if I had my familiar things around me, perhaps I would not be so shattered and desolate when I moved out of my beautiful home.

About two months ago, I had bought a long-haired, ginger kitten from a pet shop, for ten dollars, and Christian named it "Tiger." But he asked me apprehensively, "Does *Dad* know you bought a kitten? Did you ask his permission?" I laughed, "No, but I'm sure he will like the kitten, as it's so cute!" Connie did like Tiger very much.

He built a shelf over Dash's kennel, and I put Tiger in a basket up there, to keep him safe from Dash. After a few days though, Tiger jumped down and snuggled inside Dash's kennel. I found him quite safe and content sleeping on Dash's stomach. Those two unlikely pets formed a lasting bond. Dash, who was so fierce and aggressive with all and sundry, did not blink an eye when Tiger playfully snatched his bone from under his nose. It was very amusing to watch Tiger frisking around Dash all day, as he had well and truly "adopted" Tiger.

Now, I was incredibly distressed to leave my pets behind, but what else could I do, as pets were not allowed. The flat was clean, and convenient, so I signed a six months lease. My job at Social Security, secured the estate agent's instant approval.

He was quick to inform me that I got the flat because I had permanent employment. I was still weak after my last attack, and took a couple of weeks to recover.

Shirani advised me to take care, and not to get too tired. She also gave me her old Mazda, as she bought a new car after many years. The Mazda was manual, and I did not know how to drive it. But she said I could learn, and when I did, I could keep the car. I thanked her for her generosity, and hoped I could learn to drive it quickly.

The day before I left, my heart ached when I looked at Christian's face, as I loved him with all my heart. I wanted to tell him that I was leaving, but was tongue-tied and emotional. And I yearned to tell him that I had to leave because of Connie's behaviour, and not because of anything Stacy and he did. But I just could not get the words out, and so kept silent.

I can still picture Christian walking around that morning in July 1991, as I planned to leave early. Connie was at work, and I took a chance, as he sometimes came home during the day. Christian told me he was going to the city with some friends, so I was happy. But he came back unexpectedly, just as the man was loading the bed into the trailer. He asked me, "Where is he taking the bed Mum?" I replied, "He's buying it." Then the man returned later, and loaded the lounge-suite. Christian did not come back again, and I thought he may have gone to his friend's place.

Lesley arrived in her car, and I packed my clothes in large, plastic bags, dumped them in the back seat, and breathed a sigh of relief, because I was escaping for good.

A few of my friends gathered in the unit later that afternoon, and helped me unpack. They tried to boost my confidence, as they could see I was very upset, and assured me of their help anytime. After they left, I fell down on my knees, and thanked God for helping me to get away. I meant to write letters to Christian and Connie later. But right now, I was shattered once again, now that I left home; this time I hoped it was permanent.

Shirani and Nelune called in the night, and said that Connie rang them and asked where I was. They would not tell him, but when Christian asked Shirani, "Where is my Mum?" she was very upset, but replied that she did not know. A few days later, Nelune visited, and stayed a couple of days with me. We drove to Shirani's one afternoon, and Christian told me later that he saw us driving down Stud Road. He had followed with his friend, but lost us somewhere along the way.

I walked to work, as I did not know how to drive the manual car yet. This time, I was determined not to turn back, and forgive him so easily. Connie called me at work, and begged me to come home. He said he was sorry, but I told him, "Go see a counsellor, and sort out your problems, because I'm sick and tired of it all." I was emotionally drained, and cried over the phone. Heather was sympathetic, and told me, "Be strong."

I got into the Mazda every evening, and it hopped like a kangaroo, when I drove to the shopping centre car park, to learn how to drive it properly. I had a crazy time though, as the car jerked and "bunny-hopped" along. I tried to teach myself, but alas, to no avail, as I could not master the gears. It was a wonder that I managed to get it back to the flat and park it there.

The evenings and nights were bitterly cold, with only a small gas heater in the lounge, which did not warm up the bedroom. I snuggled under layers of sheets, blankets, and a bedspread, but I still shivered so much that my teeth chattered. I did not have an electric blanket, and the cold was so intense, that I stayed awake all night, wondering if the chilly presence of a ghost froze the very air.

A week passed by, and I thought I would be alright, if only I could get Dash and Tiger, as I was settled in now. I did not have to tell the agent about it, as they could stay indoors. So, a few days later, Heather drove me home, and I put Tiger in a cardboard box, Dash on a lead, and returned to the flat.

I did not know then that my actions were the talk of the family circle. News spread to Berlin that I took "everything" from home and ran away. Stacy was in Berlin then, and Cuckoo received daily bulletins from Esme, Geraldine, and Connie.

Cuckoo heard many negative things about me, as Esme, Geraldine, and Connie, gave him their versions of the situation. They told Connie to change locks in the house, as I would come back to take all the furniture away, so he changed the locks. When Stacy returned home, he told me about their malicious gossip.

I dropped in at Esme's one morning, and gave her my house keys. I did not enter into any discussion with them, as Paul was aloof, and so was Esme, but she said, "Whatever you both decide to do, good luck." I could not blame them for their prejudiced attitude, because Connie presented such a different picture of a devastated, loving husband. So they believed it was all my fault, and he was blameless.

He kept calling me at office several times. I felt very vulnerable when he cried and begged me to give him another chance to make our marriage work. I was reduced to tears every time he called, because of my emotional state, and physical weakness after the last attack. In response to his pleading, I agreed to see him one evening, and accompany him to meet Fr McKay, our previous parish priest. Connie had called him, and told him about our separation, and asked him to help us with counselling.

I gave Connie my address reluctantly, because I knew he would start visiting me, and wear down my resistance. Later that evening, he picked me up, and we met Fr McKay in Scoresby. When Father asked me what was the problem, I blurted out, "He's *always* saying hurtful things, especially after drinks, and he gets very violent with me, and Stacy. He says that from the time he met me, he has been running to doctors, because I'm sick, and that hurts me deeply because it's not my fault I'm not well. We just don't see eye to eye on anything, and argue all the time, ending in violence." Father listened quietly, and said, "Conrad, *remember,* marriage is for better or for worse, in *sickness* and in health."

Connie did not utter one word, but just sat there, absorbed in his shoes. He did not explain his behaviour, and just mumbled, "I *sometimes* take a little bit extra and say things I don't mean. I lose my temper sometimes, and I have a habit of spitting in Stacy's face when I'm angry." Other than that, he could not explain *why* he got so angry and violent, or drank too much.

I wanted him to tell Fr McKay what it was that I said or did, to make him so angry with me. But he just could not, or would not express his feelings, even when I asked him, "*Why* don't you tell me what upsets you so much?" He replied, "Nothing, I can't think of *anything* you say or do to annoy me, it's all my fault. I'm sorry. I won't drink too much again or hit Stacy or you."

Father advised, "I think it's *best* that you both see a marriage counsellor, and try to patch up your differences. Try to make a go of your marriage." Connie promised faithfully that he would do all that was necessary to make our marriage work, and that he would see a counsellor as well. Father spent a couple of hours with us, trying to find out what exactly was wrong in our marriage. When he understood there was no third party involved in our lives, he wondered why we failed to understand each other at all, and were living in such a violent, self-destructive environment.

I then said, "Connie's drinking is a problem, as he becomes more aggressive and irrational." At this, he promised to stop drinking, and I replied, "I will try to be more tolerant, and patient once again." Father nodded, "*Try* to get to know each other again, and go out *alone*, not only to visit your family Conrad, take time for each other, and try to work out your problems." The outcome of this session was reconciliation, forgiveness, and the promise to "try again."

I believed Connie, and expected him to start seeing a counsellor immediately, and told him that I would return home only on these conditions. He promised over and over again. So I agreed to return home, just like that. This time, our separation lasted over a month.

Each time I moved out, I vowed it was for good, and that I would never go back to Connie. But when I was alone, I broke down, and regretted our failure to make our marriage work. I was an emotional wreck, and being susceptible, and compassionate, I believed he would change, and treat me better, because it was his behaviour that drove me away. But saying "Sorry" was so easy for him, and though he tried hard to refrain from drinking for a day or two, he always reverted to his destructive, irrational self before too long. It was always worse than before, and he told me, "I don't trust *anyone* in this world," because he had more cause to doubt me.

He insisted that he would not bring up the past, but he was only human, and I could not blame him totally. I was unable to make a clean break from him, and not fall to pieces when we were apart. I kept things to myself, and seethed with resentment, then reached a boiling point, where I had to escape or explode.

I could not articulate my feelings of anger and frustration, without us ending in a futile argument. It was madness to keep coming back, and trying over and over again. And I asked myself, how many times do I have to forgive and forget. It was something to do with my Catholic upbringing too, because I felt guilty, and could not be at peace with myself, knowing Connie was hurting so much, when I left him. I tried to forgive him "seventy times seven" as Jesus Christ told us we must do, when someone asked Him the same question, "How many times must I forgive my brother?"

No matter how hard-hearted I tried to be, I hated the thought of causing anyone pain, not even my worst enemy. I believed that leaving him was the only solution, to make him change his ways. But somehow, it was only a temporary measure, and before long, we were caught up in the same, vicious circle.

A few days after our session with Father, Connie's brother, Paul, came in a trailer, and took the lounge-suite and bed back to Rowville. When Paul saw me, he said, "I'm happy you and Connie are back together again! The trouble with us de Sielvie's, is that we have bad mouths and tempers!"

I was back home at the end of July, and tried to resume a semblance of normalcy. Connie told his family not to mention anything about my leaving home. But Aunty, Wendy, Babs, and Cristobel, called to ask how I was. And I told them the real reason why I left again, because I knew he kept up a facade, and never accepted that he was to blame.

Once we reconciled though, we tried to forget past failures and move on. He could be very nice and loving, when he wanted to, and that was all I ever wanted from him; to treat me kindly, instead of grinding his teeth when he spoke, or barking orders at the children and me. He found it difficult to pay me compliments, or appreciate what I did. But I knew he praised me to his mother, and to my sisters and friends.

They told me, "Connie thinks the world of you, and he always says how well you do everything, and what a good cook you are etc. etc." Aunty said, "Connie will die, if you leave him because he loves you so much!" I replied, "Then why doesn't he show it by his behaviour and the way he talks to me? You'd think he'd learn a lesson by now and try to behave better?"

We were happy, and peaceful, when he did not nag or find fault with Stacy, Christian or me. I realized too late though, that he could not help the way he was born. Just like a scorpion, who cannot help stinging, Connie could not control his tongue or his anger, and did not know how to be close to me emotionally.

When he knew I was upset, or annoyed about something he said or did, he could be very persuasive and tender. And lull me into a false sense of wellbeing, so as to cajole me into having sex. Afterwards, he withdrew into his shell, and was indifferent or angry.

He bought trinkets for my birthdays, anniversaries, and Christmas' and everyone said, "You are so lucky! Connie gives you so much of jewellery!" He knew I liked rings and bracelets, so he bought me quite a few over the years. But they were not worth thousands of dollars, as I never cared for diamonds, and favoured precious or semi-precious stones.

When he behaved badly, I told him, "I don't want all these trinkets! I just want you to treat me kindly, that's all I want!" He never understood that all the gold and jewellery in the world, could not compensate for the lack of love and understanding in our marriage.

Christian was very happy when I was home again, and he brought Linda over often. And I was glad to get better-acquainted with her. Connie complained, as he did not want Christian to bring any girlfriends home. So, we started arguing about this, and I said, "Linda is a beautiful, respectable girl from a good family, and there's nothing wrong with her spending time with Christian here at home." But he followed me around, and nagged me to death, whenever they were listening to music in his room, or just chatting. Once, I was so angry that I screamed at him to leave me alone, as I could not bear his non-stop nagging any longer.

Christian heard us arguing, walked into the kitchen slowly, and said, "Mum, I don't want you to leave home again! I'll tell Linda not to come here, because she heard Dad calling her a bitch, and now she has gone off home really upset!" Christian was in tears, as he ran after Linda to pacify her. Connie was unrepentant, and I tried hard to avoid confrontation, so we tread warily around the edge of an emotional volcano.

We celebrated Christian's eighteenth birthday at a local Chinese restaurant, and Connie invited his whole family. Shirani and Ranjith did not attend that party. Some stony-faced members of his family gave me cold looks, but I put on a brave face, and got through the evening for Christian's sake. Linda was there too, so we chatted with each other and Christian.

I was very attached to her now, as she was such a warm-hearted girl. She was fond of me too, and called me "Mrs De." Once, she bought a few metres of white crepe, and asked if I could sew her an outfit, which I did, and she looked stunning in it. Christian bought some fabric from Spotlight too, and wanted me to sew a purple jacket, lined with black, quilted-satin. He looked very handsome in it, and I still have that jacket. He was interested in designing clothes, and knew how to sew and knit, which was handy.

Connie and I settled down to a shaky truce, and we decided to add a garage and fireplace to the house, now that we were secure in our jobs. I had liked the gas heater with a mantelpiece over it, in the unit I rented. So Connie decided to build an open fireplace, because I always wanted one. We applied for a loan, to build the garage and fireplace.

He was busy some nights, as he drafted plans to build a garage adjoining the house. And he cut down all the trees and shrubs in that area to make way for the building. Fiore, a local builder, was the father of one of Stacy's friends, and he agreed to do the work. Fiore wanted ten thousand dollars to build the garage, a large outdoor barbeque, and an open fireplace in the lounge, with a tiled hearth.

It looked great when it was finished, and I loved sitting there with my pets sometimes. And it was amusing to watch Tiger jump up in the air, each time crackling sparks and embers flew out. I enjoyed reading or knitting by the fireside, as it was cosy and warm. Tiger kept me amused with his antics, and was an adorable, lovable cat. Although Christian named him "Tiger" he was more leonine, and reminded me of the cowardly lion in the "Wizard Of Oz."

Cuckoo phoned frantically almost every night, complaining about Stacy, and that he kept company with drug-users. One day, he said that Stacy broke a crucifix that belonged to Regina's mother, and Cuckoo was very upset about his behaviour.

He rarely spoke to me now, and was aloof, and when I picked up the phone once, he did not even greet me, but said, "Can I speak to Connie?" He had been very close and dear to me, but now believed the worst, because I had left home.

Connie told me that Cuckoo referred to me now as, "Your *wife*," and hardly mentioned my name. It took many years for him to resume his cordial friendship with me. Stacy wrote long letters, saying he wanted to come home. I replied that it was not a good time, and advised him to travel around Europe for a few more months. But he said that Cuckoo wanted him to return home.

Stacy came back in early December 1991, and we picked him up at the airport. I was very glad to see him again after so long, and he too appeared to be happy and relieved to be back. He told us many anecdotes about his travels on the Continent. And grown more mature in some ways, as he was more patient and tolerant towards Connie.

Stacy gave me a beautiful, crystal, paper-weight he bought in the States, when he was in transit, and he still had his guitar. He spent most of his time singing, and playing it in the bathroom. When he came out, he said, "The acoustics are much better in the bathroom, Mum."

He strummed his guitar endlessly, and appeared to be alright. But sometimes he had alarming mood swings, which I now know, was due to his experimenting in mild drugs. As he did not take any now, he suffered withdrawal symptoms, because he became moody and irrationally angry.

When I came home after work, and tried to rest a while some evenings, he sat on the floor in our bedroom, and cried in frustration, "I've travelled around so many places, and now, here I am, back at square one, in the same groove! I'm so confused and lost, and so uncertain of the future!"

When I asked him what he wanted to do, he was bewildered and distressed, and burst out, "What's the *point* of doing anything! We all just die anyway!" I replied, "If all the people in the world had that same attitude, and didn't achieve anything, then we wouldn't have any of the wonderful music, art, and literature we are privileged to share in this world." He was unconvinced, and did not emerge from his depression for long periods.

I found it difficult to understand his behaviour. And I was very surprised to find he started smoking overseas. He asked Connie for cigarettes, and an occasional beer too. The children in the neighbourhood were impressed with Stacy, and listened to him playing his guitar, and singing, for hours on end. It was still very stressful between Connie and Stacy though. He was a non-conformist, while Connie was a strict disciplinarian, and autocratic in his dealings with Stacy and Christian. This led to many altercations once again.

One day, when he wanted to go to Knox, Connie barked, "Why can't you walk?" And did not want to give him a lift. I was in the car with Connie, when Stacy asked for a lift. Before he could drive off, Stacy jumped in the back seat, and questioned in a hurt voice, "Always so harsh! Why are you so harsh with me Dad?"

When we returned later that evening, Stacy had kicked a hole in the laundry door, as he was so frustrated. When Connie saw the damage, he started shouting at him. Stacy got so angry, that he grabbed the heavy paper-weight from the shelf in the lounge, and hurled it right across the room, where it gouged a hole in the wall over the fireplace.

The day Stacy arrived, he took one look at the new fireplace, and said in his forthright manner, "That's the last thing you need here, as an air-conditioner would have been better!" He made a valid point, because the weather was scorching, and in the high thirties that December. Stacy became argumentative with me too, no matter what we discussed. But I allowed him to vent his frustrations, as he just wanted to be heard.

The four of us, and Linda, went out for dinner to restaurants a couple of times, and Stacy told me, "Christian is lucky Mum, he's allowed to have a girlfriend, and go out with her, but Dad didn't even let me bring any girl home!"

Stacy was watching television quietly one evening, when Connie yelled out, "Put that volume down!" Stacy ignored him. And as Connie continued nagging him,

Stacy dashed the remote control on the floor, rushed to his room, and smashed the window in his bedroom.

The sound of crashing glass brought some neighbourhood children running over to see what was wrong. I cried helplessly, because I felt so sorry for Stacy being nagged all the time. He had no other way to vent his anger and frustration except in destruction.

It was Christmas Eve. I cried bitterly, as the whole situation was getting beyond me again. I did not know how to help Stacy or ourselves. We left him at home, and drove to Esme's. When she saw me, she exclaimed, "Your eyes are so red, have you been crying?" We told her about Stacy, and then Connie said, "Stacy has to live somewhere else, because we can't put up with his mood swings and violent behaviour." I knew Connie was partly to blame for treating him like a little boy, and nagging him constantly for the slightest misdemeanour.

Later that night, Connie asked Babs, if Stacy could stay in her bungalow for some time until he settled down. I knew it would be good for him to have some peace away from Connie. Next day, when Connie told Stacy that he had to move out, he packed up his few belongings in a backpack, and moved into a bungalow in Bab's backyard.

Babs, who was a "Born again" Christian now, introduced Stacy to several of her new-found friends, including Paul Whittaker, a bachelor in his forties, who tried his best to convert Stacy. He visited us a few times, spoke with Stacy, and took a great interest in him. Paul persuaded Stacy to accompany him to their Christian church, where Stacy met some other friends of Bab's. They encouraged him to move to Sydney, for whatever reason, I am not sure. Stacy told me it was to pursue his music, as he had more opportunities in Sydney.

Just before Christmas Eve, Babs held a family gathering, and Linda accompanied us too. Once again, Stacy told me, "Christian is lucky to take his girlfriend to family gatherings, when I wasn't allowed to!" While we were there, Christian, Linda, and I, watched a series called "Dark Shadows" which we were following for some time. Stacy commented, "Mum, that is very anti-social behaviour!" True, I would not normally watch television at a dinner party, but that night, it was chaotic everywhere. Hordes of people (some strangers too), ran around and made so much noise, that I preferred to sit quietly, and watch television, as no one missed us.

Connie was chatting to his family members, and was quite happy; Stacy played the guitar, and sang his favourite song, 'Wish You Were Here' by Pink Floyd. Jeremy and he entertained us with their music for a little while.

A few days later, I saw a letter that Stacy had written to Cuckoo, describing that party. He left the unfinished letter lying on the dining table, and after reading it briefly, I put it back. He made some very astute observations about each family member, and described Connie as being "socially inept." I did not want Connie to read that letter, so I covered it with some paper, and put it on Stacy's desk in his room. I was unsure whether he left it there deliberately, for us to read his comments.

On New Year's Day, 1992, Stacy accompanied us, and some friends to a dance. And he told me, "Mum, I became a 'Born again' Christian, and I was baptised today."

He smiled pleasantly, and I replied, "Good for you Stacy, hope you will be happy in your new-found faith. I'm glad you found God."

Geraldine and Alan were married in January 1992, and they held the reception in a large marquee in their backyard, and invited many people. She asked me to cook a meatball curry, one of her favourite dishes, so I obliged. Stacy went across to wish them too, and had a good time chatting with the guests. Unfortunately, it rained heavily, but we were dry and warm inside the marquee.

When Stacy lived in her bungalow, Bab's said he told her that he hated both of us, and Christian, and wanted to burn the house down. I wondered if he said such a thing. But she was convinced he was on drugs, because he hallucinated, and screamed out that he saw monsters around him. My poor, poor Stacy! I wish with all my heart that I was able to help him then. After Stacy's return, I persuaded Connie to see a counsellor with him, but they went only once.

Stacy told his side of the story; that Connie was physically violent and abusive, hitting, spitting in his face, and nagging him incessantly all through childhood and teen years. Connie did not say anything in self-defence, except that he believed he did the "right thing" disciplining the children, and not sparing the rod.

Towards early January 1992, someone from the Christian community asked Stacy to visit him in Sydney, as he could help further his music career. Stacy wanted to play in a band there, and we thought he would be safe with a Christian man, who was one of Bab's friends. Stacy called to wish us goodbye. And although I was anxious about him going to Sydney alone, I hoped he would be alright with her friends.

The day he was leaving, Connie took him for a movie, "Total Recall" starring Arnold Schwarzenegger, had dinner with him, and then dropped him off at the bus terminal, where he boarded a coach to Sydney. I hoped and prayed with all my heart that he would find what he was searching for, and prosper in all that he did. He told me that he had a better chance to achieve his dreams in music, if he went to Sydney.

When Stacy arrived there, Nelune met him, and took him to a motel that she booked for two weeks, until his friend organized lodgings. After a day or so however, he left with a man whom he had met at Bab's place. This man had promised to further his singing career, and Stacy, being a very naive young boy, believed in him.

We heard later that this "friend" let him down, and did not accommodate him. Stacy then found lodgings with a family in Darlinghurst. He phoned us from time to time when he was broke, and we deposited money into his bank account.

Nelune was upset that he did not stay in the motel. But Stacy contacted her a few days later, and told her he was working in a pub at Darlinghurst, and was staying with some people there. We sent him money on and off whenever he requested, but once, when he asked me $500, I refused. He told me that he had to pay a recording studio, but I was firm, as I thought he wanted it for drugs.

I should have given him the benefit of the doubt, and sent him the money, if it was indeed for a recording session. But how was I to know what his life was like over there? He seemed to be happy enough though, and did not want to return home or to Melbourne.

He sent cards to all the family members that Christmas, including overseas relatives. I hoped and prayed he was settling down, and following his dreams wherever they took him. He was twenty years old, and I thought he was mature enough to handle life sensibly.

One of Stacy's friends, Malter, whom he met in Germany, visited Melbourne in early April that year. Connie called me at work to say that Esme and Paul were bringing him over for a visit that evening. So I rushed to the supermarket after work, and bought some meats for dinner, and was ready when they dropped in. We had a great barbeque, and finished at about nine o'clock that night. Connie and Christian drove Malter back to the city, where he was staying in a motel. He said he was sorry he had missed Stacy, as he was leaving for Germany next day.

Nelune returned from a trip to London on Sunday, 12 April, and I was glad she came back safely. She enjoyed a lovely holiday with Janice and family, and was full of news.

Connie, who worked part-time at Safeway's for about one year since his retrenchment from Composite Buyers, broke the good news that he would be full-time from the 28th of April. I was happy for him, and hoped it would be more secure. In the next few years, he had a company car, and rose to a managerial position in the drawing office. He did not want to draft anymore due to chronic back pain.

I felt like a change one day, and cut my hair very short, but Connie did not like my new hair-style at all, and was annoyed when I walked out of the hairdresser's. He told the hairdresser bluntly, "I married her because of her long hair, now there's nothing left!" I knew he just wanted to hurt me, so I did not reply. Later that day, he frowned as he said, "You look queer with such short hair!"

Most weekends were busy with Connie's family, as they visited often, and stayed long. Aunty liked to spend a few days with us sometimes, as she was really troubled about Cristobel, who lived with her in a small flat in Dandenong. Aunty said she harassed her, and got into violent arguments, and on a few occasions Cristobel had even slapped Aunty in her fury.

Aunty told me, "Bella is unpredictable and dangerous, as she drinks every evening, and doesn't know what she says or does. You can't trust her because she's like a snake in the grass! She can be sweet as honey to your face and then backbite you." I sympathised with her, knowing just exactly how Connie behaved after drinks.

She did not tell Connie about Cristobel though, as she said, "If Connie knows she slapped me, he'll *kill* her! I don't want to create any trouble." And another time, Aunty told me, "Bella slapped poor Esme twice! I don't know what to do with her sometimes! She hasn't got a job, and that's why she's so frustrated without any money. Only playing bingo and gambling with her social security money."

Esme dropped in every single evening, on her way home from work. She sat at the dining table and smoked for hours, ate dinner with us, and then left at ten o'clock or later some nights. Paul hated her smoking, and so she said she "relaxed" at our place, smoking and unwinding before going home.

Connie's brother, Paul, asked us to sign as guarantors for a loan, and then was unable to meet repayments for some time. The finance company contacted Connie and demanded that we repay three thousand dollars. We refused, and he made sure Paul settled the loan eventually.

Soon after that, Esme came with Cristobel one evening, and persuaded us to get a loan of two thousand dollars for Cristobel to buy a car, saying, "I promise I will see to it she pays off the loan in full." When Connie hesitated, I said, "I'm sure it will be alright Connie, let's help her to get a car, then she can look for work."

After a few months however, Esme had great difficulty in getting Cristobel to pay the instalments, and she said, "I wash my hands off the whole thing because I'm fed up asking her to pay the money!" Connie replied, "But Esme, you promised you would make sure she repays the loan!" She did not respond, so we had to pay off that debt until Cristobel repaid us sporadically over six or seven years time. We did not receive payments for a long time, and after one year Connie told her to forget the balance thousand dollars and interest on the loan. But she told Esme, "I paid back *more* than I should have with interest!"

I was very fond of his family, and helped them whenever I could, and was always kind to them. And I treated them well whenever they visited us, and I thought they were sincere. Even when Connie complained or spoke against them sometimes, I defended them, which made him angry.

Cristobel told me, "I visit just to see you, because I hate Connie!" Connie and she clashed often and argued heatedly. He slapped her a couple of times, in the middle of their quarrels, and she hated him for that. When Paul was in his early teens, he spoke rudely to Uncle on one of their visits. Connie beat him severely, and yelled at Paul, "Get down on your knees and say sorry to Daddy, you rascal!"

Aunty and Uncle though, were not too happy, because Aunty cried out, "Connie, stop hitting Paul!" So, these two siblings had cause to be angry with Connie, because they resented his heavy-handed behaviour.

Sherone, Glenn, Valerie, and Ifti wanted to come for dinner one day, on very short notice. I took the afternoon off, shopped at Knox City, and rushed home. And Christian cleaned up the whole house, and laid the table, as he knew we expected guests. He was always very helpful, and considerate. I thanked him profusely, then rested a while before I cooked.

When I woke up on the 1st of May, I heard about the terrible night of racial violence in Los Angeles. The radio stations and newspapers were full of the appalling behaviour of people, looting and killing indiscriminately. I was shocked when I watched the news on television that night. Later, to get my mind off those dreadful scenes of death and destruction, I watched "Pollyanna" starring Hayley Mills, and enjoyed it very much.

The garage was finally completed in late May, after a few weeks of confusion and chaos due to heavy rains, and Dash being restricted in the backyard. Fiore did a professional job, and we were pleased, but we did not enclose the back of the garage, because of the extra cost more. At least the cars were under cover now.

I progressed steadily at work, and won a gazetted position as an administrative service officer, level 3. The section manager, Wayne, broke the good news to me on 2 July. But it was still unofficial, until it appeared in the gazette. I was elated, and could not believe my ears.

It was of paramount importance in the public service to be "gazetted" in a position, as staff who were paid "higher duties" could be demoted to their basic grade whenever it suited management. By now, I was accepted, and respected in the office, and acted at level 4. I was in a supervisory position, and approved work submitted by officers at lower levels.

I organised several "International lunches" at work, and soon became well-known for my hot curries, savoury pan rolls, and pastries. We enjoyed good times then, and I drew up a list of exotic foods, that every staff member volunteered to bring in. We held these lunches every two or three months, and management considered it a great team-building exercise.

I was also appointed stress contact officer, and received training in Box Hill to take on this position. Staff members confided in me, and I listened with empathy to their personal or work problems.

Shirani and Ranjith visited us in early July 1992 for the first time since 1985. He did not visit because of their marital problems, and separation. It was Rosie's birthday that day, and she called me later in the evening. We had a long chat, and I told her that Shirani and Ranjith finally visited us together after so long. She was happy for Shirani and me, as it was very difficult for us to keep visiting each other, when Ranjith and Connie were not on speaking terms.

Christian went out with Linda since he was seventeen, and she was fifteen, and they spent most evenings at home, watching videos with us or on their own. Her father, Paul, was born in New Zealand, but his father was Norwegian. And her mother, Julie, was Australian. Linda had two younger brothers, Mathew and Shane, and a younger sister, Michelle. Christian was very attached to her family, and spent a great deal of time with them, and Linda. He treated Mathew like a younger brother, and Mathew looked up to him as a role model.

We flew to Ceylon on a two week holiday on 17 December that year, and Christian and Linda dropped us at the airport. We boarded Dash in the kennels, and we were packed and ready to go by lunchtime. Christian was in a blue mood when we left, as he was sad to stay back. But he had a job that he was keen on, and could not take time off.

The flight to Singapore was good, with one night's stopover, and we arrived in Colombo the following day at 1am, local time. Nelune and Tanesh picked us at the airport. And it made me very sad to think of previous years, when the whole family were there to meet us, but now things were different.

We drove through dark, deserted roads, and arrived in Maharagama around 3am. Thathie was awake and made coffee for us, but Ammie, who had just woken up, looked very pale and sickly. My heart went out to her, as she looked so unwell. I urged her to go back to bed, and told her we could talk later on in the day, so she was glad.

I was overjoyed to be with my family once again, and really pleased when Menika arrived later on that day with her two sons, the eldest and youngest. It was almost twenty-five years since I last saw her! She had not changed very much. Menika had the same, kind, benevolent manner, and her face was unlined; her figure was still strong and slender, and her black hair untouched with grey streaks. Menika was in her mid-fifties then, and her face shone with goodwill and serenity that was part of her charm.

After many delightful hours of reminiscing about our past, which was irrevocably bound up with hers, we decided to visit Menika's village in a few days time. The poor woman travelled seven hours by bus to see me. Her eldest was sixteen, and the youngest, ten. They were bright, intelligent children, and wore clean, neat clothes. Menika too, was dressed in a snowy-white jacket, and printed sarong, with her hair knotted in a bun at the nape of her neck.

Chapter 20

The political situation was still volatile in the country, and intermittent violence and terror erupted in the north and east of the island. We decided however, to travel up-country in a car, to enjoy the scenery we loved, and drop Menika and her sons in her village. Connie hired a chauffeur-driven car a couple of days later.

We left around two o'clock in the afternoon, as Menika was anxious to get home, after her two day holiday, away from paddy fields. She told me it was imperative to be there soon, as it was sowing season, and she would incur severe penalties, if she did not work on the fields by Tuesday morning. Menika arrived on Saturday, and was restless, as she was a very conscientious worker. Ammie and Thathie looked sad when we left, and I did not realize that they would have liked to join us too, but we had no room in the car.

Connie sat in the front seat, while I sat in the back seat with Menika and her two sons. It was rather crowded, but we hoped to arrive in her village in a few hours time (Connie declared optimistically). It was depressing, and yet delightful to pass so many old familiar buildings, roads, bridges, and towns that looked so different and strange, yet remembered in my memories. A sense of déjà vu pervaded my consciousness, as we drove through steep, winding roads.

I left Ceylon twenty years ago, and soon discovered that nothing ever remains the same. It was a shock to my system, when we finally reached Kandy town around six in the evening, and I found its Babel-like commotion, chaotic. Bus loads of tourists streamed continuously, and the streets seemed very narrow and congested, with people jostling and shoving, hardly able to move an inch.

I sat in silence, wondering if this really was the once serene, and delightful Hill Capital, where as a teenager, I sat in one of the Chinese restaurant's, listening to pop songs on an old Juke Box, and idly watching passers-by through large windows. And a powerful gust of nostalgia swept over me.

We were very hungry by now, but I thought we would be lucky to get a foot inside one of those jam-packed cafes and restaurants. We parked just outside town, and Connie went off with the driver to buy some take-away rice and curry packets. It was obvious we would never make it to Menika's house in time for dinner. Just as we left Kandy town, the heavens opened every flood gate, and the deluge did not abate as we sped through incessant slanted rain that splattered the windows.

I stepped out of the car in Kandy, and stretched my legs for a few minutes, and also drank several cups from my water bottle. But Menika declined even a sip of water, and did not want to move from her position in the car. She sat there placidly, a smile on her calm face, and did not fidget, talk much or drink anything, as she patiently awaited the end of the arduous journey.

Her sons were a little more active though. They enjoyed the various stop-overs on our way, especially at one of the little tea shops, perched precariously on the edge of the high road at Kadugannawa Pass. They ate a snack, and gulped down cups of black tea sweetened like honey. The scenery was truly magnificent, and my soul soared to far-away mountain tops. I glimpsed the silhouette of the famous "Bible Rock" named for its obvious square shape, and not because of any religious association.

As the minutes whizzed by, I felt nauseous, and my head reeled at the never-ending hair-pin bends along the way. The torrential deluge continued, and when Connie told the two boys, "We will get to the village in the next hour," they burst out laughing in uncontrollable mirth. It took four hours by bus from their village to Kandy town, so they thought it was very funny that Connie expected to be there in an hour's time. They giggled and whispered to each other.

I hope I never travel again on a road so bad and fraught with so many precarious bends and sharp inclines. The narrow road disappeared into a tiny laneway in some places; and if another vehicle approached, we reversed until we reached a slightly broader stretch of road, and hugged the hill side until the other vehicle passed by.

Connie kept pressuring the driver to cover the miles in good time, and the driver expertly manoeuvred the car, as it slid at an alarming speed. He kept the car skilfully on the road by sheer force of will, I thought, as visibility was almost nil. All I saw, was a windscreen that looked like a minor waterfall, and wipers that could not wipe away the cascade quick enough.

Menika quietly observed, "It's the monsoon season, and it has been raining heavily for the past few weeks." My nausea was unbearable, and at the first sign of civilisation, we stopped the car, as I needed a soda to settle my churning stomach.

The hair-pin bends, narrow, pot-holed, and mud-encrusted roads after weeks of rain, snaked along the mountain sides. The treacherous precipices plunged hundreds of miles below towards valleys dotted with tiny shacks, and mud-huts nestling in thick mist.

It seemed as if time had stood still in this forgotten, remote region, where Menika lived with her children. Her husband (father of her three sons), was an ailing, elderly man, who died the previous year, and left her to fend for herself with three young children. The journey stretched my nerves to the limit, as the twisting laneway (mistakenly named Main Kandy road), seemed to go on forever.

I bobbed around like an orange in a tub of water, experiencing the most shaky, rackety drive in my life. When I sometimes glimpsed sheer drops on the side of the road, my heart thumped painfully, as the wheels of the car teetered almost on the edge of that rain-softened, muddy road. The slightest mis-calculation on the driver's part would hurl us down the precipice into deep jungles, to remain undiscovered forever, I thought nervously.

Around ten o'clock, when I thought my nerves would snap, we finally arrived at a modest house, situated in the middle of a clean, wide compound. I told Menika we wanted to spend the night in her house, but she insisted that we would be more comfortable sleeping at her "Aiya's" (brother's), house. He was her father's brother, but she called him "Aiya" too.

We remained in the car until Menika spoke to her relatives, and in less than ten minutes, all the lights glowed in the house. Bolts and chains were drawn away, and a tall, thin man hastened to the car with an umbrella. Menika's "Aiya" was a dignified, middle-aged man, who had a warm, welcoming smile on his benevolent face, and his short, plump wife greeted us with a toothy smile as well. Everything seemed to have been settled, and they carried our cases in quickly.

As we walked inside, I noticed long, metal strips placed across the entrance, (building material for future use), they explained, and I walked on them gingerly. My head swam, as Menika showed me to a tiny bedroom. The bed was made up with clean linen, and a warm blanket. I just sprawled across this inviting bed, unable to stay awake any longer. I caught a cold, and suffered from a bad tooth ache as well. And the winding roads made me travel-sick, so I could hardly keep my head up. It was an arduous journey, but a wonderful experience to visit Menika's "village in the mist" and to travel through some of the most breath-taking scenery, (whenever I caught a glimpse through the rain).

Voices droned on all around me, some hushed, and others loud. Menika's relatives were two young girls, one recently married, and heavily pregnant, due in a week's time, and the younger one still in her teens. The pregnant girl's husband, a pleasant young man, with a scarf wrapped around his face, was down with the flu. The young couple vacated their room to give us a bed for the night. I was filled with gratitude and guilt at this demonstration of such unselfish hospitality.

The married couple were staying with her family until the baby was born. The younger daughter smiled shyly and kept staring at me. All of them wanted to help ease my misery, and I was very grateful. But I just wanted to lie down quietly, until my head stopped spinning and settled on my shoulders once again. Even after we stopped moving, I felt like I was still travelling dizzily along that hellish road.

Connie walked into the room with a "tot" of arrack, and persuaded me to swallow it neat (alcohol was his panacea for all ailments). The fiery liquid settled my nausea slightly, and now the whole household urged me to partake in the meal. They warmed up the packets of rice and curry we brought, and soon arrack flowed freely between Connie, driver Duncan, and "Aiya."

The dining room was a long, narrow area, with paddy strewn on the floor, as it was a storage place, and it was strange to feel my feet scrunching on the paddy. The entire family waited on us. They passed jugs of hot water and finger bowls around quickly. Menika still played the role of waiting maid. She did not swallow a morsel, until we ate and settled down. Dinner was a charming, and cosy family affair. My heart went out to these simple, warm-hearted people, and very soon they arranged a folding bed for driver Duncan.

I felt slightly better after dinner, and ventured down a few rickety steps that teetered into a cellar-like room that was the kitchen. A huge fire was ablaze in a corner, and the young man suffering from the flu, sat there with his pregnant wife, warming themselves by the fire. It was a quaint old kitchen, bare and basic, but spotlessly clean. The young girls made tea and coffee next, and the fragrant coffee had an unusual blend of roasted coriander (to ward off chills), and the coffee beans were specially blended for the expectant young mother, they explained.

"Aiya" proved to be an entertaining person. He visited the United States a few years ago as an electrician, and was employed in the embassy. He regaled us with many anecdotes, and we had a very pleasant time. The rain continued without much chance of abating, and I turned in soon, as my cold was worse. But each time I woke up to go to the toilet, the entire family woke up too. The front door was unbolted, and an umbrella provided to protect me from the rain. And I tottered to the precariously situated lavatory at the bottom of the garden.

The "steps" were only muddy indentations carved into the earth, that heavy rain had washed away completely. It was with great difficulty that I manoeuvred the descent, wearing a flimsy dressing gown, head wrapped with a towel, while balancing a large umbrella.

The wind howled, and sheets of rain lanced across the compound as I sat inside the dark lavatory without a light. Connie stood at the top of the pathway, flashing a torch on the shed. I would have been greatly amused, had it not been for the fact that I was freezing, very uncomfortable, and down with a cold.

The entire family retired to bed once I finished, and so did we, but only for fifteen minutes, because my bladder strained again. It was the cold temperature, or stress. Embarrassed, I told Connie that we should go out as quietly as possible, but the ever-vigilant host and hostess were up at the first scrape of the bolt. And there I was in the limelight again, as that zealous family keenly observed, and monitored my second trip to the lavatory. I told Connie, "This won't do at all! I'll ask Menika to give me a bed pan until morning." And so, I finally fell asleep.

The following day was cold, wet, and dreary too, but Menika was up at the first light of dawn. She stood before us, smiling, and handed me a cup of coffee. The years rolled away, and I felt as if I was back in Bandarawela or Hatton, when Menika unfailingly brought a cup of tea, served with the broadest smile on her loving face. What a flashback! I had to slip out of the past with an effort, and return to the very real present. She insisted on emptying the bed pan, and I went out to the well for a hasty wash. But as relentless rain poured down, Menika brought a basin of hot water, and asked me to have a wash indoors.

After my ablutions, we sat down to a delicious breakfast of milk rice, cooked with country rice from their fields, and sambals that Menika prepared early in the morning. The sweet, delicious plantains were from their garden as well, and we completed this scrumptious breakfast with a cup of fragrant tea.

I was impatient to walk down to Menika's house, as she told me it was just a few minutes away, so I followed her children. It was a very picturesque area; ferny banks, freshly washed and sparkling-green, rose on either side. Giant trees, gnarled with age, and with massive, tentacle-like roots, stretched out thirstily, clutching the damp earth.

It would have been glorious walking along such unspoilt pathways and wooded areas on a sunny day, but it was wet and cold when we arrived at their house. A small, rectangular-shaped house constructed with mud-bricks, stood in the middle of a lush garden, abounding with various fruit trees, including jak, orange, avocado, plantains, and mango trees.

The little house was sparsely furnished, but immaculately clean and tidy, and the cosy kitchen aglow with a large fireplace. I pictured Menika cooking over the fire, without electric lights or lanterns. She kept up a sporadic correspondence with me through her children, as she could not read or write, so I had an idea of what her life was like. Her face glowed contentedly now; and her sons faces reflected similar tranquillity, rarely seen in faces of affluent people, who possess a hundred-fold more than these poor villagers.

Menika and her family treated us like royalty, and I promised to visit them again, as they wished us a fond farewell. Nelune, Ammie, Thathie, Nilanthi, and Tanesh visited them the previous year. Our hostess bade me greet them all, and remind Nelune of the "thagi bagi" (presents), she promised to send them. Nelune regularly sent Menika money to help build her house.

Menika joined her hands in thanks now, as I gave her a substantial amount of money to tide her over. And I promised to help with a monthly allowance too. She needed money to educate her sons, and told me hesitatingly, "It would be the greatest thing to have electricity connected to our humble dwelling." She mentioned earlier, that electricity would be available in their village very soon. I told her that I would send her the money to get it connected, and would also send clothes, blankets etc. as soon as I arrived in Melbourne. She was very grateful, and invoked Lord Buddha to bless me always.

I felt sad to leave Menika, but we had to return home. Before we left though, we drove to the nearest town with her eldest son, and opened a bank account in Menika's name. We met the bank manager, and explained that as Menika was illiterate, her son would act on her behalf.

The bank manager, who was very helpful, gave his phone number, and asked us to call him if there was any problem. Then I bought some baby clothes for the expectant mother, and some food items for Menika and her family. I was glad that I achieved some good out of this visit, and Connie too agreed to help that poor family.

When we drove past Menika's village, and driver Duncan looked down at sheer precipices on the side, he shivered and exclaimed, "If I had only known *how bad* the roads were, I would *never* have driven in that thick mist and rain last night!"

On our return journey from Ragala, we stayed one night at the elegant, colonial-style Grand Hotel in Nuwara Eliya. After my unusual experience the night before, I indulged in a hot water shower, and the comfort of a hotel room. The driver stayed in a comfortable guest house near-by, and had his meals there. Connie ordered drinks in our room before dinner, and when the old waiter tottered in with the brandy, I noticed that the large goblet held only a tiny tot.

I asked Connie, "Is this how much they serve, just a finger?" He nodded, "Yes, I think so." But I was suspicious when I saw the waiter's unsteady gait the second time around when he brought drinks, and concluded that he may have taken a few "sips" on his way. He reminded me of the drunken waiter in a Peter Sellers movie, who kept sipping champagne from every glass he served, until he was thoroughly intoxicated. I could not blame the old waiter though, as it was very cold, musty, and cheerless inside those huge, old rooms. The dining area was more pleasant, and we enjoyed a good dinner, and a generous breakfast the following morning.

When we passed Talawakale next day, Connie talked about his past continually to the driver; how he and his family travelled this road so many times etc. etc. I was in the back seat, lost in my thoughts. But not once did Connie talk to me, so deeply engrossed was he in sharing his reminiscences with the driver, who listened patiently, and just nodded at everything. The poor man had no choice, but to pretend he was interested. We returned to Colombo via Kadugannawa Pass, and once again, we passed some stunning scenery. Then we stopped at a few more places of interest, before arriving home late in the evening.

I missed Malcolm very much, and Ammie cried bitterly whenever she remembered all the good times with him. Indrani too was inconsolable, and cried even at the mere mention of his name. She was left with Imali now, who was shattered at the loss of her beloved step-father. Although Indrani told her she was an adopted child, Imalie knew she was surrounded by a loving family, and adjusted to her situation. Malcolm doted on her, as if she was his own daughter, and his death affected Imali very much.

Janice, Bobby, and the girls were spending a few weeks too, and we had a great holiday with them, and my family. Hannah was very ill, with a severe stomach ache, which was very worrying, especially for Janice and Bobby. So that was a troubled time, until Hannah recovered slightly.

Nilanthi and Heron returned to the chicken farm at Kottawa, and were rebuilding their lives, after the traumatic period they endured. Heron fell ill and was admitted to hospital, and Nilanthi was run off her feet, visiting him in hospital daily, and trying to entertain us as well. Connie and I spent a few days with her on the farm, and I painted some pastels for Nilanthi and Janice.

On Christmas day, the whole family met at a nice restaurant for the festive meal, and we spent a memorable afternoon. All too soon, our brief holiday came to an end, and we returned to Melbourne on 31 January 1993. Granny's parting words made me smile though, "You'll have a big New Year's party on the plane, dancing and singing!" As she had never been on a plane or a ship all her life, she thought a plane was as spacious as a luxury liner.

We resumed our routine almost immediately, as we were busy with our jobs and other matters. I bought a used, four-cylinder, Holden Commodore, in April that year as it was very inconvenient with one car. It was a pale, green ten-year old car, and cost $5000. And though it drove alright at the start, it proved to be a lemon and required several repairs over the next few years.

David, the mechanic, who lived next door to Geraldine, repaired it at a reasonable cost each time. His garage was in Croydon though, and he drove my car over when I left it at his place the previous day. Many a time, that car stalled, or stopped right in the middle of the road, leaving me stranded.

One wild, wintry evening, on my way home from work, the car stopped suddenly near Ferntree Gully road. I had no choice, but to pull over and knock on someone's door to call roadside assistance, as I did not own a mobile phone then. I was nervous, and did not want to enter the house, but an elderly man answered the door, and when I told him my car broke down, he handed me the phone. Then I sat in the car until the RACV van arrived. This was one of numerous occasions when the car broke down.

We seldom heard from Stacy, and Christian was busy working at Safeway's as a "shelf-fitter." He did various jobs for work experience, and was interested in a modelling career, and clothing industry.

Stacy called on 25 May that year, and said, "Mum, guess what? I got married!" I tried hard not to express surprise or disbelief, as I never knew when he was serious, and when he was joking, as he had a great sense of humour. So I replied cautiously, "Congratulations Stacy, who is she?" "She's a French girl, and I married her because she wants to stay in Australia." I was not at all sure if this was true or not, and he said he was still staying somewhere near Darlinghurst. We ended the conversation pleasantly.

I suffered another severe tachycardia attack in mid-July, and spent a couple of days in hospital, then rested a few more days at home. When I returned to work, I asked the manager, if Christian could work as a temporary clerk, and she agreed, because they employed temporary staff now and then.

We had a different manager now, as John left a few months ago. And in my time at Boronia, four different managers passed through those doors. The current one was quite pleasant and helpful. Christian was working part-time at Kentucky Fried Chicken, and McDonald's ever since he was fifteen or so, and involved in modelling jobs too.

I drove with Christian in the morning, and we left together in the evening. It was great spending time with him, as I enjoyed his company very much. He worked for about a month, and was very popular with all the staff. Wayne, liked him too, because he was a hard worker, and he told me, "Christian is a good worker, like his Mum. I hope we can extend his contract." But he left, as temporary staff were not kept on too long.

Linda and he were still going steady, and I was very close to her too. She liked hot curries, and pan rolls, which I made whenever she visited.

Stacy turned twenty-one that August, and we sent him a card with our good wishes, and deposited some money into his account. He was happy, and phoned to thank us, but did not talk about returning home, as he seemed to have settled down; neither did he mention anything about his marriage. So, I assumed he was joking.

I sent Menika a monthly allowance now, and several boxes of warm clothes and blankets, which her eldest son picked up from Colombo. Menika and her sons were very happy when electricity was connected to their house as well. Her letters dictated to her children, brimmed with gratitude, and blessings. She said that everything I sent was very helpful for her family to survive. She called Nelune and me her, "golden children" who made their lives so much better. Menika deserved much more for her years of love and devotion, and I was glad we could make her life more comfortable in her later years.

Our financial situation improved vastly, with Connie working full-time now, and on a good wage. So, after much deliberation, to my infinite joy, I bought a new, upright piano for $3000. It was a fine-sounding "Bernstein" (German Scale,) and made in a German factory in Korea. I always longed for a piano ever since I was a little girl, and I finally realized that dream. And I wanted to study music too.

I found a teacher in Belgrave, and started taking piano lessons. Connie wanted to learn too, and accompanied me to her place every Saturday morning, where we studied for a few weeks. She was a middle-aged, Dutch lady, and charged $15 each, and was a good teacher. I cannot recall her name, but I did not stay with her too long. I learnt a few basic notes, and she was pleased, because I practiced very hard, and was able to play easy melodies in the beginner's book. Connie found it difficult to find time to practice, and the teacher told him sternly, "You have to *practice* some more Conrad!"

Connie's sister, Geraldine, wanted my electric organ for Adam, and bought it for a couple of hundred dollars. I found another teacher, John, who taught at a music school in Boronia, which was closer to home. He was about sixty years old, and was quite a pleasant gentleman, who was impressed with my aptitude.

After a few lessons, he told me, "What a shame you did not learn piano as a child! You would have achieved great things! But, better late than never, so keep practising and trying hard." Connie stopped lessons, due to his busy work schedule.

A few months later, I was shocked to hear that my teacher, John met with a dreadful end. As he sat playing the piano in his house one morning, his stepson shot him dead, while under the influence of drugs. I was really dismayed at this terrible news, and left off learning piano for a while. That was until I found Delina, another teacher in Boronia. I went for lessons to her house after work, and began studying for exams in late 1993, and made good progress.

Christian passed year twelve a couple of years ago, with very good results, and since then he worked part-time in several places. When he wanted work experience as a graphic designer, Connie asked one of his friends at "Sign- Craft" to take him on. Christian was very talented, and skilled in graphics, so he was happy doing what he enjoyed. He applied for jobs in that field, and was called up for interviews, but nothing eventuated.

Stacy and Christian were very gifted children, as they were very good musicians, artists, and remarkably articulate. They studied various instruments in high school, and Christian played the piano beautifully. His poem, "The Moth" appeared in an anthology a few years later; he also composed songs, stories, and poetry from a very young age.

Stacy asked me to read about ten of his poems, and I was very impressed, as they were so profound and poignant. He wrote them from the age of sixteen, and left them with me. I still marvel at his talent, and depth of feeling, and am pleased they were blessed with gifts of music, art, and writing.

I was once again on part-time hours, due to health issues, and was off every Wednesday. But I was promoted to acting supervisor in the Family Payments section, and enjoyed my job very much. I interviewed many people, and heard some interesting stories about their personal lives. But it was stressful too, as some were tragic stories. However, I was there only to listen, and assist with payments, and if needed, I referred them to social workers.

My new interest now, was playing the piano, and practising as often as possible after work. It was a challenge preparing for examinations, but I enjoyed learning theory, and new melodies.

We did not hear from Stacy very often, and I always hoped he was getting on alright. I had no reason to worry too much, because I knew that if he needed help, he would call.

Connie and I flew to Queensland for the first time that November. We stayed at a pleasant place, "Aussie Resort" in Burleigh Heads, right on the Pacific Highway, on the Gold Coast. The apartment was spacious, and comfortable, and included a kitchenette. I cooked meals every day of the week that we stayed there, as eating out was exorbitant.

We called Christian often to see how he was coping, as he was looking after the house and Tiger. He said Stacy phoned, and asked for a small loan, but he did not have enough money. Connie deposited some funds in Stacy's bank account immediately. I wondered what he was doing, as he seemed to be short of funds often.

It was very scenic and warm in the Gold Coast. We rented a car and drove to Noosa Heads. And then up mountains, to view the breathtaking panorama of skyscrapers along the Gold Coast towering up to the heavens; thundering surf beaches, majestic mountains surrounding the coast, and deep-blue ocean splashed with snow-white foam. The scene was well worth the precipitous drive, up narrow, mountain roads, in an uncomfortable, lumbering 1985 Ford. I loved the hills and dales, and Glass-House Mountains looming in the far horizon. We drove out every morning, and spent all day touring places of interest.

We returned to Melbourne after one week, and Christian was happy to see us. He cleaned up the house as usual, so I did not have to worry about anything, and Tiger was looking well too. Christian was extremely tidy and methodical, and was always so, since he was a child. His room was in perfect order, but Stacy was the opposite; and whenever Connie nagged him to clean up his room, he retorted, "I like the *lived in* look."

Stacy sent cards to the whole family that Christmas, including Janice and Rosie. I was glad he was keeping well, and seemed happy. He visited Nelune sometimes, when he needed financial help. She always obliged, as she said they were small amounts of twenty dollars each time.

Christmas was hectic, with many family gatherings, and Bab's usual parties, where she announced dramatically, that she was baptised as a "Born again" Christian. She talked long about her new-found faith, as she attended evangelical churches, and decided to be baptised.

Connie was very annoyed, and kept telling them, "Daddy must be rolling in his grave to think that all of you *baptized* Catholics have gone astray like this!" He never accepted the fact that they chose to belong to other churches, because he was such a staunch Catholic. Aunty, Esme, and Connie, were the only ones who were Catholics still. But his siblings joined different evangelical churches, and kept flitting from one church to another according to their whims.

We celebrated New Year alone, after spending the previous night at Aunty's place in Dandenong, where the family gathered. Connie entertained the crowd, playing the harmonica. I was very tired, and left with Christian and Linda at midnight, but he stayed behind till early dawn. Geraldine and Clifford spent Christmas in Queensland, so Connie was pleased they were not present at family parties.

Ian, Aunty Molly's son, who was in his late thirties then, was getting married in early January 1994, to Romayne, a distant cousin from Ceylon, whom he had never met. Aunty Molly "chose" her, as she believed "Mother knew best." And she discouraged Ian from marrying a girl of any other nationality. Romayne flew to Melbourne, and the wedding was organised within a few weeks time. She stayed with Esme when she arrived, and Esme invited us to meet her.

Connie suffered from severe hay fever then, and was in a rotten mood that evening. But when he was introduced to Romayne, he grinned and exclaimed, "My hay fever was bad, but after seeing you, my hay fever has just gone!" He did not know I was standing right behind him. It was typical of his flirtatious behaviour with young girls. Romayne was of average height, thin, and dark, but with pleasant features.

When she saw Ian at the airport for the first time, she told Esme, "I could have died! I wanted to return to Sri Lanka immediately!" No one could blame her, because although Ian was an unassuming person, he looked liked a shorter, skinnier version of Mr Bean. Totally lacking in personality, he drank too much, so that his eyes were always bloodshot, and his inane, lopsided grin exposed toothless gaps.

She had no choice now, as everything was ready for their wedding. Aunty Molly asked Christian to be best man, and Linda, to be bridesmaid, as she told me, "They are such a beautiful couple, and they will look good in the photos!" Linda was very reluctant, because she was a timid, reserved girl, but she agreed, just to please Aunty Molly.

Christian was not too keen either, because he was never close to Ian, and could not understand why they wanted Linda and him, as they were not even close acquaintances. Perhaps Ian was not allowed to choose his own best man, as Aunty Molly only wanted a good-looking couple to pose in photographs (to send relatives in Ceylon).

The wedding was held at a church in Noble Park, and we were invited to the church ceremony only. The bridesmaid's dress was of emerald-green satin, and Linda looked lovely. Romayne's wedding dress was another matter though. It was way over the top, with trinkets, baubles, ribbons, flounces, frills, and bows decorating every inch of her dress. It was double-skirted, and she looked like Little Bo Peep; only a bonnet and a shepherd's staff were missing to complete her ludicrous attire. I wondered who was responsible for such a disastrous costume? Perhaps her fond mother, and relatives in Ceylon ensured that not one bauble, bow or ribbon was left out.

Linda was very upset and stressed, because of what went on behind the scenes right through the ceremony. She told me Esme and Cristobel were on her back, nit-picking constantly; and at one time Linda burst into tears, because they nagged her all the time, which was an ordeal for her.

She was in tears when she told me how Connie's sisters picked on her all through that morning, especially Cristobel. She said, "They were so bossy and irritating, bullying and treating me like a little child." I was very sorry Linda was subjected to such unpleasantness, and tried to pacify her, but it was too late to make amends.

Cristobel, Geraldine, and Esme, were over-bearing and officious, especially when they were in company. Fortunately, Geraldine was not there, as it would have been worse, if all of them ganged up on Linda. I told her not to take any notice of them, as they did not know how to conduct themselves graciously, without giving offence to others. I assured her she was a lovely bridesmaid, and carried herself well.

After the ceremony, Esme took over the proceedings completely, and shouted out to all the guests, "We're going now to take photos, but *only* the *immediate* family is invited to the reception!" Several close relatives were deeply offended. And the only "immediate family" who accompanied the bridal couple, were Esme and Paul, Babs, Cristobel, Aunty, and Aunty Molly, besides Christian and Linda, whose presence was mandatory for photographs. We just stood outside the church and watched them drive away.

The remaining relatives grumbled, and went off home in a huff, muttering to themselves about, "Cheap, stingy so-and-so's." Although she was a kindly soul, Aunty Molly's parsimony was a byword in the family. Ian was averse to loosen his purse strings too, so the wedding was a very modest affair, without a grand reception. Shiranthi and Roland invited us for a snack, and we stayed with them for a little while.

A week or so later, we were invited to the newlyweds "Home-coming" party at Wendy's and Brian's place. Once again, we were obliged to be there, but Christian and Linda refused to attend, as they were busy. They engaged a cook to make hoppers in the garage, and a crowd of about fifty people gathered in that small house. Geraldine and Clifford, who returned from Queensland, attended too, and we left after midnight.

Ian and Romayne had two girls over the next few years, and their marriage lasted ten years, until Romayne fell in love with someone else. Ian called me and explained what happened, "We were in Paris on a holiday with Mummy, and Romayne was acting very strange. She was inside a public phone booth for over one hour, and when she came out, I asked her who she was calling. She replied, 'my boyfriend' I felt like killing her there in front of everyone!" That was how she broke the news to him that she wanted a divorce.

On Connie's birthday that year, I cooked dinner for about thirty people (that was only his family). Shirani, Ranjith, and Nelune came too. Connie was in a good mood, and full of praise, "Dolly gives me a lot of pleasure, as she does so much for me!" The night passed without any incidents.

He did not usually pay me any compliments, especially in public. And he did not like anyone else paying me any either. He diffused any praise or compliments immediately, like when someone told me, "You look like a doll!" Connie immediately replied, "We *all* look like dolls where we come from!" Once, when we visited my friend, Vivian, her place was very untidy, and looked like a storm had hit it. She said, "Excuse the mess, kids have been playing." Connie piped up at once, "You should see *our* place! Don't worry about the mess!" I was taken aback, and asked him later why he said such a thing, when our house was always neat and clean, to which he replied, "Oh, I was just trying to make her happy, I know you keep our house tidy all the time."

A few days later, on my birthday, I invited some friends from work, and Shirani, Ranjith, and Nelune, to a Sri Lankan restaurant, the "Jolly-J." Connie invited his entire family too, but only Wendy, Brian, Esme, Paul, and Aunty came. Christian and Linda joined us and we chatted away happily.

It was not even remotely jolly though, as they played heart-wrenching Country and Western songs all evening. Nelune remarked, "*That* music is enough to make you want to slash your wrists!" One of my friends asked me later why Connie's family sat stony-faced, without smiling or socialising with the other guests. And she said, "For God's sake, it was supposed to be your birthday party, not a wake!"

The dinner was very very late, and Dorothea, banged plates, demanding "Food, food, I want to eat!" It was a very long, boring evening. Connie and I danced a little, as a live band was playing. When the food was finally served, tasty though it was, the guests were too hungry and disgruntled to enjoy the meal. So ended my birthday party on a very disappointing note.

Connie travelled to country stores often then, and he stayed in motels overnight, if he went to Albury or Mildura. But sometimes he drove back on the same day, from places like Portland and Warrnambool, if he was not too tired. If I did not accompany him, he took Aunty, and Aunty Molly with him, and sometimes, Roland

and Shiranthi, or Wendy and Brian. He liked company, as he said it was boring to go on those long drives. Once, Christian and I joined him to Mildura, and we stayed in a caravan park. It was a hot, arid area, and the only pleasant memories I have of Mildura, are its abundant orange groves.

A few days after that forgettable birthday party, Linda and Christian broke up. Linda was heart-broken, but their relationship ended, as he said it did not work out. She turned to me in her sadness, and I became a lifeline. Linda constantly asked me, "Mrs De, will Christian come back to me?" And all I could tell her was, "If it's meant to be, you will get back together again." The only comfort I could offer was such a well-worn cliché.

She felt it very deeply, and though so long ago, I remembered very well the angst I suffered with my unrequited first love. She was fifteen when she started seeing Christian, and she was vulnerable. I sympathised with her heartily.

Connie was very angry, and told Christian, "The next girl you bring home will be the girl you are going to marry, as I don't want a tart here!" He was annoyed with Connie, but he did not bring his new girlfriend home. Linda and I remain good friends to this day.

I trained to be section manager, Family Payments temporarily, as Gwen, the current section manager, thought it was time I developed managerial skills. So, I was pleased when she sent me to Box Hill for further training. Work conditions were good now, and I got along well with all the staff members, and I received further training as a stress contact officer.

The manager said I had excellent listening skills, which were important in that role. I always had time for anyone who needed to talk about problems at work. This extended to after work too, and several friends called me at home to discuss certain issues. Connie did not like that at all, as he said, "You should not have to listen to other peoples' problems when you are at home!"

The situation at home now dwindled to such a low point, that it was impossible to even be in the same room, without tearing each other apart. And I reached breaking point once again around March that year.

This time, I was determined to end our marriage once and for all, and vowed never to return. Connie and I were in the same old groove, with our relationship steadily hitting rock bottom again. We just did not, and could not communicate. We were not close in any way, with only arguments and tension all the time. Escape was the only solution for me once more.

I found a multitude of reasons for returning, each time I left, which included finances, insecurity, and remorse. Now I asked myself, how many more times must I keep on repeating this pattern, before we finally resolved our differences?

I had a secure job now, and enough money to pay rent, even though I still worked part-time. I saw a two-bedroom unit in Croydon about a week ago, and the landlady appeared to be very pleasant. So I paid her a bond of $500, and she did not ask me for a month's rent in advance. I had some savings, and also pawned one of my rings at a jeweller's in Boronia, to make up the bond.

When some of my friends at work knew what I was planning, they helped me to move out once again. I hired a truck to take only my lounge-suite, a coffee table, and a single bed. What I did not bargain for, was the enormous removal truck that pulled up outside. It was large enough for a few house- lots, and all I had were a few items of furniture and my clothes.

Dash barked non-stop at my friends, and the removalists. Geraldine, Alan, and George looked over the fence, just as Lesley and Heather helped to load my bags. Heather wrapped up all the cutlery, and did not leave a single teaspoon behind, as I discovered later. She was an embittered woman. And I think she gained enormous satisfaction in hurting another man, as she suffered at the hands of her ex-husband.

She told me not to leave *anything* that I could take. But I left behind everything else, including my beloved piano, paintings, tapestries etc. I took my clothes and personal belongings only. But his family spread rumours that I cleaned out the house.

While we loaded things and hurried about, Dash did not stop barking, and in desperation, I locked him under the house, where he kept up his incessant barking. Soon, we packed everything, and I left behind my home, pets, garden that I loved and tended so well, and went off to a better and new life forever (I hoped).

Connie drove to Portland that morning, and I knew he would not return till late at night, so I planned to move out on that day. Christian was out with his new girlfriend most of the time, and he was busy at work too.

Although I knew his family would tarnish my reputation as usual, it did not worry me at all, because I had to escape for my sanity, as things just did not seem to work out between us.

He stopped drinking only for a few days when we reconciled. And when he started again, it was nothing but a litany of curses and abuse. His drunken babbling, and never-ending harangue made no sense. What puzzled me most was, he did not seem to care that I had no choice, but to leave him again. Because sometimes when I told him, "If you don't change your ways, I will leave you." He yelled, "Get out! I don't care!"

Looking back on those dark days, and trying to analyse the anatomy of my dysfunctional marriage, all I can say is, that each time I left home, goaded beyond endurance, I was convinced it was the very end, and I would never ever reconcile with Connie again. Yet, when I was alone in a strange place, without my family and familiar surroundings, I just fell apart.

I found excuses for Connie's behaviour once again, and wondered if I should give him another chance to make our marriage work, and whether he learnt his lesson this time. But when we were together, I just could not handle the situation, and the only solution was always flight, as I did not want to stay on and fight. My peace of mind and equilibrium were shattered in such an environment of conflict and disharmony.

I longed to find peace somewhere, but the emotional ties with Connie always proved too strong to destroy. And over the next few months, I finally discovered a lasting truth; there is no way someone can change their intrinsic nature, and only *I* can change my attitudes and reactions to that person's behaviour.

Many well-meaning friends helped me during my troubled times. And talking to some of them, who experienced similar situations, I knew I must resolve our differences once and for all. I had to change my attitude and reaction, without getting hurt anymore. I was always driven to leave home, much against my will, but to me, it was the only way I could preserve my sanity and wellbeing. My friends were very supportive and caring; they dropped in to see me and keep up my morale. Some even gave me bits and pieces of furniture, including an old fridge and a washing machine.

I pictured the drama and confusion at home that night, when Connie returned from Portland. I left him a letter, saying this time, it was goodbye forever. The neighbours were sure to tell him I moved out, as they saw the huge truck.

When I consulted doctor, just before I left, he advised me to separate, as the stress would eventually kill me, if I did not leave home and make a life of my own. I was constantly ill, with some complaint or another then, and doctor was convinced my ill health was due to stress.

I tried to live on my own several times, but always ended up feeling guilty, and emotionally drained. Because I walked out on Connie, leaving behind the security and comfort of a home that I helped to build through the years. He would never leave home, that much I knew. And I resented the fact he drove me to the brink of endurance, even though he knew that if I reached breaking point, I would walk out on him again, and again.

He did not seem to care what he did under the influence of alcohol especially. But when he was alone, he too fell apart, and said he could not live without me. I questioned him why he did not try to treat me better, if our love was so precious to him. He never cherished me the way I wanted him to. I suppose he just could not help himself, and his behaviour reminded me of this particular story:

"Once, a scorpion sitting on the banks of a lake sees a turtle swimming across. He asks the turtle to let him ride on its back but the turtle replies, 'No, if I do, you will sting me and we'll both drown,' but the scorpion insists, 'No, I promise, I won't sting you, please take me across.' So the turtle agrees, but halfway through the lake, the scorpion stings him and the turtle questions, '*Why* did you do that, now we'll both drown.' To which the scorpion replies, 'I can't *help* myself. That's how I was born.'

Moral of story: people cannot change their nature, whatever they may say or do.

Connie consulted Anne, a naturopath, who lived in Belgrave. Anorexic Pam recommended her to me, when she knew about my heart problem. Although I stopped using her remedies now, Connie still saw her, as he trusted her in every way, and was very close to her. He often visited her on his own, and told me, "Anne is the only woman I trust." She was a serene, pleasant-looking lady in her late forties then.

When I was at work next day, Anne called and asked me what was wrong, as Connie wanted to know why I left him. I said I did not want him to call me at work, and I would not be going home again. I knew Connie persuaded her to act as go-between, and she called me a few times on his behalf.

Christian met me at work, and I told him that this time I was positive I would not return, as it was too much for me to put up with Connie's behaviour. Then Connie told his family that this time I left because I was upset over Christian and Linda breaking up. I was livid when I heard this, as I could not believe he still blamed me, and did not accept it was mostly his fault. When Anne called me again, I asked her to advise him to see a counsellor, and try to resolve his anger and drinking issues.

Stacy called me in mid-April, and said that he was phoning from a DSS office in Brisbane, as he was stuck for money. I told him I left home for good this time, and he immediately replied, "May your spirit shine Mum! I can hear the relief and joy in your voice!" Then he said, "I'm sitting here crying, and thinking of what Dad has done to me. Why was he so *bitter* and negative towards me? I think I'm becoming just like him!" And he started crying out loud.

I comforted him and said, "What you make of life Stacy, is your own responsibility. Don't blame anyone. If Dad was like that, you must try to overcome negative thoughts, and be better than him." We spoke at length, and he said, "I miss you Mum, I love you. I'll come to Melbourne soon." I promised to deposit hundred dollars, as I could not send much, because I was on my own.

I walked to the Commonwealth Bank at lunch time, and deposited hundred dollars in his account. I was so angry with Connie, that I called him that afternoon, and told him how Stacy was crying and suffering, because of all he had said and done to him, just like the way he treated me. He did not say anything, and I hung up.

Stacy called him that night, and asked for more money, as he said he was stranded in Armidale, and needed extra to return to Sydney. Connie told him, "I will deposit some money tomorrow, but don't ask any more money as I'll tell you to piss off, if you ask for money again. I have had an earful from Mum because of you!" He was intoxicated, but they spoke for some time, and Stacy ended, "I love you Dad." And he replied, "I love you too son."

Connie conveyed messages via Anne in the days that followed. I was willing to forgive and forget, and give our marriage another go, because it seemed we could not live together or live apart. But I firmly resolved that if we did reconcile again, I would try hard to change my reaction to his bad behaviour, and not let him destroy my peace of mind and my life.

Linda was a regular visitor, and spent a few days with me, as she found solace being with me, and talking about Christian. I gave her a key to the unit, and she was free to come and go as she pleased. When I came home sometimes, she would be watching television, and the heater was on, so it was warm and cosy. I did not mind, because the flat was very cold, and I wanted her to be comfortable. We shared whatever I cooked for dinner, and she stayed overnight, if she was too tired.

Linda visited Connie too, and kept me up to date. He hurt his back, and was in severe pain. She said that he took our separation very badly, but was confident we would soon reconcile, and told her, "Dolly *always* comes back! I know she will return." That made me mad, as he seemed to know just how soft-hearted and vulnerable I was.

Cristobel called me sometimes, and said that Connie told everyone I left because I could not handle Linda's and Christian's break up. I phoned Aunty and Wendy a couple of times, and Aunty asked me when I was going to return home. I told her Connie must get help, and go for counselling, before we made up.

He called me at work soon after, and spoke in a slurred voice. He said he was at his mother's place, and the ambulance was taking him to hospital, as he hurt his back and was in severe pain. I listened silently and said, "Take care." He was very emotional, and cried out loud over the phone, so I just hung up.

Nelune and Shirani visited me sometimes. Shirani was overseas for a few weeks, so she said that this time Connie could not blame her for helping me to move out.

Before returning to Melbourne, she spent a few days at Ammie's and Thathie's, and helped them around the house, and bought everything they needed to make them comfortable. They were very happy, and grateful for that time spent with Shirani. Nelune stayed a couple of days with me, and we had a good time together.

Mrs Rodrigo, who was holidaying in Melbourne, visited Shirani with her son Derek, and his wife. I drove over with Nelune to see her, and I thought she had not changed at all. After so many years, she seemed to be the same Mrs Rodrigo we knew as children, and it was such a lovely trip down memory lane. Derek was quiet, and his wife even quieter, as she did not share our reminiscences and conversation. After a couple of hours, Nelune and I returned.

Connie kept consulting Anne for various complaints, and she told me that he was seeing a counsellor; she advised him to be honest, and discuss all his problems with the counsellor, who was also a female. He told me that he always felt more comfortable with women, and would never consult a male, if he could help it. Even when he needed physio, he insisted on seeing a female. His explanation was, "I'd *rather* have a woman touching me, than a man!"

It was the same all these years, because he never admitted he was in the wrong. And even my leaving home was not his problem, but mine, so he could never address the issues. Finally, when he admitted that *he* had a problem, he started seeing a counsellor.

He promised me he would stop drinking alcohol, and try to control his violent temper. And would do his best to change the pattern of behaviour that drove a wedge between us, and forced me to leave him. When he told me about his sessions with the counsellor, he said, "I told her that I love you so much, and I can't find any fault with you!" And she had asked, "Then *why* can't you both get along?"

He never opened up emotionally, or admitted he had an uncontrollable, violent temper, a drinking problem, and insane jealousy. Without admitting these issues, how could he hope to get help? He wanted to lull me into a false sense of optimism, that he was seeking professional help. But I knew from what he told me, that the counsellor would never get to the bottom of his problems, if he did not discuss them openly. One day, he said, "The counsellor can't understand why we are not happy together, because there's *nothing* wrong with me!"

Linda won a ticket to Sydney in a competition, and her mother asked her to travel with me, so I accepted her invitation. We drove to the airport very early in the morning, as Linda stayed with me overnight, because the flight was at 6am. She drove my car very fast, and I teased, "You are a lead-foot lassie Linda!"

We took a ferry across to Mosman, and a taxi to Nelune's place, where we stayed for a few hours. Then we spent the entire afternoon shopping around. Nelune rented a car and took us to the famous markets, which delighted Linda, but she was short of funds, tired and frustrated towards the end of the day. I spent $100 on my return ticket, and did not have much spare money to give her for shopping, so she was unhappy that she could not shop to her heart's content.

That morning before we went out, I called Connie from Nelune's place to ask him for Stacy's phone number. He was amazed to hear I was in Sydney with Linda, and mumbled, "Oh Dolla, *why* do you do these things?" I did not reply. He gave me Stacy's number, and I told him I hoped to see him before I left.

I called that number where Stacy was boarded at, but they told me he was away still, and had not returned. I was sad and disappointed, as I dearly wanted to see Stacy before I left, and tell him what was happening in my life. Nelune had another appointment at two o'clock, so she dropped us off at Darling Harbour.

Linda and I were exhausted, footsore, and lacking funds to do much there, so we sat around for some time, and then trudged around wearily from place to place before we boarded a bus to the airport. Linda was down in the dumps, and hardly spoke a word until we reached Melbourne. Then we drove back to Croydon, still not speaking much. She broke the silence only to say, "Next time, I'm going to make sure I have *plenty* of money, as I love to shop in Sydney!"

I was extremely short of funds over the next week, and bought a bag of bones for two dollars, to make a pot of soup to last me a few days. I did not mind, as I liked soup. Although I tried to keep busy, and not get depressed, I could not help feeling disheartened on some days. Good Friday was one of those days. And since all the shops were closed, I had no where to go, except the cinema.

I had never been to a cinema on my own in my entire life, and being Good Friday, it was even more unusual. I thought of what Ammie would have said had she known I was going for a movie on Good Friday! She would not have believed it. In fact she would have been absolutely horrified. Anyway, I drove to the cinema in Croydon around two o'clock, and watched Walt Disney's animated masterpiece, "The Aristocats" which made me forget my troubles for a while.

On Easter Sunday, I was down with flu, and had exactly two dollars left until next payday in three days time. I bought a few vegetables, and made another pot of soup again, and lived on that and bread for three days. I did not starve, but I would not ask anyone money.

In the meantime, I kept working and getting on with my life. Connie promised faithfully that he would continue seeing a counsellor, until he resolved some issues. And said that he hoped we would reconcile soon.

In mid-May, Connie conveyed a message through Anne, asking if I would meet him, because he wanted to discuss about the house, and whether to get rid of Dash. She told me he was still seeing a counsellor, so I agreed to meet him in a park nearby.

He drove a company car now, and he asked me if I wanted his old Commodore, and to sell my car, as it was unreliable. I refused his offer, and we talked a little more. The counsellor had told him, "I can't find *anything* wrong with you." Because he maintained he loved me deeply, but did not mention his uncontrollable anger, insane jealousy, violent temper, and drinking problems. So how could she help him?

I could not believe he was still hiding behind a smoke screen, so I spoke my mind about his behaviour, his attitude, and the way he treated Stacy and me. He listened silently, promised to mend his ways, if I would come back and give him another chance. I told him I needed more time to think about it. And I did not give him my phone number or address, as I knew he would then start calling and visiting me anytime he wanted.

I bought a cute little kitten in mid-May from the pet shop, for just ten dollars. She had an adorable face, and I called her Misty, because of her unusual peach and grey fur. Misty was a beautiful little kitten, and kept me amused, so that I did not miss Tiger and Dash too much. I left her in the bathroom at nights, and she slept on my bed when I went to work. Once, she crept through the opening in the doona, and was sleeping inside there until I discovered her.

Connie told me he could not manage Dash, so he took him to the kennels where we bought him. And the breeder told him, "Best thing is to put him to sleep, if he's vicious and bites people." He was my most devoted, and adoring companion, but I hardened my heart, and did not wallow in sentimentality. So I agreed, and next day, Connie said the deed was done.

I thought of all the amusing things Dash did; when Connie was mowing the lawn once, Dash strongly objected to the noise, so he jumped up and nipped Connie's bottom. He bit Shirani's ankle, Cristobel's leg, Geraldine next door, and any other child foolhardy enough to venture near him. He was the most unpopular dog I ever owned. But whenever he looked at me, his eyes melted into pools of love and devotion. After eight years of barking his head off at the neighbours, and biting all and sundry, he was gone.

Chapter 22

I gave my phone number and address to Connie at the end of May, as I was weary of his incessant pleading. He promised faithfully that he would not visit, or call me unless I asked him to. Coincidentally, he was seeing a masseur in Croydon, just a few streets from where I lived. Very soon, we started communicating on the phone.

Connie told me that he spent every single evening with his mother, or one of his siblings. Christian lived with a friend, as he did not want to be at home, now that we were separated. I had mixed messages, and unjust accusations from some members of his family, but I did not worry, because I knew who I was. Babs and Cristobel called me at work, and asked where I was living, but I did not want to give my address just yet.

I called Aunty a few times, and she was very upset. She said, "I hope you know what you're doing, and your conscience is clear." I told her that unless Connie changed his behaviour, I would not return. She told me then that Connie broke down and said, "It's all *my* fault Mummy! I'm the one to blame for Dolla leaving me." This was the very first time he ever admitted that it was his fault. And I hoped that he finally realized what his behaviour was doing to me.

Wendy, Babs, and Cristobel were sympathetic, but Geraldine and Esme were hostile, and criticized me harshly. Connie repeated everything they said. And I realized how much they resented me; and what ill-feeling they harboured against me. Especially Geraldine, who only waited for an opportunity to denigrate me whenever she could. They blamed me solely, because they thought Connie was the perfect husband, who did not deserve to go through all this.

I wrote to my parents this time, and told them I was on my own. They were very upset, especially Ammie, as she did not like the situation at all.

Nelune called me on the 1st of June, to say that Thathie told her Ammie was in hospital, as she suffered heart failure. She was in a serious condition, and he asked Nelune to come over as soon as possible. Anthony was already there.

I was very upset and shaken, so I called Connie at ten o'clock in the night and tearfully broke the news to him, as I was very emotional. He told me that he would arrange everything for me to go home. And he said that he sold the Commodore to David, the mechanic, for $1000. Connie bought my ticket with that money. We drove my car, with Misty, back to Rowville, and he said he would look after her.

It was strange, and very upsetting to return to the house that I left vowing never to return. It looked so cold, and desolate, and not at all like the beautiful home I built. Tiger stared at me, and shied away, as if I was a stranger. That hurt deeply, but I put on a brave face as Connie drove me to the airport.

Nelune and I were meeting in Singapore, and flying together from there. Thathie did not know I was accompanying Nelune, so he would be surprised. Connie and I saw each other a few times over the last few weeks. We were trying to work out a lasting solution, to build a better, and more solid foundation. I tried to connect to him emotionally when we met, but all he said was, "I love you. Come back home."

He would not discuss all the hurtful issues and problems that simmered between us, and often erupted when he was angry, or drank too much. How much I wanted to understand his behaviour! But how could I get to the bottom of this morass, if he kept evading issues, and pretending nothing was wrong?

When he drove me to the airport, and waited till the plane took off, my heart was leaden. And I cried helplessly, as I thought of the mess I was in. I watched Connie waving from the airport terminal, and then my tears fell. Was it remorse for leaving him, or self-pity, I know not which emotion was stronger.

It was generous of him to buy my ticket, and drop me at the airport. And his care-worn face touched my heart. I was deeply distressed that we were in this unhappy situation. I was also afraid that I would not make it in time to see Ammie, as she was in a critical condition. Connie wanted to be with me at this crucial time, but due to various reasons, he was unable to join me.

Nelune met me at Singapore airport, and we had an interesting journey to Colombo, although I felt heart sick at the thought of poor Ammie not being alive when we arrived. We stayed at the Airport Gardens Hotel, in Katunayake, as the plane landed after midnight, then we took a taxi to Maharagama early next morning. I felt physically sick, when only Thathie stood at the door to greet us, looking sad and forlorn. Ammie was usually by his side, welcoming us with her gentle smile. But she was seriously ill in hospital, and unable to greet us that day.

We rushed to the General Hospital, after unpacking our bags, and were shocked at the appalling conditions there; putrid smells, and lack of proper care for a heart patient. Ammie could hardly breathe, and her legs were swollen, like two huge stumps. Nelune and I instantly decided to take her to the best heart specialist that day, but Ammie kept insisting she wanted to go home.

Anthony had arrived a few days ago, and while we discussed what was best for Ammie, she was adamant that she would not stay in hospital another day. And much to our consternation, she came home the very next day. But it was obvious that she was very ill, and could hardly breathe.

Nilanthi was employed on the farm to supervise the female workers, and was very happy now. She invited us to stay with her, as it was difficult for Ammie and Thathie to manage on their own.

Nilanthi asked Menika to come over immediately, if possible, and she arrived with her youngest son a couple of days later. Nelune and I were very happy to see her smiling face and embraced her affectionately. She immediately took charge of the kitchen, and set about preparing meals.

That was the last time I saw Menika and her children, because over the next few years, I did not receive any letters from them. The older son found a good job in Colombo, and I hoped they were financially stable now. Nilanthi wrote to her sons a couple of times, asking Menika to come over, but she did not receive a reply either. I was glad we helped her through her difficult years, and if her children were able to care for her now, that was good.

One of Ammie's acquaintances brought a mischievous, thirteen-year old girl, Champa, to help in the kitchen and garden. She was a strong, mulish, tom-boy of a girl; with ebony skin, and short, straight, black hair. Champa smelled strongly of urine, no matter how many times we asked her to bathe and wash herself, but she never got rid of her repulsive body odours. She washed and powdered her face only, and wore fresh clothes, but always reeked of urine.

Nelune discouraged her from coming too close to us, but the girl insisted on sleeping on a mat in our bedroom. She told me very solemnly that she longed to become a soldier. And she slept on the hard, concrete floor without a pillow or sheet to cover herself, as she was in "training" to sleep out in the jungles.

She had a strong, ruthless temperament, and I believed she would make a splendid soldier one day. I was sorry for her, when she repeatedly told me that she had never seen the ocean in all her life, and could I take her to see it one day. I was non-committal, but decided to do so at the very first opportunity.

Ammie scolded Champa when she visited her in hospital, as she was highly malodorous, in spite of her powdered face and new dress. One night, after Ammie returned home, I woke up for a drink of water, and I saw Ammie sitting up in the lounge, moaning and gasping for breath. She looked so ill, that the very next day, Nelune and I admitted her to a private hospital, where she was taken care of immediately.

Her sugar levels soared, as she was a diabetic, and blood pressure was just as bad. The excess fluid around her heart, made it extremely difficult for her to breathe properly. She was soon relieved of the immediate symptoms, and the cardiologist commenced long-term treatment for her heart condition.

Ammie was concerned about the hospital bill. But Nelune and I reassured her that we were more than happy to take care of the bill, and not to worry about money, as we wanted her to have the best treatment in a private hospital. She was very moved, and told Thathie, "I'm so grateful to have such loving children."

Ammie's left ventricle had failed, and she was warned to be very careful in future, because she was extremely weak, and in a dangerous condition. But she never took her condition seriously, and to her, it was just like having a common cold. Ammie had a great sense of optimism, and a total contempt for her illness, even though it was life-threatening. She did not give up her daily routine of marketing, cooking, gardening, washing, and cleaning. But it was obvious that she struggled with her chores. So it was good to see Thathie helping out in the kitchen and house work. Champa, was of little real use, as she had to be supervised constantly, because she was naughty and unreliable.

Nelune left in a week's time, and as we hired a van to drop her at the airport, I asked the driver to take the scenic route on our way back, so that Champa could view the ocean. What an ecstatic, incredible expression of delight suffused her entire face, when she gazed in wonder at the sparkling, sapphire-blue ocean, crested with snow-white frothy peaks. And the crashing, roaring, thunderous breakers, held her entranced.

I was very glad to have granted her this wish, and she thanked me repeatedly. Now (in a display of extreme devotion), she accompanied me whenever I walked up to the junction to buy groceries, or to the jeweller, where I purchased a beautiful amethyst ring for hundred dollars.

Heron suffered from high blood pressure, and was admitted to the same hospital as Ammie. They were in neighbouring wards, and we visited them daily. Rita too visited Ammie, and she was delighted to see Nelune and me. We joked about Champa's mischievous doings, and the trouble we had to teach her hygiene.

In spite of the poignant situation, with Ammie being so ill, we had some happy moments too. Menika stayed for about a week, and Nelune bought shoes for her children, as she told us they could not afford new shoes. But she never asked us for money, although we insisted on helping her.

Ammie and Thathie knew I was living away from home, and one evening, Ammie asked me, "Are you going to make up with Connie? He bought you a ticket to come and see me, and he's always been kind to us. Why don't you try to forgive and forget, and make the most of your marriage? How many times have you tried to leave him Dolly? You know you can't live alone, so when you go back, I hope you will return to your home."

This advice coming from Ammie, who endured her fair share of trouble, and domestic violence for so many years, moved me deeply. They had one thing in common though, as they loved each other very much, in spite of all their differences and quarrels.

I did not say anything, as I was not too sure of what was going to happen once I returned to Melbourne. I left at the end of two weeks, while Ammie was still in hospital, and I pleaded with her to stay there until she was well enough.

But she kept telling me that her main concern was the huge medical bill for the private hospital, which, in her mind was a small fortune. But we assured her we would take care of the medical bills. It worked out to less than fifty dollars a day, and we were more than happy to pay, knowing she received good treatment there.

All the way on my flight back to Melbourne, I had plenty of time to think about what I should do. And when Connie met me at the airport and asked me the same question, I replied, "Give me a few more weeks, and by the end of June I will give you an answer, as I don't want to rush back and get into the same old rut. I'm *tired* of leaving home too, and I want to make sure that this will be the last time."

He told me that he stopped drinking, and I tried to sort things out over the next few weeks, and weighed the pros and cons of my situation. My friends visited often, and offered me their advice.

Connie told me that Esme and Geraldine were my worst critics, as they spoke very uncharitably about me. Aunty and Wendy were genuinely concerned, and

Wendy kept asking Connie when I would return, as she missed me very much. Babs did not get involved, but when I spoke to her a few times, she wanted to visit. She said that she understood why I left Connie, and to be sure of myself, before I returned this time.

Some of my friends were not too happy when I decided to go back, and warned me that things would be the same. But I told them I expected Connie to keep his promise, and not drink again, or at least not too much. And I too promised that I would not leave home again (without telling him), no matter how bad things were.

We wanted to try and work out our problems together, because he told me, "Don't leave again Dolla, I'm not sure if I can take it again, it's too much for me to bear." I replied, "It's not *easy* for me either, but you drive me to despair, and leaving you is the only way I can keep my sanity."

When I moved back, Connie tried his best to abstain from alcohol for a few days, then he started with just one drink before a meal. And he tried hard to restrain his temper too. I avoided conflict by ignoring his behaviour, and not getting into an argument with him.

Since Christian and Stacy were not home for him to pick on, and I refused to be drawn into any brawls, we appeared to get along better. But whenever his sisters or mother visited, he took the upper hand, drank a little extra, and started an argument with me. After they left, and he was alone with me, he said, "Sorry Dolla, you know I didn't mean anything I said." That was Connie's nature, but it did not upset me as much. I learnt to live with the good and the bad.

Chapter 23

Krishan came on a holiday, sometime in August that year, and he enjoyed a great time with the family, as they all went camping near Bright. They persuaded Connie to join them too, and he wanted me to accompany him. but I said I needed time to myself, and it would be good for him to go on his own, and be with his family. So he spent a day, and one night at the camp.

Krishan was a very pleasant young man, in his early twenties now, and visited us a few times before he returned to Germany. One of his friends too, visited us later on, as he had made friends with Stacy. But we did not hear from Stacy for more than a year, and could not contact him anywhere in Sydney. We kept calling the phone number he gave us, but the people there said he did not return, and he did not leave any belongings either.

When Connie contacted the police at Ferntree Gully, one of the officers told him, "It's not a crime to go missing." We were very concerned now, as it was quite a while since Stacy contacted us, but we did not know what else to do. I hoped he would call us for Christmas that year, but the deafening silence continued. My heart ached for him, as I did not know why he was not communicating with us.

Connie wanted to move out of Rowville, so we drove around looking for a block of land. We always liked the seaside town of Frankston, as we took the children there often. And even when we lived in Nunawading, we still drove down to Frankston. We parked near the pier, while the children ran around and climbed the steep hill below Oliver's Hill. They loved to roll down the hill right to the bottom, in spite of getting mud and grass on their clothes, and they enjoyed some good times there.

The estate agent drove us around, and we ended up seeing a nice block in Heatherhill Road, Frankston. We glimpsed great sea views from the street, but as a couple of two-storey houses were already built, they obstructed sea views from our block. But we purchased that block of land for about fifty five thousand dollars. It was less than a quarter of an acre, but we bought it as an investment, with the intention of selling it later.

I applied for a job in Frankston office in 1995 at level four, although I was paid higher-duties at level five, as a section manager in Boronia (which was a temporary position). I did not have to go out to reception or counter any longer, but interviewed only "complex" cases.

I was not selected for the position I applied for, but they offered me a job at level three instead. I was not interested, as I was already gazetted at that level, and wanted to transfer out only at a higher level, as I was better off at Boronia.

I suffered a severe tachycardia attack around midnight in April 1995. I was busy all day, cooking lunch and dinner for Wendy and Brian, who were spending a couple of days with us. It was Easter Sunday next day, and I ended up in an ambulance to Dandenong hospital. Wendy was very frightened, when she saw paramedics jabbing needles in my arm, as they tried their best to get my heart beat to slow down.

I was in hospital a couple of days, and returned home feeling exhausted after the trauma of that attack, and suffered severe chest pains. The morphine gave me severe headaches. I did not tell Ammie and Thathie about all these attacks, as they would have just worried, and being so far away, I thought it was pointless to burden them.

It was now over a year since we heard from Stacy. And as we were very concerned about his continued silence, we approached the Salvation Army family tracing service, and they promised to do their best to locate him. It was a constant, nagging worry, that made me incredibly sad, as I missed Stacy dearly, and hoped he would return home any day now.

We went to Ceylon in May that year, as it was my parents' fiftieth wedding anniversary, on 15 May. A few days before we left for Ceylon, Christian had a nasty experience, as his car was stolen from some place in Rowville. It was later found torched to the frame, and he was absolutely devastated.

It was on the same day I had an interview at Frankston office, and as I was leaving, two policemen, who were parked outside our house, approached me and asked if Christian's car was stolen. He was still asleep inside, so I woke him up. And when I told him the reason why, he just burst into tears, "*Why* do all these bad things happen to me Mum?" I pacified him, and told him to go out and talk to the policemen and I left. I could hardly concentrate at the interview, but did not mention that distressing incident to the panel of interviewers.

It was a fantastic re-union in Ceylon, as most of the remaining family members were present, except Shirani and Ranjith. Aunty, and Aunty Molly joined us this time, and we stayed at the Airport Gardens Hotel on the night we arrived. The smorgasbord-style breakfast was delicious, as they had a variety of foods. We hired a van later, had lunch with Connie's relatives, where we dropped off Aunty and Aunty Molly, and finally arrived in Maharagama around four o'clock.

I can still picture Ammie standing at the gate, and exclaiming with a slow smile, "I was so *worried* when you didn't come earlier! Where were you? What happened?" I explained that we dropped Aunty and Aunty Molly at a relative's place, and were invited for lunch there.

Ammie went inside quickly, and brought out a little gift box. When I opened it, I found a beautiful amethyst ring. I hugged her, and thanked her, but before we could unpack our suitcases, she disappeared. It was 6 May that day, and as it was Rita's birthday, Ammie said we were invited for dinner at Granny's place, along with the rest of the family.

Ammie went early, as she was on medication for diabetes, and was already feeling hungry. She looked very ill, and frailer than when I saw her the previous year. And my heart felt heavy to see her in such a weak state.

Thathie was his usual, jolly self, after a couple of drinks, and we walked up to Granny's to greet Rita, who smiled happily, as she was glad to see us. During the evening, I mentioned that I would like to organise a family lunch, to celebrate their fiftieth wedding anniversary. They were agreeable, and we had to settle on a venue now.

We gave them five hundred dollars each as a present, and told them we would pay for lunch and drinks, so not to worry about the cost. In the midst of all this happy talk, Nilanthi, Heron, and Tanesh arrived, and it was absolutely delightful being together again.

Ammie was very happy about the forthcoming anniversary party, and the very next day, she started writing invitations to her nearest and dearest relatives. She was very sad though that Malcolm, and Uncle Barlow, who died of a lung disease a few months ago, were not there to celebrate.

As they compiled a list, I was vastly amused when they broached the subject as to who should be invited to the party; for instance, when Thathie wanted to invite his brother's widow, Karuna (whom Ammie did not like), Ammie objected vehemently, and vice versa when she wanted to invite someone *he* did not like.

The conversation went like this, "Raja, you can't invite Karuna to our anniversary party, because she's a *widow* and its bad luck!" Thathie's lips twisted sardonically, "Then Carmen, what about Indrani, your brother's *widow?*" Ammie sulked. Thathie drank, and muttered sarcasms to annoy her, while I tried to find a happy solution to this dilemma of drawing up a mutually acceptable guest list. Ultimately, it was up to Ammie and Thathie to decide who should be invited, as it was their party.

I was taken aback, but thoroughly amused, when Ammie showed me the letters she had written to all the relatives, saying she preferred to receive cash gifts instead of knick knacks. And she told me very seriously, "If I don't mention it, they'll all end up buying cheap rubbish from the pavements! It's much better to give us some cash!"

Ammie's honesty, and simplicity made me laugh out loud, "You can't write and ask cash gifts Ammie! Let them give you whatever they want!" But it was hilarious when a relative turned up the very next day, and presented Ammie with a brightly coloured ceramic angel. Ammie came to the room and whispered low, as she showed me the present, "See Dolly! *Didn't* I tell you what sort of things they'll give me?"

As she was getting ready for the party, Ammie said, "I can't see very well Dolly, can you apply my lipstick?" I thought then, how ill and worn-out she looked, and my heart ached. The lunch that we organised for about fifty people at one of the local Chinese restaurants, was a great success. All the invited relatives and friends turned up, including Aunty Molly and Aunty.

Granny climbed up the steep, narrow flight of steps with my assistance, and laughed as she remarked, "This is like climbing the stairs to Paradise!" Although she was in her mid-eighties then, she was game enough to climb up the long stairs and partake of a good lunch.

Nelune arrived a day later though, and so did Rosie and Christine. As we were staying for two weeks only, we held the party on 11 May. Marie and Neville arrived, and Anthony too. We enjoyed great times in the evenings, when we were together, and sang old songs, joked and laughed. Rita laughingly called our group, "The singing shit-birds."

Rosie looked slightly better, and slimmer, although she limped when she walked. One dark, rainy evening, as she tottered along in the slippery grass to visit us at Ammie's, she had a nasty fall, and was laid up in bed for a few days. When she returned to London, she became worse, and they thought the fall had an adverse effect. The tumour was growing larger, and affected her speech and mobility now. Christine nursed her constantly, and I have nothing but admiration for her amazing care and service through those harrowing years.

One of the happiest memories of that precious time with my family, was one evening, when Nilanthi, Nelune, and I sat around Ammie. We poured her tea, manicured her toe nails, and pampered her with our undivided attention and care. Thathie was napping, and Nelune joked, "Thathie should go on sleeping longer, so we can spend more time with you Ammie."

Ammie laughed happily as she said, "Now I know I'm a very *lucky* mother, to have three of my daughters around me, and only poor Shirani is missing today! But at least she spent a few days with us last year." A little attention and tender, loving care brightened up Ammie's day so much, as she was always content to stand aside and let Thathie bask in the limelight.

Connie went out every day to spend time with his mother, and other relatives, so it was good for us to be with our families.

The night before our flight we left for the hotel, and the whole family accompanied us. I sewed a few skirts and blouses for Ammie, and she wore one of them that evening, but they hung loosely on her frame, as she was so gaunt. When it was time for them to leave us, Ammie cried so bitterly, that I was deeply saddened. She was inconsolable, although I kept saying, "Don't cry Ammie, we'll come back soon." She cried even more, and her whole body trembled uncontrollably. Thathie tried to console her, "Carmen, you will end up with one of your migraines, if you don't stop crying!" That was my last memory of Ammie, crying as if her heart would break. Long after we left, I wondered if she had a premonition that we would not see each other again.

Chapter 24

When we returned home, I was busy once again with several projects, which included music, writing, and painting. I entered the Stringybark festival in Rowville, and my pastel painting of large "Poppies in the field" won first prize. I will never forget the rush of adrenalin throbbing through me, when I walked in, and saw the certificate attached to my painting. The exhibition was held at the old Stamford House in Rowville, which was over one hundred years old. It was a beautiful old homestead, with high, vaulted ceilings, and ambience of a bygone era. Connie invited his family to the exhibition, because he was happy for me.

A popular Women's magazine held a literary competition that year. And I wrote "Serendib-Isle of dreams," a romantic fiction, about one hundred thousand words long. The prize was $5000, and I told Ammie that if I won that prize, I would definitely come over for a long holiday. She was so pleased, and encouraged me, as she believed I could win.

I typed away frantically during every spare moment of my day, and sometimes during lunch and tea breaks at work too, My supervisors did not stop me from working on my novel in my own time. A few months earlier, I bought an electric typewriter, which was a vast improvement, after my 1972 portable Remington.

The idea for the story came to me in a dream one night. And when I woke up next morning, I wrote down the entire plot in one sitting. Later on, I embellished, and fine-tuned the story, until I was satisfied with the end result. I submitted the manuscript, and hoped for the best, but did not win any prizes for my novel. It was shelved in a bottom drawer for the time being. I hoped to work on it again one day, and try another publisher.

Cuckoo's daughter, Clarissa, and her girlfriend, visited Australia in August 1995, and travelled everywhere with Christian. They went to Eden, in New South Wales, and enjoyed a great holiday with the family, and Clarissa left soon after.

Christian met with a bad accident a few months later, and his car was a write off, but thankfully, he was uninjured. He was ingenious, and enterprising, so he started fixing up the wrecked car. And it was amazing how he put it all together again. He helped David to fix up cars sometimes, so he had a very good knowledge of motor mechanics. When the car was repaired, he sold it for a reasonable amount.

He decided to spend that money on a holiday. And I was surprised when he said that he wanted to travel overseas, especially to Germany and England.

I did not dissuade him, as he was old enough to travel on his own, but I knew I would miss him dearly. He was always very close to me, and very loving from his childhood days. Christian was extremely talented, clever, and exceptionally good-looking, and he also modelled clothes since he was a teenager. I was very proud, not only of his achievements, but of his caring nature, and great personality.

Stacy too, had a gentle, caring side, in spite of his troubled character, and to me, they were the most amazing children that God blessed us with. They were so intelligent, clever, and unique, and I knew they would succeed in life no matter what they undertook.

Shortly after he sold his car, Christian flew out to London, believing that he could stay a few days with Rosie and Christine until he found lodgings. Rosie told me he could stay with her as long as he liked. But he had a nasty shock when he arrived in London, because Rosie told him that she was too unwell to keep him.

Anxious and disappointed, he rang immediately from Heathrow Airport, as he was stranded in a strange city, without a place to stay. I called a chance acquaintance I met on the plane in 1994, when I was returning to Australia; she was a friendly lady, Josephine Lewers, with whom I corresponded sometimes, as we had formed a long-distance friendship.

I explained Christian's predicament, as he did not know anyone except Rosie and Janice, who lived in Dunstable Downs. Josephine said, that Derbyshire, where she lived, was very far from London. But she would ask her son to recommend a reasonable hotel, until he found long-term accommodation. Christian stayed in a motel for a few days, until he could organize something more permanent.

Before he left Melbourne, I spoke to Rosie, and she told me it was quite alright for Christian to stay with her. Anthony told me off in a very abrupt and heavy-handed manner that Rosie was very sick, and in no position to keep Christian. Rosie called a while later, and said it was all a big misunderstanding, and she wanted Christian to come there as soon as possible.

When Christian called me a few days later, I conveyed her message, and he stayed with her a few weeks. He helped them out so much with housework and shopping etc. that they were very impressed. He moved to lodgings in a few weeks time though, as Rosie was going to Ceylon, and she wanted to lock up the place during her absence.

Coincidentally, Linda was also in London then. They met in a pub, and remained good friends, but did not resume their relationship, as they were with other partners. They worked in pubs, until Christian travelled on to Germany.

Cuckoo and Regina welcomed him warmly, and he enjoyed his time with them very much. He travelled around Europe for almost two years, and worked his way through the Continent. But had trouble getting back to England, without a working visa. So he wrote that he would return soon.

Chapter 25

We celebrated our 25th wedding Anniversary on 18 November 1995, and spent a few days at Port Campbell. We dined at one of the local restaurants, and afterwards, we walked around the small tourist town, and enjoyed the scenic area. Numerous ships met their end near this rugged and treacherous coastline, and many tales of shipwrecks abound in Port Campbell. We drove around sight-seeing, and headed home after an interesting trip.

Ammie sent five dollars (a substantial amount in rupees), and asked me to buy a souvenir for our anniversary. I was deeply moved, because I knew how much she must have scrimped, to save that money. So I bought a silver-plated spoon, with a picture of Port Campbell on it. And I told that I would keep it in remembrance of her gift. She was happy to hear we enjoyed a good trip.

I secured a level four gazetted position, at Cranbourne Social Security at the end of 1995. I was keen to transfer from Boronia, as the entire work structure was changing. And there was talk of Boronia office closing down completely. Some staff were already transferred to Knox City, and Upper Ferntree Gully.

Theresa, who was a friend and colleague, appealed against my promotion. But her appeal was overturned, when they interviewed me a second time. And I was officially appointed at Cranbourne office in early February 1996. The manager, my supervisors, and most of the staff, said they were sorry to see me go, and organized a farewell lunch. I too would miss my friends, but it was time to move on.

Cranbourne was about half an hour from Rowville, and I drove there in my old car. On my very first day there, much to my dismay, I suffered a severe tachycardia attack as I sat at my desk. The manager, Chris, and other staff members, did not know me at all, or that I had a medical condition. So I phoned Connie, and he came within the hour and drove me to hospital. I did not want an ambulance to come there on my very first day at work.

I was off work for one week, but I soon settled in. And I was quite pleased, as my staff consisted of women and men in their early twenties, whom I had to supervise and "coach." I soon made friends, as I related well to them. In time, I became very good friends with the co-supervisor, Anne, an attractive Irish lady in her early forties. Evidently, she had kissed the Blarney Stone, because she was a great talker, with an adroit tongue. We visited each other, and shared many common interests. She possessed a good sense of humour, and lively manner that I found amusing. And we laughed and talked a great deal during our breaks, and in-between work.

I thought she was a nice person, and trusted her implicitly at the start. How was I to know she resented my position and popularity, as most people did not like her very much. The manager wrote in the office bulletin, "Nalini comes to us with a great reputation," and so they had high expectations.

My previous manager at Boronia gave an excellent report, regarding my work, and team-building skills. I soon organised international lunches, and other social functions, just like in Boronia office, and those occasions were great fun.

Shirani and Ranjith bought a block of land in Narre Warren south, and were building a house there. We looked at display homes for some time, and decided to build a Tudor-style home on our block. Shirani and I liked that design very much, so they decided to build a similar house.

They did not sell their house in Hampton Park then, as it was not a good time to sell. But rented it to someone they knew, and sold it a couple of years later. It was a busy, but happy time for Shirani, as the house was to be completed in early July, and she shopped around for curtains and furniture.

Shirani held a surprise party on Ranjith's fiftieth birthday on 13 March, at a Chinese restaurant in Hampton Park, and invited all his friends and family. Some people travelled from interstate as well, and Ranjith was indeed surprised, when we all turned up at his dinner party. Nelune too arrived in time for the party, and we had a great time. Anjo made a huge birthday cake, and after dinner, Roshan gave a moving speech.

Ammie fell ill some time later, and was admitted to hospital for a few days. When I called to wish them on their fifty first wedding anniversary on 15 May, Ammie pleaded to bring them to Australia permanently. It was the first time in all these years she wanted to immigrate. And she said, "We are very lonely here, and miss you all dearly."

Connie suggested that they come on a holiday first, and see how she liked it here. But Ammie became upset and agitated, and insisted that she wanted to immigrate. I told her that we would sponsor them soon. And I wanted to help them financially as well, because Thathie told me that all they needed was a little bit extra every month, to make ends meet. I was in a better financial position now, so I intended to send them fifty dollars a month.

The following week, I stopped at Shirani's on my way home from work, as they were busy packing, and buying furniture for the new house. She bought a very nice lounge-suite, and asked me over to have a look at it. I told her that Thathie called the night before, as Ammie was in hospital again with heart failure. We were very upset, and hoped she would recover soon.

Driving home at dusk, I nearly met with an accident, when the car in front of me stopped abruptly, but I jammed brakes just in time. My heart flipped in panic, but I was alright, and arrived home safely. I just stepped inside, when the phone rang shrilly. And I knew immediately that it was Thathie, with news of Ammie.

His voice was subdued, and he sobbed brokenly, "Dolly, my dear, Ammie passed away this morning!" I could not stop my tears flowing, when he described how much pain she was in, and had cried, "Jesus, take me away!" He told me, that contrary to doctor's advice, Ammie continued walking up to the junction in very hot weather, to do her shopping every afternoon. Invariably, when she returned home, she lugged two or three heavy bags of fruit and vegetables.

That afternoon was no different. But when she came home, she was in severe pain, and gasped for breath. He rushed her to hospital immediately. Connie walked in just then, and took the receiver from my hands. It was 23 May, exactly a week after their fifty first wedding anniversary.

The next day, Connie and I drove to St Anthony's church in Hawthorn, and I lit candles, and prayed for Ammie's soul to be at peace. Then we stopped at a park nearby, and I recalled all the things Ammie endured in her life. I felt utterly sad, and desolate, that she died at the age of sixty five. She could have enjoyed many more good years ahead. But it was not for me to say how many years we are allocated in this life.

None of us were able to attend the funeral, but Thathie said it did not matter, as Ammie would not know anyway. And he did not mind, as he understood our situation. He agreed that it was more practical to help financially. Shirani, Nelune, and I, paid for the entire funeral.

I did not like attending funerals anyway, as it was a pointless exercise. I would rather visit people when they were alive. And I was glad I saw Ammie the year before, and ensured that she enjoyed our last family reunion. Nilanthi helped Thathie organise the services, and alms-giving. Thathie could not believe that after all these long years, he had lost his faithful companion and wife, and he was totally devastated.

Nelune flew to Ceylon just after the funeral though, and was a great comfort and support to Nilanthi and Thathie. And she promised Thathie a holiday in Australia before the end of that year. Thathie clung to that little ray of hope, as he looked forward to visiting us again.

A few days later, when Nilanthi called to ask us about Ammie's belongings, none of us wanted anything, and we told her to donate everything to charity.

Ammie had over one hundred beautiful saris, some were never worn at all. She also accumulated umpteen bottles of perfume, costume-jewellery, etc. It was a daunting task for Nilanthi to wade through all that stuff.

I grieved silently, and deeply for my poor mother, who had suffered so much. I missed Ammie dearly now, but she would never know how much she meant to us.

I took a couple of days off on compassionate leave, and then went back to work with a heavy heart.

Thathie called sometime in early June, and sobbed brokenly, "Dolly, if *anything* happens to you too, I'll just commit suicide! Look after yourself." I was upset, and very anxious about him, and wondered how he would cope living alone. He knew I was prone to frequent tachycardia attacks, so he worried about my health now.

After Ammie's death, co-incidentally, Shirani, Nelune, and I, moved from our previous residences. Nelune bought a beautiful, two-bedroom apartment on the same street in Mosman, where she lived all this time. Shirani moved to the neighbouring suburb of Narre Warren, after nineteen years in Hampton Park. And we sold our house in early August, after eighteen years, and started building in Frankston.

Nilanthi and Heron left the farm, as he retired, and they moved in with Thathie. We thought it was an ideal solution, as Thathie needed company, instead of spending his days alone, drinking and grieving over Ammie. When they moved in, Nilanthi changed everything, and removed all Ammie's furniture and belongings. She thought that the sooner she rearranged the house, Thathie would get over his grief.

But it all backfired on Nilanthi. Thathie resented the fact that he had to share the house, because he felt like a "lodger" in his own home, as Heron tended to lord it over the place. Thathie spent his days and nights in the small back room; he told me that he could not bear to see Heron sitting in the lounge in Thathie's favourite chair, and generally behaving as if he owned the house.

Thathie bemoaned the fact that they wiped out all traces of Ammie from the house. He berated Nilanthi for not leaving Ammie's belongings alone, for him to sort out. She was surprised and hurt, as she sold all the things and gave Thathie the money. He also found Ammie's bank book, with about thirty thousand rupees in her savings account, which he used for travel expenses when he came to Melbourne.

Ammie grew begonias, and roses for sale, and whenever we sent her cash gifts, she always saved the money. She was very thrifty, and terrified of being destitute again, like the time when Thathie lost his job all those years ago. Now, when I heard Thathie's complaints, I advised Nilanthi to be patient, as he was not himself after Ammie's death.

Nilanthi made sure that Thathie ate well. But she found it very difficult when he drank heavily in the evenings, and upbraided her for "barging in'" before he laid Ammie's memory to rest. It was a distressing situation for Thathie and her, because she believed she was doing what was best for him.

Connie and I worried about Stacy constantly, as it was uncharacteristic of him to be so silent. Mother's Day, Father's Day, birthdays, and Christmas' went by, without a phone call, or a line. Every day, we hoped to hear some positive news, but the Salvation Army was unsuccessful in locating him, or finding out anything about his movements.

We believed he was still in Coffs Harbour or Armidale, and I hoped fervently that he would phone soon, and let me know he was alright. But the days moved on to months, and I was troubled. I was also upset that Stacy did not even know Ammie was dead.

On 7 July 1996, Shirani and Ranjith moved into their new house. She was so excited, that she slept there the very night they got the keys, even before all the furniture was arranged. I cooked dinner for them, and when we arrived, the carpet layer just finished, and Ranjith mopped up the tiled area. It was a beautiful house, and I was very happy for them, as it was exciting to see the completion of it. Shirani selected everything with good taste, and great care.

She employed someone to sew ivory-toned drapes, with curtain pelmets made up in the same fabric as the lounge-suite. When she decided to plant only white flowers in the garden, I suggested "Le Jardin Blanc" (the white garden), as a name for the house. She thought it was a good suggestion, and made a plaque with that name engraved on it.

A few months ago, when we inspected the Villa Tudor display home, it cost about $250,000 to build it, on your land. So we gave up the idea, as it was beyond our means. Some time later, the sales lady at AV Jennings Builders, called to say that the price was drastically reduced. And if we were still interested, she would organise the building project.

We went ahead with the loan application, and our house went up for sale, even though the market was very bad. The agent said, that a few months ago, he would have sold it for $145,000 to $160,000, but we ended up selling it for only $115,000.

We decided to build the Villa Tudor on our block of land. And in late August 1996, we rented a two-bedroom unit in Reservoir Road, Frankston, which was close to the block. It was one of ten units, situated in a secluded area, and the rent was $125 a week.

I kept Tiger and Misty locked up under the flat, as pets were not allowed. And some funny incidents took place, whenever the agents brought potential buyers (as the unit was up for sale). I rushed out, grabbed Tiger and Misty, and locked them up under the flat, where they protested loudly, while I fervently hoped the agent would not hear their mewing.

Connie and I drove up every evening to see how the building progressed. It was exciting to watch the building take shape, from the time foundations were laid, until its completion. I waited impatiently to move in to our new house, as the small unit was cramped with all our furniture, and we could hardly move around.

We left most of the crockery and cutlery in boxes in the garage, and managed in that place for about three months. Esme, Cristobel, Aunty, Wendy and Brian, visited us regularly, and sometimes accompanied us on long drives. They were very curious to see The new house that we were building. But we told them to wait until it was finished, and they could visit once we moved in.

We enquired about curtains for the house, and some companies quoted around twenty five to twenty seven thousand dollars. I decided to sew the curtains, as I always did in previous years, except this was a two-storey house, with many large windows upstairs and downstairs.

When I drove past Dimmey's Store, in Frankston one day, I spotted some velvet fabric in the window display. I quickly parked and went inside to check the fabric, which were the exact colours I wanted; deep, dusty rose, and moss-green velvet. They did not have any other colours except these two, and I was pleased that I saw the fabric. We selected carpets, and tiles already, and I knew that the dusty rose matched the two-toned burgundy carpet well. And the moss-green was perfect, with muted peach and beige tiles.

I bought one hundred and fifty metres of each colour, at eight dollars a metre, which was very reasonable; so we saved a great deal of money on curtains. Then we bought curtain tracks from Dollar Curtains, and employed one of their tradesmen to put them up, as Connie said he was too busy, and tired, to fix so many tracks.

He helped me roll out bolts of fabric on the floor, while I measured and cut drops and valances for each pelmet and window. When I finished sewing curtains for each window, I marked, and wrapped them in plastic, so all would be ready when we moved in. I enjoyed sewing them, as I knew they would look good.

Everyone who saw the finished curtains later, could not believe I sewed them, as they said they looked very professional. Only downside was, that the block-out was not too effective. So I bought thicker block-out lining, and sewed it on, which was an immense task, but was much better protection against the hot summer sun.

I applied for a few weeks long service leave in September that year, as we organised a holiday for Thathie. Once again, the three of us paid for his ticket, as we thought it was good for him to get away from all his sad memories.

One morning, in early September, we picked him up from the airport. And I was immediately struck by the enormous change in him. He was remote, and acted almost like a stranger, which was a great shock, as he was always such a loving father.

He spoke vaguely, "So, Connie and Dolly, it's good to see you both again." Not at all like his loving, enthusiastic greetings in the past. We stopped for a snack and coffee at one of the shopping centres nearby, and then drove straight to the unit. Aunty and Aunty Molly waited to greet him, as they spent the previous night with us.

I made milk rice and beef curry for breakfast, and laid the table now, and waited for him, as everyone was very hungry. But he took ages to wash, and finally joined us, with an indifferent response to the old ladies greeting. He told me later, "I would have preferred a *Western* breakfast, as I often have milk rice and curry in Maharagama." I suppose I should have known that, but it was only the beginning of his difficult and strange behaviour.

Connie dropped off Aunty and Aunty Molly later, and in the evening we drove to Shirani's for dinner, as she requested. Thathie asked me in an off-hand manner, "So, Dolly, where am I going to be deposited tonight?" I replied laughingly, "You are not a piece of luggage, to be deposited anywhere!" And I put down his uncharacteristic behaviour to grief, and emotional state. Connie took Thathie on long country drives whenever he went on business, and even stayed with him in Bendigo one night.

Thathie enjoyed the long drives, and was almost jovial, like he was before when he told me about the good times he had on those trips.

I arranged the spare room for him, and he was happy, even though we were so cramped in that unit. He walked across the busy Frankston-Cranbourne road, to the little shopping centre, to buy a bottle of whisky from the bottle shop.

Jean, Barbara, and Nancy, were three dear old ladies, who lived in the units across ours, and were quite friendly with me. Jean was a large, jolly lady, with a craggy face, short, iron-grey hair, and pale-blue, merry eyes. She was very kind and sociable, and remained good friends with us. Barbara was a tall, slender, elegant lady, well-read and cultured.

Her unit was extremely neat, and furnished tastefully, with many expensive curios and works of art. It was quite the opposite to Jean, whose unit was a jumble of old furniture and ornaments. She did not care how the place looked, as long as the television was on, and she had a comfortable chair to sit on. Jean suffered a stroke many years ago, and had a slight speech impediment, as she struggled to pronounce some words.

But these kind souls made our stay in the flat very pleasant. Jean loved Tiger and Misty very much, as she had a pet cat too. Nancy, a faded lady, with a vestige of past good looks, was in her mid-eighties, and very pleasant and chatty too.

I invited them over for a cup of tea, so they could meet Thathie, and socialise with him. But he greeted them briefly, whisked into his room, and did not come out till they left. Thathie stayed a few days with us, and then with Shirani, who took him for long drives, and one of her school plays. He told us about his troubles, saying how very unhappy he was with his home situation, and that Heron took over the house completely, acting as if he owned it.

I sympathised with Thathie, and was very upset when he said, "I'm only a lodger in my own home." I tried to convince him that it was for his own good Nilanthi moved in, but he was very resentful. He said he preferred to live and die alone, like the character in Charles Dickens' novel, "Great Expectations," alone, with nothing but cobwebs, and his memories for company.

In retrospect, I think he was out of touch with reality by then. And it was increasingly hard to please him, as he seemed to have lost part of himself when he lost Ammie. Poor Thathie, I lost *both* my parents, as he was not my beloved father any longer, whom I idolised all these years. Grief had taken its toll.

Chapter 26

Nelune invited Thathie to spend some time with her in Sydney, so we dropped him at Southern Cross Station one evening. He was very pleased, as he told me he liked long, train journeys. Just before he left for Sydney, we drove up to the Dandenong's, and he boarded "Puffing Billy" the tourist train. A photograph of him peeping through one of the windows in the train, makes me nostalgic still. Thathie was very happy in Sydney, as Nelune and her friends entertained him, and he had a great time. She also took him on tours to the winery areas, and the Blue Mountains.

Thathie made a deep impression on Mrs Jean Buchanan, Nelune's next door neighbour. She called him "Raja" and invited him for elegant teas at her place. Mrs Buchanan took a strong fancy to Thathie, but he referred to her as "The Iron Lady" as she was a very resolute lady, with a no-nonsense attitude. We became good pen-friends from then, and she wrote interesting letters in her graceful handwriting.

I got along well at work, and now we had a new manager, also called Chris. He was the best manager I worked with, as he had great people skills, and treated everyone with respect. He soon appointed me as the harassment contact officer, and sent me for training to obtain my certification, and also involved me in several projects at work.

On International Women's day, celebrated in March, Chris nominated me to represent our office at a function, which ended with lunch at Moorabbin area office. Over one hundred women from various offices attended, and I was pleased to be there. Many guest speakers talked about the important role of women in the work place, and in society.

Shortly after that, I took on the role of stress contact officer as well. Many people found their way to my desk, and discussed work issues, customer aggression, and other personal issues; they trusted me, and found it easy to communicate with me. I always gave them my time, and complete attention. And sometimes, I referred them to other resources, as being the first point of contact, my role was mainly to listen, and refer them to professional advisors, and department of human resources. I enjoyed helping people, as I was genuinely concerned about their welfare. So, the first few months at work sped by quickly.

We operated a visiting service at Wonthaggi, about one hour's drive from Cranbourne. Once a week, two officers drove down in the morning, and returned by four o'clock. We processed work in a small shop-front office, collected benefit forms, and advised customers when they dropped in for information. As all members were on a roster, I travelled with a colleague every fortnight, and enjoyed the spectacular drive through the seaside town of Kilcunda.

The name, Social Security, was to be changed soon, and staff in all offices were requested to send in suggestions. None of us cared for the name "Centrelink" though when that was selected, as we thought it was an odd name for Social Security. But in time, we grew accustomed to it, as all the logos and designs were now changed to reflect the new name.

We wanted to move in to our new house by November, and he requested the keys to be handed over on 18 November, the date of our wedding anniversary. And much to our delight, the house was completed in time, and we moved in on that day as planned. We moved in to our Rowville house on 18 November 1978 as well.

When Melissa, the sales manager, the project manager, and some of the tradesmen involved in the building, arrived that afternoon, we served them chicken and champagne, to celebrate our move. It was a memorable event, and I was truly grateful to own such a beautiful and gracious home, like the Villa-Tudor. The builders at AV Jennings completed the house competently, even though Connie pressured them to finish it ahead of schedule.

On the night we moved in, Thathie came over with Shirani and Ranjith. And as he entered the house, he blessed us, and said, "I'm so happy to see you both in such a beautiful mansion!" He presented us with a quaint clock for the mantelpiece, with the same chimes as the sound of Big Ben, which I admired in a shop window. Thathie, who was with me then, pulled out fifty dollars, and said, "Go buy it Dolly, here's some money towards it." I added the balance, and thanked him gratefully, as I really liked that clock.

I loved the open fireplace especially, and on cold days, I lit a roaring fire all evening. Sometimes, I roasted chestnuts, when they were in season. Connie's family stormed in to "check" the house as soon as we moved in. Esme phoned Cuckoo later that day, and told him, "There are toilets in every corner of the house, but the kitchen is very small!" Cuckoo was curious to know if this was true, and wanted to know every detail about our new house. Connie told him that we had two toilets, and bathrooms upstairs, and one downstairs for visitors.

Cristobel rushed in next, and the first thing she told me was, "I thought you were going to build a *small* place! Why don't you knock this down and build a cottage?" I could not believe my ears, because the Villa-Tudor was such a stunning house, and we loved the design, that was why we built it. She spent the night, and woke up early next morning, only to criticize everything around. I did not take much notice of her, as I saw her spiteful expression.

From then on, every time Connie's siblings visited, and even Aunty, they said, "We visited so and so, and their house is much *bigger* than this!" And made sure to tell us that someone else's house was bigger, and better than ours. Connie retorted in exasperation one day, "We built this house because we *love* it, not to show off to anyone, or because we wanted to have a big house. This is an investment for us." None of them were happy for us though, that we built our dream house after years of hard work.

The smallest room upstairs was now my studio. We had the floor tiled in that room, so I could paint without worrying about spilling paint or turpentine on the carpet. I had ample room now for my model, "The Enchanted Forest" that I built a few months ago. I set it out on a large piece of hard-board, about two feet by three, and I displayed it on a small table in the studio.

All the children who saw it were delighted with the details of the forest, with miniature cottages, and buildings that I made with plasticine, a mirror-pond with ducks, farms, streams, and even a witch with a cauldron, sitting under an apple tree. It was a fantasy place I wanted to build ever since I saw Barry's model village when I was a child.

One of Connie's acquaintances, Chris Del Piano, a builder/carpenter, who was a contractor at Woolworths, built picture-rails in the studio, where I hung all my paintings. Chris was Rino's son, and Connie knew Rino since he joined Woolworths. Rino was a master-builder and craftsman, and Chris was apprenticed under him.

They were excellent builders, and Rino also cleaned our block, and cut the grass before the building started. He built several houses over the years, and worked as a contractor for Woolworths for a long time. We visited him, and his wife, Pam, in their beautiful house in Langwarrin that he built. And when I complimented Pam on their house and garden, she replied, "Rino will sell this house too, as he always does after four or five years, and then he wants to build another one!" They visited us a few times when we were renting in Frankston, and we were quite friendly with them. So, it was a shock when a few months later, Pam told us that Rino was diagnosed with a brain tumour, and was in a serious condition.

She had urged him to see a doctor, as he looked very ill, and she thought it was the flu. Rino's future looked uncertain, as the tumour was too close to his brain. But she said that if they did not operate immediately, he would not last even a few months. We visited him in hospital after the operation, and when he returned home. It was sad to see how a strong, vibrant man like Rino, now stumbled about unsteadily, and spoke in a slurred voice. His vision, mobility, and speech were severely affected after the operation.

They invited us for his only daughter's wedding on 23 February 1997, as his dearest wish was to see her married to her long-time partner. It was a lavish wedding, and after a garden ceremony, the reception was held at a restaurant in Frankston. But it was pitiful to watch Rino tottering from table to table, and struggling to articulate, but he made it a point to greet every single guest. Rino died a few weeks after the wedding. Connie attended his funeral, and was very upset. We planted the rose-bush in the front garden, which Rino gave us when we moved in to our house.

The studio window looked out to the court, and I could see our driveway clearly from above. And though we did not see the ocean, if we stood on the bath in the master-bedroom ensuite, we caught a glimpse of the sea. I named the house, "Willowynde" for obvious reasons, as we planted a willow that grew into a sturdy and graceful tree within six or seven years. And it was very windy up there on the hilltop.

We also planted a mulberry tree, that spread its branches in the backyard, and produced berries abundantly every year, and I made jam and liqueur with them. As I wanted to soften the aspect of the two brick columns at the entrance of the house, I planted lichen, and trailed it along the walls.

In a few years time, the tiny plant I carefully nurtured, covered the whole front, and was so rampant, that we trimmed it down regularly to stop it creeping up to the ceiling. But the dark, green foliage clinging to the red brick walls, added so much character and beauty to the house. And to my delight, many generations of doves built their nests in its sheltered nooks.

The position of the house was such, that we did not have sea views from any of the windows. And a few years later, we built a balcony outside our bedroom sliding door upstairs. But we only had views of surrounding treetops and rooftops from there. Though we only had to walk down the street, to look at the city skyline, and Port Phillip Bay.

The three ladies, Jean, Nancy, and Barbara, kept in touch with us still, and came for dinner once. I invited Lorraine, and her ninety-year old mother, Doris too. She lived with Lorraine and Tony now, as Lorraine did not want her to live on her own since she had a fall.

Doris and Lorraine came by taxi that evening, and we had a pleasant time with the ladies. Doris joked that Connie was the only male present, and said, "Let's see who can run the fastest and catch him!" She resembled Lorraine in looks and physique, and was a pleasant, jovial lady. Lorraine and Tony complained constantly though, that she was difficult to live with. And after a couple of years, Doris went into a nursing home, where she lived till she was about ninety-five years old.

I painted often now, and I had a fair collection of paintings hanging on the walls. Esme walked into my studio one day, looked around, and exclaimed, "The best thing I like here, is the palette with all the colours in it!" I thought she was joking, but she was quite serious. Or else, Geraldine and she came in and admired all the frames, but not the actual paintings.

We enjoyed lazing by the fireside whenever I lit it, and Aunty too liked to sit there and sip a brandy. We drove around Frankston, and surrounding areas in search of pine trees, and picked up pine cones to start the fire with.

Babs visited often, and spent a couple of days and nights with us. She grew very close to me from this time onwards, as she was on her own, and her sons were grown-up.

It was a very busy time, setting up the garden, and hanging curtains in all the rooms, and Connie employed a landscape gardener to do the heavy work. I wanted a fish pond, with a rustic bridge over it, so we went to Garden World in Springvale, and bought a fibre-glass pond, with a small fountain, and a ready-made, rustic bridge. We installed an old-fashioned coach-lamp by the bridge, and it looked very nice in the nights, with the sound of tinkling water from the fountain.

I showed Thathie how to use my electric typewriter, when we were in the unit, as Connie bought a computer a few months ago. And I wanted to give Thathie the electric typewriter. He was still using my old portable Remington typewriter, so he was very happy and impatient to try the electric typewriter. It was amusing to watch him though, as he found it difficult to get used to the high speed at which it typed, and the little window that spelled out words before typing them. He stared at the machine in alarm, but I told him to keep typing until he got used to it. And it kept him busy during the day, as he tried to master the "monster" (as he called it).

I asked him to spend Christmas with us, but he was in a great hurry to get back now. Thathie seemed a little bit better, physically and emotionally, and he enjoyed good food and entertainment that we provided, in the way of outings and dinners. But he could not be persuaded to stay on, so we dropped him at the airport in early December.

I still picture Thathie standing in the doorway of the security section, clinging onto the typewriter, which he carried as hand-luggage, his thin face grave and unsmiling. He just nodded, because he could not let go of the typewriter to wave goodbye. Thathie was unaware that we could not enter that restricted area with him. And he wrote later that he was very sorry that he went inside so soon, because he wanted to spend those last few minutes with us.

A comedy of errors occurred when he arrived in Colombo, as he mistakenly took another lady's suitcase at the terminal. He hired a van next day and returned to the airport to sort out his luggage. Poor Thathie! He was so confused towards the end of his holiday, and could not even focus his attention on trivial matters. He was happy to be at home, and took several little gifts and trinkets for all his friends.

We invited Connie's family for dinner that New Year's Eve, and they all came, except Geraldine and Clifford, who made an excuse. Lorraine and Tony invited us to go trout-fishing at a farm in Warburton, the day before the dinner party. I did not fish, but the others did, and we had a barbeque later. Josephine, who stayed overnight, joined us too.

It was a scorching day, and Josephine was tired after the long drive, so when we came home, she went to her room and rested, before the guests arrived. That was the only time she stayed overnight, as she told me later, that it was too tiring for her to climb the stairs, because she had angina. But she loved the house, and kept saying, "It's so gorgeous Dolly! You have such good taste!"

She visited often, and we took her to Ballarat once, when the begonia festival was on. We booked a motel there, and she was happy staying in the adjoining room with us. Josephine loved flowers too, and she enjoyed the spectacular begonia display in the hot house, and everywhere else. Connie and I visited Ballarat almost every year, on labour-day weekend in March, for the famous festival, and each year we invited one of the family.

Aunty, and Aunty Molly came a couple of times, then Shirani and Ranjith, and another time Esme, Paul, and Cristobel. A few years later, we stopped going, as I saw enough begonias, and enjoyed all the jazz music, art and craft exhibitions, to last me a long time.

Nilanthi said that Thathie was very anxious to immigrate to Australia now, and we were happy to sponsor him again. I wrote often, asking him to be careful of his health, if he wanted to immigrate, as he was seventy years old, and required to pass a medical examination.

Nilanthi called in March, and pleaded with me to get her down on a holiday, as she said she could not cope with Thathie. Heron was ailing, and needed constant care, and she complained that Thathie refused to eat his meals, and drank too much daily. It was a very traumatic period for us, but Nilanthi bore the brunt of it, as she had to live with Thathie. When I told Nelune about it, she offered to pay half, and we bought a ticket for Nilanthi. She arrived soon after, and stayed with us.

She looked care-worn, as the strain was too much for her, and I was very sorry to see her in such a state. It was obvious that she badly needed respite from that stressful environment. I pampered her, took her out shopping, cooked her favourite food, and generally tried to make her happy. And then, without even consulting Nilanthi, Heron's children organised a surprise trip for Heron.

Just two weeks later, Heron arrived in Melbourne, and he stayed with us as well. Nilanthi was very upset, as she really needed a break from him too. She complained bitterly about his interfering children, and cried inconsolably.

Tamara visited a couple of times, and took Nilanthi to spend time with her in her flat in South Yarra. We met her after seven years, when Thathie visited the previous year, and she took him out once. And on the day we drove Thathie to the airport, we visited Tamara in her flat. He was very sad to take leave of her, as she stood crying outside. He prayed for her welfare, and told me that he wished he could see her more often, as he cared about her. We did not see her again till Nilanthi visited that year.

Nilanthi was soon stuck in her usual routine, caring for Heron, and giving him all her time and attention. After about a month, Heron complained that the weather was getting too cold, and wanted to return home soon. It was such a pity Nilanthi did not have any respite from him. He visited his children sometimes. But he stayed with us most of the time, as Nilanthi preferred to spend time with us, and he stuck to her like glue.

Christian returned somewhere in mid-March, a few weeks before they left. It was wonderful to see him again, and I was so thankful that he arrived safely, after his travels overseas for almost two years. We had great fun together, and he showed all the photographs he took in England and Europe.

I had missed him terribly. And was greatly relieved he was home, even though he kept in touch faithfully; no matter which part of the world he travelled, he sent us postcards or letters regularly. He looked well and happy, and soon set about looking for work.

Christian did not have a car then, and he walked all the way to Frankston station and back, which was a very long distance. He had several jobs over the next few months, and worked briefly at each place, until he found something that he really liked.

Nilanthi and Heron went back to Maharagama sometime in early May. And she wrote to say that Thathie enjoyed himself hugely with Tanesh and his friends, as they had plenty of drinks every evening, and he was in his element. When they returned though, Thathie reverted to his old ways of refusing to eat, and spent all his time alone in his bedroom.

Connie and I promised to help Nilanthi with a monthly allowance of fifty dollars, to buy food items that she liked and needed. She told us that Heron did not buy anything for her with the money his children sent him. I was sad to see the state she was in, as she looked worn out and thin. So, from then onwards, we sent her an allowance without fail.

I suffered a severe tachycardia attack in June, and ended up going to Frankston hospital in an ambulance. A nurse in the emergency section told me, "Did you know there is a new procedure now that doesn't require open heart surgery? You should really consider it." A few months ago, one of Connie's colleagues recommended a heart specialist, Dr Kertes, and we consulted him as soon as I was out of hospital. He was a slender young man, with black hair, and light-brown eyes, and reputed to be one of the best heart specialists in Melbourne.

Dr Kertes advised me to book in to Austin Hospital as quickly as possible. He was the only surgeon then who performed ablations at the Austin Hospital in Melbourne. He was very persuasive, and warned me that there was a long waiting list, because we did not have private health cover. I demurred, and said I would think about it. His parting words were, "You'll be back here soon, and begging me to do this operation when you get another attack!"

As we were leaving his office, I decided to register. And the nurse said, "There is a vacancy in July, you are very lucky to get in so soon." So I booked in.

Connie drove me to the Austin Hospital on 23 July, and I was admitted around eleven o'clock. Then began a series of amusing events straight out of a sitcom (I thought). I went to ward D, and Connie looked so worried, and upset, that the nurse thought *he* was the patient, because I smiled cheerfully and looked out of the window at the pleasant garden below. The ward was clean and bright, and the nurses even brighter, and very pleasant.

Audrey, one of the patients in that ward, who had suffered with polio, was a woman in her late sixties, with a rubbery, mischievous face that contorted expressively. She wheeled herself up to her bed just as I entered. A nurse brought in Audrey's battered, old suitcase, muttering under her breath, "This weighs a *ton*! What on *earth* could she have in it?"

Anastasia, a hatchet-faced, Greek woman in her late seventies, shuffled to the window near the last bed, a nondescript scarf swathed around her head. She did not speak much English. Cass, a sweet-faced, little old lady in her eighties, with long, grey hairs sprouting from her chin, occupied the third bed.

The attractive and vivacious nurse who attended me, now handed a large triangular-shaped "nappy" with two ties on either side, and remarked, "Here's our wonderful designer-bikini! Doesn't fit *anyone* though, especially the men, with their bits and pieces!" I laughed, "Who designed these nappies anyway?" She chuckled, "*Not* Versace, definitely! *That's* not the reason he was shot!" A pretty quick repartee, alluding to the recent shooting of the famous designer, Versace. I laughed with her, and was quite relaxed as she prepared me for the ablation.

I watched Audrey wheeling herself frantically around the ward corridors, eager for her lunch. She bellowed out for all the patients to hear, "*Where's* me lunch?" And said conspiratorially, "I have an *enormous* appetite you know!" Then she rummaged in her suitcase, pulled out a parcel wrapped in foil, and nibbled surreptitiously at some hidden delicacy. The nurse placed her suitcase within easy reach on her bedside chair, as Audrey's legs were paralysed.

All I can remember prior to the operation was the anaesthetist jabbing a needle in my hand. And when I emerged out of the theatre six hours later, I felt dizzy and very cold. Dr Kertes spoke to me soon after, "It was a success, and we managed to locate the secondary electrical impulse and zapped it off. You should be able to leave hospital tomorrow, all being well."

Without private health cover, they did not keep me any longer than a day, due to the shortage of beds. My inner thighs were bruised and purple, where the surgeon inserted tubes through the artery. I felt alright, except a little weak, and extremely cold, as I lay shivering in the recovery room. Dr Kertes asked the nurse to cover me with a couple of blankets, and he left the room. He was very confident and capable, and I knew he must have done his best for me.

He also asked me to take it easy for a couple of months at least, without any heavy work etc. and his parting words were, "If you don't get another attack for at least five years, then you will be completely cured. Because sometimes, in a very few cases, the electrical pathway may grow back again."

Connie stayed in hospital, and prayed in the chapel (he told me), while the operation was in progress. He came in when I was wheeled back to the ward. He looked relieved, and said, "I suffered more than you, waiting in suspense for six hours until the operation was over!"

We spoke a little, and as it was late evening, I asked him to go home and feed the cats, as they would be waiting for their dinner. He left, saying that he would return early in the morning, as the nurse was unsure if I would be discharged next day.

Back in the ward the fun continued. I dozed off, and felt groggy most of the evening. But I opened my eyes, and saw another new occupant next to me. She was a very large, short woman, about seventy-five or so. All the patients in the Coronary Ward, were elderly women and men, and I was the youngest. The new patient was dressed in a bright pink nightdress; she strutted about hiding behind an oxygen mask, attached to a long, pink hose, and a very noisy oxygen box that she brought along with her.

When I surfaced from the depths of drowsiness, I heard a strident voice shouting out to the nurse, "Jacinta! *Come* here! Come here at *once!*" The nurse breezed in, and whispered, "Keep your voice down Trish, the lady next to you has just come out of the operating theatre!"

Trish's voice dropped to a theatrical whisper now. And she wandered over to the little old lady opposite me, determined to make friends. They carried on a conversation across the ward. Trish explained that she was in for an operation for a "Lump in my tummy." Two doctors, and the anaesthetist came in just then to examine her. I heard her raucous voice bellowing, "My doctor tried to tell me that it's a *hernia,* and I told him not to be stupid! It's a *lump*! Here feel it! It's a *lump* and the silly bugger tells me it's a hernia!"

The anaesthetist spoke calmly, "I have to give you a needle in the bum." Trish shouted out, "No, you're not! I'm not having a needle in my bum! Had it before and didn't like it!" "Then I can't operate on you!" The harassed doctor sighed. This impasse continued for some time, until their voices dropped to an inaudible whisper.

After the doctors left, Trish strutted around the ward showing off her "dotted" stomach, where the incision was to be made. She went about lifting her nightdress and showed everyone the exact dotted area, "It's going to be from here to here! I'll be in recovery for more than 24 hours...blah...blah..." Her droning voice rattled on. Later that evening, she turned on her radio, then switched on the television, and in the midst of all this racket, she carried on a loud conversation with Cass, whom she addressed as "Granny."

Trish bellowed out, "Granny, I'm looking for a man around seventy years or so! I've still got a lot of kicks in me!" Cass laughed loudly. Trish continued without pause, "Granny, do you watch Danielle Steele on television? Very good stories, I like them." Cass nodded, "No, I haven't watched any of those stories." Cass looked melancholy, as she sighed, "My husband, who died recently, never went to a doctor when he was ill, as he didn't have much faith in the medical profession anyway."

I dozed off and did not know what else Cass was saying. But as I drifted in and out of consciousness, and emerged from a deep sleep, Trish's braying voice jolted me once again. Anastasia, and the other patient, also recovering from heart surgery, synchronized a cacophony of snoring all through the evening. Trish shouted out to Cass, "Listen to them two sparrows or cockatoos, with their open mouths! Someone throw a jug of water on them or jab a needle to make them stop that racket!" Trish's voice was as unmelodious as a jackdaw's and grated on my nerves, as it did on the rest of the patients, I am sure.

I could hear only her cackling voice drowning all other noises in the room. And I hardly slept, even though my eyes were heavy, and my body cried out for sleep, and more sleep (the effects of the anaesthetic). At midnight, Trish complained that she could not sleep, because of the racket the other two women made with their snoring. I shut my eyes tight, and willed myself to sleep, but remained wide awake.

Another loud commotion erupted in the early hours of morning. The nurse, who started her shift, asked Audrey to put away the bulky suitcase inside the cupboard, as it was in the way, and she could not get around to the patient next to her. This request upset Audrey very much, and she started wheezing noisily, which ended up in an acute asthma attack. She moaned and bawled out inconsolably, "You didn't consider my feelings when you said that it's in the way! *I'm* not in the way am I? Awwwwww....boo hoo hoo!"

The unhappy nurse had a very difficult time, pacifying and reassuring Audrey that she did not mean it like that at all. She meant that the *suitcase* was in the way, and not Audrey. Too late! Audrey was deeply offended. She continued wheezing, and took to her bed, sniffling and sobbing her heart out. Her operation was scheduled sometime in the morning.

I was truly exhausted by six o'clock, as I had little or no sleep, and felt only pain now. Suddenly, a loud, whirring noise jolted me. It was Trish, with a faulty electric razor. She was shaving her chin, when next moment, she flew across the room, plugged in the electric razor in the socket next to Cass's bed, and tried to shave off the long, sprouting hairs on "Granny" Cass's chin. Cass covered her face with her wrinkled old hands, "No, no, don't shave me! Leave me alone!" She pushed her away, and that virago finally left poor Cass alone, shaken and scared, as Trish went off into the shower.

I noticed that Trish bullied everyone in the ward, including nurses and attendants. A loud scream filled the ward then, and louder gibberish from Anastasia, the Greek woman. She pointed angrily to an empty bag, and babbled incoherently. With many gestures, sign language, and explanations, we finally understood that her carton of Soya milk was missing from the fridge, which her son brought in especially for her.

I did not find out what happened to the missing Soya milk, as I was quickly wheeled out for an x-ray, prior to being discharged later that day. As I sat waiting for my turn in the x-ray room, another old lady was clearly very distressed. She kept screaming in a foreign language, and pointed to her lower regions. I watched her for a few minutes, and finally understood that she was desperate to go to the toilet. So I rang for the nurse, and in a few minutes she was whisked away to the toilet. Poor woman nodded at me gratefully when she came back. We crossed the barriers of language, and I nodded back at her with a smile.

I had fluid in my lungs, and was told that Dr Kertes had to see the x-rays before I could be discharged. And I was wheeled back to the ward, and put to bed.

Chapter 27

Connie came later that day, and spent some time writing a "Thank you" card to the nurse, who took care of me. Dr Kertes was not unduly concerned about the fluid in my lungs, and said, "It's quite normal after the procedure. But take it easy, and if there's a problem, contact me or the hospital." I was discharged, and Connie drove home aggressively and very fast. He was annoyed over some issue with Christian, and complained non-stop.

I was thrown about in the car, and I told him, "Can you drive a bit *slowly* Connie, as I feel sick with all the jolting!" He slowed down, but hardly spoke to me as we headed home. I went straight to bed when we arrived, as I was exhausted after a restless night. As I required complete rest for a few more weeks, I took six weeks long-service leave, as I had exhausted all my sick leave. My friends visited me, and brought me huge bouquets of flowers from work colleagues too.

I did not hear from Thathie then, as he was going through a dreadful period. Nilanthi wrote to say that he hardly ate anything at all, and she admitted him to hospital, as he was in a very poor state. When he was discharged, he continued drinking heavily, but abstained from food.

Nelune invited me to spend a few days with her in Sydney in mid-August, as she said a change of scene would do me good. We still did not hear from Stacy, although we called his last known phone number in Darlinghurst often, and each time they said he had not returned. The Salvation Army family tracing service wrote to us sporadically. They told us that they advertised in newspapers, Centrelink, and public places, but all to no avail.

When I arrived in Sydney airport, Nelune picked me, and later that day, we drove around Darlinghurst, in the hope of seeing Stacy around, but we had no luck. I spent a quiet time with Nelune, and one of the best evenings we enjoyed, was at a play called, "Late night Catechism." We laughed so much that I had an aching face afterwards. Joanna, one of Nelune's friends, joined us too.

We had meals at a Chinese restaurant, and after about four days, I returned to Melbourne. I was in Sydney on Thathie's birthday, 21 August, but we did not call him, as we were unsure if he was in hospital or at home. Nilanthi and Heron had connected a phone to the house now, which was very convenient. They did not have to run up to Granny's house now to receive or make phone calls.

Nelune planned to visit Janice and family in early October that year, and Thathie expected to travel with Nelune as well. But we knew he was in very poor health, and unfit to travel. She intended visiting him on her way to, or from London, as she was anxious to see him.

I returned to work, but applied for part-time hours, until I recovered completely. My friends from work visited me often, and Anne came too. We were still good friends, in spite of certain issues that came up in the work place. Anne was acting Section Manager, and was very pleased that she was finally given higher duties. And I was happy for her, as we worked well together.

Rosie called early in the morning on 17 October. Nelune was in London, and Rosie told me that Thathie died in hospital earlier that day. Connie took the call, and I knew what had happened, even before I spoke to Rosie. She heard the news from Marie, who was in Ceylon then. I lay in bed, tears streaming down uncontrollably. How suddenly Ammie and Thathie had left us! Connie just mumbled something when I hung up, but he did not hold me and comfort me in my grief. He may have felt sad, but he just could not console me with a few words or a hug.

I spoke to Nelune later on, and she said that she planned to stop over in Colombo, on her way to Melbourne. But she was very distressed, because she was just a couple of days too late to see Thathie. Nilanthi and Heron organised his funeral, but Nelune, Shirani, and I paid for all expenses. I was too upset and heartbroken, to even talk about his death, as drinking destroyed him.

Aunty called to sympathise next day, although Connie told her, and his family the previous day. She spoke vaguely, "I'm sorry Dolly, anyway, he's at peace now. Esme is here colouring my hair, she'll talk to you later." No sympathy in her tone at all, and even Connie had no words of comfort. It was the same when Ammie died. I cried alone, but not once did he say, "Don't be sad Dolly, I'm here for you." He could not express his emotions, although he sent money for the funeral immediately.

As I said, to me, attending funerals is a futile exercise, especially travelling overseas. Because I would rather have visited Ammie and Thathie when they were alive. It would have been different if I was living in Ceylon, as I would have certainly attended my parents' funerals. But to spend a great deal of money, just to avoid public censure, was absurd. None of us were present at Thathie's funeral either, which took place a few days after his death. He was cremated according to his wishes, but Ammie was buried in Pannipitya cemetery.

I phoned Anne at work, and told her that I did not want to talk about my father's death, as it was too traumatic. So when I returned to work after a few days, no one sympathised, or spoke about my loss at all. I was a little surprised, but some people told me that Anne specifically asked them not to talk to me about my father's death. That explained the general indifference of the staff, and I grieved silently. I had meant that I did not want to discuss details, not that I did not want sympathy from people. But I understood why no one even offered their condolences.

It did not take long for me to notice that a subtle change came over Anne. She did not consult me on any issue, divided the team up, and took away my supervisory role.

She loaded most of the outstanding work on me, without the slightest consideration, sent me back to the counter, and in general, treated me like a dogsbody in the team.

When I spoke to the new regional manager about the unfairness of it, she said I should try to work things out with Anne. Chris, the best manager I worked with, transferred to an area office, and I was very sorry to see him go. We had Margaret now, whom the younger staff members called "Vinegar- tits" for obvious reasons; she was an unpleasant, sour-faced woman, with minimal people skills.

I was completely bewildered at this sudden change in Anne's behaviour and attitude. She harassed me constantly, pinching and nipping in a dozen subtle ways, just like a crab worrying an insect to death. If she directed me to perform any tasks in the office, in a professional manner, I was flexible enough to adapt. But it was the arrogant and malicious way that she treated me, which I found unacceptable.

I could not stand it any longer, and requested a transfer from Cranbourne to Frankston, even though I knew Frankston was one of the busiest offices, and had a very bad customer reputation. The manager tried to talk things over with both of us, but I did not make any progress with Anne, as she stuck a knife into me. Her betrayal of our friendship was very painful to bear her, and just after Thathie's death too. Anne and I visited each other several times; she had enjoyed meals at my place too, when Nilanthi visited, and we were good friends ever since I came to Cranbourne.

Now she spread malicious lies about me, and half the team members ignored me, while the other half, who knew me well enough, befriended me. Anne let "power" distort her vision, as it was the first time she was in a managerial position. She deliberately provoked me, exerted her authority to the limit, and undermined me on every possible occasion. It was probably the most traumatic period in my career, and all due to one person, who made my life impossible.

I took leave over Christmas, until the matter was resolved. And I wrote to the workplace delegate in the human resource area, requesting an investigation into the state of affairs, as another team member was harassing me unfairly. When the dust settled down, and an independent person interviewed us separately, it was decided that I should be granted my request, and transfer out, in order to avoid further confrontation.

I liked Cranbourne office very much, but as Anne would not move out of the section, I requested a transfer. Never ever did I endure such an unfortunate experience with a colleague in my working life. I bitterly regretted the fact I was so trusting.

Anne had a cunning, treacherous nature, and she told me hair-raising stories of vengeance, and betrayal back in Ireland. When I first came to Cranbourne, she told me she had no friends at all. And I felt sorry for her, when she said that her neighbour scattered nails all over her driveway. One woman in her pony club, even tried to run her off the road on her way to work.

These tales shocked me, as I thought she was being victimised. But when I knew her better, I found that Anne had a habit of talking badly about everyone. But she turned the tables on me, and said that I spoke disparagingly about other staff members. It was her word against mine. I did not want to lower myself to her standard, and get involved in an altercation with her.

As I did not want a farewell party either, I took time off before my transfer. Some of my team members, who knew what Anne was really like, visited me several times, and we went out for meals. They assured me that they did not believe any of the lies Anne spread, because they knew who I was.

The first day I started work at Frankston office, in early January 1998, one of the men asked, "Did you have your head *examined* before you came to Frankston from Cranbourne?" Frankston office had a very heavy work load, and the customers were reputedly aggressive. Rumours spread that I transferred due to a dispute, and the staff were not too friendly.

That was only the beginning of my trials. The manager, Jan, was quite polite, but the other team members watched me stealthily, like alley cats, waiting to pounce on me, if I made the slightest error in my work. Then they reported to the section manager, who did not like me right from the start, and I did not like him either. He was a sly-looking, weedy man, in his forties, who played favourites with the young girls, and depended on them to make his decisions.

I felt I was being persecuted again for no reason at all, and spoke to the workplace delegate in the area office. She advised me to record any events that could be construed as harassment. It was a very unhappy period in my career, and I did not seem to make any progress in Frankston either. I worked extremely hard to secure gazetted positions, ever since I joined the public service, and was now at the top level of an administrative service officer, level four. Then the powers that be, introduced "Broad-banding," a system in which officers at levels one and two were progressively promoted to level three, and those at level three to level four.

It was great news for officers at lower levels. But for those like me, who achieved higher positions through hard work, job applications, interviews, appeals, and the difficult process of ascending the public service hierarchy, found ourselves actually "demoted" (in my opinion).

We were sent back to counters, and to process work that was previously designated to level two and three officers. I had no choice, but to follow directions, and accept the changing situation. I still believe it was a very unfair decision, and affected many of us during the transition period. We back-tracked in our career, and were treated with little or no consideration at all. I was a union member then, but I really do not understand how the union approved that "Broad-banding" system. I was disheartened, and unmotivated to progress, because I lost enthusiasm for my job.

I was unwell for some time, and I almost fainted with dizziness, one Sunday morning at church. The young doctor at Dandenong Medical Centre, whom I consulted later that day, heard me out about the stress levels at work, and nodded, "It's just stress, take it easy, and don't worry too much."

A few days later, on the night before my birthday, Connie and I dined at a local restaurant. I still felt unwell, and had a persistent cough too. I thought I was getting the flu, although it was summer, and the weather was quite warm.

But when I tried to get out of bed next morning, I could hardly raise my head. I went back to sleep, thinking it was better to rest, than go to work. Connie drove off to work, but a few minutes later, he returned, and told me, "You better go to the doctor, and check up what's wrong with you." I dressed with difficulty, and he drove me to casualty in Frankston Hospital. He raced ahead of me as usual, while I shuffled along unsteadily. I wished that he gave me his arm to hold onto, as I felt so dizzy, but I was too weak to call out to him.

The nurse checked me out, and immediately diagnosed pneumonia, as I was running a high temperature, coughing non-stop, and had a bad headache. I was admitted to hospital, much to Connie's surprise, as he did not think I had to stay in hospital. He asked the nurse, "Can she come home by night?" She looked him in the eye and replied, "No, she's too ill to go home." He left reluctantly, and went home to pack some clothes for me.

A female doctor kept checking me while I was in the emergency ward; she took x-rays and blood tests. After some time, she walked in, and blurted out in Connie's presence, "I *think* you have breast cancer! There's something in the x-ray on your left side, you better go for a scan as soon as you leave hospital." I looked at her in disbelief. She announced such devastating news right there, without any preliminary warning or consideration. I looked at Connie and whispered, "I *don't* believe it! She must have made a mistake, and anyway, I'll wait until I do a scan."

Connie was annoyed too at the casual manner in which the doctor broke this news. I underwent a series of penicillin injections for about three days, and was discharged after a week. Whenever Connie visited me, he looked harassed, and complained bitterly about everything; what Christian did or did not do, about the cats, or his work, or some issue. I looked at him, and wondered if he had any notion of what I was going through. He resented the fact I was in hospital, while he had to cope on his own. Although he was less impatient now, he still had bouts of bad temper, but he did not get as violent as before.

He was more agitated and tired now, with his busy work schedule. And he hardly took the trouble to get close to me for months at a time. If I questioned him, he snapped, "I'm too tired! This job is too stressful!"

Aunty spent a few days when I came home, but I never stayed in bed, like she expected me to. I got up from bed and came down for my meals, even though my legs trembled, and I sweated constantly. I was very weak, and lethargic for a long time. But, I returned to work after one month. I went for a breast scan later, and was relieved to be told that I did not have breast cancer. And I was very annoyed with that inconsiderate doctor.

When I returned to work, things were slightly better, as they were sorry I was so ill. I developed complications in my lungs, which made it difficult for me to breathe at times. Then began umpteen visits to lung specialists, and dozens of various tests, to find out what was wrong. The x-rays showed a patch or shadow on the left lung, but the specialists could not diagnose the cause, or prescribe a cure for it.

I was on different types of medication over the next ten months or so, but my condition did not improve. The slightest cold or flu meant that I ended up with a lung infection. Rosie and Christine sent me some beautiful plants through Interflora, and one of them, an umbrella tree, grew into a large shrub that I planted in the garden.

Rosie called me constantly, as she was very concerned about my health. Once, the specialist sent me to Frankston Hospital for a bronchoscopy, and I was under an anaesthetic for a few hours, until the procedure was completed. I coughed up blood clots next day, but when I called the hospital, they said not to worry, as it was normal, after a scraping of lungs. And a few days later, I was relieved when the coughing stopped.

When Nelune heard about my breast cancer scare, she went for a routine check up. But she kept the results a secret from me, as I was just recovering from my bout of pneumonia, and had other health issues too. So, I was very disappointed when I did not hear from Nelune for about a week, and asked Shirani if she knew where Nelune was. She was reluctant to tell me, but when she did, I was devastated. I could not believe Nelune had breast cancer, and she underwent a double-mastectomy in March 1998.

While I was at the counter in Frankston office, Connie called to tell me that Wendy died of a heart attack that morning, on 13 July. I could not breathe, and had to leave the counter immediately. She was always very dear to me, and I was grief-stricken when she died so suddenly.

She promised to visit me after my illness, but never got round to it, as she was down with flu over the last few weeks. Connie took Wendy, Aunty, and Brian, on one of his country trips about a month ago. And on the way home Wendy said, "Dolly, we're missing you! Wish you had come with us too! I will definitely come and stay with you when I come back." That was the last time I spoke to her.

I wept unhappily, and in the middle of it, one of the officers tried to carry on a "training" session with me. Talk about insensitivity. When she finally realised I was too distraught to concentrate on what she was saying, I left work, and drove home.

Connie drove to Wendy's straight after work, and did not come home to take me with him. But he had broken down at the sight of her lifeless body, and was inconsolable, shouting and crying out, "Wenda, Wenda!" Shiranthi told me that she had to drag him away from the corpse. He came home around eight o'clock that night, and he was shattered, as he loved her dearly. I hugged him tight, and he just bawled. I told him how much I had cared for her too, and tried to console him as well as I could.

When he calmed down a little, I asked him how it happened. And he said, "She was baby-sitting Brittany," (Valerie's younger daughter, who was about two years old then). When Wendy sat on her bed, and tried to light up a cigarette, she had just fallen back dead. Brian found her lying there when he returned from the shops. It was very sad, as she just turned sixty the week before.

The funeral took place a few days later, and the Wake was held at Sherone's place. Connie and I organised a requiem Mass for her, and invited the whole family for a meal afterwards. So it was that Wendy, a very kind, and sincere person, left suddenly. She lived for the moment; eating, drinking, smoking, and playing bingo right to the end. She was very ill, over-weight, a heavy smoker, and drinker, but only harmed herself, and left behind no hard feelings or bitterness among the family.

In early August that year, Janice, Bobby, Sarah, and Hannah visited Australia, to celebrate Janice's fiftieth birthday. They stayed with Nelune in Sydney, and she drove them up to Brisbane, and all the way back to Melbourne over a couple of days. How she endured that marathon drive, I'll never know.

Nelune, with her indomitable spirit and courage, fought back her cancer bravely, and looked well now. Janice and the family stayed with us for a few days, and we had a memorable time together. The two girls were delightful, and I enjoyed their company enormously, as well as dear Janice's. Bobby's relatives came over for dinner one night, and Connie invited his family too.

We went on a few drives down the Mornington Peninsula, to Arthur's Seat, and the beaches. They liked Melbourne very much, and I told them it was a pity we could not meet more often. Janice was just the same, lovely, caring person she always was, and I just loved sharing those few days with her.

The two girls slept on folding beds in the spare room (my studio), as Christian occupied one bedroom, and Janice and Bobby the guest room. Nelune slept on the couch downstairs, but we all had a great time together, talking and laughing till late at night. Janice filled in so many details about life with Nihal, as she flicked through the old photo albums.

It was such a pleasure to have them, and we spent quality time together, although it was such a brief stay. Janice had not changed her warm, loving ways, and I missed her dearly when it was time to say goodbye. On their way to Sydney, she sent me a beautiful bouquet of flowers, and they returned to London, after about three weeks in Australia.

Chapter 28

An accidental gas explosion in one of the main plants in Melbourne, in October 1998, disrupted gas supplies, and caused two weeks gas shortage. We brought our portable gas barbeque to the kitchen, and I cooked on it. Connie carried a large pan of hot water, and filled the bath upstairs for me to wash in, as the weather was still very cold. The water was just enough for a sponge bath every evening. We had electricity, but no gas, so I bought an electric frying pan, and a small heater for temporary use.

It was very inconvenient, but most of Melbourne suffered in the same manner. Connie and Christian showered in icy cold water, and I could hear Connie's shouts and yells, as the freezing water hit him. The Premier, Jeff Kennett, annoyed everyone when he declared, "Cold showers are invigorating!"

We drove to Shirani's place on some evenings, where I enjoyed a hot water bath, as they installed an electric hot water system. A few people came to work and showered there, as the office had an electric hot water system. I missed my daily hot water baths, and morning showers very much, but had to do without them, until gas supply was resumed.

We drove up to Sydney, and the north, a few weeks later, to find out what had happened to Stacy, as we still did not hear from him. Aunty and Aunty Molly spent ten days at our place, and took care of Misty and Tiger.

It was an interesting journey, and we stopped at several places on the way. The drive brought back many good memories of trips with the children, and of that time when Thathie and Rosie visited in 1985.

We stayed in Armidale, NSW, for one night, and made enquiries at the police station there. They said they had a record of Stacy's complaint about his stolen belongings, lodged in April 1994, but could not give us any more information because of privacy provisions. We knew then that Stacy had been in Armidale, as he told us so, but we had nothing else to go by; sadly, we drove on without finding any clues as to his whereabouts.

It was late at night when we finally drove through the Blue Mountains, and arrived in Mosman. Nelune looked well, although she was half her size, and her hair closely cropped. We spent a few days in Sydney, and Nelune drove us around to Terrigal, the Entrance, and some very beautiful scenic places. Connie and I drove to Coffs Harbour via Dorrigo (a place I fell in love with), as it was breath-takingly beautiful, then back to Melbourne. The cats were well, and I was grateful to them for taking care of my pets. They said Esme, Babs, and Cristobel visited a few times, to see how they were getting on.

Before the end of that year, Tanesh came to Melbourne on a holiday, and stayed with some of his friends in Hampton Park. They visited us a few times, and I made dinner for them, and Tanesh enjoyed his time here. But he was working without a permit, and someone inadvertently spilled the beans. He was held in detention for a few months, before he was forced to return.

Redundancy-packages was a hot topic at work, as the department cut back staff. I toyed with the idea, even though I was in the department only twelve years. I was heartily fed up of the changes, stress levels, and total lack of support by management. And I struggled with health issues too, so I worked only three days a week.

I still studied classical music, and sat for five practical, and three theory exams so far, with the Australian Music Education Board, and passed with "Honours" each time. When I sat for the preliminary, the examiner smiled and said, "It's great that you're sitting for exams, as it's never too late." I was among very young children, and I was forty-two years old then. She was very impressed and encouraged me to continue.

When we moved to Frankston though, I had to look for another teacher. And I found Irene, an excellent piano teacher, quite by chance. While I was walking in Cranbourne town one day, I happened to see her music school, which she ran with her husband, Tony. She too encouraged me to keep studying music.

Under Irene's training, I sat for theory, and practical exams each year, and made time to practice, and study theory after work, or on the days I was off. Connie too wanted to learn piano, and he went to Irene every Saturday morning. But he never had time to practice, because of his long working hours, and found it difficult to play with both hands. He gave up after a few lessons. At least he tried, and found out it was not very easy to learn how to read music, and play fluently, without practising daily.

I unearthed an old manuscript I wrote in 1995 for a competition, and began revamping it. Although it was a romantic novel set in Ceylon, I re-wrote the plot, included more adventure, drama, and intrigue, and wove threads of the ethnic confrontation into the background, and sub-plot. Even though I did not win that competition, I worked very hard on my novel. So, I searched for a publisher in Australia, or intended to self-publish it someday.

Ammie was full of encouragement, when she heard about the competition, and was sure I would win. She wanted to read the manuscript too, and I promised I would send her a copy, but never got around to sending it.

A writer from Mornington, Linda Massola, ran a publishing business, Beach Box Books, and she supplied schools with educational and childrens' literature. I became acquainted with her when I read an advertisement in the local papers. She wanted books from local authors, on consignment. So I sent her a few copies of my book, "Return to Enchantment." When I discussed my next book with Linda, she suggested that I should contact University Printing Press, in Fitzroy, as their costs were reasonable

I also subscribed to the local theatre groups, "Nomad Players" and "Frankston Theatre Group," and had the pleasure of seeing some very good productions at the Arts Centre Frankston, and at the Briars Homestead in Mount Martha. We attended a great production of "The Darling Buds of May" at the Arts Centre, in early 1998, which was a memorable evening.

We also saw a production of "The importance of being Ernest" staged at the old 1812 Theatre in Ferntree Gully, sometime in the early eighties, when we were in Rowville. I enjoyed live theatre immensely, and they were all excellent productions.

I was also privileged to see Rex Harrison and Claudette Colbert, in the play "Aren't We All?" when it opened at Her Majesty's Theatre in 1986. And musicals like "Cats" "Phantom Of The Opera" and "Le Miserables" just to mention a few of the unforgettable stage productions that we saw over the years. I loved theatre, and Rosie always said that if I ever visited London, she would take me to all the famous plays, especially "Mouse-Trap" the longest running play in London, and I promised I would visit her soon.

I was also busy painting, and making handcrafts too, whenever I had spare time. My Bonsai collection grew steadily, but I neglected to prune and shape them, as I was too busy with other projects, so they did not look like Bonsai specimens now. Friends and family visited regularly, and I was known for cooking delicious dinners, especially curries, and spicy food, that our friends enjoyed. We entertained a great deal, and visited our friends often.

Lorraine and Tony were our close friends, and now, Liz and Gerry were very friendly with them too, so the four of them socialised with us often. But I was not as close to Liz and Gerry.

Shirani and I visited each other on weekends, and whenever we could, but Nelune was unable to travel to Melbourne very often, as she had medical appointments and treatment etc. Connie and I were very busy at work, and seldom took time off to travel or visit Nelune then.

On the other hand, Nelune told me that she could cope better with her illness alone, without us having to watch helplessly. She underwent painful treatments, and we could do nothing to help, except pray for her complete recovery. She was very fortunate to have close friends around her, who supported and cared for her like her own family.

In the next year or so, she developed secondary cancers, which meant further chemotherapy, and more weight loss, until she weighed less than forty kilograms. It was a painful time for us, as we rode another wave of tragedy.

Rosie took a turn for the worse, and was now hardly able to move from her bed. Christine was marvellous, as she nursed her day and night, with the utmost devotion. Rosie spoke with the greatest difficulty over the phone now, and it was very distressing to hear her struggling to articulate. She was a fighter though, and determined to keep going as if nothing was wrong with her. She believed she would beat the tumour and recover completely one day; that was how optimistic she was. And never for a moment was Christine negative about Rosie's illness.

Chapter 29

I was convinced that I had enough of working at Centrelink, by early January 1999, and spoke to the regional manager about a voluntary redundancy package. She asked, "Are you *quite* sure about it?" And I replied, "I'm positive." So the departmental wheels were set in motion.

I intended to leave just after my birthday in February. After thirteen years of service, they offered me a reasonable package. But as I was under fifty-five years, I was unable to access my superannuation contributions. Five of us applied for redundancy packages, and were given free consultations with financial advisors, as part of the deal. I knew I made the right choice, as I did not want to waste any more years in an unsatisfactory career groove.

I was very busy getting my manuscript ready for publishing through the University Press. It was called, "Serendib-Isle Of Dreams." They designed a suitable cover, based on a photograph I sent, and I printed one hundred copies.

Then I contacted local newspapers, who sent a photographer home, and ran an article about my book. This was my first attempt at self-publishing, as the earlier book was published in Ceylon under Thathie's aegis. I negotiated with a few Ceylonese shops in various suburbs, and they agreed to take a few copies on consignment.

That was how I had a phone call one morning from a local radio presenter, "Rylie" who said, "Nalini, I'm standing here in this shop in Dandenong, with your book in my hand. Would you like to come on my radio show one evening, and talk about your writing, and this book 'Serendib-Isle Of Dreams?' Please let me know when you can come over."

Needless to say, I was quite pleased, and organized a time to appear on Rylie's show, which went off very well. Next, I sent copies to several libraries in Victoria and interstate, and was happy when they purchased copies. It was all about marketing (which I was learning as I went along). Not only did I write, edit, and proof-read, but now I marketed the books as well. Linda Massola edited the final copy of the manuscript, and also wrote the blurb, as she told me she found the story intriguing.

It was a "one-person" self-publishing business, and most of my friends, and some family members bought copies, so very soon, I sold all hundred copies. Those who read the book liked it very much, and gave me positive feedback.

That book was reasonably successful, but did not make much of an impact, as I did not hold a launch or advertise widely enough. I was still a novice at this game, but was quite satisfied with the result of this second publication. I wanted to send Rosie a copy too, as I was very keen for her to read it, and thought she would enjoy the story. When I asked Christine about it, she told me Rosie was unable to read, but she would read it out loud to her.

The staff and manager gave us a good farewell lunch, with presents and speeches afterwards. The team bought me a small, Swaroski crystal cat, as they knew I loved cats. After one year in that office, some of them thawed towards me, and were friendlier. I even invited a few of them home one evening. Christian moved out that same evening, when my friends arrived after work for nibbles and drinks. He decided to share a house with a couple of friends, which was five minutes away off Heatherhill Road. He was happy, and I wished him well.

The day after I left work, Rosie called me very early in the morning. "Why have you left work Dolly? Are you sick?" Her voice was thick and slurred. When I explained that I took a voluntary redundancy package, she was relieved, and wished me well. That was the last time Rosie spoke to me, because soon after, she lost the ability to speak and lay in a coma.

Christine struggled on bravely, and kept assuring me Rosie would "Pull through" as she was a battler." She could not, and would not accept the fact that Rosie was sinking fast and told me, "When I ask Rosie a question, she can blink her eyelids, and she understands what I say, even though she can't speak."

I just could not believe what a tragic ending it was for Rosie, as she was someone who had possessed the energy of ten people! Friends and colleagues rallied round her, and Tamara, who was now living in England permanently, visited her. Christine hardly left Rosie's bedside, and we prayed for a miracle.

Tamara phoned on 27 June, to say Rosie died that morning. It was overwhelming, and her death left an immense emptiness in all our lives. Rosie was such a vital, and beloved member of our family for as long as I remembered. Christine was devastated, but bravely set about organizing a spectacular funeral, with a horse-drawn hearse, decorated with a profusion of red roses. I spent the day with Shirani, and we sent Christine a wreath of red roses through Interflora.

We consoled each other, and shared myriads of good memories of Rosie through the years. We smiled and laughed through our tears, as we recalled her mischief, generosity, and great sense of humour. So, another chapter in our lives closed, when our beloved Rosie left us at the age of just fifty three.

I wanted to be involved in community work, now that I had time. And soon after Rosie's death, I joined the Pastoral Care Workers in our parish. I found a great deal of satisfaction visiting sick and lonely people in hospital. Conzuela, a Spanish lady, was a fantastic Pastor, and she ran a short training course on pastoral care, as part of our induction. I spent a couple of hours each week visiting the hospital. And

I also met several nice people there, including Colleen, who was a pious, and regular church-goer, and we became good friends.

One day, as I was desperate about Stacy's silence, and disappearance, I persuaded Connie to take me to a clairvoyant, Kerry Kulken. She lived in the Dandenongs, and helped with police investigations sometimes, so she was well-known and respected.

Kerry was a tall, lean, scary-looking person, with very long jet-black hair, heavily lined dark eyes, and dressed in flowing flapping garments. She fluttered her hands around some Tarot cards, and mumbled, "I don't see death anywhere. Beware a female in your close circle, who is very envious of you. You will be speaking in public very soon," and finally, "You will win tatts lotto one day; here are your lucky numbers."

It was the most disappointing experience, and we were no wiser as to Stacy's whereabouts. She interviewed Connie and me separately, but she did not tell him anything more. Kerry charged fifty dollars each, but was no help at all, as she did not even mention a missing person in our lives

We continued in limbo with no news, or the faintest idea of what happened to Stacy, my precious son. I cried silently; every night I dreamed of him, and woke up with tears running down in rivulets. My dreams were so vivid, that I felt I was actually talking and laughing with him. In my dreams, he was always a young child or adolescent, never an adult. I prayed constantly, and thought, "If only you knew how much I miss you, and how very much I love you Stacy, perhaps you would have found a way to let me know you were well and happy, so I can stop grieving for you."

The only way I could cope with my grief, was to keep busy, and not have a moment to brood on my sadness. I immersed myself in music, and was very busy with music exams at the end of that year. Irene and Tony (the music teachers), held a concert in Cranbourne at the end of that year. Christian, and his girlfriend, Athena, Shirani, and Ranjith attended the concert.

I was presented with a certificate, as I passed both practical and theory exams with honours. Irene asked me to play the theme song, "My Heart Will Go On, from the movie "Titanic" and we enjoyed that evening immensely. I played an electric keyboard, as they did not have a piano. It was the first time I played in front of such a large audience, and I was quite nervous, but I managed to get through the recital.

I converted a substantial amount of my superannuation into a fortnightly pension, which was just enough "pocket money" for me. And I was happy with a secure Government superannuation pension.

I worked out exactly what I wanted to do with my payout, and the financial advisor, whom I consulted, agreed that it was the best choice. So I contributed forty thousand dollars towards the mortgage, which reduced the loan considerably. Connie borrowed seven thousand dollars from his credit union to purchase a car for Christian, and I paid off that loan too.

Financially, we were not badly off now, as Connie earned a generous wage. After so many years of hard work and struggle, I now enjoyed my time pursuing my hobbies; art, music, and writing. And I revelled in my solitude and creativity during this period; especially since I was out of the rat race, and futile politics of my public service career. It was the first time in many years that I devoted my time and energy to things that really mattered to me, instead of worrying about earning money to balance our budget.

Babs visited soon after, and asked me to sew curtains for her caravan, which she had just purchased. It was an old van, but she wanted to live in it, and parked it in a friend's backyard. Connie and I measured all the windows, and Babs bought the lace that she selected. I spent a few days sewing them, and she gave me $200 for my efforts. We spent half a day hanging them up, and Babs was very pleased with the results.

Wide-spread panic and speculation about the impending chaos of the millennium bug (inability of computers to recognize 1 January 2000), built to a crescendo. We stocked up on food items, and withdrew extra cash, as a precautionary measure against such doomsday predictions.

Christmas 1999 passed peacefully, with the usual family gatherings. But Connie's mother, and Aunty Molly, were so worried about the doomsday predictions, that Aunty phoned me and said, "Molly and I want to be with you and Connie whatever happens! Please come and pick us up!"

They were determined to spend New Year's Eve, and the next few days with us. We did not mind at all, and Connie picked them up after work. We attended church that evening, and stayed up till midnight. Thankfully, New Year dawned without any global catastrophe, and we greeted the millennium New Year 2000, without any dire events.

On the following day, most of the family came over for lunch, and later, we walked on the Frankston pier. Aunty Molly and Aunty stayed on for a few more days, until they felt comfortable enough to return to their own homes.

Chapter 30

We flew to Queensland on 19 February 2000, as a result of attending a property investment seminar. They gave us free flights and accommodation for two days, and I boarded the cats for the first time at the RSPCA Animal Shelter in Pearcedale. I felt more heartsick, and upset than the cats, who mewed piteously all the way to the cattery. And I worried about them so much that, as soon as we arrived at the motel, I called twice to find out how they were. They told me not to worry, as they were comfortable, and settled in well.

The real estate consultant drove us around, and we inspected a few units and houses along the Gold Coast, before we found a townhouse we liked, and decided to sign up the deal. It was a new, three-bedroom townhouse in Reedy Creek, about five kilometres from Burleigh Heads, on the Gold Coast.

Once we signed all the legal documents, we spent hours at Scott's office, who became our financial advisor. He was a very pleasant, helpful young man, and when I commented on the spectacular view from his window, he took my camera, leant out precariously, and removed some great photographs of the mountain ranges beyond the sea. Some time later, I painted a pastel scene, based on one of the photographs he removed. Scott was delighted with it, and immediately hung it in his office.

We celebrated Connie's birthday over there. But he was like a little child that evening, as he wanted to stop everywhere, and see everything, although my feet were killing me, as I trailed behind. He raced ahead, as he usually did, so it was difficult to keep up the pace. Connie did not want to take taxis either, and insisted on walking. He told every single person he met, "I'm fifty five years today!" And he looked at them expectantly. Because when someone said, "You *don't* look your age at all!" he was very pleased, and grinned smugly. Connie was very vain about his looks, and kept telling me, "No one can believe I'm fifty five!"

Finally, we stopped for dinner at a Chinese restaurant, after briefly visiting the Conrad Jupiter Casino, (which held no great attraction for me at all). Connie wanted to "Try his luck" there, so we just went for the experience.

I found it pathetic to watch some human beings consumed with greed and madness. They sat like robots at the clanging poker machines, staring at the "one-armed bandit" as the cold, heartless box swallowed up tons of gold coins. And some others sat glassy-eyed around roulette and card tables. Connie complained about *everything* that night; the food was no good, etc. etc. and he was not happy with anything.

He looked sheepish when he woke up next morning, and said, "I dreamt that Nihal and Thathie were beating me up, because I gave you such a bad time last evening although you tried hard to please me!" So he knew, and admitted he was difficult all through the evening. It must have been his guilty conscience that gave him nightmares.

We picked up the cats as soon as we returned to Melbourne. They were slightly disoriented, but otherwise well enough. They mewed, and followed me around before running outside to sniff familiar places.

The property settlement was finalised in a month's time. In spite of slight apprehension, we were glad to take the first step towards property investment. We hoped to get a reliable tenant to rent it now. An on-site agent managed the huge complex, so we did not have to do anything, except pay the agent's monthly fees, and it was up to him to find a suitable tenant.

Soon after that trip, I started taking Italian classes at U3A (University of the third age), at Chisholm Campus in Frankston, as I wanted to learn conversational Italian only. I was the only person under fifty at these study groups, but I met some very interesting senior citizens. One of the dear ladies asked me one day, "Have you ever read 'A Fortunate Life' by Albert Facey? If these youngsters think they have it tough, they should all read about what that man endured!"

She lent me a copy of that book, and I must admit, it was one of the most interesting books I have ever read. And I marvelled at the author's experiences that he recorded when he was in his late seventies and eighties. I bought a copy of the book, and asked Connie to read it too. And though he took his time reading it, he too enjoyed the story very much.

I spent my days immersed in the arts, writing, painting, and playing the piano, and had no time to be bored, but I sometimes toyed with the idea of finding a job. I wanted to contribute to our budget, because we had another large mortgage on the investment unit now. And being a sociable person, I missed interacting with people.

We enjoyed an excellent lunch on my last Christmas at Boronia office, which I organised with a little help from my friends. I continued the same custom at Cranbourne, but not in Frankston, as I was too ill, and not at all keen to organise any functions there. I missed all those social activities very much now.

Cuckoo called Connie often, and said he was very upset that Esme did not manage Aunty's pension properly. She gave Aunty only thirty dollars a week for expenses, bought groceries, and paid energy bills with the rest of the pension, but she did not save anything. Cuckoo and Regina argued the point that over the last twenty years, Aunty should have saved a modest amount. So he told Connie to find out what was happening with the pension money.

Cristobel called Cuckoo regularly, and upset him about this issue; and once, she even slapped Esme over an argument about it. He pressured Connie to take over, and manage her pension better. Since our finances improved, Cuckoo was confident that Connie was more capable of budgeting than Esme.

After several more phone calls, and pleas to help Aunty maintain a better standard of living, Connie agreed to manage her pension. I accompanied Connie to Esme's, and she was very angry, and bitter about the whole situation. She argued with Connie for some time, and she finally brought Aunty's bank book and flung it at him. "*Good luck* to you Connie! I did my *best* for Mummy, but it's not easy! Paul takes loans from her, and she's always giving money to Bella and Paul." She had a balance of only thirty dollars left in that account.

Aunty though, was very happy for Connie to manage her affairs, and he soon brought some order into her finances. He gave her hundred dollars a week for expenses, but she spent it all on Bingo. And that was the reason why Esme gave her only thirty dollars a week. Aunty was addicted to gambling and drinking, but no one minded, as it was her money to do as she pleased. Connie paid her bills, and bought her weekly groceries, and made sure she had plenty of good food. He kept a detailed account of all her expenses, as he told me that he did not want the family to say he mismanaged her pension, like Esme.

Aunty lived by the side of Dandenong Highway, and was burgled numerous times, so we looked around for a safer place. She said she was happy to move anywhere close to us.

Somewhere in late April 2000, the Australian Tax Office advertised positions for Tax reform Officers. The new GST (Goods and Services Tax), was to be implemented on 1 July 2000, and the Tax Office recruited hundreds of people to assist with GST enquiries. The GST 'Hotlines' were to operate from Cheltenham and Melbourne city. I revamped a previous resume, and sent it off, without much hope of being interviewed, as Morgan's Recruitment Agency were in charge of the selection process.

A few weeks later, I received a letter, requesting me to attend an interview in the city. It was a capability assessment test, and I spent about three to four hours in the city along with hundreds of other applicants. Connie dropped me, and picked me up later in the evening, and said he would spend some time with his mother until I finished.

I did not wait until results were announced. But some hopeful candidates hung around the building, anticipation and anxiety clouding their tired faces. Each person was called in after the test, and advised if they were suitable or not.

Later that evening, I received a phone call from one of the panel members, who said, "Nalini, you have been selected, and a position will be offered to you, depending on a police check and referee comments." I was elated!

I called Chris at Centrelink next day, who was an excellent manager in all the time I knew him at Cranbourne. We met a few times at Frankston office afterwards, and I told him about my bad experience with Anne. He was very sympathetic, and told me, "Several people have made negative comments about Anne. I know who you are, and what a great worker you are, so don't worry about what happened with Anne." I knew he would support me, if I requested a referee report. Chris was more than happy to be my referee, and I thanked him profusely.

When I asked my previous team leader, Mary, at Frankston office, for a referee report, she refused point-blank, and replied, "I can't comment because I didn't know you or your work well enough!" She was my team leader for about six months, but that was how unfriendly, and unsupportive they were.

Mary always looked woebegone, and one day, in response to someone enquiring after her health, and whether anything was bothering her, she exclaimed, "Look, I'm not as *unhappy* as I may seem, it's just the way my face is!" She was on the verge of a marital break-up, and perhaps that accounted for her cold, unfriendly attitude towards me. Wayne, from Boronia office, wrote an excellent referee report. But it was a few years since he was my team leader, so the panel disregarded his report.

The very next day, one of the panel members called me once again, and told me everything was fine, and I would receive a letter in the mail regarding date and place of appointment. I requested Cheltenham office as my first preference, because it was only half an hour's drive from Frankston, and hoped I would get my choice.

I called Chris immediately and thanked him again. He replied, "I only told them what was true, and that you are one of the best workers I've known! I hope you have a long, and successful career at the ATO." That was the kind of person he was. And wherever he is today, I hope he will continue to be a fair-minded, and good human being.

In a few days time, I received a letter, requesting me to attend an induction course in the city. The venue was very impressive, and about one hundred recruits gathered there that day. People from every walk of life; engineers, architects, and other professionals, who were all keen to start a new career at the ATO.

When I told Connie I was selected, and how much the annual salary was, his response was, "How *easy*, just to answer phones, and you get paid so much! *Anyone* can do that!" I replied, "It's not *just* answering phones, you have to know the right answers to the GST enquiries, and that's why we have to be trained for the job."

I met some of my future team members, Joanne, Fiona, Morag, Tina, Priantha, and Mark, just to name a few. Our team leader, Sandra, was a tall, attractive blonde lady, in her early thirties. After one month's training in the city, we commenced work on 31 July 2000. I boarded a train daily to Melbourne city, as training was at the Exhibition building.

All the people I met there, were very nice and different, compared to the previous public servants at other offices, especially Frankston and Cranbourne. These people were untainted with the "hierarchy" mentality of the public service, and I knew the working environment would be much better than before.

Everyone was very friendly, and eager to learn the new GST rules, so we could assist the public, especially the small business sector. We believed we were trained as Tax Reform Officers. And at no stage in these early proceedings did anyone even a hint that we were employed as call centre staff. But over the next few weeks, some of the trainers kept referring to us as "Call Centre" staff, which upset many. The initial contract did not mention anything about our job functions.

Janice visited Australia in August that year, and Nelune, Joanna, and Janice drove up from Sydney to spend a few days with us. It was great seeing Janice again, and I loved spending those few days with her. Nelune rented a car that Joanna drove, but when I saw Nelune's physical state, I was extremely shocked.

She was very weak, and unable to keep her food down, as she was constantly nauseous, due to large doses of morphine. This was just about the worst period of Nelune's illness, when her health plummeted rapidly. I did not upset Nelune with my tears or references to her state, but I was close to bawling out loud, each time I saw her suffering so much. I felt so very helpless watching her pain, and knowing I could do nothing to ease it. But she knew I was there for her, any time she needed to talk or visit me.

We spent a few pleasant moments with them though. And once, we had dinner at Shiranthi's and Ananda's place in Doncaster, and I invited them for dinner as well. Nelune, Joanna, and Janice left after three days, and Janice promised to visit again sometime in the future. She flew back to London a few days later, and it was a traumatic experience for her too.

I commenced work in Cheltenham office on 25 August. It was a nice, modern office, with new equipment and computers. Management treated us well, but we knew by then that we had to take inbound phone calls from customers.

Although we wore headphones all day long, we had greater freedom, and flexibility than some other ATO call centres in Melbourne. But after a few weeks, several disgruntled people left, as they did not want to work in a call centre environment. We started on an annual wage of thirty three thousand dollars, which I thought was a good wage at level three of the Australian Public Service.

In the early stages of opening, only a few calls came in daily, but soon, I was taking about fifty to sixty calls on my own, as did the others. We had technical support from some "experts" who helped us with complex enquiries. The GST rules, tax legislation, questions and answers were all on the computer, and we just had to find the correct answers. It was alright, as far as I was concerned, and the job was not too difficult.

We had a great team though, and I enjoyed some very good times, as there was always plenty to do in Cheltenham. One of the team leaders, Nancy, and I became good friends, and we remained so through the years. She was very kind, and supportive in every way, and I liked her immensely. Nancy was a fair-minded, no-nonsense person, who could be relied on to help in any way she could.

Nilanthi wanted to come on a holiday in early November, so Connie and I paid for her ticket. It was good to see her again, and we enjoyed our time together.

It was our thirtieth wedding anniversary that year, but Connie did not wish me. He left on a business trip to the country early in the morning, and rushed off with hardly a word. I thought he would remember in the evening, but he did not. It was the second or third time in all our years together he had forgotten. A few days later, when I asked him about it, he replied," So, why didn't you *remind* me?"

Connie behaved very strangely then, as I noticed he had a fixation with one of the young girls in his department. Every time we spoke about anything, he always mentioned her name, "Rosa this, Rosa that, Rosa's skin is smooth like a baby's bum etc." I asked him, "Why do you have to talk about her all the time?" and he replied, "So, what's wrong?" Whenever I baked a cake, or biscuits for his morning tea, he said, "Put some extra pieces for Rosa." So I did, but I asked him, "What about the other staff? Why only for Rosa?" He did not reply.

She gave him a tie that Christmas, and he was all excited when he wore it to work next day. Before leaving he said, "Look, I'm wearing Rosa's tie! I want to make her happy!" I told him later that he was acting silly over this girl, and not to make a fool of himself. He mumbled, "She's engaged to be married, and is leaving soon."

The day Rosa left work, he came home looking very despondent, and sat alone without watching television with me, and did not talk much either. I asked him, "What's the matter? Why are you taking this so personally?" He replied, "It *is* affecting me personally, because it will *never* be the same without Rosa in the office!" I thought he was going through a mid-life crisis, but after she left, he did not mention her name as often.

Christian and Athena surprised us when they announced they were getting married on 26 November that year. We had afternoon tea at a nearby restaurant, and met her parents, John and Dorothy for the first time. Nilanthi came with us too. They decided to have a garden ceremony at Ashcombe Maze, in Shoreham. And invited only the parents of both parties, and a couple of close family friends, as they wanted a quiet wedding.

That day was glorious, without a cloud in the sky, and the ceremony was brief and simple. Athena looked beautiful, in a long, dark-blue, silk dress, and Christian looked very handsome in a dark-blue suit as well. They made a stunning couple, and I was very proud of them.

Athena's sister, Anastasia, stood as bridesmaid, and her brother, Steele, Christian's best man. John's brother, Mick, flew over from Adelaide, and I was pleased to meet such a pleasant old gentleman. The only others present at the wedding were Dorothy's brother, and his wife, Dr Zhang, and his wife, who were long-time friends of Athena's family. We had lunch at "Gold Leaf" Chinese Restaurant, in Springvale.

In the evening, they invited us to her parents' place, and Dorothy prepared large quantities of short eats, and I spent time looking at Athena's photo albums. Christian and Athena spent some time opening their presents, and had a good time, while we enjoyed a pre-view of their wedding video. We left around ten o'clock, and Christian and Athena returned to their place later on. Before they left, we suggested that we have the family over for dinner at our place soon, and they agreed.

A few days later, we organized a dinner, and most of Connie's family turned up; and my family, including Shirani, Ranjith, Roshan, Suresh, and Nilanthi added to about forty guests.

Geraldine, Clifford, Cristobel, and Paul did not come, although they were invited. Cristobel called me a couple of days ago, demanding to know why Aunty was not invited to the wedding. I told her that only the parents of the couple were invited. But she made a big issue about it, although it was none of her business.

Aunty did not ask why she was not invited, but she may have complained to her children, because Cristobel told me, "After all, Mummy is Christian's Grandmother! He should have invited her!" I repeated, "Only the parents were invited." But she was affronted on Aunty's behalf, so she did not come for dinner.

I cooked several curries, and buriyani rice for dinner, and Shirani came early to help with desserts and salads. Nilanthi too lent a hand, while Connie attended to the drinks and music. Everybody had a good time, and we were happy that Athena met the family. But John and Dorothy were unable to make it.

I sat for my fifth grade music examination that November, and I was happy to receive good results in December. Irene, told me that she could not teach any longer, as she was going back to teach in a school. I was very disappointed. I started with her in 1996, and she was a very patient and encouraging teacher.

I looked for another teacher again, and made enquiries everywhere. Once, I went to a teacher in Cheltenham for one lesson only, and she charged $25 for half an hour, but somehow I did not take to her, so I did not go again. I kept on with my lessons, and practised daily though, as I wanted to continue studying.

By the end of December 2000, rumours grew that Cheltenham office was closing in July 2001. These call centres were set up to launch the GST; mission accomplished now, more than one hundred staff members had one choice only, which was to move on to the call centre in Melbourne. Many dissatisfied members raised objections, and disagreements flared up between management and some staff members. But most of us waited to see what would happen in July 2001.

I applied for part-time work, and my request was approved, so from January 2001, I worked three days only. The reason was that I required a couple of days, to concentrate on my music and literary pursuits.

Some interstate call centres had already closed down by early March 2001. And soon after, the manager called a general meeting to inform us that Cheltenham office would close before July 2001. He said we had no other choice, but to transfer to Melbourne call centre.

Some people who lived on the other side of the city, took up the offer immediately, and left within a few weeks. I had no intention of moving to a call centre in the city though, and neither did most of the staff. The union got involved now, and requested all staff should be considered for other jobs in Dandenong office, instead of call centres only. An impasse ensued at the union's demands. Our teams amalgamated into fewer teams, with about four team leaders now, whereas we had ten team leaders before.

When some of the people I worked with knew I published a couple of books, they wanted to read my novel, "Serendib-Isle of dreams." And they gave me great feedback, saying it was a very good story, which they found intriguing, and wanted to know more about Ceylon, also what "hoppers" were. So, on my next day off, I made hoppers, beef curry, and chilli sambal for my team, and surprised them at lunch time.

The staff were impressed, and enjoyed the hoppers and beef curry very much. I told them, "*Now* you know what hoppers taste like, they are not grasshoppers!" (That's what they kept saying, as they had never heard of hoppers before, except Sri Lankans who worked there).

My team leader, Sandra, smiled and said, "That was a very nice thing to do Nalini, very kind of you to take so much trouble. Thank you. I really enjoyed the yummy hoppers and curry." The team members too relished the unusual treat, and I was pleased they enjoyed the surprise hopper feed.

In April 2001, after much searching, I found an excellent piano teacher, Antoinette Dikeliotis in Seaford. I read her name in the Victorian Music Teachers

Association list, that Irene sent me, as I told her I still had not found a teacher. I was so keen to learn piano, that when I started work at Cheltenham, I drove to Cranbourne straight after work, just to have a music lesson for half an hour. As I was studying for my examination then, Irene suggested that I look for a teacher closer to Frankston.

I was quite happy when I drove to Seaford one day and met Antoinette. She was a petite lady, a few inches shorter than me, but with keen, dark eyes and a warm smile. She spoke with a heavy accent, and told me she was Egyptian, but was married to a Greek. Antoinette was widowed now, with a grown-up daughter, Toula, and she lived on her own. After speaking to her for a while, she asked me to call her Ninette. And I agreed to start lessons on Tuesday afternoons, from the following week. She wanted only twenty dollars for a one hour lesson, which was very reasonable.

Ninette discouraged me from sitting for further examinations, as I had already sat for six practical, and three theory examinations. She said I could learn more under her guidance. She learnt piano under a Russian teacher, and from the moment she played for me, I knew she was a brilliant pianist. She accompanied tenors and sopranos, who came to practise every week, and I was grateful to have found such a gifted teacher. Now she set about teaching me technique, and interpretation of music, as I was proficient at reading music.

Over the next few years, Ninette and I became very close, and she said, "You are like my second daughter." After my lesson, she asked me to take her to the shops in Patterson Lakes, or walk with her to the chemist or bakery. I drove her wherever she wanted to go, even to Springvale, and Chelsea for eye appointments. At this time, Toula was very busy with her work and could not visit daily, so Ninette looked forward to my visits. Sometimes, if I could, I visited her on other days too, just to take her out, or have a coffee with her.

I regarded her as my "second mother" as well, and was extremely fond of her. Connie resented my visits to Ninette's right from the start, even though it was to study music. He never failed to phone me every Tuesday afternoon between two and three o'clock, knowing I was busy with my lesson.

He asked in surprise, "*Are* you at Ninette's?" which made me so irritable, I could hardly reply politely. Then he lost his temper and demanded, "*What's* the matter, you sound annoyed?" I retorted, "You *know* I'm here at Ninette's *every* Tuesday afternoon, so why do you ask?" He hung up abruptly, and later in the evening, he picked up the same issue when he came home. I just could not understand his resentment, that I spent an afternoon learning piano with Ninette.

Once, when I mentioned I was taking her shopping to Patterson Lakes, we were surprised to see him parked there, waiting for us, just as we stopped. He grinned foolishly, "I thought I'll have a coffee with you both." Ninette replied, "No, I want to finish soon and go home." So he had to go on his way and attend to his business, and not hang around us.

Ninette asked me on the way, "*Why* is your husband so possessive? He knows you are with me, but he's suspicious eh?" I could not confide in her, as she had a good opinion of him, but this incident struck her as very odd. Connie's suspicions grew worse, because he thought I will meet Ninette's tenors, and other singers at her place.

Ninette soon introduced me to a world of music, and concerts with a famous tenor, Luigi Campeotto, one of the three Italian tenors, including Ornello Favero, and Attilio Bragnanolo. I was privileged to hear Luigi's magnificent voice at these brilliant events, and Connie was happy to attend these concerts, as he enjoyed them too.

Shirani and Ranjith went on a holiday to Ceylon at the end of March, and Connie's mother, and Aunty Molly joined them, as they needed someone to take care of them.

Cuckoo asked Connie to send Aunty to Berlin, and as she now had enough savings, due to Connie's budgeting, he bought her a ticket. Aunty Molly was keen to go with her too, as she wanted to see her relatives. Aunty was spending a few weeks there, and then flying direct to Berlin.

When Shirani and Ranjith arrived in Maharagama, they found Granny was ailing. Rita stayed with her then, but Granny was seriously ill for some time, and could hardly breathe. She was about eighty-eight, and Rita did not called a doctor. She told them, "It's *only* the flu, and she'll get over it."

But Granny died a few days later, on 3 April. Ranjith and Shirani attended to all the funeral arrangements, as no one else was available. Anthony did not come immediately, but arrived in time for the funeral. Nilanthi and Heron did what they could, and finally, she was laid to rest. Aunty told me she would visit Granny, but she could not make it before she died.

Esme decided to visit Cuckoo as well, and said she wanted to be with Aunty. The whole family, including Cuckoo, discouraged her, but she was determined to go. A few weeks later, much to Paul's annoyance, she left. And Paul told us, "Talking to Esme is like talking to a brick wall! She is very *stubborn,* just like all the de Sielvie's!"

Cuckoo told me that he enjoyed the first few weeks with Aunty very much, and they went for long walks together. But when Esme arrived, Aunty took to her bed, and behaved like an invalid, so Esme mollycoddled her. Now that she did not handle her pension any longer, she sought other ways to be in charge of Aunty.

We decided to go on a short holiday to Tasmania. So on Friday, 8 June 2001, we boarded the "Spirit Of Tasmania" at five thirty in the evening, to visit Tasmania for the first time. It was a calm crossing, and we had a very pleasant trip on the colossal ferry, and arrived in Devonport at eight thirty in the morning on Saturday, 9 June. We ferried the car across as well, and drove down to Hobart around midday, after looking around the town for a few hours.

Then we drove past some incredible scenery, and arrived at Burnie, where we stopped for fish and chips. It was a scenic coastal town, and we walked along pristine beaches. Later, we drove from Burnie to Queenstown, through world heritage areas. We beheld splendid, majestic views, including Cradle Mountain in the distance, wide silvery lakes, and sparkling waterfalls. Queenstown came as a shock, after the visual feast of unspoilt beauty all around. The ugly, rugged mountains, were bare and scarred over decades of copper, gold, and lime mining. Stark desolation stared us in the face wherever we looked.

Naked mountains, stripped of any vestige of shrubs or trees, jutted up to the sky, like blackened, accusing fingers, in grim protest at the devastation mining industry did to its forests. Sulphurous fumes belching out constantly on mountain-sides, over hundred years of continuous mining, turned Queenstown into a barren moonscape. We passed Dermont Bridge soon, as twilight streaked rosy hues over dark forests and mountains around.

The scariest part of that journey, was the precipitous drive round and round mountain sides, with roads that resembled lassoes strung around bare mountains. I was so nervous when I looked down the treacherous precipices, that I held onto my seat tightly. Our mobiles did not have any reception in these remote areas, and we did not pass another vehicle all that time. I wondered aloud, what would we do in case of a breakdown? It is one road that I will not travel again - that mountain road through Queenstown.

Hundreds of tiny marsupials, with eyes like saucers, scampered out in the gathering dusk. They sat beside the lonely road, or hopped across carelessly in suicidal mode. A few of these creatures lay flattened and splattered on the road; accident victims of previous traffic. Fortunately, we avoided knocking down any of those little animals, as we kept looking out for sudden sprinters across the highway.

Finally, around six thirty in the evening, we sighted the city of Hobart, lights glinting in the distance. Flickering, rainbow-hued lights reflected in the calm waters at the entrance to the quaint city of Hobart. Before we drove to our apartment though, we stopped to buy some takeaway dinner, and a bottle of whisky for Connie. But were disappointed to find that all the shops were shut and barred (business hours on a Saturday night were different to that of Melbourne).

But we located a Chinese restaurant, that served dinner till nine o'clock, and bought some takeaway food. But Connie had to do without a stiff whisky, which he was looking forward to (he said, after the long strenuous drive). The apartment was cosy and comfortable, and we had a good night's sleep. I woke up in the morning, and looked out the window at Mount Wellington looming nearby, with houses and buildings sprawling right up to the foothills of that grey-blue mountain. It was crispy and cold, but a bright sunny morning, so we decided to drive up to Mount Wellington (as the tourist guide brochures urged visitors not to miss that scenic view).

We stopped halfway at "Ferntree" about twenty minutes from the pinnacle of the mountain, and I was fascinated with the incredible sights there. I feasted my eyes on lush green forests, woods laced with tree-ferns, and mountains and sea views rimmed in the distance. Then we walked further up to a magical waterfall near "Fern-Tree Glade" and I removed some photographs before we resumed our drive to the mountain top. I was glad the ascent was not as steep and precipitous as the road through Queenstown, and the road inclined gradually up to Mount Wellington.

Ice still clung tenaciously to mountain-sides, and in some places, the melting ice snaked down in muddy trickles. When we reached the summit, it was a clear bright day, and I beheld a breath-taking vista across the space right down to Hobart, and the southernmost coastline of Tasmania. It was indeed the most spectacular scene I witnessed in Australia. Endless ranges of majestic, blue mountains, towered in the distance, and valleys, inlets, lakes, and forests looked paradisiacal in all its pristine beauty and glory.

What an experience! And yet, words are so very inadequate and hackneyed, to describe the grandeur of God's miracles, so evident in His handiwork around me. I could only whisper the beautiful lines of that enduring hymn, "How Great Thou Art," which sums up my sentiments exactly. "Oh Lord my God, when I in awesome wonder, consider Lord, the world thy hands have made."

We drove on to Glenorchy, but the market was closed, and all the shops were shut on Sundays, so we ended up buying a pizza for lunch. One of the independent supermarkets was open for a few hours though, so I bought some meat for dinner. And I made a hot curry, that we ate with steamed rice. Afterwards, I wrote cards and letters to friends and family, and a lengthy letter to Cuckoo. Aunty and Esme were with him then, and we sent picture postcards from Tasmania.

The following day, on Monday, 11 June, we drove up to the city central in Hobart. But shops, and other venues were closed, as it was a public holiday in honour of the Queen's birthday. We walked a couple of hours, and looked around the quaint, colonial-style city, before we headed off to Richmond and Port Arthur.

We stopped at a tea shop in Richmond near the famous old bridge, where I read several magazines about haunted buildings and the bridge in Richmond. I removed plenty of photographs of the picturesque scenery, with the imposing cathedral in the background.

We reached Port Arthur around four o'clock in the afternoon, and the sunny weather disappeared, only to be replaced by sullen, grey skies, and heavy raindrops. It was a desolate-looking, lonely, and eerie place, with a heavy atmosphere, weighed down by untold misery of countless men and women incarcerated within those gloomy prison walls.

I could hardly wait to get out of that suffocating atmosphere, and did not want to go on the "Ghost tour" I read about in the tourist office. The whole place was said to be teeming with unhappy spirits (according to the guide), and people saw or sensed their unearthly presence on dark nights.

On our return from Port Arthur, we sighted "Eaglehawk Neck" and I held my breath at the splendid sight of the vast, deep-blue ocean, edged with majestic mountains looming beyond Port Arthur. It must have been a desolate sight for convicts though, because it was naturally guarded from all sides by ocean, forests, and mountains, destroying any hope of escape from their prison.

We returned home late at night, and then rested, but I woke up bright and early next day. And once again, we drove into Hobart, and explored the city, before heading off to Richmond to see the famous "Hobart Model Village" built in Richmond around 1991. We met one of the creators of the model city there, and I was fascinated to hear the story of how they constructed the intricate details of the model city of Hobart, the way it was in early days.

The historical buildings were made to scale, and the mills had running water, with life-like statues of people, and animals, depicting the pioneers' life-style. It was very interesting indeed, and I was pleased that I saw the model.

Then we hurried off to Forcett, which was about half an hour's drive from Hobart, to visit my friend Pauline, who worked with me in Frankston. She too accepted a voluntary package in 1999. And Pauline invested in fifty acres of bushland, including a two-storey house on the land. She was happy with her two young children, Zac and Holly, and hordes of farm animals.

She was a tireless animal activist, when she lived in Red Hill on the Mornington Peninsula. Pauline tried to ban "'battery-hens." Because the appalling conditions in which those unfortunate hens were forced to lay eggs continuously, was enough to upset all animal lovers. I bought farm-fresh duck and chicken eggs from Pauline, as she ran a hobby farm in Red Hill. We kept in touch even after she left, and she invited me to visit her, if I ever came to Tasmania. And so, I made a special effort to see her this time.

It was a large, comfortable farm-house, and the property was nothing but uncultivated bushland. But she had plenty of sheep, goats, dogs, and horses wandering around. She lived just twenty minutes away from the beach, where the children and she rode their horses daily. I was happy to see her well settled and content. We spent a couple of hours with her, and returned to the apartment around six thirty in the evening. We bought fresh seafood from the wharf, and enjoyed some delicious seafood that night. The scallops, prawns, and oysters, were absolutely succulent, and were straight off the fishing boats.

The following day, we drove back to the city of Hobart, as we wanted to visit the historic places. The museum and art gallery were open, and I was very impressed to see extensive convict memorabilia, wild life displays and some exquisite paintings. It was inspiring to behold so many splendid scenes in oils and other mediums. After I enjoyed more than my fill of this artistic feast, we drove over to Sandy Bay, as we heard about the renowned "Tudor- Village" model display.

I cannot begin to describe the beauty of that incredible model village, as words are beyond me. What was truly inspiring, was the fact that Anthony Palotta, the creator responsible for this magnificent work, was crippled with polio from the age of nine years. He painstakingly created every single building, and figures all by himself, using just his three fingers, as his other hand was completely inert. It was a monumental inspiration to human endeavour and achievement.

The model village stretched out across the span of the large room, and all the cottages, church, and ruins of Glastonbury Abbey, were accurately made to scale. When lights were turned off in the room, a magical night scene appeared, with lanterns and tiny lights flickering within all the cottages, and buildings of the model village.

I was mesmerised by this fantastic model. Tiny, life-like figures of peasants, lords and ladies, King Henry V111, and Anne Boleyn, in period costumes, were true in every detail. I was reluctant to leave this exquisite miniature world, and would have spent hours there. But we decided to return to Hobart, and finish our tour of the museum, as we had hurried off from there earlier on. I had my sketch book, and pastels with me, so I made some rough sketches of the surrounding area and places I saw.

Our brief stay in Hobart came to an end on Thursday, 14 June. We woke up early, and drove off to board the ferry once again. We stopped at Launceston, which was not as scenic as Hobart, but distant mountain ranges were discernible in the horizon. After lunch at Devonport, we boarded the "Spirit Of Tasmania" in the evening. It was a pleasant voyage on our return journey as well, but the sea was slightly rough and choppy, though not too bad.

After a fairly good sleep, we arrived safely in Melbourne at about eight fifteen in the morning. I was anxious to bring my pets home, so we picked them from the cattery before midday. I was very pleased to see Tiger and Misty again. And I was certain they enjoyed returning home too, although they ignored me for a couple of hours, and pretended not to know me at all. That was payback time for boarding them, no doubt. I rested awhile, and re-lived all the amazing experiences in beautiful Tasmania.

We considered expanding our investment portfolio, so we looked around for another property. And soon, we found a neat, two-bedroom unit, in Hill Street, Frankston. It was in a good area, close to Reservoir Street, where we rented a unit in 1996, and was very "rentable" too. We bought it, and I suggested that as it was a very nice, secure unit, with about four other units in the compound, it would be a safe place for Aunty. Although he organised several improvements in her Housing Commission flat, and also installed a burglar alarm system, he too agreed that it would be good for her to move out from Dandenong.

We purchased that unit for $128,000, and decided to rent it to Aunty for $100 per week. It was not a good proposition for building our portfolio, as we should have rented it for $175 or more a week. But we were more than happy to make up the shortfall ourselves, and to make sure she was happy in a safe and better unit and area. Our financial advisor, who did not see it in that light, warned Connie against renting it for such a low rate. It was a bad investment move, but when Connie said, "It's for my mother." He understood.

The settlement was in three months time, and when Aunty saw the unit, she was overjoyed. The entire front garden was full of several varieties of roses in full bloom, and it had a well-tended backyard, with camellias, irises, ever-green shrubs, and a huge lemon tree. Aunty blessed us and said, "This is a *dream* unit, and God bless you both for letting me live in such a beautiful place surrounded by roses! I *love* roses!"

The rest of the family were not too impressed though, as they said Frankston was too far away for them to visit. Dandenong was more central to where they all lived. But Aunty, for once, was adamant to move to the unit, and they could not make her change her mind. She planned to move in as soon as the unit was ready, and looked forward to living in that pleasant, comfortable place.

Some of my happiest memories in our house in Frankston, are of Christian and Athena dropping in some evenings, or on weekends, and then sitting by the fireside, chatting away for hours. I loved those special moments. But Connie rushed in and out saying, "Excuse me son, I have to go out for a smoke." He spoke a few words to them on and off, but did not sit for long, or concentrate on any topic, as he rushed out again on some pretext or other.

I was driving to work early morning on 11 September, 2001. It was just another ordinary working day, until I heard the shattering news on the radio about the attack on the twin towers in New York. When I arrived at the office, the staff were gathered around the television set. I could not believe what they were saying, and rushed in through the door to watch the news on television. None of us could concentrate on work that day, and not much was done, although the phones rang constantly. We suffered from great shock, just like the rest of the world.

Aunty's packing was soon underway, as we hoped to settle her in by November. The days rushed past, and Aunty moved in to the unit on 7 November. We packed everything, and Connie brought Aunty Molly, and Aunty to our place, until we arranged the place. I scrubbed, and cleaned, and arranged everything just as she liked, and I sewed lace curtains for the kitchen window. Connie and I helped her to settle in comfortably, and visited her daily, until she got used to her new surroundings. Hundreds of fragrant, colourful roses were in full bloom on that beautiful, sunny day when she walked inside.

Aunty always told me that whenever she sat at her window and looked out, she prayed for us, "Bless Connie and Dolly for giving me this beautiful unit." We spent a great deal of time with her, helping her with shopping, and settling in. We took her to a store one day, and she picked furniture that she liked. As she now had enough money in her savings account to buy a new lounge-suite and a few other items.

Cristobel moved in with Aunty, and lived with her during the first few weeks and months, as she thought Aunty was too lonely there. But I dropped in often after work, and Connie visited her every day. I made dinner for her some nights, and Connie brought her over, or we went there, and shared a meal together. Aunty too invited us for meals whenever she was alone. She was happy, and every one in the family visited her during the week.

We spent that Christmas with Aunty, and took her for Midnight Mass, and then she visited the rest of the family. I spent hours shopping with her a few days earlier, and then wrapped up all the presents for her grandchildren. She liked me to do these little things for her, and said, "You're very patient Dolly, my fellows don't have patience to take me shopping and buy presents, then wrap them all up. God bless you for your kindness." I was happy to do this for Aunty every Christmas, until a few years later, she decided to give her grandchildren money, instead of presents.

Connie became completely absorbed in Aunty's affairs from then onwards. He spoke about her constantly wherever we went. Even when we walked around the block after dinner, he invariably discussed his mother's affairs, or the family situations. I walked ahead of him, as I wanted peace, without constant problems, or discussions about his family.

He grumbled about how stressful his work was now, and that it was added responsibility taking care of Aunty's affairs, and her shopping etc. But when I offered to do her grocery shopping, he replied, "*I* want to do it myself for Mummy." And once, when I was shopping, I saw him pushing a trolley and coming towards me. I said, "Hello Connie." He looked up at me vaguely, and mumbled, "Ah, Dolla?" And just walked past me, as if I was a stranger. Now on top of his busy work schedule, which involved a great deal of travelling, he still wanted to shop for Aunty. And he spent every weekend running to see what she needed, or what had to be done in the unit or garden.

Esme and Cristobel were controlling forces, and instructed what *they* wanted done in the unit, and they took over the garden. One day, Esme chopped down a mature, crepe myrtle tree, without even asking permission. Cristobel dug out all the established shrubs and plants, and turned the backyard upside down according to her whims and fancies.

Connie did not tell them anything, but he complained to me about their constant interference. Esme took down the lace curtains I sewed, and replaced them with her old curtains, and rearranged everything else.

My old Holden Commodore finally gave up the ghost, and David advised me to get another vehicle. I told him jokingly, "You know David, what I would *really* like, is a burgundy Jaguar!" David promptly replied, "I've *got* a 1983 rouge-red Jag in the garage, that someone wants to sell. Would you like to have it?" "*Really,* David? How much?" I asked, pleasantly surprised, and he grinned, "Oh, for you Dolly, I could persuade the guy to take $6000." I glanced at Connie, he nodded. We told David we would look at it, and take it for a drive.

I loved the feel and look of the old Jag, as I always admired its classic, sleek contours, more than any other car. It was in very good condition, and although not burgundy, as I preferred, rouge-red was close enough. So we bought it for $6000, and David fixed a few minor, mechanical details.

I whizzed around in my "dream" car, which caused a stir in the office when they saw little old me driving a huge, red Jag! One thing I must say, the Jag sat so solidly on the road, that I felt very safe, unlike in new cars, made of flimsy, light metal, that crushed easily like tin-foil, in an accident.

In October 2001, Cheltenham office closed down. And twenty of us transferred to the ATO office at Casselden Place, in Melbourne, where we were to make outbound calls only (so we were told), but that changed later on. I had no choice but to accept the transfer, and in December 2001, I started travelling to the city. I drove my car to the station in Frankston, and then boarded a train.

It was a pleasant, friendly environment, and we had a great manager, Margaret. Fran, our team-leader, was a friendly, chatty lady in her late fifties, and I liked the place well enough. I was happy that some of my good friends, including Joanne, transferred out with me, and we enjoyed some pleasant times at Casselden Place.

Chapter 31

In early 2002, one of our neighbours, Ivan, asked me if I would teach his six-year old daughter, Madeline, piano, as I distributed some flyers advertising piano classes. My previous teacher, Irene, encouraged me to take on some pupils, as she said, "You will be a great teacher, because you're very patient." I agreed to teach Madeline, and started giving lessons at my place in January.

Before long, another lady asked if I could teach her daughter, Jordee, who was in Madeline's class at St Francis Xavier's primary school in Frankston. Then another neighbour, Brigid, enrolled her daughter, Ellen, and before long, I had five students.

I loved teaching piano, and found it immensely rewarding to impart knowledge, and the gift of music to children. Their parents told me they were very pleased with their childrens' progress, which made me happy. But Connie did not encourage me, as he did not like the idea of my teaching piano, and asked, "Are you sure it's okay to teach them, be careful that their parents don't complain about you." And he was negative about anything I tried to do.

Whenever I had time, I played piano for more than an hour on some days. And once, when our next door neighbour, Uta, visited, she said, "Dolly, you play the piano very nicely." I thanked her, but Connie immediately broke in, "You should hear her teacher play! She is fantastic!" My neighbour looked at me, but did not say anything.

It was just his habit, to diminish any compliment someone paid me. Connie was very insensitive, and blurted out whatever came to his mind, without thinking whether it was hurtful or not. It was the same when he praised a local author one day, and a friend of mine asked him, "Have you read your wife's stories yet? You should read them, as she is a very talented writer." He did not know what to say, but looked a little sheepish.

In early February that year, we booked tickets to see "'A noble Spaniard" at the Briars Homestead in Mount Martha. We invited Aunty Molly, Babs, Aunty, Shirani, and Ranjith to join us too. It was a very funny play, and we had a good time. We thought Aunty would enjoy going for plays, and local functions now, as her only entertainment so far, was playing bingo, or socialising with her children and relatives.

The whole family came over for dinner on Connie's birthday on 19 February, but Shirani and Ranjith were unable to make it. Shirani applied for a transfer to

Cairns, and they were very busy travelling to and fro, trying to find a suitable house to rent up there. They rented a flat at the start, and Shirani was keen to start a Bed and Breakfast business, when they found the right place.

I was sad that Shirani was so far away now, but it was her dream, and she had to follow it, and see where it led her. The good part though, was they travelled to Melbourne often, as Suresh and Roshan lived in the house in Narre Warren, so they came down often to see them.

On my fiftieth birthday, we attended a "Carnivale Ball" at the Austro-Italiano club in Carrum, as Ninette was playing that night. It was great, with many people dressed up as various characters. We were not in fancy dress though, as we did not have time to get costumes. But we told the organisers that we would definitely make it the following year too, as the dance took place around this time, on my birthday. Ninette played the keyboard in the band, and we danced away the night to the sound of haunting, Neapolitan melodies, and some popular favourites as well.

On Labour Day weekend that March, Aunty Molly, and Aunty came to Bright with us. And on our return journey, Connie drove very fast, as we promised to get back in time for Ranjith's birthday party that night. When he raced to overtake a truck, a police car zoomed out of the shrubbery, and stopped us. Connie could not do much about it, as the officer read the speedometer and said, "You were doing more than one hundred and ten in a hundred zone! I will have to book you, and suspend your licence for one month." Connie was shocked, as he depended on the car for his job, but that was it. On our way home, he was gloomy and despondent, not knowing how he would manage without driving for one month.

We ended up at Shirani's around nine o'clock that night, but we did not break the bad news to them, as it was Ranjith's birthday.

We decided it would be best for him to take his annual leave for a month, and go on a holiday. And it would be a good time to visit Cuckoo, as he was ailing now, and on regular dialysis.

Heron was in Melbourne then, as his children brought him to celebrate his eightieth birthday with his family. Nilanthi was unable to join him, as Tamara bought her a ticket to spend a few months with her. And she arrived there on 10 March. We told her we would meet her in London when we stopped over for a few days.

I was happy that Nilanthi could be with Tamara, who insisted that we stay with her too, and not in a motel, as we planned. She would not hear of it, and told us that it would be great to be together, as Nilanthi was there, and Tamara had a spare room for us. As she was so persuasive, I did not want to hurt her feelings, and agreed to stay with her. She was very pleased to hear that.

Heron was very happy to spend time with his children, and they invited Shirani, Ranjith, Connie, and me to his birthday party at his son, Peter's place in Narre Warren. We had a good time with Heron and his family, and Nilanthi sent him special wishes too, which they read out loud.

Before long, we organised to board the cats for two weeks at the RSPCA in Pearcedale, and made preparations for our trip. I encountered a few problems at work, trying to get my annual leave approved. But was finally granted two weeks pro rata, and a few days "leave without pay." The manager, Margaret, was very kind, and sympathetic when she learnt that I intended visiting a sick relative, and she finally approved my leave.

Shirani and Ranjith dropped us at Melbourne Airport at one thirty in the afternoon on 7 April, and our plane left two hours later.

We arrived in Singapore at eight forty in the night, local time, and it took about six and a half hours to reach there. The flight in was beautiful, and I glimpsed the glittering harbour, with anchored ships, like tiny, toy vessels afloat on the midnight seas. Singapore city looked like a wonderland, with its towering skyscrapers shining brightly in the balmy night.

A taxi drove us to the magnificent Concorde Hotel, and the impressive building looked like fairyland, with bright lights glittering everywhere in the lobby, and circular-domed lifts floated up and down effortlessly.

Our room was on the eleventh floor, and although it was thirty one degrees Celsius outside, the hotel room was air-conditioned, and very comfortable. We quickly showered and took a taxi to the old market, now converted to an eating place called "Lau Pa Sat."

All the brightly decorated food stalls stood in a marvellous, octagonal-shaped building, with intricate, but discoloured wrought-iron decorating the railings. It was a very old and quaint, colonial-style building. We looked around quickly, but as we were very hungry, we ate rice and curry at midnight. The meal was very good value, and we had a variety of curries, including several types of fish curry.

Then we took a taxi back to the hotel, and went to bed around one thirty in the morning. I woke up early next day, and watched with disappointment, as heavy rain pelted down. It did not look too promising, and the rain continued unabated. Before going down to the dining room, we ordered a glass of milk, which cost five dollars a glass (room service included). Everything was very expensive in Singapore.

After showering, we went down for breakfast to the "Melting Pot" restaurant in the hotel, where our orders got mixed up. And Connie ended up not getting any breakfast. He was too annoyed to eat anything, but I had an omelette, toast and tea.

We went to the shopping centre in a taxi, although it was raining lightly now, and looked like it was easing off gradually. The taxi dropped us at "Mustafa's" bazaar, a garish, noisy place, over-run with gaudy glitter and full of bargain-hunters. Connie bought a camera, and a watch for Christian, as he wanted a particular brand, with a pale-blue dial.

Gold, gold, and more gold! I never saw so much gold before! And all of it fashioned in the most hideous, and ornate pieces of jewellery I ever set eyes on. The entire shop walls were covered with gold displays in every style, size, and pattern imaginable. My eyes were beginning to hurt with the glare of gold.

We spent a long time searching for a black, silk, dressing gown for Cuckoo, as he told us he would like to have one. I bought Regina's favourite perfume for her, and Connie bought a bottle of "English Blazer" after-shave lotion, which proved unfortunate, as it caused a skin allergy. He soon developed an irritating rash in his underarms, and other parts of his body, wherever he splashed lotion on.

He also bought a larger suitcase, as we purchased more things in Singapore. But the shop-keeper had trouble getting the visa card approved, as phone lines were busy, so we ended up paying cash for the suitcase. This led to a shortage of cash for a taxi and lunch. So we walked up and down the streets for over one hour, along Mustafa's shops, and Little India (as that street was called), in search of an automatic teller machine. None of the people could tell us where to find one, and they all gave wrong directions anyway.

Connie was ravenous by now, as he had not eaten any breakfast. I was footsore and weary with all the trudging around in dirty, muddy streets, not to mention getting wet in the steady drizzle that fell on my uncovered head. Hungry, tired, and raw nerves frayed almost to snapping point now, Connie craved to eat Muthu's famous crab curry, in a hotel in Little India. Finally, in desperation, we entered a travel agent's office, and were directed to an ATM location, where we withdrew enough money for lunch and taxi fare. We walked another thirty minutes until we found Muthu's Curry Corner.

Muthu had gone "up-market" since our last visit here in 1987, when it was a dingy, shabby eatery, with enormous flies buzzing around the tables. Now, it was modernised, and boasted "computerised" toilet doors, that opened at a touch; automatic entrance doors, and a very clean interior, even better than McDonalds, and other fast food outlets in Australia. The waiter wore a snowy-white cap, and brought hot towels wrapped up in little plastic bags, to wipe our fingers.

Then he laid out fragrant, banana leaves on the table, and a young man carrying containers of vegetable curries, slopped them on to the banana leaves. We ordered deliciously flavoured king prawns, and crab curry, which we enjoyed very much. But inflation had caught up with a vengeance, as it cost forty-five dollars for rice and curry. Things had certainly sky-rocketed since our last trip.

We returned to the hotel in a taxi, and I showered, after which, I sat by the pool, wishing I spent the afternoon swimming in the blue water, instead of trudging along dirty streets of "Little India." The water looked so cool and inviting, but huge drops of rain started to fall once again, and I darted inside. It was time for us to leave, and we took a taxi to Changi Airport.

The taxi drivers were most informative, and this particular driver told us he paid taxes annually, after all deductions were made for spouse, children, and parents. He said the first $7500 was taxed at four percent, and the additional $7500 at six percent. But cost of living was very high, and a chicken (the cheapest meal), cost about three dollars each.

It was certainly very interesting listening to that taxi driver, and finally, we arrived at the airport, which was busy as ever. Beautiful plants, fountains, and exotic orchids, decorated every level of the airport. The varieties of magnificent orchids that filled almost every corner of the airport, were breathtaking indeed.

It was about nine forty five in the night, Singapore time, and our flight was at eleven o'clock. We booked a direct flight to Paris, which meant we had a thirteen hour flight approximately. It was a mixed sort of day in Singapore, weatherwise; very humid, cloudy, and overcast all day, and also, it was exhausting.

Connie looked pensive, as he worried constantly about his mother, although most of the family visited her regularly. Cristobel, who was unemployed then, stayed with her too. He gave Esme enough money to buy her groceries, besides pocket money for bingo. But he still fretted about her, so he phoned her from Melbourne Airport, and again from Singapore, just to find out if she was alright. Aunty was happy we were visiting Cuckoo, and said she was not lonely at all, as one of her children, or Aunty Molly stayed with her.

He ordered a beer while waiting at the airport terminal, and one of the attendants came over to me, and related an interesting tale. A tourist once left thirty thousand US dollars on a barbecue table in the hotel. And she found the bundle of money, which she duly returned to the tourist, who was astonished at the poor woman's honesty. Her photograph appeared in a magazine, praising her for her integrity. She showed me a crumpled piece of yellowed-paper, featuring her grinning face, and the story she just related. The grateful tourist paid her a handsome reward, and she warned us to be careful of pickpockets who roamed at large.

The flight from Singapore was delayed about twenty minutes, and it was a gruelling flight to Paris. I tried to sleep, but I started to cough persistently, which kept me up. I knew I must have picked up a virus, when I was trudging in the rain on those dirty streets in Singapore.

Chapter 32

It was freezing in Paris, and although it was early April, and supposed to be spring, it was about three degrees Celsius. Distant lights gleamed, as the pale sun struggled through heavy clouds, and after thirteen hours of flying, the plane commenced descending. We flew over various provinces, and towns, like Luxembourg and Reims; towns I had seen only in picture books before. The country-side looked very green, and appealing, but Charles de Gaulle Airport, was just a drab, ugly mass of concrete, with a maze of tunnels everywhere. It was cold and unwelcoming, and made worse with building works in progress.

I thought it was chaotic and messy, with tacky, mobile toilets dumped in a few corners. The unfriendly, stony-faced Parisians did not speak English, and looked up with blank expressions, when we addressed them in English. My first impression of Paris was quite disappointing, and the drive from the airport to the heart of Paris, did nothing to change my opinion of the city either.

We boarded a coach to the hotel, but before that, we had a few over-priced bread rolls, and coffee at a small café. Paris was just as, or more expensive than Singapore. The outskirts of Paris were lined on both sides of the road with drab, dirty, old grey buildings right up to the city. The coach stopped outside the "Paris Opera" which was a magnificent structure.

A taxi drove us to hotel "La Sanguine" that Janice recommended, as it was situated in the heart of Paris. The hotel was quaint and warm, with clean, comfortable furnishings, and exuded "Rustic French" ambience. After we booked in around ten thirty that morning, they served an ample breakfast of bread rolls, croissants, orange juice, and coffee.

Then we showered quickly, and armed with dozens of tourist maps and guides, we started our tour of the famous city, as we had only one day in Paris. Our first stop was Champs Elyses, and we wandered along looking in at all the famous shops, cafes, and the Arc De Triomphe. Connie photographed all these historic landmarks, as we walked along the streets of Paris.

It was extremely cold, though spring was in the air, and I glimpsed fragrant lilac bushes, and wisteria in some gardens, just bursting into pale, mauve and purple blossoms. Fortunately, it was a bright, sunny day, unlike Singapore. I craned my neck up at all the amazingly tall, narrow buildings, and the President's Palace looked very impressive, even when viewed from outside.

We strolled along to the Eiffel Tower, and walked down to the river Seine, to enquire about a river cruise. But we decided not to go on a daytime cruise, as the guide said the night cruise was more enjoyable. We wanted to walk as much as possible, and visit the most interesting places in Paris.

Connie wanted to go right up to the top of the Eiffel Tower, but when I refused to join him, because of vertigo, he changed his mind, although I urged him to take the lift, and view the surrounding scenes from the tower. The river banks of the Seine reeked of urine, and my feet ached with all the walking. But I continued dragging my steps to another station, to visit the famous Mont Marte area, and Sacre Coeur church. The streets of Mont Marte were narrow, dirty, and full of dingy buildings, but steeped in "olde worlde" ambience.

It bustled with activity now, as all the shops were run by immigrants, especially Indian traders, who did brisk business. Crepe (pancake) makers in little mobile stalls, lurked in almost every corner. I thought Toulouse Lautrec's paintings of Mont Marte laundresses and dancers, were a far cry from the modern-day inhabitants of Mont Marte. Having always held such romantic ideas of Paris, and all that it stood for, I was very disappointed with what I saw of the city so far, and no vestige of romance could I see in these dreary streets.

The Louvre was closed, as it was a Tuesday, and I was very disappointed that I could not view the famous painting of Mona Lisa. The sight of Sacre Coeur perched atop Mont Marte, was a splendid sight indeed, and well worth the arduous journey up there. We climbed dozens of stone steps to reach the summit, and I enjoyed looking at the early spring tulips in pastel shades, and other annuals that flanked the sides.

The ancient church was awesome, and two French Padres walked around, hushing up noisy tourists inside that sacred place. More crepe and ice-cream vendors dotted the entire place, but we missed going up the side-walk, a popular place for artists.

The public toilets were an absolute disgrace, as they were smelly, unhygienic, and expensive. And cost $1.40 to visit the "Ladies'" outside Notre Dame Cathedral. The toilets near Sacre Coeur were out of order, and some desperate person had defecated outside one of the portable toilets.

Once I reached the top though, I forgot the unpleasant aspects of the climb, and enjoyed spectacular views of the whole city of Paris, and surrounding suburbs. Late afternoon sunlight glowed on domes, and white city buildings.

We boarded an underground train to Notre Dame next, and the stations were absolutely filthy, and scary. Several unsavoury-looking characters hung around aimlessly. I thought about pickpockets that the attendant warned us about. We had difficulty communicating, as hardly any of the people spoke English, and customer service at stations was appalling. But we got off at the right station, and went off to tour the famous cathedral of Notre Dame.

The famous edifice was truly magnificent, inside and out. And I cannot begin to describe the feeling of grandeur, and ancient character of the place; words are too hackneyed, and inadequate in this instance. It is a monumental tribute to human achievement, and very inspiring. I stood in silence, just absorbing the beauty around me.

The marble "Pieta" was truly amazing to behold. And the historical, religious atmosphere overcame me with powerful feelings, of past centuries embedded within these walls. Huge masterpieces adorned the walls, and the grand building was simply steeped in history and majesty. We stood beside the huge, bronze statue of Charlemagne outside the Cathedral, and removed photographs, just like all the fascinated tourists around us.

My mind dwelt on the time when Connie and I were in Bendigo, in Melbourne. I visited a smaller model of this magnificent cathedral, where I saw a replica of the "Pieta" in that cathedral. I was grateful that I had the opportunity of seeing the real cathedral in all its splendour.

I could hardly walk another step by now, as I was on my feet since morning. And I soaked up enough culture, art, history, and sight-seeing for the day. I longed to just sit down somewhere quiet, and have a decent meal, as I was heartily sick and tired of snacking on croissants and crepes.

Paris was home to some beggars too, and one Yugoslav woman squatted in the heart of Champs Elysee, while another refugee woman sat on the steps of the underground station. A young girl accosted me. "You speak English?" I nodded. She showed me a postcard, explaining that she did not have a working visa, and had no money, so could I please help her? This was another form of civilised beggary, I thought. I ignored her and walked away. She turned to follow, then thought better of it, and went off to approach another tourist.

I bought two small tapestries of Notre Dame, and St Michel, in Mont Marte, and a sketch of the Eiffel tower from one of the pavement artists by the river. As I was footsore and weary, I wanted to take a taxi, and return to the hotel, but Connie wanted to see more. So we boarded another underground train to Pigalle station.

We walked along the main streets of Paris for another couple of hours, where we bought hot, roasted chestnuts from a mobile vendor. And I finally dragged my weary feet up the steps of La Sanguine Hotel. I was totally exhausted, after trudging around Paris for more than six hours. We wanted to see as many places of interest as possible in such a short time. But it proved too much for one day, especially after a gruelling thirteen-hour flight. We fell asleep for a couple of hours, and woke up at nine thirty in the night. The tourist guide told us that the night cruise down the Seine was romantic and beautiful, with myriad neon lights reflected in the dark waters. But we decided not to go, as it was too late, and we were exhausted. After showering, we ventured out into the chilly night air, looking for a restaurant to have dinner.

We ended up at café Madeline, ordered two salad rolls, coffee and tea. And later on, we wandered around the streets, taking in Paris by night, and finally returned to the hotel around midnight. My throat felt raw and scorched, as if it was on fire, and I had difficulty swallowing food and drink. I was afraid I had caught a viral infection in Paris or Singapore, so I gargled with warm salt water before going to bed.

We woke up at 6am to the sound of a shrill ringing (wake up call), and the coach was already parked in front of the hotel, ready to take us to the airport. After a hearty breakfast, we arrived at Charles de Gaulle Airport. And I still thought it was a hideous sight even the second time around, with its concrete mazes, gigantic tubes, roads, and glass-dome tubes. The coach dropped us at terminal one. And I could not get over the cold, unattractive place, compared to the warm, welcoming atmosphere in Singapore and Melbourne airports.

It was soon time to board a plane to Heathrow Airport, London, and the flight from Paris to London was hectic. The short flight took about forty minutes, and I glimpsed the English coastline, and outer suburbs in the early morning sunlight. Connie and I were not very happy, as we bickered over something or another all morning. I sat in silence, as I did not want any more arguments.

Since leaving Melbourne, he was moody, and hardly bothered to be close to me, in any sense of the word. I was hurt, wondering why he could not be pleasant and kind, now that we were on holiday, and seeing places we only dreamed of seeing. But he withdrew into a sullen silence, so I left him alone. He complained of the rash spreading all over his groin and underarms, and was irritable, because none of the creams he applied, eased the itching. The rash had spread since we left Singapore, and I told him to get some antiseptic ointment from a chemist, but he did not listen.

The plane descended rapidly, after they served sandwiches and tea. I accidentally added salt and pepper sachets into my tea, instead of sugar. Argh! The mildly amused attendant handed me another cup. My head felt wobbly, and my body ached feverishly. The flight was twenty minutes late, as we could not land until control tower gave the "all clear" signal.

When we cleared customs and walked outside, I noticed that Heathrow Airport was at least brighter, though still not half as attractive as Singapore. And the people were friendlier too than at Charles de Gaulle Airport. It was great to see Nilanthi and Tamara waiting to greet us. But I immediately noticed that Nilanthi looked subdued and tense, and not her usual cheery self.

Tamara's husband, Gihan, was slight, short, and swarthy, but friendly and pleasant enough. They lived just twenty minutes from London, in a comfortable, three bedroom, semi-detached house. Gihan drove us there in his four-wheel drive in no time at all. He was a motor mechanic, and owned a garage.

The house was a pleasing, country-style building, surrounded by several shrubs and trees, full of spring blossoms, including apple and cherry. I thought the English countryside was very picturesque indeed, especially during spring. Tamara had furnished the house well, and everything was cosy.

Tamara showed us to a bedroom upstairs. And when I asked her if it was alright for us to stay with them, since Nilanthi was here too, she was positive that they wanted us to stay. She would not hear of us going to a motel, and assured me that she was very pleased to spend a little time with us. Nilanthi occupied the adjoining room, and the master bedroom was next to the guest- room. We shared an attached bathroom with Nilanthi, and we freshened up immediately, before going downstairs to join the others.

Christine, and her sister, Grace, whom everyone called "Acca", waited for us at Tamara's place. They drove more than twenty kilometres, to welcome us. Christine still looked youthful and pretty, but had lost a great deal of weight. Acca resembled

Christine, and had a pleasant smile on her placid face, as she joined the conversation in a quiet, unassuming manner.

We had a lovely re-union, and talked, laughed, and joked away the hours, but I lost my voice completely. Christine cooked tandoori chicken, and lemon rice, which we enjoyed thoroughly. I rested in the afternoon, as I was burning with fever, and suffered from a severe throat infection. By evening I was unable to talk or even stand up.

Tamara made lemon and honey concoctions for me, which relieved my sore throat slightly. Christine and Acca left at about five thirty in the evening. I went straight to bed, and slept through till about eight o'clock. I woke up and tried to eat some dinner, then stayed up chatting with Nilanthi, and Tamara, or rather, listening to them, as I could not talk at all.

I could hardly breathe that night, and I knew I had a chest infection, when I started coughing up green mucus. I had caught a viral infection in Paris, and came down with a severe bout of flu. Connie too was plagued with a rash that kept him up all night, as it was painful and itchy. That was one of the reasons he was so irritable, I guessed.

He was not only moody, but distant and petulant. Even though I was so ill now, he did not show any sympathy, or affection. He seemed to be living in a world of his own, and called one of his siblings, or his mother every day.

Cuckoo called him a few times, and did not sound keen for us to visit him. And told him, "There are so many other places for you and Dolly to visit in Europe, you don't have to come to Berlin." But Connie was determined to see him, as that was the main reason why we came in the first place. He went to a chemist finally, and bought some lotions and cremes for the rash. But nothing seemed to help or relieve him.

When Tamara saw how ill I was next day, she consulted one of her friends, who was a doctor, and got a prescription for antibiotics. Christine and Acca arrived at nine thirty in the morning next day, and in spite of my illness, I woke up and joined the others. And shortly afterwards, Tamara drove us to Janice's place in Dunstable. We passed beautiful old houses, cottages, and flowering cherry trees along the way, and I loved the soft greens, and pastel shades of spring time in England.

Janice and the family lived in a cosy, two-storey house, beautifully furnished in typical English style. They just extended the place, and we sat out in the conservatory, which was full of exotic plants, and comfortable outdoor furniture.

It was great to see Hannah and Janice again, but Bobby was away, and so was Sarah. Sixteen year-old Hannah was a lovely-mannered girl, and I met Vera, Janice's mother. She was frail and elderly, but a very pleasant lady. Janice said, "Mum, do you remember Nihal? Dolly and Nilanthi are his sisters." Vera replied, "*Of course* I remember Nihal! We always got on well with each other." She smiled at us, and continued chatting to Hannah, who sat close by, holding Vera's hands, as she was devoted to her grandmother. We enjoyed a delicious lunch at a Chinese restaurant later, and we chatted away happily. Janice was still the same, warm-hearted, and loving person she always was, and I enjoyed those few hours in her company. She spoke about the time Stacy visited them, and how much they enjoyed seeing him, but was sad he disappeared from our lives so completely.

Each time we discussed Stacy, a heavy gloom descended on my heart and mind. Although I tried to forget my yearning to see him again, the reality of a missing son, constantly gnawed at me. And I asked God, when would Stacy come back to me again? I felt as if I was dragging an unburied corpse around with me all the time, as I had no closure until I knew what happened to Stacy. We changed the subject, and dwelt on happier matters, as they saw how deeply it hurt to talk about him.

After a while, we walked around the town, and then Janice drove us to scenic Dunstable Downs, where I glimpsed Chiltern Mountains in the distance. Spectacular countryside, with green valleys, sweeping fields, and majestic trees surrounded us. When I asked Janice about the history of the place, she filled us in about Dunstable Downs, which had a rich and varied history.

The guide book proved interesting, with the following information:

"The prehistoric burial mounds and earthworks on the chalk hills around the town bore witness to its importance since earliest times. Dunstable Downs sits on the site of a small Roman settlement called Durocobrivis, which was established at cross roads formed by Watling Street, and the prehistoric Icknield Way, which was abandoned in Saxon times, but in 1131 Henry 1 founded an Augustinian Priory, built a palace and established a new market town. Dunstable became a place of considerable importance, hosting regular royal visits and jousting tournaments.

The town is also famous for pronouncing the annulment at Priory church of the marriage of Henry V111 and Catherine of Aragorn in the 16th century. With the advent of stage-coach travel the town became an important resting point on the run north from London, and several coaching inns remain from that prosperous period. Part of the town's original Priory church still survives with its fine Norman nave and magnificent West front, even the ancient street marker has returned to its traditional High Street South location."

I was greatly interested, and absorbed in the past as always, so I enjoyed reading about the historic significance of the place. We returned to Janice's place for a cup of tea, and when we left her after fond farewells, we realised we left our gifts for Janice, and the family at Tamara's place. Janice too called Tamara later, to say she forgot our gifts, and sent them by special courier the very next day. I asked Janice to pick up our gifts from Tamara's, because unfortunately, we did not have enough time to return with the gifts. Christine and Acca spent a few more happy moments with us before leaving that evening, and said they would come back next day, if possible. Connie and I went walking in the park in front of Tamara's place, where gnarled old willows, holly trees, spring flowers, lilacs, blue-bells, and various other flowers bloomed beside a gurgling stream; but the air was still cold and crispy.

I rested awhile when we came back from our walk, and jotted down notes in my travel diary, about the day spent in Dunstable. Dosed with Panadol, lemon and honey, and antibiotics, I was determined to make the most of our trip. Although I felt very ill, I did not want to make a fuss.

Connie called Cuckoo and told him of our travel itinerary. But he tried to persuade Connie to spend more time in London, and visit Germany some other time. But he was determined to visit Cuckoo this time, as we did not know when we would be able to make it to Europe again.

We sensed Cuckoo was reluctant to have visitors because of his illness, but Connie assured him that we did not want him to entertain us in any way. And we just wanted to spend some time with him, that was all. Connie phoned Aunty daily, as he was concerned about her, although she kept reassuring him that she was fine.

Over the last few years, Cuckoo called Aunty almost every day too, and spoke to her over an hour each time, as he missed her very much. When his health deteriorated, he said that his only consolation was talking to his mother about his youthful days in Ceylon. He usually phoned late at night. And as Aunty was in her eighties then, she told me, "I get very tired and bored, and sometimes I fall asleep, as he always repeats the same thing, and everything in the past about his youth."

He never went out any more, since he began dialysis, and he told me, "The only pleasure I now have is, talking to Mummy." It was bizarre, but Connie too told me a while back, that he was quite happy and content to socialize only with his mother, and Aunty Molly. He said, "I don't need any friends, as long as I have Mummy, and Aunty Molly, I'm happy." I could not understand his mindset at all, as I liked my friends, and socialized with a variety of people. I loved my sons, and sisters dearly too, and enjoyed their company, but did not want their companionship exclusively. So, it was difficult for me to comprehend such obsessive behaviour.

It must have been some deep, psychological need, as they were all totally fixated with their mother, except Babs. She cared for Aunty very much, visited her often, and did all she could to make her happy. But she had other interests too, and many friends, so her whole world did not revolve around Aunty. Connie and his siblings did not talk about their father as much.

I often wondered about this crippling, emotional need. And Cuckoo, with all his education, and knowledge, had nothing else to make him happy in his life, except phone calls to his mother. It was sad; but, if calling his mother daily was the only thing that made him happy, it was a case of, "To each his own." How he spent his time and money was his business.

He told us that he bought phone cards, so he could speak for hours, without running up a huge phone bill. Connie too got a phone card in London now, so he could call Aunty and Cuckoo.

Although I had loved my parents dearly, my life was not wrapped around them, as I had my own life to live. But Connie and his siblings were unable to cope without their mother. And even while on holiday with me in Europe, he continuously fretted about his mother's welfare. He called her daily, not so much as to find out how she was, but because he missed her. And he could not get close to me emotionally, or physically, because he was unable to relax and enjoy the present.

Whenever Cuckoo phoned us in Melbourne, he usually spent a couple of hours talking. And I enjoyed some very interesting conversations, as he always remembered Thathie and Nihal, and details of all their discussions. He had an amazing memory for such particulars. And when he spoke to Connie, they always talked endlessly about the family, and their past.

Gihan's step-mother, Veronica, dropped in, like she usually did on a daily basis (so they told me), and was invited to stay for dinner. She looked vixenish, and bad-tempered. She caused Tamara plenty of grief, but she tried to be on good terms with Veronica, because of Gihan and his father, who were terrified of the spiteful woman.

Every line in her heavily made up face, accentuated the malice that was evident in her looks and attitude. I could hardly bear to look at her, and my first impression was confirmed, when Tamara told me she put up with a lot of flack from her in-laws, especially Veronica, and I pitied Tamara. After dinner, Tamara and Gihan suggested we tour London by night.

It was a wonderful sight indeed, and Westminster Cathedral looked magical, with its lacy, graceful façade, and soaring spires. We drove past the impressive Savoy Hotel, and Hyde Park, then stopped outside Harrods, ablaze with thousands of lights. Buckingham Palace looked splendid under the cold stars, and we returned home close on midnight. My throat still felt raw, as if I had swallowed a ball of fire, and the chest cold and cough kept me up all night.

The next day, on 12 April, we woke up around eight thirty, to a mild, spring day, and after breakfast, we planned to visit Stratford-On-Avon. Connie was very anxious to travel to Scotland by train, just for the day. But as I was not up to it, Tamara discouraged him, saying that it was too tiring, and too far away for a day trip.

We drove up to Warwick Castle first, which was about one and a half miles from Harrow. It was truly spectacular countryside, with all the cherry blossoms bursting into white and pink flowers. It was like walking inside a pastel painting; all pale greens, soft shades of pinks, cream, lilac, and beige foliage.

We walked through the castle, where wax figures of various household members stood in each room. They looked so real that I almost expected them to start talking to us, as they were extremely life-like, and meticulous attention to the smallest detail was evident.

I beheld breathtaking views of the Avon River, from the upper windows of the castle, and gazed in wonder, as I wanted to register each detail in my memory. Although the period costumes and furnishings were Victorian, I felt we were transported back in time to the medieval era. Nilanthi and I hardly spent time together, but we walked hand in hand now, admiring the wonderful sights we were privileged to behold. We chatted briefly, and I told her I was glad she was able to visit Tamara.

She told me that she was very stressed living with Tamara and Gihan, as they were constantly at logger-heads, and she felt very uncomfortable. I did not notice anything amiss with the young couple though. But Nilanthi told me she booked a return ticket home several times, as she could not stand their endless quarrels. But they persuaded her to stay on a little longer. Nilanthi was fond of Gihan, and he returned her affection, and I thought he was a nice, quiet young man. But that was just a facade, and only Tamara knew the kind of person he was, so I was not passing judgement.

After all this sight-seeing, we stopped at a quaint old pub, the "Porridge Pot" and had lunch there, then we drove on to Stratford-on-Avon. Our first stop was Anne Hathaway's cottage, which looked very romantic, with its thatched roof, and thousands of spectacular, myriad-coloured tulips that bloomed profusely in the gardens.

The cottage faced a pleasant little park, with flowering cherry trees, shrubs, and tall trees, with masses of daffodils carpeting the slopes of the park. It was truly inspiring, and conducive to creativity, and plain to see why Anne Hathaway chose to live here. Spring was indeed a lovely time of the year to visit England.

Shakespeare's birthplace was a drab, Tudor-Style cottage of weathered, black and brown beams. The streets were lined with similar structures, and I stepped back in time to absorb the ambience of the famous village. I enjoyed the spectacular scenery once again, with its soft, pretty colours, rivers, and rivulets flowing gently along.

We stopped at a souvenir shop, and for fifty pounds (Nelune's birthday gift), I bought a hand-crafted scene of an English cottage, set in a peaceful countryside. Nelune wanted me to spend it overseas, and this was something I really liked. I bought Nilanthi a souvenir too, and after looking around the famous area for some time, we returned to Harrow in about one and a half hour's time.

Back at Tamara's place, I showered, and waited for Anthony and Barbara to come for dinner, and they arrived around eight thirty. Dinner was lively, and we laughed and joked all through the evening. Anthony invited us for dinner the following night, and we accepted. It was late when they left, and we slept after midnight. I was amazed at how much we packed into those few hours!

We woke up late next day, and headed off to Christine's place, around eleven thirty in the morning, and arrived there a couple of hours later. Tamara drove through heavy traffic, and it was a very long, slow drive. I found it very distressing, and felt strange to walk in to that flat where Rosie lived for so many years.

Many photographs, mementos, and memories of Rosie were everywhere I looked. Christine made it a point to keep her memory alive in every possible way she could. A large, framed photograph of Rosie's smiling face seemed to follow me around wherever I walked in the flat. Christine said she completed over a dozen tapestries, that hung on the walls now. She told me it was a form of therapy, ever since Rosie's death, and a coping mechanism for her over-whelming grief.

Christine and Acca treated us to a delicious Chinese meal in a near-by restaurant, after which, we shopped around in a popular shopping centre. I bought a black, chiffon blouse, and each time I looked at something, Christine jumped up to buy it for me. I refused her generosity very firmly, as I told her I had no room in my suitcase. She was so very kind and loving, and said, "I want to treat you just as if Rosie would have treated you if she been around today."

Then she drove us to Rosie's grave, and Christine's niece, Jeyan, her little daughter, Aimee, and Acca joined us too. It was a pleasant, old cemetery, with an ancient church set amid dark sighing trees, like sentinels guarding the graves. I would have loved to have visited Nihal's grave with Janice too, but as it was quite a distance, I was unable to make it due to our limited time in London. I promised myself I would definitely return someday, and visit Nihal's grave.

I stood by the grave as countless memories swept over me; it was very sad to think of someone as vital and energetic as Rosie, lying there in that quiet lonely grave. Christine had blanketed the entire grave with flowers, trinkets, and mementos, and she made it a point to visit the grave weekly or more often, just to let Rosie know she was not forgotten. What a fantastic friend and companion she was to Rosie.

In the midst of our grief, little Aimee's helium balloon disappeared without a trace. And Christine kept saying, "Aunty Rosie has it Aimee, don't worry!" We returned to the flat, feeling subdued, and I could not bear to talk about Rosie at all. Just as we were about to leave, Christine suddenly burst into uncontrollable sobbing.

I felt helpless in the midst of such violent emotion and heart-rending grief. She could hardly contain her vast emotion that burst all boundaries, as she realised the enormity of her loss once again. Seeing us, Rosie's much-loved nieces, and visiting her grave, brought back Rosie's memory too vividly, and she bawled out, "I'm *so lonely*! I *miss* Rosie so much!"

We pacified her as well as we could, and her sobbing gradually eased off. Sam, Christine's black cat, whom she adored, mewed piteously, and joined in Christine's howling, as he was clearly upset to see his beloved mistress crying so bitterly.

Janice sent us gifts via express mail to Christine's place, and Christine and Acca showered us with many gifts as well. As we said goodbye, they told me, "Dolly, your caring ways remind us so much of dear Rosie." On our return trip to Tamara's, we dropped in at Anthony's and Barbara's place around eight thirty that night. He had cooked lamb curry and fried noodles, and insisted we stay for dinner, which we did. We met Kristian, their eldest son, who was visiting, as he lived in Sydney, Australia.

He was an interesting, good-looking young man, and we chatted away for some time, and he said he would keep in touch when we returned to Melbourne. Kristian was engaged to an Australian girl, and said he loved Australia better than England. He had the heater on at thirty degrees because he hated the cold, English weather, and loved the hot climate in Australia. It was a long, emotional day, and I was extremely tired when we finally arrived at Tamara's place close to midnight.

Chapter 33

We boarded a train next day from North Harrow to Baker Street, and from there we travelled in a tour bus to Trafalgar Square. I still felt unwell, and had a chesty cough that kept me up at nights, but was determined to see as much of London as possible. We walked to Buckingham Palace, but the roads were blocked off due to the annual London marathon that was in progress. Then we strolled through St James' Park, which was stunning, with fresh, green foliage adorning all the trees. Masses of brilliant tulips bloomed everywhere, and the gardens in front of Buckingham Palace were simply astounding.

We cruised along the Thames River next, and beheld all the historical landmarks; the Tower of London, Shakespeare's Globe Theatre, and London Bridge. On the way, we heard a macabre story about "Sweeney Todd" the murderous barber; he cut his victims' throats, hauled their bodies down to a woman's kitchen, where she cooked them, and passed them on as "chicken pies" horrible thought! I decided never ever to eat minced chicken or meat pies after that story.

Our next stop was the "London Eye" and Connie went sight-seeing on his own, while I stayed down below, reading brochures and tour guides. He had a habit of dashing ahead, and never walked beside me to take in sights together, so we could discuss and share our impressions. I trailed far behind him, and sometimes I could not see where he was, as he quickly ducked in somewhere for a smoke. It was exasperating to keep looking for him, so I sat in the mild sunshine and waited for him to turn up.

We had McDonald's for lunch, then walked around for several more hours, looking at all the fascinating sights of London. Footsore and weary, I was glad when we finally returned to Tamara's place around five o'clock in the evening. I was greatly impressed with all the ancient monuments, edifices, and historical places I had seen.

Rosie always told me, "My dearest wish is for you to visit London, so I can take you sight-seeing, and to the theatres." She knew how much I loved live- theatre. When I walked around the city they had loved so dearly, I sensed Rosie's and Nihal's presence very much. They described its wonders to me so often, that I could almost fancy hearing their beloved voices, laughing, joking, and enjoying life to the fullest.

Later that evening, Connie and I walked with Nilanthi to a near-by church, and lit candles, and then spent a quiet evening with Tamara and Gihan. We had an early dinner, then I called Christine, Acca, Janice, Anthony, and Barbara to wish them goodbye, and I thanked Janice, Christine and Acca especially, for their wonderful hospitality and love.

Nilanthi was sad to be leaving, because she said she was "mothering" Gihan and Tamara. She woke up early every morning, made breakfast for them, and even made Gihan's sandwiches for lunch. He was fond of her, and would miss all the pampering no doubt.

We woke up early on 15 April, packed up quickly and prepared to leave. Tamara cooked a huge breakfast; toast, bacon, eggs, sausages, dhal curry, and chilli sambal too. We sat down to a leisurely breakfast, chatted some more, and Nilanthi became very sad and emotional to think of saying goodbye.

Tamara cried copiously, as Nilanthi too was leaving later on that day. I had a brief moment alone with Nilanthi, who explained, "I did not want to spend much time with you, as Tamara is so moody and unpredictable. She would have accused me of spending too much time with you, and not with her. I feel I'm under obligation to her as she bought my ticket. So don't get angry or feel hurt, if I was a little distant, because you know what she's like. She gets very jealous if I spend time with you and not with her."

I was sad that they still had these issues, and Nilanthi said she wanted to leave a few weeks earlier, due to the constant friction. Gihan drove us to the airport, and we arrived there at eleven thirty in the morning, and Tamara dropped Nilanthi a few hours later. Connie and I walked around Heathrow Airport, which was more welcoming than Paris, as it was brighter, and the atmosphere more pleasant and friendly.

The flight to Amsterdam took about forty five minutes, and I enjoyed the view from the plane. Colourful tulips carpeted fields everywhere I looked, and green swards criss-crossed murky canals. We landed at Amsterdam Airport around three thirty in the afternoon (local time). It was very clean and orderly, and people were helpful too, as we boarded a train to City Central Station.

I was dismayed though, to find City Central Station was very dirty, and teemed with drug-users and unsavoury-looking characters, but several police officers patrolled the area. Cuckoo told us to leave our suitcases in a locker there, as we were staying only one night and one day in Amsterdam. Numerous Algerians and Black people loitered around, just like in Paris. An Englishman approached us, and begged money to buy a return ticket to England. Needless to say, we just ignored him, not knowing if he was a drug- addict or not.

Then we walked to the accommodation centre to book a room for the night, but it was closed. We rushed off to the Tourist Information Centre, and spent half an hour there trying to book a hotel room. The receptionist informed us that a room was available in a cheap hotel in the notorious "Red Light" district, for 110 euros a night, but we thought it was not the ideal place to stay.

She checked again, and booked us in at a five star American hotel, the Crown Plaza, which was about fifteen minutes from City Central Station, for only 105 euros a night (on a special deal). I was relieved, as I wanted to rest somewhere soon, after such a long day.

We returned to City Central Station to get some clothes from our suitcase for our overnight stay in the hotel, but when we tried to lock them again, we were told we had to pay another four euros each for opening the locker. Connie was furious, as it seemed unfair to pay twice for the same locker, but we had no choice, and paid a second time. Then we took a taxi to the hotel, as one of the policemen told us that a taxi was safer than a bus.

On our way to the Crown Plaza, a luxurious American hotel, I glimpsed the Palace, where Queen Beatrix lived. And the staid Dutch architecture, evident in the square, tall buildings, narrow windows, and gables galore, was quite different to the edifices in London and Paris.

It was a well-appointed hotel, and the room was plush and comfortable, with a large, king-sized bed in the centre (very American). I enjoyed the luxury of a hot water bath, and felt much better and relaxed after the hectic pace of the last few days.

After enjoying a delicious dinner in the hotel restaurant, we called Tamara, Gihan and Cuckoo, to let them know of the next stage in our journey. Drinks were dear at 7.50 euros for a whisky, and the same for a nip of brandy. Connie switched on the television set later, and was told that the standard cost was 14 euros per room, whether you watched television or not. This too annoyed him, and we were fast coming to the conclusion that Amsterdam was an expensive place to visit.

I slept well, as the bed was very comfortable and warm, and woke up at seven thirty in the morning. The rash was making Connie very petulant and uncomfortable, and he did not try to get close to me in any way, but kept tossing and turning, unable to fall asleep. I thought that staying in such a beautiful hotel, and enjoying a delicious meal, he would be in a mellow mood, and we could be close, but I did not understand his continued moodiness. I was sorry about his rash, but that was no reason to behave like a sore bear all the time.

We sat down to an ample breakfast in the restaurant next morning, and the total bill for that one night in Amsterdam, including dinner, breakfast, two phone calls, and pay television was 210 euros. We went on a canal cruise for two hours, but it continued drizzling, as on the previous day. It was dull and cloudy, with hardly a glimmer of sunshine or blue skies. The cruise boat was heated though and quite pleasant. And as we glided along, the tour guide's loud voice bellowed out, "There are three main canals, which are 'Gentleman's 'Empress' and 'Prince's.' We are now on the Empress' canal."

Connie ignored me most of the time, as if I was a total stranger, but struck up a conversation with the young female tour guide, and spent the rest of the cruise hanging around her and asking questions.

We stopped at Rijksmuseum, and were fortunate to get in without queuing too long. Not many people were inside either, and we just rushed up to see the Dutch Masters section mainly, as I definitely wanted to see Rembrandt's great masterpiece, 'The Night Watch.' Not enough superlatives or adjectives exist, to describe the beauty and grandeur of those wonderful paintings. Rembrandt's masterpiece was stupendous, and I stood before it lost for words. Connie quickly removed one photograph, before a female guard yelled at him, "No photos allowed!"

All the paintings were incredibly beautiful, and some of them stood from floor to ceiling. How much of work, how many years to complete these Herculean works of art! Well may I ponder on that question ever after, as I gazed at the craftsmanship, genius and inspiration that must have possessed those giants of art. I was humbled and privileged, and am forever grateful to have seen those magnificent paintings.

Some of the paintings, like "The massacre of the Bethlehem innocents" were vividly sensual and erotic, and I believe, was just an excuse to paint male and female nudes in various postures. Many of the remarkable paintings were based on Biblical themes, such as "Lot and his daughters," female nudes with their old father. And another erotic depiction of an old, feeble man with his daughter breast-feeding him, as he lies starving in prison.

Then we walked to another section where several ancient pieces of Dutch furniture stood in imposing rows. I was sad to rush through quickly, as it would take more than a day to fully appreciate every thing in the Museum.

We returned to the cruise boat and drifted past most of the old buildings in Amsterdam; the "Golden Bend" where rich merchants lived, and snug little house-boats that cost around 350 thousand euros to own one. Hundreds of canals and bridges criss-crossed Amsterdam, and were originally built to transport goods to houses and warehouses. The goods were then taken in through windows of houses, as the staircases were too narrow.

The guide went on to explain that the River Amstel, was the only natural river and waterway, and there was a dam before, which was how the city gets its name "Amsterdam." The cruise was quite pleasant and enjoyable, and we stopped for a fifteen-minute break at a small café where Connie sipped a Heineken beer, and I enjoyed a cup of tea.

My impression of Amsterdam though, on such a gloomy, wet day, was that all the buildings looked drab and un-inviting. But in the night, just like every other city in the world, it looked very pretty, when myriads of coloured- lights glowed and reflected in the dark, tranquil canals, winding around like slithering, gleaming snakes around the city. It was also a city of bicycles, as thousands of them crowded the streets rather than motor vehicles.

We got off the boat close to our hotel, and after a quick wash and change, we took a taxi back to City Central Station. We collected our suitcases from the lockers, and boarded a train to Berlin from Platform 11 B. It was still light, and I watched the countryside zooming past, like a blurred dream, as the fast train whizzed by at lightning speed.

The landscape looked much the same as glimpsed from the plane, and was still wet, dreary, and dark. Spring was just stirring here, and in summer the landscape would be green and bright. But right now, only cold, bleak, wintry fingers spread out everywhere I looked. Quaint abodes, like doll-houses, dotted the country-side, but on the opposite side of the track were unsightly, square, concrete masses that housed people and offices.

Quiet, peaceful woods, little streams and rivulets, sheep and cattle in distant meadows looked picturesque. And I saw plenty of uncultivated land, with belts of green woodland and some logging areas too. We soon passed a very scenic little town, Deventer, where quaint houses lined the streets, and a large river flowed by on the outskirts of town. It looked just like a fairytale book, sprinkled with tiny houses and farms. I tried to absorb the beautiful picture before the speeding train hurtled past. We still had a fair way to Berlin, and it was only four thirty in the afternoon.

As we neared Berlin, the landscape changed. I could see distant mountain ranges, green pastures, woodland, and forests with blackened tree trunks still in the grip of winter snow; tender, green shoots appeared in silver birches and conifers. Once again, I found the scenic landscape very pleasing, with ginger-bread houses nestled beneath green woods.

Houses with A-frame, slate-grey, gabled roofs, that almost touched the ground, were a familiar sight here, and everything looked neat and orderly. A few deer leapt and frolicked in the woodlands, and broad, silvery rivers ran alongside the rail track; endless meadows, green woods, and flowering cherry trees sprang up everywhere.

We bought coffee and sandwiches on the train, as hot food was unavailable. Connie walked off to the smoking section. When he returned to the carriage some time later, a young, German girl followed, demanding cigarettes from him. Connie looked abashed, as he told me that he gave her a cigarette when he went for a smoke. When he ignored her now, she let out a stream of abuse in German, which we gathered were insults, judging from the vicious expression on her face.

She did not stop her tirade for five or ten minutes, until one of her friends came along and dragged her away from our carriage. I asked Connie, "What was that all about?" he replied, "I just gave her a cigarette, that's all." "Why was she so angry then?" I asked. He shrugged his shoulders and did not reply. A German lady sitting opposite me, who was listening, now translated, "The girl said your husband led her on, so she came to ask cigarettes." I looked at Connie in disbelief. He glared at the lady and stomped out.

He learnt to say, "I love you" and "Kiss me" in German and Italian, instead of "Hello," which would have been more to the point. He may have said that to the young girl and misled her, perhaps that was the reason why she was so angry. Connie did not venture into the smoking area again, but stood out in the corridor, and smoked now and then. I hoped he learnt a lesson, not to approach strange girls again.

We had travelled for more than five hours now, and it was quite dark outside. I could hardly see anything around, so I read a book. Just before the darkening skies clouded the views though, we passed high mountains, close to a place called Minden Station, where I glimpsed a dome-like structure perched high on the mountain top. When I asked Cuckoo about that place, he explained, "When Hammond, a German hero, conquered the Romans hundreds of years ago, that monument was built in his honour."

We finally arrived at Zoological Gartens Station, Berlin, around eight fifteen in the night. Regina, greeted us cheerfully, and she gave me a large bouquet of red tulips, and golden ranunculus. It was good to see her after more than eighteen years. She still looked the same, except that she was much heavier, but was just as friendly and warm. I hugged her, and communicated as well as I could, because she still did not speak fluent English, but we managed to understand each other.

It was drizzling, and very cold, as we walked out and took a taxi to their apartment on Wielandstrasse place. And we climbed a great number of steps to the third level. Regina carried one of the cases, although Connie wanted to carry them, but she was already halfway up the stairs.

I was sad and shocked when I saw Cuckoo, as he was very feeble, and looked much older than his sixty-six years, with his slow, shuffling gait, and head cocked to one side. After greeting us, he led us to the huge, loaded dining table, where, in spite of his frailty, he had cooked a delicious rice and curry meal. Large dishes of chicken curry, fried potatoes, dhal, beans, and yellow rice, looked tempting. And he said with a faint smile, "You both must go down on your knees and eat this meal, because I took so much trouble to cook it!" I could well believe it, and thanked him heartily.

That night, he told Connie he did not want us to see him in such a bad state, so frail and ill; and that was the reason why he discouraged us from visiting him. Poor man, all the more reason to visit him when he was ailing, I thought. After dinner, we sat around the table, and talked till past midnight. Regina and Cuckoo had gifts of perfume and books for us on the table, and a shirt for Connie, which he immediately put on, and we removed a few photographs that night. He was pleased with the black, satin, dressing gown we bought, and Regina thanked us for her favourite perfume.

I woke up after a good sleep next day, as it was warm and cosy under the feather doona. I still took antibiotics and felt better, so I did not mention I was ill. Connie was suffering with the rash though, and he asked Regina to recommend something to relieve it. She advised him to get some different cremes, but they did not heal or relieve him much, though he said it was slightly better.

I had a good look around the apartment in the morning, which was an enormous, old mansion, built in the 1800s. Stone ovens, with glazed exteriors, stood about seven or eight feet from the floor. Coal and briquettes were used to light them, and when the stones heated up, they radiated substantial warmth in each room. Food was also heated in the "oven" which had an opening, with a hot plate on top.

Cuckoo laid the table, and we enjoyed an ample breakfast of toast, sausages, fruits, and jam. We sat there chatting till about two o'clock in the afternoon that day. It was mild and cloudy, but not raining. He purchased tickets for us to tour Berlin, and paid for bus, train, and museum entrance fares too. Regina accompanied us, and we boarded a bus to see Berlin by night. It was a fantastic city, and we had a very comfortable trip around in the bus.

Public transport was well-organised, and reasonably priced too. Most people used the public transport system, and even Regina and Cuckoo never owned a car, because it was so convenient, with transport at their doorstep. We returned to the apartment very late that night, and Connie stayed up talking with Cuckoo till the early hours of dawn. He wanted to make the most of the few days we had with Cuckoo.

The weather remained much the same next day, and we had a late breakfast, then sat at the table talking till midday. Regina left soon after breakfast though, as she was on sick leave, due to a bad back, and had to see doctor. But Cuckoo did not have dialysis that day, so he was determined to sight-see with us.

We stopped at a framer's shop nearby on our way, to frame a pastel-painting of a field of red poppies that I painted for Cuckoo. A few weeks before we left, he told me, "Dolly, I want you to paint me a field of poppies before I die." So, I finished a large painting, about sixteen by twenty inches, and transported it in a plastic tube. I wanted him to choose a frame now.

He was very happy and impressed with the painting, and when it hung on his study wall, he told me later, "All my friends admire your painting of the poppies, and think it is very beautiful. Thank you for that Dolly." He also kept a small landscape of the Australian bush I painted about ten years ago, on the piano. I was pleased to fulfil his wish, as he wanted to remember the Australian landscape, and gaze upon a field of vibrant poppies.

I lent him my arm for support, as he walked very slowly. And he said, "I have not been out for a walk for five months, because I need someone to walk with me, and Regina is too busy with her work." I replied, "I'm glad to help you." We walked around the block at a leisurely pace, and he talked about the history of Berlin, and various other issues. Then we sat down on a bench while he rested, as he tired easily, and Connie ran across the street to get him an ice cream.

That evening, we relaxed, and enjoyed more conversation about "cabbages and kings," as Cuckoo liked to call these happy discussions. Regina prepared a delicious dinner, and I turned in later, but Cuckoo and Connie stayed up chatting till four o'clock in the morning.

Every night, Cuckoo talked with Aunty, Esme, or Cristobel. They called him regularly, to find out how he was, and how we were enjoying our holiday.

We waited for Cuckoo to return after dialysis next day, as he wanted us to see some places of interest in Berlin. When he returned, we walked across the street, boarded a bus, then a train, and walked a short distance to the "Place Of Remembrance," and the "Shooting Wall," where firing squads executed victims.

I saw the gruesome place, with black, blood-soaked hooks still hanging, where victims were strung up by their throats. It was a distressing, silent place, surrounded by pine and cypress trees, that seemed to sway and sigh sorrowfully at the memory of atrocities committed within those walls. The courtyard was a silent witness to untold human misery.

I was deeply moved, and subdued in that eerie place, and really wished I did not have to re-live the horror of the holocaust. As we stood in front of the bullet-riddled, blackened wall, Cuckoo prayed silently for all the tortured souls murdered so cruelly. The words on the wall read, "Dedicated to the victims murdered by Hitler the Dictator."

Afterwards, we walked back slowly to the bus-stop, and then boarded another three trains, and two buses, with Cuckoo struggling along painfully, but most determined to keep up with us. He paused now and then, for a swig of port or whisky to alleviate his pains. His legs were bandaged, as his varicose veins were infected; he had osteoporosis too, which caused excruciating pain in his legs and feet. Poor Cuckoo.

Although he was in a great deal of pain, he was very hospitable, and anxious to make our visit memorable, even though we kept insisting that we did not care to sight-see, but just spend quality time with him and Regina. We returned, feeling very tired after long hours of sight-seeing, and I was glad to just sit back and relax.

Regina cooked a delicious tomato soup, grilled sausages, and sauerkraut. And Clarissa dropped in for dinner. It was lovely to see her again after about seven years. But Krishan was holidaying in Spain, and called us the day we arrived, as he was leaving for Spain that same day. We were sorry we missed seeing him, but he planned to visit Australia soon. After dinner, we removed photographs with them, and I gave Clarissa some souvenirs from Australia. She was a sweet, delightful young girl, and I was very fond of her.

I woke up early next morning, and as Cuckoo was busy typing some urgent work, because he still translated letters for courts and private individuals, Regina accompanied us on another tour of Berlin. We stopped at the famous Opera House, museum, the American quarter, "Checkpoint Charlie" and all the other places of interest in Berlin.

We took buses and trains, and after a few hours, Regina left us, as she had to attend to some business. Connie and I continued to walk around the streets, shopped for souvenirs, then bought fresh meat, and minced beef at the butcher's, and a mint plant for Regina.

Then we headed back soon, because I planned to cook dinner. As I began preparing the food, Cuckoo shuffled up to me, tied one of his aprons round my waist, and said, "Now I will make Connie jealous, by saying that I will sleep with the apron under my pillow!" We laughed, as it was good fun when he joked, and was not in too much pain. I finished making dinner around eight o'clock.

Regina and I had a great time in the kitchen, trying to communicate. And we burst into peals of laughter, as we resorted to actions and charades to make ourselves understood. But we managed very well, and translated for each other. After a few glasses of beer, she exclaimed, "I think Cuckoo very fussy, but *Connie...hundred* times more than Cuckoo! They crazy, but we love them no?" I agreed. She was still fuming, because the night we arrived, she served rice in a round bowl, and Cuckoo nagged her to change it, and serve the rice in an *oval* dish.

Connie and Cuckoo were talking in the dining room, but he was in a great deal of pain that evening, and was petulant. I made beef curry and cutlets, which they enjoyed very much. And Cuckoo told me, "The mince is too good for cutlets, because Regina usually eats such good mince, raw."

Later that night, Esme called, and then Cristobel. Afterwards, Cuckoo came over, and asked Connie, "Why don't you stay another week or so?" Then he turned to me seriously, "You are such an experienced traveller Dolly, you can return on your own can't you? Esme and Bella told me Connie has plenty of leave, so he can remain a few weeks longer here." Connie replied at once. "Cuckoo, I won't enjoy my stay, if I had to be here alone without Dolly. We came together, so I'd like to return with Dolly. We will come back again, I promise." Cuckoo replied with a laugh, "Well, *that's* a different story, if you don't want to stay alone without Dolly!"

I did not let their interference bother me, because I knew Connie would not stay on his own. They told him Connie wanted to stay longer with him, but I was anxious to return home, due to my work. Once he understood how Connie felt, he did not try to persuade him to stay on his own. We laughed and talked for hours during that last dinner. But later, when I went to bed, Connie stayed up, as he wanted Cuckoo and Regina to watch a video of our house and garden in Frankston.

We woke up early next day, and I made meat patties for them. Connie helped to roll out the dough, and I soon made patties, as Cuckoo was very fond of them. He went early for dialysis, so we walked down to the shops, and bought some white roses for Regina (her favourite flowers), and a deep-red, flowering begonia for Cuckoo, just to say "Thank you" for their hospitality and generosity over the last few days.

When Cuckoo returned, he was surprised, and very pleased, as he relished the patties, and admired the flowers. After lunch, we accompanied them to St Konrad's church, but the doors were closed, so we stood and prayed outside. Regina asked the sacristan's daughter to open the church door, which she did, so we stood in the porch and continued to pray.

It was almost five o'clock when we returned, and we chatted a while over a cup of tea. Cuckoo asked me to play the piano, and he sang "O Danny Boy," and "Long Long Ago," two of his favourite old tunes. Then it was time to leave.

They gave us a beautiful, large book, with all the interesting places in Berlin, and he wrote on the fly leaf, "In memory of a short, but very sweet stay in Berlin." When I hugged Cuckoo, and wished him goodbye, I knew deep in my heart, I would not see him again, as he was too frail to travel to Australia in the near future. And I was unsure when we would return, so it was very sad to say goodbye to an affectionate and generous brother-in-law, and a dear, kind, sister-in-law.

Regina came with us in a taxi to Tegel Airport, a small, but clean domestic airport. We talked as we sipped drinks in a restaurant, and I thanked her once again for everything they did to make us comfortable. She was very warm and caring. I hugged her, and watched as she went back to the taxi. We walked to the gate, and boarded the small plane for a very short flight to Frankfurt Airport.

The flight-attendants had just enough time to serve a glass of orange juice, and before we knew, we arrived at Frankfurt Airport. It was quite the largest airport I ever saw, and an incredibly busy, gigantic city of terminals everywhere. It looked like a vast, sprawling city stretching out as far as I could see. A bus transported us to airport terminal one, and we stayed there a whole hour, as Connie enquired about Singapore Airlines, that we were travelling with. They told us we had to go to terminal two, which was Qantas Airlines, which would take us to Singapore.

We rushed off, and boarded the skyline train to terminal two, where the queue was so long, and with just three people at the enquiries counters. Fortunately, we arrived a few hours early, or else we would have missed the flight. It seemed an endless wait, so I sat down, while Connie stood in the long line, waiting his turn.

I wrote in my travel diary, until the queue slowly edged its way to the counter. The airport was clean and bright, with shops and bistros everywhere. Terminal two was a very large area, with overhead, steel, criss-cross domes. We arrived at eight o'clock, and our flight was at eleven fifty five that night. Before we boarded the plane, we phoned Cuckoo, and he told me, "Try to come over one more time, before I die okay Dolly?" I was very moved, and replied I would certainly try to make it again.

Chapter 34

After a gruelling, thirteen-hour flight once again, we arrived in Singapore for a few hours stopover, and finally reached Melbourne. It was great to be home, and Ranjith picked us up very early in the morning, as the plane arrived at dawn, and he dropped us in Frankston. We went to sleep immediately, as the journey was exhausting. The time difference, and jet-lag affected us for a couple of days, and we woke up at midnight to have snacks. We called Cuckoo and Regina to thank them once again for their wonderful hospitality, and I also called Tamara.

The cats looked alright when we picked them up from the cattery next day, but they were disoriented, after three weeks away from their home environment. I pampered them, but they looked at me indifferently, as if quite unused to my company. Connie could not drive for another two weeks, until he got back his licence, so I drove him around everywhere.

He made an appointment with a skin specialist in the city, and was prescribed tablets, and cremes for a bacterial, fungal infection. The cremes he used in London and Berlin, only aggravated the rash. I was glad when he finally had some relief. Through the years I knew him, he was susceptible to skin rashes, and he did not know how or why they flared up.

In the days that followed, I felt so unwell, that I could not return to work as I intended. I consulted my doctor, and he did some blood tests. The diagnosis was, type two diabetes. My sugar levels were very high, and he prescribed glucose-lowering medication. That accounted for the reason I felt so ill, combined with the chest infection. I was off work for a few more weeks, until I recovered.

Nelune visited on 1 June, but the day before, I over-exerted my right hand, cutting up some thick cardboard. And when she arrived, I was helpless, and could hardly move my hand. While I was considering whether to see doctor, Geraldine rang at about nine o'clock in the morning, and spoke to Connie for a long time.

The night before, which was Saturday, Adam, and his friend, were lighting highly explosive, banned fireworks. And he was injured when he bent over to check one of the unexploded rockets. He was rushed to casualty in a critical condition, but with no hope of survival. Connie came downstairs, red-eyed as he broke the news.

We rushed to Dandenong hospital immediately, but Nelune stayed behind, as she just arrived from Sydney, and Shirani was visiting in the afternoon.

Adam's whole head was bandaged, as he lay inert, and the family gathered around in deep shock. Geraldine was the only one who kept *insisting* he would miraculously pull through. The doctor called the immediate family to his office, and explained the extent of Adam's horrendous injuries. The explosive burst through Adam's eye, shattering part of his brain, and surgeons could not help him. He was on a life-saving machine, but all hope was gone. We were astounded and deeply grieved.

After we left Adam, one of the doctors in casualty checked my hand. He wrapped it in a sling, and asked me to rest it for a few days, as the ligaments in my palm were injured. Connie dropped me at home late afternoon, and returned to the hospital once again to keep watch with the family, and returned after midnight.

He drove back to hospital early next day, and did not come home till late at night. In the evening, Nelune, Shirani, Ranjith, and I visited Adam, but it was the same story, no improvement and no hope. Several "Born again" Christians, prayed at his bedside. And their pastor insisted that Adam would get up and walk again, giving the parents false hope. A few years ago, they too were baptised as "Born again" Christians, and were in total denial now, as they stormed heaven for a miracle.

Geraldine lost touch with reality from that day onwards, and she lived in a bizarre world, and constantly talked about Adam. She drew parallels with Jesus, the Son of God, who was sacrificed. Although Adam's injury was solely due to his own fault, lighting banned fireworks, she overlooked that part completely, and spoke as if her son was sacrificed in the name of God.

She could not speak one sentence without dragging Adam's name into it. I sympathised with her, but most of her family and friends considered her a dead bore, with her Bible-bashing, and never-ending harping on Adam's fate. I understood her grief, because I too missed Stacy dearly. But I hardly mentioned my feelings to anyone, unless they asked me about him. And neither did I dwell on my misfortune, the way she did.

On the third day after Adam's accident, the doctor called his parents, and family for a meeting. He explained that the nurses refused to dress his wounds, as gangrene set in. They were told that the life-saving machine would be turned off. It was tragic, but his parents were compelled to accept the fact that there was no hope now, no matter what their pastor told them about a miraculous recovery. So, it was turned off that day.

Nelune and I were with Aunty then, as everyone else was in the hospital. Geraldine called Aunty, and told her to say goodbye to Adam over the phone. And they told me that he heaved a gusty sigh as his life ended. The next few days were dreadful for the whole family, especially for the parents. But Geraldine said that her new-found faith as a "Born again" Christian sustained her. The funeral was held in a large hall, and she got on the stage to speak long about her faith, and said that she put her trust in God.

Aunty did not attend, as she said she could not bear funerals. It was the same when Wendy died. It seemed to me that she had a fear of death, and it grew worse as she became older. Her Catholic faith, and prayers were not enough to uphold her in this tragedy. I gave her some prayer books, and literature about life and death, but she was inconsolable.

My arm was still in a sling, and I was unable to use my hand. But Connie was at the hospital with his family day and night, until they turned off the life-support machine. I was fortunate that Nelune was with me then, as she helped me to do even the smallest task, like feeding me, and monitoring my sugar intake. She was simply fantastic, and I was very grateful to her.

A few weeks later, Geraldine told me that she wanted to give a character reference for the man who was with Adam on that fateful night, as he was responsible for procuring banned fireworks on the internet. He had to appear in court, and Geraldine asked me to write a letter on her behalf, defending that man, as she said she did not know how to write one.

I obliged her, as I always did, whenever she or one of the family asked me favours; like when she wanted me to write a letter on her behalf, in support of a job application, or sewing curtains for her flat. I never refused to help them, no matter what they asked.

One night, soon after these events, I was walking with Connie after dinner, when I stumbled on an uneven, concrete slab on the pavement. Next moment, I hurtled into a shrubbery, and hurt my back and wrist, which resulted in another few days off work. I was on leave for about two months now. After acupuncture treatment on my wrist and back, which helped me greatly, I was able to walk without pain, and returned to work.

We decided to celebrate Aunty's 84th birthday at our place, on 3 August, and invited the whole family, about forty people. I cooked a traditional Ceylonese dinner that night. But Aunty did not want to enjoy the party at all, saying she was too sad about Adam, but Geraldine tried to comfort her saying, "Adam would have loved to be here with you, so be happy with the family."

After the visitors left that night, Connie scowled and barked, "Why did Clifford kiss you? You don't have to kiss him, just because he lost his son!" He just gave me a peck on my cheek as they arrived, but Connie did not like that at all. But I just ignored him. I was weary, as I spent so much time and energy trying to please him and his family, that I did not need this added stress. At dinner though, Connie was full of praise for my efforts, and made a very loving toast, because he was happy that I prepared such a delicious feast, and finished with a tasty cake that I baked and decorated.

Shirani and Ranjith moved to Cairns a few months ago, and I was very sad to say goodbye to Shirani, but she wanted a change. They visited Melbourne a few times afterwards. They liked Cairns at the start, because of its tropical climate. But after a few months in a rented unit, and over-whelmed by the constant humidity there, Shirani decided not to renew her teaching contract, and decided to return to Melbourne shortly. I was relieved and delighted.

When she was in Cairns, we phoned each other almost every day, as Shirani missed her family and home very much. Suresh was staying on his own in the house in Narre Warren, and Roshan moved out to Kernot, near Grantville. He built a small house on the acre block of land, and was busy setting up a garden there.

When I finally returned to work at the end of June that year, I found we were going through an uncertain phase at work. And it did not come as a total surprise when management informed us that the outbound call centre at Casselden Place, was closing down that December, and we would all be re-located to the call centre in Melbourne.

A disgruntled rumble swept through the office once again, as twenty of us who transferred from Cheltenham, refused to be "dumped" in the main call centre, which was a nightmare. We were invited to have a look at the call centre in Melbourne, where we discovered that the conditions were extremely stressful for staff, who each received over one hundred calls per day. Most staff left after twelve to twenty four months at the most, if they survived that long.

Margaret, our manager, who operated from Tasmania, flew in frequently, to negotiate a better deal for us. And thanks to her intervention, the manager at Dandenong tax office, agreed for all twenty of us to transfer across to the debt collection area.

We had to apply for the positions all the same, and though we were not required to attend interviews, we were "screened" once again for job suitability, before we transferred. The outbound call centre in Casselden Place closed down in early December, and we moved to Dandenong. The department paid five hundred dollars each for "relocation" costs. Some people, who worked with me at Cheltenham, and who lived closer to Dandenong, had already transferred across from the call centre in Melbourne.

Joanne and I remained good friends till about 2014, when she left the ATO, and drifted out of my life. I was upset, because we were very good friends till then.

I met several other good friends in Dandenong though, like Joelle and Anne, who were part of our team. Anne remained a close friend until the end. She was diagnosed with ovarian cancer that spread to her liver, and in 2008, she succumbed to cancer at the age of fifty. I visited Anne with Connie when she was in palliative care, and I could not help crying when I left her, because it was heartbreaking to see how much she had deteriorated. Anne was a tall, well-built lady, but when I last saw her, she looked like a shrunken old woman. I was very emotional at her funeral too, which most of the ATO staff attended. When we spoke to her widowed husband after the service, he was inconsolable. Yet, not even two months later, he travelled to Mauritius and re-married. Perhaps he just could not bear the loneliness, as they were married for twenty-five years, but were childless.

Joelle, Joanne, Anne, and I met for coffee every month or so, at Sofia's in Frankston, or at a cafe in Mornington, and after Anne died, the three of us continued to catch up, until Joanne slipped out of my life.

Dandenong was an enormous change from Casselden Place, and the very first day Joanne went out for a walk, some foul-mouthed hooligans terrified her so much, that afterwards, she only walked out with me, or another friend at lunch time.

I applied for leave without pay from mid-December to the end of January, as I needed time off to complete several projects, besides taking it easy over Christmas holidays. Although I was on sick leave for almost two months, I was not paid, as I did not have sufficient sick leave.

I still studied music under Antoinette, whom I now called Ninette, and we developed a good student/teacher rapport. In January that year, Ninette invited Josephine, Connie, and me to her place, as the three Italian Tenors were singing there. Luigi Campeotto, a once famous tenor, had a magnificent voice, and the other two singers, Ornello, and Attilio were gifted tenors too.

We attended a few of their concerts, and soirees that Ninette organized for the tenors, whom she accompanied. Much to the three tenors delight, Josephine too joined in their singing, as she still had a good singing voice, and we enjoyed a pleasant, musical afternoon.

Ninette related Luigi's life story to me, as he recounted most of it to her. And knowing I was a writer, she asked if I would write his biography, if Luigi was agreeable. I asked his written permission to do so, and arranged a few initial interviews with him at Ninette's place. She met him in 1997, and played a major role in bringing him out of his self-imposed retirement. I found his story very interesting, and based on personal interviews, and taped recordings, I started writing his story.

I waded through hundreds of newspaper clippings, old photograph, and memorabilia he gave Ninette for safe keeping. Luigi also asked me to contact his previous wife, Margaret, and present wife, Jackie, to gather any information I required about his past. As I was always keen on biographies, it was a fascinating project. And I spent hours on the internet, researching some of the events he spoke about, and his Italian background.

I made steady progress in classical music, and of all the great composers, I loved Chopin best, and so did Ninette. She was a great teacher, and brilliant pianist, who demonstrated her special technique.

Ninette invited us to another Carnivale Ball at the same Italian club on my birthday, 23 February, 2003. We asked Shirani, Ranjith, Aunty, and Aunty Molly to join us too. I dressed up as a Spanish senorita, in a long, black lace gown, trimmed with red lace, and large, red roses, a black lace mantilla, and a red rose in my hair. Connie dressed up as a Spaniard, in full black, with a broad, red cumber band that I sewed. Aunty and Aunty Molly dressed up in the "twenties-style" and we had a great night out.

I enjoyed the Carnivale Ball very much, as the music was excellent, and Ninette played Neapolitan songs all night. Luigi was present, with several other friends of Ninette's, but he did not sing that night. He complimented me on my costume and exclaimed, "You look beautiful!" A fancy-dress parade took place later on, and Connie and I danced along in that parade, so did Aunty Molly, but we did not win any prizes for our costumes.

Connie kept twirling and spinning me round and round the dance floor. He grinned and said mockingly, "Everyone is saying you look beautiful, so turn now and parade for the judges!" I looked at him and whispered, "*Will* you stop turning me around so much! I'm feeling dizzy!" But he just kept giggling and turning me around, until I stopped dancing and went back to our table.

Ninette's neighbour, an enormous, Maori woman, sat next to Luigi at Ninette's table. She looked very masculine, with a large head, and bulging, green eyes, and she openly admitted to being a prostitute from the age of sixteen. I wondered how she came to be here with Luigi. And the story unfolded when I asked Ninette about the woman next day.

Her name was Lisa, and she noticed Luigi, the other tenors, and musicians visiting Ninette. The woman immediately decided that she was, "Going to have sex with Luigi," the moment she saw him. Those were her own words, when she boldly declared her intention to Ninette, that she wanted to seduce him.

Luigi was separated from Jackie then, his wife of thirty years, but they lived under the same roof. When the woman ogled him, and invited him in for a coffee, he accepted without a second thought. He later confided in Ninette that the woman was a prostitute, who shed her clothes quickly, and jumped into bed with him at the very first opportunity.

Ninette was astounded at the sudden turn of events, as she was very successful organizing Luigi's comeback. She even recorded two CD's of his past and present songs, and one with the Three Italian Tenors singing together. Luigi was trapped in a sordid adventure. Ninette suspected that Lisa gave him marijuana, and other drugs, as she boasted to Ninette that she habitually took "party" drugs.

The next few months were fraught with difficulty and anxiety for Ninette. She tried her best to prepare concerts, and club performances with Luigi, but his singing career was sliding back in a very obvious manner. Soon, the woman started bad-mouthing Ninette, as she was very envious, and wanted to sever Luigi's professional and friendly connections with her. Ninette was at her wit's end, as she was caught up in the middle of vicious rumours.

On 10 August, 2003, we attended a concert at Glen Eira Town Hall, which Ninette organised with the Three Italian Tenors. The first thing I noticed was, Ninette's pallid face, and sombre appearance. I did not know what was wrong, and the concert started soon after, so I could not ask what troubled her. We invited Lorraine and Tony, as they enjoyed music too. Luigi walked on stage, and sang magnificently. But half way through his performance, he broke down, and sobbed uncontrollably, and one of the musicians took him away.

Isobel Morgan, who compeered the concert, came forward and announced gravely, "I'm sorry to break this tragic news to you, but Luigi's son, Angelo, died tragically last night in a motorcycle accident in Italy." The audience were stunned into silence, but more so, because Luigi kept on singing almost to the end, when he finally broke down.

We quickly joined the throng backstage to condole with Luigi. I noticed that Lisa was there too, fussing all over him. I shook hands with Luigi, and went away, overwhelmed by this tragedy. Tony, Lorraine, and the two of us stopped at a café nearby for coffee and drinks, before we returned home. I was badly shaken, because I knew how much he doted on his only son.

Chapter 35

Luigi was absolutely devastated. Angelo, was twenty-three when he was killed. All work on his biography came to a standstill, as he lost interest in the project, and did not want to be interviewed anymore. He had a daughter, Anna, from his first marriage, and she lived in Perth with her mother. But he did not see Anna often, and was not very close to her. Luigi and Jackie went to pieces.

He wallowed in grief, hardly aware of what he was doing. And he became deeply involved with that woman of ill-repute, who plied him with drugs, to help him cope. Ninette, and Luigi's other friends and colleagues, did their best to support him and Jackie during this time of despair.

In mid-September 2003, Josephine moved into an aged care hostel, in Geelong, where we visited her quite often, until she settled down. It was very pleasant, with plenty of activities for the elderly. But Josephine was very distressed and insecure at the beginning, until she became accustomed to her new surroundings and way of life.

The staff were great, and took good care of the aged, but she complained about the bland food, because she was used to her home-cooking. Poor Josephine. I bought her a small, electric, frying pan, so she could whip up pasta sauce, or soup. She was quite pleased, and whenever I called her, she told me what she cooked in the frying pan.

She had fallen out with her family, and none of them visited her when she needed them most. Although she was an irascible person at times, she was very loving, and never treated me badly. Being a loyal friend, I visited her with Connie, called her often, and listened to her complaints, because she had no one else.

We could not do anything to solve her problems with her family though, or help them reconcile, except pray for them. It was pitiful to see a sick, old lady of eighty-four dwindling her days away, without any family to care for her. She phoned me a few times during the week and said, "Dolly, you are an angel! I love you so much! Please come and see me soon, okay?" What could I do? My heart always melted when I listened to her, or anyone who was sad and lonely. I coaxed Connie to drive to Geelong on weekends, just to take her out for a meal and shopping. He did not mind, but he was in a quandary, as he did not want to upset Paul and Esme.

They were annoyed with us for visiting Josephine, and Esme chided me, "Don't go to see her! Leave her alone! She's a wicked old woman, and is always scolding Paul, and calling him a pig!" I did not take any notice of her, as Josephine's quarrel was not with us. And I could not stop visiting her, just because Esme did not want us to.

A few months after Adam's death, Esme and Paul sold their house in Ferntree Gully, and moved to a flat next door to Aunty's. She told everyone that Connie was too busy to care for Aunty, so she was moving close by to look after her. From that time onwards, Esme took complete control of Aunty in every way, except her finances, and Aunty lost the will to live.

She had no independence at all, as Esme controlled everything she did and said. Whenever we visited Aunty, Esme rushed in, and sat beside her. And if I asked anything, or tried to converse with her, Esme immediately answered, before Aunty could respond.

Over the next few years, she shaved Aunty's head, just like a prisoner, and made her wear a cap; she kept her in a dressing-gown all day, and said, "It's easy that way, as Mummy doesn't go anywhere now, and she is better off without perming her hair." Aunty was very particular about perming her hair before, and I was sad to see her deteriorate into a vegetable state. She spent a few days with us still, but she was not the lively, happy person she was. No one could tell Esme that she was suffocating her with her mollycoddling. And she was ably assisted by Cristobel, who thought she was the only one qualified to take care of Aunty.

The sisters were at loggerheads, with constant friction between them. Babs referred to them as the "Mafia" as they did not allow her to take Aunty for a walk on the beach, saying it was too cold, and she would get sick. And they stopped Babs from giving her a tot of brandy, which she relished.

Aunty stopped cooking and entertaining, as the whole family visited frequently, cooked for everyone, and generally took over. Connie did not object, but he complained that they were running up huge energy bills, with their frequent cooking, and usage of hot water.

Rita died of a heart attack later that year. She was in her early seventies, and I was very distressed. Only a few months ago, she asked me to send her some lace-edged handkerchiefs, which I promptly did. Rita was a kind and loving aunt, and I will always remember her zest for life. She was a diabetic too, and suffered with heart problems for some time.

So many of our relatives died over the last ten years; Wije, Thathie's brother, died of liver cancer, and the irony was, he never drank or smoked, unlike Thathie, and his other brothers. Chanda died in his early forties, due to an alcohol-related disease, and Wimala too drank himself to death.

Our family had dwindled fast, and only a few relatives were still alive. Daisy Akka was frail, but in good health, and lived till her late nineties, although she was nearly blind, and suffered from dementia when she turned ninety.

I did not like working in debt collection at all. And I was getting heartily bored of the type of work I had to do there. I considered my options now.

I had a few students, who came home for music lessons, and I enjoyed teaching them very much. I held a concert for my students that December, and the parents were very impressed with their childrens' performances. I seriously considered taking on more students in future, and leave the tax office, no matter how secure the job was, although no job was secure in the current climate.

Aunty and Aunty Molly had joined us to Lakes Entrance, to spend the Easter weekend there in March. We enjoyed a good trip, and stayed in a spacious two-bed-roomed unit. Aunty spent all of Thursday, and Good Friday indoors, as she did not want to do anything, or go out anywhere, because she gave up bingo and pokies over the Lenten season (which was her usual practice). Connie, Aunty Molly, and I, walked around the shops, and went to the beach in the evening. Aunty showed a little interest on Holy Saturday, when Connie suggested playing pokies.

I did not join them, as I found it very boring. I stayed back instead, and prepared dinner. When they returned late at night, the three of them enjoyed a few rounds of whisky and brandy. Connie was in a good mood, as he was very happy talking about the past, and dwelling on his childhood memories, especially with his mother and Aunty Molly. We attended Mass in the morning, and I asked Connie to take them out for a drive or a walk, until I prepared lunch.

I brought all the ingredients from home, so I made buriyani rice and chicken curry for Easter lunch. We enjoyed ourselves, and Aunty was more like her cheery self, without Esme's constant surveillance, and whom she now referred to as "Mother Superior." Aunty Molly and she pretended to be little children, and that I was their mother. Aunty talked like a lisping toddler, which was very amusing.

As we prepared to leave on Monday morning, Christian called to say that they were at an estate agent's office in Mt Martha. And could we meet him before four thirty that afternoon, as they wanted to pay a deposit on a block of land. So we drove back as fast as we could to get there in time.

Christian and Athena were happy to see us, and he said, "They want a deposit of $1000 Dad and Mum. Being the weekend, we don't have that much on us, so can you help out, and I'll return the money next week?" Of course we agreed, as we were very happy that they found a block of land that they liked.

Connie wrote a cheque, and the deal was signed, and the agent said their house would be ready in about six months time. We told Christian not to worry, that we would help them with the deposit, so he was glad. They joined us for dinner at our place, and later, we dropped Aunty and Aunty Molly in Frankston.

I met Elvira Spaziani, and Mary Filippone for the first at Ninette's, a few days later. Elvira had written down brief sketches of her early childhood in Sicily, and composed several songs too. She wanted her story to be adapted as a stage play. When Ninette told her I was writing Luigi's story, she wanted to meet me.

We had a long discussion, and she gave me a sheaf of hand-written notes, which I had to decipher, and compile into a stage play. It took me a long time, but I charged a very nominal fee for my work. Elvira was very pleased, and from then onwards, I encouraged her to find someone to produce her play.

I applied for leave without pay towards the end of December, and concentrated on self-publishing another novel, "Edge Of Nowhere," a story of a teenager, and her downward spiral, due to substance abuse. I took two months off, during which time,

I completed my novel, and went about looking for a good printer. I wrote the outline of the story some time ago, and I only had to edit and proof-read now.

Nelune and I bought Nilanthi a ticket in April 2004, as she told me she was anxious to see us again. And she visited us when I was in the middle of publishing my book, which I hoped to launch at the end of May 2004. I found a printer in Moorabbin, and was busy proof-reading the final drafts then.

Connie carried the manuscript to and fro from the printer's, until I was satisfied that it was perfect (almost perfect). The onus was on me to ensure that the final draft was without any printing errors. So I proof-read, and edited the manuscript umpteen times, and finally ran it past another editor, just to make sure.

I joined the Peninsula Arts Society, and the Society of Women Writers Victoria recently. I exhibited my paintings at the Arts Society very often, while in the process of publishing my book. I also attended monthly meetings of the Women Writers Society in the city, so, it was a very busy period.

Connie and I drove around the countryside on weekends, looking for an ideal scene for the book cover. I wanted a remote place, with a narrow road, or path disappearing into the horizon. So I removed several photographs of a lonely stretch of road that dipped over a cliff, somewhere near Rosebud.

Once again, I contacted newspapers, who were always supportive of local authors, and more than happy to run an article with my photograph. The launch was publicised more widely, and I sent out invitations to all the people I knew. Local libraries, and book stores purchased copies of my book before the launch.

Nilanthi enjoyed a great time with us as always, and it was good to spend those few weeks with her. But she was unable to stay for the launch, as someone she met in the airport in Colombo, who wanted an English tutor for her children, promised to employ her in early May. So she left at the end of five weeks.

I invited the Mayor of Frankston to open the launch, as I thought it was a pertinent book in our drug-riddled society, especially in Frankston then. The Mayor phoned, and personally apologised for being unable to attend the launch, but delegated Councillor Macarthur (Mayor of Frankston the following year), to open the launch.

The night before the launch, Connie and I arranged the Xavier Centre Community hall, which was a very pleasant, modern building, with great facilities for such functions. I hired the hall for three hours, and it cost only $25 an hour.

On 31 May, 2004, around forty people arrived at the Xavier Centre. And my first book launch was very successful, as I sold several copies at the event, while libraries and schools purchased the rest.

Councillor Macarthur delivered an encouraging speech, and congratulated me on my achievement. It was a satisfying experience, and my colleagues and friends from work, congratulated me on my opening talk. I received great feedback about the book too, so I was quite pleased. Shirani, Ranjith, Christian, and Athena attended the launch; Esme brought Aunty, and Roland and Shiranthi came too.

Esme hurried out with Aunty just as I was signing copies. I heard Connie say, "Dolla is signing books now, let Mummy come and get a copy too." Esme replied, "You can bring a book later, we have to go home now, and cook dinner for Paul and

Lin." Connie replied, "It's only 2.30 now. You have plenty of time." But she rushed out, not in the least interested in the launch. Lin, a Vietnamese, was Paul's latest girlfriend, and she was the flavour of the month with the family.

Some of our previous neighbours from Rowville, Birdie and George, and their daughters, Geraldine and Judy, and Bronwyn and Ian, besides Pam (from Knox City Centrelink), and her mother, attended the launch too. One of Connie's friends in the sign industry, designed a large poster, with the title of the book, and he hung it in the background. That evening, Christian, Athena, Connie, and I, celebrated the occasion in a local restaurant.

A few days later, after the euphoria of the book launch subsided, I ended up being ill again. I came down with several bouts of flu during this period, that ended with chest infections and lung problems, even though I had the flu vaccine each year. This period of bad health only strengthened my resolve to find an alternative career.

In August that year, Jordee's mother, Mara, urged me to teach piano at St Francis Xavier primary school, as the piano teacher just left, and they required a teacher urgently. I considered the offer carefully, but was hesitant to take on another commitment. Mara told me that it would be great if I came in for a few hours a day each week. She had an interest in the matter, as she was the school secretary.

I spoke to Maree, the principal, who sounded very pleasant and encouraging over the phone. I worked at the tax office from Wednesday to Friday, and went for my music lesson on Tuesday, so I said I could come in on a Monday morning, and see how it worked. She was delighted, and I commenced teaching at the primary school in August 2004.

When parents heard I was teaching at the school on Mondays, ten or twelve students enrolled at school, and five students at home. The end of year concert that I held at Xavier Centre was a great success that year. Numbers continued to grow, as parents spread the word that I was a very good piano teacher, and they all told me that the children "loved" me. It was because I was very patient with them, and tried to make lessons as enjoyable as possible (with the incentive of lollies sometimes).

I was happy teaching, but I wanted them to learn as well, and it was a bonus if the children actually *liked* their teacher. I tried to build a rapport with the young children, because I wanted to instil my love of music. To some extent I succeeded with most of them, and was very pleased when they were eager to learn.

Whenever students came to my place after school, Connie rushed in after work and bustled around and interrupted the lesson. One day, he started playing scales, while Jordee stared at him with wide eyes, and he asked me, "Did you show her how to do this?" I replied, "Of course, I taught her how to play scales!" After she left, I told him, "Don't interrupt the lessons Connie, that child wasn't comfortable at all with you barging in like that." He scowled and muttered, "She was sitting there like a ghost! I wanted to help her lighten up." He may have meant well, but he was a caution. I never knew what he would say or do when the children came around.

When I gave certificates of merit to the children, to acknowledge their achievements at the end of the year, Connie asked, "Are you *allowed* to give them certificates? You'll get in trouble with their parents!" He never encouraged me in any way, and only found something to criticize. I registered as a piano teacher with the

Australian Music Education Board, because Madeline's father was anxious for her to take examinations.

Madeline went on to take examinations under my training up to grade four, and when she went to high school, she continued with another teacher till grade five. She was only seven years old when she started with me, and she passed all her examinations with honours. I was vindicated, and Connie refrained from commenting about my teaching or giving out certificates.

He was very suspicious and annoyed whenever Madeline's father, Ivan, accompanied her, to discuss her progress with me. And he demanded irritably, "Why is he coming all the time? What's wrong with her mother? Is she paralysed that she can't come with the child?" I did not bother to reply, because I could not understand why he felt so much antipathy towards Ivan.

It was the same one evening, when he came home and found a student's father parked his van a little too close to the shrubbery. Connie went out and shouted at the poor man, just as he was snacking on a pie. After that day, he stopped bringing the child over for lessons, and never contacted me again.

The parents gathered round at the end of the annual concerts, and congratulated me on being a great teacher, and said their children loved me, and enjoyed piano lessons very much. Connie bustled around and helped with the snacks and drinks that I always provided for the children and parents, besides Christmas goodies. In return, the children too gave me little gifts of appreciation, for which I was grateful. But I told them not to worry about presents, although they continued this tradition.

Christian and Athena finally moved to their own home at the end of October 2004, after more than a year of delays and frustration with the builder. It was a beautiful house in Mt Martha, and I was very pleased for them. We went over to celebrate with a bottle of champagne, and a few weeks later, they invited her parents and both of us for dinner.

Maree phoned me a few days later to say, "I hope you don't mind my giving your name to Fr Eugene Dolly, as I told him that I knew a beautiful pianist who plays quietly, when she thinks no one is listening!" I was apprehensive about playing in public, as I usually felt very nervous in front of an audience. But when Fr Eugene asked me if I could play the church organ at midnight Mass that Christmas, and on Christmas day too, I reluctantly agreed.

But now he insisted that I play at Sunday Mass *before* Christmas, and he brought all the hymn books home. Practice began seriously on week nights, and Connie sang in the choir too. We made good progress, but the only thing I worried about, was my vision at nights, which was affected when my sugar levels were too high or too low. The parishioners said they would pray for me, and not to worry. I played for the first time on the fourth Sunday of Advent, as Fleur, the regular organist, was going away. She approached me in church, and persuaded me to start playing from the following Sunday. I played a few hymns, and it was not too bad, although I was very nervous at the start.

But the great moment came on Christmas Eve, when I played all the traditional carols from eleven thirty onwards and right through all the singing sections of the Mass. Some of Connie's family attended Midnight Mass at St Francis Xavier's church that year. I wore a red, crepe jacket, with a black and red chiffon skirt. The first thing Cristobel told me afterwards was, "From where we sat, all we could see were your big boobs!" I just ignored her comments, as she thought she was being funny.

Fr Eugene congratulated me at the end of the service and said, "Don't you think Dolly played beautifully tonight? Give her a big hand!" And the congregation clapped enthusiastically. It was exhausting playing at the ten o'clock Mass on Christmas morning as well, but I survived the ordeal, and afterwards, Father commended me again, while the congregation applauded. He gave me a card, and a present to show his appreciation.

When Father asked me to play again next day, on Sunday, I told him I was spending time with my family. Then he pressured me into playing on the following Sunday, 2 January, and I agreed reluctantly, because he just did not take no for an answer.

We drove to Christian's after church, as they invited us for lunch. It was the first time I did not cook Christmas lunch in all these years, but Athena cooked a delicious roast, and I enjoyed it thoroughly. Then we went home, and I rested a while, as we were dining with Shirani and family at Narre Warren that night. Roshan, June, and the boys were there too, and we had a pleasant time.

We picked up Aunty in the evening, and drove to Woolamai next day, and we enjoyed chatting around the fireplace till very late that night.

Connie and Ranjith went fishing to the Bass river early next morning, and Shirani and I went for a long walk, while Aunty rested. I removed photographs of the beautiful scenery around, although it was very cold and gusty. Later that day, we heard of the tsunami that was wreaking havoc in Sri Lanka, Indonesia, and India. The loss of lives was enormous, with thousands left homeless. I prayed for those wretched people killed so suddenly on Boxing Day.

They returned around one thirty, but they did not catch any fish. Connie said he relaxed for a few hours though. It started to hail and rain, as strong winds roared from across the bay. We left that evening, and on our way we stopped at Cranbourne, where Aunty bought me a plant to say "Thank you" for helping her shop, and pack presents over the last few days.

After dinner, we drove around Frankston with her, as Connie wanted to show her Christmas decorations and lights along some streets and on Oliver's Hill.

Next day, Connie dropped Aunty at her place after lunch, and I painted an abstract study for Joanne, from a picture she gave me.

I picked up Ninette in the evening, and she listened to my recording of all the Christmas carols I had played in church. She said she was very proud of me, then we listened to her CD, and I could not believe what a brilliant pianist she was. She was very upset that her eyesight was failing now, and so was I. We dropped her in Seaford after nine o'clock that night.

It was a very busy time that Christmas season, and I told Fr Eugene I was going away for New Year, and could not play every Sunday either. He applied immense pressure on me to play the organ every Sunday at ten thirty, which was the children's Mass. But I could not make a commitment on a regular basis, due to other involvements.

In order to convince me, he said, "Jesus wants you to play the organ *every* Sunday at the 10.30 Mass." When I steadily refused, he replied crossly, "*Where* do you go on Sunday mornings? To the pub?" He reminded me of the nuns and priests in my childhood, who always tried to get their own way by making me feel guilty. I was strong enough to stand up to him now, and was not going to be bullied into doing something I really did not want to do.

The next time I played the organ in church, was on Connie's sixtieth birthday, in February 2005. Fr Eugene said Mass, and afterwards, Connie organised brunch for his family at one of the restaurants in Frankston.

Fr Eugene loved visiting parishioners, and sharing a meal with them, so I invited him a couple of times, and he enjoyed the dinners very much. He was quite amusing, and a good conversationalist. And I liked his company, only when he did not apply pressure to play the church organ.

Then he persuaded us to follow the "Alpha" course, which went on for ten weeks, every Tuesday night. Connie and I started in March or April that year, and it was well worth the effort, as we gained a great deal from the "refresher" course in the Gospel. We had early dinner in the hall, with about twenty other people every Tuesday night, then watched a DVD, which explained the Gospels for a couple of hours. Then we discussed the evening's topic, and it was very rewarding.

Fr Eugene pressured me to play the organ on Holy Thursday evening, and right through to Easter Sunday, and I had no way of refusing. So, I ended up playing on Holy Thursday, Good Friday, Holy Saturday vigil service, and on Easter Sunday. When I suggested that Mary Lou, another pianist, and I share the playing, he was adamant that only I played on all those days.

I was very tired after that episode, and decided not to get involved again, because he did not want Mary Lou and me to share the task. Joanne and her partner, Steve, Erika, Joelle, her mother, Celine, and aunt, Micheline, came to church on Good Friday to hear me play. They were quite impressed, and complimented me, so did the other parishioners.

After the service though, Erika told me something amusing, "Fr Eugene was getting impatient at the end, when people took long to come up to the cross and kiss it, so he started snapping his fingers and saying, 'giddy up, giddy up' to the people." We chuckled about it.

Holy Saturday vigil Mass, was another trying time, as so many incidents took place, that I was worn-out at Easter Sunday Mass, but managed to survive. During vigil Mass, Fr Eugene threw kerosene oil into the fire in the brazier inside the church, which caused sparks to fly, and accidentally landed on the back of the lady, who was reading the epistle. She shrieked and jumped aside in shock, while Father ineffectually tried to extinguish the flames. It was chaotic, and Father, who was exhausted, stumbled and almost kissed the floor! Poor man. Then when all the lights were out, the choir started singing, but I could not accompany them, as I had no light to read the music.

That was it, no more playing the organ on those occasions, I told myself. Athena made Easter lunch, and we had a great time with them. They were thoroughly amused when I recounted the incidents of the night before. We walked on the pier afterwards, and I took it easy next day.

I volunteered to help the Women's Society distribute the monthly newsletter. Athena helped many times, to get them ready for mailing. I had to pick them up from the printer in Mornington, then spent a couple of hours at their place, while we chatted and folded newsletters. I did this for a few years, until the committee members decided it was more cost-effective to send them out electronically, except to those who did not have email.

Del was Treasurer then, and current vice-president now, and we became very good friends over the years. She made sure I was re-imbursed for the printing costs in a timely manner, as I paid the printer first, and then claimed expenses from the Society. She was an excellent writer, and she helped me with practical suggestions and her support. Del also broadcast a radio show, "Writers Corner" on local radio in Mornington. She interviewed me a few times over the years, and whenever I launched a new book. We remain good friends to this day.

Chapter 36

Since we purchased the townhouse in Burleigh Heads in 2000, we travelled up to the Gold Coast every year to inspect the property. Scott advised us that a certain percentage of travel expenses etc. were tax deductible, so Connie wanted to take advantage of that as much as possible. And we flew to the Gold Coast again on 12 June that year.

We boarded Tiger and Misty at the cattery the previous day, much to their disgust, and my sadness, as I hated to leave them there. We drove to the airport around seven o'clock in the morning, and arrived there in about an hour's time. It was a two-hour flight to Brisbane, and it was a warm, twenty-two degrees when we landed. But when we picked up a rental car and drove to the main city, all the shops were closed. Parking was exorbitant, so we drove around Brisbane, and I noticed many nice parks, but no place to park in the city. Tired and hungry, we looked for a place to have a meal, and headed to the Gold Coast, as we wanted to get there before dark. We found only a Woolworths store open at Logan, so we kept on driving to Springwood shopping centre, where we bought some buns, as all the shops were closed on Sundays.

It was almost four o'clock when we arrived at the luxury resort "Xanadu" in Main Beach. It was a fantastic unit, with spectacular ocean views from the lounge and bedroom. The spacious interior was comfortable, and beautifully decorated. We unpacked and then drove to Miami around five o'clock to attend Mass, but there was no Mass on Sunday evenings, only in the morning; we decided to attend early morning Mass next day.

The only place that was open, was a Chinese restaurant, where we bought fried rice and steak for dinner. Then we drove past "Grande Florida" apartments in Miami, where we stayed the last time. After dinner, we walked along the incredible surf beaches near Xanadu, and all night I listened to the sound of thundering waves, crashing and rolling along the beaches. I was tired and fell asleep after eleven o'clock.

Next day, we woke up early, and drove to Miami for the nine o'clock Mass. The young, visiting priest, finished the service in twenty minutes, as he rushed off to say Mass at another church. We drove to Burleigh Heads later, and as Connie was hungry (without breakfast as usual), he looked for a place to have a snack, while I walked in the near-by park. It was another beautiful, warm day, with blue skies, and hordes of tourists everywhere I looked.

Then we drove to Pacific Fair shopping centre, and spent a few hours looking around, and stopped at Oasis shopping centre to buy groceries at Woolworths. When we returned to the apartment, I relaxed, and later enjoyed a spa and sauna, which was restful. I made dinner, and a small roast for sandwiches, as we found the price of takeaway food was quite expensive, even at Seven Eleven.

The glorious, sunny weather continued, and I removed some photographs of the surf beaches from the balcony. It was a little cloudy next day, but still a warm, twenty-five degrees. I watched huge breakers in the early hours and photographed them.

We drove to Reedy Creek to inspect our unit at Boca Raton. Jean, the new property manager, gave us a key, as the tenant was out. Connie removed photographs, and we were pleased that the unit was clean and tidy. We had no maintenance issues, so we returned the key to Jean, and told her we were satisfied that all was well. We stopped at a shopping centre nearby, as Connie wanted to pay City Link at a post office, then we had lunch in a park near the sea at Broadbeach, and I enjoyed splendid ocean views there. We drove to Surfers Paradise and browsed around, where I bought three pairs of shoes on a special, and some gifts for Christian and Athena.

I was very tired by the time we returned, so I had a spa, but Connie was not too keen to get into the spa, as he said he felt "squeamish" because other people used it. I felt relaxed, and after a cup of tea, I started packing up, as we had to leave early. I did not mind short trips to the Gold Coast, but I missed Tiger and Misty so much (more than they missed me I know), and could hardly wait to get back and see them again. After an uneventful flight, we were home, and I was glad to be back with my pets again.

During this time, another idea for a book was shaping up, and the embryo of "Catsville" kept niggling and growing all the time. The idea just would not leave me, until I sat down and started writing the saga about the intrepid cats in peaceful valley. By the time I finished the story, it ran to about forty thousand words, and I visualised what the cover should look like. I painted "Catsville" as an idyllic scene, in shades of pale blues, and greens. Athena photographed the painting, and designed an attractive cover for the book. I decided to launch this book at a luncheon.

I called this event a "launch-eon" and engaged a caterer to provide three kinds of roast meats, salads, and dessert at the launch that I hoped to hold at the Xavier Centre on 31 July, 2005. Although I invited Steve Bracks, the Victorian Premier then, to open the launch, his secretary called and declined the invitation on his behalf, as he was "busy elsewhere."

The Premier encouraged literacy in children, and inaugurated an award in schools, for children who read the most books in a given time, which led me to believe he would agree to open my launch. It was disappointing when he declined, as I could not find another person at such short notice.

The local newspapers ran an article about the book and launch, and a photograph of me holding my book. And I sent out invitations to everyone I knew. I designed posters and flyers, and distributed them everywhere, in libraries, schools, and shops. As the event was catered for, bookings were confirmed, and money paid in advance, which included the cost of the book and a meal. It was hard work, as I did the marketing and promotion myself.

I resigned from the ATO on 22 July, 2005, with mixed feelings, as I was fortunate to work with some very good people in my team. They gave me a wonderful send-off, and Anne, baked a delicious cake, and decorated it beautifully. The team presented me with a gold bangle, and after the team- leader gave a very complimentary speech, I left work at the end of the day, for the very last time.

Driving back to Frankston on Dandenong-Frankston road, I breathed a sigh of relief, that it was my last trip to and from Dandenong. Those five years at the ATO were eventful. But I had to consider my health, besides changing direction and concentrating on music, writing, and painting.

I suddenly felt as if time was running out, and at fifty three, my mortality seemed fragile and uncertain. It took more than twelve months to finally arrive at this decision to resign, and take the plunge into uncertain waters of the future, but I was prepared to take a chance.

The night before the launch, Connie and I arranged the tables in the hall, and I filled each vase on the tables with deep-pink camellias from our garden. The tables looked elegant, with burgundy tablecloths, and fresh camellias. Everything was ready for the caterers next day, and we left the hall around eleven o'clock that night.

Though it was quite cool in late winter, the day dawned bright and sunny, and more than eighty people turned up at the "launch-eon" including twenty of my friends from the ATO. It was great seeing them again. Athena made elegant little name-cards for each table, and Christian directed guests to their seats. Connie was in charge of the books and receipts, and I was very grateful to them for their love and support.

He invited his family, but only some of them came. Esme brought Aunty, and as usual, was in a hurry to take her back home. Roland, Shiranthi, and their children were present too, and so were Shirani and Ranjith, who were very supportive, and came to share my modest achievements. The book sold well, and many schools and libraries purchased quite a number of copies.

When one of the teacher's at school read the article in the local newspaper, she told her class about it, and invited me to talk to them about writing, which I did. I was pleased when the children asked me questions about how and why I wrote that story.

Catsville proved to be very successful, and was well received by the public and libraries. Many people suggested that it would make a great animated movie. And I seriously considered writing a script one day, as my dream was to see Catsville as an animated movie. I sent the book to the BBC, and to a local animation producer. Their feedback was very encouraging, but they said I must write a script for an animated feature, before they could take it on board. I sent a copy to Toonz animation as well, and they were quite positive. That spurred me on to follow a scriptwriting course.

Benjamin, Roland's son, and Leanne, were married in November that year, at a garden ceremony near Ringwood. We attended their wedding and reception with Christian and Athena.

Nelune and I bought Nilanthi a ticket once again, as she said she wanted to see us, because she missed us very much, and she arrived in late November 2005. We had some great times together, and drove down to Woolamai for Christmas.

Fr Eugene asked me to play at all the Christmas Masses again. But I told him I was going away, and we spent Christmas at Woolamai, and went to a nice little church in Wonthaggi on Christmas Eve. We spent Christmas with Shirani and the family, before returning home in the evening.

Just before Nilanthi left in early January, Shiranthi fell and broke her arm on 1 January 2006. She was rushing to her neighbour's place with some milk rice, when she slipped on the doorstep, and she was in hospital, so Nilanthi, Connie, and I, visited her next day. Shiranthi was in great pain, and they operated on her the following day; the bone had snapped in two, and they inserted a metal plate.

She was in a great hurry to recover soon, as Rebecca's wedding was in March that year. But healing was very slow, and she was in constant pain for the next eight months or so, until the bone healed. It was very sad that she suffered months of pain and discomfort, as the broken arm did not heal well. She never quite recovered, and in years to come, she underwent several operations to fix the problem.

Chapter 37

I was very busy writing Luigi Campeotto's biography over the last few months, and had almost finished typing the manuscript. It was very challenging though, as I had to do so much research, old photographs to be included in the book, and myriad details to take care of. Besides editing, proof-reading, printing, and marketing the book, I had to organise a book launch too.

This book was very different to writing fiction, and an entirely new project for me. And sometimes, it was difficult to curb my imagination and adhere strictly to facts, but I had to make the story readable and interesting. Therefore, I sometimes resorted to "poetic licence" when the past was too obscure. My creative writing though, did not deviate from factual sequence of events, as Luigi, Antoinette, Jackie, and Margaret had related.

I met Luigi at Ninette's several times over the last few years, in order to glean as much information from him as possible. It was a very trying time though, as Connie kept telling me, "Don't get involved with those people! Keep away from Luigi!" This was because he saw the kind of woman Luigi was having an affair with, and he was not happy about it. But I told him that it was none of our business, and I interviewed him on a professional basis only.

I asked Luigi to record as much as he could remember, so I would have enough material to work with. Every time I mentioned Luigi's book, Connie got annoyed and scowled at me. But if I asked him to take the manuscript to the printer in Dandenong, or photocopy some flyers etc. he obliged. And at the launches too, he was the first to run around, attending to sales, and helping me. It was only when he was alone with me that he aired his objections, and made negative comments about the project.

Ninette and Luigi knew many people in the Italian Community, and some were influential people in the media. I sent out invitations to over fifty people, and I thought it would be a good idea to coincide the launch with Luigi's 70th birthday on 23 August 2006. I set about organizing the launch at Robinson's Book Shop in Frankston.

Rebecca, Roland's daughter, and Reavath were married on 23 March 2006, and over three hundred guests attended. It was a warm, March day, when we went for the church ceremony at two o'clock in the afternoon. Then we came home to Frankston, and back again to the reception at six o'clock in the evening. It was a most tiring day, and we came home after midnight, but it was a lovely wedding, and everyone enjoyed themselves.

Rebecca was an attractive bride, and we were happy for her. Shiranthi was in extreme pain throughout the evening, and took several pain killers. Her arm hung down limply, and she could not move it at all. The doctors could not ease her pain either, saying she needed physiotherapy, and it would heal in time.

I was utterly shocked when Connie called me from work on 23 June, to say Cuckoo was dead, and Krishan called me later with more details. He was in an induced coma for over a week, as we knew, but I hoped he would recover. He was a couple of weeks away from his seventieth birthday. I was grieved, as I was very close to Cuckoo, and he was like a brother. He was always ready to listen and discuss anything with me, and everybody else who knew him, and was a very affectionate and sincere person. It was hard to imagine I would not hear his gentle voice wishing me, "Good morning, Dolly," or "Good evening, Dolly," before he started a conversation.

So many of my dear ones who mattered to me, left suddenly. We spoke to Krishan, and then Regina that night. She was absolutely overcome by her sense of loss, after a long marriage of more than thirty years. I spoke to Cuckoo only ten days before, and told him Luigi's book was completed, and I would be sending him a copy soon. He congratulated me as always, and exclaimed enthusiastically, "Wonderful Dolly, well done!" He always encouraged my literary efforts, and enjoyed reading my previous books.

He was not cremated for more than four weeks, due to some reason or other, and Krishan explained that they followed his last request to the letter. That night, we invited the whole family over for dinner, and just to reminisce about good times we spent and shared with Cuckoo. It was an agreeable evening with the ones who turned up, but Esme, Cristobel, Geraldine, and Clifford did not turn up.

The book, "Is this your Caruso? Biography of Tenor Luigi Campeotto" was finally ready. Athena designed an attractive cover, with one of Luigi's black and white photographs, and it was very striking. I organised the launch to be held on 24 August, 2006, at Robinson's Book Shop in Frankston. The owner, Terry Perry, was very supportive of local talent, and took care of details and catering.

The local newspapers ran a good article, including my photograph. I contacted the Italian newspaper, "Il Globo" and sent them a copy of the book. They wrote a full page article about the launch, including a great book review. And the Italian Radio station advertised the book and launch several times. Isobel Morgan, patron of the arts and opera, who was Ninette's good friend, agreed to launch the book.

Ninette, Connie, and I, visited her a few weeks before, and she told me she enjoyed reading his book very much, and would be happy to open the launch. On the day of the launch, Isobel, her husband, John, and her daughter, Michelle, came too. And Isobel made a great opening speech, as she knew Luigi well, and had held many soirees for him. Shiranthi, Tim, and Benjamin came, but Roland could not make it, as he was working.

Many of Ninette's and Luigi's friends were there to encourage and support him. Elvira and John, Con, Cornelia, Karen, Stuart, Lorraine, Tony, and friends from school, attended as well, and I was very pleased to see all my good friends. Babs missed the way, and arrived after it was all over, and so did Esme and Aunty. Esme wandered around saying, "Gosh, lot of books here!" Someone heard her and commented, "It *is* a book shop, and that's what they sell!"

Shirani and Ranjith attended too, although Shirani was down with the flu, but she turned up, just to be there for me. Some of my friends, including Joanne, made it, and enjoyed the event. Terry organized the catering, and his assistant served delicious finger foods and wine. Luigi's CD, which Terry played throughout the launch, filled the room with his magnificent voice.

We sold fifty copies of the book, and it was very successful. I invited Luigi, Attilio, and Ornello, the Three Italian Tenors, to sing "O Sole Mio" at the end of my talk. The audience loved his singing, and several people bought copies of his CD as well. Connie and Benjamin video-recorded most of the event. Later, we invited close friends, and Christian and Athena, to celebrate at Sofia's restaurant in Frankston.

It was a great afternoon, and after lunch, Connie and I drove to Ninette's place, as she invited her close friends, including Luigi and some others. Her small unit was over-crowded, but full of fun and laughter, as the tenors sang their favourite songs. Then we dropped in at Christian's and Athena's for a cup of tea, as Christian bought an electric piano, and wanted me to hear him play. It was an amazing instrument, and I too enjoyed playing it.

After such an exciting, happy day, Connie became depressed while we were at Christian's, and suddenly burst out crying, "Stacy, Stacy! I miss Stacy!" I was at a loss to know what brought on this fit of despondency. After a while, he recovered and said, "I'm sorry for crying, I couldn't help it, I just felt sad." It was late evening when we finally came home.

The book sold out, and I received very good reviews, which made it all worthwhile. As the demand for his book was great, I printed another hundred copies, which sold over the next few months. Most libraries in every state in Australia requested copies.

One of the major library suppliers in Australia, ordered several copies of Luigi's book, and my previous books, so I was quite pleased with such positive results. I was invited to talk about the book on local radio, while Luigi's CD was played several times too, which boosted sales, and increased publicity enormously.

A month later, Luigi and Jackie went ahead with their divorce, although Jackie accompanied Luigi to the launch, in spite of their differences. He continued living in the same house in Craigieburn, until she paid him his share, and he eventually moved out to a unit in Seaford.

The year ended with Nilanthi arriving on 28 December, and once again, Nelune and I financed her trip. I saved all my piano fees throughout the year, to buy her a ticket, and Nelune always paid half the fare. Every time Nilanthi cried over the phone, and said how lonely she was, and how much she missed us, my heart melted, and I immediately promised her a ticket.

Connie was unaware I saved all the piano fees to buy tickets for Nilanthi, and I never told him, so he was under the impression that Nelune was paying for her regular trips. We picked her up from Tullamarine airport very early in the morning, and it was good to see her again.

The weather was extremely hot and dry since late September, and the relentless heat kept getting worse. Temperatures soared to the high thirties without any respite or a drop of rain. The garden was parched, and the tank water ran low.

Chapter 38

We spent New Year's Eve with Shirani at Narre Warren, and enjoyed a peaceful evening. Next morning, on 1 January, 2007, Connie drove back there to pick up his mobile that he had left behind. We arranged to have lunch at "Gold Leaf" restaurant in Springvale, and Christian and Athena were to join us, but were delayed, and could not make it.

Nilanthi, Connie, and I, shopped before lunch, and when we entered the restaurant, we were surprised to see Esme, Paul, and their neighbour, Judith, sitting at one of the tables. They came over to wish us, and we chatted briefly.

Later, we drove to Southland, where I met Maree, the principal, and she was her usual cheery self, as she greeted us for New Year. We watched "Charlotte's Web" that Nilanthi and I enjoyed thoroughly, then drove back to the pier in Frankston, and walked for about half an hour. Nilanthi sat on a bench and rested though, as she was too tired to walk, and when we returned home, we stayed up chatting till late.

The following days were very busy, as Heron's family visited her, and we drove her to various places in Melbourne to visit them too. On our way to visit Ninette one afternoon, I had an unpleasant experience with the Jag, as the engine kept stalling and cutting off right in the middle of the road.

It was scary, when it stopped on Nepean Highway, just as I was turning right into Ninette's unit. Toula, who was there, told me that it could be the alternator, as she had a similar problem with her car. And she followed us on our way home, just in case the car stopped again.

Shirani asked me to drop Nilanthi at her place that night, but I told her I did not want to risk driving the Jag, until it was checked out. Shirani and Ranjith picked Nilanthi that evening. Later that night, Roland and Shiranthi dropped in unexpectedly, and had dinner with us. When I finally turned in, Christian and Athena dropped in at eleven o'clock, with heaps of clothes and knick knacks for Nilanthi to take back, as they were cleaning up all day.

January continued being a scorcher, and I prayed fervently for rain to fall on our parched land. Nilanthi spent a few days with Shirani, and with Heron's son, Peter and his family. We picked her on 6 January, as I bought tickets to see the play, "The Wizard Of Oz" staged at Frankston Arts Centre. One of my friend's, Karina Stroot, played the wicked witch of the West, and she was fantastic. Nilanthi too enjoyed the play immensely. Scenes from the original 1930s movie flashed on an enormous screen in the background, and looked very effective.

Whenever I had a moment to myself, I worked on my latest manuscript, "An Eternal Summer" that I hoped to complete, and publish before the end of the year. Athena designed my own website two years ago, and I was also moderator on a writer's forum. She suggested that I upload all my books as "E-books" (electronic books), which meant I had to save all the manuscripts onto discs for Athena to upload them as PDF files. I left the technicalities to her, as she was the expert, but it sounded like an interesting project.

I was also testing the market for an animated feature of "Catsville" and submitted outlines of the story to several local and overseas producers. Toonz animation was one of the interested parties, and I kept my fingers crossed. Their readers sent back positive feedback, which was encouraging, but ended with a predictable apology, "we are unable to make an offer at present, but are happy for you to send us any other material for consideration." I was not discouraged by any means, as I kept working at the script, and looked out for any interested party.

Nilanthi and I watched DVD's and videos on most evenings, as she too loved old movies and comedies. I had quite an extensive library of classic movies, comedies, and BBC drama series. This was a very relaxing time of the day for us, and we enjoyed quality time together. Connie joined us sometimes, if he was not too tired.

One night, I invited Elvira, John, Mary, Tony, and Ninette for dinner, and we had a great time, as Elvira sang, and Ninette accompanied her on the piano, and we finished after midnight.

Isobel, who was a close friend now, wanted to meet Nilanthi and Melissa, one of Ninette's friends, so one morning, we all drove in Melissa's car to Armadale. Isobel served a delicious lunch, but we could not stay for the dessert of yoghurt and fruit, because Melissa had to get back in time for lessons, as she was a singing teacher.

Melissa had a tragic tale to tell, regarding her missing mother and sister, and Isobel was very keen to hear her story. Isobel was very sympathetic towards me too when she heard about Stacy, who was missing since 1994. She was a very caring, warm-hearted person, and deeply involved with volunteer work in prisons.

The weather soared in the high thirties, and rose to forty, and forty one degrees, without a cool change in sight. But as we had air-condition in the bedrooms, we coped with the extreme heat. Nilanthi however, did not like to sleep with the air-condition on, and preferred the hot, humid nights, as she said it reminded her of Colombo.

Anjo and Ronald visited one afternoon, and spent some time with Nilanthi till about seven o'clock in the night. The following day, we packed up five boxes to send all the clothes and other items for the needy, which Nilanthi hoped to distribute when she went back.

After several weeks, we finally had a steady downpour, but we drove to Mount Martha in spite of the rain, to have coffee with Athena and Christian. We returned late that evening and watched "Blackbeard's Ghost" till dinner time.

A few days later, Connie picked Aunty, and brought her over to spend a couple of days with us. But she was very reluctant to stay overnight, and was anxious to return the very next day. She was not her usual happy self and was ill at ease. We were disappointed at her changed attitude, and could not understand what was wrong.

Rebecca invited us for a delicious lunch one afternoon, and later we dropped in at Joelle's for afternoon tea. Then we visited Cornelia and Con, and I gave them a bottle of my home-made cherry jam, as we picked cherries with them on Boxing Day in Redhill.

Toonz animation responded on 23 January, saying they could not take on Catsville at present, so I decided to try another studio. I was not ready to give up so easily, because I believed my story would make a great animated feature, judging from feedback I received from readers.

Next evening, Nilanthi wanted to visit the charismatic prayer group in our church, and observe how they conducted their service. It was stifling inside the small, side chapel, and the service went on for two hours. My heart beat was irregular, and I was famished. But I stayed till the service ended, so I could introduce Nilanthi. The group promised to contribute towards the church fund in Maharagama, which Nilanthi was promoting then. Christian and Athena dropped in later, and we had a great time with them.

Chapter 39

The weather was much cooler on Australia Day, 26 January, and it rained intermittently, but was hardly enough to break the severe drought. We were now on stage three of water restrictions (no watering of gardens on certain days). But I watered the garden with tank water, when restrictions applied, and the hardy native shrubs survived the drought.

After shopping at Springvale that day, we drove to Southland to watch "Happy feet," which was very amusing. And then visited Aunty Molly in Cranbourne. We listened to her tale of woe, regarding Ian's divorce, as she was very upset about the situation.

I pacified her, "You can't do anything about it Aunty Molly, and it's not your fault they decided to divorce. Try to accept the situation, and support Ian now, as the children and he need you. And don't be angry with Romayne because she fell in love with someone else."

She was very bitter towards her though, because Aunty Molly arranged the marriage. And their failure to make it work, really distressed her. She sniffed and sighed, as she said, "That wretch won't think of the children, and he moved into a new house just to please her! I can't forget that." She carried on in the same manner for some time, then rummaged in her wardrobe, and gave Nilanthi some clothes for the orphans in Maharagama parish.

On the following morning, we drove down to Woolamai, and enjoyed a barbeque with Shirani and Ranjith. Suresh paid a surprise visit, and then came back with us. Nilanthi stayed at Narre Warren, and they dropped her the following evening.

I invited Roland and family, Aunty Molly, and Aunty for dinner on 30 January, as we were leaving for Sydney on 1 February. We boarded the cats on the previous day, and I hemmed a few of Connie's shirts, as he needed them for work. He had an important interview on 1 February, for a managerial position in his department, and I wished him well. The interview was at two o'clock in the city, and he returned home around four thirty. We left home shortly after, as our flight to Sydney was at seven thirty that night. Connie was tired, but confident that he did his best at the interview.

It was a pleasant flight, and we arrived in Sydney at nine o'clock in the night. We picked up a rental car, and Connie drove through maze-like streets out of Sydney airport, and we arrived in Mosman around eleven thirty. Nelune was awake, but looked very tired, so we did not stay up too late, and turned in just after midnight. It was very humid in Sydney, and I hardly slept that night.

Nelune left at seven o'clock in the morning for dialysis, and returned after one o'clock. She looked well and rosy, and was full of fun and laughter as usual. She drove us to a Chinese restaurant for lunch, then we shopped around, and returned home late in the evening.

Joanna joined us for dinner at a Thai restaurant, and Connie ignored me completely, and hardly spoke to Nilanthi and Nelune either. I wondered what was wrong with him. We returned to Nelune's apartment quite late, and chatted and joked for a while before turning in.

I did not get much sleep that night either, and felt very lethargic next day. Nilanthi called Barlo, to ask if we could visit her on our way to Cherrybrook, as Felix and family invited us for lunch. But Barlo sounded very tired and ill, and told Nilanthi she was very busy, and unable to see us that day. We were disappointed, but it could not be helped.

The drive to Cherrybrook was marred, as Connie and I argued over something. Nilanthi listened for a while, then finally broke in, "Now, now, children, stop this fighting, and try to make up." I was sorry to upset her, so I retreated into "silent mode" for the rest of the journey. Connie was sullen, and refused to get out of the car when we arrived at our destination, and muttered, "You both go in, I don't feel like meeting anyone." Nilanthi coaxed him, but all I said was, "What will they think of you, if you sit in the car and refuse to have lunch with them?" After a while, he dragged his feet and joined us.

Connie's mood soon improved though, as he smiled and chatted to Felix and his family as if nothing was wrong. I did not look at him, as I was very upset over his behaviour, and some of the things he said in front of Nilanthi. Felix and family lived in a very pleasant, spacious house in Cherrybrook, and were very kind and hospitable. Felix's wife, Yasmin, was fair-complexioned, tall, slender, and very attractive, and she cooked a tasty meal. Their children, Sabena, Zaneta, and Adriel, were pleasant, well-mannered teenagers, and joined in our conversation good-humouredly.

We reminisced about our days in Hatton, when Nihal attended St John Bosco's college, and had formed their band, "The Blue Boys." It was great catching up with Felix, who was a very sincere friend. They hoped to visit Melbourne soon, and we left a couple of hours later.

On our way back, we shopped at Waringah Mall, and returned after three o'clock in the afternoon. Nelune bought a roast chicken, and salads for dinner, as she did not want me to cook. Joanna came over with her little dog, Bambi, later that evening, and stayed for dinner.

She asked me to draft a letter on behalf of a friend, who wanted to apply for permanent residency. Nilanthi and Nelune walked her home later, but I rested. Connie went to the Mosman RSL Club earlier on, as he said he wanted to be alone. He got dressed and told Nelune, "I'll leave you girls alone tonight and relax at the club." I was relieved when he left, as it was very tense with him around in that compact apartment. He returned a couple of hours later, but did not win anything at the poker machines.

Nelune played DVD's of her gala, fund-raising events that evening, and we were very impressed with all she had achieved. It was incredible that she organised such immensely successful events, with the help of close friends. Although she insisted that her friends helped her out, I knew it was all due to *her* brains, vision, and stamina, that made it all possible. Because she told me of her intention to help cancer patients way back in 2000.

We turned in soon, as our flight was early next morning. Nilanthi and I spent a couple of hours in the morning with Nelune, and watched more DVD's of her "Lilac Ball" in October 2006. It was spectacular, and I congratulated her on her achievements once again. Nelune was awarded the "Order Of Australia" medal that year, for her generous contribution towards improving services for cancer patients. The money she raised helped St Vincent's Hospital to provide many facilities for them, and Optus donated a van to transport patients to and from hospital.

We left Sydney airport at one o'clock in the afternoon, and arrived in Melbourne a little after two o'clock. It was a great re-union with Nelune, and I called her later, to thank her for her hospitality. Nilanthi was sad, because she told me that she did not know when she would meet Nelune again, and was down-hearted all evening.

The weather was still incredibly hot, and did not cool down, so I watered the garden till late that evening. Connie visited his mother, to see if she was alright and needed anything. Nilanthi and I watched DVD's till late.

I was anxious to pick up Misty and Tiger from the cattery, and was upset when Misty mewed non-stop as she saw me. They were disoriented, so I spent time petting and feeding them when we came home. It was thirty four degrees that day, so we took it easy in the afternoon.

When I finished teaching my students that evening, Connie drove us to Sonna's and Carol's place in Toorak for dinner. Mimi was there too, and they had cooked a feast. Mr Sam Loos, Anjo, and Ronald, arrived a little later. We enjoyed the evening, laughing and joking, as we recalled good times we shared since our childhood.

Mimi, and the others looked subdued when we mentioned Barlo, as we said we were unable to see her in Sydney. I was sad to hear she was very sick, and had lost a great deal of weight. But they were evasive as to what her illness was, and we did not press them for details. We returned home after eleven o'clock.

We drove to Hiranthi's place for lunch next day. They lived in Craigieburn, which was a suburb beyond Melbourne city. Heron's sister, Jasmine, and her husband, Emmanuel, were visiting their son, Christopher, who was married to Hiranthi. They had two daughters, who were in their early twenties, and the whole family entertained us very well. Hiranthi cooked an enormous lunch, and I simply could not eat a morsel afterwards, when she pressed me to have dessert.

I gave Jasmine a copy of "Climb The Mountain," an anthology, that the Women Writers Society just released. I contributed a few poems, and as she wanted to read my work, I thought she would like a copy.

The last few days of Nilanthi's holiday were very hectic. Many friends invited us for dinner, because they all wanted to entertain Nilanthi before she returned home.

We visited Shirani in the evening next day, and met Peter, Astrid, and Penny, who came to wish Nilanthi goodbye. Roshan just returned from a long visit to Japan, and gave us some pretty ceramic mugs as souvenirs. June and Max were still in Japan, as she wanted to get dual citizenship for Max in Japan.

On our way home, we dropped in to wish Aunty, and then drove to Mount Martha to have dinner with Christian and Athena. Athena cooked a delicious meal, and Christian made some tempting snacks too. We spent a very pleasant night, and returned home after eleven thirty.

We woke up late the following morning, as we were very tired. I cherished those last hours with Nilanthi, before she returned, and it was always traumatic for us to say goodbye. But in recent years, Nilanthi had found inner strength and peace.

She was happier now, and found solace in her faith, as she helped out in the church, and looked forward to supporting needy people in her parish; and she carried clothes, and money I gave her for that purpose. I told her to deposit two hundred dollars in a special account, and use the interest money whenever she wanted to make meals for the nuns and the poor. She said she would do so, and assured me that she would use the funds for that purpose.

I was quite stoic about these partings, because it was inevitable that her holiday had to end sometime. Much as I loved her to stay longer, the reality was, she had her own life with family, and church obligations. We arrived at the airport at two o'clock, had coffee and a snack before she boarded the plane. I made Nilanthi promise she would not shed tears, and she held up, because I told her I would send her a ticket soon.

On our way home, we stopped at Frankston shopping centre as Connie had a bad back. He wanted to buy a similar "massage mat" that Christian used on him the previous night. But after trying it out just once, he was not satisfied with the one he purchased, and returned it to Myers store next day. The house was very quiet without Nilanthi's chatter and laughter, and I missed her very much.

Chapter 40

I resumed my routine the following day, and after finishing chores, I called Nilanthi at midday. And it was good to hear her cheery voice over the phone. The flight went well, with only a brief stop-over in Singapore, and she sounded alright. I called Nelune and Shirani to let them know that Nilanthi arrived safely.

She experienced a fiasco when she brought duty-free whisky to Melbourne this time; she bought two bottles, and received another one free. Customs confiscated all three bottles, as it was over the quota. Nilanthi did not expect such a hassle, and as customs wanted her to pay full price for all three bottles, she left them at the airport.

A few days after Nilanthi left, Connie drove back to the airport, paid full price for three bottles, and arrived home late at night. That same night, Cristobel suddenly appeared carrying a potted chilli plant at nine o'clock. She did not visit for months, even to see Nilanthi, so I was surprised to see her. She said she was too busy to visit before, and finally left after midnight.

A few years ago she was in financial difficulty, with her rent in arrears. And when she asked Connie to help her out with a loan, I told him we should help her in time of trouble. Connie lent her $2000, but he wrote cheques to her landlord, and other debtors, and made sure her debts were discharged.

He advised her to budget, and wanted to handle her finances too, which was a mistake. I heard them bicker over the phone constantly, until he finally had enough. He told her to pay her bills on time, and that he would not help out again. She did not visit, or repay that loan for more than five years.

Connie was very disappointed when he was not selected for the manager's position. Instead, they chose Mathew, whom Connie trained in maintenance supervision. He was a young man in his early thirties, and I suppose they wanted a younger man than Connie, who was sixty-two then. But it was cold comfort, and Connie felt bitter and hard done by. He knew he was the best man for the job, as he did it for so long.

The reality was, that they did not give him the designation, "manager" because they had to pay him accordingly then. So they called him a "maintenance supervisor" instead, and made him do all the hard work. It was from then onwards that he became terribly disillusioned with Woolworths, and lost all enthusiasm for the work he enjoyed doing before.

He audited more stores now, about one hundred and twenty five or more, and he said he was very tired of driving to country stores. Connie seldom stayed overnight now, as he was anxious to return home on the same day. He constantly talked of retiring soon.

Whenever he was on holidays, he never switched off his mobile, in the mistaken belief he was indispensable. And that they had to contact him regarding any problems. I found it very annoying when we went away to Queensland even for a few days, because he never had a break from phone calls. I told him to stop worrying about work, because the company would not care if he dropped dead with all the stress. That he would be replaced the very next day, but he was happy to answer his mobile even on holiday. He never really had a break from work, no matter where we went.

The next few days were very busy, as I resumed teaching at school. I had a few more students at home too, and time just sped, with several projects on hand.

Chris and Peter La Ponder invited us for lunch on Sunday, 18 February, and we celebrated Connie's birthday, which was next day. She baked a cake for him, and invited four other friends as well. And they gave Connie a very nice present too. It was thirty eight degrees, and we wilted in that unbearable heat. But it was a pleasant afternoon with our good friends.

I gave him a bottle of his favourite Cognac, and made a special dinner on his birthday next day. Esme and Aunty dropped in unexpectedly, and stayed for dinner. Christian and Athena arrived after they left, and we enjoyed a very pleasant evening. We stayed up late, and they left around midnight.

On Friday, 23 February, Connie dropped me in the city for the monthly meeting of the Women Writers. Some of the members who read "Is this your Caruso? Biography of Tenor Luigi Campeotto" congratulated me, and gave me great feedback. And they also presented me with flowers, along with their compliments.

I had a very good time, and when I came home later in the day, I received several phone calls from all my friends. Nelune and Shirani called, and the La Ponders sent me a gift by special delivery. It was a busy day, and as I was tired, we ordered pizzas for dinner.

We continued celebrating our birthdays next day at Elvira's and John's, with Mary, Tony, and some other friends of John's, Arul and Rajini. We had a great evening, and enjoyed ourselves very much. It was after midnight when we returned home.

We slept in next day, but drove to Ninette's at two o'clock, as we were attending a soiree at Isobel's place in Armadale. And I told her that we would pick her at three o'clock. It was an enjoyable afternoon, and the two young baritones, Adrian and Samuel, whom David Kramm accompanied on piano, sang very well.

Isobel and Michelle prepared a delectable afternoon tea that we enjoyed very much. She introduced me to all her musical friends, and Ninette was in her element, sharing her love of music, and experiences with other guests. Several people asked me about Luigi's book, and wanted to read it, so I took down their names and addresses, and promised to send them copies.

I still drove to Mornington to collect the newsletters for the Writers Society from the printers. Then dropped in at Athena's, and she helped me with labelling. After we finished, and I mailed them, we sometimes went out for lunch to various cafes and restaurants in Mornington, where Athena's mother, Dorothy, joined us occasionally.

On one such occasion, when I drove to Mornington, Athena came with me to pick up the newsletters after we had lunch with her mother. But when I tried to stop in the car park at Mornington Central, the brakes failed, and the car went up the kerb. Fortunately, there were no on-coming cars, as I just could not stop it. It was like my re-curring nightmare, where I lost control in a car without brakes. I was shaken up badly. Athena remained calm though, and instructed me to pull the handbrake on. I jammed the car against the kerb, and stopped in time before running off to the road.

She called Christian, who came immediately, and drove the car to John's garage. He said that the master cylinder was broken. Athena drove me to her place in Christian's car, and we folded the newsletters for some time. She was really caring, and helped me a great deal. When Christian returned, he drove me home around six o'clock. I spent a bad evening and night, as I was very agitated and stressed after that experience.

When I told Connie what happened, he decided to buy me a new car, as he said that the Jag was too unreliable now. So we went car hunting on Saturday morning, 21 April, and signed up a deal at Holdens in Mornington. We selected a 2007 Barina, which was a small, four cylinder car. And they said it would take about two weeks to order the silver-grey car that I liked.

We picked up the new car on 11 May, and I was quite pleased to drive it around now, without a hassle. But I felt a pang to part with my old Jag. The dealer suggested that we sell it privately, as we would get a better price. So until then, I still had both cars in the garage.

Shortly afterwards, Peter and Chris La Ponder came for dinner, and Peter said, "Don't get rid of the Jag, you have a treasure there! Get rid of that Holden piece of junk, and restore the Jag." Peter was an auctioneer, who knew a great deal about antiques. So, I was ready to accept his advice, and hang onto the Jag.

Connie said, "You can't keep both cars, so you get rid of the Barina, if you want to hang onto the Jag." We advertised the Barina, and Christian found a buyer within a few weeks. I had it less than six months, and we lost a few thousand dollars in the process. But now, Connie wanted to restore the Jag, so he gave it to a mechanic, to clean the rust and re-paint it. I hoped it would be trouble-free for some time at least.

I started a painting of a Tuscan scene, for the cover of my next book "An Eternal Summer" as Athena was designing it this time too. I was fortunate to have Christian and Athena, who understood my concepts, and designed the book covers exactly how I imagined them. They had excellent judgement, and an eye for detail, so I had confidence in their skills.

These projects kept me very busy, and I hoped to get the manuscript finished before the end of the year, besides launching e-books. Then it was just the introduction of electronic devices for reading books, but now it is well-established. And many readers prefer downloading their favourite books onto these devices.

I invited Genevieve and Joe, Alice's parents, for dinner in late March. And though Alice stopped piano lessons, I still kept in touch with her mother, as she was a very nice person. Joe owned a rose-nursery, after leaving his regular job, and he brought me some exquisite roses that evening.

We had a great evening, as they were very pleasant people, and we discussed some issues they experienced with Alice, who was a sore trial to her parents. When they heard about Stacy's disappearance, they were very sympathetic, and we advised them to be patient with Alice, because teenagers were so vulnerable. And when I asked, "Is Alice mixing with the wrong people?" Joe replied, "I'm afraid, *Alice* is the trouble-maker!" It was very difficult for me to understand how such a quiet, pleasant child, grew into a rebellious, incorrigible teenager. After mutual commiseration, they left late at night.

Connie and I rode our bicycles on some weekends, as we bought two bicycles a few months ago. Mine was a "girl's" size, as I was not sure I could get on a big one just yet. It was exhilarating, and I enjoyed our rides down the bicycle tracks in Somerville and Frankston very much. It took me a few hours to get my balance, as I did not ride a bicycle since I was a teenager. We had good fun, as well as exercise.

Cornelia and Con called us one day, and he insisted that we accompany them to a "business seminar" in the city. It was a wintry, wet night when we arrived at their place, and Con drove us to the city in his car. I was famished by the time the Amway seminar finished at nine thirty that night. We were not interested in joining that business at all. But when we returned to their place for dinner, they introduced us to Melissa, an Amway agent, who bombarded us with her sales-pitch all night.

I was partly convinced during Melissa's sales pitch, but Connie kicked my foot under the table, and gave me meaningful looks. Later, he warned me not to get involved in any Amway business, and we left at one o'clock in the morning.

We discussed it at length next day, and I told Connie I would like to join, and see how it worked. He phoned Con and said that I decided to join up, and we drove to Keysborough to sign a contract. I was the business owner, as Connie did not want to join in his name. And he told them, "It's conflict of interest with Woolworths"

We spoke to Christian, Shiranthi, and Roland about Amway, but they were not keen on the idea at all. They knew it was not easy to build up a pyramid business. In fact, Roland said that they tried it a few years ago, but found it difficult to get others interested. I wanted to try it out in any case, and if I did not succeed, at least I tried; that has always been my philosophy, but Connie was very unhappy about the deal, and discouraged me right from the start.

When Ronald phoned on 12 June to inform us Barlo had died, I was shocked, because I did not know she was terminally ill. None of her family wanted to discuss her illness, but her husband, Clifford, told Nelune that it was cancer of the pancreas. Barlo suffered a great deal in the last few months, and in desperation she flew to Lourdes with Clifford.

She hoped the miraculous waters of Lourdes would cure her, but was hardly able to move, or eat anything while they were there. They cut short their visit and returned to Sydney, where she died in a matter of days. Mimi and the family were inconsolable, and I could not say or do anything to help them bear their heavy cross. Barlo was in her early fifties then.

Connie and I planned to leave for Queensland on 14 June, and we boarded the cats on the previous evening. It was a cold, rainy day, and Misty immediately hid in the cat "igloo" while Tiger snuggled in the basket. The cage was heated, and they were warm and dry. They looked happy, although I felt miserable leaving my pets behind.

Christian and Athena dropped in later on, and we packed our bags after they left, and had an early night. We arrived at the airport at eleven o'clock, parked in the long-term car park, then took a bus to the terminal. This time, we travelled on Virgin Airlines, which was a pretty ordinary, basic service, compared to Qantas, as we paid for drinks and a sandwich. I was glad I brought my bottle of water. The weather was somewhat turbulent over NSW, but otherwise it was an uneventful flight.

We arrived at Coolangatta Airport around two thirty in the afternoon, and picked up a rental car. Then we drove to Main Beach, and stopped at Xanadu, a luxury apartment block. It was a self-contained apartment, with a kitchen, and spectacular ocean views from every window. Christian called to say he picked up our mail, and I chatted a while, and then we went grocery shopping in the evening.

An enormous, Morton Bay fig tree spread out like a gigantic umbrella inside the shopping centre. I wanted to remove a photograph of it, but forgot to bring my camera, so I decided to come back in the morning. I also forgot to pack a swimsuit, and shopped around for another one.

We enjoyed steak and salad for dinner, and then walked along the beach late at night. Though it was cool, it was a glorious, starry night, with the sound of huge waves crashing on the white shores of the sandy beaches.

After breakfast next day, we drove to inspect our townhouse. We removed several photographs of the sea views along the way, and also of the property, which looked shabby and neglected.

The manager tried to convince us that it was because of drought conditions that the gardens looked drab and shrivelled up. But I thought it was no excuse for giant, rampant weeds, and general untidiness of the area. The beige carpet in the townhouse was almost brown, and spotted with stains all over, and many things inside needed fixing up.

We were very disappointed, and told the manager we expected better, and he said he would speak to the tenant about tidying up the interior. Then we drove back to "Tree-Tops" shopping centre, where I removed a few photographs of that magnificent tree.

We returned to the apartment in the afternoon, and I made a quick snack for lunch. I relaxed for a couple of hours before we walked along the boardwalk right up to South Port. The splendid surf beaches were pristine, and surrounding park areas immaculately maintained by Gold Coast Council. No wonder they charged us such high rates.

I indulged in a spa and swim that evening, so did Connie. What a life! We were relaxed and happy. After a light dinner, we went out walking again, as we just could not get enough of the warm, balmy sea breezes.

We attended Mass at a church in Miami Beach, on Sunday evening, and later on enjoyed a swim and spa in the indoor pool. Then packed up our bags, and after dinner we turned in early, without another long walk.

We woke up at five thirty next morning, and arrived at the airport at seven thirty, only to be informed that our flight was cancelled! Connie was furious, and demanded that they book us on the very next available flight. We boarded a plane at nine o'clock, which flew via Sydney, with a forty-five minute stop-over there. We finally arrived in Melbourne at one o'clock in the afternoon, and vowed never to fly Virgin Airlines again.

On our way home, we drove to the cattery, and picked up Misty and Tiger. I was so glad and relieved to see them. Now that they were getting on in years, Tiger sixteen, and Misty thirteen, it was becoming more difficult to part with them, each time we had to board them.

Misty though, was reluctant to come out of her igloo, and I dragged her out forcibly. She was too warm and cosy in there, and hated to be disturbed. It was good to be home again with my pets. I unpacked and cleaned up, while Connie took his car down to the car wash.

Chapter 41

Elvira's husband, John, celebrated his 70th birthday, on 25 June 2007, and invited us to his party at Rugantino's restaurant in Frankston. We picked Ninette at midday, and then spent an enjoyable afternoon. They served delicious food there, and we had a pleasant time with their friends and family, who added up to seventy guests.

We returned home late, after dropping Ninette at Toula's place in Karingal. I rested, as I was very tired after so many hours of eating and drinking in true Italian style. I did not drink wine or alcohol though, only plenty of lemonade.

Anjo invited us to Barlo's Requiem Mass to be held on 14 July, at St Jude's church, Scoresby. Shirani and Ranjith misunderstood directions, and went to St Simon's in Rowville. And as our mobiles were turned off, they were unable to contact us.

Sonna gave a very moving eulogy to his beloved sister Barlo, and I was teary all through his tribute, because he could not hold back his tears either. Mimi, Mr Loos, and the whole family looked devastated. Diana, Mr Loos's second ex-wife, and her two children, sat at the back of the church. And Mr Loos sat beside Mimi and their children at the front.

Fr Noel Mackay looked quite old and frail, but conducted the service well. I had not seen him since 1991, so when he greeted me, I was surprised he still remembered my name. When I asked him if he knew who I was, he replied, "Of course, I remember you, Dolly, and the feast you cooked for me, and the *mysterious fish*!" What an amazing memory, I thought. When he asked me at dinner that night, way back in 1979, what kind of fish I served, I did not know, so he called it the "mysterious fish."

One Friday evening, towards the end of July, Andrei called Connie on his mobile phone. He said that his father met with a serious accident, and they were on their way to hospital. Connie promised to visit him next day.

I accompanied Connie to hospital next morning, and when we saw Con at the Alfred Hospital, he was sedated, and still in the emergency ward. Andrei explained how it happened, "Dad jumped down from the ladder when a roller door was about to fall on him, because if he hadn't jumped, he would have been crushed under the door!"

Cornelia and Andrei were in shock, as it was very distressing to see Con lying there, with his broken arm and wrist. Andrei told us that he saw the bone jutting through Con's arm, and he also suffered severe injuries to his leg and pelvis. But as it was a weekend, the surgeon could see him only on Monday morning, to decide when to operate on Con.

They took x-rays, fixed the broken bone, and made him comfortable. He was sedated, so he hardly knew what he was saying, when he responded to our questions. We returned home, deeply concerned, and anxious, because he was so badly injured. We promised Cornelia and Andrei we would visit him again soon, and to keep us informed of his progress.

Con was operated on Monday morning, as soon as the surgeon saw him. And he was sent to the rehabilitation hospital in Caulfield a few days later, where he stayed until mid-November. We visited him in hospital, and rehab several times, and when I was unable to visit, Connie stopped at rehab on his way from work. The surgeon was unsure when he would walk again, if ever, and Con went around in a wheelchair, looking very dejected.

The weeks sped by, and disappeared like a flight of birds in the distant horizon. We entertained almost every weekend, or visited friends, went to plays, movies, concerts, and soirees. In between this hectic socialising, I frantically typed away at my manuscript, which I still hoped to finish before the end of December.

My writing time was usually in the evenings, when I finished my chores, and cooking. Connie came home very late, sometimes after eight or nine in the night. It was peaceful in the evenings, which helped me to get through most of my writing. I painted two landscapes for the book cover, and a sunset scene for the annual art exhibition at St Francis Xavier's school, held at the end of September.

The art exhibition was a great success as always, and one of the ladies wanted to buy my painting of a "Storm Cloud" but her husband discouraged her, "Where are you going to hang it?" She was annoyed, and told me, "It is the *best* painting in the show, so atmospheric, and I want it badly! I wish I could persuade my husband to buy your painting. Don't sell it just yet, in case he changes his mind okay?" I said I would hold it.

The art show attracted many professional artists in the Peninsula, and I loved looking at the beautiful paintings on display. Maree stayed in the background, and I wondered why, but she told me she was down with the flu. Our regular guest of honour, Peter Hitchener, a long-time, popular newsreader, and television personality from channel nine, could not make it that year, and a local member of parliament attended instead.

One morning, soon after that event, Maree broke the sad news that she was transferring to the city next year, as she wanted a change, after eight years at St Francis Xavier's. I told her I would miss her very much, as she was such a positive, and lovely person to work with.

She did not know who would be selected as the future principal, but I hoped she would be as nice as Maree. And she said, "Don't worry Dolly, I will recommend that you stay on in the school, as you are so good with the children, and it's been such a privilege to know you. We need you here to go on teaching piano." I told her that I would stay, as long as the new principal was happy to keep me on.

I contacted the producer, Roslyn, at Go-Motion animation studios in Melbourne, as I read about her work in the newspapers. She asked me to send her a copy of "Catsville" which I did. And she called me a few weeks later to arrange an interview.

Connie dropped me at her studio one morning in late September, and Roslyn spoke with me for over two hours. She liked my story very much, but wanted me to write a screenplay (with her help). She was pleasant, and helpful, and was very keen to animate "Catsville" one day.

We kept in touch over the weeks, and I said I would start work on the screen play. But I reeled when I heard how exorbitant it was to animate a story. Something in the vicinity of millions of dollars. Roslyn said we needed investors to go into production, so I looked elsewhere.

Rebecca held a dinner party at her place on 4 August, to celebrate Aunty's 89th birthday. Connie, and his friend, Graham, played their harmonicas non-stop until dinner time, in spite of Paul Maschio's grimaces and frowns. He found the continuous noise irritating, and looked at me, and rolled his eyes. But oblivious to other's sensitive ears, they kept on playing energetically.

Christian and Athena came a little later, with their friend Azzy, who had just flown in from Malaysia. We met before, and I liked Azzy's out-going personality. She was a pleasant-faced, intelligent girl, who liked reading and doing handicrafts. They came home with us afterwards, and we chatted for some time.

We attended a "Neapolitan night" at the Italian club in Carrum Downs the following weekend, and enjoyed a pleasant evening with Elvira, her family and friends. Ninette accompanied the singers, and I met a very good singer, Anna Maria, a long-time friend of Ninette's.

Nelune's annual "Lilac Ball" held in early September, was a huge success, and she raised close to a million dollars, which was a fantastic effort. I marvelled at her incredible energy and spirit. Because over the next few years, she raised a total of more than twelve million dollars, which she donated towards the cost of a new hospital in Sydney. Words are inadequate to express my admiration for my incredible sister.

One morning, when I opened the garage door to let Misty and Tiger out, I was concerned to see Misty's head lolling to a side. And she mewed in distress as she was unable to get out of her basket. I took her to the vet immediately, and he said she had suffered a stroke. He did not think she would get better, but he gave her a cortisone injection just the same. When I took her home, she lay helplessly, and I wept to see her state, as it was pathetic to watch her trying to get out of the basket.

I prayed for a miracle all day, and when I went to check her for the umpteenth time that night, she stumbled groggily out of the basket, and stood near the laundry door. I let her out, and she kept tumbling over as she dug the garden bed and tried to do her business. She fell over several times, but persisted until she finished, and then tottered back to the door. I held her close, and whispered a prayer of thanksgiving.

Next morning, she was able to hobble around drunkenly, and drink some milk and eat her food. After that, I took her for a monthly cortisone injection, which seemed to help her move around slowly, and she led an almost normal life. The vet was surprised at her recovery, and said, "As long as the cortisone works, she will be alright."

One spring afternoon, in late October, Connie was pruning, and cleaning up the garden. I was working upstairs, and came down for a cup of tea around three o'clock. Next moment, I slipped, and bumped all the way down eight steps right to the bottom! Misty screeched in pain and fear, as she was sleeping on the step, and I accidentally stepped on her. She was not hurt, but my back ached, and I gasped for breath.

I tried to call out to Connie, but no sound emanated, and I sat, unable to move, until finally, I managed to shout, "Connie" and he came inside. First thing he said was, "A glass of brandy will help," before he helped me stagger onto a chair. I was more concerned about poor Misty, as she stared accusingly, thinking I deliberately stepped on her, and disturbed her afternoon nap. A little cajoling and petting reassured her that I meant no harm.

My back was sore for a few days, but other than the shock of finding myself at the bottom of the stairs and unable to move, I was not seriously hurt, and was back on my feet soon. I kept a keen eye after that whenever I came downstairs, as I did not want to trip on Misty again.

The weeks and months flew by swiftly, interspersed with Connie's siblings, and other family members dropping in unexpectedly and late at nights. Some weekends, Cristobel and Esme dropped in for a "curry" and if I had cooked some, they stayed and shared it with us. I invited Aunty and Aunty Molly for lunch one weekend, but it was pathetic to watch Aunty in a "vegetable" state now. She hardly spoke, and just answered "Yes" or "No" in response to all my attempts to engage her in a conversation.

She seemed to have withdrawn completely, and was content to watch the world go by. This was ever since Esme found her on her knees by her bedside a few months ago, unable to move or get into bed. When Esme saw her in the same position a couple of hours later, Aunty had said, "I'm saying my prayers, I'm alright." But she suffered a mild stroke, which her family did not want to accept. An ambulance took her to hospital for a check up and observation, but from then onwards, she was totally changed, and hardly got out of bed.

We had lunch at Café 115 in Mornington on 18 November, our 37th wedding anniversary, and then visited Elvira for afternoon tea, and Mary came too. We had a pleasant time, and I asked Elvira to translate some Italian phrases for my forthcoming book. Afterwards, we drove down to Rosebud for evening Mass, and returned home late.

I was absolutely shaken, when John Howard was defeated at the elections held on 24 November, and even lost his seat of Bennelong! He was a great leader and politician, and it was Australia's loss that John Howard was gone. I did not have much confidence in smarmy, smooth-talking, Kevin Rudd. Time will tell, I knew. And time certainly did just that, when his own party members ousted him, and Julia Gillard replaced Kevin Rudd before his term was over.

Needless to say, that the back-stabbing, and dirty politics in the labour party continued over the next few years. Kevin Rudd was embittered at his betrayal. And whenever he appeared on television, he looked like he was run over by a bulldozer, as he still could not believe he was ousted.

After attending the monthly meeting of the Society of Women Writers at the end of November (Christmas break-up party), we visited Josephine in Geelong, which we usually did a few times during the year. We arrived in Geelong at about three o'clock, and took Josephine shopping. I was very tired pushing her around in the wheelchair, and carrying her shopping basket in the other hand. But I did not say anything, as she loved being out. She bought some pasta for dinner, and we returned to the nursing home, but Josephine did not want us to leave, and kept insisting, "Stay for dinner." I was worn-out, so we left soon, and it was after nine o'clock when we came home. It was a long, exhausting day, but Josephine was very happy to see us. I was glad we spent some time with her, as she was so lonely and unwell.

Frankston Theatre Group's Christmas play that year was, "Nil by mouth" at the Community Centre, Mount Eliza. It was hilarious, and I laughed all evening. We returned home long past eleven o'clock that night.

Christian and Athena were travelling to the Philippines for Christmas, with Dorothy and John. So they invited us for dinner on 15 December, and cooked a delicious meal. We spent a very enjoyable evening, before returning home very late.

I prepared many things next day for the end of year piano concert, as I had twenty four students then. It took several hours of practise and rehearsals, but they all performed well. I presented them with certificates, lollies, and little gifts. A couple of parents had difficulty paying piano fees, and when they met me afterwards, to explain their situation, I told them to forget about arrears. I knew they struggled to pay fees, as they were single parents.

A few children, who missed out playing at the concert, asked if they could come over to my place on the last day of school, and hold a "mini-concert," to which I agreed. Six of them turned up at two thirty in the afternoon on 20 December, and one parent dropped off some, and another, the rest. Charlotte organised games, and Tabitha and Sarah brought their own music. Mitchell, Jayden, and Liam, joined the girls, and played many party games, and finally they played their musical pieces. I made a large quantity of finger food and drinks, which they devoured hungrily.

After several weeks of hot, dry weather, the storm finally burst on that afternoon, and the children squealed delightedly, as they ran around playing hide-and-seek. They could not play outside, but amused themselves for a couple of hours, until their parents picked them up around five o'clock in the evening.

I phoned Ninette later on, to ask if she was alright, because over the last five years or so, I called her daily, which she appreciated very much. If I did not phone her every evening, she called to ask if I was alright. She said I was like her second daughter, and I loved and respected her very much. I also phoned Josephine once a week, because she liked to hear from me, and said she was very lonely. The least I could give these dear people, was my time, and a willing ear to listen to their woes.

On 23 December, we dropped in at Christian's, as they were busy packing for their trip. Athena cleaned up the fridge, and gave me all the perishables. I wished them a safe journey, before we headed off to Rosebud for Mass that evening. When we woke up the following day, I noticed presents, and decorations near the mantelpiece. Christian and Athena had come at dawn on their way to the airport, and left their presents for us. I was deeply moved by their love and thoughtfulness.

Connie worked on Christmas Eve, and came home late, and we went to church at six thirty for the family Mass. The church was very crowded, so we were lucky to find two empty seats. After service, we dropped in at Aunty's place, and chatted with her till about ten o'clock. Esme and Cristobel were with her, and the rest of the family were expected later, as they always joined Aunty for midnight Mass. We came home and watched some comedies till midnight.

Chapter 42

On Christmas day, we exchanged presents, after an ample breakfast of milk rice, beef curry, sambal and bananas, and later that afternoon, we drove down to Dromana for lunch. It was a pleasant, warm day, and after a delicious seafood lunch that I brought, we spent time in Shoreham, where I removed photographs of the sea and pine forest. I rested for a while in the afternoon, and then we drove to Shirani's at Narre Warren, as they were leaving for India and Sri Lanka on a three week holiday.

We dropped them at the airport by nine thirty that night, and then had coffee and a snack at McDonald's nearby. It was after eleven o'clock when we returned home, but we stayed up for a while, and watched DVD's. Christian left a message to say they arrived in the Philippines after a very long and arduous journey.

We visited Ninette on Boxing Day, and she played the piano for a little while to entertain us. She had baked biscuits and pastries, which she gave me to take home, after we ate some. Ninette liked baking, and was very good at it too. I gave her a bottle of home-made cherry liqueur, which she enjoyed, and after some shopping we returned home late.

Joanne picked me up next morning, and we drove to Morning Star winery and café in Mornington, where we had a delicious snack and coffee. Joelle joined us too, and we walked in the lovely rose gardens, and enjoyed ourselves immensely. The weather was glorious, and I was disappointed I did not bring my camera. They came home with me afterwards, and I served Christmas cake and cherry liqueur. Connie and I went back to the winery later that day, and I removed several photographs.

We went cherry picking next day to the same orchard in Red Hill, where Con and Cornelia took us the previous year. It was sad that Con was still not well enough to join us. But he was home now, and trying to get back on his feet slowly, as he was determined to walk again. We picked about five kilograms of sour cherries and then headed home.

I prepared the fruit and bottled them in sugar, then placed the large bottles in a sunny position near the kitchen window until the sugar melted, before adding pure alcohol. It was a traditional Rumanian recipe that Cornelia gave me. and was a potent, delicious liqueur.

When I told Josephine we were visiting her next day, she was very happy. The late night news broadcast that Pakistani opposition leader, Benezir Bhutto, was assassinated, shocked me. I was sickened at such hatred and violence in the world around us. In days to come the violent reaction to this atrocity, continued to ripple in Pakistan, and surrounding countries, in mindless hatred.

We woke up very early next day and drove to Geelong, although it was soaring to thirty eight degrees later. Josephine was very pleased to see us as usual, and looked quite well, even though she complained of constant pain in her hip and leg. She was very disappointed when the surgeon refused to operate on her for a hip replacement. Her heart was too weak, and she would die under an anaesthetic. She was in tears, and very depressed when she told us about this, because the last time we visited, she said, "When I get a new hip, I'm going to *run* away from this horrible place!"

When she was more composed, we drove to a Chinese restaurant in the city and treated her to yum cha. Then she wanted to shop at Myers store, as she wanted to buy some things. I pushed her around the mall in her wheelchair, while she laughed happily and said, "You are an angel Dolly! I wish you were my daughter! I am lucky to have you!" She talked in Italian, and when I asked her what she said, she translated, "I love you till I die!" Poor Josephine. All she wanted was company, and some attention from her family. Back in her room, she asked me to prepare the green prawns I bought in Melbourne. I cooked them with garlic and butter, which she relished with pasta.

She insisted that we stay for dinner. But we refused, as it was a long day, and we had a two hour drive back home. She was somewhat mollified though when we stayed till six o'clock, and we finally arrived around eight thirty. Josephine became petulant when we did not spend all day and evening with her. I knew that she did not want to be left alone, but once she knew we had to leave, she was resigned.

The night was much cooler than the sweltering heat of the day, but next day it rose to the high thirties again, and I cooked early before the heat of the midday sun. It was a scorching forty two degrees on 31 December, and we sweated through the night, as we danced at the Italian Club in Dandenong.

The hall was packed with over four hundred people, where two hundred could have danced comfortably on the modest dance floor. In spite of the heat and cramped conditions, we enjoyed ourselves, with Elvira, John, Mary, and Tony, It did not cool down till dawn, and another sizzling day dawned on 1 January 2008.

We returned home around one o'clock in the morning, and rested for a few hours. After a traditional Ceylonese breakfast, we drove to Southland shopping centre, as it was cooler there, and watched "Golden Compass" starring Nicole Kidman. It was quite good, and I enjoyed the movie, but it was still thirty seven degrees outside when we left late that evening.

My schedule was hectic over the next few days, and I also proof-read my manuscript several times before final print. The printer was closed until the first week of January, and he printed a "mock-up" cover before he closed over the holiday season. But it took him a few attempts to get the exact colours that I wanted. Finally, when I was satisfied with the finished work, I approved it, and looked forward to the publication at the end of January. I drew up a list of guests for the book launch, and designed flyers, which I sent all the libraries, and book shops.

The local newspaper sent a photographer, and a reporter interviewed me a few days before. As always, I had a great deal of organising to do before a launch. This time I chose Mornington library as the venue, and scheduled the launch on 23 February, to coincide with my birthday.

The library co-ordinator offered to launch the book, but I said someone else was launching it. When Nancy visited in late January, and we discussed the forthcoming event, she asked who was launching my book. And when I replied I did not know yet, she exclaimed, "Can *I* have the honour of launching your book Nalini? I've got some great ideas for the event, and I'd be more than happy to be the master of ceremonies." I agreed at once, as I was delighted to let Nancy launch my book. We were very close friends now, and I knew she would do a fantastic job.

A few weeks before, Joanne asked if she could buy my piano for Erika, and I agreed, as I saw another piano that I wanted. Joanne and Erika visited to check the piano, and they liked it very much, as it sounded beautiful, and still looked new. They saw several other pianos before their final decision, but Erika liked mine the best. Joanne bought my piano for $2000, and the removalist arrived on 18 January. I was a little sentimental when my treasured piano was taken away, after so many years of musical delight. But I was glad because Erika would look after it, as she loved music, and my piano very much.

We picked Shirani and Ranjith at the airport that same night around nine o'clock, and dropped them at Narre Warren. It was great seeing Shirani again, and we chatted all the way home. She enjoyed the holiday very much, and said she would show their holiday photographs when we visited them for dinner next day.

I had a dental appointment in Noble Park next morning, and after the dentist finished drilling, and filling a large cavity in my jaw tooth, we went piano hunting. The tuner, who looked after my piano over the last ten years, suggested that I visit Lyra Pianos in Bentleigh. I was glad I did, because I found a magnificent Yamaha piano for $7,500. Leon, the owner, was of Russian origin, and a great pianist too.

He was very pleasant and helpful, and asked me to play on several pianos before I decided. So I did, as I took my music with me. Even though my head felt woozy, and my mouth ached, I played Beethoven's, "Moonlight Sonata" and Chopin's, "Opus No 10" (popularly known as No Other Love), many times on various pianos, until I was satisfied that the sound I liked best, was the Yamaha.

Leon organized delivery on the following Wednesday, and he told me that if I ever decided to sell it, he would pay the same price to buy it back. But I did not think I would be selling it in the near future. I was elated, and looked forward eagerly to many hours of playing my beautiful new piano.

We had a delicious meal at Shirani's that night, and enjoyed seeing holiday photographs, and listening to travel stories. They spent a few days with Nilanthi too, and said she was well and busy. It was a delightful evening, and we came home late.

Connie drove me to Karen's place in Mornington, next afternoon, as she invited all the members of the Writers Society for afternoon tea, but only six ladies turned up. It was because most of them lived quite far beyond the city, and some even further. We read poetry and prose, and shared stories for a couple of hours, while nibbling delicious snacks that Karen prepared.

I handed out invitations to my book launch, and some of them promised to make it. Karen, who was vice-president of the Society, also offered to launch the book, but I told her I already had someone. Connie picked me up later, and we visited Christian and Athena. We spent some time chatting and listening to their ideas, as they helped me immensely with my books and launches.

I woke up bright and early on 23 January when the piano was delivered. Then spent some time playing it, and revelled in its exquisite sound, before heading off to Snap Printing at Dandenong. Campbell, the owner, was very helpful as usual, and I clarified all the details, before final print. It was always very exciting at this point, when I saw the results of countless hours of fevered writing, angst, doubt, proof-reading, editing, and finally held the finished book in my hands.

Christian and Athena dropped in later that evening, and they too liked the sound of the piano very much. Christian played a few tunes, as he never forgot his music. He was very clever at many things, and such a fine musician too. I was very proud of him, and wished he had more time to play the piano. Athena downloaded programs onto my laptop that Christian bought me. I was so grateful to them, as I could now work on the laptop whenever Connie was using the home computer.

Linda and Leo were married on 26 January 2008, Australia Day, at the Botanical Gardens in Melbourne. We arrived there at one o'clock in the afternoon, and found parking close by. The weather soared to a scorching thirty five degrees, although it was cloudy, but did not rain as predicted.

It was a very moving ceremony, and we had a great time, in spite of the extreme weather. As the reception was at six thirty that evening, we visited Anjo in St Albans. I changed into an evening dress, because I wore a summer-suit and hat for the garden ceremony. We spent some time with Anjo, before driving back to the city for the reception.

The sky was black and threatening, but the storm held up all night, and dinner was excellent, although the music was very loud. We danced, and had fun, until we returned home after one o'clock in the morning. Before we left, Paul and Julie, invited us for afternoon tea on the following Sunday.

Nancy, and her partner, Neil, dropped in on their way from Inverloch on 30 January, and we discussed the book launch at length. Nancy wanted to read the book before the launch, and they left after four o'clock in the evening.

I had an appointment with Colleen, the new principal, next day. She was very tall, attractive, and quite pleasant; we spent some time discussing mutually suitable days and times, and agreed on Mondays and Wednesdays. I was happy to continue teaching, as I liked the school and staff very much.

I invited Diana Whaley, a local radio presenter, but she said she was away on that Saturday. She was very encouraging though, and wished me well with the book, and promised to advertise the event on her radio show. Then I called Campbell and thanked him for his great work. And he said that he too was very pleased with the result, as it was exactly what I wanted.

We had a delicious afternoon tea at the Karlsens, on the following Sunday. And I was impressed with their charming home in Camberwell, that Paul built some years ago. It was on the market now, as they said it was too big for them, as all the children had moved out. They were very nice people, and we made a date to have dinner, once Linda and Leo returned from their honeymoon. Julie and Paul were babysitting Josh, and Leo's parents took turns minding him too, until Linda and Leo returned. He was a gorgeous little boy, but quite a handful and kept Julie on her toes.

First term commenced on 4 February, and it was hectic, as new children enrolled, and it was always tiring teaching beginners. I still visited Ninette every Tuesday afternoon for "Master Classes," as she wanted to teach me interpretation of the classics. I enjoyed spending those few hours with her, and learnt a great deal about technique and interpretation. Sometimes, she played for a little while, and then talked about her early days in Egypt, or her musical experiences, while we sipped coffee.

I taught a few students at home a couple of evenings, and after they left, I spent two to three hours writing until late. But no matter how busy I was, I always cooked a delicious meal, and dinner was ready when Connie came home. But invariably, he came home very late now, and did not have dinner, as he said, "I had lunch at 4.30, so I'll take it for my lunch tomorrow." And he ended up having a slice of toast, or nothing, because he was too tired, and he was quite happy with a few drinks and cigarettes.

The evenings were best for my writing, when it was quiet and undisturbed. Sometimes though, Esme, or Shiranthi and Roland dropped in late at night around eighty thirty or nine o'clock, because they chose to visit at those times. Esme did not bring Aunty now, as she was already in bed by six o'clock. Babs too visited at ten or eleven o'clock in the night, and told me, "That's the only time I'm free."

As Connie did not come home till late, I stopped my writing, or whatever I was doing, and kept company with them until he arrived. They visited a few times during the week. And no matter how much Connie told them to visit on weekends, or earlier in the evening, they disregarded him completely. And this was an ongoing issue, which caused friction between us.

To me, it was a self-imposed task, spending two to three hours a day, writing and editing, or else I would never accomplish my goals. But it was frustrating when I did not have time to write in the evenings, as I tried to make use of every single moment in order to finish my book.

The hot weather eased over the next few days, and after months of drought, heavy showers continued for a couple of days, but the drought was by no means at an end. We could water the garden only on Tuesdays, and no watering of lawns at all, so that most suburban lawns were now burnt out, brown patches. The tank filled with rain-water again, so we used that for the garden.

Jill Mitchell, the photographer from Leader Newspaper, arrived early on 12 February, and photographed me holding a copy of my latest book. She said the article would appear the following week, just before the launch. The days that followed were crowded, with several visits to the library, preparing posters, and distributing promotional flyers.

Most people said they would attend, and I expected seventy to eighty people. The library facilities were more than adequate. And Christian and Athena offered to take care of catering, and refreshments. Connie was in charge of sales, and Nancy had some great ideas regarding the launch. I was confident everything would go well.

On 16 February, we drove down to Woolamai, and took our bicycles, as we enjoyed riding along quiet roads there. We had a barbeque with them afterwards, before heading home late in the evening. It was relaxing, and we enjoyed a great time. Shirani planted several trees and shrubs, that now bloomed and flourished under her care.

We visited Cruden's farm, in Langwarrin next day, on Sunday. I saw a television advertisement regarding the owner, Dame Elizabeth Murdoch, who, at ninety-nine years of age, still ran the large farm. She was married to one of Australia's richest media magnates, Sir Keith Murdoch, and Rupert Murdoch was their son. When they were newly married, she and her husband built an elegant, white mansion on the property.

It was inspiring to watch her at such an advanced age, as she was still sprightly, and pleasant-mannered. She greeted visitors kindly, and sat out on the porch, signing copies of her book. We spent hours there, along with thousands of tourists, who arrived in bus loads from all over Melbourne, and interstate. I bought a signed copy of her book, and told her how much I admired her for her philanthropy, and life-long devotion to several worthy causes. She lived to be about a hundred and three, and was truly a great Australian lady.

Chapter 43

I picked up a copy of the Leader newspaper on 18 February. And although my photograph was not very flattering, the article about my book was very good, which was what mattered most. And I hoped that those who read the article would attend the launch.

Esme and Aunty dropped in unexpectedly around eight thirty that night, to wish Connie for his birthday next day, as we planned to go out for dinner with Christian and Athena. They stayed a couple of hours, and Connie was happy to enjoy a pre-birthday toast, and celebration with them.

It was a scorching thirty four degrees next day, but we went to Ceasar's restaurant in Frankston, to celebrate Connie's birthday, and enjoyed a delicious meal. We walked down to "Baskin Robbins" café for ice creams later on. The hot weather did not ease, but a warm, sea breeze blew over as we returned home.

Babs dropped in after ten o'clock the following night, and said she was travelling overseas during the last couple of months. And now she wanted to live in Fiji. I told her she must do as she pleased, because every time she went somewhere on a holiday, she wanted to live there. As it was very late, she stayed overnight, and left next morning.

I counted down the days, and prepared my speech for the launch. Nancy finished reading the book, and said she was very impressed, and gave some positive feedback. I called Nilanthi every week, so she was aware of all that was happening, regarding the launch. She was quite excited, and wished me well, so did Shirani and Nelune, and all my close friends.

I visited the library on the day before the launch, and helped the co-ordinators arrange tables and chairs, and made sure everything was set up for next day. When I returned home, I relaxed, and went through my speech again, and hoped it would all turn out well. It was going to be fair weather too, after all the scorching days. Nelune sent me a big bouquet of flowers for my birthday, and also to wish me "Good luck" at the launch. I was very pleased, and thanked her for the lovely flowers, and kind thoughts.

I woke up bright and early next morning, and Connie had bought presents galore. He left them on the table downstairs, but I told him I would need a great deal of time to open them all. I left it for later, as the launch was scheduled to start at ten thirty. A slight drizzle did not worry me unduly, as the sun peeped through later, and we arrived at the library in good time.

Nancy, her daughter, Danielle, and Neil, were already there. Nancy decorated one hundred tea light candles, with the date of launch, and title of book on ribbons wrapped around them; also, a large, orange candle, with title and date cut out on dark-blue paper, and pasted on it. She must have spent hours doing such a fantastic job, as they were so beautiful.

We arranged olive and grape leaves around the table, laid out with champagne, and light snacks that Christian and Athena prepared. They took their places behind the food tables, and served the guests later. The room was filled to capacity, and the library co-ordinators were impressed at the number of people who turned up. Nancy made an excellent opening speech, and launched it in her inimitable style; she asked me to light the large orange candle, and then declared the launch open.

Everyone congratulated me on this event, and on my latest book. I met Mary and Peter Hancock after about fourteen years, and they drove all the way from Croydon (over an hour's journey), to attend the launch. Chris and Peter La Ponda, and Ginny and Alan came too. I did not invite Connie's siblings, as they were not interested in my work at all, and always turned up late, missing the opening, and important part of the launch. Aunty was no longer able to move about comfortably, but she called me that morning, and wished me well.

Connie invited Shiranthi and Roland, and I did not mind, as they usually made an effort to be on time. They now helped to serve refreshments, and directed guests. Everyone drank a toast later, when Nancy announced it was my birthday as well.

Con limped in just then with a big bouquet of flowers, but Cornelia did not come, as she had slipped and hurt herself. Elvira and Mary came too, but could not stay for lunch, as we invited about twenty of our closest friends for lunch at Soy restaurant near by. Shirani and Ranjith were unable to stay, as they had to baby-sit Max.

Christian and Athena joined us, and we had a memorable time till late afternoon. I was pleased with the results of the launch, and also to celebrate my birthday with good friends. Joelle could not stay for lunch either, but Joanne, Marina, and Nancy joined us, along with Con, Mary, Peter, Chris and Peter, Alan and Ginny; and Christina Biernacki, as she always attended my launches.

The waitress asked what the occasion was, and when I told her, she immediately bought a copy of my book. I sold over forty copies that day, and within two months, I sold hundred copies, and printed another fifty. The library co-ordinators presented me with chocolates, and a bottle of wine to say "Thank you" for holding my launch there.

We visited Cornelia next day, and I was sad to see her face bruised and swollen, as she had slipped in the bathroom, while trying to clean and scrub the bath. But she was feeling better, and said she was sorry she missed the launch. On our way home, we dropped in at Shirani's, and she congratulated me once again on the book launch.

The last few months were so frantic, that I suffered with dizzy spells and frequent headaches, but managed to ward off colds and chest infections. I now felt the first irritating symptoms of a cold and cough when I went to school on Monday morning. But I rushed to Mornington library after school, to give the co-ordinators a box of chocolates, and found the library closed at two o'clock on Monday afternoons. I returned home and spoke to Nelune, as it was her birthday, and I wished her well.

Connie left next day to attend a convention in Sydney for three days. I was down with flu, but made dinner, as Christian and Athena came around to keep me company. Connie phoned at about nine thirty that night, to say he arrived safely after a long delay.

I could hardly get up next day, as I was feverish and weak, but I went to school. When I finished, I drove to the library at Mornington, and the ladies were pleased with the chocolates. And they said it was the most successful launch they saw, as a fairly well-known author sold only six copies of his book at a previous launch. I attributed the good results to the terrific advertising efforts of the library co-ordinators. The event was on all the library websites, posters everywhere on the library walls outside, and newspaper articles as well, besides all the flyers and posters I distributed.

They told me I was more than welcome to hold future launches there, and were glad to support me as a local author. I thanked them, and then we talked about the importance of publicity, and advertisement. I asked if I could have one of the colourful posters on the walls advertising the launch, and they were only too happy to oblige.

I received a large order from a leading library supplier in South Australia, the following day, and several more orders from schools, and libraries Australia wide, for which I was very grateful.

Connie returned home around ten o'clock at night three days later, and he was exhausted, as it was a hectic schedule. He could hardly stay awake, and after his usual whisky and cigarettes, he went to bed without dinner.

I promised Mary Filippone a seascape as a house-warming present, and told her I would come over to take some photographs next day, as it was beautiful and sunny. Mary served a delectable afternoon tea, and I removed plenty of photographs of Arthur's Seat, and the glistening blue ocean. We drove down to Rosebud later, and walked in the Banksia woods near the foreshore. We returned late after attending Mass at Our Lady of Fatima church, in Rosebud.

Chris and Kate, Connie's friends, who lived in Langwarrin, were selling up and leaving soon, so we dropped in to wish them farewell. Chris was Rino's son, and a carpenter/builder by trade as well. He designed and built a very nice, two-storey house on their ten-acre property. But as a main road was to be built on the boundary of their land, they decided to move on. They had a four-year old daughter, and another baby girl now. We spent a pleasant afternoon, and wished them well in the future. Chris always came around to fix anything around our place, and was a kind, helpful person, just like his father Rino.

I usually posted copies of my books to Janice, and in early March, I received a beautiful bouquet of flowers from her to thank me, and to offer her congratulations. It was very thoughtful and generous of her. I emailed and thanked her for her love and kindness, and she said she could hardly wait to start reading my new book.

Janice was a positive influence in my life, as she encouraged and appreciated my literary efforts, for which I am very grateful. She always treated me with love and concern, just like a real sister. And although Nihal was no longer with us, Janice compensated for his absence in every way she could, just as if he was still around. It is a remarkable characteristic, that fills my heart with love and admiration for this unique person in my life.

Chapter 44

Karina, the organizer of a local book club, called me soon after the launch, and invited me to be their guest speaker at dinner in her house. She said, "We chose your book as our 'Book of the month,' and would you be able to give a short talk about it?" I was very pleased, and accepted her invitation. The dinner was in a few weeks time, and I looked forward to that evening.

We still had extreme temperatures in Melbourne, and I felt it was really an "Eternal Summer" here, as mid-March (autumn), continued to be scorching. Liz, Gerry, Lorraine, and Tony came for dinner one Saturday soon after, and we enjoyed the evening. But Gerry, who had chronic pain in his feet all the time, was very irritable, and not very good company.

I worked on the large seascape for Mary and Tony whenever I could spare a moment, and was pleased when it turned out well. And those who saw it, admired the light, and colours of the ocean. The trouble was, that once I completed a painting for someone else, I felt reluctant to part with it. So, I removed photographs of all my artistic offspring, before I sent them off to hang on strange walls somewhere.

Lucille, my cousin in Sri Lanka, wanted an abstract painting, measuring two metres high, and half a metre across. I agreed to paint something, but slightly smaller in size. When I finished Mary's seascape, I started on the abstract immediately. It was one and a half metres high, and half a metre wide, so I had to stretch up high to reach the top of the canvas. I used canvas cloth for easy transport, as a friend of Lucille's, who was in Melbourne then, agreed to take it.

The painting was of tropical fruits and foliage. And I used bright oranges, yellows, earthy tones, and greens, as Lucille sent me a postcard with the colours she wanted, to match the decor of her new house. It was not my usual style, but the abstract painting turned out quite well too, and I was pleased with the results.

The days disappeared into weeks, and it was Easter before I knew it. Connie and I attended Easter Mass at St Anthony's church in Hawthorn. Then drove down to Dromana for lunch, before visiting Christian and Athena later on.

I was now busy working on my autobiography, which I put aside for a few years. Janice often asked me when it was going to be ready, and that spurred me on to shake the dust off the forgotten manuscript, and start on it again. Ever since Ammie and

Thathie died, I found it very painful to go through the manuscript. But now, I was determined to be objective about my writing. And events re-lived through distance of time, would perhaps be less painful, so I believed.

The weather changed suddenly in early April; blustery winds swept across Tasmania and Victoria, ravaging towns and land, in the wake of its fierce onslaught. Huge gums, and eucalyptus trees were uprooted and tossed around like toothpicks. I heard the news, but did not take it seriously, as we experienced similar gales and storms before. And I drove to Karingal to shop as usual. But on my way, I was concerned, when the car swayed from side to side, and I witnessed havoc along some roads. Trees, shrubs, and withered branches spun around like little twigs, and a gigantic gum tree lay sprawled on top of a parked truck.

Thunder and lightning echoed in my ears, and I dashed inside the shopping centre. The storm peaked at about five o'clock, and I waited until the worst of it was over, before I drove home without any mishap. The raging storm and furious winds shuddered and shook every corner of our house all night. But we did not lose even a roof tile, though many people lost their homes and roofs that day. Most suburbs had power cuts, but thankfully, our power supply was uninterrupted.

The violent storm continued next day too, and it rained heavily, making the situation worse, as great trees crashed around everywhere. I cancelled lunch with my friends in Dandenong, stayed indoors, and played the piano instead. Nilanthi and I chatted long, and then I continued working on my manuscript for the rest of the day.

I was pleased when the manager at Dymock's book shop, in Southland, accepted a few copies of my book on consignment, as did Farrell's book store in Mornington, and Robinsons in Frankston. Some people, who attended the launch, called me to order more copies, and I told them they could purchase copies from those book stores now.

Elvira turned seventy on 5 April, and invited us for lunch at Caesar's restaurant in Frankston. We picked Ninette on our way, and joined Elvira's family and friends for lunch. The food was delicious, and we enjoyed a few hours with Elvira, and our friends till about five thirty. I could hardly breathe, after so many huge courses, as Italians entertained lavishly.

Elvira was an attractive, kind, and caring person, and I was very fond of her. I told her I would help to produce her play one day, which I wrote a few years back, based on her life story. I edited and wrote her dialogue as a stage play, and she composed about ten songs and music for the play.

I sent copies of the play to various high schools, and they gave me positive feedback, but were unable to produce it, due to lack of time, and resources. We hoped to stage a production for St Vincent's next year (if we could). Nothing was impossible, if you set your mind to it, so I kept telling Elvira. This was her pet project, and I wanted to help realise her dream.

Genevieve, Alice's mother, dropped in early one morning, to buy a copy of my book, as she wanted to read it, before the book club met the following week. We had coffee and a chat, and I liked her very much, as she was a very pleasant, and friendly lady.

Melissa dropped in later that same afternoon, and we enjoyed chatting, and playing the piano. She was a very talented singer, and pianist, who ran her own music school. We talked about her missing mother and sister, and I marvelled at her courage and determination, in trying to bring their killer to justice. She wanted to write her story someday, and I encouraged her, as I told her it was a great form of therapy.

The meeting at Karina's place on 17 April, was very successful, and I received great feedback from all the members of the book club; they had long lists of questions about the book too, so I enjoyed the discussions, and their views very much. I found it very interesting to hear how deeply my readers related to each character, as if they were "real" people, and not just figments of my imagination.

They expressed strong opinions about each character, whether they admired or detested them. From my perspective as a writer, it was intriguing to stir such emotion over imaginary characters. We enjoyed a delicious dinner, and a champagne toast later.

Karina's beachfront house was unique, and very atmospheric. I admired the splendid views from the balcony, and told her how fortunate she was to live there. Karina walked back with me later, and waited until I drove off, and I came home after ten o'clock. Connie called me later, as he was away on a business trip in the country. It was a stimulating evening, and I was exhilarated, not only with champagne, but the satisfaction of having written a story that so many enjoyed reading.

We visited Josephine on 25 April, Anzac Day, but she was in severe pain and very petulant. She needed groceries, and we took her out shopping and for lunch. But she was very tired, and we left her around six thirty in the evening. It was a sad life for poor Josephine, but she had to make herself happy, or else spend her twilight years in misery. The choice was hers.

Mary and Tony were very impressed with the seascape, when I presented it to them. She made Tony hang it up on the wall immediately. And I was pleased they appreciated my work. And Tony said, "Your painting will have a place of honour in our house always."

We joined Elvira, John, Mary, and Tony for a dance at Nunawading Whitehorse Club on 9 May, the night before Mother's Day. Christina Biernacki, and her husband, Adam, turned up at the last minute too. Adam was quite active, and physically fit, as he danced away the night. So it was a shock, when Christina called a few months later, to say he died of a heart attack. He was in his early fifties then.

I attended his funeral with Connie, and learnt he was a very heavy smoker for many years. His family was devastated, and I was very upset for Christina, who was a good friend now. She spoke about the danger of long-term smoking, and urged smokers to give up, so they would not compromise their health.

The day before that dance, I was working all day, then took Tiger for his vaccine, and visited Aunty later, to wish her for Mother's Day. By the time I returned home in the afternoon, my back ached, so I rested awhile. But the pain worsened during the dance, with all the swirling Connie did.

I could hardly move the following day, but as we said we would meet Christian and Athena for lunch at café 115 in Mornington, I woke up with difficulty, and we drove there. The pain was very severe, and I had to curtail our time with them, as I could hardly sit up. I came home and went straight to bed, and ended up spending the next three days in bed, hardly able to walk.

I consulted doctor, and he took an x-ray, and some blood tests, but did not find anything amiss. His diagnosis was, stretched muscles, and he told me to get plenty of rest, and use a hot water bottle to ease the spasms. I missed school, but was back to normal in a week's time.

I dreamed about Ammie, Thathie, all the dead family members, and Stacy very often. The dreams were so vivid, that I woke up in the middle of the night, and forgot they were no longer with us. I dreamed, especially if I was thinking of them the previous day.

A few months ago, the police requested a DNA sample from Connie, which he gave, but they did not ask me at the same time. So I was surprised when a police officer from Frankston called me on 21 May, and requested me to come down to the police station, so they could take a DNA sample from me. The police told us that it was just a procedure, as Stacy's case would soon go to the coroner's court. I went down after school, and hung around for two hours, before they took me in for a DNA sample.

The police officer was very kind, and polite when he read about Stacy; he shook hands with me and said, "It is a very sad thing about your missing son. I hope we will have an answer for you soon." I thanked him and came home feeling depressed, as I always did, whenever the stark reality of Stacy's disappearance overwhelmed me. I dreamed that night, and my dream of Stacy was so vivid, and important to me, that I wrote it down immediately. It was towards dawn, because my dream woke me up at six o'clock.

In my dream, I was sitting at a small, outdoor table with one of my friends, who looked like Vivian, Lorraine's daughter. On the table, was a red, folded paper serviette, and it moved about in the slight breeze. Vivian said, "I believe in the occult." I touched the red serviette, and with all my heart I asked, "*Is* Stacy alive? Tell me where my son is!" The serviette dropped on the ground, fluttered around, and then travelled up my legs, until it stuck near my ear. A gentle male voice whispered, but it was not Stacy. I strained every nerve to hear that soft voice, and it said, "The Lord gives, and the Lord takes away. All things must be returned to the Lord. Remember the story of the brave mother and the robber?" The voice continued to explain the story, but I could not hear anything at all, only a murmur.

I woke up trembling. It was six o'clock, and Connie was awake already, as he had to drive through the city to Sunshine that day. I told him about my dream, and he replied, "That's just your sub-conscious, as you were at the police station, and talked about Stacy." Perhaps it was, but all day, I felt a peaceful sensation, as if it was a message of healing. I called Nilanthi and told her about it; and then Ninette, and Isobel too, as they were spiritual people, and knew there must be some meaning to it.

Ninette said that when she told Jackie and Luigi about my dream, they were moved to tears. All I can say is, that since that day, I did not dream of Stacy as often. I believe that some unseen power sent me solace, so I would not grieve constantly for my beloved son. If the Lord has taken him away, then I know he is at peace too.

I invited a dozen people on Sunday afternoon, 29 June, to "brainstorm" Elvira's stage play. And was pleased when Alan and Ginny from Nomad Players, Nancy, Christina, Melissa, Mary and Peter, John and Elvira, Mary, Christian, Athena, Shirani and Ranjith, all turned up. We sat around the fireplace, and enjoyed an enormous afternoon tea, while Elvira read her play. And the listeners commented, and gave positive feedback and constructive criticism afterwards.

I baked a cake, and made dips and savouries, Elvira brought her famous scones, and Christian and Athena made some delectable short eats. Everyone brought a plate, and after several cups of tea and coffee, creative juices flowed, and ideas kept bouncing around like rubber balls. I said I would do my best to help Elvira stage her play "Elise's Journey." We finished after six o'clock in the evening, but as it was a chilly, wet afternoon, no one complained about snuggling besides the fireplace, and indulging in "high tea."

Eastlink opened that day, and Mary and Peter drove down the new freeway, but delayed twenty minutes near Seaford exit, as a huge "bottle-neck" hampered the flow of traffic. As it was a trial run, they decided not to go via Eastlink on their return home.

Christian and Athena stayed till late, as Athena upgraded my website. She wanted to get my e-books on-line, in time for the radio show tomorrow morning. But a technical glitch delayed her, and she could not complete the task. It was just amazing how much they always supported me in my work, and I was very grateful for their time, love and generosity. Connie too helped with serving, and washing up, and we had a late dinner together.

I just managed to get some notes together the previous day for the radio show, and hoped it would go well. Sleep eluded me, as I was over-tired, and my brain ran on top gear, with revisions of Elvira's play. And mental rehearsals of the radio show, raced through my mind.

It was after three in the morning, when I finally fell asleep, but woke up a couple of hours later. After a quick breakfast, Connie drove me to the local radio station, 3RPP on Moorooduc highway, which was about ten minutes from Frankston. I met Cathy Alexander, the other guest speaker, who was a local writer, and editor from Mornington, and we started chatting away.

Del, who was the presenter, handled the interview excellently, and she made me feel very much at ease, as we discussed my books. It went off very well, and I read a few passages from "An Eternal Summer," that sparked off discussions, questions, and writers issues. Connie taped the show, which I listened to later on, and was relieved I did not flounder.

Chapter 45

New Year's Eve dance was enjoyable, and we came home long after midnight. We danced all night, and made friends with a nice couple from Mt Eliza, Ron and Marian, who sat at our table with Elvira, John, Mary, and Tony. The dance floor was over-crowded, and it was a very warm night, but the food was delicious. Christian and Athena called to wish us at midnight, while we were still at the club, and said they were enjoying their holiday. We went to sleep after two o'clock, but rested till late next morning.

After a leisurely breakfast, we drove to Southland, and watched "Bolt" an animated movie. We wore 3D glasses for the first time, and I was amazed at how effective they were. I felt as if I was *inside* the movie. The film was great, and I enjoyed it thoroughly. We visited Shirani and Ranjith in Narre Warren later, but did not stay long. And on our way home, we stopped at Aunty Molly's too. She spent New Year's Eve with her family, and went to bed at dawn, so she was very tired.

It was almost eight o'clock in the night when we finally returned home, and I was quite exhausted. Misty was still asleep inside the house, so I let her out for a little while. She seemed alright, and I was happy to see her walk around steadily. As it was a cold, showery evening, Misty preferred to be indoors. Joelle rang and thanked me for the DVD I sent her, and after a light dinner I went to bed early.

Ninette called next day, and asked me to come over, as she had baked bread and biscuits for New Year, and wanted to give me some. I took some fresh grape vine leaves that she liked to stuff, flowers, milk rice, and beef curry. Then I spent a pleasant afternoon, walked with her, and helped her with shopping.

When we returned, she played the piano for a while, and I enjoyed listening to all the beautiful melodies she played by memory. She could not read music at all, due to her failing eyesight. My eyes too felt tired after all the late nights, so I came home and took it easy. When I called Ninette later on to thank her for the home-made goodies, she asked me to visit her with Connie on Sunday afternoon. I agreed, and then got onto the exercise bike for about half an hour. Misty was a little more energetic that day, and climbed on top of my car to have a nap.

Connie was ready at six thirty on Saturday morning, in good time to play a round of golf with Pat, his work mate. By the time I finished my usual chores and routine, they returned. I served Christmas cake, cutlets, and short eats that Pat relished. He was very happy when I packed a basket of home-made goodies for his family too. He always said, "Dolly, you make the best pan rolls I have ever tasted!" Pat attended my last book launch, and gave me positive feedback, saying he enjoyed reading my book.

After he left, we drove down to Woolamai at midday. and I had a peaceful afternoon with Shirani, as Ranjith and Connie went fishing, but did not catch anything. It was a glorious, summer day, and I was glad to be out in the garden. We came home late that evening and I made dinner, as Christian said he would drop in, but he called at nine o'clock to say his car had a flat battery, and he was delayed. It was eleven o'clock when he finally arrived, and it was another late night, as we went to bed after one o'clock in the morning.

I woke up late on Sunday, and did some sewing for Christian, as he brought several t-shirts to be taken in and hemmed. Then we visited Ninette around three thirty, and Luigi was there too. While we were still there, Nelune called me on my mobile to say that Mrs Jean Buchanan had died of a stroke that morning. She was ninety-seven and a half years old. I felt very sad, as I would miss her interesting letters, and cards very much. She sent me a Christmas card that year, as usual, but she suffered a stroke just after Boxing Day, and died in hospital a few days later.

We went to Frankston church afterwards, and l lit candles for all my dear ones, especially the ones who were no longer with me. Then we dropped in at Christian's for a short while. He was very busy doing things around the house, so Athena chatted with us over a coffee, and we came home after eight o'clock that night.

The hot, sunny weather continued next day, with cloudless blue skies, and not a breeze to caress the trees in the garden. I sat underneath the Jacaranda tree, which was a mass of vibrant purple and mauve blossoms now. What a glorious sight! I spent some time editing Elvira's play that evening.

It was thirty degrees next day too, but I visited Ninette as usual. She wanted to shop at Karingal, so after playing the piano for about forty-five minutes, I stopped, as it was just too hot and stuffy inside her crowded unit. I drove her to Karingal, and then stopped at Safeway in Seaford, as she wanted to buy groceries. But the heat was intense, so we came back soon. I had a coffee with her, helped her to read some sheet music, and then drove home, as I was too tired to stop for groceries.

After my usual routine next day, I called Nilanthi, who said she hoped to visit us in mid-February (if I could send her a ticket). I said I would send her the money, so she was happy. Her one refrain was, "What else have I got to look forward to, except visit my sisters in Australia?" And I always melted at her words. Because through the years, I took on the responsibility to ensure she was comfortable, and to make her happy whenever I could.

Ninette called at midday for a long chat as usual, and repeated the same story about Luigi, and his affair with the notorious woman next door. I drove later to get groceries, and felt drained, as the heat was exhausting.

The high temperatures continued next day as well, and I woke up late, as I felt unusually tired. Then I picked some mulberries, as the tree was weighed down, and made jam. I called Nilanthi to say I received her emails, and was very happy for her to visit us soon. Then I sent her a letter of invitation, bank statements etc. for her visa application, and Connie did not mind helping me to get the documents ready. I typed the revised version of Elvira's play till late. Christian dropped in, and we had a nice long chat, and he left around eleven thirty that night.

I bottled jam next day, and after doing the usual chores, I collected some photographs at Big W, and bought summer clothes for Nilanthi, and her grand-daughter, Tia. Then I called Ninette, and she started playing some tapes for me to listen to. And I could not leave the phone, although I was very tired and just wanted to relax.

I called Cornelia the following day, and she told me that her grandchild was not born as yet, but it could be any day now. Christian called later, and I was glad he sounded alright, as he was very stressed. Shirani said she was very pleased with the sign he made for her restaurant in Woolamai. I made "thosais" for dinner, and was worn-out after standing so long to cook them; I felt unusually lethargic, and my eyes hurt too.

We visited Linda and Leo that Sunday, and I gave her a present, and the seascape I painted for her. We arrived there around two o'clock, and we had a very nice afternoon, watching their wedding photographs on DVD. Linda baked a delicious cake, and she was so happy with the painting, that she immediately hung it up on the wall in their dining room.

Then we visited Shirani briefly, as she brought some vegetables from Woolamai, and wanted me to pick them up at Narre Warren. Christian dropped in later that evening, and we had an interesting chat, and he was happy with the t-shirts I altered to fit him.

I took Misty for her cortisone injection on Monday morning, and the vet said she looked alright. I was relieved to see her walking steadily, although her head leaned sideways, ever since she had a stroke, and she was a little unsteady at times. I came home and rested, because I was drained, as I woke up a few times last night.

It was a scorching thirty-seven degrees next day. I woke up early, washed all the lace curtains, and cleaned up the house, as I could not do much in this extreme weather. I tried to play the piano for a little while, but my palms dripped with perspiration. Tiger and Misty looked exhausted from the heat too, so I kept a watchful eye on them. I worked on Elvira's play as I wanted to print some copies.

In the meantime, I submitted "Catsville" to a few more animation studios, and some responded positively. Shutterbug animations wrote back to say they were interested, but their cost was exorbitant. So I decided to produce it someday, if I acquired the skill and knowledge.

The extreme weather continued over the next few days, and in spite of it, I tried to play the piano at least one hour each day. But it was very difficult when the weather was soaring in the high thirties.

Mrs Jean Buchanan's daughter, Barbara, wrote me a nice letter, thanking me for the sympathy card and letter I sent her. I told her it was a privilege to have known such a gracious, intelligent lady. Her letters were always full of information, in elegant handwriting, and I missed her correspondence very much.

Ninette wanted to shop at Patterson Lakes centre, so I drove her there on Tuesday. But we did not spend much time there, as she wanted to get back soon. The moment we arrived there, she held onto my arm, looked around one or two shops, and said, "Let's go back now Nalini, I feel dizzy! I can't breathe here!" It was very trying, as I spent time driving all that way, and she hardly spent ten minutes looking around, before returning home. I thought her behaviour was getting more and more erratic each day.

On our way back, I saw Luigi hobbling along painfully with a walking stick. Ninette said his foot was infected, and that he still visited the woman across, where he spent a great deal of time. She was very upset about his affair, and took it very much to heart, as Luigi's musical career was at a standstill now.

Misty seemed to be very slow and disoriented, and it made me very unhappy to see her now, a shadow of her former, frisky personality. I hoped she was not in pain; she ate and drank water normally. Tiger still chased her around the garden, and she screeched when he attacked her, so I had to stop him from hurting her.

It was cooler over the next few days, and a few light showers helped the parched garden slightly. Gusty winds blew in from the ocean, and caused wild weather inland. The garden certainly looked beaten up, and would take some time to recover from the harsh weather.

I finished editing and typing up Elvira's revised play, and drove to Mornington to get some copies printed, but they told me the copies would be ready next day. While I was shopping, the printer called to say I could pick them up later that afternoon. Connie called me just then, and offered to pick them up, to save me another trip.

I contacted Chisholm Campus in Frankston, as they ran an animation course for around $814, which I thought was reasonable. It was self-paced, and would take about one hundred hours to complete, so I decided to meet the tutor and find out more details.

Cornelia's and Con's grandson, Ashton, was born on 14 January, and they were very happy when I called to congratulate them. They said they would visit us soon, as they were now busy with the new arrival.

I bought a French perfume for Ninette, as her birthday was in a few day's time. And I was sure she would like it, as she told me that she preferred French perfumes. Ninette was seventy-seven on 17 January, and she was very pleased with the fragrance when I gave it on her birthday

I picked some flowers from the garden for Ginny, as we were visiting them on Sunday afternoon. On our way there, we dropped in at Elvira's to give her copies of her play, and later at Christian's place too. Ginny looked frail, and she said she was much better, but we did not stay very long.

Shirani brought vegetables again, so I told her I would visit on Monday, as I had to buy some sheet music at Cranbourne Music Centre. I went there early next morning, as it soared to thirty seven degrees again. We enjoyed a delicious lunch, and later when I drove home, the car was like a furnace, as it was out in that extreme heat.

I did not visit Ninette next day, as the temperature went up to thirty-nine degrees, and it was too hot for me to drive. And it was a great relief when it finally cooled down in the night. I was happy when Christian visited in the evening.

On 20 January, I watched Barrack Obama's inauguration. It was such a great moment in history, when the first black man became President of the United States. He delivered an excellent speech, which was so moving that I was close to tears. Aretha Franklin sang a stirring song, "My Country." I hoped it was the dawning of a new era, and prayed that racial discrimination would be wiped out in this world. I did chores and cleaned up later, and prepared a few things, as Elvira was visiting tomorrow morning to discuss the revised play.

She arrived at eleven o'clock next day, and we worked on the play for a couple of hours, and she was happy with the revised version. It was after one o'clock in the afternoon when we stopped, and snacked on sandwiches and coffee. Shirani arrived just then, and she looked tired, as she had a very busy morning with some medical tests. She was on a heart monitor the previous night, and said it was just a routine check-up. I hoped she would be alright, and it was nothing serious.

Elvira demonstrated how to make gnocchi, and it seemed very easy (when she did it), as she was an expert chef. Shirani and I took notes. And after a cup of tea, Elvira and Shirani left around three o'clock. I took it easy in the afternoon.

Hot, gusty winds blew, and the weather soared above thirty four degrees next day. Poor Misty and Tiger felt the heat badly, and I kept them cool indoors. I watered the garden till about eight thirty that night, and just as I came in to have dinner, I was surprised to see Paul and Esme. She had a cup of tea, but Paul said he did not want anything, as they just came to see how we were. Connie was not home yet, so they waited until he arrived after nine o'clock.

Tamara phoned later to say that she was worried about some blood tests she did, but I told her not to stress until she knew the results. We did not speak long, but she emailed later that night, as her blood tests were all okay, and I was relieved to hear that.

We took Tiger to the vet next day, as he did not seem well. The vet did some blood tests, and said Tiger had several problems, including a heart murmur. Tiger screamed in pain when they inserted a needle into his neck to do a thyroid test. My heart ached to hear him scream, as he never made a fuss when he had his vaccines.

When I questioned the vet, he told me that it was because Tiger kept moving while the needle was inside, and that was why he screamed in pain. I wished they could do the test with less pain for the poor animals. Poor Tiger, he was just skin and bone now, as he did not eat too much. His once majestic mane and tail were scraggy remnants of past glory. After I settled Tiger comfortably at home, we drove to the city in the afternoon, as I wanted to see an exhibition of cat drawings by Louis Wain.

I read a review about it, and Connie agreed to drive me to the city. It was a small art gallery somewhere in Bourke Street. And about twenty drawings were for sale, with prices beginning at seven thousand pounds and over. They were quaint, whimsical drawings that I found intriguing, but not seven thousand pounds worth of intrigue anyway!

Then we visited the National Gallery for a free exhibition of fifteenth and sixteenth century European art, besides another exhibition of Egyptian artefacts. I enjoyed the afternoon very much, and we returned home late. But Connie was in a bad mood, and we had a stressful evening over some issue or another, and we argued until my head ached. He sat at the computer, sulking all evening. I watched an old movie on DVD "Chandu On The Magic Island" which was quite good.

The piano tuner, John Kellow, arrived at nine o'clock next day. Connie had a coffee with him and chatted briefly. John tuned the piano well, as he always did, and left in a couple of hours time. I did some chores, made apricot jam, and hemmed Christian's jeans.

Then we drove to Karingal at three o'clock to watch "Valkyrie" with Tom Cruise. It was quite good, and as it was still warm and sunny, Connie went fishing to the Frankston pier around six o'clock. I took it easy, replied emails, and watered the garden. He did not catch any fish, but enjoyed relaxing by the sea. I called Christian to tell him his jeans were ready, but he was busy in the garden, and said he will pick them up another time.

The sizzling weather continued next day, but we went for Mass in the evening. And after dinner we watched comedies, till Christian dropped in at about ten thirty, and we had a long chat. He left at one o'clock in the morning, and was pleased that Athena was returning from her trip to Norway in a couple of days.

We went for another movie at Karingal cinema next day, as Connie was on holidays. It was, "The Curious Case Of Benjamin Button" with Brad Pitt and Kate Blanchett. Quite an unusual story, and I enjoyed it. Then we visited Christian later on, as he wanted us to see all the work he did in the garden.

I was very proud to think he completed so much all on his own. He landscaped, did the paving, a water feature, and decking all on his own. Even Connie was impressed, and kept saying, "Perfect job, son!" And being a perfectionist, that was the highest praise from Connie. Christian came over later that night and spent a couple of hours.

We did not get any relief from the extreme heat for weeks, and bushfires raged all over Victoria, and other states. I did not go to Ninette's, as it was too hot to play the piano, so we had a long chat on the phone instead.

When I called the vet that day, he told me that Tiger had severe kidney disease. And I had to consider putting him to sleep, as he was too sick. Tiger was not eating well for some time, but drank a lot of water, which he immediately threw up. I was heartbroken to watch him deteriorate so rapidly.

Poor Tiger, I had to release him from his sufferings, no matter how terribly I would miss him after eighteen years. I drove to Karingal around four o'clock that afternoon when it was slightly cooler and came home soon. Then I tried to feed him some fresh salmon, but Tiger barely ate a few morsels.

When I called Christian to tell him how sick Tiger was, he wanted to come over and wish him goodbye. But it was too late that night, and he said he had to sleep early, as he was picking up Athena from the airport very early next morning.

The following day, 28 January, the temperature soared to forty five degrees, and we had the air-conditioner on all night, but it was still very humid and stuffy. The bright, blue skies continued to blaze, without a single cloud to usher in some showers.

Tiger drank a little water, but refused to eat at all. I coaxed him to swallow a few morsels of raw mince meat, which he threw up. Misty did not go out, but Tiger wanted to be in the garden, and hide under the Jacaranda tree. I bathed him, syringed a little warm milk into his mouth, and tried to make him comfortable. I searched for him everywhere later, and found him hiding under the shrubbery.

When we first moved to Frankston, he went missing for a couple of days, and then too he had kidney problems. And he had the same problem when we were renting in Frankston, and Thathie visited in 1996. This was the third time he ailed with kidney problems, but the vet told me an operation would not help this time. I heard cats go missing and hide when they are sick, so I kept an eye on Tiger, to make sure he would not stray somewhere and get lost.

When I finished writing the script "Catsville," I sent it to Roslyn, and she said she would meet me soon, once she finished reading the script.

Nilanthi said she was busy planning her trip in February, and she sounded very happy and excited. We talked for some time, and I looked forward to her visit.

It was thirty degrees overnight, and very uncomfortable. I syringed water into Tiger's and Misty's mouths. But Tiger could barely eat a teaspoon of raw mince now, and it made me very sad to think how greedily he devoured raw mince before.

It was impossible to get any sleep in such sizzling weather, so we watched comedies till midnight. Tiger and Misty stayed in the garden till very late, and I brought them in just before we went to bed.

I bathed Tiger next day, and fed him a little more mince. And then I knew I had to accept the inevitable, and let him go, as I could not bear to see him in such a sad state. I called the vet and booked him in at ten thirty next morning. He did not eat much over the last six days, and was just skin and bone, in spite of his long fur that made him look big and fluffy. Poor Tiger was eighteen years old now, and lived a long, happy life. It was time to say goodbye, no matter how difficult.

When I told Christian, he was very sad, and said they would drop in later to say goodbye to Tiger. It was forty three degrees, and still no rain or cool weather in sight. Misty stayed indoors, cooling down in front of the fan, but Tiger staggered to the garden, and sprawled under the trees as he always loved being outdoors.

Christian and Athena came around eight thirty, and after dinner, they spent time with Tiger and fussed over him. Even Athena shed a few tears for him, and I was surprised, as I did not know she was fond of him. She was very tired after her long flight, but I was happy to see her after a month. She brought some gifts for Connie and me, and in spite of my heavy heart, we had a pleasant chat. It was unbearably hot that night too, and the temperature was expected to reach high forties next day as well. We stayed up till about one o'clock in the morning, after Christian and Athena left, and watched more comedies.

It was 30 January next day, and I woke up at seven o'clock in the morning, as I had a restless night. I diced some rump steak and fed Tiger, but he ate only a few morsels, and drank a sip of water. He was very weak and subdued, and the heat did not help, as it was thirty eight degrees at eight o'clock in the morning.

I bathed him in luke-warm water, and kept him cool indoors, then I sponged Misty, and fed her water with a syringe. We drove to the vet's at ten thirty, and Tiger did not utter a single mew in the car. Usually, he mewed all the way to the vet's and back. But now he looked straight ahead, in a dignified, stoic manner, as if prepared for his end.

The vet took us to a small room, and the nurse explained what was going to happen. Scott said, "It's the best decision long term, as it's humane to end Tiger's pain. Sometimes, we are kinder to our pets than to humans!" Tiger sat quietly, as Scott took him to another room to insert a catheter in his leg. When he brought him back, he asked me to hold Tiger while he administered the anaesthetic.

I held my warm, beautiful pet one moment, then in a few seconds, his body went limp, slid down and lay still, his eyes hazy, and his tongue showing between his teeth. It seemed very quick, ten seconds or less, and he was no more. I was glad that he was no longer in pain, and at peace now, but the anguish in my heart was more than I could bear, and tears just flowed. I could not help crying when I saw his body lying still. Scott said, "It's okay to shed tears for your beloved pet, they are a part of your family."

Tiger was such a lovable cat, with a great personality, and I loved him dearly. He lived a long, adventurous life, and after eighteen years, it was very difficult to let him go. He brought me so much joy, just by being around, and gave me his companionship, that was what I would miss most. I will love him always, and treasure his memory. He understood when I spoke to him, and it was the same with Misty.

I was prepared to let her go one of these days as well, as I could not hold onto them forever, I know. But oh, how much I will miss Tiger and Misty when they are gone. I am thankful for so many happy years I spent with them. I do not think I can go through such pain and grief again, so I decided "no more cats" but who knows. I will be so lonely without their presence and companionship, as they were so very close to me. I hope Tiger is in "Catsville" in cats paradise.

Scott placed Tiger inside a plastic bag, and amid more tears, we brought him home. It was forty three degrees, and too hot for Connie to dig a grave to bury Tiger, so we kept him in the laundry until it became cooler. I wanted to bury him under the pussywillow tree, where he loved to laze under its shade, as he enjoyed being outdoors. I cried so much that my chest ached, and I kept seeing his beautiful face everywhere I looked, as he was always somewhere close by wherever I walked.

He had a habit of standing up in a most gentlemanly fashion, as soon as he saw me, and purred a greeting, no matter where he was hiding. If I sat to watch television or read, Tiger jumped on my lap immediately, and sprawled across my legs, and did not budge until I shook him off. No more would I feel the comfort and warmth of his fluffy body.

I gave Misty some water and meat, and kept her away from the laundry. But she sensed something was amiss, and kept standing at the laundry door and staring at me, as if she wanted me to open the door. When the grave was ready, I wrapped him up in his blanket, and laid him to rest. I noticed an unusual thing happened just then, as a ginger-coloured butterfly rose out of the grave, and flew around the garden. I told Connie I was sure it was Tiger's spirit hovering in his beloved surroundings.

Chapter 46

After the trauma of Tiger's death, I felt sick next day, when I remembered the details of his last few days and hours. It took all my will power to go about my daily routine. But all day I seemed to glimpse his dear, familiar face, hiding in the garden or his soft purr behind me.

With the dawn of another sizzling day in the high thirties, bush fires raged without any sign of abating. And after a distressing day, doing a few chores and phone calls to Nilanthi and Nelune, we drove to Cornelia's for dinner.

It was a pleasant evening, and as they loved cats and dogs too, they understood how I felt. We talked about our beloved pets, and the ones we said goodbye to, and we returned after midnight.

Sunday was slightly cooler, but the wind blew all the clouds away, and no rain followed to relieve us. I had to start school next day, 2 February, so I prepared music lessons in the evening. Misty looked very subdued (more so than usual), and I was sure she missed Tiger.

I missed my long-time students, Sarah, Charlotte, Tabitha, and Mitchell. They were some of my best students, and were such interesting characters too. A few more new students enrolled, and some from previous years. First thing I noticed that morning, was an awful stench in the room, and I saw a dead possum. The heat got him no doubt. One of the teachers removed it, and sprayed some air freshener, but it did not do much to lessen that putrid odour.

I made enquiries regarding animation courses, and the secretary at Chisholm Campus in Frankston, called to say they had a course available. And could I come for an interview on 2 February, so I agreed to meet the tutor, who conducted the course.

I finished lessons around midday, and went home to get ready for the interview that afternoon. It turned out to be an interesting meeting, and I was accepted for the course. But I said I would have to consider it, as I had to attend two days per week, for thirty two weeks. It was a serious commitment, and for the amount of money that it would cost me, I had to attend every lesson to get my money's worth. I was unsure if I could spare the time, with teaching three days at school, and my writing. And after due consideration, I decided not to enrol.

I could not help missing Tiger very much in the days and weeks that followed, and tried to keep my thoughts away from him and kept busy. Misty seemed to be looking for Tiger in the garden whenever she went out. She sat quietly, and glanced around nervously, expecting him to jump out of the shrubbery and ambush her.

A few brief showers brushed the garden lightly, but hardly enough to make a difference. Although the extreme weather continued, I visited Ninette next day, and drove her to Chelsea, as she had an appointment with her optometrist. It was still about thirty three degrees next day, so I spent time editing Elvira's play, as it was too hot to do anything else, and waited for the weather to cool down.

When I tried to start the car later, it did not work, and by the time RACV came and fixed it (some loose wires), it was four o'clock. But I drove to Karingal to get some groceries. And later that night, Christian and Athena dropped in for a little while. They too missed Tiger, and were sympathetic when I told them how sad I was.

Babs called me very early next morning, and had a long chat about a man she met recently. "I'm over the moon, and I've never been so happy in my life! I'm getting married next month!" she gushed excitedly. Although she knew him only for a few weeks, she was convinced that he was "Mr Right." I told her to consider carefully, and get to know him better, but she decided to marry him anyway, and wanted to visit with him.

That Saturday was extremely hot, and soared to forty six degrees or more, and gusty winds howled all day in scorching heat. Babs dropped in later that afternoon with Patrick O'Hara, her new boyfriend. He was a Sri Lankan Burgher, of average height, pleasant-mannered, a few years older than her, and was married and divorced three times. He lived in Adelaide, and he seemed agreeable enough, and chatted away to Connie. Babs asked if I knew of a marriage celebrant, as they intended to have a civil ceremony, and hold a small reception later. I thought of Nancy immediately, and gave Babs her number.

They stayed for a couple of hours, and I rested a while after they left, as the intense heat was unbearable. I watched the shocking news that evening about devastating bushfires raging all over Victoria. One was very close, in Narre Warren, and was deliberately lit. I called Shirani to ask her where it was. And she said they could see smoke, but it was not too close to their house, which was a relief. That day went down in history as, "Black Saturday" because they were the worst bushfires in Victoria.

It cooled down to mid-twenty by midnight, and some welcome showers in the morning cooled the parched gardens. The Karlsens invited us to their new home in Hallam, and we visited them in the afternoon. They sold their house in Camberwell, and moved to a smaller place. We had a pleasant afternoon, and on our way home, we dropped in at Shirani's for a while.

I thought of Ammie, as she would have been seventy-nine years today, the 9th of February, and said a special prayer for her. Although it was much cooler today, "Black Saturday" destroyed many homes and lives. I was stunned, as was the whole of Melbourne, to hear that Brian Naylor, a well-known television personality, and news reporter for many years, and his wife, died in Saturday's bushfires in Kinglake. Their son died tragically in a plane crash in the same area one year ago. The bushfires claimed many victims, and left hundreds homeless.

Sarah, and her mother, Tracy, visited after school on Monday evening, as Sarah decided to continue piano lessons at my place. I was happy, because she was very talented in singing and piano. Christian called to say they would drop in later, so I made dinner quickly, and we had a great time till they left late at night.

When Ninette heard me play on Tuesday, she was happy with my rendition of "Moonlight Sonata" and "Barcarolle." We had coffee, and I walked with her to the shops later. She was sympathetic when I told her about Tiger, as she called me on the day I put him to sleep. She was very fond of her dogs too, and understood the trauma of putting them to sleep.

Our neighbour's daughter, Alanah, commenced piano lessons shortly, so I was busy teaching in the evenings too. A few more students enrolled that week, and now I had ten at school.

I noticed Misty sitting in all the usual places where Tiger sat in the garden, and looking around for him. I was sure she missed him just as much as I missed my beautiful Tiger. My grief was still very raw, and I could not think of him without getting teary.

It drizzled slightly that night, but was hardly enough to quench the bushfires raging uncontrollably. The late news said that thirty one bushfires burned out of control at present, and even though we had some light rain, it did not fall where it was needed most. Every summer, it was the same tragic news of destructive bushfires, but the worst part was, that some of them were deliberately lit.

Nancy called to say that Babs met her regarding the wedding, and she agreed to be their celebrant, also that she set a date to meet Patrick too.

I drove to Mornington next day to collect newsletters for the Women Writers, and mailed them as usual. Then I bought books and gifts for Valentine's Day, and Connie's birthday.

Misty was still sleeping when I came home, and it was distressing to see her so inactive, and unlike her frisky self. But she seemed content, and that was the main thing. When I spoke to Nilanthi later, she was very excited at the prospect of spending time with us.

It was twenty eight degrees on the 13 February, and still very warm and humid, but I went shopping, as I wanted to buy some seedlings, and a few more gifts for Connie. I was worn-out with the heat when I came home, and had chest pains, which I did not take seriously. I was rushing around all day, and knew it was just tiredness. But my heartbeat was erratic, and I decided to take it easy.

I sent copies of my script to a few more producers, and replied emails before making dinner. The bushfires still raged out of control, and I prayed for rain, but it was expected to be another scorching day tomorrow.

We exchanged cards and gifts next day, on St Valentine's Day. Connie visited his mother after breakfast, and to do her shopping. I called Josephine, and she was very happy when I told her that we would visit her soon with Nilanthi.

In spite of Esme telling me off, and to keep away from Josephine, I decided I would see her whenever I could, because Josephine did not do me any wrong. It was Esme's and Paul's quarrel with her, not ours. But Connie did not want to upset his sister and Paul, so he warned me not to tell them whenever we visited Josephine.

Ever since Esme phoned a few months ago, and was very rude to me, I lost all respect. When I said we visited Josephine out of charity for a lonely old lady, she scoffed, "All *bosh! What* charity! You are interfering in our lives, don't visit her! She's a wicked old woman, and doesn't want us to come for her funeral, so leave her alone!" Anyway, she carried on in the same abusive manner, until I told her firmly that I would visit Josephine whenever I wanted to.

The day after that abusive phone call, I was surprised when she came rushing home to apologize for her behaviour, and the things she said. But it was never the same again. She said some very hurtful things, when all I did was give some time and companionship to a lonely old lady.

We attended Mass on Sunday evening, and I asked Maureen if I could take Holy Communion for Ninette, as she did not feel well enough to attend Mass. She gave me a blessed host, as I told Ninette I would bring Holy Communion whenever she wanted. While I was watering the garden that evening, I saw Mitchell at Madeline's place. And they came over to have a chat, and to tell me all about their new school, as they were in high school now.

On Monday,16 February, we arrived at the airport at six o'clock in the morning. Nilanthi's plane was scheduled to arrive at 6.30am, but it was delayed by one hour, and we picked her up two hours later. I was glad to see her once again, and she was very happy too, although she was worn-out with the delayed flight. She enjoyed the lunch I made, and we rested afterwards. I had students at four o'clock, so I was busy till late, but we enjoyed a great evening, and turned in early that night.

I drove Nilanthi to see Aunty next day, and it was depressing to see her vegetable state. She wore a skullcap that covered her shaven head, was very vague, and did not talk much. Then we visited Ninette for a little while, shopped at Karingal, and came home in time for piano lessons. Christian and Athena dropped in later that night, and after dinner, Athena sewed cushions till midnight.

Connie took time off next day, and we drove to the city in the afternoon to extend Nilanthi's visa, as she was given a visa for one month only. They gave her another two weeks extension, and we came home late, after walking around in the city. Nilanthi was happy to stay longer, as Heron was staying at her friend, Chandani's place. Chandani and her husband cared for him, so she knew he was alright.

It was Connie's birthday next day, so we went to Southland with Christian and Athena to have lunch, and see a movie. We enjoyed yum cha, and after window shopping, Christian and Athena left, as they had to work. The three of us watched "Ghost Town," which was a good movie, and I enjoyed it very much.

It was almost seven o'clock when we returned, and I was about to serve dinner, when Roland, Shiranthi, Geraldine, Esme, and Paul dropped in unexpectedly at nine o'clock. I invited them for dinner, and it was a very late night when they finally left.

We drove to Geelong early next day, and thankfully, it was cool and cloudy. Josephine looked well, and we took her out for lunch to an Italian restaurant on the waterfront. Then she wanted to shop at Myers, and after dropping her, we returned after 7.30pm. Josephine was very happy to spend the day out, and we always treated her for lunch, for which she was very grateful. We also bought her whatever she needed, and she said, "You are like my daughter Dolly! I'm so lucky to have you for my friend!" When we came home, we relaxed and watched a movie till late.

Connie went out early next morning, on Saturday, and did not return till late evening. Shirani and Ranjith dropped in for a little while, and I took Nilanthi shopping afterwards. In the evening we watched, "The Man Who Knew Too Much" with James Stewart and Doris Day. Nilanthi and I loved watching old movies, and it was something we enjoyed sharing, as I owned most of the classic movies on DVD.

We shopped at Karingal next afternoon, and when we returned, Sherone, Glen, and family visited around four o'clock. We went for evening Mass, and Esme wanted us to drop in afterwards. We stopped there for a little while to see Aunty, and it was after eight thirty when we came home.

It was my birthday on Monday, but I was in school. Nilanthi boarded a bus to Frankston shopping centre that morning, and spent a couple of hours there. And Connie picked her up in the afternoon. It was a busy day at school, and I was tired when I came home. Connie and Nilanthi gave me presents, and as usual, he bought a few trinkets, earrings, a necklace, and perfume etc.

We dined at Rugantino's restaurant in Frankston, where Christian and Athena joined, and they came home with us afterwards. Athena sewed cushions till past midnight again, as she wanted to finish them soon. Connie went to bed as he was tired, but Nilanthi and I stayed up chatting with them, and had a late night.

I took Nilanthi out for lunch next day, with Athena and Dorothy, at Onde's Cafe in Mornington. We shopped later, but I came back in time for Alanah's lesson. Roland and Shiranthi dropped in unexpectedly around five o'clock that evening, and stayed for dinner. They brought a toy kitten in a basket, which looked very life-like. Misty settled down beside it and purred away. Connie thought it was real and asked, "*Why* did you bring another kitten? we don't want it!" We had a good laugh when he found out his mistake. After they left, Nilanthi and I watched a few episodes of "Bewitched." I felt weary and dizzy that night.

It was Ash Wednesday next day, so Connie and Nilanthi joined me for the 10am Mass at Frankston Church. I was in school, and the children attended Mass at 12 o'clock. It was another sizzling day, as the temperature soared to thirty three degrees, and I came home by two o'clock. We called Nelune to wish her for her birthday, then I watered the garden till late.

The next few days continued to be blistering and windy. Pat and Brian invited Nilanthi for a few days, and they picked her up on Friday evening. I had an early night, as I was very tired after a busy week.

Connie went out on Saturday morning to organize our trip to Queensland, as Nilanthi was keen to travel there. I spent a quiet day, then took it easy in the evening.

I played the piano for a while next morning, as Connie was still resting upstairs till late. I did not get much time to play the piano now, due to the extreme weather, my busy schedule, and entertaining Nilanthi. When he came down a little later, he bustled around, then started hammering nails in the store-room under the stairs. I stopped playing, and went to see what he was doing.

"Why do you have to hammer that *now* when I'm playing the piano?" I asked him reasonably. He rushed out with hammer in his hand and yelled back, "*What* other time do I have to do this?" I was taken aback at his fury, and asked, "Is that so important right now, can't you wait till I finish playing?" He ground his teeth and started shouting at the top of his voice. His temper was uncontrollable.

I was shocked at his animosity and violence for no reason at all. He looked so furious, that I thought he would strike me with the hammer, as he gnashed his teeth and scowled angrily. My heart thumped rapidly, as tears started. What made him so angry? I went upstairs without a word, grabbed my handbag, and rushed out of the house, and into the car. I drove off not knowing what I was doing, or where I was going, as my head was spinning.

I cried all the way to Karingal, as I did not know where else to go. When I stopped there, I sipped a coffee, and waited till I felt calm enough to return home. My mobile rang. It was Connie. "*Sorry*, Dolla, I didn't mean to shout at you! Where are you?" "I'm at Karingal, and I'm too upset to come home right now. What made you shout and carry on like that? I don't deserve to be treated like that." He mumbled, "I'm so stressed out at work, and I have too much on my mind. I didn't mean to take it out on you. I'm sorry Dolla. Come home now."

When I returned after an hour or so, he was repentant, and tried to pretend nothing was wrong, but I felt sick and dizzy all day. He was ready to go to church at five thirty though. I asked Holy Communion for Ninette, which I usually gave her on Tuesday.

When I woke up next day, I was very dizzy, and my head felt heavy. I wondered if my blood pressure was high, as I stayed up watching a movie till late last night, just to unwind, and Connie went to bed.

I made an appointment to see Dr Khelil that morning. I told him how I felt, and what brought it on, as I was extremely stressed. My blood pressure was very high, and he prescribed medication. He advised me on how to deal with such situations, and to avoid conflict with Connie, especially if he was violent and aggressive.

I came home early from school, as Connie was flying to Sydney on business that afternoon. I rested a while, and did exercises for vertigo, but nothing helped, and the dizziness was very severe. Pam and Alan dropped Nilanthi that evening, and I served some nibbles and drinks, and we chatted till late. After they left, I told Nilanthi what happened on Sunday morning, and that I was not feeling too well. She was upset and very concerned.

The following day was cloudy and warm, with gusty winds, but not too hot, so we visited Ninette. She walked with us to a Chinese shop nearby, after my lesson, and bought two sun-hats and scarves for us. And she also gave me one of her piano recordings on a CD for my birthday. After Nilanthi and I did some shopping, we came back in time for piano lessons.

I did not feel as dizzy that day, thank goodness. Christian and Athena dropped in later, and they gave me a large microwave for my birthday. I was very pleased and surprised. Christian set it up, and then we had a nice time chatting and laughing over dinner. I did not tell Christian what happened with Connie, and how my blood pressure was so high that I was on medication now.

The weather cooled down over the next few days, with strong winds and showers at times. It was about nineteen degrees, which was quite pleasant. Peter, Astrid, and family visited Nilanthi one evening, and left around eight o'clock. Connie said he would arrive home around nine thirty that night. When he came home, he said he was exhausted, and after a few drinks, he went to bed early night. He did not want any dinner, as he had stopped for a snack on his way. Nilanthi and I watched a movie till late.

We finally had good rainfall, after nearly three months of scorching, dry weather, and it was pleasant and cool. I drove to Springvale with Nilanthi, as she wanted to look around there. When we returned, Penny visited in the evening. I made dinner after serving them some snacks and tea, and they chatted for a couple of hours.

Although the weather was much cooler, and we had some heavy rain, bush fires still burned in Victoria. Josephine wanted to know when we were visiting her again. And I told her we were going to Queensland for a few days, and would try to see her when we returned. She was very disappointed, and said, "I'm longing to see you again, Dolly. Come soon." I promised I would, and spoke to her for some time.

I bought groceries and items that Nilanthi wanted, besides shoes, and clothes, then packed a few boxes to send before the end of the month.

We visited Elvira and John next day, on Saturday, and enjoyed a delicious afternoon tea, as she baked scones and biscuits. Then we dropped in to see Christian and Athena. Nilanthi too was very impressed when she saw the work he did in the garden. On our way back, we walked on the boardwalk and pier in Frankston.

We drove to Woolamai on Sunday afternoon, and had a great time, as we enjoyed a barbeque, and relaxed a couple of hours. It was very pleasant and warm, and we came back by late evening. I made jam with peaches from Elvira's garden, and jelly, with passion fruits from Christian's garden. Then we watched a movie till late, and Connie stayed up for a while, but said he was too tired and went to bed.

Labour Day, on Monday, 9 March, was a public holiday, so I rested late. It was beautiful and sunny, and Nilanthi sat under the jacaranda tree, watching Misty ambling around slowly in the garden. Connie made chilli sambal, and pounded with the pestle in the mortar.

We went to Dromana after breakfast, and Connie drove past Mount Martha, to show Nilanthi the block of land on the hill top, that we considered buying a few years ago. When we returned, I made thosai and beef curry for dinner, and Christian and Athena dropped in around nine o'clock. After we enjoyed a pleasant evening, they left around midnight. I went to bed too, as we were too tired to watch any movies.

I took Misty for her cortisone injection early next day, and we visited Ninette in the afternoon. She made a light snack for lunch, and we had a good time laughing and chatting with her. And after some shopping, we came back in time for piano lessons. Misty looked subdued after her injection, but I was happy to see that she was moving around alright.

I was busy at school on Monday, and in the evening, Christian and Athena dropped in, and we enjoyed dinner with them. Christian broke a couple of toes while doing Tae Kwondo a few days ago, and his foot was injured too. I was very concerned, as he was in a great deal of pain. But he did not complain, and never did, no matter how badly injured he was. But I was very upset, as I did not want him to get injured doing Tae Kwondo.

I steeled myself to leave Misty in the cattery the day before we went to the Gold Coast, on Saturday morning. I was extremely sad to leave her, as she was in such a pitiful condition, but the cage was heated. And she was content to snuggle up in her basket and go to sleep. She hardly mewed on the way to the cattery, which was unusual, because she was very vocal in her protests when boarded. I tried to forget about her, and decided to make the most of the next few days on the Gold Coast with Nilanthi. Nelune said she would join us there, instead of flying to Melbourne to see Nilanthi. So we looked forward to seeing her.

We arrived at Coolangatta airport around two o'clock on Saturday afternoon, and the weather was great. After checking in at our apartment in Xanadu, we drove to the shops to buy groceries. Nilanthi loved the warm weather and holiday atmosphere. And we enjoyed a spa and sauna in the evening. I cooked beef curry and rice for dinner, and later, we walked along the beach for a while.

We drove to Brisbane city next morning, and kept driving around, as parking was difficult and very dear. It was not a very pleasant day, and the city looked dreary. We had lunch outside the city, in Springwood Centre, and then came back to the apartment. After shopping at Pacific Fair Centre, we enjoyed a spa and sauna in the evening. Then after dinner, we walked on the beach, as the nights were so warm and balmy.

We went to pick Nelune at Coolangatta airport next day, but she arrived on an earlier flight, and was already waiting for us. She looked well, and I was so happy to see her again. We stopped for lunch in a Chinese restaurant at Surfers Paradise. And Connie gave the waiter a hard time, demanding everything that was not on the menu!

He argued with the hapless waiter, and complained to the manager, while Nelune, Nilanthi, and I, looked on with amusement. Connie refused to be pleased in that restaurant or anywhere else. Nelune gave me two hundred dollars to give Nilanthi once she left. And said, "I don't want to see Nilanthi crying, because that's what she'll do when I give her money, so please wait till I'm on the plane, before you give her the money." And true to her word, Nilanthi's tears gushed, when I gave her the money, and told her what Nelune said.

Con and Cornelia were holidaying on the Gold Coast too, and they invited us for dinner that night. But we declined, as we had to drop Nelune at the airport, and it would have been very late. It was a lovely sunny day, but suddenly, the skies turned black. A severe thunderstorm approached, followed by heavy rain around six o'clock in the evening.

We dropped Nelune at the airport, but the plane did not take off till very late, due to bad weather. I removed some photographs from the balcony of the spectacular cloud formations, just as the storm broke out. I never witnessed such a fierce, tropical storm before. I went for a swim and a spa before dinner, and Nilanthi enjoyed the spa as well.

We had leftovers for dinner, but Connie insisted on a pizza. It was still raining very heavily, but he told us, "I'm going to find a pizza parlour somewhere around." He returned with a pizza, a couple of hours later, and said, "The only place open, was in the red light district, so I had to stop there to get a pizza. All sorts of kinky people were staring at me." I did not respond, as I knew he was just being perverse as usual, wanting to eat something that we did not have. I said, "It would be good to finish all the cooked food, so we can clean up the fridge, but now there's more leftover pizza."

Connie raced ahead at the airport, and left us trailing behind, till he attended to the flight details. It was very tiring keeping up with him. I was glad to be returning, and looked forward to seeing Misty again, as I was very sad about her. We arrived in Melbourne around midday, and went to pick up Misty that afternoon, as I was very anxious to bring her home. She seemed alright and well-cared for, but I was sure she was glad to be back in her familiar surroundings. Christian and Athena dropped in later, and I made a quick dinner, and after a pleasant evening, we went to bed late.

I was at school next day, but came home early in the afternoon to take Nilanthi to Ninette's, as she wanted to wish her goodbye. Luigi was at Ninette's, and Nilanthi met him for the first time. He was quite interested to chat with her about spiritual matters, and asked her to come back again. Then we drove to Karingal for some last minute shopping.

Nilanthi gave me some red roses, and a "Thank you" card, as she said she appreciated everything I did to make her welcome and happy. I had to drive to Mornington to pick up newsletters next day, but the car would not start again. And it was around eleven o'clock by the time RACV came and fixed it. When I returned shortly afterwards, Roland and Shiranthi were there, and they told me all about Bab's and Patrick's wedding, which we missed, as we were away on the 17th. They showed all the photographs taken at the reception. I was surprised to see Babs in a sari for the first time.

They stayed for lunch, and then I drove to Shirani's for a brief visit. Shirani insisted we have dinner at five o'clock, as Roshan, June, and the children were there too. We came home and took it easy, and watched some comedies till late. Christian and Athena dropped in too, and Connie drove Nilanthi to see Aunty, as she wanted to wish her goodbye.

Nilanthi left next day, Friday, 20 March. Shiranthi and Roland dropped in again, and left before we drove to the airport in the afternoon. I felt very sad to see her leave, and she always cried so much, that I had to be very strong and not break down. I told her she could look forward to another holiday next year, and not to weep so much.

I gave her half the airfare each time she left, and told her I would send her the other half, when she was ready for her next trip. This consoled her, as she knew she would be able to return soon. Christian and Nelune gave her many mobiles, laptops, and other items that she sold, and collected some money towards her expenses. And I collected knick knacks, and electrical items for her too.

Connie always wanted to know how many students I had, and how much money I earned, because he wanted me to deposit everything into our joint account. He did not like me to keep any of my wages, so I deposited most of my earnings into our joint account and saved some of it.

Whenever I called her, Nilanthi told me how homesick she was for us, and how much she missed us. And this time she said we had so much fun and laughter over the last five weeks, that it was very sad to return to her mundane and tiring life, looking after Heron. As Chandani, and her husband, cared for Heron at their place, until Nilanthi returned, she enjoyed a good break, without worrying about his welfare.

We came home after six o'clock in the evening, once she checked in at four o'clock. I hoped she would have a safe journey home.

Chapter 47

Nilanthi called early next morning to say she arrived safely, and I was relieved. Although I missed her, I had to get through several chores, and was busy all day. It was another sizzling thirty three degrees, and I did not get much sleep that night. I woke up at two o'clock in the morning, had a warm drink, and then rested on the sofa downstairs. I finally fell asleep around three o'clock. I packed a few more boxes, with all the clothes and items that Nilanthi was unable to take. Connie taped them up, and took them to the freight company next day.

The following days were busy, but Nilanthi and I called each other a few times during the week. I posted home-made jam, and Christmas cake for Nelune, and she sent me some pretty cardigans by mail. I spent the next few evenings typing up the manuscript for "Wild Poppies," a collection of short stories and poems that I wanted to publish at the end of the year.

I consulted Dr Khelil a few days later, as I did not feel too well. He checked my blood pressure twice, and said it was too high, and asked if I was stressed or worried. I told him ever since that day, when Connie behaved in that violent manner, I was prone to severe headaches and dizziness, and did not sleep very well. He asked me to take it easy and try to relax, but said he would increase the medication, if my pressure continued to be high.

We drove to Waneet on the weekend, a place that we often passed on our way to Woolamai, but never stopped to look around. But it turned out to be a horrid little place, full of mosquitoes, and derelict buildings by the seashore. We did not stay long, as I wanted to get away from the buzzing insects as quickly as possible.

Then we drove to Shoreham and Rosebud, and walked on the beach, and we returned late in the evening. I did some chores next day, and hemmed Connie's slacks, but the headache persisted. I tried meditation, hoping it would ease, and my pressure would come down, but to no avail.

When I visited Ninette the following Tuesday, I took my blood pressure on her monitor, and it was still high. But I stayed with her a couple of hours, and we listened to some music that she recorded.

The students came for piano lessons, and I was very pleased with Sarah's progress, as she was doing very well. She learned several pop songs on her own, and sang while she accompanied herself. I was getting tired though, and looked forward to school holidays at the end of March. And I worked on my manuscript for a few hours every evening.

Nilanthi asked me to paint the Assumption of Our Lady, for their flag, when the annual procession took place there. I told her I would try, and so I started sketching from a holy picture. When Christian dropped in later, I was very concerned, because he injured his feet and arms at Tae Kwondo again! We had a long chat, and he spent some time with me, as Athena was at work.

I started painting for about two hours next day, and hoped to have it finished in a few weeks. Christian said he would screen print the painting onto a heavy, plastic material that they could use for a flag.

I attended to my usual routine on the weekend, as Connie woke up at midday, and then went out to visit his mother, or do her shopping. He lost interest in the garden, and did not weed or mow the grass for weeks. All he did on weekends was sleep half the day, and then visit his mother and siblings. I did not mind, as I enjoyed the peace, and finished my tasks without him to worry me. As he was unable to communicate with me, without flying into a temper, it was best to leave him alone.

The weather was much cooler now, and daylight saving ended on Sunday, 5 April, which was Elvira's birthday. I called to wish her, and we chatted for some time, then discussed her play, which we hoped to stage soon.

The painting turned out better than I hoped. But I did not want anyone to see it until it was completed, not even Connie, as I did not want to hear any negative comments.

Nilanthi's relatives, Emmanuel and Jasmine, were returning after a holiday in Melbourne, and were prepared to take the painting and the flag. As I painted it on canvas cloth, it was easy to roll it up and the flag too.

In between my work, I kept painting a few hours each evening, until my eyes grew too tired.

One of Connie's acquaintances from Sri Lanka, Bro. Leander, visited Melbourne on 8 April. He was now an ordained Catholic priest. Roland and Connie wanted to meet him in Craigieburn, and bring him down to meet Aunty. Connie drove early in the morning, and called me at about eleven o'clock to say he was bringing his friend and Roland home. But I told him I was shopping in the afternoon. Then he called again to say they would visit his mother instead.

I was not particularly interested in meeting their friend Leander, so I spent some time at the shops, and came home after two o'clock. Christian and Athena dropped in later that night, and Connie came home after ten o'clock. He drove back to Craigieburn to drop his friend off, and told me that he gave him hundred dollars as well.

I could not understand Connie at all. Because, all through the years, he told me that when he was in the novitiate, Bro. Leander had a reputation for paying unwanted attention to young boys. And once, when he had a rash on his upper thigh, Bro. Leander wanted to apply lotion. But Connie refused him, and told him off quite strongly.

Connie complained to his superior, and told him that he wanted to leave the novitiate, because he thought that a religious Brother should not behave like that. But the superior persuaded him to reconsider his decision. Connie told me very often that Bro. Leander tried to fondle him too, while pretending to apply lotion on his thigh. So, I had the impression that the man was a paedophile.

I asked Connie why he took so much trouble and time to please this man, who had such a dubious reputation. To which he replied, "*That* was all a long time ago, and he was very happy to meet us and Mummy."

A few weeks later, Connie received a letter from Leander, addressing only him, and not a word about me. He sent his good wishes to Connie's mother and siblings, ending with a request for more money. I told him I did not see why he should send him money at all, and do not know if Connie complied with his request or not. But I found his behaviour quite inexplicable.

I woke up at two o'clock on Good Friday morning, as Misty was full of beans and very frisky. I was happy to see her so active, but it was too early in the morning to enjoy her frolics, so I left her in the garage till about six o'clock. We went to church at two thirty in the afternoon, for Good Friday services. And I met Jordee my past student, her mother, Mara, and grandmother, Nellie. Jordee looked very grown-up now, and we spoke for a little while before they left. We walked on the pier later, and came home before too late.

Connie was furious next day, for some reason or other, and we had another pointless argument, which made me feel heart-sick and desolate. I wished I knew the answer to our continuous quarrels and arguments, and wondered what to do. He went out at eleven o'clock to play golf, with his friend Graham. I called my friends, then Josephine, Ninette, Nilanthi, Shirani, and Nelune, and wished them for Easter next day.

We drove to Woolamai in the afternoon, when he returned from his game of golf, as it was a pleasant day. The renovations in the restaurant looked great, and Shirani did a terrific job with the interior. We spent a little time there, and then drove to Wonthaggi, where I bought twenty four, earthy- coloured cups to match the restaurant decor. We dropped in again on our way home, and I gave them to Shirani, who was very pleased. It was late evening when we came home.

It was beautiful and sunny on Easter Sunday, and we attended morning Mass, where I met some friends from school and my piano students. I packed steaks, sausages, and snacks, and we drove down to Dromana for a barbeque. We visited Christian and Athena on our way, and came home late.

My pressure continued to be high over the next few days, and although I tried to relax, paint, and play the piano, it did not come down.

I saw doctor again, and he prescribed a different medication, which I bought, and then visited Shirani in Narre Warren. We spent a pleasant afternoon, and I told her the reason I was so stressed, and why my pressure did not come down. She was very sad and concerned, but I had no way out of my present situation. I was unable to sleep at nights, and woke up feeling worn-out the next day.

When I searched on the internet, I found an animator in Sri Lanka, who said he could animate "Catsville" for a very reasonable cost. I posted some cat pictures to him, and hoped something positive would come out of this. He was very impressed with the story line, and wanted to take on the job. And he also asked if he could translate the story into Sinhalese. But I did not give him permission to do that until my project was completed.

I woke up at two o'clock next morning, and wrote down all the titles of short stories and poems for my forthcoming publication. I called Dymocks at Southland later on, to find out if they sold any more copies of my book. They did not, but were happy to stock them for as long as I wanted.

I painted for a couple of hours on the weekend, and then we drove to Berwick, to look at eleven display homes. Connie constantly badgered me now to sell the house in Frankston, and move to a larger block, where he could grow lavender when he retired. He dreamed of a lavender hobby-farm, and told me that he was not interested in maintaining the garden, or the house in Frankston any longer. We started looking around for a large block of land close to the sea.

We drove to Mornington on Sunday, 19 April, and looked at real estate shops there. I browsed through a local newspaper and showed Connie an advertisement; newly released, large blocks of land for sale in Mount Martha, close to Elvira's and John's place. After a cup of coffee in Main Street, we drove to that area. The views were magnificent, and the street aptly named, "Waterview Drive." The agent drove us to a block, which sloped to a reserve below.

A few houses were already built there, but mostly they were vacant blocks. And the one he showed us for three hundred and sixty thousand dollars, had great views. We made an offer, as he said the owners were keen to sell. I hoped we could purchase it, because it was such a superb area. We attended evening Mass at Frankston, and came home at seven o'clock. Connie liked that block of land very much too, but he said he would not go beyond the offer he made. So I hoped for the best.

It was the first day of term two next day, and not many students started that week. I came home early, as Connie took time off to meet a financial advisor in Mornington, regarding the land purchase. We drove to the block again, and watched a beautiful sunset over the ocean. I wished with all my heart we could build a house on this splendid block, but I left it in God's hands.

I still did not sleep well, and was awake till three o'clock in the morning. This insomnia was taking its toll, but I drove to Ninette's next day, as she wanted to shop at Patterson Lakes. We did not spend more than twenty minutes there, and after I dropped Ninette, I came home at three o'clock, but Connie was still out. When he arrived a little later, we drove to Lyndhurst to look at more display homes, and returned late in the evening. Christian and Athena dropped in, and brought some fish that Connie had left behind in the fish shop at Mornington earlier that day. He had told them to pick the parcel before the shop closed.

I woke up at three thirty next morning, and could not go back to sleep, because I had a vivid dream of Stacy again. He kept saying, "Open the door Mum, I can't get inside the house!" His hair was completely grey, and he wore a cap. Every time I dreamed of Stacy, it left me with an aching heart. And it took me a while to get over my vivid dreams, because I tried to interpret their meaning all day. I wondered if he was thinking of me, and trying to send a message through telepathy.

I spoke to Nilanthi that day, and when I told her the painting was almost finished, she was very pleased, and said that the parish priest too was eager to see it and the flag. I continued painting that day, as Christian wanted to take a photograph of it, and screen print it onto a flag.

It rained next day, and was very cold, but the rain was welcome after the drought and heat wave over the last few months. Elvira called to ask about the play, and we set a date to meet and discuss the project. Then I phoned Mary to ask how Tony was, as I heard he was unwell.

Connie went out early in the morning that weekend, to play golf with a friend. I tried to ride the exercise bike, but I got tired very easily, and was short of breath, so I did not do thirty minutes like before. When Connie returned, we drove to Pakenham to look at more display homes in the afternoon. But we did not like any of them, and were not impressed with the Jennings Homes.

One of the ladies, Leanne, remembered us when we met her to discuss building the Villa Tudor back in 1996. She asked us now, "*Why* are you thinking of selling that beautiful home?" and I replied, "We love the house very much, but want to build on a larger block of land." But she shook her head in disbelief, as none of the current display homes could compare with the appealing design, and grandeur of the Villa Tudor.

We attended Mass on Sunday evening as usual, and Maureen asked if I would like to be a special minister, and take Holy Communion to sick people. I agreed, as I was already taking it for Ninette.

Babs and Patrick went to Sri Lanka for a couple of weeks after their wedding, and on their return, they went their separate ways. He, to his house in Adelaide, and Babs, to emergency housing in Melbourne. She called me and said that her marriage was a "big mistake" as he was an alcoholic. And he was not sober from morning till night when they were in Sri Lanka. It was a shock, but I knew she rushed into marriage, without getting to know him better. When she visited a few days later, she elaborated on the details. I sympathised with her, because she believed he was the right one this time. Some family members ostracized her for this unfortunate mistake, and treated her with contempt. She came over often, and stayed with us, as I pitied her for being taken in so easily.

Chapter 48

The next few days were freezing and wet, and I wanted to buy a heat lamp for Misty, as she slept in the garage where it was very cold at nights. I could not find one anywhere, so I bought an oil heater, as it was safe to leave it on all night. Misty was warm and cosy now, and loved dozing in front of that heater.

Although I still felt tired and dizzy most of the time, my blood pressure was low, and I had a persistent dry cough that would not go away. When I saw doctor next day, he said I had a chest infection, and prescribed antibiotics.

Nilanthi was happy when the boxes arrived at the end of April, and she kept thanking me for sending so many things. I was glad, because I wanted her to have all the things she liked, in the way of clothes, shoes, and food.

I received Alice Landau's autobiography, "Snippets from my family album" that day. She belonged to the Society of Women Writers too, and was a lovely person, who had an interesting story, about her escape from Europe to Australia during World War Two. I started reading it immediately, and enjoyed her story of survival, and settling down in Australia.

Next day, I spoke to her, and told her I was enjoying reading her story. She was pleased, and invited me to one of her famous "high teas" as she was an excellent chef. I said I would try to make it, but she lived very far away over the city, so I had to find some time.

The bank sent a valuer that afternoon, and after he left I went out to get some groceries. Although my chest was still painful, I did not want to stay in bed, as there were too many things to do. I was up all night, as the cough was worse. And I got out of bed at three o'clock, to take some hot lemon and honey.

An estate agent appraised our house next day, as we had to sell it first, in order to proceed with the new house in Mount Martha. We met a nice lady, Badiha, who stayed till late evening, then had a coffee afterwards. She promised to get a fair price for our house, as she exclaimed, "It's beautiful and immaculately kept, so it should fetch a good price." After she left, Connie went to shop for Aunty, and came home a few hours later.

I offered to do her grocery shopping many times, as he had too much to do with his job, but he insisted on doing it himself. He came home angry and tired every time he shopped for her, and said, "That *wretch* Bella is staying with Mummy, and she criticized *everything* I bought, saying it was the wrong brand, or Mummy didn't like that particular item. I lost my temper and wanted to slap her, as she was so nasty and annoying!" I did not say anything, because I knew it was no good telling him to ignore his sister, as they were constantly at loggerheads.

The year before, on Melbourne Cup Day, we drove to Rosebud to enjoy a relaxed day, when Cristobel called Connie and said, "Connie, go to Mummy's place *immediately*! She's alone, and wants to bet on a horse!" He did not refuse or ask me, but drove to her place at once. When we got there, Aunty was sleeping, and not at all interested in the races, or placing a bet on a horse. But we stayed a couple of hours, and she said, "What nonsense, I'm not lonely! Molly will be here soon, and I was just resting a little."

I slept in on Sunday, as I felt weak with the cough and chest infection, but we went for a drive in the afternoon. I dropped some warm clothes, and food items at the church, for St Vincent's Charity appeal. Shirani called later to say she had nine customers for dinner, and I was very pleased for her, as she worked very hard to promote her new restaurant.

The persistent cough lasted a very long time, and I just had to put up with it and the insomnia. Connie worked from home on the computer till almost three o'clock in the afternoon, and after he left, I did chores, and then called Ninette. She was very upset, as her dog Max, had died suddenly the night before, on 3 May. She said it just dropped dead, but I knew he was ailing for some time, was totally blind, and thirteen years old. The poor dog was at peace, but I understood how she felt, and tried to console her. She was already talking about getting another dog, as she was very lonely without a pet.

When Sarah came for her lesson, Misty was very frisky, and poked her nose into Tracy's handbag, then jumped all over the chairs. I could hardly believe she was the same ailing cat, but was glad that the cortisone injections were helping her.

When I visited Ninette next day, I did not play the piano too long, as I felt unwell. But I just went there for a chat, as she was so depressed about her dog. When Alanah came for her lesson that evening, I gave her some blank canvases, as she liked to paint, so she was very happy. I started clearing up unwanted things from the studio, and bedrooms, in preparation for the sale of the house.

We got some documents signed and witnessed at the chemist's, on 6 May, and later that afternoon, Connie rang to say that the bank approved the loan for the land purchase. I was elated! I thanked God for his blessings, because I really liked that beautiful area in Mount Martha.

Christian called to say that Athena's job was made redundant, and they were very disappointed. When Nancy rang, I cancelled coffee next day, as I was feverish, and down with flu. Christian and Athena dropped in for a chat that evening, and we stayed up late. I hoped she would find another job soon, because she was happy going out to work these last couple of months.

The painting was ready at last, and I wanted Christian to draw the halo around Our Lady, because he had a very steady fist, and an excellent eye. He did a perfect job, and finally, it was finished. Athena too was impressed with the painting, and they took photographs of it for the flag.

Nilanthi called to say she picked up the rest of the boxes, but was very tired and stressed, as it took all morning to clear them at customs. All the items arrived safely though, and she was happy to distribute clothes, food, and cash to the poor. She said they blessed me, and sent thanks, but I did not want any thanks, as long as I could help the needy in any little way.

Josephine called on Thursday night, to ask if we were visiting that weekend. When I told her that we were, and taking her out for lunch, she was very happy. I visited Ninette on Friday afternoon, and gave her a potted chrysanthemum plant, and chocolates, for Mother's Day on Sunday. She was still upset about Max, and said that she was very depressed. I spent some time with her, and when I came home a couple of hours later, Misty was still sleeping indoors, from about nine o'clock that morning. I let her out for fresh air, but she seemed to love her warm basket in the garage, as I kept the oil heater on whenever she was there.

Josephine called again that night, and asked what time we were coming, and I said around lunch time. But she always said, "Come in the morning, and stay till dinner time." And she always got annoyed when we left in the evening. But she did not understand how tiring it was to drive to Geelong, spend all day with her, and then return home late at night.

On our way to Geelong next morning, Connie was in a foul mood, and when I asked him what was bothering him, he shouted, "I want to take Mummy around in a wheelchair, and spend time with her! We're doing all this for a stranger, when I should be doing it for my own mother!" I replied, "But you do enough for your mother, and she has all her children around her, to take her out and do her shopping. Josephine is so lonely, with no one to visit her, and spend time with her."

But he continued arguing, and yelled at the top of his voice so angrily, that I felt sick at heart, just listening to his pointless arguments. My head started throbbing, as it always did when he shouted, and used foul language. Once again, the argument was over something quite unreasonable and futile.

He did not want to spend time with anyone else except his mother and siblings, that was the sore point, I understood. As it was, he visited his mother almost every evening and weekend. And he dropped in to see his siblings on his way to or from work, so I did not know how much more time he wanted to spend with them.

I did not speak to him till we arrived, as I did not want to hear any more abuse. But he changed his attitude when we reached Geelong, as Josephine looked so frail and ill, that I could not help feeling sorry for her. She smiled and said, "You are an *angel!* You have come to see me, and I'm going to have a happy day! Connie, you are so good to me! Better than my own sons!" I looked at him, and he did not meet my eyes. I hoped he was ashamed of his outburst.

We took her out to lunch, and then shopping, and I pushed her in the wheelchair around the shops. Connie tagged along, shame-faced, as he tried to talk to me, and mumbled, "I'm sorry Dolla." But I knew it was just meaningless, as he would only repeat his bad behaviour. Josephine was turning ninety on 13 May that year, so we treated her to a delicious lunch, then took her on a shopping spree, and paid for all the items she bought at Myers, as a birthday gift.

When I wished Josephine goodbye, I wondered if I would see her again, as she looked very tired and ill. She blessed me, and said in Italian, "I will love you till I die." It was sad to leave her, but we rushed to Caroline Springs before five o'clock, as we wanted to look at some display homes there.

We barely made it, as it was ten minutes to five when they closed the centre. But we had a quick look around, and did not find anything we liked, so we drove back, and arrived home by seven o'clock. I was exhausted, and did not think I could go through such a day again; to travel all the way to Geelong, starting off with an argument, and putting up with Connie's foul language and black moods along the way.

I woke up early on Sunday, Mother's Day. Shiranthi and Geraldine called to wish me. And Connie took time to phone all his sisters, and nieces to wish them. We drove down to see Aunty later, and I gave her a bouquet of flowers and chocolates, and Connie gave a bottle of brandy. Then we went to Christian's, and they made a superb lunch, that I enjoyed very much.

Athena made a delicious chocolate mousse to finish off the meal, and we had a great time laughing and chatting. We drove to the block of land afterwards, and I removed some photographs. It was late evening when we came home.

I drove to Karingal early next day, to get some snacks for tea, as Elvira was visiting that afternoon to go through the play. Connie worked from home till about two o'clock, as he woke up late now, worked on his computer, and then came home after eight or nine o'clock almost daily. That afternoon, as he drove out of the garage, without looking back, he reversed straight into Elvira's new car that was parked in our driveway. He was sorry, and apologized to her, but she said not to worry about it, as it was a small dent on the side of the car.

I felt very bad and upset about it, but she was very nice, and did not make a fuss. Anyway, after he left, we settled down, and finished a fair amount of work on the play, before she left in a couple of hours time.

When Sarah came for her lesson that evening, I asked her if she would like to take part in the play, and she said she would consider. Christian and Athena said they would drop in later, so I quickly made some dinner, but it was after eight o'clock when they arrived.

We drove to Mornington on 12 May to sign documents for the bank loan, then to Berwick, and met Leanne, at Metricon Homes. Although they had some good designs, they were not too flexible about any modifications to the plans, so we did not select anything there. We came home late, and I was very tired, but I watched news, and the budget speech. And I was appalled to hear the budget deficit was now in the billions! Not very good news for Australians.

Although I still felt the after effects of flu, I went to school on Wednesday, but stayed in on Thursday, as I was getting chills and sweats. I hoped I was not catching a cold again. Christian said he could do the banner that week, and I was happy.

I did some chores on Saturday morning, then made sausage rolls and pastries. Connie said he had to fix taps in Aunty's flat, and left in the morning, and did not come back till four o'clock in evening.

He was pottering in the garden when he returned, and I asked him, "Why did you get so late? We have to go for the play before seven." He yelled back at the top of his voice, "What do you *think* I was doing? Sitting on my mother's arse?" I replied, "Don't shout, all the neighbours can hear you." He did not care, and rushed around while I got ready.

We left home at six forty five, for the play that was going to start at seven thirty, at the Briars in Mount Martha. I was always so stressed whenever we went for a play or concert, as I knew they would not wait for us. But he just did not make an effort to be punctual.

We met Elvira and John at the play, as I asked them to come for it too. Connie told them he would get his insurance to fix Elvira's car, but they refused, as John said his insurance would take care of it. Connie admitted it was his fault, and in the end, his insurance paid for repairs. Karen and Stuart came too, and I stopped to chat with them during interval. The Nomad Players were very good, but the leading character, Napoleon, needed a great deal of prompting.

Ginny told me later, that the person who was to play that part fell ill, and the understudy stepped in. It was an original play," From Roses To Poison" by a local playwright. And it was about Napoleon's exile, and his connection with the original owners of the Briars, in Mount Martha.

We left home in the afternoon next day, to see more display homes in Narre Warren South. And we saw a Porter Davis house that we liked, and wanted to discuss the cost etc. so we made an appointment with the agent. We returned home late.

Shirani was in Woolamai, as she had lunch and dinner bookings, so we did not visit her that day. She was doing a great job at the restaurant, and I was very proud of her efforts. We attended evening Mass, and Maureen asked us to be special ministers on the following Sunday, to which we agreed. I watched television for a while, and Connie worked on his computer till very late that night.

He never came to bed before midnight, and sometimes, he played music so loud, that I told tell him to lower the volume, as I was trying to sleep. He liked to sleep in on weekends, and wanted me to do the same. But I did not want to waste time sleeping during the day, when there was so much to do. So, we did not have much of a sex life now, which dwindled to once in six months, and then petered out to every twelve months or so.

Dr Khelil prescribed Viagra for his erectile problems, but he did not want to take any medication, give up smoking, reduce his alcohol intake, or take up exercise. He was moody, irritable, and ready to flare up at the slightest provocation, and without any reason most of the time.

I hoped a change of scene, and something to look forward to, with the building of a new house, would make him happy. Frankly though, nothing on earth could make him happy, as I knew by now. Why I persisted in thinking he would be pleased about this move, I did not know.

Esme and Paul dropped in often at eight or nine o'clock in the night, and Roland and Shiranthi too, always visited late at night, when Roland finished work. It did not matter to them, if Connie and I were tired after a busy day. And as he usually came home very late, they stayed till he arrived, had dinner with us, and left at midnight. Esme and Paul did not stay for dinner though, as they ate early, and came for a coffee or a drink.

When I asked Connie to tell them to visit us in the afternoon, or at a reasonable time, when we were not so tired, he replied, "I've told them, but they don't listen to me. Why don't you tell them not to come so late at night?" This was a constant source of irritation, and I dreaded the evenings, when one of them barged in to disturb us. Babs did not come as often now, but when she did, she stayed overnight and left next day.

Once, when Babs stayed overnight, and woke up in the morning, we started talking. And she asked me if Connie still drank a lot, because every time she visited, he drank heavily and argued with her. I replied, "He drinks every night." He walked in on our conversation just then, and told Babs off for talking about him. She said it was just in passing, as she wanted us to get along and be happy.

He was really annoyed with me too for telling Babs about his drinking. I said, "There's no need for me to say anything, because she can see for herself how you behave when you've had too much." He stormed off, and did not talk to me all day.

I took Misty for her cortisone injection on Monday, 18 May, then came home and prepared the newsletters for posting. Connie was still working at home on the computer, and left at three o'clock, when I returned.

I visited Ninette on Tuesday afternoon, but I cancelled piano lessons with my students that evening, as we had to sign documents in Mornington for the loan settlement.

I was at school on Wednesday in spite of being unwell, and most of the children were down with coughs and colds too. I thought I had picked up a virus, and came home early. Then Connie and I drove to Narre Warren at one o'clock to meet Lara, regarding the Porter Davis house.

She took us through the luxurious house that we were interested in. I hoped we could build that house with a few slight modifications, as it was a good, practical design. We dropped in at Shirani's later, but she was out walking, so we stayed till she returned, had a cup of tea, and then came home.

I drove to Mornington Library on the 21st, to participate in the "Biggest Tea" celebrating local authors, which the library organized. It was a great event, and I met some very interesting local authors, including Marika, who wrote the play, "From Roses To Poison" that we recently saw at the Briars. Cathy was an editor for a local newspaper, and I enjoyed chatting to local celebrities. Then I drove to Main Street Printers, to get more copies of Elvira's play.

Another sleepless night, and I woke up before dawn and took more lemon and honey, as the cough was so irritating, especially at nights. I slept in late next morning, then spoke to Nilanthi, Nelune, and Ninette. Then I spent some time cooking curries etc. for tomorrow's dinner for Con and Cornelia.

It was Ammie's thirteenth death anniversary, on 23 May, so I said a special prayer for her. I still missed Ammie very much, and thought of her life with sadness. It was a pity that she never came on a holiday to enjoy some luxuries and pampering.

I spent the day cooking and cleaning up, and was about to rest for a while, when Babs dropped in unexpectedly. I was sorry for her when she related all her woes, and how she had to manage on her own now. She said Patrick lied to her about having property in Sri Lanka. He posed as a wealthy man, but owned only a very old, weather-board house in Adelaide.

She was very disillusioned, to say the least, but the Housing Commission gave her a one-bedroom unit in Brighton, so she had a place to stay. She left late, and I could not rest, as Con and Cornelia came just after six o'clock. We had a pleasant evening, and they left after midnight.

I woke up feeling feverish, so I took it easy next day. Emmanuel called to say he could take the painting on 3 June. Connie agreed to drop the banner and painting at Craigieburn, where they were staying.

I did not go to school next day, as I was very ill and coughed all night. When I saw doctor, he told me to stop taking pressure tablets, as they sometimes caused a dry cough, but he did a blood test as well. Connie worked on the computer at home, and in-between, he shouted at some contractor or another over the phone. He told me, "Be quiet, and don't play the piano because I'm on the phone." I loved playing the piano for at least an hour when I could, but now I had to be as quiet as possible until he left.

We argued about that too, as I told him that he should work at his office, as I had to play the piano, and do my usual work at home. But he did not listen, as he stayed home till very late in the afternoon, and then drove to work, where he stayed till night.

He was just impossible to talk to, and I asked him to shut the study door when he was on the phone, so I did not have to hear him yelling. But he never did, because he liked to stand in the middle of the kitchen or dining room and shout at the top of his voice.

Sarah came for her lesson that evening, but I spoke to Ninette later, and cancelled Tuesday's lesson, as I was too unwell. I stayed home on Tuesday, as the cough was no better, and I was awake all night. Connie stayed home again, and worked till late. Alanah came for her lesson, and Denise's daughters, Victoria and Steph, were to start that evening, but they forgot. When Nancy called to say she would visit me on Thursday afternoon, I was pleased, as we always had a pleasant time. I went to school on Wednesday, although I did not feel too well.

Cornelia called that evening to say she found a white kitten in the paddocks close to the nursery where she worked, and asked if I would like to have it. I agreed gladly, and called Connie to ask him to pick up the kitten after work.

When Connie brought the kitten, all wrapped up and hiding in a cat cage, I loved it immediately. It was so tiny, just a handful, with beautiful, blue eyes staring fearfully at me. I did not know if it was a male or a female. It was so nervous and scared that my heart melted.

Cornelia said she gave it a bath, shampooed and blow-dried it, as its long white fur was almost grey, and it was full of fleas. I kept it warm in the laundry, and left some milk and cat food, and away from Misty, who sniffed around disdainfully, and made threatening noises.

I woke up early next morning, to see how the kitten was. It ate all the food and drank the milk. But I did not see the messy carpet where it did its business, and stepped right on the soiled carpet! Although I left a litter tray, the kitten did not use it, and I hoped I could train it to use the tray soon.

I washed and cleaned my shoes and carpet, and thought, oh, the joys and trials of a new kitten! I took it to the vet later that morning, but he saw me at twelve o'clock, as they had an emergency. I was vexed, as I had to get back before one o'clock because Nancy was visiting.

The vet checked the kitten out, and said it was a female, about six weeks old, and in good health. He gave her vaccines, and flea treatment, then handed me a bill for $150. And he said he would see her again in three months, to see how she was doing, and de-sex her then. I did not hear one single mew from the time she was brought home, but now she emitted a weak, little sound that resembled a mew. At least she was not mute. I brought her home, fed her a little more food and milk. And although she hid in her basket, she looked more relaxed and settled.

Nancy came just after one o'clock, and left a few hours later. It was good to catch up with her, as she was such a lovely person, and we got on well. I rested a while after she left, and then went to the laundry to see how the kitten was doing. But she was not in the basket. I looked under the washing machine, and everywhere, but there were not many hiding places in the laundry. I was puzzled at her disappearance.

Then I pulled the curtain aside and looked up, and there she was, perched on top of the curtain track. She looked down at me with her bright, blue eyes, as if taking pleasure in my perplexity. She was adept at climbing up curtains, and sitting on top of the track. I did not name her yet, so I called out, "Here Puss, come down at once!" She ignored me, and was quite comfortable up there, so I let her be. She was beautiful, with medium-length white fur, pink nose, and blue eyes.

I baked two cakes next day, to take to the play, as I told Ginny I would. We were to help back stage, and serve refreshments during the evening production. Christian and Athena dropped in, and brought the banner for Nilanthi. It was excellent, as Christian did a perfect job. We packed it up carefully, and the painting too, so they were ready for Emmanuel to take them.

Connie went to Bairnsdale on business for the day, and came home after nine thirty that night. He was very tired, and did not talk much, as he wanted to sleep early. I stayed up a little while longer, and chatted with Christian and Athena.

I went to the dentist on Saturday, and later on, we dropped in at Cornelia's, as she wanted us to see some display homes in Lyndhurst. We had a look there, but none of the houses appealed to us. We dropped Cornelia at Laura's place in Dandenong, and it was late afternoon when we returned home. I iced the cakes, and we drove to the Briars around five thirty, in time to prepare refreshments and the props. We had a good time talking with the other volunteers, and actors during their breaks. And we came home after ten o'clock, once we finished washing up, and cleaning the kitchen. Two other volunteers stayed back as well, and Ginny was very grateful for our help.

I took it easy on Sunday, as I was exhausted. The new kitten was very cute, but impish, as it liked to hide in the most unusual places. I could not find it anywhere once again, and only when I heard a faint mew did I locate it under the fridge grill. Connie went out that morning, and came home late, but he went for evening Mass, as he had to read the lessons. I stayed in, as I was too tired, and I also had to make dinner.

I named the kitten Mishka, because she looked exotic, and the name suited her perfectly. She was more comfortable around me now, and started playing furtively at the beginning. Then she grew bolder, as she ventured out of the laundry to explore the kitchen, and the rest of the great big world in the living areas. Mishka tried to get close to Misty, but she bared her teeth and hissed at her. I hoped the kitten would be good company for Misty, but she did not want to know the intruder at all.

Poor Misty was very sick, and kept vomiting. She was not eating too well either, and I wondered what to do about her, as I hated to think she was in pain. When I called Ninette later, she told me that she got another dog on the weekend, and she was very happy. And she called her dog, Fido. Sarah was amused with Mishka, and played with her after her lesson.

I visited Ninette next day, and liked her frisky new dog, as it was a playful, eighteen-month old Maltese, crossed with a Poodle. She wanted to go to the post office later, so I dropped her there, before I went shopping. Christian called in the evening to ask if I could help Athena sew a costume for her boss's 30th birthday party, to which I immediately agreed.

They were flying to Tasmania for the party, and she wanted to dress up as a waitress in a fifties' Diner. They came in the evening, and he cut out the pattern, which took him a couple of hours to get it perfect, so it was after midnight when they left.

I woke up next morning to find we had no hot water! It was some problem with the gas hot water tank. I went to school after a quick, cold water wash. It was a busy day, so I rested when I came home. Christian and Athena came at eight o'clock that night, and continued sewing her costume.

I helped with the frills on the skirt, and Christian sewed the piping very neatly on the apron and cap. Athena sewed the shirt, and we stopped after midnight. We still had a little more to do, but we were very pleased with our efforts.

The plumber came early next morning to fix the hot water unit. When he finished, and the hot water came on again, Connie and I drove to North Cranbourne, as we had an appointment with a consultant at Porter Davis Homes. It was quite comprehensive, and we finished after midday. When we came home, I rested a little, before I went out for a haircut.

Christian and Athena came in the evening, and I made some dinner. Then we sewed away till late, and finished on the stroke of midnight! Athena tried it on, and she looked gorgeous in the dark-blue and black outfit. After they left, I had a good sleep, and did not wake up till late morning.

One of Connie's friends at Woolworths, offered a ginger kitten in a few weeks time, as it was not yet six weeks old. He emailed Connie a photograph, and it was so cute, that we agreed to take it. We thought it was like Tiger, but it was short-haired, and not the same breed as Tiger. Still, I could not resist taking another kitten, as Misty was so poorly now, and I knew she would not last too long. Mishka was doing well, and settled in happily.

I called Nilanthi and Josephine, and was sad to hear Josephine say that she was in severe pain. She complained about everything non-stop, and asked, "When are you coming to see me Dolly?" I replied, "I will try to visit you very soon Mamma. Hope you feel better soon." She spoke for about half an hour, and was reluctant to hang up.

Ninette was very upset, because Fido escaped from her garden the night before. But fortunately, one of her neighbour's found it, and brought it back. She was worried it would escape again, and wanted to secure her backyard. I told her not to worry, as Fido was safe now, but she sounded very anxious and upset about it.

I watched "Notebook" with James Garner that night. It was a good movie, and very poignant. And it made me think that it was a good idea to write down our memories when we can remember them, because one day, we may forget everything that happened in our lives.

I did some gardening next day, and planted cuttings in pots, as the weather was mild. Then I played the piano, with the soft pedal on, as Connie was still resting at one o'clock in the afternoon. He said he was always tired now, and slept in till very late on weekends. When he woke up that day, he went out, saying he wanted to do some shopping for Aunty. I told him not to delay, as we were going out for dinner with the La Ponders, to Onde's Cafe in Mornington.

The dinner was an Italian six course banquet, which was held annually, and we made it a farewell dinner for our friends, as they planned to move out of Mornington soon. The food was delicious, and we had a pleasant time with Chris and Peter, and came home late. They sold their house, but had not decided where to buy their new place.

We drove to Cranbourne North next day, to have another look at a display home that we saw before. Then we visited Mary and Tony, and were happy that he was much better, as he was ill for some time. And from there we drove straight for evening Mass.

It was Shirani's 59th birthday on 8 June, so I baked a cake, and we visited her next afternoon at Narre Warren, and enjoyed a pleasant time.

Ninette wanted to go to Patterson Lakes again the following week, so I drove her there after my lesson. But when we got there, she did not want to stay long. She looked around for five minutes only, and told me, "I feel dizzy, too many people and things in this shop, let's go home now!" She was getting worse with her panic attacks, and did not like to be in crowded places now. I found her behaviour quite strange, but tried to be patient.

The students came for lessons after school, and Christian called to say they arrived safely the previous night. They enjoyed the party in Tasmania very much, and said they would visit us soon. He said that it was freezing in Tasmania, and they caught colds, and I told him it was no better here, as it was icy, with rain, and hail storms.

School was chaotic on Wednesday, and I moved the piano to another room, as the hall was occupied. I finished early, and then drove to Karingal to meet Connie, as we had an appointment at the bank.

When the students came for their lessons, I asked if they would like to take part in Elvira's play. Sarah, Julia, and her elder sister, Jessica, agreed. I was happy, as we were meeting at Elvira's on the weekend, to read the play and hold auditions.

Christian called to say they would drop in later, and I invited them for dinner, as I was just making some. We had dinner, and they left early, as they had bad colds.

I worked on the manuscript "Wild Poppies" for a few hours next day, and was pleased that I was almost finished. Mishka was doing well, but Misty was still not friendly towards her. It was a shame, as Mishka seemed to think Misty was her mother, and tried to cuddle up to her, but Misty did not tolerate such familiarities.

I called Nilanthi to ask about the painting, and she said that she was very happy with it, so was the parish priest, who was going to email me to thank me for the painting and banner. She said they could not believe how beautiful the painting and banner were, and the priest wanted to hang the painting in the church. He said he could not stop gazing at the painting, because it seemed as if Our Lady was looking right through him. I was glad they were pleased, because it was a very difficult task to accomplish that painting, and thanks to Christian as well, for making such a fantastic banner.

I woke up early on Saturday to do chores, and work on Elvira's play. Connie went out on some errand or another. Misty had another episode, and I was very distressed to see her tumble over helplessly. Poor little thing! I hoped she would recover, and not suffer another major stroke. Then I typed for a few more hours in the afternoon.

We drove to Elvira's on Sunday afternoon, and some of my students were already there; Sarah, Julia, and Jessica, who agreed to take part in the play. We had a very interesting time, and the girls read their parts well. John and Connie went to pick olives at one of John's friend's place, and they returned late. John invited us for dinner at Rugantino's in Frankston, so we came home soon, then I attended to Misty, made her comfortable, and turned on the heater in the garage. She seemed alright, and did not tumble over, but was very unsteady on her paws. I kept Mishka in her basket in the laundry, and we went out for dinner.

Chapter 49

I took Misty for her cortisone injection on Tuesday morning, but the nurse jabbed her right on her spine, and she screamed in pain and fright. I was very distressed about it, as the vet was usually very gentle with her. Connie was at home, working on his computer till late afternoon, and I visited Ninette. When I returned after some shopping, he had left.

I saw doctor next day, as the dry cough persisted, and he prescribed a cough mixture with codeine. After one dose that night, I had a good sleep after a very long time, and I wished he had prescribed it before.

Mishka was cute and entertaining, and kept me amused with her antics. But Misty was still hostile because she was unwell, and felt threatened whenever the kitten jumped around and followed her everywhere. She thought Misty was her mother, and tried to cuddle up to her, but Misty just hissed and spat at her if she got too close.

We drove to Cranbourne to meet Lara, the consultant, on the following Saturday, and had another good look at the display home. When we finished there, it was late afternoon, so we stopped at Cranbourne Centre and had a snack for lunch.

We told my sisters, and Christian and Athena about the block of land we had purchased, and about our plans to build on it. But Connie said it would be best if we did not mention it to any of his family, until the house was built. He did not say anything even to his mother, which was surprising, because he usually told her just about everything.

He told me that some of them were very negative, and envious, so he kept it from his siblings. I was happy to move out, as it was open house any time of day or night. But I regretted leaving such a beautiful house, and only the thought of living a peaceful life in Mount Martha, was very appealing. That night, Elvira called and asked if I could drop in next day, as she wanted to discuss something about the play.

Sunday was busy, and after the usual chores, we dropped in at Elvira's. She was very excited, because her son had found a producer, who was interested in the play, and she wanted me to accompany her to a meeting with him in Brunswick next Saturday. I was happy for her, and said I would. Then we dropped in at Christian's for a coffee. They drove with us to the block of land later, and were happy when they saw the ocean views, and agreed it would be a good move. We returned home after six o'clock.

Connie drove to Pakenham on 22 June to pick up the kitten. I came home a little early after a busy day at school, as Connie said he would drop the kitten at home, and then go to work. When I saw the cute little ginger kitten, I was very happy. He was not at all timid, unlike Mishka, and was quite content to sit on a chair, and look around curiously with large, tawny eyes. He was a little over four weeks, and very friendly.

Connie said his friend's little daughter hid the kitten in a shoe box, and left it under her bed, because she did not want to part with it. Mishka started to hiss and behave very nastily to the newcomer, but Misty was more tolerant of the little kitten. Perhaps it reminded her of Tiger with his ginger coat, who knows.

I had a hectic time now, with two little kittens, and an ailing, old cat to care for. Mishka got excited whenever she saw the new kitten, and did her business in the lounge. She still ran after Misty, trying to make friends with her, but Misty was just too grumpy and ill to stretch out a paw in friendship.

I drove to Onde's in Mornington on Friday, to have coffee with Christina, but she did not turn up. So, I did my usual shopping, and emailed her when I returned home. She forgot and apologized profusely, but I did not make another date, as I had too many things happening then.

Elvira came around nine thirty in the morning on Saturday. She parked her car on the street, and as John was busy that day, he could not drive her, so Connie drove us to Brunswick. I settled all three cats; Misty in the garage, and the two kittens in a basket in the laundry. I named the ginger kitten, Simba. He was very placid, and ignored Mishka's hissing, and settled inside the basket, oblivious to her threatening glares and grumbles.

We arrived in Brunswick in an hour or so, and met Tom Padula, the producer, in his "theatre," which was an old, crowded, untidy room. He was brusque, and quite rude at the start, when I made any suggestions, as he thought he was a "big shot" and knew it all. He told us he had a small segment on Channel 31 every week, where he read his own poetry and stories. And he said he could get the play televised on Channel 31, if he produced it.

Elvira wanted to raise money for St Vincent's with the proceeds of the play, but Tom objected to that notion. He said that *all* the ticket money was his, and he would pay the actors whatever *he* thought was fair. He thawed a little towards me at the end of the interview, and his farewells were more effusive than his greetings.

I had my doubts about the project though, and told Elvira and Tom that I did not want to be involved any longer, once he took over. But Elvira and he *insisted* that I continued to be a part of it, as I wrote the stage play. He made arrangements to hold a reading the following week, and then we left.

We shopped at a few Italian places, where Elvira bought some groceries, and then we had lunch at an Italian restaurant. It was late afternoon when we returned, and Elvira left after a coffee. I was tired and rested a while, but Connie went to do some shopping for his mother in the evening. I worked on my manuscript later, and when I finished, I played with the kittens, as they tumbled, tossed, and chased each other tirelessly.

The days were busy, taking care of Misty, and the two little kittens, teaching piano, and working on my manuscripts. Wherever Connie went out in the morning or afternoon, he returned in time to go for evening Mass on Sundays, and if I was tired or unwell, he went on his own.

A few days later, when I called Josephine one evening, her daughter-in-law, Yvonne, was with her, and she had a long chat with me. Yvonne said, "I'm very angry with Paul, as he didn't even stay till Josephine cut her birthday cake on her 90th birthday!" Connie and I visited her a few days prior to her birthday, which was on 13 May. Yvonne thanked me for that and said, "My mother-in-law loves you with a passion!" I replied, "I'm very fond of her too."

Christian and Athena dropped in one night soon after our trip to Brunswick. And when I told them about the play, and how Elvira wanted Tom Padula to produce it, they said it would be best if I did not have anything to do with the project.

They thought it was not very nice of her to go to another producer, knowing how hard I tried to help her produce it. And especially after spending so much time brainstorming with all my friends, a reading, and finding some players too,

I called Sarah, Julia, and Jessica to say that the venue was now in Brunswick. But their parents' said it was too far away to go for rehearsals, and I understood their reluctance. So, we lost those players. When I spoke to Sarah, Charlotte and Tabitha were there too, and I had a nice chat with them, and Charlotte's mother, Jackie.

I told Elvira the girls did not want to travel so far, and also, that I did not want to be involved any more, as Tom did not need my help. She accepted my decision, and I was relieved to step aside. I only wanted to stage the play for Elvira's sake, and worked very hard at writing it.

I visited Ninette the following Friday, as she needed help sorting out her DVD's, and reading the television guide etc. Then I drove her to Woolworths at Seaford, before doing my shopping on the way home. When I came back, I was happy to see Mishka and Simba still sleeping in the same basket, and settling in well.

When I wore my beret and said, "I'm going out now, stay in the basket till I come," they seemed to know they had to sleep in the basket the moment I put my beret on. Such intelligent little kittens, but oh so naughty and frisky! Whether they tumbled out of the basket and played till I came back, I am not sure. But they were always sleeping inside it when I opened the door.

Connie went out early on Saturday morning, to play golf. I was happy when he relaxed with his friends and played golf, instead of sleeping half the day, or spending hours shopping for his mother.

He admitted he was very slow at shopping, as he had to pick out each item carefully, so Cristobel did not criticize the things he bought. He visited his siblings and nieces on his way to work, and very often did not mention that he did. Shiranthi sometimes said, "Connie dropped in today on his way to work." When I asked him why he did not tell me, he replied, "I don't have to tell you everything I do!"

I noticed Mishka was acting strange the following Saturday; she rolled over, mewed loudly, as if she was in pain, and I did not know what to make of her. I petted her and held her until she calmed down a little, but I was at a loss to know what ailed the poor little thing.

We drove to Hoddle Street, in the city next day, to look at fireplaces for the new house, then to Dandenong, but the shop was closed. We came home, and I rested awhile. Mishka still behaved as if she was very distressed, so I decided to take her to the vet next day.

The vet said that Mishka was in heat, and had to be spayed soon to prevent her getting pregnant. She was hardly three months old, but I booked her in, although I felt sorry for such a tiny kitten to be spayed.

I stayed home on Monday, as it was a student-free day, but Sarah came for her lesson in the evening. I lit the fire and waited for Christian and Athena, who came later that night. They found a 4wheel drive on the internet for Athena, and Christian was flying to Brisbane early next day, and driving the vehicle back to Melbourne. I was very anxious because he was driving from Brisbane on his own.

When I came home from Ninette's next day, I called Athena. And she said he left Brisbane at two o'clock, so I hoped he would arrive safely. I was very relieved to hear he returned without any problems.

Ron and Cynthia visited in the afternoon, and brought a cat cage with them. It was very well constructed, and I was happy to have it, as I could keep the kittens in there overnight, instead of in the laundry. Ron painted a sign inside, "Catsville," and it had two shelves for their baskets. A couple of Ron's workers came along to set it up, and they left late in the evening. I kept Simba and Mishka in the cage that night, as I had to take Mishka to the vet next morning. Joelle called to say she would visit me next day.

I got Mishka out of the cage at seven o'clock next morning, and took her to the vet by eight o'clock. She mewed in distress when I left her, and I was upset. But the vet called at midday to say that she was fine, and recovering well, so I could pick her up that evening.

Joelle arrived just after midday, and brought me a calendar, and a tea-cloth from Canada, as she always brought me souvenirs from her travels. We had a pleasant time chatting about her trip and experiences, and she left in a couple of hours time, then I drove down to pick up Mishka.

The vet told me to keep her quiet, and not let her run around for a few days. But when I let her out at home, she just whizzed upstairs and down as if nothing was wrong with her, then sat and pulled at the stitches in her stomach. She was like a little tornado running around the house.

I kept her in the laundry, hoping she would settle down, but she mewed at the top of her voice, and I found it hard to ignore her. The moment I opened the door, she ran and jumped on the chairs, thinking that I was playing with her. I had a difficult time keeping her quiet, until I finally locked her in the laundry for the night.

I kept Simba in the cat cage, where he was quite content and cosy with extra warm blankets, and cushions in his basket. Misty waddled around in a daze, as she gained considerable weight due to the cortisone injections. And I could not believe she was once such a lithe and active little cat.

She still glared at the kittens in a most unfriendly manner, and did not let them come near her. Mishka played non-stop, and was hyper-active, as she was friskier than Simba, who knew when to play, and when to sleep. I kept Mishka with me when I went to bed or·sat down to read, and Simba in the cat cage, until Mishka was better. I did not want them to play around too much, until her stitches were removed.

We drove to National Tiles in Port Melbourne on Saturday, 18 July, to choose tiles, before the colour selection appointment. We spent some time there, and at last found some neutral-toned tiles, and it was late afternoon when we returned home.

It was gusty and chilly next day, so Simba stayed inside the igloo in the cat cage, and was quite happy there. We drove to Mount Martha later, and looked at the block of land again, before attending Mass at Frankston. I kept Mishka in the cat cage with Simba that night, because she would be restricted, and not run around.

It was the same busy routine at school on Monday, and the students came for lessons in the evening. Christian and Athena dropped in later, and Athena invited me on Thursday, to teach me computer drawing. I was interested to learn how, and said I would come in the afternoon.

I altered Christian's shirts the evening before, as I wanted to take them on Thursday. Athena was very good at instructing, and I learnt a great deal about photo shop, and computer drawing. It was late evening when I came home.

I woke up with vertigo on Saturday morning, and was hardly able to move around. It usually came on when I was stressed or did too much. I took it easy and rested, but when I felt better in the afternoon, I made some pan rolls for Athena and Christian. Dorothy came with them in the evening, but they did not stay long. The vertigo was still severe that evening, so I rested, and later watched an old movie, "Spitfire" with Katherine Hepburn.

I let the kittens out early on Sunday morning. They were already out of their baskets, and stared through the window to see if I was awake too. I brought them inside the house for a while, and was glad to see them settling down well. We drove to Chadstone later, as Shirani gave me a gift voucher for my birthday, to spend at "Border's" book shop. Then we drove to Southland, but could not find a parking spot, so we came back to Mount Martha instead, and returned late.

I did my first computer drawing of some poppies that evening, and enjoyed utilizing this new skill. The next few days flew past, teaching at school and at home, visits to Ninette's, socialising with friends, getting my manuscripts ready, and all my other involvements.

I took Mishka to get her stitches out, and for her last vaccine, two weeks later, on 30 July. She was alright, and the incision had healed well, in spite of her trying to rip out the stitches with her teeth. I dropped her at home and went out to do my grocery shopping.

The vertigo was easing, and Joanne visited me on Thursday afternoon. We had a pleasant catch up, and she left after a couple of hours, saying she would visit again soon.

I did chores on Saturday, while Connie went out to do his "thing" as he told me. I called Aunty sometimes, but it was a one-sided conversation now, as she did not converse at all, and only replied in monosyllables, "Yes" and "No." It was sad to think that such a garrulous person dwindled into a vegetable state now. Then I called my sisters, and enjoyed a nice chat as always. But when I called Lorraine and Josephine, they did not answer. I wondered how Josephine was, as it was unusual for her not to answer her phone in the evenings.

Mitchell wanted to start music lessons after school, and I told him I would be happy to teach him again.

I woke up feeling exhausted on Sunday morning, as I did not sleep at all. These frequent bouts of insomnia left me feeling lethargic all the time. We visited Aunty to wish her, as it was her birthday next day, the 3rd of August. I took a bouquet of flowers and a card, and Connie gave her a bottle of brandy, but she was not communicative at all.

Esme barged in as always, and when I tried to engage Aunty in a conversation, Esme replied on her behalf, as she took on the role of Aunty's mouthpiece as well. We left after a strained conversation, and drove to Mount Martha, and then to Frankston for evening Mass.

When I was at school on Monday, Connie drove to Frankston hospital for a stress test, as he constantly complained of chest pains. Sarah, and the other students came for their lessons, and later that evening, I worked on my manuscript "Wild Poppies." I was pleased that it was almost finished, and had only a few more chapters to edit and proof-read, before it was ready for publication.

I was too tired to visit Ninette next day, so I stayed home and took it easy. Connie went for the second part of the stress test in the morning, and came home late afternoon. In spite of bad weather, we drove to Mount Martha, and then to a display home in Cranbourne, to check out a few details. It was pouring down by the time we came home. Alanah and Steph cancelled their lessons, as they went for a concert. I had another sleepless night and finally fell asleep around three o'clock in the morning, and was worn-out next day.

School was very demanding, and I finished early next day. On my way home, I posted a card for Joelle's birthday tomorrow. Christian and Athena visited that evening, and we had a great time, chatting and sharing our interests, and they left late that night.

Christian picked up my Jag next day to check out the tyres, as one had a slow leak. Connie went to the opening of a new Woolworths store in Beaconsfield, and brought home two large, fresh snapper. And Christian dropped off my car in the afternoon, after getting the tyre fixed. We had a cup of tea and a chat before he left, then I worked on my manuscript till late evening.

Whenever Connie was home, and I worked on the computer, he yelled out, "Dolly, are you on the *internet*?" Or he crept up behind me and said, "I hope you're not going to those chat sites, like all these women do!" This really annoyed and frustrated me, as I never wasted my time on such activities, but he had a morbid suspicion that I would do so. I retorted irritably, "I'm working on my manuscript! *Why* do you ask?" he mumbled, "I heard about this man, whose wife found another man on the internet, and he caught her chatting to him!" So, *that* was the reason for his suspicions, as he stared and growled at me, as if *I* was that guilty woman. I could never convince him that I was not interested in meeting any other man on the internet, or anywhere else, but he was more suspicious as he grew older.

I took Misty for her cortisone injection on Friday morning. And when I returned home, in spite of severe pains in my neck and shoulders, I bottled fifteen bottles of sour cherry liqueur. It was tiring work, filtering and bottling, but worth the trouble. I usually ended up giving them away for Christmas, as I did not drink any, because it was too sweet and strong. Then I typed for a few more hours, and watched an old movie in the night, "Birds," which was a scary movie.

It was pleasant on Sunday, and I was glad to see the two kittens settling down cosily. Misty was scared they would hurt her, and did not let them come anywhere near her. She snarled and hissed at them, which was a shame, because they were so tiny, and mistook her for their mother. I watered the garden, and took it easy, as my muscles ached. I was weary, so I did not go to church that evening, and Connie went on his own.

We attended a "Tender" meeting at Porter Davis Homes in Berwick next day. And it was late afternoon when we finished. Then we drove to the display home in Cranbourne, to check a few more details in the plans.

I visited Ninette next day, who was getting over a kidney infection, and looked quite unwell. I was sorry to hear that, and stayed a couple of hours with her, but she kept saying, "Stay a little more, do you have to leave now?" I said I had students, and I had to go home in time. But only one student came that evening, so I had extra time to work on my manuscript for a few hours.

When I came home on Wednesday, I was glad to see that Misty was steadier on her paws, after the last cortisone injection. After relaxing awhile, I spent a few hours on my manuscript. I still suffered from insomnia, and did not get to sleep till early dawn on most nights, and did not know what to do to get a good night's sleep. I read till late, until my eyes closed in weariness, but I still could not fall asleep. And I refused to take sleeping tablets, as they were habit-forming.

Nilanthi was very excited about the painting and banner, as they were carrying it in procession next day, the feast of the Assumption of Our Lady. I was pleased to hear everyone admired the painting and banner, so it was worth my trouble.

Christian and Athena visited that evening, and stayed till one o'clock in the morning. They set up my personal email on the laptop, so I could work on it when Connie was on the computer at home. They did so much for me, and I was very grateful. He went to bed early, as he was very tired. I read for a couple of hours after they left, but I was still not sleepy.

Connie left early next morning to play golf, and to do some shopping for his mother afterwards. We went to Cornelia's for dinner in the evening, and had a good time. Florica, Cornelia's mother, always sat next to me at table, and chatted away in Rumanian for hours, even though I did not understand a word she was saying. But Cornelia or Con sometimes translated, so we got by.

When Florica kept beating her chest repeatedly, Cornelia said, "My mother says it doesn't matter about language, she can feel in her heart you care for her, and that's enough." I smiled and nodded, and her lips stretched happily. Language certainly was no barrier, when love bridged people, so she continued chatting away happily. It was a wild, stormy night, and when we came back at midnight, I read till two o'clock in the morning.

The windstorm continued next day, and the kittens were scared of the noise and blustery weather, so I took them inside, where they played around merrily. We drove to Oakleigh next day, to select carpets, and stopped at Shirani's on our way back. Although it was such a cold, wild day, we drove to Mount Martha before coming home. We could not walk around the block, as it was too wet, but Connie wanted to check a few details.

I called Nilanthi, as it was her birthday next day, the 18th of August, and we had a long chat. Then I visited Ninette, and took a phone card, so that Ninette could wish Nilanthi too, and they chatted for awhile. We walked to the local shops later, before I returned home after grocery shopping.

I finished early on Wednesday, as I took Simba to the vet for a check up. Scott examined him, said he was in good health, and could be de-sexed soon. Christian picked up the computer to upgrade it, and said they would come in the evening, once it was done. I dropped Simba at home, and drove to Karingal to buy some meat for dinner. When they came a little later, we had a good time, and the computer ran much faster now. After they left, I prepared some things, as we had to leave at eight o'clock next morning for an appointment in Port Melbourne.

I settled the cats early next morning, as Misty had to be fed, and kept warm in the garage, and the two kittens in their basket in the laundry. They shared one large basket, and cuddled up to each other to keep warm. I fed them dry, and tinned food now, which they relished. Mishka liked raw chicken wings, but not Simba. Once the three of them settled down, we left soon, and arrived in the city around ten o'clock. It took almost two hours to get there through heavy traffic and rain.

We finished both appointments by two o'clock, and then drove to National Tiles. But they told us we had to make *another* appointment, which was very annoying, to say the least. We had hoped to finalise the tile selection on the same day.

We returned home late that evening, and I was exhausted. I tried to unwind and read a little, but at eight o'clock, Babs was at the door. She stayed for about one hour, and then Roland called Connie at nine thirty, and they were on the phone for a long time. I went to bed and read till late.

We drove to Southland on Saturday, and watched "3D Coraline" a clever animated film, which was very enjoyable. It was quite late when we returned home, and then Connie worked on the computer. I watched a very good movie, "Kate and Leopold" later that night.

It was Stacy's 37th birthday next day, 23 August. I felt very down-hearted that he was missing for so long, and wondered where he could be. Then I said a heartfelt prayer for him, and hoped he was happy and safe wherever he was.

We had lunch with Chris and Peter, at Soy restaurant, Mornington, that afternoon. It was a farewell meal, as they were moving to Tea Gardens in New South Wales. I was sad to say goodbye to our dear friends, as we had enjoyed many pleasant times together. We came home late, and as I was too tired to go for Mass, Connie went on his own.

It was freezing and gusty on Monday when I drove to school, and I did not feel too well. I hoped I was not coming down with flu again. Sarah came for her lesson, and Mitchell called to thank me for his birthday card, and gift. Athena said they would visit that evening, and I was happy, as I loved having them around, because we shared so much, and talked about so many things.

I bought harnesses to train the kittens to walk, and it was very amusing to watch them keep in step sedately. And they soon learnt how to walk with a harness on. I did not let them out in the garden, because they would jump the fences and get lost. So I took each one out for a while, and let them sniff around in the garden, until they were familiar with their surroundings. I continued working on my manuscript every evening, as I wanted to finish it soon, and launch it early next year.

It was blustery and chilly next day, and I caught a cold in school, so when I came home, I rested. Christian dropped in later with my shoes, that I wanted re-soled. He gave them to a cobbler in Mornington, who charged reasonable rates, and we chatted over a cup of tea before he left.

Con gave a DVD about the Rumanian Communist Party under a dictator, and I found it very interesting. But Connie said he was too busy, and did not have time to watch it, although I told him it was a worthwhile documentary.

Nilanthi was well and happy when I called her next day, and she said she framed the painting, as the priest wanted to hang in the church. I went grocery shopping later, although I was unwell. When I spoke to Ninette in the evening, she kept me on the phone for almost an hour, with her usual complaints. It was sad, because most of her ailments were imaginary, and all the blood test results were clear. But she did not believe what the doctors told her, and was convinced that she suffered from multiple illnesses.

It was Christian's 36th birthday on Saturday, 29 August. How quickly the years have flown! I made patties for afternoon tea, as Christian was very fond of them. And when I called to wish him, he said they would drop in later. We had a great time chatting, and discussing various issues, and they left in a couple of hours time. We went for evening Mass, and Mary Lou played the organ that evening, and we caught up later. She said that she made a commitment to play at Mass every Saturday evening, and I was glad she could do that.

Sunday was a pleasant day, so I cleaned the oven, and did all the chores inside and out. I wanted everything to be clean and tidy, in preparation for the sale of the house. Connie mowed lawns, and did some weeding after several months of avoiding the garden. He said he did not feel like doing anything, now that we were selling up. But as we had to maintain the garden and keep it neat, he grudgingly spent a couple of hours cleaning. When we finished our chores, we drove to Karingal that afternoon and watched a funny movie, 'The Ugly Truth' and returned home late.

I was feverish and down with flu, so I did not go to school on Monday. But we had a contract meeting with Porter Davis at Berwick that afternoon, which we had to attend. It was late evening when we finished. And Connie was very annoyed when they told us that we had to apply for town planning approval, which we thought was their responsibility. I called Ninette to say I could not visit next day, as I was unwell.

Connie drove to Mornington Council next morning, and they told him he had to wait twelve weeks for applications to be processed, due to a backlog. He was livid, and wanted to cancel the contract with Porter Davis immediately. I had to calm him down, and told him that we would lose a couple of thousand dollars, if we cancelled the deal at this stage.

I too wanted the new house to be built soon. Porter Davis promised that construction would start by October that year, and the house would be completed in April 2010. But with a twelve week delay, just to get the town planning application approved, it was not going to happen. I told Connie we had to be philosophical about it.

Alanah came for her lesson that evening, and Ninette called to ask how I was feeling, as she was very concerned. I did not go to school on Wednesday either, and rested most of the day. But I made marmalade jam in the evening, to send Nelune, as she and Joanna relished my home-made orange marmalade.

The next few days continued to be very gusty, but with sunny breaks, so I walked the kittens with their harnesses on. They were well trained now, and much to my amusement, they walked really well. I asked Connie to remove a photograph of the kittens walking with their harnesses on, which he did.

I was relieved when the optometrist told me all was well with my eyes, when I had an eye test on Friday, as my vision was sometimes blurry.

It was mild and pleasant on Saturday, and I finished chores before calling Shiranthi. I thanked her for visiting Nilanthi, as Roland and she were on holiday there, and she gave Nilanthi twenty dollars for her birthday. Then I spoke to Nilanthi for some time, before we went for Mass. I enjoyed watching a 1958 movie, "Touch Of Evil" that night.

We drove to Springvale next day for yum cha at Gold Leaf restaurant, where we were meeting Christian, Athena, her parents, and John's brother, Uncle Mick, from Adelaide. It was so crowded, that they hurried off customers, in order to give all the people in the queue a chance to eat.

Connie and I drove to Mount Martha later, where we walked on our block and enjoyed the splendid ocean views. We came home late, and I worked on my manuscript for a couple of hours.

I went to school on Monday, but I came home early and rested, as I was still unwell. Sarah and the other students came for lessons in the evening, and I was very tired by the time I finished. I spoke to Ninette for some time, and I said I would visit her tomorrow, so she was happy. Josephine called in the night, to tell me that Yvonne's mother died the week before. She was in the same nursing home as Josephine, and was in her late eighties or so. I said I would send Yvonne a sympathy card.

Ninette was pleased with my musical progress, when she heard me play next day, and I had a good lesson. We spent some time talking about music, and she played a few melodies after we had coffee. I loved to hear her play songs like "Granada" and other Neapolitan classics, which she played beautifully.

The piano was wheeled to the front room again on Wednesday, as building works started in the school library that morning. Colleen said, "You never complain Dolly, no matter how many times we move the piano around!" I replied, "No point in complaining Colleen, as it serves no purpose, and it can't be helped, while the building is in progress." She was happy that I did not make a fuss about the constant piano moving.

Christian brought an external hard drive for my laptop, and they stayed till late, uploading all my files. They always helped me with computer updates, and technical issues. I could not fix any problems on the computer, without their assistance. We had an interesting time, as I always learned something new from them.

I drove to Frankston pathology for my annual blood test next morning, and came home after eight o'clock, then rested a while after breakfast. I called Ninette later that day, and she was happy, because she said it was like having company, whenever we chatted on the phone.

Ranjith called Connie that night to say that their dog, Tyson, was put down, as he was very sick. He was very upset, and said that the dog could not be saved, as he could not bark or breathe. He was grossly overweight, and his paws could hardly bear his bulk, poor dog. Ranjith over-fed him, and through the years, the dog grew enormous, until he was very unhealthy, and too fat to even move around comfortably.

I woke up early on Saturday, to make Christmas cake to send Nilanthi. It was a stormy day, and after baking the cake, I took it easy in the evening and watched a movie, while Connie worked on the computer till late.

It was the same busy schedule at school on Monday. Sarah and Alanah came for their last lessons for the term that evening. They made good progress, and I told their parents that I was very pleased with them.

I visited Ninette next day, and once again, it was a very good lesson, and she was happy that I played well. I was pleased, because she was meticulous, and wanted only perfection in piano playing. We walked the dog for a while before I had coffee with her, and then came home.

The school held a mini-fete on Wednesday, and I bought a few videos and books. It was a fine, sunny day, and twenty five degrees, so it was good being outdoors. I met a few of the parents, Merian, and Sam Keily, Isabella's mother, and spent some time chatting with them. I walked the kittens when I came home in the afternoon, as they loved it; and they sat patiently while I harnessed them. I thoroughly enjoyed watching them walking sedately.

Chapter 50

I consulted doctor next day, and he said that my glucose, cholesterol, and blood pressure were high. And he advised me to do a stress test, because I told him I had chest pains, while riding the exercise bike. I agreed to do so within the next couple of days.

The town planner wrote after two weeks, to say that they required some amendments to the plan, which meant further delay in approving the application. It was very annoying, and Connie was extremely frustrated over the whole business.

Nilanthi wanted food items, and some things for Christmas, so I bought them in time to send a box before the end of the year. Esme called that evening, and had a long chat, and I wished her, as her birthday was next Monday.

It was Nihal's 30th death anniversary today, and I said a special prayer for the repose of his soul. It seemed like only yesterday when he was around, and made us laugh with his never-ending jokes. I could still picture him making funny faces, and talking like Jerry Lewis, or mimicking someone. I miss him dearly still, and he lives forever in my memory.

Connie went out early on Saturday morning to shop for Aunty, and he came back very late that evening. He never told me what he did, or where he went, so I did not ask him, as he only shouted at me if I questioned him. If he was happy doing his "thing," I just accepted this phase in his life. We watched an old movie that night, "The Glenn Miller Story" starring James Stewart, which I enjoyed very much.

The weather was pleasant next day, and I walked the kittens in the garden before making some pan rolls.

Esme called that afternoon to say Josephine died that morning, 20 September. I was deeply distressed, as her death was so sudden. She spoke to me only a week ago, and had sounded quite well. Josephine ended the phone call with her familiar Italian phrase, "I will love you till I die!" And I promised to visit her again very soon. But when I called her a few days ago, she did not answer the phone. Esme said, that while standing on a stool, she lost her balance, fell over, and suffered a massive heart attack.

She turned ninety that May, and could have lived a few more years, I thought. I would miss her talks over the phone, and our visits to Geelong. But I prayed she was finally at peace, without her constant refrain, "I'm so *lonely*! Please come and see me Dolly!" What a sad end.

When I called Shirani later, she was very upset about the situation in her school. She tried very hard to get ahead there, but did not seem to make much progress, and she was tired of the politics. I told her not to get stressed about it, and I wanted to visit her. But Connie was working in the garden, so I did not want to bother him. We went for evening Mass, and I lit candles for the repose of Josephine's soul.

I visited Ninette on Monday afternoon, after calling Nilanthi, as I had a stress test on Tuesday. Ninette wanted me to walk with her to the shops, after my lesson, as she liked to browse in the charity shops. I had a look in there too, and found a denim dress and jacket, which were ideal for the western play at the Briars next month. The audience had to dress up, and participate in a "Whodunit" mystery play, which I thought would be interesting. Christian and Athena dropped in later that evening, and we had a pleasant time.

I walked the kittens next day, and then I let Simba climb up the willow tree, because Mishka was at the top, showing off to him. He was timid, and did not climb too high. A bird flew past just then and scared Simba so much that he fell off the branch and landed on my face, as I was standing right beneath looking up at him. Two scratches on my nose, and a scratch from eyebrow to my cheek, bled copiously. But I thanked my lucky stars he missed my eye. I rushed inside to wipe the blood off my face, and washed the scratches with disinfectant. Fortunately, they were not very deep, and they healed well, except for one that scarred the side of my cheek.

Connie drove me to the Peninsula hospital later for the stress test. And after about seven minutes of exercising, I was tired, and had to stop. The specialist thought I could have angina, and booked me in for an angiogram at Frankston hospital. I rested when we came home, as I had chest pains, and felt very tired. Christian and Athena came over in the evening, when I told them what the specialist had said. They were concerned about the stress test, and also when they saw the scratches on my face.

I invited them for dinner next day, and we enjoyed the evening, and they were glad to see the scratches were healing. Christian wanted to give his old mobile to send Nilanthi, as I was sending her a box for Christmas.

I settled the three cats on Thursday, and prepared a plate of antipasto for lunch at Christina's holiday house in Rosebud. Her friend, Irena, who lived in the city, picked up Ninette on her way. Christina picked me up at eleven o'clock, and we drove down in light rain that started early in the morning. We had a pleasant time chatting and laughing, and I helped Christina to wash and clean up later. Irena and Ninette brought platters of food too, and Christina dropped me home in the afternoon. Christian brought his old mobile, and some other knick knacks later that day.

I was surprised when Babs called that evening, and said that Aunty was admitted to hospital in the afternoon, as she was unable to move and was disoriented. I said, "It sounds like a stroke." But she replied, "I'm not sure what's wrong with Mummy." So I called Connie, but Esme had told him, and he knew already, and he went to hospital straight after work.

She told Connie later that night, that it was Josephine's funeral that day, but she did not attend. Only Paul, his brother, and family were present. Esme did not tell me when the funeral was going to be held, and I was very sad, as I would miss Josephine very much. My consolation was that Connie and I visited her often when she was alive, and needed company. So it did not matter, if we were not present at her funeral. She was so angry with her sons, and daughters-in-law, and constantly told them, "I *don't* want any of you to come to my funeral!" Ironically, only her sons, and Yvonne, were the only ones present.

I took Misty on Friday morning for her cortisone injection. And after I returned home, I settled her in her basket, and drove to Mornington to meet Mary Lou, as she wanted to have coffee with me. We spent a couple of hours at a cafe in Main Street, but as it was wet and gloomy, I came home soon, after shopping at Mornington Safeway. Then I called Babs to ask how Aunty was, and she said she was heavily sedated, as she was in a great deal of pain. But she still could not tell me what exactly was wrong with her.

Babs asked me to let Aunty Molly know what was happening, so I did, and then I spoke to Ninette. Around nine thirty that night, Babs was at the door. She said she was feeling down-hearted, and wanted to stay overnight, as it was too late for her to drive back home.

She said she was very appreciative of all that Connie and I did for Aunty through the years. And that we should be happy we made her comfortable, especially over the last few years; she had a beautiful unit to live in, and seen to it that she lacked nothing, as Connie managed her pension carefully. Babs said, "You gave Mummy dignity in her old age, and she was always saying how much Connie and Dolly have done for her, and she blessed you both daily for giving her such a beautiful place to live in." She gave Connie a bottle of whisky, and a nice indoor plant for me to say, "Thank You" for all we did.

After she had dinner, and settled down a little, Babs said, "There's some ill-feeling between the rest of the family and me, because you know what control freaks my sisters are. They dictate what everyone else must to do, regarding Mummy, and they're just like Mafia!"

They also resented us for whatever we did to make Aunty happy and comfortable, and were always ready to criticize.

Babs knew how much we did, because she had spent a great deal of time with her mother, and Aunty Molly, and taken them for long trips and holidays. She said, "Mummy used to say that she had enjoyed the happiest times with both of you, when she went on all those trips over the past years. So think of the good times you shared with her and be happy." After chatting a little longer, we went to bed long after midnight.

I woke up early next day and had breakfast with Babs, and she left around midday. Connie taped the box I packed for Nilanthi, and dropped it off in Dandenong, in time for the next shipment at the end of the month. As soon as he returned, we visited Aunty in Frankston hospital. She was very frail and vague, but when I kissed her, she said in a drowsy voice, "I love you." I replied, "I love you too Aunty." And I held her hand, as she drifted into a deep sleep.

She was heavily sedated, and the doctor told Connie she had renal trouble, and suffered a mild stroke as well, so they were just keeping her comfortable. After we left hospital, Connie agreed to drive down to visit Shirani and Ranjith.

It was wet and stormy, and gusty winds ripped trees savagely when we drove down to Woolamai. I was amazed to see the restaurant, as Shirani did a marvellous job transforming the old shed, and I told her it was a great renovation. We spent a couple of hours there, and arrived home late in the evening. I was weary, but made dinner and then took it easy.

We visited Elvira on Sunday afternoon, as Connie wanted to meet John. She made scones, and we enjoyed a delicious afternoon tea. Then we drove to look around the block of land, before returning home in lashing rain.

I took Simba for his vaccine next day, and Christian dropped in later to say he visited Aunty, and she was in a very bad way. I was glad he saw her, because she was so weak, that I doubted she would go back home. I asked Christian to come for dinner with Athena, and made a quick meal, but he called to say it was too late for them to come that night.

Ninette asked me to visit early next day, as she wanted me to sort out some of her videos, and then walk with her to the shops.

After doing odd jobs and helping her out, I went to the medical clinic to get a referral to see Dr Kertes. I decided it would be best to get a second opinion from him, before I went for an angiogram.

Shirani said she would visit, and I was ready early next day, but she called to say she had a few bookings, and could not make it. Christian and Athena dropped in later. They stayed a couple of hours, updated the computer, and helped me with a few technical issues. We chatted till late, and had a pleasant evening.

When I called Nilanthi on Thursday, 1 October, she said Heron was very ill, and she was exhausted looking after him, as she had no help from anyone around. She broke down and cried, as she said she had had enough. I felt very sorry for her plight, and tried to comfort her, but she was inconsolable, and kept asking, "How much *longer* do I have to bear this burden!"

Connie called a little while later, and said he had to attend a family meeting at the hospital that afternoon. Because they wanted to know where to admit Aunty, as they would not let her go home again.

When he came home that evening, he was very agitated and stressed, because his siblings were divided, and objected to Aunty going into a nursing home, or palliative care. Roland, Geraldine, Esme, Cristobel, and his brother, Paul, wanted Aunty sent back home. And only Babs and Connie agreed that she would be better off in a home. So they argued and quarrelled with each other, until Connie was fed up with the bickering.

Each one of them wanted total ownership and control, as they were all very possessive of their mother. I sympathised with Connie, but the hospital would not keep Aunty much longer. And if the family could not decide what to do, they said they would admit her to palliative care. When I went shopping next day, Connie met me at Karingal for a coffee, as he wanted to discuss what was happening with the family.

I booked Misty to have her teeth cleaned, because I thought her teeth were causing pain, and that was the reason she was not eating well. Misty was up early next morning, mewing her head off. She was hungry, because she had nothing to eat since the night before. The vet told me that she needed to fast from midnight, because of the anaesthetic.

When Connie heard her mewing so loudly that morning, he let her out of the garage. And she waddled into the kitchen and tucked into the food in the kittens' bowls. I only hoped she would not be sick during the anaesthetic.

It cost more than three hundred dollars to clean her teeth. I saved half, and paid the other half with the credit card, as Connie would have strongly objected, if he knew what it cost to clean a cat's teeth! After dropping her, I came home feeling anxious about the poor little thing.

When I called the vet at midday, he said Misty was doing alright, and I could pick her up in the evening. I went to Onde's for a coffee with Karen later, and we had an interesting conversation for a couple of hours. Then I picked Misty on my way, and was glad that she looked fine. The vet said her teeth were not too bad, but they cleaned them up just the same, and did not extract any. Christian called to say they would drop in later, and they stayed a couple of hours, so we had an enjoyable time as always.

Connie visited Aunty in hospital on Saturday, 3 October, but I did not go, as I wished her farewell on my last visit. And I did not want to see her so helpless and under sedation. We drove to Moorabbin that evening, to a restaurant called, "Silky Dragon" to celebrate Sherone's fiftieth birthday. Paul Maschio wanted a lift, and to drop him home later, as Esme needed the car to visit Aunty in hospital. She did not want to come for Sherone's birthday dinner, so he came with us. We left the restaurant after ten thirty, and dropped Paul on our way home.

The last time we visited Con and Cornelia, they asked if I could teach their six-year old, step-grandson, piano. And I agreed, if they brought him over on a Sunday afternoon. He was Andrei's partner's son from a previous relationship. Con said he was very keen to learn piano.

But he called early on Sunday, to say that they could not bring him that afternoon, due to some problem with his mother. I asked them over anyway, as I baked a cake, and made some finger food. It was a pleasant, spring day, and they came later that afternoon.

But unfortunately, they had some issues with their son, Andrei, and his partner, who decided to break up. Cornelia was very upset, and the two of them bickered non-stop from the time they arrived. I felt very uncomfortable when Con swore at Cornelia in his frustration, and he used four-letter words freely. We suggested a drive, just to get their minds off their troubles. And we spent a couple of hours walking on the beach, after looking around in Mount Martha, and the houses being constructed near our land.

We chatted for a few more hours when we came home, and I was glad that they calmed down, before they left late that evening. I had no idea they could get into such a state, especially Con, who was violently angry, and verbally abusive, because she tried to exonerate Andrei's behaviour. She did not want him to break up with his partner, as she was very attached to the little boy.

It was the start of term four next day, and I was very busy at school, and also with the students, who came home after school. So the next few days passed quickly.

Connie spent time with Aunty after work, and made several trips to Mornington council, before going to work. It was a very trying time for him, especially with so many issues. Christian and Athena visited on Wednesday, and I drove there next day, to learn more computer skills from Athena.

Connie met the social worker in the hospital on Thursday, 9 October, as they moved Aunty to palliative care the night before. I called Nilanthi and Ninette in the afternoon, and told them what was happening with Aunty, as they were concerned. When Connie returned home late that evening, he looked exhausted, and very stressed, and he wanted to go for a walk on the pier. When he came back later, we watched a few comedies together, as I wanted him to relax and take his mind off the on-going drama with his siblings.

The phone rang at four o'clock on Saturday morning. We expected that call anytime, as we knew Aunty was not going to last too long. When Connie answered the phone, I woke up too, as I heard Cristobel screaming at him, "Mummy isn't dead *yet* and you are going to sell her unit! I curse you and hope you die and *rot* in hell!" She slammed the phone down, and we looked at each other in disbelief.

What on earth possessed her to say such things, I do not know. We could not go back to sleep, as we were very upset. I was sorry for Connie, that at a sad time like this, his youngest sister should curse him for no reason. I made a cup of coffee for him, and Esme called within the hour to say that Aunty died a few minutes ago. I held him close and comforted him, saying, "You have done your best for Aunty always, so you have nothing to regret."

When Connie told Esme what Cristobel had said, she replied that she came to the unit when Geraldine and she were taking down some pictures from the wall, and jumped down their throats too. They told her they wanted to clean up the place, as Connie would be selling the unit when Aunty died, so that was the reason why she had screamed at him. Cristobel told her sisters later, "Why can't Connie mortgage his house, and keep this unit, so I can come here to grieve for Mummy?" She was absolutely clueless, and ignorant about financial affairs.

Connie had no support or sympathy from *any* of them, except Babs. And he turned to me solely during this traumatic time, when they should have comforted and helped each other. After a quick shower, he rushed to the hospital, but I did not want to be there, as it was very distressing. I wanted to remember all the good times only, and how Aunty was in the past. When Connie came home at midday, he made an appointment with the funeral director to visit us that afternoon.

When we pre-paid our funerals in 2001, we organized Aunty's too. And she discussed her last wishes with the representative, regarding her funeral service. Roland and Cristobel called several times now, to dictate what Connie should do about her funeral. His brother, Paul, wanted some of Aunty's ashes, as he said he wanted them to remember her. Connie refused to do so, and said that Aunty's request was to scatter her ashes in the sea, and he did not want to divide the ashes.

Roland and the others called Connie, and told him there was nothing wrong in giving Paul some of the ashes, and so the petty squabbling went on. After the funeral director left, we went to Mount Martha, and walked around Waterview Drive. Then we visited Christian and Athena, who were very supportive and sympathetic. Connie told me that he was glad he had the three of us to help him get through this time. And he was very disappointed with his siblings' behaviour and attitude. My sisters, and all our friends called to offer their condolences.

I continued to console Connie constantly, and told him that Aunty led a long life, as she was ninety-one. And he was always a very loving and dutiful son, as long as I had known him. In the last ten years, his priority was work, then Aunty's welfare, so he had nothing to regret. But I knew he was emotionally bereft, as he was very close to his mother, and would miss her greatly.

My mind went back to what Anne, the naturopath, told me about fifteen years ago. "You are going to have a very difficult time when Conrad loses his mother, because he is very dependent on her emotionally." No one knew that better than I.

I typed a list of family members' names, to send the newspapers next morning. Connie could hardly concentrate on any of the mundane details, and he asked me to write Aunty's eulogy, and program for the service. I replied, "Connie, you know I loved Aunty very much, and don't mind doing that, but she was *your* mother! You should write sincerely what is in your heart! I will type it for you, and help you with the program, but you must try to write what you feel." He replied, "You knew her just as well for so long, and you can write it for me, I can't think properly, too many things on my mind."

I said I would write a draft, and he could add or delete whatever he wanted. He then asked me to write a poem, to include in the program at the end of the service, and said, "But don't put your name, as the family will be upset and make a fuss, because you wrote a poem for Mummy." I did as he asked, as I wanted to ease his burden and grief, so I went along with whatever he said. It was the first time in many years that he turned to me, and depended on me to see him through this trauma, as his siblings turned away from him completely.

We picked up Judy Bartosy from Carrum next day, on Sunday, and drove to Hawthorn for Karen's book launch, as I told her I would attend. When I asked Connie if he was alright to drive, and attend the launch, he said he did not mind. I was glad, as I knew it would take his mind off the immediate problems and sadness, if we went out for a while.

It was a good turnout in an old hotel, and I bought a copy of her first book, which was a collection of stories, and I looked forward to reading it. We dropped Judy later, and Connie went to meet the priest at Frankston. And I drove out to get groceries. When I came home, Connie had returned, and was on the phone to one of his siblings. He was busy organizing funeral details, and the phone did not stop ringing till midnight. I was worn-out hearing the constant bickering going on between Connie and his siblings, and longed for a break.

I was at school on Monday, but Connie stayed home to attend to several matters. Once the students finished their lessons after school, I took it easy. We drove to Port Melbourne at six o'clock next morning, for the tile selection. After we finished, we stopped at the funeral parlour in Cheltenham, to organize leaflets for the service, and preparations for the rosary that evening. I rested a while, before going to the chapel in Cheltenham at six o'clock, as it was a long, tiring day.

The whole family, and some close friends were already there. Cristobel saw us as we parked the car, and she scooted off in the opposite direction. Esme came up and said, "Bella is going around telling everyone that the coffin is a cheap one, and I told her who cares about that, as I want to be buried in a wooden box!"

We were shocked at Cristobel's behaviour at such a place and occasion. Connie told Esme, "Mummy chose that coffin, as she knew she was going to be cremated, and told us she was happy with her choice." Esme replied, "I know what Mummy was like, and she couldn't have cared less, if it was an expensive coffin or not."

The coffin stood in the middle of the chapel, and was covered with a dark-blue, velvet cloth, and Cristobel peeped under the cloth to see what it looked like. Connie and I ignored her, as she sidled up to Sherone and Valerie. Geraldine was at loggerheads with Shiranthi, so Clifford and she sat on one side of the chapel. They did not speak to Shiranthi or to us, neither did Paul and his wife Sanit. Joelle, Celine, and Micheline came too. I spoke to them later, and told Joelle what was going on, as all the siblings ignored each other and the two of us.

Wednesday was a student-free day, so I had time to prepare for the funeral. The phone rang from early morning. Roland called first, to tell Connie that he wanted to "upgrade" the coffin. He spoke to the funeral director about it, who then called Connie to say he could not do anything, without Connie's permission, as he was executor of Aunty's will. Connie told the funeral director not to move his mother's body, as he did not want the coffin to be changed.

Connie asked Roland, "How *much* do you want to spend, and *who* will pay for it?" Roland replied, "Benjamin will pay five thousand dollars on his credit card for a better coffin!" Connie lost his temper, and told him off, as he knew they did not have that kind of money to throw. And what annoyed Connie most, was that Roland did not mind Benjamin getting into debt, just because he listened to Cristobel.

Then Geraldine spoke to me. And I thought she was really off this planet, as she kept me on the phone for forty minutes, saying, "You were so lucky you stayed with Mummy in Ceylon, and she looked after you, and she kept you in the convent." And she kept on about how much they had done for me when I stayed with them. That was way back in 1970. So I said, "I have repaid Aunty and Uncle a hundred times over in the last forty years or so, for all what they did for me then." I could not understand where she was coming from, or what brought on this conversation.

She spoke accusingly, as if she resented the fact I had stayed with her parents, and she became very argumentative. I held my tongue, as I did not want to get involved in a useless squabble. It was not the time or place for this conversation, and finally, I excused myself, saying I had to get ready for the funeral. I told Connie about her blabbering, and he too was at a loss to understand why she carried on about the past on a day like this.

Before the funeral started, Cristobel strutted up to Connie, with Roland in her wake, and said that she wanted them to play some songs she chose. Connie said the hymns were chosen already. She retorted, "Mummy *loved* this song, "Wind Beneath My Wings." *I* know what she liked, better than you!"

Connie asked the funeral director to play that song just to appease her, but they did have not Bette Midler's rendition, only the instrumental version, so she was unhappy. On the previous night, she argued with Connie about the hymns, and told him she would not attend the funeral, if he chose traditional hymns, which Connie said Aunty always loved to sing.

To my utter surprise then, Roland brushed past Christian, Athena, and me a few times, and ignored us completely! I wondered what he had against us, and why he was so rude. But when his cousin, Lena, walked past, he grabbed her, and exclaimed, "Hello *darling*!" And he was all over her, like a rash, hugging and kissing her excitedly. He barely spoke to Connie either, as he, and the rest of the family sat on one side of the chapel.

Connie told them he would read the eulogy, but Roland wanted to read a lengthy tribute too. Roland told the funeral director that all the grandchildren planned to do a few readings. But the director said the service was scheduled for forty-five minutes only, and they could not fit in so many readings, as well as the priest's sermon.

Connie's siblings looked utterly miserable, not just with grief, but with all the underlying issues and rancour towards Connie and me. We paid about eight hundred dollars, to cater food and drinks for the Wake, and did our best to make sure it went off without any confusion. Connie warned Ifti and Glen, to keep an eye on Cristobel, in case she started to make a fuss there. They were more than happy to do so, as they all knew she was quite capable of creating an unpleasant scene.

I was glad to see Mary, Elvira, Joelle, Celine, Micheline, Lorraine, and Tony, besides all Connie's colleagues, and boss, Mathew. I spoke to them afterwards, and Mathew said the service was well organized. Connie asked Esme to select some photographs of Aunty, taken over the last few years, and they showed them on a screen after the service.

The priest had other duties to attend to, so he kept his sermon short. Connie read the eulogy well, but he became emotional at times. Christian, Athena, and I sat with him during the service, and he was glad, as he was very disappointed with his siblings.

Just before we left, Lena stopped to exchange a few words with me, and Connie walked past, barely acknowledging her. When we went to the car, he asked, "Who was that woman you were talking to?" I replied, "Didn't you recognize your cousin?" He mumbled vaguely, "She doesn't look *anything* like Aunty, I didn't know who she was." I could not blame him, because she was extremely over-weight, with sparse, frizzy hair, and dressed in drab clothes.

We stopped at a cafe on our way, and sipped coffee, as Connie was still very distraught after the funeral, and came home later. Christian and Athena spent the afternoon with us, so we decided to have dinner at Rugantino's restaurant. It was good to unwind for a couple of hours, and they drove off from there. We returned home, tired, and emotionally drained. At least the funeral was over now, and Connie only had to scatter the ashes in the sea on Saturday. He was exhausted, and I told him to have an early night.

He was grateful for all I did and said, "Thank you Dolla, for everything you do. I couldn't have written the eulogy better. At such a time like this, I thought my brothers and sisters would support me, but I'm sick and tired of their bickering over petty things. Poor Mummy would have been so sad to think her children behaved like they did at her funeral." I replied, "It's the least I could have done during this sad time. I'm happy the service went off well, even though your family didn't behave the way they should have." And I told him how Roland ignored Christian, Athena and me.

He woke up early next day, to meet the priest, and arrange a service prior to the scattering of Aunty's ashes. I had an appointment with the heart specialist, Dr Kertes, at his Knox clinic that afternoon. We drove there, and after examining me, he said he would perform an angiogram at Austin hospital, and to cancel the booking at Frankston hospital.

We stopped at Lorraine's briefly on our way, and thanked them for attending the funeral. Then we had a look at Dimmey's in Dandenong, as we had to get a few more items for our costumes for the play. Christian and Athena dropped in later, and we had dinner together.

It was torrential next day, but I went shopping in the afternoon, and Connie was busy organizing the service. He called all his family members to tell them the time and venue, but Roland, Cristobel, Paul, and Geraldine said they were not attending the service.

I did not feel too well on Saturday morning, so I did not accompany Connie, but Christian and Athena went with him to the rocks near Oliver's Hill in Frankston. Afterwards, Aunty Molly, Babs, Jeremy, Christina, and their two children came home, and had lunch with us. Now that everything was finished, I hoped we could have some peace, without any more bickering and arguments with Connie's siblings.

Shirani and Ranjith were unable to attend the funeral, as they were busy with bookings, so they visited on Sunday afternoon, and brought a huge bouquet of irises from her garden in Woolamai. We attended evening Mass and spent a quiet time later.

Chapter 51

After the hectic weekend, I was exhausted on Monday, and when I came home after school, I fell asleep for a couple of hours. Dr Kertes wrote to say he had booked me in for an angiogram at the Austin hospital on 26 October, and to do an ECG and blood test prior to the procedure.

Sarah and Mitchell came for piano lessons in the evening, and Sarah, who had a beautiful voice, sang and accompanied herself. She learnt new songs every week, and I was very proud of her, and encouraged her to keep on singing, and learning piano.

After walking the kittens around the garden next day, I locked them in the cat cage, and Connie drove me to the pathology clinic at eight o'clock in the morning. We came home within the hour, and I took it easy, but when I tried to do my usual chores, I felt light-headed and tired. I visited Ninette briefly in the afternoon, but came home soon, and relaxed before the students came for lessons.

I tumbled down again as I came downstairs next day, but it was not too bad this time, except for a sprained ankle and sore back. I went to school in spite of the pain, but limped painfully. It was a pleasant, sunny day, and I did some shopping later, but my back and ankle ached all evening. Christian and Athena said they would drop in, but he called later to say they were too busy, and would come some other time.

The weather continued to warm up, and the kittens were so excited to walk out in the garden. I still did not let them wander off alone, in case they got lost. Mishka loved being outdoors all the time, and both kittens looked so forlorn when I locked them up in the cat cage.

We drove to Mount Martha on Saturday, and saw the "Sold" sign on our block. Then we hurried to Karingal to watch the movie, "Mao's Last Dancer," which was excellent, and I enjoyed it very much. We came home early, after some shopping, as I wanted to prepare a few things for the angiogram tomorrow.

I fasted from nine o'clock the previous night, and woke up feeling famished, at five o'clock in the morning. I let the kittens play, then walked them for twenty minutes, before locking them in the cat cage. Misty was alright inside the house, as she slept all day, and did not get up to any mischief, unlike the two kittens. I hoped they would be alright till evening. Connie munched on fruit loudly all the way to the hospital. And I wanted to tell him he was making me feel hungrier, but I refrained from saying anything.

He looked subdued and vague when he told me that he soiled his pants the night before, and was afraid he was losing bowel control. But I told him it could have been a one off thing, and not to worry about it. We arrived at the hospital at eight o'clock, and a very pleasant nurse, Peter, looked after me.

The cardiologist, Dr Logan, said he would be performing the procedure that day, as Dr Kertes would be observing only. Dr Kertes came out of the theatre a little while later and told me, "The ECG shows you have had a heart attack, and some of your arteries are hardening with some deposits too. We have some new drugs now that we can use to help you, so don't worry." Connie went to one of the near-by Woolworths stores, as he said he wanted to do some work on the computer, until I was ready to go home.

After the angiogram, Dr Kertes told me, "When you had a heart attack, there was a blockage in your main artery, which dissolved because you are on asprin, but I have prescribed something stronger now. Take it easy, and don't get stressed. I'll see you again in a few month's time."

When Connie came to pick me up, instead of asking how I was, and what the doctor said, he sniffed around, stared at me, and barked, "What's that bad *smell*? Did they wash you?" I replied, "What smell? They didn't have to wash me, as there was no need to." But he kept sniffing the air around, and muttered, "I can get a bad smell here."

Once inside the car, I tried to tell him what they found, and that I had suffered a heart attack. But he hardly paid any attention, as he mumbled, "It must be the smell of sewerage outside the hospital. I thought you had gone out in your pants, and that was the bad smell, because I soiled my pants last night, and I thought you must have done the same."

I looked at him in disbelief. It was difficult to understand why he said such things to me. But I knew he felt bad about soiling his pants, so he wanted to make me feel equally bad. I was just told that I had suffered a heart attack, and all he could do was talk about bad smells.

I was very upset, to say the least, and did not speak all the way home, and he did not ask me what the doctor found out, or how I felt. When we came home, I went upstairs to rest, and asked him to walk the kittens and feed them too, as I was too tired.

He stormed into the room a few minutes later, and shouted, "You be *thankful* you have a husband who takes you to hospital! Other husbands wouldn't do all that for their wives, and look at your attitude!" I was too weary to argue, but asked, "What attitude? You hurt me, when all you could talk about was a bad smell, and not even care when I told you I had suffered a heart attack." He growled, "You didn't talk to me all the way home!" Then he muttered under his breath and fumed off.

I stayed in bed next day, and Connie worked from home till lunch-time. But he did not have anything to say to me, and did not even come up to ask if I needed anything. Ninette said she would visit me on Thursday afternoon with Toula. Then I spoke to my sisters, and they were relieved when I said I was alright, but had suffered a mild heart attack. Christian and Athena visited in the evening, and I was happy to see them. But I felt light-headed still, so I had an early night.

I felt much better on Wednesday, and walked the kittens in the warm sunshine. I could not drive to the shops that day, so I asked Connie to buy some summer shoes that were on sale at Rivers Store in Mornington. He said they had sold out my size, but drove to the store at Somerville, and bought four pairs. I thanked him, as it was good of him to drive to Somerville, and they were pretty shoes.

I stayed in bed that day, read, and hand-stitched some hems, as I still had chest pains and a headache. Dr Kertes sent the prescriptions via email, and Connie said he would get them in the evening. I started taking blood- thinning medication instead of asprin from then on.

I was up every hour or so that night, running to the toilet, but did not know if it was due to the new drugs, and felt very weak next day. But as Ninette and Toula were visiting, I kept some Christmas cake and biscuits ready for tea, and then cleaned up the place. They arrived at about three o'clock, but did not eat or drink anything, as they said it was too hot. It was about twenty eight degrees, and still very warm. I took the cats walking after they left and then rested.

I called the nurse at Austin hospital next day, as I did not feel any better, and she said that if I still felt the same over the next couple of days, it was best to check with my doctor, or go to emergency. I felt so weak that I could hardly play the piano. And when I called Nilanthi, she was concerned when I told her I was still feeling very tired and weak. Connie came home early and we went shopping, as I did not want to drive on my own. It was a very warm night, and a fierce storm broke out suddenly. I was worried about the cats, but they hid inside their igloos and seemed alright in the cat cage.

We drove to Dandenong next day, Saturday, to do our tax returns, and the accountant advised us not to sell the two units, before Connie's retirement, because of capital gains taxes. But we decided to sell the unit in Frankston, as we could not afford to keep it, and build a new house in Mount Martha as well.

It was still sizzling at thirty degrees that evening, but I walked the cats and then prepared to go for a play at the Briars at seven o'clock. We had a great time solving the murder mystery in a western called, "The Good, The Bad And The Stinky," which was hilarious. Connie and I dressed up as a cowboy and cowgirl. The play was performed in the old shed at the Briars, and was not really comfortable, but it was a fun night.

A severe storm broke out during the play however, and it was so noisy that at times we could hardly hear the actors speak. Ginny and Alan seemed much better after there recent ailments, and they could not believe it when Connie told them I suffered a mild heart attack only a couple of weeks ago. Ginny said, "But you *look* so well Dolly! I can't believe it!" I was very tired next day though, so Connie went to church on his own.

I still felt weak, dizzy, and listless, over the next few days, so I called the nurse again, and she advised me to see my doctor. He was not in till the following Thursday, but I made an appointment to see him anyway. I continued with my usual routine though, and invited Christian and Athena for dinner. When they came, he said he hurt his back doing some work at home, and was in a great deal of pain, but he never took pain killers. He always worked so hard, that I told him to take it easy, when he was in so much pain.

When I saw doctor, he said I could be suffering from possible side-effects of the new medication, but nothing was wrong with me, just flu symptoms. He told me to take it easy, and not to stop taking the medication. The weather continued to be warm and in the mid-thirties, so I enjoyed walking the kittens in the garden.

I was surprised to hear from Yvonne, Josephine's daughter-in-law, that day. She was effusive, and exclaimed, "Congratulations, I couldn't put down Luigi's book! It's the best book I have read in a long time! Thank you so much!"

I gave Josephine a copy, and while clearing up her room, Yvonne found it and started reading it. I thanked her for her feedback. When she attended Aunty's funeral, we spoke briefly. Now she repeated, "My mother-in-law loved you with a passion! Thank you for all you did to make her happy." I replied, "She was very dear to me as well, and I do miss her very much."

Chapter 52

The scorching weather continued over the next few days, and it was too hot to do anything. I did not visit Ninette on Tuesday, as it was still sizzling. Christian and Athena dropped in the night before, but as it was too hot to eat spicy food, we just chatted and spent some time together.

Babs, Aunty Molly, and a couple of their friends dropped in unexpectedly that afternoon, and spent some time with me. Aunty Molly was very dejected over Aunty's death, and sobbed, "I miss my sister so much! I can't get over her death!" I pacified her, and invited her to stay with us whenever she wanted to, and she said she would come over soon.

Connie took Simba to get him de-sexed on Friday morning, 13 November, and I picked him up later in the afternoon. He was still a little groggy, but he was alright. And I watched him over the next few days, to make sure he did not pull out his stitches.

We drove to Karingal on Saturday afternoon, and watched, "A Christmas Carol" starring Jim Carey. It was in 3D and very well done, but I thought it was too gimmicky for my liking, and preferred the old version. On our way home after the movie, we drove to Mount Martha, and walked around for a while. We were impatient for the building to start soon, but due to the planning delays, it did not look as if the house would be ready in April 2010, as promised.

The council did not approve of the proposed cut and fill, which was about two metres deep. Porter Davis said they could not build the house we selected, unless they dug two metres deep. It was an impasse, and Connie spent hours negotiating with the council authorities.

We visited Christian and Athena next day, and wished her for her birthday on Monday. And after walking on the pier and coffee at Dromana, we attended Mass in Rosebud.

I watched a documentary about Audrey Hepburn's life that night, and it was very poignant. She was one of my favourite movie stars; I just loved all her movies, her inimitable elegance, and stunning looks. She lived her life well, and was productive to the end of her days. I admired the work she did for several charities.

School was chaotic next day, with builders everywhere, and the noise was intense; drilling, hammering, and banging going on all around. I could not find a quiet place for the piano. And Colleen moved it to the corridor, where it was very hot, and the noise unbearable. I wore my hat and sunglasses, as the sun streamed into the corridor. I could hardly wait to come home and rest, as I was worn-out with the heat and noise.

Connie took one week's leave, starting that Monday, and he was out when I came home, so I took it easy until the students came for piano lessons. I invited Christian and Athena to drop in, and they enjoyed the special dinner I made them.

Connie left at seven o'clock next morning, to meet John at the block, and get the grass and shrubbery cleared. I picked up Ninette at midday, and drove her to Mount Martha to visit her niece, Helen, who lived in a beautiful house, in a bushland setting. We spent a pleasant afternoon, chatting to Helen and her teenage daughter and son. Ninette was very happy to see them, and we left in a couple of hours time.

I dropped her around three o'clock, and when I came home, Connie told me that our application was still not approved. He was very angry, and kept saying that the builder should attend to all this, without letting him do all the hard work. We wondered what would happen now, in case the council rejected the application, which meant we would have to go through another builder. Because Porter Davis builders were inflexible, and built only their display homes.

I kept some presents, and a card for Connie on the bench top next morning, and he too left presents and a card there. I wished him a happy anniversary, and then went to school.

It was thirty two degrees that day, and builders were everywhere, making a great deal of noise. The piano was out in the corridor still. I finished early and left after lunch. When I came home, I walked Mishka first, as she was mewing her head off.

I did not feel like going out for dinner to celebrate our anniversary, as I was exhausted with the heat. I watered the garden later, and we spent a quiet evening. Connie met with the town planner, and Porter Davis the following day, to discuss options.

The sweltering weather continued, and went up to thirty six degrees next day, and he left early. I called Nilanthi and we chatted for some time. She still complained bitterly that it was very difficult caring for Heron. And she asked his children to admit him to hospital. I hoped they would do something soon, as she sounded exhausted. I did some grocery shopping later on, then Christian and Athena dropped in, and we enjoyed a pleasant time. Connie came home late, and was very annoyed because he had to go back to the council next day.

When he met the council officer again, Connie said he was frustrated with all the clauses and conditions. And he doubted very much that Porter Davis would start building until the following April. It was so close to Christmas, and builders did not work from early December to late January.

The weather was much cooler on Monday, at twenty degrees, which was a great relief after the heat wave. I noticed that the Jag had a flat tyre, before I drove to school that morning. And I waited twenty minutes, until RACV came and changed it. It was chaotic still, with on-going building at the school, so I came home early. When Connie returned, he drove the Jag, and checked all the tyres.

It was still the same at school on Wednesday, as the builders were expected to be there for a long time. When I called Nilanthi that evening, she said that Heron lingered helplessly, as he could hardly move now. We chatted for a while, and I comforted her. I told her to be strong, as everything comes to an end.

A severe thunderstorm broke out that evening, after the extreme hot weather, and the deafening noise crashed non-stop. I called Christian and Athena, to wish them on their ninth wedding anniversary, and they wanted to drop in later, in spite of the bad weather. They came around ten o'clock, and left within the hour, as they too were tired. But it was great to spend even a brief time with them. I had a restless night, and was awake till early dawn.

It was the Women Writers last meeting for the year that Friday. Connie drove me to the city in the morning, and went to one of the Woolworths stores nearby. I enjoyed a few hours with the group, as it was the Christmas break up party, with readings, and competition prizes as well. When Connie picked me up in the afternoon, we stopped for a coffee on our way, before coming home.

We drove to the Community Centre, Mount Eliza, on Saturday evening, for Frankston Theatre Group's annual Christmas play. It was always a farce, and this year, "Not Now Darling' was hilarious, and we enjoyed it immensely. Ginny, Alan, Peter, Penny, and Louise, from Nomad Players, sat at our table too, and we laughed all through the evening. It was after eleven o'clock when we came home, and then we stayed up and watched a couple of episodes of "Father Ted" on DVD.

I had another strange dream about Stacy that night; a short, dark, young man, tapped on our door, and introduced himself, and then said, "Stacy has been bitten by a shark! Nine wounds!" I did not see Stacy in my dream though. I woke up feeling very sad and weary, as I wondered what these dreams meant.

I wrote merit certificates next day, which I gave my piano students at the end of year concert. I kept busy, and tried not to think too much about Stacy, or what the dream signified. We attended Mass in the evening, and by the time we returned, the heavens opened.

Poor Misty looked very frail, and was not eating much, and I felt helpless, as I watched her deteriorate. I knew she could not last too long, and could not bear the thought of losing another much-loved pet.

The new kitchen in the school was completed on Monday, 30 November, and it looked very nice. All the students who were performing at the end of year concert, said that their parents and families would attend next Sunday. I asked Christian and Athena for dinner that night, but they could not make it, as they were busy working. I invited them whenever I cooked their favourite dishes. And if they were not too busy, they were glad to spend a few hours with us.

I did not fall asleep till dawn once again, and it was a very disturbed night. These bouts of insomnia were very exhausting. But I visited Ninette, and enjoyed a pleasant afternoon, listening to music. Then I walked with her to the shops before I returned home.

I held a rehearsal at school on Wednesday morning, and listened to all the children playing their recital pieces. They seemed confident enough, even the beginners, so I was pleased. I stopped at the church office after school, to pick up the keys for the hall. But when I came home, I realized I did not have the key to the piano, which was locked.

I spoke to Nilanthi and Shirani, then called Babs, to wish her for her birthday tomorrow. She was pleased, and we talked for some time. Christian and Athena dropped in later, and spent a couple of hours doing updates on the computer. We chatted for a while when they finished, and had a pleasant evening.

I picked up the key next day, and played the piano for a while, as I wanted to check if it was tuned, and it sounded alright.

I took Misty for her injection the following day, and told the vet that she hardly ate at all. And he said that the injection may help her to regain her appetite. Then he checked her, and took her blood pressure, and said she was not too bad. When I called Nilanthi later, she said that Heron was still the same, as doctors could not do much for him, and just made him comfortable.

I made final preparations for the concert that afternoon, and Christmas treats afterwards, as the children looked forward to the party and presents. Madeline came over, and told me that she passed Grade Four piano examination with honours. I was very pleased that she progressed so well. She thanked me for teaching her, and I told her to keep practising daily.

I organized last minute details on Sunday morning, and we drove to Xavier Centre one hour before the concert started, at two o'clock. I arranged all the food on the table, and Connie set up chairs, and moved the piano. The concert went very well, and I was pleased to see my past students, Charlotte, Tabitha, and some others. The hall was packed with all the students' families and friends. My past students looked so grown-up in just one year, especially Charlotte, who looked very pretty, and used make-up. Sarah played and sang beautifully, and all the other students did their best. The parents thanked me for my hard work, and I wished them all a Merry Christmas. We cleaned up the place, and came home by four o'clock. At last, I could take it easy, now that it was over (until the next time).

It was hectic at School on Monday, and I visited Ninette next day. I finished the last lessons for the year on Wednesday, and took cards and gifts for my friends. I came home early though, as I expected Christian and Athena later.

Grade six graduation ceremony took place on Thursday,10 December. I went to church at six o'clock, and was happy to meet the parents of past students. And I could not believe that Alice looked so grown-up at seventeen. Her mother told me she was more settled now, and they did not have as many issues with her as before. I was pleased to hear that, as I was fond of Alice, and hoped she would overcome her teenage problems.

Joelle and Joanne met me for afternoon tea at Onde's, that Friday. And later, Joanne and I window-shopped in Main Street, as Joelle left early. I bought an antique telephone for Connie, and hoped he would like it, as I paid a substantial sum for it.

While vacuuming on Saturday, I caught my finger in the powerful vacuum cleaner, and skinned it badly. It was very painful, and took a while to heal. Then I had a very bad morning, as Connie was annoyed over some issue, and he just kept on arguing, until my head started to spin.

I was so weary of these constant altercations, because he flew off the handle over such petty issues. But I knew that his anger stemmed from something more deep, which he did not want to discuss. He was very stressed at work, and kept saying they put constant pressure on him, and he had too much to do. He was also very upset with his siblings, who did not visit or contact him since Aunty's funeral. He grieved deeply for his mother too, and he broke down many times, and sobbed brokenly, especially after a few drinks. The slightest irritation though, triggered his simmering temper.

He attended several town planning meetings, and the whole process of building a new house, was just too much for him. I knew he was under a great deal of strain, as he told me many times, "I can't think straight." It should have been an exciting, and happy time, to build again in such a beautiful place like Mt Martha. But everything was too much for Connie to handle now.

The unit in Frankston sold within a month, and the settlement was in early January 2010, which was one less burden.

We spent most weekends driving down to the block, or display home in Cranbourne. But the builder would not start now, as most of them closed till mid-January. So we just had to be patient.

When I drove Ninette to Patterson Lakes the following Tuesday, I went over the curb accidentally. And the car made such a loud noise, that I was worried until I came home. I asked Connie to book the Jag, and we drove it to John's garage in Mornington next day. He fixed the exhaust pipe, which had broken off, and he joked that I must not drive on the curb again. Athena and Christian visited in the evening, and she fixed some problem on my laptop.

I was busy making Christmas cake and shortbread biscuits on 19 December, when Shiranthi and Roland dropped in suddenly. Connie opened the door, and I was very surprised to see them. Shiranthi said that Roland wanted to apologise for his bad behaviour at Aunty's funeral. They blamed Cristobel, and the other siblings for causing all the unpleasantness, but when I asked Roland why he ignored Christian, Athena and me at the funeral, he had no answer.

But I knew it would take some time for Connie to forget his siblings' appalling behaviour, and grief for his mother. I could never be on the same affectionate terms with any of them again, as they showed their true colours. Esme and Paul dropped in that evening too, and we had a late night.

I packed presents for Shirani and the family, bottled cherry liqueur, and then we visited her at Narre Warren on Sunday. And I was happy to see Roshan, June, and their two boys as well.

The weather was sweltering, and Sarah forgot to come for her piano lesson on Monday evening. Tracy called to say that she would come on the following day, and I told her that was alright.

Before going to Ninette's next day, I dropped Christmas cards at all the neighbours' houses. Some of them were home, and I chatted to them before I drove off. Ninette made bean soup and salad, and invited me to have a snack with her. Then

I listened to her playing Neapolitan songs, and later, she wanted to shop at Safeway in Seaford. I was relieved when she said she did not want to go to Bayside shopping centre in Frankston, as parking was impossible during these festive days.

Madeline and Mitch dropped in around nine thirty that night, as it was still very warm, and I was out watering the garden. They chatted for a while, and said they would visit again next day. They were lovely children, and I was very fond of them.

I went to church at ten thirty next morning, for general reconciliation, and came home as soon as service was over, because it was thirty seven degrees. Babs called to have a long chat, as she was still very depressed over her latest marital fiasco. She said that some family members treated her badly because of that.

Mitch and Madeline dropped in that afternoon, and stayed for a while, as they played piano duets, and kept me company. It was slightly cooler on Christmas Eve, and drizzled all day. I made a special dinner for tomorrow, as Christian and Athena were spending Christmas evening with us. I packed presents, called Lorraine, and wished Tony for his birthday, then spoke to Ninette, and some other friends. We went to church at six o'clock in the evening, half an hour before Mass began, but the church was packed already! I was happy to meet all the parents and past students, and chatted with them after Mass.

We woke up late on Christmas day, and I was relieved that it was much cooler. Connie and I exchanged presents and cards, and after an ample breakfast of milk rice and beef curry, we drove down to Dromana for lunch. I packed some steaks, salad and prawns, and we enjoyed a barbeque by the sea.

I walked the cats when we came home, called my sisters, and then prepared a few more dishes for dinner. I had a great time with Christian and Athena as always, and they left after midnight. They gave us some lovely presents, and liked theirs too. Connie cleaned up after they left, as I was very tired. I took it easy on Boxing Day, and after I did some chores, we relaxed that evening.

Connie went out to play golf next day, and I painted for a couple of hours. Then I washed the windows, and cleaned up, as I wanted everything tidy before New Year. I noticed that Misty was not looking too good, so I called the vet, and Scott was in. He said he could give Misty another dose of cortisone, and see if that helped, so I took her down in the afternoon. Even after the injection, she kept faltering around in circles, with a glazed look in her eyes. It was very sad to watch her, and my heart felt leaden when I brought her home.

I made her comfortable, and tried to feed her some tinned food, but she hardly ate. Then I syringed some warm milk, which she swallowed reluctantly. I went out later, and did some shopping. And as I returned, Babs dropped in around eight o'clock, with home-made sweetmeats.

I fed Misty next morning, and once again syringed some warm milk. She was still going around in circles, as she could not walk straight, and looked dizzy and disoriented. The vet told me I had to consider putting her to sleep, if there was no improvement after the second dose of cortizone.

It was heart-wrenching to let her go, but I could not bear to see her suffer, because no matter how traumatic, it was worse for my poor Misty. The vet told me she was not in pain, just wobbly and disoriented all the time. But she was a pathetic sight. And it made me very sad to watch her going around in circles, stumbling and falling over, each time she tried to dig a hole to do her business. I could not stop worrying about Misty, and how I could bear the pain of putting her to sleep.

The temperature soared to thirty five degrees next day, and I watered the garden, and then walked the kittens. Christian said they were driving to Sydney that night to spend New Year there.

I woke up early on 31 December, to check Misty. And she still looked dazed as she stumbled around in circles in the garden, then mewed loudly when she tried to pass water. I fed her, and gave a little warm milk, then spent all morning cuddling and petting her, before walking the two kittens.

Misty wrapped one paw around the guava tree, and then kept going round and round the tree for a long time, until I felt dizzy just watching her. I was on my feet most of the day, keeping an eye on her.

After that day, I could not bear to watch Misty suffer any longer, and knew I must be strong and put her to sleep. She could not focus at all, and when I tried to feed her, she just kept rolling over to a side and falling in a heap. I settled her in comfortably, before going to Elvira's for dinner.

We left home around seven o'clock, and picked up Ninette on our way. Elvira made a delicious meal, and we had a pleasant time, as Mary, Tony, Daphne, a few other friends, John, Elvira, and Ninette were good company. Ninette played the keyboard, and Elvira sang for a little while, and we came home around two thirty in the morning.

Christian called, and then sent text messages to wish us; he said they watched the fireworks, and had enjoyed a good evening. As we came home, I ran in to see if Misty was alright, and then called her upstairs, as I wanted to see if she was any better. But she was still disoriented, and kept falling over every step that she climbed so laboriously.

I rested till late next morning, then fed Misty, and walked the kittens. We drove to Woolamai in the afternoon, and stopped at San Remo to get something that Shirani wanted. The restaurant looked really great, and they gave us a delicious meal. We spent a couple of hours, and I told her I was very proud of her achievements. After we exchanged presents, we drove to Mt Martha, and walked around.

I decided to take Misty to the vet next morning, as I knew it was not fair to keep hanging on to her, when she was suffering. The ache in my heart was unbearable, as I could not stop thinking how much I would miss her.

Misty was still the same on Saturday, 2 January, though a little steadier on her paws. But I called the vet, and made an appointment in the afternoon, and then I fed her some meat, and she drank a little milk. I noticed that she did not have a bowel movement for about four days, and I wanted to ask the vet to give her a laxative. Before taking her down, I let her out in the garden, and she still walked around in circles, and kept leaning on the trees. When the vet examined her, and told me she was blind, I knew the time had come to let her go.

She had gone blind when she had the last stroke, and now I understood why she stepped into her food and water bowls, and walked around in circles. The vet jabbed a pen in front of her eyes, and she did not even blink. This young man was another vet, who was very blunt about her condition. And I was sorry, because Scott treated Misty for a long time, and was very empathetic, and great with my pets, especially Misty.

I thought I would get a laxative for Misty, and bring her home again. But when he told me she was blind, and her condition would only worsen, I had to let her go. So I held her close, right up to the last moment, when the vet injected the lethal dose, and she went limp. Then we brought her lifeless body home. Misty was gone in less than twenty seconds, and my heart froze with pain.

I could not stop crying, as I sat alone in the bedroom and bawled my eyes out, because I missed her so much already. She was with me for so long, and now she was gone. I loved Misty very much, but my only consolation now was, she did not suffer anymore. No matter how heartbroken I was, Connie never offered me any comfort, as I sat alone for hours, and cried my heart out.

I tried to excuse his lack of sympathy, because perhaps he thought it best to leave me alone. But it hurt when he did not come up all evening and offer any words of comfort. Yet, only a few days ago he told me, "When I visited Esme, she was so upset, and was crying, because Bella had fought with her, and I hugged and comforted her, and told her not to cry." If he could be empathetic towards his sister, why did he fail to understand how sad and upset I was over the loss of my beloved pet.

Connie buried Misty next to Tiger's grave, under the pussywillow tree, and I could not explain my grief to anyone. I hurt so much, that it was a physical pain. I could not think of Misty without tears rolling down uncontrollably. When one of his siblings called that night, I heard him say, "Dolla has been crying all day over Misty, she's very upset." But still, no words of comfort did he offer me.

We dropped in to see Shirani at Narre Warren next day, and Nelune called, as she was very concerned about me, when she knew I lost Misty.

It felt so strange over the next few days, not hearing Misty mew in response, whenever I called her in the morning, or to see her sleeping on her favourite chair near the window, and basking in the warm sunshine. Chris called me, as I emailed her about Misty. She understood just how I felt, as she had to put her beloved dogs to sleep as well.

We spoke for a long time, and it was a comfort to share our mutual grief for our beautiful pets. I still cried, whenever I looked at Misty's familiar places in the house and garden. She was my constant companion for sixteen years, and I cried and grieved, as if I lost my dearest friend. I grieved so much for Tiger, that I thought I could not hurt so much again, but I was wrong.

The year started sadly for me, and although I had two kittens to cheer me up, a large hollow in my heart told me that I would never forget my little Misty, or Tiger. Even writing about that traumatic time when I lost her, still hurts after all this time.

Chapter 53

I was busy preparing to launch "Wild Poppies," a collection of short stories, and poems in early March, which Del Nightingale agreed to present at Mornington library. Del compeered a weekly "Writers Corner" on local radio 3RPP, and she interviewed me a few times regarding two of my books published in the last few years. And our friendship flourished over the years. Christian and Athena helped me with the book cover. Athena photographed my painting of red poppies on a black background, and she designed a terrific cover.

The next few days were extremely hot, and soared to thirty nine and forty one degrees. I still cried for Misty whenever I thought of her, and missed her at every turn. But I had several tasks to do, and life went on, in spite of heartache and loss.

We drove to Southland one weekend and watched "Bright Star," a great movie, based on the life of poet, John Keats. It was beautifully photographed, and I enjoyed it very much. The temperature rose to forty one degrees that day, but we visited Con and Cornelia afterwards, and then Lorraine and Tony.

I gave Ninette one of Andre Rieu's DVD's for her birthday. But I visited her a couple of days before her birthday and had lunch with her, then took her shopping. She was very pleased with the DVD, flowers, and chocolates.

When I came home, I walked the kittens, but could not help missing my beloved Misty very much. I talked to Tiger and Misty whenever I was in the garden, and it eased my pain to think that they were still there, and listening to me. I could not help myself, as they were such close companions for so long, and it was habitual, talking to them daily.

Connie left early on Saturday, 16 January, to help John clear up the block. Before he left, I specifically asked him to leave a couple of acacia trees, as it would be good to have some shady trees in the back yard. But he did not listen, and told John to cut down every single tree and shrub! I was very disappointed, and annoyed when he told me what he did, but it was too late. He did not care, even when I told him that it would take ten years or more for trees to grow to that height.

Mishka wanted to go out to the garden all the time, but much to my amusement, Simba wanted to sit beside me when I played the piano. He walked gingerly on the keys, and made "mewsic." When the students came, Simba jumped onto their laps, eager to show off, as he walked on the keys. The children were vastly amused at his antics.

Nelune arrived next morning, and we picked her at the airport. And after a coffee at Gladstone Park shopping centre, we drove straight to Woolamai, which took one and a half hours. We had lunch there, and enjoyed a pleasant afternoon. Then we drove to Mt Martha on our way back, and showed Nelune the block of land. She liked the area, and great ocean views very much.

Christian, Athena, and her parents, came for dinner that evening, and we had a pleasant time. When they left, Connie and I drove Nelune to the Windsor Hotel in the city, where she was staying for a couple of days, as she was in Melbourne on business. After dropping her, we came back in about one and a half hour's time. I was exhausted, as it was a hectic day. Connie stayed up and washed dishes, although I told him I would do them in the morning.

We drove down to Woolamai again on the following day, Monday, because Felix, Yasmin, and their children were visiting Shirani. We had a great time and enjoyed reminiscing; Felix had an amazing memory, as he vividly recalled mutual friends, people and places in Hatton and Bandarawela.

We stopped at Grantville on our way home, as Connie wanted to smoke. When I came home, my head was spinning, as I was worn-out with all the driving and visiting, so I rested a while. Connie went out again in the evening, and when he returned, he said he had to check the unit, and see Esme. He did not tell me where he was going before he left, but now he said that he distributed Shirani's restaurant cards to his siblings.

He also said, "I sat on the rocks near the pier, and had a beer and talked to Mummy." Ever since Aunty's death, he went there often, and told me that he communed with his mother. I knew he missed her and grieved deeply, and if it comforted him to sit on the rocks where Aunty's ashes were scattered in the sea, that was his business.

The following days were very busy, as I finalised my manuscript for printing. The weather continued to soar, and rose above the high thirties almost every day. In the midst of my work, I had severe chest pains and back aches, and hoped it was not another heart attack, due to the extremely hot weather. Besides all the running around involved in publishing another book, and organizing a launch.

And it did not help, with Connie behaving like a sore bear most of the time either. With all the stress of selling the unit, building a new house, and coping with his job, if I so much as disagreed on anything, he lost his temper, and roared like a wounded animal. I was utterly fed up with the constant bickering and arguments. And I knew I suffered chest pains and dizziness because of the constant stress.

I was still negotiating with Roslyn, the producer, as she had enjoyed reading "Catsville" very much, and was keen to turn it into an animated feature- length movie. Connie drove me to her place in the city on 28 January. It was a positive meeting, and we finished in a couple of hours time. She said she would contact some interested parties, to invest in this project.

I gave the final copy of the manuscript to the printer, and waited for proofs and mock-up cover now. Joanne and I met for coffee at Onde's next day, and walked down Main Street later, just window-shopping and enjoying the warm weather.

After playing golf in the morning, Connie took Simba to the vet to insert a micro chip, on 30 January. I met him in Karingal that afternoon, and Simba was in the cat carrier on the front seat. When Simba saw me, he started mewing loudly, and appeared to be very distressed. I asked Connie to take him home soon, without leaving him in the car, as I was going back immediately.

Simba became very nervous, since that trip to the vet, and I wondered if they hurt him during the procedure. From that day onwards, if Connie so much as approached Simba, he bolted for dear life, which annoyed him, as he could not understand why. But Simba associated Connie with a painful trip to the vet, and his placid personality was seriously affected.

It was one year since we put Tiger to sleep. And I still missed his dear presence very much, and kept seeing his beautiful face behind shrubbery. Misty and Tiger lived on in my memory, and I felt their presence keenly in the garden, that they had loved to laze in.

It was sizzling hot, and soared to the high thirties next day, but we drove to the Italian club in Dandenong, to organize Connie's birthday dinner. He told me that he wanted to invite only his close friends, John, Elvira, Tony, Mary, Con, Cornelia, and Ninette. He did not want any of his siblings to come because of their bad behaviour and attitude when Aunty died. Connie said he wanted to do something special, even though it was his sixty-fifth birthday, and not a milestone. We spent some time with the manager, and chose a delicious menu, and he was happy to organize everything for Connie's celebration.

Christian and Athena came around nine o'clock that night to check the mock-up and manuscript, and Athena corrected a few things before the final print. They helped me a great deal with the publication, and I appreciated their help and input.

I met the printer next day, as a few errors in page numbering had to be corrected. Christian picked up the final proof a few days later, and I was satisfied with the results.

In the meantime I worked on the script for "Catsville" as Roslyn wanted it soon. She charged one thousand dollars for editing, which I paid in advance at our last meeting, even though the script was not ready yet.

The next few days flew past quickly, with school, piano students in the evening, and preparing for the book launch. The settlement for the Frankston unit went through without any hassles. It was a relief, as Connie did not have to worry about maintaining the place any longer.

As the weather continued to soar in the high thirties, without any relief, I hoped we would not have any more devastating bush fires like last year. But unfortunately, several fires were rampant in every state. Ninette called to say she had to put down her eighteen-year old dog, Solita, and she was very sad. The poor dog was ailing for some time, and should have been put out of her misery a long time ago. Still, I knew how she felt about her loss, and sympathised with her.

Ron and Cynthia visited the following Saturday afternoon, and we had a good time. They asked me to play the piano, and Cynthia sang, "O Sole Mio." When I played Chopin's study, popularly known as "No Other Love," she cried heartily. And she said, "Thank you for that beautiful music Dolly. My father loved that music, and it was very touching." After they left, I made some pan rolls, as Connie enjoyed them for lunch and snacks at work.

We drove to Nancy's at Sandringham next day, as she had an "Open Garden" event. She worked very hard to set it all up, and I was very impressed with the beautiful display of plants. Danielle helped with the sales of seedlings, and home-made soap.

We spent a couple of hours there, and I was pleased to see a large number of people walk through the gardens. It was thirty one degrees though, and very hot outside. But we dropped in at Shirani's later, at Narre Warren, and I enjoyed a pleasant time with her. I expected Christian and Athena that night, but they called very late to say they were held up, and would visit another day.

Roslyn wanted to meet me in a few weeks time to discuss the draft script, I agreed, and then visited Ninette on Tuesday. She was alright, but she said she missed her dog, Solita. It was thirty three degrees that day, and I could not play the piano too long, as my palms were drenched. I stopped playing after a little while, then we had coffee and I came home soon after.

The weather did not ease all week, and continued to soar in the high thirties, with no sign of rain. I spent most evenings watering the garden with tank water, as tap water was restricted. The days flew past swiftly, with preparations for the book launch.

The microwave packed up one night, and the very next day, Christian walked in with a new microwave. He gave the other one for Christmas two years ago, and it was still on warranty. Christian was very loving and generous, and always ready to help me.

A sudden change in the weather was most welcome. But it was the loudest clap of thunder I ever heard, before the rain poured down in torrents and lasted all night. I was happy that the garden was soaked through. Connie was home till late afternoon on Friday, and I could not play the piano until he left.

I called Ginny, but she was unwell, and cancelled her 70th birthday party. I was sorry to hear she was poorly once again, but hoped she would recover soon.

I received the final proof of my book that day, and was happy that everything looked professional, without any printing errors.

We exchanged gifts and cards on Sunday, 14 February, Valentine's Day, then drove to Southland for lunch. Then we watched a good movie, "Tooth Fairy" with Julie Andrews and Billy Crystal.

We drove to Mt Martha later, and I was sad, because all the trees were cut down, and the land was bare. Connie did not leave a single tree, like I asked him to, and that upset me. But he just said, "There are *enough* trees in the reserve, and I don't want any snakes creeping in the garden." The wind was very strong and gusty that day, so we came back soon.

That night, I started writing another novel, "Dark Shores," a sequel to "Serendib-Isle of dreams." And in between school, piano lessons, and socialising, I typed a few chapters each night.

Athena, who had enjoyed reading "Serendib" very much, kept asking me, '*When are you going to write a sequel?*" That spurred me on to re-visit my story, and I hoped to publish the sequel next year.

It was Ash Wednesday on 17 February, and I went to church with the school children at midday. As it was still scorching, with no chance of a cool change or rain, I came home early, walked the kittens, and took it easy.

When the students finished their lessons, I quickly made dinner, and finished by eight o'clock. Christian, Athena, and their friend, Azzy, visited soon after, and we had a good time laughing and chatting. Azzy gave me a patch-work soft-toy she had made, and it was after midnight when they left.

The following day was thirty five degrees, and the intense heat made me feel dizzy, and my heartbeat was erratic. I fitted the harness on Mishka, then left her alone in the garden for a few moments until I walked her. But she took it into her little head to jump over the fence and explore the neighbourhood. I ran to the neighbour's garden, and caught her just before she wandered off. She was very frisky, and I had to watch her all the time.

I gave Connie a gift-voucher, and a bottle of Cognac on his birthday. He stayed home till midday, and went to work after lunch. It was still extremely hot that day, and I finished watering the garden after eight. Esme and Paul dropped in at nine o'clock in the night to wish Connie. I just came out of the shower, and was preparing to have an early night, when Shiranthi and Roland stepped in, then Babs walked in at eleven o'clock. I cooked enough food, and they all had dinner, before leaving at midnight. And I went to bed after one o'clock in the morning.

It continued to be very hot on Saturday as well, but I made a rainbow-coloured butter cake for Connie's dinner party tomorrow. I wanted to surprise him, as it was his favourite cake, so I iced it, and prepared everything for the evening.

The relentless heat continued day after day, and rose to thirty three degrees next day. I was heartily sick of the hot weather, and longed for rain and cooler days. We left home at six o'clock that evening, and picked up Ninette on the way. I was relieved when the weather changed slightly, and was much cooler. We had a pleasant time with our friends, and the food was delicious. The band played great Italian music, so we danced, and enjoyed the night, before leaving at ten thirty, as we had to work next day.

The phone started ringing from seven o'clock in the morning on my birthday, and I had a splitting headache by afternoon. Connie gave me a small video camera and jewellery. He knew I liked to photograph the cats and scenery, so I was happy with it. Then Birdie called to thank me for her birthday card, and to greet me as well. Her birthday was on the 24th of February, and I never failed to send her a card.

The printer said he encountered a slight problem with the art work, so I asked Connie to pick the mock-up cover in the evening. Christian said Athena would fix the problem, and they would drop by soon. We had dinner at Rugantino's with Christian, Athena, and Azzy that night, and they came back home with us. Athena soon fixed the art work problem, and I emailed the file to the printer later that night. I hoped it was the last correction, and the printing would not be delayed. I went to bed after midnight.

It was beautiful and sunny next day, and the weather was much cooler at twenty three degrees. I was busy at school, and with students in the evening. But once again,

Esme and Paul dropped in after nine o'clock that night, with a card and present, and left in an hour's time.

Connie drove me to the city to meet Roslyn a few days later, and it was a very good meeting. I was very excited at the prospect of seeing "Catsville" as an animated movie. We talked at length, and Roslyn was very enthusiastic about the project as well.

We stopped at Bab's place in Brighton, on our way back, and she invited us for lunch. We left in a couple of hour's time, after walking with her to see the community garden nearby. Babs was very happy in her snug, one-bedroom unit.

A thunderstorm broke out early next morning, cooling the parched earth. It was a pleasant twenty five degrees, for which I was thankful, and I prepared some curries etc. for dinner. Linda, Leo, Josh, Julie, and Paul arrived at six o'clock in the evening. Linda was due to have her second baby in a few weeks time, and she was very tired and uncomfortable, poor thing. They brought a delicious dessert, and we enjoyed a great time together, but as Linda was exhausted, they left around nine o'clock.

It was much cooler next day too, and I took it easy. Felix called to say that Victor Melder, President of the Burgher Association in Melbourne, was a good friend of his, and wanted to promote my books. Victor requested copies of my books for his library, and I posted them next day. The printer called on 3 March, to say the books were ready. He was happy with the finished product, and said his partner was very happy about it too. I told him Connie would pick them up next day.

The books looked great, and I was very pleased. Christian and Athena visited that night. And Athena fixed a few problems on my laptop and computer, as she was excellent at fixing problems; my technical knowledge of computers did not cover a pin head.

I was busy organizing the launch, and printed flyers for local distribution. Then arranged an interview with a local newspaper, and liaised with libraries. Most of them ordered my previous publications, and were always interested in forthcoming books. It was a hectic period, but on Saturday, we drove to Southland and watched "Alice In Wonderland," with Johnny Depp and Anne Hathaway. It was in 3D, and although it was full of gimmicks, I quite enjoyed it. It rained heavily on our way home, and I took it easy that evening, because I did not have to water the garden.

I let the kittens out next morning, but Mishka jumped the fence, and climbed on top of the roof. She was a mischievous little cat. Simba just observed her with a shocked expression, as he sat sedately in the garden, like a quiet little gentleman.

I brought Holy Communion for Ninette, after Mass on Sunday evening, as she liked to receive the Host whenever she could. And I usually took it to her on Tuesdays.

Del visited next morning, to discuss the launch, which she was presenting. We had an interesting discussion, and went through her introduction etc. After Del left in the afternoon, I visited Shirani briefly, and she gave presents for our birthdays. When I came home, the weather turned stormy, and gusty winds wreaked havoc in Melbourne that evening.

The photographer from the local newspaper, wanted to come on Tuesday evening, so I visited Ninette in the afternoon, and came back by three o'clock. He arrived as soon as I parked the car, and he removed a few photographs of me sitting inside, and standing out as well.

The printer gave me hundred flyers, free of charge, as he said I was a good customer. Christian and Athena dropped in later that night, and I went to bed after midnight.

It was always a very busy, exciting time before a launch, and I was fortunate that Christian and Athena helped me in so many ways.

I was extremely busy next day, as I had to make many phone calls. And Frankston library asked me to organize a book signing event, sometime in April.

Roslyn arrived the following morning to continue discussions about animating "Catsville." It was a positive meeting, and I gave her a copy of "Wild Poppies." She started reading some of the poems immediately, and was very impressed. And she said, "I've got goose bumps, when I read your poems! There is so much of emotion!"

Then we listened to a recording of the songs she had sung for "Catsville." I wrote the lyrics, and she arranged the music. Roslyn's voice sounded great, and she sang very well. I paid $500 for the recording in a studio, and she asked me to write an extra scene, profiles for the characters, and a few more songs. Roslyn was very encouraging and positive about the whole project, so I was happy. I started to write a whole new scene, profiles, and two more songs after she left. I was that keen!

I packed up a box to send Nilanthi on Saturday, and then made some pan rolls. We were visiting Christian and Athena, and I wanted to surprise them with a treat. They were busy when we arrived, as they were expecting guests. So we did not stay too long, but had a cup of tea, and they enjoyed the pan rolls. We drove to the block, as it was a pleasant, sunny afternoon, and we met some neighbours there.

Connie gave them a bottle of wine, as he told me they offered him a drink of water, when he was clearing the block with John. I enjoyed walking there and looking at the ocean, blue as Ceylon sapphires, glistening in the sunshine. And across the sea, the pale blue outline of the You Yang ranges in Geelong, Mount Macedon, and city skyline, were visible on a clear day. Only a few houses down Waterview Drive were built then, and it was mostly vacant land around. Star-shaped, pastel-hued, wild-flowers covered the block, and I gathered a pretty posy sometimes. After we returned home that evening, I worked on the screenplay for a couple of hours. I had a sleepless night though, thinking of lyrics for the songs I composed.

Connie drove to Albury early in the morning, on 17 March. But I was surprised to see him walk in at nine o'clock, as he forgot to take his mobile phone, and he turned back after driving one hour.

It was St Patrick's Day, and school was busy, as they held many events, and celebrations. I finished early, and took it easy in the afternoon.

The kittens were used to staying indoors whenever I went out, and now slept in the laundry till I came home.

That evening, I watched an Australian opera called "Bliss," which was full of bad language, and obscene scenes. I switched it off, and watched a classic movie instead. It was incredible that such material slipped the censors.

When I spoke to Isobel and Ninette about it next day, Isobel said that some people in the audience walked out after the first scene. I said I did not blame them, because it was not entertainment, just lewd behaviour, and foul language on stage.

I posted copies of my book to the State and National libraries later. Jackie, Charlotte's mother, called and said she would attend the launch with Charlotte, so I was pleased, as most people accepted my invitation. Connie returned from Albury at about seven o'clock that night, and was exhausted, so he had an early night.

I prepared some dishes for lunch the day before, as Peter and Mary were visiting on Sunday. Connie complained of severe pains in his head that morning, and went to emergency in Frankston hospital. I did not hear from him all afternoon. Finally, he called me at five o'clock in the evening, and said that he was still waiting to see a doctor! I thought he must have been somewhere else all day, and gone to the hospital only then, as they would not have kept him waiting in emergency so long.

Mary and Peter arrived at one o'clock, as they missed their way, but we had a good time, and enjoyed the afternoon, and they left in the evening. We drove to Mt Martha later, as it was still sunny and pleasant, and we walked around there.

I listened to Del's radio program on Monday morning, and she gave a very good review of my book, and advertised the launch. I was pleasantly surprised later, when Wayne (my previous boss at Boronia), called me. He received my invitation to the launch, and congratulated me on my new book, but was unable to attend. And he told me that Michelle (from Boronia office as well), was his partner for the last nine years, which was news indeed. We had a long chat, and he said he was thinking of retiring from Centrelink, to get away from stress. He was in his mid-fifties now, and wanted to travel, and enjoy life, which I told him was a very good aspiration.

Christian and Athena dropped in later that week, and he looked so troubled and down-hearted, that I was very concerned about him. But he did not tell me what was wrong. I had a bad night worrying about Christian, and could not fall asleep. So, I jotted down some notes for the sequel, "Dark Shores."

I went out next day, after preparing a few more things for the launch. And then distributed more flyers at local book shops, and handed some to individuals at shopping centres too. As I walked past the pet shop in Karingal, I saw the cutest, long-haired, ginger kitten playing in a cage. He looked exactly like Tiger did at that age, and I watched him in fascination.

I could not resist going in a few minutes later, and enquired how much the kitten cost. The sales-lady said, "$160, as he has a micro-chip, and has had all his vaccinations. He is just eight weeks old, and you will have to de-sex him later, that's all." The kitten was just adorable! And he was born on 26 January, Australia Day.

I said I would think about it, and then phoned Connie. He said, "Do what you want, but *how* are you going to look after *three* kittens?" I did not answer that. But I finished shopping, went back to the pet shop, and bought the little kitten. It was very friendly and placid, and hardly mewed inside the small cardboard box, as I drove home.

Mishka and Simba were not impressed at all, and started hissing and snarling when they saw the intruder. But the new kitten just ignored them, and followed me around. Christian dropped in later, and he liked the new kitten very much, because it reminded him of Tiger. He did not look as harassed today. But when I asked him what was wrong, he said he was just stressed out over some business issues.

Tigger (as I named him), was a cute, handful of fluff, with mischievous, green eyes. And together with the other kittens, he helped to fill the emptiness Misty and Tiger left behind. Connie liked the kitten immediately, and took to keeping him on his lap, whenever he watched television in the evenings.

As Tigger grew bolder, he was like a little monkey. He raced up and down the stairs, or in the garden, and whizzed up the willow tree like a tornado. He was delightful, and kept me on my toes. The three kittens entertained me continuously, and kindled smiles whenever I looked at their adorable little faces. Kittens are certainly, "Angels With Whiskers" as someone aptly observed.

Tigger was delightful, and mewed softly whenever I cut meat. I gave him a few morsels, and he just gobbled it all up. I could see that he relished raw meat, and Mishka was partial to raw chicken wings, but Simba ate almost anything that was in his bowl, and had no marked preferences.

I prepared a few last minute things for the book launch on the day before. And then practised my speech a few times, as I wanted to keep it under ten minutes. Chris, Peter, Ginny, and Alan were visiting on Sunday, so I prepared some dishes on Friday. I had an early night, and hoped all would go well at the launch tomorrow.

I settled Mishka and Simba in the laundry, and Tigger in the cat cage next morning, and then we drove to Mornington library at ten o'clock. Del was already there, and had everything in hand for her presentation. We attended to a few last minute details, while Connie arranged chairs around the long tables. Most of the people I invited turned up, and a few others, who just walked in to see what was going on in that room.

Genevieve, Alice and her sister, Jackie, Charlotte, and some other parents came as well. Christina brought a friend, but Cornelia was admitted for a gall stone operation the day before, and Con phoned to say they could not make it. Cynthia was unwell too, but about forty people turned up, including Elvira. The launch was very successful. Del's presentation was excellent, and read a few excerpts from my book. Athena told me later that Del's reading was very entertaining.

I sold about thirty copies at the launch, and received several orders from libraries nationwide, so I was glad it all went well. Del did a marvellous job, and I was very grateful to her. We celebrated with Christian and Athena afterwards. They organized the catering, and several other details involved in a book launch.

Chris, Peter, Alan, and Ginny came around midday on Sunday, and we had a pleasant time. They all attended the launch, and congratulated me on its success. It was great to see Chris and Peter especially, as they were in Mornington for a few days only, before they returned to Tea Gardens. They all fussed around Tigger, and said he was the cutest little kitten they had seen, and were as captivated as I was. They left around four thirty, after a few pleasant hours.

We drove to Dandenong hospital that evening to see Cornelia. I was glad that she looked alright, even though she was fasting all day, until they operated her on Monday morning. She was not too pleased about it, but as they did not operate on weekends, she had to fast till next morning. It was torrential all the way back, and we came home around eight o'clock. I went to bed early, as it was a long tiring day.

The next few days were very busy, visiting friends, or entertaining them on weekends. We forgot to turn the clock back on Sunday, 4 April, and when we went to church in the morning, the early Mass was still going on. We followed that service, then drove to Dromana, and walked along the foreshore for a while. Esme and Paul dropped in at eight thirty that night, and stayed for a while.

When we drove to Mt Martha the following Sunday, 11 April, we were pleased that the water was connected. And we hoped they would start building soon. It was stormy, and gusty winds tore across the bay while we were driving. We did not stop to walk around, instead, we dropped in at Christian's. I gave them some flyers to distribute, for the book signing at Frankston library next week. As the weather cleared up slightly, we drove down to Dromana, sipped coffee by the bay, and returned a couple of hours later.

I enjoyed watching Tigger frisk around, as he was such an energetic kitten. He had an amusing habit of running ahead of me, whenever I put food in his bowl; then he sniffed cautiously, and if he did not like it, he started pawing the floor to bury the food. It was very funny, and never failed to amuse me, as he continued that habit even when he was older. It was his way of telling me what he thought of the food in his bowl.

I did some last minute preparations, and rehearsed my speech once again next Friday. Del emailed a copy of her introduction, and I expected some of the school staff, and others to attend the book signing next day. Ninette said she would give the flyers to her friends too, so I hoped it would be another successful event. Christian dropped in that evening, and we had a long chat, as he was very troubled about some business issues. I was restless, and spent an anxious night worrying about him.

I was ready for the book signing next morning, Saturday, 17 April. It was a beautiful day, and a warm, twenty seven degrees. Nancy, Peter, Mary, Liz from school, and her friend, attended, besides a few strangers. Del did a great presentation and reading once again, and all went well. The library staff, especially the duty manager that morning, were well-organized, and very helpful. He thanked me for holding a book signing in the library, and offered the library facilities any time, if I held another event.

My friends and I had a great time, and we drove to Mornington later to have lunch with Christian and Athena at Soy restaurant. Then we drove past the block, to see if they had begun site works, but nothing was done as yet. We were disappointed that they were still dragging their feet, as we had waited so long for them to start.

Mary invited us for lunch next day, at Rugantino's restaurant, as it was Tony's seventy-third birthday. I accepted her invitation, and she asked for a copy of my book as well. Elvira and John came too, and we had a pleasant time with our good friends. We finished around four thirty, and spent a quiet evening. Judy Bartosy rang to apologize for not attending the book signing, but wanted to know how it went, and requested a copy.

Liz told me that she enjoyed the event very much, when I met her in school on Monday. I thanked her for attending with her friend, and she said she started reading "Wild Poppies," already, and looked forward to finishing it soon.

The evening news was all about the underworld gangster, Carl Williams, who was bashed to death in Barwon prison. Channel Nine ran a special documentary on Melbourne underworld gangsters, and the drug scene. It was very chilling, as they showed the bitter rivalry and violence among the Morans and Carl Williams.

The site works finally began on 20 April, after all these long months of waiting. But it rained heavily that day, followed by thunder and lightning all evening. The rain eased slightly over the next couple of days, and Connie drove to see how much they had completed. We were glad that the land was cut and levelled.

When I booked Tigger for his vaccine, they said Scott did not consult anymore, as he was semi-retired, which was a pity. He was a very good vet, and he reminded me of James Herriot, the renowned vet. He wrote a best- selling book about all the animal stories, which went on to become a popular television series.

It was twenty eight degrees that Thursday, 22nd, and we drove to the city, as Roslyn wanted to meet me again. Connie dropped me at her place, and drove to Pascoe Vale, to Pam and Alan's place to give them a laptop, which they offered to take for Nilanthi soon. Christian gave his old one, which was still in excellent working order.

I was not too keen when Roslyn wanted to re-write the entire script, loosely based on my book. I said I had to consider it, once I read her version of the script. We left it at that, and I was disappointed, because she already charged me thousand dollars to edit my script. Instead, she now wanted to re-write the entire script, and she said thousand dollars was not enough for her work.

When I asked to see the edited version she had worked on so far, she did not want to give that either. I could not believe I paid so much for nothing, as it was difficult enough to save that amount of money. I was beginning to have doubts about Roslyn now, as she did not play fair. I was sad and disillusioned, to think I was so easily taken in with her promises that were not going to eventuate. We did not sign an agreement, and she did not give me receipts for the money I paid for editing and recording either. I did not mention any of this to Connie, because he would have said, "I told you so, don't just trust people!"

On our way home, we stopped at the building site, to see how much further they had progressed, but nothing much was evident, since our last visit. Then we visited Christian, who was busy building a fence at his in-laws place, so we did not interrupt him. He did a great job as usual, and we chatted briefly before returning home.

Lorraine and Tony were coming for lunch on Saturday, so I cooked a few dishes the day before. They said they would catch a train to Frankston, and Connie would pick them. At eleven o'clock on Saturday morning, they were already in Frankston, and Connie picked them up. And he drove them all the way to their place in Wantirna after lunch, and returned a couple of hours later. He was very tired, but we enjoyed the afternoon, and they were very pleased that Connie drove them home.

He left early to help John clear up the rest of the land on Monday 26, Anzac Day. John hauled the trees and shrubs away before the building started. When Connie returned in the evening, he saw the mother of one of my student's parked on the lawn. He yelled at the poor lady, "Get your car off the lawn!" She was very embarrassed, and kept saying, "I'm sorry, I'm sorry!" I felt really bad, and asked him later why he was so rude. He shouted, "I work so bloody hard to keep the lawns nice, and these people have no sense to park on the lawn!" He was so angry, that I did not say anything to aggravate him further.

Connie drove to Wangaratta early next morning, for two days on business. The student's mother called me in the evening, and I apologized to her for Connie's behaviour. She replied, "Olivia was quite shaken up, as she didn't know why your husband was so angry!" I told her that he was under a great deal of pressure. But she did not come again, as her daughter stopped lessons after that incident. Connie rang at ten o'clock that night, and said that the drive was very tiring, and he was going to bed early.

I was at school next day, and when I came home in the afternoon, Christian dropped by, and we had a long chat. Connie called at nine o'clock in the night, and said he was leaving early next day, and hoped to get home before too late.

I took Tigger for his vaccine the following morning, and also asked the vet for an exemption letter, to de-sex him at six, instead of three months, as council required. He gave me a letter, and said it was alright for a male cat to be de-sexed at six months.

When I spoke to Nilanthi later, she said she was exhausted looking after Heron, as he was almost bed-ridden, and she had to do everything for him. Poor Nilanthi, I told her to look after herself, and hoped she would have the strength to carry on. She cried heartily, as she did not know how long she would have to care for him on her own. I comforted her, and said I would call again. And I told her to ask Heron's children to employ someone to care for him, and help her with chores.

Connie came home by six o'clock that evening, and was very tired and irritable. He said it was getting too much for him to be driving so far now, and his constant cry was, "I wish I could stop this bloody work and retire! I'm sick and tired of it all!"

In spite of being exhausted, he went to work next day. And he dropped me off in the city for the Women Writers monthly meeting. It was now held at a new venue, the Wheeler's Centre, in the State Library, instead of Ross House on Flinders Lane. The room was quite nice, but the chairs were very uncomfortable, as my legs hardly reached the floor. I bought a few books from other members, and sold about six of mine. Connie picked me up in the afternoon, and we came home without delay, as he said he was worn-out and went to bed early.

Mishka kept jumping fences, and I did not know how to stop her from wandering around the neighbourhood. I coaxed her back into the garden that morning, and then kept her indoors for the rest of the day, as we went to Cranbourne to measure windows in the display home. I wanted to start sewing curtains as soon as possible, so they would be ready when the house was completed. We stopped at Mt Martha on our way back, as they said the site was ready for concreting on Monday, 3 May.

I could not help feeling down-hearted next day, 2 May, when I thought of Misty, as it was now four months since she was gone. I felt a lump in my throat, each time I thought of her beautiful little face. And I missed her so much, even though I had three naughty kittens, who kept me on my toes. How very true, that our pets leave indelible paw marks in our hearts!

It was a pupil-free day on Monday, and it was beautiful and sunny. Connie stayed home, as an electrician came to fix the grill in the oven. After the children finished lessons that evening, we drove to Mt Martha. But the concrete was not poured, so we were disappointed, as it was a sunny day, and they did not take advantage of the weather, before the rain started again. I took some pan rolls for Athena and Christian, but they were not in, and we came home in a couple of hours time.

When I visited Ninette on Tuesday, she gave me the sheet music for a beautiful piece of music called "Le Lac De Como," that I heard her playing, and wanted to learn. It is one of my favourite pieces to this day. She said that several of her friends called to give positive feedback about Luigi's book, "Is this your Caruso?" I was pleased to hear that.

I sent a copy of "Wild Poppies" to Joanna by express mail, as she was leaving for Poland on Friday for a long holiday, and asked if I could send her a copy before she left. I got caught in a severe storm on my way home, and when I stepped out of the car, I caught my right hand in the door! It was painful, and I hoped my fingernails would not bruise. Christian called to say they would drop in later. And a few minutes later, it came down in torrents. It was unlikely they would pour the concrete slab next day.

Nancy was visiting that Friday, so I prepared some dishes for lunch in the morning. Although she called to say she was running late, she arrived just after midday. We had a pleasant time, and an interesting discussion, before she left late in the afternoon. Connie came home early that evening, and started drinking till late at night. He had too much, and began arguing as usual.

I could not get any sleep, as he turned up the stereo volume to the maximum, and played spiritual songs till midnight. I had a splitting headache, but he would not turn the volume down, even when I asked him to, and the noise continued till after one o'clock in the morning. He did it on purpose, just to irritate me, because he knew I could not stand loud noise.

I planted geranium cuttings in pots next day, as I wanted to take some to the new place. When I spoke to Nilanthi later, she said she collected the box, and also that she enjoyed the wedding, which she attended on her own, as Heron was too ill.

Mishka jumped over the fence again, and did not come back, no matter how much I called her. Connie drove around the neighbourhood, then chased her back over the fence into our backyard. I was anxious till she came, as I did not want her to get hurt or lost. But she was incorrigible.

It was Mother's Day, on Sunday, 9 May, and Connie gave me perfume, a card, and a rose from our garden. We drove to Spotlight in Frankston after breakfast, and checked some curtain fabric, and then to Dollar Curtains in Mornington. We had fish and chips at Dromana, and then drove past the land, and were pleased that the concrete slab was poured, and timber was on site, ready for framework to start tomorrow. Connie made dinner that evening, as he wanted to give me a break.

The framework started next day, and Christian and Athena dropped in later that evening. One of my student's mother, came with a nun, who was visiting them, Sister Zita, from a convent in India. I met her once before, and now I gave her a small donation, and a copy of my book. She was happy, and asked me to email her whenever I could. Sister Zita was a nice person, and I promised I would keep in touch.

The following days and evenings were busier than ever, as I worked on my manuscripts. I was re-publishing "Serendib," and the sequel "Dark Shores," at the same time. I signed a contract with AuthorHouse UK, who were publishing my books this time. I also negotiated with a few local book stores, who agreed to take my previous publications on consignment.

When we visited the site on 15 May, the ground floor timber frame was constructed, and we removed some photographs. Then we walked around the streets there, as it was very peaceful. We drove to Spotlight in Fountain Gate later, where I found the exact shades of fabric I had in mind; sage green for the tiled section, and a dusty, rose-pink for the bedrooms and lounge, to match the aubergine carpets.

The damask fabrics were coated with block-out too, and I ordered a hundred and forty seven metres in total, for upstairs and downstairs windows. It was a great deal of cutting and sewing I knew, but I liked sewing curtains.

We visited Christian and Athena on Sunday, and then attended Mass in Frankston.

When I was at school next day, Connie called to complain that the kittens jumped on the dining table and broke a crystal bowl. It was a souvenir from Tina's wedding in 1987. I came home and cleared the mess, but what else could I do, when three frisky kittens got up to mischief.

I suffered severe vertigo over the next few days, because I was exhausted rushing around and doing several things. It was worse when I put my head down, and nothing relieved me, although I tried a few exercises that doctor recommended for vertigo.

Christina was meeting me for lunch at Onde's on Friday, 21 May. I arrived there on time, and I waited for her, but she called to say she could not find her way, and walked around in circles, before she finally arrived. She was hungry and stressed at the start, but relaxed later, after lunch. We spent some time there, and later, I dropped a few books at Farrell's book shop in Mornington. On my way home, I drove to the site, and was pleased that the second-storey framework was completed. I had a good look around, before I went home.

Chapter 54

We drove to the site next day to check some measurements, and met Jarrod, the estate agent, who sold us the land. He said he was building a house on the same street, just a few blocks below. Then we hurried back, as Elvira invited us for dinner that evening.

We arrived there at six o'clock, and waited for another couple, but they still did not turn up by eight o'clock. And when Elvira called, they said they got the dates mixed up, and thought it was the following Saturday. So, we had too much food, as Elvira cooked for eight people, but we enjoyed ourselves, and came home after midnight.

It was Ammie's fourteenth death anniversary on 23 May. I could hardly believe the years had disappeared so swiftly. I said a special prayer for the repose of her soul, but did not feel too well to go for Mass that evening. Connie went on his own.

I felt very dizzy, as the vertigo was bad, but I drove to school on Monday morning. And I did not feel any better by Wednesday, so I rested till late, and went to school a little later. The children just finished "Sorry Day" events, and Margaret was disappointed I did not see the dancing, or heard the story-telling. I told her I did not feel too well. I was groggy, had a splitting headache, blurred vision, and felt as if I carried a heavy rock on my head. So I came home, took a panadeine, and rested for a few hours.

When I called Nilanthi a couple of days later, she said Heron was sinking rapidly, and the family did not expect him to last much longer. Pam and Alan were holidaying in Sri Lanka then, and supported her. I called her again next day, and she said he was unable to speak or move, and they were taking him to hospital.

In spite of being so ill and at death's door, he did not change his ways at all, and continued being nasty to Nilanthi right up to the end. The only thing he did a few days before he died, was to say he was sorry. That was an iota of comfort for her. I called Shirani and Nelune, and we hoped he would die peacefully.

I woke up at five o'clock in the morning on 3 June, and thought I heard the phone ring a few hours ago. But I was too sleepy to answer, as I still suffered from vertigo. I checked my mobile. Nilanthi had sent a text to say Heron died at eight thirty in the night, Sri Lankan time. He received the last rites in the evening, and died peacefully at home, with Pam, Alan, and Nilanthi by his bedside. Peter and Penny called us very early, to tell us the same news.

I offered them my sympathy, and they said the whole family were going to Sri Lanka to attend his funeral. Then I called Nilanthi later, and she said that her friend, Chandani, Tanesh, and Petunia were with her, and she had great support from friends and neighbours around, which was comforting. After a long chat, and assurance that I was always there for her, I made an appointment to see doctor next day, as the vertigo did not ease.

When doctor saw me next day, he took some blood tests, and also advised me to go for a gastroscopy, to check for ulcers. I called Nilanthi a couple of days later, and she said the funeral went well, with many people attending the service, and that Heron's children were there too. She was more settled now, and I told her that it was a new chapter in her life, and to be happy that Heron was at peace, and she could visit us again soon.

We drove to Woolamai on Sunday, as I wanted to wish Shirani for her sixtieth birthday on 8 June, which was a few days away. I gave her a large, potted cyclamen, and a few presents. It was good to see Roshan and his family, and Suresh too.

I called Shirani to wish her on the 8th, and around ten thirty that same night, one of Connie's siblings left a message on his mobile, to say Aunty Molly's son, Ian, died suddenly the day before. He was fifty-four years old, and had suffered a heart attack. Poor Aunty Molly! She was devastated, as he was her favourite son. Ian was to marry another distant cousin in the next week or so. And the bride-to-be (a divorcee), flew in from Ceylon, with her sixteen-year old son from her previous marriage.

I joined another group of writers, "Authors Australia Inc." in May that year. And the first meeting was on Saturday, 12 June at Federation Square, Melbourne. We drove to the city in the afternoon, and I met the founder of the group, Peter Frederick, and the president, Dan Stoj, another writer.

We had a very interesting discussion about the difficulties that self-published authors had to find distributors. And we came up with several good ideas and suggestions. I bought a couple of books Peter had written (his memoirs), and gave him copies of my books too.

Our main focus was to get more members to join the group, so we could help each other with distribution, and other matters related to self-publishing. I said I would let the Women Writers Society know about this new group, and ask if any of the members were interested. We planned to meet once a month at this same venue, as it was a great idea to support each other. On our way home, we stopped at the building site, and were pleased to see that the roof, and some of the brick work was completed.

When we came home, Mishka jumped over the fence into the next door neighbour's garden. She was petrified of the dog, who barked his head off to see a cat in his domain. I asked our neighbour to take their dog in, and Mishka finally worked up enough courage to jump over the fence, and come into our back yard. I hoped that would teach her not to trespass, but she was undaunted.

No hot water next morning, as the unit was broken again. Connie called a plumber, who said he could not come till the following Tuesday, as Monday was a public holiday. I boiled a pan of water, and some in the electric jug, and managed to have a wash, as it was too chilly to have a cold water shower.

We visited Aunty Molly in the afternoon, who was staying with a relative. She was shattered, and totally lost, as she could hardly focus on anyone or anything. We gave her a bottle of brandy, and I tried to console her. But she just bawled and moaned non-stop, completely overcome with grief.

Ian's prospective bride looked very timid and lost, as this sudden calamity rocked her world. I was very upset for Aunty Molly, and told her we would visit her again soon, and then we left. The small flat she was staying in, was over-flowing with people I did not know, and I could hardly breathe in that suffocating atmosphere.

Then we drove to Peter's, in Narre Warren. He showed some photographs of the funeral, including Heron's corpse, which I thought was morbid, and did not want to look at them. We visited Shirani in Narre Warren too, before we came home late in the evening.

Connie dropped Shirani and Ranjith at the airport on 15 June, as they were travelling to Ceylon for a couple of weeks. The plumber came on Tuesday morning, but could not fix the unit. Connie called another plumber, who came later that afternoon, but he too was unable to fix it, and said we would have to replace the whole hot water unit. Another evening of getting by with basins of hot water, instead of a hot bath. I wondered why the unit broke down in winter, and not at the height of summer, when a cold shower in forty degree heat, would have been refreshing.

It was chilly and rainy next day, and I had a "cat wash" again, while Connie had an icy cold shower. I heard him yelling out loud, as he jumped out of the shower as quickly as possible. Another plumber checked the unit that morning, and I hoped he could fix it this time, as it was very inconvenient, to say the least.

When I came home that afternoon, the hot water was still not turned on, so I called Connie immediately. He contacted the plumber, and he said to turn on the tap outside, and let the water run, which I did. And at last, the water started to heat up. I indulged in a very long, hot water bath that evening. Christian and Athena dropped in later, and Shirani called to say they arrived in Colombo. A severe storm hit Melbourne that night, and I was glad we had hot water again, as it was freezing cold and wet.

We drove to the site on 19 June, and the bricks were laid halfway up the first storey. It was messy, and muddy there, so we drove down to the beach at Mount Martha, and walked there for a while.

I baked a cake, and made some cutlets for afternoon tea on Sunday. Christian and Athena dropped in a little while later, but Athena looked very stressed, and did not talk much. We went for Mass after they left.

It was Winter Solstice on Monday, 21 June, and it became very dark by five o'clock in the evening. I worked on my manuscript for a few hours, and then called Ninette to invite her for lunch next day. She said she would be happy to come over, and we chatted for some time.

Toula dropped her at midday, and Ninette enjoyed the cutlets, and home-made soup. She asked me for the recipe, as I made stock with marrow bones, and the soup was rich and flavoursome, with leeks and vegetables. I dropped her around two thirty, and stayed awhile to write some letters for her, and check her correspondence.

As I came out of Ninette's unit, a distraught, elderly woman ran out of the opposite unit, crying out, "Can you *help* me *please* to switch on my television? No one to help me!" She looked very upset, and was crying out loudly. I tried to take her to Ninette's place, but she did not want to go in there. Then I told her to call one of the neighbours to help her, as I was getting late for piano lessons with my students. I phoned Ninette later, as I felt bad about not helping that distressed woman. She told me not to worry about her, as she was a little crazy, and sometimes asked people for money.

Christian and Athena visited on 23 June, and told us that Athena's father, John, had suffered a heart attack, and was in hospital. Her mother, Dorothy, was very upset, as she did not know what to do when he came back home. John was a very stubborn man, who did not listen to doctors, and refused to take medication.

Athena and Christian offered to take him to their place, and look after him for as long as he needed to stay there. Dorothy had to work, and as Athena worked from home, she said she would be able to keep an eye on him, and see that he followed doctor's orders. Dorothy was very relieved that John would be cared for, while she was at work.

Connie came home a little early next day, Thursday, and went out to practise golf, as he was playing with friends on Saturday. But he came back after an hour or so, complaining about chest pains, and that he had pulled a muscle. He worried and stressed about it all night, and complained non-stop, so I told him to see doctor.

The evening news was surprising next day, to say the least! Kevin Rudd, the Prime Minister, was ousted, and Julia Gillard, was the new Prime Minister! Kevin Rudd was very emotional and bitter at this betrayal, and shed a few tears as he addressed the nation. Federal politics were absolutely topsy turvy during this period, and elected leaders were no longer secure in their positions, as the removal of Kevin Rudd proved.

Connie saw doctor on Friday, and all the tests were clear, but he had pulled a muscle. Although it was painful, at least he did not suffer a heart attack, as he kept insisting that he had. He played golf as planned, on Saturday.

We visited Christian and Athena on Sunday afternoon, and I took them some patties. John was discharged the day before, and was staying with them. Red-eyed and distressed, Dorothy cried non-stop, and kept moaning, "What will happen to *me* if your father dies!" When I heard her, I tried to pacify her, "John is out of danger and needs rest now, and you're lucky Athena and Christian are there to help and look after John so well." But she was inconsolable. We left them shortly afterwards, and drove past the site, but nothing more was done, due to bad weather over the past week.

The next few days were busy, with several visits from friends, including Del, and Cynthia and Ron. We drove to Mt Martha every weekend, to see how the house was progressing. And we hoped to move in before the end of the year, if the house was completed according to plan.

Christian wanted to build a new website for me, and as usual, he did a fantastic job that took him a great deal of time. He scanned some of my paintings to add to the website, and I was very impressed with his skill in everything he did.

Heron's children invited us to a memorial service, to be held in a church in Narre Warren on 3 July. We drove there in the morning, and I found the service very moving, and well organized. Peter's eulogy though was distressing. He broke down helplessly, when he recalled how Heron went with Nilanthi, and abandoned his family.

He spoke about tough times without a father, when Peter was not even in his teens. I felt it was hardly the time and place for such painful memories, but he just let his emotions flow. He said Heron was a very good father, until he left his wife and family for someone else. His sisters were all in tears, and the grandchildren sobbed hysterically, although Heron was never close to them or a part of their lives.

It may have been that they wept for lost time, and a sense of having missed out on having a grandfather. It was a relief when Peter stopped his blubbering, and the service ended. I was pleasantly surprised to meet Una, who was at school with us in Hatton. Her sister, Bertha, had married Patrick, the boy who acted with me as Henry, in that funny song, "Hole In The Bucket." We reminisced about our school days, and the people we had known. It turned out that Una was a good friend of Pam's, and was so from her days in Hatton. We exchanged addresses, and promised to keep in touch.

We drove to the site later that day, and saw scaffolding and bricks laid half way through to the second storey. Then we walked down the streets in the area, before returning home.

Ron and Cynthia visited us next afternoon, and left a couple of hours later. We visited Shirani and Ranjith at Narre Warren, as Roshan's wife, June, just came home after an operation, and was staying with them until she recovered.

Christian completed my website, and dropped in to show me what he had done. He had excelled as usual, and I was very pleased with the new website.

I drove to Dandenong a few days later, and had lunch with Joelle at a nice cafe. It was more than seven months since we met, so we had a great deal to talk about. Joanne did not join, as she hurt her leg, and was on crutches. The streets in Dandenong were messy, with building projects and road works going on everywhere, but I managed to find parking close by.

Christian dropped by in the evening with some business cards that he designed and printed for me. I thanked him for all he did, as he was such a great son in every way, loving and generous, and always helpful and supportive in whatever I did. I hoped and prayed he would succeed in all his endeavours.

Mary invited us for a dance at the Furlan Club in Thornbury, on Saturday, 10 July, as it was their wedding anniversary. Con and Cornelia promised to join us too, but when we went to pick them up at six o'clock, only Con was ready. Cornelia did not even come out, as she was painting the house all day, and got some paint on her hair. He told us she could not get rid of the paint, so she did not want to go out.

It was a freezing, gusty, and wet day, and did not improve by evening, but we had a good time with our friends, and after dropping Con, we came home by one o'clock in the morning. I was drained next day and stayed in, as my foot hurt badly. An enormous lady accidentally stomped on it while we were dancing on the crowded floor.

Connie took two weeks leave, starting from Monday,12 July, as he was worn-out with work. I encouraged him to go fishing and play golf, but all he did was sleep most of the day. And then he drove around visiting one of his siblings, especially Esme, who now filled the void that his mother left. Connie visited her often. His two younger siblings needed a mother figure in their lives as well, and they spent time with Esme.

When I left Ninette's on Tuesday, I transferred funds to AuthorHouse, as I decided to publish my book with them. I fervently hoped it was not a scam, as so many charlatans abounded, who did not scruple to swindle people, especially struggling authors keen to get their work published. James, a publishing consultant from AuthorHouse, called that night, and Connie answered the phone.

I could not speak to James or call back, and he said he would call again later. If Connie knew I paid that much money, he would have told me it was a rip-off, and would have been very negative about it. I just said that I was thinking about publishing with them. If, and when the book was printed, then I would tell him, not before, just in case this turned out to be a scam.

I invited Liz for lunch one Monday afternoon, and we enjoyed talking about books, and spiritual matters, as she was a very interesting and supportive friend. Liz introduced me to the teachings of Bruno Groening, a great healer, and I was very interested in reading about his life story. She also gave me a DVD with documented evidence, regarding the miraculous healings he achieved in his lifetime. From then onwards, I firmly believed in Bruno's healing powers, and told Ninette about him too.

It was still raining, and wintry in mid-July, but we drove to the site and noticed that the insulation was delivered, and tradesmen were busy inside. We did not go inside, but walked around the building, then drove to Dromana for a coffee before returning home. I was glad when Connie went out to play golf next day, as he needed to unwind.

We visited Cornelia on 17 July, as it was her birthday, and I gave her chocolates and books. It was a pleasant evening, as she invited family and some other friends for dinner too. Her mother, Florica, looked very frail and worn-out, as she broke her arm when she fell down the stairs. Poor lady! She spoke non-stop to me in Rumanian all evening, and I asked Cornelia to translate. It was after one o'clock in the morning when we returned home.

Judy Bartosy said that she always felt very lonely on Sundays, ever since her husband died, so I said I would bring her over to my place for a visit soon. Christian printed some striking posters of my book covers, but did not want payment, as he said they were a gift.

It was a frosty, rainy day, on 21 July, when I drove to school. Margaret said she was ill, and still grieved for her younger brother, who died suddenly of a heart attack. She said she found all his photographs that she kept on a table, thrown on the ground last night, and did not know what it meant. I could not interpret that incident, so I told her not to think about it too much, as grief was making her sick. Athena said they would drop in with John, as Dorothy was working till late.

They came around seven o'clock that night, and I had a very interesting conversation with John, who was well-read, though very self-opinionated. And they left after ten o'clock that night. Although I felt lethargic next morning, we drove to Dandenong to meet Michael, at Retire invest, as Connie had to sign some superannuation documents. He was a very pleasant young man, and told us that his surname "Krivonos," meant, "crooked nose" in Russian. But his nose was very straight, and not at all crooked (I observed).

Cornelia, Con, and Florica were coming for dinner on Saturday, so I was busy cooking that day. They arrived around seven o'clock, and we enjoyed a pleasant evening as always. I was happy that Florica was looking much better, and her arm was healing well. Cornelia fell asleep on the sofa, in front of the blazing fire, as she loved to doze by the fireside. Con woke her up with great difficulty, and they left after midnight.

When we drove to the site next day, the plaster boards under the house were done. After walking around for a while, we attended Mass in Frankston.

Nilanthi wanted to come on a holiday soon. I posted all the documents she required to get a visa. But due to a postal strike over there, she did not receive them. Connie faxed all the information to her once again, and she was happy to receive them safely. We promised to send her a ticket, as I knew it would be a good change, after the trauma of dealing with Heron's illness and death.

We picked up Ninette, and then drove to Armadale for lunch at Isobel's place on the following Sunday, 1 August. Michelle and her husband, Greg, were there too. John and Isobel looked well, but John needed a hip replacement soon. Isobel cooked a really delicious meal, and everything was very elegant as always. We enjoyed a lovely afternoon, and after dropping Ninette, we came home around six o'clock in the evening.

I came down with a cold the following week and did not visit Ninette on Tuesday, but felt slightly better by the end of the week. I started painting a seascape for the book cover, as I was now in the middle of publishing "Serendib." And the consultant at AuthorHouse asked me to send any sketches or ideas for the cover. Ninette asked if we were going to church that evening, as Luigi was holding a memorial service for his son, Angelo. But I said we were not going that evening, as Connie was out, and I did not know what time he would return.

Roslyn called to say she was very excited about the recordings she made for "Catsville." The songs sounded great, and she wanted to give me copies of the recordings soon.

I met Roslyn at her place in St Kilda, on 12 August, and listened to her recordings of "The Power Of Dreams," and "The World We Knew," which I wrote. She sounded fantastic, and I felt shivers down my spine and was almost moved to tears. Her voice was powerful, and the arrangement with a musician, Neil, was great. Connie dropped me and went to a store, so he did not hear the songs then, but when he came to pick me, I asked him to come inside and listen to the songs.

He said, "That's good." That was the *highest* praise from him for anything I did: "good" "okay" and "not bad." But I could think of nothing else except the music all day. On our way home, he wanted to drop in at Bab's, and we had a snack with her before we came home.

We dropped the Jag at Mornington in mid-August, as John said he would fix whatever was wrong. John's health was much better, and he was back at work now, as he said he hated to be idle. We drove past the site later, and were pleased that the staircase was installed. It was quite exciting to watch the progress of the building. And now that they started the interior, we hoped it would be completed soon. We came home soon, after doing some shopping, as I was down with a cold and cough, and Connie did not feel too well either.

I finished the seascape a few days later, and it was ready to be photographed, scanned, and sent to the publisher.

I could not go to school on Monday, as I was dizzy and nauseous. I coughed a great deal, and felt as bad as the time I had pneumonia, so I saw doctor that afternoon. He said I had a high temperature due to a chest infection, and prescribed antibiotics. I came home and rested, but Connie visited Con that evening, as he was very ill with the flu. Connie drove him to Con's doctor, and came home after eight o'clock in the night, after dropping him at home.

On Thathie's birthday, 21 August, I thought of him, and prayed for the repose of his soul. And I spent some time looking at old photographs of Thathie, when he visited us, and they brought back happy memories. At least we enjoyed some great times together.

It was general elections that day, and we went to cast our votes in the afternoon. Then we drove to the site, and saw them still busy on the interior. We walked down the street for a while, and then went to Spotlight in Frankston to buy curtain tracks, and then to Lincraft. We watched election results till late in the night, and were disappointed when Tony Abbot lost to Julia Gillard, and she was elected a second term. Politics in Canberra was fast becoming the Australian version of "Game Of Thrones."

I spoke to Ginny next day, and she said she was alright now, but Alan was going through a bout of depression. It was sad that these dear people had so many health issues. It was now three weeks since I came down with a cough and cold, and I was heartily sick of the persistent cough.

On Stacy's thirty-eighth birthday, on 23 August, I thought of him as always, and prayed for him, wherever he was. It was always worse on his birthdays, as the pain of not knowing where he was, hurt more than usual. I made the same fervent wish, to see him again soon.

When I went to school that morning, the children were busy, as it was "Book Week," and they were all dressed up as their favourite story book characters. The teachers too were in costumes, and it was a fun day to watch them parade.

I was relieved to hear that Christian and Athena returned from Adelaide in the morning, as they drove there a couple of days ago. Christian dropped in that evening, and I asked them for dinner next day. And they helped me with some technical problems, and he fixed some computer issues I encountered.

Chapter 55

We planned to hold a book signing at St Kilda library, when we had the monthly meeting of Authors Australia Inc. I suggested that we promote our books at a prominent venue, and Peter said he would negotiate with the co-ordinater at St Kilda library. Del agreed to present this event as well, so I was very busy organizing this event sometime in October.

Peter and I agreed to talk briefly about our writing and publishing experiences, and hoped to sell some of our books too. Connie agreed to drive me to these meetings on a Saturday afternoon. And he liked to browse around various shops in the city till we finished. Our members spent some productive and pleasant times there, and Peter treated us to afternoon tea sometimes.

Initially, only four of us attended; Peter Frederick, founder, Dan Stoj, president, and Margaret Pearce, secretary. We discussed self-publishing, writing, and distributing books. Peter said, "Nalini, you have launched your sixth book, so we would like you to share your experiences with distribution and how you do it."

I told them it was very hard work negotiating, networking with libraries, and book stores, and it was very challenging. But once you establish a good network, then it becomes easier with every publication. Dan was still in the process of publishing his first book. Peter had published two books so far, which he was promoting, and distributing through several outlets. We put on our thinking caps and brain-stormed.

I made patties and a cake for Christian's birthday, which was next day, on 29 August. We drove there in the afternoon, and Christian was busy in the garden. But he stopped for a while to enjoy his favourite snacks, and we had a good time.

Ninette asked me to drive her to Chelsea for an appointment with her optometrist, after my lesson. I walked with her to the optometrist's, and then I shopped till she finished. We window-shopped later, and she bought a few groceries at the supermarket before we returned. She was grateful to me for spending time, and driving her wherever she wanted to go, and I was happy to oblige, as I was very fond of her.

I spent all day cleaning up the house in early September, and put away unwanted clothes and goods, as our house was going up for sale soon. I made Connie a delicious seafood dinner of crayfish and prawns, the night before Father's Day, which he enjoyed.

I gave him a card and a present on Sunday. And afterwards, I made pan rolls and a cake, which I took to Christian's and Athena's, for afternoon tea. It was a blustery, wet day, but we drove to the site after tea, though it was too wet to get down, and it poured down heavily. The four of us stopped at a coffee shop in Mornington, and spent some time together, which was very nice and relaxing.

Connie flew to Sydney for a three day conference on 8 September. He called me at ten o'clock in the night to say he had a hectic time, as the conference lasted all day, and he was exhausted. After he complained about the bland dinner, second-rate hotel, and his demanding job, he hung up, as he said he wanted to sleep early. I spent a few hours editing "Catsville," as I was publishing a second edition, in time for the book signing in October.

When I called Nilanthi the following day, she was very depressed, and cried bitterly when she talked about her sad life with Heron. And she kept saying, "I can't understand why he was so cruel to me right to the end." I tried to comfort her. But I said I had no answers for the way other people behaved and treated us. After a long conversation, I urged her to cheer up and go forward now, as that chapter was closed.

Then I worked on my manuscript till about eleven o'clock, and was glad when I finished editing it. Connie called around eleven thirty that night, and said he went out for dinner with his colleagues, and that was why he was calling so late. He was after a couple of drinks, and was in a better frame of mind, as he giggled and related events of the day.

I was very concerned about Nilanthi, because she sounded so morbid and depressed. So I called her again next day, and was relieved when she sounded much better. She said she would plan her trip in November, and we chatted a while longer. When I came home after shopping that evening, I could not find my mobile anywhere, and I thought I dropped it at the centre.

I called Connie to let him know I lost my phone, so he suspended it immediately, as the account was in his name. I searched everywhere at home, and went through my coat pockets later. The phone had slipped through an opening in the lining of the pocket, and I was relieved to find it.

Nelune called to say that the "Lilac Ball" was next day, Saturday, 11 September. I wished her all the best, and knew it would be another great success.

I took Tigger to the vet very early in the morning on 16 September, to get him de-sexed. And when I called at midday, the vet said Tigger was doing fine, and I could pick him up later that day. We visited Lorraine and Tony in the afternoon, then picked Tigger at four o'clock on our way home. He seemed a little groggy, and slept through the evening.

I spent all day cleaning the house again, while Connie mowed lawns and tidied the garden, as the estate agent was coming soon to value the house. We decided not to put the house on the market, until the new house was completed. And I told Connie that we should ask for a sixty-day settlement, as the transition would work out well. And we could move into the new house at once, instead of renting, like we did before. It all depended on the sale of the house within our time frame, so I hoped for the best.

I spent some time composing my forthcoming talk at St Kilda library. Then we attended evening Mass, and I got Holy Communion for Ninette. I lit candles for all the departed souls. And I remembered Josephine especially, as it was one year since she died. Christian and Athena were in Sydney for a couple of days, and he called in the night to say they arrived safely that morning.

Chris Del Piano came over a few days later, to fix and paint the timber panels outside. And once he finished, the panels looked almost new.

I visited Ninette on Tuesday and gave her Holy Communion. Then I walked with her to the post office to pay bills, and shop at Seaford. Poor thing, her eyesight was getting worse, and she needed a great deal of help with everyday tasks.

Connie and I drove to the site a few times each week, as we wanted to keep an eye on every stage of the building. So, when we drove there that evening, we were happy to see that the house was almost completed.

The printer said he encountered a problem with the manuscript, so I fixed it, and emailed it late at night. And he said the books would be ready in a day or so.

We stayed in and continued cleaning on 22 September, and the agents arrived that afternoon. They were very impressed with our beautiful house, and said it would sell easily, as everything inside and out was so clean and tidy. They could hardly believe that the house was fourteen years old, and were quite enthusiastic, as they said they never had such a stunning, Tudor house on the market in this area before.

They kept saying it was a unique house, and would fetch a good price. We told them we would not consider offers below five hundred and eighty thousand dollars, and they said they would try their best.

The only negative aspect was, that although the house was in a good area in Frankston South, buyers would not pay too much, if they could buy within that price range in Mount Eliza, which was the next suburb. But we stressed the point that a Tudor house in Mount Eliza would cost twice as much, and Badiha, the agent, agreed. She seemed to be a nice person, and stayed to have a coffee, while her partner left soon after the appraisal.

Connie wanted to visit Esme, as it was her birthday yesterday, so we stopped there for a while before going to the display home in Cranbourne. On our way home, we bought a bottle of brandy, and dropped in to see Aunty Molly, who looked depressed and disoriented. She was thin and haggard, poor thing. I felt very sorry for her, when she started crying her eyes out, and talking about, "My poor son Ian," and I tried to comfort her. We stayed with her for a while, and promised to drop in again.

Christian and Athena visited a few days later, and said they met Nelune while in Sydney, and had enjoyed a good time there.

We drove to Oakleigh the following day to select carpets, as they did not have the one we selected previously. We chose a light aubergine tone, and then stopped at Spotlight to buy curtain tracks and rods. Connie picked up my books from the printer, for the book promotion next day. I took care of some last minute preparations, so we had a pizza for dinner.

We left home early on Saturday, 25 September, and arrived at the library around ten forty-five. I looked around at the drab meeting room, and was thoroughly disappointed, as it was such a dreary place compared to Mornington, and Frankston libraries. A few disinterested characters wandered around the library, and Christina and some friends arrived shortly afterwards.

Unfortunately, we organized this event on the wrong day, as it was footy Grand Final that Saturday. And not many people visited the library, as most of them were all at the match, or glued to their television sets at home.

I spoke to Hemal a few days ago, and he told me he would like to interview me, and film the book promotion, as he worked for Channel 31, and would try to air the event.

He arrived shortly afterwards with his wife, Rathna, a pleasant lady, and a prominent actor in a Sri Lankan theatre group; she had performed in many productions, and I was interested to hear about her theatrical performances, as I thought she would like to take part in Elvira's play. When I spoke to Rathna after the event, I mentioned the play to her. And they agreed to visit one weekend, and I said I would invite Elvira and John as well.

Del was great, and did a splendid job as usual, with her presentation and readings. Peter and I talked about our writing and our books. But Dan and Peter Whelan, the other two authors, who came to the event, were not very helpful in setting up the place, or getting anything ready for the promotion. They did not want to get up and talk about their work either, but just sat there impersonating two sacks of potatoes.

Peter Whelan was a dejected man; he spent a large sum of money on publishing a book that he was desperate to sell, but was unsuccessful so far. To start with, the book cover was an unattractive pea-soup green, with brown lettering. And even though his story may have had potential, he did not realize the importance of an eye-catching, well-designed cover.

Peter Frederick and I, with Del's help, did everything, and it was very disappointing, as we did not sell many books. I worked hard to organize this event, but the venue left a lot to be desired, so we decided not to re-visit this place. Hemal interviewed me, and recorded the event, and said he would do his best to get it aired. Christina, Peter Frederick, Connie, and I, stopped at a near-by cafe for a snack and coffee afterwards.

I woke up with a bout of vertigo and felt very sick next day. I knew it was due to stress on the previous day, and preparing for the book promotion. Yesterday's Grand Final resulted in a draw, so they played again on the following Saturday.

It was a beautiful, spring day, and just twenty degrees, so I cleaned up and did some washing before visiting Christian and Athena later. It came as a complete surprise when they decided to lease their house in Mt Martha, and rent a place in the city, because of their business. I was incredibly sad to hear they were packing up, and putting their furniture in storage until they moved to the city, but it was their life and their choice.

When we visited them that evening, they were busy packing up, and getting rid of unwanted items. I felt a pang as I watched them, as I knew Christian worked extremely hard, building a pergola, fences, and a beautiful garden, all on his own. He took so much pride in keeping a spotless house and garden too. But they decided it was the best option, so I could only wish them well in whatever they planned to do.

It was ironical that our house was just about ready, and I looked forward to living closer to them, as I loved their regular visits, and our interesting conversations by the fireside. We always discussed so many topics, and whenever I had an idea about my writing or any other interest, I sounded it out to them first. They had so much to contribute, and I valued their input. It was all going to change once they moved so far, and I knew I would not see them as often.

They were staying with Athena's parents, until the apartment in the city fell vacant in mid-January. And they planned to go overseas with her parents for a few weeks in December. Christian asked if they could stay with us for a couple of weeks when they returned. I said that would be fine, as we hoped to be in the new house in January 2011.

It seemed like only yesterday that they moved in to their house, and now just as our new house was ready, they were leaving. But if it was in their best interests, I did not tell them how sad I was to see them packing up. They gave me some books, and items to sort out, and put away if I did not want them, and then we came home. I felt very depressed just thinking about them moving out.

Our house was on the market only a week or so, when the estate agent called on 27 September, to say he was bringing some people over. I rushed around cleaning and mopping, and putting out cat litter trays, even though I still had vertigo. Later that afternoon, about ten people (all from one family), walked in with the agent. It was a rainy day, and they trailed in with muddy shoes onto the tiled areas. I hoped they would not walk on the carpets with their dirty shoes on.

The people were very impressed, and liked the house very much. I was in the lounge, so I heard them discussing plans to knock down walls, and extend the garage etc. etc. I thought it was quite amusing that they talked as if they already owned the house! The lady told the agent she would come back again with her husband.

I started cutting out fabric and sewing curtains for the new house over the next few weeks. After I sewed for a couple of hours, I felt very tired, as it was fourteen years since I last sewed that many curtains. I did not realize how arduous it could be, but I enjoyed the project.

The agent brought the same people next day. They inspected the place thoroughly, and by evening, the agent called to say they made an offer of $540,000 for our beautiful house. Connie was enraged, and told the agent we would not consider anything less than $580,000, and not to bother bringing people, who could not pay what we wanted.

I baked a couple of cakes on Friday, to take to the Briars next day, as we were helping Ginny and Alan with refreshments and props backstage.

I cleaned up on Saturday morning, 2 October, as it was "Open Day" from 11.30am to midday. Two couples came, and one was a Chinese couple, who wanted to look at the site plans. And after glancing at them, they left immediately, as they did not like the "pointed" shape of the block (bad feng shui).

I took it easy after they left, and we went to the Briars that evening to help out the Nomad Players. It was a good night, and the audience enjoyed the play, and we came home around ten o'clock after we cleaned up.

We forgot to turn the clocks forward, as daylight saving began next day. The agent called at nine o'clock to say she was bringing more people over that afternoon. I was in the garden with the cats, when a family with three children arrived with the agent. The lady was completely bowled over by the house and garden. She told me she had a dream a few nights ago that, "There was a willow and a mulberry tree in the garden, and now I see that there *is* a beautiful willow and a mulberry tree in your garden! I can't believe it!" She thought it was a good omen, and this was the house of her dreams.

I lit the fire, and all her children sat on the sofa in front of it, as if they were already quite at home. Even the agent smiled as she said, "Don't they look comfy sitting there!" Before five o'clock that evening, the agent called to say they made an offer of $578,000. But she said she would be able to get a little more, as they were very keen to buy our house.

We were at Christian's place then, but we drove back to the agent's to sign the forms, as we thought it was a good offer. The agent was jubilant, and said, "This is the *highest* price we have ever had in that area, and the only house like the Villa Tudor, so you should be very happy with this offer!" After we signed the paper work, we came home and hoped for the best. Christian and Athena dropped in later that night, with a better computer than our old one, and they left after one o'clock in the morning, once they set it up.

The agent brought another couple on 7 October; this time, an elderly American couple, who liked the high ceilings and "space." They knew it was under contract, so did not make an offer, although they were very impressed. My piano students, and their parents were sad when they saw the sign in front of our house, and asked me if I would continue giving lessons at home. I replied it would be better for them to find another local teacher, as some of them did not want to drive to Mt Martha in the evenings.

Christian dropped in briefly that evening, and he was very stressed and busy with his work, and moving out in a few weeks. Their agent had already found a tenant for the house, and he was trying to get all their things into storage soon.

I cut more fabric and sewed all afternoon next day, even though it was very demanding. But I wanted to have them ready by the end of the month, when we got the key to the new house. It was "Open Day" once again on Saturday, as the agent said they had to follow rules, even though it was under contract. Only one couple turned up, and they were not interested when they knew it was under contract, but the American couple told the agent they would like to know if the house would be up for sale again, in case the previous offer did not go through.

I made some savoury sausage rolls later, and we drove to Christian's and Athena's place in the afternoon. They enjoyed them very much, as Athena liked the spicy rolls, then we drove to see our new house, which was almost complete. It looked very elegant inside, with new fittings, and carpets laid out. We walked on the secluded beach at Mt Martha, before returning home.

We attended a charity lunch at the Angler's Club in Frankston, on Sunday, 10 October. Elvira's brother, Angelo, was one of the organizer's, and we had been there a few times before with Elvira and John. This time, we asked Con and Cornelia, and they came with their son, Andrei, and his current girlfriend, Lucy. We had a good time, and the seafood was delicious as always.

When I was at school on Monday, I heard the tragic news that Tess's father had died of a heart attack at the age of forty-six. When Tess came for her piano lesson, I comforted her, and she murmured, "I'm going to miss my Dad very much." She was only nine years then. Some of my students, who came after school, cancelled their lessons, when they knew I was moving out. But Ellie, a new student, was very keen to learn piano, and was upset when I told her we would be leaving in the New Year.

We picked up Shirani early morning on Tuesday, 12 October, and drove to the city, as we had an appointment with a notary at ten o'clock. Shirani, Nelune, and I agreed to grant Nilanthi power of attorney, in order to sell part of the land in Maharagama, so she could be independent, and use the money for her living expenses.

It was a very long, complicated process, as we found out to our cost. The notary charged us forty dollars each for his seal and signature. Then we walked to Casselden Place, and Lonsdale Street, and it brought back many happy memories of my time at the ATO, when I worked there in 2002. I met some very nice people there.

We took our place in the queue at the Foreign Affairs department, where a woman was very unhelpful, and Shirani called the embassy in Canberra for some information. After we finished all the paperwork and red tape, we dropped Shirani at Narre Warren by midday. On our way home, we bought a bottle of brandy, and stopped at Aunty Molly's place to wish her, as it was her birthday that day. She was still very despondent, and grieved over Ian's death. We spent some time listening, and consoled her before returning in time for my students' piano lessons.

Christian and Athena dropped in later, as she wanted to fix something on the computer. I knew I would miss them both very much, once they moved to the city, not only because of all their help and support, but because they were such caring and loving children. I enjoyed their company very much, and we had great times together, but I had to accept the choices they made.

Chapter 56

The building works at school were finally completed, and it was open day on 13 October. I went early, but the car park was full, and I had to park at the Xavier Centre and walk to school. Colleen was in the middle of her speech. I sat at the very last row, and was taken aback when Colleen said, "I know you're sitting there at the back Dolly, and I must say that Dolly has the patience of a saint! She never complains, and always with a smile, even if she couldn't find the piano sometimes, as we had to move it around so many times! So I thank you very much for your patience Dolly."

It was very nice of her to say so, even though there was nothing much I could have done during the chaotic building period, when I had to be flexible. I thanked Colleen afterwards for her kind words, and she repeated them with a smile. After chatting to some of the parents and staff, I came home a few hours later.

Connie was at home, as Chris Del Piano was still busy fixing the walls etc. I went out shopping to buy some plants, and when I returned, I planted some petunias around the pond, and trimmed a creeper near the mulberry tree. Ninette called in the evening and told me about an awful nursing home she visited on Sunday. She could not believe that such gloomy, unpleasant places existed for old people, and was sorry for her old friend, who had no- where else to go.

I spent the next few days cutting and sewing curtains, in between other appointments, and visits to Shirani's and Ninette's. I was in touch with Nilanthi regularly too, as she was visiting us soon.

Chris came again to finish the touch-up jobs etc. later in the week, and left in the afternoon. The house looked new inside and out, as Chris did a great job fixing the panels, and one of the interior bedroom walls where I found a wasp's nest.

Christian was still moving their furniture into storage, but dropped in briefly to say their tenant would be moving in soon. And I kept on sewing curtains till late each night.

The agent came again on 16 October, but this time, she did not have anyone with her to inspect the house. She was very impressed, now that the panels were done, and the walls gleamed with new paint.

We went for a play at the Briar's that evening, "Death On The Nile," which was very good, and we had a great time as always. Karen and Stuart were there, but Ginny was too unwell to attend. It was after eleven o'clock when we came home. Christian called, as he was driving past Frankston, but did not visit, as he said he was too tired.

It was thirteen years since Thathie died, on 17 October, and when we went to church that evening, I lit candles for him, and all my dear departed ones. Fr Denis announced that St Mary McKillop, Australia's first saint, was canonized today. But I knew about it already, as the newspapers and television covered that special story. It was a great day for everyone, and the congregation offered special prayers of thanksgiving for the first saint to be canonized here.

When Connie's siblings visited some days later, they were very surprised to see the "For Sale" sign outside our house, and kept asking where we intended to move. We decided not to tell anyone we were building a new house, until it was ready, as we did not want any negative vibes from them. But they were extremely curious, and kept phoning daily to find out what was going on. Some of them thought we were in financial difficulty, and were forced to sell our "mansion" (as they called it).

Connie's brother, Paul, drove past our house with his wife, Sanit, to "show" her our house, but they did not visit us all this time. And even Esme drove past with Yvonne and Armando to "look" at our house and did not come in. I thought it strange that they drove past our house, just to show people where we lived.

We did not enlighten them regarding our intentions, so they wondered and pried, but we kept our plans to ourselves. Connie did not blurt out anything for once. He told me he lost all confidence in his siblings after their dreadful attitude when Aunty died, and their bad behaviour at her funeral too. They said and did some things, that made him realize how envious they were of our achievements.

The agent called on 20 October, to tell us that the buyer's loan was approved, and they would make the final inspection next day. We were relieved, as it meant we did not have to keep the house open for inspection any longer. Our house was on the market for only two weeks when we had this offer, so we were very pleased, and so was the agent.

Everything was going according to plan, and we requested a settlement in ninety days.

The building inspector and valuer came two days later, and finished in one hour's time. But Badiha, stayed behind to have a coffee with me, and we sat outside, as it was a sunny day. She told me of her early days, and how her marriage was arranged when she was seventeen years old. Her parents took her out of school at fifteen, and she had no choice in the matter.

I told her it was amazing how far she had come now as a successful business woman, in spite of being a divorced, single mother, who brought up a child on her own. I told her I admired her very much, and we remain friends to this day. We enjoyed sitting out in the balmy weather, and Badiha said she would be in touch.

After she left, I went to the optometrist for my annual check up, and was relieved when he said there were no significant changes. Connie got over a bad cold, but I was still down with it a week or so later. I called Nilanthi that night, and she became very emotional over her financial situation.

Heron left her destitute, as he did not arrange his pension to be transferred to Nilanthi after his death. It was a very sore point with her that he did not care how she survived without an income. Unfortunately, our efforts to give her power of attorney, failed due to some bureaucracy over there.

We posted all the required documents to Nilanthi, but because Nelune's documents arrived a week later, the solicitor in Sri Lanka did not accept hers, as all the dates did not match! Shirani and I could not believe it, as it was the most absurd thing we ever heard. We were not prepared to go through the whole rigmarole again with various departments here, and spend more money on legal fees, which were exorbitant. So, we had to think of another option to help Nilanthi financially.

Chris agreed to fix all the curtain tracks in the new house for $500, and Connie and I would hang the curtains as we did before. We saved a small fortune on curtains once again.

I finished editing "Serendib" and sent off final corrections to AuthorHouse, and hoped the book would be published by the end of the year. But I just did not have time or energy to plan another launch, and decided to distribute the book to libraries and book stores. I was in contact with a nationwide supplier, who ordered substantial copies of my previous books for libraries, and requested my latest publication too.

Ninette called the following evening, and complained about the seating arrangements at next Saturday's dance that Elvira organized. She said she wanted Connie and me to sit at *her* table, with Luigi and Jackie. But I told her not to worry about it, as we did not mind where we sat. But she was not happy at all. She said that Luigi too did not like us sitting at another table, and would not attend the dance, if we sat somewhere else. So she was going to insist that Elvira changed the seating arrangements. I did not understand why she made such a fuss about it, but that was Ninette's way. She wanted us to sit at her table, and not with strangers.

We drove to Mt Martha early morning on 28 October, for final inspection, and hand-over of the keys. I was happy and excited, and loved the new place, but Connie found fault with everything. And he kept saying the finishes were not very good. And his constant refrain was, "In our house that *Jennings* built, they did a fantastic job! Their work was *perfect!* I'm not happy with the finishes here!" The project manager replied in a tightly-controlled voice, "Why don't you write out a list of all the things you are not *happy* with Conrad, and let me know within three months."

Connie kept criticizing and grumbling non-stop, as he checked everything thoroughly before we drove to Porter Davis in Narre Warren that afternoon. The consultant, who dealt with us during the whole project, handed us the keys, and a gift of herbs in a terracotta pot. I spent most of the following days sewing curtains, as there were many windows in the new house too.

It rained heavily on Saturday, 30 October, and I spent a few hours cutting out more curtain fabric. Then I rested a while before going to Elvira's "Charity Dance." Luigi and Jackie picked Ninette on their way. We arrived at the Rosebud club around seven thirty, and sat at Ninette's table, with Jackie and Luigi. Ninette was happy, as she told Elvira to re-arrange the seating. Ninette accompanied Elvira and Ornello on the keyboard.

One of the teachers from school, Judy, and her husband, came too, and I chatted to them whenever we stopped dancing. Luigi and Jackie did not dance much, and he sat there looking morose all evening. It was Jackie's birthday, so after dinner, Elvira surprised her with a delicious cake that she had baked. We enjoyed the night, and came home after midnight.

When we got down from the car, we stepped into a few inches of water! The heavy rain flooded the area outside the garage for the first time in fourteen years. We were concerned, because the buyers were coming for final inspection next day.

It continued raining heavily on Sunday too, and Connie cleaned the drain outside the garage door, and mopped up most of the water before the buyers arrived. I thought they were a nice family. Her name was Deanna, and she told me they had three girls, and two boys. But one of the girls was overseas, and so only four of her children, and the two of them were going to live here. They did not take much notice of the wet garage floor, but Connie mentioned that the drain was blocked, and the water had overflowed.

They could hardly believe that the house was so spotless after fourteen years, and were excited to move in sometime in early January. After they left, we drove to Elvira's place, as Connie wanted to give John the house plans. We had coffee, and then drove to the new house to measure curtains for hemming, as I sewed most of them, and they only needed to be hemmed.

Just as we were getting ready for bed, around ten thirty on Monday night, someone started banging on the front door. Connie peeped from upstairs, and said it was Roland and Shiranthi. But he was too tired to entertain them, as we had a long tiring day. So we just ignored their banging and shouting, and went to bed. Then the phone rang non-stop till after eleven o'clock, and Roland left umpteen messages. I could not believe their persistence at this time of night, when most people were in bed. Connie too was quite irritated at their lack of consideration.

I dropped in at Robinson's book shop next day, and was happy to hear they sold some of my books, and handed me a cheque. They were very helpful, and said they would order more copies, once they sold the rest.

Connie drove to the new house early morning on Saturday, as Chris was fixing curtain tracks. He called a little later, and asked me to come over and adjust the curtains and valances, as he did not know how. I stopped sewing and drove there to show Chris how to fix the rods and tracks, then returned home in the afternoon, and continued cutting and sewing, as I had quite a few curtains to finish. I baked a Christmas cake later, as I wanted to have it ready when Nilanthi arrived, and it always tasted better, after a month or more.

We drove to the new house again next day, and hung more curtains, and finished all the windows downstairs. I was relieved that I now had only the upstairs windows to finish, and was glad I sewed most of them before we moved in.

We visited Linda and Leo, on 13 November, and Linda prepared a delicious dinner. We enjoyed the evening, and Julie and Paul dropped in for a chat later. Zara was seven months old now, and cute as could be, and Josh was a very interesting little boy. It was after ten o'clock when we came home.

Next day we drove to Mt Martha, and hung a few more curtains. They looked very attractive and elegant, and was well worth my trouble. We came home after six o'clock, but at least we finished hanging a few more curtains.

Connie tried to negotiate a reasonable price for concreting and retaining walls, as the few quotes we received so far were exorbitant. We had to get fences done as well, as we wanted the backyard enclosed, before we moved in. The problem was, that being so close to Christmas, most of the trades- people wound down, and were not too keen on taking new jobs, especially small, domestic ones.

AuthorHouse sent me the mock-up cover and proof on 15 November. I was pleased with the presentation, as it looked very professional. I emailed to let them know that everything looked good, and to proceed with the final print. Some students came for lessons still, and Sarah returned from overseas. It was good to see her again, and she looked well. But Tracy said that when I moved to Mt Martha, Sarah would not continue piano lessons, and I was sorry to lose her, as she was a very good student. At least she had a good knowledge of music now, and I told her to continue music lessons at school. When I returned from Ninette's on Tuesday, I sewed for a few hours, and was pleased that I had completed ten windows so far. It took me about four hours to cut and sew curtains for one window, as they were very large floor to ceiling windows.

Athena's birthday was next day, and they visited quite late in the night, as they were busy working. We gave her a card and present, and Christian bought her a 1978 Leggo set, that she just loved and played with it till after midnight! She asked me to keep it at our place, as most of their things were in storage.

It was our 40th wedding anniversary on 18 November, and Connie was determined to move in to the new house by then. But the garden was a mess, with no fences or retaining walls, and the concrete paths around the house had to be done as well. So, we decided to wait till New Year, until all that work was completed. He gave me jewellery and perfume, and I gave him a bottle of Johnny Walker whisky, after shave lotion, and his favourite marzipan chocolates. We planned to have dinner out that night, but Connie said he was too tired, so we ordered a pizza instead, and then watched an old movie.

I called Nilanthi next day, and she said she was arriving in Melbourne on 26 November. Connie and I sent her a ticket, and she was very grateful, and kept thanking me for another holiday. I told her that it would be nice to see her again, and spend a few weeks with her. I arranged her room, and cleaned up, before sewing for the rest of that day.

We drove to Mt Martha on Saturday, and hung a few more curtains. It was very strenuous work, cutting, sewing, and hanging, but we finished most of the windows now, so it was good. We came home after seven o'clock that night.

Elvira, John, Hemal, and Rathna were visiting next day, to discuss her play. Connie went to church in the morning, but I stayed home to clean up and vacuum. Elvira came a little earlier, but Hemal and Rathna arrived around four o'clock. They were very pleasant, and helpful people, and Rathna was happy to take part in the play. She said she would get a few male actors from her drama group, and we were pleased that it was a positive meeting. They left after six o'clock, and we hoped for the best. Elvira and I found a few people, who were interested in taking part in the play, and we wanted to start rehearsals, as soon as we had the whole cast.

I typed flyers and advertised for actors, stating it was an amateur production, although Rathna was a professional actor. Elvira wanted to donate all the money to St Vincent de Paul, so we advertised it as a charity event.

That was the beginning of our venture, and we were happy to get started soon. Elvira and I tried to stage her play for a long time, but we did not have the required actors. I told her that once we had the whole cast, I would organize the meeting room at St Francis Xavier's church, or the community centre for rehearsals every second Sunday.

The concreter started work on 22 November, and said he would finish all the footpaths around the house, driveway, and al fresco area in a few days time. It was going to cost over sixty thousand dollars, but he was the most reasonable out of four or five concreters.

I wished Marilyn, our neighbour, for her birthday, and gave her chocolates and a card. She told me she was organizing a farewell party for us with our other neighbours. I said that was very good of her, and I looked forward to it. I sewed for a few more hours afterwards. Christian dropped in later, so I gave him some pan rolls to take for Athena.

It was a scorching thirty four degrees on Tuesday, and very uncomfortable at Ninette's, so I did not have a long lesson. But I stayed for a coffee, and after doing a few tasks for her, I came home and cut up the rest of the fabric, as I now had only a few more windows upstairs.

Marilyn dropped in on Wednesday evening, to tell me that drinks and nibbles at her place were at seven o'clock on 3 December. I thanked her, and then continued sewing for a few more hours. It was another hot day, but was expected to cool down tomorrow. Unfortunately, it rained heavily over the next couple of days, so the concreter had to stop.

I took a break from sewing, as I was exhausted, and spent a couple of hours playing the piano instead. I could hardly wait to resume my daily playing, once all this sewing and moving house were over. Then I cleaned and arranged fresh flowers in the guest room. I looked forward to spending some time with Nilanthi, as it was one year and nine months since her last visit. This time, I asked her to spend at least three months with us, as she did not have to worry about Heron anymore. She agreed, and we made plans for her to visit Heron's family, Shirani, and all her other friends before she left.

Chapter 57

We arrived at the airport early morning on Friday, 26 November. The plane was due to land at ten o'clock, so we were surprised when Nilanthi walked through customs at ten fifteen. But she looked very tired after the long flight. We drove straight to Shirani's place at Narre Warren for a quick visit, and then came home for lunch. It was great to see her again, and we chatted for a while, but I insisted that she rest for a few hours as she looked worn-out.

She brought gifts of clothes, and food items for us, and was impatient to distribute them first before she went to bed. While she was resting, I sewed for a couple of hours, and then Christian and Athena dropped in that evening. It was their 10th wedding anniversary, so I asked them to stay for dinner, and we enjoyed a great evening.

It poured down non-stop next day, and Nilanthi slept in, as she still suffered jet lag. Connie and I cast our votes that day, before we went to Mt Martha. When we arrived there, the surrounding area was very muddy, with puddles of water, as the driveway was not concreted yet. We hung a few more curtains, and came home after five o'clock. Nilanthi said she felt better, so we relaxed after dinner, and watched some comedies.

She was very sad that we were selling up this house though, and kept asking me, "With what a heart can you leave this beautiful place!" I replied that she would like the new place better, as it had great ocean views, but she remained unconvinced.

It continued raining on Sunday, so I cleaned up my wardrobe, and put some clothes away for charity shops. Then we attended Mass in the evening, and stopped to do some shopping before we came home.

I held rehearsals on Monday, as the annual piano concert was on the following Sunday. The children were all prepared, and I was pleased that they knew their recital pieces well.

The school staff organized a morning tea for volunteers and helpers next day. I went there at ten o'clock, and came home within the hour. Then we drove to Ninette's, as she wanted to see Nilanthi. We had a good time, and returned home late afternoon.

Marilyn came over later and offered me some pretty hats, as she was cleaning out her wardrobe. We went outside to chat, and next moment, Nilanthi accidentally shut the front door behind her, locking us both outside. I had no way of getting in, so I asked Chris, Marilyn's husband, to try and open a window in the kitchen area.

He managed to get a fly screen out, pried it open, struggled through the window, and opened the front door. What a drama! The window-frame was slightly damaged, and I was upset about the dent; just when we had to move out, as I wanted everything in the house to look nice and in good condition.

The rain continued incessantly on 1 December, first day of summer, but it was warm and humid. Once again, the concrete works were held up due to bad weather. They said it was the heaviest rainfall since records began. Just our luck, when we needed good weather for the concreting.

Nilanthi boarded a bus to Frankston Centre some times, and was enjoying each day. She liked watching old movies, and "Columbo," so we relaxed and watched them most evenings.

Just as Nilanthi and I left the shopping centre next day, we got caught in a severe thunderstorm, and drove home in torrential rain. We took it easy after dinner, when Esme and Paul breezed in unexpectedly around eight thirty. They were surprised to see Nilanthi and wanted to know, "What's happening with the house? *Where* are You moving to?" And were disappointed when we did not tell them what our plans were, or where we were moving to. Connie said, "We *may* be moving to Queensland to live in our unit for some time till we decide what to do," And their faces just dropped. Esme screwed up her mouth and exclaimed, "I *hate* Queensland! All those cyclones and cockroaches in the heat! I love Melbourne! I will never leave to go to another state!"

Just after they left, Babs came at nine thirty, so I served some dinner for her, as she had not eaten yet, and we chatted for a while. She left at midnight, and I was very tired and agitated, so was Connie. I just wanted to go to sleep, but I was restless, and woke up at three o'clock in the morning to have a warm drink.

I woke up late next day, as I was worn out, but I sewed for a couple of hours, as I still had a few more to finish. Nilanthi was happy to watch movies in the afternoon while I sewed. When Connie came home that evening, we went to Marilyn's around seven thirty, and we had a good time with all the neighbours. Marilyn and the others kept asking us about the people who bought our house. But I told them I knew nothing about them, except that they had four children, and appeared to be nice people.

Marilyn prepared several platters of finger food, and we enjoyed a glass of champagne before coming home in a couple of hours time. We parted on good terms, and everyone promised to keep in touch, and visit us in our new home, as they said we were good friends and neighbours for so long.

When Marilyn's nineteen-year old daughter, Shannon, was found hanging from a door in her flat a few years ago, I visited Marilyn daily, and made soups and meals, as she was absolutely shattered. It was a shocking incident, as they did not know what made their beautiful young daughter commit suicide.

Shannon had spoken to Marilyn only the night before, and had sounded happy and carefree. But early next morning, her flatmate discovered her lifeless body hanging from a door. They never got over that tragedy, and Marilyn mellowed over that period. We attended the funeral, which was a harrowing time for the family. I was quite close to her since then, and we got along without any problems.

So, I was taken aback, when a few days later, Marilyn and Chris came over and said that they were very upset, because the new people were "Jews" and we did not mention it. She said, "We saw the man and the little boys with their caps on," I replied, "What *difference* does it make? As far as I'm concerned, they're just nice, ordinary people, who bought our house."

But unfortunately, it did seem to make a big difference to them. I never knew they were so prejudiced and racist. Because a few months after we left, they decided to sell, and move out too. She said they could not stand the noise and all the "Carrying on" every Saturday night. It was unbelievable.

Nilanthi woke me up at midnight, to say that she had a sore back after riding on the exercise bike, and could I apply dencorub. I did so immediately, and she went back to bed feeling more relaxed. It was very warm next day, but Connie drove to Mt Martha to fix some curtain tracks. Nilanthi rested, while I cleaned up my wardrobe, and packed more bags for the charity shops.

We went to the Community Centre in Mt Eliza that evening, and watched a play "Funny Money," and had a great time. Ginny, Alan, Elvira, John, Karen, and Stuart sat at our table, and we enjoyed their company, as well as the very funny farcical play. It was after eleven o'clock when we came home, and we went to bed after midnight.

We rested till late on Sunday morning, then Brian and Pat picked up Nilanthi around midday, and took her out for lunch. Connie and I drove to Mt Martha in the afternoon and continued our work there. It was a sunny but blustery day, and we were happy to see the concrete was poured around the house, but the driveway was not finished as yet. Pat and Brian dropped Nilanthi later that evening, and she said she enjoyed herself for a few hours.

Connie drove to Lakes Entrance on business on Monday, 6 December, and was due back next evening. After I finished school that day, I stopped at Xavier Centre to check the piano, as it was being tuned later that day. Vicki, the parish secretary, said they had a microphone set up for Sarah, and she gave me the keys to the hall and piano, and wished me well.

The students came for lessons after school, and we held a rehearsal. Sarah sang beautifully, and I was very pleased with her piano playing too. Christian and Athena dropped in later that night, and stayed till after midnight. We had a great time laughing and chatting.

Nilanthi and I visited Ninette on Tuesday afternoon, and were surprised when Elvira, Mary, and Daphne dropped in too, as Elvira wanted to sing a few songs especially for us. We had a pleasant afternoon with our friends, and then did some shopping at Karingal. But on our way home, we got caught to a severe thunderstorm again. When we returned, I sewed for a few hours, and then watched old movies with Nilanthi in the evening.

I finished at school on Wednesday, 8 December. Then I went to the Xavier Centre to check the piano again, and after playing for a while, I was pleased that it was tuned well. I stopped at church for a brief visit, and by the time I came home, it began to rain heavily.

Nilanthi was depressed, and cried all evening, but did not want to tell me what was worrying her. She rested a while, and seemed to be more cheerful when she woke up, and then we watched movies. I knew she was going through depression and anxiety after Heron's death. Because he left her with nothing, and her future was very bleak and insecure. I sympathised heartily with her, and kept telling her that I would always be there for her, and not to worry too much.

Christian and Athena dropped in the following evening, with a new laptop for me, and set up my old one for Nilanthi. Christian always gave me his laptops and mobiles whenever he upgraded them. They finished with the laptop around one o'clock in the morning, and I went to bed immediately after they left.

I invited six past students for a Christmas party at home on the following Saturday, and spent most of Friday getting some things ready for the party. I catered for six children, and had plenty of food and drinks, but only Sarah and Tabitha turned up at two o'clock.

Nilanthi wanted to go shopping, so she boarded a bus to Frankston Centre that morning. I expected the students to come anytime in the afternoon, but no one else turned up by three o'clock. Still, I had a nice time with Sarah and Tabitha, and we listened to Sarah sing and play the piano. Tabitha's mother, Marina, and Tabitha's sister, Astrid, came to pick them up at five o'clock. Nilanthi returned just before, and chatted with the girls, and Sarah promised to attend the piano concert next day. I took it easy after they left.

It was chilly and overcast on Sunday, and I hoped it would not start raining. I had all the food, certificates and presents ready, and went to the hall by one o'clock. Connie arranged the chairs, and Nilanthi helped me lay the tables with nibbles and drinks.

All the children, their parents, and friends, arrived on time. Madeline was my guest performer that year, and in spite of a few slips, she played very well. Sarah and Jamaeka played beautifully too, and I awarded Sarah the special performance award, with Jamaeka in second place. All the children and their parents were happy, and stayed till about four thirty, chatting and enjoying the goodies. Then we cleaned up, and came home in an hour's time. It was tiring and a great deal of hard work, so I was relieved that the concert was successful.

I drove with Nilanthi next day, to hand the keys to Vicki, then visited the chapel and lit candles. And later, we drove to Frankston Central, as Nilanthi wanted to buy some things she had seen there. It was a warm, sunny day, so it was pleasant to be out. When we returned, I relaxed a while before sewing for a few hours.

I picked up Ninette on Tuesday, as I invited her for lunch. We had a good time, as she played the piano and entertained us with her funny stories. Toula picked her up a couple of hours later, and after they left I continued sewing till late evening.

Connie stayed home next day, and worked on his computer till nine o'clock in the night. I went to church with Nilanthi in the morning, and stopped at school, as

I wanted to give cards and presents to the staff. Later, we went to Frankston Centre to exchange a pair of shoes I bought the day before, but they did not have my size. When we returned, I rested a while, before sewing, and then watched movies with Nilanthi in the night.

I ran short of fabric for one last window upstairs, so I went to Spotlight and managed to buy a few more metres of the same fabric, and fortunately, it was the last bolt they had. The electric jug packed up that afternoon. I drove to Karingal and bought a new one, then came home and found I had left it behind, so I had to drive back again to get it. Christian dropped in later to say they planned to go overseas for Christmas with Athena's parents.

Shirani and Ranjith visited briefly on Friday, while I was busy preparing dinner for my guests tomorrow. Nilanthi helped to make dessert and chilli sauce. Later, I cut the fabric, and hoped to finish the last curtain in a few days time before we moved in.

I cleaned up the house, and cooked the rest of the dishes next day, and lit the fire in the afternoon, as it was cold and wet. Con, Cornelia, and her mother came around seven o'clock, and Elvira and John a little later. We had a very pleasant evening, and after dinner, Cornelia fell asleep on the sofa in front of the fire as usual. Her mother kept trying to wake her up, but she was oblivious. They left after midnight, and Connie washed dishes till two thirty in the morning, even though I told him to leave them, as I would wash them in the morning.

Next day, Nilanthi and I drove to Southland in torrential rain, to buy shoes and other items for her. Connie went to Mt Martha to fix curtain rods, and Chris put shelves in the garage that day. I packed a few boxes for Nilanthi, as she had many things to take back, including food items. Del visited that morning and stayed a couple of hours. And as she enjoyed the Christmas cake very much, I asked her to take a few slices home.

Ninette was not well on Tuesday, as she had a kidney infection, so we did not stay too long. When we came home, I packed up the rest of the boxes for Nilanthi, and at long last, I finished the last lot of curtains! It was such a relief, as it took much longer than I thought.

Ron and Cynthia arrived at seven thirty next morning, on 22 December, and I was still in my dressing gown. They brought two helpers to dismantle the cat cage and transport it to Mt Martha, as the concreted areas had set by now. Nilanthi helped me to pack some crockery, as I started packing the kitchen items already. I washed the lace curtains in the kitchen and toilets, then cleaned the kitchen shelves, so everything looked bright and fresh.

Christian and Athena dropped in on the 23rd evening, as they were leaving for the Philippines early next morning. They brought a bottle of champagne for us to open in the new house. He was sorry they could not be with us on that day, so was I, as I would have loved to have shared that special time with them.

On Christmas Eve, I started packing a few more boxes with crockery. And I cooked dinner later, then made milk rice for breakfast on Christmas Day. Connie was working right through, and unable to help with the packing at all, so it was up to me, with some help from Nilanthi. We went to church at six o'clock that evening, as soon as he came home after work. It was packed already, but we managed to get seats right at the back. Mass finished by eight o'clock, as it was the children's service, and then we came home and took it easy.

We enjoyed an ample breakfast on Christmas Day, then drove to Tooradin, where we spent a couple of hours, and enjoyed a barbeque in the park by the river. It was a warm but overcast day, so we walked over the bridge and alongside the water's edge, as it was very peaceful there. We drove to Woolamai later, to wish Shirani and the family. Roshan, June, and the boys were there, but Suresh had left by the time we arrived. We spent a few hours with them, and drove back in the evening. Nilanthi and I packed the ornaments and knick knacks on the dresser, which took ages.

We slept in late on Boxing Day, and then drove to Mt Martha to hang the last of the curtains. Nilanthi stayed back, as she said she would come to the new house once we moved in there, and not before. Connie drove his car, and I drove the Jag with some light boxes and bags. When we were returning, Connie reversed the Jag over the hump on the new driveway. I knew from the loud, jarring noise, that the bottom of the Jag scraped the concrete.

The petrol started to leak, so we called RACV. It took them one hour to get there, and the mechanic advised us to leave the car, and not drive it until we had it checked. It was very frustrating, as we were delayed till seven o'clock in the night.

Nilanthi looked very depressed when we came back, and when I asked her the reason why, she said she wanted to take a bus to the Centre. But buses did not run on Boxing Day, and she was bored staying on her own, till we returned. I explained what happened with the car, but it did not make much difference, as she continued being miserable all evening.

This was a different side of Nilanthi's personality that I was seeing for the first time. I understood what she went through, but I told her that she should be so relieved, now that her burden was taken away. She had cried so bitterly when Heron was alive, because she had to care for him, without respite. It was difficult to comprehend her behaviour, as she was very insecure after Heron's death. I tried my best to cheer her up, and even bringing her on this holiday was to boost her morale. But she was determined to be unhappy.

Peter picked her up next morning, and she wanted to stay there until we moved to the new house. I continued packing all the books and kitchenware till late evening. Connie drove to Mt Martha, as a mechanic was checking the car, and I hoped he could fix it.

I spent all day packing and cleaning up the fridge next day, the 28th. We had pizza for dinner, and the cats were frisking around everywhere. Simba preferred to get inside empty boxes and hide there. They sensed something was in the air, with boxes everywhere, and their routine was thoroughly upset.

We wanted to move out on the 29th, as the new owners wanted to move in on 7 January. That meant we had a few days to clean the house, and shampoo the carpets, before handing over the keys. I kept an eye on the cats and walked them early, as the removal van arrived at 7.30am, and loaded the truck till midday.

They returned at 1.30pm to take a second load and all the pots and plants. I packed my clothes and shoes and took them in small loads in my car, so the removalists transported only heavy furniture and white goods. When all the furniture was gone,

I did not have a chair left. So I sat on the staircase with the cats, who ran around, looking quite upset over this state of affairs. I fed them and waited for Connie to pick us. We left the Jag at Mt Martha after the mechanic fixed it, so I did not have my car.

I warmed the pizza in the oven and it got burnt. I ate burnt pizza, as I sat on the stairs and waited till Connie finally came at nine o'clock! He was busy arranging furniture in the new place, and said he forgot the time. The cats mewed a little, as we drove there but they were not too bad. We came to the new house around ten o'clock. The cats felt very strange and disoriented, especially Mishka, who mewed loudly at the top of her voice.

She continued mewing all night, and did not stop till daybreak. Tigger and Mishka slept on the bed, and Simba hid under the bed. Poor little cats! It was very traumatic for them, as I did not let them go out in the garden at all, except when I walked them on a leash.

I was exhausted next day, and more so, trying to settle the cats, as they were following me around, and mewing all the time, especially Mishka. Simba and Tigger settled down gradually, and slept quietly during the day.

We spent all day arranging furniture, and unpacking boxes. Connie wanted to pack and bring all the glasses and drinks from the bar, which was all that was left in the old house now.

It was forty degrees on New Year's Eve, and we drove to the old house in both cars. I packed more bags, boxes, and my sewing machine in the Jag, and I could hardly see the rear window. But I managed to drive safely, and parked outside the house on the street. I did not want to drive the Jag down the driveway again until the concreter fixed the hump on it, which he promised to do next week. I do not know how I did it, but I unloaded all the bags and boxes in that scorching heat, and made about twenty trips up and down the driveway and into the house.

We hardly had time to relax, as we had told we would spend New Year's Eve at Mary's and Tony's place. Connie went to pack up the glassware and drinks in his bar, and it was eight o'clock in the night when we arrived at Mary's place. Elvira, John, and another couple were already there, and we had a good time seeing the New Year in. We watched fireworks from their balcony, and then on television till countdown.

I wrapped dollar coins in red tissue paper, tied them with gold ribbons, and at midnight I gave them to everyone including Connie, as a symbol of good luck. We came home after one o'clock in the morning, and I was worn-out. I left the cats in the laundry, and they were alright when we returned. And for once Mishka slept without mewing her head off.

Chapter 58

I spent New Year's Day unpacking, and when I looked at the numerous boxes, it was daunting, and seemed like a never-ending task. As I packed everything indiscriminately, without discarding unwanted items, I now went through each box carefully, and put away five boxes of pots, pans, and crockery I did not need.

We stopped unpacking in the evening, relaxed a while, and then enjoyed a delicious dinner of crayfish and salad, with a glass of champagne that Christian and Athena gave.

The curtains looked very elegant, so I was pleased, and even Chris Del Piano said, "You have done a very good job with the curtains, as they look very professional." The colours blended well with the carpet and tiles. Now, it was a matter of turning this house into our home. And I hoped we would enjoy many years in this beautiful place and surrounding area.

I kept thinking about Misty on 2 January, as it was exactly one year since she was put to sleep. Time muted the pain, but the poignant memories of her last days still lingered. I drove the Jag to Frankston later that afternoon, as I still had a few more clothes and items to transport. And I spent the morning cleaning kitchen cupboards. Then shampooed and vacuumed the carpets, and everything looked clean and fresh, ready for the new owners.

Connie drove to Narre Warren that day and picked Nilanthi from Peter's and Astrid's place. She said she was very busy with her relatives, and had cooked for them every day. Although she was tired, she helped me to dust and clean the cupboards, before we drove back to Mt Martha. We stopped in Mornington, as she wanted to buy a loaf of bread and salt, to bring into the new house, (a symbol of prosperity).

When she entered the new house, she exclaimed, "This place is full of light! I thought I will miss the Frankston house, but this house is very beautiful too, and I hope you will be happy here." Nilanthi was very upset when she knew we were selling the old house, as she loved it very much, and kept asking me, "*How* can you even think of leaving such a beautiful house Dolly?" I replied that Mt Martha was a more scenic area, with spectacular ocean views. But she was very sad until she walked around now, and could not believe her eyes when she saw the superb ocean views from our garden.

We spent the next couple of days unpacking, moving furniture around, and putting things in order. One afternoon, Nilanthi and I drove to Rosebud, and dropped five bags of clothes, ornaments, and five boxes of pots and pans at a charity shop there. Then we shopped at K-Mart, and had a snack in the shopping centre before heading back.

The final inspection was on 5 January, as the new owners were moving in on the 10th. We drove to the house late evening, and met Badiha and the buyers there. They were very impressed with the cleanliness of the house, and thanked us profusely. I told them that I hoped they would be very happy in this beautiful home. We left the firescreen, some other cleaning implements to reach the high ceilings, besides all the shelving in the garage, which they thought we would dismantle and take with us, so they were pleased. Badiha and Nilanthi chatted as if they were old friends.

The settlement went through on 7 January, and we were relieved. Connie spent all day at the old house till nine o'clock in the night, still cleaning up! He said he transplanted about twenty saplings from the garden, as he wanted to plant them in the new place.

I was still very busy unpacking, and arranging rooms upstairs next day, when Nilanthi decided to go downstairs to get something. And halfway down, she turned to say something to me, instead of watching where she was going. Next moment, she slipped down a few steps and hurt her ankle badly.

She was lying in a heap on the landing, and was in a great deal of pain by the time I went to her aid. I applied an ice pack on her ankle, and then some dencorub, but she could not move her foot. So I made her soak her foot in a basin of warm water. She cried non-stop, convinced that her leg was broken, but it was not bruised, only a swollen ankle. From that day onwards, she lost interest in doing anything, or going out with me. And just wanted to rest in bed all day, and watch DVD's on the laptop.

My hands were full now, as I had to walk all three cats a few times a day, because the fences were not done as yet. Connie paid three and a half thousand dollars in advance to a tradesman, to put up the fences before Christmas. But that man never turned up, and he could not be contacted on his mobile either. We learnt that he did the same to many people; took money upfront, and then disappeared.

Connie complained to Consumer Affairs, and they sent an officer to interview him at home. The officer said it would be a court case, and Connie would have to appear in court. Meanwhile, we lost all that money, and still no fences! I could not understand why Connie paid the man upfront, before the job was done. But the man wrangled money out of all his victims, before the job was done, as that was how he operated.

The swindler was eventually caught and charged, but he declared himself bankrupt, so no one recovered their money. Connie found a reliable local tradesman, a few weeks later, who had good references. He promised to finish the fences by the end of January.

Shirani, Ranjith, Roshan, and family visited on Sunday afternoon, 9 January, as Shirani was concerned when she heard about Nilanthi's sprained ankle. She was disappointed when Nilanthi refused to go to Woolamai, as she had promised to help out in the restaurant. Now, she did not want to go anywhere, and was impatient to return home, as she said she had more faith in native treatment there.

While we chatted and laughed, Connie rushed around looking very agitated, as he wanted to attend Mass in Rosebud. He kept saying, "Dolla, we *have* to go to church *soon!*" So Shirani and the family left, but Nilanthi wanted to stay home, as she complained that her ankle hurt badly.

We rushed at five o'clock for the five thirty Mass. Connie drove the Jag because he said he wanted to give it a "Good run" on the freeway. He failed to notice that from the time we got on the freeway, a policeman was right behind us. A siren sounded ten minutes later, and Connie pulled aside.

The policeman walked over and said, "Sir, I was following you all this time, and you didn't move to the left, but stayed on the right hand lane all the way. Can you see the sign that says, *keep left unless overtaking*?" Connie mumbled, "You cops just pick on us drivers, when you should be out catching the real criminals!"

When he returned to his car to check Connie's licence and write a ticket, I told him," *Don't* be rude to him, otherwise you'll make it worse. You know you were in the wrong, so be quiet!" This annoyed him more than ever, and he barked out angrily, "*Why* don't you take *my* side, instead of siding with the cops? He's just being cussed, and I have only three points left, if I lose any more points, that's it, I will lose my licence!" When the policeman came back he said, "That's two demerit points, and a fine of $119." He handed Connie a ticket and walked away.

We arrived just in time, but Connie could hardly breathe, he was that angry. After much grunting and fidgeting inside the church, he whispered, "I *can't* follow Mass now, I'm going outside!" So, after all that rushing and commotion, hurrying Shirani and the family away, he now waited outside till Mass finished. We argued all the way home, and he blamed *me* for getting a ticket and fine!

He kept insisting, "I got a ticket because of *your* attitude!" I demanded incredulously, "*My* attitude? Not because you were on the wrong side of the road?" But he continued to blame me, as he was worried sick that he would lose his licence, with only one demerit point left. And I was his punching bag, as usual.

When we arrived home, I went outside to walk the cats, but I heard him complain to Nilanthi, "Bad enough I got a ticket, but Dolly *never* takes my side, and that makes me so angry!" I walked in and asked, "*How* can I take your side, when you do something against the law?" It was a very bad evening, with him furiously berating me on one side, and Nilanthi in tears, complaining non-stop about her broken leg and ankle.

I applied dencorub and bathed her ankle in warm water, but all to no avail. So, I asked her if she wanted to see a doctor next day, but she did not want to, and still kept saying her bones were broken. She called Petunia next day and sobbed, "My bones must be all crushed *inside*, it is so painful!" I tried to tell her that she would not be able to walk, or stand up, if she had broken bones, but she was unconvinced.

The builder came with his assistants at seven o'clock in the morning next day, to start work on the retaining walls. But I was surprised when they packed up and left two hours later, as they said they had another job to go to. The builder was a lame, elderly man, and he had a young girl and a boy to help him. The three of them spent a great deal of time over their morning tea break. And after the old man perused the newspapers leisurely, and hobbled around slowly to do some tinkering and hammering, they were gone for the day.

Nilanthi spent the next few days in bed, and looked very unhappy. She kept saying she wanted to go home sooner than planned, as she wanted to try native treatment on her ankle. She was due to leave in mid-February, but she told me that she could not wait that long. Every morning, she limped downstairs, crying bitterly, and looked very miserable.

I was sad to see her in this state, as she was not spreading any cheer in our new home. I sensed a subtle change in her attitude, because she was resentful of everything and everyone. Ever since Heron's death, her financial security vanished, and I sympathised heartily. But I could not reach her, as she cocooned herself in a bubble of self-pity and misery.

Her sprained ankle compounded her unhappy state of mind, and I never knew she was so fussy, and not a very easy patient. She complained of pain constantly, but did not want to see a doctor, or try to help herself in any way. This was another aspect of her character I did not perceive before.

Christian sent a text message on the 12th, to say they would be arriving on Saturday, 15 January.

Torrential rain caused havoc, as some areas in Queensland were flooded, and some lives were lost too, with several houses going under water. The news each day was tragic, and I hoped the rains would ease soon, and bring relief to the poor victims.

Although Nilanthi's foot was much better, she did not want to go out anywhere now, and preferred to stay home and watch DVD's. I applied anti-inflammatory creme on her ankle, and she said it brought some relief for a while, and then she seemed alright.

But the following Saturday morning, I found her crying and very upset, as she sobbed, "I *can't* stay here any longer! It's *boring* stuck here in the room with my bad foot! I want to go home!" I tried to pacify her, and said that it was only a few more weeks till February, and to try and enjoy the rest of her stay. But she was adamant, and wanted to leave early, so I refrained from persuading her to stay.

I just could not understand what was worrying her, so I said she was free to leave whenever she wanted to. When she was in Sri Lanka, she complained how lonely she was, and how desperate she was to be with us, as she loved it here in Melbourne. And when she was here, after a week or so, she always fretted until she went back. This was her usual pattern, I thought, and did not let it bother me.

Christian and Athena arrived safely, and said they would come over later that evening. Ninette and Eric visited that same day around five o'clock. She was happy to see the new house, but she told me, "I liked your old house better Nalini." She could not see very far, and so did not appreciate the ocean views or tranquil area around. But I said I liked it here much better, although I knew what she meant, because the Villa-Tudor was a gracious and unique house. The new house had more living space, with well-planned spaces though.

I was really glad to see Christian and Athena when they came around seven o'clock, and they settled in the second spare room upstairs. It was late when we went to bed that night, as we sat up chatting and laughing. Connie paced up and down irately, as he was stressed about losing his licence. He kept nagging me about various things; the cats, the noise, the money he lost to the fraudulent fencing man, his job, the bad workmanship in the new house etc. etc. until my head was spinning with so many issues. I just wanted to unwind quietly in a hot bath.

I locked the bathroom door, and tried to relax in the spa, but a few minutes later, Connie banged on the door and shouted out, "*Open* the door at once! I want to go the toilet!" I replied, "There are *three* other toilets in the house that you can use, *why* do you want to come in *here*?" He did not stop banging on the door, until I opened it and he growled, "I *want* to use this toilet! Why are you locking the door?" "Because I want some *privacy* and quiet here!" I replied irritably.

He did not understand my need for space, and quiet time, while I had a bath, but repeated the same behaviour on two more occasions, shouting and banging on the door until I opened it. Finally, after the third time, I told him to stop behaving so stupidly, as Christian, Athena, and Nilanthi were staying with us, and I did not want them to know how badly he was behaving. I was stressed on every side, and did not know how to find some peace. The tension was incredible whenever he was at home.

I woke up early next day, and walked Tigger and then the other two cats. We drove to Dromana with Christian, Athena, and Nilanthi on Sunday. And after walking for a while along the seashore, we stopped to have a snack and coffee before coming home a couple of hours later. I made pasta for dinner afterwards. Athena set up her computer on the kitchen bench-top, with plugs and wires spread across the floor. Connie complained about that too, as he said he did not have any place to relax.

I told him he could work on his computer in the study, or anywhere else in this huge house, but he was just being difficult as usual. Most evenings, when we sat around chatting, he smoked and sipped a drink outside, as he seldom joined in the conversation, but preferred to be alone. He watched television in the living area sometimes, while Athena worked on her computer in the kitchen. And Nilanthi, Christian, and I, enjoyed chatting and laughing over some funny incident he related.

I was relieved when the fencing man arrived on Monday, 17 January, because I could walk the cats in the garden, without them wandering off to the adjoining vacant land. It was Ninette's birthday, so I wished her and chatted for a while. Nilanthi said she felt better, so we drove to Mt Martha village, and walked for a little while before heading off to Main Street, Mornington.

She decided to go back in early February, and I wanted to make the most of our time together. Christian and Athena worked on their computers till late at nights. When Nilanthi went to bed, I did crossword puzzles, while Connie prowled outside, smoking and nursing a glass of whisky.

Nilanthi promised to help Shirani in her restaurant for a few weeks at least, but now she did not want to go to Woolamai at all, because of her sprained ankle. It was unfortunate, as Shirani was really busy, and would have appreciated her help.

The workmen were still busy doing the retaining walls, and all I could hear was their blaring radio from seven in the morning, and not much work was done. They seemed to be taking a very long time, and blamed the rain and wet ground.

Christian drove Nilanthi to Pam's place in Pasco Vale on the 19th, as Pam wanted Nilanthi to spend a few days with her, and visit other family members too. He returned late, and I spent time with Athena, as the computer was down, and she could not do much until she fixed the problem. I was relieved when the cats settled down after a few weeks, but Mishka still had little "accidents" whenever she got excited, and then she wet the bathroom rugs.

Mary and Elvira came for afternoon tea on the following Saturday, and Athena helped to serve tea, and washed up later. Nilanthi stayed at Pam's place a few days, and I spoke to her every evening; she said Alan and Pam would drop her on the 23rd. When she returned, she told me she was happy to be back with me, and in her own room, as she was not very comfortable moving around to different places.

We drove to Mornington next day, and I bought more anti-inflammatory creme, which relieved her ankle. Although the swelling was down, she complained of severe pain still.

Con and Cornelia visited on Australia Day around four thirty in the afternoon, and brought champagne and chocolates. We enjoyed the evening, and they left after seven o'clock in the night. Christian called to say the townhouse in Carlton was vacant, and they could move in soon, so I was happy for them.

He left a set of golf clubs inside the empty wardrobe in the spare room, saying, "Dad can use them, so I'll leave them here." When Connie saw the clubs, he told Christian, "There's no room here, so better take them with you." Christian just looked at him in disbelief. So many empty wardrobes and spare rooms, and he said there was no room! I told Christian not to mind what Connie said, because he was just being difficult, so he took the clubs with him.

Joelle, Celine, and Micheline visited on the following Friday evening, and stayed a couple of hours. They were happy to see Nilanthi again, and it was good to catch up with Joelle and her family too.

We dined at Elvira's on Saturday, the 29th, as she wanted to wish Nilanthi goodbye before she left. She took a great deal of trouble to prepare a delicious meal as always, and we had a pleasant evening. It was close to midnight when we returned. Nilanthi was very tired, and too full of pasta! She complained that she was sick and uncomfortable, as she drank too much red wine, and ate too much pasta. I gave her a quick-eze tablet and hoped she would rest well.

Shirani and Ranjith visited with Max and Will on Monday evening, to wish Nilanthi goodbye. Max found it amusing to walk Simba on a lead, and enjoyed playing with the cats. They stayed a couple of hours and left after seven o'clock.

Ninette invited us for lunch on Tuesday, and we had a light snack with her before doing some last minute shopping at Karingal. The evening news showed cyclone "Yasi" approaching Cairns, and causing untold havoc in its wake, but I hoped it would not wreak too much destruction.

The maintenance man from Porter Davis came on 2 February, to fix a few things, as the three-monthly check up was due. Some of the interior doors did not shut properly, so he fixed the locks, and a minor leak in the garage ceiling. I collected some holiday photographs for Nilanthi to take back, but she stayed home, as she said she was too tired to walk around the shopping centre. That night, Nelune, Shirani, Ninette, and some other friends called to wish Nilanthi goodbye.

She was up very early next day, all packed up and ready, before I even woke up. We arrived in the city at midday, and had lunch with Christian and Athena at a restaurant called "Spicy Temptation" in China Town. Connie enjoyed the super hot chilli dishes. Then we drove to the airport by two thirty, and had a coffee with Nilanthi, before she checked in at four o'clock. I was sad to see her leave, but she was very anxious to get back and attend to her sprained ankle.

We came home two hours later, and I was exhausted. Cyclone "Yasi" had ripped through north Queensland last night. But so far, no lives were lost, only total destruction of houses, banana plantations, trees, and buildings. It was very distressing to watch the chaotic scenes on the news.

Sarah, Janice's daughter, was staying with Nelune in Sydney for some time now, as she was travelling around Australia. She was in Melbourne for a few days visiting a friend, and called to ask if she could visit us. I was very happy, as we missed seeing her in 2002, when we were in London. Christian agreed to drive her over, as Athena was busy working. I waited all afternoon, and he called at three o'clock to say they would be here for dinner. So I raced down to the shops to get some groceries, came home soon, and prepared steaks with mushrooms.

A terrific storm was imminent in Melbourne in the wake of cyclone "Yasi," and the non-stop deluge spread a thick mist all around, so that nothing was visible; and unfortunately, Sarah was unable to even glimpse the ocean when they arrived at about eight thirty that evening.

It was lovely to see Sarah again. She was very friendly and pleasant, and we chatted away happily. I was sorry she could not spend more time with us. We had a great evening, and I invited her to visit us again soon. Connie arrived at about nine thirty, and I was glad he met Sarah too. After Christian and Sarah left, we did not get any sleep till after two o'clock in the morning, as his phone rang constantly; some stores were experiencing leaks, floods, and power outages due to the severe storm.

They finally delivered the two new sofas we ordered in October last year, on Saturday, 5 February. And said they could not deliver them earlier, although they had assured us we would have them before Christmas. They blamed the storms, as the warehouse was flooded. Anyway, I was pleased, as the sofas looked attractive and elegant. We re-arranged the furniture in the family area, and I was happy they fitted in well. I called Nilanthi that night, and she still complained about being unwell, and very tired after the long journey.

I expected Chris and Peter La Ponder for afternoon tea next day, but Chris rang to say their car was in the garage, and they were unable to make it. I was disappointed, as I had looked forward to seeing them again, as we had not seen each other for some time.

Connie went for morning Mass on Sunday, but I stayed back to prepare tea for Isobel, John, Michelle, and Greg, who were staying in a holiday home near by. They arrived around two o'clock, and we had a very pleasant and interesting afternoon, and they left a couple of hours later. Ninette invited them that evening, and she asked Connie and me to join them for drinks and nibbles too.

We went there at seven thirty that night, and enjoyed a great musical evening. Isobel sang, Ninette played the piano, with Dora accompanying on mandolin, and Angelo on the piano accordion. They played beautiful, Neapolitan melodies, and I could have listened to those haunting songs all night, but we returned home two hours later. Dora and Angelo were good musicians too, and got on well with Ninette. They visited her a few times during the year to play wonderful music together, and Ninette always invited me on those occasions. Dora usually brought large quantities of pasta, and pizza, that everyone enjoyed after the musical evening.

Although the new fences stood six feet tall, I was concerned that the cats would escape through some large gaps underneath. So, I still walked them on leads, although I was sorry, and knew they were longing to wander off unrestricted. But I wanted to play it safe and get them used to the area, as I did not want them to get lost in the reserve, or in the lonely neighbourhood. Only a few houses were built then, and most of the blocks were overgrown, with the likelihood of snakes slithering in from the bushland.

Chapter 59

I stopped to light candles after school on 9 February, as it was Ammie's birthday. It was habitual to light candles, and pray for the souls of the departed, especially my parents, Nihal, relatives and friends, as it was my way of remembering those dear, precious people.

Elvira wanted to learn piano, and asked if I could teach her, and she would teach me spoken Italian in exchange. She came one afternoon for her first lesson, and I tried teaching her the fundamentals. Her fingernails were about one inch long, but she told me she would not trim them even a whit!

I showed her how to play scales, and she jabbed at the keys with one fingernail. She taught me Italian for about half an hour afterwards, and we had fun teaching each other. I saw something strange creeping around the garden that evening; it was an echidna from the reserve, who had lost its way. I quickly videoed it hiding behind a flower pot.

The building next door started, and the endless hammering and drilling assaulted my ears from seven o'clock in the morning till late evening. The owner, and his brother were building it themselves, so they stayed as late as possible. I fervently hoped they would finish soon.

I was deeply saddened and shocked to hear that Christine's sister, Acca, had died the day before. Janice told me that Acca was suffering from lung cancer for some time now, and was seriously ill during the last few months. I called Christine immediately to offer my condolences, and to comfort her. But her grief at losing her beloved sister was too much for her to bear, and she could hardly speak. It was too traumatic to even think of such a tragedy, as Christine nursed Rosie and Acca through their worst days.

We asked Fr Denis to bless our new house, and he agreed to visit after morning Mass on Saturday, 10 February. Connie picked him up, and they arrived around ten thirty. I served morning tea, and he stayed a couple of hours chatting to us. He was a very interesting and approachable priest, who genuinely cared about his parishioners. He said he enjoyed spicy food, so I said we would invite him for dinner soon.

Then he said a prayer in each room, and went outside to bless every area of the garden. Connie dropped him in Frankston later on, and we went to Rosebud for evening Mass. I fed stale bread to the gulls on Dromana pier, then we had hot chips, and walked on the pier for a while before returning home.

Fr Eugene left the priesthood a few years ago, due to health problems, and was undergoing treatment for mental issues. He was under a great deal of pressure, as he did not have an assistant priest to help him. When I attended his farewell Mass, I was upset to watch him break down in tears, as he explained what he went through. He appeared in the local papers too, with a scathing attack on the lack of support from his superiors.

A few months later, he married one of his parishioners from his previous parish. We exchanged Christmas and Easter cards for a while, but then we lost touch with him.

He was a lively character, and I remember some of his wacky comments; like the time when he saw us in church after some time, he came up to me and said, "Where have you been? I thought you had died, and I missed your funeral!" Another time, he muttered, "I've forgotten what you look like because I haven't seen you, must take a photograph!" When I told him that we sometimes attended Mass at Rosebud or Dromana, and did not always come to Frankston church, he grunted, "You are two spiritual butterflies!" His comments were always forthright.

Once, when he asked me to play the organ on Holy Thursday night, I replied I would have liked to, but we were leaving for Warrnambool that night for the long weekend. And he immediately retorted, "Yes, you want to play, but the devil won't let you!" So now, we had a more conservative priest, who did not suffer any mental health issues. And it was easier to communicate with Fr Denis.

We drove to Springvale next day, and had yum cha at Gold Leaf restaurant. On our way home, we dropped in at Shirani's place in Narre Warren, and I enjoyed catching up with her.

The fencing man said he would come on Monday and finish the side gates, so Connie stayed home, but the man did not turn up. I gave Connie chocolates for Valentine's Day, but he said he was too busy to remember. But he went out later, and bought a card and a bottle of perfume. I told him he did not have to give me presents, because I did not expect gifts.

The workmen turned up after two weeks, and dragged their feet all day, and did not make much progress with the retaining walls.

I took Holy Communion for Ninette on Tuesday, and met her sister-in-law, Arlette, for the first time. She was a friendly, outspoken lady, and asked if she could share the Host with Ninette, which she did, and was happy. When I came home in the afternoon, I was glad to see that the side gate, and fences were completed at last.

I returned the communion "pixel" to the church office on Wednesday, as I had to organize communion for Ninette at Mornington church, now that we belonged to that parish. Fr Denis and Sr Diedre were there that morning, and I had a pleasant conversation with them. Before I left, I said I would let him know when we could invite him for dinner, as Connie was very busy with his job at present.

Elvira came for her piano lessons every week, and I had Italian lessons too. She was not making much progress though, but at least I showed her how to play scales, and recognize notes. And I did not make much progress in Italian either, as I found pronunciation challenging. But I did learn a few basic phrases and words.

Marilyn, our previous neighbour, worked at Targets store in Mornington Central, so I dropped in there after shopping next day. I was taken aback though when she looked annoyed, and spoke very rudely to me, "You *didn't* tell me that the new owners were *Jews!* They make such a big noise in the night, and they have people dropping in at all times of the night, we don't get much sleep!" I was surprised and replied, "It was unimportant to tell you they were Jews, as they are just ordinary people." She was not pleased at all, and I was disappointed at her blatant racism. I wished her, and went off to Benton's Square to do some shopping.

We drove to the city at midday on Connie's birthday, the 19th. He wanted to have lunch with Christian and Athena at the same restaurant in China Town, that he had liked so much. It was a gusty day and quite cool, but after lunch, we walked to Federation Square, for my monthly meeting with Authors Australia Inc.

Christian and Athena strolled along with us, and spent some time browsing in the shops until the meeting was over. And later, we drove to Carlton to see their new place. It was a nice, three bed-room townhouse, and they were settling in alright. On our way back, we stopped at Ikea and had a look around, but did not find anything we liked.

Next day, we drove to Townsend Furniture in Dandenong, and bought a desk for my laptop. Connie ordered a custom-made liquor cabinet, as we did not find anything suitable in the store. When we came home, I took the cats out walking, and left Mishka alone just for a moment. She jumped over the fence and Tigger followed suit. But as Mishka ran to the adjoining block, I managed to pull her lead and get her back. Tigger was on the fence with the lead dangling over, so I yanked it and made him jump back into the garden. They were a caution, the pair of them, but Simba was not as wild and mischievous, and just looked askance at the two miscreants.

The plumber arrived next day with two enormous rainwater tanks in his truck, and he spent all day setting them up. We could be certain of enough water for the garden (when it was established).

I completed the sequel to "Serendib," and was busy editing it now. I wanted AuthorHouse to publish it soon, because they did a very good job with the first book.

Sarah was still keen to continue lessons, so she came on Monday evenings. I was very proud of her achievements, as she was a very good student.

On my birthday next day, I had an enjoyable day at school. The staff gave me a card, and Liz organized a delicious cake and morning tea, and they all sang happy birthday. I visited the chapel and lit candles later, and then had coffee with Liz at Karingal.

When I came home, Townsend Furniture delivered the desk, so we took it upstairs, and set up my laptop. Connie was working from home all day, and he continued till late evening. All my friends and family called to wish me that evening, and later we went for a walk on Mt Martha beach. We ordered a pizza, as we were too tired to go out for dinner. Birdie called to thank me for her birthday card, and to wish me too (as she always did without fail).

It was the Women Writers first meeting for the year, on the last Friday in February, and Connie drove me to the city. The traffic was very heavy, so we arrived there at eleven o'clock. It was good to catch up with all the other members, and I had an interesting time. I left after two o'clock, and we came home within the hour. I wished Nelune for her birthday that evening, and we had a long chat.

We went for a dance at the Dromana club on Saturday, and Elvira surprised me with a cake that she made. And during the night, she requested the band to sing Happy Birthday. Mary, Tony, Connie, John and Elvira joined in the singing. We had a pleasant evening, but while I was dancing, my heart beat was very rapid. I had to stop for a while, although Connie wanted to dance all night.

I rested till late next morning, and let the cats out on their own, as they were getting used to the garden now. And when I called, they came reluctantly. I stopped them from jumping into the reserve because the council culled foxes and feral cats there. They requested that all cats and dogs be kept indoors during this period. So I made sure they did not wander off to the reserve.

Christian dropped in next day, and asked if he could park his 4wheel drive in the garden, as he did not have enough parking space for two cars in Carlton. I said it was alright, then I drove him to Mornington to pick up his car, and he drove back to the city.

I had a very bad time that night because Connie was in a foul mood. He was not happy at all because Christian parked his vehicle in the garden. He nagged and complained so much, that I had a severe headache, and did not get much sleep. It was always the same. I had to listen to his nagging, because he did not say anything to Christian or to anyone, but unleashed his bad temper on me. I had chest pains and shivers all through the day.

The men finished building the retaining walls on Wednesday, 2 March. It took them almost three long months, and finally the job was done. They looked good, and now all we had to do was landscape the garden.

I painted a seascape for the book cover, "Dark Shores" and almost finished editing the manuscript, as I wanted to have it ready by the end of the month.

Connie stayed home on Tuesday, and was on the phone from eight o'clock onwards. I was happy that the piano was in a separate room now, and I could close the door and play without disturbance.

Ninette was not feeling well when I visited that day, but I read her letters out loud, checked the television guide, and bills etc. She said she was very tired, and had panic attacks, so I stayed a couple of hours with her, then went to see Dr Khelil. He wrote a referral to Dr Kertes, as he wanted me to consult him because of chest pains.

Connie drove to Albury on Thursday, 10 March, and stayed overnight. I enjoyed a peaceful evening, and edited my manuscript till midnight. And was glad that it was almost finished.

We visited a few nurseries in Mornington next Saturday. Tony's brother, Angelo, owned one on Nepean Highway, so we looked in there, and found his prices were very reasonable. We told him we would buy all the plants we needed from him.

I watched a good movie on television that night, "Marnie" with Sean Connery and Tippi Hedrun. It was very interesting, and next day I checked it on Google, because I wanted to know more about that film and background. It was not a box office hit, but I found the story intriguing.

Luigi agreed to pay for the second publication of his book, "Is this your Caruso?" So I signed a contract with Melrose Books, UK, for it to be published in early 2012. I had a few projects going on then, as his book had to be edited all over again, and many more photographs included in the second edition. I selected about forty old photographs from Luigi's album, and then emailed them to Melrose Books.

I also finished editing "Dark Shores" and sent the manuscript to Author- House, as Christian fixed the problem in my laptop the day before. Melrose Books confirmed that they received the first instalment, and would start work on Luigi's book soon.

After visiting Ninette the following Tuesday, I stopped at Woolworths in Seaford to get some things, and I heard Connie's voice. He was standing in the bakery, so I waited for him to finish talking on his mobile. He was preoccupied, and greeted me perfunctorily before rushing off to attend to his work in the store. For some reason or another, he was in a bad mood that night too, and we ended up arguing.

I felt drained, and was sick of this non-stop bickering. Nothing seemed to make him happy or please him. And he found something to complain about, and nagged me over every little thing he could think of. It made me very sad to think that he could not be content in this beautiful place we worked so hard to build. Instead, he wallowed in his misery, and wanted me to be just as miserable. How true that saying, "Misery Loves Company."

It irked him to see me busy and happy, just following my pursuits, because he constantly said, "Don't get involved in that!" Especially Luigi's book, because he did not want me to have anything to do with him. But I told him it was my work, and I enjoyed writing his biography. Or else he snapped at me, and spluttered angrily, "You...you...go write another book!" And made it sound as if it was a nefarious criminal activity.

Elvira continued piano lessons, and I learnt a modicum of Italian too over the next few weeks. It helped whenever she came, because I practised a few sentences with her, and learned correct pronunciation.

I communicated regularly with Melrose books, and the manager, Jill, was constantly in touch via email and phone. They appeared to be genuine publishers, so I hoped Luigi's book would be a success overseas.

When Judy Bartosy called me, I told her I was unable to attend the next monthly meeting, as I was busy that day.

When Peter Frederick emailed me on 24 March, asking if he could nominate me as the next president of Authors Australia Inc. I was very surprised. He said that Dan was stepping down, and Peter could not do everything on his own. He wrote, "You are the best person for the role, as you have a lot of experience in publishing, and you could help our group very much."

I replied I would consider it, and thanked him for his confidence in me. After a day or so of mulling over it, and what it would mean, with all my other commitments, I was hesitant to take on this added responsibility. But on the other hand, it was a worthwhile venture, and several authors were interested in joining our group. I decided to accept the nomination. Peter was very pleased, and said they would hold an election, and let me know the outcome soon.

I watched an old movie with Elizabeth Taylor, "Cat On A Hot Tin Roof" on 25 March, and then remembered she died only a few days ago, at the age of seventy-nine. She was a great actress indeed, and I was sad that another Hollywood legend had left us.

I drove to Chelsea on Saturday, to meet Rathna and Hemal regarding Elvira's play. Elvira followed in her car, as I had some shopping to do afterwards. Connie left early morning to play golf with some friends, for which I was glad, as he needed to unwind, without working so hard.

We had a positive meeting with Rathna, and after she read it, she was very keen to play a lead role. She said that some young people in her drama group were interested too. Elvira and I were happy that at last we were getting somewhere with the play. She was very disappointed when Tom Padula dropped the whole project after a couple of weeks, saying he could not undertake to produce it.

Christian and Athena were unimpressed, when Elvira turned to me once again, and asked for my help. They thought it was unfair to go ahead with another producer, and then ask me to help, when he dropped out. But I told Elvira I would help on one condition, that she did not change her mind and find another producer again. She agreed.

Hemal and Rathna were very kind and hospitable, and we spent a couple of hours discussing various issues regarding the play. Later, I drove to Spotlight, as I wanted to buy some lace curtains for the front windows. Elvira went home, well pleased with the outcome.

I edited Luigi's book all weekend, as I had to send the manuscript to Melrose Publications before the end of that week. Elvira still came every Wednesday to learn piano, and sometimes she delayed to come, but never apologized for being tardy. I had to put everything on hold till she came and spent a couple of hours, as I continued with Italian lessons as well.

I spent the following Saturday afternoon cooking and cleaning, as Lorraine, Tony, Liz, and Gerry were coming for lunch on Sunday. Connie picked up some plants from Angelo's nursery, and was busy planting them till late evening.

It was gloomy and quite cool next day, when our guests arrived at eleven forty five in the morning, while I was still preparing things. And they left after four o'clock in the afternoon. We had a pleasant afternoon though, and they brought some cuttings from their gardens.

The following Wednesday, I cooked buriyani rice, and chicken curry for the staff, as I finished lessons for the term. They enjoyed it very much, and I liked to cook something special every term, as they all liked spicy food.

I spent several hours browsing through Luigi's albums, and selected quite a few, as he wanted some special ones included as well. I was excited about this project, as it meant global exposure of his book. The production manager called me several times, and said they hoped to have the book ready by late November that year.

Gusty winds and rain caused havoc on the weekend. Connie was kept awake all Saturday night, answering phone calls from stores, due to problems caused by the wild weather. I was disturbed as well, with the continuous phone calls, and did not get to sleep till three o'clock in the morning. Then we were up at seven next morning, as a tradesman was coming to measure and quote for a security gate at the front.

As the bad weather continued, I kept the cats indoors, as it was too stormy and windy to keep them in the cat cage at nights. They were very happy, as they played upstairs and downstairs, but their noisy antics woke me up before dawn.

Peter Frederick emailed me on 11 April, to let me know I was elected as president of Authors Australia Inc. unanimously, and I was elated. I hoped to achieve great outcomes for our group. And Peter was very pleased that we would accomplish some positive results now. He told me that the previous president did not show much interest or initiative at all.

I took a break from my routine over school holidays, and Elvira too did not come for piano lessons. But I still visited Ninette, as I did not stop my lessons with her. She usually needed a few little tasks done afterwards, like hemming skirts, reading her mail and television guide, etc. When I finished, we walked to the shops, and she sometimes took Fido too.

A few days later, she called to say she was very upset, as she played at a nursing home, and the piano there was out of tune. So she said she could not play well, but I pacified her, and said that she was still a fantastic pianist, and people would not blame her if the piano was not tuned. But there was no pacifying her, as she was devastated about it.

I "skyped" Nilanthi often now, and she was happy we could communicate via skype on the computer. She said she just returned from a pilgrimage to Kandy with a group of friends, and had enjoyed herself very much. Her ankle was healing too, but she still applied some herbal balm for the pain.

We drove to the city early on Saturday, 16 April, to a meeting with Authors Inc. I asked Christian and Athena to meet us after the meeting and have coffee.

It took us long to get to the city that day, as traffic was very heavy on Hoddle Street. Peter handed me some documents to sign, and then proclaimed me president of the organization. We had an immense brain-storming session that afternoon, and the other members congratulated me, and said they were happy to work with me.

We finished around three o'clock, and then had coffee with Christian and Athena, who arrived just as the meeting finished. We delayed getting home, as we had to wait another twenty minutes, because the parking meter was broken, and Connie had to find a parking meter attendant to fix it.

Next day, I prepared afternoon tea for Mary and Peter, then waited and waited. Mary finally phoned around two thirty and said they lost their way, but were almost in Mt Martha. They came half an hour later, and we spent a lovely afternoon together, as there was always fun and laughter with Mary and Peter. They gave us an exquisite, crystal bowl, as a house-warming gift and they left after five o'clock. I took it easy after cleaning up, and Tony helped Connie to plant some lavender in the garden.

Chapter 60

Connie did not tell his siblings where we were, since we moved to Mount Martha. We agreed that until fences and gates were installed, and we settled down in the new house, we wanted peace. They had his mobile number, so they communicated only with him.

At first he was quite agreeable to wait until we completed the garden, and surroundings before inviting them. But lately, he was very unhappy about this situation. One evening, when he came home from work very late, he was very annoyed. He threw his briefcase on the kitchen bench-top, and started banging things around.

After a while he muttered, "Esme called and said she and Bella were driving around Somerset Drive, in Mt Martha, and wanted to know where our house was." I asked him, "*Why* are they driving around looking for our house?" He exploded! "They're calling me *daily,* and asking me where we are, so they can visit us!" I replied, "Is it unreasonable to ask them not to come so late at night? Why don't they visit on weekends in the afternoon, when we're not busy and tired?" He shouted, "Why don't *you* tell them! They don't listen to me!".

We started arguing over this issue, as I wanted a few more weeks of peace, until everything was finished in the garden, and inside the house. When we moved here, I hoped our relationship would improve, and we could be happy, without any interference. I did not want to spin on the same old merry-go-round. I had no sleep that night, as I was so upset. He drank too much, and kept jabbering nonsense even in his sleep. My chest felt heavy, and I woke up at two o'clock to have a cup of Milo and relax. I felt ill and drained next day.

I tried to change my attitude, and not care about what he said or did, because I hated to feel so sick, emotionally and physically. Our arguments were now because of his siblings, who did not leave us alone, but pestered him daily as to our whereabouts. I knew it was just curiosity, and not because of any concern for us. But they badgered and annoyed him.

Nancy visited next day, and I cooked prawn curry, lentils, and rice, as she was a vegetarian. She arrived after one o'clock, and enjoyed lunch very much. And we had a great catch up till late evening. Connie took the day off, and helped Tony to dig up and clean the backyard.

We drove to Woolamai on Good Friday, and brought some seedlings, and a cutting from the willow tree in their garden. Shirani looked well and happy with her new life-style, and we enjoyed our time together.

The weekend was busy, as I cooked a few dishes for Easter Sunday, while Connie and Tony worked in the garden till late.

We attended morning Mass at St Macartan's, and the church was packed, but we got a seat right at the back. Elvira and John were there among our other friends, and we chatted for a while. Then we stopped for a snack and coffee in Main Street, before we came home. I sewed Connie's jacket, and hemmed slacks for a couple of hours, then planted herbs in the garden. And after calling to wish everyone, I took it easy.

Hemal, Rathna, Elvira, and her grand-daughters, visited on 26 April. We had a stimulating discussion about how to produce the play. Elvira was musical director, and I agreed to produce it. Tony and Connie were busy in the garden again, and Connie drove to Bunnings a couple of times, to buy pipes etc. And after greeting everyone briefly, he was in the garden till late.

The business of finding actors though was difficult, and I suggested that we advertise in the local paper and church bulletin. Rathna knew a couple of young men, who had expressed interest in the project, so we set another date for our next meeting. They enjoyed the spicy rolls, and high tea very much, and left after five o'clock.

I watched Prince William and Kate's royal wedding on 29 April. Although I am not a royalist, it was entertaining to watch such a lavish wedding, and she was a very beautiful bride. The pageant was just what people liked; so they too could pretend they were living inside a fairy tale, and escape mundane life.

I started painting a seascape on the weekend, which was to hang in the corridor at the front entrance. I sketched a few preliminary drawings of the sea, with the Yo Yang ranges in the distant horizon, then spent a few hours on it over the weekend. I wanted to finish it soon, and paint another seascape for the long corridor.

Connie drove to Bright on business, on 3 May, and was away for a couple of days. I made an appointment with an upholsterer, to give me a quote to re-cover the old lounge suite. I waited all evening, but she called at six o'clock to say she could not make it, and re-scheduled the appointment. Christian and Athena visited that night, and we enjoyed a pleasant evening chatting about various issues, and I was very glad to see them.

It was the first day of term two on 4 May, and I was very busy at school all day. The upholsterer arrived at six thirty, and I was still selecting fabrics, while she worked out a price. Connie came around eight o'clock that night. She gave me a fair quote, and organized to pick up and deliver the lounge- suite within a fortnight. Connie was very tired and irritable, and complained about everything non-stop. I was worn-out just listening to him.

It was Mother's Day, on Sunday, 8 May. I wanted to go for a movie in the afternoon, but when we came home after morning Mass, Connie started to move some mulch, and worked in the garden all afternoon. Christian called to wish me, and after watching a few comedies, I had an early night.

Tony arrived very early next morning on his bobcat, and continued work in the garden, and it was very noisy all day. The editor at Melrose sent me the manuscript for final proof-reading and editing, so I was busy doing that in the evenings.

I was sad to see Ninette looking very frail and down-hearted, and she said she was not feeling well all the time. But nothing was physically wrong with her, as she went for many tests, and her doctor told her that she was fine. She insisted though, that she had several health problems, and worried about her health constantly.

Connie gave his siblings our address, because he said they pestered him daily. He told them we were building a house, and when everything was finished, we would invite them. Esme was impatient, and very curious to see where we were living, and insisted on visiting us immediately. I told him I had hoped to have a few more months of peace. But it was too late now, as I knew what would happen, and he could never stand up to them.

When he came home that night, he had a big lump on his forehead, and he said he accidentally banged the boot lid on his head! I had a vexing evening with him, because he complained about the pain, and everything else, till he finally fell asleep. When doctor checked his forehead next day, he said it was just bruised, and not serious. I was relieved, because Connie insisted that he suffered a major injury and had concussion.

I finished both seascapes that weekend, and waited till they dried to hang them up. When we went to church that evening, I spoke to Sr Gen, and asked if I could take Holy Communion for Ninette. She was very nice, and said she would organize it for me.

We watched "Thor," starring Chris Hemsworth, in Karingal cinema next day. It was very entertaining, and I enjoyed it very much.

Mary visited on Saturday afternoon, and had a long chat. She was quite uptight over some domestic issues with Tony, and told me that she was on medication for depression. I was sorry for her, as she was on medication for a very long time.

Fiona and Ivan, (Madeline's parents) dropped in unexpectedly. They were visiting their friends, Stuart and Vicki, who were their neighbours in Frankston. It was quite a coincidence that we now lived opposite each other. Fiona and Ivan spent a little while chatting with us, and said they would visit again. I asked them how Madeline was doing with her piano lessons, but they said she had stopped. I was disappointed, as she was a very good student, and told them to encourage her to continue.

I hung up the two seascapes that evening, and Christian liked them very much as they were in pale blues and greens.

When I saw Liz in school on Monday, she gave me a beautiful card, and said, "Congratulations! I enjoyed reading 'Serendib' very much, and look forward to reading the sequel." She was very encouraging, and always gave positive feedback on my writing. I appreciated her comments, as she was very well-read and an avid reader.

I just finished reading Thomas Hardy's "A Pair Of Blue Eyes," and found it a very poignant, unhappy tale, so we discussed his writing at length. I enjoyed sharing "book reviews" with someone as knowledgeable as Liz.

Connie stayed home on Friday, and helped Tony, as he was digging and levelling the backyard still. I bought some prawns for dinner, but as usual, Connie complained they were "old" and not fresh, so we had heated words. I told him that he always complained about food, and never appreciated anything I made. What was new anyway, as he was very critical, and impossible when it came to food.

I watched a great series "Downton Abbey," on Sunday, and could hardly wait for the next episode. It was a period-drama, set in the early 1900s. I enjoyed it very much, as it was beautifully photographed in some spectacular English countryside, and the costumes too were exquisite. The actors were just perfect in the roles they depicted, and the series went on for five very successful seasons.

Christian and Athena dropped in around nine o'clock in the night next day, and I felt very sad to see him looking stressed and tired. He had laryngitis, and could hardly speak. But Athena chatted as usual, and she said they were going to Sydney next week.

The council was culling foxes and feral cats in the reserve again. So I had to walk Mishka and Tigger on leads, as they jumped over the fence into the reserve. As Simba stayed in the garden, I let him out on his own. But I had to watch Mishka and Tigger for more than two weeks. And in spite of my vigilance, and walking her a few times a day, Mishka escaped when I opened the door. And she jumped over the fence, before I went to school on Wednesday. Although I called her till I was hoarse, she did not come home.

I was very distressed all morning, thinking of the danger she was in, and thought of phoning the ranger, to tell him that my cat jumped the fence. But I did not, and came home straight from school around one thirty. And much to my relief, Mishka was at the door, staring at me with her blue eyes gleaming mischievously. I thanked God, as I was so anxious, and that night, after walking her, I made sure she would not escape again.

It was muddy and messy outside, except for the concreted areas around the house, so it was very inconvenient to be walking the cats for the next two weeks.

Connie came home after nine thirty in the night next day, as he attended an office dinner in the city. He was very tired, as he went there straight after work.

Mary invited us for a dance at the Springvale club on 10 July, to celebrate their fortieth wedding anniversary, and I said we would be there.

I organized a book promotion at Dymocks Store in Southland, on Saturday, 18 June, and Connie drove me there. The store manager was very helpful, as he wanted to promote local authors. Five members from our group represented Authors Australia Inc. as we had a fast growing membership now. We could not have too many authors at this promotion, so the manager agreed that five was a fair number. I sold a few of my books that day, and the manager took some on consignment. Nancy, Liz, and Del attended, and spent some time conversing with the authors, and browsing through our books.

I was pleasantly surprised when Maree, the previous principal of St Francis Xavier, walked into the store. She congratulated me on my work and achievements, and then we had a great conversation. As that event was very successful, I asked the manager if we could hold regular book promotions, to which he agreed without hesitation. We finished our promotion after three thirty in the afternoon, and I was quite pleased with the outcome of that event. Connie planted some trees, and worked in the garden till late.

The weather turned gusty over the next couple of days, and the new plants were battered in the blustery conditions. He stayed home the following Tuesday, and spent all day in bed, saying he was exhausted. I visited Ninette, and when I came home after shopping, he was still in bed at five o'clock, and did not get up till late that night.

He saw doctor a few days ago, and doctor said he suffered from depression. Perhaps it was because he was so tired, slept most of the weekend, and lacked energy to do anything. Connie came home after nine o'clock on most days, so naturally he was tired. He did not have any time to unwind in the evenings, but he did not try to finish work and get home early.

The bad weather continued over the next few days, and the cats did not even venture to put their noses out in such turbulent conditions. The front security gate was still incomplete at the end of June. But they promised to finish the job in a week's time. I was relieved, as no one would be able to walk into the garden, once the gate was closed.

When I spoke to Cornelia at the end of June, she told me that her mother was still in hospital. And would have to go into a nursing home, because it was unsafe for her to be on her own. She fell down the stairs a few weeks ago, and hurt her back badly. I was sad to hear about dear Florica, and invited them for dinner in a few weeks time.

Ninette was very anxious and upset that Toula was going overseas in early July. But I told her I would take her shopping, and visit her a few times a week, to make sure she was alright. She was slightly mollified, then I helped her with her correspondence, bills, and television guide, as she wanted the names and dates of some programs written out in large letters. When I spoke to Toula later, she said she was very happy, and would be grateful if I could take Ninette shopping once a week, and visit her a few times, just to keep an eye on her.

We visited Cornelia's mother at the Valley Hospital in Dandenong, on Sunday, 2 July. When we arrived there, we realized we did not know her surname, to find out which ward she was in. I only knew that her first name was Florica, but Connie lost his temper, and started blaming me for not finding out her surname. I told him to call Cornelia or Con and ask them, instead of just yelling at me.

They did not answer their mobiles, but their son, Victor, picked up the phone, so we were able to locate which ward she was in, and spent about an hour there. She had early onset of dementia, but she knew who we were, and she even kissed my hand. I was very distressed to see her looking so old and frail, but she smiled broadly, when I kissed her, and told her we would see her again very soon.

On our way back, we stopped at Joelle's place, as she was away on holiday, and I told her that I would visit her mother and aunt, to see how they were getting on. Although they had visitors when we arrived, they were very happy to see us, and thanked me for visiting. And we spent about half an hour before coming home.

The stormy weather continued that night, and we had no peace at all, as Connie's phone kept ringing till after midnight, because some stores had major problems. He just tumbled into bed, utterly exhausted, at one o'clock in the morning. I did not fall asleep for hours afterwards, so I got up at five o'clock to have a warm drink.

I organized the first rehearsal at the community hall in Frankston that afternoon, and as I had the keys, I had to go early to open the doors. Shirani and Ranjith paid a visit just as I was going out. I was sorry to leave, as they did not get much time to visit now. But they understood, and said they would have coffee with Connie, and go for a drive later. We finished rehearsals after five o'clock that evening, and I was happy to see a few more actors there. But we still needed some young males, as the female roles were easier to fill.

I took Ninette shopping on Fridays, as promised. She was happy, and thanked me, "You are like my second daughter. I'm very lucky I have you." I replied she was like my mother too, and I was glad to help her in any way.

We celebrated Mary's and Tony's fortieth wedding anniversary at the Springvale club on 10 July. Connie and I danced a little, but as I was very tired and breathless, I did not want to dance too much. Elvira, John, and some other friends sat at our table, and we enjoyed the night very much, and came home after midnight.

I wrote to the council, because I felt very strongly about them using poisoned bait, shotguns, and traps in the reserve. The ranger replied that they used "humane" methods to catch feral cats and foxes. But I was still unhappy about it, as I thought their methods were cruel. I decided to keep phoning and writing to them, until they found a better way of culling those poor animals.

Shirani lent me a book that she said was very good, and I started reading "Angela's Ashes" by Frank McCourt that night. And once I started, I could not stop reading, as it was the most pathetic, funny, and disturbing book I had read. I tried to tell Connie about it, but unfortunately, he did not have time or the patience to read it. He read my book "Catsville," only halfway through, even though it was such a short novel. He kept telling me that he wanted to finish it, but did not have time to read, as he was too sleepy at nights. The only one of my books he finished reading was "Edge Of Nowhere," in 2004.

I took Ninette shopping on Thursday, but she said she felt dizzy and claustrophobic there. I had to steady her, as she clung to my arm and said she was not feeling well at all. It reminded me of the time I shopped with Josephine. I was distressed to think of the way old age ravaged people. Her vision impairment frustrated her, as she could not see too well.

When she wanted to shop at Woolworths in Seaford, I drove her there, and later helped to sort out bills, letters, and television guide, before I came home. It was very tiring, as she became more demanding now, but she could not help it, and I was happy to help her.

Joanne visited me in mid-July. We met after eighteen months or so, and I was sorry to see her looking very stressed. She said she was selling up, and moving out with her eighteen-year old daughter, Erika. I could not believe time had slipped by so soon. Erika went for her driving licence, but failed the first time, and was going to try again soon.

She spoke to me on the mobile, and said she would like to visit me, and I said she was welcome any time, as she was a pleasant and polite young girl. Jo and I had a great time, and she promised to visit again, but she never did. And much to my regret, she has drifted away. I was upset, as I liked her very much. It made me muse that most of our friends go out of our lives sooner or later when the time comes, as nothing lasts forever.

We drove to the city on Saturday for another meeting, and this time a few more members turned up. We discussed about holding more book promotions, and also to represent our group at the Writer's Festival in August. And how we could showcase our books in some of the stalls at that venue. It was a positive meeting, and we came home late.

Cornelia called next day, to say that her mother was now in a nursing home, and she was very sad about it, as she missed her very much. Then I called Celine to see how she was, and she said Joelle was coming home soon, and they were getting on alright.

A few days later, I drove Ninette to Patterson Lakes, and then to Seaford. But she was very nervous now, and did not let me out of her sight, as she exclaimed, "Nalini, I *can't* see! Don't go far from me!" And then she did not spend more than ten minutes in one place before saying, "That's *enough*! I feel dizzy, let's go home now!" It was very tiring to take her shopping, but I felt very sorry for her, and was as patient as possible.

Joelle, Celine, and Micheline visited at the end of July, and she brought me a souvenir, and her holiday DVD that we watched. I enjoyed some breath-taking scenes of Switzerland. They liked the butter cake very much, and wanted the recipe. It was good to see Joelle again, and she looked well and happy. They left after a couple of hours, and we promised to meet again soon. Then I made dinner for Con and Cornelia, and they came around six o'clock in the evening. We had an enjoyable evening, and they left after midnight.

I contacted one of the local newspapers, as they were interested to know about Authors Australia Inc. and wanted to interview me, and a few other authors to talk about our books. The reporter asked me about my work, and we set a date for an interview. Connie drove me to Martin Davey's place in Frankston, on 26 July.

Martin was a middle-aged, local author, who had just joined our group, and the photographer from Frankston Leader newspaper was already there. Martin lived alone in a one bed-room apartment on Oliver's Hill, which commanded splendid ocean views. But his place was extremely untidy and chaotic, with hardly an empty space to sit comfortably. Connie and I came home after the photographer left.

I had an appointment with Dr Kertes at Knox Private Hospital at four thirty that same evening. Although we were there early, he took me in an hour later. After he examined me, he asked me to go for a stress test, and that he would take it from there. It was late when we came home, and I had an ear ache. I warmed a clove of garlic and held it in my ear, and after a while, the ear ache eased. It was an old remedy, but I found it quite efficacious.

Connie went to Springvale next day and bought some green chilli leaves, and asked me to make a mallun (spicy dish), with the leaves. After dinner, I suffered severe diarrhoea from about eight thirty onwards, and ran to the toilet about twelve times, till two o'clock in the morning. The leaves obviously disagreed with me, and I was certain they were toxic.

So next day, I threw it all out, as I did not want to eat that mallun again. Connie did not suffer indigestion, but we thought it was best not to eat it again. I felt drained and weak after that bout of diarrhoea, and could only stomach vegetable soup for dinner.

Chapter 61

Connie drove me to Knox Hospital, on Monday morning, 8 August, where I underwent a stress test till midday. Dr Kertes said he would contact me, if necessary. On our way home, we visited Lorraine, but Tony was away, so we had a cup of tea with her, before we came home.

Lorraine called the following Saturday morning, and said she left a message a few days ago inviting us for dinner that night. But I did not get her message. Anyway, we drove there that night, but did not make it before seven o'clock, as Connie was busy doing something else. I told her not to hold up dinner, because they usually ate at five o'clock.

When we arrived, they had finished eating, but we enjoyed a pleasant evening, as Liz, Gerry, Dorothea, Ian, and some of Lorraine's neighbours were there too. I sipped a glass of red wine, then nibbled at a slice of roast pork, and vegetables. But immediately afterwards, I was violently sick, and threw up in the toilet all evening. The diarrhoea started again, so I was running to the toilet a few times, before we left at ten o'clock. When we came home, I sipped black tea with ginger, and went to bed exhausted.

I did not feel any better next day, so I thought I must have caught a stomach bug. It was the second time I had felt so sick, after eating at Lorraine's place, and I was unsure what disagreed with me. Although I was still unwell that afternoon, I picked up Elvira, then her grand-daughters from Mount Eliza, before going for rehearsals to Frankston.

We delayed a while, and found Myra and Rathna waiting for us, as I had the keys to the hall. Rehearsals finished after four o'clock, and later, Hemal discussed my forthcoming book promotion, at one of the Sri Lankan events that he organized regularly.

Connie was on one week's leave from 17 August, as he wanted to finish planting and setting out the garden. But as it was so wet and muddy, he could not do much outside. We drove to the city on Friday, the 19th, as it was the annual general meeting of the Women's Society, and I had an interesting time with Del, and the other members. Karen did not attend that day, and I heard she resigned as vice-president, due to her other work commitments. After the meeting, we met Christian and

Athena, and had lunch at "Spicy Temptation" once again, as Connie really enjoyed the very hot food there.

Then we walked through the new Myers complex with them, and had coffee later. Connie was on the phone for some time, and told me that Esme wanted to visit that afternoon. He had said we were in the city, and did not know what time we would return. When we came to the car park, we found that parking was forty five dollars for three hours! It was exorbitant, and Connie was annoyed that we had not parked somewhere else, as he did not read the parking fees notice properly.

When we came home that evening, someone had left two CD's in the letter box, without even a note. Cristobel called Connie in the night to say she had driven past, and left them for him. I was agitated all evening, as I knew they would start the same old routine. He kept saying, "What can I do? They want to visit us now, and I can't tell them not to come."

Esme called Connie three times next morning, as Paul and she wanted to visit us with Geraldine and Clifford. I went out shopping around one o'clock, but in my hurry, I forgot to take my mobile. They arrived while I was still out, and had tea with Connie. I came home after five o'clock, and he said they had seen my mobile at home, and were disappointed they could not call and ask me to come home soon. He said Paul was a misery, as he complained non-stop about his diabetic condition.

I painted for a couple of hours in the evening, then took it easy on Sunday, and spent the afternoon painting again.

Sarah and Tracy visited on the following Monday, and I was delighted to hear Sarah playing the piano and singing beautifully. I was very proud of her talents, and urged her to continue playing and singing. Then we walked in the garden, and they spoke to Connie, who was busy planting all the fruit trees. They left soon after, saying they would visit again very soon.

It was a spectacular sunset, and a lovely evening, so I removed several photographs, till the sky darkened and melted into dusk. I told Ninette I could not visit next Tuesday, as I expected Christian.

I thought of Stacy on his thirty-ninth birthday on 23 August, and said a special prayer for him. Thinking of him so much on his birthday, and praying that he was safe somewhere, made me very emotional, as I would give anything to see him again soon.

Christian spent some time fixing the computer, and we had an interesting afternoon chatting and sharing. He was always a comfort to me, and compensated in every way. I was glad I had one caring, and loving son at least.

Liz wanted to visit Ninette with me one afternoon, so I arranged a date. Luigi was with Ninette, when I called and wished him for his birthday, which was yesterday, the same as Stacy's. It was his son's birthday today, and a very sad occasion for him and Jackie, as they remembered their son's tragic death on the eve of his 21st birthday. I spoke a few consoling words, and told him I would pray for Angelo's soul.

We went for a dinner dance on Saturday, the 27th, at the Dromana Bowling club. When we walked in at six thirty, we noticed we were the first arrivals for once! I told Connie to try and make an effort to get there on time, as we were always late, so he did. It was seven o'clock when Elvira, John, Mary, and Tony arrived. It was a pleasant night, and we came home before midnight.

The next day, we drove to Burwood Hall, at five o'clock in the evening, as Hemal was hosting an event. He arranged some of my books on a table in the foyer, and about fifty people wandered around the large hall. When Hemal finished his speech, about the purpose of this evening (an eminent Sri Lankan was giving a talk), he introduced me. And I spoke briefly about my writing, and recent publications.

A few people came over and conversed with me later. Some bought copies of "Serendib," and were interested to know about my other books too. It was a good evening, and I thanked Hemal for inviting me. I met a nice lady, Shelagh, who had lost her only daughter to cancer, and was now battling with the disease herself. I bought her book of poignant poems written to her daughter, and I told her how sad I was to hear her story, and wished her well.

The following Tuesday, the 30th, Connie and I went to Mornington police station, to give DNA samples in connection with Stacy's case. They took about one hour to complete the procedure. And the officer who interviewed us was very kind and sympathetic, when he heard how long Stacy was missing, and said he hoped we would have answers soon.

Connie dropped me home afterwards, and I visited Ninette, as Liz was coming to meet Luigi and Ninette. She came around two o'clock, but Luigi could not make it. Liz brought Ninette a beautiful bouquet of flowers, and a bottle of strawberry champagne. We spent some time chatting, and Ninette played the piano afterwards. Liz said she was going for Peter Hitchener's mother's funeral on Friday, as she knew Peter well. He was a pleasant, friendly man, and a popular newsreader on Channel Nine. He compered some fund-raising events at the school, where I met him a couple of times.

We invited Elvira, John, Mary, and Tony for dinner on the following Saturday, and they arrived around seven o'clock, and stayed till almost midnight. It was an enjoyable evening, and we had a great time. Connie washed up till late, but I was exhausted, and went to bed at midnight.

It was Father's Day, next day, and I gave Connie a card, lottery tickets, and a bottle of whisky. After breakfast, we attended Mass at Mornington, where we met Elvira and John, then we took it easy, and spent a quiet evening.

It was blustery and chilly on Tuesday, and the cats did not want to go out, so I tried to sleep from about six thirty in the morning. But Connie's mobile kept ringing non-stop, and he stomped in and out of the bedroom, without going to another room to take his calls. Whenever the weather was stormy, he did not get any rest, as stores called him all through the night, due to various problems because of the wild weather.

I was irritable, as I wanted to get some rest. But he disturbed me so many times, as he kept saying "Goodbye," about ten times, and still did not go, but kept talking on the phone. I was impatient and said, "*Stop* coming in *ten* times to wish me goodbye, as I'm trying to get some sleep!" He got annoyed and went off in a huff, shouting out, "I'm *sick* and *tired* of this damn job! I wish I could retire!" It was the same old catchphrase, so I just ignored him, and finally he drove off, and I got some much-needed sleep.

He picked up his new company car that day, as they upgraded them every three years. And I always told him that he should be grateful for all these benefits he received, and for earning a good wage. But he was tired of working now, and constantly talked of retirement.

I visited Ninette in the afternoon and had a pleasant time, as her friend Liliana was there too, and we had a few laughs, as she was a very amusing lady. The winds did not ease by the time I came home, so the cats were still reluctant to go outside.

Tony arrived on his bobcat at seven thirty next morning, as he was still helping in the garden, digging out a pond, and levelling the backyard. I went to school that day, and came home early. At about seven o'clock that night, Babs called Connie, saying she wanted to visit later. I heard him say we were both tired, and to come on the weekend, but she replied that she goes dancing on weekends, and can only come on week nights. Then she wanted to speak to me, but he told her, "Dolla doesn't want to give her mobile number to anyone." But as she insisted, I spoke on Connie's mobile.

Connie consulted doctor next day, as he complained of severe back ache. He did not go to work till late the following day, and then went to see doctor once again. He told me that doctor advised him to take it easy, stop smoking, and cut down on drinking, but he exclaimed, "Smoking and drinking are the *only* pleasures I have in life! I *don't* want to give up either." I just looked at him in amazement, because it was pointless to tell him that there were so many other pleasures, and means of enjoyment in life. He never knew how to enjoy life, no matter how many blessings he received.

The following Saturday, Connie planted three flowering-cherry trees on the nature strip, that he bought from a nursery in the Dandenongs. In the evening, we dined at Cornelia's. I missed dear Florica very much, as this was the first time we visited, since she was admitted to a nursing home. They had renovated the house, and it looked very nice with newly polished floors and freshly painted walls. We had an enjoyable night, and came home after midnight.

We held another rehearsal at Frankston on Sunday, 18 September. This time, Catherine, a member of the Frankston Ladies Choir came too. She had the main role, as she sang beautifully. Elvira's two grand-daughters dropped out, and we were still looking for more actors. That evening, we finished by five o'clock, as we had snacks after rehearsals. Elvira and I supplied cakes and biscuits for the cast, and we enjoyed unwinding, after a few hours of serious work.

I never knew that in producing a play, I had to deal with so many issues; smoothing out rough patches, soothing ruffled feathers and egos. I could not imagine how these amateurs would have behaved, had it been a professional production at a famous theatre.

Everyone had their own opinion, and how things should be done, so it was hard work to make them listen to Elvira, the musical director, and do what she wanted. The male actors were not so bad, but the females were more dominant and demanding. I was weary when I came home. Connie had planted more trees, and the backyard was beginning to take shape, more like a garden than a paddock now.

I called Judy to say I would visit her the following Tuesday afternoon, as she was recovering from a fall. After I finished my lesson with Ninette, I drove to Carrum about three o'clock, and I knocked on her door, but no answer. I was concerned, as I did not know if she had fallen again. So I kept calling her on the phone, until she finally opened the door.

She said she was on the phone, and did not hear me knocking. I gave her some flowers and chocolates, and then enjoyed an interesting conversation over a cup of tea. Judy told me she had suffered a very bad fall and she was bruised all over. She tried to show me her bruises, but I could not see any discolouration on her back, so I supposed the bruises must have healed.

It was good to see Judy though, and I promised to visit her again soon. She wanted me to read and edit a few chapters of her memoirs, and I said I would do so very soon, and get back to her. As she was a member of the Women Writers Society too, I wanted to help her in any way I could. I encouraged her to publish her memoirs, which she was working on for some time. I made some pan rolls in the evening, and it was quite late when I finished.

A few nights later, I dreamed that I was in Ammie's and Thathie's house in Maharagama, and I was bawling my eyes out over them. When I woke up, I felt a deep sense of loss and desolation, to think they were no longer with us. I felt depressed all day, and could not shake off my feelings of loss and grief.

I called Nilanthi often, as she was going through bad days, and sometimes told me, "I wish I could end it all, as I'm so lonely and depressed." I tried to console her, but it was inevitable that she rode the highs and lows of life, just like the rest of us.

I baked a Christmas cake in time to send Nilanthi for Christmas, and Christian brought some clothes and mobile phones for her too. A few days later, I had another dream about Ammie. This time I dreamed I was electrocuted, when I tried to connect a television, and was dying. I called out to Ammie. She was dressed in her favourite, multi-coloured, polka-dotted housecoat that she frequently wore around the house when I was a child. She was walking very fast, but turned to look at me, unsmiling, and said, "Go and lie down," and walked away, just like that. Thathie appeared briefly, and asked me for two varieties of soup. I woke up wondering why I dreamed of them so often, and what these dreams meant, if anything at all.

When I visited Ninette later that day, I was very concerned to see that her left eye was red and swollen, but she said it did not hurt at all. Poor thing, I felt sad to see her in such a sorry state. I told her she should consult her doctor next day, and she agreed to go with Toula.

Del visited next day, and we had afternoon tea. I was happy to see she looked well, in spite of some health issues, and she told me she was going for an eye operation on 22 October. Del left after a couple of hours, as she did not want to drive back in the dark due to her vision problems. We always enjoyed stimulating discussions about literature, our writing, and projects that kept us busy. She always encouraged me in my endeavours, and I was very grateful to her for her valuable input.

We had lunch at the Frankston Yacht Club, on Sunday, 2 October, as Elvira's brother, Angelo, was one of the organizers of this annual charity lunch. Mary and Tony came too, and we had a pleasant time. Connie's previous boss, Norm Tindall, and his wife, Pat, were there too, as Norm was a long-time member of the club.

Pat said Norm almost died of pneumonia a few months ago, but he was alright now, although he was diagnosed with early dementia. It was sad to see him looking very frail, and we said we would visit them soon. When we left there, we visited Shirani in Narre Warren.

Joelle asked if I could pick her up at Chelsea on the following Monday, as she was getting her car serviced there. I met her around one o'clock, and we drove to Sofia's restaurant in Frankston for a coffee. Later, we walked on the pier, and enjoyed a pleasant time, before I dropped her at the garage in Chelsea around four o'clock.

When I saw Ninette the following Tuesday, I was glad to see that her eye was much better, and the infection had cleared up. I walked with her to the bank, and helped her with some shopping. Then I spent some time listening to her playing the piano before I came home.

We drove to Garden World in Springvale on the weekend, and bought a wisteria plant. I asked Connie to plant it near the side of the house, as I wanted it to climb on the wall and fence, then I planted some ferns in pots.

I came down with another bout of flu next day, but I went to school and came home early, then took it easy in the afternoon.

Chapter 62

Over sixty new members joined Authors Australia Inc. by mid 2011, with more potential members making enquiries regularly. When Dan stepped down as president, I was unanimously voted in as the new president. And although it was a privilege and an honour, I did not expect or want the office, as I now devoted a great deal of time, and energy to promote our group. I organized several book signings, and promotional events at various venues, including Frankston and Rosebud libraries.

Peter was the driving force behind our group, until his health suffered, and he stepped down, leaving all the responsibility to me. Margaret was in her early eighties, but did an excellent job as secretary. Del kept in touch, and was a great support too, promoting our group on local radio, and at the Women Writers meetings. And at one of our meetings in the city, we awarded her a lifetime membership.

I was still keen to write a screenplay, and adapt my book "Catsville." So, in late October 2011, I enrolled in Open Colleges NSW, to follow a two year on-line course in scriptwriting. It was a great course, and I enjoyed the assignments immensely. I had an excellent tutor, who spent a great deal of time guiding my first steps along this fascinating path.

It was money well spent, and I applied myself enthusiastically to the task. I finished the course before the two year period, and was awarded a certificate in screenwriting in early 2013. Armed with this newly acquired skill, I busied myself with writing a script for "Catsville." Sometimes, when he was in a mellow mood, Connie asked me, "How is the writing going? *When* are you going to get it done in animation?"

This was not easy, because I approached a producer some time ago. And although she liked the concept, and everything was promising, it fizzled out to nothing, as she wanted me to finance the whole project. I could not afford the exorbitant amount of money, even to come up with a five minute pilot for an animated film. But I do not despair, and believe I will eventually find someone, who will take on this project, and make my dream a reality.

We had to attend a charity dance in Rosebud, on 15 October, as Elvira was raising funds for St Vincent's. Connie went out early that morning, to hire a costume for his conference in Sydney the following week. He was going as an Elvis impersonator (and so were five others in his team).

When he came home with the outfit, I shortened the slacks to fit him, and we had a good chuckle when he put on an Elvis wig, and with sideburns included. He told John he would help to set up tables, so he drove to the hall at five o'clock, and then came home to pick me in time. Fortunately, it did not take more than twenty minutes to Rosebud from Mount Martha.

I was very ill with flu, but dosed myself with panadeine and dragged myself to the dance, but it was boring, as I could hardly stand up to dance. I donated one of my paintings, and a very large, ornate, Chinese vase for a raffle, which Daphne (Elvira's friend), won, and another very happy lady won the landscape.

On Monday, I was still bad, so I saw doctor that afternoon, then visited Sarah and Tracy, as Sarah invited me the day before. Mitch and Tess came too, and Tracy baked a delicious cake. I was delighted at the sight of a magnificent liquid amber in their front garden, which spread its branches over the entire garden. I just could not get over the enormous girth of its trunk. I enjoyed a couple of hours with the children, who played the piano for my entertainment. Sarah sang a few songs, and I encouraged her to continue singing and playing the piano.

Although I was still very weak, and had a persistent cough, I visited Ninette on Tuesday afternoon, and then went for an eye test afterwards. I could not read the chart very well, so the optometrist asked me to come again, when I was better. Connie came home early that day, as he had to leave at four thirty, to catch a flight to Sydney.

He said he was not at all keen to go, and was in an irritable mood as usual. When he called me the following night, he told me that he missed his flight, as he left home late, and had to take a later flight. He said his colleagues teased him about his tardiness, because everyone knew he was never on time for anything.

Connie nagged Christian to remove his 4Wheel drive that he had parked in our backyard a few months ago. So I picked Christian at Frankston Station, that day, then drove to Mt Martha, and he drove his vehicle back. Fortunately, it started without any trouble, and now Connie would have one less reason to complain about. I called Nilanthi, and we had a long conversation.

Connie returned at nine o'clock that night, and was exhausted. He went to bed early, but next day, he showed some photographs they removed of him, and the other Elvis impersonators. And he said it was quite good, as they all enjoyed themselves.

We drove to the city on Saturday for another meeting at Federation Square. Connie dropped me, and then went off somewhere for a couple of hours. We spent a profitable time, discussing how to distribute our books, and how to set up an online bookstore. Christian volunteered to upgrade the existing website, and already worked on it for many hours.

He said he would attend one of our meetings to display the new website, once it was completed. Pauline, who joined recently, appeared to have some knowledge of setting up an online bookstore, and made it quite obvious she wanted to be in sole charge of it.

She was a loud, aggressive, and dominant woman in her fifties, and her repugnant personality matched her looks. I tried to be polite and patient, and said that we should wait until the new website was completed, before we went ahead with the book store.

She talked of charging members a "commission" for selling their books online. I intervened immediately, as the whole point of our organization was to help writers, without ripping them off further, like most book stores, who gouged huge commissions on each book. Ours was a "non-profit" organization, with the sole intention of helping self-published authors promote and distribute their books. Pauline wanted to manage the online store for a forty percent commission on each sale.

Naturally, no one liked the idea, except the ones who were desperate for sales. I knew she was going to be trouble right from the start, and mentioned my concerns to Peter, who said, "You are the president Nalini, you make the decisions, you don't have to take her ideas on board, if they don't help the members." I decided to be very firm with Pauline, regarding any commission she hoped to charge.

I read an entry made in my diary on 23 October, "One year of celibacy!" It was hard to believe we were not intimate over the last twelve months. He came to bed long after I had fallen asleep, gave me a peck on the cheek, and mumbled, "Goodnight Dolla," and that was about it. I never asked him the reason why, as he would just get angry, and shout out that he was too tired, and that I should help him to relax.

Although I felt uncomfortable to ask him why he did not want to have sex with me anymore, I could not keep silent any longer. So, that night, I casually said, "Do you realize how long it has been since we made love?" He retorted, "So, what are *you* doing about it?" I was annoyed and replied, "*I'm* not the one with the problem! You know that doctor told you to stop drinking and smoking, and do regular exercises, but you don't even try, and you don't want to take any medication either."

He scowled and muttered, "*You* have to *help* me to relax! My job is so stressful, and I'm so tired at the end of the day!" I left it at that, but a few days later, he did make a feeble attempt. It was too much of an effort for him though, and unsatisfactory for both of us, so we did not talk about it again, and neither did he try to get close after that.

I drove to Elvira's place for rehearsal on Sunday afternoon. She asked Simon, a talented pianist, to set her songs to music. He was the musical director of the Frankston Ladies Choir, and although he said he did not play classical music, he was a superb pianist.

The music sounded great on the keyboard, and he made a couple of CD's for Elvira. A few ladies came over to practice the songs, and we had a good rehearsal that afternoon. Mary, Elvira's sister, and her husband, Peter, who lived in Queensland, were here on holiday, and they joined us afterwards, and we had a pleasant time.

Connie was very restless, and moaned all through that night, as he was coming in for a cold. I wanted to go upstairs and sleep in the spare room, but was too tired to get up. I fell asleep finally towards dawn, and did not get up till nine o'clock next morning. He stayed home and rested all day, as he was too sick. Although it was just a head cold, he made such a great noise, that I went in constantly to see if he was alright. He asked for something or other every time he saw me, and I was worn-out by the end of the day.

Ninette was very depressed when I visited her on Tuesday, so after my lesson, I walked with her to the shops, and helped her to pay her bills and do her shopping. She was becoming more anxious and dejected now, I noticed, and she was very cantankerous too. I thought it was because of her aches and pains, so I did not take much notice of her crotchety moods. I phoned Judy on my way home, to say I was unable to make it that afternoon, as it was too late, and I would visit another time.

I spent over an hour studying on-line each evening, as I really enjoyed the scriptwriting course. I had to read, and comprehend a great deal of material, and then write a ten minute script at the end of the first lesson.

Rathna wanted to listen to the songs before next rehearsal, so I posted a copy of Elvira's CD, but she did not receive it for over a week, which was strange. I called Rathna to ask how she was doing, and she said she received the CD at last, and was learning the songs.

I read "Lord Of The Rings" and "The Hobbit" almost every year. And even after umpteen times, I was still spellbound with the magic of Tolkein's masterpiece, and could not put the book down until I read one more chapter till late into the night. "Pride And Prejudice" was another book I read over and over again. And I could read P.G Wodehouse, and Georgette Heyer's novels, without ever tiring of them either.

It was one of the joys in my life, to keep reading those stories time and again. This year was no exception, and I lost myself in the intrigues and adventures of Tolkein's "Middle Earth." And I was very pleased when famous film producer, Peter Jackson, adapted those books to movies, as more people could appreciate Tolkein's genius.

Liz, Gerry, Tony, and Lorraine came for lunch on Sunday, 30 October, and stayed till after five o'clock that evening. Before they left, Liz already made a date for a meal the following year, as she wanted to fill her diary with lunch or dinner dates! We had a good time though, and I said we would visit them soon.

I submitted my first scriptwriting assignment on 31 October. But before doing that, I had to watch a movie, "Brothers," and write a critique. The movie (in my opinion), was two hours too long, with strong violence, and a great deal of rant. But it was quite good, and I had to comment on certain scenes etc. I learnt to watch movies critically, after that first lesson.

Simba jumped the fence for the first time that evening, as he saw a stray cat and started chasing it. I called him for ages, as he ran onto the road, but did not come back. Finally, I managed to get him, but now I worried that he would start jumping the fence and run onto the road.

In early November, I applied for a credit card in my name, as Liz brought up the issue when they visited the last time. I told her that I did not make any purchases via internet, and sent international money orders whenever I needed to. She urged me to get my own card, as it was cheaper, and more convenient to pay by credit card. Connie became very agitated over this conversation, as he never used his credit card for internet purchases, and did not want me to use it either.

I sometimes purchased books and DVD's online, but he had an intense fear of using our credit card online. And as I paid AuthorHouse international banking cheques, which cost me a fortune in bank charges, I thought it was a good idea to have a card in my name.

Connie was very annoyed, and dead set against the idea of my having my own card. But I went ahead anyway, and met a customer officer at the bank, who turned out to be a helpful and interesting person. After I told her I was a writer, and explained why I needed the card, she said she had written a children's book too, and would like my opinion on it. I told her about Authors Australia Inc. and asked her to consider joining us, and encouraged her to publish her book.

My card was approved that same day, and she said she would email me her manuscript. I was happy, and elated about my card, but when I told Connie, he was very displeased, and grumbled about it. He said he would change our home loan etc. to another bank, as he did not want to bank with Westpac anymore.

The Jag was giving trouble for some time now, and once, at the corner of Forest Road, and Nepean Highway, it just stopped dead. I called RACV and as Connie was home that day, I called him too. He came over and I drove his car to Frankston, while he waited for RACV. The water in the radiator was empty, so the mechanism just locked up as a safety measure. He took it to the same mechanic, who fixed it earlier, and I hoped it would run smoothly (until the next episode). Connie talked about getting me another car, as it was costing a fortune to repair the Jag.

I finished reading "Lord Of The Rings," over the next few weeks, and felt sad when I came to the last chapter, as I wanted the story to go on and on. It was one of the most fascinating books I have read, and will always remain a favourite, as I never tire of the story no matter how old I am.

We drove to Heronswood gardens in Dromana on the first weekend in November, as it was open day. I enjoyed seeing the beautiful flowers and magnificent trees, especially the desert ash, and gigantic willow. We spent a couple of hours walking along the paths, then sat on a bench under the wisteria bower, from where we saw breathtaking views of the ocean and city scape.

The following afternoon, we watched a movie in Karingal "Anonymous," the real story of Shakespeare, and it was very enjoyable. We came home late in the afternoon, and I was just taking it easy, when Con and Cornelia dropped in. It was getting late, and they were still sipping wine, so I served them a snack of mixed rice vermicelli and beef curry. I made it for dinner the night before, as Christian and Athena stayed overnight, and then went to a friend's place for a picnic lunch that day.

Our guests were still there at dinner time, so I served fried sausages, with bread and salad, as I did not have anything else to offer. And they finally left after eleven o'clock, as we had to work next day. Con and Cornelia were very nice people, but they bickered non-stop, which was very tiresome.

I made fried rice and chicken curry for the staff next Wednesday, and Maxine and Claire wanted the recipe, as they liked spicy food very much. That same afternoon, when I was returning home around three thirty, the Jag stalled and stopped dead, just as I was making a right hand turn from Nepean Highway into Forest Drive! Cars turning behind me tooted horns, but I could not budge. I turned the hazard lights on, and they veered round me to do a right hand turn.

It was a scary moment, as traffic was very heavy at that time of day, and I was holding up all the cars turning right. A few minutes later, I got out of the car and walked across the highway to the opposite side to a bus shelter, and phoned RACV once again. One of the cars driving past stopped, and Kim, a neighbour, asked if I wanted a lift home. I thanked her and said I was waiting for RACV.

It took them forty five minutes to arrive, and then tow the Jag home with my groceries still in the boot. The driver asked me to climb up to the front seat of the tow truck, and I came home feeling tired and frustrated because of these frequent breakdowns. When we came home, the mechanic organized to tow the Jag to a garage in Mornington. I unloaded my groceries before he towed the Jag away.

I expected Christina for lunch next day, but she called at one o'clock to say she did not know how to get to my place. I gave her directions over the phone, and she finally arrived an hour later. We had a nice afternoon and she enjoyed the lunch, before leaving at six o'clock.

That morning, before he went to work, Connie was in a very bad mood. And while I was still resting, he started making a big noise, dusting the sheets and pillows, until I said, "Can't you see I'm trying to rest?" He scowled and barked at me, "*Resting*! What resting! I'm *dusting* all the cat furs here!" I replied, "There's no cat fur, you're just disturbing me." He mumbled and banged the bedroom door behind him and stomped off in a huff.

The Jag could not be fixed until Friday, but on Friday morning, it still was not ready. I worked on my scriptwriting assignment all afternoon, until Connie picked me up at five o'clock. He drove the Jag back and I drove his car home. He said the radiator was still leaking, and they had not fixed it properly although they charged a huge amount for repairs. He was very annoyed, naturally, and I too was tired of this on-going saga with the Jag.

On Saturday, 12 November, we watched "Mousetrap," Agatha Christie's famous play, which was performed by a local theatre group at Rosebud Hall. I asked Elvira, John, and their friend, Daphne to join us.

Connie went out that afternoon and came home after five o'clock, and I was anxious, as the play started at seven, and he always took ages to get ready. We made it just in time, and I was irritated, as it was always such a rush whenever we had to go out, because Connie never ever tried to be punctual, and I was the opposite.

Anyway, I enjoyed the play very much, and so did Daphne, but John slept through it all, as he said he was tired after a long day's work, and Elvira said she found it boring, because there was a great deal of dialogue, which had to be followed through carefully. Connie did not say whether he liked it or not, but we came home after eleven o'clock that night.

Elvira and I drove to Chelsea Heights to Rathna's and Hemal's place next afternoon, as she invited a few more people, who were interested in taking part in the play. It was a good meeting, and a young man, Misaka, and his brother-in-law, Daham, were enthusiastic about the production. Misaka had a very good singing voice, and loved acting, so he agreed to play one of the main parts.

Chapter 63

After the last traffic offence, Connie was left with only one demerit point. And in late October, he was caught speeding again, and lost that last point, and he knew his licence would be suspended for three months. When he came home looking absolutely dejected that night, and told me what happened, I said, "*Knowing* you had only *one* point left, why couldn't you stick to the speed limits?" He barked angrily, "You *don't* understand! I'm on the road all day, not like you, just driving short distances now and then!" "All the more to be mindful of the speed limits." I replied, to which he shouted back angrily, "I have to get to places in a hurry!"

No matter how much I told him we all had to stick to the rules, he thought he was above the law, and he had the right to drive faster than legal limits. We never saw eye to eye over this, because his excuse was that he was on the road all day.

Anyway, he could not argue the point with the authorities, and soon received a letter, stating that his licence was suspended for three months. Mathew, his boss, came home with Connie on 14 November, and drove the company car back, as he thought Connie would be foolish enough to drive without a licence.

He could not do anything about this situation, so he applied for long service and annual leave for three months. That evening, he spent a long time phoning his siblings, and acquaintances and gave them his new mobile number. He had to give up his company mobile too, so he bought a mobile and paid the monthly bill.

He said he would do the garden, and complete things around the house during his enforced leave. And he talked about going on a long holiday, but I was not prepared to go overseas with him again, as I did not enjoy that last holiday at all. It was very stressful travelling with him, and I had enough to keep me busy at home. I was quite content doing my work, but I dreaded three months with him staying at home, without a car. I found out about the community bus, and told him he could take it whenever I was not home to drive him around, but he said he would cycle to the shops if he had to.

We drove to Rosebud next day, and left the Jag at a garage there, then came home in a taxi. I called Ninette to say I could not visit her that day, as I did not have my car. She was disappointed, as she told me she looked forward to some shopping, and wanted me to do some little tasks for her. We took a taxi to Rosebud that afternoon and picked up the Jag, then drove to Bentons Square.

Connie had to appear in court at Frankston, regarding the fencing scam, as the man was to face charges, so we left home early on Wednesday morning. Just fifteen minutes after we got into the car, he shouted, "I have to go to the toilet!" I stopped near Woolworths at Mount Eliza, and asked him, "Why didn't you go at home before we left?" He did not reply, but just sulked all the way. When we arrived in Frankston, I dropped him at the Court House and then went to school.

Colleen asked if I would come back to teach next year, and I replied, "Gladly, as I love teaching piano here." Then she asked if I would teach at St Macartan's in Mornington too, as her daughter Tess attended that school, and she wanted me to teach her. I said I would not mind, so she said she would speak to the principal there.

Connie walked up to school after the case finished, and we drove home by two o'clock. Shirani called in the evening to say that her restaurant would be featured on Channel 31 on "Vasili's Garden Show," as he had interviewed her that day. I was very pleased for her, and looked forward to watching it on television.

On our forty-first wedding anniversary, on 18 November, I wished Connie, and gave him his favourite chocolates, and some tatts lotto tickets, but he did not give me anything, and did not even wish me. I cleaned and vacuumed the house, cooked, and then took it easy in the afternoon.

Chris Del Piano came over, and was busy with some odd jobs that Connie wanted him to do, then John and Christian dropped in, so it was quite busy. Connie was very subdued all evening, and did not even talk to me, or try to get close to me, but just went around ignoring me, as if I was a total stranger.

When his mother was alive, he talked to her, and reminisced about all the things she did before our wedding day; how she made my bouquet, and all the details of the night *before* the wedding. But he never reminisced about that day with me. And in all our years of marriage, he did not talk to me about our wedding day, the way he did with his mother, which I found hard to understand.

At six o'clock in the evening that day, he wanted me to drive him to Bentons Square to buy some liquor. When we got there, he told me to park in a disabled spot close to the centre, as it was torrential, but I refused to park there. He grumbled and growled as he ran out, but I was not going to break any rules for him, and end up getting a ticket.

Once we came home, and he enjoyed a good fill of whisky, his mood mellowed. And when I was in bed at eleven o'clock in the night, he asked, "Are you tired?" I replied, "It has been a long busy day, and I'm worn out." He stayed up listening to music, and did not come to bed till very late.

This was just the beginning of a really dreadful time, as I drove him everywhere. I did not mind driving him around, but he vented his anger and frustration on me whenever I was driving. And it was now habitual to holler at me at the top of his voice, if I so much as disagreed with him one iota, or ventured to give my opinion about anything.

I could not understand his hostile behaviour, and as we stopped being intimate many months ago, I wondered if that was the underlying problem. We slept in the same bed like two strangers, back to back. Only a peck of a goodnight kiss, and that was all. Sometimes, he tried to put his arm around me, then complained of aches and pains in his arms and shoulders, and could not sleep on his side. Our lack of intimacy was an excuse to fly off at me over the slightest irritation.

Connie was reluctant to admit he had erectile problems since 2009 or earlier. Doctor advised him on how he could help himself. But he was not willing to try any medication, or follow doctor's advice. Our sex life was non-existent, and dwindled from six monthly, to once a year, and then full stop.

He blamed his job, and said that the only pleasures in his life, was drinking and smoking. I could not help him in any way, as he was impossible to reason with, especially after drinks. He told me later that those three months were the worst period in his life, but he did not foresee how much worse was to come.

Con, Cornelia, and Laura came for lunch next day. It rained heavily in the morning, but by the time they arrived at midday, it cleared up slightly. Cornelia brought more seedlings from the nursery where she worked, and it looked like I had a great deal of planting to do. She brought petunias and flowering begonias, which I liked very much.

They enjoyed lunch, and afterwards we walked next door to have a look at the house that was up for sale. The owner wanted 1.4 million dollars, and we inspected the luxurious mansion. It was not to my taste though, as it was ultra-modern, in a flashy, Hollywood-style. But the ocean views from all three levels of the house were worth millions.

When we came back, they asked me to play the piano, and I played "Moonlight Sonata," which they enjoyed listening to, and then pop songs on the digital piano. Laura looked tired, and said she had to work next day. But Con and Cornelia were in no hurry to leave, as they chatted and drank till nine o'clock.

The neighbours across the street started playing loud music from six o'clock till midnight. And after our visitors left, as it was too noisy to go to bed, I watched an old movie "Darling Lili," with Rock Hudson and Julie Andrews.

We attended morning Mass and met Elvira and John, so we chatted for a while before coming home.

Roslyn emailed, asking for a three-year free option on my book "Catsville," as she wanted to write the screenplay. I replied I would consider it, but I was reluctant to hand over my book, and for her to write a script the way she wanted to. I suppose all writers are protective about their literary offspring, and have no wish to see their work mutilated.

I cooked fried rice, and chicken curry for the staff on Monday, and was happy when they all enjoyed lunch.

In preparation for the end of year concert, I urged my students to practise daily, and was unimpressed when some of them did not play fluently. Anyway, I encouraged them to try their best, and that was all I could do.

Christian said he was in Mornington, and would drop by in the afternoon with some jeans that needed hemming. He brought ten pairs of jeans, and I said I would try to finish them on the weekend. He stayed a couple of hours and we had a nice chat.

Roslyn called that night, and tried her best to persuade me to sign an agreement regarding optioning my book. I told her I would let her know soon, as I was still undecided. I understood that optioning my book meant I could not submit my screenplay to anyone else for the next three years, and she could re-write the story any way she liked.

When I got ready to visit Ninette on Tuesday, Connie wanted to come with me too, as he wanted some things from Woolworths. I dropped him at Seaford store, and, he walked to Ninette's place at about three o'clock, and had coffee with us. She played a few songs, and then we drove to Karingal to pick up my new glasses. On our way, he wanted to get some things at Bunnings in Mornington, so we stopped there as well, and it was after six thirty when we came home. I was exhausted, and relaxed in the spa for about half an hour.

David, who sold me the Jag, told Connie that he would check it, because it stalled and stopped in the middle of the highway once again on the previous day. Ninette was very concerned when I told her about it, and she called to ask how the car was. When Connie called, David was not home, and his wife, Eileen, said he was in hospital, so we had to wait until David recovered.

I watched the final episode of "Spicks And Specks," and was disappointed it was off the air after seven years. It was a very entertaining show, and full of musical trivia, which I enjoyed very much.

Now that Connie was home all day, my routine was disrupted, and I felt unsettled, as I could not concentrate on my work. If I was writing, or playing the piano, he interrupted me without any consideration, and asked me to drive him to the shops to get something. And I had to be ready to leave at a moment's notice. He spent some time planting trees and shrubs in the garden. We asked John to build a fireplace with a gas burner in the lounge room, and a deck as well. Connie wanted these things done before he went back to work. Chris Del Piano agreed to build a pergola at the side of the house.

Christian and Athena stayed overnight on Friday, the 25th, as they were attending a friend's wedding in Mornington next day. They came at six thirty in the evening, and brought me a lovely bouquet of roses. We spent a happy evening, and Christian showed me a new program on the laptop, to record music from the digital piano. It was very interesting, and I was always happy to learn something new.

It poured down next morning, when Christian and Athena left at six o'clock, and the torrent continued all day. I worked on my scriptwriting assignments later, and spent a couple of hours trying to master the format.

Connie wanted drinks and cigarettes in the evening, so I drove him to Bentons Square in the incessant deluge. I bought a pair of shoes for Cornelia, as she admired the pair I wore on their last visit, and I wanted to surprise her.

Shirani and Ranjith visited next morning, and brought lunch for us. It was good to see her after some time, and she asked us to watch her interview with Vasili, on channel 31 next Wednesday. I said I would definitely record the program. We attended evening Mass in Frankston, where I met a few friends afterwards and chatted awhile.

On Tuesday, Connie wanted me to drop him at Frankston, and after I completed a few tasks for Ninette, I picked him up at Harvey Norman's. He said he bought a sound system, and had to pick it up in a few day's time.

I made the students practise repeatedly next day, until they were confident enough, and then picked up the keys to the hall and piano. I stopped at Karingal on my way, and then came to the dentist at three thirty. That evening, I watched and recorded "Vasili's garden." Shirani was very composed and demonstrated some recipes very well. I was very proud of her, and happy that her restaurant was getting this publicity.

My jaw ached next day because of the dental work, and I had a headache, but I drove Connie to Frankston, as he wanted to pick up the sound system. I bought a white coffee table for the morning room upstairs, and it looked very nice. He was busy setting up the system all evening, and played loud music till late at night.

Elvira called next day to ask if we would spend New Year's Eve at her place with Mary and Tony. I agreed, as Connie said he did not mind.

On Sunday, 4 December, I woke up early, and we left home at midday to prepare for the concert. Sarah and Tracy arrived half an hour before, and helped me arrange the snacks and set up chairs. Sarah brought a microphone, and everything was ready by the time the other children and their families arrived.

I was relieved when the children performed well, and no major hiccups, after all their practise and preparation. Sarah sang beautifully, and played well, and everyone was very impressed. Liz came too, and she was surprised to see so many students and parents there. We had a great time later, and the children enjoyed the treats and Christmas presents at the end of the concert. They gave me presents too, and the parents thanked me for their childrens' progress. They said the children really enjoyed their lessons, but I stressed on the fact that they had to practise more diligently. I derived much joy and satisfaction in the knowledge, that my greatest achievement was the gift of music I imparted to these children.

Chapter 64

We drove the Jag to a garage in Mornington a few days later, as it was obvious that David was not keen to work on it at all. Also, it was inconvenient for us to drive to Rowville, and then find our way back to Mount Martha. So we looked around locally, and as this garage specialized in Jags, and similar cars, we thought we would try them. The mechanic seemed to know what he was about, and he gave me an old Saab, as a courtesy car, because he said it would take a couple of days to work on my car.

I found the Saab a little awkward to get used to it, but drove it without any mishaps. On our way home, Connie said he was hungry, and told me to stop at McDonald's for breakfast. I had a coffee while he ate, and afterwards, we stopped at Mornington Village, where he did some shopping.

John came later that day, to start work on the fireplace and deck. I had a severe headache when we came home, and it got worse with the noise of drilling and hammering. John broke down part of the wall, and removed some bricks to build the fireplace.

One of the parents called to say that her friend's son wanted to take piano lessons. I told her I would like to speak to the boy's mother first, before I agreed. The mother called me soon after, and said that her fifteen-year old son studied piano for a few years. During our conversation, I had a distinct feeling that she was keener than her son, so I said I did not take students at home anymore. I knew from experience, that some boys of that age had "attitude," and were smart alecs. And I told her to look for another teacher closer to Frankston.

Peter Frederick emailed, that due to ill health, he was resigning from Authors Australia Inc. altogether, and left me in sole charge to carry on. I was very disappointed with this news, and knew it would be difficult without him to help the organization, as we now had over one hundred and sixty members. I composed a warm tribute, thanking him for his great contribution, and for founding our group, and wanted to read it at our next meeting.

Connie arranged for an electrician to come on Tuesday morning, to set up the sound system and install speakers in the ceiling. I visited Ninette that afternoon, and was sad to see her looking very tired and frail. Poor thing, she said it was her nerves, and that she had severe panic attacks. But she was losing a great deal of weight too, and was less than fifty kilograms then. I came home around three o'clock, and we drove to pick up the Jag.

The mechanic handed us a huge bill of $2500! Connie was very annoyed, to say the least, and told me that they must think we were made of money. The man said they replaced several parts, but the labour cost heaps more than parts. Christian dropped in later to pick up his jeans, and then Connie wanted me to drive him down to Mount Martha Village to post some bills.

I dropped the keys at the church office, and gave Vicki a box of chocolates, and a card, as she was always nice and helpful. It was busy at school, and when I finished, Liz, Jacintha, and I, lunched at a pleasant place, which was an old nursery on Beach Street, that was converted to a restaurant. It was a delightful setting, with huge Robinia trees that dappled the gardens in golden light, and we relaxed there a couple of hours.

When I came home, Connie wanted me to drive him to the chemist at Mornington, then Bunnings, and Woolworths, and we came home after eight o'clock. I was really exhausted, and wondered how I could survive another two and a half months of this driving around. I escaped to have a long spa bath for one hour.

John was at the front gate at seven thirty next morning, and he phoned from the street, as he came to work on the fireplace. I tried to rest upstairs, but the noise was deafening, as he kept hammering and drilling to remove the bricks.

The maintenance man from Porter Davis came to fix a few locks and taps that were not closing properly, and to check the house. He finished inspecting quickly, and said the rest of the house was okay, and no further issues.

I showed him the bumps and lumps in the carpet in our bedroom and upstairs, and his response was, "That's nothing! I've seen worse!" I was disappointed, as it was obvious that the carpet was not laid properly, but they were not prepared to fix the problem. As it happened, the carpet had to be re-stretched in the bedroom, as the bumps got worse over the years.

Next day, it was the same noise and hammering from early morning. But John took out the bricks by midday, and started the next stage of the building.

The following days and weeks continued in the same way, driving Connie wherever he wanted to go, and doing all my other work in-between, besides school. He came with me on Tuesdays, when I visited Ninette, and told me to drop him off at Frankston, and I picked him when I finished.

On our way home, he wanted to stop at the golf range in Mornington, to practise golf before he played with his friends next time. Then he told me to stop at Bentons Square to get a few things, and it was after five o'clock when we came home.

I understood his frustration, and sympathised with him wholeheartedly. It was very difficult for him to be house-bound, and unable to jump into his car and drive around like he did. But what hurt me was, that he vented his anger on me. And acted like an angry grizzly bear, because he was restricted, and unable to go where he pleased.

From the moment he got into my car, he fidgeted non-stop, just like a two-year old boy. He distracted me with his pulling, pushing, banging, and complaints about every single thing imaginable. And then he instructed me on what to do, and how to drive etc. I could hardly concentrate, as he started a heated argument, and yelled at the top of his voice. My head spun around every time this happened, and when I asked him to be quiet, and let me drive in peace, he became angrier.

He was not at all sorry about his traffic offences, instead, he blamed the police, and abused them for "picking" on him, when all the real criminals got away with murder. So he justified his offences, and I had to listen to him constantly, without saying anything, as I did not want to argue or contradict him.

Cornelia and Laura visited early on 14 December, as we planned to visit the Mornington Market. It was a cloudy day, with a few sunny breaks, but it did not bother us. I served them some pan rolls and coffee, before the three of us left, as Con and Connie wanted to play golf till we returned. We walked the length and breadth of Main Street, and bought shoes, plants, and knick knacks. I was hungry and tired when we finally came back at two thirty.

Andrei had driven Con to our place, but left by the time we returned. They did not play golf, so we decided to visit Heronswood at Dromana instead. We had lunch at home, and then spent time walking in the gardens till about five o'clock. The flowers were magnificent, and they liked Heronswood very much too. We walked everywhere in the gardens, and they were astounded at the sight of the gigantic willow tree. We stood underneath that willow, and removed many photographs there and among the shrubberies. When we came home, we had more snacks, and they drank their home-made red wine, before leaving at eight o'clock.

John was busy working on the fireplace and deck again next morning. Connie wanted me to drive him to the shops in the evening, and it was late when we returned.

Mr Loos, Anjo's father, had died on 14 December, at the age of ninety three. I called Anjo next day, the 16th, to offer my condolences. We reminisced about the old days, when Mr Loos was in his heyday, and were sad that it was the end of another era. I told her we would visit soon.

I wished Shiranthi on her birthday that day, and I thought it was strange that she and Roland had not visited yet. Only Esme, Geraldine, and their husbands had come so far. Even Babs said she was too busy, but would visit soon. Later that day, Connie wanted me to drop him at the golf range in Mornington for a couple of hours, so I arranged to have coffee with Karen at one of the cafes in Main Street.

We had an interesting discussion about our writing, and Karen's next book, which she hoped to publish soon, then I picked Connie at four o'clock. We did some shopping, and I made mango chutney in the evening.

That night, after more than fourteen months of abstinence, Connie tried to get close to me. Although he could not perform satisfactorily, at least he tried to be intimate. And that was a change, after all his shouting, negligence, and resentment over the past months.

I told him not to worry about our lack of intimacy, and we should try to be close, without constant tension and his bad moods. I tried to be as patient as possible with him, and he tried to be kinder for a few days. But soon slipped into his usual sullen and hostile behaviour.

John came very early on Saturday, to continue work. He brought a young apprentice this time to help him with the deck. I watched an old movie "Misfits," in the evening, and found it very disturbing, as the horses were treated brutally, and it revolted me.

We visited Shirani next day, and I was happy to see her after some time; she presented me with a beautiful terracotta pot with herbs, and I gave her some perfume and other goodies.

I gave my friends cards and chocolates on Monday, and Colleen had chocolates and a card for me too. She said she appreciated all that I did, and for the delicious food too. Colleen wanted me to come again next year, and I said I would be pleased to continue teaching.

We visited Ninette next day, and Connie stopped at Woolworths to get some yeast for her, as she wanted fresh yeast to bake her traditional bread and biscuits for New Year. I gave her a bottle of brandy and some chocolates. And she was very pleased when Connie brought her a big block of fresh yeast, which he got from the bakery at Woolworths.

The phone was still not working next day, and Connie spent one hour on his mobile to Telstra, trying to find out what was wrong.

I drove down to the post office and picked up a box of my books, "Dark Shores," and was surprised to get them before Christmas. The cover was beautifully done, and the production was exceptional, as AuthorHouse was very professional. I was very pleased with the art work and printing. The publisher did a great job, and I emailed the project manager immediately, and thanked her, as she worked closely with me right up to final print.

I drove to Mornington Market on Wednesday, to pick up thirteen pots of hydrangeas, and a pair of shoes that Cornelia put on a lay-by at one of the shops there. Later, I sipped a coffee in the courtyard at Onde's, where it was lovely and quiet. I enjoyed peace and solitude for an hour before going home. Gerry, the cafe owner, said he sold some of my books, and would settle the account later.

When I came home, Connie had not returned from golf, as he went out with some friends that afternoon. It was good to spend a couple of quiet hours, and get some things done before he came back.

I went to the Commonwealth bank next day, to add my name, as one of the signatories to Authors Australia Inc. account, as the treasurer was the only other signatory. I did some shopping later, and came home soon to put up Christmas decorations, and arrange the table centrepiece.

I followed a cooking show "My Sri Lanka," by Peter Kuruvita, a Sri Lankan chef, and I enjoyed watching some regions in Sri Lanka that I had never visited. He was travelling along the east coast that evening, and I felt very nostalgic, seeing such beautiful scenery.

John was still working on the deck on the 23rd, as he said he would not be able to start again till after Boxing Day. I picked up another box of my books, and wondered if I would be able to hold another launch early next year. It required a huge amount of work to organize a launch, and I had too much going on then. But I would have liked to promote, and market the sequel to "Serendib" although most libraries had ordered copies already.

Christmas Eve was scorching, humid, and sunny, and rose to thirty one degrees. I made about seventy five patties in the afternoon, which took me three hours. I could not work any faster in the intense heat. I finished around four o'clock, and then took it easy, before going to St Macartan's for the seven o'clock Mass.

The church was packed, but we found two seats right at the back. We came home by eight thirty, and watched "A Christmas Carol" (animated version), as I always liked to watch that at Christmas time.

I heard my mobile beeping at four o'clock in the morning, and it was a very loving message from Christian. Then I went back to sleep, and woke up a couple of hours later. We had milk rice, beef curry, and sambal for breakfast, and later exchanged gifts; a bottle of Cognac for Connie, gift vouchers, and perfume for me. We drove to Dromana later, as it was still very warm, and walked on the pier for a while, then sipped coffee in a cafe by the sea.

It was still very hot when we returned, and I could not do much, so I washed windows. And it was the first Christmas I spent washing windows! Nelune and my friends called, then I spoke to Nilanthi and Shirani. Connie talked to his siblings and relatives on his mobile all evening.

Christian said they would visit later that night, so I made some curries and waited for them. They arrived around nine o'clock, and Athena looked stunning in a pretty summer dress, and she wore a black necklace. Christian's skin had cleared up, and he looked much better too. We had a great time, exchanged gifts, then stayed up chatting till late. They left after midnight, as they were busy next day, and could not stay overnight.

Connie wanted me to drive him to the chemist, Bunnings, and Woolworths next day, and we came home very late. The Telstra technician finally arrived on the 27th, and connected the phone line, but it was very crackly, and he said he could not make it sound any better.

Con and Cornelia arrived early next morning, to go cherry picking with us to Redhill orchards. But before that, Cornelia wanted to buy clothes at Mornington Market again. Con and Connie went to check the tyres in Con's car, while Cornelia and I went to the market. We arrived in Redhill around two o'clock, and finished picking cherries a couple of hours later. It was a lovely sunny day, and the trees were loaded. And as we were very hungry, we ate heaps of cherries, while filling up our buckets as well.

It was after six o'clock when we sat down to a late lunch (or an early dinner). I was famished, and wondered how I lasted so long. By the time they left after nine o'clock, I was exhausted, as it had been a long tiring day. And after cleaning and washing up, I went straight to bed.

Now that Peter resigned from Authors Australia Inc., I had a load of extra work dealing with changes, as he left me in charge of everything. I knew Peter took care of all these details when Dan was president. But now he turned over the entire management to me, including the website, which cost me an annual fee. None of the members contributed towards it, which seemed somewhat unfair. So, I decided that all members should pay ten dollars annually, towards the website and other expenses. I suggested this to the committee members, who said this motion would be carried through at our next meeting.

We were spending New Year's Eve at Elvira's, and I made cutlets the day before, as they liked them very much. I washed windows once again, as it was sweltering that afternoon. We arrived at Elvira's around eight o'clock next day, and had a pleasant time with our friends. At midnight, I presented each of them a dollar coin, wrapped in gold paper, and tied with a red ribbon. But they forgot to exchange coins, and even Connie did not bring coins. I did not mind at all, as I did not expect anything in return. I just liked to follow that old tradition of exchanging a coin, which was supposed to bring good fortune.

Christian called to wish us, and we had a long chat. As we were leaving Elvira's, I tripped on a metal bolt near their gate, and twisted my ankle. It was painful and kept me up till dawn.

We woke up early next morning, and enjoyed a traditional Sri Lankan breakfast. Then we attended Mass, and afterwards greeted Elvira, John, and Fr Kevin. On our way home, we shopped at Bentons Square, and came back after one o'clock. Shirani and Nelune called, and I phoned Nilanthi, then I took it easy in the evening.

It was a relief when the weather finally cooled down, and a slight breeze whipped up across the sea that night. So ended the first day of 2012, and another New Year to look forward to. I fervently hoped that it would be a better and happier year.

Chapter 65

The weather soared to thirty eight degrees next day. We decided to keep cool and go to the cinema. But when we arrived at Karingal, the queue was so long, that it was too late to see "Tin Tin," at two thirty. We drove to Frankston Centre instead, had coffee there, and decided to come another day, when it was less busy at the cinema. The temperature reached forty degrees by the end of the day, and we were sweltering, as the car was over-heated. That was a worry, because the mechanic said he replaced the cooling system in the car.

One of Connie's colleague's, James, who was an engineer, checked the deck and fireplace that evening, and had a beer with Connie afterwards. James said everything looked fine, and John did a very good job.

The Telstra technician arrived next day to fix the phone again, but then we did not have internet connection! He said it would take about ten days to fix the internet problem. This was very tiresome, as I could not send emails or submit my assignments. He said they were trying to resolve the problem, so there was nothing we could do about it.

The concreters, and John, arrived at seven o'clock next morning to work on the deck and driveway, as it had a few cracks already. Connie wanted the concreter to fix them. It was very noisy, as they cut the concrete where it was cracked, and poured new concrete again. The deck was almost complete, and it looked good.

I slept upstairs that morning, but the noise was still deafening. Then I worked on my assignments, but could not submit them via email, as internet was still down. I watched the final episode of Peter Kuruvita's cooking show that evening. And he was in Jaffna, on a tiny island off the coast there. I felt nostalgic, when I saw those places.

John continued work on the following Monday. Connie was very restless the night before, and started an argument over some trivial issue. He seemed to be vague sometimes, and whenever he made a mistake, his constant refrain was, "I'm not thinking straight!" He made all the financial decisions on his own. And in retrospect, I knew he spent unnecessary money setting up the garden etc. But he did not heed my advice, as he thought he knew what he was doing.

I was very tired and upset, and rested till late next morning, and did not come down. Then I worked on my assignments till late afternoon, but the internet was still down. Connie wanted me to drive him to Bunnings at five o'clock that evening, and when we came back, I continued working on my script.

The following days continued in the same manner. I visited Ninette on Tuesdays, and he came with me without fail. As internet was still down on 11 January, we went to Telstra at Mornington, and bought a temporary connection. But when we returned, internet was connected, so we did not have to use the temporary connection, which was a waste of money.

Ninette and Toula visited next day, because Ninette wanted to listen to Luigi's CD on the new sound system. Connie turned up the sound to maximum volume, when a sudden, loud explosion frightened us and the amplifier blew up! I asked him why he turned up the volume so loud, but he just ignored me, and complained about the player being no good. So no more music now, until he bought another player.

I gave Ninette a card, and hundred dollars for her 80th birthday, as she told me that she preferred to buy something that she wanted. She was happy with the money, and said she did not want any trinkets that were of no use to her. She reminded me of Ammie, who said the same, when we were planning their anniversary party in 1995.

John, and his helper, Peter, arrived early on Friday, and worked on the deck all day. Then James, and one of his colleagues, dropped in later for final inspection. They assured Connie once again that John had done a very good job, as the deck was sturdy, and well-constructed. That evening, Connie wanted me to drive him to Dick Smith's store at Karingal, but they said they could not replace the amplifier, so he had to buy another new player.

It was after seven o'clock when we came home, and my legs ached, with all the walking I did at the centre, so I went to bed early. He stayed up till midnight listening to music, and still turned up the volume so high, that I could hear the noise in the bedroom at the other end of the house.

I was very pleased next day, when I got the results for my script assignment number three, a distinction. The tutor wrote a very encouraging and complimentary report, and I was keen to finish the last three assignments before the final exam. I showed Connie the report and the results, and he just mumbled, "That's good." He did not share my elation and satisfaction though.

We got tickets to watch the movie "Tin Tin," at Karingal that weekend. It was spectacular and entertaining, but I had a severe headache all evening, due to the extremely loud noise throughout the movie. I tried to call Nilanthi many times over the last few days, but her phone was not working. So I was pleased when she called that night, and we had a long chat.

I drove the Jag to the garage in Mornington *again,* as something else was wrong with it, even though we had spent such a huge sum of money the last time.

John arrived early next Monday morning, to finish off the deck. And he said that one of his friend's would paint it for a reasonable cost, as Andrew, a contractor that Connie knew, quoted a very high price the week before. We picked up the Jag later that evening, and paid another large sum of money for repairs. It was thirty three degrees that day, and was expected to be in the high thirties tomorrow.

I did not visit Ninette that Tuesday, as it was her birthday, and she was going out for lunch with her family. I said a prayer for her though, and called her later in the evening. John was still working on the pergola on the side of the house, and it was very noisy with hammering and drilling going on all day.

When I visited Ninette next day, I gave her a bouquet of silk roses, but she was very uptight and anxious all the while I was there. She asked me to search all her cards and letters, to find someone's name and address. Poor Ninette. She was pleased when I finally found what she was looking for, but she was getting more and more difficult now, as she said she had panic attacks over the slightest thing, and was easily upset. When I came home, John was still there, and Connie was helping him. After John left, Connie still kept hammering in nails for over two hours.

John started work from about seven o'clock in the morning next day, as he cut a hole in the brick wall to install the fireplace now. I tried to rest upstairs, but it was still too noisy. I just had to put up with the racket, as the work had to be done, and finished soon, I hoped. I wanted to work on my script assignments in the afternoon, but Connie wanted to go to a factory in Dromana to pick up a flue for the fireplace. I left my work and drove him there, and then to Mornington.

All the way to and from home, he kept nagging me about something or another. His attitude really puzzled me, because he behaved as if *I* was to blame for the loss of his licence, and for everything else that went wrong in his life. When we came home he said, "*I'll* reverse the car into the garage!" As if I did not know how to reverse my car. I wanted to retort, but then as John's truck was still in the driveway, I held my tongue, to avoid confrontation. I tried to concentrate on my script in the evening, and later made hoppers and beef curry for dinner.

Melrose books emailed to let me know that Luigi's book would not be ready till the end of February. I hoped they would be ready earlier, as I had to organize a launch at the Furlan Club soon. But I just had to be patient till they finished the final publication.

A few days later, Connie wanted me to drive him to Tyabb, to get the flues powder-coated at a factory there. He had a screaming fit on our way, and he shouted at me so violently, that my head throbbed alarmingly. I could not concentrate on driving, and asked him to be quiet. As we got into the car, he demanded, "*Why* are you so quiet? Is it because we don't have sex now?" I replied, "Is this a time to start about that? Can't you see I'm trying to concentrate?"

He was so aggressive, that I was goaded to retort, "If you *ever* try to say 'sorry' to me again, I'll slap you, because you don't *mean* it! You're just like a parrot repeating 'sorry' 'sorry' a hundred times, and not meaning it one bit!" I was so angry that I felt sick in my stomach. He did not appreciate anything I did for him, especially now, driving him around whenever and wherever he wanted to go.

He used his present situation as an opportunity to constantly pick on me, and treated me like a punching bag to vent his frustration on. I do not know how I managed to focus on the road, and get home safely. I hated to be yelled at for no reason at all, and was relieved to get home, and find some peace and quiet alone. Connie stayed out in the garden till late, and we did not speak at all, which was better, as we would only end up arguing.

Next day, on Saturday, Barry, another contractor Connie knew, and his wife Shirley, visited in the afternoon, to give a quote on some asphalt work. As the concreter wanted an extra ten thousand dollars to do the side of the house, Connie decided not to concrete that area.

Barry quoted nine thousand dollars to do the job, and Connie agreed. I could not understand his reasoning, as it would have looked much better, if the whole area was concreted for an extra thousand dollars. I could never reason with Connie, once he got an idea into his head.

Babs told Connie she would visit that afternoon, so we waited for her. But she did not turn up till about six thirty, just as we were leaving to attend Mass. She came with a man who drove a black sports car. I told Connie we could go to church next day, if he wanted to stay and chat to her. But he did not want to, and Babs said she would visit another time. I spoke to her briefly, and she left with her friend.

The following night, from about eight o'clock, Connie started shouting and groaning in severe pain, so I looked up a 24 hour clinic, and called an after hours number. A doctor rang back at nine o'clock, and said that if the pain was very severe, to admit him to emergency. I could do nothing to relieve his pain, as he could not tell me exactly what he felt. I gave him a couple of quickeze tablets, thinking it was indigestion, but nothing helped, and he was groaning constantly. I called the ambulance at ten twenty, but they arrived after one o'clock in the morning.

The paramedic told me it was a very busy night on the Mornington Peninsula, and they had to attend a few accidents first. After the paramedic examined him, he told Connie that he suspected it was kidney stones. They gave him some tablets to relieve the pain, and told him to see a doctor first thing in the morning. At least we knew what was wrong, and we finally went to sleep a few hours later.

Next morning, I drove him to Medical One. And the doctor who examined him told him to do a scan. I took him to the radiology clinic in Frankston, and then back to doctor's. The scan showed several stones, big and small, and doctor told him to see a specialist next morning.

Then I drove him to Tyabb and Mornington to attend to some things, and finally came home utterly exhausted, as it was thirty three degrees. I called Shirani and Ninette to tell them about Connie, and Elvira too called to ask how he was doing.

The following morning, I drove Connie to Mornington to see the specialist, where he explained that the procedure would "crush" the stones, or he could try some tablets first, which would dissolve the stones. Connie wanted to try the tablets first. Then the specialist drew a diagram, explaining just exactly how the procedure would work; instead of surgery, they would insert a tube through the penis and blast the stones.

But because we did not have private health insurance, the procedure would cost almost $5000. Connie was reluctant to spend that much money, and told him he would ask his doctor to get him into Frankston hospital as a public patient. He wanted us to come back in the afternoon, to give us an exact cost at a private hospital, in case tablets did not work.

I dropped him at Frankston centre on my way to Ninette's next afternoon, as he wanted some things there. When I finished my lesson, I picked him up at three o'clock and drove to the specialist's office. Connie said he would try tablets first, as he could not afford to pay $5000 or more. The specialist said he would put him on a waiting list at Frankston hospital, to which he agreed.

We picked up the prescription and got the tablets, as he wanted Connie to start on them immediately. When we came home, the bricklayer had completed work outside, after installing the fireplace, and now only the flue had to be connected. It was still a very hot thirty five degrees that day, so I watered the garden, then took it easy.

The man came early next morning to start painting the deck. And Frankston hospital called that afternoon, to say they could admit Connie on 1 February, which was six days away. That was good, as he did not have to wait too long.

It was Australia Day on Thursday, the 26th, and Tigger's second birthday. I gave him a special treat, after which, he jumped over the fence to spend the day in the reserve with his possum friends (I suspected). I helped Connie to rake some mulch in the backyard, and then did some planting. The painter came early, and was still there on Friday, as he gave the deck two coats of paint. He charged over $3500 though, and was not as reasonable as we expected.

Toula invited us to celebrate Ninette's 80th birthday at her place, on Sunday 29 January, although her birthday was on the 17th. But Toula was unable to organize the whole family before then. We went there around three o'clock, and met her family and friends, and enjoyed a pleasant time. Toula had prepared heaps of delicious food, and as it was thirty five degrees, she made an ice cream cake, which we relished. The Jag was driving alright, but I was concerned about the cooling system, as it was so very hot, even when we returned in the evening.

The cool change finally brought long-awaited showers on Monday, and the weather was much more bearable at twenty eight degrees. I planted tuberous begonias at the side of the house, and Connie took it easy, as he was very tired. Christian and Athena said they would drop in, so I made dinner, but they could not make it, as Christian hurt his neck, and was seeing a doctor that day.

Tuesday was much cooler, and I woke up around six o'clock in the morning, as I had some strange dreams. I saw Stacy again, and I was asking him to show me how to play chess; I heard a constant noise around me, and whirring of machines near my bed, as Connie was sewing. I tried to speak above the noise, but no sound came at all, even though I was shouting as loud as I could. I could not understand such a strange dream.

John arrived early to finish fixing rails on the deck. It was now five weeks since he started to build the deck. And he still needed to fix rails, as he was unable to get them before, because some factories were closed till mid-January.

It was the first day of term one on Monday, 1 February, but it was a student-free day, so I did not have to start till mid-week. It worked out well, as I had to drive Connie to Frankston hospital early that morning. I had a very bad night, and was up till dawn. The plumbers and John arrived at seven o'clock in the morning, and started their noisy work, as John was finishing the pergola roof.

We drove to the hospital at nine thirty, and after attending to the paper work, I left him around eleven o'clock, but the car just would not start! After all the times it had been in the garage, it still did not work, and I was so frustrated and tired. I called RACV, and then went back to the hospital to use the toilet. When I looked in the waiting room at one o'clock, Connie was still there.

He was busy texting away, and was not listening, when I told him about the car. I went out and stood near the hospital entrance, waiting for RACV in the burning sun, but they did not turn up for one and a half hours. So I went back to the hospital again, and waited with Connie. I could see the Jag from the window, and thought I would go down when I saw the RACV van.

The mechanic put in a new battery, but it still would not start, so they organized a tow truck to take it to the garage in Mornington. I called the mechanic there, and he said to bring it in right away.

So there I was, on a tow truck again. When we arrived in Mornington, the mechanic said he would have a look, and he gave me a loan car. Christian was in Mornington, to see his orthodontist that day. And when I told him what happened, he offered to give me a lift home, but I said it was alright as I had a loan car.

Connie stayed overnight in hospital after the procedure, and when I spoke to him in the evening, he told me they did not find any kidney stones. I asked him then why they kept him overnight. But he was confused, and did not know what was going on. He said Esme and Paul visited him in the evening, and I asked him how they knew he was there, but he was vague and elusive. I knew he sent them text messages, as he was busy texting, when he was in the waiting room.

I called Shirani, Nelune, and Christian, and told them Connie was staying overnight in hospital. Elvira and John offered to drive Connie home next day, if I needed a lift, but I told them I could manage, as I had a loan car. I woke up a few times that night, and was out of bed by six o'clock in the morning, and opened the security gate for the painter, who came an hour later.

Connie called at eight thirty in the morning, to say he was still in a great deal of pain. And complained about the treatment, or lack of it, to ease his discomfort. Later, when I was in the shower, the power went off at nine thirty, and did not come back for another hour or so. When I called the energy company to ask why the power was off, they could not explain the reason for the power outage, and said they would send an electrician soon. None of the neighbours were affected, just our place, as I happened to ask Angela next door, and she said they had power.

Two workers arrived within the hour, and said power was disconnected, but still could not explain why. I told them that the bill was paid in time, and I was very annoyed at the inconvenience. They re-connected power, and much to my vexation, went off without giving me a reason. I called the energy company again to ask what had happened, and they said they would look into it.

Some friends, and Connie phoned me, and when I asked him what time he would be discharged, he said they were keeping him another day. They took more scans and x-rays, to check if there were any more stones left, because he was in so much pain.

I drove down to Mount Martha Village, and saw Tony walking there. He asked me about Connie. And when I told him that he was in hospital, he said that he too suffered from kidney stones often, and it was very painful. But to tell Connie that it was normal to feel pain for some time.

The mechanic called to say the Jag would be ready to pick up next day, and that the starter motor had conked off. When Shirani called later, I had a long chat with her, and with Nilanthi too. Then I sent Christian a text to say that Connie was still in hospital, but he was alright.

Melrose sent the final proof of Luigi's book that day, and I was happy with it, so I signed the approval form to go ahead with the printing. It was a long day, and I was worn-out. I spent a quiet evening, and had an early night.

I called the hospital next day, and then spoke with Connie, who said he would be discharged that afternoon. When I called the mechanic to ask when I could come over, he said the Jag would not be ready till the following Monday. So I drove the loan car (an old Ford Station Wagon), which was difficult to handle, after getting used to power-steering, and picked Connie at one thirty in the afternoon.

He was very groggy, and in severe pain still. The nurse told me they "blasted" the kidney stones, but there could be some residual, which was causing him pain. They told him to continue taking tablets, to clear up any left over stones. On the way, he was very sick, and vomited, so he rested when we arrived home. But when I told him I had to go to Mornington to get some things, he struggled out of bed, and insisted on coming with me to get some more tablets, although I told him I would get them.

I did not stay too long, as he was in extreme pain, and I wanted him to go home and rest. He kept telling me they did not find any stones, and he still had severe pains, and he was sure the stones were still inside. I could not convince him that this was not the case, as the nurse told me they had blasted the stones during the procedure.

Elvira asked if they could come over that evening, and they visited at eight o'clock. John joked, "You are okay now, so no need to call the priest eh?" He was resting in bed, and just smiled at John. After they left, he had a few dry biscuits, as he could not eat much, due to pain and nausea, and then rested till about ten o'clock that night.

He was quite shaken, because it was the first time in his life that he was in hospital. And he kept telling everyone that he had "surgery," even though I told him it was only a *procedure,* and he did not have an operation, because there was no incision. But he always referred to his procedure as a major operation, and took a long while to recuperate. He was lethargic, and slept most of the time, and told me that he never felt the same after that procedure.

That first night at home, Connie was restless all night, and kept waking up every hour. He got up in the dark, did not switch on the bedside lamp, and walked right into the wall. He ended up with a small bump on his forehead, and a bad headache.

Everyone called to ask how Connie was, and his siblings rang him on his mobile every day. I cooked his favourite curries, and he ate well after a few days. We took it easy, and watched Peter Sellers in "Return Of The Pink Panther." I wanted him to relax, and stop thinking about his major "surgery," and get over this episode quickly.

I baked a butter cake for afternoon tea on Sunday, as he liked that very much. Although it was still very warm at thirty one degrees, it was gusty and stormy that day. Ninette called later to ask how Connie was doing, and she said he must drink plenty of water to get rid of the stones.

A couple of days later, I drove Connie to see doctor. Although he was getting better, doctor told him to take it easy for a few more days. And then we drove to Mornington to pick up the Jag. The bill was $950! The mechanic said the starter motor cost $550.

It was getting far too expensive to maintain this car, and we were spending huge amounts of money, each time something went wrong with it. Connie was in an awful mood, and had been so from the previous evening. He yelled and complained about everyone and everything, until I asked him if he could please shut up, as my head was simply throbbing with pain.

When we returned home, he spent a long time on the phone, trying to sort out the problem with the energy company, who kept saying we were not registered at the address in Mount Martha! That was strange, as we had been paying energy bills for the last twelve months. So he was screaming at them over the phone, and telling them to get their act together. It was indeed an odd situation with the energy company. But I knew there must be some rational explanation, and they would get to the bottom of it soon.

Ninette called to say that her grand-daughter, Nadine, gave birth to a baby girl. She was very pleased, and I was happy for her. John came around later in the evening to pick up the cheque for all his work. He had a beer and a chat with Connie out on the deck, before he left.

The fireplace, deck, and pergola cost close on twenty thousand dollars, and the painter charged another three and a half thousand. But at last, all the work was completed, and we were pleased, as John did a great job.

Chapter 66

I counted the days, and so did Connie, until he got his licence back, as it was a very difficult time for us. He had only a couple of weeks left now, and I could hardly wait until he started driving again. I went to school on 8 February, after staying home for one week, and taking care of Connie.

After school, I dropped in to give Ninette some sheet music I photocopied, and she was very happy. She said, "I wish you can visit me every day, as I'm very lonely!" Poor thing. I spent an hour with her, and when I came home, Chris Del Piano was busy hanging wardrobe doors in the two bedrooms upstairs. He did a great job as usual, and the rooms looked much better, and complete now.

The next few days were very busy, driving Connie around everywhere he wanted to go. He woke up early on Monday, 13 February, as he was due to start work that day, and get his licence back in a couple of days too. One of his colleagues picked him up at seven o'clock, and gave him a lift to the office.

Connie called me twice during the day, and asked me to pick him at Frankston in the evening, as he was working on his computer at a store. The phone and computer were down again, and when I called Telstra, they said they were fixing new cables in our area.

I was out in the front garden that day, when Liz and Gerry happened to drive past, and dropped in unexpectedly. They had attended a funeral in Mornington, and just wanted to visit me on their way home. Liz was in a strange, unfriendly mood, and made rude comments about why we were living in such a big house, and whom were we trying to impress? I could not believe she was so ill-mannered; I told her, "we moved here because we like the area, and built a house we enjoy living in, and not to impress anyone." They had a cup of tea, and left shortly afterwards. I was disappointed, that a so-called friend could be so spiteful. I picked Connie around six o'clock that evening, and he wanted me to stop at Mount Eliza to get some things.

I was very interested in a new television series called "Revenge," which they showed every Monday night, and looked forward to seeing it each week. But they changed the program, and I was disappointed, as I had to wait a whole week for the next episode.

I dropped Connie at Frankston again next day, then took a sandwich for lunch, and had it at Ninette's. And she started relating her childhood days, over coffee. I was amazed that she had survived so much of trauma at such a young age. Through the years I had known her, she related snippets of her childhood days, but she delved deep into her memories that day.

Her mother died in her early thirties, when Ninette was only twelve years old; she was so unhappy in her marriage, that she wanted to get sick, and sat out in freezing temperatures, that ended with a fatal case of pneumonia. Her father beat Ninette, and her mother at the slightest provocation. And he brought women to the house even when his wife was still alive. The day after her mother's funeral, he installed his mistress in their home.

Fortunately, her grandmother looked after Ninette, and her two brothers for a few years, until she got a job and was independent. She nursed her younger brother through a bout of hepatitis, but he died at the age of seventeen, and she still grieved for him. Since she married, and left Egypt in her early twenties, she said she never kept in touch with her father. I was very disturbed by her revelations, and hugged her warmly before I left.

I bought a silver frame, and a card for Nadine's baby, as Ninette told me a frame was a good present. Then I picked up Connie from Frankston after six thirty, and was worn-out by the time we returned home. He gave me a fresh rose, and a bottle of perfume, and I gave him a bottle of whisky, as it was Valentine's day. It was very difficult to buy any other present for Connie, as he was very critical of anything I bought for him, like clothes or a watch. The only thing he did not complain about was a bottle of whisky, or his favourite after-shave lotion, Old Spice. I tried giving him other brands, but he did not like any of them.

AuthorHouse called me at midnight, regarding my forthcoming publication with them, and I finalised payment over the phone. I could not get to sleep that night, as Ninette's story was fresh in my mind, and I was very distressed to think of her traumatic childhood.

Connie got his licence back on Wednesday, 15 February, and I fervently hoped he would drive more carefully in the future, and not speed again. He was such an impatient, aggressive driver, and just did not care about consequences when he was behind the wheel. John gave him a lift at seven thirty that morning, and I went to school. I waited anxiously for Connie to get home that evening, but it was after nine o'clock when he finally arrived; he said his car had a flat battery, and he waited for RACV to replace it.

Chris Del Piano, and the builders arrived early next morning to continue work on the fireplace. The three cats hid under the bed, as they did not like the noise and strangers inside the house.

When I finished at school, Liz and I had lunch at the same cafe on Beach Street Frankston. We sat under majestic, golden Robinia trees, as it was thirty three degrees that day, and was much cooler and pleasant out in the shady garden.

I did not hear from Christian for a few days, and was concerned, as he was very stressed the last time I saw him. And I just returned home from Benton's Square, after distributing flyers, regarding Elvira's play, when he called me at last. I was relieved to hear that he was alright, but he had been very busy. He said he would try to meet us in the city after my meeting with Authors Inc. tomorrow.

The traffic was very heavy on Saturday, due to road works, and we were delayed, so it was after two o'clock when we arrived in the city. We had a good meeting with six members, who turned up, and made some positive decisions regarding the future. Christian and Athena met us at Federation Square afterwards, and we had a snack and coffee with them.

They looked good, and I was happy to spend a little time with them after a long spell. It was still very hot when we came home in the evening, so I watered the garden till late at night. Simba heard a stray cat mewing in our garden, and next moment he jumped over the fence to the new house next door. I went around and coaxed him back home. He can only clamber over the fence, but cannot jump back into our garden, as he is too tubby. So he just sat patiently, until I brought him through the front gate.

It was Connie's birthday on Sunday, and we went to Mornington for Mass, where Elvira and John wished him afterwards. Christian, my sisters, his siblings, and his friends, called later in the day. Ninette called too, and the La Ponders left a message. I gave him tatts lotto tickets, and Old Spice after-shave lotion. He said he did not want to go out for dinner, so I made his favourite food, and we spent a quiet night watching comedies.

Christian and Athena said they would visit on Monday afternoon, so I waited from about one thirty, but no sign of them. He sent a text to say they were on their way, and would be here soon, and finally arrived after six o'clock in the evening, as they were held up somewhere. I was very happy to see them though, and they fixed my laptop afterwards, as it was giving trouble again. But they could not stay long, due to work commitments and left soon after.

When I visited Ninette on Tuesday, I was happy to see Liliana there too, and she said she had to have a heart operation soon. I gave her a small gift, as Ninette mentioned that she would visit on Tuesday too. She was pleased, and said, "You are so thoughtful dear Nalini! Thank you very much!"

Ninette looked very frail, and down in the dumps, so I walked to the shops with her after Liliana left. When I stopped at Karingal later, I met Toula. We had a long chat, as she too was concerned about her mother's health, and did not know what was wrong with her.

It was Ash Wednesday next day, and I woke up early, as I had a strange dream the night before; I was in a hospital, and was looking for a room to rest in, and found my way into a dark room. There I saw a figure lying on a bed, and covered with a white sheet. I stumbled and fell into an open coffin near the bed. I started screaming for help to get me out of there, but no sound emitted, and I could not move a muscle. It was a very scary dream, and I woke up bathed in perspiration.

Connie came to school unexpectedly around ten thirty that morning, and said he went for Mass, after seeing doctor. He did not stay long, as I was busy teaching, then I too attended Mass with the students at midday. Marg was back after a few weeks holidays, and we had an interesting chat during recess.

It was my sixtieth birthday on the 23rd, and I woke up early, as it was very warm, and soared to twenty nine degrees. Connie had left a card, and some gifts on the kitchen bench-top, with flowers from the garden. His mood had improved slightly, ever since he got his licence back, and he returned to work, for which I was grateful. It was a dreadful time over the last few months, with constant tension between us.

When I went to school later, balloons and streamers decorated the piano. Liz made two pavlovas, and a fruit platter, and she gave me a card with some beautiful, inspiring words that she wrote. We had a delicious morning tea, and the staff sang "Happy Birthday." I felt blessed, and was grateful to have such good friends.

I visited Ninette later in the afternoon, as she told me she wanted to see me that day. I had coffee with her, and she gave me a pretty bracelet, saying it was from Toula and her. While I was there, Luigi phoned and sang "Happy Birthday," then chatted a while. I told him that his book would be ready soon, and I was organizing the launch at the Furlan Club, so he was pleased. She made me listen to his CD afterwards, and then played the piano for a little while. I enjoyed spending those few hours with her, listening to music, and her reminiscences, It was after four o'clock when I returned home.

It was still very warm, so I sat out in the garden. I had several calls that evening, from friends, my sisters, and Christian. Shirani said Ranjith flew to Sri Lanka the night before, as his good friend, Gabo, was seriously ill. Anjo called and wished me late at night, and said that her son's wife, gave birth to a baby girl the day before. I was very pleased to hear that, and wished her for her birthday tomorrow.

Nilanthi called next evening to say Ranjith visited her, but he was unable to see his friend before he died. He was very upset, as Gabo and he were friends for a very long time. I called all the actors that evening, to remind them of rehearsals on Sunday afternoon, and they said they would be there.

The temperature soared to thirty seven degrees on Saturday, and it was very humid. I called Nelune in the morning, and wished her a very happy birthday, then Elvira rang, regarding rehearsal at her place on Sunday. Connie went out at lunchtime, and did not come home till late evening. I wondered where he had gone, as we were dining at Cornelia's place that evening. He never told me what he had been doing, or where he went, as his usual explanation was, "I'm going out to do my thing." Laura was already there, by the time Connie and I arrived around seven o'clock. We had a very enjoyable time, and left after midnight.

I was too tired to go to church next morning, and as I had to go to Elvira's place in the afternoon, Connie went on his own. We had a good rehearsal that afternoon, and were pleased to meet a few more new actors. Misaka was a very talented young man, with a good singing voice too. He was a friend of Rathna's, and was happy to be in the play, as it was for charity. We finished around five o'clock, and I came home soon after.

Thankfully, it rained all night, after the hot and humid weather. Christian dropped in later next day, and stayed for a brief chat. He had to attend to some business, and could not stay long.

I made spinach and cheese pastries while I watched evening news, and was amazed to hear that Julia Gillard defeated Kevin Rudd in the leadership challenge, with 71 to 31! What a fiasco in the Labour Party! Nothing changes for the people though, while politicians play their sordid game of thrones. The rain continued steadily all day, and drenched the parched earth, so I did not have to water the garden for a few days.

I was very pleased to get the results for my next script assignment, another distinction. But I still had a long way to go, to complete the course, and become proficient at scriptwriting. Still, I enjoyed the challenge immensely, as I loved to learn something new all the time.

Ninette was very tired and anxious when I visited her that afternoon, and I was sad to see her getting worse. I was so close to her after all these years, that I looked on her as a second mother. And now it was very upsetting to watch her decline so rapidly.

I picked up Luigi's books at the post office on 1 March, and was extremely disappointed with the quality, and skimpiness of the book. The cover looked alright, but the printing was not the best, and they had left out the last page of the manuscript. When I came home, I emailed Melrose and told them not to go ahead with the rest of the printing, until they included the final page, which was very important, as it was a page of acknowledgements.

I did not hear from them till next day, but they agreed to re-print the books *if* I paid the extra amount! I pointed out that it was *their* mistake, and in the end, we compromised; they would correct their mistake, but I had to pay an extra sixty pounds towards cost.

We visited Liz and Gerry on Sunday, and I was happy to see Lorraine, Tony, Dorothea, and Ian there too. Their house was up for sale, as they had decided to move into a retirement village in Knoxfield. After lunch Connie and I dropped in at Cornelia's to give their holiday DVD, which Gerry copied for them.

Cornelia's mother was there for the day, but she looked frail and slightly disoriented, although she recognized me, and smiled as she spoke to me in Rumanian. I hugged her and asked her how she was, to which she shrugged her shoulders, and said she wanted to be home with Cornelia. It was very sad, but she did not understand that she could not stay at home alone. Cornelia felt very guilty and upset too, when she told her that she had to go back to the nursing home later.

I showed Ninette a copy of Luigi's book next Tuesday, and she was pleased with it; she wanted me to drive her to Luigi's place in Seaford and show him the book too, as he did not have his car then. Luigi was quite pleased with the book, when I showed him all the extra photographs they had included in this second edition. We left shortly afterwards, and when we returned, I helped Ninette to write out a list of songs from some old tapes, as she wanted Toula to make a few more CD's in time for the book launch.

On my way home, I stopped at Karingal to deposit the final instalment to Melrose Books, when I saw Connie and his boss, Mathew, at Woolworths. I just said hello in passing, and continued shopping, as they were busy discussing some issue.

When I saw Dr Khelil the following week, after some blood tests a week earlier, he said my sugar levels were high, and that I should go on insulin. I kept telling him I did not want to, but to increase tablets instead. The sugar level was about 8.1, and not very high (I thought). He prescribed a higher dosage of tablets for now, and hoped that would help.

The Woolamai Food Festival was held on Sunday, 11 March, and Shirani organized lunch at her restaurant for a large group. She invited us too, and we arrived there at midday. Shirani looked very attractive, in a red and gold sari, and a huge crowd milled around, including Roshan and family. We enjoyed the delicious food, and had a pleasant time before returning home late afternoon.

Lorraine called next day to say she was enjoying reading "Dark Shores" very much, and I thanked her for the feedback.

A few days later, I received all of ten pounds, as royalties from AuthorHouse for "Serendib." I knew they made a reasonable amount of money on sales, but paid me less than one pound royalties on each sale. In spite of this drawback, I still went ahead with the publication of "Edge Of Nowhere" with them. Because the quality of their publications was very good, though royalties left much to be desired.

Next Sunday, Linda, Leo, the children, and Julie came for afternoon tea. Paul was down with flu, and did not come. I baked two cakes on Saturday, but as the oven was too hot, they were burnt. I managed to salvage one of them, and prepared other finger foods. But there was plenty to eat, besides, Julie brought a delicious cake as well.

It was a scorching day, so after they left, Connie and I decided to walk down to the Esplanade, to see how long it would take us. Going downhill was easy, but coming back was another matter. And it took us over one and a half hours to get home, as we climbed uphill slowly in the blazing hot sun.

The next few days were busy organizing the book launch at the Furlan Club. I negotiated with the manager, regarding payment, catering etc. Luigi asked me to invite one of his friends, Ivano Ercole, a radio presenter on Radio Italiano, to open the launch. I wrote to him, then helped Ninette to compile a list of songs on Luigi's CD, which Toula was preparing. But Ninette asked me if Christian would design the covers for the CD, as she knew he was very clever at designing. When I asked Christian, he said he was happy to do so, and came up with an excellent cover.

Connie picked up some seedlings from Cornelia's place, as I wanted some winter flowering plants. He came back late that night, and for no reason at all, started an argument over nothing. I ignored him, as it was pointless trying to reason with him, when he had too many drinks.

The next morning, I woke up feeling emotionally and physically drained. But when he woke up, he behaved as if nothing was wrong, and by evening he was ready to go to church. I went with him, as what else could I do, but pray for patience.

The following Sunday, 25 March, Connie and I picked up Elvira and Catherine, another actor, as we were rehearsing at Rathna's place in Chelsea. Road works on the Nepean Highway, delayed us, and it took one and a half hours to get there, which should have taken us only forty minutes. We had a good rehearsal though, as a few more actors turned up. Connie dropped us, and drove off to Springvale. I called him when we finished, and he picked us up at five thirty. He had bought some crabs from Springvale market, and I made crab curry for dinner.

Chapter 67

Connie did not go to work the following day, as he said he was too tired, and slept all morning. He made an appointment to see doctor that afternoon. Shirani called to say she finally decided to retire from her teaching job, and handed in her resignation, as she wanted to concentrate on the restaurant; and she said she was relieved to stop teaching after forty years. I was happy for her, as it had been a long stressful career, and now she could do what she enjoyed doing.

I woke up to find Mishka on our bed that night. I tried to pat her, but as it was dark, and she did not see me, she got such a fright, that she scratched my hand and jumped out of bed, and ran away to hide somewhere. I had two deep scratches on my hand, and I washed with disinfectant. It was my fault, as she did not know who was trying to pat her. So I learnt a lesson, that one must never pat a nervous cat in the dark.

When I visited Ninette that day, she wanted me to take her to see her great grand-daughter after my lesson. I drove to Mount Martha, and found that Nadine's place was very close to Christian's house. I did not stay long, as Ninette was getting a lift back to Seaford. When I came home, I read numerous emails, regarding Authors Australia Inc. I spent a couple of hours replying them, as several authors were keen to join, and others were sending in membership fees.

Ivano Ercole called me on 28 March, while I was still at school. He sounded very nice and friendly, and said he would be honoured to accept my invitation to launch Luigi's book. He also told me that he knew Luigi for a very long time, and was happy to help in any way to promote the launch, book, and CD, on his weekly radio program. I said I would post a copy that week, as he wanted to read the book soon.

Christian was working very hard to get some flyers ready, and the CD cover too, so he called to say he would have everything ready in a couple of days. When I came home, the sun was just setting, and it was a spectacular sunset, so I removed several photographs for my collection of sunsets.

I was busy cooking on Friday, as Con and Cornelia were coming for lunch next day. I was still busy with last minute preparations on Saturday, but they had not arrived yet at two o'clock. Finally, they turned up at four! They were busy with something else, and thought it was alright to come late, and Laura arrived at five o'clock!

I thought I had told them it was *lunch*, but obviously our wires must have got crossed, because they came for an early dinner. Anyway, we had a pleasant time, and as it was windy and gloomy outside, we lit the gas log fire for the first time.

They enjoyed dinner very much, and stayed till after eleven o'clock, but Laura left earlier, as she had to work next day. I was exhausted, so Connie did the washing and cleaning up, as I went to bed soon after they left.

Next day was Palm Sunday, and the end of daylight saving. We attended Mass at Mornington, and I spoke to Elvira and Myra afterwards. Myra sang in the church choir with Elvira, and had agreed to take part in the play too. When we came home, I asked Connie to take some cutlets for Elvira and John, as he was going there later to check something with John. Then I took it easy, as I was still worn-out after yesterday.

The following Tuesday, Toula sent a text to ask if I could stop at Nadine's and pick up some CD's for Ninette. When I went there early, Toula was already there, and she thanked me, because it saved her a trip to Seaford. After my lesson, I helped Ninette with the titles of Luigi's songs, and it was very tiring, as she could not see well at all, and she became very frustrated when she could not read them herself. I found it difficult pronouncing Italian words, but in the end we managed to sort out the titles, and she was happy.

When I drove home, the Jag was leaking water and coolant badly. I was worried that it would grind to a halt, or something would burst. But I came home safely, and wondered what else needed fixing.

We drove the Jag to the garage next morning, and he dropped me back. I typed up the list of songs for Luigi's CD's, and read them out loud to Ninette over the phone, and she was happy with the list. Then I called Elvira and asked if she could pick me up at three thirty, as we had planned to have coffee and cakes at Onde's, to celebrate her birthday next day.

She came shortly afterwards, and we had a nice time, and I treated her to a delicious cake and coffee. John gave me some freshly picked lettuce from his garden, and chestnuts from his farm. I had no news of my car by evening, so obviously it was not ready that day.

We picked it up the following morning, and the mechanic said one of the hoses were loose, and he fixed it, free of charge. *That* was very generous of him (I did not think), considering they were supposed to have fixed the hoses last time, and jolly well should not charge us again for their careless work. Joelle called to say she would visit with her mother and aunt tomorrow.

Connie stayed home till late afternoon on Friday, and the weather turned blustery and stormy. Joelle and family arrived at five o'clock in the evening, and we enjoyed a pleasant time. I baked a butter cake that they all liked very much, and they left a couple of hours later. I was disappointed that the skies were so overcast, and they could not watch a beautiful sunset.

The heavens opened just then, and it was torrential all night, as a fierce storm broke out, and gusty winds blasted across the ocean till morning. The windows and doors rattled and creaked so violently, that I wondered if the house could withstand such a buffeting. I read till midnight, while the squall lashed furiously.

I started painting a large sunset scene for Cornelia that weekend, as she admired the one I painted for our study. I wanted to complete it in time for her birthday in July, so I painted for about three hours and then rested. Next day, after Mass at Mornington, we had lunch at Tanti Hotel, as Connie had been there before, and he raved about the "atmosphere" and great food.

But it was just a cold, basic room, and the food was just awful and over-priced. I asked him, "*How* could you say that the *atmosphere* and food were *great* here, when it's obviously so horrid! I can hardly finish this meal! We have been to much nicer places than this before, and I don't want to come here again." He just mumbled that it was nice before, and perhaps it was a new chef.

We drove to Dromana later, and walked on the pier, but it was very crowded, so we had coffee, and drove back, as it was very gusty. I planted some seedlings before the winds increased.

The car was running very rough when I drove it to Ninette's on Tuesday, and the engine kept cutting off a few times. I was afraid I would not get home safely, so Connie booked it in for a service on the following Monday. I was getting so very tired of this on-going saga with the Jag. It was showing its age unfortunately, and every time I drove it, I ended up returning in a tow truck! I was just about fed up by now, and Connie was more annoyed because of the large sums of money we paid for repairs. It came close to a thousand dollars each time, sometimes more, and was getting to be beyond a joke.

In mid-April, the workmen came early, and poured bitumen on the side of the driveway, and at the back. It was very noisy, and I had no rest until they left at four o'clock in the evening. Then the computer was down again, and when I called Christian, he said he would come soon as he was near-by.

Christian said that it needed a new part, so he went out to get one; it was just before five o'clock, and he was able to get one and fix the computer. I was very grateful, as I needed the computer for my work, and emails especially, and had to contact actors for rehearsals, and members of Authors Australia Inc. I gave him some pan rolls to take for Athena, and he enjoyed a couple before he left.

We dropped the Jag at the garage on Monday, and picked it up in the evening. This time the bill was $550! I wondered if they really did anything at all, because so many things went wrong, ever since they started "fixing" it. We drove to the city on Saturday, 21 April, for another meeting with Authors Australia Inc. Christian came too, and displayed the new website, as he was working on an updated version, which was excellent. All the members commended his voluntary work.

Pauline, though, wanted him to incorporate her online book store into the new web design. But Christian preferred to design something more compatible with his new website. Some lively discussion took place about this issue, and I said I would consider Pauline's request. Athena arrived later on, and we stopped at Chinatown to have a spicy meal before heading home.

I watched an interesting movie that night "St Louis Blues," with Nat King Cole, Ertha Kitt, and Ella Fitzgerald - it was the life of composer, William C Handy, and I enjoyed it very much.

We attended Fr Kevin's 80th birthday and farewell, at Padua College hall, next afternoon. He was retiring as parish priest of St Macartan's after many decades. More than one thousand people turned up, and we found seats next to Elvira and John. The service and speeches finished at four o'clock, and we stayed a while to chat with parishioners, and enjoy a slice of delicious cake. It poured down heavily as we got into the car, but when the rain ceased in the evening, I planted a few more seedlings.

I noticed that Ninette's moods and panic attacks were worse each time I visited. She was highly strung, and I watched what I said, as she was easily upset. It was not a pleasant visit anymore, as I found her behaviour very stressful. She was peevish, and not at all like the pleasant, friendly lady I knew. It was very upsetting to watch her petulant fits. And I put it down to her nerves, and the fact that she always complained about aches and pains. But it was hurtful, when she made me the brunt of her ill-humour.

On my way back from the podiatrist on 26 April, I stopped at Karingal to distribute some flyers for the launch. When I turned on the ignition, the car did not start again! I called RACV, and they came an hour later. Then I called Connie, and as he was still in Mulgrave, he drove to Karingal.

The mechanic started the car, but he said that another part in the starter motor was not working. He advised me not to drive it home, and to get it fixed immediately. I drove Connie's car, and followed him home, as he drove the Jag. My chest was paining with all this unnecessary stress, as it was very frustrating, and I was utterly fed up with so many break-downs.

The next morning, we took the Jag to the same garage, and they said they would look at it. Connie dropped me at home, and I did my chores, but my right hand and arm were aching badly. I did not know what was wrong, so I applied some ointment and massaged it, but the pain continued all day.

When I checked my emails that night, another ten members had joined Authors Australia Inc. I walked in the garden later that night, and glimpsed a very bright red moon sinking over the horizon in the sea. It was majestic, and I gazed at the splendid sight for some time.

I believed in the healing power of Bruno Groening, and invoked him to heal my wrist, which ached all night. The pain eased by morning, and I knew Bruno answered me.

Connie drove me to Bentons Square, as I did not have my car yet. When we returned from shopping, Esme wanted to visit. Connie told her to come around three, as we were going for a dinner dance at six o'clock. She came with Paul, and stayed for about an hour.

The dance at the Rosebud Italian Club was pleasant, but I was tired, and my wrist started aching again, so I did not enjoy it as much.

We had another good rehearsal at Elvira's place next day, and we were pleased that the actors did well.

Lorraine left a message to say that Tony was in hospital. When I called back, she said he was alright, and would be home in a day or two. His pelvic bones were fractured when he fell off his bike. I asked her what happened, and she said, "He told me he was ogling a female cyclist riding in front of him, and wasn't watching where he was going and took a tumble!" It became something of a joke. But Tony was not in the least embarrassed. He delighted in repeating the story about the woman's shapely bottom, and how he could not keep his eyes off her. Lorraine cancelled lunch at their place until he was better.

We picked up the Jag early morning on 1 May, and I drove it home. Then I visited Ninette in the afternoon, and helped her again with the list of songs for Luigi's CD. When I tried to start the car to go home, it was dead again! I was so very very frustrated with this saga. I called RACV, and they came at three thirty; not a mechanic, but a battery van. And the man said that it was one way they made money, replacing batteries, even when a new one was not required.

He could not get the car started though, so he phoned a tow truck, and I went back to Ninette's place until the truck arrived. Ninette made a cheese sandwich, as I was very hungry, and she was concerned about the car too.

I rode in the tow truck to the garage in Mornington. And when they checked it, the mechanic said that one of the electrical wires was pulled out accidentally, while they were fixing another problem. Anyway, they got it working soon, and I drove home without further incident.

One of Elvira's distant relatives from Italy, was visiting for a few months, and he agreed to take part in the play. She was very happy, as the young man was just right for one of the roles. His name was Alessandro, a nice young man in his early thirties. He hoped to work in Australia, as he wanted to apply for permanent residency. Alex (as we called him), was a qualified architect. He wanted work in that field, so he could obtain the required points for permanent residency.

Christian did a perfect job on the cover, and Ninette was very pleased. But she told me that as she had the master copy, Christian should not make any CD's. I tried to explain that he would not do so, because he was only designing the cover. But she was very possessive about Luigi's CD's, and had a morbid fear that other people would copy them.

No matter what I told her, she did not believe me, and refused to sell any of his CD's. She said that people would make copies and sell them to others. We went around in circles, as she was very difficult and argumentative now. I had a splitting headache by the time we finished talking on the phone. But I still failed to convince her that no one was going to copy his CD's anyway. She did not understand that the whole purpose of the launch, was to promote and sell his book and CD's.

Chapter 68

We talked about buying a new car after the last fiasco. And much as I loved the Jag and wanted to keep it, we could not afford to restore it completely, so as to make it reliable. So far, we had spent thousands of dollars repairing it, but it still needed more work done. I had to make up my mind to part with it, although it drove beautifully at times (when nothing went wrong).

In early May, on a wet, gloomy Saturday morning, we went car hunting in Mornington. After looking at a few models, I chose a Hyundai i30. The salesman offered a very low trade-in for the Jag, but he said we could leave it there, and sell it privately for a much higher figure. Connie said he could not be bothered to wait that long, and agreed to trade it in for a great deal less than its value.

The new car was $19,000, on a special deal, as it was marked down from $24,500, so it was a good deal. But I did feel a pang when I left my old *unreliable* Jag for good, and hoped I could now enjoy trouble-free driving for some time.

We completed the paper work that same day, and paid the whole amount, but had to wait till Tuesday to pick up the car, as it was the weekend. I drove the new car to Mount Martha, and back to Mornington with the salesman, and Connie in the back seat. It was very comfortable, and I was happy, especially as it came with a seven-year warranty, and the first service was free of charge.

On Sunday afternoon, Connie drove me to Frankston for rehearsals. Elvira was very upset, because her grand-daughter did not want to be in the play. Alex came though, and was a big hit with the others, as he was so polite and friendly, even though his English was limited and stilted. We had a good rehearsal and came home late evening.

On Tuesday morning, 8 May, we drove to Mornington Hyundai, and picked up my new car "ZAS 075." I chose a silver-grey car, with a dark-grey interior, which was very nice. It felt so good to drive a new car, after all those years of driving an old Holden, and the Jag, that broke down umpteen times.

It was marvellous driving it to Ninette's later that day, and she christened my car "Holy," saying I would always be safe in it. That was nice of her, and I was relieved to see that she had settled down somewhat, about the CD's. She understood that Christian was doing only the art work for the cover, and nothing else.

On 13 May, Mother's Day, Connie gave me perfume and flowers, then we went to Harvey Norman's and bought a new fridge. The old one, that lasted more than twenty five years, was not working properly now. They said they would deliver it the following Saturday, and take away the old fridge as well. The day before, we had looked in at the new super store "Masters," a chain of stores that Woolworths just opened, to compete with Bunnings stores. We bought a barbeque, and a chimnea (outdoor wood fire burner), for a very good price there.

I was busy organizing book promotions for Authors Australia Inc. members then, and the first event was at Frankston Library. Luigi's book launch was scheduled at the end of June, and I still had several details to finalise regarding these events.

I asked Luigi to sign fifty copies of his books, that I hoped to sell at the launch. And we planned to promote his CD's and books at the same time. I also had to complete my scriptwriting assignments, besides organizing fortnightly rehearsals.

It was my responsibility to get the actors together, which was not always easy, as everyone could not be there at the same time on some Sundays. I took my portable CD player for rehearsals, and tried to keep the actors focussed, and avoid clash of egos and tempers, as so often happened.

I was "prompter," and "problem-solver," as they all expected me to sort out every little hiccup, and iron out numerous difficulties that came up as we progressed. As producer, I had to ensure that everything ran smoothly. But it was daunting sometimes, as tempers flared, and some young children threw tantrums, because they were easily bored. And it was not easy to keep up the momentum even among adults.

Joelle, and her partner, Beat, came for one rehearsal. And I hoped Beat would come aboard, as he was quite good when he read the part. But he said he could not make a commitment, as he was going away on holidays soon. I usually took some cakes and biscuits for afternoon tea, and sometimes Elvira baked scones for the actors. So much was going on in my life then, that I had little rest and relaxation.

I noticed that Ninette was getting more confused and irritable these days, and she picked on me for no reason at all. I was quite fed up, and losing my patience. It was very sad, as I loved her like a "second mother," and she too said I was like her "second daughter." Although her personality changed, I continued to do my best to please her, and was patient, because I loved and respected her. But unfortunately, she grew worse and more cantankerous each time I saw her.

One night, at the end of May, I was just getting ready to watch a movie, when Connie, who was in a bad mood, and more annoying than usual, started banging things around, and made a big noise in the kitchen. I heard a loud crash. He dropped his bowl of soup and bread all over the kitchen floor. By the time we cleaned up that mess, I was not in a mood to watch a movie, so I went to bed. His awful moods were inexplicable.

Fr Kevin said his last Mass on Sunday, 27 May, and afterwards, we had finger food and soft drinks in the community hall. We wished Father farewell, and then chatted to the other parishioners, before we drove to Narre Warren to visit Shirani.

Suresh's dog, Kaluwa, had died suddenly the night before. He was only one and a half years old, and they did not know the cause of his death. Suresh was not home, as he was very upset and gone for a drive.

David, the editor of Rowville's local newspaper, called me next day. He said he would like to interview me, regarding Luigi's forthcoming book launch, Elvira's play, and Authors Australia Inc. promotions. I told him that I would let him know when I could drive up to Rowville.

Luigi suffered from severe back and leg pains, and was going in for an operation on 31 May. I hoped he would be well enough to attend his book launch, or else I would have to postpone the event, if he could not be present.

Connie played golf with Pat and Graham the following Saturday, and I made pan rolls and cutlets for them. When they returned in the afternoon, they enjoyed eating them straight out of the oven, where I had kept them warm. Pat was very complimentary, and he said, "Dolly, you make the *best* pan rolls in the world!" He said that every time he tasted them. But I was pleased to see them enjoying the food. Pat left soon after, but Graham stayed chatting till after five o'clock.

I drove to Frankston on Sunday afternoon, and was glad when everyone turned up for rehearsals, except Misaka. We were pleased that the actors were making good progress with their lines, and the songs sounded great.

The next day, Mary, Elvira, and I, checked the stage and seating at the community hall in Mornington. We were happy with the place, and decided to stage the play there.

Elvira said she would request council to give us a concession rate for the hall, because it was a charity production. Then we had coffee at Onde's cafe, and I dropped Mary home later on. It was such a pleasure driving around in my new Hyundai, that just whizzed along delightfully "trouble-free!"

I did not miss a single episode of "Revenge," on Monday nights, and I looked forward to that one hour. But as Connie did not follow it, he made it a point to disturb me, or start some discussion *exactly* at eight thirty, when I wanted to watch my favourite show.

We had many arguments, but on Monday nights especially, as I told him to leave me alone for just *one* hour. But he never listened, and shouted, "Is that *more* important than listening to what I have to say?" and I retorted, "You can wait until I *finish* watching this, then you can talk." Then he mumbled, and banged things around in the kitchen until the program ended.

It was very annoying, because when we drove somewhere, or I tried to talk to him at home, he was always too busy to listen, and ground his teeth when he had to answer just "yes" or "no." I had to repeat his name ten times, till he even looked at me. If I tried to talk in the car too, he ignored me, turned up the volume, and barked, "I'm listening to the radio!" So, I questioned him as to why it was *only* at this *particular* time on a Monday night that he needed to talk to me? As usual, he had no rational explanation for his behaviour.

Connie drove me to Stud Park shopping centre, Rowville, to meet David, the editor, on Friday morning, 8 June. He was a pleasant, interesting man, and interviewed me for one hour, after which we had coffee. David said he would print the article next week, and also advertise Luigi's forthcoming launch. I thanked him for his support, and introduced him to Connie when he came to pick me up.

Then we drove to Lorraine's, and Tony was home too, and they were happy to see us. It was quite late when we came home, but I was pleased with the interview, as we would get more publicity for Luigi's launch and Elvira's play.

We picked Ninette on the following Sunday morning, and drove to Isobel's place in Armadale. They were lovely people, and we had a very interesting time, chatting and listening to music. Her daughter, Michelle, and her husband, Greg, were there too, and Isobel made a delicious lunch as always, that we enjoyed very much.

John was turning eighty-four next day, but he was still full of verve, and with a delightful sense of humour. When the music started to play, he asked me to tango with him! But I had to decline, as I was not feeling too good, and I was afraid it was too much for him. He was partially blind, after a failed cataract operation, and had glaucoma too. But he was still great company, and very interesting to talk to. Isobel could not attend the launch, as they were going away. But she wished me well, and hoped it would be a great success. We came home late, after dropping Ninette.

Elvira visited on Monday morning, and said they would be away for four weeks, as they were leaving for Italy on 12 June. She told me that she depended on me to ensure that rehearsals continued until her return, as we hoped to stage the play in October.

David sent me the article for approval that evening, and as it was all good, I emailed him to go ahead with the printing.

A reporter from "IL Globo" the Italian newspaper, called me while I was at Ninette's. She wanted to interview me, as she was writing an article about Luigi's book, and launch at the Furlan Club. Radio Italia too promoted the launch, so it was great publicity, and I hoped many people would attend.

Erica, one of John's relatives, arrived from Italy on holiday, and was staying with them. She was eighteen years old, petite and very pretty, and she came to watch rehearsals. When Elvira's grand-daughters dropped out of the play, Erica agreed to play the main role. She had a charming Italian accent, and spoke a little English. But she was very intelligent and talented, with a beautiful, singing voice. And it was very impressive how quickly she learnt her part, and sang all the songs so well. We were very pleased, as it was one of the main roles in the musical.

A few young men, Misaka, Daham, Luis, and Chris, devoted countless Sunday afternoons to rehearse. Young male actors were difficult to find, especially ones who could sing and act, and at times, we despaired of ever getting the play on stage. Alessandro was perfect for an important role, as he too had an Italian accent, and spoke limited English. At first, he agreed to take part, and then due to work commitments, he left for Sydney suddenly, which was quite a disappointment to everyone.

Elvira told me that when Mary and she were at one of the cafes in Mornington, she appraised likely young male waiters, for the role Alessandro was meant to play. And fortunately, she spotted a suitable young Italian waiter, who agreed to take part. And so finally, we had all the actors we required, and booked the Peninsula Theatre for 22 October, and hoped all the actors were ready by then.

We meant to hold two performances, but as time drew near, Misaka, and his wife, Theji, went overseas for five weeks. Then Rathna's father was ailing, and she travelled to Sri Lanka a few times to see him. By the time October drew near, we hardly had enough time for two or three rehearsals, and a dress rehearsal, before opening. Elvira and John left for Italy, and were due back in early July. It was difficult without a director to take charge, and we had a situation where everyone did as they pleased.

I suggested that until Elvira returned, they were to learn their lines and songs, and be ready. Some of the ladies had huge egos, but the young men did not try to take over, and were more compliant. Rathna was a professional actor, so her input was helpful. She told me how the play should be directed, and I took her suggestions into account.

In the meantime, I finished editing "Edge Of Nowhere." and submitted it to AuthorHouse on 19 June. That same night, a severe earthquake hit the country town of Moe, and some surrounding suburbs. Connie was on the phone all night, as stores in Moe, and immediate areas, suffered enormous damage. Elvira left a message to say they arrived safely in Italy.

The book launch at the Furlan Club was advertised widely in the Italian community via radio and newspaper. Lorraine called to say she saw the article in Il Globo, and Ornello too called Ninette with the same news. Ivano Ercole interviewed Luigi on radio, and all was going ahead as planned.

Elvira called a few times over the next few weeks, as she wanted to know how the play was progressing. I told her rehearsals were going well, and not to worry, but to enjoy her holiday.

We picked Ninette at ten o'clock on our way to Thornbury on 24 June, and we arrived there within the hour. I was surprised to see Tony and Lorraine walking down from the car park, as they drove, and did not take a train and bus as she intended to. The weather was not too bad, but it was freezing, so it was good to be inside the warm and crowded Bistro where we had lunch.

Ninette started panicking, as she did not want to get late, but I assured her that we had plenty of time till the launch started at two o'clock. Del offered to sit with Ninette, and reassured her, as I was busy attending to last minute details. Christian arrived early, but Athena was unwell, so she did not come. Con, Cornelia, Christina, and most of Ninette's friends were there too. Jackie accompanied Luigi, as he was still on crutches after a knee operation. Christina presented me with a large bouquet of exquisite, pale pink roses.

My friends and staunch supporters, Del and Liz from school, and several others attended as well. I invited a couple of Italian journalists, who had known Luigi in the past, and they came too. Christian did a great job taking care of details, and he played Luigi's CD's in the background while recording the event.

Ivano was a very friendly person, and his presentation was excellent. After he finished speaking, he asked me how I came to write the book, and he read a few chapters from it, saying, "You have recaptured a forgotten period of Italian history in meticulous detail, and I thank you for the wonderful story about Luigi's life." He was very complimentary about the book, and promised to keep promoting it on his radio show.

I spoke briefly about how I met Ninette. And how she asked me to write Luigi's story, as she knew he had led a very colourful life, and was a brilliant tenor as well.

Egilberto Martin, another journalist, was very helpful too, and gave me a list of several Italian clubs overseas, who would be interested in Luigi's book. He wore a tweed jacket and a felt hat, and was a good looking, middle-aged man, who for some reason reminded me of Gregory Peck. A couple of years later, that kind man was struck down with cancer, and much to my dismay, he died shortly afterwards. Luigi too was very shocked when it happened, as he was a good friend of Luigi's for a long time.

Luigi was in great pain that day, and he stood up on crutches, as he made a shaky tearful speech. But the audience understood he was just after an operation. And listening to Ivano reading some painful passages in the book, especially about the death of his only son, was too much for him to bear. The launch was a great success though, and we sold many copies of his book as well as his CD.

Connie was in charge of sales, and he kept an accurate record. We handed Luigi all the money from the sale of his books and CD's at the end of the launch. Luigi and Jackie gave Christian a bottle of champagne, and the same for me, with a bouquet of flowers.

We had a drink with Con and Cornelia afterwards, and spent some time chatting with them, as they made an effort to attend. It was a pleasant afternoon, and I was grateful it went well. I was also pleased that Luigi's countrymen came to support him, and acknowledge his great voice.

We left after three o'clock, and dropped Christian on our way. Then we stopped at Toula's place to drop Ninette. Just before we left Toula's, Connie was getting something out of the boot, when next moment, we heard him yell out. He had banged the boot lid right on his forehead, and it was bleeding! Very soon, a large lump appeared on his forehead.

We returned home very late in the evening, and I put some ice on his forehead. When I asked him, "How on earth did you do such a thing?" He replied, "I don't know!"

I spent next day writing out "Thank You" notes to Ivano, and all the others who had helped to make the launch a success. In the weeks that followed, Ivano interviewed Luigi on radio again, and promoted his book and CD's as often as he could.

Ninette talked about Luigi so much, that Ivano invited her for an interview too. She went to the station on 18 July, and had a very good interview with him. When she came home, she called to say she was very happy with the way Ivano interviewed her, and had even played one of her CD's, so I was pleased for her.

Del and Judy came for lunch a week later, and enjoyed my pasta dish, with kransky sausage, red peppers, parsley, and olives. After lunch, Judy read a few chapters from her memoirs that she hoped to publish soon. In spite of the gloomy, chilly afternoon, we spent a lovely time together. But Del left at three o'clock, as she did not want to drive in the dark.

Christian dropped in later to show me what the new website for Authors Australia Inc. looked like. I was very impressed, as he did a superb job, and I was sure the other members would like it too.

Ninette told me that I must not sell any CD's to people with restaurants and cafes, as they would copy Luigi's CD and sell them! She drove me crazy, as she went on and on about it for forty minutes on the phone, at the end of which, my head was spinning, as I just could not reason with her. I left it at that, and wearily said, "Don't worry, I'm *not* going to give anyone his CD!"

She called a few more times about the same issue, demanding to meet the person I had sold a CD to, as I unwittingly mentioned he had a cafe. It was a comedy. And I asked myself *why oh why* did I get involved in this situation with Ninette and her CD's! I took on unnecessary headaches, trying to help Luigi and her.

I drove my car to Mornington Hyundai for a service on 11 July, and they gave me a courtesy car, which was handy. I came home and attended to some work, and my car was ready to be picked up at two o'clock that afternoon. It was very convenient, and I breathed a sigh of relief because I had a trouble-free car now.

We rehearsed every Sunday over the last couple of months, instead of fortnightly, and the actors were almost ready. I told them when Elvira returned, we would hold a dress rehearsal, just before the final week. We had to make sure the costumes were right, even though they were simple outfits, based on 1950s styles.

Elvira and John returned on 19 July, and we had coffee next day, to discuss how the play was progressing. She gave me two small ceramic cherubs she bought in Italy. It was good to see her again, and I told her that when she resumed the role of director, she must be very firm with some of the actors, as they all wanted to do things their way. I had reiterated it was Elvira's play, and she knew exactly how it should be presented.

We drove to the city on Saturday afternoon on 21 August, as it was the annual general meeting of Authors Australia Inc. I had the flu, but I still went, as it was important for me to be there. Peter came too, but he did not contribute much, as he preferred to be in the background now. Christian was there, and did an excellent presentation of the new website.

All the members thought he did a great job, and I reminded them he spent untold hours working on it without charging us. And he could not be expected to do all the extra work required to finish it, without reimbursement.

But the *troublesome* member, Pauline, did not agree, and was on his back throughout the presentation. She had umpteen questions and suggestions to move her current online store across to the new website, and get it going as soon as possible. Christian's ideas were far more advanced. And being a perfectionist, he wanted the website to look as professional as possible, not a mish mash of Pauline's existing online store. He told me that her website was not practical, or user-friendly, and that was why he wanted to design a better system.

It was obvious that Pauline wanted to run the show, and none of the other members contradicted her. I said that I would consider her suggestions, but I wanted Christian to finish work on the website first, before we sold books online. It was plain to see she joined our organization with the sole object of personal profit, as she wanted forty percent on the sale of each book. But we formed this group to support and promote each other's work, and not for one person's benefit. I was exhausted when we came home, so I relaxed in the evening and watched some comedies.

I did not feel too well on Monday. Connie too said he was tired, and decided to stay home. Ninette asked me to email Ivano, and thank him on her behalf. Then I responded to numerous emails from authors, who wanted to join Authors Australia Inc. which kept me very busy. Because I was committed to organize promotional events at libraries for our group, I hardly had a moment to pursue my other interests.

I watched the final episode of "Revenge," season one that Monday night. And it had so many loose ends, that I knew they would have a few more seasons to tie them up.

I still felt unwell on Tuesday, so I did not visit Ninette, and Connie stayed home again. In spite of feeling feverish on Wednesday, I went to school, and got through the day somehow. Ninette called that evening and asked me to read the list of all the songs on Luigi's CD's *again*! She could be very inconsiderate at times, as she knew I was not too well. But I spent one hour listening to her, and reading out names on the list.

I organized the book promotion at Frankston Library, on Saturday, 28 July. Peter designed several great posters for the event, and when we arrived there, he was busy hanging up posters with his daughter, Christine. She was a very pleasant, helpful young lady, and we had an interesting conversation. The library staff too were very helpful. We set up posters in one section of the room, and displayed our books on tables that the staff set up.

Seven authors from our group, and two local authors, who were non-members were present. Elvira and Karen came too, and we stayed a couple of hours talking to other authors and readers, who came to browse or buy our books. Peter was pleased that I organized this event, and we talked about holding similar promotions in other libraries too.

I drove to Frankston for rehearsals next day, and was pleased to see one of my piano students, Lili, was there with her mother. Lili agreed to take part too, and I was happy when she proved to be very good at acting. She was nine years old, but a delightful, cheeky character, who was well-fitted for the role. When I took Mishka for her annual check up, I was disappointed when Camilla, the usual vet, was away. And her partner, Josh, examined Mishka instead. She was so nervous and timid, that I felt very sorry for her. Josh *insisted* she was deaf, and told me that *all* pure white cats were born deaf. But I had to contradict him, as Mishka could hear perfectly well, even if she was right down at the other end of the garden. I did not like his attitude at all, and made a mental note not to consult him in future.

Elvira visited on 3 August, and asked me to complete the council application forms, in order to hire the theatre. We spent some time over that, and then discussed the play, and it was a long, constructive afternoon.

I called Nilanthi a couple of times a week, and hoped she had settled in to her new way of life now. Nelune was very busy with her job, besides her involvement with on-going fund-raising events, and sometimes I did not hear from her very often. But she was always there for me whenever I needed her.

Shirani too was very busy establishing the restaurant, and was getting several bookings. So, whenever I called her, she was either cooking or doing something in the house and garden. I knew it was not easy for her, running a business and two households. But sometimes, I could not help feeling emotionally isolated, no matter how very busy I was, and how full my life was with work and all my interests.

Everyone was so busy with their lives, and so pressed for time, I mused sadly. And yet, I do not keep count of the numerous hours I spent listening to others, and being there when they needed me. I have never stinted on my time, which I think is the *most* precious commodity we could expend.

I went through an immensely difficult period with Connie then, as he was becoming almost impossible to live with. I did not know whom to turn to, or confide in, because on the surface, we appeared to get along like any other normal, married couple. I kept busy just to maintain my sanity, or else he would have driven me insane, with his bouts of violent temper and hurtful behaviour.

Whenever I visited some of my friends who lived on their own, either widowed or separated from their partners, I toyed with the idea of renting a room, until I found a place of my own. But I resisted the urge to leave home, as I knew it was not the right answer to our problems. I tried leaving him before, but returned to the same merry-go-round. I would not let him drive me away from my home again, that much I knew.

We watched "Dark Knight Rises," at the cinema that weekend, and I found it very loud, with non-stop action. And although it was a good movie, I came home with a splitting headache, as the noise was deafening.

I printed two hundred and fifty tickets, and picked them up from Curry Printing in Mornington, as we had to start selling them now. Elvira said she would re-imburse me for printing costs, once all the tickets were sold.

I packed a box to send Nilanthi in early August, which Connie was dropping off later. But he rested till one o'clock, and then said he was going out to put tatts lotto. We were dining at Laura's place at six o'clock that evening, and he came home just one hour before.

Laura lived in an old, weather-board house in Noble Park, and it was very overcrowded. She crammed bulky furniture into this tiny living area, which made it very difficult to even move around. We sat at the dining table loaded with bread rolls, lamb chops, sausages, and cabbage rolls. And as there was not much room to get up and stretch my legs, I just sat there all night feeling claustrophobic, and nauseous, at seeing so much fatty foods.

Con and Cornelia came too, and showed us their holiday DVD. Cornelia joked that Laura took a whole day off work to prepare such an enormous dinner. I noticed that Connie was in a pensive mood that night. And as he sat next to me at table, every time he said something to me, he jabbed my arm with his elbow, until my arm was sore. I whispered, "Stop doing that Connie, my arm is hurting." He scowled at me and barked, "You stop your whinging! Enough whingers around me!"

He did not care whether the others heard him or not, but I was embarrassed, as I did not want to be shouted at in front of our friends. They hardly took notice of his behaviour though, and we continued watching the holiday DVD. We came home at midnight, and I had a stomach ache all of next day.

When I went for rehearsals on Sunday afternoons, I encouraged him to play golf or go fishing. But he seemed to be quite happy just sitting at his computer. And some days, when I came home at five thirty or so, he would still be sitting in the same position, as when I left home. That Sunday after dinner at Laura's though, he came to church around five o'clock, and dropped in to see how rehearsals were going. He spoke to the actors for a while, and then said he was attending evening Mass. Elvira came with me, so I drove her home afterwards.

It was Elvira's and John's 25th wedding anniversary on 15 August, so I posted them a card. But they invited us for dinner at the Hyatt hotel in the city on Friday, the 17th. I was ready by five o'clock that evening, and waited for Connie. I called him earlier and reminded him about dinner, and he said he would leave work early, and drive to the city in time. But he was running late as usual, drove too fast, and nearly jammed into the car in front of us. I shouted out, "*Stop,* you're going too fast!" which annoyed him, and he sulked all the way, without uttering a single word.

As we entered the underground car park, he did not look where he was going, drove too close to the wall, and scraped the side of the car on the passenger side. He was furious, but he could not blame this accident on me. But he started picking on me over some minor issue, and barked out, "Why didn't *you* warn me I was too close to the wall?" I replied, "You were driving, and you should have been more careful." This led to more recriminations and grumbling, and he entered the hotel foyer in a huff.

He stood in the middle of the hotel, looked around, and then asked the receptionist if this was the Hyatt! The big neon sign outside clearly showed it was the right place. I pointed this out to him, and he snapped back angrily, "You are just like that woman in that comedy, nagging me!" I was taken aback and asked, "You call that nagging?"

It was not the first time he insinuated that I nagged him, and I was really angry. We exchanged more harsh words, and walked into the dining room without speaking or looking at each other. He said, "Don't mention about the accident to anyone." I did not reply, as Elvira and John were waving us over to their table. Tony, Mary, John's brother, Rino, and his wife, Betty, were already there.

I could hardly speak to Connie, as I was so annoyed that evening. But dinner was delicious, and we were in good company, so I smiled and pretended nothing was wrong. Later on, I told Elvira about the car, and that he was upset about it. He tried to talk to me across the table, but apart from polite replies, I just ignored him. I still fumed at his unjust accusations.

On our way out of the hotel lift, about an hour before midnight, I watched two young girls tottering out. One was very drunk, and kept mumbling, "I love this girl," over and over to her friend. Another young man looked at us and muttered, "Too much cheap drink." He got out of the lift with his companion, and said, "*Where's* the red Ferrari, or did we bring the *black* Ferrari today?" He thought he was being very funny. Such interesting characters lurk in the city after dark, I mused. On our way home, I sat in the back seat, as I could not open the passenger door, and we argued all the way home. I wondered if it was just fatigue that caused his lack of concentration and bad temper.

I was awake till morning with umpteen visits to the toilet, and did not sleep at all, as I was very upset about his behaviour and attitude. And when I asked him why he kept saying I nagged him, when I just asked him anything, he did not respond, but went off on a tangent, which made me angrier still.

He said hurtful things to me, but could never explain the reason why. I was very unhappy at home over these last few months. And in spite of all my projects and work, I often thought I *had* to get away, or go mad in this oppressive, unhappy environment. But I could not think of a solution, as there was no way I could leave again. I kept busy constantly, just to avoid thinking of the pain and stress in my life. Immersing myself in writing, music, and art, and now preparing for the stage play, was a coping mechanism.

Chapter 69

In mid-August that year, I held two more promotional events in Rosebud and Frankston libraries. And was now in the process of organizing more events, as our membership increased to one hundred and sixty five. I was doing more than I should to keep the group functioning, without financial help, and support from other members. Peter paid for the old website, and all other expenses, and I found myself in the same position now.

What precipitated my decision to resign from the group, was that on 22 August, I received a nasty, offensive email from Pauline, regarding the new website Christian was developing. She said she wanted the website to be in line with her previous one, and with her on-line book store.

We exchanged a couple of emails (hostile ones on her part), over the next few days. And at the end of it all, I decided to resign as president, as I had enough stress with the whole issue. I understood that Pauline's hidden agendas went deeper than website issues. So I asked Christian not to waste any more time with the website, and to shut it down. Now we did not have a website, as Peter, who designed the original one, shut down his site as well. When I called to tell him of my decision, Peter was shocked and disappointed, as he wanted the group to succeed, with me at the helm.

He called me a few times over the next few days, and tried to persuade me to change my mind. I said I was sorry, but I just could not cope with any more stress in my life. Pauline then offered to resign, *if* I wanted to stay on, but it was my final decision, and she could stay or leave as she pleased. Peter said he was aghast, because one obnoxious woman single-handedly decimated a great organization like ours.

He spent a great deal of time and energy setting up the organization, and he was reluctant to see it shut down. But as none of the other members wanted to be nominated as president, I had a prolonged case with Consumer Affairs, to wind up the group. We had $450 dollars in our bank account, collected from members towards website fees etc. I was advised to donate this amount to charity when the organization closed, and could not believe I had to jump so many hurdles to wind it up.

We considered all these matters at the last meeting. And although Margaret, the secretary, and some others, urged me to reconsider my decision, I was adamant to leave the group. I told them that I did not want any part in this cloak and dagger business. No matter where or what, politics *always* destroy many a well-meaning organization, I thought. And I shelved that experience as another one of life's lessons. I did not want any more conflict in my life, and that Pauline was one of the strangest, and most aggressive women I ever knew.

To celebrate "Book Week," children's author, Ian Billings, visited our school on 23 August. He was very funny and entertaining, and I enjoyed his talk very much, and spoke to him afterwards. He told me that he travelled all over the world, visiting various schools, and encouraging children to read and write.

Just after I resigned as president, I attended another book promotion in Rosebud library on Saturday, 25 August, as part of Book Week activities at the library. When I organized this promotion initially, a few of the members were to attend this event. But now, I was the only one, with a couple of local authors, who were not members of our group.

The library was festooned with colourful balloons, and many people walked through all morning, since I was there from about ten thirty. Connie helped to set up my posters and table with books and flyers. I had an interesting time conversing with other authors, and some interested readers, who stopped to browse through our books. I bought books from other authors, and sold a few of mine that day.

I picked Lilli next Sunday afternoon, and drove to Frankston for rehearsals. A few more young men came along too, so we had the whole cast, and we finished by five o'clock.

Christian and Athena dropped in that evening, and we gave him a card and gift for his birthday, which was in a few days time. We had a pleasant time, and they left a couple of hours later.

I was at school on Christian's birthday, so I sent him a text to wish him, and said a special prayer for him as always.

Ninette posted one of her CD's to Ivano, but after a week or so, he failed to acknowledge it. She asked me every day why he did not call to thank her, and to write him a letter, and send another CD by registered mail this time.

Once she got an idea into her head, she was obsessive about it, and spoke of nothing else. I wrote to Ivano, and asked if he received the CD, and registered the letter and CD. I fervently hoped that was the end of it, because she hounded me, and gave me no peace until I did what she wanted.

That same day, I received an email from Open Colleges; I graduated with distinction, and would receive my diploma in the mail soon. The tutor gave great feedback, and ended with, "I wish I could meet you and shake your hand for pursuing this course, and for your hard work. You will make a fine scriptwriter some day." That was so very encouraging, and I was elated. I showed Connie the email and the results, and after a cursory glance, he mumbled, "That's good."

Nelune emailed photographs of the opening of the "Nelune Centre" in Sydney, with Prime Minister, Julia Gillard, congratulating her. I was very excited and proud of Nelune, as she achieved such an amazing target. I sent her a congratulatory message. She replied that she was very happy, but quite over-whelmed too, that after so many years of hard work, raising funds, she realized her dream.

Elvira and John invited us, Mary and Tony, for dinner to Rugantino's restaurant on 31 August. Erica said she missed her parents, and boyfriend very much, and looked tearful, but we had a pleasant time in spite of the freezing weather. We came home close to midnight, and Connie had the air-conditioner in the car all the way home, so that I was chilled to the bone. I could not get warm, even with the electric blanket on, and shivered through the night.

I woke up with a sore throat, and head cold next morning, but finished the soft-toy rabbit for the play, until we found a better one.

Nilanthi wanted a warm jumper, as she was going up-country on a trip, and asked if I could send one through Shirani, to which I agreed.

I dosed myself with Panadol and attended Sunday Mass next morning, as it was Father's Day. I gave Connie lottery tickets, and after-shave lotion. When Mass was over, I was very surprised to see Erica outside the church, bawling her eyes out, and Elvira trying to comfort her. I thought something bad must have happened, as Erica was so very upset. But when I asked Elvira what was wrong, she replied, "She's missing her parents and home very much, especially as it's Father's Day today." Poor girl, she continued sobbing for some time, and they left shortly afterwards. She was a very emotional young girl.

We did not have rehearsals that afternoon, so we drove to Shirani's later that day, and she was happy to take the jumper and chocolates I bought for Nilanthi. It was good to see her, Roshan, June, Max, and Will too after a long time. Suresh acquired another dog, "Astro," a very boisterous puppy, who jumped and slobbered all over me.

They left for Sri Lanka on 4 September, and Shirani called next day to say they arrived safely, for which I was thankful.

Christian said our computer needed to be upgraded. So Athena and he came that evening, and he installed a new hard-drive. Their friend, Christy, who lived near-by, dropped in for a chat too. She was a nurse, and a very nice, friendly young person, and we chatted until the installation was completed.

Connie was tired, and went to bed by eleven o'clock, as it took a long time to transfer the data, but we stayed up till after one o'clock in the morning. I hoped the new hard-drive would work faster, and better than the old one.

Severe storms and gusty winds tore relentlessly over the next few days, and the poor cats were very unhappy, as they hated going out in the howling wind. They sat near the windows staring out, and then glared at me accusingly, as if *I* was responsible for such horrid weather. I was still down with a head cold and cough, and sipped umpteen cups of lemon and honey.

Lorraine and Tony invited us to a Sri Lankan restaurant in Wantirna, to celebrate their fiftieth wedding anniversary on Saturday, 8 September. It was wet and cold when we drove there around midday. And just as we arrived there, the store manager at Mountain Gate called Connie. A water pipe had burst in the car park, which needed to be fixed immediately. So, after greeting Lorraine and Tony briefly, he excused himself and drove off to organize a plumber.

Liz and Gerry were there too, but she was cold and aloof, because I forgot to keep our lunch date last month. I usually wrote down every appointment in my diary, but after her last phone call regarding the date, it slipped my mind completely. She was offended, and made sure I knew that she was displeased. I explained that because I was involved in so many projects, I genuinely forgot about it, but she remained unconvinced. So I left her alone and chatted to Lorraine's family instead. Vivian asked me, "What's wrong with Liz? She looks so grumpy!" I shrugged my shoulders and replied, "Who knows?"

I went back with Lorraine, as Connie still did not return at two thirty, and all the guests left by then. He arrived at Lorraine's a short time later, but did not want to eat anything, and just had a cup of coffee. We returned home late in the evening, and Lorraine gave him some leftovers. He barely tasted the food, before he pushed it aside disgustedly and said, "*Yuk*! No taste at all! *That's* not Sri Lankan curries!" Indeed, the curries were very watery and tasteless. And knowing how critical Connie was, I did not blame him for not eating that food.

The rehearsals went well next Sunday afternoon, as the whole cast turned up, and Erica played her part without any problem. She was just perfect for the role, and sang beautifully too. I was amazed at how quickly she learnt all the lines and memorized the songs. Elvira and I were very pleased that Erica turned up when she did.

Christian and Athena travelled to Japan on 11 September, to celebrate a friend's wedding over there. I was extremely worried till they arrived, as it was the eleventh anniversary of the terrorist attack on the twin towers in the States. I fervently hoped there would be no more incidents. And I was extremely relieved when Christian sent me a text that evening, to say they landed in Kuala Lampur.

I attended the final meeting of Authors Australia Inc. on Saturday, 15 September, to officially tender my resignation. Peter said he would not be present, but wanted a full report of the proceedings. Pauline came, and about five other members, and the atmosphere was frosty and hostile. Margaret, the secretary, asked me once more, "Would you reconsider your decision to resign?" I replied, "No, my mind is made up, but please ask if anyone else wants to step in as president."

She asked everyone present, "Is there anyone here who would stand up as president?" No one showed any interest at all, even though Margaret emailed all the members, asking for nominations. So, the few members who were present, voted to wrap up Authors Australia Inc. because no one wanted to be president and assume responsibility.

Connie and I visited the National Art Gallery afterwards, as a "Napoleon" exhibition was on. It was excellent, and I really enjoyed seeing artworks, costumes, memorabilia, and everything related to Napoleon and that era. I emailed Peter that night, to inform him of the members' decision to wrap up the organization. He was thoroughly disappointed, but not surprised, as he said none of them wanted to take on the responsibility of the job, but just wanted to enjoy benefits only.

I was worn-out next morning, so Connie went to church on his own. I rested till late, then picked up Lilli for rehearsals in the afternoon. We had another good session, and as we were getting close to the performance, everyone put in one hundred percent.

Elvira sounded very upset when she called on 17 September, and asked if she could see me. She was in tears when she arrived shortly afterwards. The council told her, that due to major repairs, we could not use the theatre at Mornington, and they would advise her of another venue soon. This setback was unfortunate, as we just sold tickets, and printed flyers with the venue as Peninsula Theatre, Mornington. But I told her not to worry, as we could re-print flyers, and advise the people who already bought tickets, that the venue was changed.

The council called her that very night, and said the venue would be Mount Eliza Theatre. So we arranged to meet there, and have a look around. I re-printed more flyers, and made a few phone calls to people who bought tickets. Elvira phoned her friends too, so we handled the situation without too much difficulty.

Then we pasted large posters on the Peninsula Theatre doors, advising the change of venue, in case people turned up there on the day. This was all part of show business, I thought, and we had to be prepared to deal with disappointments and emergencies. It was a stressful day, but in the evening, I made buriyani rice, chicken, prawn, and potato curries for lunch at school next day.

Nelune said they raised one and a half million dollars at the "Lilac Ball" on the weekend, so I congratulated her on another brilliant effort.

After visiting Ninette next day, I met Elvira and Erica at Mount Eliza. Mary came too, and we checked the theatre, which was very nice, and more modern than the one in Mornington, so we were pleased. I came home and typed new flyers, and emailed them to Connie, to print a few more.

When I came home on 20 September, after closing Authors Australia Inc. bank account, I saw a large envelope lying in the garden. Fortunately, it was not raining, because it turned out to be my diploma! I was elated that I completed the course successfully, and was very happy to receive the diploma. But not too happy with the postman, who flung the envelope so carelessly into the garden.

Shirani called next day to say they returned from Sri Lanka a couple of days ago, and were staying in Woolamai. She also said that Nilanthi enjoyed her trip up-country very much. I drove to St Vincent's charity shop in Mornington later that day, and gave them a cheque for $480 from Authors Australia Inc. and the volunteer was very glad to receive such a generous donation. Then I distributed flyers at Onde's cafe, and other venues in Mornington.

Sarah and Tracy dropped in on the following Monday, and Sarah played the piano and sang well as always, and she agreed to perform at the end of year concert too. We had an enjoyable time, and I was happy to see them again. They said they would come for the play, and visit again soon.

When I visited Ninette next day, she was very upset over something that her brother Eddie said, when he spent a few days with her. She was always distressed over something or another now, and how she coped with these constant issues in her life, was beyond me. She became very confused whenever she was in this agitated state of mind, was paranoid, and talked of nothing else, but that particular issue that worried her then. I noticed she was getting worse now, and it was not a very healthy sign.

Nelune called on 27 September, to say that the "Nelune Centre" (the new cancer hospital) was opening that night. I congratulated her on such a great achievement, and told her how proud I was of her amazing work.

Mary called later that evening, to say her mother had died, so we cancelled afternoon tea on Saturday. Instead, we drove to Mary's on Saturday afternoon, as I made some soup for them, and wanted to give her a sympathy card too, but they were not home.

We drove down to Dromana, as Connie wanted to put tatts lotto, and then came back to Mary's just as they returned. Elvira and Erica dropped in at the same time, and Mary was very pleased with the pot of soup, and kept thanking me. We did not stay long, as we had to attend Mass that evening. Rehearsals were on again next day, and we were pleased, and relieved that all the actors were good and ready.

Next morning, 1 October, we attended Mary's mother's funeral, at Rosebud church. It rained steadily, but with intermittent sunny spells, and even though we were not going to the cemetery, I was glad for those who were, that it would not be too wet.

Mary was very uptight, as they were flying to Italy that evening, and planned it months ahead. They paid for their tickets already, so they could not cancel or postpone their trip. I wished her well, and then we came home by late afternoon.

I still had some loose ends to finalise, regarding the winding-up of Authors Australia Inc. Consumer Affairs wanted me to sign a statutory declaration, stating the *reasons* why I was closing down the organization! So many formalities, that I regretted getting involved with that group in the first place, as I now bore the brunt of it all on my own.

When Peter handed over formalities, I had no idea that I was solely accountable, and he never warned me what to expect either. No wonder that the rest of the group were so reluctant to stand as president.

A few days later, Nilanthi asked if I could send her a warm blanket, as she was feeling very cold at nights. I posted a very light, fleecy blanket, and she called a few days later to say she received it, and was collecting the box of clothes and food as well.

Misaka was very good with computers, and asked me to find some old photographs that we could use as background slides. And he found some of Colombo Harbour, and various other scenes too. This was because we had a segment with a Sri Lankan dancer (a little girl). In the play, the ship stops in Colombo, and the main character sees the dancer in a surreal way. Misaka agreed to be in charge of background scenery (on slides), and Elvira's brother lent us a projector. I checked all the props and slides, and ensured we had everything we needed. John constructed a wooden platform with rails, that looked like part of a ship's deck.

I was happy driving around in my little car now, and I was at rehearsals almost every Sunday afternoon. Connie stayed home working on the computer, in spite of my urging him to go fishing, or play golf with his work mates, Pat and Graham. He preferred to sleep till midday, and then sat at his computer, attending to work-related emails until I came home. And when I returned, he nodded a cursory greeting, then continued working till late at night.

I usually came home around five thirty or so, and then cooked dinner. Once or twice though, I was surprised when he turned up at the hall, in the midst of rehearsals, and said, "I thought of going for Mass here, so I came to Frankston." He chatted briefly to some of the people, and then went to church.

I drove to Dandenong on 8 October, and met Joelle and Jo for coffee. It was good to see them, and I gave them some flyers too. Joelle said she would be there with Beat, but Jo was not too sure, as she had other plans on that day.

One week before opening, Rathna's father was critically ill, and she rushed to Sri Lanka, just in time to wish him goodbye.

Hemal called to say that her father died on the 13th, but she would be back in time for the play. I was apprehensive, as she was one of the main characters, and if she did not return in time, then Elvira had no choice but to play that role. We hoped that she would not let us down, though it would not be her fault. I understood that it was more important for her to be with her family, and follow the usual traditions of burying her loved one, than taking part in a play.

On Sunday, the 14th, rehearsals were well underway from one o'clock, as we had a dress rehearsal. I was glad to see that everyone turned up except Rathna. Misaka and Theji, who were overseas for a month, were more than ready now. I was quite weary dealing with the antics and egos of some of the players. And for some reason, that day of all days, Erica was moody, and very difficult.

The lighting and sound man, Pat King, whom the council recommended, rushed in for ten minutes, just to say he was unable to do the lighting, and we had to find someone else! This setback, only one week away from opening, was unfortunate. But he quoted a very high figure for his services, and Elvira said we could not pay so much.

The following Tuesday, Elvira, John, and I, met the sound technician at the theatre. He told us that the microphones would be suspended above the stage, so they would not be in the way, which was what we wanted, and paid him for. That week was certainly hectic, as I had so many last minute details to organize.

On Saturday, the 20th, I made platters of food for the cast, and some more props. I was in charge of production, prompting, stage-managing, props, and all the minor details involved in such an ambitious, though amateur project. Unfortunately, we had minor altercations with some of the actors, who wanted to direct the play according to their liking, and I was usually in the middle of disagreements, as they brought these issues to my attention. They did not approach Elvira. But looked upon me, as the "chosen one" to pour oil on troubled waters. And to keep the cast happy, when tempers were frayed, and first-timers suffered jitters as the approaching performance loomed on the horizon.

Elvira's brother, Dario, agreed to film the play, as he was a professional cameraman, working for channel 2. Hemal was filming it as well, and we thought we had everything under control. I asked Connie to collect the ticket money at the front door, to which he agreed. That was the most useful task he could do that day, instead of trying to help backstage.

I woke up early on the long-awaited day, Sunday, 21 October. It was mild and cool when I drove to Mount Eliza at ten o'clock in the morning. Connie said he would come an hour before the play started at two o'clock. To my surprise, thousands of cyclists pedalled along Nepean Highway, as it was the annual ride to the city! They slowed down traffic considerably, and the cars dragged behind them. But I arrived there in good time, as we scheduled a dress rehearsal before the play began.

Simon, the accompanist, came early too, and we stood outside shivering in the cold. Elvira had the key, and she was not there as yet. I did not bring a warm coat, thinking the hall had heating, and now braved the cold. I was relieved when Rathna turned up in time for the dress rehearsal, and we had just enough time to fine-tune everything with the entire cast.

The sound technician disappointed us greatly. Because he set up five microphones on stands right in front of the stage, and did not suspend them as he said he would. He had all sorts of excuses, and said he did not have an assistant for lighting either. And he told us at the eleventh hour that he could not get anyone else, and whether one of us could manage the lights. He charged $450 for doing absolutely nothing! Elvira's son, Louis, agreed to control the lighting, and the man gave him a crash course. We just hoped for the best.

Some of the actors came early, and Rathna had returned from Sri Lanka only the night before, after her father's funeral. She looked calm, and assured me she would be fine to go ahead, as she learnt her lines on the plane. She had an important role, and one song to sing as well.

The audience streamed in from one thirty onwards. Connie arrived a little earlier, and sat in the foyer looking distant and stressed.

When I went up to discuss something, he looked at me vaguely, and greeted me briefly. I asked him what was wrong, and he said some work issues came up, and he was on the phone all morning. Also, that the cycle marathon was in progress down Nepean Highway, and he was delayed getting to Mount Eliza. I told him that I too was delayed about twenty minutes, but arrived in good time, and so had he, so to stop worrying and relax now.

I left him to his task, and went around greeting friends I knew and others who were now drifting in. Shirani and Ranjith arrived about half an hour early and took their seats. We were very pleased to see over two hundred and fifty people in the audience, waiting to be entertained, and we kept our fingers crossed. The dress rehearsal went well, and everyone was pretty confident. When the curtain went up, and the music started, the audience relaxed, and so did the actors, as they slipped into their roles effortlessly.

Simon played the piano superbly, and Erica sang like an angel. In short, we were very proud of our actors, because they did their very best that day, and I did not have to prompt one single line, which was truly amazing. During intermission, many people came over to tell me how much they enjoyed the first act, and could hardly wait for the second act to begin.

The president of St Vincent's Society came too. And all Elvira's brothers, and her sister, Mary, sat in the front row; one of her brother's, and his wife, flew in from Queensland. Some of my friends, just to name a few who came, were Liz, Vanessa, Tracy, Sarah, Joelle, Beat, Con, Cornelia, Karen and Stuart, Mary and Peter, Christina and her friends. And they were full of praise for the actors.

The hall was packed, and we knew it was a success right to the end, when the audience applauded the players enthusiastically. We worked so hard, and it was well worth it. Elvira made a speech at the end, and a quick counting behind scenes, totalled to an amount of $2500 on ticket sales, which she promised to donate to St Vincent's, after deductions for hall hire etc.

Then she asked me to step forward, and said, "And I'd like to introduce this special lady, because without her, it wouldn't have been possible to stage this play today." I thanked her briefly for her kind words, but did not say much, as Elvira already mentioned the players' great work.

Once the crowd left, we celebrated with a couple of bottles of champagne, and nibbles I prepared. More than two years of planning, and rehearsing finally paid off, and we could not have been happier. I thanked each one of the actors profusely, as they were the ones who carried the day, performing to the best of their ability. Even John, who was persuaded to act as grandfather, and an uncle, did a creditable job.

When I came home in the evening, I could hardly stand, as I was on my feet from ten o'clock in the morning, without sitting down even once. I felt as if I was walking on broken glass. Though I wore wedge-heels, the shoes pinched my aching feet. Now I knew how the little mermaid must have felt! I spent the evening soaking my feet in warm water, and applying Chinese ointment.

The phone rang constantly all evening, as many friends wanted to congratulate me. Shirani said it was much better than most of the school productions she had seen, so it was a great feeling to achieve our goal.

We picked up the statue of Our Lady from Elvira's next day, as one of the parishioners lent the statue to anyone who wanted to have it in their home for a week.

Elvira and I planned a "Thank You" lunch for the players, who devoted so much of their time and talent for so long. I said I would have high tea on the same day, so we could all meet at my place, and watch the DVD of the play that Dario had recorded.

When I was at school on Monday, all those who came to the play, commended me, and said they really enjoyed the afternoon. I sold tickets to some ladies, Carol and Billie at Bentons Square shops. They too were enthusiastic about the play, and asked if I would stage another production soon, and I replied, "Wait and see."

Ninette left a message in the evening, asking me to call her back. Elvira and I did not discuss the play with Ninette, as she was negative about it, when Elvira asked Isobel to help produce it. I just mentioned briefly, that Elvira was staging the play, but she did not know of my involvement in the production. When I called Ninette back, she said Luigi's daughter, Anna, died of an overdose last morning. She was only forty-two years old, and was on drugs for the last eighteen years or so.

Jackie drove from Craigieburn at midnight, to pick Luigi and drop him at the airport, as he flew to Perth for the funeral. I was shaken to the core at such shocking news. I met Anna a few years ago, when she stayed with Ninette for some time, and I invited Ninette and her for lunch. Anna mentioned her troubled past whenever we conversed, and how she never got on with Luigi, who left her mother when Anna was only two years old. I had a very disturbed night, thinking of these tragic people.

Ninette told me that Luigi returned in a couple of days time, as the funeral could not take place until the autopsy was finalised. I said a decade of the rosary in front of Our Lady's statue, as I did ever since we brought it home, and prayed especially for Anna's soul that day.

Luigi flew back to Perth to be there with the family, and Anna's funeral was finally arranged for 1 November. Jackie accompanied Luigi to Perth the day before the funeral.

I was at school on Thursday, 1 November, and when I came home, Chris Del Piano, and his brother, Andrew, were fixing the ceiling on the pergola outside. He did a perfect job as always, and waited till Connie came home to collect his cheque. I served them coffee and biscuits inside, as it was very gusty, and the wind did not ease till next day.

Chapter 70

Connie's behaviour was stranger than ever, towards the end of October that year. He told me that he was constantly agitated, and lost his temper with contractors and his boss. He was always aggressive, but it was more evident now at the slightest provocation.

He drove to Albury one day, and returned that same night, and said that he lost patience with a contractor on the way, and yelled at the top of his voice, until he felt ill. When he arrived in Albury, and had to do a presentation at a store, he could not talk. The manager brought him a glass of water, and waited until he regained his composure. I replied, "You shouldn't lose your temper so easily, and try to stop yelling so much. I'm sure you must have damaged your vocal chords, when you shouted so loudly at the man." He just scowled and did not reply.

Some people started to notice that his speech was slurred, and when we visited Shirani, Ranjith mentioned that Connie's speech was not normal. I did not notice it particularly, as he only slurred over certain words, and it was more noticeable when he drank too much. When I told him this, he became angry. But I knew that when he drank too much, and became agitated, then his speech was slurred, so I did not worry about it.

Con and Cornelia came for dinner on 3 November, and left after midnight, but Laura said she could not make it, as she was busy constructing a pergola at her place with some friends.

Connie played golf with Pat and Graham next morning, and when they came back at midday, I had pan rolls and cutlets warming in the oven, which they enjoyed very much.

When we attended Mass at Frankston that evening, some friends, Dean and Emilia, congratulated me, and said they enjoyed the play very much.

Bishop Elliot said Mass that evening, as the Youth Group invited him to give a talk afterwards, but we did not stay to hear him.

I visited Ninette after school on 7 November, as she was very depressed, and said she needed company, so I stayed with her for an hour. That night, when I watched the news, I was very glad to hear that President Obama was re-elected! He would have more time to do all he promised to do (hopefully).

After many weeks, I received a letter from Consumer Affairs, saying that the cancellation was now in effect, and Authors Australia Inc. was no more. I was relieved, as it took them so long to send me this cancellation letter. That matter was settled now. I could put it behind me, and concentrate on my own pursuits, without unnecessary stress and trouble with egocentric, obnoxious people.

We attended a charity lunch at Frankston Yacht Club on Sunday, 11 November. Mary and Tony came too, and we met Connie's old boss, Norm, and his wife, Pat, once again. She said Norm was very ill, and found it difficult to remember things, as he was about ninety or more then. We had a pleasant afternoon, and on our way home, we dropped in at Billie's place in Mornington, and returned Our Lady's statue after one week.

Connie drove to Albury again the following day. He called me twice that night, because he was annoyed and said, "I'm tired of driving so far, and sick of this job!" I just listened to him complaining about everything and everyone, and went to bed after midnight, as I had many things to do. I edited my manuscript "An Eternal Summer," as AuthorHouse was publishing a second edition.

When I left Ninette's place next afternoon, a lady from Bright called me on my mobile. She said that she was browsing through my website, and liked my painting of "Bright In Autumn" very much, and could she print it in a local magazine for a fee? I was very happy to hear that, and she asked if the painting was for sale, and how much it would cost. I said I would get back to her, and felt quite elated at such an offer.

I emailed her a picture of the painting, with the price tag, and waited for her response. She emailed a day later, saying she found another picture for the magazine, and did not want to buy the painting either. I suppose she was reluctant to spend any money on it. As she owned a hotel in Bright, she wanted to advertise her place using my painting. I did not care, as I really did not want to sell that painting, which was one of my favourites.

On our forty-second anniversary, on Sunday, 18 November, we watched "Hotel Transylvania" at the cinema in Karingal. I enjoyed the animated movie very much, as it was very funny, with Adam Sandler's voice as Count Dracula.

We held the "Thank You" lunch, and high tea for the cast, on Sunday, 25 November. Elvira cooked pasta, and I made rice and curry for about twenty people. We enjoyed lunch and the great company, then around three o'clock we all drove to my place for high tea. The ladies helped to serve food, and pour tea and coffee.

It was a lovely afternoon, and later, we all crowded into the music room to watch the DVD of the play. Even Connie sat quietly, and watched the play with us. The only disappointing aspect though, was the poor sound quality and crackling noises, as the microphones were not suspended. But we had a great deal of fun and laughter that day. I thanked everyone for their great contribution, and Elvira gave them each a copy of the DVD.

When I visited Ninette on the following Tuesday, Connie dropped in unexpectedly around three o'clock, just as I was leaving. Ninette was surprised to see him too, but as she was tired, she did not invite him in for a coffee. As we walked to the car I asked him why he did not call before he came. He got annoyed and started yelling, "So, what's wrong? I don't have to call anyway!" He felt embarrassed because Ninette did not invite him in for a coffee, but he did not want to admit he was in the wrong.

When he arrived home, I told him that it was not right to just drop in, as Ninette was not very well, and did not like to be surprised. He started shouting at me again, as if I was in the wrong. But that evening, I heard him call Ninette, and he apologized for dropping in without phoning first. Then he told me that she said he was welcome, just as long as she knew when he was coming, as she got very tired and needed to rest in the afternoons. He was somewhat mollified, and calmed down after that.

As days went by, I noticed that his slurred speech was getting worse. From then onwards, he consulted several doctors, including Dr Khelil, who referred him to specialists, as doctor suspected he had suffered a mild stroke.

Even his colleagues commented on his speech now, and joked about it, saying, "Hey, Conrad, have you been to the pub?" That made him very angry, as he said he never drank while at work. When we drove down to Woolamai on 1 December, Ranjith and Shirani noticed that Connie's speech was worse, and they too thought he had suffered a stroke.

The end of year piano concert was on Sunday, 9 December, and I woke up the previous day with vertigo and nausea. But I felt much better by Sunday, so I prepared last minute details.

It was a mild day, and while Connie arranged the chairs, I went out to cut some hydrangeas for a vase that I wanted to arrange on top of the piano. I left the door keys on the table inside, and did not realize that Connie too went outside. Too late, the door slammed behind us, and we were locked out, with only half an hour till starting time! The two priests were out too, and we were unable to contact anyone else who had a spare key. He started to grumble, "I *always* keep the keys in my pocket, this has never happened before! *Why* didn't you give me the keys?"

The children and their parents arrived shortly, and when I explained our predicament, they tried to find a way in. The kitchen window, which was the only window that was slightly ajar, was very small. But one of the little boys somehow managed to wriggle through and opened the front door for us. To my relief all went well, even though we were a few minutes behind schedule, and Sarah, who was the guest star, performed well.

Fr Denis arrived just as we finished, and when I told him about our mishap, he laughed it off, and did not mind the forced entry through the kitchen window. But he said, "You will be on the security camera!" So, that was the first and last time I experienced such an unfortunate incident. Connie was subdued right through the proceedings, and did not speak much to anyone, as he was self-conscious about his slurred speech now.

I attended the Christmas break-up party and farewell to Sue, one of the teachers, on 14 December. Maree, the previous principal, came too, and we had a long chat. She was concerned to hear about Connie's speech problem, and told me she would say a prayer for us. It was good to see many familiar faces from the past, as they all came to wish Sue farewell.

Elvira invited us to spend New Year's Eve at her place again. Erica's parents and boyfriend were due to arrive from Italy soon, and were staying with them for a month or so. We accepted her invitation, as Mary, Tony, and Daphne were coming too, and it would be a pleasant evening.

Elvira and I were sipping coffee at Onde's just before Christmas, when a lady walked in and bought a copy of my book "An Eternal Summer," which Gerry had placed on the shelf inside. When he introduced me, the lady was very happy, and asked if I would sign the book, which I did.

I watched Nelune on television next day, as she stood with the Governor General at the cancer hospital. I called her later and congratulated her on her marvellous achievements.

When we attended Sunday morning Mass on the 23rd, we saw only John. He said Elvira and their guests were resting, as it was a long journey and they were up all night. I greeted Myra, and wished her for Christmas, but when I tried to speak to Billie, she was very abrupt and rude. I was surprised at her manner, and did not say anything as I left, but wondered how people could behave like that, especially in church.

That evening, Billie called, and kept apologizing for her rude behaviour. I did not know what was wrong with her, so I replied, "It's alright, I wasn't offended." But she was hysterical, and kept saying, "I'm so *sorry*, I don't know what came over me." I listened patiently, but when I hung up, I wondered what made some people tick. They cloak themselves in religious ardour, and somewhere along the way, lose touch with reality. And they forget how to live in *this* world, as they are too busy scrambling for a place in the next.

I cooked all the traditional Christmas favourites on the weekend, then spent about four hours making pan rolls. We left home at four thirty, for the children's Mass at five o'clock on Christmas Eve, as we expected Christian and Athena for dinner that night.

Although we managed to get two seats at the front, because we were there early, the church soon became so crowded that some people sat outside on the lawn as well. Connie gave up his seat next to me, and then went outside, so I did not see him till Mass was over. We came home by six thirty, and I took it easy and waited for Christian and Athena.

They arrived around nine thirty in the night, although they said they would try to get here an hour earlier, but were delayed. We enjoyed our time together, and had a pleasant night, in spite of Connie's non-stop harping about his speech problem. That was his only topic of conversation, and we listened sympathetically right through dinner, and until they left. We knew he was very worried, and confused about what was happening to him.

His speech was worse now, and it was difficult to understand some words. Christian and Athena urged him to consult a specialist as soon as possible, to check if he had suffered a mild stroke. I told them he had already seen a few doctors over the past month, but none of them were able to diagnose his condition.

All the specialists were away till mid-January, as it was Christmas, so we were unable to do much until then. But I told him that he should see a speech therapist, because many people regained normal speech after a stroke. But the doctors he consulted so far, were unsure if it was a stroke or not, even though he went for several tests. We had to be patient now, until he saw a specialist in the New Year. I tried to reassure him, and help him through this difficult time.

He told me that he felt a tightening in his stomach, and he could not breathe, which resulted in his speech problems. I tried to comfort him, saying that once we knew the diagnosis, he should see a speech therapist to help him regain normal speech. But he was more depressed than before, and very unhappy about this unexpected situation, which added to the problem.

Christmas day was pleasant and sunny, and in the mid-twenties, so we drove down to Woolamai at midday, and enjoyed the afternoon. Roshan, June, and the children were there, and so was Suresh. Connie did not let up about his speech problem all afternoon, and they too urged him to see a specialist as soon as possible. Shirani advised him to go into the emergency section, and let them do all the tests, instead of waiting to see a specialist in late January. He agreed to do so, and we left after five o'clock.

I had a slight headache by the time we came home that evening. When I called Shirani to thank her for lunch, she said she enjoyed the pan rolls too, and told me not to worry too much about Connie. I watched some comedies and took it easy. But Connie was very restless all night, and groaned and moaned in his sleep. I had no rest, and woke up at five o'clock in the morning. When I asked him what was wrong, he said he had nightmares all night.

We drove to Keysborough to visit Con and Cornelia in the afternoon, on Boxing Day. They told him that their Rumanian doctor was very good, and Connie should consult him soon, so he agreed to see their doctor. On our way home, we dropped in to wish Ninette, who seemed slightly brighter, and in good spirits. I made mango chutney when we came home, as mangoes were in season, and I bottled quite a few jars.

Connie was due to start work on 27 December, so he was unable to go to emergency that morning. Mathew, his boss, refused to approve his leave over the holiday season, and told him to take time off later on in the year. Connie was very annoyed over that, and complained bitterly about how unfair Mathew was. In past years, he always took a week or two off during Christmas, because it was not a very busy time of the year. He drove to work on the 27th, and then told Mathew he was feeling unwell. So, he went to the emergency unit at Monash Medical Centre in Clayton.

I was unaware of his intentions till later that day, and tried calling him on his mobile all afternoon to see how he was doing. But it was diverted, and Mathew answered. He asked me, "Is there any news from Conrad, as I don't know where he is!" I told him I had not heard from him either, and that was the reason why I rang his mobile.

Connie called at six o'clock, and said that they kept him in hospital all day, and did various tests on him. But discharged him in the evening, as they were positive he did not have a brain tumour, or suffered a stroke. I was very relieved, so was he, but we still had no answers as to why his speech was slurred.

Instead of coming home then, he told me he was visiting his Aunty Ella in Clayton. I did not ask why he wanted to visit them so late in the evening, without coming home and resting. But quite honestly, I did not understand what made him tick, as he seldom visited his aunt and uncle (as far as I knew), unless he saw them on his way to work and did not tell me. He was not very close to them at all. It was after eight o'clock when he finally arrived home, and he did not talk much. The hospital staff had advised him to consult a neurologist as soon as possible.

He was too tired to go to work the following day, and stayed home. That afternoon, we watched part one of "The Hobbit" at the cinema in Karingal. The queue was very long, but we had pre-paid tickets, so we were able to get in without delay. The movie was great, but too many battle scenes for my liking, and the screenplay was not exactly like the book. Still, it was a fantastic adaptation, and I enjoyed it very much. And I looked forward to seeing the second part, which was due in a couple of years time.

We decided to see "Skyfall," next Saturday afternoon, as Connie did not want to miss new releases. So, we watched it on the following weekend, and I found it to be a very violent, noisy movie right to the end. I failed to understand why the reviews said it was the "*best*" Bond movie yet. It was all hype and no substance. I was disappointed, and so was Connie.

In the meantime, his speech grew steadily worse. When he was on the phone to colleagues and contractors, they joked, "Are you at the pub Conrad? You *sound* like you've had a few!" He found this very upsetting, as he did not like people to think he was drinking on the job, especially as it was Christmas time, and some of them did enjoy a few beers during working hours.

Bishop Dennis Hart celebrated Sunday morning Mass on 30 December, as Fr Joe invited him to consecrate the new marble altar. It was a very long, tedious service, and we came home after one o'clock. I swept away all the cobwebs inside and out, in preparation for New Year, like I faithfully did every year. Thathie always cleaned out cobwebs before the start of New Year, because he said it was bad luck to have cobwebs in and around the house.

Sherone and Glen visited with Valerie, Amber, and Tristan, just before five o'clock that day, although they said they would be here an hour earlier. It was their first visit here, but they were quite taciturn, and did not comment favourably on the new house, or splendid ocean views. One of them looked out of the backyard and said, "*All* the houses look into each other's backyards!" I replied, "We don't mind, as we all have great views anyway." They did not stay long, as they wanted to attend evening Mass at Frankston, but they were concerned about Connie's speech, and thought he had suffered a stroke.

I did some shopping on the 31st afternoon, and then wished Nilanthi, as we were spending the evening at Elvira's place. Then I made fried rice to take there for dinner, and milk rice and beef curry for breakfast next morning. We drove down at eight thirty, and had a barbeque out in the gazebo, and everyone enjoyed the fried rice too.

Erica's parents and boyfriend did not speak English at all, but we had a good time anyway. We played "fun bingo" from eleven o'clock till midnight, then toasted with champagne. Everyone sang "Auld Lang Syne" as we greeted the New Year, and finally returned home after ushering in 2013.

Chapter 71

After an ample breakfast in traditional Sri Lankan style, we watched "Le Miserable" in the afternoon at the cinema in Karingal. It was excellent, and I enjoyed it very much, but I was very tired after preparing meals, and staying up late the previous night. So, I was content to put my feet up and take it easy. But Connie was in an irascible mood all evening, and kept complaining about everything. He was unhappy, because we did not entertain or visit anyone that night.

Sometimes, when his siblings called him, he did not tell me what they discussed. But if he spoke to one of them, he was annoyed and irritable with me for the rest of the day. I gathered that they gossiped about some family matter, which he did not want me to know.

When I served fried rice and beef curry for dinner, he demanded angrily, "Is *that* all we're having for *New Year's* dinner? We should have gone out!" I replied, "What *more* do you want? We've been out last night, and this afternoon, and this is a *good* meal. *Thank* God, and eat your dinner without complaining!" He muttered and cursed, as he banged pots and pans around, and he was just impossible that night.

I tried very hard to be patient, as I knew he was very worried about his health. He was irritable all the time, even worse than he was before. But we could not do anything until he saw a specialist, who could diagnose his condition.

When I returned from Ninette's the following afternoon, Connie was weeding and cleaning up the garden. He stumbled inside a few minutes later, rubbed his back, and blurted. "I lost balance and fell over backwards!" I was concerned and said, "May be you had a touch of dizziness? *Don't* stay out in the sun, it's too hot." He mumbled, "No, that's not it, I just slipped and fell. I wasn't dizzy, I don't know what's *wrong* with me, I don't have *strength* to even pull out the weeds!"

I felt very sorry for him, as he was always so energetic, and enjoyed gardening before. So I said, "Don't worry about the garden, till you feel better." I did not get much sleep that night, as Connie was very restless, and kept shouting in his sleep. His voice sounded hoarse and guttural now, and it was very distressing to hear him groaning. I asked him what was wrong, but he just muttered, "I don't know!"

It was forty one degrees next day, so I stayed in, as it was too hot to go out. Connie took it easy too and stayed in bed, as he was tired after a restless night. We ordered a pizza for dinner, as I did not want to cook, even though it cooled down slightly. He still behaved very strangely, and I did not know why he was more aggressive than ever before.

I hoped he would see a specialist soon, because he was very frustrated, not knowing what was wrong with him. I felt very upset and down-hearted, to see his behaviour getting worse than ever, and was unable to understand the reason why. He was irrational, aggressive, and totally devoid of any sensitivity towards me, more so than before.

Del was visiting on 11 January, but she had an accident, and drove into a brick wall because of a faulty accelerator. Fortunately, she was uninjured, but she said she would not have a car for some time, so I was very sorry for that mishap. I called Judy and said I would visit soon, as she was not in good health, and I did not see her for some time.

I drove to Mornington on Saturday morning to service my car, and came home in a courtesy car, then picked up mine a couple of hours later. Connie went out too, but called to say that Esme wanted to visit that afternoon. I was cleaning and vacuuming when he called me, and much to my annoyance, the vacuum just packed up. So I swept and mopped the kitchen area instead. Esme, Paul, and her brother, Paul, Sanit, and their four-year old daughter, Yasmin, came around four thirty.

Sanit did not speak English well, but she managed to communicate with me through sign language and a few words. After a while, Esme and Paul told me that Clifford had made lewd phone calls to Sanit, which she recorded, and scandal was widespread in the family. Struggling to explain in broken English, Sanit said, "He want sex with me!"

When she told Paul about it, and he confronted Clifford, Geraldine visited Sanit, and told her off severely. And she accused Sanit of "leading" him on. Sanit was very upset, and told me, "*If* Jenny Christian woman, I *happy* I Buddhist!" While this conversation was going on, Connie was not interested at all. He was concerned only about his speech problem, and wanted everyone to focus on him.

Paul and Esme told me repeatedly, "*Don't* have anything to do with Clifford, and don't entertain him in your house! We have heard a lot of things about him, and what he's been up to. if Jenny wants to turn a blind eye, that's her business." We attended evening Mass when they left, and came home late. I had a bout of vertigo then, and hoped it would not get worse, as the situation with Connie was getting too much for me.

We visited Mary and Tony next day, before driving to Dromana in the afternoon. Connie wanted to look at houses for sale, and we walked around for a long time. He said we should buy another place before he retired, so we could sell our current house and move into a smaller place in a few years time. So we looked around for suitable houses.

Although he made an appointment with a specialist on 15 January, Connie consulted Dr Khelil again. When he came home that evening, he went on a rampage; abusing, accusing, and behaving like a wounded bull. Then he blasted the CD player so loud till one o'clock in the morning, that I thought the amplifier would blow up again. He did not tell me what was wrong, but raged like a tormented soul.

I saw doctor next morning, as I thought my pressure was high. And I told him how stressed I was with Connie's situation, and not knowing what was wrong with him. He said he hoped that the specialist would have some answers soon, and asked me to take care, as he knew I was undergoing a great deal of strain.

When I came home after visiting Ninette on Tuesday, he had returned from the specialist's in Dandenong. He said they did a MRI scan, but failed to find any sign of a stroke; the specialist suspected it was a problem with his vocal chords, and referred him to *another* specialist in Frankston.

Nelune called on 18 January, and said that the temperature soared to forty six degrees in Sydney, the highest in one hundred and fifty years! She said that it was unbearable outside, but quite cool inside her apartment, so I was relieved, and told her to take care.

We drove to Harvey Norman's in Mornington on Saturday morning, and bought a vacuum, as the old one was beyond repair. On our way home, he was irritable as usual, and lost his temper when a female driver whizzed past us. And he barked out, "*Women* drivers are the *worst* drivers! See how that woman overtook me!" "You can't say *all* women drivers, it's only *some* women who are bad drivers," I replied reasonably, as it was true, but I was shocked when he shouted at the top of his voice, "*You*....you....! *Why* do you *always* disagree with what I say?" And on and on, accusations, insults all the way home.

My head throbbed, as I listened to his non-stop tirade, but I did not reply, as there was nothing to say. I had a severe headache all evening and next day, so I did not go to church, but he went on his own. This church-going was his *panacea*, no matter how badly he behaved, he had to go to church on Sundays. But I resented his incongruous behaviour, which was not Christian-like at all. He failed to see anything wrong in the way he treated me, as if the whole world and I were to blame for his misery.

I finished editing "An Eternal Summer," and submitted the manuscript to AuthorHouse on 24 January. I was relieved to finally finish it, as I worked on it for a few months. I caught up with a few friends over the next few days for coffee at Mornington or Frankston.

We watched "The Life Of Pi," at the cinema on 27 January, and I enjoyed the movie very much. It was about a young Indian man shipwrecked with a Bengali tiger as his companion. It was beautifully photographed, with the two unlikely survivors in a small boat.

Elvira invited us for a coffee, so we dropped in there after the movie, and Connie told them what a great movie it was, and they should see it too. Alessandro was there on a short visit, as he now lived in Sydney. He too was concerned when he heard Connie's slurred speech, and wanted to know what was wrong. Connie replied, "Something wrong with my throat muscles."

Shirani, Ranjith, Roshan, and the children visited next day, and we had a good time, as we did not see Roshan and the children for more than one year. Connie sipped a beer outside, and he told them how he shouted at a contractor in October last year, about the time his speech was affected. He shouted so loud to demonstrate, that Roshan and the children were worried and looked shocked. Connie laughed and said, "*That's* the way I shouted at him, and from that time I think I must have damaged my vocal chords!"

Babs visited later, and she arrived just after Shirani and family left at four o'clock. She looked very tired and haggard, and told us that she was in the early stages of multiple sclerosis. But I sincerely hoped not, as she was such an active person.

She told Connie, "You mustn't look so miserable son, whatever it is, you must *try* to look pleasant, because the world has to look at your face!" She could not have spoken a truer word. I nodded in agreement, as he looked so *very* miserable all the time, and scowled for no reason. When she left, he mowed the lawn, after several weeks. Physically, he looked robust, and it was only his speech that was getting worse.

Cornelia, Con, and Laura were coming for lunch on Wednesday, 30 January, and visit the Mornington market too, so I was ready from nine o'clock. It was a beautiful, sunny day with blue skies and sea. Although I expected them to come early, they arrived at midday. We had cutlets and coffee, then went to the market around one 'clock.

Con and Connie stayed back, as they wanted to play golf at Mount Martha golf course. When we returned in a couple of hour's time, they were still at home, and decided not to play golf. We finished lunch after five thirty, then we sat on the deck and enjoyed the lovely weather. They left after seven o'clock, and I was very tired, but pleased that they enjoyed the day.

Connie consulted *another* doctor in Dandenong, on Saturday, 2 February, as Con recommended him. He visited Roland afterwards, and came home in time to go for evening Mass. He was very disappointed, as that doctor could not diagnose what was wrong with him either.

After visiting Ninette on Tuesday, 5 February, I drove back on the new Peninsula Link freeway. And it took about fifteen minutes from Karingal to Mount Martha, which was excellent. I liked the new freeway very much, and used it regularly after that, as it was much better and quicker than travelling on Nepean Highway.

Connie was on annual leave from 8 February. Mathew told him that he hoped his speech would improve by the time he returned from leave, as they had trouble understanding him in the last few weeks. From the first day of his leave, he went out in the morning, and came home late in the evening. But I did not ask him where he went, as he just shouted at me, whenever I asked him anything.

Joelle, Celine, and Micheline visited on Saturday afternoon, but Connie went out just before they arrived, and did not see them. We had a pleasant time, and as they left, Elvira came at three thirty, to practice a few songs for the choir. She sang for one hour or so, and then he came home in time to go for Mass.

I accompanied Connie to Frankston on 12 February, to get the neurologist's report, as he did more tests on Connie. The results were alright, and once again he assured him. "No sign of a stroke or brain tumour, but the throat muscles seem to be affected. I will refer you to another neurologist in Monash." I asked him, "Do you think speech therapy would help?" He replied, "Yes, after Conrad sees the neurologist at Monash, he can start speech therapy."

As we left the surgery, Connie turned to me and said, "I'm *sure* I must be having multiple sclerosis, as *something* is definitely wrong with me!" I was very upset, and replied, "*Why* can't you be thankful you haven't had a stroke, and you have no brain tumour, instead of thinking you have MS? Anyway, wait until you see the other neurologist, and then you can start speech therapy."

I was convinced he must have hurt his throat muscles, the way he shouted all the time. And fervently hoped that with rest and speech therapy he would be cured. We dropped in at Shirani's place in Narre Warren afterwards, and she pressed us to have lunch, which was delicious. We enjoyed some time together, and when I told them what the neurologist said, and how Connie thought he had MS, they too urged him not to be negative, and to hope for the best.

Then we drove to Dandenong for an appointment with the financial advisor, and he gave us an honest appraisal of our current situation. Unfortunately, Connie did not realise that when he turned sixty-five, he was not covered for any disability, or death benefits by his employer. This came as a severe shock to him. He had always assured me that in case of illness or death, his company would pay a substantial percentage of his wages, because he contributed to this insurance policy since 1991.

He did not have enough superannuation either, to draw a comfortable income in retirement. When the cards were on the table, the financial planner said Connie had to apply for the age pension, if his health did not improve, and he was compelled to retire. We still had to pay off the house in Mt Martha, and the unit in Queensland. Now we decided to sell the unit, even though it was not a very good time to sell. When we came away from that meeting, we were very worried, and Connie looked dejected.

I knew the future looked shaky, but was confident that we would find a solution. I could not believe that Connie would be forced to retire, and what would he do for the rest of his life? Then we drove to Karingal and met the bank manager at Westpac. We asked him what we should do about our repayments etc. and received some worthwhile advice.

It was after six o'clock when we came home that day, and I was mentally and physically worn-out, as it was a very long day. Connie had a few drinks as usual, and we watched some comedies in the evening. We did not discuss our financial matters that night, as we were too distraught to think clearly.

After he consulted the neurologist, Sue, at Monash a few days later, he did not ask me to accompany him when he went for the results. When he came home though, he said that Sue had asked, "Conrad, where is your wife? I would have liked her to be here with you today, as I'm very sorry to tell you that you have progressive supra-nuclear palsy; a very rare condition affecting one in a hundred thousand Australians."

Connie was sceptical when he told me about the diagnosis, as we had never heard of this disease before. He immediately decided to get a second and third opinion, as he wanted answers, and a quick cure for his speech impediment. When I read about it on Google, I was devastated, as no treatment or cure was available for this terrible disease.

David Niven, the famous actor, succumbed to a virulent form of the disease, and died within one year. Gradual loss of speech, and movement was inevitable. Connie manifested most of the symptoms, including sudden falls. I now began to understand his increased aggression, irrational behaviour, and personality changes, as he could be suffering from early onset of dementia too.

Patients diagnosed with this condition, usually lived up to five or six years. Perhaps Connie was already in an advanced stage of the disease, as he had manifested some symptoms for a few years now, but was diagnosed only when his speech was affected.

Connie read about the disease too, but remained unconvinced, and did not want to accept her diagnosis. Instead, he consulted two more neurologists, and a throat specialist, desperately seeking some other diagnosis, and a cure. I was very distressed to hear him slurring badly now, as if his tongue was swollen, and he could hardly articulate. I fervently hoped and prayed he would be cured with speech therapy.

Physically, nothing else seemed to be wrong at this stage, except his speech; and for someone who talked non-stop, it was the worst possible thing that could have happened. It was heart-breaking to hear him struggle to say even a few simple words coherently.

The weather was scorching, as a heat wave continued day after day, with temperatures reaching high thirties, and no relief in sight. In the meantime, I kept very busy as usual, trying hard not to dwell on this calamity.

Even though I showed Connie every ounce of sympathy and love, and was as patient as possible with him, if he was difficult to live with before, it was ten times worse now, as he battled with this unknown disease. And fear drove all reason out of his mind.

I understood his frustration, anger, and disbelief, that he was struck down with such a rare and terrible disease. But he went into total denial, and believed he would get better, and return to work soon. So he consulted several specialists, and I understood how desperate he was for answers.

I suffered from on-going dizzy spells, and head colds then, even though the weather was so hot. And I was extremely stressed with the whole situation, as I bore the brunt of Connie's frustration and anger at what had happened to him. He was sore as an injured bear most of the time, and very rarely showed even a glimmer of sympathy for me. He did not acknowledge, or understand how difficult it was for me to watch his pain, and to be totally helpless to alleviate his suffering.

Sometimes he said, "Sorry Dolla," when he knew he had gone too far, and hurt me for no reason at all. But I was fed up with his apologies, because within minutes he reverted to the same old behaviour. The only time we relaxed together, was when we watched a movie or comedies in the evening. He laughed and enjoyed himself, and forgot his worries for a little while.

His siblings started visiting regularly now. Roland and Shiranthi, who did not visit since we moved to Mt Martha, and Geraldine, who was never close to Connie before, now called constantly, sent text messages, or visited.

Roland and Geraldine, "self-appointed emissaries of the Messiah," now promised Connie he would be "miraculously" healed, as nothing was wrong with him. Instead of helping him to face reality, they encouraged him in his denial, and to disbelieve anything doctors said. Geraldine told him, "Doctors are all devils! Don't listen to them!"

They visited whenever I was at school, but Babs, Esme, and Paul, dropped in on some weekends when I was home. They sympathised with me, whenever Connie lost his temper and yelled at me in front of them.

Elvira visited often on weekends, with home-baked scones or cakes, and was a great support. Shirani, Ranjith, Roshan, and family, visited a few times on Sundays, as Shirani was busy with the restaurant, and came to Narre Warren for a couple of days only. They were concerned that Connie's speech was worse now, and to hear what the diagnosis was. But Connie pretended that doctors still did not know what was wrong with him.

Many mutual friends started visiting almost every weekend, and he had medical appointments every week. One Saturday, after he saw another doctor in Dandenong, and visited Roland afterwards, he came home in time to attend the five thirty Mass in Frankston. As they held a healing Mass there every three weeks, I suggested we attend that. Because he now wanted to attend healing services held in "Born again" churches. Roland and Geraldine constantly urged him to attend their churches.

Since he was on leave, Connie went for several medical appointments over the next few days. He woke up early on that first Monday morning when he was on leave, and drove out somewhere, and returned home late in the evening. And this pattern continued all the time he was on leave. He did not want to stay home, relax, go fishing, or play golf with his friends any longer. All he wanted to do now was visit his siblings. As some of them, who were "Born again" Christians, convinced him that he would be miraculously healed, if he attended their churches, and followed their beliefs. He clutched at straws now, though prior to his illness, he always denounced his siblings for breaking away from the Catholic faith.

I was an outsider now, as he became more and more distant, and he did not think it necessary to tell me where he went or what he did, which was very hurtful. But I avoided conflict, as I did not want to make him angry, or be shouted at.

We lived separate lives. I had my work, and interests to keep me busy, and as he had nothing else to devote his time to, except visit his siblings and relatives, I left him alone. Some years ago, he told his relatives that when he retired, he would spend all his time visiting them. So, he was doing what he liked best, and if it made him happy, so be it.

I worked on a stage play, *and* a screen play of "Catsville," so I escaped upstairs to my "retreat area," and buried myself in work; writing was always therapeutic when I wanted to get away from problems. He sometimes climbed upstairs, looked over my shoulder, and demanded, "*What* are you doing, are you on the Internet?" I replied irritably, "I'm *writing*!" Then he asked me to do something for him, anything, as long as it took me away from the computer and my writing.

He went out early on Ash Wednesday, 13 February, and returned at five thirty in the evening. As usual, he did not say where he went, or what he did for so long. I was ready to go for Ash Wednesday service at Mornington that evening, and he said he came home in time to go to church. It was still very warm that night, and when I watched a movie later on, he joined me, although he did not say much. And I was pleased to see him relax for a couple of hours.

I spent Saturday morning cooking, as Julie, Paul, Linda, Leo, and the children were visiting next day, 17 February. We drove to Hampton Park that evening, to watch a Sinhalese drama at the local theatre. Rathna was acting in it, and sold me a couple of tickets. During interval we bought some snacks, and I bit on a vadai (spicy lentil cake), that was gritty, and one of my fillings came out. I was uncomfortable all night, but had to put up with the pain till I made an appointment with the dentist on Monday.

Our visitors arrived at midday, and we had a pleasant time as always. Linda and Leo did all the washing up, and Julie wiped and put the dishes away. It was after four o'clock when they left, and then Elvira dropped in soon after with home-baked goodies. She stayed and chatted a while, and then I took it easy, as I was worn-out after a late night and cooking.

The weather continued to soar, and it was thirty six degrees on the 18th, the day before Connie's birthday. I was at school on Monday, and stopped on my way home to get a gift voucher and card for him, and also to post Nelune's birthday card. When I came home I rested a while, as I was exhausted with the unbearable heat.

I wished Connie, and gave his presents next day. He told me he wanted to go out for lunch and then see a movie. But now he said, "I asked Tucko and Shiro to come over, as they wanted to wish me." I replied, "Did you tell them we're going out for lunch and a movie?" "Yes, they'll come early and leave soon." I was doubtful, as I knew we would not make it to the movie anyway, because they never came on time. It was his birthday though, and he could do whatever pleased him.

Just as I thought, it was after one o'clock when they arrived, and brought Benjamin's three-year old daughter with them. They stopped for take-away rice and curry in Dandenong, and by the time we finished lunch, it was well after two o'clock. When they left, Connie and I drove to Karingal, but his mood changed completely. He did not want to watch a movie, so we drove to Frankston, then came home, as he did not care to do anything else. We watched an old movie till late that night.

I made an appointment with the dentist next day to fix my broken filling, but Connie wanted to drop in at Esme's first, as she invited him. When we went there, she pressed us to have lunch, although we had eaten already. I had coffee, as she did not take no for an answer. Then we drove to the dentist at Mornington, and I had a headache all evening, after the local anaesthetic and drilling.

A few days later, we met the bank manager at Bendigo bank in Mornington. He advised us about an equity access loan, and made an appointment with one of their consultants. It was similar to a reverse mortgage, but much better, as he advised us against reverse mortgages. Connie dropped me at home after that, and returned after four o'clock in the afternoon. He had lunch at the Tanti Hotel in Mornington, which he liked very much, and said it was a great place.

I dropped him at Frankston hospital at six thirty that evening, as the specialist wanted him to do a sleep apnoea test. Connie complained about breathing difficulty at nights, and he snored very heavily too (although he refused to believe it). Whenever he snored loud, and I woke him up to ask him to turn over, he scowled and retorted, "So, *you* also snore, *I* don't snore!" I drove to the hospital at seven thirty to pick him the following morning. He said he hardly slept at all, and as soon as we came home, he went straight to bed.

It was my birthday that Saturday, 23 February, and we went for a dinner dance to Dromana bowling club, with Mary, Tony, Elvira, John, and Erica. While we were dancing, Connie stopped suddenly in the middle of the floor, and could not move his legs. Looking a little confused, he said, "I've forgotten *how* to dance!" I replied, "Let's go back to our table, I'm tired anyway."

When we sat down, he tried to make light of it, "It's some time since I danced and I've forgotten the steps." I thought he was just tired, and let it pass without further comment. None of the others noticed what happened, and we did not say anything.

Elvira baked a delicious cake for me, and she asked the band to sing "Happy Birthday," as we celebrated both our birthdays that night. I noticed that Connie did not look too good, as he seemed disoriented, and could not co-ordinate his movements. We left around ten thirty, and he drove back, as he did not want me to take over, even though I asked him if he was alright to drive.

It was another scorching thirty three degrees next day, and I watered the garden before going to Elvira's for a barbecue in the evening. It was Erica's farewell dinner, and she was returning to Italy in a few day's time. We had a great evening, and I asked Erica to come back again soon. She said she would love to, but missed her boyfriend and parents very much, as they had already left for Italy a few weeks ago.

After the sweltering weather we had endured, the heavens opened finally. And the welcome deluge continued, just as Connie planned to play golf with Graham and Pat. So he cancelled the game.

Early next day, he drove off to consult another specialist, and I did chores until he returned after three o'clock in the afternoon. He looked very subdued, but did not say much. The specialist did more tests, and told him he would let him know, once the results came back.

Erica was leaving on 1 March. On the day before, I dropped in after school to wish her, and gave her a little gift and card. She was happy, and very emotional, as she embraced and kissed me. I became very attached to her, as she had an outgoing, friendly personality. And I told her that I hoped to see her again very soon.

Connie hardly exchanged a few words with Erica all this time, and had nothing to do with her at all. But when I came home, and mentioned that I stopped to wish Erica, he immediately dialled Elvira's number, and told Erica, "I didn't know Nalini was going to visit you or else I would have come too!" He could hardly speak clearly now, and she found it difficult to understand him, but he still did not like to be left out. He visited anyone he wanted to on his own, but he disliked me visiting anyone without him.

We watched "Lincoln" at the cinema, on 1 March, and I enjoyed it immensely. Connie too said it was alright, but on our way back, he got into one of his cantankerous moods, and started to complain about everything; how *unfair* it was that his speech was affected, and he became very angry. I replied, "Just think positive, what else can you do now. You've been to so many specialists, be patient." He yelled back furiously, "*You* just don't get it do you?" I did not bother to ask him what he meant, and get into an argument. So, as usual, I kept silent all the way home, and let him rage against the unfairness of his fate.

My head throbbed. It always ended like this whenever we went out. And sometimes, I felt as if my brain was cudgelled persistently, when he barked and yelled at me. He did not show his anger to anyone else except me. I was told that it was natural he should lash out at the person closest to him, because he could not vent his frustration on anyone else.

After years of coping with his impossible behaviour, it now escalated to a crisis. I suffered insomnia almost every night, dizziness, and tightness in my chest, and knew I was very very stressed.

I tried my best to reach out to him, to show him I cared and sympathised, but it was not enough for him. He wanted an *instant* miracle, and clung desperately to some of his siblings. They promised him one, if he listened to faith healing CD's all day long, and attended their services.

I sometimes tried to reason with him, "As Catholics we should be *submissive* and ask God *humbly* to heal you, *if* it is God's will." But the "Born again" Christians *demanded* a miracle, and said they "claimed" the right to be healed (whether God willed it or not). I found such incredible arrogance in dealing with the Almighty, hard to accept. But Connie gradually drifted towards their church, and prayer meetings, hoping he would be cured.

We drove down to Woolamai on Sunday afternoon, 3 March, as Laura, Con, and Cornelia wanted to have lunch at Shirani's restaurant. It was Laura's birthday on the 28th, so we celebrated that special occasion. She brought another friend, Victor, along with her. We had a pleasant time, and after lunch, we drove to the old pub at Kilcunda for drinks and coffee. It was a beautiful, sunny day, and the deep blue sea sparkled in the warm sunshine. We enjoyed those few hours spent outdoors, and chatted away happily.

Connie was on leave again from Monday, 4 March, for a couple of weeks. He drove off in the morning as usual, and returned home late in the evening. A couple of days later, when he went out again, I asked him to bring a pizza for dinner, as it was sweltering, and I was too tired to cook. I had to work on a manuscript, so I started on that after he left.

He called me around five o'clock in the evening and said, "I slipped and *fell* on the concrete pavement on Main Street in Mornington, and I'm here in the medical centre, because the store manager saw me and brought me here. I fell on my face and hurt my forehead!" I was very concerned to hear that, and asked if he was alright to drive home. He said he could manage, and not to worry. When he came home that evening, the top half of his head was bandaged, and dark bruises appeared around his eyes.

I was upset to see his injuries, and made him sit down and relax in the evening and watch some comedies. I joked, "You look like the phantom of the opera, with your head all covered up." He giggled. These sudden falls were typical of his condition, and also the inability to control his emotions any longer; he giggled helplessly, or cried out loud, but no tears fell.

He was losing facial muscle control, and sometimes when we were in church, he could not stop giggling when the priest started to preach, and I told him to cover his mouth with his handkerchief. He wanted me to explain to the priest and our friends, that he was not being rude, but he could not control his giggling. Of course they understood when I told them about his illness, and were very sympathetic.

The morning after his fall, I expected him to rest and take it easy, but as I was getting ready to go to school, he woke up, and removed the bandage. His face looked terrible when he took the bandage off, as it was swollen and badly bruised. The area under both eyes looked puffed and blue.

The wounds were not deep, but he had severe bruising, and the skin was peeling off. He told me, "Take me to doctor's, and I'll get Esme to pick me and drop me home." I replied, "Why don't you wait till tomorrow, then I can take you and bring you home without troubling anyone." "What are families for, if they can't help at these times," he muttered. Perhaps he wanted them to know how badly he was injured. So I dropped him at the surgery, and then went to school. When I came back at four thirty, he was not home yet, but returned about an hour later. He said he drove down to pay bills at the post office in Mt Martha.

The doctor dressed his wounds, checked him again, and told him the swelling would last for some time, as he did not apply an ice-pack immediately. I was very sad to see his state, and hoped this jinx would disappear from his life soon. We watched a movie that night, and he seemed relaxed. But around ten thirty, he wanted me to call an ambulance, as he was concerned about the swelling and pain.

I told him that doctor saw him only that morning, and dressed his wounds, and it was only natural to feel pain. I gave him a couple of panadeines, and he settled down slightly. He was always a very bad patient, as he could not tolerate pain; even the slightest cut or injury made him impossible to be around. Although I knew he was in a great deal of pain now, he moaned and complained every few minutes. I hardly had a wink of sleep, and suffered with him through the night.

His breathing was very heavy and wheezy, because he caught a cold a few weeks back and it still lingered, so he snored very loud, and struggled to breathe. And although doctor urged him to stop smoking completely, he still smoked a few cigarettes a day. Two courses of antibiotics did not clear his chest, and I told him he should see doctor again about his chest infection.

I planned to have tea with Joelle and her family on Friday, 8 March, and as I did not want to cancel our date, I drove my car to Keysborough. Connie wanted to come with me too. But he did not want to drive his car, as he said, "If the cops see me bandaged like this, I may get a fine." I was unsure of the way, but I thought he could direct me, as he drove there before.

I missed the turn, and when I asked him directions, he replied, "I'm confused, I can't think properly!" I stopped on a side street, and looked at the street directory. But in a few moments he said, "Drive back there, I remember the street you have to turn into." I did so, and we made it to Joelle's without further mishap.

They were very concerned to see Connie's injuries, but Micheline told him, "A few years ago, a handbag thief bashed me when I was walking on the street, and my face looked worse than that. So don't worry, as the bruising will disappear slowly."

He wheezed and coughed all through the afternoon, and told them, "I have a lot of phlegm in my chest, which I can't get rid of!" They were very sympathetic, and hoped he would get better soon. When we returned home in a couple of hours time, he went straight to bed, as he was exhausted.

I could not help thinking he would have been better off, if he had stayed home in bed, as I had no opportunity to enjoy a pleasant chat with Joelle and the others. But as usual, he did not want to miss out on anything, and did not like me visiting anyone on my own.

The clinic phoned next morning, to remind him that he had to change the dressing. He drove to Frankston, and returned late that evening, and said they had to change the dressing every other day.

The scorching weather continued another week, with no rain in sight. Shirani and Ranjith visited on Sunday, and brought lunch. They were very concerned when they saw his injuries. Connie removed photographs of his face, and sent them to some friends, and to the council, because he *insisted* that the pavement was uneven, and he tripped over a bump.

It was another sizzling thirty seven degrees on 12 March, and Chris Del Piano arrived early, to put up picture hooks to hang my latest painting, a seascape of Mt Martha beach that I finished a few weeks ago.

Although it was unbearably hot, I drove to Ninette's that afternoon, and shopped later. Since June last year, I stopped master classes, and I visited her now because she needed me to do little tasks for her, as her eyesight deteriorated rapidly.

She sometimes wanted me to thread a few needles with different coloured cotton, in case she needed to sew something; or I mended her clothes, sewed a torn frill in her bedspread, or hemmed a skirt. Mostly, it was to read television programs, letters or bills. Toula was tied up with various jobs, and could only take her shopping once a week. So, Ninette asked me to drive her to Patterson Lakes or Karingal, whenever she wanted to shop.

I did not mind obliging her at all, as she was very dear to me. But it grieved me to notice how her personality was changing for the worse now. She became more neurotic, and obsessed with a certain issue. And she was paranoid about it, until she made herself sick with worry and anxiety.

When I came home later that afternoon, Connie was not there, and he came after seven o'clock. I asked him where he had been all day, and he replied, "I went with Jenny and Clifford for a prayer meeting at Lysterfield." He did not mention this to me before I left, so I asked him how he drove with his injuries. "Clifford drove us, I left my car at their place."

I was very surprised he visited them on his own, as he never did that in all these years. He told me that he never wanted to visit them, and especially not with me. I could not believe his attitude was changing so much, as he was angry with his siblings for breaking away from the Catholic church.

I reminded him how he always said, "Those 'Born again' Christians are a bunch of *hypocrites!*" And he told his siblings constantly that they were baptised into the one, true, Catholic church. And argued with them endlessly about their fickle faith. I now wondered how he could turn to their self-appointed, so-called 'pastors' hoping for a miracle?

We watched many documentaries on television, about such charlatans. They made people pretend they were lame or ill, and then claimed to work *miracles* and "heal" them, without medical proof whatsoever. I asked him now, "Why can't you go to healing services in our church in Frankston, instead of driving so far to their 'Glory' house?"

Connie was well aware of all the deceptions and scams in these cult religions. But now he did not pay any attention, even when I asked him, "How on earth can you visit them, and get Clifford to drive you, when you have never been close to them all these years, and didn't want to have anything to do with them?" He did not answer, and I was very indignant that he did not show any concern for my feelings.

It was hurtful when he ignored me so blatantly, and I was angry to think of all the years he made me suffer, because of his insane jealousy, and anger towards Geraldine for having married him. Even though he knew about Clifford's scandalous behaviour with Sanit, and some others, it did not seem to bother him at all. It was then that I understood how this disease was affecting him, and how his personality was changing completely for the worse.

I read all the available information about his disease, so I could cope with his behaviour. And it was very interesting to read that the patient loses all inhibitions, as the disease progresses and affects the brain. They were prone to early onset of dementia, aggression, absence of logic, and many other negative aspects, too frightening to even consider.

When Liz knew about Connie's disease, she gave me a DVD, with documented evidence of Bruno Groening's miraculous healings. She asked me to watch it with Connie, as he was known to cure people, who just watched the DVD. Although Connie sat through the documentary with me, he was not communicative at all.

After a while he mentioned that Geraldine and Clifford were having marital problems, due to his behaviour with Sanit. Geraldine told him that she did not believe what anyone said, and Connie advised them to "stay together, no matter what."

I did not comment, as I was uninterested in their never-ending problems. I was annoyed with Connie for driving off, without even telling me where he was going, especially to visit them. And then attend prayer meetings at some self-proclaimed pastor's house, who claimed to be a 'miracle worker' without any evidence to back him up.

The next day, a consultant from Bendigo bank visited, and gave us some information about a Home Safe loan. It was to help older couples stay in their homes, and whenever the home was sold, the loan was repaid at an agreed percentage made prior to the loan. We considered this option now, as we wondered how else we could pay the mortgage, if Connie did not return to work soon. At this stage, I still believed that speech therapy would help him, even though I knew what the disease was, but I still hoped for a positive outcome.

The bank consultant was very informative, but as we still had the unit in Queensland, she suggested we sell that first, pay most of the mortgage, and then approach the bank. We were disappointed with this result, as it would take a long time to sell the unit, and prices in Queensland were stagnant at present.

I told Connie, "Everything happens for the best, so let's try to sell the unit now." He did not reply, but I could see he was very worried. I called Shirani later, and then wished Ranjith, as it was his birthday today.

We drove to Frankston later, to consult another neurologist, Professor Butler. He was tall, lanky, and very friendly, and he examined Connie thoroughly. The neurologist in Monash recommended him, as he was based in Frankston hospital.

She said it was more convenient for us to visit him, than having to drive to Monash. Prof. Butler went on to explain the nature of progressive supra-nuclear palsy, and ended with, "You will get *worse* Conrad, unfortunately, there is no cure and no treatment for this disease, but I'm going to prescribe some tablets to relax your throat, neck, and shoulder muscles."

Connie complained of severe neck and shoulder pain, and Prof. Butler said, that as the muscles gradually tightened, they would get more painful. He told Connie, "Think positive, and keep as active as possible, so you will be able to use your legs and arms for as long as possible."

Connie was downcast all the way home. I knew he did not want to believe anything Prof. Butler told him. He was blind to reality, and desperately wanted to believe a miracle would happen soon.

Then we stopped at the chemist, and bought the prescription pills. One of my piano students was at the chemist's, as she had fractured her wrist, and her mother was getting some pain killers for her. I was concerned when I saw her, and said, "Oh, no, Sabrina, you won't be able to play piano for a few weeks till your wrist heals." She replied, "I know, it's so upsetting." I chatted to her mother later, and she wanted to know what was wrong with Connie, and was very concerned when I explained about his illness.

I asked Connie to take the tablet after dinner, which he did very reluctantly, saying, "I *don't* believe in these tablets anyway." I replied, "But it's just to *help* you relax your muscles, what's the use of going to doctors, if you won't listen to them and take what is prescribed!"

I was so frustrated, as this was the usual outcome after spending time and money consulting doctors, he always found an excuse not to follow their advice. He had his usual glass of whisky and cigarettes, and said, "*This* is a better way to relax!" I ignored him, and made a banana cake to take to school next day. The more I tried to help him, the more obstinate he became.

Chapter 72

When I was at school next day, 14 March, we heard the news that Pope Francis was elected, as the previous Pope resigned, due to ill health. We prayed for the new Pope, that he would be blessed in his role. A great deal of laughter and chatter filled the staff room that morning, and everyone enjoyed the banana cake.

The weather turned slightly cooler, after weeks and weeks of scorching temperatures, even though it was autumn now. But I watered the garden, as everything looked so wilted and dry. Spending time in the garden was another way of unwinding, so I did not have to listen to Connie's non-stop complaints whenever he was around.

I tried my best to lead as normal a life as possible, under the circumstances. But when he took a few drinks, he followed me around, and if I was watching television or reading, he muttered irritably, "*You* don't care what I'm going through do you?" "What do you want me to do?" I asked in exasperation. But he just scowled angrily, and muttered under his breath. He wanted me to commiserate with him constantly, and wallow in his misery. And he did not want me to spend any time away from him, as he became more demanding and unreasonable.

I did my best for him, and treated him compassionately, as it was very distressing to see him struggling to speak. But I could not do anything more to make him happy, as he became increasingly miserable, and impossible to get on with. I knew he wanted me to suffer with him, so he made sure I was unable to do anything that would make me happy. In other words, I had to stop living, and go down with him.

He snarled angrily, if I happened to be doing some work around the house, or watched television. "*Why* are you quiet? You get out of here, if you're not happy! Go and find a *stiff* one!" The absence of sexual relations in our marriage was still a very sore point with him, and he lashed out to hurt me at the slightest provocation. What saddened me more, was that even though his speech was worse, he still shouted and said such hurtful things to me for no reason at all.

When we visited Con and Cornelia a few weeks before, Con sat next to me to show their holiday photographs. But as we drove home later, Connie was very angry with me all the way back, and shouted, "I didn't *like* the way Con was sitting so close to you! You better be careful! Why does he have to be so familiar?" I replied, "He was just showing me their holiday photos, what's wrong with that?" But he did not stop nagging till we reached home. I just had to get away from him before I exploded, so watering the garden was my escape.

Tigger was still a worry, as he jumped over the fence into the reserve, and stayed out till all hours of the night and early morning. I sat up waiting for him to come home, and did not get to sleep till two or three o'clock in the morning sometimes. Then I went upstairs, and slept in the spare room, to get a few hours sleep before getting up at seven o'clock to go to school.

We had a few rainy days, as the cool weather finally drifted in, much to everyone's relief. I spent some time working on the script, and played the piano whenever I was home. I told myself I had to keep busy, and not let Connie worry me so much, as my health was affected with so much stress. Although I managed my sugar levels as well as I could, my pressure was high sometimes, and the dizzy spells and insomnia were more frequent.

When I was at the end of my patience, and sometimes told him, "I will get sick, if you don't stop worrying me like this! Don't you know I'm not all that well, with diabetes, high blood pressure, and heart condition?" He looked at me blandly and did not reply. He was always egocentric, and it was evident now that he focussed *only* on himself, and it did not matter one iota what I went through.

Although Connie's leave ended, he stayed home on Monday, 18th March, as he said he was too tired to go to work. I was at school, and when I returned home at three o'clock, Connie was on his computer doing emails, and he did not stop till late that night.

Joelle, Celine, and Micheline went on a cruise to New Zealand, and she sent me a text to say that the ship would pass Mt Martha around eight o'clock that night. I watched through binoculars, as the beautiful cruise ship, ablaze with myriad lights sailed past, and the decks were clearly visible. I sent Joelle a text message immediately, and she replied that they were aboard that ship, and were already enjoying the voyage. I told Connie to have a look through the binoculars, and he came unhurriedly, but viewed the ship as well.

One of the best things in Mt Martha was seeing ocean liners sailing by in the evenings and nights, under starry skies or in the moonlight. They looked so magical, with faint lights gleaming in the mist, that I spent some time watching ships disappear through the Heads, and out into the open seas.

I visited Ninette next day, and when I came home, Connie said Roland dropped in unexpectedly. I knew that he brought "Born again" propaganda, and CD's for Connie, so I did not say anything. Lately, Connie sat huddled in the evenings, watching endless healing CD's that they gave him.

Christian visited next day, and I was very pleased to see him. I made some pan rolls for him and Athena, so he had some, and I gave him Athena's share to take, then we had an interesting chat. Connie was happy to see him too, although he did not talk much, but just sat with us, and sipped a glass of whisky.

The next few days were stormy and gusty, and I felt feverish and unwell, but I stopped at Bentons Square after school to get groceries. As I finished shopping and passed a cafe, I was very surprised to see Esme and Cristobel having coffee there! I asked, "What are you two doing here?" Cristobel retorted, "Why, aren't we *allowed* to come here?" I ignored her, and Esme came over to greet me.

Cristobel said, "Forget the past and have a coffee with us," I said I was very tired, and had to go home soon before it started to rain. That was the first time I saw Cristobel since October 2009, when she caused all that trouble when their mother died.

Connie insisted that I have nothing to do with her, and told me repeatedly, "Don't you *dare* open the door if ever that wretch tries to visit! She is nothing but trouble!" I was aloof, but polite, and walked away without stopping for coffee, as I did not have time. When I came home, I told Connie I met his sisters, and he started to giggle, and said, "Bella sends me text messages every night, saying she's praying for me." I was taken aback, because he never mentioned that before, as he was not on speaking terms with her since 2009. I thought she was probably trying to make up for her bad behaviour, now that he was sick, and let it go.

A national upheaval took place that night, when Kevin Rudd challenged the Labour leader. It looked like Julia Gillard would be ousted, but she held onto her job, only just! The world of politics was a dizzy roller coaster ride, no doubt. But the lack of stability in the present government did nothing to restore confidence among the people.

Connie attended a "healing Mass" at Berwick Catholic church next morning, and he told me he had a phone hook-up with his bosses later that day. I did not go with him, as I was down with flu. I made pepper soup, which was certainly strong enough, with plenty of garlic, ginger, and coriander, to get rid of any virus. After a few cups of that potent brew, I rested a while.

He looked very dejected when he returned home that afternoon, and said, "Didn't go too well at the phone hook-up. They want me to provide a medical certificate from the specialist, to say I'm fit to work, as they think I've had a stroke, and that's why my speech is affected." I thought to myself, there must be an answer to all these problems. What on earth would we do, if Connie could not work any longer? How would we manage? The future certainly looked bleak. But I still hoped there would be a solution to all these troubles and woes.

Ninette invited us to an Italian festival at Thornbury, on 7 April. But the way things were going, I told her we would have to wait and see how Connie's condition was. I did not promise to take her there, as she wanted us to drive her, and spend the day with her, but I knew it was quite unlikely.

The next day was freezing and blustery, with storms that hit north of Victoria very badly, and caused enormous destruction.

The site manager in Queensland called to say that our unit was re-let to another good tenant. And that we did not lose any rental income in the transitional period when the previous tenant left after several years. That was a relief to know the unit was leased for another year. After I finished some work on the computer, we went to Mornington for evening Mass.

In spite of the flu, I was at school on Monday, 25 March, and Connie drove to see the specialist in Frankston, the one who first saw him in January. Later that morning, I was very surprised to see him at school, and waving a letter at me. "The specialist gave me a medical, to say I can return to work tomorrow!" He was happy, and I was relieved, as we knew he could not afford to stop work just yet, until we sorted our finances.

Nelune visited on Good Friday, 29 March, and Christian and Athena picked her at the airport, and arrived here by midday. We had a great time, as Nelune came after three and a half years, and it was her first visit to our new house in Mt Martha. Connie was very distressed that afternoon, as his speech was worse than ever, and he said, "I don't want to upset Nelune when she sees me like this." He bawled his eyes out. Christian, Athena, and I, were very sorry for him, as he sobbed brokenly, "After all the years I worked for that company, look what has happened to me!"

After Christian and Athena left, he drove us to Woolamai later that afternoon. Although his speech was slurred, he did not seem too bad physically. We had a pleasant time with Shirani, and returned after seven thirty. We were tired, especially Nelune, so we went to bed by ten o' clock.

Connie and I drove Nelune to the airport the following afternoon, and he seemed alright. But he was very vague, and ignored me whenever I tried to speak to him. When we returned home, we took it easy, and watched comedies in the evening.

Those rare times on some evenings, were the only moments when we had a semblance of normalcy, and enjoyed laughing together. But as soon as I served dinner, his mood changed completely, and he found something to criticize about the food. Very seldom did he say he enjoyed the meal, and now he was getting fussier. He did not like spicy food, so I made different dishes each night to tempt his palate.

The following day, on Easter Sunday, we attended morning Mass at Mornington, and the church was overflowing. We wished our friends, including Elvira, John, Myra, and Vanessa from school, and afterwards we drove to Gold leaf restaurant in Springvale for yum cha. Connie enjoyed the meal very much, as he liked steamed dumplings, with prawn and coriander especially, so did I.

Cornelia had a knee operation a week ago, so we drove to Keysborough to see her. And we stopped at Parkmore Shopping centre, to buy some roses for her. She was resting her knee, as she said it was still sore, and we spent a couple of hours there before we returned in the evening.

It was a public holiday next day, so Connie was home. I spent some time hemming Ninette's skirts. Then I called Nilanthi, before I watched "Revenge." Connie did not follow that series, so I asked him not to disturb me for one hour, until the episode was over. But would he mind me, oh no, because every ten minutes or so, he burst into the room, and demanded, "Is it over yet? *When* are we having dinner?" Or start complaining about something or someone, until I became irritable and retorted, "Can't you just be patient for *one* hour until this is over and not disturb me?" He stomped off angrily, muttering and grumbling, "Is *that* show more important anyway, than listening to what I have to say?" So, it was the same old story every time.

The following days were quiet, once Connie returned to work, and I kept busy with my writing. It was Elvira's birthday on 5 April, and she invited us to Rugantino's Restaurant in Frankston. When Connie came home after work, we drove there at about seven o'clock. He was subdued and hardly spoke a word, as he was very self-conscious about his speech now, and he knew people found it difficult to understand him at times.

I was very upset to watch him eating quietly without talking, because previously, he would not have stopped for a breather all evening. Our friends noticed his silence, and sympathized with him. We tried to cheer him up, saying he would soon be alright, and speak normally, once he started speech therapy.

Tigger did not come home till late that night, and I could not fall sleep, so I stayed up calling him till I was hoarse. He strayed from evening till early morning now, and it was very stressful, as I could not sleep until he came home. I hoped that he would settle down soon, like Simba and Mishka.

Although I waited till two o'clock in the morning, Tigger did not come home. I was very worried, thinking he was injured in the reserve. About nine o'clock in the morning, Connie and I walked through the reserve, calling Tigger, but he was nowhere to be seen. I invoked Bruno to bring him home safely.

After a while, I stopped and waited for Connie to catch up, as I went ahead, and stood watching him amble towards me. I noticed then that he leaned to one side, and looked a little wobbly on his feet, as he dragged them awkwardly. I took his arm and walked slowly with him, to make sure he did not stumble.

Tigger padded in nonchalantly at six thirty that evening, his fur full of thistles and twigs. When I admonished him, he looked sheepish, but was unrepentant, as he was off again next day! I was so thankful to see him safe now, but I told him off soundly before giving his dinner.

I met Del on Tuesday at Judy's place in Carrum, before I visited Ninette, and it was lovely to spend some time with them. They were very concerned to hear about Connie's illness, and were supportive as always, offering me any assistance during this troubled period. These dear friends were a great comfort, with their kindness and concern. What a blessing true friends are, especially at times like this.

I visited Nancy a few days later, and spent a very enjoyable afternoon with her too. She served home-made pasta and sauce for lunch, which I enjoyed very much. Her garden was beautiful, and she did an amazing job looking after it. She called me later, to ask if I arrived home safely, because of the road works on her street. That night, I watched a colossal cruise ship sailing by, and Joelle called just then to say she was in Rosebud with her mother and aunt, watching that same ship.

Elvira and I had coffee at Onde's next day, and discussed Connie's health issues. She assured me that John and she were there for us anytime, day or night. I thanked her for their kindness, and told her we were fortunate to have such good friends. Elvira replied that she appreciated our friendship very much too, because of everything I did for her.

When I spoke to Nilanthi later that evening, she said she wanted to visit us soon, as she was very sad to hear that Connie's speech was worse. I told her I would speak to him and get her down at the end of the year. Then I asked her to pray for him, and not to be too sad. But she started to cry, and was emotional when she spoke about his kindness towards her over the years.

It was true that he had always been generous and affectionate towards her, and she wanted to tell him how much she appreciated his kindness. He tried to talk to her on the phone, but she could hardly understand him, and was very upset to hear him struggle to speak.

Connie prepared the usual documents that she needed to get a visa, and although he was very slow in his movements, he did all that was required. I said I would post them to Nilanthi on Monday. Esme and Paul turned up unexpectedly that day and stayed for about an hour.

We visited Lorraine and Tony in mid-April, and Dorothea dropped in too. She talked non-stop in her loud, boisterous way as usual. Tony could not understand what was wrong with Connie, and was distressed to watch him struggle to speak. We returned home after a couple of hours.

Mary called next day, and invited us for dinner at the RSL club in Rye, on 18 April, which was Tony's 76th birthday. I said I would let her know if Connie agreed, as I knew he was self-conscious now, and avoided company. But he was not averse to the invitation, so I told Mary we would be there.

I caught a head cold, and had flu symptoms *again,* so I dosed myself with panadeine, and drank several cups of pepper soup. Then I rested a few hours, and hoped I would feel better soon.

It was wet and frosty next day when I was at school. I finished early, then rested for a while, before driving to Rye around seven o'clock. Connie did not enjoy the dinner at all, and said that his chicken Kiev was "too dry," but I liked the delicious grilled fish and vegetables. Elvira, John, and some other friends of Mary's and Tony's came too, so we had a pleasant time, and returned home before midnight.

Elvira and Alessandro visited on the following Saturday afternoon. I baked a cake, and we had an enjoyable time before attending evening Mass. They were delightful people, and even Connie joined in the conversation, as much as possible.

When he returned to work in early April, management asked him to consult their company doctor as well, before he could continue working. His speech deteriorated so much, that most people found it difficult to understand him. The company doctor requested him to bring along a family member.

I was unaware of this request, because Connie did not ask me to accompany him. But before his appointment on the following day, he told me at ten o'clock in the night, "I have asked Tucko to come with me to the specialist." I had school on Monday, but I would have definitely changed my schedule to be with him. So I was very upset that night, and I asked him, "Why didn't you tell me what the specialist said?" He replied vaguely, "I thought family member meant my brother or sister." I told him, "Family member means your *wife* or *son*, not your brother, as we're still alive, and your next of kin!"

Honestly, he was very trying, as I knew he pushed me further away, and turned to his siblings increasingly. I tried to understand his personality changes, and ignored his behaviour. But his siblings took advantage of the situation, and were full of self-importance, as they influenced him, and undermined me.

A day or so later, when Esme and Paul dropped in, I told them how he asked his brother to accompany him to the specialist. And Paul admonished him, "Connie, your *wife* and you are a *team,* and you come *first* in each other's lives! Brothers and sisters come *after*! You should have asked Dolly to accompany you, not your brother!"

Connie looked a little sheepish, but I do not think he cared, because he did what he wanted.

His boss took him off phones, and he was at the computer all day in the office, attending to emails and not visiting sites anymore. Connie did not take holidays over Christmas that year, as his boss was on leave, and except for a short break in March, he worked through till April.

When I watched television on some nights, he had early dinner in the dining room and went to bed, saying he was very tired. It was best that he rested, as it was an effort now to get up early and drive to work daily.

Isobel called, and we had a long chat, as she was a counsellor, as well as a very perceptive, intelligent lady. She explained about some of the symptoms Connie displayed, and was very comforting. Isobel asked me to call her anytime I needed to talk to someone. I found her advice very helpful, as she had vast experience dealing with people suffering from dementia, and other mental diseases.

I drove to Woolworths head office in Mulgrave, on 23 April, and arrived there at midday. Connie's boss asked me to be present during the phone hook-up with management, including the occupational health and safety officer in Sydney.

The first thing I noticed when I walked in was how cheerless the office looked, compared to the bright, bustling place it was so many years ago when we were in Rowville, and I had visited a few times. Connie was sitting very quietly at his desk, and I felt a sharp pang to see him there alone, looking forlorn in his little corner. He had lost some weight in the last few months, and his gaunt appearance was unhealthy.

How very distressing it was for him to be stuck inside the office, just doing emails now, and unable to communicate on the phone or verbally. When he saw me, he got up at once, and took me to the canteen, where we had sandwiches for lunch. He introduced me to some of his colleagues, and we sipped coffee, until it was time for the phone hook-up at one fifteen.

When the introductions were over, we could see everyone's faces via Skype, and the OHS officer read the medical report aloud, and said, "Conrad, you will have to take medical leave as from today, until your speech improves. Don't worry, your job will be here for you when you come back. If there is no improvement, we'll find another role for you in the company. Main thing is to get better, and start going for speech therapy as soon as possible." Connie just mumbled, "Yes" in a very thick voice, and once or twice he asked me to explain some issues to the managers.

They were sympathetic and positive, but it was very painful and difficult for me to watch Connie sitting there so helpless, and unable to communicate properly. Afterwards, he walked with me to the car park, and I hugged him, and said, "Don't worry, at least they understand what's happening, and you can do with some rest, until we see the speech therapist." He did not respond, so after wishing him goodbye, I drove home with a leaden heart.

I felt very dejected on my way, but I could not do anything, except wait and see what would happen. In the evening, I called Christian, Nelune, and Shirani to let them know how the phone hook-up went, as they were concerned to know what would happen with Connie's job. They were very sad about the whole situation, and as always, ready to help in anyway. Nelune even offered financial assistance, if it came to the worst, but I told her not to worry, as we would sort out our affairs accordingly.

He brought all his personal belongings that evening, but Mathew told him to leave his computer and mobile phone behind, because someone else would do his job until he returned. We had a very quiet evening, and did not discuss the future at all.

Tigger came home at eight o'clock that night, after wandering off at seven the previous morning! At least he was home safe, the incorrigible little cat. Connie woke up around nine o'clock next morning, and said he wanted to consult Dr Yap, a general practitioner in Dandenong. His brother and family consulted him, and Connie saw him a few times when we were in Rowville, but Dr Khelil was our family doctor now. I asked him why he needed to see another doctor, and he replied, "I have more faith in Dr Yap." He left shortly afterwards, and I went to the skin clinic in Mornington, to check out some sun spots on my neck.

I came home around four o'clock, and started making dinner. Connie returned a couple of hours later, looking annoyed and in a very bad mood. I knew he had visited Roland, when he picked on me immediately, even though he saw I was busy. His first complaint was that I did not accompany him to visit his family. I replied, "You can visit them whenever you want, and I have never stopped you from seeing your family." But he *insisted* that I should go with him too! I reminded him of all the times I spent visiting his family over the last forty three years. And it was only in the last couple of years that I did not go with him as often, because I was involved in so many other activities and my work.

In the past, we spent one whole Saturday or Sunday, visiting all his relatives, until I grew tired of driving around all day; besides, I had so much to do on weekends now with all my interests. The next grievance was that Christian did not call, and had not visited for some time. I told him to stop complaining, as Christian called me a few times weekly, besides dropping in whenever he could spare time from his work. He sent Connie text messages now, because Connie could not speak on the phone now.

Whenever Connie visited his siblings, he came home in a foul mood, which led me to believe they discussed these issues. And especially his brother, who told Connie that his children cared for them so much, they were always visiting, and helping them financially. Connie told me that he was sorry for Roland's children, who did everything for their parents, because they were financially unstable. I was annoyed that he picked a quarrel over such trivialities.

He became very nasty then, and growled, "Now don't go and *repeat* what I'm saying to you about Christian, because you have a habit of repeating everything. Stacy told me." I really lost my temper then and asked him, "*Why* are you bringing in Stacy's name when he isn't here? And when did Stacy say such a thing, because I don't believe he said that!" One thing led to another, and recriminations over just about everything followed next. He was so angry, that I did not understand what really bothered him. I tried to excuse his behaviour, thinking that he was forced to take sick leave now, and was worried about his job, and his speech problem.

Also, when he asked Dr Yap to refer him to a throat specialist, doctor told him to make another appointment. But Dr Khelil had already told Connie it was pointless seeing a throat specialist, because his diagnosis was PSP, and a throat specialist could not help him.

When I went to bed that night, I thought to myself, *this is only the first day of his sick leave, how am I going to cope if he behaves like this?*' He sipped whisky all evening, and played loud music well into the night, which he knew irritated me. I could not fall asleep with such deafening music blaring through the house on surround-system speakers.

Elvira brought scones the following Saturday, and we enjoyed the afternoon. But Connie became very emotional; one moment he was giggling and laughing, next minute he bawled out, but no tears fell, only distressing noises. Elvira was very upset, and did not know what to do or say. I told her that he was unable to control his emotions now, which was part of the illness, but it was very painful to watch Connie.

Karen held a book launch on Sunday, 28 April, at a hotel in Hawthorn. We left home just after midday, and arrived there at two o'clock. Del was already there, and about thirty people gathered in a small, upstairs room in the hotel. Plates of assorted sandwiches, tea, and coffee were arranged on tables. I bought a copy of her book 'Torn,' and explained briefly about Connie's illness to Karen's husband, Stuart, as Connie started giggling helplessly at the most unexpected times.

Karen and Stuart were very sorry to hear about it, but we did not have much time to talk, as she was busy. And when it was over, I chatted to Del, before we left. I told Shirani I would visit her at Narre Warren, so we went there later, and after a brief chat over a cup of tea, we returned home. I started reading Karen's book that very night, and found it very interesting.

I was at school next day, and came home at five o'clock, after finishing the last lesson with Tess at four thirty. Connie was home for a change, and as I was walking in the garden trying to "de-stress," I saw Babs at the front gate, shouting and waving. Connie said she phoned to say she was visiting, and that was why he stayed at home.

When she came in and saw my mobile on the kitchen table, she asked my number, but I told her, "Don't give my number to anyone, because I don't want nuisance calls." She promised faithfully, but in a few weeks time, she called to say she gave it to Connie's brother, Paul, as he wanted to speak to me.

All through these trying days, I played the piano at least one hour, and still kept this up no matter how stressed I was. I closed the door, and tried to forget all my troubles and lose myself in music. Connie rapped on the door sometimes, and demanded something or another. I replied irritably, "Can't you wait just a little while, until I finish?" Then he banged the door shut, and stomped off angrily, muttering and grumbling under his breath.

Ninette was full of complaints when I saw her the following Tuesday, and repeated a list of her ailments constantly. I had heard it before, but she kept adding to the list, even though her doctor told her she did not have diabetes or thyroid problems.

When I saw Carol, the podiatrist, later, she complained about her nasty daughter-in-law, who gave her son a very hard time. On my way home, I mused that the world is full of people with their share of troubles to bear, and it was all part of our human condition. Connie's illness had to be endured now, as it was predestined in the grand scheme of things. How else can we cope, if we do not find some comfort, in knowing we are all susceptible to whatever misfortune life holds.

Connie began speech therapy on 1 May, and I accompanied him to Rosebud rehab centre. The therapist, a young woman, spent time with Connie from three o'clock till about four thirty that afternoon. She asked him to read short sentences, and then told him to try and speak in short sentences, and not long-winded ones, and gave him reading exercises to practise. It was good to get started, and I encouraged Connie all the way home, saying he must think positive now, and hope his speech would improve.

I still visited Ninette every Tuesday afternoon, without fail, as she depended on me to do a few things for her, and sometimes just to keep her company for a few hours. I did not mind doing all this for her, as her eyesight was getting worse. But now she suffered from hypochondria, and spent all her time complaining about various symptoms, and visited doctors often, to get relief for her imaginary ailments.

I enjoyed my visits very much in the past, listening to her playing the piano (which she seldom did now), and it was a pleasant afternoon. But now, with Connie at home complaining non-stop about his illness, and Ninette on the other hand, my head was spinning by the time I went to bed.

But I did not stop visiting Ninette, because I felt very sorry for her, as it was a tragedy, that such a brilliant pianist should be losing her eyesight. And if I could alleviate her loneliness for a little while, I was happy to do so. I knew she was very lonely, and enjoyed having me to listen to her complaints for a couple of hours, as she said, "Nalini you are a good listener, so very patient. Thank you for visiting me."

We met the financial advisor again on Friday, 3 May, and was with him from ten o'clock in the morning till after one o'clock. He was very helpful, and suggested strategies for our future, in case Connie's speech did not improve. It was a positive outcome, and when we finished, Connie wanted to visit Roland. Shiranthi insisted we stay for lunch, and it was late when we drove back. Then we stopped in Mornington to get pills for his neck and shoulder pains.

He took the tablets that Prof. Butler prescribed only once, saying, "They make me drowsy." And now he complained he could not move his neck, as it was very painful, and wanted to take some other pills.

Linda called to ask how Connie was doing, and said she would visit often, as she was very sad to hear about his illness. Mary and Peter visited that Sunday afternoon, and we had an enjoyable time. They came all the way from Croydon, as they were very concerned about Connie, and hoped that speech therapy would help.

The following Tuesday, as I was getting ready to visit Ninette, Esme called Connie, and said she was visiting him that morning. I left early, as I had to buy some flowers at Bentons Square on my way, and I came home by five o'clock. It was a brilliant evening, so I removed some photographs of a spectacular sunset. He did not mention anything about Esme's visit, and I did not ask either.

I drove Connie to Rosebud on Friday, 10 May, as he said he was too tired to drive. The wheel was set in motion now, and a wide network became involved in Connie's case, as there was plenty of support for patients diagnosed with motor neuron disease. The physio checked his arms, legs, and neck, and made him walk up and down. The social worker spoke to us later, and gave a list of various support groups who would help Connie.

We returned after three o'clock in the afternoon, and as he complained of severe neck pain, I drove back as well. On the way home, he was his usual ill-tempered self, and very nasty to me, as he raised his voice at the slightest thing. I felt sad and angry, that in spite of his speech difficulties, he still shouted at me for no reason. He was very pleasant and polite to the physio and social worker, who were young women, but showed his nastiness only to me.

He was angry, because they told him that his condition would deteriorate, and he shouted out, "They are all *negative!* That's why I go to the 'Born again' prayer meetings, because they are positive that I will be *healed!*" I did not argue with him, as it was pointless. It was another beautiful evening, which closed in with a magnificent sunset, so I removed more photographs. I collected a whole album of these splendid sunsets in Mt Martha, as it seemed they were more spectacular each evening.

I finished my usual chores on the following Saturday, and then baked a butter cake, Connie's favourite, and waited for Cynthia and Ron to visit that afternoon. Several mutual friends visited every weekend now, as they were all concerned about Connie. These two people knew Connie since 1980 or so, as they worked for Woolworths on contract. We had a good time, and later attended evening Mass at Mornington. I made pepper steaks, and pumpkin soup for dinner, which he ate without making a fuss.

Misaka and Theji visited the following evening. Theji was expecting her first baby in July. And they wanted to see Connie before she had the baby, as they knew it would be a busy time for them. I was very pleased to see them, as they were a nice young couple.

Esme wanted to visit that evening too, but I told her we had visitors, so she did not insist on coming. It was raining heavily when they left at about six o'clock. Connie stood at the front door and said, "Hold her hand, in case she falls," as the driveway was very steep. They smiled and thanked him for his concern.

I washed and cleaned up dishes, and attended to the cats, then had an early dinner. Connie went to bed around nine thirty, saying he felt dizzy. He groaned and struggled all night, as he found it difficult to breathe, so I hardly had any sleep, and was worn-out the next morning. I told him to stay in bed and rest, as he hardly slept the night before. But I drove to school a little later, bleary-eyed and exhausted.

When I came home around five o'clock after grocery shopping, Elvira called and invited me for coffee next day, as her sister from Queensland was there. Ninette wanted me to come early and have a snack with her, so I told Elvira I would come afterwards.

I printed the group photograph of all the actors in Elvira's play, which I removed when they came for tea. And I was about to leave, when Esme and Paul dropped in unexpectedly at ten thirty that morning. I was very surprised to see them so early, and said I had to leave soon. They stayed for an hour, and when I drove off, they left as well, although I asked them to stay and keep Connie company. But Connie said Roland was visiting later. At least he had company, so that was alright, I thought. Little did I know about Roland and Geraldine's insidious intentions to brain-wash him into joining their cult religion, and confuse him further. His reasoning was becoming more irrational now. But they failed to understand the nature of his illness, and did not acknowledge his disease at all.

I attended to some little tasks for Ninette, and she asked me to play a piece of music that she wanted to practise for Ornello. She could still play by memory, and had a very good repertoire, but she found it very difficult to read notes now. Then I did some shopping at Seaford, and came to Elvira's around three thirty.

She told me Connie dropped in earlier to return a carry bag John gave him, and he was unable to stop giggling. He had stood at the door giggling helplessly for about ten minutes. I told her that he could not help it, and he did not mean to, but had no muscle control now. She was very sorry and concerned about him. He knew I was going to Elvira's for coffee, and that was why he made it a point to drop in, on the flimsy pretext of returning a plastic bag.

Elvira's sister, Mary, and her husband, Peter, were nice people, and I liked them very much. I stayed for about an hour before I came home. Misaka had posted a CD with all Connie's favourite Sinhalese songs, as he said he would. And when I came home, he was listening to that CD.

Chapter 73

Wild winds howled across the ocean, and heavy rains lashed all morning on Wednesday, 15 May. I accompanied Connie to Rosebud that morning to meet the dietician, and the speech therapist later in the afternoon. The dietician recommended more protein in his diet to build up muscles, as she said his muscles would be affected progressively, and he needed to exercise daily too. When the dietician finished, we had coffee and sandwiches at the hospital canteen, and waited till the speech therapist was ready to see us. That session with the speech therapist was positive, and she made Connie repeat words and speak short sentences very slowly.

We discussed the best ways to help Connie to communicate with me *first,* and then with others. I told her it was very frustrating for both of us, when he tried to tell me something in his usual, long-winded manner, that I could not understand.

We came home after two thirty, and the weather was still wild and stormy. I spoke to Shirani, who was very upset, because Suresh was causing problems. We had a long discussion. and I tried to comfort her, but it was a very difficult situation. When I called Ninette later, she sounded alright, and said she looked forward to my next visit.

The turbulent weather continued to be wet and stormy over the next two days. I baked a cake, and made pan rolls for our visitors on the weekend. Connie drove to Berwick church at five o'clock that evening, for a healing service at seven thirty in the night. I had a few phone calls that evening, and the La Ponders wanted to visit on Sunday morning, instead of the afternoon, due to a change in their plans.

Cornelia rang to say her mother died earlier that day, and I was very distressed to hear about Florica's sudden death. She said the funeral was on the following Monday, and asked if we could come for the pre-funeral service at Springvale on Sunday evening. I told her I would let Connie know, as he could drive us there.

Then I tried to take it easy and watch a movie, and Connie returned home after ten o'clock. I wondered what kind of healing service it was, to keep sick people up so late. But I did not bother to ask him why he was so late. He hardly spoke, but said he had dinner at Roland's place, and went to bed immediately.

I woke up early on Saturday, and prepared everything for Linda and her parents. They arrived before midday, but Leo did not come, as he was busy studying. They stayed for a couple of hours, and we had a pleasant time catching up. Linda and Paul enjoyed the pan rolls, but they were too spicy for Julie. I took it easy before making dinner. At seven o'clock that night, Connie drove to a church in Narre Warren for another healing service.

I watched "Inspector General," with Danny Kaye, and enjoyed it very much, as it was very amusing. Then I went to bed around eleven o'clock, and wondered when he would get home. He finally returned at one o'clock in the morning! I could not believe he was staying at these services so long. But I understood he went back to Roland's place, and that was why he delayed, as he had dinner there, and spent time with them.

He had no consideration for me at all, as it appeared he had forgotten he was married and had a wife. And his siblings encouraged him to stay out so late at nights, under the pretext of attending healing services. They had no qualms at all in disrupting our lives like this, when I was going through such a traumatic time with Connie. I was too angry to even ask him why he was behaving so uncharacteristically, as he never stayed out till so late in the past. He should have drawn closer to me, instead of disregarding me so completely, and together we would have coped with his illness.

I woke up early next morning, and was ready for Chris and Peter when they arrived at eleven o'clock. We had a pleasant time, and it was great to see them again. But they were very concerned when they heard Connie's speech, and kept asking me if it was a stroke. I explained that he was diagnosed with PSP, and they were very sorry when I told them how it affected patients.

I made vegetable soup, with marrow bone stock, and I served it with hot bread rolls, which they enjoyed very much, and they left after two o'clock. I hardly had time to rest afterwards, although I was very tired. We left home soon in time for Florica's pre-funeral service at five o'clock. Connie drove and when we arrived there, the funeral parlour chapel was crowded with their friends and family.

Florica lay in a white, satin-lined coffin, and although I could not bear to look at corpses, I did not find her repugnant. She looked sweet and peaceful, but I did not touch her hands. I prayed for the repose of her soul, and went back to my seat.

We did not understand the words, as the whole service was in Rumanian, but it was very solemn and dignified, and everybody was quiet as was expected. So it was embarrassing when Connie had a fit of giggles, when he saw the Rumanian priest, with his elaborate head-gear. He could not stop giggling loud, as he pointed at the priest.

I whispered to him, "*Cover* your mouth with your hanky." He tried hard to stifle his giggling, but he just could not help himself. And he told me later to explain to Cornelia's sons, who were sitting in front of us, that he was not being rude, because this was part of his illness. When I told Victor and Andrei, they were sympathetic, and very sad for Connie.

Cornelia had prepared short eats, and the table was loaded with a great deal of food. We stayed for a little while, sharing good memories of her mother, and had a few snacks. I told her I could not attend the funeral next day, as I had to be at school, but Connie would definitely be there. She understood, and we came home after seven o'clock that night.

I drove to school next morning, Monday, the 20th, and Connie left at nine o'clock to attend Florica's funeral at Springvale cemetery. The weather was dreadful, and it rained heavily, with cold, gusty winds that howled non-stop. After a busy day, it was almost five o'clock when I returned home, as Tess finished her lesson at four thirty.

It still rained heavily, and the stormy weather continued all evening, as I started making dinner. Connie returned home around six o'clock, and said he went for the wake at Cornelia's place, and then somewhere else, before he came home. He was out from early morning till now, and I wondered how he could go on without resting.

I was busy in the kitchen, while he stood near the bench-top opposite me, trying to explain how the funeral went, and who was there etc. as he liked to relate everything in detail as usual. I listened, while I was stirring the pot, when next moment, without any warning, he flipped over and fell backwards. I watched helplessly, just like in a slow-motion movie.

I could not get to him in time, as I was standing opposite him with the bench-top in-between. He hit his head on the side table, and then fell on the tiled floor. A trickle of blood spread under his head, but he managed to struggle up to his feet. When I asked, "What *happened*?" he replied, "I tripped on my shoe." "*How* can you trip on your shoe, when you were just standing there talking to me?" He frowned and did not reply. I quickly checked his head and saw a deep gash, so I applied an ice-pack to stop the bleeding, washed the wound with some disinfectant, and bandaged it. Then I made him sit down, and gave him two panadeines. When I tried to call an ambulance, he became really angry and shouted, "*Don't* call an ambulance! I don't want to go to hospital!" I cleaned up the floor where a pool of blood was congealing, and mopped up the area while he sat quietly in the lounge.

I served his dinner, which he ate slowly, and then sat with me for an hour while I watched "Revenge." He went to bed early that night, and I was glad he did not wake up till morning, as he was exhausted and suffering from mild shock after that sudden fall.

I refrained from telling him that it was too much for him to be out all day, besides keeping up till dawn over the last few nights, attending healing services. Whatever I told him, did not seem to penetrate his mind.

I knew that loss of balance was part of the disease, and he knew it too, as the neurologist explained this to us. But he *never* admitted his falls were due to the disease, and kept blaming something else, like tripping on his shoes, or on the tiles.

I left at midday to visit Ninette next day, and Connie seemed alright, as the wound had stopped bleeding. But he said he wanted to see Dr Yap again, as he was not happy with Dr Khelil. This was because Dr Khelil always told Connie hard facts, and he did not like to face reality. So he kept consulting various other doctors to hear what *he* wanted to hear. He made an appointment to see Dr Yap at two o'clock that afternoon, but before I left, I asked him why he did not see Dr Khelil instead. He lost his temper and started shouting that he was fed up with him, and wanted to see Dr Yap.

Ninette started relating all her symptoms and ailments from the moment she saw me. She was totally engrossed in her health issues, and paid very little attention when

I told her about Connie's fall. It was very sad to watch her becoming so self-absorbed, but I supposed it was all part of growing old. I fervently hoped I would never become a hypochondriac, or be a nuisance to others when I grew old.

After I left Ninette's, I stopped at the post office around four o'clock, when Connie called me. He was sobbing over the phone, and I thought he was feeling sick, so I asked him, "What's wrong?" "Dr Yap didn't see me! He told me to go back to my own doctor! I don't trust *any* doctor, I only trust God! I know God will heal me soon! I'm going with Tucko for a prayer meeting tonight. Babs called just now, she wants to visit. I told her you'll be home soon." I asked, "*How* can you go anywhere tonight, when you're not well after your fall? Why don't you come home now, if Babs is coming?" He hesitated, then said, "I'll come home in a little while, I'm going to Tucko's place now." And he hung up.

I came home shortly after, feeling very distressed, not knowing why Connie would not come home and rest, without driving around at night. I knew Roland and Geraldine were responsible for this change in Connie, because he was so vulnerable now. When I reached home, I saw Babs and Aaron parked outside the gate, waiting for me. I invited them in, and they had cake and coffee. Aaron said he was managing a holiday resort in Cambodia, and was visiting briefly. It was good to see Babs and him. I told her what happened the night before, and how Connie went to healing services regularly now.

She once belonged to a 'Born again' church, but left after some years, and she told me the reason why. "Those fanatical cult religions try their best to break up families, and in the name of God, they divide families!" So she found out, and was really annoyed with her siblings for what they were doing to us. She said she would speak to Roland about taking Connie out so late at nights. I tried calling his mobile to ask him if he was coming home soon, but he did not answer. Babs and Aaron stayed till about seven o'clock, and he still had not returned.

I was tired, and went to bed around ten o'clock, as it had been a long day, and I expected Connie anytime. But I could not fall asleep, as I was worried, wondering whether he was alright driving home so late. It was unlike him not to call and let me know when he was coming home.

I fretted till way past midnight, and still no sign of him. I heard the car at 12.30am, and got out of bed to find out why he was so late, and why he did not even call me. When I saw him stumbling through the door, I asked, "*Why* didn't you call me? And why are you so late, especially after your fall last night? Don't you know I was worried about you, wondering what could have happened?" he replied, "My mobile wasn't charged." I was so angry, and asked, "How would you like if I told you I went for a prayer meeting so late, and didn't even call you?" he mumbled, "I would say, 'alleluia, praise the Lord!'"

I became angrier still. "*Why* are you talking like those 'Born again' Christians? Why are you behaving like this?" he retorted," *You* go to Ninette's!" Then I lost my temper. I could not believe that he resented my visits to an elderly lady, and used that as an excuse for staying out so late. "What do you think I go to Ninette's for? She is my piano teacher, and I don't go out visiting her at midnight anyway!"

We argued for about twenty minutes, and I was really disgusted that he used my visits to Ninette as an excuse for his midnight excursions. I did not speak anymore, and he stayed up for a while before he settled down.

I felt tired and upset next day, thinking about Connie's behaviour and resentment because I visited Ninette, an elderly lady, who needed help. Ever since he started going to prayer meetings with his brother and sister, his behaviour towards me was worse. He was more aggressive and bitter. And behaved as if I did not matter in his life anymore, and did not care about my feelings at all.

I found solace playing the piano for a while next morning. And then attended to book orders, correspondence etc. as Luigi asked me to send copies of his book, and CD's to various people, and I had to write some letters on his behalf.

The occupational therapist, Claudia, a resolute, no-nonsense lady, arrived at one thirty that afternoon, to assess Connie. I told her about his fall the other night, and how he was out driving till after midnight. She was very concerned, and had a long talk with him. Then she said, "Conrad, I have seen a few patients like you, and you have to expect your mobility to get worse, that is the nature of this disease. I'm going to assess whether you need a walker very soon, to prevent these falls. Also, no more driving at nights! Only short trips to Mornington and back, for your own safety, and other drivers." He did not reply, and looked vague, as if he did not hear what she was saying or chose not to hear.

She checked his hands, legs, and mental alertness. I was relieved to hear her say he could not drive at nights, because I knew it was becoming too risky. His brother and sister were constantly assuring him that "God will protect you, and you will be okay." So, he could jump in front of a train, and God would protect him. That was how fanatical these evangelists were.

Before Claudia left, she told him, "I will come again next Monday, and we're going driving to the shops, to see how you can cope with getting about. Also, we will get a special pillow to help your breathing." This was because his chest was congested, and caused him a great deal of discomfort, especially at nights. She left after an hour, then I did some grocery shopping and returned soon. I made dinner, and we watched a movie. He was subdued, but he said, "Claudia is very negative!" I did not reply, because I knew that anyone who told him the truth about his illness was being "negative."

When I went to school next day, Connie stayed home, and I knew he was exhausted, as he was still resting at nine o'clock. I hoped he would settle down, and try to enjoy life with me, now that he was not working, instead of running to his siblings, or going to their prayer meetings.

The weather was better, and I saw the building on our left, rising higher and higher. It would cut out a large section of ocean views from downstairs, but it was inevitable, I supposed. I was sad, as the sea view from the living and dining areas was one of the advantages here. Elvira invited me for coffee, so I visited her briefly after school.

I told her what was happening, and she too was very concerned about Connie's behaviour. And she could not understand his siblings, who did not show any concern for his safety or well-being, or even asked me if it was alright for Connie to be driving so late at nights. She was incredulous that they did not respect me as his wife, and influenced a sick person so adversely.

I told her that they had no consideration for me, as they just wanted to convince Connie that he would be miraculously cured at their prayer meetings. Poor man. He was so desperate, and ready to believe anything they told him. As someone told me, "The 'Born again' followers descend like vultures on vulnerable, sick people, who can't think straight, and they claim to have converted them!"

When I returned home, I made dinner, and later we watched a comedy show on television. At least he seemed to be slightly relaxed, as his mind was occupied watching something entertaining, and not constantly dwelling on his illness. The show went on till almost midnight.

He said Geraldine called and asked him to attend another prayer meeting that night. Honestly! What utter gall! But he told her I was very angry with him for going to those meetings so late at night, and that the occupational therapist told him he could not drive at nights any more. I did not reply.

Connie then told me that Geraldine was dead set against all medical advice, and told him not to take any medications, or listen to doctors, as they did not know anything, and only God had the power to heal. She failed to understand God can work miracles *through* doctors, and patients need to follow a doctor's advice, if they wanted to be cured. Roland and she had no idea what this disease was about, and although I believe in miracles too, I have faith in doctors, knowing they have skills and drugs to heal.

I was home on Friday, and busy with my writing, as I wanted to enter a scriptwriting competition held by the Australian Writers Guild, and that kept me busy for a few hours. Connie drove to Rosebud in the afternoon for an appointment with the physio. He said he was alright to drive during the day, and did not want me to drive him, so I stayed home. I called Shirani to see how she was coping, and was sad that she had to deal with so much of stress. Then I made some curries for our guests on Sunday.

Connie returned home by six o'clock, and seemed more calm. He said he walked on the beach after the appointment, and the physio made him exercise his legs and arms, and told him to do those exercises daily. She also told him that riding an exercise bike would be beneficial for his leg muscles.

The bike was upstairs in the spare room, so I encouraged him to ride it for at least twenty minutes daily. He said he would try. And I stressed how important it was, as the physio explained that the only way to delay the progression of this disease, was to strengthen his muscles.

I served his dinner, and he ate without complaining, which was unusual, because he was very difficult, and fussier than ever with meals. He could not chew meats, so I made sure everything was cooked until very tender.

We watched "Inspector General" (again), as I told him it was a funny movie. He laughed and enjoyed it too, so it was good to see him unwind.

I cooked a few more curries and buriyani rice, and a few mild dishes for Lorraine on Saturday. And I was worn-out by the time I finished, as I was coming in for a head cold again. Then I cleaned and vacuumed the house, before resting for a while.

Connie went out that morning, saying he needed a pair of shoes. I called Nilanthi, and she said she was planning to come before the end of the year (provided we sent her a ticket). I promised I would help, as she said she was anxious to see us.

Connie phoned in the afternoon and left a message, "Dolla, don't worry, I'm out looking at cars." He planned to buy a new car, in case they took away his company car soon. Although I was not too happy about him buying a new car, I did not want to discourage him, as it was something he looked forward to. He came home by four o'clock, and we were too tired to go for Mass that evening. Lorraine called to ask directions, as Tony was going to drive next day.

I woke up early next morning, knowing that they always came well ahead of scheduled time. Connie went out again at eleven o'clock, as he was not happy with the shoes he bought, and wanted to exchange them. Lorraine and Tony arrived fifteen minutes later, and it was just as well I was ready, and lunch was prepared too. Connie returned about an hour later, and we enjoyed a pleasant afternoon. They left around two thirty, as Tony wanted to get home before too late, due to his poor eyesight.

Elvira wanted to drop in later, and I said it was fine. Then Joelle called to say that one of our colleagues, John, at the tax office, died of a brain tumour the week before, and the funeral was last Friday. John was a very nice, friendly person, and I was sad to hear about his death, as he was in his early fifties. Elvira and John came soon after, and she brought freshly baked scones, which we enjoyed.

We had a good chat, and then I played some songs for her, which she wanted to practise, and they left after five o'clock. I cleaned and washed up all the dishes, as I did not want Connie to do anything. He was losing his grip (literally), and dropped things often, and broke a few glasses and crockery over the last few months. He took it easy, and watched television till I finished cleaning up.

Although I went to school next day, I did not feel well at all, as I had a head cold and a slight temperature. I came home early, and Claudia took Connie to Mornington that afternoon to see how he coped with shopping, and also to observe his movements. The therapists were very thorough, and good at their work; ever since Connie was diagnosed, the network of therapists and services they provided were excellent. I rested till Connie returned at four o'clock.

He said he did not buy the special pillow, which was $100, and told Claudia, "My wife can sew a pillow like that! I'm not spending so much for a piece of foam!" He said he was tired, but she assessed him as being able to manage going to the shops at present, which was good. Then I watched "Revenge" in the night, and he went to bed soon after.

Early next morning, Connie told me Roland was on his way here. Shiranthi was holidaying in Sri Lanka then, and he was at a loose end, not knowing how to spend his time. Geraldine also called to say she was visiting that afternoon, but he said he had a doctor's appointment at three o'clock.

I was weary of these two people, and their determination to drag him to their prayer meetings and convert him. I wanted to give them a piece of my mind, for keeping him out so late, even after his fall. But they cunningly intruded whenever I was not at home, so they could brain-wash him. So I told Connie I was fed up with their behaviour, but he started shouting, and lost his temper. And we ended up arguing because of them, as usual.

Between Roland and Geraldine, they bombarded him with their fanatical beliefs, and prevented him from accepting his illness patiently, and following doctor's advice. That was what made me livid. They brought dozens of so-called "healing" CD's and urged him to listen to them all day long, over and over, in the way people were indoctrinated. He always looked more desolate, and was hostile towards me after they visited him, which made me wonder what was going on.

When they did not visit, they phoned, emailed, or sent text messages with the same propaganda, so they completely controlled and manipulated Connie. They drove a wedge between us, and took the upper hand, now that he was weak and incapable of rational thinking. Geraldine slithered into our lives with false promises of miracles.

I was so stressed about this situation, that I left before midday to visit Ninette. I told him that it was very annoying I had to leave early, just because his brother wanted to visit early in the morning. I returned at four thirty, and Connie came home an hour later, as he said he visited Esme after seeing doctor. I did not say much, and he sat at the computer all evening.

I was upset to think how Connie wasted his time now, instead of pursuing all the things he said he would, when he stopped work. He never read a book, or enjoyed being at home. All he did now was listen to healing CD's or visit his siblings.

Nelune called, and we chatted and laughed, which was good, because I felt so weary of all these problems. As if I did not have enough stress dealing with Connie's illness and bad behaviour, I now had to endure his siblings' interference and intrusion as well.

I watched Bill Gates on Q & A on ABC, and found it really interesting, as he spoke so well on important issues that we faced today. It was enjoyable, but Connie did not watch it with me, as he was still working on the computer. I started reading George Eliot's "Adam Bede" that night, and hoped it would take my mind off my worries.

It was sunny, but very gusty next day, and my cold was worse, so I did not accompany Connie to the speech therapist that afternoon. We had trouble with the landline, and the phone was out of order again. Christian called on my mobile to say that Athena and he would visit that night.

I was happy, as they were very busy, and could not visit for some time, so I quickly made a couple of curries, and then relaxed a while until they arrived a little later. We had a good time chatting and laughing, and I was very glad to see them. Connie too sat at table, and tried to join in the conversation now and then, and they left after a couple of hours.

I washed up and was about to go to bed, when the drama began. Connie complained about severe stomach pains, and said it must have been the dinner. I asked him what was wrong with the meal, as we all ate the same food, and none of us suffered indigestion. I suggested that he take a quick eze tablet, or some raw ginger to help indigestion.

He got into bed, and told me to bring some ginger, as he was in extreme pain. I did so quickly, and he chewed the ginger and took a quick eze tablet. But at about one o'clock in the morning, he said the pain was so severe that I should call an ambulance. He got up and struggled to the kitchen, and while I was on the phone to the ambulance, he stood there and let his dinner explode all over the kitchen floor! And instead of going to the laundry or toilet, he stood near the bench top and splattered his dinner everywhere.

I told the person on the phone that he was vomiting violently now, and she said the ambulance would arrive soon. Then I made him sit down, and told him to try and relax, while I mopped and cleaned. I said, "*How* am I going to get up in time to go to school tomorrow?" and he mumbled, "Don't go to school, stay in and rest tomorrow."

I kept looking outside to see if the ambulance was there, and they finally arrived at two o'clock in the morning. They were busy with other emergency calls, and were delayed. When they checked Connie, they could not find out what was wrong with him. He told them he took four panadeines already, but they gave him another pain killer, and said they would take him to Rosebud hospital to keep him under observation. I told him I would call the hospital in the morning, and pick him up if they discharged him. I was exhausted, and went to sleep a couple of hours later.

A nurse from Rosebud hospital called me at eight o'clock next morning, and said they were discharging him, as they could not find anything wrong with him. And they would send him in a patient ambulance. I waited till they dropped him off at nine thirty, and I was ready to go to school. But I told him to rest in bed until I came home. It rained heavily, so I hoped he would stay in till I returned.

I had a busy day at school, and stopped to get some groceries later, so it was after five o'clock when I came home. Connie was sitting up, and watching one of the "healing" DVD's. As he saw me, he started complaining of severe pains again. I said, "The hospital didn't find *anything* wrong, so what do you want to do now? Do you want to see Dr Khelil tomorrow?" he did not reply. And when I went to bed, I could not sleep a wink, as Connie lay tossing and groaning in pain all night. Finally, around six o'clock in the morning, I tottered upstairs to the guest room, and flopped into bed, as I was desperate to get a few hours sleep.

Connie woke up early next day, 31 May, and made an appointment to see Dr Khelil, and left home at 9.30am. My head cold still lingered, and I felt rather lethargic. Christian called to say he would drop in around three o'clock, as I told him about the drama with Connie, after they left that night. Then I did some chores, and called my sisters to tell them what was happening, and they were very concerned to hear about Connie.

I played the piano later on, and I felt very sad, wondering how much longer I could hold on, as Connie was getting worse. I would never leave him, now that he was so ill. But because he knew that, he behaved worse than ever. I put it down to his illness, as it was easier to be patient and tolerant that way.

At about one o'clock that afternoon, Elaine, the secretary from St Francis Xavier church, phoned me and said, "Conrad is here, and he's behaving very strangely. The other ladies here and I, are very concerned about him driving, as he doesn't seem too well at all. When we told him we were going to call you, he shouted, '*Don't* call my wife!' He wanted to know when the healing service was at Frankston, but I told him we did not have a service that day."

I told her he was referring to the monthly, healing Mass on Sundays. Then she said he was getting aggressive because they tried to keep him in the office until they spoke to me. I said he had a doctor's appointment there, and he was supposed to be at the clinic, then I thanked Elaine for calling me, and told her not to worry, as he was alright to drive himself home.

I was upset, wondering why he was behaving aggressively to outsiders, especially to those nice ladies in the parish office, and waited for him to come home. Christian came around three thirty, and I told him what happened, and he could not understand his behaviour either. Connie returned an hour later, and said he had seen Dr Khelil, and waited for x-rays and scans. In the meantime, he went to the church office to find out about the healing services.

I told him Elaine called me, because she was concerned about him, but he was very annoyed with her for calling me anyway. Dr Khelil said that Connie had a few small kidney stones, which were causing him pain, and to drink plenty of fluids and water to help pass the stones, also to take panadeine forte. He went to bed immediately, as he was exhausted, without much sleep the previous nights. After Christian left, I walked in the garden for a while, and then worked on the stage play.

Connie woke up later in the night, but did not eat much. I spent some time writing. And as always, immersing myself in writing, music, and art was the panacea for my problems. If I did not keep my mind busy, I knew it would drive me crazy, with all that was going on around me; writing gave me something else to focus on, and helped me to look at everything in perspective. I was thankful I had this coping mechanism all my days, as we all have our own ways of coping; some turn to alcohol or food, or any other outlet that obliterates the problem even for a little while.

My head cold still persisted, and I felt weary, but I followed my usual routine. Shirani asked if they could drop in that afternoon, so I was happy to see them, although they could stay only for an hour. They were very worried when they noticed how much Connie's speech had deteriorated since they last visited. After they left, we attended evening Mass at Mornington. Cornelia wanted to visit tomorrow morning, and Elvira too rang in the night to ask after Connie. We watched a comedy till late, and he relaxed a little that night.

I slept upstairs in the guest room over the last couple of nights, as I told Connie I needed to rest, due to my head cold, and also to prevent him from catching it, as he already had trouble breathing at nights. He did not mind, and agreed without making a fuss, which was good, as I thought he would start shouting at me because I wanted to sleep alone.

I woke up early, and waited all morning, but Con and Cornelia failed to make an appearance, and did not even call to say what had happened. Anyway, I took it easy, and Connie rested too, as he was still feeling very tired and in some pain, although it was not too severe. He thought he may have passed the kidney stones, as the sharp pains subsided, for which I was glad. Then I wrote for a couple of hours, made dinner and took it easy. I slept much better upstairs, and was glad for the few hours of undisturbed sleep.

After a busy schedule at school next day, I did some shopping and returned home at about five o'clock. Connie said Roland visited, and he looked very subdued, and hardly spoke all evening. Whenever Geraldine and Roland visited, Connie was distant, and immersed himself in "faith healing" CD's and DVD's they brought him every week.

He clutched at straws desperately, and I was very sorry for him. But I kept telling him God will work a miracle *if* God wanted to, and to try and be submissive to His will. And not to believe that just listening to CD's and going for prayer meetings was going to heal him. They had convinced him it was the *only* way, and unfortunately he believed them. I watched "Revenge," and then read till late.

I visited Ninette next day, and had a snack with her, then later on, I dropped in at Shirani's place at Narre Warren to wish her for her birthday, which was on 8 June, and came home around five o'clock. The reason I did not want to come home early was, that I needed respite from Connie, as he started complaining about something from the moment he saw me. He was watching "faith healing" DVD's again. I made soup for dinner, and then watched television for a while, as he was in the other room watching his DVD's.

Chapter 74

I accompanied Connie next day, the 5th of June, to Woolworths store in Mornington, to meet Mathew, and his boss, Robert, from Sydney. Mathew asked me to be present at the meeting too, as Connie decided to retire at the end of June that year. He knew he could not drive far, and his speech did not improve with therapy.

When Robert spoke via Skype, I explained what was happening with Connie's health, and his decision to retire. He said, "Conrad, *if* you are able to take on another role, which doesn't involve driving, or verbal communication, we'll find another job for you in the company. Would you consider that?" Connie shook his head and replied, "No, no," quite emphatically a few times.

Robert then asked, "What about driving?" I replied, "He is allowed to drive only short distances, and not at nights." Then Robert asked Mathew to pick up the company car at Connie's convenience. and Connie said they could pick it up next Friday. When all these matters were settled, Robert told Connie how sorry he was to hear of his health problems, and thanked him for all his hard work over the years, at which, Connie broke down and cried helplessly.

I was very upset to watch his distress, knowing how difficult it was for him to make this decision. His bosses understood that he was unable to control his emotions, and sympathized with him. I tried to console Connie and hugged him, as I felt incredibly sad and felt his pain deeply, but was helpless to alleviate his sufferings. Words are so inadequate to describe the sadness, heartache, and confusion we both endured. And I can hardly begin to convey the utter desolation and emotional tsunami that swept over us.

We stopped at Mt Martha later to get some groceries, before returning home late afternoon. He was still very emotional, and I tried to comfort him as well as I could, but I knew he was shattered. His work was his priority for more than thirty years, and to be forced to retire, because of his health, was a bitter pill to swallow. Christian and Shirani called that evening to ask how the meeting went, and were very distressed when I told them about the outcome.

I finished school early next day as a few students were away, then I drove to the sunspot clinic in Mornington. But they did not see me till an hour later, and I finished at three thirty. Then I stopped at Bentons Square to get my pills, and as I came out of the chemist's, who should be hanging around there, but Cristobel! When she saw me she burst out, "I was *praying* to meet you here, so I could explain why I behaved like that when Mummy died."

I was extremely surprised, and did not want to listen to her excuses. But she held onto my shopping trolley, and spun her usual excuses and stories, trying to justify her deplorable behaviour. "When I saw Esme and Jenny pulling down the pictures, and packing up everything, because they said Connie wanted the unit cleaned up so he can sell it soon, I was so angry! That's why I called him that morning." I replied, "That is *no* excuse for the way you cursed Connie. You told him he will crawl on his knees, and should die and rot in hell! Are you *happy,* now this has happened to him?"

She immediately reverted to the past, and some incidents when we lived in Nuwara Eliya. "We know how jealous Connie was of you, and I visited only because of you, as I *hated* Connie! Now it's different, and I'm sorry he's so sick." She kept going on for nearly forty minutes, and then said, "I'll come and take Connie in a wheelchair, if you want to go out anywhere." I replied, "He's *still* able to walk, thank God. When that time comes, we'll see. And I never go out anywhere on my own, especially during weekends." I knew she wanted to take over, and be in charge of Connie, just like she controlled her mother. Then she said, "We're *family,* we want to spend quality time with him."

I asked, "How come you didn't visit him over the past seven years or more, when he was well and able to talk? You and Connie have been at loggerheads as far back as I can remember, and you told me how much you *hated* him. But if you want to make up now, and spend time with him, you are free to visit him. I have to go now." I walked away, as she was absolutely annoying, and I knew just how insincere she was.

Even Aunty warned me a few times, saying, "Be careful of her, she's like a snake in the grass!" Her mother summed up her character precisely. She could make up with Connie for all I cared. But I despised the way she insinuated herself into his life now, just so she could manipulate him.

When I told Connie about the encounter, all he did was giggle, and did not say anything. I made dinner, then watched television till late, and was almost asleep when he came to bed. But instead of sleeping, he sat up texting in bed for about half an hour. He had an old mobile, not an iphone, so every time he pressed a button, it beeped, and this went on and on.

I did not ask who he was texting at midnight, but I said, "Why don't you go somewhere else and text, because you're disturbing me!" He did not pay any attention, and just kept on texting for a few more minutes. The next day, he told me that Geraldine and Cristobel sent him prayers and messages every night.

He showed me Geraldine's messages sometimes, as she copied long passages and quotations from the Bible. His siblings always stayed up till the early hours of dawn, and now they kept Connie up too, especially Geraldine, with her excessive Bible-bashing even via text messages.

I woke up around three o'clock on Friday, 7 June, and went to sleep upstairs, as Connie was very restless, and kept me up with his tossing and groaning all night. Finally, I fell asleep a couple of hours later, and although I was worn-out, I was ready when Mathew and Joel came to pick up the company car around ten o'clock. They brought a large hamper of fruits from Connie's colleagues, and chatted to him for some time. After they had biscuits and coffee, they left within the hour, and said they would visit regularly with his other colleagues.

Connie drove my car to Rosebud in the afternoon, for his appointment with the physio. I took it easy after he left, then made some cutlets for our guests next day. Later on, I spoke to Shirani, Nelune, and Ninette, as they wanted to know how Connie was, Then I walked in the garden for a while, as it cleared up after heavy rain. Connie said that when he finished with the physio, he drove to Frankston hospital to do a MRI scan. I made dinner, and worked on the computer till he returned.

I prepared some more dishes next morning, but Con called at one o'clock and said they were delayed, and would come at four o'clock. Elvira brought home-made scones a little later, and left in an hour's time. Con and Cornelia finally turned up at five o'clock. They said they waited for his mother to pick their grandson Ashton, and that was why they were delayed.

We had a pleasant evening, although I was very tired after waiting for them all day, and they left after eight o'clock. But a few minutes later, Con drove back, saying Cornelia could not find her car keys. We searched everywhere, but they were nowhere to be seen. He went off, and then called a little later to say they found her keys in the car.

I was drained, so I enjoyed a long spa bath, then watched "Avatar," for the first time. It was a good movie, but went on till midnight, because of all the commercial breaks. Connie typed his letter of resignation till late, so I read a little, and tried to unwind.

We attended Mass at Mornington next day, and took some fruits from the hamper for Elvira and John, then came home around midday. It was a pleasant, sunny day, so Connie decided to mow the lawns, but when he tried to get it going, the mower did not start. He was very annoyed, and wanted to buy a new mower from Bunnings.

I spoke to Chris La Ponder for some time, as she asked me how Connie was, and then I called Mary. Mary was going for an operation next day, to lift her drooping eyelids. I wished her well, and hoped she would be alright. Then I worked on the stage play for a few hours.

We watched "The Great Gatsby," starring Leonardo Di Capri, at Karingal cinema the following afternoon. He was excellent in the role, and I enjoyed it thoroughly; it was beautifully filmed, very atmospheric, and the 1920s period was re-created skilfully.

Connie did not enjoy the movie though, and when I asked him why, he said the music was too loud. We came home by six o'clock after some shopping. I tried to call Janice in the evening, as she emailed me regarding Connie's health, but she was not home. Janice called next day, and we had a long chat. She was very upset to hear that Connie's condition was worse.

Whenever he watched television now, he sat on three cushions, as he said his stomach felt tight, and he could not breathe. He spent a long time trying to make himself comfortable, then complained the sofa was no good. He lost a great deal of weight in the last three months, which was quite noticeable now. And when he walked, he dragged his left leg and leaned to a side.

I visited Ninette next day, and she invited me to share a bowl of soup with her. When I returned home around five o'clock after grocery shopping, Roland's car was parked out on the street. So I drove back to Mornington, as I was not in a mood to have a discussion with him. While I was driving there, Connie called to ask where I was. I told him I was in Mornington, and would get back within the next hour. Then Roland took the phone and asked, "*Where* are you? *What* are you doing?" I replied I had to finish some shopping, and would be home later.

I was tired and uptight, as I wanted to get home and relax. When I came back an hour later, his car was gone, so I drove into the garage. Connie said he came at one thirty, and they watched religious DVD's till six o'clock. It was not that I minded, or cared how long they stayed, it was Connie's behaviour *after* they left, that upset me. I could not understand *why* he was so hostile, agitated, and depressed after their visits.

Connie was becoming utterly confused now, because they told him nothing was wrong with him, and he would be cured soon, as God would work a miracle. The neurologists and therapists told him otherwise, and what was actually happening to his body and mind, as they tried to prepare him for the inevitable.

I went along with the doctors, and tried to help him accept the unavoidable as well. But he thought I was negative, and that I should deny the truth, like his evangelical siblings. That was one of the reasons for his hostility, I supposed. But I just could not shut out the truth and be blind, even though I prayed earnestly, that if God willed, to heal Connie soon.

Being optimistic and realistic were very different, and Connie did not face reality at all, as his "Born again" siblings did not *allow* him to accept his disease. He was angry with me, and resentful that he was going through this terrible situation; losing his speech, gradually getting weaker, and told he would lose all mobility soon. He turned on me in his fear and frustration, as I was the only one he could vent his anger on. Although I tried hard to be patient with him, it was very difficult to tolerate his behaviour at times.

Mathew left a message on my mobile, asking me to contact him. And when I spoke to him, he said he wanted Connie to re-phrase, and edit a few sentences in his letter of resignation. His letter implied that Woolworths had *forced* him to retire, which they did not. In fact they offered alternative employment, where Connie did not have to communicate with contractors or stores, and just work on a computer. But on a lower wage, and no company car either, because no travelling was involved. That was why Connie decided to retire, rather than work under those conditions. When I told Connie what Mathew said, he sat at the computer immediately and edited his letter.

We drove to Rosebud the following afternoon, for his appointments with the speech therapist and dietician. The speech therapist continued with his exercises, and also watched him drink water, and munch on a biscuit, to see how well he could swallow. She said that as the throat muscles became weaker, he was liable to choke on food and drinks. At present he swallowed without any difficulty, but the dietician was concerned with his rapid deterioration, and weight loss.

His chest was badly congested, and his breathing very difficult. So they referred him to a doctor there, who advised him to go to Frankston hospital that very evening to check his lungs and breathing problem.

It rained heavily all day, and the weather was miserable when I drove back a few hours later. We waited at Rosebud rehab centre till they organized a bed at Frankston hospital, and they told us to go straight into emergency, and Connie would be admitted without much delay.

On the way back, and at home, his mood changed rapidly. He was hostile, shouted, or ignored me completely, when I asked him anything. What hurt me most was, that he was very pleasant and friendly to all the ladies and staff at the rehab centre. And they all said how well he was dealing with everything, but it was another story with me. I wondered what went on in his mind, as he was so rude and uncaring towards me now. He did not seem to realize how exhausted I was, after spending the whole day driving him to Rosebud and back, then sitting with him till evening.

When I asked him to get ready before it got too late, as I did not want to drive back in the night in such bad weather, he growled angrily, "I *don't* want to go to hospital!" As he could hardly speak clearly now, he had a small notebook, in which he wrote brief messages and instructions for me. I reminded him to take that notebook to hospital, and then I packed an overnight bag. At about four thirty, he was still dawdling, and refused to get ready.

I kept telling him that he should listen to doctor, and check out his lungs, as he always complained about how difficult it was to breathe, especially at nights. It took a great deal of cajoling and convincing, and we left home around seven o'clock. I drove, as it was dark now and still pouring down heavily, and he said he was very tired.

I explained to the nurse in emergency that Rosebud hospital called earlier to arrange a bed for him. And she said it would not take long, although she had no record of such an arrangement. I was very surprised, as we waited for hours at Rosebud, till they finalised Connie's admission that evening.

I told her that Connie had a speech problem, but he could write, and understand what was being said, then he told me that he did not bring the notebook with him. I had one in my bag, so I left that with him, and drove home in such torrential rain that I could hardly see the road. It was after eight o'clock when I arrived home, and I was exhausted after such a long, trying day, especially dealing with Connie's bad behaviour.

I went to bed early and slept well, and I drove to school next morning, feeling refreshed. When I called the hospital around nine o'clock, they put me through to the ward. Cristobel answered the phone, and she said, "Esme spent the night with Connie and left in the morning; if you are too busy, Esme and Paul can drop off Connie." I replied, "Of *course, I* will pick up Connie, when I know what time they will discharge him. Don't worry about it." I found her tone of voice, and insinuation that I was "too busy" to pick up my husband, very offensive, to say the least.

Connie had sent Esme a text message at ten thirty the previous night, asking her to bring him a sandwich, as he was hungry, and did not take his wallet with him. They kept him waiting in emergency till after midnight.

The nurse asked me to call back in the afternoon, as they could not tell me what time he would be discharged. I finished school early, did some shopping, and came home at about three o'clock. Just as I arrived home, the nurse called to say he was discharged, and I could pick him up now.

Connie sent me a text message too asking me to come "immediately." I drove back to Frankston, and found him standing outside the hospital with Cristobel holding his arm. I helped him in, and he waved at her saying, "God bless you, thank you *very much*." He had nothing to say to me, and we drove back in silence, as he did not utter one single word all the way. When we came home, he sat at the computer and typed a whole page, to tell me what happened the previous night.

He wrote, "I was hungry and asked Esme to bring food at ten thirty. She came again in the afternoon, so did Tucko, Jenny, and Clifford to see me. Jenny had come to Mt Martha and asked Tucko where I was, so they all came there. The hospital couldn't find anything wrong with my lungs, but told me to see my doctor and take some antibiotics for the congestion."

I put away the groceries, and later replied emails on my laptop, as he was still on the computer all evening. But he slept alright that night, and was still sleeping when I woke up at three o'clock in the morning to let Mishka and Simba out, as they were impatient to run out.

The rain eased slightly next day, but it was still very cold and gloomy. I did my usual chores, and then called Esme to let her how Connie was, and gave her my mobile number, in case she needed to contact me. She said that when she saw Connie in hospital, he wrote, "I give Dolla a hard time," because he must have realised how much he stressed me that day. I explained what happened, and how stubborn he was, when it came to following doctor's instructions. She replied that she knew what he was like, and was sympathetic.

Babs sent a text message to say she would visit on Saturday. And Elvira invited me in the afternoon, but I told her I was too tired, so she said she would drop in instead. She had baked rock-cakes, and brought them over in the afternoon, and stayed for about an hour. We talked about all the issues I faced with Connie, and his siblings, and she was very concerned. He was busy on the computer, and only stopped to have a rock-cake, and a cup of tea.

I rested a while after she left, then walked in the garden, as it was a pleasant evening, although storm clouds hung heavily, but patches of pink swept the skies, and cold stars gleamed high above. I watched a funny movie that night, with Will Smith and Kevin Kline "Wild Wild West," and afterwards "Air Force One," with Harrison Ford. It was a very good movie too, but Connie did not watch television that night, and went to bed early, saying he did not get much sleep the night before.

I felt a surge of energy next day, so I weeded the garden, cleaned the house, hemmed Ninette's skirts, and then waited for Babs, but she did not turn up all day. I spoke to Nelune, and then took it easy before working on the stage play. The draft of the last act was nearly finished, and it was satisfying to see the end of it, as I spent a great deal of time and energy on it. I watched television for a while before going to bed, and then read for some time. Connie turned in early, as he was very tired.

I made some pan rolls after lunch next day, then Esme left a message on my mobile, saying they would visit, and arrived at about two o'clock. I had not finished frying the rolls yet, but I served them a few. They were just leaving a couple of hours later, when Paul, Sanit, and Yasmin dropped in, and stayed for an hour. We were ready to go for a healing Mass at Frankston, at five thirty, so they did not stay long. I gave Yasmin $20 for her birthday, and $50 for Paul's birthday at the end of the month.

It poured down that evening, but Connie insisted on driving. After Mass I spoke to Donna and Harry, who led the prayer group, and they prayed over Connie. When Fr Denis anointed Connie, and the other sick people, Connie started to bawl out loudly. I explained about his illness, and they all said they would pray for him.

I was really stressed when we drove back, as it was dark, and raining heavily, and Connie's driving was erratic. Next moment, he swerved the car and drove on the wrong side of the road. I shouted out, "*Connie,* you are on the *wrong* side of the road!" The driver of an on-coming vehicle flashed his lights, until Connie cut back onto the right side of the road, and steadied the car. I was a nervous wreck, but I did not say anything. I knew he would only shout at me, as if it was my fault.

His speech was thick, and incoherent now, and whenever he was angry, he made terrible, growling noises, like an animal in distress. And it was extremely painful to listen to him. So I tried my best not to say anything, because he hated to be told he was in the wrong. We came home safely by seven o'clock, and I finished frying the pan rolls in an hour's time. Then I had a long, hot spa bath, and went to bed early, as I was drained.

I woke up around five o'clock next morning, and let Simba and Mishka out, then went back to bed. When I called Simba later, he was nowhere to be seen. I walked around the garden, calling out, but there was no sign of him. I was very upset, as he could not climb or jump fences, because he was too tubby, and his back paws were not very strong. He was like that ever since he was a kitten, and could not climb trees as nimbly as the other two.

When I visited Ninette that afternoon, I told her how upset I was about Simba, and that I was invoking Bruno to bring him home safely. It was my habit to invoke Bruno now, no matter what the problem was, and many times I had evidence of his help.

Ninette too believed in his miraculous powers, and constantly asked for his help, so she told me. When I came home that evening, there was Simba, sitting nonchalantly, as if nothing had happened at all. I was so relieved to see him, that I called Ninette immediately, and told her Simba was back safely, and she was happy too, and said that Bruno answered me. I never found out where Simba went that day, or how he came back, unless he had a secret hiding place in the garden.

Next day, 19 June, we drove to Frankston for Connie's second appointment with Prof. Butler. He checked Connie thoroughly for about forty minutes, his throat, arms, legs, and neck. Then he turned to me and said, "Conrad's facial muscles are stiffening, and as you can see, there isn't much expression in his face, is there? There'll come a time, when he won't be able to keep his eyes open either, as the eyelids will start drooping. His hands will lose strength, and he won't be able to grasp things, besides losing the ability to walk. I've seen similar cases, and I'm sorry to say you will be in a wheel chair eventually."

I looked at Connie, who did not pay any attention to him, and looked ahead vaguely, as if he did not hear him at all. But he wrote in his notebook, "Is there any medication I can take?" Prof. Butler replied, "Unfortunately, there is no cure or treatment Conrad, but I will prescribe some tablets to help relax your muscles, as the pain in your neck is due to tightening of the muscles around that area. Take one a night, and see if it helps you." Then we left, after I made another appointment in a few weeks' time.

Christian called on our way home, to ask how the appointment went, and I explained briefly what the neurologist had said. He was very upset to hear the prognosis, then he spoke to Connie, who just grunted in reply.

He was in a foul mood all evening, and started raving over nothing, shouting at me, and making those horrible, guttural sounds in his throat. My head was spinning. I was so weary of this burden; as if it was not enough I drove him around for all his appointments, and shopping etc. I had to put up with his foul moods as well. He was so frustrated that he could not speak, and I understood that, but what more was I supposed to do to help him. After hearing the professor's prognosis, he lashed out at the unfairness of his fate, and naturally, I bore the brunt of his anger.

No matter how sympathetic and understanding I was, he vented his frustration on me. I needed the patience of a saint to keep my mouth shut, and told myself repeatedly that he could not help it, as it was a terrible illness. But he did not make it any easier by accepting the inevitable, instead he fought angrily against his fate.

It was very pleasant and sunny next day. I cleaned and vacuumed the house, as Linda and her parents were visiting tomorrow. Then I baked a cake, before taking it easy in the afternoon. Joelle wanted to visit the following afternoon, and I said it was fine. I enjoyed her company, and her mother and aunt were very nice people too.

I spoke to Del later, and she was very comforting and sympathetic as always. Her husband, Jack, was diagnosed with cancer, and was not too well either. So we shared our burdens, which was very helpful.

The evening turned out to be very pleasant, and I walked in the garden for some time. Then I worked on the stage play as I was home alone.

Connie said he was driving my car to Springvale in the afternoon. He came home after six o'clock in the evening, and said he went to Mornington instead. But I did not ask him what he did so long.

Linda sent a text saying she was unwell, and could not come, but her parents were still visiting. Julie and Paul arrived around eleven o'clock, and we had a pleasant time. Paul was very helpful, and attended to some things around the garden. And he said he would visit again with Linda and Leo, so they could help with some gardening jobs. Julie baked a cake for afternoon tea, and they had lunch when Paul finished outside.

They enjoyed the pasta I made with chorizo sausages, and Julie wanted the recipe. It was a beautiful, sunny day, and we spent some time outside.

I was grateful to all my dear friends, who were very concerned about Connie, and wanted to help in any way they could, and enjoyed their company whenever they visited. After they left, Joelle, Celine, and Micheline arrived around three o'clock, and stayed for an hour. I was tired, but we attended evening Mass in Mornington. Shirani called that night to ask if they could visit tomorrow afternoon, and I said I would be happy to see her.

Sunday was another beautiful, sunny day. I relaxed and played the piano until Shirani and Ranjith arrived around one o'clock. But they did not stay long and left within the hour. We enjoyed a good chat though, and after they left, Connie drove to Mornington Bunnings to buy a new lawn mower. He gave the old one to Roland, as it was too difficult for him to use it any more. Now he wanted one with a key start, so he did not have to use too much pressure to start it.

I walked in the garden and enjoyed the pleasant weather. Christian called to ask how Connie was. And we had a long discussion about the future, and what the specialist told us, as I did not like to discuss his illness when he was around. He was very worried, and sad to hear what would eventually happen to Connie.

It was another spectacular sunset, and I removed more photographs. Connie came home around six o'clock, and asked me to help him get the new mower out of the boot. I was annoyed and asked him how he expected me to lift such a heavy load. It was still in a box, and was very very heavy. But I managed to unload it, as he had no strength in his arms at all, and could hardly lift it. Eventually, we got it out of the boot with great difficulty, and I hoped I did not strain my back and shoulders. I replied emails later, and edited the stage play for a couple of hours.

Chapter 75

Mathew called and asked if I had any suggestions about a farewell gift for Connie, as they had only two choices so far, a pen or a watch. They were organizing a farewell party in the canteen at Woolworths head office in Mulgrave, on 28 June. I was at school when Mathew called me, and it occurred to me then, that as Connie scribbled on notepads, and bits of paper whenever he wanted to communicate, an ipad would be more useful than a pen or a watch. Mathew was very happy with my suggestion, and thought it was a good idea.

I thought about an ipad after our last visit to the speech therapist, as she showed us a program with a robotic voice, that read back whatever was typed on an ipad. It would be a great way for Connie to communicate. But I did not mention that Mathew called, as I wanted him to be pleasantly surprised.

Connie told me Roland was visiting early that Monday morning, and when I came home around five thirty, he was not at home. I thought they went for a drive. But I was very concerned, and upset that he did not leave a note to say where he had gone, because he usually scribbled a note to tell me what he was doing. I relaxed in a spa bath, and I heard them coming in a little later. Roland was talking to Connie, so I stayed in the bath till he left half an hour later.

When I came out, I asked, "Why didn't you leave a note to tell me where you were?" he replied, "I sent text." And when I checked my mobile, I saw a message at five thirty, sent half an hour before he came home. He said they had looked at cars. He never mentioned anything about looking for cars, and did not even ask if I wanted to go with him, but went with Roland, and then visited Paul and Sanit.

I just looked at him in disbelief. I wanted to tell him that his wife should be involved in an important decision, like buying a new car, and not his brother. But I did not want him to get angry and shout at me, so I refrained from saying anything, and went upstairs to do some writing and emails.

I visited Ninette next day, and walked with her to the shops, before I went for my appointment to the podiatrist, then shopped, and came home around five thirty. Connie was very unpleasant, and ignored me completely when I greeted him, and then just grunted when I asked him how he was feeling.

I was at the end of my patience and wondered, *how much longer Lord, how much longer*? That evening, he gave me a really hard time. He waved a pension application form in my face, and *demanded* that I complete it. Next moment, he grabbed the form from me and tried to fill it. After a few minutes, he shouted and banged his fists on the table, yelling out that he could not complete the form. I asked him, "Do you want me to help you fill the form or not?" He flung around furiously and got into a frenzy, threw the form and pen on the floor and shouted at me angrily.

I could not stand his aggressive behaviour any longer, as he was acting like a raging lunatic. I asked, "Is *this* your idea of Christianity, to be so rude to me for no reason?" He began growling like an animal, and looked so furious, that I left him alone. I thought he was having a fit, the way he twisted and swayed around.

I walked out of the room, as my chest started to hurt so badly, I could not breathe. I went out to the deck and sat down on a bench, then cried so hard and begged God to help me bear this burden, as his behaviour was getting worse each day. The chest pains continued all evening and night, and I thought I would suffer another heart attack, if I had to bear the brunt of Connie's aggressive moods any longer.

He sat at the computer that night, and typed one whole page saying, "I'm sorry Dolla, but I was getting so frustrated at all the questions in the form, and that's why I never wanted to go on an age pension, if I could have helped it. I didn't mean to take it out on you."

When I read what he wrote, I was so sad, that I just hugged him and said, "I understand how you feel, and if you want, I will go through the form and help you to complete it. You know I'm here for you, so try not to get so angry. It's not good for you, or for me." He was calmer afterwards, but I was afraid he was becoming more irrational and frustrated. And I did not like being caught up in the firing line all the time.

Mathew called again next day, to ask if Connie finished typing his farewell speech, as Connie wanted Mathew to read it out loud to his colleagues. I said I would ask him to email it as soon as it was ready. Connie wanted me to read his draft first, and correct any mistakes. Then I typed his speech quickly, and he emailed it to Mathew that same afternoon. I completed the pension application form later, as Connie's writing was very shaky now, and he did not want to make mistakes.

It was a very depressing sort of day, although the weather was mild and sunny. I did some chores, played the piano, and then called Nelune, as she was always cheerful and comforting. Then I edited the stage play for a while, before I made dinner.

I was at school next day, on 27 June, but finished early, and had lunch with Liz at a cafe in Frankston. We ordered a pizza, that turned out to be half-baked, with very sparse fillings. Liz was not happy at all, and complained to the manager, so they brought another pizza, which was no better.

I stopped to get groceries on my way, and came home around five o'clock. When I reversed into the driveway, the first thing I noticed, was a patch of dark blood stains at the bottom of the driveway, and thought, *oh no, Connie must have hurt himself again!*

Sure enough, when I walked into the kitchen, he stood there, holding tissues to his bleeding forehead. "*What* did you do?" I asked, and he replied, "I wanted to help you bring in the garbage bins, and I slipped and fell." I was so annoyed. "You know Claudia told you *not* to walk up the driveway, as it's too steep or drag bins?" he did not answer.

I made him sit down, and asked him what time he fell, and he said it was about twenty minutes ago before I arrived. I put an ice-pack on the bump, as it was swelling up, and his eye was bruised again. He said his shoulder hurt where he knocked it on the concrete. I dressed the wound on his forehead, and went out to wash the driveway.

The last time Claudia saw Connie, she specifically told him that he should not go down the steps to the garden, or walk up the driveway, so as to avoid falling. I was very annoyed, because he did not pay any attention to what was being told for his own good.

Christian called in the night, and when I told him about Connie's fall, he was very worried. He asked if he should get their friend Christy, a nurse, who lived close by, to have a look at him. But I told him not to worry, as the bleeding had stopped, and it was not a deep wound, just a nasty bump on his forehead, and he had a black eye.

Connie sat quietly and watched television while I prepared dinner, but once again, I was so stressed and tired that I had chest pains all evening. He complained of pains in his shoulder, so I applied dencorub on his neck and shoulders before he went to bed. Sometimes, when I was so upset with him, I told him that the stress would kill me·first, if he did not listen to doctors and therapists, but continued to flout their advice and ended up falling and hurting himself.

It was unfortunate that he fell and hurt himself just one day before his farewell, because his forehead and eyes were bruised and badly swollen. Mathew called the previous day, and asked me to bring Connie at least fifteen minutes earlier to the office, just so he would be prepared, as two of his bosses were flying in from Sydney.

I told him I would see to it that Connie was there in time, so I woke up early next day on Friday. Connie seemed to be alright, as he woke up around ten o'clock. He sat down at the computer after breakfast, and I reminded him from about midday to get ready, as we had to be in Mulgrave by one forty five.

He ignored me completely, and did not care as time ticked away, until I got so frustrated and said, "Can you please get ready soon?" he shouted back, "*Don't* rush me!" He took one hour just to shower, and could hardly put his socks on or button his shirt. I said, "*Knowing* how long you need to get ready, why don't you start *early*?" he just growled angrily. I sat there all dressed up, waiting, and waiting.

Finally, I helped him to button his shirt, and put his socks and shoes on, as he could not do it. Then it took him about ten minutes to get into the car, as his lumbering movements were very very slow now. It was ten past two when we left Mt Martha, and Christian called at two forty five to ask where we were, as I told him to be there with Athena on time. It was three o'clock when we finally arrived at Mulgrave. I was so frustrated, because I liked to be punctual, and had promised Mathew I would be there early. But with Connie, it was always a rush to get anywhere on time.

Everyone gathered in the large amenities area, where photographs and posters of Connie with his colleagues at various conventions, and functions decorated the walls. In one poster, Connie, and a few others were dressed up as Elvis Presley impersonators, and everyone had a good laugh when they saw them.

From the time we got down from the car, Connie wanted to hold on to my arm, and walked up to the room slowly. But when they saw him, plenty of ladies, and his mates wanted to help him around. They all asked in disbelief, "What *happened* to you Conrad? Did your wife beat you up?" he giggled, and I explained that he fell the previous evening.

Christian and Athena removed many photographs, and every single contractor, and colleague that Connie knew over forty years or more, were present that day. They all asked me what was wrong with Connie, and he told me to explain his condition, as he was just able to say, "Thank you very much," to his bosses when they finished their speeches. And when Mathew read out Connie's farewell speech, all those present were very moved. He did not get emotional, and I was relieved. Because it was just terrible when he started bawling and crying helplessly.

He received many presents from those who attended, and at the end of the speeches, Mathew presented him with an ipad. Connie was very happy with it, and showed his paper notepad he used, and they all laughed. Over one hundred people came to his farewell. And I was happy to know how much his bosses and colleagues appreciated his hard work, and long years of loyal service. They all acknowledged his dedicated contribution to the company. Christian and Athena too were impressed to see so many people, who gathered to wish Connie farewell, and a happy retirement.

We stayed chatting to some of the people we knew well, like Con, Cynthia and Ron, Chris, Barry, Graham, Lorraine, and many others. They all promised to visit us often, as they told me they knew Connie for so many years, and would miss him very much. And they held him in high esteem, because he did his job well, and even his bosses said they commended his dependability and "tenacity" when it came to getting a job done to everyone's satisfaction.

Finally, we left at about five o'clock, and came home within the hour. Christian and Athena drove back to the city, as they had to work, but I was really pleased they came, and although Connie did not say much, I knew their presence meant a great deal to him. When Christian and Athena were introduced to one of his bosses, he said, "Conrad, I hope you enjoy retirement with your beautiful family." He did not respond, but just looked around vaguely.

I was exhausted when we came home, and so was Connie, as it was a very emotional afternoon, especially for him. They gave photographs of him dressed up as Elvis, and every time he looked at them he giggled helplessly. So I said he should hang them in the study, where he could look at them and be happy recalling fun times.

The following day, Suresh called unexpectedly, and said he wanted to visit. He arrived before midday, and when he saw Connie's state, he just burst out crying. He stayed a little while, and said he would visit again. Suresh kept saying, "He has been a good uncle always, as he helped me to get a job at Woolworths." I was glad that Suresh remembered, and was grateful.

Con and Cornelia were visiting that day, and we expected them anytime, so I made over fifty meat patties. Babs phoned and asked if Damian and Jeremy could visit too. I said we would be happy to see them, as Connie always asked her to bring Damian along. Con and Cornelia arrived at about four o'clock, and they enjoyed the patties with their home-made wine.

Babs, Damian, and Jeremy, came an hour later, and they too enjoyed the patties, especially Damian, who kept saying, "These patties taste just like the ones in Ceylon!"

Then Connie started playing Elvis's Christmas CD. And one of the songs "It Won't Be Like Christmas Without You," was his favourite one, as he said it reminded him of Stacy. Now he started bawling out loudly, "Stacy, Stacy," and was very distressed. I told Babs that he always got emotional when he heard that song, and she replied, "Why don't you *chuck* that CD away for heaven's sake, if it upsets him so much!" I could not understand why he played that CD now, because it was not even Christmas, and we were entertaining friends. Con and Cornelia looked upset, but I explained the reason why, and they understood.

After that futile incident, they all stayed on till about nine o'clock, but I did not have anything cooked for dinner, except soup, so I could not ask them to stay. I did not expect them to wait so long, and I kept plying them with more patties, until they were all finished. Connie and I had a bowl of soup and pan rolls after the visitors left, and watched television for a while before turning in. I was very tired, but read for a while.

I slept in late on Sunday morning, and did not go to church, as we were both too tired. Then I called Nilanthi, and we had a long chat. I made a few more patties in the afternoon, with the left-over filling. Elvira wanted to come over, as John had to fix the lock on the back gate.

She brought some delicious biscuits she baked, and I served them some patties, which they enjoyed, as they liked savoury food. John fixed the lock, and they left after five thirty. It was drizzling slightly, but I walked in the garden for half an hour. It was another tiring day, and we relaxed, watching television for a while before going to bed.

We had to go to Mornington Centrelink that Monday afternoon, 1 July, to lodge an application for the age pension, as Connie's last salary was paid to the end of June. I slept upstairs the night before, because Connie was very restless. He asked me to phone RACV, and his Credit Corp, and change personal details. Then he wanted to see doctor, because of his breathing difficulties.

I made an appointment with doctor at two o'clock, but he kept dawdling without getting ready. And then he became angry, saying he could not get ready by one forty five, as I said we had to leave by then. So he told me to cancel doctor's appointment, which I did. Felix called just then, to say he was flying to Melbourne on Saturday, and would visit.

I drove Connie to Centrelink at two o'clock, as he was very unsteady, and did not want to drive. We had a long wait, but finished in an hour's time. Then he wanted to shop at Karingal to get a new razor, so I drove him there. He never took any notice of how tired I felt. He was aloof most of the time, and acted as if I did not exist. He ignored me whenever I spoke to him, not even bothering to reply. It was very hurtful, as I did my best for him, and tried hard to be patient and understanding. But he was just so difficult, and getting worse each day.

When I tried to hold and steady him at the shops, he pushed my arm away, and held on to a shopping trolley instead. I supposed he felt more secure holding on to a trolley. Usually, he would have insisted on driving, but he said he did not want to drive back home either. I could see he was weak and shaky on his feet. When I came home, I called Ninette, as she expected me to call her daily, and also to tell her I was visiting tomorrow.

I spent a pleasant afternoon with Ninette next day, and listened to her playing the piano, then came home around five thirty after some shopping. Geraldine and Clifford were driving off, just as I drove into the garage, and Connie stood at the front door waving at them.

A few minutes later, she returned, and stomped inside the house, saying, "I saw you driving in, and wanted to talk to you, because I want to ask you something." I replied, "I hope you're not going to start *preaching* now, as I'm very tired," Because I knew what her conversation was like. Some of the family called her an "utter bore," as she had only two topics, Adam and Bible-bashing.

She smiled in an ingratiating manner, "No, I want to ask you to write a book about Adam." I could not believe my ears. Aunty told me that Adam was expelled from a couple of schools, due to some serious misdemeanours. And he died violently, while setting off banned fireworks and explosives. But she always carried on as if Adam was a *martyr*.

I replied, "I'm *not* interested in writing a book about Adam, and also I'm not very comfortable about this situation with you and Clifford. I heard what's been going on, as Sanit told me everything. I would appreciate it very much if you don't come here with him in future. I'm also very angry that you got Connie to drive to a prayer meeting in Berwick, after he had a bad fall. And you still send messages telling him to go for those meetings."

She immediately blamed Roland, "Tucko *shouldn't* have done that! I didn't know, and anyway, no one knows what my life is like with Clifford. I know what the family thinks, but I do what God wants me to do, I'm praying that Clifford will be healed from his sins."

Connie always said that they were a "weird couple," and he felt uneasy with them. I felt negative vibes in her presence now, and one look at her haggard face, was enough to convince me that she had no inner peace. The family shunned Clifford, but only Roland and Connie accepted him now, and overlooked his scandalous behaviour. Geraldine condoned her husband's behaviour as well, because she was too insecure to live on her own. And no matter how many times he strayed, she clung to the belief that he would be "healed" from his infidelities.

I could see nothing spiritual or serene about her; dark circles smudged her sunken eyes. She looked like a demented harpy, with bleached blonde hair that frizzed around her swarthy face.

After more gibbering about God, faith-healing, and her marital problems, she finally left. I was irritated that she barged in, and forced me to listen to her raving, when all I wanted was some peace at home. I asked Connie, "What's going on?

Knowing about the scandal regarding Clifford and Sanit, why are you encouraging him in our home, when you tormented my life for the last forty two years because of him! And you told me that you wanted nothing to do with them."

He wrote on a piece of paper, "She's not negative, and wants me to be healed." I asked, "*Who's* negative? We *all* want you to be healed, but you must do as the doctors ask you, and take the medication they give you." Then he went to the computer and typed one page about how he felt, and how he had changed his attitude regarding Clifford.

I could not understand why he was so weak now. But he thought he would be miraculously healed, as he believed them implicitly now. They took it in turns to visit a few times a week, and manipulate him. I could not convince him that it was delusional to think that listening to CD's all day long would heal him. He desperately *wanted* to believe in them, and the miracle they promised, if he followed their beliefs. They well and truly infiltrated into our home and lives, when he was so vulnerable.

They never dared to try and convert us all these years. That was the sore point, as they slithered into our lives when he was weak. Now, Geraldine kept telling Connie, "Don't trust doctors, *I* don't take any medicines, so trust in God, and don't take any medicines!" I was very upset about this situation. I made dinner, and then watched a comedy series "Soap" on DVD. Connie sat with me for a while, and watched it too.

I was also annoyed because whenever they visited Connie, he was more depressed, and hostile towards me. I was unaware what mind games they played with him, as he huddled in a corner, ignored me, and listened to healing CD's all night. But he was not cheerful or positive, for all the good they did him. If their propaganda helped him, I would not have minded so much. But I believed he became more confused, and for some reason, his anger was directed at me.

Babs and Esme were the only ones who were sympathetic, and understood what I endured. They were aware of Connie's difficult and stubborn nature, which became worse with his illness. His other siblings had no clue as to what I went through, because Connie was on his best behaviour with everyone else except me.

Not only did I have to suffer Connie's irrational and aggressive behaviour, but his siblings' interference made my life with him worse than ever. I had no support from them at all. And as I said, only Babs and Esme showed any understanding of the situation, and they did not try to convert him either. Esme was still a Catholic, and Babs left that cult religion some time ago, as she found out how they destroyed families.

It was pleasant and sunny next day, so I took it easy and pottered in the garden, and then played the piano for a while. Esme called to say she would visit tomorrow.

I drove Connie to Frankston for his appointment with the sleep specialist, at three thirty that day. When the specialist asked him why he did not take the tablets that Prof. Butler prescribed, Connie became angry, and raised his voice, "They have *side-effects,* that's *why* I won't take them!" He could not convince Connie to take the tablets. But he prescribed a mild sedative, and recommended an oxygen mask, to wear at nights to ease his breathing.

The specialist said we could hire one from the sleep clinic at Frankston hospital. He wanted to see Connie again next week, to see if the sedatives and mask were helping. When we stopped at the chemist's at Bentons Square, I met Alan and Ginny after a long time. They were concerned to hear about Connie's illness, and said they would visit next Saturday afternoon.

I was busy next day, and as Connie took a sedative, he slept through the night, which was good. But he was very annoyed, saying he felt drowsy all day, and would not take the sedative again. Esme and Paul came around two o'clock, and stayed for an hour. I took it easy before we went to Elvira's for dinner that evening. It was a wild, stormy evening, with gusty winds, and I drove, as he said he was tired.

Before we left home, Connie was very agitated, and cried out loudly for no reason at all. He shouted out, "I'm going to buy a car and *drive* to Berwick for the prayer meetings! I *want* to go tomorrow night!" Poor man. I understood his frustration. But I did not want to tell him that he was incapable of driving again, and it was pointless to buy a car. When I told him he should listen to the doctors, he shouted at the top of his voice, "You are *negative!*"

Now I understood why he was so angry with me. He wanted me to pretend that nothing was wrong with him, and lie to him, that he was going to be well again. I could not lie though, as I accompanied him to all the therapists and specialists, who all said the same thing; that his condition was deteriorating rapidly. And I saw him weakening before my eyes. His siblings were not there to hear the weekly reports of the medical team. And Connie did not want to believe anything they said, because his evangelical siblings influenced him adversely.

I braced myself to face the worst now, as I knew he was mortally afraid of what doctors told would happen to him at the end. And I understood perfectly why he was deluding himself, because the truth frightened him out of his wits. When I read more about this disease, I found out that David Niven, the famous actor, died of a similar condition, which was so virulent that he had lasted only twelve months after diagnosis. The disease progressed slowly in some patients. And they lived a few years, as they became immobile gradually, but in Connie's case, it was incredible how quickly he weakened mentally and physically.

His "Born again" siblings assured him that he was "healed" and sent him cards and messages saying, "We thank God for your healing! Praise the Lord, alleluia! You have been touched, and healed in His name!" I did not mind them being optimistic and hopeful. But I was sad to see how he clung to such a doubtful promise of a miraculous cure.

Although it was perfectly normal to be hopeful in such a situation, Connie was in total denial, which was a tragedy. He was manipulated and brain-washed relentlessly, so that he was totally confused. If they left him alone, he would have come to terms with his illness, and we would have borne this burden together, with mutual love and support. But their constant interference deprived us of any peace.

On our way to Elvira's that evening, he did not fasten his seat belt, and it beeped all the way. Then he turned on the radio volume very loud, so as to drown out the beeping, and my ears and head ached with all that noise. But to avoid an argument, I refrained from saying anything, till we arrived there in less than five minutes.

During the evening, I mentioned to John that he wanted to drive to Berwick on Friday night for a prayer meeting, and to please talk him out of it. John's daughter,

Kay, and their friend Daphne, were present too, and we enjoyed a pleasant evening. Before we left, John said, "Conrad, *promise* me you won't drive in the night, and not so far by yourself tomorrow?" Connie did not reply, but just smiled vaguely. We left around nine thirty, and I drove home.

The next morning, Connie wrote a brief note, "I'm sorry for bad behaviour last night, and I won't drive at nights to go for prayer meetings again." I hugged him, and told him I understood what he was going through. And that I knew how frustrating it was for him, but he could drive and go anywhere, once he got stronger and better.

Then he started to bawl and cry out loudly. It was heartbreaking to watch him. No matter how badly he behaved, when I saw him break down and cry like that, my heart melted, and all my anger and irritation left me. I was full of compassion for him, as my husband, and a suffering human being. But I was helpless in this situation, and only wanted to live with him, as normally as possible under the circumstances.

That was the main reason why I resented those zealots, who interfered in our lives constantly now. They did not allow Connie to come to terms with his illness, and leave us alone to cope with this challenging time. They ignored the fact that he had a wife and son, as they wanted to be in control.

I tried to tell him that if God wanted to, he would work a miracle any time, any place, not just in a church in Hallam or Berwick. And I said, "Even Jesus Christ prayed to God to take away his suffering, *if* it was God's will, and said, '*Thy* will, not mine be done.' So, you *must* try to submit to God's will and be patient." He listened, and did not reply. These were the only times that I could try to reason with him, when his mind was not confused by their relentless onslaught.

Now I understood how religious fanatics all over the world create so much disruption and destruction within families, all in the name of God. But in reality, for selfish ends, to drag vulnerable people into sects. Except for Babs, not one of his siblings even asked me how *I* was coping, and whether I needed any support. *That* was the true extent of their Christianity.

The strong winds still blew gustily, and the front fence crashed down! The garbage bin lid also came off its hinges. I called council, regarding the bin, and they said they would replace it soon. Then I phoned the fencing man, who said he would come as soon as possible that morning, and brace up the fence. But he could repair it only on Monday, as it was Saturday next day. I said it was alright, as it could not be helped.

Connie drove to Rosebud for an appointment with the physio that afternoon. I cleaned up, and did some chores till he returned around three thirty. He did some exercises, and she asked him to ride the exercise bike daily, to strengthen his leg muscles. I told him to follow their advice faithfully, and to exercise ten or fifteen minutes on the bike. Then I went to get some groceries, and returned soon, and baked a cake for our visitors tomorrow.

I prepared everything the following morning, and expected Felix and Yasmin around midday. But they arrived after two o'clock, as they were delayed on the roads. Yasmin's cousin drove them, so they could not stay more than half an hour. I prepared lunch for them, but they were due to have lunch at her cousin's place.

Anyway, they enjoyed the butter cake, patties, and cutlets, with a cup of tea, and said they would visit again.

Felix brought some blessed oil from a church overseas, and said a prayer, as he applied it on Connie's lips. He was a very sincere friend, and so was Yasmin. I was sorry they had to go early, but just as they were leaving, Alan and Ginny arrived.

We had a pleasant afternoon with them too, and they left a couple of hours later. Although I was very tired, we attended Mass at Mornington, and I drove, as the weather was very bad. When we came home around seven o'clock, I opened the garage door to go inside, and then I heard a loud crash. I rushed back to the car, and found Connie down on the floor! He was lying on his back, unable to get up, and kept struggling to stand.

I tried to help him up, but he was so heavy, that I was unable to get him back on his feet. So I brought the step ladder, and told him to try and raise himself by holding onto the handles. It took him about half an hour, with me helping him. My arms and shoulders were aching, as he clung onto me. But finally, we managed. I helped him inside and made him sit down.

That was not the end of it, because he felt dizzy and wobbly on his feet, so I had to fetch and carry all evening. He wrote down instructions on how to mix his drinks, and what he wanted for dinner. By the time he went to bed, I was drained. It was going to be a real challenge now, as he was getting weaker, and not very steady on his feet. Each time he fell, he found it more difficult to get up, as his legs became stiff, like wooden stumps.

I was even more upset that night, because although I called Simba till midnight, he did not come home. I left the cat cage door open, and went to bed. When I woke up early next morning, there he was, fast asleep in his basket inside the cage, as if nothing was amiss. They were such a worry at times, the three naughty cats.

Hemal and Rathna visited on Sunday afternoon, and they brought lunch from a Sri Lankan restaurant in Dandenong, as they told me not to worry to cook anything. The food was delicious, and tasted just like home-cooking. I enjoyed it very much, and even Connie said it was good, and he ate well. We relaxed and chatted later, but it turned out to be a busy afternoon. Graham and Lorraine arrived around two o'clock, and were still there when Elvira, John, Mary, and Tony arrived an hour later.

They told me they would visit today, and although it was hectic, I did not mind at all. They were very kind and supportive friends, and we had a pleasant time. Connie wrote little notes, and joined in the conversation as much as possible.

I asked him to get the ipad connected soon, so he could type instead of scribbling notes. He said he was waiting for one of his colleagues to come over and connect it. Mary and Tony left within the hour, but John and Elvira stayed a little longer. John brought the exercise bike down, and set it up in our bedroom, as Connie said he was finding it difficult to climb the stairs, and preferred the bike to be in the bedroom.

We arranged the arm chair behind the bike, in case he fell backwards, and tried to make it as safe as possible. I told him he should get on the bike daily, as he had no excuse now. I cleaned and washed up dishes after they left, and then we watched a few comedies till late.

The fencing man came early on Monday morning, and finished around eleven thirty. He wanted to know what was wrong with Connie, when he saw him standing at the door and waving at him, but not saying anything. I explained what the illness was, and he was quite concerned, as he had never heard of such a disease in his life.

I drove to Mornington after the man left, as I was meeting Nancy at Onde's. We had a pleasant time, but Nancy did not eat or drink anything, except her home-made juice, as she was on a "cleansing diet." She drove me to Mt Martha afterwards, as she wanted to see Connie too.

When she saw him tottering unsteadily, she was surprised and told me, "He will need a walker soon to help him, as he looks very wobbly." Connie did not hear her. I asked him whether he would like to drive back with us, as my car was parked in Mornington. He agreed, and said he wanted to feed stale bread to the sea gulls, and walk on the pier.

Nancy drove us back, and I picked up my car, then drove towards the yacht club in Mornington, where plenty of ravenous seagulls hovered around. Connie got out of the car, and tottered along a few steps towards the pier. He could hardly walk straight now, so I asked him if he would like to walk any further. But he just emptied the bag of stale bread near the car, and said he was too tired to walk any further and wanted to go home. I thought the last fall must have affected him more than he knew. Because overnight, he was weaker, and dragged his legs painfully when he walked.

I visited Ninette next day and took a chocolate cake for tea, and I was happy to see Liliana there. We were fond of each other, and sometimes, she made it a point to visit on a Tuesday when I was there as well. I stopped to get groceries on my way, and returned home around six o'clock. He said no one visited him that day.

I typed a few letters later in the evening, to enclose with Luigi's books and CD. He asked me to send copies to several prominent figures in Melbourne and Sydney, as he wanted someone to sponsor him and organize concerts. But so far, they never acknowledged receipt of the books or CD's.

Shirley Whiteway, one of the members of the Women Writers Society, just published her first book, and sent me a copy. It was a very interesting story, so I wrote her a note of congratulations, and a cheque for the book, then finished my correspondence by late evening.

I cooked fish and chips, and steamed vegetables for dinner, as Connie preferred mild food now, without too much spice. He still enjoyed a couple of drinks before dinner, but added more ice cubes than before. We watched television together, and he seemed a little more calm, which made me happy. He was not confused, aggressive, or in a depressed mood, like he was whenever the evangelists visited.

I drove to doctor's next morning, as I was getting chest pains often, and also to check my pressure. Roland told Connie they were visiting, and bringing lunch. I did not stay, as I had a busy schedule, but it did not matter to him at all, because he was home all the time.

When doctor asked if I was under any stress, I told him how very demanding and tiring it was, dealing with Connie; his falls, his behaviour, and how difficult it was for me to pick him up, as I hurt my shoulder and arms the last time I helped him to get back on his feet.

He had a long chat with me then, about how Connie was going to get worse, and would need 24 hour medical attention, which I would be unable to provide. He said he would eventually have to go into a nursing home, but I would have a great deal of help and support. I would not have to deal with him on my own, so not to worry too much about it at present.

Then he told me that the first step was to get him assessed by the Aged Care Assessment team, so that Connie would get help at home. The Carer Support team would assist me with advice and respite care, if I needed to go out, and was unable to leave Connie on his own.

He faxed the paperwork while I was there, and told me they would contact me shortly to make an appointment. Then he told me to take care, in order to prevent another heart attack, with all the stress I was going through. I explained how some of his siblings were trying to convert him, and influenced him so much, that he would not listen to doctors' advice or take medication.

He understood how much pressure I was undergoing then, but advised me on how to deal with Connie. I felt slightly better afterwards, knowing there was support for me too. After shopping at Karingal, I drove back to the chemist at Frankston, as I forgot to pick up my medicines.

Connie could not clip his toe nails now, so I spent time doing that for him in the evening. He had a fungus in his thumb nail that I treated daily with anti-fungal medication, as he was very worried about it. He fussed greatly, each time he saw the discoloured nail, although it was not painful.

Elvira called the following day, 13 July, to say they would pick us up at six o'clock to go to Mary's for dinner, as it was their anniversary on 10th July. It was chilly and rainy, and I rested a while, after making pan rolls in the afternoon. Connie still enjoyed them very much, and that was why I made them almost every weekend.

They arrived just after six o'clock, and John almost carried Connie and settled him in the front seat. Janet and John, Tony's relatives, came too, all the way from Whittlesea, and they prepared a great amount of food. Elvira had made a pasta dish, which she said was especially for Connie, as it was soft and easy to swallow. I was distressed when Connie sat still, and just listened to everyone talking, as he could not join in. And I hoped that the ipad would help him to communicate to some extent. We had a pleasant evening, and came home around nine thirty.

I took it easy next day, but Con and Cornelia dropped in unexpectedly around midday. They said they were passing by, and wanted to see how we were. I served pan rolls and cutlets, with a bowl of soup for lunch, and they stayed till about five o'clock. Connie was restless, and kept writing notes, "We have to go to church soon!" So they left shortly after.

We attended Mass at Frankston, and when we came home, Janice called to say they were going away on holiday, and just wanted to know how Connie was doing. I had a nice long chat with her, and Connie managed to say "Hello" in a thick, guttural voice. Janice was very upset when she heard him struggling to speak, and could not believe his condition deteriorated so rapidly.

Christian called later, and said he was busy sorting out some issues that were causing him a great deal of stress. I was very worried, but he said he was alright now, and would visit soon.

It was the first day of term three at school on Monday, 15 July, and after a very busy day, I came home around five o'clock.

Shirani and Ranjith went on a two week holiday to Sri Lanka, so I missed talking to her, but was glad that she had a short break from her hectic schedule. I spent a quiet evening, and watched "Mrs Brown's Boys," a BBC comedy, as Connie was on the computer.

He told me later that Claudia, the occupational therapist, was visiting him at one thirty next day, and so was Roland. I drove to Ninette's, and after some shopping, I returned home around five thirty. Connie said Claudia wanted to see me on Friday, but did not say why. After doing some chores and making dinner, I watched a few more episodes of "Mrs Brown's Boys," till about one o'clock in the morning, as he went to bed early, but I wanted to unwind.

I went to bed and fell asleep, but only for a short while, because an hour later, Connie made distressed noises, and shouted out loud, "Arghh, arghh, arghh," and looked very frightened. When I asked him what was wrong, he just kept on shouting, and thrashing his arms and legs about.

I got out of bed and said, "I don't know what's *wrong* or what you *want!* Did you have a nightmare? I'll bring your note book, and you can write down what you want me to do." When I gave him the notebook, he scribbled, "Turn off the electric blanket, I'm too hot." I replied, "*Why* didn't you turn it off before you fell asleep, or when you just woke up, without making such a big fuss? I thought something was really wrong with you!"

He went back to sleep after I switched it off. I was really puzzled as to why he behaved like that over such a trivial matter, like feeling too hot. He gave me such a fright, as I thought he was having a fit, or was in severe pain.

Chapter 76

The Aged Care Assessor, Lindy, called me a few days later to make an appointment, and she arrived around one thirty on 17 July. I was busy all morning, trying to format a screen play, which was challenging. But I was determined to get it right. Just before Lindy arrived, I prepared Connie for her visit, and said that it was all part of the system, to assess him.

He wrote "Claudia has already assessed me," I replied, "This assessment is through Aged Care for future needs." But he was not happy, and did not look pleased at all when she entered the room. He scowled at her when I introduced him, and then ignored her completely.

She asked him several questions, then explained her role. And she said that because of his progressive illness, he would soon require care in a nursing home, and also a carer at home, to assist with showering, because I would not be able to cope looking after him. He became very angry, and scribbled, "I have family, and my brothers and sisters will come anytime, I don't need a carer!"

Then he stomped off to the study to get something, and I explained to Lindy about his "Born again" siblings, and she said, "Don't talk to me about those cult religions! I've seen enough of that in my time! They *always infiltrate* when people are sick and vulnerable, to get them in their clutches and create disruption in families!" I was pleased that she knew what I was talking about.

I mentioned about the night he woke up, as if he was having a fit, and looked disoriented, just because he was too hot, and wanted me to turn off his electric blanket. She said that he could be suffering from early onset of dementia, judging by his irrational behaviour, as dementia was part of PSP in most patients. Then she completed a form, and said that from what she observed, he would require "high care" very soon.

She also told me that it was very important to organize medical and financial power of attorney before he got worse, and said she would send me the necessary documents. Connie was quiet after she left, but later he wrote "Do you want me to go into a nursing home? You know how they treat people there!" I did not reply, as it was pointless. He was convinced that all nursing homes were bad places, and perhaps some of them were. But they could not all be condemned, on account of some bad ones.

He wanted to go to Benton's Square afterwards. And on the way, he told me to stop at our neighbour's place in Somerset Drive, and give him an invoice for fencing costs. I could not find parking on the busy road, and drove up and down for some time, before I finally parked on the nature strip. I felt drained and stressed by now, and then he wanted to stop at Main Street Mornington, to buy something there.

I stayed close to him, because he was very unsteady on his feet. And each time he pulled out his wallet, he fumbled, as he was unable to take his card or money out. His fingers were stiff and losing flexibility. I realized then that it was no longer safe for him to be out on his own.

It was an unusually warm, twenty two degrees next day in the middle of July, and it was very pleasant. I was at school till about two o'clock, when a sudden thunderstorm broke out, followed by torrential rain. So much for the Indian Summer! I came home straight, as Connie had an appointment with Dr Gupta at Rosebud hospital that afternoon. The receptionist called at two thirty to say that the three o'clock appointment was cancelled.

I drove down to Rosebud with Connie anyway, as he had to see Fleur, the physio, at three thirty. She made Connie do some exercises as usual, and showed him how to get up, if he had another fall, because I told her how difficult it was to get him back on his feet.

She demonstrated how to roll over and kneel first, and then hold onto something to brace himself. Then she checked his legs and hands, which were losing strength, as he could not grip anything too well. She said, "You are going down quite *rapidly* Conrad, and because you have had a few falls now, it's best that you use a walker to steady yourself, even inside the house. You can rent one from here for five dollars a week."

She then brought a walker, and got him to use it around the exercise room. He did not make a fuss, but listened to her quietly. We put the walker in the boot of my car, and drove back in the pouring rain.

On our way, he asked me to stop at Chemist Warehouse in Safety Beach. But when I parked there, the place was closed, and looked as if a fire had raged through the building. I asked him if he wanted to go to another chemist in Mornington, but he wanted to go home, as he was exhausted, and so was I. We came home and I took it easy, before replying some emails, and then we watched television for a while.

It was a wintry, rainy morning on Friday, 19 July, and after attending to all the chores, I played the piano for about an hour, to get my mind off my troubles. I worked on the computer downstairs later, as I was finishing off a screenplay that I wanted to enter in a competition. Connie kept barging in every few minutes to see if I had finished, because he wanted to use the computer at the same time as well.

I was getting irritable at the constant interruptions and said, "You have *all* week to do whatever you have to do on the computer, whereas I have to wait for a free day to attend to my work!" But he did not care at all, as he just kept on distracting me, fidgeting, banging things around, and making a big noise.

I was so upset and exasperated with his behaviour, and wished there was an end in sight, because I did not know how long I could go on like this. He behaved just like a spoilt and demanding child, who thought the world revolved around him. No matter how sorry I was for him, and looked after him as well as I could, he just wanted more and more attention, and I was physically and emotionally drained.

Claudia came around two thirty that afternoon, and said she was happy to see me. After the routine check up, she spoke of Connie's changing needs now. And she was relieved when she saw him using a walker and said, "You have to see about fixing hand rails in the shower and toilet too. Council will provide them, and the maintenance person will fix them for a nominal fee. I will bring a chair for the shower, and a prop that goes under the mattress, so that Conrad can brace himself up when he gets out of bed." Then she chatted about other safety issues, such as not going down the steep steps in the garden, or taking bins up the driveway.

As for driving, she was very firm, "*No* more driving for you Conrad, because if you do, doctor will advise Vic Roads to cancel your licence. It's not a joke if you drive and then lose control, you will end up killing others, as well as yourself." He did not comment, but listened stony-faced, as he did not want to hear or believe what she was saying. She left soon after, and I went upstairs to rest a while, as it was still raining heavily.

He could not climb stairs now, because his legs were too weak. Claudia also warned him not to use the iron, as his responses were very slow, and if he touched the hot iron, he would be unable to withdraw his hands in time. Gradually, he had to give up doing everyday tasks, and I did almost everything except shower him. He was still able to get in the shower slowly, but needed help drying, as he could not wrap the towel around him. Before he went into the shower, he wrote, "Keep a very careful eye on me till I finish showering and help me out." I stood at the door to see that he did not slip or fall in the shower.

Next day was no better, as the rain did not ease, and it was still very chilly. I finished the script, and sent it to the Australian Writers Guild Competition that afternoon. These projects helped me to keep my sanity, and I was happy writing, or immersing myself in creative arts. Alan and Ginny dropped in unexpectedly around two o'clock that afternoon, and Elvira called to say she would not come, if we had visitors.

Penny and Steve arrived a little after Alan and Ginny, and we had a pleasant time chatting. Although Connie sat with us and scribbled little notes, I did all the talking and entertaining, which was very tiring now. Steve tried to set up the ipad for Connie, but he was unable to connect the voice function, so he told him to ask Christian to connect it. As if on cue, Christian called just then, and said he would come down soon to connect the ipad.

Ginny and Alan left after four o'clock, and the others an hour later. I washed and cleaned up, as I did not want Connie to do anything. The last time he tried to wash a saucepan cover, he dropped it, and it smashed to smithereens. I knew he could not grip things too well, so I told him not to worry about helping me with the washing. After our visitors left, he went to the study, and sat at the computer doing emails. We did not go to church, as it was freezing, and poured down heavily still.

I did some chores next day, before driving Connie to the chemist in Mornington. He wanted to buy some things at Woolworths as well, so he pushed a trolley around slowly, as he insisted on doing it himself. I sat outside the store and waited till he finished, which took him over two hours to get what he wanted, and then I stopped for petrol on our way back.

It was very difficult getting him in and out of the car now, besides storing the walker in the boot. I was exhausted, because he wanted to stop several times, and I had to help him. But as he was determined to get about as much as possible, and liked to shop and buy what he wanted, I helped him. I understood how he felt, as he was such an active man in the past, who hardly sat still for a moment. He was always on the move, constantly driving around and doing as he pleased.

I told him that if he wanted to attend the healing Mass at Frankston that Sunday evening, I would drive him there. He agreed, and we went there at five o'clock. All our friends, including Maureen, Harry, and Donna were there, and they prayed over Connie. He got very emotional during Holy Communion, and Fr Denis, who had returned from overseas, anointed us and all those who needed healing.

When he said a special prayer for Connie, he started bawling and crying out loud, and everyone looked distressed to hear him. I explained that Connie was unable to control his emotions anymore, so they were very sympathetic and said they would pray for him.

We returned home after seven thirty, then I made dinner and had an early night, but Connie stayed up watching television till very late. He was very subdued all evening, so I left him alone, as he seemed to be lost in another world.

On my way to school on Monday, I stopped at the church office to book the community hall for Elvira's musical afternoon in October, but the hall was unavailable on that date. When I told her she had to choose another date, she said 13 October was alright. So I booked that date, and told her that it was confirmed. She was raising funds for St Vincent's, so they charged a nominal fee for the hall. I always supported her, and attended these events, as it was for a worthy cause.

It was a long, busy day at school, and I finished after four o'clock, then stopped to get groceries before returning home at five thirty. Claudia dropped the shower chair, toilet aids, and a prop, which she inserted under the mattress, so Connie could hold onto it and steady himself. Ninette wanted to know what time I was visiting tomorrow, and then I made dinner.

I drove to Ninette's at midday, then visited Judy at Carrum. Del was there too, and we enjoyed a very pleasant time. Del's husband, Jack, was worse, and she was his sole carer, so we had a great deal to talk about, and shared our troubles.

I came home around six o'clock after shopping, and he said that Roland, Shiranthi, Esme, and Paul visited. I had a spa bath, and was about to relax and watch television, when his brother, Paul, was at the gate at seven thirty. He called Connie on his mobile to say he brought him a box of yoghurt, and to open the security gate.

When he came inside, he said, "I was going to jump the fence, if you didn't open the gate!" I replied, "*Better* not do that, as the neighbours will think you are a thief!" I was irritated, because after a busy day, I liked to take it easy in the evenings.

He stayed with Connie, and they watched a healing DVD till after eight o'clock, while I worked on my laptop upstairs. Although I told him that Connie could not eat a whole box of yoghurt, and to leave just a few tubs, he left a dozen behind, and then went off. I watched television later, and I heard Connie shouting in the bedroom. When I asked him what he wanted, he stood in the middle of the room, and pointed to his track pants that he pulled down.

I could smell it, as he had soiled his pants. So I took him to the shower, helped him undress, and waited till he washed himself. He wrote a note later, "I had a loose tummy all day. I *don't* want to eat *any* yoghurt that Paul brought, I don't like those flavours! Throw them away!" I said I would give them to someone, and not throw them out. I knew his siblings wanted to bring something when they visited Connie. But I wished they would first ask us what he wanted, as there was absolutely no need for them to provide any sort of food for him.

I went upstairs at one o'clock in the morning to try and get some sleep, as Connie was very restless, and made loud noises. But I was restless and anxious, as I did not know how long this situation would continue. I did not want to end up getting sick, because I did not sleep well at nights, with constant tension, and Connie's aggression. A change for the worse was evident now, as somewhere in the nebulous regions of his mind, I was just a punching bag in his life. I finally fell asleep a couple of hours later.

I went for a dental appointment next morning, and had two fillings done, then I visited Elvira. She was very sympathetic, and understood what I was going through. When I came home, I ate a banana, as I could not chew anything else for a few more hours.

Later that day, I drove him to the sleep clinic in Frankston, which was next to the hospital. It took him ages to struggle with the walker, but we made it finally. He did not want me to hold the walker, or help him along, because, stubborn as always, he *insisted* on pushing it alone. But I was concerned that he would lose balance when crossing the gravel pathway to the clinic.

The nurse showed me how to secure the oxygen mask on Connie, and told him he should wear it all night, to see if it helped his breathing. It was on loan, as she said it was best to try it first, before buying one. Then we stopped at Karingal and had a snack, as I was hungry. He ate a burgher at McDonalds and drank a cup of tea. Christian called later, and we had a long chat. I told him how Connie was worse now, and he was sad to hear about him falling often. He said he would visit soon.

I got ready to go to school, on 25 July, and Connie got up too, as he wanted a cup of Milo. Suddenly, I heard a loud thud and bang in the kitchen. I rushed to find Connie on the kitchen floor! He was not hurt, as he fell on his buttocks. I told him, "Remember what the physio told you about trying to get up? Roll over on to your knees, and let's see if you can raise yourself up by holding onto the walker." It took a few minutes, but he went on his knees, and then braced himself on my arm and walker, and got up.

He was shaken, but no bruises. I was worried to leave him on his own though. So I called Elvira before I left, and asked if she could drop in later that morning to see if he was alright. I told him to have his breakfast, and then sit at the computer or go back to bed, without walking about too much. He told me not to worry as he was alright. Even with the walker, he was too unsteady, and he said he was making a cup of Milo when he fell down. Once again, he had an excuse, that the walker got in the way, and that was why he fell.

When I called later, Elvira said she dropped in, and he was sitting at the computer, and seemed alright, so not to worry. I thanked her, and said I would be home soon. I finished early, but visited Ninette briefly, as I sent Toula a text to tell her I would come for a while.

Ninette was agitated when I arrived, as she just came home after shopping with Toula. She was very flustered, and wandered around saying, "Next time, *phone* me the day *before,* so I know you are coming." And every time I tried to converse with Toula, she kept interrupting, and was so restless, that I regretted for having dropped in.

I needed a short break, before going home to listen to Connie's demands, but this did not help me at all. I decided that it was the last time I visited at short notice. When I came home around six o'clock, he said Geraldine and Clifford spent the afternoon with him. He sat huddled in the television room, zombie-like, and watching a faith healing DVD. I wondered why he looked so depressed, miserable, and aloof.

The whole kitchen smelled of pungent curry and fenugreek, which Connie could not abide in curries, because of its strong, unpleasant odour. I usually made his lunch, and kept it in the fridge whenever I went to school, or to Ninette's. I asked him now, "*What's* that *horrible* smell in the house?" he wrote, "She brought lunch." I was really annoyed that she came with her husband again, especially after I told her that he was not welcome here. I said, "Dial her number *now.* I want to speak to her." So he did, and handed me the phone.

When she answered, I told her that I was not happy she came here again with Clifford, and she pretended not to understand. Then I said, "I came home to find Connie looking troubled and depressed. Can you please stop trying to convert him to your religious beliefs, as he believes in the Catholic faith, and always has, so why are you trying to take him to your church? You are confusing him with your promises, and telling him not to take medications or listen to doctors! In future, if you want to visit Connie, you can come on your own."

She just did not listen, but kept talking over me, so I hung up, as I was so irritated. I did not know how much clearer I could make myself, because she was impervious to what I said. I told Connie, "It's unfair for her to put me in this situation, as I don't want to have these discussions with her." We had a serious argument then. He scribbled notes to tell me how he felt, while howling and shouting all the time, which was too distressing to listen to.

I called Esme, and asked her to talk to Connie and try to calm him down, as he was shouting at the top of his voice and carrying on like a madman. She told him, "Listen to Dolla, Connie, if she has told Jenny not to come with Clifford, then she shouldn't bring him. Tell her to come on her own."

Esme and Paul did not want Clifford to visit their place either, as they told me some scandalous stories about him. They insisted we discourage him from visiting us. Then I called Babs, as I was so annoyed at Geraldine's arrogant behaviour in flouting my wishes. They understood how difficult the situation was for me too, not just Connie.

After Esme and Babs spoke to him, he calmed down a little. I told him I would not tolerate Geraldine's behaviour, as she must respect my wishes. He must listen to what I told him, as his wife, and not let them interfere in our lives. I reminded him of all the difficulties we faced in our lives. And this was the greatest challenge that we must bear together, without letting his siblings come between us. He did not respond, but watched healing DVD's till late. I wondered how they would have liked, if *I* interfered in their lives and behaved the way they did.

I was very agitated that night, and experienced severe chest pains. In the morning, I called Roland, and asked to speak with Shiro, but he said she was resting, as she had a bad back. I told him I was not happy with all the faith healing propaganda they bombarded Connie with, because he was very depressed, agitated, and more hostile towards me whenever they visited. He pretended not to know anything, and queried, "Why is that?" I asked him very politely then, to refrain from visiting too often, and to give him time to come to terms with his illness.

I said, "You can help him better, if you told him to be submissive to God's will, and be patient. We will all rejoice, if he is miraculously cured by prayers and supplication. But to *pretend* nothing is wrong with him, and to convince him that he is already healed, is just absurd, when we can see how rapidly he's going down." He did not comment, and I hung up after wishing them well.

I played the piano for a while, and tried to unwind later, and then spoke to Nelune. I told her what was going on with his impossible siblings, and she could not believe such inconsiderate behaviour. Shirani was still in Sri Lanka, and called to find out how Connie was. And she was very concerned to hear that he was getting worse. She said that torrential rain prevented them from getting around, and she was not enjoying her holiday at all. And the chance of catching dengue fever was great.

I drove Connie to Rosebud that afternoon for his appointment with the speech pathologist. She checked him as usual, and observed his swallowing and chewing, which she said was still alright. But he complained that he bit his inner cheeks each time he chewed food, so she looked at his mouth and found a few ulcers. She told him to ask doctor for something to relieve the ulcers, and we came home soon after. I was weary, so I rested.

Chris Del Piano came on Saturday afternoon to do some odd jobs, and he left after four o'clock. I prepared some dishes for lunch next day, and then we attended evening Mass in Mornington. It was late when Connie went to bed that night, but I fitted the mask, as he could not do it himself. It had a small monitoring machine set up on the bedside table, and he took a sedative before I fitted the mask. So I thought we would get a good night's sleep. But, I woke up an hour later when he started making loud noises, as if he was in agony. He tried to pull the mask out violently, and I said, "*Don't* try to rip it off, I have to take it off carefully." After I took the mask off, he wrote that it suffocated him, and that he could not breathe, when it was supposed to do the exact opposite. Anyway, I said he would have to try it tomorrow night too, until he got used to it. He was supposed to use it all night for one week at least.

The Karlsens arrived around ten thirty next morning, and it was cold and windy, but Paul got the new lawn mower started, and mowed the lawns. Linda, Leo, and the children, came a little later. They weeded the garden, and Leo mowed the back lawn. I really appreciated their kindness and generosity in helping out. We had lunch around one o'clock, and Connie was reasonably calm. He joined in the conversation with his little scribbled notes, and thanked them for their help.

Linda and Leo washed up all the dishes, and Julie helped to put them away. Paul set up the ipad, and he tried a few voices, but he could not activate the voice program. Connie was happy though, as he did not have to scribble notes any longer. They left after three o'clock, and I rested upstairs.

Paul phoned at six thirty in the evening to say he forgot to "re-engage" the remote control on the garage door, and it would not have worked when I tried to open it. He instructed me on what I should do, and although I tried to follow what he said, I found it very difficult to lift the heavy roller door, and re-engage it.

I managed to re-set it after several attempts, while Connie just stood at the door and watched me struggle to lift the heavy door. He did not write down any instructions on how to get it to work, although he knew exactly what needed to be done.

Chapter 77

When I returned from school on Monday, 29 July, the Aged Care Assessment was in the mail, and it said that Connie was eligible for high care in a nursing home. He did not want to read the report, but I did, and was relieved to know he was eligible. Dr Khelil told me that when the time came for him to go into a nursing home, I would not have to deal with the inevitable end on my own.

When I visited Ninette on Tuesday, she was very neurotic, and in a strange mood. She constantly harped about her non-existent ailments, but I walked with her and the dog up to the shops. I came home around five thirty after shopping on my way. Roland and Shiranthi, who had come at one thirty in the afternoon, were still there.

I offered tea and biscuits, but they said they already had some. I was weary, and wanted to unwind, but they stayed till seven o'clock. Christian sent a text message to ask how things were, and I told him what was going on with his siblings. He was very indignant to hear about their interference, and that they were such a nuisance.

After they left, Connie read the Aged Care Assessment report, then tottered up to me, looking absolutely furious. He shouted angrily, and pointed to something Lindy wrote. "On-going conversion to Born again faith, influenced by brother and sister." He typed an angry message on his ipad, and I pacified him. "Lindy came to that conclusion because you told her you didn't want to take medications, and that God will heal you."

Then he wrote, "You want me to go to a home?" I replied, "I did not make the assessment that you need high care, and if that is for your welfare, you must listen to them."

He sat down and typed a long letter to Prof. Butler, as Lindy mentioned she sent him a copy of the assessment too. He wrote, *"I'm proud to be a Roman Catholic, and will remain a Catholic until I die!"* I kept out of his way till bed time, as he was in such a violent temper. I served his dinner, and I went to bed, as I was exhausted. I wondered how much longer I would have to endure this stress.

Shirani and Ranjith returned from Sri Lanka, so I had a long chat to Shirani next day. I was very worried and upset, because Christian sent me a message late last night to say that he suffered a severe electrical shock, while working on the old wiring system in the premises he was renovating. Thank God he was alright, but he was in shock, as he was thrown right off his feet.

I told Connie about it, but his face did not register any emotion, perhaps that was because his facial muscles were very rigid now. Later that morning, I drove him to Frankston for another appointment with Prof. Butler. As we sat in the waiting room, Connie started to giggle helplessly, and pointed at two overweight ladies. I whispered, "*Don't* point Connie, they'll think you are being rude." He wrote, "Go and tell them I can't help it. They remind me of Jenny and Esme." And he went on tittering.

I walked over to the ladies and apologised, saying it was part of his illness, and he could not help it. They said they understood, and not to worry about it. A few days ago, I heard him chortling loudly in the bathroom. When I went in, he was shaving, and pointed to his reflection in the mirror, and giggled uncontrollably. I asked him what was so funny, but he giggled all the more, and could not stop. Later, he wrote, "I can't help giggling."

When Prof. Butler checked him, he told Connie that his condition was getting worse, and he must take the medication he prescribed, in order to relax his muscles, and relieve the pain in his neck and shoulders, because they were so rigid now, and the pain would get more severe.

Then he told Connie to walk up and down the room, and observed that his walking was not very steady. Lindy's report was on his desk, and Connie gave him the letter he typed the night before. He wrote on his ipad that he disagreed with Lindy's statement about his "on-going conversion to Born again" religion. Prof. Butler did not comment, but reiterated that eventually Connie would have to be in a nursing home, as he required high care, due to his many falls, progressive swallowing difficulty, and loss of mobility.

He said, "Your wife is not medically qualified to care for you, and you are going to need 24 hour medical attention, which only a nursing home can provide." Connie's face had a stony, stubborn look, but he did not write anything in response. I brought the documents Lindy sent, regarding medical power of attorney, and I gave them to Prof. Butler. He told Connie, "It's a good idea to complete this form while you can still write, as your wife will be responsible for your care when you can no longer make decisions."

Connie filled the form, and Prof. Butler signed it jointly with another doctor in the same clinic. Then he said, the waiting period for nursing homes was sometimes as long as two years, so it would be a good idea to start looking around, and put his name down at a few places. We saw the sleep specialist later, as he was in the same building.

That specialist too, advised Connie to continue with the sedatives Prof. Butler prescribed, and also to use the oxygen mask for one week. Connie raised his voice, growled at him and wrote, "They make me drowsy during the day, that's why I don't want to take them!" The specialist tried to convince him that it was good for him, as it would help relax his muscles, but Connie just kept growling angrily.

When we left, he told me to stop at Hungry Jack's, as he wanted a hamburger. We spent forty minutes there, till he ate very slowly, and then stopped at Karingal, as he wanted to buy drinks. Then he wanted to get something at Chemist Warehouse in Mornington. He did not realize how very tiring it was for me to get him in and out of the car so many times. And his walker too, which had to be folded and stored in the back seat each time.

Connie did ten things in one go when he drove, but I was unused to so much driving, and the extra work involved now, so it was too exhausting for me. I asked him why he could not attend to one thing at a time, without getting me to stop several times, as it was too much for me. We came home after five o'clock. After feeding the cats, I just flopped into bed for an hour, as I could not stay awake any longer. When I woke up, I made dinner, then spoke to Shirani, and mentioned what the doctors said.

While I was talking to her, I heard Connie shouting loudly, "Ah, ah!" When I came down, he typed, "I want to read the power of attorney document, as I didn't read it before." I took it upstairs and filed it in my desk drawer earlier on, so I brought it down and handed it to him. He went to the study and sat there reading the form carefully, then he left it on the kitchen bench top. I filed it away, and then had an early night.

I was very busy at school next day, and I was weary when I came home, as Connie fell again the previous night, just as he was trying to get into bed at midnight. He rolled around helplessly near the bed, and it was very distressing to see him struggling to get up. I helped him to get on his knees, and brace himself onto the bed. He did not hurt himself, but every time he fell, he seemed more unsteady and disoriented afterwards. He fell asleep soon after, and was still resting when I left home. I sent him a text later to ask how he was, and whether to ask Christy, the nurse, to visit him, but he replied he was alright, and not to worry.

I came home early, and he said that Esme, Paul, Sanit, and Jasmine visited around three o'clock. When I called Ninette and Shirani later on, they too were concerned to hear he fell again. Christian called that night, and I told him about Connie's fall, and that I wanted to ask Christy to check him. He said Christy would come anytime, if I needed professional advice or help, which was good to know.

I made ox tail soup with vegetables, for dinner, and he had a bowl of it with some bread. He did not like to eat rice any more, as he said he could not chew too much. I fitted the oxygen mask on him later, and he took his medication at eleven o'clock, and seemed to fall asleep soon after. His breathing sounded much better, and he was not wheezing and groaning through the night.

It was freezing, wet, and blustery next day. After doing some chores and playing the piano for a while, I prepared some savoury and sweet snacks for Connie's colleagues, who were visiting that afternoon. Mathew, Brent, and Joel, spent a couple of hours with him. And Brent loaded the voice program, "speak it" on to the ipad, where a robotic voice read whatever was typed.

Brent selected a flat, mechanical female voice, and we found it amusing, especially Connie, as it sounded like a robot giving orders. But over the next few weeks I came to dislike that metallic voice immensely, as it jolted me each time I heard it barking orders at me.

He tried a few male voices too, but as they had peculiar accents, Connie was satisfied with the female voice, who had an Australian accent. They sipped a few beers with Connie afterwards, and said they would visit again soon, and left around four thirty. I took it easy after they left, before preparing our dinner, and lunch for tomorrow's visitors.

We watched a few comedies in the evening, and that night I read "Ann Frank's Diary" again. It moved me very deeply, to think of such a young girl and her family living in that attic room for more than two years. And it helped me endure my present situation with Connie more patiently.

I prepared a few more dishes next morning, and Con, Cornelia, and Laura arrived at about one thirty, carrying many things. Cornelia made her favourite eggplant dip, and we had that with a freshly baked French stick that they brought as well. Laura brought four bottles of home-made wine and cherry liqueur, and Con presented me with a huge bouquet of pale-pink roses. Cornelia also brought heaps of seedlings, pansies, and Flanders poppies, as I told her I liked them very much.

They were very kind, generous people, and I did not mind cooking plenty of curries for them, as they enjoyed spicy food very much. We had a good time as always, and they left after six thirty, as Cornelia wanted to visit her elderly aunt on the way. After they left, I washed and cleaned, while Connie stood by the kitchen bench and watched me. He wrote on the ipad, "Unfortunately, I can't help you wash up Dolla," which the robotic voice barked out.

I went up to him, hugged him and said, "It's okay, as you have done enough washing up in the past. Just relax, and take it easy now." Later, we watched a few episodes of "Soap," a very funny US comedy series, popular in the seventies. He enjoyed it as much as I did, and giggled happily.

I rested till late, as I was up at five thirty in the morning to let Simba out. Shirani and Ranjith visited at midday, and shared a snack with us, and we caught up with all the news from Sri Lanka. When they left a couple of hours later, Elvira said they would come around soon. And just as they were leaving at five o'clock, Chris Berman dropped in, as he phoned me the day before to ask if he could bring some herbal pills for Connie. We had an enjoyable time, chatting and laughing at his jokes. The "miracle cure" herbal pills sold at $60 for thirty tablets. But I told Connie that if they helped him, the money was unimportant.

Chris gave a spiel on the marvellous, medicinal properties of this pill, and how several people were cured of various ailments. Connie wrote, "Chris, you are a God-send! Maybe I will be cured with these pills." Chris was a serious-minded, spiritual young man, so I asked him to say a special prayer for Connie, before he commenced taking the pills. He did that, and he left in an hour's time. I went to bed a few hours later, feeling worn-out.

I had a splitting headache at school on Monday, as it was a very hectic weekend, and I hardly had any time to relax. I sent Connie a text message around midday to ask if he was alright, but he did not reply. I was worried, thinking he may have fallen, and was lying helplessly on the floor, so I came home straight after school.

Thankfully, he was alright, and reading his prayer book in the television room, while listening to faith healing CD's. When I asked why he did not reply my text, he wrote that he did not check his mobile, and looked depressed, and weary as he huddled on the sofa. He did not say much, and I left him alone.

It was icy that evening, as wild winds blew across the ocean, and continued all through the night. I made dinner and watched some television later, and continued reading "Ann Frank's Diary." It was a poignant story, with so much to learn and admire in that young girl's character.

The pest control man from Term guard, arrived next morning to check the house for termites, and much to my relief, he found none. The last time the Karlsens visited, I showed Paul some black insects that fell through gaps under the window, and I was concerned they were termites. After the man left, Connie told me to make an appointment with Dr Khelil, to check his lungs, a rash on his back, and he had a cold.

I called the clinic, but the receptionist said doctor was away on holiday. Connie was very annoyed when I told him that, but he did not want to consult another doctor. I visited Ninette at midday, and after doing some little tasks for her, and walking with her to the shops, I stopped to get some groceries.

Esme called at five o'clock, to say Connie sent her a text to pick him up from the medical centre in Frankston. I told her that he was home when I left in the afternoon, and I did not know how he went to doctor's. I said I would call her when I got home, and not to go to the medical centre till then. When I arrived home fifteen minutes later, he was sitting at the computer. I asked him to text Esme and let her know he was home, and not at doctor's.

He was getting stranger every day, and behaved very aggressively whenever I asked him anything. So I left him alone, as he did not communicate with me, except to order me around to do things for him. Sadly, he did not use the ipad to say anything positive, good, or kind to me, only constant complaints, and demands to do something.

I grew to hate that barking, robotic voice on the ipad. I wished it sounded more gentle and kind, since I did not hear Connie's voice being tender anymore, not that there was any tenderness in his voice for a long time. Once, I asked him to write exactly how he felt, and any symptoms before he fell. As PSP was a rare disease, it would help others to understand the condition better, but he was stony-faced and wrote, "No symptoms before I fall." So I left it at that.

It was rainy and stormy next day, and I let Simba out at five o'clock in the morning, as he was up early, and then I rested for a while longer. After my usual routine, I called Shirani and Esme. And when I told her Connie had an appointment at the sleep clinic that afternoon, she asked us to drop in for coffee.

I drove, as Connie found it difficult just getting into the car, let alone drive. He used the mask only a couple of times, and did not want it any more, as he wrote that it suffocated him, and he did not take the prescribed sedatives either.

I told the nurse he did not want the mask, and she said some people were not comfortable with it, and it was alright. Then we dropped in at Esme's, but she was out, and only Paul was there. Although he offered us a drink, Connie did not want to go inside, because Esme was not there. We went to Karingal, as he wanted to shop, and he finished an hour later, at five o'clock. These trips with Connie wore me out, as it was very difficult getting him into the car, which took a long time, as his legs were stiff as wood now. Besides dragging the walker in and out as well.

He wanted to get in the car by himself, and pushed me away when I tried to ease him gently to the seat. I wanted to make sure he did not knock his head on the roof of the car. But because he was so stubborn, and thought he could still do things by himself, it took a long time for him to struggle in and out of the car. He bought two cases of beer that day, and the salesman loaded them into the boot. I asked Connie, "*How* on earth can I carry such heavy boxes into the house?" The man suggested, "Cut the boxes and carry a few bottles in at a time."

It was still pouring when we came home by seven o'clock. I opened the cases and took in six bottles at a time. I stacked some in the large fridge and in the bar fridge, and a few in the cupboard. He wrote, "They were on special and that's why I bought two cases." Then he wrote, "Jenny is getting dropped off tomorrow afternoon." I did not comment, or ask him who was going to drop her off. I thought I made it quite clear that her husband was not welcome in our home.

It was still wet and cold when I went to school on Thursday. Maree visited that day, and she had a long chat with me. She was sorry to hear about Connie's illness, and said she would pray for us. I was very fond of her, as she was such a warm, friendly, and caring lady. I finished teaching around two thirty, and came home straight, and found Connie huddled in front of the computer.

He did not look at me, or acknowledge my presence, even when I greeted him and asked how he was. He just ignored me, and was uncommunicative all evening. I did not ask him if Geraldine came, but I knew she had, because I found some rubbish, and tea bags in my rice container, which she used as a garbage bin. I asked him to show her where the dustbin was next time, and not to dump rubbish in my rice container again.

He still did not respond to anything I said, so I went about doing my chores. I made a vegetable soup, with beef bone stock for dinner, and served him a bowl when he sat to watch television. He hardly tasted it, before he began shouting and jabbing the spoon violently into the soup bowl. I took it away before he spilt it, and asked him to write down what was wrong.

He stomped off to the kitchen and typed, "Too much liquid in the soup, I dribble when I try to drink it." I replied, "But I made soup, thinking it was easy for you to swallow the tenderised vegetables." As he kept on shouting, I strained the soup, and gave him only the vegetables with some bread. He calmed down slightly, then ate slowly. But he was getting violent and agitated over the slightest thing now, and his fits of temper were uncontrollable. I went to bed and continued reading "Ann Frank's Diary." So much to learn from such a young girl, as her humour, passion, and love of life just burst through the pages, and it was distressing to think of her tragic end.

I slept in next day, as the turbulent weather did not ease, and heavy rain and gusty winds howled all night and morning. Connie seemed to be very tired, and slept till twelve thirty. I asked him, "How did Geraldine come here yesterday?" he wrote, "Clifford dropped her and picked her up. He stayed in the vehicle and didn't come inside." I thought she was brazen to come with him still, and make him sit outside.

Although I have never been intolerant of people or their beliefs, I burned with indignation at the injustice of Connie's behaviour towards me, because of their influence. She was on a ruthless crusade to convert Connie, so Roland and she took turns to brainwash him persistently.

That was the reason why he was so tired and depressed after their visits, and became more aggressive towards me, because he knew I did not believe in their faith healing meetings. They did not do him any good at all, except to confuse and drain him. If they were not so intent on converting him, they had no other reason to visit so often, and spend hours with him. Geraldine left two unwashed mugs in the television room, and I knew they were watching those all that time. They forced him to watch faith healing CD's and DVD's, especially when I was not home.

He kept those CD's hidden away behind some other DVD's on the shelf, and I counted over twenty five of them. That evening, Connie was on the computer while I made dinner. He hobbled to the kitchen, and gave me a piece of paper on which he wrote, "I think this is truly you," and he opened the Bible, and showed me the Book of Proverbs.

It was the passage about the "good wife," how she kept busy all day, and her husband was proud of her etc. etc. I said, "Thanks for the compliment." It was the first time after a long spell, that he showed any appreciation for all I did for him, and had done in the past. I slipped that piece of paper inside the Bible, intending to read it again later. Then he wrote, "Pat Egan wants to visit on Sunday, can we go for Mass on Saturday evening?" I agreed, as Pat was a good friend and colleague of Connie's.

I took Mishka to the vet in Mt Martha next morning, as she was due for her annual vaccine. She mewed all the way there, as if she was being strangled. The vet said she was fine, but she had lost a few grams since the previous year, which was nothing to worry about. When I came home, I did some chores, planted seedlings in pots, and tied one of the trees that blew down during the gusty winds.

It was pleasant and sunny after the bad weather, and Connie sat out drinking coffee, and having a smoke. He seemed relaxed and calmer today, for which I was glad. I cleaned and washed up later, but Connie did not want to go to church that evening, as he was too tired. He said we could go to Frankston on Sunday evening, so I said it was fine with me.

Pat arrived around eleven o'clock on Sunday morning, and he enjoyed the pan rolls very much, so did Connie. I cut the roll into small pieces for Connie, and he managed to chew and swallow slowly. Pat said, "Dolly, you make the *best* pan rolls in the world! I'm a *connoisseur* of pan rolls, because I've eaten them at many places, and no one makes them so tasty!" I laughed and replied, "Thanks for the compliment, nice of you to say so." Every time Pat ate them, he never failed to say they were the best he had tasted. Connie smiled and nodded in agreement, as he too said I made the best pan rolls.

After Pat left at midday, I took it easy for a while, and then drove to Frankston for evening Mass. Fr Denis greeted us, as Connie hobbled with the walker up to the front pew. Maureen and Bernie chatted after Mass, and they helped Connie, and bundled him into the car. We came home around seven thirty, then watched a few comedies in the night.

I drove to Karingal after school next day, to get some documents certified at the chemist's, then posted them to Centrelink, because they requested more information, with regard to Connie's application. I came home around five thirty, and I spent a quiet evening.

But when I served dinner, he did not want to eat rice, and wanted macaroni instead, so I boiled some. Then he sat beside me while I watched television, and started jabbing his fork angrily into the bowl. I tried to ignore him, because he behaved just like a spoilt child throwing a tantrum.

He did not write what he wanted, or what was wrong with the dinner, but did his best to annoy and upset me. I knew his behaviour was not normal now, as Lindy said in her assessment that his behaviour was typical of early dementia. So I did not take any notice of his annoying behaviour, and watched a few comedies before going to bed, and then read a while.

Whenever I visited Ninette on Tuesdays, Connie came up with some demand or another. He said he wanted to see Dr Khelil that day, because his neck and chest were paining, and he had difficulty breathing. I could not see the point of him going to doctors every time, as he never listened to them anyway. He did not take any medication, or try to help himself at all, like using the oxygen mask. I did not say anything though, and told him to get ready, and I would drop him at the clinic. He wrote that Esme would pick him up later, and bring him home.

I made an appointment at twelve o'clock, but he was reading prayers and not getting ready in time. Knowing he needed at least two hours to shower and get dressed, he just dawdled around, until I reminded him a few times to get ready, and finally, we left at eleven forty. I became so frustrated waiting for him to get ready. He was always late, and was never on time for any appointment in his life, and now he was worse than ever. I held my peace though, as I did not want a scene, and I went in with him to see doctor.

After doctor examined him, and told him what the neurologist wrote, he advised Connie to consider entering a nursing home very soon, as he was getting worse and falling too often. Connie wrote on his ipad, "I don't want to go to a nursing home." Doctor explained that he could not be looked after at home, and I could not help him when he fell, but he remained adamant, and ignored doctor.

When we left, Paul Maschio was waiting outside to pick Connie. I went to Ninette's, and as Arlette was there too, I stayed till about three o'clock, and enjoyed a pleasant afternoon. Then I drove to Karingal to get my medication, and as I left the chemist, I saw Esme, Paul, and Connie, walking up towards me. They offered to take him home, when I said I still had some shopping to do, and as Connie was getting tired, he did not want to wait till I finished.

I was worn-out that evening, so I went to bed around ten o'clock. He stayed up watching faith healing DVD's, and tottered in around one o'clock in the morning. But before he could reach the bed, he fell in a heap and landed on his bottom. Fortunately, he did not knock his head or injure himself, and I managed to help him on his feet with the greatest difficulty.

As he struggled and wobbled towards the bed, he fell down again by the side of the bed. This time, my back really ached, as I helped him up a second time, and put him to bed safely. I thought it was because he had a very tiring day, going to doctor's, then to Esme's, and the shopping centre, but to fall twice in one night, was not a very good sign.

Looking back over the last ten years or more, he often complained of back, neck, and shoulder pains. But since he became ill, it was even worse. He wanted me to rub voltaren or dencorub on his body every night, which I did, hoping it would relieve him. He also complained of itchiness, but did not have a rash on his back. Dr Khelil said it was due to dry skin, and prescribed a soothing lotion for it. I applied that lotion on his back as well, before he went to sleep.

I did not fall asleep till three o'clock in the morning, as my back ached constantly, after lifting Connie twice last night. I was so weary and upset about this situation that I could not fall asleep, wondering how much longer I had to endure this. He was so helpless when he fell, and shouted angrily in frustration, as he rolled about and struggled to get up, but unable to move a muscle.

It was really painful and heartbreaking to watch his helplessness, as it was humiliating for him to struggle and roll around so weakly. I tried to understand, and be patient with him. And I knew it was terrifying for him to lose his independence so rapidly, because he was always such a dominant man.

After a restless night, I went upstairs at five thirty, to try and sleep for a few hours. After finishing the usual chores, I played the piano for a while. Sometimes, he left me alone when I played the piano, but if he was angry, he opened the door, glared at me, made garbled noises, or pointed to a scribbled note. And I told him, "Wait till I finish playing, and I'll see what you want." Usually, it was a trivial matter, or more complaints about his aches and pains.

I became frustrated too, because I asked him, what was I supposed to do when he did not listen to doctors or take any medication for his aches and pains. He shouted loudly and banged the door behind him. When I was home, that was what he was like, non-stop complaints and tantrums.

How much I wished he sat quietly and read a book, to get his mind off his illness. But apart from doing emails on the computer, reading "Born again" propaganda, or listening to faith healing CD's and DVD's, he just did not try to be as happy as he possibly could in his situation. The only time he enjoyed doing something together, was when we watched comedies. Then I was pleased to hear him chuckling away for a little while, and forgetting to complain about something.

I baked a butter cake for afternoon tea, as Misaka, Theji, their newborn baby, Thamika, and Chris Berman were visiting. I invited Elvira and John to meet them as well, and they arrived just as the others came around three thirty.

The baby girl was really cute, and we all fussed over her, and enjoyed a very pleasant afternoon. Connie joined in the conversation via his ipad with the "speak it" program on. They left after six thirty, and I was tired, as I did not sleep well the previous night. But I cleaned and washed up, and then took it easy. The winds picked up by seven o'clock and blew in gustily across the sea. It rained all day, and still showed no sign of easing, as the stormy weather continued to rage all night.

When I drove to school next day, it was still stormy. And when I saw Colleen later, she asked me how Connie was doing. I told her that he was getting worse. She was very sympathetic, and offered any assistance, if and when I needed it. I thanked her, and when I finished lessons, I drove to the chemist's to get a nasal spray for Connie, which doctor prescribed, to ease his breathing. Shirani called while I was there, so I told her what was happening, and how he fell twice in one night.

When I came home at four thirty, Esme was still there, but Geraldine had left. Paul picked Esme an hour later, and she said she would drop in again on Monday. Geraldine came with Clifford again, but Connie said that he dropped and picked her up. I told Esme how worrying it was to leave Connie on his own, because he fell more often now. She offered to stay with him on the days I went to school. That was a relief to know he would have someone to stay with him, and also, Esme was more realistic about his condition, instead of being in denial.

Lindy, the Aged Care Assessor, advised me about Carer Support, and to contact them if I needed help. I wanted to get respite care soon, and hoped I could engage a carer to stay with Connie on the days I went out. In the meantime, I was relieved that Esme agreed to stay with him on those days., Connie got into a bad mood after they left, and started shouting and banging things around.

He hovered around in the kitchen while I made dinner, and wrote on his ipad, "Esme did my toe nails, and applied balm on my feet. She applied dencorub on my back." I replied, "But I cut your toe nails and finger nails not so long ago? I would have done them for you if you asked me." He wrote, "She had the time to do it." He glared angrily, as if I did something wrong.

After all the extra work involved in taking care of him, without ever complaining or making him feel he was a burden in any way, he now implied I did not have time for him. And that evening, I noticed his attitude was more hostile. He was spiteful, and played childish games with me, but I could not understand why he wanted to hurt me for no reason. From then onwards, every time his sisters visited, he got them to cut his toe nails and finger nails, massage him, and apply dencorub.

I did not want to get into an argument, as he just shouted and threw a fit. He was becoming increasingly irrational, and was maniacal if I contradicted him in any way, or wanted an explanation. I shut my mouth, and prayed to hold my tongue, *"As with a bridle,"* like the Good Book says, and refrained from saying anything to provoke or upset him.

When I was in bed that night and trying to read, he stomped in and threw the nasal spray on the bedside table. I asked, "Don't you want to use it? You complain of not being able to breathe, and doctor asked you to try a spray." He scribbled on a piece of paper, "How do you open it?" I got up and opened the stopper for him, but then he left the spray in the bathroom and did not use it at all.

It was still gusty, wet, and freezing next day, but a little gleam of sunshine burst through darkening clouds in the afternoon. I took it easy, and played the piano before I drove Connie to Rosebud for his appointment with the physio. He was getting late as usual, and when I asked him to hurry up, he started shouting. So I told him to stop raising his voice, and shouting at me, every time I asked him something. He just glared at me and kept making loud guttural noises in his throat.

Fleur examined his legs and arms thoroughly, and when I mentioned his falls, she said, "Conrad, it looks like you are not safe *even* with the walker, and may have to use a wheelchair to prevent falling again. You are lucky you haven't broken your hips or injured yourself seriously so far." He was not happy at all and wrote, "I don't want to use a wheelchair."

When we left the rehab centre, he pointed at McDonalds, and wanted me to stop there. It took us a while to get inside, as he shuffled along very slowly with the walker now, and he wrote his order on a piece of paper, chips and chicken nuggets. I sipped a coffee till he finished eating, and when we came home, I rested a while. Then I made a vegetable soup for dinner, and strained the liquid, and served Connie only the soft vegetables with bread. Later, I made curry powder for Joelle and Jacinta at school, as they liked it very much.

Chapter 78

It was still blustery and wet next day. Joelle and Celine arrived at midday, but not Micheline, as she was unwell. We had a very pleasant afternoon, and they left in an hour's time. As soon as they left, Connie gave his mobile phone to me and dialled a number. I did not know who he was calling, but Amber answered. She said they were on their way to our place now. I said, "Alright, we'll see you soon," and then rested for half an hour.

Sherone, Glen, Valerie, Brian, and Amber dropped in soon after, and stayed for about two hours. Connie joined in with his ipad and wrote, "I won't be able to dance at your wedding Amber." And she replied, "You will get better Uncle Connie, have faith." After they left, I made some pan rolls, and finished around seven o'clock.

I woke up late on Sunday, as I was very tired physically and emotionally. I followed my usual routine, and played the piano for a little while. Ninette, Toula, and Frank arrived around three thirty, as Ninette told me the day before that they would visit. They enjoyed a slice of butter cake with a cup of tea, and left after a brief chat. We offered to drop Ninette in Seaford before attending Mass at Frankston, as Frank and Toula were visiting his parents in Mornington.

Frank helped Connie into the car, and also showed me how to fold the walker, and store it in the boot instead of the back seat, as it was very difficult for me to store it in the back seat. It fitted better in the boot, and I was able to take it out easily. We dropped Ninette at her place, and when I tried to park outside the church, Connie shouted and growled at me. And he pointed frantically to the ramp at the front entrance of the church.

Maureen told me to park on the ramp, as it was easier for Connie to go up with his walker. So I turned the car around and drove up to the space where he wanted me to park. The ladies helped him after Mass, and he got into the car without making a fuss, and we came home about seven thirty.

I watched a few episodes of "Soap" after dinner, then switched off, and was just coming out of the television room, when he stomped in angrily and started shouting and pointing to the television. I asked, "What do you want? Stop shouting and write down what you want to say." He fumed off, and then scribbled on a piece of paper,

"I wanted to watch 'Soap' too, why did you turn off the TV?" I replied, "If you want to watch it, why don't you sit down and watch it, without shouting at me?"

I was exasperated, because his outbursts over such trivial matters made no sense at all. He switched on the television, and watched the comedies on his own. I was at a total loss to understand his behaviour, especially as he was so insistent to go to church every Sunday, and then when he came home, he behaved so badly.

The weather continued to be wild and stormy, as gusty, damaging winds swept across the state. I looked at the fences apprehensively, wondering how long they could take this battering, as it was blowing non-stop for a few days now. I went to school early that day, but the "Book Fair" was in progress, and the library was occupied till eleven o'clock. So I read the newspapers, and had a cup of tea until the activities were over.

It was a little distracting in the library all day, as the children were very noisy when they came in to choose books. I finished at four thirty, and came home an hour later, after the usual grocery shopping. Esme and Paul were sitting at the dining table with Connie, while loud music blared throughout the house over the speaker system. Connie went to Benton's Square with them, and she gave him a crew cut, which made him look like a convict. Esme did the same with her mother, as she shaved her head and made her wear a skull cap, so that the poor thing looked liked a prisoner.

I told Connie, "It looks awful, you look like a convict!" He just giggled, and Esme said, "He wanted it cut short." They left shortly afterwards, and I asked Connie to reduce the volume, as my head was spinning, after a long, busy day teaching. I thought to myself, *when* will I get peace and tranquillity in my own home again? I could not go anywhere else to relax, as this was my home. I usually walked outside for half an hour to get some peace, but because of a sudden hail storm and heavy rain, I could not go to the garden. So I just stood out in the al fresco area, breathing in fresh air, as the house was stuffy, with the heater running full blast as well.

I cannot begin to describe the feeling of suffocation and tension pervading the house at such times. I wanted to scream and scream, just to get some relief, but I controlled myself, went upstairs and replied emails. Then I prepared Luigi's books to mail out tomorrow, as I received a few orders.

It was another blustery day on Tuesday, and I did not feel too good. My head ached, and felt as heavy as a rock, a sure sign of another bout of vertigo, when I was stressed. I invoked Bruno to help me overcome my headache, as I did not know how I could cope with Connie, if I was unwell. He wanted a soft-boiled egg, and toast for breakfast, and after I made it for him, I left around midday.

Ninette made bean soup, and she asked me to have a bowl with her, then we walked up to the chemist to buy her medicines. On our way back, we got caught in a heavy downpour, and sheltered under her umbrella for a while until it eased. Elvira invited me for coffee later, and she gave me mandarins, and some lovely orchids from their garden.

When I came home, Connie wanted to go outside for a smoke. I helped him to put his jacket on, and held his arm till he went over the step of the sliding door. I left him near the cat cage, as it was still drizzling, and went back into the house, when

I heard a loud crash. I rushed outside. He had fallen over backwards, and knocked his head on the brick wall.

I managed to help him to his feet, and he held onto the walker. Then I checked him, and saw a small cut at the back of his head, but he was more shaken and wobbly than hurt. So I made him sit on the chair outside, while I cleaned the wound with disinfectant, then helped him inside the house slowly. His legs buckled inwards and were very shaky. I lifted his legs one at a time over the step, until he steadied himself.

By then my back and arms ached after dragging him up. I made him a cup of tea, which he sipped, and I left him sitting in the television room watching the news. After a while I went to see if he was alright, and asked him, "Do you want a drink?" He just glared at me angrily, and made a growling noise, as he pointed to the ipad. I looked to see what he wanted, and my head started to spin when I read what he typed. "You let me fall! You pushed the walker."

I was sick in my stomach and felt dizzy, as it was such a shock to read that. I cried out, "That's a wicked lie, and I want you to apologize for your false accusation! I was nowhere near you when you fell!" he wrote, "I've been in that spot many times, and didn't fall before." I replied, "Can't you understand that you lose balance without warning?" I was trembling with anger and shock.

I left him sitting there, and I called Shirani. I could not help crying when I told her what he accused me of. She could not believe what he wrote either, and tried to comfort me. When I called Esme later, she said, "Oh don't worry, you know it's not true, just ignore him." But I could not, as I was worried about what other false accusations he would start making against me now. When I went to check him later, he pointed to the ipad again, and he wrote, "I'm sorry. I appreciate all that you do." But it did not appease me at all. I was deeply hurt that he could write such a lie, after all I did and continued to do for him, with so much love and compassion.

It was late that night, but I went upstairs to phone Carer Support Help Line, as I could not fall asleep. The lady at the other end listened patiently to what I told her and said, "It's typical dementia, when they start getting paranoid about the ones closest to them, and imagine they're being ill-treated or they are being harmed. Don't worry about it at all, but see your doctor, and tell him what happened, as you will then have a record of the incident." I decided to follow her advice.

It was very bad next day, as Connie was so weak and tired, that I had to wait on him all day. He kept asking me for various things; do this, do that, fetch and carry, and rub his back. And finally, when he got into the shower in the evening, he left the shower door open, so the whole bathroom floor was flooded. I mopped and cleaned, while keeping an eye on him, as I did not want him to fall in the shower.

I went to school at ten o'clock on Thursday morning, but it was "Book week" still, and the children were busy in the library all morning. I made an appointment to see Dr Khelil at eleven o'clock. I told him what took place the day before, and how difficult it was for me to take care of Connie now, besides picking him up every time he fell.

He advised me about my health issues, and warned me that I would end up getting another heart attack, if I did not look after myself. Then he told me to call an ambulance the next time he fell, as I mentioned that I hurt my neck and shoulders, lifting him up so many times.

As to Connie's accusation that I let him fall, doctor said that most patients with dementia were paranoid, and imagined the worst things about their spouses. He gave an example of a husband shouting at his wife, "You are a devil, you want to kill me!" He said no one would take Connie's words seriously, if they knew he had dementia. And he said the next step was to get Connie assessed.

Because he kept refusing to go into care willingly, he would have no choice, if he was assessed as suffering from dementia. When I mentioned his irrational behaviour, doctor was convinced that he had early onset of dementia. But I could not get him assessed, without his consent. So I left it at that, knowing he would get worse progressively, as Prof. Butler had said, and in the meantime I had to be strong.

I felt slightly better after seeing doctor, and went back to school. I finished early and then drove to Narre Warren to see Shirani. She was very concerned to hear what was going on at home, and how much I had to endure with Connie.

When I came home around five o'clock, Esme and Paul were still there, and they said they wanted to wait till I returned. Roland had visited as well, and brought a bulky old walker from a charity shop. I wondered why he brought it, when I told Connie it was better to hire one, as he may need a wheelchair soon. He told me to return the walker to the rehab centre when we went there next time. The whole house vibrated, as he blasted spiritual music at the highest volume on the surround system once again. Roland had brought the chair down, that I used at my writing desk, and rearranged the dining area, with my chair at the head of the table.

Connie said it was better for him to do his exercises, sitting on that chair because it had arms. The whole place smelled, and when I asked him why, he wrote, "Esme rubbed my back with dencorub." I put things back in order, and asked him to lower the volume; he did not communicate with me all evening.

It was Stacy's forty-first birthday next day, 23 August, and I prayed for him as always, wherever he was. I did not say anything to Connie, as he was totally self-absorbed, and nothing else mattered except his welfare, and comfort. Dr Khelil told me that Connie was in "survival mode" which patients like him often resort to, and I should not be too upset if he behaved as if I did not exist

I woke up feeling nauseous and dizzy that morning, then vomited, and felt so weak that I could hardly stand up. I hated these dizzy spells, which made me so helpless, and I could not walk, without holding onto walls and furniture. So I went back to bed, and rested till late. After a shower, I had a slice of toast, but felt so dizzy that I could not keep my head up at all, and slumped back into bed. I kept invoking Bruno to take away this dizziness.

When I felt slightly steady on my feet, I dialled the emergency Carer Support Unit, and told them how sick I was. I said that it was getting too difficult to leave Connie home alone, because of his falls, so could they please help me with a carer on the days I was out. The lady at the other end was very helpful, and promised to send a carer on Monday, 26 August, from nine in the morning till three thirty.

We discussed several other issues, and they were concerned about my health, when I told them I injured my shoulders and neck picking him up. They advised me to get an ambulance the next time he fell, and said that one of the Carer Support counsellors would call soon, and make an appointment. I was very relieved, as Connie would be in good hands with a trained carer, and I would not have to trouble Esme to stay with him.

I felt very sick all day, and did not come downstairs till about six o'clock in the evening. Connie was sitting at the computer, and did not show any concern at all. So I asked, "Do you know I've been very sick all day, and if I can't get out of bed, how will you manage to make something for you to eat? You haven't even asked me how I'm feeling."

He did not look at me, but wrote, "I know you are not well, are you better?" I nodded, and went about my work, and prepared dinner. It was still raining heavily, so I could not walk outside, and the cats could not go out either. I called Shirani afterwards, and told her I was unwell, and about a carer coming in on Monday, and she was happy to hear I would get some help soon. Before I went to bed that night, I told Connie about the carer, but he did not respond.

I woke up feeling tired, and I was hoarse next day. Con rang early morning to ask if they could drop in around two thirty that day. I told him I was not feeling too well, and he thought I had a cold. Connie tottered to the kitchen just then, leaning heavily on the clumsy old walker Roland brought. It was not as good as the one we hired, but he wanted to use it.

He looked very angry, and glared at me as he wrote on his ipad, "I don't want a strange woman in the house keeping an eye on me! Cancel the carer on Monday! I can look after myself!" I did not respond, but I was not going to cancel the carer. I was taken aback though, and tried to reason with him that he could not be left on his own, in case he fell.

He was in a violent temper, and trembled all over, shouting and making awful guttural noises as he wrote, "Why are you so negative?" I said, "What do you mean by *negative*? I'm only doing what's best for you, to see that someone is here to take care of you, when I'm not at home. How is that being *negative,* because you don't know when you may have another fall."

That made him angrier still, and he wrote, "What is she going to do when I'm resting? She'll be going through all my personal things, and do you know what nursing homes are like? You want me in a home? They don't treat old people well." I gave up. His use of the word "negative"was something I did not understand, because whenever I spoke common sense, he did not want to listen. He wanted me to be delusional like his fanatical siblings, who told him, "*Nothing* is wrong with you, you will talk again, and walk like before."

They did not want to admit it, or tell him the truth that was staring us in the face, that he was going down rapidly, and there was no medicine to cure him. That was why he became so angry with me, when I told him he needed someone to be with him all the time. He continued typing about all the negative things he heard about nursing homes, and insisted he did not want a carer. I ignored him, as I wanted the carer here on Monday, no matter what he said.

Con and Cornelia came around three thirty, and we had a pleasant afternoon. I made chilli sauce, so Cornelia could watch me, as she wanted the recipe, and I gave her a bottle of sauce to take home. They enjoyed pan rolls with chilli sauce, and a bowl of macaroni with patty mix, which I made often, as it was Connie's favourite dish then. After relaxing and chatting for some time, they left a few hours later.

It was a spectacular sunset, and I removed several photographs, then I rested, as I did not want to end up with dizzy spells again. Bruno helped me I knew, as I felt much better. The dizziness usually lasted days or weeks, so I took it easy, as I knew it was due to stress.

I rested till late on Sunday morning, as I was still slightly dizzy. We enjoyed a pleasant afternoon when Mary and Peter came. Mary brought a lemon cake, and it was amusing to watch Connie's face pucker up when he took a bite, as if he sucked on a lemon. He pushed it away, because he did not like anything acidic now.

I told Mary it was delicious, but that Connie could not eat it, as it was lemon-flavoured. She laughed, as she understood, and they left a couple of hours later. I washed and cleaned up slowly. He did not communicate much, except to ask me to fetch and carry, and later in the evening, to rub voltaren on his back.

I woke up early on Monday morning, as the carer was due to arrive at nine o'clock. Connie got out of bed soon after and followed me to the kitchen, where he started typing on the ipad. "I don't want a stranger here in my house! She'll go through all my personal belongings! Cancel her at once!" I ignored him, and went about getting ready.

My head was spinning, as I was so stressed out with Connie's nagging behaviour; even with an ipad, he managed to nag, and tried to control me. Liz, the carer, arrived at eight forty five, and I met her outside the gate to explain that Connie did not want her here, and how very troublesome he was.

She said she understood very well, as she had vast experience dealing with difficult patients. She was a pleasant lady, in her mid-fifties or so. She came in, and I showed her where everything was, and gave her a list of emergency numbers, in case he fell or choked while eating or drinking. I told her that his lunch was in the fridge, and he could warm it in the microwave oven when he was hungry. She said she knew what to do in an emergency, and she brought sandwiches for her lunch, so not to worry, as he would be fine.

When he saw Liz, Connie scowled and stomped off to the bedroom, and banged the door behind him. He pretended to be asleep when I left soon after, and did not respond when I wished him goodbye. I worried about the situation all day, and hoped he would not be too rude and upset the poor lady. I could hardly wait to finish at school and get home.

I stopped at Bentons Square to get some groceries on my way. Someone from the Carer Support Agency called me at four o'clock, saying Liz was concerned, as she was supposed to stay only till three thirty. I said she could leave now, as I was on my way home. But she replied that Liz could not leave Connie alone until I returned. I apologized for getting late and hurried home.

When I returned half an hour later, I was very surprised to see Liz and Connie seated side by side snugly on the sofa. Connie giggled and laughed happily. It was such a relief, and Liz said, "Conrad and I had a good day. We watched one of his faith healing DVD's and he wrote a lot of information about himself and his family." I said I was happy they got on well, and she left soon after.

I could never understand his erratic and unaccountable behaviour. After all the nagging and hassle about not wanting a carer, he was quite happy sitting next to Liz, and behaving as if she was an old friend. I was relieved that I overcame the hurdle of having a carer now.

Next morning, when I was playing the piano, Connie wrote, "Drop me at Esme's, and I will come back with them." So I stopped there on my way to Ninette's in the afternoon. She was not too well, but we took Fido for a walk to the shops and back later. I received a note from Philip Brady, a radio personality on 3AW, thanking me for the book and CD that Luigi asked me to send. Philip wrote that he would like to interview me later in the year, to talk about Luigi's career.

When I told Ninette about it, she was very happy, and said that Luigi would be pleased too. I came home around six o'clock, after my usual shopping etc. Esme called to ask if I was home yet, as they did not want to leave Connie alone. And they came in just as I was putting away the groceries. Esme said Connie fell in the shopping centre. Although he was not seriously injured, he complained of pain in his arm and shoulder, as a couple of men grabbed him and helped him to his feet.

He wrote, "They were very rough and pulled my arm. It hurts now. You will have to rub some voltaren." I said I would, and when they left, I massaged his shoulders and arm with voltaren. Then I took it easy after dinner, and went to bed early, as I started reading George Eliot's, "Mill On The Floss" again. And as it was such a thick book, I knew it would take me a while to finish reading it. It was one of the books I read umpteen times in senior school for the final exam, and I still appreciated the poignant story very much.

I felt much better, as my vertigo eased next day. And as it was very pleasant and sunny, I planted poppy and pansy seedlings near our bedroom window. I thought it would please Connie when he looked out, as I did not walk with him in the garden anymore, since that day he accused me of letting him fall. But he went out to the garden with his siblings whenever they visited, and I was not home.

I drove to Mt Martha village to post another CD to 3AW, that Ninette wanted me to send, and I walked around for a few minutes. Connie wrote that he felt tired and weak after his fall at the shopping centre last evening, and was resting, after I applied voltaren on his neck and shoulders. At least he typed, "Thank you."

Before going home that day, I looked in at Andrew Kerr nursing home in Mornington. It was very pleasant and cheerful, and in response to my query, they said I had to make an appointment with the manager, to add Connie's name to a waiting list. When I returned home, I went upstairs and rested a while. Connie was still asleep till about three o'clock, and then woke up in a very irritable mood. He started picking on me for the smallest thing (nagging via the ipad). It was so very annoying to listen to that robotic voice barking out Connie's orders in that flat, metallic monotone.

The agency sent another carer, Glenda, on Thursday, 29 August, which was Christian's birthday, so I said a special prayer for him. Glenda arrived at nine o'clock, and seemed pleasant enough. We went through the same discussion, and I gave her a list of contact numbers before I left for school. He was in the kitchen, and when I introduced Glenda, he did not respond or acknowledge her.

When I returned home at three o'clock that afternoon, I found Glenda sitting alone in the lounge. And when I asked her where Connie was, she said his sister, Geraldine, brought lunch at midday, and she was with him still. I noticed unwashed, takeaway containers on the dining table.

Geraldine was seated close to Connie in the television room, and watching a healing DVD. She was holding Connie's hand and mumbling something, when I walked into the room. His eyes were closed, and he repeatedly said, "Yes, Yes" to everything she said. Evidently, it was some kind of indoctrination, because she jumped up guiltily when she saw me, and tried to cajole me.

I asked, "What are you doing here? The carer is sitting by herself." I did not say anything else, as Connie was in a daze, and did not even look at me. I walked out of the room, and apologized to Glenda, for his sister barging in and taking over, and letting her sit on her own. She said that it was alright, but before she left, she asked me, "I wondered why he needed a carer, when his sister was here?" I replied that his sister would not come so early in the morning, and he would be alone until one of them visited in the afternoon.

I was afraid that if Glenda mentioned his sister was with him, that would jeopardize my situation to get a carer in future. I was fuming, so I called Elvira, and she asked me to come over for a coffee. I spent a few minutes there, and tried to unwind over a coffee. And I told her about his interfering siblings, who did not leave us alone, and drove back an hour later. I was relieved to see that Geraldine had left, so I walked in the garden, and tried to take it easy.

I called Shirani and Ninette later that evening, and then wished Christian for his birthday. I asked Connie to send Christian a text message, but he wrote that he would do so later. When Nelune called that night, I told her what the situation was like, and she too was very indignant at such interference. I asked Connie later, why he did not mention that Geraldine was visiting, as the carer sat alone all afternoon. He wrote, "I forgot."

When I drove Connie to Rosebud that afternoon, he was so weak that he could hardly get out of the car and walk. I returned the walker we hired, as he now used the old one, which was bulky and clumsy, so that it scratched my car badly.

The physio tried to use a brace on his legs, to make them firmer, but could not find the right size, and he could not walk with them anyway. She told him once again that it was best to use a wheelchair now, because I mentioned his frequent falls. But he was adamant, and refused to use one. On our way home, he wanted me to stop at Bentons Square to get some things. It was very tiring, as he could hardly walk back to the car, and he stood on the pavement shouting loudly, so that people stopped to see what was wrong.

A kindly gentleman stopped and asked me if he needed help, then held onto Connie's arms and helped him totter up to the car. I spent a long time getting him inside the car, and then the walker into the boot. A lady parked next to me, was watching us all that time. She came up and asked, "Has your father had a *stroke?* He *really* should be in a home, and you did well getting him into the car. You see, I'm a nurse, and I work in a home."

When I explained the nature of his disease, she shook her head and repeated, "You *can't* look after him, he should be in a home!" I doubt Connie heard our conversation, as he was sitting inside the car, and the windows were up. When we came home, he was so weak, that it took a long time for him to get out of the car once again. I was exhausted that night, waiting on him all evening and serving his dinner, which he ate very slowly.

It was a beautiful spring day on Saturday, and after playing the piano for a while, I planted more seedlings in pots and near the study window. Christian said they would visit tomorrow, on Father's Day, and I was happy. I called Nilanthi, and we had a long chat. She said the rash on her hands was still bad, and she did not want to visit until it was healed.

Connie slept till midday, then wanted a soft-boiled egg and toast. When I served it, he started shouting and jabbing at the dish with a spoon. I asked him what was wrong, and he wrote, "The egg is over boiled, and I can't swallow when it's like that!" I threw it away, and boiled another egg for two minutes. He ate it without a fuss. Honestly, he could still eat McDonalds burghers and chips, which he swallowed without a problem, but fussed over an egg that was just a little over boiled.

I cleaned and vacuumed the house, then went upstairs and rested a while. A couple of hours later, I heard him warming up his lunch in the microwave, and I did not come downstairs until he finished eating. He invariably threw a tantrum, and complained about the food if I was around. When Nelune called later, we had a good laugh as always, because she told me about some strange people she had to deal with too.

It was once again a brilliant sunset that evening, and I removed photographs. But it was impossible to capture the grandeur and true colours of those splendid sunsets.

The first day of spring, Sunday, 1 September, was a pleasant, sunny morning. I gave Connie a card, tatts lotto tickets, and some of his favourite chocolates, and he seemed calmer. He ate a late breakfast, and sat at the computer till Christian and Athena arrived that afternoon. They spent some time after lunch, but left early, due to their work.

Elvira wanted to drop in later, but I told her we were going to Frankston for evening Mass. When I asked Connie if he wanted to go to church that evening, he wrote, "I'd love to go for Mass today." When we arrived there, I parked near the ramp. And after Mass, Maureen and her daughter helped Connie into the car, and then packed the walker into the boot. We returned home around seven o'clock, and he relaxed as he watched television, so we spent a quiet evening.

He woke up early next morning when I got out of bed, and complained of severe pain in his arm, and wrote, "The man who pulled me up when I fell in the shopping centre was very rough. Apply voltaren on my arm before you go to school." I did so, then asked him to rest in bed till I came back, as I was unable to organize a carer that day.

It was another beautiful spring morning, and it was exhilarating to be driving on such a glorious morning. When I saw Colleen, she said she was feeling dizzy and nauseous all week too, so I wondered if it was some kind of a virus. Tess did not turn up for her lesson, so I left early, and just stopped at Karingal to post the ballot papers. I requested postal votes, due to Connie's mobility problems. It was about four o'clock when I came home, and Connie was sitting at the dining table having lunch. No one visited him, and he wrote that he rested in bed till two o'clock. He still complained of pain in his arm, so I applied more voltaren.

Then I walked in the garden, and watched another splendid sunset. That was one of the things I was so grateful for, to witness the amazing panorama of the skies so often.

I made ox tail curry that evening, as it was Connie's favourite, and simmered it till it was so tender, that the meat just fell off the bones. And I did not make it too spicy, as he could not eat hot food now. He wanted macaroni with the curry, and I chopped the meat into small pieces, so he could chew and swallow easily. He ate without a fuss, after sipping his usual whisky, mixed with plenty of ice cubes. I was thankful that there were no complaints or tantrums (for a change).

When I got ready to visit Ninette next day, Connie wrote, "Bring another tube of voltaren on your way." I said I would, and was very surprised to see Esme dropping in at ten thirty with a tube of voltaren. She said Connie sent her a text to bring one. I was irritated, and asked Connie why he got Esme to come all this way with the voltaren, and then tell me to bring one as well. He did not reply. This was either forgetfulness, or dementia, as he was manipulative now, to convince his siblings I did not do anything for him.

I told Esme to check with me in future, if Connie asked her to bring anything, as he was now very forgetful. I had an appointment with Ruth, from Carer Support, at Frankston that afternoon, so I drove to Ninette's first, and spent a little time with her.

Then I was with Ruth for over an hour, and found her to be very supportive and caring. She understood exactly what I was going through, and it was good to unburden to a professional counsellor. Ruth said that their main concern was for the carer, as most of them ended up getting sick, doing their best for patients, and then getting "burnt out." It was their role to support and help in any way they could. But she said that she could not do anything regarding a regular carer for Connie, and suggested I ask for council help.

When I contacted council previously, they said that because Connie was assessed as requiring "high care," they did not have experienced carers who would be responsible for such a patient. Ruth told me that it was imperative to admit him to a nursing home soon. I came home at about five thirty, feeling very tired and depressed, and was busy getting dinner ready, when Roland dropped in after six o'clock, and said he was just visiting.

Connie and he went to the television room, and watched a faith healing DVD for a couple of hours. He said Shiranthi was home alone, after a neck operation. Obviously, his priorities were awry, as he should have been home taking care of his wife, and helping her, and not watching a DVD with Connie for two hours. Shiranthi told me later, that she could hardly manage to do anything for herself. And yet here he was, driving so far, when it would have been more charitable to help his wife. I cut some orchids, and gave a box of chocolates for Shiranthi, and asked him to give her my best wishes. He left soon after.

I still felt slightly dizzy, and these stressful situations did not help. I could not fall asleep that night, so I went upstairs at about one o'clock in the morning to try and get some sleep. And I finally fell asleep a couple of hours later.

I felt drained, but woke up early, as it was a nice day, and rose to twenty six degrees, though it became windy and overcast.

He complained about his teeth constantly, so I made an appointment at twelve o'clock that afternoon. He took ages to get ready, as usual, and at eleven forty, he wrote, "Can you make soft-boiled egg and toast for breakfast?" I replied, "Can you eat in ten minutes, and be ready for your appointment?" He became angry, and started shouting and banging things around. He carried on like this whenever I tried to reason with him, because he always wanted to have his own way.

He ended up having cereal for breakfast, and we arrived there in time for the appointment in Mornington. One of his back teeth was chipped, and cut into his inner cheek, which was the reason why he had ulcers in his cheek. The dentist filed the jagged end, and cleaned his teeth. When we returned, I made his lunch, and he wrote, "Thank you for all you do." I said, "It's alright, and you don't have to thank me. You know I will look after you."

Claudia was due at two o'clock that afternoon, but arrived forty five minutes late (as usual). And after she checked his movements and mobility, she advised him about various other issues, and left an hour later. I went to Bentons Square for an eye test soon after she left. It was the first time I saw this optometrist, John Old, and though he was quite elderly, he was very efficient.

After examining both eyes, he told me that my right eye was not too good, and I would need to have a cataract operation soon. He wrote a referral to an eye surgeon in Mornington. But I wanted to consult my previous optometrist for a second opinion. Because I wondered how I could have a cataract operation, without a carer to help me with Connie.

Chapter 79

Before I went to school next day, he wrote that Geraldine was visiting at midday, so I did not have to organize another carer. It was a wet and dreary day, but I arranged to meet Elvira at Andrew Kerr nursing home at three o'clock, as I decided to put Connie's name on their waiting list.

Elvira wanted to be with me, as I was apprehensive to go on my own. I had to organize this without Connie's knowledge, as he was adamant that he would not go to a home. But the way he was deteriorating so rapidly, his doctors and therapists urged me to put his name down, because the waiting lists were so long.

The first thing the manager wanted, was the Aged Care Assessment, and power of attorney documents. Then he showed us around, and Elvira and I agreed that it was very pleasant, but he said the waiting period was more than two years. I put his name down anyway, then we went back to her place and had coffee. I came home at five thirty, and was relieved that Geraldine had left by then, as I found it increasingly difficult to be polite to her any longer. Because she had such an adverse influence on Connie.

I walked in the garden for about half an hour before making dinner, and tried to unwind. It was not easy visiting the nursing home, and seeing all the helpless inmates there.

Connie's grip weakened so much now, that he could hardly hold an object without dropping it. He asked me to pour him a drink every evening. And I carried his bowl of soup or plate, and kept it safely near him, so he would not drop it. Sometimes, he wanted to sit in front of the television and have his meals. Then he needed three big cushions to sit on, saying his stomach was getting cramped, if he did not sit up that high. I told him it was better to sit at table, but he insisted on sitting in front of the television.

I asked him to open all the jars and bottles in the past, because I could not open them. But now he was so helpless, and it made me very sad when he watched me opening his bottle of whisky. Connie was more demanding than usual that evening. I ran at his beck and call, as he asked me to bring various things, until I could not cope anymore. I told him, "I will die before you, if you keep worrying me like this, and not giving me any peace!" No response, just a sullen expression.

When he could not take the bins out anymore, he stood at the front door and watched me wheeling them up the driveway. And when I came in, he wrote, "All these years when I took the bins, I left them on the concrete path. You have left them on the grass. Go and put them on the concrete." It irritated me, because he still wanted to tell me what to do, even in such a trivial matter, because one wheel was sitting on the grass.

The following day, on Friday, 6 September, I felt very depressed, and wanted to speak to Dr Khelil about Connie's deteriorating condition. Connie wanted to see doctor about his arm, so I made an appointment at midday. Before we left, Connie started shouting and banging things in the bathroom. When I went in to see what was wrong, he had dropped his electric razor, and could not fix it again, so he was frustrated and shouted at me.

I was very upset to watch his pain and frustration, as he just could not hold onto the razor. I tried to help him, but he pushed my hand away angrily, and was determined to fix it himself. Finally, he gave up, and got ready, with half his chin unshaven. I told him we could get another razor on our way home, and gave him a disposable razor to finish shaving. I could not do anything more to help him, but I felt his pain deeply.

When I made the appointment that morning, I asked to speak to doctor on the phone. I told him that it was becoming increasingly difficult to cope with him, as he was so demanding and irrational, and asked him if there was any way he could advise Connie about going into a home. Although doctor was sympathetic, he could not do anything, unless Connie agreed to go into care. He told me, "The only thing I can suggest is, that if he has another fall, get the ambulance to take him into hospital."

When we went in, Dr Khelil was very abrupt, and appeared to be annoyed with both of us. He said, "Conrad, it is plain to see you are now getting so weak that you *can't* manage alone at home, and Nalini can't look after you. So you must think of going into a home, where they'll look after you 24 hours." Connie looked stony-faced and mulish. He wrote, "Not at this moment," and ignored doctor's advice completely.

When we left the clinic later, he could hardly walk steadily, as he held onto the ramp rails, and shuffled his feet along sideways in a crab-like fashion. He dragged his left leg, as he could not lift it up even to take small steps. It was a very distressing sight, watching him inching his way down the ramp, and it took him over twenty minutes to walk such a short distance to the car. I was weary when we came home, so I took it easy, then made dinner. I made sure he ate it all, as he was so weak.

He was losing weight rapidly, as he did not eat big meals anymore. Doctor advised him to go on a high protein diet to build up his muscles, so did the dietician. Although he took supplementary protein drinks, his weight dropped at an alarming rate.

I was upset that evening, because my laptop malfunctioned, and I did not back up all my manuscripts, especially the script I was working on. I hoped Christian or Athena would be able to retrieve all my files, otherwise I would lose all my work. But I could not do anything till they came, and that worried me a great deal. My writing was one way of dealing with stress, and an escape to fantasy worlds without all this trouble and woe. To lose all my manuscripts would be an irreparable loss (to me), because of the countless hours I spent on them.

After my usual chores next day, I took it easy, as Connie still rested at midday. When he woke up, he wrote, "Can you buy a bottle of scotch, as I feel too tired to go anywhere today." I drove to Bentons Square, and bought a bottle of whisky and came home soon. Chris Berman called the day before, and asked if he could visit that afternoon with a friend, who was a nurse. He thought it was a good idea to introduce us to his friend, who lived in Frankston.

They arrived around two thirty, and Moira, who was in her early forties, appeared to be very friendly. She said she usually worked late night shifts in the pathology section in Frankston, and Mornington hospitals. Connie finished his shower, and dragged himself to the table. Then he wrote on his ipad, "Open the bottle of scotch." I did, and poured drinks for him, and our guests.

Moira enjoyed a couple of drinks, and became even more exuberant and kept us amused. Connie giggled happily, and wrote about how we met in Ceylon, and all the incidents there. He wrote, "We have been married for forty three years this November, and we have been very happy together."

Then he wanted his lunch, and ate slowly, but finished the whole bowl of macaroni and patty mix. Chris was happy, and said, "That's a *good* meal, and he enjoyed it!" He asked Connie if he took the herbal pills still, but I told Chris that he took them only a few times, and complained they were too large for him to swallow. Chris was disappointed, but I told him that Connie had swallowing difficulties. After they left, we relaxed, and watched election results till late. The Liberals won, much to our relief, and I went to bed and read for a while.

I woke up around five thirty next morning, on Sunday, and let Mishka out. Then I went upstairs and slept till about nine o'clock. Then I heard Connie grunting and making loud noises. And I thought it was his usual moaning and groaning, trying to get out of bed, so I did not worry about it.

But when I came down ten minutes later, I found him rolling on the bedroom floor, unable to get up, and the walker upturned near the door. As I did not see him fall, I did not know if he knocked his head, or was badly injured. So I did not touch him, and said, "I'm going to call an ambulance, as I can't lift you up anymore."

In the meantime, I put a pillow under his head, and covered him with a sheet, as he wore only a t-shirt. I comforted him, and told him not to worry, as they would examine him for any bruises, and he would be alright. The ambulance arrived within ten or fifteen minutes. And the paramedics told me that it would be safer to take him into emergency, as it was difficult to say if he was hurt or not, and they needed to x-ray his head.

I agreed, and they took him to Frankston hospital. I sent Moira a text message, asking her to stay with Connie until I arrived. She had told me that she was working there the previous night. When I arrived at the hospital within the hour, after showering and breakfast, she was sitting by Connie. I thanked her, and she left soon after.

The medical team started asking him a series of questions while examining him, with Connie getting angrier. He wrote, "I was opening the door to go out and get a cup of Milo when I tripped on the carpet." He still would not admit he lost his balance. One of the doctor's said they would take an x-ray shortly, and till then he was not allowed to eat or drink anything. The nurse fixed a stiff brace around his neck, which he tried to wrench out, and wrote, "This is the worst contraption they have invented, and I'm choking!"

I asked the nurse to loosen it, as he was very uncomfortable. She replied, "You don't have a *neck* Conrad, that's why it's not fitting properly. I'll see if I can find a smaller collar." But she could not, and I had to listen to him shouting and groaning non-stop. Then he wanted to pass water, so I asked the nurse for a bottle. One of the male nurse's gave me one, and told me to hold it in position for him. When I tried to do that, he pushed my hand away roughly, and held the bottle himself.

I asked doctor if I could speak to her in the next room, as she wanted to know what was wrong with him. I gave her a full history, his frequent falls and rapid decline. Prof. Butler worked in this hospital, which was good, but when I saw Connie a few minutes later and told him, he wrote, "I won't stay here, because Dr Butler will use me as a guinea pig." I replied, "Delete that at once Connie! Don't write things like that." He deleted the sentence, but was still very angry and wrote, "Take me home now! Bring the walker when you come back."

I cleaned his face with a moist tissue, and told him to be patient, that I would get him something to eat and drink as soon as they took an x-ray. Then he wanted to go to the toilet. I got a wheelchair, as his legs were wobbly, and he could hardly stand up. The nurse settled him on the toilet seat, and I stayed with him. But he did not have a bowel movement, so the nurse carried him to the wheelchair, and lifted him onto the bed again.

They took long to attend to Connie, and it was after one o'clock when they wheeled him to the x-ray unit. I stayed in the ward until the results came, and was happy when they said he had no head injuries. And they removed the annoying collar from his neck. I asked the nurse if he could eat something, as he missed breakfast. She brought four small sandwiches, and an orange juice. I took the sandwiches out of the plastic wrap and gave him one at a time. Then he held one out to me, but I said, "No, don't worry about me, you have them, and finish the drink too."

He appeared to be slightly mollified, and did not shout now, but wrote, "Bring the charger for my mobile and ipad, as these are the only means of communicating. Call Esme and tell her to send Paul to pick them and bring them here." I replied I would do so as soon as I left hospital, and promised to bring whatever he needed.

The doctor came in, and much to his annoyance said, "Conrad, although the x-ray was clear, you are very *weak,* and can hardly stand up, so we have to keep you overnight, until the specialist examines you tomorrow morning, because he's not here on weekends."

He scowled at the doctor, and then at me, and wrote, "I don't want to stay here, I want to go home." She looked at me and beckoned, so I went out to the next room to have a word with her. "He's not *fit* to go home, and it's not safe for me to discharge him, so you have to convince him that it's for his own good we have to keep him here till tomorrow at least." I went back, and told him to be patient till tomorrow. And then I wished him, and left after three thirty. He was busily texting away before I even left the ward.

As I got into the car Esme called, "Dolly, Bella just called me to say Connie needs the charger for his ipad and phone. Paul will come there to pick them up." I replied, "I was going to call you when I got home. I know that already, and was going to send them through Paul." She said Connie sent Bella a text as soon as I left him, and she was with him now, as she was working in the hospital that day.

Paul came at five o'clock, and asked me what happened, and I explained everything. He too agreed that Connie should really consider going into a home, as it was plain to see I could not look after him at home. And he said, "The way he dribbles all over when he's eating and drinking, and he can hardly walk now. It's the best thing if you admit him to a home soon."

As Connie's facial muscles became weaker, he found it difficult to eat or drink without dribbling copiously, and used up dozens of tissues at every meal. It was a very distressing sight to watch him eating and drinking now, and they had seen him during those times.

I did not know what the doctors would say tomorrow, but whatever happened, I hoped it was for his own good. I made a few phone calls that evening to inform everyone of what happened. And I sent Mathew a text, as he told me to keep him informed. He replied immediately, that he and his colleagues would visit him next day.

I left early on Monday morning, and visited Connie on my way to school. He sent me a text late last night, saying he needed a pair of shorts and toiletries. He glared at me angrily as I went in and typed, "I want to go home! How long do I have to stay here?" I replied, "The doctor will see you today, and we'll know then." It was a busy and stressful day, as I was exhausted after yesterday's events. I worried about Connie constantly, and how I would cope, if he came home again, and kept falling over like this.

I went home around five o'clock and tried to take it easy, but several friends called all evening. Then Christian, Nelune, Shirani, and Ruth, called as well. Ruth advised me that it was best now to let everything take its course, because it was highly unlikely they would send Connie home, without a care program in place.

My head ached, and I went to bed after eleven o'clock. Then I had a text from Connie, saying that Esme and Cristobel visited him, and to bring a birthday card for Cristobel, as it was her birthday next day. He also wrote, "Mathew, Brent, and Joel dropped in after work."

I visited Ninette on Tuesday afternoon, and she too wanted to know what was happening, so we discussed at length what could eventuate now. While I was still there, a doctor in Frankston hospital called, and asked if I was able to care for Connie at home, if they discharged him that day.

I explained how I hurt my neck and shoulders picking him up several times, that I had a heart condition, and suffered a heart attack a few years ago. I also told him that the treating specialist told Connie he needed high care in a nursing home, but he would not agree to go into a home. Then I said that the Aged Care Team assessed him as requiring high care, and there was no way I could manage, if he was sent home that day.

When he asked about a carer, I told him I looked after Connie on my own, with no help, except for two days, when carers stayed with him when I was out. But the worst part was when he fell, and I had to help him get up.

He listened, and said all they wanted to do was to establish if Connie could go home or not. They were short of beds, and he would have to be moved to Rosebud hospital for some time, until they decided what to do. He also mentioned that the social worker would contact me that day. When I was driving home later, the social worker called, and tried to convince me I should take Connie home, because he *wanted* to be at home.

I told her exactly what I told doctor, that physically and emotionally, it was impossible for me to care for him at home any longer, *even* if a carer came for a few hours. I could not lift him up when he fell down, and he was very weak now. I said that my doctor was very concerned about my health and wellbeing too. Because I was not medically, physically, or emotionally capable of taking care of Connie.

But she refused to understand my situation at all, and was very keen to send him home as soon as possible. Obviously, she did not understand the state he was in. She said that he wrote, "I can look after myself, and do everything at home by myself." He was in denial, and far removed from reality, which I gathered she did not perceive.

I found out later, that due to shortage of beds, the hospital would do *anything* to send patients home as quickly as possible. And they used social workers to persuade people to care for patients at home, even if they had debilitating illnesses like Connie.

I was very annoyed with that particular social worker, as she only wanted to please Connie, because he kept saying he was alright and wanted to go home. I could not believe she overlooked his physical and mental state, and thought he was capable of looking after himself at home, without a carer. She showed no empathy or concern for me at all.

I paid some bills later, and collected a bank statement that Centrelink requested. Then I went for another eye test at the medical clinic in Frankston. He said my eyes were not too bad, and cataracts were not a problem as yet. I did not know whom to believe, as I knew Peter for more than twelve years. But the other optometrist was positive that I needed a cataract operation soon.

I was relieved though to hear that my eyes were alright at present. I drove to the hospital and met Ruth, as she was going to speak to the social worker regarding Connie's future. Ruth was waiting for me in the foyer, and we talked at length, as she had seen Connie earlier.

She was very supportive, and told me that I must be very strong, and not let Connie or the social worker *bully* me into taking him back home. It was obvious he needed 24 hour high care, given the state he was in. She told me that the hospital would do their best to pressure me into taking him home, without any consideration for my welfare whatsoever. Carer Support was there to *ensure* that carers were looked after adequately, as well as the patient.

Ruth said it would take time, and money to organize a carer package, if possible, but it was apparent to anyone that Connie required high care. And she was annoyed with the social worker too, when I told her about her uncaring attitude. It was good to have Ruth's support, and then I went in to see Connie, while Ruth and the social worker held their meeting.

Esme and Cristobel flanked him on either side, and he was propped up in bed. I greeted them, and went over to Connie. Esme said, "I brought his dinner." I looked at her in surprise. "Why, don't they serve meals here?" She wrinkled her nose and said, "Their food is yucky! I brought congee and gravy for Connie." So, he refused to eat the food they served.

He glared at me, and Esme said, "Connie, you want to be alone with Dolly, so we'll go out for a little." She sounded *so* patronising the way she said it, as if I was a visitor, and not his wife. This was just the beginning of a dreadful time with his siblings. So far Esme was understanding and supportive, but her attitude changed overnight, as she and Cristobel took over.

I gave him the card, but he typed, "You write something soon before she comes back, as I can't write very well." I asked him to sign the forms for Centrelink, which he managed to do, but continued scowling and looking miserable.

I felt hurt, because I did all I could to please him, and attended to practical issues now; dealing with Centrelink especially, and all the other tasks that fell on me. But he just did not show any gratitude or appreciation, so I asked him, "Why aren't you responding to anything I say?" he typed, "Thanks." I hugged him then, and wished him good night, and left forty minutes later before his sisters came back. I felt emotionally drained when I returned home, so I relaxed and had a long bath. Several friends called again, to ask how things were, and it was very late when I went to bed.

Connie sent a text around ten o'clock next morning, "I'm sitting in the foyer and thought I'm coming home, but they are taking me to Rosebud hospital now. Are you responsible for this?" I replied, "I have nothing to do with the hospital's decision, but they said they are short of beds, and that's why they're taking you to Rosebud." He did not respond to that.

I drove to Mornington Centrelink that afternoon and lodged more documents for Connie's application, and the evening was very busy once again. Ruth called to find out what was going on, and she said it was good that he was moved to Rosebud hospital, as they had a rehab section there. And she spoke to the social worker, who wanted to get patients home quickly, due to a severe shortage of beds, and staff in Frankston hospital.

Ruth was very concerned about my health and wellbeing, and understood I was incapable of caring for Connie now. Shirani and Nelune called later, and so did Christian, as they were all very anxious about Connie and me. Christian said that Athena fixed my laptop, and managed to retrieve all my files. I was so relieved, and thanked them very much. It was fortunate that the files were not deleted. He said he would drop it off next day.

When I was at school on Thursday, 12 September, the occupational therapist at Rosebud hospital called to ask more information, as their team were assessing Connie. I told her that he had been seeing all the therapists in Rosebud over the last few months, and they should have his details there, but I answered her questions anyway.

I finished at school early, and drove to Karingal to get a third opinion regarding my eyes, as I wanted to be certain what was going on. Christian came there, and we had a coffee and snack at Degani's cafe. He brought the laptop, and advised me to get an external hard drive, to back up my files in future, just in case it happened again.

Then he went to Dick Smith electronics, and bought an external hard drive for me, and we spent about an hour discussing the present situation. He agreed that the best place for Connie was in a nursing home now, as it was impossible for me to take care of him any longer.

I came home around five thirty, and Connie sent a text, saying that Sherone, Valerie, and their families visited him the previous evening. I called Sherone to let her know what was happening. And she said that Cristobel told everyone, "Connie is on his death bed, and everything was shutting down." They were concerned, and rushed down to see him.

I could not get over the drama queen, calling all the family and spreading such a falsehood. I reassured Sherone, and told her if there was any change in Connie's condition, I would definitely let her know. Then I called Esme, but Paul said Cristobel picked her up and they were with Connie.

Cynthia, Cornelia, and a few others called that evening, then I relaxed before going to bed. It was a strange feeling being alone. And although I was very distressed that Connie was in such a bad way, I knew he was well looked after in hospital, and that was a relief. It was very quiet though, without his constant growling and barking orders at me.

Simba woke me up around four thirty next morning, scratching and scraping the door, as he wanted to go out. He was one cat who suffered from insomnia, as he could not sleep after four o'clock in the morning. I called Shiranthi and Roland, and told them about Connie, and that I was visiting him that afternoon. Then I attended to some emails and checked bills that had to be paid, before driving down to Rosebud.

I did his laundry from the time he went to Rosebud, knowing he was very fussy about his clothes. So I took a change of clothes, and brought his soiled clothes home, as he did not want the hospital to wash them. When I saw him, he was sitting by the bed, and typing on the ipad. He had just finished lunch and wrote that he wanted to go to the garden.

When I told the nurse, she came and helped him into a wheelchair, and I took him to the canteen first, as he wanted a cappuccino. When they served him, he wrote, "Too hot," and scowled as he handed me the cup. I sat down until it cooled, and he finished sipping it slowly. He was still able to hold a cup then, and drink slowly without any help.

As I wheeled him out, several nurses and staff members greeted him, "Hi Conrad, good to see you!" He giggled and laughed as he waved back at the female staff. I was glad to see him being pleasant, and hoped he would settle down, until the doctors decided where to send him.

He wrote, "Could I use the walker and go for a walk under supervision?" But the nurse replied, "No, Conrad, you *can't* use the walker, *only* the wheelchair, as we don't want you falling again." He was very upset, and displeased I could see. He wrote a string of complaints about the hospital; the nurses were too noisy, and he hardly slept at nights, his back was itchy, and his neck and arm were paining. I applied lotion on his back, and voltaren on his neck and arm.

Then he wrote, "Pay all the bills that are due end of this month." It meant he accepted the fact that he would not be home to do it. I asked him to sign the forms for Centrelink, as I had to post them immediately, and he managed to do so. He wrote, "Esme and Jenny visit from 5 to 8 daily." I asked whether he meant Cristobel, then he wrote, "Esme and Bella, not Jenny."

I replied, "It's good that you have company, and they have time to visit daily, but you know I have to work, look after the house and garden, and attend to everything by myself. I will visit every other day, and take your laundry home, but I can't visit daily, and not at nights especially, because of my eyesight. It's too much for me." He just stared down at the ipad, but did not write anything in response. I left at about three o'clock. He wanted me to stay with him all the time, every day, but it was impossible. I needed to get on with my life, and do practical things that had to be done.

I was loving and compassionate right throughout, as I understood what he suffered. But apart from doing everything possible for his comfort and welfare, I could not sit by his bedside all day and night. If his siblings had so much time to spend with him, I was glad he had company, and that was that.

This unfortunate period was not a competition or a game, to prove how much I cared for Connie, by spending all my time in hospital. If that was their intention and mentality, I could not care less. I knew all that I did, and continued doing for Connie's welfare, and that was all that mattered.

When I wanted to connect the television in his room, and asked if he wanted me to do it that day, he refused to let me do so. He still kept hoping he would return home soon, and wrote, "I don't know how long I will be here for. Don't pay for one whole week." So I let it be.

I stopped on my way to post the documents to Centrelink, and came home soon. Then I called Ninette, and we had a long chat. I read a little when I went to bed. But felt very emotional and sad about Connie's condition, and this sudden misfortune that turned our lives upside down.

I wanted him to understand that I still cared for him very much, and I had not abandoned him in any way. So I sent him a text saying, "I love you, and don't worry, try to rest, see you soon." He replied, "Thanks for all you do. Love you very much. Take care." It made me immensely distressed, to think of him being so helpless and unable to communicate verbally, but I tried to fall asleep nonetheless.

It was a mild, beautiful spring day on Saturday, and Simba woke me up at three o'clock in the morning. I decided to lock him up in the cat cage tonight, if I wanted to get some sleep. Then I cleaned the house, and washed Connie's clothes to take them next day.

I drove to Bunnings in the afternoon, as it was such a pleasant day. And I bought two native hibiscus plants for the front garden, as it was bare, and needed some colourful shrubs where the fence fell down. I spoke to Nilanthi when I came back, and she said she was still unwell, with eye problems and a rash on her hands.

It was Nelune's fund-raising "Lilac Ball" that night, and I called her the night before to wish her well, as she expected to raise enough money for the completion of the hospital. Every time I looked at the garden, and saw the spring flowers in bloom, I grieved for Connie, because he could not enjoy any of this beauty.

Even when he was at home, he stopped "looking out" in every sense, as he became totally immersed in his pain and misery. Last night he sent me a text. "Hope this nightmare ends soon." Poor man. This was his destiny, and no one could bear his pain or help him, except God.

No matter how rude or unreasonable he was to me, I tried to understand that he lashed out at me, because I was the only one who would take it from him, and no one else, and he knew it. I baked his favourite butter cake for tomorrow, as I told him I would bring his change of clothes. And I thought he would like to have a slice of home-made butter cake. I felt weary that evening, as I did so much work, and watched a movie to unwind.

It turned out to be another beautiful day on Sunday. After the usual chores and routine, I iced the cake with some very light, lemon-icing, and drove to Rosebud in the afternoon. Roland, Benjamin, and all his three children were visiting. I asked the nurse if I could take Connie to the garden, so she helped him into a wheelchair.

We sat in the quiet little garden enjoying the sunshine. Roland and the others left after a while, and I spent some time alone with Connie. He wrote that Con visited the previous afternoon, and connected the television for $49 a week. I said that it was good of Con, but when I asked him before, he told me he did not want it connected. He seemed somewhat calmer when I wheeled him back to the room.

Although he was not allowed to stand on his own or use the walker anymore, he looked alright, but was very tired and feeble. Before I left, he wrote, "I miss you." I held him close and comforted him, saying, "I miss you too, take care, and I will visit soon." I was very upset as I drove back on the freeway, and came home burdened with a weight in my chest. I told myself I had to be strong now, and I had to keep telling him that I could not manage to care for him at home.

One of his siblings visited him daily, and he was well cared for by the nursing staff, so I did not have to worry about him, I told myself all the time. I spoke to Shirani later, and told her how Connie was. She was pleased he was in hospital, and told me not to worry. Then Nelune called to say they raised $1.8 million at the Ball last night. I was delighted for her, and congratulated her on another marvellous effort, then we chatted for some time, and she was very comforting too.

Chapter 80

It was wintry and rainy on Monday, and on my way to school, I stopped at church to light candles, and spoke to Fr Denis and Vicki later. When I told Fr Denis that Connie was in hospital, he said he would visit him soon. Although we now belonged to Mornington parish, he said he did not mind visiting Connie in Rosebud, as he knew us for some time. Then I booked the community hall for 15 December, for the annual piano recital. Vicki and the other ladies in the office were concerned, when they heard about Connie's condition, and that he was in hospital now.

One of the nurses in Rosebud hospital called that afternoon to say Connie fell after his shower, while he was being dried. She sounded very upset, and said he fell a second time in the bathroom, but she managed to stop him before he hit the floor. Although he knocked his head, he was not injured, and were taking him for an x-ray soon. I sent Connie a text immediately to ask how he was, and that I was sorry he fell again. He replied some time later, "The nurse was clumsy, and the chair was too high, that's why I fell."

It was typical of him to still find excuses for his falls, so I did not respond to that message. It was about five o'clock when I came home, and I was drained. Connie sent me a few more text messages that evening and night, saying he was alright, and I told him to try and rest well. He knew I did not drive at nights because of my vision, so I said I would visit him soon. Then I watched the final season of "Mr Selfridge," which was a very good series, and turned in later.

I made several phone calls next morning, including the financial advisor, Adrian, from Retire invest. He was very helpful, and advised me on what needed to be done now. The social worker at Rosebud called to ask if I could meet her to discuss Connie's future, and I agreed to meet her at one thirty the following afternoon.

After attending to my daily routine at home, I drove to Westpac Bank at Karingal, where the lady was very kind, when she heard about Connie, and helped me finalise some issues. I visited Ninette later, and took some butter cake for her, then we had pasta for lunch, and I walked with her to the chemist. I did some tasks for her later, and left around three o'clock, as I had an appointment with the podiatrist.

When I returned home, I called Ruth, and told her about the appointment with the social worker tomorrow. She advised me, and told me not to let her pressure me into taking Connie home. Then I spoke to Shirani, and replied some emails. Christian called in the night to ask how I was, and what was happening with Connie. I told him I had a meeting tomorrow, and would let him know the outcome.

It was another wet and gloomy day on Wednesday. After a few more phone calls regarding Connie's pension, and usual tasks, I drove down to Rosebud. I met the social worker, Marissa, a young lady in her mid-twenties or so. She told me she was the relief person, as the permanent social worker was away.

Marissa walked with me into the room, and Connie just glared at me angrily. She introduced herself, and said, "I'm here to discuss your future program Conrad, as you may have to go to rehab at Mornington very soon, because you can't stay in hospital indefinitely." He seemed oblivious to what she was saying, and wrote, "Bella is coming at two o'clock to shower me, as male nurse is clumsy. Esme and Bella shower me. My sister is a nurse at Frankston hospital."

I told Marissa his sister was a patient care assistant, and not a registered nurse. I did not know where he got the notion she was a nurse, unless she told him so. She would have convinced him that she was a nurse, and therefore was able to care for him. The cake I brought him was still in the container, untouched. I asked him why he did not eat it. He wrote, "I don't like the icing." I asked him why he was so angry with me, and was it because I did not visit him daily?

I said, "You know I have to go to school three days, besides all the other things I have to attend to on my own." He wrote, "She works too." I replied, "Yes, I know she works a few part-time hours. This is not a game, or a competition to see who comes every day and who doesn't. You know better than anyone how much I have to do, looking after the house and garden, three cats, teaching at school, and taking care of all your affairs and bills now, and doing your laundry, and bringing them here every other day. I know you have visitors *every* day, and you are well looked after here, you are not on your own."

But he continued to glare and growl at me, and was so nasty that I could not stand his attitude any longer. Whenever I visited him, I felt physically ill by the time I left, because it was so very stressful. If he was kinder, I would have tried to visit daily. But I just could not cope even with visiting him every other day, as I felt my head pounding, and my chest ready to burst with anxiety.

When he was at home, he saw how much more extra work I had on my hands now, as he was unable to do anything to help me. I knew he wanted to hurt me, because I did not take him home. All his text messages ended with, "When am I coming home?" He did not realize how difficult it was for me to keep saying, "No, you can't come home just yet." It made me feel violently ill, when I had to tell him the same thing over and over, knowing how much he wanted to come home. But unfortunately, it was impossible for me to take care of him any longer.

I did not say anything more after that. The social worker spoke to him about the rehab program they planned, and he agreed to it. After she left, I told him I would not stay long, if his sister was coming. I felt sick in my stomach to think he asked Cristobel and Esme to shower him. How could he get his sisters to shower him, and not a male nurse or his wife, as I was with him at the time. If he had asked his brother to shower him, I would have understood, but his *sisters*?

It made me realize his condition was worse, because I read that this disease made him lose all inhibitions. But what made me livid, was to think that his sisters were so devoid of modesty, that they even agreed to shower him. It seemed deviant to me, and I found the situation sordid and nauseating.

Bitter tears stung my eyes, as I hurried down the corridor and thought of his behaviour towards me; to not even taste the cake that I baked especially for him, was very hurtful. But even more, was his attitude regarding his sisters. Marissa saw me in tears and stopped.

I explained everything to her, and said I was hurt and disgusted that his sister was coming to shower him now, knowing I was with him. He could have asked me instead of his sister. She said this was typical behaviour of a patient with dementia, as they turned on the one closest to them, as I told her that he was nice to everyone else except me.

Marissa advised me, and told me to put it down to his illness. And not to get hurt, no matter what he said or did, as he was not responsible for his behaviour anymore. Then I spoke to the head nurse, who was just as surprised as I was, that his sisters were showering him. She said it was against hospital rules, and if he fell in the shower, they would be held responsible for his injuries. I asked her how this could happen in a hospital, and why the nurses did not stop them.

She promised to look into it, though it was difficult for them when nurses changed their shifts. When I came home, Ruth called, and she was just as surprised, and appalled to hear what his sisters were doing in hospital. And told me the same thing Marissa said, that I should not blame Connie, as he did not know what he was doing.

I spoke to Shirani, Nelune, and Ninette, and they were just as shocked as I was. Ninette especially was outraged, and asked me, "What *kind* of shameless women can be so low, and without any decency to shower their own brother, when his wife is still living?" Her sense of modesty was outraged, and she could not get over it. And she kept asking me the same question, as to why his sisters behaved like that. She told Luigi too, and he was just as surprised as Ninette, because they never heard of such a situation before.

None of my friends and family could believe or understand how his sisters could behave so. All they had to tell Connie was, that it would be best for the nurses, or his *wife* to shower him. But they were puffed up with self-importance, because Connie asked them instead. They were lost to all sense of propriety in their scramble to oust me out of Connie's life, and take over completely. I often wondered how they would have reacted *if* they were in my shoes, and it happened to their husband.

I woke up around two thirty on Thursday morning, and could not fall asleep till dawn. I was exhausted and felt down-hearted, and although I tried hard not to think about yesterday's events, I felt sick each time I thought of Connie's attitude. And how he wanted his sisters to shower him, even though a male nurse was on duty, and I was with him too. It distressed me very much, but I tried to get on with my daily work.

He sent a text early in the morning, asking me to bring more clothes, although I took his washed clothes only yesterday. it was just an excuse to get me to visit him, even though he knew I was at school that day. I felt much better as the afternoon progressed, although it was chilly, and rained all day. Three of my students were absent, so I left school early, attended to a few things, and then came home around four thirty.

Ruth called to say that she had a discussion with Marissa. And she advised me to take one day at a time, and try not to worry too much about the future, as everything would fall into place. She was a very caring person, always encouraging and supportive, so that I did not know what I would do without her good advice.

During this time, not one of his siblings contacted me, to find out how I was coping, except for Babs. Esme changed completely, since Connie went to hospital. Cristobel and she behaved as if they were in complete charge of him, and I was an outsider. Esme called a couple of times only to ask me to bring something for Connie, as if I did not have enough text messages from him, whenever he wanted anything. This was another one of his manipulative games to punish me.

He told his siblings to do things, or get things for him that he already asked me, and pretended I did not do anything for him. They sympathised with him, and believed I did not care about him at all. I was aware of what he was doing, but I thought his siblings knew me better. I did whatever I could to make sure he was looked after well. And as long as my conscience was clear, it did not matter what they said or did, or what falsehoods Connie conveyed. Because I knew he was angry with me for not bringing him home.

Ruth kept telling me to be strong, and not to let him manipulate me, or let the hospital pressure me into bringing him home, as he definitely needed to be in a nursing home now. She saw his state when she visited him in hospital, and was shocked that the social worker there had insisted I should take him home. I tried to unwind in the evening and forget my troubles.

I packed his clean laundry, and drove to Rosebud on Friday morning. When he saw me taking out his tracksuit pants to hang in the cupboard, he typed, "You have washed my clothes with the towels, there's fluff on them. All these years I washed my clothes and didn't get fluff on them." I did not get annoyed, but took a deep breath, knowing that he just wanted to pick on me, because he was so unhappy.

Then he started picking at imaginary fluff in the pants, so I tried to look at the funny side of this situation. Here he was, helpless and incapable of doing anything for himself, and he was concerned about fluff on his tracksuit pants. I replied, "I will brush the fluff away, and you know I don't wash your clothes with towels anyway."

Just then Roland came panting into his room, carrying an electric shaver. And when he saw me, he exclaimed, "*You* are here?" I did not know what he meant, the way he said it, as if it was such a great surprise to find Connie's wife with him. But I just ignored his remark, and told him Connie was picking on me about fluff on his clothes. So he took a look at them and said, "No, where is the fluff? I can't see any."

I asked him why he was rushing down here to shave Connie, and whether the nursing staff did not do it. He replied, "They are very rough, Connie doesn't want them to shave him." It was apparent that when Connie pulled the strings, they danced like puppets to his tune. They did not know him as well as I did; how very controlling and demanding he was, and still wanted to be in charge. None of them were aware of the nature of his disease, or that he had early onset of dementia, because they were all in denial.

I asked Connie to sign the pension concession card, and he did so with great difficulty, because his hand was very unsteady. He wanted me to write a card for Esme, which he asked me to bring, as it was her birthday next day. When lunch was served at midday, I told him I should leave, because the hospital rule was that patients should not be disturbed during meal times. He did not seem to mind, and did not start shouting and throwing a tantrum.

But I stayed a while longer, and he seemed to enjoy the food, as he ate without fussing. He was still able to use cutlery and feed himself at that stage. Before I left, I spoke to the head nurse again, and told her what was going on with his showers. She said she understood the dynamics with his siblings. And told me that she would ensure all staff adhered to hospital rules, and not let his sisters shower him in future.

I was hungry by then, so I went in to the canteen, and had a snack and coffee before I drove back to Bentons Square to get my medication. I was amazed at the substantial savings with a pension concession card. When I arrived home, Joelle called to say she would visit tomorrow. Then I rang the energy companies to apply for concession rates. I spoke to Shirani and Nelune later on, as they were concerned about me, and wanted to know how I was.

The outside windows looked grimy, due to strong winds blowing dust everywhere. So I spent a few hours washing them, then took it easy, and spent a quiet evening watching an old movie.

It turned out to be a very pleasant, sunny day on Saturday, and after doing my usual chores, I waited for Joelle. They arrived around two thirty, and brought some savoury pastries, and I served them butter cake, which they really enjoyed, and wanted the recipe. Celine and Micheline walked in the garden, as it was quite warm and not windy. We had a pleasant time, and they left within the hour, as they had another appointment.

Del phoned later, and we had a long chat about my situation now. She gave me good advice, as her mother was in a nursing home, and she knew what the process was like.

I replied some emails later, and then walked in the garden for a while. In the evening I watched "That's Dancing," which Ninette copied for me on a DVD, and I enjoyed it very much. Then I read till late, as I found it difficult to fall asleep. When Connie did not send any disturbing or demanding text messages in the evening, I knew that one of his siblings were with him, and he was too occupied to send me messages. It was a relief to get a break from his constant demands, especially the on-going pressure to bring him home soon.

Sunday was a warm, sunny day, so after I finished my tasks, I drove down to Rosebud in the afternoon with his washed clothes, and a few more items he wanted. Esme and Geraldine were there, attending to his finger nails and toe nails at the same time, as he had a fixation about them.

Esme looked up, and said in a peremptory voice, "Here, take his dirty clothes home Dolly!" Then grabbed the bag of fresh laundry from me, and started hanging them up in the cupboard. She did not even greet me, or ask how I was. I did not take much notice of Geraldine, as she continued fussing around Connie.

I found Esme's tone and attitude offensive, issuing orders as if I was a laundry maid. So I did not reply, and she said, "Connie sent me a text to come and shower him, so I came this morning and showered him, and I came now with Jenny and a friend." I was very surprised that the nurses had allowed her to shower him still, even after speaking to the head nurse about it.

Connie was his usual sullen self with me, and did not type anything on the ipad, not a word of greeting or any other communication. I brought his electric shaver as he asked me, but he wrote, "Take it back home as Tucko left his shaver here." Then I wheeled him to the garden in a wheelchair, and his sisters and their friend followed us.

Geraldine acted idiotically, as she rattled non-stop about her faith, and Adam: two topics she dwelt on constantly, just like a broken record stuck in the same groove. My head ached, because she would not give it a break even for a moment, so that I hardly had a peaceful time alone with Connie. She talked so loudly and monotonously, that it grated on my nerves. I found it difficult to be even slightly polite to her, knowing how intrusive she was, to invade our home and lives over the last few months.

His siblings were in their element now, because they could hang around the hospital any time they liked, and stay as long as they pleased, because the staff were not too strict about visiting hours. Connie sat in the sunshine with his eyes closed, seemingly oblivious to all that was going on around him. Esme broke in at last, "Come Jenny, we must go home now! I spent half the morning and afternoon with Connie!"

Geraldine was reluctant to leave, as she was still Bible-bashing, and bombarding her friend with all the details of Adam's death. I was relieved when they finally left, and I stayed a little longer in the quiet garden. I removed some photographs of the wisteria in bloom, which he planted two years ago, and I showed them to him on my iphone. He blinked and wrote, "I can't see them because the sun is too glaring," I said he could look at them when we went inside.

I tried to communicate with him, and held his hands, saying how difficult it was to do everything by myself, and that I missed him. But he did not even look at me or respond in any way, so I wheeled him into the room and drove back. I felt so drained each time I visited Connie, and it was very tiresome when his siblings were there too, because their behaviour and comments irritated me, and I could see how much they influenced him.

I could not reach him wherever he was, and if he was distant before, he was now a million light years away from me, or so it seemed. He looked weaker each time I saw him. And I was deeply distressed that he could not be at peace with himself and with me.

It was pleasant and sunny on Monday too, and Suresh came around ten o'clock in the morning to mow the lawns, like he said. But after he mowed the top section, he could not get the mower to start again. And this was the new mower Connie bought, and never used, except when Paul and Leo mowed the lawns once. I paid

Suresh fifty dollars for petrol, and for doing some of the work. He left soon after, saying, "Sorry Dolly, I will come back and cut the rest of the lawns when the mower is fixed." I thanked him for visiting and trying to help me.

I made several phone calls and replied emails, and then I thought of checking our wills, and other documents. But I just could not locate them, although I searched the whole house for hours. I invoked Bruno to help me find them. I thought I would search the filing cabinet once more that evening, and there they were in a white, unmarked envelope. Every file had a label except the one I was looking for.

I spoke to Shirani, Nelune, and Ninette, and told them about Connie, and they were concerned at his rapid deterioration. I sent Connie a goodnight message later, but he did not respond.

Next day, I contacted an estate agent in Queensland, and told him to market our townhouse in Reedy Creek. Because it was very difficult to pay the mortgage without Connie's regular wage coming in. I tried to tell Connie that the agent said it was a good time to sell. But he did not show the slightest interest in the matter. I had to make some decisions now, and do what was best.

The agent said they would market it around $270,000, but were not hopeful of achieving that price, due to the slow movement in property over there. I agreed, as Connie wanted to sell it for $250,000 in January 2013. I disagreed then, as it was too low. But I agreed to sell now, due to our changed circumstances.

The agent was very proactive, and sent me regular emails and called often. While I was visiting Ninette the following Tuesday, the solicitor called to say that they could not proceed with the sale, unless I had financial power of attorney. I told the agent that Connie was in hospital, and unable to speak or write, so I said I would attend to it as soon as possible.

As I had the necessary forms with me, I decided to take it to hospital next day, and ask Connie to sign them. My laptop was down again, and I was exasperated, as it delayed my work. I did not know why it kept doing that, but as everyone knows, computers and machines have minds of their own. I felt very stressed, worrying about all these financial matters, and now the added stress of selling the unit in Queensland.

I did not fall asleep till late that night, and then Simba wanted to go out at four o'clock in the morning. So I had no sleep till after six o'clock, then fell into a deep sleep, and forgot to text Shirani to say I was alright. She sent me a text at about nine o'clock, asking if I was alright. I told her I was sorry, as I overslept, but she was relieved to hear that I was okay.

The speech pathologist called in the morning, to say they were holding a meeting at eleven o'clock tomorrow morning, regarding Connie's assessment. I said I would be there with my son. Then I drove to Rosebud in the afternoon, and told Connie I needed to have financial power of attorney, in order to attend to financial matters. I was sorry I omitted to get that document signed at the same time as the medical power of attorney, but he did not refuse. So I asked a nurse to find two doctors to witness Connie's signature.

Fortunately, Connie's treating doctor was in the ward then, and when the nurse called him, he came immediately. He explained to Connie that I needed this document, as I could not attend to our financial matters otherwise. Connie typed, "I trust my wife to do what's right with my financial affairs, and hand over full responsibility." When he read this, the doctor was satisfied. He completed the form, then called another doctor to witness the signature. It was a great relief to get that important document in my hand, before he became completely helpless.

A few months later, when I read our wills, which we made in 2001, we had completed financial, and medical power of attorney for both of us, in the event of either one of us being in a situation such as Connie was in now. With all the stress and worry, I did not go through those documents as carefully as I should have done. But the main thing was, I could now fulfil the current requirements, in order to sell the unit etc. I wheeled him to the garden afterwards, as it was sunny though a little windy, but he wanted to come inside.

Instead of going back to his room, I wheeled him around the different wards. And he was relaxed, as he smiled and waved at everyone who passed by and greeted him. Then I tried to communicate with him, and repeated that it was very difficult doing everything by myself now, but no response at all. He typed a list of complaints, and what things he wanted me to bring next time. But not one word of concern, or how I was coping.

I failed to understand why he treated me like this, as he responded and communicated with others, but not with me. He appeared to be utterly unconcerned about whatever I told him, and pretended not to even hear what I was saying. But when his siblings visited, he communicated to them whatever I told him. I found out about this, as Roland and Esme mentioned certain matters I discussed with Connie. When I came home, I took it easy and had a quiet evening.

Chapter 81

On Thursday morning, 26 September, I drove to Rosebud for the meeting with the panel of doctors and therapists. Christian said he would be at there at eleven o'clock, in time for the meeting. I was happy to hear that he could make it, as it was a long way from the city to Rosebud.

When I went in to the room, the physiotherapist wanted to wheel Connie to the meeting room. But he started making loud aggressive noises, and insisted on using the walker. And he hobbled down the corridor with great difficulty, while the physio walked close behind and kept an eye on him.

The social worker, dietician, speech pathologist, head nurse, and one of the treating doctors were already seated in the meeting room. Christian arrived shortly afterwards, and pulled up a chair next to me. Connie was at the other end of the table, and we waited for the specialist, as he was running a few minutes late. The meeting started twenty minutes later, and went on for almost two hours, because it was very difficult to get Connie's attention.

He did not look up or make eye contact with anyone, and kept typing brief sentences in response, and behaved as if he was on another planet. The specialist gave his opinion on Connie's condition, and strongly recommended that he should be admitted to a nursing home soon, and all the therapists who were involved in his case agreed unanimously. Only the social worker, a young, over-powering female, disagreed, based on the fact that Connie did not want to go into a nursing home. She said no one could force him into a home without his consent.

All the therapists and both doctors said that Connie's condition had deteriorated rapidly since he was admitted here. And if he was not under 24 hour supervision in a nursing home, he was at great risk of falling and injuring himself fatally. But he still did not respond to their questions, as to how he was going to manage at home.

Christian told the panel, "My Mum is physically and emotionally incapable of taking care of Dad due to her own health issues." And I reiterated that it was impossible for me to care for him at home now. Then the whole team agreed he was getting weaker and not improving, in spite of regular physio and speech therapy.

Finally, he typed, "I guess I'll have to agree to go into a home." He was too weak to walk back, so the physio wheeled him to the ward. His lunch was served, so we left him to eat undisturbed. I was drained at the end of that meeting. He had no idea how difficult it was for me to keep saying I could not take care of him, and it made me physically ill each time I had to tell him the same thing. He did not realize that it was impossible for him to come home, the way he was. And I could not comprehend the social worker's attitude at all. Because all she wanted to do was send Connie home, irrespective of who was going to care for him, or whether it was for his own good or not.

Christian and I wished him before we headed home, and as we were very hungry, he stopped to get some takeaway lasagne, as I did not have anything prepared at home. I asked him to change the ink cartridge on the printer later, but although he washed it and put it back, it still did not work. So he said he would get a new cartridge when he came down again. He was a great comfort, as he understood exactly what I was going through with Connie, and his siblings, and was very supportive.

Strong gusty winds blew across the sea, when I drove out later to attend to some banking and shopping. I took it easy when I returned. Babs called in the night to say she visited Connie that evening, and he seemed happy and calm. He typed that Christian and I came for a meeting, and what was discussed there. She too told him that it would be best for him to be in a home, given his weak condition. At least she realized how frail he was, and that he needed full time care.

I met Elvira at Onde's for coffee next day, and we had an interesting chat. Gerry, the gregarious owner, entertained us with anecdotes about his guided tours to Italy, as he had just returned, and we watched some of it on a screen. After attending to some business matters, I came home and took it easy, and Nelune called to say she would visit soon.

I was busy next day, as I took Simba to the vet for his annual check up and vaccine. The vet said he was a little too heavy, and should lose some weight. Then I mailed some documents by express post to the estate agent, and solicitor in Queensland.

When I came back, I started making Christmas cake, as I wanted to have it ready in time for Nelune's visit. Ninette called and had a long chat as usual, then Moira, who kept me on the phone for almost two hours. I delayed baking the cake because of that long phone call.

Ever since Connie was admitted to hospital, Moira called me at the most unexpected times; late at nights, or early in the mornings, when she finished her shift. It was getting very tedious now, as her conversation was always about her failed relationships, and love life. And I found her free and easy attitude towards the opposite sex quite distasteful. I did not want to pick up the phone now, but she either sent a text, or called my mobile if I did not answer the landline.

I gave her both phone numbers, thinking it would be useful in an emergency. But now, she made an absolute nuisance of herself, and gave me no peace. When she called that morning, she insisted that I join her and spend the day at the beach. "We could sip wine, and read or just talk all day! Please do come!" I had a hard time refusing her invitation, as she refused to take no for an answer. But finally, she got the message that I was not interested, and I finished baking the cake. Then I attended evening Mass at Mornington, because I wanted to take Holy Communion for Connie, and for Ninette. He sent me a text late last night, asking me to bring Holy Communion on Sunday.

Nelune phoned to say she would be here some time next month, as she was too busy at present. I watched an old movie on DVD, "Rhapsody"' with Elizabeth Taylor, and enjoyed it very much. This was my way of unwinding, and forgetting all the stress in my life at least for a few hours.

I finished all my household tasks, and drove to Rosebud on Sunday afternoon, and hung his clean laundry in the cupboard, also some new t-shirts he wanted me to buy. He seemed alright, but as usual, was uncommunicative with me. I gave him Holy Communion, and spent some time wheeling him around the ward and garden. When the lady served him a cup of Milo, he took one sip, then poured it all on the ground. I said, "Leave it on the table, if you don't like it Connie, why do you have to throw it like that?" no response.

The television was on, and I asked, "Who connected it?" he typed, "Bella, because I wanted to watch the Grand final match." I replied, "You didn't want me to connect it, when I asked you if you wanted the TV, so why did you have to ask her?" he did not respond.

He phoned Cristobel late on Friday night, and asked her to connect the television, giving her and everyone else the impression that I did not want to connect it. She complained to her siblings that she did not have money to connect television, which was $49 a week, and she used her credit card. I just could not understand Connie's behaviour at all.

I decided to connect it next week without asking him, so he would not trouble anyone else, and make them think I did not care, or want to connect the television. I learnt that this was typical of his manipulative behaviour. He wanted to convince his siblings I was not concerned about him, and that they were the only ones who cared for him. Once again, I was advised to ignore his behaviour, as it was obvious he suffered from dementia.

Just before I left that day, he showed me a long passage he typed on the ipad, "I want to go to the glory house in Hallam for two weeks, because Tucko and Jenny will take care of me there, and I will be healed through a miracle."

When I read that, I was very upset and shaken. He did not understand that he could not just leave rehab now, and expect them to take him back in two weeks time. What kind of people were they, to even suggest such an absurd thing. It was cruel to give him hopes of a miraculous cure, when there was no guarantee whatsoever.

After two weeks they would just dump him back at home, and undo all the work the medical staff had achieved in convincing him to go into a nursing home. I replied, "You can't leave this place for two weeks, just like that. Because what will happen when you have to come back? Why are they interfering in our lives, and causing all this trouble?"

He started shouting and howling at the top of his voice. The two patients in the same room stared at him in consternation, thinking he had gone mad. He trembled violently as he tried to type, "You don't believe I will be healed! I will end up in a home till I die!" I replied as calmly as I could, "Connie, if you really believe, God can work miracles *anywhere*, and he can heal you in this place. God is not only in that Hallam church." He giggled for a moment, and then started howling again.

I walked out and spoke to the head nurse. She said she would make sure the doctors were aware of what was going on. And they would keep an eye whenever those two zealots visited, in case they tried to take him out of rehab. I was really too distressed and stunned at their audacity. They upset Connie with such a scheme, without first asking me if it was possible to remove him from this place or not.

As they did not seem to have a clue regarding Connie's real condition, they just encouraged him to have impossible expectations of a miraculous cure that could be achieved only in their glory house. I was furious, and drove back on the freeway, feeling thoroughly upset as angry tears streamed down.

When I came home, I called Roland, and asked him what this was all about. I told him they just upset Connie, and I was very annoyed with Geraldine and him for putting such ideas into his head. And I said, "I have a good mind to restrict Geraldine's visits, because she upsets Connie constantly, which is not doing him any good."

He replied at once, "It's all *Jenny's* idea, and just her talking. You know how she carries on, don't be upset now Dolly, I told her I can't take leave to look after Connie. Have a cup of tea and settle down, we won't be able to do such a thing."

He sounded so insincere, and I did not believe him, because Geraldine and he planned it all, and now he denied any involvement. It irritated me more to think that they played with Connie's emotions and my feelings, without any concern for consequences.

Instead of pacifying Connie and keeping him calm, as I tried to do all this time, they just disturbed him every time they visited, and in turn, he vented his frustration on me.

Then I asked Roland, "Why do you discuss these things in front of Connie, knowing he's a patient, and is so weak now, physically and mentally? He has difficulty rationalizing anything, because he just wants to come home. I understand how Connie feels, because no one wants to go into a nursing home, but unfortunately, he has no choice. You can tell Geraldine to stop interfering, otherwise I will definitely restrict her visits." He did not reply, so I said, "Tell Connie you cannot look after him in their glory house even for two weeks. And can you please leave Connie alone, so he can accept his situation, and don't upset him with your false promises of a miracle." Then I hung up.

Roland was definitely absent on the day spines were handed out, and now proved just how weak he was. He went along with whatever Geraldine and Cristobel told him to do, and when confronted, he backed off, and put the blame on his sisters.

I had a very bad evening, thinking of his siblings' interference in every way, and not letting Connie have peace of mind. And he in turn, vented his anger and frustration on me. That night I sent him a text saying, "Sleep well, and God bless you. All my love." But he did not respond.

I woke up feeling exhausted on Monday morning, as I spent a very restless night, thinking of the traumatic time I endured with Connie yesterday. His frustrated howling echoed in my ears constantly. I called Shiranthi, Babs, and Esme, and told them to warn Geraldine that I would take an intervention order against her, if she did not stop upsetting Connie with her interference, and talk of miracles through faith healing in their glory house.

I watched several documentaries exposing charlatans, who paid healthy people to come in wheelchairs. They got them to walk, then pretended they were healed, and claimed they worked miracles. Connie was so vulnerable and desperate now, and it angered me to think they exploited his weakness. Nelune and Shirani were very sympathetic when I told them what happened.

I called Rosebud hospital to speak to the social worker, but she was not in. When I told the head nurse last afternoon about how his siblings upset Connie, and were trying to take him out of rehab for two weeks, she told me they would assess Connie. As they wanted to find out if he was capable of making any decisions, so as to protect him from any such situations in future.

The doctors and medical staff told me that as I had medical and financial power of attorney, I was responsible for Connie's welfare. But only the social worker seemed to think that Connie still had the right to make decisions, which was highly debatable. Because in all respects, he was devoid of logic, as the disease progressed and affected his brain.

I was exhausted by evening, as I was so troubled and emotional over these issues. They had no idea how much difficulty they caused me. It was bad enough dealing with Connie's condition, without them adding fuel to the fire, and antagonizing him against me. It was incomprehensible what they wanted to achieve, because all they did was upset and alienate him. I was restless as I listened to howling winds raging across the seas. It was a wild night, and the storm did not abate all night.

Next morning, I woke up to find the side fence in the backyard had blown over during last night's gale. And about twenty metres of fencing was down. I called RACV to find out when they could come over, as I wanted to claim it on insurance. When I phoned the owner of the vacant block next door, he was reluctant to pay half the cost. He grumbled about the cost involved when the front fence came down before, and was not prepared to pay again.

I drove home straight from Ninette's place, expecting the fencing man to come over to give a quote, but he finally arrived at eight o'clock in the night. I kept an eye on Simba constantly, as he tried to sneak over the fallen fence to the other side. The man did not bring temporary metal fencing either, but he said he would come around seven thirty next morning to put up a temporary fence.

I locked Simba in the cat cage at nine o'clock. Then I watched a few episodes of "Soap," later, and finished reading "Mill On The Floss" that night. What a tragic story. I pondered long on the unhappy tale, before finally falling asleep after midnight.

I woke up every hour from about four o'clock in the morning, as I wanted to be up when the fencing man arrived. Later on in the morning, I sent Connie a text, telling him the fence fell down again. But he did not respond to what I said, instead he wrote, "Bring my socks and more track suit pants." He was not concerned about the fence, or anything that happened at home or with me.

The man arrived around eight o'clock in the morning, and set up a temporary metal fence, and left a couple of hours later. It was adequate for the moment. And he told me that RACV had to send an assessor first, and then they would advise me if the claim was approved or not.

I was unsure how long all this would take, but hopefully, it would be done in the next couple of weeks. I laid some of the damaged timber against the metal fence, to discourage Simba from creeping under the gaps. Then I braced the remaining fence with some posts, as strong winds continued to blow gustily all day and night. When I spoke to Nilanthi later, she said she hoped to travel at the end of the month. We were very happy at the prospect of being together, especially during this difficult time.

I watched a movie later, and the cats were out, so I went to the garden to get them in at about ten o'clock. While I stood on the deck and called the cats, I heard someone shouting, "Dolly, Dolly!" I was greatly surprised, because it was so late in the night, and still very gusty and rainy. I asked, "*Who* is it?" "It's me, Bella," "What do you want?" I demanded sternly.

She walked along the metal fence on the neighbour's side, And peeped through it. "I brought something for you." I was taken aback, because she had not visited us for over six years, and why she came at this time of the night, was beyond me. So I called back, "Leave it in the letter box," and went inside quickly. I was really surprised, not knowing what her intentions were.

I went upstairs to see if she went away, as I did not open the security gate. Her car was parked outside for about fifteen minutes, before she finally drove off, when she knew I was not going to open the door for her at this late hour. I was appalled at her audacity, turning up like that, and shouting from the other side of the fence. If I was not in the garden, I would not have heard her, and it would have been better, as I could not fall sleep. Because I was very disturbed at her behaviour, especially as she sat outside for so long instead of driving off.

I called Christian and told him what happened, and he said to just ignore her, and it was good that I did not open the gate so late at night. She was so unpredictable, and there was no way I would trust her again. Around midnight, I looked out to see if her car was still there. And then went to the letter box, to see what was so urgent that it had to be delivered at this time of the night.

I thought perhaps it was something from Connie. But inside the letter box was a card, saying, "Thinking of you," and a box of paper serviettes with a floral design. I read her mawkish words, and then tossed them in the bin. I was wary of her peace offerings, and did not want to have anything to do with her, knowing her nature. And I was especially repulsed at the way she had assumed the role of Connie's "substitute" wife.

When I woke up in the morning after a restless night, I still wondered what her motive was in coming here so late at night. I spoke to Nilanthi again, and we had a long conversation, and she too was surprised at what took place last night.

I drove down to Rosebud later that morning, and Connie looked subdued. He was not so distraught and angry as he was the last time. I showed him photographs of the flattened fence on my iphone, and he glanced at them off-handedly. After a while he typed, "How did the cats manage?" Nothing about how *I* managed, but the cats. I said it was very difficult to keep them inside, and he just giggled.

When they served his lunch, he tried to eat with a teaspoon, then dropped the spoon a couple of times, and found it difficult to hold it. He complained that the cutlery was too heavy, and he could eat only with a teaspoon now. I cut up the braised steak into very small pieces, and watched him eat slowly. Then he typed that he wanted macaroni and patty mix for lunch, and I said I would bring some on Saturday, and then I left.

I drove to Karingal, to send Nilanthi some money via Western Union, but the system was down at the post office, and they said the nearest one was at Langwarrin, just ten minutes down the road. I hurried down there, and sent the money without a hassle. Then I sent her a text saying to collect it that very afternoon, before driving back to Karingal to finish grocery shopping. I was very tired by evening.

Ninette called and asked what was happening. And when I mentioned about his sister turning up the previous night, and all the issues with Connie and his siblings, she broke in abruptly, "Nalini, we've discussed all this before, you are repeating yourself!" I was hurt, as I listened to her complaints all these years, without once losing patience. And she repeated the same stories a hundred times over.

I had to remember she was getting old, and I should not take offence. But she always wanted to know what was happening, and that was why I explained those incidents. But now, I decided I would not discuss my problems with her anymore, even if she asked me what was happening. I took it easy, and watched a few more episodes of "Soap" till late.

Friday was a pleasant, sunny morning, and relatively quiet. I made a few phone calls after breakfast, and attended to the usual household tasks. Elio's cousin was mowing their lawns, so I asked him if he could mow our lawns too. He came around when he finished next door, and quoted $40 to cut the lawns, which was reasonable. I asked him to mow the lawns as soon as possible, as the grass was overgrown. He said he would come next week, which was a relief.

Then I started a painting of a sunset in Mt Martha, and spent a few hours immersed in it. I could not finish it though, and left it to dry, then made some marmalade jam, and patty mix in the evening.

On Saturday morning, I drove down to see Connie, and took macaroni and patty mix in one container, some grated cheese, and a fresh salad separately in two other containers. I hoped he would enjoy his lunch, as I took a great deal of trouble to prepare it. When I went into the ward, a nurse was dressing him, as he was unable to dress himself now. She said, "Aren't you lucky to get a nice home-cooked meal!" he did not respond, but wrote, "Heat it in the microwave in the canteen," which I did, and kept it on his table.

He took a few mouthfuls, and I said, "There are notices outside, that visitors should leave patients alone at meal times, and I think I should leave you while you eat." That's all I said. But once again, he started howling and shouting, and became very angry. He pushed the lunch aside and wrote, "Esme and Bella bring me food and stay here till I eat. Other gents wives spend hours feeding their husbands, not me!" I replied, "But you can feed yourself, you don't need me to feed you. I'll come back when you finish eating, as I'll go to the canteen and get a snack."

I did not want to upset him any further by saying that his siblings did not care about observing rules anyway, and they flouted them all, with scant regard for regulations. And I did not mention about his sister visiting me the other night either. I was certain she would have told him about it anyway, and not cared about upsetting him. They did not show any consideration for his mental or physical welfare. Then he wrote, "Take the food back home, I've lost my appetite." I asked him if he wanted to eat something else, and wheeled him to the canteen.

He wanted a sausage roll and a cup of coffee, and I sat with him until he finished eating and drinking. Then I took him back to the ward, and left at about two o'clock. Before I left, I asked him why he was so angry with me, and that I took a great deal of trouble to prepare his favourite meal, but he did not look at me or respond.

I spoke to the nurse and told her what happened, and she said, "Unfortunately, *all* patients with dementia take it out on their closest family members." And that Connie's unreasonable behaviour and anger were evident of dementia. I always felt emotionally drained whenever I visited Connie, as I was uneasy all the time, not knowing when he would start shouting and howling at the slightest thing.

Alan and Ginny called the day before, to ask if they could visit me that afternoon, so I rushed back, in case they had arrived already. But they came around two thirty, and we had a pleasant time. Ginny was still unwell, due to her nervous condition, but she seemed to cope alright. Alan took good care of her, as he was very kind and patient with her. Being a carer was very difficult I knew, and I admired him for his dedication.

I felt weary after they left, so I took it easy, but before I went to sleep, Connie sent a text wishing me goodnight, and saying, "Sorry about lunch, I was agitated. Don't worry, I had dinner." Same behavioural pattern as always; hurt me without any concern, and then say "Sorry." That was how he always was. I replied that it was alright, and wished him goodnight too.

I slept in late on Sunday, and the Karlsens arrived just after eleven o'clock. Linda did not come, as she cancelled their trip to the Maze in the Peninsula, due to stormy weather. Paul and Julie stayed for a while, and I served pasta, mixed with kransky sausage, parsley, red peppers, olives, capers, and some other ingredients, which they enjoyed very much.

They left around two thirty, as they wanted to visit Connie before they returned home. Mary dropped in a little later, and stayed a couple of hours. She said she was feeling down, because of her marital woes, as Tony was very harsh to her sometimes. I listened, and comforted her as well as I could. And she said she felt better by the time she left, poor Mary.

I was weary, as I did not have a moment to myself all weekend. Connie did not care or understand what I was going through at home, and dealing with his aggression was becoming too much for me to handle. Later that night, Julie called to say that Connie communicated via his ipad. He thanked them for visiting, and coming such a long way, but they were distressed to see him in such a weak condition.

It was the first day of term four at school, and as usual, most of the children had forgotten all they learnt over the last few terms. So I just revised all the previous lessons with them. I was very disappointed, when one of my promising students dropped out, as his mother punished him by taking him out of piano classes. He told me that he was naughty, and because he loved piano so much, his mother stopped his lessons. I was surprised at such harsh punishment, but it was up to the parents, not me. He was very gifted, and I was sorry to see him go.

It was a long day, and when I left school around four thirty, Roland phoned to say Shiranthi and he were at the hospital. And Connie's ipad was not working because a nurse spilled yoghurt on the keyboard. He said Connie was very angry and frustrated, and wanted to know if I could do something about it. I said, "Ask the speech pathologist to have a look, because he knows about such things and may be able to fix it." I did not hear from him again. I had my doubts that a nurse spilled yoghurt, as he would have done it himself, but did not want to admit it to his siblings, and blamed someone else as always.

Tuesday was a warm, twenty eight degrees, and I visited Ninette in the afternoon. She was very agitated and nervous, and said she was in severe pain. Although she had a sore back, she wanted to walk to the shops. On my way home, I stopped to buy some things that Connie wanted and came home soon after.

Elio's cousin did not turn up to mow the lawns, and now the grass was really overgrown. One of Connie's friend's told me that his brother-in-law, Ron, a retired gentleman, mowed lawns now and lived in Dromana. He asked me to contact him, as he would be able to help me, so when I phoned Ron, he agreed.

I drove down to Rosebud on Wednesday afternoon, 9 October, as they wanted to tell me about the results of Connie's assessment. I spoke with the neurologist first, and he told me that according to the analysis, Connie was "capable of making decisions," and so, they could not hold him against his will, and would have to send him home.

I was distraught, as I kept asking, how on earth was I supposed to look after him? I told him there was no way I could cope physically or emotionally, and it was not safe for him to be at home on his own. But he replied, "Look, if he wants to take a risk and falls down and injures himself, that's of his own free will." I could not believe my ears, but I could see that it was pointless arguing. I found out later that this superficial "analysis" was not really as comprehensive, as testing for dementia, which they should have done then.

All they wanted was to send him home, to make room in the rehab ward. When the social worker told Connie a few weeks ago that they would move him to rehab in Mornington, he was quite agreeable. And he sent a text saying, "Bring my black slacks and red shirt for me to wear when I go to rehab in Mornington." But that did not happen, and they kept him on at Rosebud rehab for some reason.

The doctor walked with me to Connie's ward, and although he told him about the assessment, he added, "It's best in your own interest to go into permanent care, because your wife is unable to look after you at home." Connie was very angry and stubborn, as he glared at me and wrote, "You and the doctors are conspiring against me. I will take an ambulance and go home." The doctor replied, "Your wife may not be there, as she may go and live with your son." He typed, "I will divorce you!" And scowled at me, as he made angry growling noises. It was pointless staying any longer, as he was so aggressive. The doctor left, and after a while, so did I. My mind was in a whirl, not knowing how I could cope with him at home.

I made a few phone calls when I came home. Then Babs and Roland called in the night, to say that Connie sent text messages to the whole family, saying he had to go into permanent care. And once again Babs told him that it was the best thing to do in his situation. She told me later that although he did not want to hear it, all his siblings agreed that he needed to be in a home now, with full-time medical care and supervision.

I felt mentally and physically exhausted, and drowsy all day, due to lack of sleep as well, and rested for a while. Roland phoned in the evening to say he saw Connie, and he typed everything that was discussed with the doctor and me, and how he wrote that he would divorce me. Roland asked him, "So did Dolly say, go ahead and make her day?" And Connie started giggling at that. Obviously, he knew what he wrote me, and remembered it too.

But the only positive outcome was, that he finally accepted the fact that he had to go into permanent care from rehab. I was relieved, but knowing Connie, I was unsure what his mood would be like at tomorrow's meeting. I could understand his fear, and the darkness that clouded his mind, thinking I was abandoning him. I also knew how much he hated nursing homes, due to adverse things he heard about them. But he could not go unattended to the toilet now. So I knew I could not look after him, no matter how much he wanted to come home.

I wished he could see my point of view, but that was impossible, as he was in full "survival mode" and only his comfort and wishes mattered. Even if he was a less difficult person to live with, there was no way I could have looked after him at home. And like a broken record, I kept saying this, and so did all the medical staff. Ruth advised me to keep on saying the same thing, and not allow the social worker, or Connie to pressure me into bringing him home.

Christian picked me up on his way to Rosebud on Friday, 11 October, for the meeting with the entire panel of therapists, doctors, social worker, and chaplain, at eleven o'clock. When we went to the ward, Connie was typing. "I agree to go into care, provided I can inspect premises first." The social worker appeared to be in full control of the meeting, and she assumed he did not agree to go into care. So she said, "Conrad will be sent home, and I'll organize a carer package, to help you out for a few hours a day."

I was stunned, and replied, "What about the evenings and nights, if he has to go to the toilet or has a fall, how am I going to help him when I'm not physically strong enough to lift him, or carry him on to the toilet seat? In any case, Conrad has agreed to go into care, please read the ipad." She changed her tune then, and said, "You must start looking for a home *immediately*, as he can't stay in rehab too long after transition care. If you don't find a place locally, he will have to go to the first available place anywhere in Melbourne, or will be sent home."

I could not believe how insensitive she was regarding my welfare. She was an overpowering, officious young female, who did not seem to have much empathy for the carer. She only harped about Connie's rights, and that he could not be forced to do anything, because he could make his own decisions.

Listening to her, Connie took advantage of the situation, and I knew he would definitely find fault with any place I found, as he would try his best to postpone going into care. He then wrote that he wanted a private room here, as it was too noisy with three others; staff were very noisy too, and he could not sleep, and had not slept ever since he came here.

The doctor said he would do something about it, and I was taken aback, as Connie and I did not have private health insurance. He was not in a position to demand a private room, but he did. In the next couple of days, they moved him to a room with one other patient. But he said he still could not sleep, because the other person had his television on all the time at a very high volume.

After the meeting, Christian and I spent some time with him in the ward, till he finished his lunch. Then he asked Christian to get him a new keyboard, which he said he would bring as soon as possible. I told him Nilanthi hoped to visit at the end of the month, and he put his thumb up, which was now a sign of approval, and to say "yes," and thumb down if he did not like anything or to say "no."

He seemed to be more settled, and we left soon after. Christian dropped me at home and headed back to the city, after which, I spent a few hours ringing up every local nursing home in and around Frankston. Craig Care in Mt Martha had a vacancy in high care, and they said I could come over to have a look.

I was very relieved, and called the social worker immediately to tell her about it, but the first thing she said was, "Conrad must be involved in selecting a place for him." I felt frustrated, because how on earth was Connie going to move around inspecting homes, when it was such a problem to transport him.

Anyway, I drove down there soon after, and it was quite pleasant, and close to Craigie road, which was about ten minutes from home. It was ideally located, and the room was large and comfortable. I said I would confirm by next Friday, as my husband had to inspect the place too. The lady was very helpful, and photocopied all the relevant documents.

I woke up with a head cold next day, and felt weary and fed up of the whole business of looking for a home, especially because of Connie's obstinacy, and the social worker's unhelpful attitude. After finishing my chores, I made several phone calls, and I told Ruth about the social worker. And she too could not understand why she was so insensitive towards me, as a carer.

She said she would follow it up with the social worker, and find out what was going on. I sent Connie a text in the afternoon saying, "I'm down with a cold," and he replied, "Take care," that was all, but at least he responded. I watched the second half of an old movie, "Thank Your Lucky Stars," and rested early.

I was very busy on Sunday morning, as I had many phone calls. Moira kept me on the phone for one and a half hours, then Ninette, and Mary. Moira was a nuisance, as she related every sordid detail of her messy marriages and two divorces. And she assumed that I had nothing better to do than listen to her distasteful stories. I came to the conclusion she was not quite stable, and I was apprehensive about her trying to get too close to me, as we really did not have anything in common.

She was just a chance acquaintance that Chris Berman introduced, and I did not have the time or inclination to socialise with her. She persisted in inviting me to night clubs, or spend the day drinking alcohol in her beach box at Mornington. She refused to take no for an answer, and I was tired of trying to convince her that her idea of fun was not my scene at all. She was about twenty years younger than me, and why she wanted me to hang out with her was beyond comprehension.

Roland called that afternoon to say Rebecca would buy a keyboard for Connie, as he asked her to get one too, although Christian ordered one and paid for it already. I could not believe how meddlesome Roland was, and he did not seem to understand that Connie suffered from early dementia. Because he either forgot that he told Christian to order a keyboard, or else he wanted to show we did not care to get him a keyboard. This was the start of many problems. Connie manipulated his siblings in order to convince them that Christian and I did not do anything for him.

Connie was far removed from reality, and did not seem to know what was going on anymore, because of his self-absorption. I told Roland that Christian had paid for it already, and would bring it as soon as he got it. He sounded sulky and replied, "I will ask Rebby to return it then." I told him to do whatever he wanted to. But in future, to please let me know, if Connie requested anything, before going ahead and buying it.

Chapter 82

When I was at school on Monday morning, 14 October, I phoned Janine at Craig Care nursing home, to ask if Connie's placement was confirmed. She said she would call me back, and I waited anxiously for her call. And she called around one o'clock, to say everything was fine, and not to worry, as the room was still available. All I had to do was come in to sign the admission papers.

The social worker, Melissa, called me later, and I told her that everything was fine, and I found a place for Connie, but he had to inspect the place before it was confirmed. At about four o'clock, Amanda from Craig Care called to say she was sorry, but they could not give the room, as they just got a new manager, who decided not to admit Connie.

I was very upset, to say the least, because it was very unethical what they did; to promise they would take Connie, and then do a complete turn around. Tess came for her lesson just then, and it was very difficult for me to be patient, as she did not practise at all. I was very annoyed and frustrated at what happened with Craig Care.

When I came home, I phoned Ruth, and she was just as surprised, and said, "It's not very professional what they have done, and I will call them to find out the story. Don't worry too much. There are other places, I'm sure." I was worried all evening, then called everyone to say that Craig Care changed their mind. I had an early night, and tried to fall asleep, as I was exhausted.

Christian arrived early next day, on Tuesday, as he said he would accompany me to meet the manager at Craig Care to find out why they changed their mind. Shirani and Ranjith dropped in too, as Ranjith took the lawn mower to get it fixed, and brought it back. They met Christian after a long time, and I was happy that they had a good chat. In the end, we decided that it was pointless meeting the manager, because if that was their decision, it was unlikely they would change their minds.

Melissa called soon after, and said she would follow up with Craig Care, and then the pastoral care worker from Frankston hospital called to say she would speak to them as well. So I decided to leave it to them, as there was nothing else I could do about it. It was a very busy day, and I took it easy in the evening.

I drove down to Rosebud on Wednesday morning, to meet a counsellor, as part of the Carer Support Program, and Ruth recommended that I attend a few sessions.

I was there at eleven thirty, and we discussed all the problems and issues I faced with Connie, and some of his siblings, who did their utmost to convert him to their cult following, with promises of instant miracles.

The counsellor said it would benefit both of us, if Connie too would attend the next session, so he could listen to my side of the story, and how his siblings' and his behaviour affected me. I told her that he would not consent, as he was very obstinate.

After the session, I went in to see Connie, and took his washed clothes and the new keypad that Christian bought. I thought he kept the one Rebecca bought, but he typed, "No, Tucko took it back." He was very hostile towards me as usual. And when I gave him a card that one of our friends sent him, he took it and threw it in the bin without even looking at it or opening it.

Then I told him to ask the speech pathologist to fix the new keypad, instead of waiting for Christian. I hardly finished speaking when he flew into an uncontrollable rage. He started shouting loudly, his legs and arms jerked angrily as if he was having a fit, and he typed. "Christian said he will come and fix it!" He made such a loud racket, and howled as if I was attacking him, that I left the room in tears. I could not understand why he shouted like that for no reason at all.

I spoke to the nurses, as they were in the canteen close by and could hear the noise he made. And once again they told me not to take any notice of him, as all dementia patients took it out on their nearest relative. I did not feel like going back to his room, but after a while, I went in to say goodbye. He just glared at me, and did not respond. I drove back, burdened with an immense weight in my chest.

When I arrived home, Ron had cut the lawns, but he grumbled about how difficult it was, as the grass was so overgrown; he was very grumpy, and rude when I asked him how much it would cost to mow the lawns regularly. He wanted $85 that day, and said he must cut the lawns fortnightly, for $60, so I agreed, though reluctantly, but he did a good job.

I made a few more phone calls to nursing homes in the area, and as there was a vacancy at Baptcare in Frankston South, I drove there immediately. Melanie, the manager, was a young lady, in her thirties. I told her how disappointed I was at the way Craig Care let me down, and she assured me they would not change their minds, once they confirmed a booking.

It was a very pleasant place, and the room was airy and bright, and looked out to the road, with lavender-bordered gardens. We spoke at length, and she photocopied all the relevant documents prior to admission. I told her I would organize his brother to bring Connie to have a look around, and if he was satisfied, I would sign the contract.

I also filled her in about his siblings, and how his sisters showered him in Rosebud hospital. She was shocked, and replied, "That won't be happening here, as only our staff will be providing care and showering him, so don't worry. You have full financial and medical power of attorney, so his siblings won't be allowed to take him away anywhere, without your permission."

I was very pleased, and hoped this would be the right place for him. The staff seemed very caring and friendly, and there were no unpleasant, stale odours around either.

When I returned home, I showered quickly, and drove to Elvira's for dinner. I spent a pleasant time there, and told them about the nursing home I saw, and they too were happy about it. They visited Connie often in Rosebud, especially John, who told me that he met his siblings there a few times. Mary and Tony visited him once as well. I returned home around eight o'clock, and took it easy, before going to bed, as it was a very long day.

After a busy day on Thursday, I left school around two thirty, and then stopped to do some shopping. I phoned Roland later that evening, and told him that I saw a nice place, and asked him if he could take Connie to have a look. Because I could not transport him in and out of the car, as he had to be carried now. He agreed to take him next day, and let him inspect the place.

I thought I was doing the right thing, because Connie was so hostile towards me now, that no matter which home I found, he would have refused to go there. But I knew he would listen to his brother, and all that mattered now was to find a comfortable place for him.

In hindsight, I made the biggest mistake in letting Roland take Connie there. Because from then on, Connie was under the impression that Roland, Cristobel, and Geraldine were in charge of his welfare, and that they found the place for him. Because they were the ones who took him to inspect the home, not me. And Roland did not tell Connie I found the place. They had no idea of the stress and hassle I underwent, or how many homes I called before I found a place at Baptcare. Christian, Nelune, and Shirani, called to find out what was happening, and they too hoped that Connie would agree to go in to that home I found.

It was sunny, but very gusty on Friday, 18 October. I called Roland in the morning, and he said he would take Connie around one o'clock. Then I rang Melanie at Baptcare, and told her that his brother would bring Connie that afternoon, and she said she would be happy to show them around.

I was apprehensive all day, wondering what the outcome would be, and whether I would have to keep on looking for nursing homes, until Connie was satisfied with one. Christian called around three o'clock, and he was very upset, as he got a speeding fine. He was worried that he would lose his licence for one month. But as it happened, he paid only a fine, so he was very relieved.

I did not hear from Roland all afternoon, and I wondered what happened, as I told Melanie that I would let her know in the evening, whether he liked the place or not. He finally called after four o'clock, to say Connie agreed to go into that home, as they all said it was convenient for them to visit him there, and it seemed to be a very nice place. He said he took Shiranthi and Geraldine with him too, and they were now at Esme's place, as Connie was hungry, and wanted to eat something.

I said the hospital expected him back by six o'clock, and not to keep him out too late, as he would be very tired by now. He did not say anything. I called Melanie immediately, and said I would come in to sign the paperwork that evening, and she said they could admit him next Tuesday.

After I signed the contract, and finalised the paperwork, I breathed a sigh of relief, and thanked God for this mercy. Now, I only hoped it would go well without any more problems. Later that night, I called Christian, Shirani, Nelune, and Ninette, and they were all pleased and relieved too. I spent some time outside, and watered the garden till about eight o'clock.

It was sunny but very gusty next day, and Esme called in the morning to say, "The nursing home is very nice, with lavender bushes under his window, have you seen the place at all?" I replied, "How else could I know if it was a good place or not, if I didn't go in to see it, and meet the manager? I'm the one who found the place."

I could not believe that after I did all the hard work finding a home, Roland did not mention it to Esme or the others, that I requested him to take Connie to inspect the place. Obviously, he gave them the impression that he was responsible for finding a home, and perhaps Connie believed it too. I did not care anyway.

Esme went on to say, "It was *so* difficult yesterday, to bring Connie to my place, and we left him outside in the garage, as we couldn't carry him inside the house. He said the food I served was tasteless, and I had to put some gravy in it. It's really the best thing he's going into a home, because I won't be able to take him to my place even for a visit." So, they found out how difficult it was to manage Connie.

I drove down to Rosebud rehab that afternoon, and stayed with him for a couple of hours. But he did not communicate with me at all about his thoughts on the home or how he felt. He only asked me to do this, that, and the other all the time I was there. I spoke to the nurse on duty, and she said his brother brought him in after seven o'clock last night, and he was very angry, and extremely tired too. He threw his medication on the floor, and gave the nurses a hard time, till they put him to bed.

He seemed calmer today, and I did not say anything at all, in case he started shouting at me again. I watched him totter slowly with the walker to the power point, and struggle to put the plug into the socket, but his hands were so weak that he did not have the strength to push the plug in. I observed him for a few more minutes, then walked over and said, "Let me do that," and I plugged it in. He did not start a commotion, and I left soon after.

He typed a list of things for me to buy; more t-shirts, track pants, toiletries etc. to take with him to the home. On my way, I stopped at Rosebud Plaza to get some things. I noticed there was no bedspread on the bed at Baptcare, and wanted to get something nice and cheerful. So I bought a deep blue, fleecy blanket, that could be used as a bedspread for the time being, as they did not have any other suitable ones. And It was after five o'clock when I returned home.

Although it was thirty degrees on Sunday, it was overcast and windy, and after finishing some chores, I packed up Connie's fresh laundry to take down in the afternoon. Then I tried calling Nilanthi, but no answer, so I sent her a text. She replied that the phone lines were down, due to bad weather and heavy rain, and she would let me know when the phone lines were fixed.

Ninette, Christian, and Nelune, called to see how things were going, and they were all pleased about Connie's admission into the home next week. I spoke to Esme and Paul in the afternoon, and told them what was happening. They too agreed that it was the best outcome for Connie now.

Shirani returned from a Yoga retreat, and was very impressed with her experience there. We chatted for some time, and I was very happy that she was following her dreams and aspirations.

While I was at school on Monday, I was very anxious all day, wondering if Connie would refuse to go to the nursing home. But thankfully, I did not hear from him all day. I finished lessons by four thirty, and when I came home, I had several phone calls all evening. The nurse from Rosebud rehab called to ask about Connie's discharge tomorrow. They were organizing an ambulance to take him to Baptcare, once I signed his discharge papers. And I told her I would follow the ambulance in my car.

I kept my fingers crossed that all would go well next day. Christian called late at night, to say he had severe gastro, and would be unable to come to the nursing home with the television set as promised. But he would try to get there on Wednesday, if he was better. I was sorry to hear he was unwell, but I knew Connie would not be too happy, when I told him that Christian could not bring the television on Tuesday. Poor Christian. I hoped he would get better soon.

I drove to Rosebud at nine thirty in the morning on Tuesday, 22 October. Just as I walked into the ward, he sent a text, "bring box of chocolates for the nurses and two big suitcases to pack my clothes." I told him I would get the chocolates another time, and that I brought a few bags, but not suitcases. He did not get angry or start shouting. He was subdued, did not acknowledge me at all, and he looked very depressed. I did not say anything, and a nurse helped me to pack all his clothes and personal effects, while another nurse helped him to the toilet.

He wrote, "Get a card for Tucko and put fifty dollars that was in my wallet inside card. He deserves it." I was very surprised that he remembered he had exactly fifty dollars in his wallet, the day he was admitted to hospital. I nodded and replied, "Okay." The ambulance was ready at ten forty five, and they wheeled him out of the hospital, and carried him inside it. I drove behind it through incessant rain.

I felt incredibly sad as I watched the ambulance in front of me, because I knew he hated going into a nursing home. But he did not understand that it was impossible for him to be at home now. He was going to be very unhappy, but there was no help for it. I told him many times that he could choose to be happy and accept the inevitable, or go through life being miserable and discontented, fighting against fate. He replied that I did not understand the hell he was going through, and it was impossible for him to come to terms with his situation.

Christian sent a text, saying that he was still feeling bad, and did not think he could make it that day. I said it was alright, and not to worry. I arrived five minutes after the ambulance stopped, and he was already seated in his room. It was pleasant enough, and the window looked out to a nice garden and the main road, so he could look out and watch the traffic. He sat morosely and fidgeted with the ipad.

I had to complete and sign a great deal of paper work, and the head nurse asked me umpteen questions about Connie, while she took notes. Then she said, "We have regular outings, would you like to join?" He put his thumb up, and I was glad, as they would take him out on supervised excursions near by. The staff were pleasant and friendly, and seemed to be very caring people. But as soon as the nurse left the room, he started grunting and making loud, aggressive noises, and wrote, "This chair is not comfortable."

Lunch was served soon after, as it was almost midday. It smelled delicious, and I opened the covers to show him a chicken casserole, an orange juice drink, and dessert. He tasted a few mouthfuls, pushed it away, and started shouting and swaying about in his chair. I asked him, "What's wrong?" he wrote, "No taste in the food." I tried to add salt and pepper, and he typed, "I don't use salt and pepper in my food." I asked him how he expected it to taste good, without salt and pepper, but he kept on shouting and refused to eat anything.

It was the worst day for him and for me, as I understood how miserable he was, now that he faced the reality of being admitted to a home, much against his will. He behaved just like a little boy, throwing a tantrum now to punish me. While he sat typing more messages, I arranged his clothes in the narrow cupboard, and spread the blue blanket over the drab sheet on the bed.

He did not take any notice of me, but a little while later he wrote, "Send armchair and the other upright chair now." I asked him how I was going to do that in this heavy rain, and who was going to bring them. He wrote, "Tell John to bring the chairs. He can carry them, he's strong." Then he giggled a little. I said, "I'll call John when I get home, and ask him if he can do that in the evening."

I was drained by the time I left after three o'clock, and dropped in at Ninette's for a coffee, as she wanted to know how the move went. While I was there, Elvira called to say that Connie sent John a text, asking him to contact me. I told her that he wanted the chairs brought over that evening. She said John was prepared to take them, whenever I was ready, so I said I would be home within the hour.

John arrived at four thirty in the deluge, and he covered the chairs with sheets of plastic he brought. He asked one of the neighbours down the road to give him a hand to load the armchair on to his truck. It was very kind of him, and I thanked him profusely. The rain did not ease, and he drove off to Baptcare a little later. From then onwards I had several text messages from Connie demanding, "Where did this blue blanket come from?"

I did not respond immediately, because he did not say anything about getting the chairs, or a thank you for all I did, especially that day. But instead, he wanted to know where the blue blanket came from! I was irritated, and ignored his messages. But as he kept on texting the same question about five times, I finally replied, "I bought it," and he sent a text immediately, "Why wasn't I told about it before you bought it?" I replied, "Because you were so upset and angry over the food and everything else, I thought such a trivial matter like a new blanket wouldn't interest you."

He stopped texting after that. I could not believe he was so unreasonable, and wondered why he was carrying on about the blanket. He was getting worse, and impossible to deal with. I hardly slept that night, thinking he would text me any time with some ridiculous demand.

I called RACV and the tax agent etc. next morning. Then I called all the other nursing homes and requested them to take Connie's name off the waiting lists, as he was now in Baptcare. They all said I was very lucky that I found a good place so soon. Then I spoke to Shirani for a while, and prepared things to take to the home that afternoon.

I tried to play the piano, to unwind a little, but my mind was in a whirl, as I just could not understand Connie's irrational behaviour. The rain did not ease, and it was still very wet and miserable. I was at the home by two o'clock, and Christian arrived a little later. He did not look too well, but he came nevertheless, as he knew Connie was waiting for the television, and would keep harassing me, if it was not set up immediately.

He did not write anything, or acknowledge Christian and me in any way. Christian went about setting the television, and we made everything comfortable for Connie to watch it. It was a very nice set, and just the right size for the room. I noticed the blue blanket was rolled up, and left on a chair, and an old drab, brown blanket was on the bed.

I asked him if he did not want the new blanket, and who brought that raggedy old thing. He wrote, "Bella brought it last night. Bella said it belonged to Mummy. Leave the blue blanket there." I did not say anything, because I doubted it ever belonged to his mother, and was just another instance of her interference. I thought, if he did not care how his room looked, then I should not bother either.

John had placed the armchair in a corner, but there was no way he could sit on it, as he could not move around, so all that trouble to get it there was not for him, but for his siblings. We stayed with him for a couple of hours, but he did not thank Christian, or write anything at all when we left. I told Christian not to mind him, as he was just being nasty and wanted to hurt us for some reason, so we had to ignore his behaviour. Christian still looked pale and weak after the gastro attack, so we stopped at Karingal, and had coffee. I thanked him for all his trouble, and hoped he would get better soon.

As I was getting some groceries, Shiranthi called around six thirty, and asked if they could drop in for coffee, as they were with Connie. I said I was out, and it would be late when I returned, so not to visit that night. I was exhausted, and tried to unwind before going to bed.

I finished at school late next afternoon, then came home and cleaned up the place, and prepared the guest room for Nilanthi.

Elvira said she would take me to see her solicitor in Pearcedale tomorrow morning, as I wanted to discuss some legal issues with him. I did not receive any more text messages from Connie that night, so I hoped he was settling down.

Chapter 83

I went to Elvira's around nine o'clock next morning, and she drove us to Pearcedale in her car. Bill, a long-time friend of theirs, was retired now, but he was very helpful, and did not charge me anything for that initial consultation. His house was situated on a pleasant rural property, with a large lake, fringed with willow trees. After a long discussion over a cup of coffee, he gave me the name and address of one of his colleagues, if I needed a solicitor in future.

I told him about my concerns regarding Connie's siblings, and how they invaded our lives suddenly, to take over completely, because Connie was so vulnerable. They had convinced him that they were the only ones who cared for him, and Connie treated Christian and me like two outsiders.

I was suspicious of their motives, as they were capable of manipulating Connie for financial gain, especially Cristobel and his brother, Paul, who were always in financial strife. The two of them constantly told me how much they detested Connie. And over the last forty three years, never maintained a close relationship with him. So I did not trust their motives, as they wormed their way into Connie's affections now.

Roland worked differently, as he would use a different approach to get Connie's sympathy, and Connie would repay him financially for his care. When Connie told me to give Roland fifty dollars, because "He deserved it," that roused my suspicions. It was exactly what his siblings wanted him to believe, that they were the only ones who cared about him, and antagonized him towards Christian and me.

Bill listened sympathetically, and when I finished, he said, "It's always the same story; when someone is too ill to know what they're doing, family members infiltrate like vultures, to take their pickings. Make sure you protect your son's and your interests against any of them, as your husband seems to be totally irresponsible, and doesn't know what is what anymore, if he has early onset of dementia." I thanked him very much for his good advice. He told me what steps I should take to ensure that Christian and I were legally protected from any financial disadvantage.

On our way back, Elvira stopped at their farm in Pearcedale, which was a peaceful property, with a nice house on the block. We walked around, looked at the dam, and all the work John had done there. When we came back to her place, we had coffee, and then I spoke to John about the fences. And he said he would ask someone to have a look at them.

I was weary when I came home, and all through the evening I had non-stop text messages from Connie, "Food is horrid," "I'm starving," and so on. I did not respond to them, and wished him goodnight, but he ignored my message. I made some curries for lunch tomorrow, then vacuumed the guest room, and arranged a bunch of lavender in a vase, as I knew Nilanthi liked them very much.

Early next morning Connie sent a text, "Find another home, this place is useless, service very poor." I could not help being amused, even though I was exasperated. He seemed to think it was as easy as finding another hotel. I replied, "It's not easy to find another place so soon, as you have to wait two years to get in. Try to be patient with the staff. I'll speak to them when I come."

I hated the sound of the mobile when text messages came, as I knew there was nothing but negative messages from Connie. I also found out later that Cristobel and his other siblings criticized the place right from the start, and made him more unhappy, instead of helping him to settle down and accept the inevitable.

It was just like them to make mischief, because they thought they knew better than anyone. Cristobel told the family that *she* wanted to find a better home for Connie. And Roland should not have listened to me and admitted Connie to this "Useless place." I could not get over her audacity and ignorance, as Baptcare was around for a long time, and had a very good reputation.

I had every legal right as his wife, to find Connie a home, so where did she get the notion that she was in charge of Connie, and had the right to find a home for him? She was deluded that she was his "substitute" wife, ever since he asked her to shower him. I wanted to tell her that it was none of her business to interfere in this matter, as he was going to remain in Baptcare, no matter what he said or did.

The home was undergoing a period of staff changes and management, and if they had problems with the staff, no doubt they were being addressed. Connie thought he was in a hotel, and the nurses should jump to it whenever he rang the bell. And he could not understand why they took a little long to answer his summons. His siblings ganged up on the nursing staff, and encouraged Connie's discontent.

Christian and Athena arrived with Nilanthi around lunchtime that day, and we had a pleasant time together. It was great to see her again, especially during this trying period in my life. After lunch, the four of us visited Connie, but he was not alone. Esme, Sanit, and Paul were there, and when she saw me, Esme was all over Connie, fussing and carrying on. They took him out somewhere in the wheelchair, and Sanit was hanging his jacket in the closet. All Esme said when she saw Nilanthi was, "You have cut your hair short!"

When Connie saw Nilanthi, he started to bawl loudly, and made distressing noises. After Esme and the others left, we spent some time with him, and after a while, he wrote, "Welcome to Australia, how are Tanesh and them?" Then he played the voice function on the ipad, and it started relating his biography that he typed when he was at home. "My name is Conrad de Sielvie. I was born in Talawakale in Sri Lanka. I have got PSP.....etc. etc." Christian said, "Dad, Nilanthi *knows* who you are!" But he ignored us, and kept playing the voice function all the time we were there.

I hung his new clothes etc. in the closet, and arranged the food items he asked for, Milo, sunshine milk, and Sustagen. We left him soon after, and I hugged him and said, "Try to be patient, and eat the food they give you here." He did not respond. Nilanthi was exhausted after her long flight, so she went to bed as soon as we returned home. She too was very upset to see Connie's condition. Christian and Athena drove back to the city a little later.

Nilanthi and I rested till late next day, Sunday, and we got ready to visit Connie again. Just before we left, he sent a text asking me to bring macaroni and patty curry for lunch. I did not prepare any, and it would have taken time to make it, so we went there without the macaroni.

He looked very miserable, and did not acknowledge us, and typed, "Tell Christian to connect internet, and I want a recliner chair, like Josephine's." I knew instantly where this was coming from, as Esme told me that he needed a reclining chair, as he could not sit on the armchair.

I told him I would see to it as soon as possible, and he kept typing, "Get the chair from Rosebud rehab, that was comfortable," and I said I would speak to the physio about a comfortable chair for him. It was now a case of him wanting everything *immediately*, without any thought of how much time, and effort it took to organize what he wanted.

Then he asked where the macaroni was, and when I said I did not have time to make it that afternoon, he became angry. I offered to get Kentucky fried chicken, but he refused. He looked at the washed clothes I brought and wrote, "There are fluff balls on the track pants. All these years I washed my clothes, there were no fluff balls."

I was getting so upset by now, I could hardly breathe, so I left the room. Nilanthi sat close to him, talking and thanking him for all he did for her through the years, and she was in tears. But he did not respond to her at all, and kept looking at her vaguely, as if he did not know who she was. I took a card with fifty dollars inside it for Roland, as he requested. He struggled to write, "Happy birthday, love Connie" Then he typed, "Leave the card inside the cupboard." We left after some time.

I felt hurt and upset, as he was very nasty to me, and although I tried to ignore his behaviour, it was very difficult not to get hurt. In the night he sent me a text, "You hurt me today," I was so surprised, and replied, "*How* did I hurt you, when you picked on me about fluff balls on your clothes?" He did not reply. But I supposed it was because I did not take macaroni for him. I told him to let me know the day before, so I could prepare it in time.

I was getting ready to go to school next day, on Monday, when I had a text from Connie, "Come here immediately," I replied, "I'm on my way to school, I will come in the evening." I called Esme, and left a message to ask if she could visit Connie, and see what he wanted. But she did not reply all morning.

I kept getting umpteen text messages from Connie all day, "You don't care what I'm going through here," and when I sent a pacifying reply, he wrote, "You don't have a clue what's going on here," and so on, until I was exasperated with his messages. I had to teach right through this stressful time, and wondered what I should do.

His text messages drove me up the wall. I knew he wanted me to get him out of the home, and he thought if he complained non-stop and nagged me, I would give in. I hated the sound of text messages coming in on the phone, as I knew they were nothing but complaints. I came home feeling exhausted, like I did most days now. Nilanthi was feeling rested after a good nap, so we had a long chat, and walked about in the garden.

Esme did not reply my message, so I thought Connie was alright, as I was too tired to drive to the home that evening. I knew if there was a problem, the nurses would call me anytime. We had an early night, and I was relieved when my phone did not "ping" to announce another text message.

I took his washed clothes on Tuesday when I visited him, but Nilanthi stayed in the car, as I did not want to stay too long. And she did not want to come in again, as she thought Connie would be upset to see her, thinking I was having a good time with her, while he was in a home.

As I walked in, Melanie, the manager, said she would like to speak to me. And she said, "His siblings are here all the time, and I can see they're adding fuel to the fire, because they won't let him settle down at all. He has not been out of his room to the community area so far, and is always in his room. One of them was here till eleven o'clock last night, and she stopped the duty nurse in the car park, and tried to get medical information about Conrad. Now, this is unacceptable, and you have to let me know what the boundaries are. We're not like a hospital, and don't have strict visiting times, but we expect residents to be in bed at a reasonable hour, so the nurses can wash them and put them to bed."

I was taken aback, and replied, "All his doctors have advised me that he shouldn't be having more than one or two visitors at a time, for about two hours daily, and he must have a good rest by eight or nine o'clock at the latest, for his own benefit. As it's too tiring for him to sit upright on a chair all day long. I will write a letter to his sister, and ask her not to visit so late at night. And to take turns to visit, instead of them all coming in at the same time."

Melanie said she was happy for me to do this, but in retrospect, I think that as manager, she should have set boundaries, without involving me. She knew exactly which way the wind was blowing though, and sympathised heartily, as she could see how they took over. Geraldine pasted religious placards in his room, then brought a portable CD player, and faith healing CD's. She did not stop to ask me, or let me have the privilege of decorating my husband's room, the way he wanted.

She wrote a long list of instructions for the staff, regarding Connie's care. And the manager said that if I did not put up that list, or approved of it, I had all the right to take down whatever others pasted there. Because no one else had a legal right to give the home instructions, except his wife.

When I went into the room, Esme was feeding him yoghurt. I told her what the manager said, and she replied, "Bella was working late last night, that's why she got so late." I told her, "Don't take away his independence just yet, let him feed himself, as long as he's able to." But she ignored me, and kept on feeding him, saying, "He gets frustrated when he can't feed himself properly, and keeps spilling the food." I hung his clothes, and did not stay long, as I was so infuriated with them.

I met the bank manager later on, and explained what was going on. And he immediately suspended internet banking, so no one could take advantage of Connie, or influence his financial decisions. I was relieved once this was done, because of the manner in which his younger siblings suddenly latched on to Connie.

When he was in rehab, one of his siblings asked me if Connie kept any money in his room, and to make sure Cristobel did not have access to his finances. She complained that Connie always asked her to buy Kentucky fried chicken or McDonalds, and she did not have any money to spend on him. I was unaware of what was going on then, or else I would have asked Connie why he made his siblings buy food, when I would have brought anything he liked. It was just another example of how he made them believe I did not care to do anything for him.

When I left the nursing home that day, we drove to Shirani's at Narre Warren, and had a pleasant time. Shirani said they would come early next morning to pick Nilanthi, and go down to Woolamai for a few days. We did not visit Ninette, as she had an appointment with a specialist, but I spoke to her in the evening, and she sounded alright.

Shirani and Ranjith arrived around nine thirty next morning, 30 October, to pick Nilanthi. They had a cup of tea, and left soon after, as they had several tasks to do at the restaurant.

I drove to Rosebud in the afternoon for my appointment with the counsellor, Marlene, and the meeting went well. Marlene was happy that Connie was in a good nursing home, and that I now had some respite. She was very nice and helpful, so I was glad I spent some time at these sessions.

I needed strength and patience to deal with his fanatical siblings. When I mentioned what the manager told me, Marlene said it would be a good idea to write a letter to Cristobel, and outline boundaries, regarding late night visits, for the good of her brother. And to advise the manager, and send her a copy of the letter as well. I was glad to have professional advice, before I took any further steps.

When the meeting was over, I stopped at Rosebud Plaza, and bought some jeans, and a fleecy blanket for Nilanthi. Ron arrived at three o'clock to mow the lawns, as we reached a mutual agreement regarding his charges, and he said he would come every three weeks during summer. Then I spoke to Elvira, and she said she took gnocchi for Connie on Monday evening, as he sent John a text requesting some. But he did not write about all that to me, as he was very secretive. He only typed non-stop complaints and negative comments about the staff and nursing home.

I continued to do my best for him; washed his clothes, and visited him every other day, as he needed fresh laundry, and any other items he asked me to bring. But it would have been more hygienic for the nursing home to wash them daily; soiled clothes sitting in a laundry bag for a day or two, stank to high heaven. I held my nose when I sorted them out, but I told myself I should not expect him to show any tenderness or gratitude. He would not admit it, but he was incontinent now, and soiled his pants, and then blamed the nurses for not taking him to the toilet in time. I decided to talk to the head nurse about getting incontinence pants for him immediately.

Elvira said that when she and John visited on Monday evening, Roland, Shiranthi, and Geraldine, were there too. Connie had typed that he wanted his brother to stop work and take care of him. Shiranthi had said that if she was not so ill, she would have looked after him gladly. I was thoroughly upset when I heard about it. And a few days later, when I asked Shiranthi about what she had said, she denied it completely. She blamed Geraldine, who had replied, "Yes, that's a good idea Tucko. Why don't you stop work and look after Connie?"

It was because I told Connie that the nursing home fees were very expensive, and I paid his full pension, plus an extra two thousand dollars a month. He and his siblings calculated the high fees, and thought that one of them could get that money, if they looked after him.

Esme called and told me the same thing, and she had asked Connie, "Where is Tucko going to keep you in their crowded flat, inside a box?" I just could not believe they were scheming to get Connie out of the nursing home, and gave him false hopes that they would care for him in their homes. They played power games with me, promising to take Connie out of the home.

I consulted doctor next day, as I was very stressed and felt ill, then deposited money for the fence repairs. Before I returned home, Connie sent a text, to say he did not eat lunch, and no one was answering the bell.

I called the home, and the nurse said she would check up and call me back immediately, which she did. And she told me that he had not touched the meal that was served, and the tray was still in his room. She also said he was in a bad mood, and threw his orange juice all over the floor. I apologized, but she said, "Not to worry, we know how to handle difficult patients."

I came home feeling weary and upset, then Roland sent me the same text from Connie, without writing a message. I replied that I read Connie's text already, as he sent it to me, and that I spoke to the nurse. In a few minutes, Esme sent me the same text from Connie. Obviously, he sent all his siblings the same message. Connie manipulated them, because he knew I would not fall for his games.

I asked Esme why she forwarded Connie's message, as I received it already. She replied, "I want you to find out how the home is caring for him, after all the money they are getting paid," I sent a text back saying I spoke to them already, and Connie was just being difficult. And to tell him that he was not getting out of there, as I could not find another home so quickly.

I posted a letter to Cristobel, and a copy to the manager that day, regarding visiting hours etc. and my head ached all evening with these unnecessary problems. I mistakenly thought that once he was in a home, the situation would improve, but oh how wrong I was. I called my sisters, Christian, and Ninette in the evening, as it helped to talk about what I was going through with Connie.

It was a lovely sunny day on Saturday, and on my way to visit Connie, I stopped at Bentons Square to get some things he wanted. When I went into his room, he appeared to be subdued after yesterday's complaints. I wheeled him around the home, and in the garden, as it was twenty eight degrees then. I made him a cup of Milo, and later stored all the items I brought, then hung his washed clothes in the cupboard, and stayed for some time. He did not write anything, or respond when I hugged him, and told him to eat what was served.

I dropped in at Ninette's on my way back, and stayed a while listening to her complaints, and it was after six o'clock when I came home. Julie left a message, so I returned her call, and we had a long chat, then spoke to Shirani. That night, Connie sent a text, "Thanks for all you do. Goodnight 143." The numbers, 143 represented "I love you," that he always wrote, or said, instead of the actual words. I replied, "Thank you for all you have done for Christian and me. Have a good rest. I love you too."

I hoped and prayed he would settle down gradually, and accept his fate, without fighting against it, no matter how difficult it was for him. When he had moments of lucidity, he seemed to realize how much I did for him. But at other times, he became hostile, when he was under the influence of his siblings, and I bore the brunt of his ill-humour.

It was a school holiday on Monday, 4 November, the day before Cup Day, on Tuesday. Christian arrived around midday, and he drove us down to Woolamai in my car. We spent a pleasant afternoon with Shirani, and left a couple of hours later. Elvira called to say she would visit, and also that Connie sent John a text, asking him to bring the bar fridge from home. I told her he could come anytime, and she said John would pick it up next day.

Then she told me that his siblings were there again when they visited Connie the previous day. Shiranthi had said once again, that she would take Connie to their home, and she would look after him, if she did not have problems with her neck and arm.

I was very disturbed to hear such things, but I was helpless to prevent them from upsetting Connie. And I wished they would not discuss these issues in front of him when they visited. That was the reason why he was so angry with me. He thought I admitted him to a home, when his siblings were prepared to care for him in their houses. They convinced him that only they could take care of him. Tamara called late that night, to ask if she could speak to Nilanthi. I told her she was at Woolamai and would return tomorrow. I did not talk long, as I was very tired and distressed.

I visited Ninette next day, after John picked up the bar fridge in the morning. And I walked with her to the shops later. On our way back, Shiranthi called, as I left a message that Christian would step in, if they did not stop scheming to take Connie out of the home. She denied everything vehemently, saying, "How could I do such a thing, when you, his wife, are still alive? I *never* said anything like that, and I don't want Christian to get involved in this matter. It was Jenny, who went on about how we always looked after sick people in Sri Lanka."

I had my doubts, so I told her, "My friend, Elvira, heard you say that, and she wouldn't lie." But she went on and on, insisting that she did not say such a thing, until I called off. I drove to Narre Warren afterwards, as I said I would pick Nilanthi. We had an early barbeque at Shirani's place, as Roshan, June, and the children were visiting too, so it was nice to see them.

I was slightly relieved after Shiranthi's phone call, because according to her story, they would not take him out of the home. It was all talk, just to show Connie, and my friends that they were such caring people. It made me irate to think how inconsiderate they were of Connie's mental and physical condition. It was absurd to discuss about taking him out of a nursing home and care for him in their house, when anyone could see that he needed twenty four hour supervision and medical care.

Ninette said she wanted to visit Connie, so I picked her on the following Wednesday, and Nilanthi joined us too. We arrived there at about two thirty in the afternoon. But he was in a bad way, as he looked very unhappy, and scowled at us. He did not write anything when he saw Nilanthi and Ninette with me. And he did not acknowledge us at all, even though Ninette and Nilanthi tried to talk to him, he just ignored us completely.

I heard some music in the lounge room, so I asked him if he would like me to wheel him there. He did not respond, but struggled to his feet, grabbed the walker, and dragged himself to the lounge room, but I walked close behind him, in case he fell. So far, his siblings did not give him the opportunity to move around the home, and get acquainted with other residents, and communicate via his ipad.

I was told they confined him to his room whenever they visited, praying over him, and brain-washing him relentlessly, until he was mentally and physically exhausted. And when I visited him on some days, he was ready to sleep by six o'clock. Sometimes, they wheeled him around the garden, and I found out later that they even took him in his wheelchair across the busy Moorooduc Highway, to have McDonalds or Kentucky fried chicken.

At this stage, he was still able to grip the sides of the wheelchair, even though he was losing strength in his hands. It was very unsafe for him to be wheeled across a busy highway, in case he lost his grip and fell over. His siblings did not comprehend he was getting weak very rapidly.

One of the resident's, a ninety-two year old lady, was playing the piano, so we sat down to enjoy some rag-time music. Connie was alright, and even giggled a little, when Ninette said she would like to come here to play the piano, and accompany Luigi. She kept on saying what a lovely place the home was, and he was very lucky to be here. But he did not even look at her, or respond in any way.

We were there about ten or fifteen minutes, when the entertainment finished, and a nurse came over to take Connie back in a wheelchair. But he absolutely refused to get into it, and started shouting at the top of his voice. She tried to calm him down, but he screamed at the top of his voice, as if someone was skinning him alive.

All the other residents looked at him curiously, as he looked like he was having a fit. He started shaking uncontrollably and frothing at his mouth. I tried to hold his hand, but he pushed me away, and would not stop screaming. The nurse said, "Stop shouting Conrad, you are upsetting the other residents!" He trembled and shouted, as he angrily wrote, "I want to use the walker! I don't want a wheelchair!"

She managed to wheel him back, in spite of his shouting, and although he lowered his voice, he still kept growling and moaning. He glared at the nurse while she read what he wrote. "You were very rough with me, and you hurt my shoulder!" The nurse did not respond, but she brought some papers over and read out, "The doctor has stated that you mustn't walk more than a few feet with the walker, to avoid any more falls, and that you must use a wheelchair for longer distances. That was the reason why I brought you back in a wheelchair. I'm sorry if I hurt your shoulder."

He did not write anything else, and after settling him down, and applying dencorub on his arm and shoulders, I said we had to leave. Then he wrote, "You should be here feeding me." I told him the staff would see to it that he was fed, when I could not be there in the evening. I just wanted to get out of that room as soon as possible, as my stomach was churning and knotted up with anxiety. On our way out, Ninette was very upset, as he did not even acknowledge her presence, neither Nilanthi or me, for that matter.

He wanted to hurt not only me, but those who were close to me as well. Ninette said she never witnessed anyone behaving the way Connie did, and the way he shouted non-stop, was very traumatic for everyone around. I was very distressed and disturbed all evening, as the sound of his screaming echoed in my ears.

That night he sent me a text, "Goodnight. God bless. I love you." I replied, "I love you very much too. Sleep well." I was relieved he had settled down, and must have realized how much his behaviour affected us. But unfortunately, he could not control his emotions at all.

Chapter 84

The man arrived at seven thirty next morning, and started repairing the fence at last. On my way to school, I stopped at the church office and picked up the hall keys for Elvira, as she was holding a charity concert there. Nelune arrived in the morning, and Christian picked her from the airport and drove her down.

When I came home around midday, Alan and Pam were just driving off down the street, as they had visited Nilanthi. I parked the car, and they walked over to greet me. We chatted a few minutes, and I was pleased to see them. They asked me how Connie was doing, and said they would visit soon.

It was great to see Nelune, and we had a leisurely lunch, chatting and enjoying being together, and Christian left a couple of hours later. The fence was nearly done by late afternoon, but the man said he had to come over next day to finish it.

I called Elvira later to find out how she was, as she saw her doctor that morning. She was distraught, as the tumour on her forehead was malignant, and she was having it removed on the following Tuesday. I comforted her, and said I would like to visit her that evening, if she did not mind. She replied she would be very happy to see me, so I bought some flowers on my way, and dropped in. She was distressed, but said she trusted in God, and she would be fine. When I returned home a little later, Nelune and Nilanthi were chatting away, and laughing over Nelune's droll stories. It was good to have my sisters, sharing and caring.

We drove to Woolamai next day, and returned home late in the evening, after spending a pleasant afternoon with Shirani.

Nelune, Nilanthi, and I visited Connie next morning, because they wanted to see him, and spend some time with him. We found him looking very angry, and the floor was sticky with some liquid he had spilled. Nilanthi and I immediately started cleaning the floor with paper serviettes, and damp towels, as we could not walk on the sticky surface. He did not acknowledge us, as we continued to clean up the floor.

After about twenty minutes, he typed, "I'm not ignoring you Nelune and Nilanthi. I had a horrid morning." When I asked him why the floor was so sticky and dirty, he wrote, "They did a shoddy job cleaning it." But when I spoke to the nurse, she said he threw a cup of orange juice on the floor, as he was in a bad mood that morning.

Esme, Paul Maschio, and Sanit, were there too, and they stopped outside his room to chat with Nelune and Nilanthi. I took macaroni and patty curry, so I tried to feed him, but he could not swallow well. He wrote, "Put it in the blender next time, as I can't swallow macaroni."

Once again, I cooked his favourite dish for nothing, as I took it back. Christian and Athena dropped in that evening to pick Nelune, and they left after an early dinner. Nelune promised to visit again soon, as she was concerned about me, and upset over Connie's condition.

Elvira asked me to pick up a platter of sandwiches she ordered from a cafe in Mornington, before we came to the concert next day, on Sunday. It was very disappointing to see the platter though. The cafe let her down, as they made a dozen club sandwiches, instead of cutting them up into bite size ones, much to Elvira's chagrin and disappointment. Nilanthi and I cut them up, and rearranged the platter, which was slightly better.

I offered to make a couple of platters of sandwiches, but Elvira said she did not want to trouble me, and the cafe would help out. The Frankston Ladies Choir was very good, and Elvira put on a brave face, as she sang for the next hour or so. But I was concerned, because I knew she had to go for an operation on Tuesday, and she did not tell anyone else about it. A few other ladies, Nilanthi, and I, helped to wash dishes and put away the crockery afterwards.

Elvira's operation was successful, and they removed the tumour, but she had radiation daily for the next two weeks. She was relieved to know there was no danger of the tumour spreading.

The next few days and weeks passed by in the same manner; visits to the home, putting up with Connie's tantrums, and constant interference from his siblings.

Elvira said that when John and she visited Connie once, Geraldine started talking to her, and told her, "Don't trust in doctors, they are devils! Don't go for radiation. Just listen to these CD's and God will heal you." Elvira had replied, "I trust in God, but I will follow doctor's advice." She was stunned that Geraldine could say such a thing to her, a total stranger. And now she understood how she influenced Connie, as he refused medication and behaved so badly.

I was too busy with visits to the home and school etc. and did not have much time to write in my diary for about a week, until 18 November, which was our forty-third wedding anniversary. I sent Connie a text to let him know I would bring his favourite food for dinner after school, and hoped he would be in a mellow mood. When I saw him, I hugged him, and wished him a happy anniversary.

He was in a calm mood, and wrote, "I love you with all my heart." I replied, "I love you too, and thank you for all you have done for me. Be strong, and patient, and we'll pray that you will recover soon, if God wills it." I pureed the macaroni and patty mix in the blender, so it was smooth and easy for him to swallow. This time he ate it all. I stayed a little longer, and left him in a quiet mood, and ready to rest.

That was about the last time he was a little close to me, because soon after, Cristobel showed him the letter I sent her, and he sent me angry messages late at night. "How dare you restrict Bella from visiting me. She can come any time day or night. Take off restriction." I replied that I would discuss it when I visited him next.

After I wrote to the manager, and spoke to Dr Lyall, his treating doctor, he wrote the following instructions to the home: visiting hours should be two hours at a time, with no more than two visitors in the room, bedtime should be nine o'clock the latest, and he is not to be taken out of his room anywhere without his wife's permission. They had put up a notice on Connie's door with these instructions.

One morning, soon after, I was very surprised to read Roland's text message, "Dolly, I'm here to feed Connie breakfast. Are you coming here now? We as Christians have to take care of our sick brothers. If you are *unable* or *unwilling* to care for Connie, don't stop us!" And then a long harangue about how he worked in a hospital, and knew everything, whereas I did not know what was going on in the home. Now I knew why Connie sent me messages, saying I did not have a clue about what went on there.

This was the first of several offensive text messages from Roland. They had no idea that the nurses and doctors were in constant touch with me, and resented the fact they were not involved with the medical staff. It was difficult for them to comprehend that Christian and I were next of kin, and were under the mistaken notion that they had the right to be in charge of Connie's welfare.

Cristobel and Roland wrote those text messages together, as she was very angry with me, because I did not open the gate on the night she intruded.

Dr Lyall left a message on the phone a few days earlier, asking me to meet him, as they had problems with Connie at the home. And he could not take care of him, because he would not heed his advice. When I met Dr Lyall, I explained that Connie's aggression towards me, was because his siblings were instigating him to stay in their church in Hallam, where they promised he would be miraculously healed.

Then he said, "Although I prescribed pain-killers and muscle relaxants for him, he refuses to take them and throws his medicine on the floor." I replied, "I'm paying more than seventy dollars to the chemist for medicines every month, and it's not worth it, if he's not taking them."

The staff told me that he was the "Worst patient" they knew, and his family was the "Most interfering lot" too. Because they never met such intrusive people in their lives. Dr Lyall then said, "His brother, Roland, called me a couple of times, to ask about his condition, because Conrad had said he was constipated, and Roland wanted to know what I'm doing about it."

Then doctor told Roland that he was in touch with Connie's wife, who was next of kin, and as far as he knew, the nursing staff were looking after Connie very well. Roland was very unhappy about this, as he and Cristobel wanted to be in sole charge of Connie, in the mistaken belief that they were more qualified than the doctors and nurses.

And Geraldine was determined to convert him, and remove him to their glory house church. Between the three of them, they did him more harm, and hastened his decline, as they confused him, and wore him out mentally and physically.

Connie was in very high danger of choking over his food or drink, and had to be under medical supervision 24 hours a day, doctor concluded. When the nurse called to give me a daily report, she said that according to Connie's daily records, he had regular bowel movements, and there was no problem about that.

When I visited Connie the following morning after his text message, I asked one of the nurses to stay in the room with me, while I explained to him why I wrote that letter to Cristobel. Otherwise, he would have howled and shouted, without listening to me. In any case, he still howled, but not very loudly. I told him they should not keep him up till late at night, as he needed to rest, and Cristobel stayed till after eleven o'clock. He typed, "I don't want to sleep early. I can stay up as late as I please."

We went on and on, while I tried to explain, and he typed angry replies. Then I said, "Cristobel should not try to get medical information from nurses, as she is not the next of kin, and should not be showering you either." She recently bragged to Elvira that, "The nurses don't do a good job showering him, so *I* still have to come here and shower him." As if it required a highly skilled specialist to shower a patient.

I did not relent however, as I told the staff and manager, that Cristobel should not be allowed to visit at ten and eleven o'clock in the night, as Connie needed to rest. He complained constantly that the chair he was sitting on was uncomfortable, and to get him another chair. I spoke to the physio about it, and he said he would order one soon.

Then his brother, Paul, started texting me about a circulation booster for Connie's feet, as his legs were swollen. Connie texted, telling me to give Paul money to buy this booster that they advertised on television. I told Paul I would get one, because he said he did not have money to buy it, even though Connie told him I would reimburse him.

Paul texted, "After all, he's my brother, and if it was your sister, you would want to do the best for her." He insinuated that they had to do things for Connie, because I did not want to. It made me very angry to read his messages, and I sent a text saying not to worry, that I would get the booster soon.

When I spoke to the nurses, they said it would not help at all, as the swelling was due to his kidneys, and the circulation booster was just for tired, sore feet. But because Connie was so adamant, I went to the chemist to buy one, and the chemist said it would be best to hire one for a month, and see if it was effective, as they cost more than three hundred dollars to buy one.

So I hired one, and Nelune paid hundred dollars for the first month, as she said she wanted to do something for Connie. I took it to the home straightaway, and then he asked me to massage his feet. He seemed pleased with the booster, as he put his thumb up when I asked him if it helped his feet.

I lifted his legs, one at a time, and placed them on the booster, because they were like wooden stumps, and he could not lift them at all. Then I knelt down every time he wanted the speed adjusted or to move his legs, which was very tiring. But I was glad he got some relief from it.

I received a letter from Cristobel towards the end of November, in response to mine. It was such a vitriolic missive, that I asked Nilanthi to read it for me. At the end she threatened that if she could not visit Connie anytime in the night, she would take "action" against me. I was fed up with such threats, and her attitude. I took the letter to my solicitor next morning. And after listening to me, and reading the letter I sent Cristobel, and her response, he drafted a letter to be sent to all Connie's siblings, stating that I would restrict their visits, because of their adverse effect on him mentally and physically.

He said, "Your letter to his sister is reasonable and logical, in consideration of your husband's illness. So I'm not sure why they can't understand why you want them to visit during the day, and let him rest at nights." It was beyond me too. But I told him that it was just a power struggle with me, as they wanted to be in sole charge and control him.

Nilanthi accompanied me to the solicitor's office, and she said she was sad that I had to waste money on legal fees, just because of Connie's interfering siblings. But I did not mind paying exorbitant fees to the solicitor, in order to protect my rights.

After considering the matter for a few days, I knew Connie would be more upset when they showed him that letter, as they had no qualms about distressing him, just to vilify me. I did not post the letters as I intended to, but decided that if they interfered any further, I would not hesitate to send them.

In the middle of this ordeal, Philip Brady called, to request an interview, regarding Luigi's book and CD. I said I would be happy to arrange a time, and he asked me to email some of the key points in the book, so we could discuss them at the interview.

A week later, on Friday night, when Nilanthi was still here, Philip interviewed me on the phone, for about twenty minutes. Luigi and Ninette listened to it too, and Ninette taped the interview, and so did I. It went well, and they played a few of Luigi's songs on the show. The interview was recorded on u-tube, and several people called to say they enjoyed listening to it. Ninette and Luigi received positive feedback from their friends as well, who had listened to the interview.

Whenever I visited Connie over the next few weeks, Geraldine was there, and she started arguing with me about various issues. On one occasion, Connie typed he did not have breakfast yet, so I went to the head nurse and asked her. She came in to the room at once, and in front of Geraldine she said, "Conrad, you *had* your breakfast this morning, oats and milk." Connie did not write anything, but looked down, totally devoid of any interest. It was typical of his "forgetfulness," or attempts to show his family he was being starved.

When the nurse left, Geraldine said, "They don't puree his food well enough, and he can't swallow their food, unlike when I puree it at home, then he eats everything." I told her that the nurses knew what they were doing, and to stop criticizing the staff in front of Connie. She did not care, because she carried on saying, "He needs a full-time carer here, to give him tender loving care, because the nurses don't have time." I replied, "He's in a nursing home with qualified nurses, therapists, and doctors to take care of him. Why would he need a full-time carer to sit here all day with him? And can you please stop filling his mind with these prayer meetings, as he keeps texting me that he wants to go to your glory house in Hallam."

She strutted about arrogantly, and retorted, "*I* don't tell him, Connie receives *divine* messages about the prayer meetings!" I just looked at her in disbelief. When he was at home too, she sent text messages about scheduled prayer meetings, and unsettled him. That was when he became really agitated, and argued with me, because he wanted to drive to their meetings.

I just looked at her and said, "You don't seem to understand that he's very weak, physically and mentally, and you shouldn't be upsetting him." She barked at me, "Nothing is wrong with him!" I asked, "Have you seen people being cured with your own eyes, or just watched manufactured miracles on DVD's?" "Of course, I have seen *worse* people than him getting cured through miracles!" "Then why don't you just pray for him, and get the miracle workers to come here and see Connie, instead of trying to drag such a sick person to Hallam? Doctor says he shouldn't be moved without medical supervision." She yelled at me, "Get the doctor to meet *us*! It's always, doctor this and doctor that! *Why* can't we take him out every morning and bring him back at night?"

I left the room, because I could not take it any more, but she followed me, arguing at the top of her voice, just like a common fishwife. I walked away as fast as I could, with her in full pursuit, until a nurse stopped her and said, "Can you keep your voice down, because you are disturbing the other patients here. You must settle these issues privately."

I was fuming when I left, because she said all those things in front of Connie. She had no consideration for a sick person, which showed the extent of her so-called love, and lack of Christianity, the way she argued with me.

The nurses told me that he manipulated everyone, just so he could get out of the home. And they reassured me that they would not ask him to leave, as that was what Connie and his siblings intended. But they said they knew how to manage him, and sympathised with me, because his siblings were controlling Connie and vilifying me, because I did not let them take him out of the home.

Every morning or night, and sometimes during the day, one of the nurses called, and gave me a full report, as to whether Connie ate his meals, if he had rested, and any other issues. By this time, they knew he was incontinent, and he used special underpants, which was better for him, and for the staff. I was always apprehensive when I received these calls from the home, not knowing what was wrong.

The nurse on duty sometimes said that he threw a tantrum, because he wanted some left-over food in the fridge, that had no "use by" date. And because she refused to feed him that, he howled and threw things on the floor. The staff told me that any food from outside, had to be labelled with a "use by" date, and what ingredients were in it, as a precaution against frequent bouts of gastro occurring in the home.

I always made it a point to label the containers of food, stating ingredients, and "use by" date, but his siblings never bothered to follow these rules. And just like that, a severe gastro outbreak raged in the home shortly afterwards. A nurse called to say it would be best if I did not visit Connie for a few days, until the gastro was controlled. Connie escaped the gastro outbreak because he never left his room. But the nurse told me that his brother, Paul, and Sanit visited, even though a notice on the front door warned visitors to stay away during this period.

I picked Ninette on Saturday, 30 November, and we drove to Isobel's place for lunch. She invited Nilanthi too, before she left in a few days time. On our way, a nurse called to say that Connie was very weak, and refused to eat his lunch. The nurse said that doctor would see him on Monday, and they would let me know the outcome. It was very sad, as I knew Connie was getting weaker by the day. But he just would not listen to doctor, or take his medications to ease the pain.

In spite of my writing down directions to Isobel's place, I missed the way, and had to turn back a couple of times. We finally arrived there at two o'clock, after leaving home at eleven in the morning. Ninette sat in the front seat, and was worse than a child, as she kept asking, "Are we there yet? *Where* are you going now? Is this the right way?" She drove me crazy with her constant questions, fidgeting, and frantic directions.

I held my tongue, and drove in silence, till we arrived at Isobel's. We had a pleasant afternoon, although we were so late for lunch, and Isobel was very comforting. She listened to all that was going on with Connie and his siblings, then advised me on how to cope with the situation.

I dropped Nilanthi at Narre Warren next day, as Shirani and Ranjith were driving her to the airport on Monday evening. When I returned home, I prepared some food, pureed it, and took it for Connie in the evening. He appeared to be calm and wrote a few things he wanted me to do, "Put the booster on, wipe my nose, get this, get that," and finally, when I did all he wanted, he wrote, "Paul is bringing dinner," and did not want to eat the food I brought. I left it in the fridge, and said he could have it next day.

Roland sent a text early morning on 4 December," Dolly, I'm here with Connie, and he's crying to go to the glory house church in Hallam. Tell me if I can take him, and I'll arrange everything." He often sent me similar messages, with this same request. And I was tired of it, because I heard it was at Geraldine's instigation, that Roland pressured me to take Connie out of the home.

I told Nelune about it, as I just could not stand this stress any longer. She called Roland immediately, and asked him to stop harassing me with these requests, as they should understand Connie was too weak, and could not be moved from the home. She also told him, "Dolly is not having a ball on her own, so don't give her any more stress at this time." She was firm, but polite and he hung up on her.

When I arrived there on Sunday afternoon, Connie was not in his room, and nothing was written in the visitors register either to say who took him out. Though the staff looked everywhere, they could not find him. I stood outside for about twenty minutes, and then I saw his brother, Paul, wheeling him back to the home.

I asked him, "Where did you take him, without even letting the staff know?" He grinned foolishly, "He wanted to go to McDonalds for an ice cream." I told him, "It's not safe to wheel him across such a busy highway, as he could easily fall off the chair, because he can't grip the sides very well." There was no pedestrian crossing, and the traffic zoomed past at hundred kilometres an hour. Paul had no idea how risky it was to push Connie across in a wheelchair, when he was so feeble.

I spoke to the staff later, and told them Connie should not be taken in a wheelchair across the busy highway, for his own safety. They explained that the problem on Sundays especially, was that the home operated on skeleton staff, and were unable to keep an eye on every patient. I hoped Paul would use common sense in future, and stop endangering Connie's safety, and at least inform the staff before taking him out, even if it was only to the garden.

When I visited Connie, one of the staff members would be feeding him, and he did not make a fuss, because he ate without any trouble. But at other times, when he was in a bad mood, because he was frustrated being confined in a chair, and unable to speak or move his body at all, he refused to eat, and was very difficult.

From about the beginning of December, Connie kept texting me the same question a few times during the day and night, "Are you taking me home for Christmas? If not, Tucko wants me to come to Rebby's for lunch. What are you going to do?" I replied, "I will spend Christmas with you, like we've always done, and Christian and Athena will come too." But this did not make him happy, because he kept on sending me the same text.

I wondered why Roland suggested taking him to Rebecca's for Christmas, without first asking me what my plans were. Connie and I had always spent Christmas with Christian and Athena. This was a new development about going to Rebecca's, as they never celebrated Christmas all these years. Because they did not believe in traditional celebrations according to their Born again beliefs.

Why Roland upset Connie, and told him that if I did not take him home, he would take him to Rebby's, was something I could not understand, as if Connie did not have a family. Although I tried to ignore Connie's texts, it was annoying to get the same message three or four times a day.

It was just another ploy to disturb Connie, because once he got a notion into his head, he became obsessed, and demanded to know if I was taking him home or not. This total fixation with one idea, was another symptom of dementia, and I wished they would mind their own business and leave us alone. Christian and Athena were in Japan for some time, and he called to say they would be home in time for Christmas, and we could spend the day with Connie.

Connie sent a text early morning on Sunday, 8 December, to ask why he was not allowed to go out with Esme. I replied she could take him to the garden and premises, but not across the highway. When I visited him in the afternoon, he had written a long passage, "Dolly, I can go anywhere I want with my brothers and sisters; for a walk on the beach or a coffee in a cafe, and I am now totally committed to the Lord. I won't take any medication, because I trust in the Lord."

I knew straightaway from the wording and style, that one of the zealots wrote that, because he always called me "Dolla," even now when he wrote anything, and not "Dolly." So I said, "I'm not reading what someone else has written, because that's not you." He just scowled and glared at me. But I did what I had to do, put his clothes away, took his soiled clothes, fed him dinner, and left after a couple of hours, feeling exhausted as always by the time I came home.

It poured down all day on Monday, and I finished school after four thirty. When I came home, I had a text from Connie, "Dolly, use my hard-earned money to get a full time carer for me. I'm weak." I did not respond to that, but later on, I sent him a goodnight message, and he responded with his usual message. I knew once again that his irresponsible siblings were filling his mind with all this nonsense, and constantly upsetting him.

It was infuriating to think they influenced him so much, because Connie never once mentioned anything about using his, "hard-earned money" to get extra care.

Geraldine, Cristobel, and Roland, were the ones who put that idea into his head, as Geraldine told me so in front of Connie, when she confronted me.

I just could not understand their mentality, as they were obviously trying to manipulate him about his finances now. Connie knew I paid very high fees to the nursing home every month, and we had a huge mortgage, besides ongoing bills and expenses. So where did he get this sudden notion that he had so much extra money, to employ a full-time carer to stay with him at the home?

Chapter 85

The solicitor called in early December, and said that the unit was sold unconditionally. That was good news, as the nursing home deemed that unit an asset, and charged high fees because of that. He also wanted to know why my middle name was not on my birth certificate. I explained that it was my baptismal name, so he wanted a signed affidavit, and more proof of identity. It was such a nuisance, but I said I would attend to the matter as soon as possible.

I looked up the address of a local Justice of the Peace, and found one in Mornington. But when I drove there, I just could not find the place, as there was no such address. So I drove to Frankston police station, and the JP there signed all the documents, but he stamped the original, instead of the copy. I hoped they would not reject the document because of that. Then I sent them by express post, and hoped the sale would go through without a hitch.

Cristobel told her siblings that I should sell our unit in Queensland, and pay for a carer for Connie. So I did not mention the sale to Connie, as it would not have bothered him in the least. He was beyond caring about anything else other than his immediate comfort. But he would have written about it to his siblings, who would have dictated what he should do.

In the meantime, he sent me two text messages, asking me to bring lunch although it was late afternoon. I came home after five o'clock, as I dropped in at Shirani's place in Narre Warren for a brief visit. When I sent him a goodnight text later, he did not respond.

A couple of weeks before Christmas, Mary and I visited Connie one afternoon, as she had a small crib to give him. I asked Elvira and John to hang some holy pictures in his room, because he did not want me to bring anything, or decorate his room. But I still took a pot of artificial lavender that he bought for me some time ago, and left it on his table, as he liked lavender.

I was upset that he did not want me to decorate his room or make it cosy. He did not want to be there, and rebuffed any effort to make his room look pleasant. I wanted to hang a few prints of sunsets, and seascapes on one bare wall, for him to look at when he was alone. But it took a few weeks to hang them one day, when he was not looking.

When Mary and I entered the room that day, he did not look at us, as he was busy typing. A tub of ice cream stood on his table, and I tried to feed him some, but he turned his head away, growling and scowling at me. Then he looked at Mary and pointed to the ipad, so I read it too, "My wife doesn't trust me. She thinks I'm a liar. Tell Tony that my wife doesn't trust me." I asked him what he meant, but he kept typing similar messages. I replied, "You have been scheming with your brothers and sisters to get out of the home, that's why I don't want you to leave this place." He wrote, "Get me out of here soon, otherwise I will kill myself. I will starve to death."

Mary tried to pacify him, "Don't get upset now, try to eat your ice cream." And she fed him a few spoons, which he ate without fussing. I went out of the room, as I wanted to speak to the head nurse. She told me he behaved very badly, threw his food and drinks on the floor, and refused to take his medications. I said that I paid a substantial amount of money to the chemist every month for those pills, and it was no good if he refused to take them. She said, "I can see a lot of family interference here, and Conrad thinks if he behaves badly, we'll ask him to leave, but don't worry, we know how to handle him."

I went back to his room, and he was still typing away. I hugged him, and we left soon after. I was very distressed, as I knew he was not wholly to blame, because his mind was affected. His siblings were the culprits, as they would not leave him alone to accept his illness, and deal with it as he should. Instead, they upset him, and denigrated the nursing staff, and encouraged him to complain constantly, so that he could get out of the home.

Even his treating doctor was losing patience, as he left a message on the answering machine a day later saying, "Mrs de Sielvie, your husband, Conrad, is making it impossible for me, and the nursing staff to care for him, as he refuses to take any medication, and will not listen to my advice at all. In fact he asked me to 'get lost' when I told him what to do, to ease the muscle aches and congestion in his chest. I would like to talk to you soon, if possible, as his brother has been calling me too, and asking me for medical information, which I refused to give him because of privacy reasons. His brother was not happy, when I told him that the staff and I deal with you only, as Conrad's wife, and no one else."

I met Dr Lyall soon after, and I sympathised with him, because he was very perturbed too, as Connie was so stubborn. We had a long discussion about what was best for him now. And he found it incredible that his siblings discouraged him from taking medication that would help relieve his aches and pains. And doctor insisted that he was not to be taken out of the home at all, because he was so weak, and liable to choke on his food or drink, if he was not supervised constantly.

I was busy preparing students for the end of year piano concert on Sunday, 15 December, and was happy when it went off well. Some of my previous students attended, and played as guest performers too. All the parents wanted to know about Connie, and were concerned when I told them how ill he was. The priest, and pastoral care workers visited Connie regularly, and took Holy Communion for him. I came home feeling very tired, but was glad the concert was successful.

Connie sent several text messages every single day now, asking me the same question, "Are you taking me home for Christmas? Tucko wants me to come to

Rebby's if you won't." My reply was the same, that I would spend the day with him, and Christian and Athena would be there. But he did not stop asking me the same question, stuck in a groove, like a broken record.

It wore me down, but I knew it was impossible to bring him home, without a qualified nurse on hand. I was unable to lift him and take him to the toilet, and it would be very bad if he fell again and hurt himself. The worst part would be, when I had to take him back. I knew he would refuse to go, and create an ugly scene, which I could not handle.

Cristobel phoned at three o'clock in the afternoon, on 24 December, but I did not answer. She sent a text, saying she wanted to take Connie for a walk in the gardens. I called the nurse on duty, and told her it was alright for her to take him around the premises, but not across the highway. Cristobel replied immediately and thanked me. After a while, she sent a text, saying she would like to have coffee with me sometimes, as she and Connie missed me very much. She wished me for Christmas, and I sent a text wishing her too. I prepared a special lunch for tomorrow, and pureed Connie's meal in the evening.

When I woke up next morning, I sent Connie a text and wished him, but he replied, "Bring breakfast drink, Milo, Sustagen." I was very sad, as he did not even wish me. I went there around eleven o'clock, and he appeared to be in a very bad mood. I wished him again and hugged him, but he wrote, "Wipe the snot from my nose. I can't breathe." After I cleaned his nose, I asked, "Why didn't you wish me for Christmas?" He just ignored me, and kept writing various demands. I was worn-out by the time Christian and Athena arrived.

I fed him pureed rice and curry, and he ate without fussing, then we wheeled him to the garden, as it was sunny and pleasant. Christian showed him photographs of Japan, and explained about the places. And he told him what they were doing there, but he did not show much interest. I asked him if he would like a chocolate drink from the machine, and he put his thumb up, so I brought him one, and he sipped it slowly.

After a while, he typed, "What about internet connection on my ipad?" I told Christian I was very suspicious of his request, because he could hardly use one finger to type on the ipad. And even his text messages were erratic, and getting worse as his fingers stiffened. I did not know why he was so keen to get internet, unless his siblings had ulterior motives.

He could not access his bank accounts now, but still, there was no saying what went on in his mind. Christian said he would connect it next time, and he was quiet. He did not communicate after that, and the three of us sat around, just chatting with each other, and trying to interest him, but he remained distant.

When it was almost three o'clock, we wheeled him back to the room. I was famished, as I did not have lunch, or even a snack since morning. When he was back in the room, he typed, "Can I go to Rebby's now?" He looked so weak and miserable, that my heart ached. But I had to be strong, so I replied, "No, Connie, the doctor said you are too weak to be moved, and there are no nurses to look after you, if you leave the home." He typed, "Tucko can take care of me." I kept repeating the same thing, and he started howling at the top of his voice, as he shook with violent, uncontrollable spasms.

It made my stomach churn and flip to see his misery. Christian and Athena stood by the bed, watching him in dismay. I could not pacify him, as he kept howling like a wounded animal. It made me very unhappy to cause him so much distress. I blamed his interfering siblings thoroughly for having put these notions into his head. We would have spent a quiet day otherwise, and he would have been calm. And one of his siblings would have visited him in the evening.

I went out of the room and asked one of the nurses to come in, as he just would not stop shouting and crying out. I explained what happened, and she reassured me, "Don't worry, he'll settle down, we'll look after him. No, you are right, he's in *no* condition to leave here, especially as he's liable to choke on anything, as he has difficulty swallowing even liquids now."

We had a very subdued meal at home, and afterwards, Christian did several odd jobs around the place, and some updates on my phone and computer. They too were very upset to witness Connie's behaviour, and I told them that whenever I visited, he lost his temper over the smallest issue, and waited for a chance to start shouting and throwing a tantrum. When they left a few hours later, Elvira called to wish me, and then related all the stories Cristobel told her the previous evening.

She said that when they visited Connie, Cristobel was still there. And she told Elvira that I should visit Connie more often and feed him, as I visited him once a week for ten minutes only. Elvira replied, that I was there just the day before, with the circulation booster. I returned the hired one, and bought one, and spent a couple of hours with Connie, trying the new one. She also mentioned that when I visited with Mary, and tried to feed him, he refused to let me feed him. Connie had typed, "I was angry then." He told his siblings, and everyone else who visited him, that I came once a week for ten minutes only. Naturally, I was very upset, but that was his dementia, and he was not to blame. But his siblings believed whatever he told them, as they did not have a clue about his mental state. He had convinced them that Christian and I did not visit him, and we did not care for him.

Elvira knew I was doing Connie's laundry, and took them to the home every other day. And that I spent time feeding him, and doing everything he asked me to do. So she did not believe that story about my visiting him once a week for ten minutes only. Then she told Elvira that Christian visited only three times so far. Elvira said that was because he was in Japan, to which she replied," *I* didn't know Christian was in Japan!"

Connie knew Christian was overseas, because I told him so, but whether he really forgot, or he did not want to remember, I did not know. Then Cristobel said, "Connie, you may be my brother, but I have to tell your friends that you have been very hard on Dolly." She then told Elvira that Clifford was my boyfriend before I met Connie. And that was the reason why Connie was so jealous, and hard on me etc. etc. I was absolutely stunned, to think she had nothing better to do than gossip about me.

I wished I did not have to hear all this from Elvira, especially on Christmas Day, after the traumatic time with Connie. But she went on to say that Cristobel mentioned about the night she visited, and how I did not open the gate. She wanted their address, so she could post them a copy of the letter she sent me. John gave her their address, and I was apprehensive, knowing she would somehow inveigle her way into their house, and talk more nonsense.

I warned Elvira about her devious character, and how his siblings would somehow try to slither into their lives, and influence them too. Then Elvira said, "Remember, I'm on your side Nalini, I'm not going to believe whatever she has to say about you." I replied that I had nothing to hide. And if Connie wanted to let down Christian and me to his siblings, they could believe whatever he said, that was their choice.

I told her that I knew who I was, and my conscience was clear. I did everything for Connie, and would continue to do my best for him. It did not matter what they said, or what the world believed, because it did not change the person I was. It was just a matter of their opinion, and I did not care a whit.

That Christmas was definitely the worst one ever, and I went to bed with my heart weighed down, and a sick feeling in my guts. But I did not cry, as I was angry with his siblings, not with him. I said a prayer that he would have a peaceful night, and sent him a goodnight text, but he did not reply. Esme said she went with Cristobel that evening, and spent some time with him, so that was why he did not respond.

Mary visited two days later, and after she left, I took Connie's dinner around four thirty. He was subdued and did not type any messages, except, "Put the circulation booster on." He ate all the food, and when I tried to feed his ice cream from the tub on his tray, he turned his head away, and typed, "Go to the kitchen and bring ice cream in a bowl." So I did, and they just opened a tub of ice cream, and spooned it into a bowl, which he allowed me to feed him.

It was the same every time, as he demanded something of that sort. I could not understand why he wanted the same ice cream in a bowl, and not from a tub. I applied dencorub on his shoulders and arms, as he typed that they were sore. When I asked him why he did not take his medication for the pain, he ignored me.

Then I hung his washed clothes in the cupboard, and took the soiled ones in a plastic bag. By now the stench of his soiled clothes was so bad, that I held my nose, and the whole car smelt of stale urine. Dirty clothes left in a bag for two days, reeked badly. And I thought it was better for the home to do his laundry daily, instead of keeping them in his cupboard for a couple of days, which made his whole room stink. Still, he would not hear of it, so I continued doing his laundry.

When Nilanthi visited in October, she helped me label all his clothes, and I sewed the labels on the machine, but she hand-stitched some. This did not prevent clothes getting mixed up though. And I found Connie dressed in someone else's ill-fitting t-shirts or pants sometimes.

Con and Cornelia invited me to go cherry-picking to Red Hill on Sunday, 29 December. I was ready by seven o'clock in the morning, and we went there around ten o'clock. We had a good day, but I was famished by three o'clock, as they still did not finish picking cherries. I prepared some curries, and fried rice, so we had a very late lunch around four thirty, and they left a couple of hours later.

It was very peaceful and relaxed on New Year's Eve, and I stayed up till midnight to see the New Year in, and watched the fireworks display on television.

I went at eleven thirty next morning, and took pureed milk rice and beef curry for Connie. Although I sent him a text earlier and wished him, he did not respond. So I asked him why he did not even wish me, and he pointed to the ipad. He had typed, "Happy New Year. God bless my wife, Christian, Athena, and my brothers, and sisters and grant them good health."

He was subdued, and ate all of it. Then typed his usual demands, "Do this, and do that." After eating, he typed, "Thank you for bringing lunch. Happy New Year, and hopefully it will be a good year for both of us." I felt incredibly sad when I read those words, and hugged him close and long. He seemed to be in severe pain, and looked very frail. It was very difficult to watch him deteriorating rapidly each time I saw him. He struggled to even lift his finger to type. I left around two o'clock, worn-out and overcome with sadness.

Ever since Geraldine confronted me, and made such an ugly scene, I did not want to face her again. And each time I drove along the highway and turned in to the home, I felt so apprehensive, that it made me physically ill. My stomach started to churn, not knowing what was in store, and who would be visiting him.

Chapter 86

The following days continued without any change, teaching, visits to the home and Ninette. As I walked in to the room once, he typed, "How are the cats?" A day later, when I visited him, I showed him some enlarged photographs of all three cats that I pasted on an A4 poster, and he giggled a little when he saw them.

Before I left, I hung that poster on the wall, as he smiled when he looked at the cats. I returned home after seven o'clock that evening, as it took very long to feed him the dinner I took. Sometimes, he watched television while I was there, and seemed a little more settled now. He did not type any more demands to take him home, or to get a carer.

Con, Cornelia, and Laura visited the following day, Saturday, and we planned to have a barbeque. But the weather turned cold, so I cooked the meats indoors, and we had a pleasant afternoon. They left after five thirty, and I was very tired.

Christian dropped in later that evening, to set up my new mobile that Nelune sent me. But the sim card was not right, so he could not do anything, but he said he would bring another one soon.

On my last visit, I asked Connie if he would like roast beef and potatoes, and he typed, "Yes, that would be nice." So I made it for lunch on Sunday, pureed it well, and he enjoyed it very much, as he ate everything. Afterwards he typed, "It was nice, I could taste the roast beef." He still harped on getting internet connection, and kept typing the same request. I said Christian would come down soon, and evaded the issue, as I did not want him to throw another tantrum.

The home underwent some changes, and the previous manager left early in the year. A new manager took over, and he seemed very efficient. I spoke to him on the phone once, and then met him personally a few days later. I explained about the on-going difficulty with his siblings, because of their schemes to take him from the home, and he was very understanding.

He told me, that in his experience as a manager, there were always some issues when the family demanded to be involved. If they visited Connie with altruistic intentions, it would have been different. But they all had ulterior motives, in their continued determination to control him. Except Esme perhaps, who was just manipulated by Cristobel and Connie.

I told him of their plots to get him out of the home, and care for him, thinking they could get the fees instead of the nursing home. And he advised me to seek legal advice regarding financial matters, in case some of them were after monetary gain. He said because dementia patients did not fully comprehend what was going on around them, family members usually took advantage.

I mentioned that Connie insisted on getting internet connection. But the manager did not think it worth while, considering his frail condition, and inability to type even with one finger now. He was of the same opinion, that his siblings had some ulterior motive in trying to get internet connection for him.

Another matter of concern was, that although Connie did not use his mobile to make phone calls, only text messages, I received a bill for $144. I showed him the bill and asked," Who has been using your phone?" He looked at the bill vaguely and typed, "Pay it." I had no doubt at all that his siblings were responsible for this bill, but he did not care at all.

I was very surprised, and annoyed one morning when I had a text from Shiranthi's mobile saying, "Dolly, go and feed Connie lunch, as I have to go to work today." I called Shiranthi, and asked what she meant by that peremptory order, and she replied that Roland used her mobile to text me. I asked her what business did he have, to order me to feed my husband. She apologized, and told me not to worry.

Then next morning, I had a call from Connie's phone. It was Roland, saying, "Thank you for feeding Connie." But I did not feed him lunch, because as usual, I took his dinner last evening. Now I knew why Connie's mobile bill was so high, because they used it whenever they visited. Connie was very vague and forgetful now, and he could not remember when, or who fed him any longer.

I woke up at five o'clock in the morning on Monday, 6 January, to the sound of a beeping smoke alarm. It was time to change the battery again.

I was emotionally and physically drained after last evening's visit to the home. More than two hours of fetch and carry, "Do this, do that," and with no word of thanks, or any concern for me at all, was very distressing.

He never asked how I was, or how I coped, as it was all about his needs and welfare now. Nilanthi was amused whenever I had a short nap before I visited Connie, as I found the visits so exhausting. And she said it was the first time she heard of someone needing a nap, before visiting a patient.

After feeding him last evening, I applied voltaren on his neck, shoulders, and arms, and massaged his back. Then arranged an extra pillow at his back, because he complained non-stop about the chair, and how uncomfortable it was. I said I asked the physio a few times to get him a good chair, and was still waiting for him to order one. My back ached by the time I came home, and it was the same again when I visited him a day later.

I felt depressed, and exhausted by the time I finished doing the chores, feeding him and making him comfortable. He could not understand that it was not only the chair that made him sore. But that his whole body was weakening, and the pains became more severe as his muscles stiffened. That was the reason why Prof. Butler prescribed relaxants, and told him he would get worse with painful muscles. But he still did not take medication, because of Geraldine's influence.

It was scorching over the next few days, and when I watered the garden, I saw Angela sitting on the balcony, so we had a long chat. I was very happy to hear that her cancer was in remission, and she was recovering slowly. Then she asked me about Connie, and said, "It's a terrible disease to have, and I'm sorry to hear he's getting worse." I thanked her, and she said to let her know if they could help in any way.

The nurse called at nine o'clock on Saturday morning, 11 January, to say that Connie was unable to sit up when they tried to shower him, so they put him back to bed. She wanted to admit him to hospital, but I told her not to, and just to make him comfortable. Because the doctors said they could not help him, and he was better off where he was, rather than in a hospital.

I dropped in at Elvira's later, and gave her a large holy picture to hang up in Connie's room. She agreed to do so, when they visited him next time. Then I came home and made macaroni and patty mix for his dinner. But when I arrived there at four forty, Geraldine was still feeding him a very late lunch, or a very early dinner, I did not know which.

This was another of her games, knowing that I brought his dinner around this time on certain days, she made it a point to feed him a meal just before his dinner. I did not speak to her, but waited in the reception area until she left.

When I went in, I found Connie in a very weak state and propped up in bed, and he could not even type on his ipad. He looked exhausted, and was very drowsy. He did not want dinner, as he just finished eating. As I wrote the date and contents on the box, I left it in the fridge for his lunch or dinner next day. He seemed ready to sleep, and did not want the television on. So I left around seven o'clock, after making him comfortable, because he looked drained.

I knew Geraldine bombarded him with faith healing propaganda, until his brain was overwhelmed. And I was tempted to take legal steps to prevent her from this relentless brain-washing, as I could plainly see that she wore him out, and hastened his decline. She did not seem to understand, or accept the fact that not only was his body deteriorating, but his mind was very fragile too.

John told me that when he visited Connie on several occasions, he found her playing those CD's over and over again. He switched off the player, and turned on the television to give him a break. Because he said that Connie was definitely being "brain-washed," as he looked like a zombie after Geraldine visited him. And he agreed that constant indoctrination made people do anything.

I understood the reason why Connie always looked depressed and exhausted after Geraldine and Roland visited him, as it was the same at home. He also said that he spoke to Roland, about them visiting Connie at different times on different days of the week. So that one of them would be there once a week or so, as they all descended on him at the same time on the same day.

But Cristobel continued visiting him late at nights, and keeping him awake, while he sat upright on his chair for hours on end. If she had any concern for his comfort, she would have ensured he was in bed by nine o'clock the latest, and visited him in the afternoon.

I hardly slept that night, but I woke up early on Sunday morning, as I wanted to attend Fr Denis's farewell, at eleven thirty in Frankston. The hall was filled to capacity, and it was great to see that everyone turned up to wish him. Although people thronged around him, eager to get his attention, he spoke briefly, to inquire after Connie. And said that I could contact him, if I needed him to do anything for Connie. Then I visited Shirani for a short time at Narre Warren, and returned home in the afternoon.

Christian and Athena dropped in to see Connie that same afternoon, as I told them how weak he was the day before, and that they wanted to admit him to hospital. They visited me around eight o'clock that night, and told me that his brother, Paul, was there too. And he asked the nurse to put Connie in his chair, which the nurse did. I was very surprised, as they told me that he could not sit upright yesterday, and was lying in bed when I saw him. Christian attended to my mobile, and we had an interesting evening, catching up with events.

The next few days were unbearably hot, as temperatures soared above forty degrees. I had a head cold, and my throat was on fire, but I visited Connie on Wednesday, and fed him some pureed food that was in the fridge. When he finished eating, two staff members lifted him onto the bed, wiped his bottom, and changed his underpants. I was very very distressed, to watch him being handled like a baby. His weight dropped from sixty five to about forty five kilograms, and he looked skeletal.

After they left, he typed, "Switch TV and lights off, and close the door." He seemed comfortable, but very drowsy, so I left around seven o'clock. When I came home, I called Nelune, and we had a long chat, as I was very upset. But there was nothing anyone could do for him now, and I had to be strong.

The scorching weather continued without respite over the next few days. And the temperature rocketed to forty three and forty four degrees, before the cool change finally swept in. I was down with flu, and was feverish, while the cats felt the heat badly too. I kept them indoors, and ran the air conditioner. It was forty three degrees on 17 January, Ninette's birthday.

When I called to wish her that evening, she said she enjoyed the day with Toula, so I was pleased to hear that. Connie sent a text early that morning, after a couple of weeks. I was under the impression he could not text anymore, as his fingers were too weak. But he wrote, "This chair is killing me." I replied that the physio was seeing him soon, and he said that he would get a good chair for him.

Then I called the nurse to ask when the physio could see Connie, as I expected him to attend to this matter a few weeks ago. And she replied, "He's seeing Conrad today." When I asked about a chair, she said the physio would contact me, and I had to speak to him about it. I also requested the hairdresser, who visited the home, to cut Connie's hair, but so far, she did not give him a haircut. I reminded the nurse again, and she said she would follow up with the hairdresser.

I waited all day for the physio to contact me, and finally he called around four o'clock. He said he would organize a comfortable chair as soon as possible, and I could rent or buy one as I wished. He said the "Princess chair" cost about $2500, so I told him I would hire one. Then he said that from next week, another physio would see Connie two or three times a week, to try and manage his pain.

I visited him the following Sunday evening, and took roast beef and potatoes for dinner once again. But he was not hungry, which made me think that one of his siblings must have fed him a late lunch. He never once asked how I was, even though it was plain to see I was very sick, coughing, and sniffling. I did not want him to catch a cold, as it would have made his congestion worse, so I avoided getting too close to him. I put the circulation booster on, applied voltaren on his neck, arms, and shoulders, and then I left after seven o'clock, feeling drained.

I slept in late next morning, but was determined to watch the last of the series of Peter Jackson's adaptation of Tolkein's masterpiece, "The Hobbit," part two. I looked forward eagerly to the "Lord Of The Rings" trilogy, and Connie and I enjoyed watching all three movies. Now I felt sad that he was unable to watch the last of the series, because he would have liked this one too.

I was feverish, and my head throbbed when I drove to Karingal in the afternoon. But I did not have to queue up, as I purchased a ticket a few days ago. It was a fantastic movie, and the 3D visual effects, were absolutely stunning. But whether it was due to my being so unwell, two hours of deafening battle scenes made my head spin. I came home with a splitting headache, and rested a while. It was the second time in all these years that I went to the movies alone. I did not mind though, as it was very relaxing, because very few people were at a matinee on a Monday.

I visited Ninette next day, and was happy to meet Liliana and Luigi too. We had a pleasant afternoon, chatting and listening to music. When the others left, I walked with Ninette and the dog. I still coughed, but was getting better. When I came home, Judy, from Bendigo Bank called and said that I did not meet the criteria for a "home safe loan," as the block of land was not worth sixty percent of valuation. They had some very strict rules, and although the house and land were valued over a million, the land had to be worth more, so I thanked her, and said I would look at other options.

I visited Connie around four thirty next day, and took pureed macaroni and chicken curry. After I fed him, he wrote, "Not chilli hot enough." I asked him what he would like next time, and he wrote, "Hot beef curry and congee." I noticed then that he was sitting on an old chair, with its arms wrapped up in some fleecy fabric. I asked him where the other chair was, and he typed, "Esme took it home. This is her chair."

I asked him why she did not speak to me first, or leave the other one outside, so John could bring it back home, as it was my desk chair. He wrote, "She left a message on your phone. She said it was too crowded in here." I replied I did not receive any message, and asked him to text her to bring back my chair, and leave it outside his room. I was irritated, because she brought an old chair, when I asked the physio to get a "Princess chair," which was due that week.

I was exhausted by the time I left after doing so many things, as he was very demanding that day, and kept me on my toes. His legs were stiff and heavy, like wooden stumps, and getting his feet onto the circulation booster was very tiring. And when he was not happy, he made growling noises and scowled at me, until I adjusted his legs to his satisfaction.

It was a warm, thirty three degrees next day, 23 January. Del called to say her husband was admitted to palliative care, as his cancer had spread, and his days were numbered. Poor Del, she was very busy running around and taking care of him. We gave each other moral support, and hoped to catch up soon.

I made fried rice, chicken curry, and some cutlets for lunch on Friday, as Felix and Yasmin were visiting. They were staying in the city, and taking a train to Frankston, and asked me to pick them, and drop them later. Although I recovered from the flu, my cough was worse at nights, and kept me up till dawn.

It rained slightly on Friday, when I picked them up at eleven o'clock from the station. We had a very enjoyable afternoon, and Felix advised me about the house etc. He gave me a small cross, and holy water from Mother Mary's house in Turkey, where they toured a few weeks ago. I dropped them at the station at three o'clock, as they had another engagement in the city. Then I attended to some banking on the way, and came home feeling very tired. I was feverish all through the night, and the cough persisted.

Nilanthi called on Saturday afternoon, and was very excited at the prospect of visiting us again in early February, as she had an open visa for one year. She said she sold the mobiles that Nelune and Christian gave her at a very good price. And Nelune and I subsidised the difference for her ticket.

Ninette called that evening to say that she was very upset, as her niece's husband had died, and she attended the funeral that morning. He was in his early fifties, and was battling cancer for some time. I visited Ninette's niece with her in Mt Martha not so long ago, so I was sorry for the young family.

I made a hot beef curry for Connie next day, and when I arrived there at five o'clock, Elvira and John were still there. They had come at two o'clock, and were doing some things for him. She looked glamorous in a black outfit, and said she came straight from singing in the choir at a citizenship ceremony in Frankston, as it was Australia Day that Sunday. I fed him, and did the usual tasks he wanted, then Con and Cornelia dropped in half an hour later.

Cornelia did not visit him before, and she was upset to see his state now, as he was so weak, that they hoisted him out of bed and into the toilet. It took two people to manage him, and I wondered how Cristobel could brag that she showered him, and put him to bed because the nurses did not do a good job.

Connie could hardly move his fingers now, and he was getting very angry and frustrated, as he could not type properly or use his mobile phone to send text messages. He kept howling at the top of his voice, and swayed from side to side, until one of the nurses looked in to see what was happening. She told me, "It is very frustrating for you and for him to communicate now, but the speech pathologist is going to see him about using pictures to communicate. She will contact you and show you both how to use the picture cards."

I was grieved and heartsick to see him struggling so, and Con kept going on and on, telling him what to do to try and communicate. But it did not help, and Connie kept moaning and howling desolately. They intended to visit me afterwards, but something was wrong with their car, and they left early to check it out.

I drove home feeling depressed and physically sick, and prayed very earnestly that God would release Connie soon; either heal him, or end his sufferings, because it was too traumatic now to watch his frustration and helpless state. The last shreds of human dignity were gone, and the way he howled helplessly like a tormented soul, was too much for me to endure.

A few weeks ago, when I spoke to Esme and Babs, they told me they too prayed for Connie's sufferings to end soon, either way. But Cristobel or Geraldine conveyed that to Connie. And once when Con visited him, he typed, "Some of my family think it's better for me to be dead." Babs, who visited him a couple of times, said he was very unpleasant to her. Esme too mentioned that he just glared at her, and she did not know the reason why.

It was a public holiday next day, on Monday, so I visited Ninette, and had a snack with her. Luigi was still there, after his usual singing exercises, and we chatted a while. It was thirty five degrees, so I came home soon after, and watered the garden in the evening. I watched comedies till late, as it was still too hot to go to bed.

Around eleven o'clock the head nurse, Debbie called, and she sounded very upset, and in tears as she explained what happened earlier on. She apologized for calling me so late, but I said it was alright, as I was not in bed yet. She said, "Another nurse and I went in at eight thirty to dress Conrad's pressure wound on his back, and Cristobel was still there. So I asked her to leave, because we had to dress his wound. She asked me, 'can I stay and watch?' I said, 'no, it's not appropriate, as you are not the next of kin.' At this, she got very angry and demanded, 'does his wife know about the wound?' I replied, 'of *course* she knows, because we keep his wife informed of everything about him.' Then I asked her once again to leave the room till we finished."

Cristobel stomped off in a huff, and they thought she left for the night. But she returned an hour later, after the nurses switched off the lights and put Connie to bed. Then she stormed past, pushed the nurse aside, and tried to get back into the room. Debbie told her that he was in bed, and should not be disturbed so late. But she shoved the nurse aside, and dashed inside shouting out, "Connie, they are trying to keep us apart!" Debbie then warned her that she was going to call the security guard, if she did not leave quietly.

I asked Debbie how Connie reacted when she stormed in screaming like that, and she replied that he started howling and shouting frantically.

I was just stunned. Was this how she showed love for her brother, not caring a jot if she upset him, and no consideration for his welfare at all. Then Cristobel turned nasty and threatened Debbie, hinting that very soon everything would change here, that it was a "useless home" with a "bad reputation" etc. etc. Debbie said she did not want to lose her job over this incident, and admitted, "It's my fault, as I have been too lenient with Cristobel, allowing her to come any time, and stay as late as she pleased."

Debbie was shaken, and she told me she never encountered such a person or situation in her entire career.

I pacified her, and asked her if she made a report, and whether the other nurse witnessed it. And she replied that she and her colleague made incident reports. I said I would meet the manager, and discuss what should be done about Cristobel's unacceptable behaviour, and late visiting hours.

I was so shocked, that I called Nelune, but she was very tired and drowsy, and I felt bad for disturbing her so late. I could hardly sleep that night, as I wondered how Cristobel could behave in such an uncivilized manner with an outsider. Her family was well aware of her erratic behaviour, but this came as a total surprise, and Debbie said she strongly suspected she had been drinking. And then I understood, as that would account for such offensive behaviour.

It was scorching next day, and soared up to thirty nine degrees, with the extreme danger of bushfires, as gusty winds lashed out all day. Christian said he had a new keyboard for Connie's ipad, and would fix it that afternoon, as Connie did not like the previous one he bought. I explained what happened the previous night, so Christian said he would speak to the manager. I called the manager a few times that morning, but he was at meetings, so I told the duty nurse about the incident.

Christian came home around three o'clock, and said he met the manager, and discussed the issue with him. And he was dealing with it through occupational health and safety, as Debbie was on sick leave for some time. He had said they would restrict Cristobel's daily visits, if she continued to upset the staff and Connie.

Del called later, and suggested ways and means to communicate with Connie, as she had experience dealing with similar patients. We talked at length, and I felt better afterwards, as Del was a very positive person.

Connie could not use his mobile to send text messages any longer. I decided to take his phone home, as I did not want anyone to run up huge phone bills.

It was slightly cooler next day, and I visited Connie at five o'clock. I took him dinner and fed him. But he was very troublesome, howling and shouting at every little thing, when I could not understand what he wanted me to do.

I did not say anything, and was very patient, as I knew how frustrated he was without being able to communicate. I stayed a couple of hours, and then noticed that my chair was still not there. But I did not say anything, as he would have got upset. I spoke to Christian about it though, and he said he would call Esme.

The following day, Christian said he spoke to Esme. And she told him that she could not bring the chair back, as Paul refused to put it in his car. I wondered how they took the chair in the first place? Then she told him to ask John to pick it up from her place, but I could not impose on him any further. Christian then replied that he would pick up the chair soon. I thanked him for his trouble, but I was irked with her for causing unwanted hassles.

Chapter 87

It was another sweltering thirty five degrees on Saturday, 1 February, so I was reluctant to drive in such hot weather to meet Liz in Mornington. And she understood when I re-scheduled the date. Then I made dinner for Connie, and drove there in the evening. I noticed that Elvira had put up the holy pictures in his room the previous day. But he did not type anything about their visit.

I woke up with severe muscle pains, and felt exhausted that morning. But I fed him, and I gave him two tablespoons of whisky mixed with iced water before he ate. I asked him, "Did you enjoy the drink?" He wrote, "Not sitting comfortably to enjoy."

Then he pointed to what he had written; he wanted to see the specialist at Monash, that I did not respond to his requests, so he told his siblings to call me, and ask me to take him to the specialist. It made me very angry to read what he typed, as it was just his manipulative behaviour to show his siblings I did not care. I restrained my exasperation, and told him that the specialist was on leave, but I would make an appointment soon. When I spoke to the manager about it, he said I had to accompany Connie in a patient transport ambulance.

Although I was willing to humour him, I told Connie that the specialist in Monash could not do anything more. She had referred him to Prof. Butler, who looked after him now. And he explained several times that there was no cure, but prescribed medication to manage the pain.

He did not listen to me, and was very petulant as usual, and did not type a word of thanks or goodnight when I left. After visiting him, I always came home feeling as if my chest was crushed with pain. I asked myself, why was he so unkind to me even to the bitter end? Did he think he was going to live forever? I was afraid he did not prepare himself spiritually to meet his Maker, as he persisted in being so nasty to me.

Chris Del Piano called, and said he would like to visit Connie, and offered to do any odd jobs at home, if I needed anything done. I thanked him, and said I would let him know.

The temperature soared to thirty nine degrees on Sunday, with no respite over the next few days. I could only hope that we did not have any bushfires in Victoria, like the ones we experienced on "Black Saturday" a few years ago.

Anjo called that evening, to invite me for Ronald's sixty-second birthday. I asked her, "How am I supposed to come to St Alban's on my own?" and she replied, "I invited Shirani and Ranjith too, so you can join them." But Shirani told me they were not going either, as it was such a long way from Woolamai.

It was the first day of term one on 3 February. The weather still sizzled, and peaked at thirty seven degrees. One of my students stopped lessons after three years, which was a pity. But only a very few children continued till grade six, because they had too much to do.

The internet connection was down for a few days, so the Telstra technician arrived at nine o'clock next morning. He told me that the old modem was dead, and replaced it without extra charges, as it was still on warranty. And he assured me that internet would be fine now.

I visited Ninette later that afternoon, and spent some time with her. She was very frail, and not very pleasant, as she complained about constant pain in her spine. I was sorry for her, but could do nothing to relieve her, so I left soon after.

I took Connie's dinner the following evening, and now that he was unable to text anymore, it was slightly less stressful than before. I did not dread the sound of my mobile going "ping" at all times of the night and day, asking me to do this, that, or the other; or his never-ending complaints, and demands to take him out of the home.

I was busy cleaning and cooking over the next few days, and prepared for Nilanthi's visit on Saturday, 8 February. Christian and Athena picked her at the airport, and they arrived at midday. We enjoyed the afternoon, and they left after four o'clock. Nilanthi and I attended evening Mass and lit candles, thanking God for her safe arrival, and for Ammie too, as it was her birthday tomorrow.

When I visited Connie on Sunday, Nilanthi did not accompany me, as she did not want him to get upset, if he saw her again. Every time I visited him now, I could see how quickly he was deteriorating. And I could only watch him sadly, because this was no way for a human being to exist. When I entered the room, the whole place stank of stale urine, and I had to hold my nose. I looked everywhere to see where the smell came from, and found a pair of soiled underpants in the bathroom.

I spoke to the nurse in charge, and told her that it would be best to wash his clothes in the home daily. It was very unhygienic to keep smelly clothes for a couple of days, until I took them home. She agreed with me, and said that the enormous fees I paid the home, included laundry charges as well, so I may as well make use of the facility.

She removed the notice on the cupboard saying that I did his laundry. I told her I labelled all his clothes previously, so they would not have to label them again. It was a relief to sort that out, as Connie was unaware of what was going on now, and could not complain that his clothes were washed in the home.

The chair that the physio ordered was very good and comfortable. When I asked Connie how it was, he wrote, "Very comfy" and I was pleased. It cost $40 a week to hire it, and they wanted a substantial deposit, because it was an expensive chair. The leather was soft and supple, and the chair designed to mould to the body's contours, which was ideal for Connie. He could recline or sleep on it, if he wanted to. The nurse said that sometimes he did not want to be moved onto the bed at nights, as he was quite content to sleep on the soft "Princess chair."

At least I would not hear about the chair "killing" him any more. It was a pity the physio took so long to get it, but he told me that he ordered it a few weeks ago, but they delayed sending it. To be fair, he had tried a few chairs, but Connie found them all uncomfortable, so I was very pleased he could rest easily now.

The days passed quickly, visiting Connie, and teaching at school. I enjoyed having Nilanthi with me, as she was comforting, especially when I came home after visiting Connie. She could see how upset and drained I was, and sympathised with my tribulations.

When I visited him on Wednesday, 12 February, the manager came in to the room, and had a long chat with me in Connie's presence. He said they would do everything to make him comfortable. As it was all about caring for him, and making him happy, irrespective of what his siblings or anyone else wanted.

Then he said, "You may get a call from a lady, who works for the Elder Advocacy. She visits the homes whenever she has to investigate complaints." I asked him, "What sort of complaints?" he replied, "She'll explain everything to you, I just wanted to tell you not to worry if she phones you. I have already spoken to her, and she just wants to touch base with you." I came home wondering what was going on, and who could have complained to the Elder Advocacy, who mostly investigated elder abuse cases.

Next day, Judy, from Elder Advocacy called. And she said, "Nalini, I have received a complaint from Roland, Geraldine, and Cristobel, about Conrad's care at the nursing home, and we're holding a meeting on 18 February, and I'm calling to ask if you would like to be there?"

I was astounded, because I just could not believe what those meddlesome people did to make more trouble. After my initial surprise, I opened up to Judy, about how much they interfered in every possible way. And how they made my life extremely difficult; they turned Connie against Christian and me, besides upsetting him constantly, with promises of a miraculous cure, if he went to their churches.

She listened to me and said, "Unfortunately, these things happen in families when someone falls ill. But my role is to ensure that the sick and elderly are not neglected or abused, and that's the reason I have to meet the manager, and Conrad's siblings, who have complained about the home."

I told her I did not want to face Roland, Geraldine, and Cristobel, because I felt physically ill whenever I saw them, as I found their behaviour absolutely disgusting. I also mentioned about the incident with Cristobel and the nurses recently. And told her that I would ask my son to represent me at the meeting, and she was happy with that.

When I told Christian about it, he too could not believe to what extremes they went to meddle and control Connie. My sisters and friends too found their interference totally objectionable. Why they did not behave normally, and just visit him to comfort him and not upset him, was something I could not understand.

Connie was so used to getting his own way, and he was always unhappy, no matter what. He thought by manipulating everyone, and complaining persistently about the home, I would find another place or take him home, which was his constant request.

Mary dropped in on Saturday afternoon, and Nilanthi and I visited Elvira later. And then we attended evening Mass in Mornington. I took Connie's dinner next day, the 16th, and before feeding him, I broke half the Host, soaked it in water, and gave him Holy Communion. I told him I would visit him again on Wednesday, his birthday, and I would bring him something special for dinner.

He did not type anything, as it was very difficult, now that he did not have arms on the new chair to support him while typing. The physio asked me to buy a television tray that he could keep on his lap, and place the ipad on it, and I said I would bring one on my next visit.

On Tuesday, 18 February, Christian attended the meeting at Baptcare with the manager, physio, chaplain, and his three siblings. When Christian went into Connie's room, Roland was there. And when he read what was written on the ipad, he was really annoyed. Because someone (it was not Connie), had typed, "When I can't make decisions any more, I want my brother Roland and sister Cristobel to do what is necessary." (necessary was misspelt).

Christian had exclaimed, "Dad, that's illegal what is written! You can't do that, as Mum has financial and medical Power of Attorney." Roland frowned at him and demanded, "What do you mean illegal?" Christian did not reply, but he removed a photograph of that message, as he wanted me to see what they were capable of. It was not Connie, as he could not type so many words then. We knew it was either Roland or Cristobel, who were trying to get Power of Attorney for Connie.

Christian told me that the three of them were puffed up with self-importance, as they carried little note books, with their trivial complaints jotted down. First thing they asked was, "Where's his wife, and the doctor? We thought they will be here too." And when they saw Christian, they shut up.

He said it was unbelievable what petty issues they raised. Geraldine's complaint was, "The nurse said my brother lied about not eating, and my brother is not a liar. When I was there once, he went out in his pants and the nurse didn't answer the bell for forty five minutes." Had I been there, I would have told her that anyone with a grain of common sense would have called the nurse, instead of letting her brother sit with wet pants for so long.

Roland's complaints were, "We weren't allowed to take him out for Christmas. Connie says he has enough money in the bank to get a full-time carer for him." The manager replied, "If Conrad has assets, then he would be paying a very high fee here, and he is being cared for 24 hours here, so why would he need a full-time carer in a nursing home? As to taking him out of the home, you can take him by all means, but you are *fully responsible* if he has a fall in the toilet, or chokes to death." And Roland asked, "Can't we take him out, without the responsibility?"

The manager replied, "No, you can't take him out, if you are not prepared to take full responsibility." That shut him up, and Judy said, "Christmas is over now, and that's not an issue here, as it's not a case of neglect or abuse." Then Cristobel piped in, "The nurses don't straighten his t-shirt at nights, and he couldn't sleep with it all bunched up." The manager replied, "We will take note of that."

Christian was surprised when she suddenly turned on him and had a go at him, "How often do you visit your father anyway?" To which, the manager said, "That has no bearing on this meeting, even if Christian visits only once a year. I understand he has been overseas for some time." And so on with several petty complaints, that obviously Connie wrote some time ago, and which they compiled. Food was another issue, as they said it was not pureed well enough for him to swallow.

The manager said that he would make a note of it too, and any other genuine concern. Judy told them at the end that she could not find any evidence of neglect or abuse. And as the manager would address the issues that were raised, there was nothing further to be discussed.

The manager concluded that he did not mind them visiting at reasonable hours, as long as they did not interfere with the nurses' routine and care of Connie. When Judy asked Christian if he had anything to say, he replied, "Mum doesn't want to have any further communication with them, and they are to respect that."

I told him to mention that at the meeting, because I did not want to associate with them at all. Christian said Connie remained vague, and hardly typed anything at all during the entire meeting. It was just an unwanted drama, and to me it was all about power games. They thought they were in control, and just wanted to impress Connie.

Christian said he had a long conversation with the manager afterwards, and he had told him that he would address any genuine issues that were raised. Then Judy walked out with him to the car, and was very understanding and sympathetic, regarding Connie's condition. She asked Christian to convey her best wishes to me.

When he came home to tell me of the outcome, poor Christian was very stressed, and when he showed me the message on Connie's ipad, I just froze. I could not believe Connie wrote those hurtful words. Nilanthi said I turned ashen, and thought I would faint. After Christian left, I phoned the solicitor and made an appointment to see him once again.

The last time I saw him, he drafted a letter to send Connie's siblings, setting out boundaries, and warning them of repercussions if they did not abide by them. After he sent me the draft, he called and told me that in his experience, it was likely that they would show Connie the letter, and he would take it out on me.

He said it appeared that his siblings had no consideration for Connie's feelings or welfare, and would do their best to make matters worse between us. But he told me that if they persisted in trying to take him out of the home to their healing houses, then I could send them the letters anytime I wanted. I thanked him, and said I would consider his advice and hold back, until they forced my hand.

Then I asked him if Connie could change the Power of Attorney by just typing something on his ipad, even though I did not believe he typed those words. Roland had acted suspiciously when Christian read it, and questioned Connie. The solicitor told me that it would be unacceptable in courts. Because independent witnesses, and a qualified medical practitioner, who had to assess Connie's mental state, must be present, before such a message could be proved legal.

I was relieved, but I just could not get over Roland's audacity, to talk about Connie's financial affairs. What did they want to achieve in the end, I wondered. All this legal advice was costly, but at least I knew they could not do anything to take charge of Connie's finances or welfare.

I visited Connie around five o'clock next day, on Wednesday. I took cards that friends and family sent him, and his favourite macaroni and patty curry, and a card from me. It was drizzling slightly, but fairly warm. When I went in to his room, Geraldine was feeding him, and Connie was bare-bodied, with the overhead fan whirring away. She said, "He was feeling too hot, so I took off his t-shirt."

I wanted to tell her, "Don't you know he could catch a chill under the fan? Put his t-shirt back on, as his chest is very weak." But I did not say anything, as the very sight of her repulsed me. The healing CD's were going on and on, and she took a long time to finish, while I sat out on the porch, until she left. She deliberately fed him at this time of day, knowing I was bringing him dinner. I just could not understand why she fed him lunch at five o'clock, completely disregarding his wellbeing. He would be hungry later at night, as this was neither lunch or dinner at this time.

An elderly lady sat on the porch, and she looked very unhappy, so I smiled at her and said, "How are you? Isn't the rain nice, after all the hot weather?" she frowned, and then burst into tears. "I want to jump over that fence and run home! My family put me here! I hate it here!" I did not know what to say, so I sat there silently.

Shortly, a car pulled up, and Cristobel scrambled out carrying a bunch of flowers. She waved and said, "Hi Dolly." I did not reply, but I went back to Connie's room, gave him the cards, put the food in the fridge, and told him, "I will visit you again when you are alone, as you have visitors now, okay?" I wished him, and left quickly.

Debbie spoke to me earlier, and said that when Cristobel saw her, she either ignored her or smirked haughtily, as if she had won a battle over the home. But Debbie tried to smile and be polite to her, as she told me that she was a professional nurse, and would never treat people rudely. I asked her to disregard her completely, and not to get upset over her behaviour.

As I walked along the corridor, Cristobel strutted over and tried to stop me, but I went out to my car. I heard footsteps crunching behind me, "Dolly, Dolly!" But I walked faster, and wondered which part of, "I don't want to have anything to do with you," could she not understand. I wished she would leave me alone, without being such a persistent nuisance. I was relieved when I drove off, as the last thing I wanted was to be in the same room with them.

I was very upset though, because I wanted to spend a quiet evening with Connie on his birthday. It was very spiteful of Geraldine, because she knew I visited him on Wednesday evenings with his dinner. She could have come earlier and left by five. But she told her siblings that if she wanted to visit Connie on Wednesdays, she would do so anytime of the day, whether I liked it or not. I had a splitting headache by the time I arrived home, so I relaxed for a while, and then chatted with Nilanthi.

It was good having her with me, as she was such a comfort. And I was blessed to have Christian, loving sisters, and staunch friends, who supported me in every way, calling and visiting regularly, to make sure I was coping alright. I saw doctor on Friday afternoon, to check my pressure etc. as I had a persistent headache, and I told him about all the stressful issues that still went on. He listened, and gave me sound advice as usual on how to deal with Connie, and other matters.

Mary and Elvira met us at Onde's cafe on Saturday, and we had a pleasant time, and in the evening Nilanthi and I attended Mass at Mornington. We drove to Southland next day, on my birthday, and had yum cha, which Nilanthi really enjoyed. As we walked there later, I met Maree, and we had a nice chat, and she was very sympathetic when I told her about Connie. She said she would pray for us, and hoped all would be well for me.

While Nilanthi was window-shopping, I walked to the fishmonger's and bought the last blue-swimmer crab, as I told Nilanthi I wanted to have crab curry that night. She started laughing when she saw me carrying the crab, because she found it very amusing to see me carrying a solitary crab.

On our way home, we stopped at Ninette's, as she wanted to wish me, and the poor thing was very flustered, as she was trying to wrap a present for me. It was a nice brooch, shaped like a grand piano. After we had coffee with her, and spent some time there, we drove back. I made crab curry for dinner, and Nilanthi enjoyed it very much, so did I.

It was still sweltering, and soared to thirty four degrees next day. We called Nelune to wish her on her birthday on the 25th, then visited Ninette, as she invited us for lunch. Then we drove to Narre Warren later, as Shirani wanted Nilanthi to help her at the restaurant, because Ranjith was away in Sri Lanka for two weeks. We did not stay long though, as Shirani was already packed and ready to drive to Woolamai, and she was impatient to get there before the heavy traffic started. Tigger decided to stay out till midnight, and I could not sleep till he came back. It was a long day, and I dropped off to sleep very soon.

It was milder next day, and in the low twenties, which was a relief, after the heat wave. I felt extremely sad, when I thought of everything Connie wrote and did all these months. But I tried to unwind, and played the piano for a while, and felt a little better afterwards.

When I took his dinner, I found a birthday card for me. He had written in a very shaky scrawl, "Darling Dolla, love with all my heart" I thanked him, and hugged him close. And he giggled when I said, "You remembered my birthday?" It was heart-wrenching to think what a struggle it must have been to scrawl those few words. And I could not imagine how he managed to hold a pen, as his fingers were bent like claws now.

He was quite placid until I finished feeding him, and then he started to get frustrated, because he could not write what he wanted on the ipad. I bought a small cushioned table to keep on his lap, but he could not manage, as his hand kept slipping down. I told him I would look for another table, and left around seven o'clock. When I came home, I called Ninette, Nelune, and Shirani. Then Christian called later, and we had a long chat. He too was distressed to hear how bad Connie was now.

When I went to school next morning, the staff organized morning tea for me, and gave me a lovely bouquet of flowers. I had a pleasant time, and enjoyed the delicious cakes etc.

Christian said he would pick up my chair from Esme's place and drop it off in the evening. Isobel and John were visiting tomorrow morning, so I vacuumed and cleaned up, but when I read her email later, it was the following Friday, and not this week. That was alright though, as I had several things to attend to that day.

Christian arrived at five thirty in the evening, and he carried the chair upstairs where it was before. It was stinking of urine, although Esme told him she cleaned it. I told him to leave it in the bathroom upstairs, as I would have to wash it with some strong detergent to get the stench off, as the smell had penetrated right through the fabric.

He stayed for a while, and then I dropped him at Frankston station, as he left his car here, saying he would take it to the garage next week. It was almost eight thirty when I returned home, and I was very tired.

Tigger stayed out all night once again, and I called him till three in the morning, but the naughty cat did not come home. He sauntered in at eight o'clock next morning, and looked cheekily at me, as if to say, "What's your problem? I can stay out all night if I want to!"

I kept him indoors, and rubbed butter on his paws, and hoped that would keep him busy, and stop him wandering off in the night. Then I spoke to Mary Hancock and Nancy, as they wanted to know about Connie, and how I was coping.

The physio rang to say that Connie was getting very angry and frustrated, as he could not use his ipad any longer when he sat on the new chair, because he could not sit upright. I said I would get a "stable table" and hopefully Connie would find it better. But the reality was, that he just slumped in his chair, unable to sit upright, or use his fingers any longer because he was so weak now.

Chapter 88

Mary dropped in on Saturday afternoon, and left after four o'clock, and I was too tired to visit Connie. But I went for evening Mass, and got Holy Communion to take him next day. Liz, Gerry, Lorraine, and Tony visited on Sunday afternoon, and stayed a couple of hours. I told them I had to take Connie's dinner, so they left around four o'clock. When I saw Connie, he looked very dejected and feeble, and my heart ached to see him like this.

I set up his ipad on the "stable table" I bought, and he typed very slowly, "Bella bringing dinner...." I replied, "You can have it tomorrow. I have brought your dinner now, and I will feed you." He did not make a fuss, ate all the food, and had ice cream for dessert. I always felt depressed whenever I visited him, even for a couple of hours. As I could not bear to see him slumped like a sack, so helpless and miserable.

I went to church with the school children on Ash Wednesday morning, and got some ashes for Connie too. When I spoke to Fr Raj afterwards, he said he took Connie some ashes the day before, and anointed him as well, so I was glad to hear that.

I took his dinner, Holy Communion, and the blessed ashes at four o'clock, but Geraldine was still there feeding him again. She made it a point to feed him late afternoons, knowing I was bringing dinner. After she left, I asked Connie, "Did you forget I was bringing your dinner and Holy Communion today, as it's Ash Wednesday?" He did not look at me or bother typing anything. I fed him the Host soaked in water, and made the sign of the cross on his forehead with the ashes.

I spoke to the manager later, and he said Connie needed extra large t-shirts to make it easier for him, as he could not raise his arms. I said I would bring some on Friday. Then I mentioned that although his siblings knew I visited on certain days, Geraldine persisted in coming on those particular days, and fed him just before dinner time. So he could not eat what I brought him, and she did not let me spend time with him alone. He said, "Send a text and remind them, so they won't visit at the same time."

Isobel, John, and Greg visited on Friday morning, and we had a very pleasant time, but Michelle drove back to the city for another appointment, so I missed seeing her. Isobel was very supportive, when she heard about all the issues I was facing, and she gave me positive advice as always.

Before she left she told me, "Nalini, you know this won't be forever? From what you have told me, I don't think Conrad is going to last much longer. So be brave and patient." After they left, Elvira wanted to come over to practise a new song for the choir, and it was after four o'clock when she left. I made some patties in the evening, as Christian was dropping in next day, and I knew he enjoyed them.

It was almost midday when Christian arrived, and we drove to Woolamai in the afternoon. We did not stay long, and left within the hour, as Shirani was very busy cooking for customers that night, and everyone enjoyed the patties with a cup of tea. On our way home, Nilanthi complained that she was exhausted, after ten days of cooking and was glad to have a rest.

Ranjith returned from Sri Lanka that morning, and although he asked her to stay for a few more days to help out, Nilanthi said she did what she could to help Shirani, and wanted a break. We took it easy when we came home, and Christian cleared up some things in the garage before he left. He fell down a few nights ago while doing some renovations, and bruised his rib cage badly. And was still very sore and uncomfortable, so I hoped he would get better soon.

I drove to Mornington with Nilanthi next day, to get some eye drops from the chemist, as she complained of eye strain. It was a lovely day, and the temperature rose to thirty two degrees, with clear blue skies melting into the sapphire sea. We stopped to admire the view, and when we came back after shopping, I rested a while, before visiting Connie. Nilanthi found it amusing, as she said it was the first time she knew of someone, who needed to rest before visiting a patient.

But she knew it was not easy, because Connie was so demanding, and when I returned home after visiting him, I was physically and emotionally exhausted.

When I arrived there at five o'clock, he was alone for a change, so I fed him and attended to his needs. It was very draining, and depressing to watch him struggling, as he was so frail and could hardly type now. His fingers were almost frozen stiff, and he did not have strength to raise them to the keyboard. I applied voltaren on his shoulders and arms, and massaged his fingers before I left.

It was a public holiday on Monday, Labour Day, and I took it easy, but Elvira visited in the afternoon to practise songs again. We had coffee later, and enjoyed a long chat.

Nilanthi and I visited Ninette next day, and shared a pizza with her before shopping afterwards.

When I visited Connie on Wednesday, he was very weak, and unable to type anything on the ipad anymore. I fed his dinner, and he wanted two serves of ice cream. He just made guttural noises, and frowned at me to make me understand what he wanted. I had to keep asking, "Do you want this, or do you want that?" until he got what he wanted. It was very difficult to watch him getting so feeble now.

On Saturday, 15 March, Con, Cornelia, and Laura came for lunch, and though it was a warm twenty nine degrees, it was very windy. We barbequed the meats, but brought the food indoors, as it was too gusty to sit out. And they left after five thirty in the evening.

When we visited Ninette the following Tuesday, Elvira dropped in and sang a few songs, and then Luigi came later. We did not stay too long, as Nilanthi and I had to do some shopping on our way. Sofia, my neighbour's nine-year old daughter, was starting piano lessons that evening. She was quite keen to learn, and I looked forward to teaching her.

When I visited Connie next evening, and fed his dinner, I was upset to see that he was incapable of typing now. It wrenched my heart to see him looking so desolate, unable to communicate via the ipad now, even though he used it to write only negative comments. And he seldom wrote something kind and positive. I came home with a splitting headache, because it was very traumatic to watch him in that state even for a couple of hours, and he was worse each time I saw him.

After I finished school on Thursday, I drove to Frankston Station, and bought a Myki card to take a train to the city with Nilanthi. She wanted to experience a train journey, and spend a day in the city.

Ninette invited us on Friday evening, as Ornello was singing, and she thought Nilanthi and I would like to hear him. We spent an hour or so enjoying Neapolitan songs, and left around five o'clock, as we wanted to come home soon and watch "Thornbirds" on DVD, that I bought the other day. Nilanthi was keen to watch it, as she just finished reading the book while she was in Woolamai, and was really interested in the story.

Joelle and Celine visited on Saturday, and we enjoyed a pleasant afternoon. They gave Nilanthi hundred dollars to buy food for some poor people in Maharagama, and said they were happy, as they knew Nilanthi would use the money for that purpose.

Cornelia asked me to write a short speech for the "Mother of the groom," as Andrei was getting married soon, and she had to make a speech. I typed a few paragraphs, and read it to her over the phone. When I finished, she was moved to tears, as it was exactly what she wanted to say. I asked her what she liked to tell Andrei, and based the speech on her sentiments.

I was glad she liked the speech, and told her I would post it to her work address, as she did not want Con to know about it. Just a few days before, Con asked me to write a speech for "Father of the groom," so I wrote both their speeches.

Shirani and Ranjith dropped in on Sunday afternoon, and spent a little time with us, as Nilanthi was leaving soon. I finished typing Cornelia's speech and posted it next day. They told me afterwards that everyone congratulated them on their great speeches, but they did not tell each other or anyone else that I wrote them. As long as they were pleased, and the speeches went down well, I was happy for them. We went to church in the evening, then took it easy, and we watched an old movie.

I wished Colleen a safe journey when I saw her on Monday, as she was going overseas for seven weeks. Tess was stopping piano lessons until they returned. I hoped she would resume lessons later, if she was still interested.

I was too weary to visit Ninette next day, as I had to do several things. Then I spent the afternoon cooking curries for lunch on Sunday, and prepared Connie's dinner to take next day.

Liz and Andrew, who was a leader of Bruno's circle of friends, visited on Wednesday afternoon. He talked about Bruno, while playing some reflective music in the background. Andrew wanted Nilanthi to spread the word in her parish, but she said she did not know how the priests would react to this movement. She said she would have to ask them first, even though she was quite impressed with the story of Bruno's life, and his documented healings. Christian dropped in that same afternoon, and cleaned up the garage. He took the exercise bike, as I told him I did not need it anymore.

I visited Connie around four thirty, and found him so frail, that he could hardly sit up. But he ate all the food that I fed him, and he had some ice cream too, which he seemed to relish now. After spending a couple of hours, and settling him for the night, I hugged him, and spoke a few words of comfort and love. I hoped he understood that I wanted him to be at peace with himself and me.

The next day, Nilanthi and I had lunch with Liz at Sofia's restaurant in Frankston, as she wanted to share some of her spiritual experiences with us. We drove to Joelle's place later, and as we turned into her street, I saw Joelle's car just behind us, as she left work early. We enjoyed a pleasant afternoon with them, and came home quite late in the evening, as Nilanthi wanted to have a haircut.

I woke up feeling dizzy, and had a severe headache on Saturday morning, so I invoked Bruno to heal me, as I still had to cook a few more curries. I made cutlets and fried rice in the afternoon, and by late evening, the dizziness subsided. I felt much better on Sunday, so I thanked God, and Bruno for healing me.

Anjo and Mimi arrived around eleven o'clock in the morning, as Anjo lost the way, and it took them three hours to get here from St Alban's. We had a good time though, and they left after three o'clock. Nelune called that night and said she would visit next Thursday.

When I saw Connie the next time, he was weaker than ever, but he ate all the food I fed him without making a fuss. I spent some time attending to his needs, and came home by seven o'clock in the evening, after he was settled in. I made a few more curries for lunch tomorrow, as I did not want to be cooking when Nelune was here.

We picked Nelune at midday in front of the old library in Main Street, Mornington. She came in the airport bus, and was quite pleased with the service, although it took two hours from Tullamarine. It was great to see her again, and Christian dropped in later to spend some time with us.

He attended his friend Izzy's father's funeral that day, and was upset that he died after a short battle with cancer. After Christian left, the three of us spent a quiet evening, and we had an early night, as Nelune was very tired.

We drove to Woolamai next day, and spent some time with Shirani. I ate a few grapes after lunch without washing them first, and by the time we came home, my lips were itchy and swollen. I did not know why, but my lips were numb for a week or so. We took it easy in the evening, and watched a couple of movies with Peter Sellers, and enjoyed a good laugh together.

on Saturday, we decided to watch a movie at Southland, but we did not find one that we liked. So, after enjoying yum cha for lunch, we did some window-shopping, and then came home. That night, we spent a couple of hours once again, laughing at Peter Sellers in the "Pink Panther" series.

We dropped Nelune in Mornington after lunch next day, and the bus arrived around one thirty. After seeing her off, Nilanthi and I went to church and lit candles, and we met Fr Kevin in the hall. Sr Gen celebrated her 80th birthday that day. So we

907

joined the crowd, and had tea and cakes in the hall, then chatted to the parishioners, and I wished Sr Gen all the best.

Nelune called around seven thirty that night, to say she arrived home safely. But the airport bus took even longer on the return journey, as it went on a circuitous route to pick up other passengers. She was not impressed, and did not think she would travel on that bus again.

It was Elvira's birthday on Monday, the 5th, so we met Mary and Elvira for lunch at Onde's, and enjoyed a pleasant afternoon. Gerry kept us amused with his jokes, and travel anecdotes. Then we did some shopping at Mornington Central before we returned home.

Ninette invited us for lunch on Tuesday, and Liliana came too. We drove to Patterson Lakes later, as Ninette wanted to buy a frame for a photograph. Luigi came around just as we were leaving, to wish Nilanthi goodbye. He gave her a boomerang, and said, "Hope you come back again soon."

Although I had a headache, and was still feeling slightly dizzy, I visited Connie next day, on Wednesday. The speech therapist called earlier, and asked me to meet her at four o'clock, so I went there a little early. As I climbed up the steps, I saw an elderly couple coming out of the home. I was surprised when the lady said, "You must be Dolly!" I recognized Liz and Peter Jones then, but thought they looked much older than the last time I saw them several years ago. I said, "Liz and Peter? How nice of you to visit Conrad!"

I could not talk long, as I had an appointment, but they said they left a note for me with the nurse with their mobile number. And asked me to contact them anytime if I needed anything. One of Connie's previous colleagues told Peter about him, and that he was in Baptcare nursing home. When I saw Connie later, he looked slightly better, and seemed a little more alert, when I mentioned that I saw Liz and Peter.

Peter was completely bald now, and Liz told me she showed Connie a photograph of him when he had hair, as she thought Connie did not recognize him. When the nurse gave me their note, I told her that they were very old acquaintances, whom we had not seen for about twenty years or so, and they came all the way from Chirnside Park to visit Connie. He was listening to me, and I asked him, "That's where they live isn't it?" But he could not even lift his thumb to say "yes" any more.

The speech therapist then showed me a picture book with a window, and told me how to use it to communicate with Connie. She said she would show it to his siblings too. After she left, I explained to Connie how it worked, and he seemed to be listening. I pointed to the words, and then to the window that said "yes" and I told him to look at the window if he wanted to say "yes."

His eyes moved to that window, and it was some small consolation to know that he would be able to communicate slightly with this method. It had pictures of food, toilet etc. and "yes" and "no" in the windows. It was an arduous and frustrating means of communicating, but anything was better for him than the heartbreaking silence he was locked in.

It poured non-stop the following day, so we cancelled our plans to take a train to the city. Nilanthi did not want to get wet and catch a cold, as she was due to return home soon. I called Cynthia, and Liz and Peter Jones, to thank them for visiting. Peter was sympathetic, and offered his help, if I needed anything.

Christian said he would drop in to pick up his jeans that I hemmed, but he could not make it, as it became too late that evening. It continued to rain incessantly all day and night, so we could hardly step outside.

Elvira invited us for lunch on Friday, and Mary came too. We had a nice time, and when John came later, he gave us some walnuts and prickly pears from his garden. We drove to Karingal later, and I bought the full set of the BBC series, "Pride And Prejudice" that I knew Nilanthi would like. I did not realize it was over five hours long. But we enjoyed it so much, especially Nilanthi, who had not seen the series before, that we stayed up till one o'clock in the morning and watched the entire series.

Shirani and Ranjith visited on Sunday to wish Nilanthi goodbye, but they did not stay long, as they had something else to attend to. I still felt dizzy when I woke up, but it could not be helped, and I just had to endure it. Nilanthi wanted to stay home on Monday, and call her friends to wish them goodbye, so I drove to Bentons Square in the afternoon to do some shopping.

I met Alan and Ginny, who were having coffee there. They inquired after Connie, and said they would visit me soon. Karen's husband, Stuart, happened to be there too, and I told him I was unable to attend Karen's book launch in Hawthorn, but to save a signed copy for me. He said he would let Karen know. But they were travelling to Italy, soon after the book launch, so he did not know when she would be able to catch up with me.

Nilanthi and I spent a quiet evening, and I told her I would miss her company very much. She was such a great help and comfort over the last few weeks especially; always ready to listen, pour cups of tea, and sympathise, when I came home after visiting Connie. Only she witnessed the trauma I went through with him, and my grief at seeing him getting weaker all the time. I was very grateful, and appreciated those times spent with her.

On Tuesday, 15 April, Nilanthi woke up early, and was packed up and ready to go, as she did not want to delay going to the airport. And although I kept telling her she had plenty of time and not to panic, she was a bundle of nerves. I was sad to see her leave, but she had to return some time, as she had her own life to live.

We had breakfast and waited for Christian, who arrived at twelve thirty. He had a quick snack, and they left by one o'clock. Nilanthi was a nervous wreck, thinking they would be too late, in spite of us reassuring her that they had plenty of time to get to Tullamarine. I noticed with each visit now, Nilanthi became more anxious and nervous.

After the first few days of shopping, and requesting me to buy everything on her list for friends, and her family, she was impatient to return home. It seemed as if her trips were becoming more of a shopping expedition now. She did not want to stay a few more extra weeks, even though she knew I would have appreciated her support during this difficult period in my life.

I visited Ninette later that day, to wish her for Easter. One of Luigi's old acquaintances emailed me a letter, which she wanted me to give him. So he dropped in for a little while, and was happy to receive a letter from such an old acquaintance in Perth. It came about after the radio interview on 3AW, as she listened to the interview, and heard about Luigi's whereabouts.

Christian and Nilanthi spoke to me while I was at Ninette's, and said they arrived at the airport at two fifteen, so Nilanthi was relieved, as she kept saying they would be too late. She wanted to be there three hours before the flight, and check in without a problem. Christian helped with her luggage, and to check in, so she was very grateful to him. I wished her again, and then came home after grocery shopping.

It was a glorious sunset that evening, and a total eclipse of the moon was taking place at six twenty five. I watched the skies for some time, but as it was very cloudy, I did not even glimpse the moon. It was a pity, as I looked forward to seeing the eclipse. I called Nelune and Shirani to let them know Nilanthi arrived at the airport in time. It was very quiet that night, and I missed her company. I prayed she would reach home safely.

I thought of re-arranging the television room for some time, and decided to start that evening, just to keep busy. And it was eleven o'clock when I finished. I moved the shelf to the study, although it was very heavy, but I raised it onto a rug and then dragged it slowly. It was easy enough on the tiled floor, but I had to work really hard to drag it on the carpeted areas. I did not want to strain my back or chest, so I applied dencorub before I went to bed.

Nilanthi called at nine o'clock next morning, to say she arrived safely and enjoyed a good flight. I was relieved to hear that, and we had a quick chat.

I trimmed and pruned the lavender hedges and shrubs in the backyard later. I wanted to attend to all these chores around the house and garden, and was determined to get them done soon.

After a brief rest, I visited Connie at four thirty, but he was not in his room. I looked around, and the nurse said they wheeled him out to the lounge area, where he now sat looking around at the other inmates.

When he saw me, he smiled slightly (for the first time in all these months), and tears trickled down his cheeks. I did not know if he really cried, or he could not control his tears, but I held him close, and said I brought dinner. He did not finish all the food though, but ate two serves of ice cream.

I wheeled him back to the room afterwards, then I soaked the Host in a little water, and gave him Holy Communion, which he swallowed very slowly.

Tears kept rolling down his cheeks all the time. I held his hands, as I did not know what he wanted, and my heart was heavy to see him so feeble. He rolled his eyes around and stared at the ceiling, then he started to howl and looked very distressed. I kept asking him what he wanted, and pointed to various things, then tried to sit him up straight, rubbed his legs, turned on the fan, and dimmed the lights. But he just kept on howling, until I became as distressed as he was, not knowing what he wanted.

He did not stop moaning until I left a few hours later, and I told the nurse I did not know what he wanted, as he would not stop howling. She said she would change him and put him to bed soon, and not to worry, as they would see that he was comfortable.

I was very upset and grieved as I drove back. These visits were draining, as there was nothing I could do to help Connie. I prayed fervently that God would release him from his sufferings soon. After unwinding a little, I spoke to Nelune and Ninette, and it eased my pain slightly, to share my burdens and to be comforted.

I spoke to Nilanthi a few days later, and was glad to hear Tanesh and Petunia were staying with her for a couple of days. At least she had company, and it helped her, as she said she would not miss us so much when she had the children around. I did some chores and drove to Bunnings in Mornington that afternoon, to look for shelves to organize the DVD's, but could not find anything suitable there. So I bought a couple of small DVD organizers at a storage shop in the Home Centre, and then returned home.

It was a beautiful sunset once again, with brilliant red skies. I removed some photographs, and then spent the evening arranging all the DVD's. I let Simba and Tigger out after their dinner and prawns at six o'clock, and when I called them around nine thirty, Simba did not come. I heard a thud near the side of the house, and a scrambling noise. And I thought it was a possum, or a stray cat jumping over the fence. I stayed up calling Simba till three o'clock in the morning, but there was no sign of him.

I had an anxious time fretting about him, and woke up at six o'clock in the morning on Good Friday. I walked up and down the street calling Simba all morning, but to no avail. I felt sick and disconsolate, as I wondered what could have happened to him. Then I drove right up to Forest Drive, parked the car on the side street, and walked around calling him for about one hour, but still no sign of him.

When I came back, I cried helplessly, and prayed to Bruno to bring him home safely. Then I spent all day calling him, walking up and down the street, and went to the reserve three times, but he was nowhere to be seen.

Del called, and I spoke to Ninette, and Nelune in the morning, and they understood how I felt, because I loved Simba, and the other two cats so very much. They were not just pets, but vital, close companions. Nelune called me a few times during the day to find out if he had returned. They told me cats found their way home, and not to worry.

But Simba was such a gentle, docile cat, who did not know how to survive outside. Whenever he saw a bird, he started mewing loudly, so that the bird (given fair warning), swiftly flew away; he was not a skilled hunter, and had no chance of survival in the wild. That was the reason why I grieved when he went missing.

I told myself I must be strong, but my heart was leaden, as I worried and invoked Bruno to help me. Joelle called at six o'clock in the evening, and then Isobel. They told me stories of cats returning home after missing for several days, and I took heart. I was hoarse after calling Simba so long all day, but I trusted Bruno to answer me, and bring him home safely. I had dinner, and around nine o'clock I thought I would go out to the front garden and call him once more. And to my utter relief, I saw him sitting patiently near the front gate, still as a statue. He looked at me inquiringly, as if to ask, "What's all the fuss about?"

He came running up to me when he saw me, and I carried him inside, hugging him, while scolding him at the same time, "You *naughty* cat, where did you go?" I gave thanks to God and Bruno on my knees, before I attended to Simba. He looked exhausted, and disoriented. I fed him a few prawns and gave him some milk, which he lapped up thirstily. And then he just flopped on the kitchen floor, breathing very fast, with tongue hanging out. What adventures he had gone through, I would never know. But oh the relief and joy of seeing my beloved pet home safely, was great indeed. When I called Nelune soon after, she was very pleased for me, and glad that Simba was safe.

Chapter 89

I had a good night's sleep and was delighted that Simba was alright, as he did not have any scratches or injuries. He still looked disoriented the following day, so I kept him indoors. Then I spent some time composing songs and melodies for the stage play "Catsville" and enjoyed a few hours of creativity. I called some of my friends later, and then spoke briefly to Nilanthi, who was settling down after her trip. And she was happy that she took so many presents for her friends and neighbours.

I finished pruning and tidying up the garden in the afternoon, and ended up with a sore back, but I was glad when it was all done. Cornelia, Nancy, and Ninette called later, and they were happy to hear Simba came back safely, as they all knew how much I loved my cats. And I would be devastated if I lost one of them.

When he recovered his strength by evening, Simba wanted to run off again! So I took him out walking on a leash, and then locked him in the cat cage for a while until he settled down. That night, I watched "The Bible," on DVD till late.

I woke up early next day, Easter Sunday, then called Nelune and Shirani to wish them. I attended morning Mass at Mornington, where I met Elvira and other friends. My neighbours, Angela and Elio were there too, and I spoke to her mother, Maria, and his mother, Christina.

Christina chatted to me in the car park for some time, and told me how her husband died ten years ago when he was only sixty eight years old, because Frankston Hospital gave him the wrong drugs. She still cried when she told me about it, and I told her I was very sorry to hear her story. She invited me to visit her sometime and gave me her address, and I said I would try to drop in soon.

I came home and had lunch, before visiting Ninette in the afternoon, as she told me she would be alone, and wanted to see me. When I went there though, she was fast asleep on the couch, and was very petulant when she opened the door. She behaved strangely too, because when she served some biscuits, and I helped myself to one more, she said, "Be careful not to eat too many sweets, as you'll put on weight slowly."

I was embarrassed and surprised, and did not want to eat the biscuit anyway. I was just being sociable, and wanted her to know I enjoyed her home-made biscuits. Now I wished I had stayed home, and spent a quiet afternoon, as she was still in a crabby mood when I left her. I did not know why she behaved like that sometimes, and thought it must be old age.

I walked Simba on his leash later, and watched the rest of "The Bible," till almost midnight. I would have enjoyed it, if not for the extreme violence and gory scenes, as it was well filmed. And that was the first Easter Sunday I spent alone, after so many years.

I woke up to a turbulent day on Monday, and the stormy weather continued all day with gusty, destructive winds getting stronger towards evening. I did not want to drive that day, so I did chores, and spent a relaxing time afterwards.

Daham called to wish me, and said that Misaka and Rathna were acting in a Sinhala drama, and whether I wanted to see it. I told him I would have liked to, if possible, but it depended where the venue was, as I did not like driving too far in the night. He said he would keep me posted.

When I spoke to Shirani later, we discussed some of the issues she was facing with Suresh. I felt very sad for her, as it was not easy taking care of a patient with mental issues. It was tragic to watch Suresh wasting his life away, and not motivated to get ahead. And I thought it was definitely some divine power that gave Shirani courage and patience to deal with some really confronting moments with him. It helped when we shared our burdens, and encouraged each other with mutual love and support.

When I called Ninette that evening, I told her I would not be able to visit her on Friday, as I was having friends for tea. I was taken aback when she said, "Tell your friends to leave by four, so you can visit me." I replied that I could not promise, but I would try. I was not too keen to visit her so soon, just in case she was in a crotchety mood again. Then I made beef curry, and mint sambal for dinner, as I thought Christian and Athena would visit. It was wet and windy next day too, and I waited for Christian till late afternoon, but he came at five o'clock in the evening, as traffic was heavy, and he was delayed on the freeway.

We started cleaning up straightaway, and he did an amazing job tidying up the television room and re-organizing the DVD shelves. He bought a smaller shelf unit that looked much better, and I arranged most of the DVD's on that. We did not stop for dinner till nine o'clock, and then continued again till eleven. But he did all the hard work, and loaded the old stuff into his car to drop off at charity shops. It was very late when he left, and I went to bed soon after.

I called Joelle, and some other friends on Wednesday, the 23rd, and then spoke to Ninette, as she left two messages. She said the musical get-together with her friends was on Saturday afternoon, and invited me for coffee. I said I would come for a short time. I visited Connie around four thirty that day, and found him in the general lounge room again.

He looked gaunt and miserable, with his mouth drooping to a side. I wondered if he had suffered a mini stroke, so I spoke to the nurse later, and she said she would mention it to doctor. I told him I did not bring dinner, because he did not eat the meals I brought over the last two weeks. The nurse said he ate all the food there, and took his medication without a fuss these last few days.

If only his siblings had not meddled so much, and allowed him to settle down, he would have been stronger, and eaten the nourishing food that was served daily. After the novelty wore off, it was obviously a chore for them to prepare meals and feed him. Especially, when Esme went away for a few weeks on holiday, and was unable to bring him meals.

I fed him a bowl of soup, pureed fish, vegetables, and later some dessert, then he had one and a half cups of thickened cordial. Had he eaten like that from the start, I was convinced he would not have deteriorated so rapidly, and would have been stronger, without losing so much weight. Cristobel did not visit him for over three weeks, Esme was away on holidays, Paul and Sanit were in Thailand, and Geraldine had gone away too. So Connie was forced to eat the meals they served here.

He was skeletal, and his face looked like a cadaverous mask. When he finished eating, I said, "I'm happy you ate all the food. I love you very much, and hope you are comfortable. Christian and Athena send their love too." Then I hugged him close, and massaged his hands and shoulders before wheeling him back to his room. But there was no response in his face at all, which was devoid of emotion. He did not even look at me, as his head was bent low, and he had difficulty moving his head.

They held Anzac Day celebrations in school next day, as Friday, the actual day, was a public holiday, and I was very busy. Later that morning, one of the nurse's called, to say Connie had another centimetre long pressure sore on his bottom. She said they dressed it, and he was comfortable now, and not to worry as they would keep an eye on the wound to make sure it did not get worse. I thanked her for calling me, and told her that he ate a good dinner the previous evening. And the nurse replied, "He has been eating better now when we feed him."

I kept Simba inside the cat cage that evening, because he was restless, and kept eyeing the fence covertly, hoping to jump over and wander off on another adventure. I watched the movie "Mama Mia," on television, and enjoyed it, as it was very good and quite enjoyable.

Friday, Anzac Day, was a sunny, almost perfect day, with no wind at all. I did some chores, iced the cake that I baked, and waited for my guests. In the meantime, I called Shirani and Nelune to let them know how Connie was doing. Daham and Uma arrived at four thirty, but I had expected them half an hour before, so when I called them, they said they were just around the corner.

They were a nice couple, and Uma was a pleasant young lady. They both loved cats and dogs, so we had fun swapping cat tales, and sharing experiences. But I was sad when Daham told me that his father died of a cardiac arrest eleven years ago, at the age of fifty four.

After they left a couple of hours later, Ninette called, and kept me on the phone for half an hour or more, relating the same stories over and over again. Poor thing, I had to be patient, so I just listened to her, as she wanted to talk about her past, and go over the same old stories. Then she asked me to come around three o'clock tomorrow. I said I would be there, but not to worry about food, as I would come home in time for dinner.

I woke up late next morning, as I stayed up reading till midnight, then drove to Bentons Square in the afternoon for coffee with Mary and Elvira. I invited them, as

Elvira and John were going overseas for a month. It was after two o'clock when I came back, then I fed the cats some prawns (entrée), and drove to Ninette's at four o'clock.

Angelo, Dora, Ornello, Luigi, and Brigida, (Ninette's neighbour), were already there. Ninette looked happy playing the piano, with Angelo and Dora accompanying on piano accordion and ukulele. I enjoyed listening to the haunting Neapolitan melodies, and to Ornello's singing too. But I did not stay for snacks, and left before six o'clock. When I came home, I walked Simba on his leash, and brought him in early, as I did not want him going on a "walkabout" again, but he was not too impressed.

It was a clear, sunny day on Sunday, and I woke up early. After finishing some chores, I played the piano for a while, and then waited for Christian to bring a van to transport the television set to Lorraine's place, because Tony wanted it. But he called at five o'clock to say he could not get his friend's van, and would have to come another time. I told him it was alright, and to organize it whenever it was convenient.

Then I called Ninette to say I enjoyed the musical evening very much. But she was in a cantankerous mood once again, and was difficult to converse with, as she cut me short at every sentence. And nothing that I said seemed to please or interest her.

I pruned a few more shrubs, and cleaned up the garden till late, and watched another spectacular sunset. Then I took it easy in the night, and watched the last episode of "Downton Abbey." I was reluctant to wish the characters farewell, because they were so real, and were like good friends I did not want to leave behind.

It was just thirteen degrees on Monday morning, although it was expected to be a pleasant twenty two degrees. I was very busy at school, as l had a new student as well. But it was tiring to teach a seven-year old, who was not keen to learn piano at all. It was after two o'clock when I left school, then I stopped to buy a large canvas, as I wanted to paint a forest scene for the television room. Elvira came at four o'clock to practise a new song, then I spoke to Shirani and Ninette later.

I stayed in the garden with Simba from six o'clock in the evening till seven thirty. He was still restless, and wanted to jump the fence and investigate the front garden, in the hope of finding a stray cat there.

It was freezing next day, 29 April, and rained heavily. The manager, Michael, called me around eleven thirty in the morning. He said that Connie did not eat or drink anything from the previous night, and was in a very bad way. The doctor was with him at the moment, but Connie was adamant that he did not want to be fed through a tube in his stomach.

When he was able to communicate, he wrote on the ipad, "I don't want to be cut up and a tube inserted into my stomach." And doctor told me that Connie became very angry whenever the subject was brought up. He warned Connie that when he could not swallow anymore, that was the only option.

I discussed this issue with Michael now. And he said that if Connie had stated he did not want to be tube-fed, they could not go against his wishes, and I agreed. He said it would be best for me to come over that afternoon, as he needed to discuss some administration affairs, and they would start giving Connie morphine.

I just started painting that morning, but I dropped everything, and drove there soon. Before I left, I called Christian and Nelune and told them what was happening. Christian said he would come down as soon as possible. I arrived at the home just after one o'clock, and was relieved that none of his siblings were present. It was important to spend these last few moments with Connie, before he slipped into unconsciousness once they administered morphine.

I felt incredibly sad, to think he went down so rapidly, as he weighed less than thirty five kilograms now. And when I saw him lying in bed looking so gaunt and feeble, I found it very hard to bear. I would not have liked any human being to endure what Connie went through. And no matter how nasty he was to me, it was his illness that made him behave the way he did. So it was not difficult for me to understand and forgive him.

His siblings did not give him any peace of mind, or support me in any way to bear this terrible situation. After stirring so much trouble and dissension between us, and hanging around him like vultures, they now stayed away, because they could no longer influence him, and upset him with their fanatical notions. Cristobel stopped visiting him for over a month, now that he could not communicate at all. All their efforts to manipulate, control, and get him out of the home had failed, and this was the inevitable end.

My deepest sorrow was that he did not convey any comforting words of peace and love for me, after all our years together. When he could use his fingers, he did not type any positive or loving messages, just negative, hurtful messages right to the end. Now that his end was near, and he was unable to communicate his feelings, I wondered, if at last he was resigned to his fate.

When I saw him, his mouth was open and drooped to one side. Michael walked in with me and said, "Conrad, your wife is here to see you. Isn't that nice?" His eyes moved towards us, and I held him close. When he left the room, I fed Connie a few teaspoons of a chocolate drink that was on the table, which he managed to swallow very slowly. Michael told me that he did not want even a sip of water.

I wiped his face with a damp towel, then sat beside him, held his hands and tried to comfort him. I prayed aloud, and recited the rosary. And I kept telling him to be brave, and to have faith, because God would take care of him, and not to be afraid, as I would stay by his side.

His eyes were full of fear, and he did not look peaceful at all, as he kept moaning and groaning softly. I spoke to him gently, and thanked him for all his hard work, and for taking care of me and the children. But he looked around in confusion, as if he was disoriented. My heart was heavy when I left a few hours later. Michael wanted to talk to me about the various issues involved, now that Connie was almost at the end of his journey.

I said I would bring the documents he needed on the following day. When I came home, I called the parish secretary at St Francis Xavier's, and asked if Fr Raj could visit Connie and give him the last rites. She said that he already visited him, and anointed him the week before, and on Ash Wednesday too. I was glad to hear that he received the last rites according to the Catholic faith, which Connie stipulated in his will.

When Lilli finished her piano lesson that evening, Sofia was delayed, and turned up at six o'clock. I told her it was too late, as I was worn-out mentally and physically.

But it was disappointing when I called Ninette, and told her about Connie, she was not really concerned. And all she said was, that she was very depressed. I listened to her and tried to pacify her, but she would not be comforted.

The weather was still cold, but sunny next day, on Wednesday, and Ron mowed the lawns in the afternoon. I tried to unwind later, and spent a couple of hours painting, to get my mind off Connie's impending death, then I visited him later. He was heavily sedated, and did not open his eyes, but I kept talking to him, and held his hands as I recited the rosary.

Michael met me when I left his room, and I gave him the required documents to contact the funeral parlour, when the time came. He told me Connie would not last long, the way he looked. And he also said that Roland visited last afternoon just after I left.

He told Roland that he expected his siblings and him, to behave respectfully, and not to make a fuss in Connie's room, if I happened to be there. He had reiterated that it was all about keeping Connie comfortable in his last hours. Roland had replied, "I won't say anything to his wife, I have nothing against her." Then Michael said that it was a matter of waiting now, as they would increase the morphine gradually.

When I returned, I sent Mathew a text, and to other friends too, as they asked me to keep them posted. Then I called Cornelia, and cancelled lunch on the following Saturday, as I did not know what would happen. She understood, and was very upset to hear about Connie. I told Ninette too that I could not visit her next day, as I had to go to the home. Christian and several other friends called, so I was on the phone till late evening.

I was at school on Thursday, 1 May, and then visited Connie around four thirty. Mathew and his colleagues were in the room, and looked very subdued, and I noticed that Steve and Penny were there too. I greeted them, and we spoke in whispers.

When I touched Connie's forehead, it was clammy with sweat, as it was stifling in that small room, with so many people. I wiped his face with a tissue, and moistened his lips with some water. His eyes were closed, but I whispered in his ears that his friends were all around him, but he did not open his eyes.

Just then Geraldine barged in, and screeched in her high-pitched voice, "Hi, *lovely* to see you guys again!" And she grinned at Mathew and company, as if they were her long-time bosom pals. I ignored her, and she did not look at me. But she pushed her way through, fell on her knees by Connie's bed, and shouted, "*Darling, I'm* here!" She fussed and carried on, as if she was in charge and I was an outsider. I found her behaviour ridiculous, as she lacked decorum even at a time like this.

I could not bear to watch her antics, as she tried to impress Mathew and the others. So I walked out to the dining room with Penny, where we had a quiet chat. Penny asked me, "Who is that silly woman?" When I filled her in about all the grief that she and her siblings caused me over the last few months, she could not believe her ears.

Although I waited outside until Geraldine left, she would not budge. I thought that even to the very end, she did not have any consideration to let me spend some time alone with Connie. I did not want to talk to her or ask her to leave, because I knew that soon all this would be over. The best thing was to leave them to heaven, as they would have to answer for their actions one day.

Christian visited Connie later that evening, and told me that he was asleep, and did not wake up, although he spent some time by his bedside. Geraldine and her husband were still there at six o'clock, and she did not give Christian the opportunity to spend time alone with Connie either. She was busy directing staff, and told them she had to be there, to help Connie relax. And she kept playing doleful music on CD's all the time Christian was there. Well, they did not have long to carry on their drama, because when he was gone, they would have to find another victim to brainwash.

That same evening, Christian brought his huge television set home. And I asked Elio, my neighbour, to help him move it to the music room, as it was very large, and too heavy for me to carry it with Christian. Elio spent some time chatting with us before he left. He was upset to hear that Connie was at the end of the road, and offered to help in any way. I thanked him, and said he had enough on his plate, looking after Angela and the kids, and that I had Christian, my sisters, and good friends around to support me.

It was past ten o'clock when Christian left, after setting up the television and doing some other odd jobs around. He took his television set out of storage, as it had a very large screen, and he said I would enjoy watching DVD's on a big screen.

Elvira called earlier, and said that she visited Mary in hospital, who just had a stomach operation, and she was recovering well. I was happy to hear that, and said I would visit Mary soon. Elvira and John were flying to Italy next day, and she was really upset that she could not be there for me when Connie died. She said she would have postponed their trip, had they known his end was so near.

I told her not to worry, but it was ironical that Mary was in hospital, Elvira and John were going to Italy, and even Joelle and her family were in Queensland. But that was the way things happened, and I knew their thoughts and prayers were with me.

Chapter 90

I was very busy on Friday morning, the 2nd, as I had several phone calls and text messages from friends, Shirani, and Nelune. Then I called the funeral director and changed the service to St Francis Xavier's church, Frankston, instead of their private chapel. They charged extra for the upgrade, but I knew it was the right thing to do. I wanted Connie to have a Catholic ceremony in church, and not a brief service in a funeral parlour chapel.

When I called the home later, Michael said that Connie was resting comfortably, and he would call me, if there was any change. Then I drove to Frankston to pay some bills. And when I came home, I had several phone calls once again, as everyone wanted to know how Connie was. Del called that night, and said that Jack was at the end of his journey too, and would not last long. So we comforted each other, and prayed that their end would not be traumatic.

Saturday was a wintry day, and while doing my usual chores, I waited anxiously to hear from the home. I called them a few times during the day, and the nurse said he was very weak, but comfortable, and they increased the morphine once again. It was a strange hollow feeling, waiting to get that phone call anytime, and I hardly slept. I was very restless, and had a premonition that the phone would ring any moment that night.

On Sunday morning, 4 May, a nurse called at six o'clock, and said that Connie died ten minutes ago. I said a prayer for his soul immediately, as it was a merciful release from his torment. But I regretted that I did not have the consolation of hearing his last words. Some dying people, even Heron, asked Nilanthi's forgiveness, and told her that he loved her before he died. But this was my destiny. It was indescribably traumatic for me to watch Connie linger, especially these last few days.

I wished they had eased his suffering quickly, instead of him struggling, and clinging to life for more than five days after the first dose of morphine. The nurse then said, "Some people are in his room. I think it's his brother and sisters, who are already cleaning and packing up his clothes into bags." I just could not believe it. I told her to inform them that his wife and son would attend to his belongings, and to leave his clothes, until his body was removed at least.

It grieved me deeply, because of the lack of respect they showed for the dead, to start packing his things while his body was still lying in the room. Not only did I have to deal with Connie's death, and all the practical matters involved, but this last instance of their interference, was unpardonable. When I hung up the phone, I just could not get over their determination to be in control until the end. I heard that Cristobel packed his clothes in garbage bags, and ordered the assistants around.

How they stormed the home so early in the morning, was a mystery, until I found out that Roland, and his son, Timothy, visited the home at midnight, and spent the night there. Shiranthi was after an operation on her neck, and needed help more than ever. But instead of taking care of her, he left her alone all evening and night, while he and his son hung around the nursing home till dawn.

He wanted to ensure that he was in charge of Connie right to the end, and called Cristobel and Esme with the news, and they rushed there without delay, ahead of Christian and me. Esme sent a text a couple of hours later, "At least he's at peace now." No condolences, not a word to ask how I was, and if she could do anything, that was all. I had more sympathy, love, and understanding from my friends, than from his family.

And his brother, Paul, who was holidaying in Thailand over the last month, sent a text later, "It's the best thing for everyone that Connie is gone." Not one of them asked how I was coping, or offered their sympathy. They were the only two text messages that I received from his siblings and family.

I felt strangely calm and relieved though. I knew I had to get used to the idea he was no longer there, and that life would change for me now. And I felt as if I was holding my breath for a very long time, and was finally able to exhale a sigh of relief mingled with sadness.

I sent text messages to friends, and then called my sisters. The nurse called Christian too. And as I sipped a cup of tea a little later, Christian called to say that he and Athena would go to the home that afternoon, and clean up the room.

Michael, the manager, called to offer his deepest sympathies. He was very comforting, because he knew the trauma I endured, not only with Connie's illness, but with his siblings' interference in every way, right up to his death. He asked me if I could remove Connie's belongings as soon as possible, as they had to clean the room. And he also said that the doctor had been notified, and would arrive sometime in the afternoon to write his report for the coroner. He informed the funeral parlour as well, so everything was under control.

I spent the morning attending to all the practical side of things, then visited Mary at the Bays Hospital in Mornington, and spent an hour with her. She was so surprised and grateful, and could not get over the fact that I visited her, even though Connie died only that morning. I told her there was nothing more for me to do there, as I did not want to visit the home again. I already said goodbye to Connie a few days before he died, and that was enough. Mary was doing fine after the operation, and hoped to go home in another week or so.

When I returned, I called Nilanthi, who started crying when she heard the news. She just could not believe he was gone, and was upset that he died only a couple of weeks after she returned home. And said that she wished she was with me at this time, but I told her I was coping alright, and not to worry. I had not cried yet, as I resigned myself to the inevitable a long time ago. Although I sighed deeply, and my heart felt leaden, the relief that only tears can bring, eluded me.

But no one can imagine the pain and grief I endured, watching Connie suffer, trapped in a helpless body, with only his mind ticking slowly, but erratically. I watched his complete regression into boyhood, and how his siblings instigated and encouraged his negative behaviour towards me. These thoughts swirled endlessly in my mind, as I tried to come to terms with the finality of his death.

Christian and Athena returned from the home around four thirty that afternoon. He said that Athena broke down and cried, when they removed Connie's name tag from the room door. They brought the television, and bar fridge from Connie's room, so everything had been removed from there. Then they helped me to clean and clear up some things at home as well. We talked till late evening, and after they left, some friends called, and asked if they could help in anyway.

I decided it would be best if I went to school next day, as I did not want to stay home, thinking about all that had happened. And also, I had to meet Vicki to book the church for the funeral, which I hoped to organize on Friday, the 9th, depending on Fr Raj's availability.

I called Fr Denis earlier, as I wanted him to hold the service, but he had another funeral on the same day. And he said it would be impossible for him to get down to Frankston in time. He was very sorry about it, but he told me he would pray for me, and for the repose of Connie's soul. He had known us for some time, and he understood all the problems I went through over the last few months.

Vicki arranged the funeral Mass at two o'clock on Friday, the 9th, as I requested. She said Fr Raj would meet me before then to select the readings, and also to get Connie's biography. We made a time for Tuesday, and then Kingston Funerals called, asking if I could meet the director at four o'clock that evening, to discuss arrangements. I agreed and hurried home, but the director, Terry, had already arrived fifteen minutes earlier.

We spent about two hours going through every detail, and he asked if I had a suit for Connie. I said I gave away his suits when he was admitted to the home, because he lost so much weight. But I said Christian would drop off a suit at the funeral parlour next day, so that was settled.

We talked about several other issues, and when I told him about his siblings, he replied he heard many stories about these evangelical zealots, who tried to control sick people. And he said, "Not to worry, because my staff will ensure that no unpleasant 'scenes' mar the service." That was a relief, as I knew how they behaved at their mother's funeral. I felt drained after he left, but I still had to make several phone calls.

When I told Christian about the suit, he said he would get one immediately. He bought a designer label suit, shirt, and tie, and dropped them off at the parlour next day. He was a great source of comfort and support during this time, as he and Athena did their best to help me sort out everything. I spoke to Mathew, and told him not to send flowers, but to send any donations to help research motor neuron disease. He apologized, as he said they already sent flowers to my address. When

Janice called that night, I told her the same, as donations to research would be more beneficial, and she agreed.

I met Fr Raj next day, and he chose the readings, but asked me to select the hymns. I selected all Connie's favourites, and the final hymn, "How Great Thou Art," which he had loved to sing. It was two thirty when we finalised everything. And he asked Vicki to print one hundred copies of the program, (which turned out to be insufficient).

When I saw the podiatrist later, and told her about Connie's death, she was very nice and sympathetic, and we had an interesting chat. But it was very painful when she cut my ingrown toe nail and dressed it. I limped back to the car, and came home directly, as I had many things to attend to. Sofia did not turn up for her piano lesson, as Angela was in hospital again, but Lilli was punctual as usual. Her mother, Jackie, and Lilli, were sad to hear about Connie, and asked if they could help in any way.

Christian arrived around six thirty that evening with a new printer, and a shelf unit from Ikea to arrange the DVD's. I was surprised when he assembled the unit in no time at all, and he worked hard till nine o'clock, then we stopped for dinner. He set up everything perfectly, and we organized the DVD's till about eleven o'clock.

I was concerned when he left, as he looked very tired, and had worked so hard, but he said he did not mind at all. I was happy we finished organizing the room finally, and I went to bed after midnight. I spent time doing practical things, as it was better than dwelling on the past, and regretting circumstances beyond my control.

I visited the home next day, and gave the nursing staff some flowers, and chocolates. Michael was pleased to see me, and thanked me for the small tokens of appreciation. He knew what a difficult task the staff had, and how seldom patients or their families appreciated their dedication. He spoke very pleasantly, and offered his condolences once again, and asked if they could do anything to help.

The pot of artificial lavender from Connie's room now stood on the front desk, and I was pleased to see it there. It was tragic to think of how much he suffered mentally and physically over the last six months. If only he had accepted his illness, and submitted to God's will, he would not have fought so desperately against the inevitable.

I burned with indignation, when I recalled how Geraldine confronted me at the home several times. And when I asked her what guarantee she could give that Connie would be healed in their glory house, she shouted, "I *claim* his healing!" They actually *demanded* miracles from God.

I drove to church afterwards, and gave Fr Raj a donation, then met Vicki, and checked the booklet and hymns, so she could print them in time. Then I dropped in to see Ninette briefly. She told me that Ornello, Luigi, and Jackie were bringing her to the funeral, and Toula, Frank, and Erik, would attend too. I asked her to thank them, as it was very good of them, especially Jackie, who had to drive from Craigieburn.

Once everything was confirmed and finalised on Wednesday evening, I sent text messages to Esme and Shiranthi, regarding funeral details. Then I called Aunty Molly, who sounded vague and confused, and then started to cry about her son, Ian, saying, "He was only twenty-five when he died!" I replied, "Ian was fifty-five Aunty," and she said, "Ah yes, I forgot." But she was unable to attend the funeral, unless someone picked her up. I told her not to worry, and to just pray for Connie's soul.

When I called Valerie later, she was aloof, and did not even offer her sympathy. But said petulantly, "We were *wondering* why it was taking so *long* for the funeral." I replied, "Connie died on Sunday morning, and today is only Wednesday. I had to organize many things, as I was trying to get our previous parish priest to say Mass." But I was very disappointed at her coldness, and thought that strangers were kinder, and more sympathetic than these family members. Then I left a message for Sherone and Cornelia.

I was always very fond of Sherone and Valerie, and their families. And treated them with unfailing love and kindness all through the years. So I could not understand why they were so indifferent now.

I heard that Cristobel denigrated me with her malicious stories, that I visited Connie once a week for ten minutes only, and did not care for him. If Sherone and Valerie did not know who I was, there was nothing much I could do about it. But it was hurtful, when they showed me no sympathy or concern. And though I sent them Christmas cards when Connie was in the home last Christmas, they did not reciprocate.

I was in school till about three o'clock next day, and on my way home, I stopped to get some things for tomorrow's Wake. I baked a few cakes, and iced them, before arranging them on platters. Liz Newland sent a text at seven thirty next morning, asking in which paper was the death notice advertised. I told her to check the Herald Sun, then she said a strike was on, and it was not in the papers. I wondered what I was supposed to do about it.

Nilanthi and Shirani called, and Nelune said she would be coming for the funeral, but could not stay overnight, as she had a medical appointment the next morning. I told her it was quite alright, as it was great that she was coming over for a few hours at least, just to attend the funeral. Then Anjo called to offer any help, and said she would bring a few platters of sandwiches.

Christian and Athena offered to make finger foods and sandwiches too. Vicki and the parish committee provided most of the food, and some of my friends at school made fruit platters. The school staff were very helpful and supportive as well. I was fortunate that I had so much of help and support from all my friends.

Joelle and her family were in Queensland still, and were returning a couple of days after the funeral. But she called me a few times, to let me know they were thinking of me, and had offered a Mass for Connie too. Elvira called all the way from Italy, and left a message to say they would be thinking of me on Friday.

Mary said that Tony, and their neighbour, Mulwina, would attend the funeral, but she was still unable to move comfortably. She was sorry she could not be there, but I told her not to worry, and to get better soon. All my friends called to say they would be present tomorrow. I thanked God for my family, and good friends, and was relieved when everything was organized.

Del called early morning on Friday, 9 May, to wish me well, and I wished her the same, as Jack's funeral was at eleven o'clock that morning. We spoke briefly, and said we would catch up soon. I arrived at the church by one o'clock, and arranged the food platters on the tables in the hall. The committee ladies did a great job with the catering, and three or four ladies were ready to serve tea and coffee. I thanked them profusely, then stood outside to greet my friends.

Christian and Athena arrived soon, then Shirani, Ranjith, and Suresh. Shirani brought a few platters as well. Nelune called just after one o'clock and said that she was still on the train, but not to worry, as she would take a taxi to the church. All my friends, and Connie's workmates came, and more people kept streaming in, until the main body of the church was packed to the last pew.

Shiranthi, and her children, Rebecca, Benjamin, and Timothy, spoke to me for some time. She did not look well at all, and I was sorry to see her so worn-out. Cristobel, Geraldine, and Esme, were nowhere to be seen, but Babs, Jeremy, Christina, and their sons were there. They were very caring, and said they would visit me soon. Babs was very supportive too.

Someone said that Esme just popped in to look at the coffin, and vanished before the service began. I could not help wondering what their problem was, as she and Paul did not attend the funeral, or even offer condolences to Christian, Athena and me.

Nelune arrived at two o'clock, just before the service began, and sat with Shirani, Christian, Athena, and me at the front pew. I noticed that Ninette, her friends, Toula and Frank, were seated just behind me. Even Alan came, but not Ginny, as she was unwell. Tony and Mulwina, and John's brother, Reno, with his wife Betty, were there; Elvira's brother, Silvio, and his son, Tony, came too, and Tony spoke to me before the service. He offered his condolences, as he worked for Woolworths, and had known Connie a long time.

Nancy was very comforting, and spoke to me at length, as she came very early to help me. Liz, Margaret, Claire, Jackie, and Vanessa from school, sat close by. Tracy, Sarah, Merian, and some of my students and their parents were present too. Hemal came, but Rathna was unable to make it, and I was happy to see Misaka, Theji, Daham, and Chris Berman as well. Christina Biernacki gave me a huge bouquet of beautiful roses, which I arranged in the church.

In fact, just about all our mutual friends who could make it, turned up to say farewell to Connie, besides every single contractor who knew him at Woolworths. Mathew, and his colleagues were present, and Connie's previous boss, Bill, and his wife, Sue, came as well, and they spoke to me later. Peter and Liz called the day before, and said they were sorry they could not attend the funeral, and offered their condolences, and asked if I needed any help.

The coffin was covered with a red, velvet cloth, with a beautiful bouquet of red roses on top of it, and the church was decorated with lovely flowers too. Con and Cornelia sat next to us, and Cornelia cried all through the service, as she said she became very emotional at funerals. Linda, and her parents were there, and all the young people who took part in Elvira's play.

I was overwhelmed to see so many of my dear friends there. Meryl, from the Women Writers Society, attended Del's husband's funeral at eleven o'clock, and then rushed to Frankston, to attend Connie's funeral.

Fr Raj performed the service in a very dignified and solemn manner, and the beautiful service was very impressive. Christian delivered the eulogy well, although he became emotional at times, but finished his brief tribute without stumbling. The funeral director, and his helpers carried the coffin and drove to the crematorium afterwards. But we did not follow, as it was a private cremation, and we had to collect the ashes later.

Most of them stayed for the Wake until about four thirty, and I spoke to all my friends. Mary and Peter, who drove all the way from Croydon, Bronwyn and Ian, long-time neighbours from Rowville, Liz, Gerry, Lorraine, and Tony. They were all very caring, and told me that the service and Wake were very well organized. Mathew, his wife, Janine, Bill and Sue, and Ron and Cynthia, all came around, and asked if I needed anything, and to call them anytime. Chris Del Piano, and his wife Kate were there too.

Connie's many acquaintances and colleagues held him in high regard, and they all told me that they had known him for more than thirty years, and how good he was at his job. I was glad to see that they all came to pay their last respects. Babs, Christina, and Jeremy spent some time chatting to us at the Wake, and she too was surprised that her sisters did not turn up.

Geraldine and Clifford however, had arrived almost at the end of the service, and missed the most important parts, so they did not hear the eulogy, or the sermon. Someone saw her skulking at the Wake, where she made an ugly scene with Valerie. But they never offered condolences, when Christian, Athena, and I, stood outside in the church foyer, as Fr Raj instructed us to do. As he wanted people to come up in an orderly manner, and offer condolences after the service.

Shiranthi, Roland, and their children offered condolences, so did Valerie, her girls, Sherone, Glen, and their children. Brian was there too, and Valerie's mother-in-law, Arlene, but Ifti was unable to make it. When Roland came up to me, mumbled condolences and kissed my cheek, I barely acknowledged him. Because I could not pretend to be friends, when he had behaved so badly.

Christian and Athena drove back to the city, as they had their work schedule, and Shirani, Ranjith, and Suresh returned to Woolamai. I dropped Nelune at the station, as she preferred the train journey. Although Anjo, Ronald, and Christian, offered to drop her at the airport, but she did not want to trouble anyone.

I helped the ladies to clean up, and so did some of the others, before I drove Nelune to the station. On the way, she said that she would have liked to have told Connie that she was very grateful for all he did for her, and regretted she was unable to. But I said that I was sure he knew how she felt, and not to have any regrets.

Athena told me later, "I'm very impressed Dolly, because you were so strong and dignified right throughout the afternoon." I did not shed any tears and make a scene. My grief was a private affair, and I hated to make a spectacle of myself, and there was time enough for tears and sadness when I was alone. I drove home after dropping Nelune, and did not stop anywhere.

I was physically and emotionally exhausted. But I felt a sense of relief, now that Connie was finally laid to rest, and I prayed he was at peace. So began another chapter in my life. I mused, that fortunately, I was eased into my single state from the time Connie was admitted to hospital last September. So it did not come as a shock to my system, to realize that I was well and truly on my own now.

Chapter 91

I woke up early next morning to a wet and wintry day, and reviewed yesterday's events, and the last few months of my life. I felt I was tossed in a tsunami of emotions. And I now had to gather my thoughts and life together, and continue living as normally as possible. I always believed that the panacea for all my troubles and sorrows, was to keep busy. And not to feel sorry for myself, or waste time and energy on useless regrets, and think of what "might have been." Everything happened the way it was destined to happen, and no matter how tragic the past was, I still hoped to live the rest of my life to the fullest, and to find peace and contentment.

I called some friends, my sisters, and Ninette. She told me how impressive the service was, and exclaimed, "Con was treated like a Prince!" She wanted to convey how dignified the funeral was. And she liked all the hymns too, as Ornello sang along. Christian said that Athena and he would visit on Sunday, Mother's Day.

I was filled with relief more than ever now, knowing I did not have to witness Connie's suffering any longer. I prayed for his soul constantly, and hoped he was resting in peace at last. I did not dream of him that first night, but afterwards, he was there almost every night; it was always a good dream though, as he was trying to tell me something, and talking about various everyday issues.

I attended Mass at Mornington next day, then stopped at the Centre to get some groceries, and had bacon and eggs for "brunch" when I returned home. Christian and Athena arrived around four o'clock, and dismantled the big old television, so they could load it onto the van, as I told Lorraine they would drop it off that evening.

But even after they removed part of the television, it was still too big and awkward to fit in the van. Christian had to re-assemble it, and I called Lorraine to say they would bring it another day. He said he would hire a trailer in a few day's time, and transport it to Lorraine's. Poor Christian, he did so much for me that evening, and it was quite late when they left after dinner.

It was twenty degrees, and quite sunny when I drove to school on Monday morning. I called Centrelink later and notified them of Connie's death, and to cancel his age pension. Then I dropped in at the church office and collected ten extra booklets Vicki had printed, as Nilanthi, Janice, and Christine, wanted copies of the service.

One of the authors I met through Rathna, invited me for her book launch on the following Saturday. I said I would have liked to attend, but it was quite a distance, and I did not want to drive so far. I read her book, and she asked me to write the introduction, which I did. It was a very good story set in Sri Lanka, and I commended it highly in my introduction, so she was very happy. Mary was still in hospital; I called her and we had a long chat, then I spoke to Nelune, and other friends. It was quite late when I finished dinner, and I had a good sleep that night.

When I visited Ninette on Tuesday, she told me once again that the funeral was very well organized, and, "Con was like a Prince!" She found the Mass inspiring, with all the beautiful hymns. And the solemnity of the memorial service impressed her very much. We chatted for some time, and when I returned home, I attended to my usual chores. Then called the bank to make an appointment on Thursday, as I had to re-organize the loans.

Lilli and Sofia came for their lessons, and Angela and Elio visited that evening. They brought some delicious cakes, and we chatted till about eight o'clock. Christian came soon after, and Elio helped him to load the television onto the trailer. And he left soon, as he had to return the trailer before ten thirty that night. I was weary by the time I settled down and had dinner, but I was glad he took the television to Lorraine's at last, as I wanted to rearrange the living area.

I prepared some short eats and cakes for Joelle, Celine, Micheline, and Noelle on Wednesday. Mary called to say she was going home that afternoon, so I was happy for her. I walked Simba in the front garden on his leash, but I slipped on the grass and landed on my bottom. I did not hurt myself, but was a little shaken.

My visitors arrived in the afternoon, and brought me a lovely bouquet of roses. I received a few bouquets from the staff at school, and some friends too, who did not know about my request regarding flowers. But it did not matter, as they showed how much they cared, and I was grateful.

We enjoyed a pleasant couple of hours, and when they left, I spoke to Ninette for some time. Mary called to say she was glad to be home, but had to rest another three months, until she was fully recovered. I told her to take care, and let me know if she needed a lift or anything else.

The skies were magnificent that evening, with streaks of crimson and orange shining through grey clouds. I spent some time out on the deck, enjoying the spectacular sunset. It was peaceful and relaxing, just gazing at the panorama overhead and the distant blue ocean. I thanked God for all the beauty around me, and especially for the tranquillity in my life now.

Jacinta, one of my friend's at school, gave me a beautiful pink cyclamen when I went to school that week, and Liz left a stunning anthurium plant on my desk. I thanked them profusely for their lovely gifts, as they knew I loved plants and flowers.

I met the bank manager after school and advised him of Connie's death. He gave me some positive advice on how to re-arrange the loans in the best possible way. Christian dropped in while I was away, and left some timber and concrete bags to do the pathways in the backyard. I was sorry I missed him, but he said he would come down soon to finish the work in the garden.

I spent Friday morning writing "Thank you" notes to all the friends who sent flowers, cards, and attended the funeral, especially the ones who came from a long way off. Then I called Nilanthi, and we enjoyed a long chat. I told her not to worry about me, as I had plenty of support from Christian, Athena, Nelune, Shirani, and my good friends.

But she said that she was very sorry she could not be with me, and bemoaned the fact she left just two weeks before Connie's death. Nelune and Christian called later, and I chatted for some time, then had a bowl of soup for dinner. That was three nights in a row, as I did not feel like cooking anything special. The soup was fine (comfort food), and it was a nourishing meal.

I visited Mary on Sunday afternoon, as I did several chores and clearing up on Saturday. She was recovering well, and we had a pleasant afternoon chatting and discussing many issues. When I came home, I decided to make a beef curry for dinner (after days of not cooking), then watched some comedies before going to bed.

It was a warm, twenty two degrees on Monday, and I arrived at school a little late. Colleen, who was overseas for seven weeks, came that day. She stopped to chat when she saw me. But when she asked about Connie, I became emotional, and could not help crying, as I told her about his last few days, and how terrible it was to watch him waste away. She was very kind, and sympathetic, and offered to help in any way she could. While I was still at school, Michael, from Retire invest called to condole, and he too offered his assistance in sorting out financial issues.

I felt a little dejected that evening when I thought of Connie, because last night I dreamed of him. It was the first of umpteen vivid dreams over the next few months. In last night's dream, he was at home and looking for an address, as he said he wanted to thank someone for attending his funeral. He rushed around the house, like he did before his illness, and stubbed his big toe, and it was injured and swollen. So I had to take him to doctor's. It was so vivid, that I wrote it down in detail in the morning.

I attended to some banking after school, and felt drained when I returned home. When I called Shirani, she was very busy, as Misaka was there selecting some songs he wanted to sing at the opening ceremony of her Ashram in June. Nelune, and then Felix, called later, and we chatted for some time.

I met Joelle in Dandenong on Tuesday, 20 May, as I had an appointment with the accountant there. It was around eleven o'clock when I arrived at the tax office, and saw Joanne hobbling on crutches towards me. She said she could not join us for lunch, but would visit me soon. Joelle and I enjoyed a delicious snack and coffee at a Polish cafe nearby. On our way back, we met Bobby and Priantha, who were walking back to the office. We chatted a while, and then I went for my appointment.

After I finished, I stopped at the Sri Lankan shop "Colombo," to buy some spices before returning home. It was torrential that afternoon, so Christian was unable to drive down and work in the garden. I spoke to Nelune and Shirani as usual, before Lilli and Sofia came for their lessons in the evening. After they left, I spent a few hours painting, and immersed myself in a creative vortex, which was relaxing.

I told Ninette that I would visit her after my appointment on Wednesday. And when I saw doctor, he was very sympathetic, and spent a long time advising me on how to cope with my changed circumstances. He said all the blood test results were good, so I was relieved.

When I dropped in at Ninette's, she was busy recording some music, as she wanted to take a few CD's to Anna Maria's place in Mornington tomorrow night. She said that Erik, Luigi, and she were invited for dinner, and was vague and flustered, and not very conversational, so I did not stay long. But I had a cup of coffee with her, before returning home after shopping and banking. Mary left a message, and when I called her, she said she was feeling much better, and wanted to catch up for coffee. Liliana too left a message, offering her condolences. I spoke to her and said I would meet her at Ninette's soon.

I bought a new vacuum cleaner, as the old one lost suction. Then I cleaned and vacuumed my bedroom, as I was getting a new bed and dressing table, as I wanted to brighten up my room. I chose an elegant, white, bedroom-suite, which they were delivering on Friday. Christian took the old bed head away. I was too tired to cook by the time I finished cleaning up, so I had steak and steamed vegetables for dinner.

Ron arrived at midday on Friday to mow the lawns, and left within an hour. He was very thorough though, and weeded the place as well, so the garden looked nice and tidy now. They delivered the suite just after Ron left, but to my dismay, they were all in packing cases. I managed to unpack them, but could not set up the dressing table and mirror, as they were very heavy, so I left it for Christian. Then I spent some time cleaning, and took it easy in the evening.

Saturday was mild and cool, and I spent the day doing household tasks. Then I cut out the quilted fabric, and started sewing a new bedspread in the afternoon. It was difficult, but it was good to keep busy, and I wanted to complete all the projects I put on hold for so long. I made cutlets, and a chicken curry later, as Cornelia and Con were visiting.

I attended Mass in Mornington on Sunday morning, then stopped at the Centre to get some groceries. When I came home, I felt a little down-hearted, so I called a few friends in the afternoon. Del said she was very busy sorting out her affairs now, so we did not talk long. She had to deal with many issues, and faced a challenging time ahead. But she said she would visit soon, once she sorted out Jack's business affairs.

Then I spoke to Judy and Nancy, and I thanked Nancy again for everything she did for me, and for her on-going support. It was good to talk with her, as she was very comforting. It was a pleasant afternoon, and I walked in the garden for some time, then weeded for about half an hour, before replying emails.

Two students were reluctant to come for piano lessons on Monday, as they said they were too busy doing another project. Cheeky little things! I insisted that they did their piano lessons first, so they sulked all through their lessons, but I did not take any notice of their moods.

On my way home after school, I shopped around for a white bedside lamp, and found one that I liked at Harvey Norman's. It was interesting to change old furniture, and erase all the bad memories of Connie's last months at home. I wanted the bedroom especially to look different, from what it was when he was sick and so miserable at home. When we built this new house, we planned to do many things.

But everything was put on hold when he was diagnosed with PSP, and he lost interest in doing anything. I wanted to accomplish those projects as soon as possible now.

When Nilanthi told me that Heron's ex-wife died the previous week, I sent sympathy cards to Penny and Pam, and asked them to convey my condolences to the rest of the family. They called to thank me, and said that their mother was in her early nineties, and suffered from dementia. But that did not make it any easier for them, as they said they would miss her very much.

Ninette told me that she had enjoyed the evening at Anna Maria's place, so I was happy for her, as she sounded better and in good spirits. After months of suspense, the series "Revenge" was nearly at an end, and I could hardly wait to watch the final episode.

It was wet and gusty when I visited Ninette next day, and we had a snack before I helped her sort out some CD's, and then wrote down their titles. She looked very frail, and was depressed as usual, poor thing. Her vision impairment was worse, and she could not read anything now, and depended on someone to help her. It was part of the reason that she was so depressed and irritable, so I tried to be patient with her. I returned home in a couple of hours time, as I expected Christian, and he arrived soon after.

Lilli and Sofia came for lessons on time, and Christian soon assembled the new dressing table and mirror, which was very nice. The room instantly looked brighter now. I was concerned because he looked very tired and pre-occupied. He said he suffered another anaphylactic attack the day before, which always wore him out. I prayed he would not get another attack again. He did not want any dinner, as he was not very hungry. But he ate a few cutlets and left late, after loading packing cases, and old furniture in the van he borrowed.

It was stormy once again, and rained heavily on Wednesday, 28 May. Isobel called to condole, and we had a long conversation. She comforted me, and offered good advice, as she was a very warm-hearted, professional counsellor. And I was very grateful to her. She said they returned from their trip a week earlier, due to John's failing eyesight. Poor John, I was so sorry to hear of his ill-health. We said we would try to meet soon, and I wished them all the best.

I drove to Frankston Power Centre later, and shopped around for a television unit, and they said it would take two weeks to deliver the one I selected. It was torrential when I returned home. Mary left a message again, and when I called her, she said she was very depressed, so I said I would visit her soon. Then I spoke to Nelune for some time, and Ninette, before making pork curry for lunch on Saturday. I cooked progressively now, as I found it less tiring, and the menu was almost complete.

The accountant called me at school next day, and said I had to pay $1700 for Connie's last tax return. That was unexpected, and I thought, *bills, bills* and *more bills!* And there seemed to be no end in sight to all these unexpected expenses. When I came home, I walked in the garden, and all three cats trailed behind me. They loved to play in the garden when I was around to watch them, because they liked to have an audience to enjoy their antics.

It was very cold but sunny on Friday, so I finished my chores and drove to the dentist's in the afternoon. I needed to have two fillings, and although he was expensive, at least I could chew my food without discomfort now. Then I stopped at the council offices in Mornington to pay rates, and notified them of Connie's death.

I walked down Main Street afterwards, as it was very pleasant to stroll in the sunshine, even though it was cold, and I came home feeling refreshed. Then I cleaned, vacuumed, and cooked buriyani rice, before I called Mary and told her I would visit her on Sunday afternoon. I was happy to hear she felt much better now.

I woke up early on Saturday morning, and rushed around getting everything ready for lunch. But Cornelia called to say they got up late, and would be here between one and two o'clock. So I waited, *and* waited, and they finally arrived after three o'clock! As usual, they said they had to go somewhere else on their way to pick up some wines, and brought a dozen bottles for me too. It was a very good chardonnay, and we enjoyed it, but it was after four thirty when we finished lunch.

Cornelia was very tired and wanted to go home by six o'clock, and I was exhausted too. After they left, I took it easy before washing and cleaning up. I felt a little depressed, as they went on and on about Connie not being with us any more, and wallowed in sentimentality, especially Cornelia. Here I was, trying to go ahead now, as it was a new phase in my life, and wished they would realize that too. I was determined not to think about the negative aspects of the last few years. But Cornelia became very emotional, especially after a few glasses of wine, and kept talking about her mother as well, who died one year ago.

Much as I sympathised with her, I was never one to exhibit my emotions in public, so I found it a little too much when she would not change the subject. I wanted to tell her to "live in the moment," because all our regrets and tears will not bring back the dead, and we had to be happy living in the present. After they left, I enjoyed a quiet evening watching an old movie till late.

It was Ascension Sunday next day, and I attended Mass at Mornington. Fr Gerald, the assistant priest, was leaving the parish, as he was transferred to Donvale, and they had a farewell tea afterwards. I stayed for a while and spoke to some of the parishioners, and wished Fr Gerald all the best, then stopped to buy some flowers and visited Mary.

She was feeling better, and happy to see me, but I stayed only for an hour, and came home to unwind. I sewed till late evening, as I wanted to finish the bedspread soon.

It was wintry next day, so I kept the cats indoors, and they were happy and cosy inside. I took rice and curry for Maxine and Claire, because they enjoyed hot curries, and I had enough food left over from Saturday's lunch. When I came home, I felt so cold, that I started shivering for a long time and could not get warm.

I was feverish and came down with a head cold next morning. But I had an appointment with the optometrist at three o'clock, and had to go out in the freezing weather. He said I needed new glasses, and charged me over four hundred dollars. I considered getting a second opinion regarding my cataracts, as he kept saying not to worry, that my eyesight was fine. And he just kept prescribing new glasses, which was very expensive.

On my way home, I stopped at Bentons Square, and sent Shirani flowers through Interflora, to congratulate her on the opening of the Ashram. Joelle sent a text to say that her uncle, who was battling cancer, died that evening. I sent them my sympathies, and called her later.

I was down with a head cold and felt very feverish. So I dosed myself with ginger tea, neurofen, and cold tablets, as I did not want to get any worse. The nights were bad, as I shivered continuously, and was frozen to the marrow all the time, even with the heating on. I called Bupa health insurance next day and joined up, in case of serious illness. Connie opted out of private health cover more than thirty years ago, and because of that, they imposed a life time loading on my premiums.

It was already one month since Connie's death, and I could hardly believe time had passed so quickly. I had no time to indulge in self-pity and regrets, as I had so much to do, and I was thankful that my life was full and rewarding.

When I visited Ninette next day, Luigi was still there, as he just finished his singing exercises. He was in severe pain, and very grumpy, and I felt sorry for him. But he said he did not take any pain killers, because he did not believe in them, and just complained about constant pain. I had to listen to his woes, no matter how cantankerous he was, but it was tiring. Ninette wanted me to walk with her and Fido, and I did not mind, as the sun was just coming out, and I liked walking. It was more enjoyable to be outdoors than in her cramped unit.

Shirani called to thank me for the flowers, and we had a long chat. Suresh was causing her a great deal of anxiety, and now he was determined to fly to Spain on a holiday. She could not stop him, and he went ahead with travel arrangements. We thought it would help, if he had a change of scene, and hoped that he would be alright on his own.

I had a very bad night, due to my head cold and coughed all night, but I went to school next day. I wished Jacinta, and gave her a box of chocolates, as it was her birthday, and gave Frank, a bunch of fresh watercress. Frank was a ninety-year old Austrian gentleman, who came once a week to teach children how to play chess. And he related some very interesting, but atrocious stories of his early days under Nazi rule, and how he escaped the holocaust. Frank was a popular local man, and he visited most of the schools in the area, to teach chess, besides contributing to various charitable causes in the area. He showed me an article about him in the local papers, as he was honoured for his community work, and was invited to Government House in Melbourne for "high tea." During our conversations, he told me that he liked watercress for salads, but could not find it anywhere. So he was happy when I bought him a bunch from Woolworths.

When I came home that afternoon, I fed the cats and went straight to bed for a couple of hours. I called my sisters later that evening, and then spoke to Ninette, as she wanted to know how I was. I made pepper soup for dinner, and then took it easy, as I felt lethargic and feverish.

It was pleasant and sunny on Friday, but I rested till late, as I was up coughing all night, and felt weak and unsteady on my feet. I wished I could get rid of this flu soon, because I did not like being ill, and unable to attend to my usual work.

I spoke to Joelle and Nilanthi later, then called Micheline to wish her for her birthday, but she was out, so Celine had a long chat with me. Then I attended to all the paper work, and signed up with Bupa, but I had a twelve- month waiting period, before I could claim anything. It did not worry me, as I had peace of mind now, and only hoped that I would not get seriously ill in the meantime.

Nelune said that her dear friend, and previous neighbour, Mrs Bradridge, died a few days ago, at the age of ninety-nine and three months, and she had attended her funeral that afternoon. She was a lovely lady, and Nelune was very close to her. We spent some time talking about Mrs Bradridge, and what a beautiful person she was. I tried to comfort Nelune, as she was very sad.

Although I still coughed and felt weak, I felt slightly better by Saturday. And as promised, I visited Ginny and Alan in the afternoon, and took a cake and some flowers for her. But when I saw them, I felt very sorry, as it was obvious they needed help, because of their poor health. Ginny's son, Craig, was just leaving as I arrived.

Alan said he was Ginny's carer, but he had several health issues as well, and being over-weight did not help either. I thanked him for attending Connie's funeral, and for his concern, which I appreciated very much, knowing he had to deal with so many other problems as well.

Ginny was beset with anxiety and depression, and she told me that she could not remember certain things. But I encouraged her to play the keyboard, as she said Craig was helping her to read notes. We chatted for a while, and I left around four o'clock. I said I would keep in touch, and visit them again.

When I returned home, Mary Hancock, Nelune, Christian, and Ninette called. I was over-whelmed with so much love and concern from my family and all my friends, and was very grateful to them. I spent a few hours sewing the bedspread, and was happy to see that it looked very attractive, but I still had to finish it.

I slept in on Sunday, as I was too tired to attend Mass, and the cough was still keeping me awake at nights. When I called Shirani to wish her on her birthday that morning, 8 June, she was busy giving cooking demonstrations. And although I tried a few times in the afternoon, she was still busy.

It was lovely and sunny next day, but I slept in after letting the cats out early. Shirani called later, and we had a long chat. She said that Suresh was still determined to travel, and she was apprehensive, but hoped for the best.

The cough still lingered, but I did not want to take antibiotics. So I made more pepper soup, and after drinking a large bowl of it, I took it easy in the afternoon. I finally finished sewing the bedspread that evening, and was very pleased, as it looked elegant and brightened up my bedroom.

When I visited Ninette next day, she invited me to have a bowl of soup with her, and Luigi dropped in just as I was leaving. I did not stay long, as I had to send Nilanthi's allowance through Western Union. When Nilanthi came last year, Nelune and I told her that we would send her an allowance, so not to worry too much. Nelune deposited her share of the allowance into my account, because it was difficult for her to find time during working hours. And I made sure I sent the money via Western Union.

I cancelled piano lessons that evening, as I felt too tired. Christian dropped in around six thirty in the evening to store a few boxes that he had packed from their house. He had a quick snack before leaving shortly.

I did not go to school on Wednesday, as I was exhausted, and had a dull headache. It was Joelle's uncle's funeral today, so I sent her a text to say that I was thinking of her and the family. She was very close to her uncle, and would miss him very much. When I called Shirani later, she said that Suresh was still very unsettled, and they were trying to find a way to help him. But it was very difficult, as she could not find any support groups around to help cope with him, and help him overcome his problems. I called Anjo and asked her to wish Mimi, as it was her birthday yesterday.

And although I was still unwell and the cough persisted, I went to school next day. But I came home early and rested.

They delivered the TV unit, and nest of tables on the following evening, so I spent some time arranging CD's and DVD's in the new unit. Then I called Nilanthi, who was very excited about her trip to the Holy Land that August. I sent Christian a text to wish him well at his examination, to upgrade his qualifications in TRX and fitness. Ninette left a message to call her, and when I did, I was pleased to hear that her cold was getting better.

After a busy day, I wanted to unwind and watch a DVD that evening. But I accidentally pressed the wrong button, and locked the television, and it kept asking me for a password. I sent Christian a text, but he was driving, and said he would get back to me, and try to tell me how to unlock it. It was very annoying, but I could not do anything about it.

Chris Del Piano and Kate said they would visit, so I waited for them on Saturday afternoon, but they did not turn up.

I was annoyed that the television did not work, and kept invoking Bruno to help me. Then I said a prayer and switched it on, and to my surprise and relief, the television and DVD just came back on! So I was able to watch an old movie that night. When he called me later, Christian was happy that the television worked.

I had a long conversation with Del next day, and she said that she was still very busy sorting out Jack's affairs and paper work, and it would take a long time to finalise everything. But she said she would visit soon.

Then I called Mary, who said she was unwell, and sounded very depressed. I knew she went through bouts of depression, even though she was on medication, so I tried to cheer her up. She was seeing a psychologist, who was very helpful, and after listening to her for some time, I said I would visit her soon. Shirani called later, and said they suffered a traumatic incident with Suresh that day, and she was still distraught. Poor Shirani. They sorted matters out though, and hoped they could find a lasting solution to his problems, as it was draining her. I fervently hoped and prayed he would be healed soon.

Chapter 92

When I spoke to Shirani on Monday, she said that Suresh was admitted to hospital, and would undergo treatment until he improved. It was very upsetting, as he kept phoning Roshan and asking him to take him out of hospital. I was very distressed, and hoped that the medical staff would find a long-term solution.

Ninette left a message, and when I called her, she said that she did not feel too well, and her cold was still not better. Then I listened to her usual complaints, but told her that I could not visit her tomorrow, as I had another appointment. I was weary of her erratic moods, and I felt stressed to visit her now, as she was becoming more cantankerous.

Lilli's mother rang to say that Lilli was down with a cold, so she would not come for her piano lesson. Sofia did not turn up for her lesson either. I sent Angela a text, but I did not hear from her, so I hoped she was alright, and not back in hospital.

Christian called on Wednesday night, and said he would drop in next day to store some of his furniture here.

And when I came home on Thursday afternoon, he had left already, as he had come with a friend to help him. My dining table was in good condition, but Simba chewed the cushion edges, and I was waiting to get rid of the chairs. Christian took the table, as well as the chairs, and left his black dining room suite.

But it did not matter, although the rest of my furniture was walnut brown. I called and thanked him for the dining suite. He stored his lounge-suite in the "den" upstairs, which had been empty. And as they were paying a substantial amount of money for storage, they could save some money now.

I spoke to Julie, and Shirani later that evening, and was sad because Shirani was still very upset about Suresh. We spoke for some time, and discussed various issues. Then Ninette called, and I told her I would try to visit her next week. But she kept me on the phone for a long time.

I cleaned and vacuumed on Friday, and I baked a cake in the afternoon for my visitors on Saturday. Then I removed some photographs of the damp spots in the ceiling in the al fresco area, as Porter Davis asked me to send photographs of the area, before they decided if it was my problem or theirs. My new spectacles were ready, so I went to Frankston to try them on, and they seemed alright, as I could read better with them.

When I returned home, I had a few phone calls till late, then Ninette left a message at eight o'clock, asking me to call her back urgently. When I asked her if she was alright, she said, "I'm very worried about Luigi because he has the flu, and I'm very upset about him." And when I told her, "Don't worry, he'll be alright." She got upset, and retorted, "It's my *nature* to worry, I can't help it!"

I spoke about something else for a while, to make her change the subject, but she persisted in the same manner for a long time, until I said I had to have dinner, as she did not get off the phone. I cooked pasta with kransky sausage for lunch tomorrow, and then took it easy.

Julie and Paul arrived around one o'clock, and said they had lunch already. She brought a delicious orange cake that she baked, so we enjoyed that for afternoon tea. Linda, Leo, and the children, arrived a little later, and Paul and Leo did several odd jobs around the house and garden. We had a pleasant time, and they left after four o'clock. It was a lovely afternoon with no wind or rain, and I rested a while after they left. I phoned Lorraine to ask how she was, as I did not speak to her since Connie's funeral. She sounded vague and distant, and said she had a headache, so we did not talk long. I wondered what was wrong with her, as she was quite unlike her garrulous self. And I felt sad that some of my friends succumbed to the ravages of old age and dementia.

It was a beautiful sunny morning on Sunday, and Mimi called to say she was at Anjo's, and would visit me soon, as she wanted to help me in the garden. She was a delightful lady, so I thanked her, and said I was looking forward to seeing her. I removed some photographs of my "new look" bedroom, with the bedspread I sewed, and sent them to Nilanthi, as she was keen to see how the room looked now.

I visited Mary in the afternoon, and gave her the circulation booster as a present, because she had problems with her feet. And I took some butter cake too. She was very happy with the booster, and they enjoyed the cake. Tony offered to mulch the nature strip, and fix a remote control door bell soon. I called Shirani and Nelune later, as I always enjoyed a good heart to heart talk with my sisters.

Strong, gusty winds ripped through that night, and continued next day too, but much to my relief, the fences were still standing next morning.

When I dropped in at the church office to pay for Connie's memorial plaque, Vicki said that a man was just putting it up. Connie wanted his plaque to be placed next to his parents' plaque, so I was glad when it was done. I went to school later, and finished early as two students were away.

My cough still irritated me, and I felt nauseous when I coughed. So I stopped to get some cough drops and syrup on my way home, and hoped that would help. The cats looked very unhappy, as they could not run out to the garden in such stormy weather, which continued to be blustery and freezing.

When I called Shirani that evening, she sounded better, and not as stressed, for which I was glad. She hoped that Suresh would receive proper treatment now, and improve with the new medication.

The stormy weather continued on Tuesday as well, and gusty winds ripped a native hibiscus from the roots, which I had just planted, and liked so much. One of the trees in the backyard too was blown over to a side, and chairs on the deck were upturned. I looked over, and noticed that the pool fence and large umbrella on the deck next door, had blown over as well. I sent Angela a text message, but they were not at home. She replied that they had seen it, and not to worry, and thanked me for my text.

When I drove to Ninette's that afternoon, an accident on Oliver's Hill forced me to detour and take a circuitous road, which delayed me twenty minutes. Ninette stood on the road waiting for me, as she said she was very worried because of the bad weather.

I did a few small tasks for her, and as I was leaving, Elvira called to say they returned from Italy last afternoon, and I said I was glad they were back safely. I invited them for tea tomorrow, as it was John's birthday today, and I wished him all the best. By the time I came home in time for Lilli's lesson, the wind dropped slightly, but we expected more of the same wild weather over the next few days.

Mary, Tony, Elvira, and John, came for afternoon tea next day, the 25th, and we enjoyed a pleasant time. Elvira gave me a pretty ornament from Italy, and we spent an enjoyable afternoon, chatting away till they left a couple of hours later, as Elvira and John were expecting visitors that evening. Tony said he would install a remote control door bell on the letter box in a day or so. I asked Connie to do that from the time we moved here, but he kept putting it off, saying it was a big job. Tony said it was easy, as he had a similar doorbell. And I was pleased, when a few days later, he installed one at last.

The blustery winds continued all night with no sign of abating, and it was just as turbulent next day. On the last day of term two, I told some of the students that I would not be teaching them next term if they did not practise daily, because they were just wasting my time and their parents' money. I decided to talk to their parents, as I was losing patience when students did not apply themselves and failed to progress.

I drove home through a deluge, after stopping at the supermarket. The windstorm caused enormous damage in Victoria, and once again, I worried that the fences would blow down. And the squally weather did not abate by Friday. I kept the restless cats indoors, as they could not go out at all in such turbulent weather.

Fr Raj called to make an appointment, regarding the memorial service for Connie, and I met him at two o'clock next day to organize readings and prayers. I set the date for 26 July, so that Mary, Tony, Elvira, and John, could be present, including Christian and Athena. Christian agreed to scatter the ashes in the sea, according to Connie's wishes. Then I finalised Connie's credit card payments at the bank, and drove home through torrential wild weather that showed no sign of abating.

The violent storm continued on Saturday, and it was now six days or more since the windstorm began. I prayed fervently that the gale would cease, as the strong winds were so destructive.

Shirani sent a text asking me to wish Suresh for his birthday, as he was home now, which I did. He replied immediately and thanked me. I hoped and prayed he would improve, and make a go of his life soon.

Then I spoke to Nelune, and Nilanthi, who said Tanesh was admitted to hospital with dengue fever, and she was very worried about him. I said I would pray for his quick recovery, and not to be too anxious. She was so upset, as she did not deal too well with sickness.

I finished the painting I was working on for a couple of months now, and hung it in the television room. It was a forest scene, with a rugged pathway over-shadowed by tall trees and leading towards a sun-filled vista. I liked it very much, as it depicted light at the end of shadows and darkness. Although it rained heavily, followed by a hail storm, the winds dropped slightly by late afternoon that day. I breathed a sigh of relief, and thanked God that the fences were still standing.

I took it easy, and read one of my favourite author's, Georgette Heyer's novels for the umpteenth time. Those novels never lost their appeal, although I read them so many times; pure escapism, and I was glad to lose myself in Regency England for a few hours.

The weather eased slightly by Monday, and the winds were not so strong, although it poured steadily all day. I dropped some blankets at the RSPCA charity shop in Main Street, and then went to Centrelink to lodge some forms. They kept me waiting for one and a half hours, and I recalled that coincidentally, on 1 July last year, I was here with Connie, to lodge his application for the age pension. By then he could not speak at all, and I had talked to the officer at the counter, while he just looked on, or scribbled a few words on his notebook. I could not believe how soon one year went, and here I was, dealing with Centrelink again.

The days flew by swiftly, with many things to attend to, and in between, Christian, my sisters, friends, and Ninette called. Ninette though, was becoming very difficult now. One evening, she told me that she was trying to call me several times, but my phone was engaged, so she could not get through. She argued about it for a long time, and was very upset because I did not answer immediately. I did not know how to deal with her at times like these. And I tried to tell her that if my line was busy, not to keep dialling over and over, but to wait a little while and try later. But she did not want to do that either, as she wanted me to answer the phone at once.

I drove down to Rosebud sunspot clinic on 3 July, to check some spots, and was relieved when the doctor said they were not cancerous. He burnt off a few spots and tags on my forehead and underarms, and my skin was stinging for a long time. On my way home, I stopped at Rosebud Plaza to get a reading lamp for my bedside table.

Christian called late that night and said he had an accident. He was riding his bicycle, and had stopped at the traffic lights, when a car knocked him down, and he landed on his back. And although he wore a helmet, he was bruised and badly shaken when he somersaulted. His bicycle and mobile were damaged beyond repair. But I was very relieved to hear that he did not have any broken bones.

The passers-by called an ambulance, and took down the number of the offender's car. I was very concerned, and told him I would come to the city next day, and have lunch with him and Athena. The driver of the car said he would pay for any damages, but it turned out to be a long-drawn process. Christian was not paid any compensation for his expensive bicycle or mobile, as the man did not have adequate insurance.

I drove to the church car park early next day, parked the car there, and told Vicki I would leave it there till late afternoon, and she was fine with that. I was relieved, as I knew my car would be safer there than in the station car park. It was sunny but gusty as I walked to the station, and I had a pleasant journey to the city, which took about an hour.

I felt nostalgic at times, as I looked out the window and glimpsed some of the old suburbs, especially Ormond, where we first rented a flat in Leila Rd. It seemed like another lifetime ago, and how very quickly life flashed by! It was exactly two months since Connie died. And here I was, passing through suburbs where we first started our lives in Melbourne.

I changed trains at Flinders Street Station, and Christian met me at Melbourne Central. Although he looked tired and shaken up, he was never one to complain about aches and pains, and bore up his discomfort stoically. I was glad to see him, and very relieved to see him walking steadily.

The city looked so different now, compared to the times when we walked through the streets in the seventies and eighties. We arrived at their studio, and I was amazed to see the results of his handiwork. Christian renovated the place, with Athena's help sometimes. It was just incredible that he did so much work, and I was very proud of him.

I felt sad because Connie missed seeing how much Christian achieved here, as he would have been very proud and impressed too. He always talked about Christian's perfect workmanship, as evidenced in the pergola, decking, and fences he built at their place in Mt Martha. Athena joined us a little later, and we walked up to a restaurant nearby, "Tea Garden" and had yum cha for lunch.

Christian travelled with me up to Seaford, as he had to pick up his car from a garage there. We had an enjoyable time chatting, and when we passed through Ormond, I showed him the street where we lived in our first flat there. The cinnamon-coloured block of flats was still standing, but showed its age.

Although I was a little tired when I came home, I was happy that I saw Christian and Athena. Ninette left a message as usual, so I called her in the evening, and when I told her about Christian, she was very concerned about him too. Nilanthi left a message as well, and I was relieved to hear that Tanesh was better and back home, which was good news. We chatted for a while, and I told her I took a train to the city to see Christian and Athena. She said that she missed those good times with me.

Strong winds whipped up once again that night, and it rained heavily on the weekend. I could not light the gas log fire heater, so John recommended a plumber to look at it. And he turned up at ten thirty on Saturday morning. John drove up too, just to make sure the plumber would not over-charge me.

But after a cursory look at it, the plumber said he could not fix the problem, and to call the service people, so that was a waste of time.

Although it was freezing and gusty, I spent some time weeding the back yard, and then started painting another landscape, as it helped me to unwind. When I called Mary later, I was glad to hear she was getting better, and would visit me soon.

Ever since Connie was admitted to the home, I sent Shirani a text every morning, to say I was alright, and that was our security system. But I over-slept that Sunday, and at about eleven o'clock in the morning, Shirani called to ask if I was alright, as I failed to send her a text. I apologised for causing her anxiety, but at least we knew that our system worked. Because if she did not hear from me by midday, she called me.

I had a strange dream the night before. Connie's arms were wrapped around me so tight that I could hardly move or breathe, and he said, "You have to start *living*, not in fantasy!" I felt such a heavy burden on my shoulders, that I could not breathe or turn around. It was only a dream I knew, but the actual heaviness weighing me down felt so real, as if some immense force held me down.

After finishing my usual chores, I played the piano, and then baked a cake. I called Nancy in the afternoon, and we had a long chat. And as soon as I hung up, Ninette called me. She was in a very cranky mood, because she demanded, "Why was your phone busy all this time? Do you know I tried to call you for the last thirty minutes, but it was busy, on and on! Why didn't you answer me?" It was pointless telling her that I was talking to someone else, and that she should stop dialling my number for a while, to give me time to finish my call. But she just kept dialling non-stop, and became really frustrated when my line was busy.

Although she tried my patience sorely, I held my tongue, as I thought it was just cranky old age kicking in, and nothing ominous, like dementia. I was weary of her demanding ways, as she was so possessive now. She thought I had to keep the phone lines open all the time, and sit by it to answer her immediately. And she harped about it endlessly, until my head started to spin. I tried to unwind, but was so uptight, because I was forced to curb my tongue for half an hour.

I made about thirty patties later, and all that thumping and kneading pastry, helped to ease stress. I read somewhere, that before vacuum cleaners were invented, Victorian housewives beat the hell out of their carpets and rugs, which was a great way to "de-stress" (apparently). Quite true, I thought, as I looked at the chastised lump of pastry that I flattened so ruthlessly.

The weather improved at last, and it was a beautiful sunny morning next day. When I spoke to Elvira later, she said she was going to Ninette's to cut her hair in the afternoon. Sarah, Mitch, Tracy, and Merian visited in the afternoon, and we had a very pleasant time. I was happy that they enjoyed the cake and patties. Sarah and Mitch were such beautiful, well-adjusted children, that I complimented their parents. Sarah played the piano and sang a little, and it was delightful listening to her. They said they would visit again soon, and left after a couple of hours.

I called Elvira and John later, to ask about the gas plumber, and John said this plumber would be able to fix the problem. We arranged a time and day for him to come over.

I expected Shirani on Tuesday morning, but she called to say she had bookings, and was busy cooking that day. So I visited Ninette in the afternoon, and Liliana was still there waiting for me. She had come at ten o'clock, so it was very good of her to wait so long. We had a pleasant time chatting and laughing, as Liliana was always full of good humour and funny stories.

On my way home, my right eye was sore, and I found it difficult to see the road as both eyes were very blurry. It was hard to drive, and it worried me greatly, so I decided to get a second opinion about the cataracts.

Although it was stormy and poured down non-stop, I drove to Mornington next day to meet the ladies at Biscottini, but Mary was sick, and only Elvira turned up. I bought a pizza and we shared it, and then spent a couple of hours chatting.

When I returned, I called Ninette, and she said she was feeling very down-hearted. So I listened to her complaints, and the same stories for forty minutes. Poor thing, this bad weather did not help. Later in the evening, I made dhal curry, and devilled potatoes for lunch on Friday (progressive cooking again). I had to make two more curries tomorrow, and that was it.

It was wintry and blustery on Thursday morning, and I waited for the gas plumber till ten o'clock. But when he tried to ignite the heater, it would not start, and he said I should get it serviced through the manufacturer's agents. He did not charge me for the ten minutes he was here, because he said he did not work on it. What a waste of time again.

This was getting to be beyond a joke now, as a few plumbers came and went, and did nothing at all. I called the manufacturer in South Australia, and managed to get their contact details in Melbourne. Then I made an appointment with their plumber for next Tuesday morning, and hoped they would fix it soon. When I called Ninette later, I was glad that she sounded a little more cheerful. And later that evening, I cooked cabbage, and Atlantic salmon curries.

Although it was chilly and stormy next day, it did not rain, and Nancy arrived around eleven o'clock in the morning. We enjoyed discussing several issues, and sharing our interests. And just talking about "cabbages and kings," was very pleasant. She liked the curries very much, as she was a vegetarian, and relished the different flavours.

Nancy spoke about a technique she learnt, which was "tapping" on various points in the body, to remove negative thoughts, and we had an interesting "tapping" session. I gave her some bottled cherries in liqueur, and plenty of fresh celery from the garden, which she was pleased to take. And it was almost four thirty in the evening when Nancy left, and said she would visit again soon.

The same stormy weather continued on Saturday, but I went out in the afternoon and consulted the optometrist at Bentons Square. He was very thorough and examined my eyes for half an hour, then gave me a referral to see an eye surgeon in Mornington. He also said that I would need reading glasses, not multi-focals, so I ordered a pair from him.

I called Shirani when I came home, and she said she was okay, but quite busy with the restaurant and dealing with Suresh. We chatted for some time and she said she would visit soon. Then I weeded the garden, and tied up some trees that had to be braced after the wild weather.

I watched "Maleficent" with Angelina Jolie, at Karingal cinema on Sunday morning. It was very good, and I enjoyed it thoroughly. When I came home, I took it easy, as my cough still persisted, and I felt very tired. The treated skin tags and sun spots were still stinging, but most of them had dried up. After I called Nelune, Nilanthi, and a few friends, I prepared lessons for next day.

The first day back at school was demanding, and I had to wait till four thirty till Tess finished her lesson. She still did not practise enough, and made very slow progress, but was keen to plod along at her own pace. I came home straight from school and rested a while.

Another gas plumber turned up at eight o'clock next morning, when he was supposed to come at ten o'clock, so I got ready quickly and let him in. He was a know-all, and started to criticise the installation and the flue outside; everything was done *incorrectly,* he said, and disconnected the electrical unit until it was "fixed properly."

I found his attitude very annoying, but agreed to fix whatever needed to be done. And he said that according to safety and building regulations, the flue should be raised at least another foot, so the smoke would draw better. Then he replaced a small part in the unit and charged an exorbitant amount for it. I spoke to John afterwards, and he said that he would organize the same plumber who installed the unit, to raise the flue, and attend to the other details.

After Lilli and Sofia left, I replied some emails, made a few calls, and left a message for Christian, as he was still not too good after the accident. He suffered post-accident trauma. And he told me that he had recurring nightmares of being thrown off his bike; landing on his face, and then he had no face at all! Poor Christian. I could not imagine how scary it must have been. He was just stationary at the lights, doing the right thing, when that careless driver knocked him down.

I visited Ninette next day, as she wanted to go to Patterson Lakes shopping centre. We were there just twenty minutes, when she said, "I want to go home now Nalini! Too many people, and too crowded here!" She became very nervous and uptight in public places now, and she said it was because she could not see very well. I spent an hour or so with her until she settled down, and then I left.

On my way, I stopped at Karingal cinemas, and bought a ticket for Andre Rieu's live concert in Maastricht that was to be broadcast on 27 July. It was the first time his live concert was to be shown on the big screen, and I looked forward to that gala event very much.

Elvira invited me to dinner on Thursday, as Daphne was there too. She cooked a delicious meal, and we enjoyed it very much. I stayed till about eight o'clock, but I noticed that Elvira was a little uptight and pre-occupied that evening. When I asked her about it next day, she said she had a headache all evening, because Daphne talked non-stop about everything. Daphne was in her mid-eighties and had a very sharp mind. I found her very interesting, intelligent, and witty, and not at all cranky like Ninette. I was surprised that Elvira was irritated with her.

Chapter 93

The plumber arrived early on Friday morning to check the flue, and said he would send me a quote in a few day's time. Then I drove down to the skin clinic at Rosebud that afternoon and had to wait an hour, although I made an appointment. The television was blaring, but I did not pay much attention, except when I heard the tragic news flash that the Malaysian airlines plane, MH17, was shot down.

All two hundred and ninety eight people on board were killed. I was very distressed to hear such dreadful news, and it preyed on my mind all night, and the next few days. The media dwelt constantly on the tragedy, so there was no way of forgetting about it. The sun spots that doctor treated, were stinging badly, and quite painful for a few hours.

Ninette called later that evening, and said she was feeling very depressed after visiting Athelio in a nursing home with Luigi and Ornello. She said the poor man was in a very bad way, and she did not think he would last very long. I was saddened too, as I remembered many pleasant times when we enjoyed some great musical afternoons, when the three Italian tenors performed.

Athelio was never the same, since the last concert in 2003, as he suffered a nervous breakdown soon after. I tried to console Ninette, and told her to remember all those good times. But I knew it was very difficult to come to terms with the closure of each chapter in our lives.

Ninette grieved deeply, because she would never organize any more concerts with the three Italian tenors, now that one of them was at the end of life's journey. I remembered Athelio as a quiet, placid gentleman. And Ninette, who knew him for a very long time, told me he was very kind and generous too, besides being an excellent tailor. She showed me some impeccable suits and jackets he made for her, and I was very impressed.

The rain ceased, and the gusty winds dropped at last on Saturday, so I drove to Bentons Square and picked up my new reading glasses. Then I stopped at Elvira's to give John the heater installation instructions for the plumber. I came home after a coffee, then did some gardening, and planted African daisies on the nature strip. It started to drizzle again, so I had to stop planting and run for cover. I made a vegetable soup, with marrow bone stock later on, and then I took it easy and had an early night.

Around four o'clock in the morning, I woke up with severe cramps in my stomach and felt nauseous, but did not know what upset me. Then I wondered if the marrow bone stock was too rich, because I usually avoided fatty foods.

I sipped ginger tea with lemon several times, and ate a few slices of toast all day, and felt slightly better by evening. Then I spoke to Nilanthi, and Mary for some time. Christian called to say he would pick up Connie's ashes on Tuesday, and I said I would be home that afternoon.

It was very foggy that night, and I could hear ships sounding fog horns out on the bay, as they were unable to navigate into Port Melbourne. The mournful strains continued through most of the night, as the hazy blanket covering the ocean and surrounding areas did not lift at all. I ate a couple of slices of toast for dinner, and then went to bed early, as I felt weak.

When Christian arrived around four thirty on Tuesday afternoon, he brought the box containing the ashes inside the house. But I told him to leave it in his car, as it was a strange feeling, to think that only Connie's ashes returned home. He was so angry with me for not bringing him home, that as a final act of remonstration, he somehow returned home, even though it was only in the form of ashes.

Christian thought I wanted to see his remains, but when I told him my reasons, he took the box to his car immediately. Then we talked about the memorial service and scattering of the ashes. He was a lot better, and after he snacked on a few patties and drank a cup of tea, he drove back to the city. The students came for lessons later, and Ninette called in the evening as usual. When I told her about the ashes, she agreed with me, that she too did not like the idea of keeping anyone's ashes in the house.

John arrived at eight o'clock next day, to remove photographs of the flue for the plumber. I left the gate open, so I did not hear him coming in, and he had left by the time I woke up.

I visited Ninette and took some chicken curry, vegetable soup, cherry liqueur, and bottled cherries. She was pleased, and said that she would have the curry for dinner, because she liked my chicken curry. Luigi and Toula came too, and we had a pleasant afternoon. Then I walked with Ninette and Fido to the shops and back before I came home.

When I was at the bank in Karingal, I saw Chris, my neighbour from Frankston. He told me that he heard of Connie's death only recently, and offered me his condolences. He said that Marilyn too was sorry to hear about it, and would contact me soon. They sold their house, and lived in Karingal now, close to the shopping centre.

It was a wintry, rainy day on Saturday, 26 July, and I drove to St Francis Xavier's church at midday. Elvira and John were just behind me when I parked. Christian and Athena came earlier, but parked on the other side, so I did not see them until they came up to the front entrance of the church. Mary and Tony arrived ten minutes later, and Fr Raj was ready to begin the memorial service.

Christian placed a few ashes in the small silver box I bought. Then he dug a hole in the garden, and placed the box in it, while Fr Raj recited burial prayers. This was in accordance with the Catholic Church's requirements, as Father told me that ashes had to be buried, not scattered, even though Connie requested it. But he agreed for a small portion of ashes to be buried, and the rest to be scattered in the sea.

All those present joined in the prayers, while Christian covered the hole with earth. I gave Fr Raj a generous donation for holding this special service, which was very moving. I was relieved when Connie's remains (at least a small portion), were finally laid to rest. But he wanted his ashes scattered in the ocean, so now we had to fulfil his last request.

It poured non-stop, and a cold, gusty wind ripped through all the time we were near the rocks. John and Tony stood out with Christian, while he clambered onto some rocks, and gently emptied the ashes on the lapping waves. I prayed for Connie's soul to be at peace when his ashes were finally scattered in the sea.

Athena and Christian hurried back to the city, as they had to work, so they could not stay for lunch. But the rest of us went to Sofia's restaurant near the pier, and had a delicious lunch. John sipped a beer in Connie's memory (he said). And he told me later, that he sipped a beer near the rocks whenever he could, and raised a glass to Connie. It was after three o'clock when I came home, but I was glad everything was finally over.

I drove to Karingal the following afternoon to watch Andre Rieu's concert on the big screen, which began at three o'clock. It was his tenth anniversary concert in his home town of Maastricht, and was an unforgettable, fantastic experience. I was transported to a beautiful place, and totally lost in soul- stirring music, until it finished two hours later. And to end a perfect day, I watched a glorious sunset when I came home. The sky turned ruby red till nightfall, and billions of stars studded the dark skies. I never tired of watching this eternal panorama in the brilliant heavens above.

Liz and I lunched at Sofia's on Monday afternoon, and we shared a pizza, then she dropped me at school to finish the rest of my lessons till four thirty. Nelune called that night, and said she had laser treatment for glaucoma, but was alright now. I told her to take care. When I called Shirani later, she said she was still going through a very difficult time with Suresh. I prayed that she would have strength to bear this burden, and was disappointed to hear how little help was available for people with mental issues like Suresh.

As the stormy weather continued, with gusty winds and heavy rain, I could not get through to Nilanthi on the phone that evening. Then I told Ninette that as I had an appointment with the eye specialist, I could not visit next day.

I drove to the specialist's office in Main Street, Mornington for my appointment next day, and Dr Renehan was very thorough. He said that although the cataracts were quite advanced, I could manage for another twelve months. This was because I told him that I just joined private health insurance, and had one year's waiting period. It cost about $2500, without private cover. He advised me not to drive at nights, and said that I would have problems differentiating certain colours, especially blue and black.

I was relieved that I could postpone the cataract surgery for one year at least. When I came home, Christian dropped in for a little while, and had a cup of tea before heading back to the city, as he had to work that evening. I thanked him for all that he did for me, and was very grateful for his love and support.

Lilli and Sofia came for lessons in the evening, and just after they left, strong winds gathered force, and increased all though the night. The windstorm continued over the next few days, with no sign of easing till Saturday. I lost a few more shrubs, and had to drag them down to the back yard. I was sad to see such big shrubs torn from their roots. So I tied up the trees near the side fence, and braced them up as well as I could. But the wind was just too strong, as it was so close to the open seas here.

I watched "Mrs Brown" the movie, on Sunday afternoon at Karingal. It was mildly amusing, which was disappointing, and I did not find it as hilarious as the sitcom episodes. Anyway, it was relaxing, and I came home before it got too dark.

Con and Cornelia were visiting next Saturday, and I was just preparing a few last minute dishes, when he called at eleven o'clock, to say they were running late (as usual), and would arrive around three o'clock. Ninette and Mary called, then Elvira invited me for lunch on Wednesday. I waited all afternoon for my guests, who finally arrived at four o'clock!

I made pan rolls for Mitchell's birthday, and planned to drop them that evening. But I had to call Merian now and ask her to pick them up, because I had guests. Merian came just as they arrived, and she was happy to take the rolls for Mitchell, as he was very fond of them. She did not stay too long however, as she knew I was busy getting lunch ready. We finished lunch more than an hour later, then I heard the door bell. And I was very surprised to see Ivan and Fiona (our neighbours from Frankston), at the front door.

They said they were visiting their friends opposite my house, and wanted to visit me, as they heard about Connie. I invited them for a drink, and they stayed for a while. Ivan said that his father too suffered from the same illness as Connie, and died a couple of years ago. They chatted for some time, and said they would visit again, then left shortly after. But Con and Cornelia stayed till nine o'clock. I was exhausted, so I left the washing up, and rested soon after they left.

Every time I invited Con and Cornelia for lunch, even when Connie was alive, they turned up in the evening, and then stayed till late at night. Although I specifically invited them for *lunch,* they continued turning up at three or four o'clock, as time did not seem to matter at all.

I found it tiring to wait all day, and then entertain them till night. I liked them very much, but I found their lack of consideration irksome now. It was different when Connie was alive, as he talked to Con, and helped me with the chores. But now that I had to cook, entertain, and clean up all by myself, it was too much for me.

I spent next day washing and cleaning up, and then dropped in next door to see Angela and Elio. And I gave them some chicken curry and buriyani rice, which they enjoyed very much. Then I took it easy that evening, and had an early night.

It was curriculum day on Monday, 11 August, so I had a day off, for which I was thankful. Later that day, I was shocked to hear the news that one of my favourite comedians, Robin Williams, committed suicide, and was found hanging in his bedroom. It was such terrible news, and I wondered what could have driven such a talented and successful actor to take his own life.

Christian dropped in the following afternoon, and did some odd jobs around, then checked water and oil levels in my car before he left. That evening, all the channels showed tributes to Robin Williams, and I watched "Mrs Doubtfire" for the umpteenth time, as it still made me laugh.

Mary, Elvira, and I had lunch at Beach Street cafe in Frankston next day, and we enjoyed the afternoon. I dropped in to see Ninette afterwards, but she was in her usual depressed and anxious state of mind, so I had a quick coffee with her and came home soon.

Nilanthi travelled to the Holy Land for ten days with a group of pilgrims, and was due back that day. I missed talking to her all these days, and hoped that she enjoyed her trip, and returned safely, as there was always warfare in the Middle East. She repeatedly told us that her one dream was to see the Holy Land. So Nelune and I helped her realize that dream. She sold some of the items we gave her on her last trip, and Nelune made up the shortfall towards her ticket and expenses.

I sent Nilanthi a text next day, and she replied that she had returned safely, so I called her, and we chatted for about half an hour. She was ecstatic when she described the wonders of the land she had so longed to see. I was very happy that the trip exceeded her expectations. Nilanthi promised to send some souvenirs, as she wanted me to share them with my friends here. Then I called Ninette and Mary to let them know Nilanthi had returned, as they too were concerned about her safety.

It was a perfect day on 15 August, although it was only fifteen degrees. I was glad that the piercing wind had dropped, and spent all afternoon planting cyclamens in the front garden. While I was gardening, Paul de Sielvie sent a text asking me if I had any photographs, items, or letters from his parents. I replied that I did not have anything belonging to his parents. And he answered, "Sorry to bother you, just thought I'd ask." Later, I cleaned up old documents and photo albums, as I wanted to break the shackles of the past and move on. Discarding things I did not want now, was therapeutic.

It was a perfect sunset once again, and I enjoyed watching it till the last rays of the sun vanished over the sea. I called Nilanthi in the night, and we had a long chat, and enjoyed sharing, and laughing over some funny incidents.

I stayed in on Tuesday, and did not visit Ninette as I felt weary. After several years of neglect, I finally sat down with my notes and diaries, and re-commenced work on my autobiography. It was very difficult at first, because recalling some past events was painful. But once I started, I kept on working for a few hours, until my fingers and eyes ached at the end of my task.

I visited Ninette the following day, as she insisted that I drop in, and I had a bowl of soup with her. She wanted me to write some letters afterwards, and to check something on the internet, as she was unsure of a song that was featured in an old movie. I searched on "Google" as soon as I came home, and called her to say that "Stranger In Paradise" sung by Tony Bennet, was from the musical "Kismet," so she was pleased. Sometimes, when she remembered an old movie or a song, she did not rest, until I found out all the relevant information for her.

It was Thathie's birthday on 21 August, so I said a special prayer for the repose of his soul, and remembered all the good times we enjoyed as children. In spite of his failings, he was a very loving father most of his life, until he changed completely after Ammie died.

I was busy at school, and became impatient with some slack students, who did not practise as much as they should. Marg visited at recess, with her son, Rocky, and we had a good time chatting and laughing. When I came home, I rested a while, and then started writing till late.

The next few days were mild and pleasant, with temperatures around nineteen degrees, so spring was definitely here, as early blossoms filled the air with fragrant perfume. It was Stacy's forty-second birthday on the 23rd, and as usual, I felt sad and missed him very much. But I prayed for him, and hoped he was well wherever he was.

I shopped at Frankston Centre next day, and bought four timber bar stools. I had looked for them for some time, and they said they would deliver them next Tuesday. When I came home, I felt drained, and my legs ached. I noticed that I tired very easily now, and did not have as much energy as before. And I had to force myself to accomplish tasks around the house and garden.

Christian visited a few days later, and we had a nice long chat, and he did some odd jobs around before he left. They delivered the bar stools that afternoon, and I was pleased that they looked good. I planned to have lunch with Mary on Wednesday, so I told Ninette I would visit her next week.

Then I picked Mary, and we had lunch at a cafe in Main Street. It was market day, so we spent some time walking along the street and looking at all the stalls, but did not buy anything. I did not mind walking, as it was a lovely sunny day, but after dropping her around four o'clock, I came home feeling worn-out, so I rested a while.

When I finished school on Thursday afternoon, and shopped in Karingal, I noticed a young man smiling and waving at me, as if he knew me. He came over and introduced himself as "Shane," a nursing aide at Baptcare. He was very sorry about Connie, and said, "Conrad touched my heart, as he always greeted me with a big smile, as if he was relieved to see me." I thanked Shane for taking care of Connie, and he said they all enjoyed the delicious chocolates I gave them. I felt sad to think how nice Connie was to everyone else except me, during those last few months.

I wished Christian a Happy Birthday on the 29th, then said a special prayer for his good health and welfare. He was so hard-working and enterprising, that I hoped he would realize all his dreams one day. He was an amazing person in every way, and I was very proud of his achievements. Then I called Nilanthi and told her that Suresh was going to Spain on a holiday, and she too was happy that Shirani would get a break.

Nelune was very busy preparing for the "Lilac Ball" in a week's time, so we chatted briefly, and I wished her success once again. Then I pottered around in the garden for a while, as it was a pleasant sunny day. Ninette asked if I could visit her next day, Saturday, but I told her I was attending a musical at the Arts Centre in Frankston.

I was ready by five thirty next day, and Jacqui picked me up at six o'clock. Lilli and Ruby were in their costumes, and had bizarre make-up on, which made me smile. It was a space-age drama, featuring all the students of Padua school, as every student took part, and it was a huge production. I enjoyed the music and story very much. And later on, I was introduced to Dharshani, the producer, and drama teacher. I congratulated her, and then we chatted to some other people whom I knew.

My neighbours, Angela and Elio were there too, and she offered me a lift home, instead of Jacqui coming back again. I agreed, and we came back after midnight. It was an interesting evening, and I was happy I made it. I slept in late on Sunday, then took it easy.

Shirani called on Tuesday morning, and said that Suresh was travelling on Thursday. We both hoped that he would have a good trip, and enjoy his holiday in Spain. John called later to say that the gas plumber and he were coming around midday to fix the flue outside. I told him I had to go out at twelve o'clock, but I would leave the gates open. Then I drove to Ninette's, but did not stay long, as Luigi dropped in to practise singing.

When I came home, I called John to thank him for fixing the flue, as it looked much better now. He said they were unable to check the carbon monoxide from the heater, as they did not go inside the house, and would do that another time. Then I rested a while before cooking lunch for the staff on Thursday; chicken and dhal curries, and ghee rice.

They enjoyed lunch very much, and said they were famished, when the spicy aromas drifted down the corridors. I called Shirani that afternoon, as they dropped Suresh at the airport at ten thirty last night, and the plane left at two thirty in the morning. She was relieved that he went on a holiday, and waited to hear that he arrived safely in Spain.

Then I spent a few hours working on my manuscript. And it was very harrowing revisiting the previous year's events, and the traumatic time I endured with Connie, and his siblings' interference. But now, it seemed as if it was someone else's story, and I told myself that he could not hurt me anymore. I hoped that time, and distancing myself from those events, would eventually ease the hurt and resentment I felt.

Ron and his partner, Monica, arrived on Friday afternoon to weed and mow lawns. They did a good job, and I was glad to see the garden tidied up. When they finished, I invited them in for a cup of tea and biscuits, and we chatted a while. And later that afternoon, I spread some pine bark around the hydrangeas and pottered around for a little while, as it was such a beautiful sunny day. Christian called in the evening, and we had a good long chat. He was much better, physically and mentally, as the trauma of the accident gradually eased.

Shirani called on Saturday afternoon, 6 September, and said that Suresh sent a text, saying, "See you soon." He was supposed to stay there for six weeks, so she was concerned. We chatted for some time, and I told her not to worry, as he would be alright. Mary and Nelune called later, and Nelune said it rained heavily in Sydney over the last few days, and it was miserable, while we enjoyed some sunny spells in Melbourne.

I called Nilanthi later, and we chatted for over half an hour. She was settling down after her trip, and now talked of seeing us soon. Later that evening, I sprayed the shrubs with oil and vinegar, as some fungus attacked them. Then spent a few hours on my manuscript, as I did every day.

It was another splendid day on Sunday, Father's Day, so I drove down to Bunnings in the afternoon, and bought a pale pink magnolia bush that I planted in the backyard. Christian and Athena called later, and we chatted for a while. It was only twelve months ago, on 7 September, that Connie enjoyed a good time with Chris Berman and Moira, and eaten well after a good shot of whisky.

Time certainly did not stand still. And I told Christian that it was so important to make the most of each day, and never put off anything for tomorrow, because tomorrow, sometimes never comes. I enjoyed the beauty of another breathtaking sunset in the evening, and gave thanks to the Almighty for such splendour.

Monday was warm but gusty, and I finished school early, as Tess did not turn up for her lesson at four o'clock. Margaret asked for volunteers to wash some table cloths and tea towels, so I brought nine table cloths, and a dozen tea towels. She was very grateful, and thanked me for my help. I thought about Connie more than ever that evening, because it was exactly one year ago that he was admitted to hospital after his fall. I was on my own since then, and was accustomed to my new way of life.

Chapter 94

The next day was stormy, and strong winds lashed out fiercely all through the night. I prayed that the fences would not come crashing down once again, as these frequent windstorms wreaked havoc in the land. Mishka was restless from about three o'clock in the morning, and mewed nervously. I woke up then, but did not let the cats out, as it was too wild and blustery. A torrential downpour followed soon after, with a hail storm thrown in for good measure, and then an incessant deluge. I did not blame Christian for not driving down in such turbulent weather.

I was surprised when Lilli arrived at five o'clock though, because the rain eased only slightly. When they were leaving, Jacqui spotted armies of snails crawling all over the flowering cherry trees on the nature strip. She told me coffee powder was a good deterrent, but I sprinkled some salt, and they fell off the trees immediately. I never saw so many snails in one spot before.

The wild stormy weather continued next day, but the rain eased by the time I arrived at Ninette's. I stayed for a couple of hours only, but helped her with some mending, reading the television guide, and writing a couple of letters. When I stopped at Karingal, I saw a small white occasional table that I liked, so I bought it for my bedroom, as it was exactly what I wanted.

I spoke to Nilanthi briefly that evening, before I called Shirani. She said Suresh was staying with a host family in Madrid, but he was unhappy there, and wanted to come home soon. She tried her best to convince him to stay for six weeks, but he was adamant, and wanted to return as soon as possible.

When I took the washed table cloths and tea towels, all ironed and folded neatly to school on Thursday, Margaret was very pleased, and thanked me profusely. But I told her that it was such a small task, and I was glad to help out. I dropped in at Elvira's after school, and came home soon, as I was tired after a busy day.

I was drained, and felt lethargic next day, as if I had fever, and did not know why I tired so easily. In the last twelve months or so, I was susceptible to frequent colds, coughs, and influenza, even though I had the flu vaccine. And my energy levels plummeted easily.

John called and said that the plumber would be here in a couple of hours time. And he accompanied "Ollie" the plumber, who was here before, but he could not fix the heater, as he did not know how to connect it. This was absurd, with so many plumbers coming in and out, and then saying they could not fix it. I gave John six stubbies of beer for all his trouble, and they left soon after.

Isobel called on Saturday morning, and we chatted for some time, and she was very pleased to hear that I was coping alright on my own. Then Mary called and said she felt a great deal better, and was able to get back to her routine. It was Nelune's "Lilac Ball" that night, and I sent her a text wishing her well, and hoped she would raise plenty of money to complete the hospital wing.

I spent a quiet day on Sunday, then called Nilanthi in the afternoon, and we talked for some time. When I spoke to Shirani later, she said that she still had a difficult time with Suresh, as he called her umpteen times a day asking her to get him back immediately. She was under a great deal of pressure, and was in a quandary, as it meant she had to change his date of travel and pay extra. So she tried to convince him to stay there for six weeks.

When I spoke to Nelune on Monday afternoon, she said they raised two million dollars, which was a fantastic effort. I told her that I was very proud of her achievements, and all the hard work that she and her helpers put in for such a worthy cause.

I called "Heat and Cool" plumbers on Tuesday, as they had the required part to finally get the heater working. Christian dropped by in the afternoon, and did a few more odd jobs for me. Then he fixed towel rails in all the bathrooms, as the suction cup rails kept falling down. The ones I bought needed to be screwed in, and he was very handy at doing all these jobs, so I was very grateful to him.

I visited Ninette on Wednesday afternoon, as she asked me to have a bowl of soup with her, that she made with the home-grown celery I gave her. As we finished, Luigi dropped in for practise, so I left shortly afterwards.

I told Nelune I would send Nilanthi's allowance through Western Union on her behalf, so Nelune deposited the money into my account. But when I went to the post office, the computer was down, and the poor lady was on the phone for forty five minutes till they sorted it out. The money transfer went through in the end, although it took so long. I sent Nilanthi a text to let her know she could collect the funds immediately.

When I called Shirani later that evening, she said that Suresh was arriving at five o'clock next morning. I spoke with Nilanthi later, and she was very happy to receive her allowance in time, and said that she planned to do her shopping next day.

I rested a while after school next day, as I was fatigued. Christian called and we had a long chat. I hoped and prayed that he would resolve all his issues soon. I spent a quiet day on Friday, and then spoke to Nilanthi, who said she was very homesick and wanted to see us again.

I asked her to apply for a visa, if she wanted to visit next March, and that I would send her the required documents and a ticket, if I had enough students next year. She was very happy, and then several friends phoned to ask how I was. Elvira called as well, and said that John would drop in when the plumber came, as he thought they took advantage of me, knowing I was on my own.

When I called Shirani on Saturday, the 20th, she said Suresh was back, and was subdued after his overseas experience. He said Spain was not what he expected, and the reality jolted him out of his delusional state. She could only hope that he would settle down now, and I prayed hard too.

I started making Christmas cake in the afternoon, which took some time to prepare, and three hours to bake. It was very hard work, and I was weary at the end of the day. I called Nelune and told her that I still used the electric hand-mixer she gave me for Christmas, in 1974, and she could not believe it still worked.

I took it easy on Sunday, and played the electric piano, as it was great fun playing pop songs with all the various sounds and accompaniments. And it was a change from the classical music I usually played on the upright piano. Then I sat on the deck, and watched another spectacular sunset that evening.

It was perfectly beautiful next day, with no wind, and went up to twenty two degrees. The plumber said he would be here at nine o'clock tomorrow morning. I told him not to come any later than two in the afternoon, as I had another appointment. Then I spent some time applying stain to three outdoor benches, as they had faded in the sun. It was strenuous work, but they looked much better after I finished.

Shiranthi called, and was on the phone for one hour or more, as she had so many issues with her in-laws as usual. She told me that Geraldine and Cristobel did not speak to her or Roland, since Connie's funeral. But Esme was still on good terms with them. I replied that I was very glad and relieved that I had nothing to do with them now, especially when I heard how nasty they were to her.

When I called Ninette later, she was so miserable, that I felt depressed just listening to her. She could not help it, as it was part of growing old, and being on her own, so I told myself. But many old people were very cheerful, and not at all cantankerous, like her. Daphne, for example, was a delightful lady in her late eighties, and I seldom heard her complain about anything, even though she had her fair share of health issues.

It was just the character of a person, I supposed, as Ninette was always a finicky, anxious person. And old age just magnified these characteristics. Nelune, Shirani, and Christian, called that evening and time passed quickly.

The plumber arrived at nine thirty on Tuesday morning, and John drove up at the same time too, when I called him. It was very good of John to watch him at work, and to make sure he did the right thing. But still, the plumber charged me an exorbitant amount to replace the electrical unit, and I hoped the heater would work. He managed to get the unit working at last, and showed me how to re-start it, in case I had problems.

Finally, after more than $600 worth of plumbers fees, the unit worked. I thanked John for all his trouble over this matter, and told him I was very grateful. He replied, "Anytime, as I don't want these tradesmen ripping you off!" I went for my appointment with the podiatrist at three o'clock, and came home straight afterwards. And when Ninette called later, I said I would visit her next day.

I arrived at Ninette's around one o'clock, and she played the piano for a little while. But after twenty minutes or so, she said she was too tired to play any longer, and wanted to walk to the shops although it drizzled slightly. We walked briskly and came back soon, as I wanted to leave before it started raining heavily. It poured down by evening, and did not cease, welcome spring showers though. Ninette called that night to say she would visit me on Friday.

Christian asked if I could do a pastel drawing of his friend's Dalmatian puppy, and I agreed. So I spent some time sketching it out from a photograph that he emailed me. I did not have pastel paper to start the drawing, as I could not find any in the local art shops. I asked Christian to bring me a few sheets next time, as he said they were available at an art supplier's in the city,

I picked Ninette at midday on Friday, and enjoyed driving in the good weather, as it was pleasant and sunny. But she was very weak, and complained non-stop about her real, and non-existent ailments all the way to my place. I felt depressed just listening to her. She seemed to derive great pleasure in dwelling on her ailments. And listed them one by one on her fingers every single time, like reciting a litany of miseries.

I made pasta with kransky sausage for lunch, but she said there was too much in her bowl, and then ate it all. When I served chocolate ice cream for dessert, she said, "No, that's too much, I can't eat so much!" And then proceeded to finish the whole bowl of ice cream as well.

After lunch, she wanted to see the garden, but came inside almost immediately, saying, "I feel dizzy, I can't see very well." By this time, I knew I had made a grave mistake in trying to entertain her, as she just could not relax, or settle down to anything. I asked her to play the piano, but she said she felt too weak.

Toula arrived at two o'clock and stayed only a few minutes, as Ninette was anxious to get back. I told Toula about Ninette's restless behaviour, and Toula said she was getting worse by the day, as she did not want to socialize or visit anyone now. My whole day was gone, just for that little time with Ninette. Anyway, I knew she would not visit again, as she was too unsettled, and suffered extreme anxiety and panic attacks.

It was four months since Connie's death on Saturday, the 4th, so I drove to Frankston, and planted a miniature, red rose under his memorial plaque. Then I visited the chapel and said a special prayer for him. I stopped and attended to various matters at Karingal.

When I called Shirani later that evening, she said Suresh was alright, and she was relieved that he was home safely. Then I spoke to Cornelia, and said I would organize lunch soon.

It was Grand Final day on Saturday, 27 September, and I wanted to watch some of it, because Tom Jones, or "Sir" Tom Jones, was singing after the game. It was the first time in all these years that I actually watched the entire match. I started making patties, just to while away the time, as I did not have any interest in the game whatsoever. I did not understand footy rules, but I did not want to miss hearing Tom Jones sing.

I ended up watching the whole match from start to finish, and Hawthorn won against Sydney. Tom Jones sang a few songs, and he looked trim enough. His voice was still good, but his hair and beard were snow-white. I could not believe that this was my erstwhile teenage idol. And if he was rounder, he would have looked just like

Santa Claus, belting out a sexy rendition of "Your Kiss." But that is what the years do to everyone, without exception.

Julie called that evening, and we spoke for some time. She broke her ankle while holidaying overseas, and she said she would not be able to move around for about six or seven weeks. I told her to take care, and we would catch up, once her ankle was better.

I started reading the life story of actor, Elizabeth Taylor, next day, and found it absorbing.

The weather turned stormy by Tuesday, and once again gusty winds lashed non-stop, followed by torrential rain. Christian could not drive down as planned, as he was unwell and was seeing doctor. I was concerned and told him to take care, as he was prone to bronchitis.

When I tried to switch on the gas log fire heater that day, I could not believe it when it did not ignite! I called the gas plumber immediately, and he came around midday. I told him that I would call him every time it did not work, as I spent so much money getting it repaired, and the new part he replaced, was on a thirty day warranty as well. He tinkered around for a while and got it working, and then he told me I had to hold the re-set button until it fired up. I was very annoyed, and told him that I hoped it was the last time I had to call him.

I watched "Cleopatra," with Elizabeth Taylor and Richard Burton that night. It was an excellent movie, and I enjoyed it very much, although it was very long.

It poured down next day, and was still blustery, but cleared up slightly by the time I left home to meet Elvira and Mary at Onde's cafe. We had a good time as usual, and Gerry kept us amused with his constant chatter and anecdotes. When I went up to pay, he said, "You *always* pay!" I replied that I liked to treat my friends, and did not keep an account of whose turn it was to pay the bill. He replied, "We Italians are like that too."

Then I stopped at Bunnings to get another tin of stain, and a rhododendron plant for the back yard. And when I stopped at Bentons Square later, I met Alan and Ginny there, so I stopped to chat. Ginny said she was getting better, and I invited them over whenever she felt up to it.

When I called Ninette that evening, she kept me on the phone for a very long time. I was weary when she finally hung up, as it was draining listening to her constant complaints. But the poor thing just wanted someone to listen to her, so all I could do now was just give her my time. I called Shirani later, as I did not hear from her for a week. She was very stressed with everything that was happening, and I knew it was a traumatic time. But we had a hearty chat, and I told her that I hoped Suresh would improve soon.

I was surprised when Simba slept till eight o'clock next morning. So I had a good rest after a long time, and hoped he would settle down and stop getting up too early in the morning.

It was gusty and overcast that day, and I did some chores around the place. Ron said they would clean up the garden and mow lawns tomorrow afternoon, as the weather was not the best today. I planned to drive to Dandenong to meet Joelle and Joanne, but I told them I would make it another day, when the weather improved. Then I spent a few hours painting, as I wanted to finish the landscape I was working on.

It was very pleasant and sunny when Ron and Monica came next day, so they cleaned up, and took the rubbish to the tip as well. Ron mowed the lawns afterwards, and as they did such a great job, I gave him six cans of beer including his payment, and a bottle of wine for Monica. We had a cup of tea later, and chatted a while. Then Christian called and said he was getting better, but would get blood test results next week. I was relieved to hear that his health was improving.

I invited Laura, Con, and Cornelia, for lunch on 24 October, and Cornelia was depressed all through the afternoon, as her knee was very painful. She said she needed to have an operation, and I was sorry to see her in pain. I hoped the operation would relieve her.

Misaka said they would visit that afternoon, so I asked Elvira and John to come over too. John said he would fix the lock in the toilet window as it was getting stuck. Theji, Misaka, and baby Thamika, arrived around three o'clock and we had fun playing with her, as she was a cute baby. And they left at six o'clock, but John and Elvira left earlier once he fixed the window.

When I tried to switch on the gas heater in the night, I could not believe it when it did not ignite again! It was very annoying, but I had to wait till Monday morning to call the plumber.

It was the first day of term four at school on Monday, and although it was going to be twenty six degrees, it was a cold morning, and drizzled non-stop. I wore a summer dress, and shivered all day, but I should have known better than to trust Melbourne's weather.

When I called the gas plumber later, he said he would come on Tuesday afternoon. Christian said that he did not have his car, so was unable to come on Tuesday. I started reading "Claire De Lune," the life story of composer, Claude Debussy, once again. It was so very interesting, especially since "Claire De Lune," was one of my favourite tunes that I enjoyed playing on the piano.

I waited for the plumber all morning, and he called on his way, to ask what was wrong. When I told him that the heater would not ignite, he said to push the re-set button, and hold it down for a few seconds. I did so while he was on the phone, and the darn thing worked! He did not have to come after all, but he said that if the problem continued, I would need to get a new pilot ignition, which cost $220. I could not believe it, and I told him that I would think about it.

Angela asked if I could teach her son, Anthony, piano too, so I waited for him that evening. But only Sofia turned up, and said that her brother did not want to learn piano. Lilli missed her lesson, and Jacqui called to say she would come next week. I noticed that after the first year or so, the students lost interest when they found new activities. And I expected Lilli to stop soon, as I knew she was not very keen to practise.

I drove to Mornington market on Wednesday afternoon and bought a yellow rose plant, as I wanted to start a rose garden in the backyard. As it cost $18 each, I thought of buying one or two plants at a time, and I wanted certain varieties only, so I ordered a couple more plants from the grower. Then I visited Ninette, as Toula called and said they were back after shopping. I took some cake for her, and we spent a pleasant afternoon.

Ninette wanted me to post Luigi's CD to Phillip Brady, at 3AW radio station. I said I would do so tomorrow, as I had to write an accompanying letter with the CD. When I returned home, Liz sent a text asking me to look outside later, as it was going to be an eclipse of the moon.

I went out to the deck at eight o'clock, but could see only a reddish glow, then later in the night, I glimpsed a silver rim surrounded by a red glow. It was an amazing sight. When we spoke next day, Liz said she was unable to get a good view in Langwarrin. I told her it was an incredible sight, and I was so pleased that I saw it. We planned to have lunch at Sofia's next day, and I looked forward to another interesting talk with Liz.

I posted Luigi's CD that afternoon, then came home and rested a while, as the dry, irritating cough started again. Then I painted for a few hours, and hung some other paintings in my bedroom, that I had recently framed.

When I tried to change television channels on the remote control that evening, everything froze for some unknown reason. I could not get the DVD to work, so I watched news on the other set, and hoped that Christian would visit soon, so he could re-set the television. These hiccups were so frustrating, as I had to wait for Christian or someone else to fix them.

I waited for Liz till after one next afternoon, as she was held up at school, but we shared a pizza, and had a long chat. It was always interesting to discuss similar interests, especially mysticism, as Liz was very much into spirituality. And I learnt about some inspiring people she came across in books and on television.

Christian called later that evening, and told me how to re-set the television, and it worked! I did not watch any movies on DVD though, as I was too busy, and switched on only to watch the news.

When I took Simba to the vet on Saturday morning, he said that he had lost only three grams. And he wanted him to lose another five grams at least, as he was over-weight. I told the vet it was difficult to monitor Simba's food intake, because he scoffed up whatever the other two cats left in their bowls. I needed to watch him carefully, and restrict his meals, if he had to lose weight.

It was warm and cloudy that day, and I spent a few hours applying stain on the outdoor benches. But it was strenuous work, so I took little breaks in-between. Cornelia called and said that she got fifteen varieties of roses from a wholesale nursery at a very reasonable cost. But she said she did not want payment, as they were a gift. I thanked her for her generosity, and she said they would drop in with the plants on Sunday afternoon. I made some cutlets in the evening, as they liked them very much.

it was a chilly morning, although it was expected to go up to twenty nine degrees. Con and Cornelia arrived around four o'clock, and we had a pleasant time. I served cutlets, and fried some spring rolls too, which they enjoyed with my chilli sauce. They left a few hours later, and Ninette left a message saying she was worried, because she did not hear from me that evening. I told her that I had visitors, but she was uninterested, and said she could not talk as Luigi was on the other line.

When I came home after school on Monday, I started digging beds for the roses. But the ground was rock hard, and I was exhausted after digging up one bed. I relaxed in the spa with bath salts that evening, and hoped it would ease the muscle aches. Christian said that Athena needed the car next day, so he could not visit. I told him not to worry, as they had things to do and places to go, and I understood that it was difficult to manage with one car.

I dug up another garden bed next day, and prepared a third. It was very hard work, but I was determined to do it myself, even if it took me long to dig and prepare each bed. Nilanthi called back after I spoke to her earlier, and said she felt very down-hearted. I comforted her, and said I would get her down some time next year. Then I took it easy, and watched "Fiddler On The Roof." It was such a great movie, that I did not mind watching it several times.

I drove to Mornington market on the following Wednesday, and bought two more rose plants that I ordered. Then I stopped at the centre to get a bouquet of roses for Elvira, as I was going there for lunch. Mary and her neighbour, little Mary, (who was not so little), were already there, and so was Margaret, Elvira's next door neighbour. Margaret was an elderly Polish lady in her late seventies, who monopolised the conversation all through lunch.

She wanted to know the recipes of every single dish that Elvira served in great detail. And she talked continually about food and recipes, so that my head throbbed by the time I left. I was bored, as I could hardly converse with the two Marys, or Elvira, because no one else could get a word in or change the subject. When I came home after shopping, I rested a while, and then planted a few more roses.

Toula sent a text on Thursday, and said they were home. So I visited Ninette after school and had coffee with her. Toula left soon, as she had other appointments. Ninette was in a better mood, but I listened to the same complaints for one hour before I returned home.

I planted a few more roses, and by evening, I managed to plant all fifteen rose bushes, so I was very pleased. Every evening I soaked in the spa to soothe my aching muscles, as I was unaccustomed to such strenuous physical exertion.

Shirani sent a text in the evening, and when I called her back, she sounded very excited, and said that she went to a house in Endeavour Hills, to see the miraculous statue of Our Lady, that constantly oozed oil. But no one could find the source, or explain why it oozed oil. Shirani experienced a great sense of peace, and felt light-hearted when she knelt in front of the statue. She wanted me to visit that place soon, so I agreed, as I wanted to see it too.

My muscles felt very sore next day, but I managed to carry 40 litre bags of mulch in the wheelbarrow, and spread it on the new beds. Then I dug out the last bed, and planted three more roses, as the weekend was going to be very hot, and I wanted to get them in the ground soon. Finally, they were all in, and I watered down the plants after mulching. I was exhausted by evening, so once again I relaxed in a hot spa.

Elvira asked if she could come over to practise songs on Saturday afternoon, and I agreed. She spent a couple of hours, and had a good practise session. I was worn-out with all the digging and planting, so I took it easy on Sunday.

Julie called to thank me for her birthday card, and we spent one and a half hours on the phone, as we had a great deal of catching up to do. Then I copied the stage play "Catsville" onto a memory stick, and typed a letter to the drama teacher at St Macartan's school. I almost finished reading "Claire De Lune" that night. And I was totally absorbed in the story, even though I read it a couple of times before. It was a fascinating, but tragic life story.

I dropped the memory stick and letter at St Macartans next day, but I did not meet the drama teacher, as she was not in. Then I drove to Frankston and watered the rose bush in the memorial garden. It looked alright, and I hoped it would survive the heat and dry weather.

When I went into the church office later, I met Vicki and Renata, and we had a nice chat. It was ten forty five when I arrived at school that morning. I took an antihistamine tablet for hay fever, and although they were supposed to be non-drowsy tablets, I felt very sleepy. Some of the students were still the same, unmotivated lot, and I told them that if they did not practise regularly, I would not be teaching them anymore.

I called Ninette after six o'clock that evening, as she left a message. But she was very agitated, and said that she was busy talking to Luigi on the other line. I told her that I received a nice letter from Phillip Brady from 3AW, thanking me for Luigi's CD, which he enjoyed listening to immensely. She was pleased to hear that, and said she would convey it to Luigi.

Shirani said she would visit on Tuesday, and I was happy that I would get to see her after some time. I tried calling the drama teacher several times, but she did not answer, so I left a message. Christian dropped in unexpectedly at midday, but he did not stay long, as he had to leave in time for a dental appointment in Mornington.

He bought me a DVD player and set it up quickly, which was really good of him. And he liked the pastel painting of the Dalmatian puppy very much, and thanked me for doing it so quickly. Shirani visited briefly, but I asked her to have some lunch before she left. And I was sorry that she could not stay longer, but at least we spent a little time together. She was constantly worried about leaving Suresh, even though Ranjith was with him.

Jacqui said that Lilli would not continue piano, as she had too much homework, and did not have time to practise. I expected this for some time, so I was prepared. But I would miss her, as she was an interesting and amusing child. Sofia turned up at five thirty, late as usual.

It was very warm next day, and Elvira dropped in at one o'clock to practise songs again. I went shopping after she left, and came home in a couple of hours time. Then I watered the roses, and was relieved to see they were alright, even in such hot weather.

After a brilliant sunset, the skies turned bright red that evening, and I spent time on the deck, just enjoying the wonderful panorama. I finished reading Claude Debussy's biography, which had a very sad ending. And it made me ponder on the tragic lives of so many gifted people.

I dropped in at St Macartan's again on Thursday, this time with a hard copy of the stage play. But the drama teacher was still unavailable, so I left it with the receptionist. I walked out and stopped to look around the school. My impression was of large, cold grey buildings, without light and warmth inside and out, unlike St Francis Xavier's Primary school.

After finishing at school that afternoon, I dropped in at Ninette's just as Toula was leaving. Jackie and Luigi arrived a little while later, and he looked very ill. One leg was inflamed, and she had taken him to the doctor. Jackie was very compassionate, and I admired her for being so concerned about Luigi, even though they were divorced. We chatted for a while, and I left soon after. When I came home, I walked in the garden, and pottered around before I made some curries for lunch on Saturday.

They arrived by one o'clock for once, and Con fixed the loose hinge on the outside gate. Cornelia brought two more rose bushes, and they were impressed with all the work I did to set up the rose garden. I played Andre Rieu's DVD on the new player, and Con was happy listening to music, while Cornelia and I chatted. It was eight o'clock when they left, and I was exhausted.

I took it easy next day, and then planted the last two roses in the evening.

Chapter 95

A severe storm broke out last night, and it was the loudest thunder I ever heard. The cats darted under the bed, and then crept on top, where they snuggled all through the deafening noise.

On my way to school in the morning, gusty winds roared across the sea, followed by torrential rain. But by late afternoon, a few sunny spells broke through the incessant deluge. I came home after five o'clock, as Tess finished late.

I started reading a very interesting book in the night that Liz lent me, "Masters Of The Far East' by Baird Spalding. It was a spiritually challenging book that opened up whole new ways of thinking. I read the first few chapters and found it quite absorbing.

Christian said he could not come next day as planned, as he still did not have a car. I looked forward to seeing him, as I enjoyed his visits, and our talks, so it was disappointing, but I knew he could not help it. The last thing I wanted to do, was apply pressure on him or anyone else to visit me. I had to get accustomed to being on my own, and doing things for myself.

When I visited Mary next afternoon, I mentioned that my eyes were getting very blurry now, and I needed to have a cataract operation before next June, even if I had to pay for it. She immediately replied, "Nalini, if you need money, I have some savings, and am happy to lend whatever you need for the operation." I thanked her profusely, as I was overwhelmed by her generous offer. But I told her that I could manage, and not to worry about lending me any money. She was a kind person, and I was fortunate to have such a good friend.

I drove to Frankston police station after school next day, to get some documents certified by a Justice of the Peace. All this hassle was due to my middle name not appearing on my birth certificate, but was on my passport and driver's licence. I had to prove that I was the one and same person, with or without the middle name. Then I dropped in at Ninette's place for a while and had coffee with her, and I was glad that she was more placid, so I had a pleasant time.

When I came home, I moved another two bags of mulch and spread it around the rose plants. Then I called Nilanthi, and we spoke for some time, and she said she looked forward to seeing us again very soon. Later that evening, Felix called and said that Yasmin and he would arrive here on 27 of November, and they hoped to spend five days with me. I said I would be very pleased to have them. They were very nice people, and Felix was a childhood friend from our days in Hatton.

Shirani called at ten o'clock next morning to ask if I was alright, as I over-slept, and did not send a text as usual. She told me that Suresh was flying to Brunei on Sunday to spend one week there, and she was concerned about his safety. He got these notions, and became restless, until he went wherever he dreamed of going. I too hoped and prayed that he would be safe and enjoy a good holiday there. It was thirty degrees that day, and very hot by afternoon, so I watered the roses and hoped they would survive.

When I spoke to Dr Renehan's receptionist that day, she said that he could not see me until 13 January 2015. I told her that my eyesight was worse, and to let me know if there was a cancellation. It was very difficult to see clearly now, especially when driving in rainy or foggy weather. One eye was worse than the other, so I hoped to have the cataract operation soon. But I could not do anything else, except wait until January.

I drove to Mornington Home Centre in search of a picture framer there. But I could not locate the factory, although I drove around, and then walked in circles looking for the place. So I ended up in Main Street, where I found a very good, but expensive framer, and left two paintings there.

Saturday turned chilly and blustery, and I could not believe it after yesterday's hot weather. It rained most of the day as well, so I stayed in and did my usual chores. I called Babs in the afternoon, and asked if she received my text message the week before. She said that she wanted to call me all week, but she was unwell, and complained that she suffered from severe heartburn. I told her to avoid spicy foods, and see her doctor.

Then I worked on my manuscript for a couple of hours, before going to church at six o'clock, as it was All Saints day. Later that evening, I enjoyed watching "La Boheme" on a DVD that Ninette gave me, which she said was a very good production.

On Sunday, I started an oil painting of "Water Lilies" from a photograph in a magazine, of a swamp covered with water lilies in the Northern Territory. I relaxed a few hours, totally immersed in my painting.

When I called Shirani in the evening, she said that Suresh left for Brunei that afternoon. And she hoped he would be happy, as he was in a better frame of mind. A few friends called in the afternoon, and said they would visit soon.

It was a school holiday on Monday, the day before Melbourne Cup Day, so I took it easy, and played the piano for a little while. Then I spent a few hours painting in the afternoon.

When I spoke to Shirani that evening, she was very upset. Because Suresh called, and wanted to return home immediately, as he did not like the place at all. Poor Shirani ended up paying extra to change his ticket, and arrange a flight back in a couple of days.

I advised her to discourage him from travelling overseas again, as it was costing her a great deal of money. Besides, it was unsafe for him to travel on his own, until he was more stable. She agreed, and we discussed what options she had in future. And I was very upset about all these issues. I prayed that Shirani would have the strength to cope with him, as she was unable to get any professional support at all. I called Nilanthi later that evening, and we had a long chat. She too was sorry to hear about the difficult time Shirani had with Suresh.

It was Melbourne Cup day on Tuesday, and I enjoyed a quiet time at home. The weather was pleasant, although a little gusty, and I watched the Cup race at three o'clock. But I was very distressed to hear that two of the horses died straight after the race; one of a heart attack, and the other was put down, after suffering injuries at the gates. I thought it was tragic that those magnificent animals had to suffer and die, just for the sake of a race.

After school on Thursday, I stopped to water the rose plant in the memorial garden, before going to Karingal for a haircut. My regular hairdresser was away, so I cancelled the appointment and dropped in at Ninette's, as she expected me. Toula was still there after shopping with Ninette, so we had a good chat over coffee.

Ninette said she felt much better, because Luigi was back home, after being in hospital all day. She worried about him constantly, and took it very much to heart whenever he was ill. When I told her not to worry so much, she replied that she could not help it, as it was her nature to be anxious and concerned about her friends, especially Luigi.

It was a scorching thirty four degrees on Saturday, but I drove to Mornington to pick up the paintings. They did a very good job, and I was pleased. As soon as I came home, I hung up the two paintings in my bedroom.

When I attended Mass that evening, I met Fr Gerald, who was visiting with Bishop Peter from Kerala, India. After Mass, they showed a short film about the plight of the poor in the Bishop's parish, as they did not have drinking water or transport to schools. The arid scenes evoked memories of Polonnaruwa, and when he said they needed funds to build a school, I offered to make a donation.

Mary and Elvira dropped in for afternoon tea, and we had a pleasant time. When they left a couple of hours later, I called Daisy Akka, as it was her ninety-third birthday. She was very happy to hear from me, and we chatted for a while, and she kept asking when I would visit her again. I told her that I did not have immediate plans, but hoped to see her soon, and that cheered her up. Then I called Nilanthi, as she sounded very depressed the previous evening, but was more cheerful today, and chatted away happily.

I woke up with a dull headache on Monday morning, because I dreamed of Connie all night. They were not scary dreams, but he gave me orders non-stop, just like he did all his life, especially when he was ill. First, he wanted me to take him to several appointments, and then he told me to have another funeral at St John Vianni's church. (I did not even know if such a church existed near-by).

When I told him I had a headache, and could not drive around to so many places, he started growling and shouting, like he did at home, and in the hospital when he got angry and frustrated. He started to re-arrange rooms, and put his clothes back in his wardrobe. And my dreams were so real, that I thought he was back home.

I forgot to send Shirani a text once again, and she called me at eleven o'clock when I was at school, to ask if I was alright. She became quite anxious whenever I forgot to text her in the morning, so I told her that I was very sorry, and would call her when I went home.

I called Shirani as soon as I came home, and told her that I was very tired that morning, and related my dream. She said that it was due to all the harrowing experiences with Connie that still worked in my mind, so it was only natural to have such dreams.

Christian said that he still did not have the car, so he could not drop in tomorrow. Also that his friends loved the pastel portrait of their pet, and I was pleased to hear that.

I spent some time next day patching up the areas around the towel rails and holders in the toilet, and was glad Christian fixed them so firmly. The drama teacher at St Macartans finally called that day. She said she did not read my play as yet, but would get back to me as soon as she did. She sounded nice, and we had a brief chat, but I never heard from her again.

I drove to Frankston on Wednesday and watered the rose plant, as it was twenty eight degrees, and I did not want the plant to wither. Then I prayed for Connie's soul to be at peace, and spoke to Fr Raj later. I asked if he could bless my home, and also mentioned that I dreamed of Connie almost every night. He replied that it was only normal, as he was my husband for such a long time. Then he asked me to email my address, or leave details with Vicki, and he would get back to me.

I told Ninette that I could not visit her tomorrow, as I was going to Narre Warren to see the miraculous statue of Our Lady. She forgot about it, but was alright when I reminded her, and I said I would try to visit later in the week.

I arrived at school by ten o'clock next morning, as the staff organized a farewell tea for Fr Nicholas, the assistant parish priest, who was transferring to Keilor. When I finished, I drove to Narre Warren at about one thirty in the afternoon. It was a scorching thirty four degrees, as Shirani drove us in her car to the modest brick-veneer house close by.

A few cars were parked on the street outside the house, and the backyard was very nice, with a fountain and flower beds. The family had renovated the garage where the miraculous statues and pictures were. As we entered the room, I felt happy in that peaceful atmosphere. Then we knelt in front of Our Lady's statue, and prayed devoutly for our intentions. Next to Our Lady's statue, was one of Jesus, which the daughter explained, had bleeding palms only on Good Friday.

The daughter was a serene lady, and she related how it all began a few months ago, when they noticed the statue oozing oil, while they prayed in front of it. And on Good Friday, the statue of Jesus started bleeding from the palms as well.

When we looked at the statue closely, oil oozed constantly from the face and hands of the statue, where it stood in a basin of oil. But the statue of Jesus did not bleed then. She said the oil had miraculous properties, and had cured some illnesses. And she asked us to take a few swabs of cotton dipped in oil, that they gave away at no cost.

When we returned, Suresh was at home, and he asked me how I liked the sacred shrine. I replied that I was very impressed, and asked him if he would like to visit it too, but he was non-committal, and just smiled vaguely. Before I left, I told Shirani that I hoped our prayers would be answered soon, and that Suresh would be healed. I drove home feeling happy, because I visited that special shrine.

Ron and Monica arrived at three o'clock next day, and finished mowing and weeding within an hour. I invited them for a drink, and they enjoyed a beer and a glass of wine. They wanted to look around the house and my studio later, and admired my paintings greatly. It was after six o'clock when they left, as they shared some very interesting stories of their life experiences. And as always, I enjoyed listening to other peoples' stories very much.

I spoke to Nilanthi almost every day, because she seemed to suffer bouts of depression when she recalled how unkind and heartless Heron was to her. I advised her to take care, as it was easy to become chronically dejected, and urged her to exercise her brain and body regularly. When she dwelt on the past, I kept saying, "You can't change what has happened, and you must move on." But it was difficult for her to cope at times, and I was very sorry for her plight. It could be draining though, trying to lift Nilanthi's spirits all the time. So I was glad when Nelune said she hoped to visit at the end of the month. We enjoyed a pleasant chat and laughter as always.

It was much cooler on Saturday, and after doing my usual chores, I called Nilanthi again, as I was concerned about her, and missed her too. We always enjoyed good times whenever she visited, and she said that it was good to share and support each other, especially now when she was down-hearted.

Justin Peters sang in the choir at Mass that evening. I spoke to him afterwards, and bought his CD. He had a powerful, well-trained voice, and his singing moved me very much. I listened to his CD on the way home, and enjoyed the spiritual songs. He sang at Mass regularly, and I found out that he attended St Francis Xavier's primary school many years ago, where I now taught piano. I took his CD to school one day, and the staff enjoyed listening to it as well, as some of them knew him as a student.

I sent Linda a text message the following day, and she said she was spending a few days in Tasmania with Julie, and that Paul's step-father had died yesterday, so I sent my condolences to Paul and the family.

That evening, I watched "Sunset Boulevard," with Gloria Swanson and William Holden. It was a classic movie, which I enjoyed watching several times, as it was a fascinating story

When I called Ninette on Monday evening, the first thing she asked me was, "What's the time now? I have to call Luigi!" She was fixated with him, and called him three times a day, sometimes more, just to ask how he was.

Her behaviour was very strange now, but what could I do. It was her life, and if she wanted to spend her days worrying about Luigi, so be it. She did not speak long, as she was very distracted, and anxious to phone Luigi, but in the past, she would not get off the phone for ages, and talked non-stop. I wished her goodnight, and then spoke briefly to Nilanthi.

It was our forty-fourth wedding anniversary on Tuesday, 18 November. And it brought back sad memories of so many wasted years, that could have been so much better. But I did not want to spend precious time on useless regrets, so I busied myself as usual.

Christian said he was held up in the city, and would be late, but as I had an appointment with the podiatrist at three o'clock, he said he would try to make it tomorrow.

Nancy was pleased when I called her, as I did not hear from her for some time. She said she was very busy with her mother and her sister, who had a few health issues. We had a long chat, and said we would catch up soon. Then Ninette called, and said she would be home tomorrow, if I wanted to visit her any time. But I told her that Christian was visiting, so I would see her next week.

It was a sunny, sizzling thirty degrees on Wednesday, and Christian arrived around one o'clock. He did several odd jobs around the place, then set up the new CD player, and radio he bought me, which sounded very good, so I was pleased. He checked my car, changed light globes, and then started building the retaining wall in the backyard. How he sweated! Poor Christian. I held a beach umbrella to protect him from the scorching sun, and he dug the rock-hard ground non-stop until he completed the work.

I felt very sorry to see him sweating and getting sunburnt, but he did a perfect job as usual, and I was so proud of his handiwork. He relaxed a while before he left, and said he would attend to the other little tasks next time. I thanked him heartily for his great work, and for taking time to come over, because I knew he was very busy with his work and business.

I called Ninette after Christian left, and told her it was too late to visit, and I would come another day. She did not complain about it, so we chatted for a little while. I was relieved, as I never knew what sort of mood she would be in now.

When I spoke to Mary later on, she said that Tony was down with bronchitis. I asked her to give him my best wishes, and hoped he would recover soon. I was very happy when Nelune said she would visit on the following Saturday. Then I called Nilanthi and Shirani, and chatted for some time before making a few curries for lunch on Saturday.

After school on Thursday, I stopped to send Nilanthi's allowance, and pay some bills, before visiting Ninette. I took Holy Communion, and some holy oil from Our Lady's statue in Narre Warren. She was very pleased, and listened intently, when I related the story about the bleeding statues. When I returned home, I cooked a few more curries for Saturday.

I spent most of Friday cleaning and vacuuming, but when I finished upstairs, the vacuum packed up! It was very annoying, as I had to sweep and mop downstairs. Then I made three kinds of sambals, to have with string hoppers on the weekend. And in the evening, I watched another one of my favourite movies "North By Northwest," featuring Cary Grant.

On Saturday morning, I woke up early, and waited for Nelune. When I called her at nine o'clock, she said she would phone me as soon as the train reached Cheltenham, which she did, and I picked her at ten thirty. We had a leisurely lunch, and enjoyed a lovely afternoon. I was happy to see her again, as her last visit was in May, when she came for Connie's funeral.

After she relaxed a while, we drove to Woolamai, where we enjoyed a pleasant time with Shirani, and left around four o'clock. Nelune drove back, and as we arrived home, Nilanthi called, and Tanesh spoke too, as he was visiting her.

We had patties with a cup of tea, and later that evening, we watched "Columbo." But Nelune was so tired and drowsy, that she did not wait to see the end. I stayed up till eleven thirty though, and watched the whole episode. And I slept well, after a long day.

It was warm and sunny on Sunday, so I drove Nelune around Mt Martha, and showed her the panoramic view down the road. When we returned, we had lunch, and after chatting for a few hours, I dropped her at the station around three o'clock.

I stopped at Karingal on my way and bought a new vacuum cleaner, and when I came home, Mary and Julie had left messages. I called them back, and we chatted for a while. Julie said they would visit me soon, and Mary was relieved that Tony was better.

Nelune called to say she was in the city, and would let me know as soon as she arrived in Sydney. Then I spoke to Nilanthi in the evening, and she sounded more cheerful, so I was glad.

A severe thunder storm broke out on Monday morning, followed by torrential rain, which did not ease till late evening. It was hectic at school, and Tess came after four o'clock, so it was late when I finished. I spoke to Ninette and Shirani later. And Nelune said she arrived in Sydney at six o'clock yesterday, and it was very late when she reached home. Christian did not say if he could visit tomorrow, so I did not know if he had the car yet.

I spent most of Tuesday cleaning, washing, and vacuuming, as I prepared for my guests, Felix and Yasmin, who were arriving on Thursday. I aired the blankets, and arranged a vase of fresh lavender from the garden in the guest room. Christian did not visit that day, and when I called him at five o'clock, he said he was busy working all day.

When I spoke to Nilanthi that evening, she thanked me for the money, and said it was raining heavily, so she could not go out at all. The bad weather always depressed her more. Because she said that electricity supply was affected, and she could not watch television or movies on the DVD player. I cooked a few more curries later that evening, and then took it easy.

The staff held a "Thank You" morning tea for all the volunteers, and Margaret, who organized it, invited me too. When she thanked everyone for their work, she said, "You contribute a lot to the school Dolly, not only teaching piano, but in many other ways." I appreciated her kind words, and had a very enjoyable time, chatting with all the other volunteers and staff members, and came home around twelve thirty. Then I waited for Felix and Yasmin, as they said they would be here by midday. I cooked a few more curries the previous evening, so everything was ready.

I waited all afternoon, but it was five o'clock when they finally arrived, due to heavy traffic at that time of day. We chatted for some time, and then they decided to go for a walk down the street, as it was a very warm, pleasant evening. I indulged in a spa bath and relaxed till they came back a couple of hours later.

Felix said, "We enjoyed our walk very much, as the people are all so friendly. They smiled and greeted us, as if we were old friends." We had a great evening, as Felix loved to reminisce. And we talked of old friends, and good times we shared as children. They finally turned in around eleven o'clock, but I stayed up till after midnight, waiting for Tigger, who was still out loafing in the bush. It was a very long day, but it was great to have such long-time, dear friends, with whom I shared so many happy memories.

Friday was another sunny, pleasant day, and went up to twenty four degrees. I was still resting, when Felix and Yasmin left around nine o'clock. They had breakfast, and left a note saying they wanted to see a movie in Frankston, and would be back in the afternoon. I rested a while longer, and was busy doing chores later. My guests returned at two o'clock, and said they enjoyed a good movie, and were very happy and relaxed.

I warmed up all the food earlier, so we had a late lunch, and when we finished, Felix wanted to clean up the kitchen sink. He had bought a bottle of "Jiffy" to clean the mark on the wall upstairs, when he accidentally knocked their suitcase. I told him not to worry about it, but he spent ages trying to clean it. As the wall was dented slightly, the mark could not just be wiped away with Jiffy. I said that I would touch it up with some paint, and not to bother about it.

They rested for a while, and when they woke up a couple of hours later, I warmed up some patties for a snack, which they enjoyed very much, with a cup of tea. As they were going out for dinner to a friend's place, they left around six o'clock. I flipped through my family album later, as Felix wanted to see some of the old photographs. I could hardly believe how swiftly the years had flown and whizzed past like a whirlwind.

I woke up early on Saturday morning, and drove to Mornington to cast my vote, then to Mt Eliza to meet Mary and Elvira for lunch. Although they were late, we spent a couple of pleasant hours, and I gave them two tickets for tomorrow's play.

I missed the road on my way back, and drove round in circles, trying to get back to Nepean Highway. My eyes were so blurry, that I could not read the street directory even with my glasses on. And it worried me, that my eyesight had deteriorated so much. It was four o'clock when I arrived home, after a few more wrong turns, as I kept winding up in the same cul-de-sac.

Felix and Yasmin dropped me at church that evening, because they wanted to take me out for dinner afterwards. We dined at a restaurant in Mornington, and came home around eight thirty. Then we chatted, and looked at the family albums for a while before turning in.

I left after lunch next afternoon, and my guests went to Tyabb, as they had heard about the antique warehouse there. They bought me a cute little ceramic cat holding a quill. And Yasmin said, "We thought of you, because you are a writer, and you love cats." They were attending a friend's wedding at three o'clock, so we all had our plans for the day.

Elvira and Mary were late for the play, and came in a little after the curtain went up. Mary had forgotten about it, so when Elvira went to pick her, she had to wait till she got ready. The play was very amusing, "Whose Wives Are They?" And I laughed a great deal. We enjoyed ourselves, and I came home after five o'clock. It was a warm, humid day, and I found the air-conditioner turned on full speed, so I assumed that my guests had switched it on. I turned it off, and after unwinding, I had an early night, but I heard them return after midnight.

Felix had a sore back next day, and they went out to get pain-killers from the chemist. When they returned, I asked him about the air-conditioner, and he replied that they did not turn it on at all. I thought it rather strange that it came on its own, as it never did that before.

Shirani arrived around eleven o'clock, as I invited her for lunch, so she could meet them too, and stayed for a couple of hours. We had an enjoyable time, then Felix wanted to drive to MKS Asian shop in Dandenong, to buy spices etc. so I rested till they returned a few hours later.

Elvira said that John and Tony would do the pathway at the back next morning, as I wanted them to spread crushed rock on it. so I cleaned up the backyard, and the cats mess, as they had to work in that area.

Yasmin came down while I was cleaning, and walked in the garden with me, and we had a nice long chat. She was a lovely lady, and I liked her very much. Felix was lucky to have married her, and she too was fortunate, because he was obviously a very caring husband, who loved her very much. I told her so, and she agreed that Felix was a good husband and father.

We spent a quiet evening chatting, and looking at the old albums. Felix asked me to send copies of the ones with him and his brother with Nihal, and all his old school mates. I said I would scan them and email them to him soon. Then we had a late dinner around nine thirty, before they turned in a little later. I stayed up and watched a few comedies, as I needed to unwind after a busy day.

Around three forty five in the morning, the heater and cooler started at the same time! I was awake from that time, and wondered what was going on with the air-conditioner. When I told them how it came on again, they too were surprised. Felix said it was best to get someone to look at it. Then they had breakfast, and left at about six forty five. They thanked me for my hospitality, and said they would visit again very soon. John and Tony arrived an hour later, to start work on the pathway.

They worked till about half past ten, then I served them coffee and biscuits. John did ten trips up and down to Mornington, to pick up ten loads of crushed rock, while Tony levelled it with his bob cat. They said Christian did an excellent job with the retaining wall at the end of the pathway, and were quite impressed. I called RACV emergency assist, and they sent a gas plumber in the afternoon.

He checked the air-conditioner, and then referred another plumber, as he could not find out what the problem was, and said that the other plumber would get here tomorrow afternoon. John and Tony finished by one thirty in the afternoon, and they did a great job. The pathway looked neat with crushed rock, and I thought it would be easier to control weeds now. I thanked them profusely, and wanted to pay them for their time and labour. But John said that I had to pay only for the crushed rocks, and not their labour, as they wanted to do that job for me.

I spoke to Shirani later, then Christian called to say he had a meeting, and was unable to make it that day.

When they arrived in Sydney, Yasmin called and thanked me once again for my hospitality, and I told her that I emailed the photographs to Felix earlier. But I did not hear from him, which was strange, as he was always very prompt in acknowledging any correspondence.

Chapter 96

Although it was cloudy, and rained intermittently next morning, it was expected to reach twenty seven degrees. I waited all day for the gas plumber to turn up. But he called at four forty in the afternoon and said that due to the rainy weather, it was unsafe for him to climb the roof. And he would come early morning on the following Wednesday. Then I called Mary and Elvira, and asked them to thank Tony and John for their hard work. Mary said Tony's cough was very bad, and he went to see doctor. Nilanthi left a message, and I returned her call later that night.

I drove to Mornington Hyundai on Friday morning to service my car, and they dropped me home in a courtesy vehicle. Then I spent time writing Christmas cards, while Ron and Monica mowed lawns and weeded the garden. I invited them in for a cup of tea and biscuits when they finished. Ron said they were going away for a few weeks in the new year, but he would cut the lawns after Christmas, before they went away.

My car was ready at three o'clock, and they called to say someone would pick me soon. Although I waited outside for fifteen minutes, the courtesy service they offered was still quite convenient. I watched an episode of "Columbo" in the evening, and then had an early night.

I attended Mass on Saturday evening, and later that night, I watched a few episodes of "Downton Abbey" on DVD.

I took it easy on Sunday, as the dry cough still persisted, and my muscles ached, as if I had the flu. Nelune said that Christian and Athena planned to spend the following weekend in Sydney, but she was going to Brisbane that weekend, and was unable to see them. In the evening, I cooked fried rice, and chicken curry for the staff.

It was seven months since Connie's funeral. And I felt down-hearted when I thought of those final days and weeks before he died. It still distressed me to think of the terrible illness he endured, and the way he died. All I could do now was pray that his soul was at peace.

There were times when I thought of past evenings, when we watched a good movie, or a comedy and laughed together. Those moments became very rare over the last couple of years. And the times that I felt my widowed state most was, when I could not share something funny or interesting with Connie. I was never lonely, as my life has always been full, and rewarding, no matter what I endured. There is a vast difference between *loneliness,* and being *alone.* And although I was alone, life was still a wonderful gift, and I was determined to make the most of my life.

One of the plumbers arrived very early in the morning next day, and the other one a little later. Then the two of them checked the thermostat, and found nothing wrong with it. They climbed on the roof to service the heating and cooling systems, and finished in less than an hour, and handed me a huge bill. I was stunned, and very annoyed that I had to pay so much, as they did not tell me initially how much the service would cost. Another rip- off, I thought, and that was the last time I engaged those plumbers.

I spoke to Fr Joe at St Macartan's about blessing the house, and he arrived that same morning around eleven o'clock. Although he came, he was recovering from a bout of pneumonia, and I could see that he was still unwell. He blessed the rooms downstairs, but gave me some holy water and asked me to sprinkle it upstairs, as he was too weak to climb the stairs. Mary arrived soon after, but they did not stay for a coffee, as she wanted him to bless their house too, so they left shortly.

I visited Ninette after school on Thursday, and Luigi was there too. He looked much better than when I last saw him, and was in a more congenial mood, instead of his usual grouchy self. And he told me that he finally picked up his four-wheel drive from the garage, where his friend, Geoff, had tinkered with it for more than one year. Ninette lent him her car for twelve months, because she did not drive anymore, but he was very happy to have his own vehicle now. I stayed for about an hour, and then headed home after some shopping.

As I had severe hay fever, I took an antihistamine next day, and rested a few hours.

I attended Mass on Saturday evening, and afterwards, I stopped at the pizza place where Connie and I had a pizza on some Saturday nights, and I ordered a small pizza. Later that night, I watched "Song Without End," the life of Franz Liszt, the composer, and enjoyed it very much, although it was a very poignant story.

Nelune called on Sunday, and said that she ran into Athena in the toilet at Sydney Airport, just as she left to catch her plane. They laughed at the coincidence, and so did I. Then I spent a quiet afternoon pottering in the garden and cleaning up. I watched season two of "Downton Abbey," in the evening, and I enjoyed that series very much. It was so beautifully photographed in some very scenic locations, not to mention the elegant period costumes, and gripping storyline. It was one of my favourite series, and even though I was familiar with the plot, it was just as engrossing, watching it a second time. I bought the complete series on DVD, so I could revisit Downton Abbey whenever I wanted to.

I slept in late on Monday morning, as I had a few lessons only in the afternoon. On my way to school, I posted all my Christmas cards, and then stopped at the church to water the rose plant, as it was warm and humid, although it was only twenty six degrees. The plant looked very dry, and I thought of planting another rose in winter.

I spoke to the ladies in the office, and gave Vicki a card, and some chocolates. The children were watching a movie, so a couple of them missed lessons. Colleen gave me a bottle of champagne, and a card, and I gave all the staff and Colleen home-made mango chutney, and cherries in liqueur.

It rained heavily the night before, and gusty winds persisted all day, with thunder and lightning booming and crashing all evening. I told Ninette I did not want to stay on the phone too long because of the lightning, and that I would visit her on Thursday, instead of Tuesday. Then I stayed in, and took it easy. And I enjoyed watching more episodes of "Downton Abbey," till very late in the night.

Karen visited next afternoon, and we had a great time discussing our writing, cats, various projects, and her physic powers. Before she left, she told me, "I feel Con's presence very strongly here, which is the reason why you dream of him every night. I also think that your son, Stacy, is not alive, and met his end in foul play." I did not know what to believe, as it was just too much to take in about Stacy, and my heart felt numb long afterwards. Ninette left a message, and when I called her back, she spoke for a long time, not realizing that I was drained.

It was torrential just as I left Ninette's next afternoon, but I had to stop at Seaford to get groceries, and it was after five o'clock when I came home. I had a severe headache, and was exhausted that evening, so I rested a while before making dinner. When Christian called later, we had a long chat, as I did not see him for a while.

That Friday, I watched the horrifying news on television, about eight children, who were stabbed to death in Cairns. They did not know the reason why as yet. But it made me sick to think of such inhuman crimes, especially against little children. Sometimes, I wished that I did not watch news, just to learn of such horrendous crimes, as it made me very depressed, and I could not fall asleep at nights.

Christian and Athena were spending Christmas day with me, so I made some cutlets in the evening, and some traditional dishes. Elvira invited me to dine out on the 20th, and I accepted.

It was quite mild that Saturday, and I took it easy before going out with my friends. I settled the cats, and kept them indoors, and was ready when Elvira and John picked me at six o'clock. When we arrived at Rugantino's restaurant in Frankston, Mary and Tony were already there. But we waited for Alessandro till about seven thirty, as he had spent the day in the city and was delayed catching a train back.

He had lost a great deal of weight, and was very lean, compared to the last time I saw him, but he was just as nice and friendly as always. We enjoyed a delicious meal, and had a good time laughing and chatting. Elvira drove Mary and me back, and John went home with Tony and Alessandro, as they planned to play cards at John's place till late.

Elvira drove us around the neighbourhood to see Christmas decorations, and it was almost ten o'clock when I came home. I was tired and glad to get back, because I worried about the cats being left indoors all evening. But they were alright, and did not insist on going out at that time of the night.

I rested till late on Sunday, and then made some patties in the afternoon, as Christian and Athena enjoyed them very much. Then I spoke to Shirani and Nilanthi for some time. I told Ninette I would visit her on Monday when Liliana was there as well, and she was alright with that.

Although it was overcast on Monday, the temperature reached twenty eight degrees, but it was quite pleasant. Liliana was already there when I arrived, then Arlette dropped in too. We had a good time laughing and chatting, as Liliana joked constantly, and amused us with her anecdotes.

I stopped on my way to send Nilanthi's allowance on Nelune's behalf, as she deposited the money into my account already. After I attended to that, I drove to Narre Warren to visit Shirani, but I was delayed, due to road works and heavy traffic all along the way. Shirani and I exchanged gifts, and she gave me a huge bouquet of beautiful gladioli from her garden in Woolamai.

Suresh was at home too, so I gave him some money for Christmas, and he rushed out immediately to buy beer. When he returned, and drank a few cans of beer, he started getting loud and boisterous, so I did not want to stay too long. Shirani told him to be quiet several times, but he just went on talking aggressively.

Poor Shirani had such a difficult time with him. I was disturbed at the way he had behaved, because it was so unexpected, and I had a headache when I returned home. Not only was I upset about Suresh's behaviour, but it was also very tiring driving through heavy traffic. I was sad though, because I meant well in giving Suresh some pocket money, not knowing how he would behave.

I felt exhausted, and my muscles ached continuously, so I had to push myself to cook a few more curries, and fried rice for lunch on Christmas day. On the 24th evening, I finished all the chores early. Then settled the cats before leaving an hour early for the children's Mass at five o'clock at St Macartan's. Although I went early, the church was already crowded, but I managed to get a seat at the front.

An elderly gentleman sat next to me, and asked me where I came from. And then he started chatting about Sri Lanka, as he said he had visited there a long time ago in the 1950s. I answered him politely, but I wanted to follow the service, instead of talking about Sri Lanka, as it was not the time or place to listen to his reminiscences.

They served cake and wine in the foyer after Mass, but I did not want to have any, and I came home without delay. Nelune called later that evening, and so did Cynthia, and all my other friends, to wish me for Christmas.

Christian and Athena arrived at midday, and we had a great time together. We exchanged gifts after lunch, and among other things, they gave me a huge box of pastels. I could not help but remember the previous traumatic Christmas. And how upsetting it was to watch Connie's irrational behaviour, all because of Roland's interference.

The memory of Connie's distress as he howled and threw a tantrum, was still fresh in my mind. And at such times, I felt a surge of resentment, as they destroyed what little peace and harmony existed between us in those final months. What a peaceful afternoon it was, compared to that dreadful time last year.

Christian spent time cleaning some of their things in the room upstairs. Then he cut and trimmed down the retaining wall posts, and they left quite late that evening.

I enjoyed a very tranquil night, as it was the first Christmas I spent without any stress, and it was very peaceful. As I ate very little at lunch time, I had an early dinner, and then walked in the garden. Then I watched a few comedies, and one of my favourite movies "It's A Wonderful Life," with James Stewart. I went to bed after midnight, and slept soundly till morning.

I spoke to Nelune and Nilanthi next morning, as I felt somewhat down-hearted, now that all the Christmas preparations were over. But I kept busy, and tried not to think too much about the past, and all the sad memories it evoked. When I drove out to buy groceries later that day, I was glad that the shopping centre was not too crowded. On my way home, I had such a severe headache that I was concerned about getting back safely. I took a panadeine when I came home, and rested a couple of hours until it eased.

When I spoke to Mary on Saturday, the 27th, she told me that Tony's eighty-three year old sister, who lived in Griffith, NSW, had died of a heart attack that morning, and they were driving up there for the funeral. I condoled with them, and she said that all their plans for New Year's celebrations were cancelled. Poor Mary. She had looked forward to the festive season very much, but was now stressed over the sudden death of her sister-in-law. I attended evening Mass, and came home by seven o'clock. And later, I watched another classic film "Miracle On 34th Street."

Some friends, and Nelune called next day, and we spoke for some time, as Nelune wanted to know how I was coping. That same afternoon, Cornelia called and said that Con was in hospital since the 24th, as his heartbeat was very rapid. She was very stressed, so we talked at length, and I tried to comfort her.

Babs said she was sorry that she did not call earlier to wish me, but thanked me for the cards I sent Jeremy and her. I told her not to worry, as we all had things to do, and it could get hectic over this time. Then Julie spoke for over one hour, and said they would visit the following Sunday.

I listened to Ninette's complaints for about forty minutes, but there was nothing much I could do to cheer her up. She said she was in severe pain, as her sciatica was worrying her. But she did not want to be comforted, as she wallowed in her misery. It was very warm that night, as it soared to thirty one degrees during the day, and did not cool down much throughout the night.

Ron and Monica arrived at midday on the 29th, although it was overcast and gusty. It drizzled slightly by the time they finished and left, but I drove to Karingal to do some banking and pay bills etc. Then I bought a large canvas, 150 by 60 centimetres, as I wanted to paint a landscape to hang in the lounge-room. It was a painting depicting a river, stream, and a lake, with a forest in earthy tones of the native bushland in the background. It was an ambitious painting, and I was keen to start it immediately.

The canvas was so long, that I had to slide it across the front seat of my car, and it partly obscured my vision from the side mirrors. I drove back very slowly, and removed it from the car before I drove into the garage. Later that evening, I called Ninette to ask how she was feeling. And after one hour's conversation (a monologue on her part), I felt weary just listening to her complaints. But I was sorry that she was still in pain, and told her I would visit soon.

Then I started painting at about six thirty, and stopped after nine o'clock, as I wanted to finish as much as possible, because my eyesight was getting very blurry.

But I did not want to put off painting until after the cataract operation. It continued to rain all evening and night, and I fell asleep to the sound of heavy rain.

I slept in late next morning, as Tigger kept me awake all night, mewing and jumping around, trying to go out. I let him out at about one o'clock in the morning, and was relieved when he came back safe and sound an hour later. I did not know the reason why he was so persistent to go out though.

When I woke up at that time in the morning, it was very blustery, but a beautiful, half-moon hung over the shimmering bay that glowed like a sheet of silver. It was a wonderful sight, and I drank in the beauty of the early morning before going back to sleep.

I called my sisters next morning, and after a long chat with each of them, I painted for about three hours. At the end of that stint, I was happy to see my landscape beginning to take shape the way I envisioned it.

Nilanthi was going through a very difficult time I knew, so I called her almost every day. And she said it cheered her up, just talking about her troubles, because she had no close family or friends, except Tanesh. After I spoke to her on New Year's Eve afternoon, I did some shopping, and when I returned, I painted for a few more hours till late evening.

I stayed up till late to usher in the New Year, and watched Andre Rieu's gala concert on DVD. Christian and Nelune called me at midnight, and then I lit a whole packet of sparklers. I sat on the deck later, enjoying the sight of the brilliant moon shining on the bay.

Melbourne City, and Sydney, spent millions of dollars on fireworks. And although I watched the spectacular displays on television, I always thought it was a shameful waste of money. Instead of burning up money on fireworks, so much good could be done for the poor and homeless. I even wrote to the newspapers expressing my opinion, which they did not print. Few people really cared about depressing issues that interfered with the superficial enjoyment of the "silly season."

I felt very strongly about the plight of homeless people, and wrote to politicians and other groups, to start doing something about resolving this deplorable situation in our country. According to the responses that I received from the local member of parliament, relevant organizations were allocated funds to alleviate homelessness in Melbourne. I can only hope that a lasting solution will be found soon. In affluent countries like Australia, England, and America, I believe it is a blot on these societies, to allow unfortunate people to exist in sub-human conditions. Before I went to sleep that night, I thanked God for his blessings and goodness. And for letting me enjoy a peaceful, stress-free evening, compared to previous years.

I called my sisters, and friends, to wish them a Happy New Year. Christian phoned in the afternoon, and we wished each other again, and hoped this year would be a good one for us. I made some cutlets for Saturday's lunch, and watered the garden till late.

It soared to thirty eight degrees next day, and when I drove to Bentons Square at eleven o'clock in the morning, it was already thirty degrees. When I returned, I cooked some curries, and fried rice before it got even hotter. But it was scorching by evening, and remained at thirty degrees throughout the night.

I was very distressed to see so many bushfires raging around Victoria, and as always, I worried about one starting around here, because of the adjoining reserve. That was the reason I kept a watchful eye there, and listened to the weather forecast daily. The cats did not want to come in till late that night, and I could not blame them. It was cool in my bedroom though, so I slept comfortably, without the air-conditioner on.

Cornelia called at about nine thirty on Saturday morning, and said they would get here around two o'clock. Nelune wanted to know how I was coping with the extreme weather, as it was going to reach forty one degrees that day. But it became cloudy and blustery during the day, which helped a little, and my guests arrived just after two o'clock. Con looked alright after his heart attack, and operation to insert a pacemaker.

Cornelia told me about Con's frightening experience, as he had collapsed at home, and turned blue as he lay helpless. And their son, Victor, saved his life. He gave Con mouth to mouth resuscitation, while the paramedics instructed him on the phone until they arrived. Laura came soon after, and they relaxed on the deck, as it was cooler there, with sea breezes blowing across the bay, and we enjoyed the afternoon.

Con tired easily though, and after watching news, they left around six o'clock. Elvira called just then to say she would drop in on Monday afternoon for a coffee. I spent a quiet evening, and was relieved when it started drizzling slightly, and the night turned cooler. I stayed awake for some time, listening to the welcome sound of rain. It poured down heavily all night, and the weather was milder on Sunday.

I prepared everything for afternoon tea, and Paul and Julie arrived at about one o'clock. Paul did a few odd jobs around the house and garden, before we sat down for afternoon tea. We enjoyed a stimulating discussion about various global issues etc. It was good to have such great friends, and I considered myself truly blessed, to have some very sincere, helpful friends around me. After they left that evening, I made a few phone calls, and told Anjo I would visit her soon. Laura called that night to give me the recipe for Italian salami, as I had enjoyed her home-made salami and sausages.

On Monday morning, I prepared some short eats for afternoon tea, and was taking it easy, when I remembered I had some urgent business to attend to. I drove to Mornington, finished there, and came home in time for my visitors.

Elvira brought vegetables from her garden, and Mary gave me some biscuits. After they left, I called Shirani and Ninette. Christian phoned that night, and we had a long chat about some business issues. He said he appreciated everything I did for him, and I thanked him for being so helpful as well. He said he would visit soon, and I was glad to hear he was feeling better.

I visited Ninette around three o'clock the following Tuesday, and she said Toula took her to Frankston pier, to watch the Greek water festival, which was a big event in their community. She was in a better frame of mind, and I was relieved when she talked about music, and Luigi's past glories, involving concerts and performances, without too much complaining about her aches and pains.

On my way home, I saw an overturned car near Woolworths in Seaford, and the traffic was held up for about twenty minutes, so it was almost six o'clock when

I came home. I called Nilanthi that night, and we talked for some time, as I was anxious, and felt down-hearted over some issues Christian faced. I had a bad night, and did not fall asleep till about four o'clock. But I took down the few Christmas decorations, and cleaned up the house next day.

The weather turned extreme once again, and went up to thirty five degrees that day. I waited for Christian all day, as he said he would visit, but he called at four o'clock to say it was too hot to drive down. We had a long chat instead, which was good, as I was really concerned about him. I advised him to look after his health, as stress was harmful to anyone's wellbeing.

A cool change was unlikely till tomorrow, although heavy rain and thunderstorms battered some parts of Melbourne, and brought much needed relief to the fire-fighters battling bushfires.

I drove to Karingal cinema on Thursday, and bought a ticket to watch "The Hobbit" on the following afternoon, as I did not want to stand in a queue. It drizzled steadily on my way home, but I was relieved, because we needed the rain badly.

I settled the cats early, and gave them some prawns, before I left next afternoon. The movie finished at six twenty, almost three hours long, but I enjoyed it very much, as it was a fantastic production. After two and a half hours of very loud noise, and crashing battles, I ended up with a slight headache though.

I liked the peaceful scenes better, as they were beautifully photographed. And I thought that Peter Jackson, the producer, had concentrated mostly on "The Battle Of The Five Armies," resulting in non-stop bloody violence, and destruction. What a shame that the real story, as depicted in the books, could not be told, without so much violence, noise, and gimmicks. Anyway, that was the last of the epic series, and I was happy that I watched them all. It rained steadily all through the evening, and was a welcome sight, although it meant I could not walk in the garden.

Linda said they would arrive around midday on Saturday, and they enjoyed the cutlets I had kept warm in the oven. The children were happy with their Christmas goodies, and I gave Linda and Leo a box of chocolates too. They did not stay long, as they had to go somewhere else. Still, it was very nice of them to visit, as I knew they were very busy young people.

Shirani and Ranjith dropped in next day, and we spent a couple of pleasant hours together.

The scorching weather continued, but Monday was slightly cooler, as it reached only twenty nine degrees. Nelune said that she posted mobile phones for Nilanthi before she left for Brisbane a few days ago, but I told her they had not arrived as yet. Then she called again to say that they tried to deliver them last Friday, and as I was not in, they had said they would deliver them on Tuesday. So I told Shirani that I would drop the mobile phones at Narre Warren when I got them on Tuesday.

Ninette kept me on the phone for over forty five minutes, repeating the same old stories, and dwelling on her past as usual. Her behaviour was very erratic, and I had to be very patient with her, as I was sad to see her deteriorating. Not only was her eyesight failing, but she was hard of hearing too, which made it extremely difficult to converse with her now, so it was better just to listen.

Luigi too was losing his hearing, and everything had to be repeated a few times, before Ninette and Luigi understood. But they were obstinate, and refused to wear hearing aids, saying their hearing was just fine, and that it was my fault. Ninette said, "You speak too softly Nalini, I can't hear you!" When they were together, and I tried to converse, it was exhausting to repeat the same thing, and talk very loudly, until they heard and understood.

I waited all day on Tuesday for Toll Express to deliver the phones, but they did not come. Christian said he would visit before midday, but neither he nor the delivery truck arrived by lunch time. I called Nelune, and she said they would be here after four o'clock. I had an appointment with the surgeon at three o'clock, so I asked her to cancel the delivery, and re-schedule it for another time. Christian called at two o'clock, and said he would be here in forty five minutes time, but I told him I had an appointment.

It continued to pour down in torrents, and turned out to be such a rush. Christian had only five minutes to drop off a laptop for Nilanthi, before I left for my appointment. After all that scurry, Shirani said to drop in on Sunday, instead of that evening, due to the bad weather.

I made it in time for my appointment, and when the surgeon checked my eyes, he said, "You have left it too long, and now I will have to use a sledge-hammer to get the cataracts out, as they are so hard!" He was quite funny, and made me laugh. Then he said that the earliest date he could book me in for an operation, was 10 February.

I had no choice, but to book it in, and he said he operated at the Bays Hospital in Mornington. Later that evening, when I spoke to Mary and Elvira about it, they said not to worry, as one of them would take me to the hospital, and pick me afterwards. When I told Nilanthi and Shirani what was happening, they too were concerned. It was an exhausting day, and I was glad to unwind in the evening.

When I visited Ninette on Wednesday, Toula was there too, and she invited me for afternoon tea next Saturday, as it was Ninette's eighty-third birthday. I planned to take chicken curry, and fried rice for Ninette, as she told me that she would be on her own. But Toula had already organized tea, and said she would be happy if I picked Ninette, and brought her around three o'clock to her place. I said I would be glad to do that.

Nelune called later that evening, and said that she would come over when I had the cataract operation, as they told me someone had to stay with me overnight. It was very good of her, and I told her that I appreciated it very much. Christian sent a text next day saying he tried to call me several times, and was concerned I did not answer. I did not have any missed calls, and told him my mobile must be playing up.

Anyway, he offered to stay overnight when I had the operation, as he said that it was too much for Nelune to travel all that way, just for one night. I thanked him, and told him that it would be good if he could organize it. And also, that Mary or Elvira would take me to hospital, so not to worry about that.

I picked Ninette on Saturday afternoon, and drove her to Toula's. And I gave her a bouquet of flowers, chocolates, and a bottle of brandy, and a bottle of champagne for Toula. Ninette's grand-daughters, and their partners, greeted us briefly when we came in, and then talked among themselves. Ninette whispered, "The young ones are to themselves always, so we'll have a good chat eh? She sat next to me, and indulged in a tête-à-tête all afternoon.

Toula was very hospitable, and kind, and tried her best to make Ninette happy. Frank and Erik, who were caught up in a photographic frenzy, removed numerous photographs of Ninette, her grand-daughters, and her two great grand-daughters. I left at five o'clock, as Toula said she would take Ninette home later. I had a slight headache by the time I came home, and although it was very blustery that evening, I walked in the garden for a while.

I hardly slept that night, as the neighbours were very noisy, banging car doors non-stop. So I woke up late the following morning, and felt very drowsy. Some children were visiting next door, and they ran in and out of the house shouting boisterously, not knowing they were disturbing anyone. I felt lethargic all day.

Isobel called, and we had a nice long chat, and she said she would visit soon. Then I spoke to Cornelia, Judy, and Nilanthi. When I called Ninette that evening, she did not keep me on the phone too long, as Frank and Toula were visiting, and she was busy. I wanted to finish the landscape soon, so I spent a few more hours painting.

Another sleepless night, as I just could not unwind, and slept fitfully after three o'clock in the morning. Shirani said they would drop in after lunch and pick up the laptop and mobiles for Nilanthi, as Peter agreed to take them for her.

I waited all afternoon, and they finally arrived at two thirty, but stayed outside for five minutes only, as they had to rush back for an appointment before four o'clock. I painted for a few hours after they left, and then called Mary Hancock, Elvira, and Mary. They all offered to help, if I needed anything after the cataract operation.

I drove to Bunnings next day, and bought some bougainvillea plants, and a peppercorn tree that I planted in the back yard. I hoped that the bougainvillea plants would thrive, as I wanted some colourful plants on the balcony and deck. Nelune was visiting that weekend, as she wanted to see me before the operation.

When I saw Ninette on Wednesday, Luigi was there too, but he was in severe pain, and very grouchy as usual. I was glad when he did not stay long. Although I felt sorry for him because he was in pain, it was very depressing to see him looking so dejected, and I was relieved when he left. Ninette and I watched "The Eddy Duchin Story," that Toula recorded for me. But she kept asking, "Is it over yet? What's happening? I can't see very well…." And so on, right through the movie.

I was glad I watched it alone at home, and only agreed to see it with Ninette, because she told me that she wanted company, as she did not like to watch movies on her own. But unfortunately, her eyesight was so bad now that she complained of blurred vision constantly. I did not mind watching that movie again, because of the beautiful piano music, and the narrative, which was based on a true life story. Toula dropped in just before I left, and watched the last few minutes of the movie. She liked it very much too, although she had seen it before.

When I came home, I touched up the toilet walls with a second coat of paint, and later on, I hung the finished painting in the lounge-room. Nilanthi called to say that Peter dropped in and gave her the laptop, and two pairs of shoes that I bought for her, so she was happy and thanked me. I was glad that she received the parcel safely.

I drove to Rosebud clinic next day, to freeze a few more sun-spots on my neck and shoulders. The doctor was thirty minutes late, and after he treated some, he asked me to come a few more times, as he could not freeze too many at once, as it was very painful. On my way home, I dropped in at Farrell's book shop in Mornington, to order Karen's book. Then Joelle called, and we had a long chat, as she had a day off and was at home. I made mango chutney, and beef curry for Saturday's lunch that evening.

Elvira, Mary, and I, drove to Tyabb Antique Warehouse on Friday, the 23rd. Elvira drove, and we had a great time wandering in a labyrinth of forgotten treasures from yesteryear. It was a truly fascinating place; acres of beautiful antique furniture, crockery, paintings, books, etc, and it would take more than a day to see everything at leisure.

Some of the items, like the old Singer sewing machine, with a foot peddle, evoked memories of the one Ammie had. I learnt to sew on that machine when I was a teenager. The last time I visited in 1995, Ammie still had that old Singer machine in her bedroom. And as the bulky, ornately carved Victorian furniture was similar to the ones I had seen in some houses in Sri Lanka, it was a nostalgic afternoon for me.

We stopped at the cafe, and I bought cakes and tea. Elvira saw some quilted fabric that she liked very much, and asked if I could sew cushions with it. I agreed, so she was pleased and bought the fabric. It was late afternoon when we finally returned, and Elvira wanted to get back soon as she had guests that night. I was glad to have visited that place, and we planned to go there again soon.

I did not get much sleep that night, as the lights went out around eleven forty, and I woke up every hour to see if the power was on. Then at about three thirty, I started worrying about the food in the fridge going off. I slept fitfully, and by the time I woke up at six o'clock, I was exhausted. But at least the power was on again. I had a shower and waited for Nelune to call me, then picked her at ten thirty from Frankston station.

She looked well, and very pretty in a floral summer jacket, and white jeans. We spent a lovely afternoon together, and she enjoyed lunch, then I dropped her at the station around four o'clock, as she had to get back to the city in time to watch the tennis. Later that evening, I watched "Rhapsody In Blue," the life of George Gershwin, which was an interesting story. But it had a poignant ending, as he died at the age of thirty-nine.

I felt much better next morning, as I had a good sleep, and woke up at six o'clock. It was gusty, but cooler on Sunday. Nelune thanked me, and said she enjoyed the few hours we spent together, and the delicious meal very much. She said she was leaving Melbourne at four o'clock that day, and would visit again soon. It was always a pleasure to spend time with Nelune, no matter how brief, and I looked forward to her next visit.

I expected Elvira and John for afternoon tea, as she told me John would fix the kitchen tap, but they did not turn up. When I called Nilanthi that evening, we talked for some time, and she said that she enjoyed the dinner party with the Dias family.

Elvira called next day, and said that John would come over to fix the kitchen tap that afternoon, as he was held up yesterday, and she would come for a coffee as well. I spent some time painting in the morning, and they came around four o'clock. John had a beer when he finished fixing the tap, while Elvira and I enjoyed chatting over coffee.

After calling Ninette, I watched the late news, and a new Prime Minister was elected in Greece, precipitating fears of global impact. Then I followed an interesting story about a meteor that dropped in Rumania a few years ago.

I drove to the eye clinic in Mornington on the 27th, and they examined both eyes thoroughly, before removing photographs, then I completed all the paperwork. They said that because of the anaesthetic, someone had to stay with me at home, or else I would have an overnight stay in hospital, which I did not want to do. When I came home, I called Christian, and my sisters, as they were anxious to know what was happening.

Elvira came at one o'clock next afternoon to practise songs, and stayed for an hour, then we had coffee, and a nice long chat. After she left, I visited Ninette briefly, stopped for groceries, and came home by six o'clock. Imagine my annoyance when the garage door, and the gate would not open! I thought the batteries were flat, so I drove back to Bentons Square to buy new batteries. But all the shops were closed, except Woolworths, who did not sell those particular batteries.

I was at a loss, but I drove home, and prayed hard all the way. And when I tried again, both remote controls worked! Then it struck me that the power must have gone off (again). I was very tired and anxious when I went inside the house, especially because the cats were all in, and waiting to be fed and let out. When I spoke to Mary later that evening, she wanted to visit Tyabb Antique place again next Friday, so I agreed.

I felt exhausted, and woke up late on Thursday morning. When I called Elvira later, she said she would like to go to Tyabb as well. I drove to Rosebud clinic at two o'clock, and doctor saw me forty five minutes later (once again). After he froze a few more sun-spots, I told him I would see him again after my cataract operation.

When I came home, I spoke to Shirani, Joelle, and Mary. Then sewed Elvira's cushions for a few hours, and finished four of them by seven thirty in the night, and hoped she would like them. It was fiddly work with the quilted fabric, and to get the scalloped edges the way she wanted. But I managed to sew them neatly, and they looked pretty.

It was a mild day when Elvira picked me around eleven thirty next morning. She was very happy and surprised when she saw the cushions, so I was glad she liked them. We picked Mary later, and then drove to Tyabb and had a very pleasant time. Mary paid for lunch at the same cafe, and I bought a pretty table lamp for $120, as I was looking for one for the side table in the lounge.

We noticed Elvira admiring a set of porcelain cups and saucers, so we bought them for her birthday, which was in a few week's time. We enjoyed the sunny afternoon, and each other's company very much. Elvira invited us for coffee, before she dropped me home around five o'clock. I relaxed in the evening and watched "A Song Of Love," the life story of Robert Schumann, for the second time, as it was a very moving story of this musical genius.

I slept in next day, as I was weary, and when I spoke to Nilanthi later, I was glad to hear she was well, and not depressed. That afternoon, I was surprised to read an email from one Jackie Jilla, asking me if I could contact Kassi, her father-in-law, and she gave his mobile number. I called him later, and enjoyed chatting to him, as he remembered that Connie and I spent our honeymoon with them in Trincomalee.

I told him about Connie's illness and death, and then he broke the tragic news about Terri, his wife, (Connie's cousin), who had died last Saturday, and the funeral was next week. He gave me details, in case Connie's relatives, or I wanted to attend the funeral.

When I asked him what happened, he said, "Terri was in a coma for a month after she caught fire on 20 December. She always lit tea light candles when she prayed, but that night, her dressing gown caught fire, and I tried to put the flames out, and burnt my hands and feet too. I'm still unable to walk properly, as my burns haven't healed. She was only seventy-nine years old, my poor wife!"

I was shocked, and sympathised with him deeply. He said that his daughter-in-law saw my website, and got my email address from there. We spoke for some time, and he asked me to call him whenever I could, as he liked to recall old times, when we visited them so long ago. Ever since then, he sent me Christmas cards, and I reciprocated.

Chapter 97

When Nancy heard about my cataract operation, she offered to come over on 12 February to take care of me. I thanked her, and said I would be alright and not to worry. But she said she would still visit me a day or so after the operation.

I did not sleep too well at nights, and felt very lethargic and drained most of the time. And as my eyes were blurry and getting worse, I could hardly wait to have the cataract removed in one eye at least, which would give me better vision (I hoped).

The days passed swiftly, with my daily routine of painting, writing, and teaching at school, besides visiting Ninette, calling my sisters, and friends, or getting calls from them. Christian spoke to me almost every day too, and time just slipped away.

All my friends called on Sunday, the 8th, to wish me well. And Nelune was still prepared to come over, in case Christian could not be with me on that night. I thanked her, but said he was certain that he could drive here after work. It was Ammie's birthday next day, so I said a special prayer for the repose of her soul, and remembered our childhood days, and how well she cared for us.

I woke up at five o'clock on Tuesday morning, 10 February. Then I let the cats out for a while, and enjoyed looking at the beautiful starry skies, with a half-moon shining so bright, that it almost looked like daylight. I rested for a little while more, and was ready when Elvira came at seven o'clock.

We arrived at the Bays Hospital in fifteen minutes time, and they took me in straightaway for several check-ups, and put eye drops every five minutes. I almost fainted with hunger, as I sat in the waiting room, because I fasted from the night before. Elvira stayed with me until the paperwork was done, then I told her to keep my handbag, as the hospital said they would contact her when I was ready to go home.

It was almost quarter past ten, when they finally wheeled me into the operating theatre, where they administered a mild anaesthetic and sedative. And I woke up in half an hour's time. The nurse left me sitting with a group of patients, who all had patches covering one eye. I could not believe that the surgeon performed so many operations that morning.

I kept telling the nurse I was absolutely famished, and they served sandwiches, and a cup of tea at about twelve fifteen. I had to wait a while longer, as my blood pressure was low, and it was after one o'clock when Elvira picked me. My eye was still covered with a patch, and I wore sunglasses, as I could barely face the glare when I walked out, and except for a slight headache, and light-headedness, I felt alright.

Shirani was home already, and as she had a spare key, she let herself in, and was sipping a cup of tea when we arrived. Nelune called soon after, and was happy to hear that I was alright, then Christian said he would see me later that night. Ninette and Mary left messages, so I called them back to say the operation went well. I saw double for some time though, and when I removed the patch from my eye, everything looked very bright and blue.

I rested after Elvira and Shirani left, although they were reluctant to leave till Christian arrived. But I assured them I would be fine, and not to worry, as I would rest and not move around too much, except to feed the cats and let them out later.

I woke up at about seven o'clock, as I fell asleep, and when I switched on the television, the glare was still too intense, but the double vision had settled. While waiting for Christian, I watched "House Of Hancock," the fascinating story of Gina Rinehart, mining magnate, and one of the richest people in Australia. I could now understand the reason behind the legal battle with her children. She worked like a Trojan to build her empire, and did not want her fortune to be squandered.

Christian sent a text at eleven o'clock, to say he was held up, and was just leaving the city. I waited till half past twelve, and then called to ask how far off he was, as I was concerned about him driving here after working all day. But though he said he would be here shortly, it was one o'clock in the morning when he finally arrived.

He looked so drained, that I was sorry I asked him to come, because I would have been alright on my own. But it was very good of him to drive over, and he immediately started to fix a few things on the computer that needed to be done. It was after two o'clock when he went to bed, after sipping a cup of tea. Although I was worn-out, I woke up at five thirty to let Simba out, and was ready at eight thirty to see the eye surgeon for the post operation check up. Christian was ready too, but we did not have time for breakfast, and he drove me to the eye clinic at Mornington.

The surgeon checked my eye, and said the operation went well, and my eye was alright now. But to continue using eye drops three times a day, for the next four weeks. And he said I could drive in a few days time, if I was confident enough. When we returned home, we had breakfast, and after attending to a few more things around the house, Christian left at midday. I was very grateful for his concern, and for all he did. Elvira, Ninette, and my sisters called during the day to find out how I was.

Nancy arrived at lunch time next day, and brought a delicious, home-made pumpkin soup. We enjoyed a pleasant afternoon, and walked in the garden later, as it was a nice warm day. I had the benefit of Nancy's knowledge and advice, as she was an expert gardener. The grapes were almost ready, so I cut a few bunches for her.

The glare was still too strong, and even with sunglasses on, my eye started to hurt. After Nancy left that evening, Liz called to thank me for her present and card that I left on her desk at school, as it was her birthday today. All my friends, and sisters, called me once again, and Christian spoke in the night. Ninette too left a message, to say that Toula and she would visit me soon. I was overwhelmed with everyone's concern, and counted myself extremely blessed to have such caring people around me.

I took it easy over the next couple of days, and spent some time writing, painting, and playing the piano. And except for the intense glare, I could see much better now with one eye, but the other one was very blurry.

I rested on Saturday, as it rained all morning, and in the night I watched "The Student Prince" on DVD, which was just splendid, and I enjoyed the music very much.

Tigger was not too well on Sunday, and the poor cat kept vomiting a few times. I gave him a teaspoon of olive oil, to help relieve his nausea, as I thought it must be fur balls. He slept under the car in the garage all day, and I thought I would take him to the vet, if he did not improve.

That afternoon, the shower upstairs started dripping very badly, so I called RACV emergency assist. The plumber arrived within an hour, and fixed the washer in the shower, which was the problem. I was glad that I did not have to bother anyone to fix it. Later that evening, I watched the next episode of "House Of Hancock," which was just as interesting.

Elvira called on Monday morning, and said she would drop in for a coffee. And when she did, she brought vegetables from their garden, and the same quilted fabric, to make three more cushions. After she left, I cut out and sewed two cushions. It was quite challenging to get them right, because of the pattern of the fabric, but they turned out well, and I was pleased.

Everyone called during the day to ask how I was, and I expected Ninette and Toula on Tuesday. But Toula sent a text to say they would visit on Wednesday instead.

Joelle said that her aunt, Noelle, was hospitalized, as she was in a diabetic coma. She took too much insulin, and her sugar levels dropped to one. Although she was recovering slowly, she had to be closely monitored, because she kept forgetting to check the correct dosage of prescribed insulin. Joelle said it was such a worry, as she was responsible for Noelle, as well as Micheline, and her mother, so I was very sorry for her.

Elvira told me not to worry to sew cushions, until my eye was healed completely. But I wanted to surprise her, so I finished sewing the last cushion, and was glad they turned out well.

Ninette and Toula visited on Wednesday afternoon, and Ninette wanted Toula to order the same book of Chopin's music that I had, even though she had umpteen copies of the same music. Twenty minutes later, after sipping a glass of water, she wanted to go home. Toula hardly had time to finish a biscuit and a cup of coffee, before Ninette became very restless and anxious until they left.

Toula said that Ninette was getting worse with anxiety and panic attacks, and she would have to get her assessed soon, as it was obvious she was not the same as before. I was sad to see Ninette looking so vague, and unable to concentrate on what was being said. But I thanked them for visiting, even though Ninette was impatient to leave so soon.

I told Elvira I would drop in for a coffee later that afternoon. And when she saw the cushions, she was surprised and delighted with them, so I was pleased. Elvira did so much for me, that it was just a minor favour to sew the cushions. I stayed for half an hour only, and she kept pressing me to come for dinner that night. I thanked her, but excused myself, as I said I wanted to rest, and be ready for school next day. That evening I watched an interesting documentary on the "Bronte Sisters," on television, and then turned in early.

My eye felt sore all day, even though I put eye drops three times daily, and I had to teach ten students that day. I was weary by the time I came home, so I rested a while. Ninette called in the evening to ask if she had left her sunglasses at my place, because she could not find them anywhere. I looked around while she was on the phone, and told her they were not here. She was not convinced, and insisted they must be here, as she was positive they were not with her. I said I would keep looking.

My eye was still irritating and teary, but we planned to go out for dinner on Saturday, to celebrate my birthday, which was next Monday. Elvira and John picked me at six o'clock, and we drove to Villa Adriana in Dandenong. Mary and Tony arrived there a few minutes later. We were disappointed to learn that the club had changed managers, and it was not the same as before. The food was quite forgettable, and their service too was very slow, but we enjoyed each other's company.

The live music, a Latin-American Band, did not start till after nine o'clock, and we left then, as we decided to have dessert and coffee at Elvira's place. Mary and Tony dropped me home later, and I thanked them for a very pleasant evening. The cats were in the garden still, and I was relieved that Simba did not jump the fence.

The staff organized a cake for morning tea, and sang "Happy Birthday" on Monday morning, and I had a pleasant time with my friends. When I drove back, my eye started to hurt, and I found it difficult to keep it open, as I just wanted to close it, due to the unbearable glare.

I had several cards, text messages, and calls from everyone that day. Janice sent me a lovely card, with beautiful sentiments as always, and Christine called in the night. Ninette left a message again, and when I called her, she said she still could not find her sunglasses anywhere, and whether I was positive they were not here. I replied patiently, "I've looked everywhere Ninette, they are not here. Try looking in your pockets or in your kitchen, as I'm sure you wore them when you left here." She was unconvinced though.

Chris La Ponder called to wish me too, and we had a long chat. She told me that a lout pushed Peter over on the street, and he hurt his head when he hit the concrete pathway. I spoke to him briefly, and he said he was much better now, poor man. He was almost eighty years old, and I was just as disgusted and shocked as Chris, that Peter should have been a victim of such anti-social behaviour.

When I visited Ninette after school on Thursday, Toula was there too, and they gave me a pretty bracelet for my birthday. I had a cup of coffee with them, and then drove to Cranbourne music centre, to pick up some sheet music. I came home at five o'clock, after attending to a few other matters, and the cats were impatient to go out. Later that evening, I prepared for my trip to the city tomorrow, and turned in early.

I left home at eight o'clock next morning, parked in the church car park, then walked to the station. I boarded a train forty minutes later, and reached Flinders Street Station within an hour. I walked through Elizabeth Street to Flinders Lane, and arrived at Ross House before ten thirty. When I walked into the room on level three, which was not the usual venue, none of the other members had arrived as yet.

We had a good meeting though, and I caught up with all my friends there. It was an interesting morning, discussing our writing, and some members' recent book launches. Del and I chatted away as usual, and she said she was pleased to see me looking well after the cataract operation.

When the meeting finished, I stood outside Ross House, where Christian and Athena met me around one fifteen. We had coffee and a snack, before I boarded a train back to Frankston, and I came home around five o'clock. I spent some time cleaning and vacuuming the house later on, as I expected visitors next day.

It was a very hot thirty four degrees on Saturday. Con called at nine thirty in the morning, and said they would be here by eleven o'clock, which was good, as they always turned up late in the afternoon or evening. Elvira dropped by later with some fresh beans from their garden, and it was twelve thirty when she left, but my visitors still did not arrive.

They finally turned up at one thirty, and Laura's son, Cristian, came too, as it was Laura's birthday. I gave her an orchid plant, and a card, and she had a gift voucher for me. Con and Cornelia too brought a lovely bouquet of flowers, and a bag of expensive bath products. We had cutlets and coffee, before we headed off to Tyabb Antique Warehouse.

After walking through a labyrinth of memorabilia and antique furniture, we stopped to have lunch at the cafe there. Con and Cornelia were not pleased with the meal at all, because it was over-priced and insufficient. They ordered steak with salad, and what they served up was a huge plate of salad, with a few strips of meat, that were difficult to unearth in the depths of so much greenery. And twenty five dollars was too much for a plate of greens (we all agreed).

My friends wanted *quantity*, as they were used to hefty steaks, and relished meat more than greens. Con complained to the manager, who replied, "The menu reads, *100 grams of steak,* and that is how that particular dish is served." And he did not do anything about it. Laura and Cristian though were happy with the meals they ordered. And I did not complain either, as 100 grams of beef strips were sufficient for me. As it was Laura's birthday, I paid for everyone's lunch, which I think smoothed their ruffled feathers somewhat.

I must admit though, that the meals were over-priced, and not the tastiest food either, and decided not to eat there in future. Later, we walked around the warehouse again till five o'clock, and they enjoyed that part of the day very much. Laura and Cornelia wanted to visit the place again.

By the time we came home, and had a few drinks and nibbles, it was after seven o'clock when they left. A fierce storm broke out about an hour later, and Angela, my neighbour, sent a text asking if I was okay. I replied that I was fine, and thanked her for her concern. Then I kept candles in every room, but thankfully, the power did not go off. The cats stayed indoors too, so I had an early night.

It was much cooler on Sunday, and I did some chores around before relaxing in the afternoon. Nilanthi called, and was full of complaints about the hectic time she had looking after Heron's elderly sister, Jasmine, and her husband, Emmanuel, who were holidaying there. They decided to spend a few weeks at her place, because she could "care" for them.

Jasmine was very frail, and had cancer. And Nilanthi said she expected to be waited on hand and foot, so she was exhausted, as the cranky old lady was very demanding, and worse than Heron. She said she was looking forward to some respite when they left, and swore she would not be forced to look after old people again, as she did enough for Heron and Thathie. Nelune called later to ask how I survived the severe storm last night, and was relieved that there was no damage in my garden or surroundings.

When I drove to school next morning, I found the glare almost unbearable, and found it difficult to drive, so I decided to ask the eye surgeon about it. Ninette called in the evening, and said she found her missing sunglasses in her laundry, of all places! She left them on the washing machine, and did not think of looking there, and found them quite by chance. I was glad that the mystery of her missing sunglasses was solved.

I had an uneasy night, and could not fall asleep for some reason, as bad memories, and negative thoughts whirled through my mind endlessly. I forced myself to think happy thoughts. But my mind was determined to torment me, and re-play every single sad memory.

I felt somewhat dejected next day, but tried to busy myself as usual. When I called Nilanthi in the evening, we talked for a long time, and I felt better for sharing similar experiences. Then I worked a few hours on my manuscript, but my left eye was getting tired, so I had to stop.

When I finished at school on Wednesday, I visited Ninette briefly, and had coffee with her before shopping at Woolworths in Seaford. Christian called, and we spent some time chatting, as he had some great new projects in mind. That evening, I watched an interesting program called "Walking Through History," presented by Tony Robinson, (who acted as Baldric in the Black Adder series). It was an excellent program, as he journeyed through some of the most beautiful places in Britain, and talked about famous people, like Jane Austen, and the Bronte sisters, to name a few, who had lived in those towns.

Nilanthi complained about a bad ear ache the last time, so I called to ask how she was. She said the doctor syringed it, and she felt much better, but was still busy running around looking after her elderly guests, and could not wait to see the last of them.

I went for my appointment with the eye surgeon that afternoon, and he told me that my left eye was really bad now, and I should have the cataract removed as soon as possible. The right eye had healed well, but I told him the glare worried me still. He asked me to buy a pair of good sunglasses, and wear them whenever I drove or went outdoors.

The earliest appointment he had was at the end of June, so I booked my next cataract operation on 30 June. I drove to Bentons Square later, and bought a very good pair of Polaroid sunglasses, which really helped to reduce the glare.

I called Chris Del Piano that evening, and asked if he could paint the outside ceiling, as it was mouldy and looked dirty. He said he would get here by nine o'clock next morning to give me a quote for the painting, and a few other odd jobs around the house and garden.

Chris arrived promptly next morning, and said he could do the painting etc. next Monday, as it was a public holiday, and he was free. I told him that would be fine, then Ron and Monica arrived shortly afterwards. Elvira dropped in at midday to practise some hymns for Sunday. When she left after an hour or so, Joelle, Celine, and Micheline arrived at two o'clock.

Ron and Monica returned just then, after taking all the green waste to the tip, and the garden looked very nice and tidy after the big clean up. I enjoyed a pleasant afternoon with my visitors, then I relaxed after they left a couple of hours later. It was a busy, but agreeable day.

After I finished my chores on Sunday morning, I raked the crushed rock from the pathway in the backyard, as Chris agreed to do the timber-edging there. Ninette invited me on Monday afternoon, but I told her I could not make it, as I was getting some work done in the garden. Then I made some patties in the evening.

Chris arrived early on Monday morning, and started doing all the odd jobs; he filled gaps under the window in the dining room, painted the al fresco ceiling, replaced rusty shades, and finally set up the timber-edging.

Shirani said they would drop in for a little while, as she had a doctor's appointment later. I spent an hour writing till they came, but they did not stay long, and left in half an hour's time. Chris finished around three o'clock, and he did a perfect job as usual. It was worth paying him, as his rates were very reasonable too.

Tuesday was a warm, pleasant day, and Ninette visited with Toula in the afternoon, and she stayed for about an hour, which surprised me. I coaxed her to play the piano, and that kept her busy for a while. After they left, I did some cleaning up outside, and raked the crushed rocks evenly, now that the edging was completed, and it looked tidy. Then I picked figs for Maxine and Christine at school, as they liked them very much.

I woke up with severe pain in my right eye around four o'clock on Wednesday morning, and I was concerned that it was infected. And as I had finished the eye drops, I did not have anything to soothe my eye. When I looked in the mirror, my eye was very red and swollen, and tears streamed down constantly. I bathed it gently with some warm, salt water, and got ready for school.

I do not know how I drove, as I had to shut my right eye to avoid the pain, and I could barely see with my left eye, because it was so very blurry. When I arrived at school, the pain was severe, and I could not keep my eye open. Margaret looked at me and said, "I think you better see your doctor Dolly, your eye looks awful!"

I drove to the Medical Centre close by, but Dr Khelil was busy, and another doctor saw me. He advised me to see the eye surgeon immediately, as my eye looked very sore, and he did not want to do anything. But when he tried to open my eye, I did not let him even touch it, as it was so very painful.

I made an appointment with the eye surgeon, but he could not see me before three forty five. Then I drove to Karingal to get some eye drops, but the chemist was reluctant to give me anything, until I saw the specialist. So I drove to Mornington, where they kept me waiting till about five fifteen, as the surgeon was so busy. The nurse put some eye drops, until Dr Walland saw me, as Dr Renehan had already left for the day.

When he finally saw me, he said it had nothing to do with the cataract operation, but was an inflammation, and gave me a prescription for some anti-bacterial eye drops. I drove to Bentons Square quickly to get the eye drops, and came home after six o'clock.

The cats were still inside the house, and waiting patiently for their dinner, but they were alright. I fed them and let them out, then put some eye drops before going straight to bed, as I could not keep my eye open. I spoke to Christian, Nelune, and Shirani later, and told them what happened, and they were very concerned.

The intense pain eased slightly next morning, and the swelling went down too. But I was drained after enduring constant pain for two days, so I rested all day. Maxine called to ask how I was, and said that Margaret, and the others were all concerned, and hoped I was better. I thanked her, and said my eye was healing, and not so bad now.

I called Nilanthi that evening, and later Nelune and Shirani phoned again to see how I was. I left a message and told Christian I was much better, but as he worked till late, I did not hear from him that night. I managed to get out of bed by late evening, fed the cats, and let them out. I was unable to look at the television screen the previous evening, but I watched the late news now, as the pain had eased considerably.

My eye was still red and swollen, though the pain was not as severe, and I kept putting eye drops four times daily. I did not know how it became so inflamed, unless some dust or dirt got into my eye when I raked rocks in the pathway. Ninette and Elvira called later, and then my sisters, who were relieved to hear that I was much better, because they were worried.

Elvira asked me to accompany her to a dinner dance at Rosebud, on Saturday, 14 March. She said John had to work at the club bar all night, and she would be alone, so she persuaded me to go with her. Mary called, and said I really should not go out that night, as my eye was not healed completely, and that I should be careful. But I said I had promised Elvira, and I had to go. John had left early, so Elvira picked me around six thirty, and we drove through pouring rain.

When we arrived at the club, Elvira's brother, Silvio, and his wife, Anne, and some other good friends of hers, were seated at the table. So really, there was no need for me to be there at all, I thought. Elvira did not dance though, as John was busy. And I sat there all evening, just trying to converse with some of them above the loud music. John came around to chat now and then.

I was weary, as my eyes were strained, but we left after eleven o'clock, and by the time I came home and settled the cats etc. it was well after midnight. I decided not to go for another dinner dance, as it was very boring sitting there alone, when all the others were couples. And I did not want to dance with any of their husbands either, although John told Elvira that he would dance with me, if I wanted to.

Chapter 98

A few more days passed, before the eye inflammation healed completely. And I refrained from doing any more gardening jobs, although there was still plenty to do.

It was hectic at school on Wednesday, 18 March, as I kept adjusting my times to fit in with some students, who were busy doing other projects. During the course of the day, Liz told me the tragic news about Roscio, Sabrina's and Dakota's mother, who was dying of breast cancer, and nearing her end.

I was very distressed, because I knew Roscio fairly well, as I taught the two little girls piano for some time now. But I did not know she was seriously ill. Dakota was only seven years, and Sabrina ten, so my heart ached for them. They did not have a father to take care of them, as Roscio was a single mother. I just could not get her out of my mind all day, and I grieved for them. Liz said she was visiting her in hospital at lunchtime, so I asked her to convey my love, and tell Roscio my thoughts and prayers were with her.

I visited Ninette after school, and Luigi was there too, as he wanted to discuss something about his book. I was very upset about Roscio, and told Ninette about her. But it did not make an impact on her at all, because she replied vaguely, "Well, Nalini, what can we do? My mum died when I was only nine years old."

That night, when I called Nilanthi, and told her about the poor mother who was dying, she was sad too. The worst part was, the children had no one else to care for them, so Roscio requested her best friend to adopt them, and give them a secure home. They were leaving school to live with their foster- parents in another suburb.

When I saw doctor next day, he advised me on various issues, as he always had time for his patients; he was very caring, and talked of mental and physical wellbeing, as he was a philosophical man too. Just as I was leaving the clinic, I met another friend, Melissiah, whom I did not see for some time. We had a long chat, and she said she would visit soon.

I saw the dentist next day, and he told me that I needed to have four fillings. I said I would do two at a time, and he agreed.

I drove to Mount Eliza Community Theatre, on Saturday, 21 March, to watch the play "Dimboola," and the audience dressed up as wedding guests. I wore a mauve and cream chiffon suit, with white hat, gloves, and shoes. It was good fun, as most of the ladies took trouble to dress up elegantly, and a few of the men did too. Some older men, and a few ladies, complimented me on my outfit, especially my elegant white hat.

I laughed, and enjoyed myself thoroughly all through the play, and so did most of the audience. But I heard a hatchet-faced female at our table complaining about the noise, bawdy language, and behaviour of the players, forgetting it was only a play, and that they just acted their parts. In between acts, they served a three-course meal as part of the entertainment, and it was after five o'clock when I came home.

Although I was tired, I enjoyed every moment of that hilarious play. After doing some chores, I spread a few buckets of potting mix on the lawn, to fill up some bare patches. Then I relaxed in the evening.

When I was at school on Monday, I heard the sad news that Roscio died a couple of days ago. I tried to comfort Sabrina and Dakota, and gave them a card, and a small ceramic angel playing a harp, as a farewell gift. And I told them as their mother always wanted them to learn piano, they must continue for her sake, even after they left this school. Then I hugged them both, and told them to be brave. Poor little girls, my heart went out to them. The funeral was tomorrow, and Liz and some of the staff members were attending it. It was chaotic that day, because the students did "Way of the Cross," at different times, and I had to wait for each class to finish the stations of the cross outside.

When I dropped in at Ninette's later, she was busy preparing her dinner at three o'clock, so I did not stay too long. She said she ate early, and went to bed around four o'clock, listened to the radio, and then talked to Luigi. This was her mode of living now, and I was sad to think of her dwindling away.

Then I rushed to the post office before five o'clock to send Nilanthi's allowance, which she picked up that day. She was very happy when I called her that evening, and thanked me for sending the money in time. She wanted me to send her allowance a week or so earlier, due to several public holidays over there.

The weather was very turbulent on Thursday afternoon, 26 March, but I let Simba out at four thirty that morning, as he mewed to go out. When I woke up later and called him in, I could not see him anywhere in the garden. Although it rained heavily, and gusty winds lashed across the sea, I walked up and down the street calling him, but no sign of Simba.

I rang Nilanthi in the afternoon, and told her that Simba was missing again, just like he did last year on Good Friday, and did not come back for more than a day. I prayed fervently, and invoked Bruno to bring him home safely.

Then I called Nilanthi again at ten thirty that night, as Simba was not back yet. And she said she would keep praying too. I could not relax or watch television, as I was very upset. I went to bed, but woke up every half an hour, and went to the front door and called him continuously. I woke up again at twelve thirty, and opened the front door. And I called him loudly, because it was still blustery and raining.

Suddenly, he was there! Mewing and panting, his tongue hanging out, as he wobbled through the door. Another miraculous return I knew, and went down on my knees to thank God and Bruno for bringing back this errant cat safely. He did not know what a great deal of anxiety he caused me. But I was so relieved to see Simba, that I hugged him and carried him inside.

He looked exhausted and disoriented, but wherever he wandered off to, he somehow found his way home. I fed him a few prawns, which he gulped down greedily, and then lapped up some water for a few minutes. He looked groggy, and just flopped down on the floor, where he lay panting heavily. When I called Nilanthi with the good news, she was very happy for me. At last I could fall asleep, without worrying about Simba.

He was still very weak next day, and could hardly stand on his paws, as they seemed to be very sore. I massaged his paws, after soaking them in warm water, and then gave him a bowl of milk, which he lapped up greedily, but was still famished.

What a night and what a day! I did not let him out that whole day, and he slept right through, only getting up to eat as much as he could, and drink plenty of water. He did not mew to go out that night, as he still looked disoriented. I relaxed and watched "Annie," which was the old version with Carol Burnett, and I enjoyed it thoroughly.

I did not let Simba out till eight o'clock next morning, and he was content to sit on a chair outside, without wandering around in the garden. I knew he was still exhausted, and his paws must have been sore. I attended evening Mass, and got Holy Communion for Ninette. And as it was Palm Sunday, the service took longer than usual, and was quite late when I came home. I made sure that Simba came in before too late that night. Then I watched a very moving story "A Farewell To Arms."

Ron and Monica arrived at noon the following day. He went fishing last week, and brought me some fresh Snapper fillets, and in return, I gave him six beers, and a bottle of wine for Monica. They enjoyed a cup of tea and cake afterwards, and we had a long chat, as we were on friendly terms now, and I liked them. I called a few of my friends, and Nilanthi that evening, but when I rang Cornelia, she was busy making wine, and said she would call me tomorrow.

Monday was a school holiday, so I drove to Karingal in the afternoon, and watched "Second Best Exotic Marigold Hotel," starring Maggie Smith, Judy Dench, and Richard Gere. It was a good story, and very enjoyable.

I went out with Mary and Elvira for lunch next day, 1 April, to celebrate Elvira's birthday, which was on the 5th. We had a pleasant time, and Elvira invited me for dinner that night. On my way home, I stopped at Bunnings, and bought twenty metres of plastic mesh to nail on the back fence, which I hoped would deter Simba from climbing the fence again.

It was about six o'clock when I drove to Elvira's, and Daphne was already there. After dinner, when I mentioned that I had to get my fringe cut next day, Elvira insisted she would trim it for me. I asked her not to cut it too short, as I wanted just a very little off, but she was not listening, and went snip, snip, snip, until half my forehead was exposed! Anyway, she meant well, and only wanted to help me. I thanked her, and said it was okay, though much too short.

I dropped in at Ninette's on Thursday, and gave her Holy Communion, and a box of chocolates for Easter. Toula was there too, so we had a good chat. She was now Ninette's official carer, as she had applied through Centrelink. Toula spent more time with Ninette, because she closed down her driving school business, and Ninette was happy. She visited her almost every day, and Ninette did not depend on me anymore to take her for a drive or shopping, and do all those little tasks like before.

I spent a few hours cleaning and vacuuming upstairs on Good Friday. But I stopped at noon, and at three o'clock, to pause and offer a prayer in remembrance of Our Lord's death. Then I cooked a few curries for lunch on Sunday, and rested a while.

Next day, I cleaned and vacuumed downstairs, and then prepared a few more dishes, and that was it. Although I was exhausted, I looked forward to enjoying a pleasant day with Christian and Athena.

Christian called around nine o'clock on Easter Sunday morning, and sounded very groggy. I was very worried and shocked to hear that some hooligans attacked Athena and him outside a Seven Eleven store in Richmond, around two o'clock that morning. They were walking home after visiting some friends. And although a few people were around, those thugs attacked from behind, and threw Christian to the ground.

He was badly bruised, and had fractured ribs, and a broken finger. There was no way they could visit that day, as he was in emergency for a few hours. To say I was distressed, does not even begin to describe how I felt. But Athena reassured me that Christian was alright, and just needed to rest. I was very disappointed that they could not visit, but it was more important for him to rest, and recover soon.

I drove to Frankston station, and picked Nelune around ten o'clock. Then we stopped at Bayside Shopping Centre in Frankston, as she wanted to buy a pair of boots. We spent a couple of hours looking around there, then came home and relaxed. And in the evening, we watched a few comedies, but Nelune too was very concerned about Christian, and hoped that he would get better soon.

I dropped Nelune at the station after lunch next day, and then drove to the Power Centre in Frankston to buy a new vacuum, as the previous one lost suction. I bought a Hoover on a special, and also a small, white, occasional table for my room.

Babs called the day before, and said she would meet me at Karingal for a coffee that afternoon. So I drove there and waited almost forty minutes. When she did not turn up, I sent her a text. And she replied that she forgot, but would leave at once, and get here by two o'clock. It was late by then, and I was tired, so I told her we could catch up another time, as I did not want to wait any longer.

When I returned home, I spent some time digging out the pond in the backyard. The soil was rock hard, and it was difficult to make much headway, but I was determined to dig it out a little at a time. Tony used his bobcat to hollow out most of it, but it needed form, and more depth, before I could line it with plastic and set it up. Nelune called around seven o'clock that night to say she arrived safely, and had a good flight back.

I collected all the newspaper clippings, books etc. on Tuesday, 7 April, and prepared for a meeting with Duane, Luigi's friend, at Ninette's place tomorrow. He was in the entertainment and media industry, and said he would promote Luigi's book and CD.

When I spoke to Christian later that day, he said he felt a little better, but was still in severe pain, as his ribs hurt, and his broken finger was very sore. I prayed for him, and hoped he would get well soon. He never took pain killers, and always bore up the worst pain without complaining.

I arrived at Ninette's at one thirty next day, and Luigi was already there, but he was in a bad mood because his leg and back were sore. After a cursory greeting, he limped outside to wait for Duane. Ninette could not sit still from that moment on, because she wanted to go out with Luigi too. Although I tried hard to engage her in conversation, her mind flitted elsewhere, and she kept saying, "I *have* to go out to keep Luigi company." I was quite stressed by then, as she was so agitated.

Duane breezed in an hour later, and I saw him walking around the units looking for Ninette's place. As Luigi and Ninette were visually impaired, they did not see him, or recognize him until he was at very close range. Duane turned out to be a bombastic, over-confident Italian, who promised Luigi the moon and the stars! He was short and stocky, with pleasant features, sparse grey hair, and in his early seventies. He had a boundless store of his shenanigans, which I found mildly amusing.

I presented him a copy of Luigi's book, promotional material, and all the newspaper clippings. He promised to promote the book and CD, saying he could easily sell over one thousand copies of the book. Then he added, "Only thing, I'm going overseas for the Eurovision contest, and will be away for a couple of months, so I will do something once I return." I left soon after, but he stayed on till late that night.

Ninette told me next day, that Luigi and she thought Duane was full of hot air, and did not expect anything to eventuate from that meeting. It was a pity, as I hoped he would promote Luigi's book and CD.

When I left Ninette's that afternoon, I stopped at Clark Rubber in Frankston to buy some glue for the pond lining, as Shirani told me she glued two sheets of lining together, and it had held. I rolled out the lining in the evening, and pasted them together, then left it to dry undercover outside. It was very strenuous work, rolling out the heavy lining and pasting them together, so I hoped it would bond firmly.

Elvira dropped in at eleven o'clock next morning, to practise some songs, and she brought heaps of vegetables from their garden, and some home-made biscuits. After an hour's singing, then coffee and a chat, she left in a couple of hours time. Then I drove to Mornington library to look at some paintings of horses by Tea, the mother of one of my piano students. She was very gifted in modernist and abstract painting, and her large paintings hung in the library foyer, where a few people walked through.

On my way, I stopped at a garden supplier on Race Course road, and bought twenty small rocks to arrange around the pond. A pleasant, helpful young girl loaded them in the boot, and I drove back very slowly with my heavy load. I was happy that I found the limestone rocks I was looking for at a very reasonable price. It was after four o'clock when I returned, as I stopped at Bentons Square.

The pond lining did not bond together very well, so I glued it again, and hoped it would work this time. Then I carried the rocks, one by one down to the pond and arranged them around it. But they were not enough, and I needed another twenty or more rocks, which meant another trip to the garden supplier.

When I spoke to Ninette that evening, she was very upset, as Duane was very rude and abrupt on the phone that day. He criticized the CD list, saying there were mistakes in the names of the composers. I pacified her, and told her not to worry, as Ivano Ercole edited the list, and he was an opera buff, with vast musical knowledge. She calmed down a little, but was upset because she could not believe Duane spoke to her so rudely, especially after he spent all those hours, wining and dining with them the day before.

I visited Joelle on Friday afternoon, and Celine and Micheline were very hospitable while we waited for Joelle to return home from work. Joelle too was a very kind and sincere friend, and I was very fond of her. I spent a pleasant afternoon with them, and came home around six o'clock in the evening. Then I did a great deal of work in the garden, and set up the pond with the lining.

When I filled the pond with water on Saturday morning, it did not fill up right to the rim, which was disappointing, after all my hard work. The seam was leaking. I decided to get a whole sheet, without having to glue two sheets together. I spoke to Christian in the evening, and he said he was still very sore, poor Christian. I hoped he would recover soon, as his injuries affected his daily work and wellbeing.

Later that evening, I spoke to Nelune and Shirani. Then I called Badiha, the estate agent, as I saw our previous Tudor house in Frankston, advertised for only $493,000! When I asked her why the price dropped so much from when we sold it, she replied that the people who bought it from us neglected the place so badly, that they dropped the price drastically, just to get rid of it. She said, "You wouldn't like to see it now, compared to how it was when you sold it." It made me very sad to think of that beautiful house being neglected so badly. But it was not my house any longer, and I tried not to care.

My muscles ached next day, as I did so much of work in the garden, so I took it easy. Later on, I called everyone as usual, and wished Ninette, Laura, Con and Cornelia, as it was the Orthodox Easter, one week after the Catholic celebration of Easter.

Second term of school commenced next day, on Monday, the 13th, and I had a few new students. It was busy, and a long day, as I had to wait for Tess till four o'clock.

The next day, Isobel's daughter, Michelle, called and said that Isobel was very sick with a virus that she picked up on their last cruise, and that John suffered a mild stroke a few days after their return. She called to thank me for the Easter and birthday cards I sent Isobel, as she was too weak to call anyone. I was very concerned, and told Michelle that I was sad to hear such bad news, and to convey my love to them.

When I called Nilanthi later, she was frantic, as she said that due to heavy rains, the roof leaked badly, and she had to place buckets everywhere. I was very upset, and assured her that I would help financially, and to get a quote and start on repairs immediately. She was relieved and very happy. And then I told her about Isobel, and that I wanted to send her some flowers through Interflora that afternoon, as I could not visit her soon. She told me to convey her best wishes to them too.

After I sent Isobel a card and a bouquet of flowers, I came home and rested. I was exhausted whenever I exerted myself now, and had to push hard to do any physical work. This unusual fatigue made me think I was overdoing it in the garden, so I decided to take it easy for a while.

Ninette told me that Michelle called her too, and when I mentioned that I sent flowers, she demanded, "*Why* did you do that? I know Isobel *longer* than you!" I could not answer her question, so I replied that I wanted Isobel to know I was thinking of her. But she sounded very annoyed, and asked me who would pick up the flowers etc. etc. Sometimes, she could be very trying, and lately, she was very cranky.

I had the flu vaccine after school next day, then stopped at Clark Rubber to buy the pond lining, but they did not have the width I required. I dropped in at Ninette's, and Toula was waiting, as she ordered a DVD for me on Amazon, and I wanted to pay her for it. When I came home, I rested, but thankfully, I had no reaction to the flu vaccine.

Nilanthi called next day, as she said there was a special phone rate over Sinhalese New Year period, and said she needed about $450 for the roof repairs. I told her that I would send her the money next day, and she was very pleased, as she said that the roof leaked for some time. I drove to Bunnings later, where they stocked durable pond lining, five metres wide, which was exactly what I needed.

It was expensive, but at least I knew it would work this time. I tried hard to set up the pond, and after some expenditure and failures, I hoped this lining was the right one. It was not easy doing it myself, but I did not want to give up.

That night, I started reading a very interesting book "The Shell Seekers," for the third time, that Thathie sent me in 1993. He wrote an inscription on the fly leaf, "Don't be misled by the title-it's a very good book." And it really was a very moving, excellent story, with several thought-provoking passages.

I sent Nilanthi the money next day, and she replied a little while later, to say she collected the funds from Western Union, and bought the materials already, for the workmen to start immediately. She was very pleased, and kept thanking me profusely. But I said that I just wanted her to live in a comfortable house, and there was no need to keep thanking me. When I checked the pond that evening, I was relieved to see that the water did not leak through, which meant the lining was good. So I filled it to the brim.

Nelune called on Saturday morning to say that she wanted to pay half the cost towards Nilanthi's roof repairs. And had deposited the funds into my account already, which was very generous of her as usual.

Then Marg, my friend from school, phoned me. And I was very concerned when she started crying, and asked me to loan fifty dollars, as she did not have any money to buy food that weekend. I told her to come over immediately, but not to delay, as I had to go out that afternoon.

When Marg arrived at noon, I was upset to see that she was very distraught, because her husband of ten years walked out on her. She said they had problems for some time, but she did not expect him to leave her. As she said she had no food in the house, I packed up some food items, including frozen meats, eggs etc. Then I gave her fifty dollars, which she promised to return within a couple of weeks time.

While Marg was still there, and I was trying to comfort her, Isobel called to thank me for the lovely bouquet of flowers. I spoke briefly, and told her I had a friend with me, who was very upset, and I would call her later that evening. When I came back from the study, Marg had settled down a little, and stopped sobbing as we walked in the garden.

She looked around and exclaimed, "What a lovely place you have here Dolly! I will come and stay with you for a few days okay?" I did not respond immediately, as I was unsure what her husband would say or do. And being on my own, I did not want to get involved in her marital disputes. I said, "You can visit me whenever you want Marg, but wait and see if John comes back home. I'm sure he will return soon."

A week later, when I tried calling her, she had turned off her mobile, and she did not return any of my calls or messages. That was the last I heard of her, and it was another lesson in life; never lend or borrow money from a friend, because she had no intention of returning my fifty dollars.

After Marg left, I drove to Bentons Square and bought a bottle of Galliano for Tony, as it was his birthday that day, and I told Mary I would drop in to wish him. I stayed there for about an hour, and after a pleasant chat I came home and unwound, as it was a busy day. Nilanthi called to say that the roof was almost completed, and it was very good, as there were no more leaks, so I was glad. I cleaned up and vacuumed, as Badiha said she would visit me next day.

I woke up feeling exhausted on Sunday, and my neck and shoulders ached badly. I wondered if I strained them at the dentist's, because I had stayed in one position for more than half an hour on Friday, while he did two fillings. It was wet and chilly, and Badiha did not turn up that evening. She said she was held up with a client, and made another time next week.

When I called Ninette on Monday evening, she was on the phone to Luigi, and sounded quite off-hand, as she wanted to talk to him and did not want to be interrupted. I said I would call her tomorrow and hung up.

Simba jumped up on the fence again, and sat there looking at me triumphantly. It was amazing, as the fence was six feet tall, and he somehow managed to clamber to the top. I coaxed him, and after a few minutes consideration, he decided to jump down on the right side of the fence into my backyard, and not the reserve. He swished his tail defiantly, and condescended to follow me inside.

I drove to Dandenong on Tuesday morning, as the accountant required all files relating to Connie's last tax returns. And I was tired by the time I came home, as the traffic was very heavy. I did not stop at the Tax Office to catch up with my friends, as I wanted to get home early.

After school on Wednesday, I stopped at the parish office to speak to Fr Raj about holding a memorial service for Connie. But the office was closed, so I could not organize anything, and had to do it another day. Then I visited Ninette, who was in a very cantankerous mood, due to her back pain, and did not want to talk much, or be pleasant. Toula, Luigi, and Eric, dropped in too, and I did not stay too long, as I was anxious to go home. I stayed in the garden keeping an eye on Simba, as he took to climbing the fence at nights, and I did not want him wandering off again.

I called RACV emergency home assist again next day, as the laundry tap was leaking badly. They sent a plumber within the hour, and he fixed it without any charges, which was good, as it was only the washer that needed replacing.

Badiha was running late, and while waiting for her, I cleaned the cats litter tray in the laundry. Mishka was getting under my feet, and shadowing me as always, so I tried to put her out. When I came inside, I banged the fly screen door as hard as I could, because it did not shut properly sometimes. Next moment, I yelled out, "Oh God!" as the corner of the door gouged my foot.

I was in so much pain that my head started to spin. Mishka, who thought I was yelling at her, glanced at me reproachfully, then darted out nervously. My foot bled, and I could see the deep wound turning purple. When Badiha arrived around three forty five, I could hardly stand up. I told her that I hurt my foot, so I elevated it on a foot stool to stop the bleeding.

We had a pleasant time, in spite of my being in severe pain, and she said if ever I wanted to sell my house, she would help me. After she left, I cleaned the wound with disinfectant, and bandaged it, but my foot was throbbing all night. When I spoke to Christian and Nelune later, they were worried, and asked me to see doctor next day.

The wound was still bleeding and very painful next morning, so I called Dr Khelil, but he was fully booked. I saw another doctor at one o'clock, and he said I should have come immediately, as the skin had folded over the wound, and although he tried hard to pull it over, he could not. He gave me a tetanus injection, and asked me to keep it dry, and see him again on Monday to dress the wound.

It was very annoying, as it was such a silly accident, and I was in so much pain now. Anyway, I had things to do. On my way home, I stopped at the same garden supplier to get more rocks, and the kind lady loaded them into the boot once again. I bought some flowers too, and dropped in at Elvira's afterwards, as she was down with a cold, but she said she was feeling much better. I told her how I had banged the fly screen onto my foot, and she was concerned.

When I came home, I rested a while before unloading the rocks on to the wheelbarrow. Nilanthi called, and sounded frantic, as I did not respond to her text messages. I told her I did not receive them till about five thirty that evening. Then Nelune and Athena called to ask how I was, and they were relieved that I saw doctor, and had a tetanus injection. The doctor called it a "dirty" wound, because the fly screen was a metal door, and the wound was more prone to get infected.

I limped around in the garden, and saw Simba sitting up on the fence again! And when I called him, he had the sense to jump down on the right side at least, before sauntering off, upright tail swishing disdainfully, in protest of the ban I imposed on his "walkabout."

Chapter 99

Saturday was torrential, and I was sorry, because Anzac Day celebrations would be spoiled. When I returned Felix's call later, he said they hoped to be in Melbourne sometime in May, and would visit me around lunch time on Sunday. I told him they were most welcome, but I did not know what I would be doing on that Sunday, so I would call him closer to the day of their arrival.

Dr Khelil examined my foot again, after cleaning and dressing it on Monday. He prescribed antibiotics, as the skin around the wound was very red and inflamed. And he wanted to see me again in a couple of days to change the dressing. When I came home I relaxed a while, before planting violets, and some other plants around the pond. The ground was not too hard, as it rained over the last few days.

I saw doctor again on Wednesday after school. It was very painful when he tried to pull the folded skin over the wound to close the gaping hole. But he was unable to do it, as the skin had grown hard already. When I saw the ugly red gash, I could not believe I had inflicted such an injury on myself. It was extremely painful, and although my foot throbbed all evening, I did not take any pain killers.

I spent most of Thursday cooking curries for lunch on Saturday. But Laura said she was unable to make it, because she was busy looking for a new house, as she just sold hers. I was pleased for her, and wished her good luck, so it would be just Con and Cornelia on Saturday.

When I saw doctor on Friday morning, 1 May, he said that the wound was healing, but he wanted me to continue taking antibiotics, and to see him again next Monday. Then he dressed the wound with a waterproof bandage, and told me to take care, and keep the wound dry. When I came home, Ron and Monica had already arrived, though he told me they would be here at two o'clock.

When they finished cutting the lawns and weeding, I invited them for a cup of tea, and gave Monica a couple of bottles of fig jam. They spent an hour or so chatting, before they left. Then I cleaned up, and finished cooking curries for tomorrow's lunch.

Con called next morning, and said that he had to work late, and they would come when he finished. Christian, and my sisters, called to ask how my foot was, and were relieved when I told them it was healing. Then Con rang again at three o'clock, to say he was still working, and could they come for lunch next day, as it was getting too late. I said it was alright, because I could not refuse, even though it meant my whole weekend was messed up.

The monitor stopped working, and I called a computer technician to have a look at it. It did not take him even ten minutes to switch the standby button on and off, and it worked! He charged me twenty dollars, but at least it was working now, and I was glad, as I needed the computer for my work.

That night, I watched "'Come September," on DVD, starring Rock Hudson, Gina Lollobrigida, Bobby Darrin, and Sandra Dee. It brought back great memories in Hatton, when we rushed to the cinema to watch it many times.

Con and Cornelia arrived around one o'clock next afternoon, and we had a pleasant time. Laura kept calling Con a few times, as she found a house she liked, and wanted his advice, and it was after five o'clock when they left. It was a tiring day, so I took it easy, and watched a beautiful sunset that evening.

Monday, the 4th, was a student-free day, so I went to church at eight thirty that morning, and spoke to Fr Neil about Connie's memorial Mass, as Fr Raj was unavailable. It was one year since Connie died, and I could not believe how quickly the months had flown by. Mary, Tony, Elvira, John, Joelle, and Celine, attended the memorial service. It was brief and meaningful, as we prayed for Connie's soul, and Father said a few special prayers for him too.

Everyone had things to do later, so they left soon after Mass. I saw doctor again that morning, and when he examined my foot, he was pleased that the wound was not infected. Then the nurse dressed my wound, and doctor said he would see me again next week. When I returned home, I made a few phone calls, and Ninette mentioned that Michelle, Isobel's daughter, had an accident.

I called Isobel to find out what happened, and she said that Michelle fell over while she was at Isobel's place, and broke her knee cap. Now she had to visit John in one hospital, and Michelle in another. Poor Isobel. I was very sorry for her, and also for Michelle, who needed an operation on her knee.

The next few days were very gusty, and rained non-stop, and much to their annoyance, the cats were forced to stay indoors.

The rain eased slightly by Friday, but it was still blustery and overcast. Ron and Monica arrived just after one o'clock to spread mulch in the garden, although I told them I would be at doctor's, and to come after two o'clock. Because the wound was slow to heal, doctor wanted to see me every week, until it was completely healed.

Ron and Monica did a great job, and the garden and nature strip looked very neat when they finished. I invited them for a cup of tea later, and they said they would finish mulching the rest of the garden, once the weather cleared up. We had an interesting conversation on various subjects, and they left after an hour or so.

Simba escaped again for a couple of hours on Saturday morning, and went on a "walkabout." But to my great relief, he turned up by late afternoon, looking quite jaunty and nonchalant, so I kept him indoors that evening.

I was busy cooking and cleaning, as I expected Christian and Athena for lunch on Sunday. But towards late morning, the power went off, and I thought it affected the whole area. I waited an hour, but the power was still down. When I called the emergency number, they asked me to check the power board outside, and to switch it on again, as I told them I checked it before, and one switch was off. I followed their instructions, and the power came on again. I did not know why it cut off, but it was very frustrating when these little things happened to inconvenience me. But I was learning a few things all the time, and to get by on my own.

Christian said they were held up, and would be a little late. But when he called again at four o'clock to say they were still running late, I told him not to worry, as it was getting too late for them to drive down. And as they were busy, they would have to rush back again in a couple of hours time. So he said they would come down another time.

It was a long, busy day at school, as I waited for Tess till after four o'clock, and I was vexed, because she did not practise regularly. She made as much progress as a turtle in a marathon race. But whenever I spoke to Colleen about her lack of practise, all she said was, "Tess has a lot of homework to do. But I will try to get her to practise more often, because she loves piano, and she loves you." That was not good enough, because I really wanted to see my students progressing reasonably well.

The accountant, Charles, needed more information about Connie's Woolworths shares, in order to finalize his tax returns, so I said I would bring the documents in next day. Then I told Ninette that I would visit on Wednesday, as I had another appointment on Tuesday.

I drove to Dandenong next morning, and Charles worked out an approximate figure for capital gains tax on the Queensland unit. He said it would not be over twenty thousand dollars, but he still had to calculate the sale of the shares, before arriving at the final figure. I was relieved, as I expected it to be double that amount.

On my way back, I stopped at Vel Spices in Carrum Downs, and bought some takeaway food for lunch, as I was famished. When I returned home, I called Charles to ask if nursing home fees were tax deductible as well. He said he would let me know next day. My foot ached and throbbed all night, as I was on my feet all day.

I had an appointment with doctor on Friday, 15 May, but Ron said he was already on his way to finish the mulching, as they had loaded it on the trailer. They arrived just as I was leaving, so I left the gate open. It was gloomy and started to drizzle, but they were determined to finish the job. Doctor said that as my foot was still swollen, I should use an elastic bandage to ease the pressure, but otherwise, it seemed to be healing slowly. When I returned home shortly afterwards, I was pleased to see that they did a great job, and the garden looked very neat.

I invited them for a cup of tea as usual, and we chatted for a while before they left. They told me a great deal about themselves, and some of their problems and issues over the last few months. I listened and sympathised, but did not offer any advice, because they had to resolve their difficulties. And I knew that sometimes, they just wanted to share their burdens, and did not expect answers.

I invited Mary and Elvira for afternoon tea on Saturday, and had everything ready for them. But Mary said she did not feel too well, and Elvira was catching a cold, so she did not want to come over either. I put away all the short eats and nibbles, then took it easy.

Lucille sent a text that afternoon, asking me to call her. And when I did, she was in a nostalgic mood, and reminisced about our childhood days with the whole family. She was in Brisbane for six months to mind her grand- daughter, Michelle's baby, and said she was missing Mohan very much. After a very long conversation, I told her to keep in touch, and to call again before she left. I walked in the garden later on, as it was a pleasant day, after more than ten days of wet weather.

I had a restless night, and was up almost every hour, so I felt drained next day. But I drove to Frankston in time to attend the special Mass for forty children, who were receiving First Holy Communion that Sunday. The children were from St Augustine's and St Francis Xavier's schools, and the church was packed. It was a very meaningful service, and later I met Liz and other staff members.

Liz said she would have liked to have coffee with me, but she had to drive to the city to visit a friend. I told her it was alright, as I wanted to go to Harvey Norman's to buy an appliance that was on a special. It was a glorious day, and I enjoyed driving home in such pleasant weather. Several friends, Nelune, and Shirani, called in the evening, to find out if my foot was better.

When I saw Carol, the podiatrist, on Tuesday, she dressed the wound again, after trimming off "dead skin." She said the wound was not healing properly, and that was the reason it looked so red and inflamed. Carol told me that she had a great deal of experience treating wounds. And in her opinion, the skin should have been cut off completely, for the wound to close up and heal well. It was a painful procedure, as she tried to rearrange the fold of the skin to close the wound, and she wanted to see me again next week. I came home and rested my aching foot, which felt as if it was on fire.

Later that evening, I called a few friends, and my sisters. Elvira was due for a cataract operation next day, so I wished her well, and offered to do anything, if she needed help. Christian called later, and said they found another apartment, and would be moving soon.

I suggested that Ninette should consult my eye specialist, as she kept complaining that her vision was very blurry. Although she had macular degeneration, I told her that if her cataracts were bad, that could cause blurriness too, so she decided to consult him that afternoon.

I tried calling Elvira several times in the evening to see how she was, but the line was busy. Then I told Mary that if she got through to Elvira, to let her know I tried calling. Mary called at eighty thirty that night, and said that she spoke to Elvira, and she was recovering well. So I was glad that Elvira was alright.

When I saw doctor again on Friday, the 22nd, he said my foot was healing well. I mentioned that the podiatrist had treated it and dressed it. Then he said my blood test results were good, but kidney function was low, and sugar levels were a little high. I was relieved that everything else was good. Chris La Ponder said they would meet me at Biscottini's cafe in Mornington on Saturday, and I told her I was looking forward to seeing her again. I watched the semi-finals of Eurovision that night, and found the contestants were very talented and entertaining.

I arrived at Biscottini's around eleven forty five next morning. Chris and Peter came after midday, as they had visited Anne's mother, Irene, at Corowa nursing home in Mornington. It was lovely to see my dear friends again, and we just chatted away the hours. Anne arrived a little later, and we enjoyed a delicious lunch. Elio (my neighbour), was working that day, and he said they were very busy, but they would visit me soon.

When I left, I drove to St Macartans's church to light candles, and said a special prayer, as it was Ammie's 19th death anniversary. It was incredible how time had flown by so swiftly, because the memory of that last holiday with Ammie and Thathie in 1995, was still so vivid. When I returned home, I pottered in the garden, and walked around with the cats, just enjoying their frolics.

When Simba came in around eight o'clock on Monday morning, I saw a dismembered possum on the lawn. And I had the disgusting task of getting rid of possum bits scattered everywhere. It looked as if a fox, or feral cat had attacked it, because it was quite a large possum; such a sad, and sickening sight, but I wondered how the remains ended in my garden.

Sarah said she would drop in for a little while that evening, as she was in the neighbourhood, and arrived around six thirty in the evening. Although I was tired, and not quite ready for her, it was very good of her to find time to visit me. We chatted for about forty minutes, before she left, and said she would visit again soon.

She had turned out to be a lovely, well-balanced young girl, and I was very proud of her, and all her achievements. I knew her since she was about eight or nine, and she was eighteen now.

Linda invited me for her fortieth birthday party, but I had to decline, because I could not drive in the night, due to my vision problems. She understood, and was fine with that, but we hoped to catch up soon. I had a severe headache that night, which started in the afternoon, and I felt very dizzy.

The headache persisted all day at school on Wednesday, but I dropped in at Ninette's afterwards, as Toula had three DVD's for me, that she copied from my old videos. Ninette was very anxious and upset, because her keyboard was not working, and she did not know when it would be fixed. She just would not be pacified, and I felt sorry for her, as she was getting worse with her panic attacks. I came home and rested, as my headache did not ease, and the dizziness continued all evening.

I was up from about three o'clock in the morning, and could not go back to sleep. The wind howled, and I woke up with vivid dreams of Connie; he was moving around the house, and looking for his things.

When I spoke to Ninette later that morning, she said that she felt much better, as Frank took the keyboard for repairs. She chatted a little while, and sounded almost like before. My head still ached, but not as bad, so I walked in the garden, although strong winds continued to blow across the ocean.

I watched "Forever My Love" (Sissi), that Toula copied onto a DVD. But this time, the movie did not seem as beautiful as I thought it was in 1967, when I saw it for the first time at the age of fifteen. It just proved that time altered everything, especially romance and sentimentality of youth. And the dubbed voices sounded artificial and discordant. When I read up about the movie, I decided it was best to get the original version with subtitles, and not with dubbed-in voices. But the Austrian scenery, and period costumes were still breath-takingly beautiful.

Ninette decided to go ahead with the cataract operation on 2 June. The surgeon told her that removal of cataracts would improve her sight marginally, but the major problem was still macular degeneration. Still, she hoped it would help her, and I was glad she decided to have the cataract operation. I called her the day before and wished her well. Then I asked Nilanthi to say a special prayer for Ninette that her vision would improve, and she said she would.

I woke up early on Tuesday, and prayed fervently for Ninette to have a safe operation. When I called Toula around midday, she said they were back home, and Ninette was alright, as everything went well.

Mary wanted to drop in later, although it was chilly and stormy. And when she came after one o'clock, she stayed a couple of hours, just letting off steam, as she was very uptight about something Tony said.

Toula said they were expecting me later, so I cut some roses from the garden, and arrived there around three thirty that afternoon. She had to go home and get some things, as she was staying the night at Ninette's. I stayed with her till about five o'clock, until Toula returned. She complained non-stop all the time I was there. And said that she felt she had "sand in her eyes," and wondered if the operation was successful, as the eye drops burnt her eyes etc. etc.

I tried to convince her that she would be fine in a few days time, but she was very negative, and determined to think the worst. I was surprised at her hostility towards me, as I was only trying to help her. And I hoped for her sake, that the removal of cataracts would improve her vision even slightly. But she became really annoyed each time I said something positive, and snapped back irritably, "*You* and Elvira can see better, because you don't have macular like me! I will *never* get better, because my eyesight is very bad!"

I refrained from any further attempts at pacifying her, until Toula arrived. It was dark and cold, although it was only five o'clock in the evening. I was relieved to come home, after such a stressful time with Ninette.

It was another wintry, wet day on Wednesday, and only thirteen degrees when I went to school. I sent Toula a text to ask if she wanted me to do anything for Ninette, in case she needed to go home for a little while. Toula replied that it was best to let her rest that day, as she was exhausted. They saw the surgeon at nine o'clock that morning, for the post-operation appointment, and he had assured Ninette that her eye was good, and the operation was successful.

I called Linda to wish her on her fortieth birthday, and she thanked me for my card and gift. Then I spoke to Ninette, and tried to cheer her up, but she was still very negative and snapped, "I have a *sick* eye, and I won't get better!" Then she recited a whole list of all her illnesses, real, and imaginary, and went on and on, repeating the same list of complaints I had heard umpteen times before.

She said that she did not believe the surgeon, even though he had assured her that the operation was successful, because she still could not see well, and the eye drops hurt her eyes. It was such a shame that she was so negative, and did not want to believe she would get better. It was impossible to cheer her up, so I wished her well, and prayed for her.

The next few days were very busy, with several things to do, and in between, I called Ninette, and all my other friends. Elvira had her second cataract operation, and was also recovering from a cold, so she did not want to go out until she was better. Ninette still called me every evening, and if I was not home, she left a message asking me to call her back immediately.

I cooked lunch for the staff on Monday, and was glad they enjoyed the curries, and buriyani rice, with home-made mango chutney.

Ninette kept me on the phone for over an hour that evening. She was in a chronic mood, and more negative than usual, and argumentative about everything. I was exhausted, and soon developed a severe headache. She contradicted everything I said, and repeated the same ailments she thought she suffered from. And finally, when I did not say anything, she demanded, *"Why* aren't you saying anything? Why are you quiet?" I was losing patience with her, and felt sad and frustrated at her strange behaviour. But it was obvious that something was definitely wrong with her now.

A few days later, Alan called, and said Ginny was diagnosed with dementia. I wondered about Ninette, as she displayed similar symptoms.

Angela, my neighbour, dropped in on Tuesday afternoon, and brought some delicious cakes. She looked well, and told me they were going away on a cruise for two weeks. I was very pleased to see her looking healthy, and getting better.

Christian brought a new monitor, as the old one was on the blink. I was glad to see him after some time, as he was unable to drive far due to his injuries. His finger and neck were not healed completely, and he still had treatment. I noticed that he had lost a great deal of weight too. It was good to see him though, as he was such a caring and helpful son always. And I hoped his injuries would heal soon.

After he left, I called Nilanthi, and told her I would post the necessary documents for her visa application. She told me how much she missed us, and wanted to come on a holiday, even for a few weeks. Nelune and I agreed to send her a ticket towards the end of the year, so she was very happy and excited about it.

I consulted the eye surgeon again on 17 June, and completed the paper work for my second cataract operation. He checked the one he had operated on, and said that he was pleased, as it was very good. But the other eye was now so bad, that he could not believe it deteriorated so rapidly. I was impatient to have that done too, because I could see perfectly well with the other one.

Cynthia and Ron dropped in on Saturday afternoon, and we had a pleasant afternoon. Ron hurt his back and hand while doing some work, and was not very comfortable, as he was still in a great deal of pain. He told me about his collection of teddy bears, and said that he had over two hundred bears in all shapes and sizes.

I was putting away a couple of Christian's old teddy bears, and two bunnies, so I asked him if he would like to have them. He was like an excited little boy, as he hugged the teddies and bunnies affectionately. I could not imagine that a man of seventy-six, could be so fond of teddy bears. Cynthia demanded irritably, *"Where* are you going to put *another* four stuffed toys?" And he replied dreamily, "Oh, I will find a nice spot for them, don't you worry."

When I came home from school on Monday, Ninette had left a message. And when I called her back, she kept me on the phone for one hour, until six thirty. Luigi was in Craigieburn, and no doubt she was lonely, and missed calling him in the evenings, so she kept talking and repeating everything. I just listened, and did not say much, as she still kept contradicting whatever I said.

When my piano students played at assembly on Wednesday, everyone was impressed. Steve, the vice-principal, thanked me for my hard work with the children, and it was good that none of my students were nervous, as they all played well. That evening, I drove to Elvira's, as her sister, Mary, and her husband, Peter, and Daphne, were there too. It was John's seventy-eighth birthday, and I gave him a bottle of his favourite drink, Galliano. It was past eight thirty when I came home, but it was an enjoyable evening.

I watched "Britain's Got Talent," next evening, and was moved to tears, when some of the very young children sang like angels. I could not help feeling emotional to hear such beautiful voices, and hoped they would achieve their dreams someday.

I finished all the chores, and heavy work, on 26 June, as I would be unable to do them for a couple of weeks, after the second cataract operation. As it was a lovely sunny day, I cleaned all the windows too. And in the afternoon, I took it easy, and read a book for a few hours, which was sheer luxury. Nothing like curling up with a good book, and getting lost in wonderful places, and meeting interesting characters, even for a few hours. As someone once said, "When we read, we live a thousand lives," which would be impossible for any of us to experience in one lifetime.

After Mass on Sunday, John and Elvira invited me for lunch at a new Italian restaurant that was previously the "Coolstore," on Moorooduc highway in Frankston. We had a pleasant time, and the pizzas we ordered were very good. It was after four o'clock when I came home, as I stopped to get groceries. I had text messages from Joelle, and Mary Hancock, wishing me well for my cataract operation.

When I called the clinic on Monday, the 29th, they told me to be there at seven thirty in the morning, and to fast from midnight. Mary called to say she would take me to hospital, but I told her that Elvira had offered already. They were so helpful, and I was fortunate to have them around.

I called Judy again, as I tried calling for several days, and could not get through. When I asked Del if she had heard from her, she said that Judy was admitted to a nursing home in Mulgrave, after she had a few falls.

Del gave me her number, and when I called, Judy sounded subdued. But she said she was very well looked after, and had settled in comfortably, as there were many activities, and she attended daily Mass in the chapel. When I asked her about her cat, Danny Boy, whom she had doted on, she said her son was looking after it, and did not sound overly concerned, or sad about her pet. I felt somewhat depressed, when I mused on how quickly life changed with old age and sickness.

That evening, Ninette was impatient to call Luigi, and did not stay on the line too long, which did not worry me now. I was used to her erratic moods, and understood she was not too well. Elvira said she would drop me at the hospital, and not to worry. Then I cleaned and vacuumed the place in the evening. Shirani said that Ranjith and she would visit tomorrow afternoon, then Christian and Nelune called to wish me well too.

I watched the shocking news about Greece that night, as they were in dire straits economically. What a shame. I only hoped they could overcome their financial downturn.

Elvira picked me at seven thirty on Tuesday morning, 30 June, and I went in ten minutes later, to complete paperwork etc. The nurse put eye drops every fifteen minutes till about nine o'clock, then I changed into a hospital gown and bath robe. And I sat in the waiting room till eleven o'clock! The anaesthetist gave me an injection, before they wheeled me to the operating theatre, and Dr Renehan came fifteen minutes later. I sat with the other patients afterwards, and had sandwiches and a cup of tea.

My recovery was delayed, as the nurse said they could not discharge me until I "blinked" first. I did not realize my eyelid was still shut tight, and I panicked, as I called out to the nurse, "I *can't* see at all nurse!" She came over and replied, "That's because your eye is still closed!" I had to laugh with the others, as I was relieved to hear that. While I waited, I chatted to Mary, a pleasant lady in her eighties, and she told me some interesting stories about her early days in Melbourne. Then Elvira picked me up at two o'clock.

Shirani and Ranjith had arrived already, and had a cup of tea before they left, when Mary came at three o'clock. Elvira went home a little later, but Mary stayed till about five thirty, until I went to bed. It was so kind of them to stay with me, and Elvira brought me dinner as well. I had a few calls and text messages from everyone, asking how I was. My left eye was very foggy still, and I could not see anything with it, which was a little worrying. I watched television (with my good eye), and slept soundly that night, relieved that it was all over now.

Chapter 100

Mary picked me up early next morning, and drove me to Mornington for the post-operation check up. My eye was still very blurry, but the information booklet said that it was quite normal to have blurred vision for a few days. And when he saw me, Dr Renehan said, "Your cataract was like a *rock*, and my machine kept bouncing back! You left it too long, as they were very very bad!" But he was happy with the result, and said my vision should improve soon. Mary and I stopped to have a snack and coffee in the cafe downstairs, before returning home.

I spoke to my sisters, who were pleased to hear it went well. Toula and Ninette dropped in later, as she too saw Dr Renehan earlier that day. And she told me that her next eye operation was in two weeks time, and seemed calmer. I was pleased when she said, "I hope I can see better when my other eye is done too."

I rested till late next day, as my eye was very sore and red, and still very blurry. I did some light housework later, and knitted for a few hours. Linda sent a text to say they returned from Bali, and that she spent my birthday present on some silver jewellery. Then everyone called again that evening to ask how I was.

I still felt very tired on Friday, so I took it easy. Elvira asked if I needed anything from the shops, but I said I had everything, and not to worry. I noticed the lights next door were on last night, and knew that Angela and family had returned from their holiday. I sent her a text, and she replied that they had enjoyed themselves very much.

Nilanthi said she received the documents I posted for her visa application, and would attend to that soon. Mary was very busy, as they expected visitors that night, and they were staying till Sunday. But she told me to call her anytime, if I needed anything. I thanked her for her kindness, and said I appreciated it very much.

My eye was much better by Saturday, and not so blurry, but as it was a chilly, wintry day, I stayed indoors. When Julie called later, I told her that my sugar levels were very high. And she said that sometimes eye drops affected sugar levels, if there was cortizone in the drops. I said I would ask my doctor about it when I saw him next. Then she said that they would visit in a couple of weeks time. I made pan rolls, as I wanted to give Elvira some, and the rest for Linda, when she visited.

I called Lucille on Sunday, as she was still in Brisbane, and had a long chat with her and Mohan too, who had arrived a few days ago. I invited them to visit me, but they said they could not make it this time, and would try next year. Elvira called again to ask if I needed any shopping done, but I told her I was alright, and hoped to drive in a couple of days time.

Elvira dropped in with flowers and oranges from their garden on Monday afternoon, and stayed for about an hour. Mary was resting, as she had a sore back, and was tired after entertaining ten guests over the weekend. I gave Elvira some pan rolls, and she was pleased, because she said that John and she liked them very much. Then everyone called me in the evening, except Ninette, which was unusual. I did not call her though, as I was too tired.

Elvira picked Mary and me on Thursday afternoon, and we had lunch at the Coolstore restaurant in Frankston. We enjoyed a delicious meal there, and spent a pleasant afternoon. And later, they stopped to shop at Fella Hamilton in Mount Eliza, as they had a sale on. Elvira invited us for coffee, before she dropped us at five o'clock that evening.

Mary and Peter visited on Friday, and they took me out for lunch to Onde's in Mornington. Gerry was his usual chatty self, and talked about his gourmet tours to Italy. Peter and Mary were quite interested about that tour, and Gerry said he would go again two years later, in 2017. As his business partner, Annette, did not work at the cafe any longer, he said it was difficult for him to go on tours now.

When we returned, we had "high tea" and enjoyed a lovely afternoon. They were very caring people, and I was lucky to have such sincere friends. Peter asked me to make a list of all the odd jobs I needed done around the house and garden, and said he would help me when they visited again. I thanked them profusely, and they left by late afternoon.

The Welsh Choir, and Frankston Ladies Choir, were performing at the Arts Centre in Frankston, on Sunday, 12 July, and I was attending it.

I woke up feeling exhausted that morning, as I did not fall asleep till about three o'clock. My sugar levels were high ever since the eye operation, but as I thought it could be due to the eye drops, I was not overly concerned.

It was wintry, and poured incessantly when I drove to Frankston. I parked near the church, and walked to the Arts Centre. John, and his daughter, Kay, were already there, and the foyer was packed. I enjoyed the beautiful music, and when the ladies choir finished singing, they wound up with Elvira's song "Australia." Simon, the musical director, and accompanist, mentioned that it was Elvira's own composition. Elvira came forward and took a bow, and I was very pleased for her.

I drove to Narre Warren on Tuesday afternoon to drop off a laptop for Nilanthi, as Ranjith was going to Sri Lanka soon, and I took a bouquet of flowers for Shirani. I spent some time with Shirani, and we had a good afternoon. Later that evening, I spoke to Ninette, and wished her well, as she was due to have her second cataract operation tomorrow morning. She was vague, and not very optimistic, so I did not say anything positive, as she would have contradicted me immediately.

I bought Harper Lee's long-awaited novel "Go Set A Watchman," and started reading it that night, and hoped it was as interesting as her first novel "To Kill A Mockingbird."

It was chilly, and raining heavily when I drove to school on Wednesday, and the hall was freezing, even with the heater on. I sent Toula a text at midday, to ask how Ninette was, and she replied that she was well, and at home already.

After school, I stopped at the post office to send Nilanthi two hundred and fifty dollars for her visa application, as I told her I would send it that day. Toula said she had another appointment on Thursday morning, and could not stay with Ninette. So I agreed to drive Ninette home after her post- operation appointment.

On Thursday morning, I drove to the clinic at eight o'clock, and they arrived at half past eight. Toula was pleased to see me, and she left soon after. I stayed with Ninette, and went in with her to see Dr Renehan. He was very pleased with the results, and said, "Fantastic!" as both operations were successful. I drove her home afterwards, and stayed for a while, until she settled down. But she kept complaining that her eyes were still very blurry, and she would never regain her sight. I tried to convince her that she would see better soon. But she was just as negative as ever, and I felt drained by the time I drove home.

The same chilly, wet weather continued on Friday as well, and I could not do much work outdoors. I started painting another landscape, and did not stop till after five o'clock. I called Julie to confirm next Sunday's lunch here, and then spoke to Cornelia, as it was her birthday that day. We spoke at length, and she said they would visit soon.

When I called Ninette later, she still sounded very "nasal" and vague, and did not talk long, as she wanted to call Luigi, which was all she cared about now. Poor thing, her fixation with him was getting worse.

Nilanthi called that night to say she would lodge the visa application as soon as she collected the money from Western Union, and thanked me for sending it so promptly. She had hurt her back lifting something, and when I hung up, she called again immediately, to say she missed me very much, and looked forward to seeing me again.

Although it was good to share our thoughts and experiences, as we were now on our own, I discouraged her from dwelling on the past too much, as it could not be changed, and told her not to waste time on vain regrets. We suffered deeply in our unhappy marriages, but we had to move on now, and enjoy the peace and freedom we had today.

I spent a few hours watching the original production in German of "Sissi" (Forever my love). The scenes were breath-takingly beautiful, and I enjoyed the story very much, even though I had to read subtitles.

I woke up with muscle aches, and severe pain in my left armpit, on Saturday, 18 July. The aches started last Thursday, and I applied some anti-inflammatory creme a few times, and thought it must be a swollen gland, due to the gardening jobs I did. Although I ached all over, I vacuumed and cleaned, then made some pasta for lunch next day. I had a warm bath in the evening, and then watched another episode of "Sissi," as the whole series was six hours, two episodes on each DVD.

Sunday was a pleasant morning, and I prepared last minute things before Paul and Julie arrived. We had a very agreeable time, and I was glad they enjoyed the pasta. Paul wanted Julie to take down the recipe, as he said it was the first time he tasted pasta with kransky sausage, parsley, red peppers, olives, and capers. I told them it was a very easy, but tasty dish, and wrote down the recipe for Julie.

Then Paul set the ducted heating zone for downstairs only, and fixed a few things around the place before they left. They were such genuine friends, and were very helpful as always. Before they left, I told Julie about the swelling under my armpit, and she advised me to see doctor about it without delay.

It was a brilliant sunset that evening, and I sat outside enjoying the panorama until the sky turned dark. I called Shirani later to ask about the event at her Ashram, and she said that a large crowd turned up, and everyone enjoyed lunch, and the guest speaker's talk. I was pleased for her, as she worked hard to organize that event.

It was freezing on Monday, and only two degrees at eight o'clock, when I drove to school. Tess finished her lesson at four thirty, and I came home after five o'clock, so it was a long, tiring day.

Ninette called as soon as I arrived home, and complained that her keyboard was still not ready, and that Toula should push them to repair it quickly. She sounded as if she still had a bad cold and cough, but she told me it was just "hay fever." I listened to her for over forty minutes, and tried to pacify her, saying that the keyboard would be ready soon, and not to worry, because Toula did her best. And she could not do much, as the parts had not arrived from overseas as yet (so Toula told me). But she did not want to listen, as she enjoyed complaining, and feeling aggrieved. I enjoyed a warm, spa bath later, as my muscle aches did not subside.

When I woke up next day, my lower back was very sore, and I thought it must be due to vacuuming and cleaning on Saturday. And when I saw the podiatrist that afternoon, she looked at my foot, and was not very happy with the way the wound had healed, and said, "It's an angry, red scar, and there's probably a cyst inside." When she pressed it hard, I groaned, and told her it was very painful. She was all for cutting it open again, to let it heal properly, but I absolutely refused, as it was too sore. Elvira called that evening to say she would join us to the city on Thursday, then Mary confirmed as well.

I had a very strange dream last night, and I remembered it distinctly when I woke up on Wednesday morning, as I kept repeating, "God is everywhere, God is in this house," and a muffled voice kept muttering, as I chanted these words. I was saying it out loud, and suddenly, Mishka jumped out of bed, as she got scared when she heard me talking aloud. It was about three o'clock in the morning, and I fell asleep after that.

I arrived at school after ten o'clock that morning, and then visited Ninette briefly when I finished in the afternoon. She looked very weak and vague, and seemed to forget things easily. I had to keep repeating everything ten times, before she understood what I said. I thought it was her hearing problem, poor Ninette. It was very difficult to have a normal conversation with her now.

Nilanthi called to say that her visa was approved, and she was overjoyed. Nelune wanted to contribute half towards her ticket, so she was very excited at the prospect of visiting again. Isobel left a message, but it was too late in the evening to call her back.

Elvira picked me at nine o'clock on Thursday morning, and then Mary. We drove to Frankston station, but could not find parking there, so we drove to the next station at Kananook instead.

We enjoyed a pleasant train journey to the city, and walked for some time, till we found the wig shop that Elvira wanted to visit. But she did not find any suitable wigs there. Then we stopped at St Francis's church, where we said two decades of the rosary with a prayer group, and then lit candles. And we spent time looking around in Myers, before we had lunch in the food court. Elvira paid for pizzas and coffee, and then we boarded a train back to Kananook station. I was home by four o'clock, and as my back ached non-stop, I relaxed in a hot bath again. I spoke to Nilanthi at ten o'clock that night, and said I would send her the money for her ticket tomorrow.

And when I did next day, Nilanthi thanked me, and confirmed the date of her arrival as 6 September, and her visa was for five weeks. Nelune called later and said that she already deposited half of the ticket fare into my account. I thanked her for her generosity, as she did not have to contribute, because I had promised Nilanthi a ticket. But Nelune always paid half towards Nilanthi's tickets, and other expenses.

My spine, and rib cage ached constantly now, and it was worse by Saturday. The continuous pain was annoying, as I had chores to do, back ache or not. Con asked if I expected them for lunch that day, as Cornelia forgot the date, but I told him to make it the following Saturday, as I had not cooked anything for them.

The cats did not go out on Sunday, as it was icy cold, and fierce winds howled across the bay continuously. When I told Nilanthi about my aches and pains, she said to try massaging with boiled "goraka" and salt, as her neighbour used it on Nilanthi, and she found relief. I said I would try this home-remedy, and see if it relieved me. Later that evening, I applied goraka with salt water, and massaged with a hand towel, hoping the pain would ease, but although I tried this remedy a few times, I did not get any relief.

Two new boys in prep started piano on Monday, and it was very difficult trying to teach them fundamentals. I called their parents in the evening and told them I would try, but I did not think they were ready as yet, and it would be best to wait another year or so until they were older. But the mother was very keen to get them started immediately. She sounded very demanding, and I told her once again that I would try a few lessons, and see if they had any aptitude.

Then I called Ninette, as she had left a message. She said she was very upset and worried about Luigi, as his back was very bad, and she feared he would end up in hospital. I tried to calm her fears, but as usual, she worried herself sick over Luigi.

I drove to the eye clinic on Tuesday, and was relieved when Dr Renehan said my eyes were fine now, and there was no need to be concerned. Ginny and Alan were there too, as Ginny was considering a cataract operation. But she was very anxious, and scared. And she told me that even though her vision was very poor because of cataracts, she was afraid to go through with the operation. Then she said she was diagnosed with dementia, but she remembered my name, and we spoke for a few minutes, before she went in for her appointment. She looked very frail and bewildered, and I felt sorry for her. When I stopped at Bentons Square later, and was just driving off, I saw them walking outside again. I only hoped she would have the operation, and overcome her fear and panic attacks.

Christian called that night, and we had a long chat, but he said he was still not feeling too good, so I said I would visit them next Friday.

Mary invited me for afternoon tea on Thursday, but the weather was so wild and stormy that I was reluctant to go out. When I called to say I would drop in for a little while later on in the afternoon, she said they were going to the city, and if they returned early, she would call me.

The wind did not ease all day, and when Mary called me at three forty five, I told her it was getting too late, and the weather was too stormy. She understood, and we planned to catch up another time. Then I made fried rice, and curries for Saturday's lunch. I cooked progressively, so I would not get too tired, but the aches and pains did not ease.

I drove to Frankston on Friday morning, parked in the church car park as usual, and told Vicki that I would be back before four o'clock. I caught a train at eleven o'clock, and I enjoyed the journey, just gazing out of the window at familiar suburbs and scenery, besides watching different passengers getting on and off stations, in a never-ending stream of activity. It reminded me of the "Friendship Train," where all the friends we meet in life, board and get off at various stations along our journey; some stay on board till the end, while others stay on for a few stations only.

It was midday when I arrived at Melbourne Central, and I had to change trains at Richmond Station, as it was going to Flinders Street, and not via the city loop. I called Christian when I arrived at Central Station, and he said he would meet me in fifteen minutes time. But he arrived about forty minutes later, as he had to go home after work and change his clothes. He looked very thin, and unlike his usual cheery self, and I was sad to see him like that. We walked to their studio, and I was amazed to see all the renovation work he did on his own.

The place looked fantastic, and I told him I was very proud of him. Athena came a little later, and I was surprised, as she was honey-blonde! I preferred her with dark hair, but it was alright for a change, and she liked it, that was the main thing. They said there was a good restaurant further down the street, so we walked for about fifteen minutes, and had lunch there. It was good to spend a couple of hours with them, before I returned home around five o'clock.

I was glad I saw them, as I was very worried about Christian. It would take time for him to recover from his injuries. But I hoped he would be alright, as he told me that he still had nightmares about his accident, and the cowardly attack that left him injured and traumatised. I was very upset, but could not do anything to help him, as only time and nature would heal.

Chapter 101

Cornelia, Con, and Laura, arrived around one o'clock on Saturday, 1 August, and they enjoyed the ox tail curry and fried rice. Cornelia wanted to know how to make ox tail curry, as they never tasted it before. I wrote down the recipe for Cornelia and Laura, and we spent a pleasant afternoon before they left at six o'clock.

The next day, Ron and Monica mulched the rest of the garden and mowed lawns. When they finished, and had a cup of tea, I got ready to attend a play that afternoon. They said they enjoyed live theatre too, and would like to see the next play, which was later on in the year. I told them I would book tickets for them, and left shortly.

The play "Something To Hide," was very enjoyable, and I came home by five o'clock. It rained heavily all evening, and I could not walk in the garden. So I took it easy, and then returned some phone calls.

The weather was dreadful on Monday, as the morning started with a hail storm, gusty winds, and then torrential rain all day. I finished late, then stopped to post Joelle's birthday card, and bought bread for Wednesday's lunch, as it was my turn on the "soup" roster at school.

When I came home, Ninette had left two messages, asking me to call her back urgently. Although I was weary, I called her, and she talked for forty five minutes, because she was very upset and worried about Luigi. He fell while he was in rehab, and they transferred him to Frankston Hospital for observation. His problem was alcohol (I knew), as he drank too much. But I did not understand how he fell while he was in rehab.

Ninette just wanted to talk and talk, and would not stop, so I listened patiently, until she finally got off the phone. When I tried to unwind and have dinner, Mary rang at eight o'clock, so it was a late evening. The children's "Spelling Bee" was on, and I enjoyed watching that, as some of them were such excellent spellers.

I made spicy lentil and vegetable soup, with marrow bone stock, which the staff enjoyed with hot bread, especially as it was a blustery, chilly day on Wednesday. When I dropped in at Ninette's after school, Toula was there too. And as it was Toula's birthday in a couple of days, I gave her a card, a knitted shawl, and a necklace. We chatted for a while before she left.

Ninette was still upset about Luigi, and called the hospital a few times a day. And she told me that the nurse asked her, "Are you his *wife,* that you call him so often?" She was oblivious to the hint, and replied, "No, I'm his colleague, and I'm very worried, as he is alone."

When I returned, I was too tired to make dinner, so I had scrambled eggs on toast, which was just fine. The phone rang at nine thirty that night, and Joelle left a message thanking me for her card, but I did not talk to her, as I was already in bed.

When Cornelia and Con visited the last time, they gave me two picture postcards they wanted me to paint; one was a winter scene of Central Park in New York, and the other was of the High Country in Victoria, with an old shack on a hill top. I told them I would try, as the scenes were challenging, especially the snow scene. Cornelia wanted a very large painting of the High Country, measuring 190 by 90 centimetres, which I had trouble loading into my car.

I started painting the snow scene on Sunday, and spent a few hours on it. But I never worked with such a limited palette before; white, grey, black, deep-green, and a splash of bright yellow, depicting lights reflected on frozen water. It was a very challenging project indeed.

It was rainy and wintry next day, and I finished lessons by four thirty. When I returned, Ninette had left a couple of messages as usual. I sipped a cup of tea and relaxed, before I called her. And as always, she was very upset about Luigi. She wanted to see him next day, as he was back in rehab at Frankston. And he had told her that one of the nurses wanted a copy of his book. Ninette asked me to drop it off at her place after school. I said I would, and she was happy.

I was tired next morning, as I woke up a few times during the night. I dreamed that Connie was in the house, looking for "snacks," and told me to make cutlets for him. Elvira dropped in around midday, and I gave her a card, and a bottle of Riccadonna for their anniversary next week, on 15 August. We had a long chat, and after she left, I spent a few more hours painting. It was coming along quite well, and I hoped they would like my work. In the evening, I enjoyed watching David Attenborough's fantastic documentary "Madagascar," which was about Limas in bamboo forests.

Mary and Elvira had never tasted yum cha, so I told them about a restaurant in Southland where they served yum cha, and we decided to go there on Thursday. Elvira picked us, and we had a great time window-shopping at Southland. But when I looked for "The Bamboo" restaurant, I was very disappointed to learn they closed down permanently.

We ended up at David Jones cafeteria, as they served delicious food there. It was very clean and nice, and we enjoyed the meal. Mary and I paid for Elvira, as it was her anniversary next week. After we walked around for some time, we came home by five o'clock, and I had a persistent headache all evening.

Elvira called next day, and invited me for dinner on Saturday night, but I told her I was going out for lunch, and it would be late when I came back home. She was very insistent, and would not take no for an answer. But I was firm, as I knew it would be too tiring for me to be out all day, and then go out in the evening as well.

When Mary called, I told her that I was not going for dinner to Elvira's, and she understood. Tony and she were invited, and some other friends too, but I had made plans already. I spent a few hours painting, and was happy that the snow scene turned out well.

I drove to Laura's around eleven o'clock next day, and it took me only thirty five minutes to Carrum Downs on the freeway. She had bought a really nice place, and I was happy for her. It was a spacious, single-storey house, and at last, Laura had plenty of room to arrange her furniture, without being cramped.

Her son, Cristian, cooked a barbeque lunch, and they had too much food. Con and Cornelia arrived at the same time, and we finally finished lunch after five o'clock. I was weary by the time I came home, and there was no way I could have gone for dinner as well. I relaxed in a warm spa bath, as my spine, shoulder blades, and rib cage still ached badly.

I took it easy on Sunday, as no one visited, although Mary said she would drop in that afternoon. I spent a few hours painting, and then sketched the second one, as the snow scene was almost finished. I called everyone in the evening, and then returned some phone calls.

Shirani sent a text next day, and when I called her, she said she was waiting to hear from her doctor, who was admitting Suresh to hospital for treatment. We spoke long, and I hoped that this doctor would help Suresh in the long term. Then I wished Nilanthi for her birthday tomorrow, as general elections were next day, and I knew it would be difficult to get through. She was very happy, and said that she was counting the days to visit us.

I woke up several times that night, and felt worn-out by morning, so I rested late, and then took it easy.

I tried Nilanthi's number that afternoon, and was pleased when I got through, so I wished her once again. When I spoke to Shirani later, she was waiting for an ambulance, because Suresh refused to go to hospital. Poor Shirani. I hoped that the health system could do something this time, as she did not have any support, and it was a struggle.

Nilanthi called that night and said that she too was very concerned about Shirani. But she was pleased to get a text from Shirani, wishing her on her birthday. She was apprehensive though, because the UNP political party won elections in Sri Lanka, and she said the future was very uncertain.

Just as I was selecting a birthday card for Christian on Wednesday, he called me. And we had a long chat about a business proposition that one of his friend's told him about. I asked him to consider it carefully, before he committed to anything.

I dropped in at Ninette's later to pick a DVD that Toula ordered for me on Amazon "The Miracle Of Marcelino," and I wanted to pay her for it. We talked for a while, and I was sad to see Ninette looking very frail and vague. She only spoke about Luigi, and was waiting impatiently to call him soon.

When I spoke to Shirani that evening, she said Suresh was admitted to Traralgon hospital. And she was relieved that he was in good hands there. I was pleased too, and we both hoped that he would receive proper treatment.

When I took Mishka to the vet for her annual check up next day, she mewed her head off as usual, because she hated being in the carrier. The vet said she was fine, and gave her the vaccine, flea and worm treatment. She was subdued, and stopped mewing on our way home, but stared at me warily all evening. Once I gave her some prawns, all was forgiven, and she was friends again.

It was a pleasant, sunny day, and after resting a while, I started making Christmas cake. I wanted to have it ready when Nilanthi arrived, so she could take back her share. When I spoke to Nelune later, she too was relieved that Suresh was admitted to hospital.

Then I phoned Monica to ask how Ron was, as she told me that he went for some tests. She said that the melanoma was malignant, and he needed another "bit" removed from his ear. Ron called me later though, and said he would clean up the garden next Saturday. But I told him not to worry, and to wait till he was fully recovered. That evening, I watched "Miracle Of Marcelino," and found it just as moving, as when I saw it as a child of seven or eight years.

I visited Toula at her place on Friday afternoon, and we had a good, long chat over coffee, as it was impossible to converse when Ninette was around. Because she was paranoid, and kept demanding, "What are you saying? What did you mean?" And it was worse, as she was hard of hearing too, and we had to keep shouting and repeating everything several times.

Toula had serious concerns that Ninette was getting dementia, and she said she would need to get her assessed soon. Ninette's behaviour was erratic and irrational, and she was getting worse, as we could see. I shopped at Karingal afterwards, and deposited some money for Christian's birthday.

Saturday was a pleasant day, and Ron arrived with Monica around eleven o'clock, and they finished in about two hours time. They had tea and biscuits later, then Ron fixed the tap washers in the powder room. He looked alright, and said he was fine. But it was a shock when they told him the melanoma was cancerous. He said, "It's *my* fault, as I spent all my youth outdoors, without a hat or sunscreen!" I told him to take care, and they left soon after.

Lucille called on Sunday, as they were returning to Sri Lanka next Saturday. And she said that they would definitely visit me next time, as she had other relatives in Melbourne too, whom she wanted to see. We spent a long time chatting, and I told her I was sorry I did not meet her this time.

When I went to school on Monday morning, I was surprised to see Elvira sitting in the foyer! She said her car broke down near Mount Eliza, and she did not have her mobile with her. But a passing motorist stopped, and let her use his mobile. So she called John, as he was working locally that morning.

John dropped her at church, as she had to meet Vicki to book the hall, and then she walked down to the school to see me. He took her car to the garage, and was waiting for him to pick her. We chatted briefly, before I started teaching.

I told Colleen I could not wait for Tess that evening, because I was very tired. And I felt drowsy, after taking an antihistamine for hay fever the previous night, so I left early. When I spoke to Shirani later that evening, she still had to meet the doctors, as they wanted to assess Suresh, and start him on new medication. I fervently hoped there would be a turning point for him soon. Then I spent a few hours painting till late, and almost finished the landscape for Cornelia.

A few days later, Shirani said that Suresh would be discharged soon, due to a shortage of beds, which was very disappointing. It was the same old story with the public health system. But this time, she said that a medical team, who proved to be helpful so far, would continue to see him regularly, and ensure that he did not stop his medication.

When I called Ninette on Friday evening, she was very abrupt. And she said she was waiting for Toula to call her with the phone number for Frankston Private hospital, as Luigi was admitted there again. She called me twenty minutes later, because when she rang Luigi, he was very rude, and asked her why she kept calling him so many times.

She was very upset and annoyed, but I told her that he must be in severe pain, and not to take any notice of his moods. I could just imagine him driven to distraction, with a dozen phone calls a day from Ninette, when he was in acute pain. But Ninette believed she was doing him a favour, because he was lonely. Talk about crossed wires!

I was busy doing chores on Saturday, when Elvira called and said that she had some spicy, Italian sausages that she bought in Brunswick, and to pick them up if I could. I dropped in for a little while after grocery shopping, and came home after four o'clock. Then I made cutlets till about seven thirty in the night. And later, I watched one of my favourite movies "My Big Fat Greek Wedding," on television, and laughed out loud.

Isobel left a message on Sunday to call her back when I could. Then Shirani sent a text to say she was in Narre Warren, and Roshan, and his family were there too, if I wanted to visit. So I drove there in the afternoon, and it was good to see Roshan, June, and the children, whom I did not see since Connie's funeral. And I spent a pleasant afternoon with them.

Isobel was not in when I called her later, so I left a message, saying I would call tomorrow.

It was a lovely sunny day on 1 September, the first day of spring. I did some spring-cleaning, and washed all the outside windows too. Shirani said Suresh was back home, but very subdued, as he was on new medication. We chatted for some time, and I was sorry for her. She had so much on her plate, dealing with Suresh, on top of all her other work, and running a restaurant too. I prayed daily, that God would give her strength and courage to bear her burdens. She was so strong and patient, and I hoped there was a lasting solution to this problem soon.

Charles called and said that he finished with all the files, and I could pick them up anytime, so I drove to Dandenong on Thursday. He had a long discussion, and told me how much capital gains tax I had to pay, before the end of next June. I spoke to Nilanthi that night, and wished her a safe flight, as she was due to arrive on Sunday.

The next day, I made some curries, and an ox tail curry too that Christian liked very much, as they were picking Nilanthi at the airport and bringing her here.

Elvira said that Alessandro was visiting on Saturday, and to drop in, if I was free that afternoon. Isobel also called, as John was very ill after a few strokes, and they inserted a pacemaker, as his heart was very weak. She did not think he would last very long, as he was in his last stages, which made me very sad.

Michelle was still on crutches after an operation, as her knee was not healed as yet, so Isobel was feeling very dejected. And she was unable to meet Nilanthi this time, as she spent her days visiting John and Michelle in two different hospitals. I said I understood, and not to worry, as we would catch up when things were better.

It was good to see Alessandro again, and I spent a pleasant afternoon with them. But I came home around four thirty, as I still had to cook a few curries for lunch tomorrow, and I wanted to finish the painting too. I kept everything ready for Nilanthi, and arranged a vase of fresh lavender in her room. It would be great to spend some time with her again, and I looked forward to her visit very much.

It was almost midday when they arrived on Sunday, and Nilanthi looked well, but was weary after the long journey. Christian and Athena picked her at the airport around eleven o'clock, and she said that she waited about forty minutes after checking out.

They enjoyed lunch, as I made it extra special, to celebrate Christian's birthday too. We had a great deal of fun, laughing, and chatting, and afterwards, Christian did a few odd jobs around the place, before they left in the evening. Nilanthi rested a few hours, while I did some chores, and then I took it easy. Shirani and Nelune called in the evening and spoke to Nilanthi when she woke up feeling refreshed.

I went to school on Monday morning, and Nilanthi said she preferred to rest until I returned, as she still had jet-lag. We spent a quiet evening, just chatting, and catching up, as she wanted to know how the last year or so was after Connie's death. I told her about those last few awful days in detail, when he lingered for almost a week after they administered morphine.

We visited Ninette on Tuesday afternoon, and she was pleased to see Nilanthi again. That night, I watched the grand final of the childrens' "Spelling Bee," and Nilanthi was quite interested to watch it too.

We spent the next few days just chatting, walking, shopping, and watching old movies, and episodes of "Columbo," in the evenings. Nilanthi felt much better and rested after the first week. And on Saturday, Con, Cornelia, and Laura came for lunch. We had a great time, and they left late in the evening. Linda asked me to visit with Nilanthi, as they had just moved to their new house in Blackburn.

We drove there on Sunday, 13 September, and as I travelled along Springvale Road, it brought back so many memories of our first years in Nunawading. I showed Nilanthi the street where we lived, Luckie Street, and how we walked to Forest Hills shopping centre every Friday evening.

I thought it was such a coincidence that Linda's and Leo's house was just one street ahead of Luckie Street. It was a very nice, new house, and everything was modern and attractive. Linda made some cakes for afternoon tea. And we had a pleasant time chatting, and sharing stories, while the two children, Josh and Zara, kept us amused with their antics.

We returned home late evening, and I told Nilanthi that I still had severe pain in my rib cage, and felt very sore when driving back. I could hardly move or sit still, as the pain was extreme, and I could not breathe easily, as it hurt to take deep breaths. She kept saying to massage with goraka paste, and that she would do it for me. But I told her not to worry, and just applied deep heat, which did nothing to ease the pain.

Anjo pressed us to visit her in St Alban's, and said that she would pick us at Southern Cross station. So we boarded a train from Frankston station, on Monday, the 14th. Nilanthi liked the train journey very much, and we had a great time recalling our numerous train journeys in Sri Lanka. Anjo picked us at the station, and it took another forty minutes or so to get to her place through heavy traffic.

Mimi was very happy to see us too, and we had an enjoyable time, laughing and chatting with them. Mimi had decorated her bungalow in her own inimitable style, with about hundred plastic birds on the shelves, holy pictures, and ornaments everywhere. She seemed happy enough, but she told me that she wanted to do "heaps of gardening," which was not allowed, because of her weak heart.

Anjo took a great deal of trouble to cook a delicious meal for us, and Ronald dropped in briefly, as he had to go out to work again. I told Anjo not to worry to drive us back to Southern Cross station, as the traffic was just too bad. And it was much better to take a train from St Albans to Flinders Street, and then to Frankston. I had a time convincing her though, because she wanted to drive us back to Southern Cross station again, but she agreed in the end. It was much better, as we did not have to battle through heavy traffic.

On our way home, I could hardly breathe, as the pain was so severe, and got worse each day. I thought it was my bra rubbing against my ribs, that hurt so much, and could hardly wait to remove it at home. It was an effort to sit up, or lie down in bed at nights, as the pain did not subside. I took some panadeine, which did not do any good either. So I kept on applying deep heat, and everything else, but to no avail.

Nilanthi tried the goraka paste too, and massaged my back and shoulders, but honestly, it did not relieve the pain at all. Although I was in constant pain, I did not make a big fuss about it. Because I wanted Nilanthi to have a good holiday, and not worry about me. I made light of it, saying it was some sort of sprain, or strain that caused all this discomfort.

Although it was cloudy and cold, we took a train to the city again on Friday, the 18th, as Nilanthi wanted to collect some religious booklets etc. from St Francis's church. So we stopped there for a while, before meeting Christian and Athena at their studio. Nilanthi too was very impressed with Christian's handiwork in the studio, and could hardly believe he renovated the interior so well. Then we enjoyed a delicious lunch at a near-by cafe, and boarded a train back to Frankston by late afternoon.

Laura invited us for lunch next day, and Con and Cornelia came too. She prepared a huge meal, and with heaps of barbequed meats too. Nilanthi was amazed at the size of the steaks! Con joked that they were "elephant" steaks. After spending a few hours with them, we drove home late evening.

The next few days were very busy, as Nilanthi and I visited my friends, or I took her shopping during the day, when I was not at school. Shirani was unable to visit often, as she had to look after Suresh, besides running the restaurant, but they visited just before Nilanthi left.

I picked Nelune at Frankston station on Friday morning, 2 October, and we spent an enjoyable time together. Then we drove to Dromana for coffee in the afternoon. As I was in a great deal of pain, Nilanthi kept saying she wanted to foment me. And Nelune joked that I was not a fruit, to be "fermented." I tried to laugh it off too, but the constant pain wore me down. Nelune turned in early, as she was tired, but Nilanthi and I watched the animated movie "Frozen" on DVD.

It was the footy Grand Final on Saturday, the 3rd. And after lunch, the three of us watched the game, even though I was not a footy fan (none of us were). Nilanthi made such droll comments about the players, that Nelune and I were thoroughly amused. We took it easy later on, and watched a couple of episodes of "Columbo."

After a late and leisurely breakfast on Sunday, we dropped Nelune at the station, and then drove to Joelle's place for afternoon tea. They prepared a delicious "high tea" and we enjoyed a pleasant afternoon, before we came home after five o'clock.

I was back at school on Monday, and thought how hectic it was over the last four weeks or so with Nilanthi; socialising, travelling by train to the city, and to Anjo's, shopping etc. We enjoyed ourselves thoroughly, and now it was almost time for her to return home. I wanted to make her holiday memorable, and took great pains to make sure she ate everything she wanted. She liked lamb especially, so I roasted a leg of lamb, with potatoes, and vegetables for dinner on Monday.

Nilanthi enjoyed red wine too, and I had a good stock, as Con, Cornelia, and Laura gave me a few bottles of their home-made red wine. As she ate dinner, and sipped a glass of wine that night, she felt very nauseous, and next moment she threw up in the toilet. It was a shame, as she looked forward to the meal. After she settled down, we watched "Air Force One," as she enjoyed Harrison Ford's Indiana Jones movies over the last few weeks. And I told her that she would like this particular one too.

We visited Ninette next day, because she wanted to wish Nilanthi goodbye. Toula and Luigi were there too, and he gave her a boomerang as a farewell gift, and Nilanthi brought rosaries, and crucifixes for him as well. She wanted a light meal that evening, and said she liked fish curry. I made a hot curry that she enjoyed, and at least she was not sick. But I told her to avoid red wine, because I knew that all the rich food, and wine, must have upset her stomach.

After school on Wednesday evening, we went to Elvira's for dinner, and Mary and Tony were there too. We had a good time, and came home after nine o'clock.

Mary and Elvira dropped in next day, as we planned to watch "The Miracle," with Roger Moore. We had Christmas cake, and nibbles, then spent a pleasant afternoon watching the movie. It was another one that I saw as a young child, and it left a lasting impression on me.

Toula dropped in next morning with her two grandchildren, and gave Nilanthi a nice scarf, and said, "This is from Mum and me." She could not stay too long, because of the little children, but she had a coffee before she left. Elvira dropped in for a little while that afternoon, and returned a book that she borrowed, "Biography Of Elizabeth Taylor."

I called RACV emergency home assist on Saturday morning, as the shower upstairs dripped all night, and I wondered where the noise came from. The plumber came at midday, and replaced washers in the shower, and the dripping stopped. I was relieved that it was nothing more serious. Nilanthi was up very early, all packed up and ready to go by the time Christian and Athena arrived at two thirty.

Nilanthi panicked, and could not settle down, although we kept reassuring her that there was plenty of time. She was a nervous wreck, and I noticed that each time she came now, she got more anxious and tense, until she went to the airport. She was very upset and emotional all morning, as usual, and cried continuously. I told her that she would make herself sick, if she did not stop crying, and that she would be back again soon.

Christian and Athena had a very quick snack, and left shortly. He called me in less than two hours, and said they arrived at the airport, and she had checked in, so all was well. I spoke to Nilanthi, and she was very emotional, and kept thanking me for everything I did to make her holiday memorable. She left a brief note thanking me, and a few flowers from the garden on my bedside table before she left.

I wished her a safe journey, and then said a prayer for her, before resting for a while. I called Nelune to say all was well, and that Nilanthi arrived at the airport in ample time. It was very quiet on my own again, but I enjoyed walking in the garden, as it was a warm, beautiful night.

Chapter 102

The next four weeks or so after Nilanthi left, was just a blur of relentless, excruciating pain. When I was in the spa one evening, thinking it would relieve my aching bones, I could not get out when I finished. The pain in my shoulders and spine was so severe, that I was unable to raise myself up. I cried, and shouted out loud, although I knew there was no one to hear me, then implored God to help me. I rolled onto one side, and then inch by inch, I managed to raise myself and get out of the bath. Ever since then, I was afraid to get into the bath again.

When I told Nelune about my severe aches, she said to try neurofen tablets, as they were strong painkillers. I tried them for a few weeks, and the pain eased very slightly. Finally, I saw Dr Khelil, as I thought there must be something wrong, for these pains not to ease by now, even if I injured myself lifting heavy bags of potting mix a couple of months ago.

The severe pains started in early September, and I felt so helpless at times, that I just howled out loud. I could not even turn around in bed, without sharp, shooting pains in my ribs and shoulders. I felt as if jagged objects twisted inside my bones. Then I noticed that my left breast was swollen, and twice the size of my right one. And the lump under my arm felt bigger, and harder too.

When I told doctor about these new developments, and the excruciating pain, he sent me for a mammogram to Beleura Hospital in Mornington. I did not have a mammogram since 1998, as the procedure was very painful and uncomfortable. So I was reluctant to go for regular check ups since then.

I drove to Beleura hospital on Thursday, 12 November, and the nurse who did the mammogram was very good, as I did not feel much pain. She said they would send the results to doctor that very evening. The pain was now so severe, that I could not sneeze or cough, without holding onto something. Because my chest and shoulders exploded with incredible pain, and I could hardly stand up straight.

The very next day, I saw Dr Khelil again, to get results of the scan, and mammogram. He read the reports, and assured me everything was alright, and said, "You don't have cancer, that's for sure." But he said I had to see a breast specialist, to find out why one breast was swollen. And he said that my kidney function was down to twenty percent.

But I was elated, and so relieved that there was nothing insidious to worry about, as doctor assured me I did not have cancer. I drove to Rosebud in a happy frame of mind that afternoon, and went to an upholsterer. Then I selected the same tapestry fabric, to re-upholster the lounge-suite, as I thought of doing it for some time. When I called Nelune that evening, she asked me about the scan results.

I read it out loud to her, and when I said "carcinoma" (an unfamiliar word to me), she said it was another word for cancer, and that she would like to see the report. So I emailed it to her directly. But I told myself that I must remain positive, until I did all the other tests, and consulted the breast specialist. The only problem was, that the constant, gnawing pain was getting me down, and nothing seemed to help. And doctor told me to stop taking neurofen tablets, as they affected the kidneys, so I had no relief from them either.

I tried to clean and vacuum on Saturday, as Nelune was visiting on Monday. But I never felt so weak, and ill before. And I shivered, just as if I had a bout of flu. I sat down every few minutes while I vacuumed, and I wondered what on earth was the matter with me. The pain in my spine, shoulders, and chest was agonizing. But I managed to finish vacuuming, then rested a few hours, as I could not even stand up.

I felt exhausted, but pushed myself to finish cleaning and vacuuming downstairs on Sunday morning. The pain in my shoulders, and left side, was indescribable, especially when I lay down. I could not turn from side to side without experiencing the most piercing pain. And the intensity of sharp objects being driven into my bones, was more severe and constant now, without a moment's respite. And the worst part was, that I did not get any relief from applying decorub or deep heat. Because the pain was not muscular, and I could not reach the source of that knife-like pain in my bones.

When I went to school on Monday, I spoke to Colleen about my health issues, and she was very concerned about me. I told her that I had to do further tests, and would keep her informed. When I finished at school, I picked Nelune at the station around three thirty. It was great to see her again, and have her with me. I was utterly drained with constant aches and pains, and prayed I would be rid of them and be healed soon.

The breast specialist's appointment in Frankston was on Tuesday morning, 17 November. Shirani and Ranjith were already there when Nelune and I arrived, as they drove from Narre Warren. Ranjith stayed in the car, but Shirani and Nelune came in with me.

Amanda, the specialist, said that she could not tell me anything definite, until I had more scans, and a biopsy. But she went on to say, "There's something going on in the lymph nodes, or in your blood to cause the swelling, and you have definitely got breast cancer, but we need to do a biopsy to find out what *type* of cancer it is." A few weeks ago, I noticed a large lump at the base of my neck near my throat as well.

Amanda said she had a bad back, and did not show much empathy towards me at all, even though I told her I was in constant, acute pain. She just dragged herself around, with one hand pressed to her back. I was surprised that she did not prescribe strong painkillers to relieve me, until I did further tests. And I was very disappointed at her attitude as well. After the consultation, her receptionist made appointments for the biopsy a week later, and scans in two days time. She said that Amanda would see me in about two weeks time after the biopsy, as she was very busy.

Then the receptionist called Dr Khelil, and asked me to speak to him about stopping my blood-thinning medication a week before the biopsy. But when I spoke to doctor, he told me not to stop the medication. So she re-scheduled the biopsy to an earlier date.

When we left the clinic, I still felt positive, and believed that it was little more than an inflammation, that would go away in time. If only I had some pills to relieve the pain now, that was all I wanted. Elvira and Mary called in the afternoon to ask how it went, and I said I needed to do more tests. Shirani brought lunch for us, and they came home later to spend time with me. I felt truly blessed to have such caring sisters, and friends around me.

Nelune and I decided to see a movie, to take our minds off these issues. So we watched "The Dressmaker," at Karingal next day, and enjoyed it very much.

I drove with Nelune to the Bays hospital in Mornington on Thursday morning, and she took a taxi to Frankston station from there. I wanted to drop her, but I could not, as the scan was at nine o'clock. I drank three glasses of foul-tasting liquid one hour before the scan, and then had an injection.

After the first scan, they told me to come back later in the afternoon, to do the bone scan. I came home, had a snack, and drove back to Mornington. I stopped to get some groceries afterwards, and rested when I returned home. Nelune was amazing, and extremely caring, and supportive from the start of my journey into this unknown territory, that she travelled in 1998, when she was diagnosed with breast cancer.

Shirani too was there for me every step of the way; she brought meals, called me daily, and offered help in any way. Christian too called me every day, to find out what was happening, and was always positive, and encouraging. I was overwhelmed with their love and concern, especially during this time.

When Nelune called that afternoon, to find out how I was, I told her that I was alright, but my back, and breast area ached constantly. Elvira, who was in Queensland with John, called to ask how I was, and whether I knew the results of the scan as yet.

Petunia sent a text message on Friday, 20 November, saying that Nilanthi was down with dengue fever, and was admitted to hospital. Poor Nilanthi. She would have been very scared, as it was a dreadful fever that was sometimes fatal to the elderly, and very young.

I noticed when she was here the last time, that she was extremely paranoid about her health. If it was slightly windy or cold, she wore a thick jumper, even if it was thirty degrees, and stuffed cotton balls in her ears to avoid an ear ache. I teased her about it, but she said, "I'm very very careful because I don't want to get sick." I replied that I would pray for her quick recovery, and to convey all my love and good wishes.

Shirani and Ranjith visited me on Saturday, 21 November, and she brought enough food to last me for a week or more. I thanked her for her love and concern, as I knew how busy she was with the restaurant etc. Roshan, Max, and Will came around three o'clock as well, and spent a couple of hours with me. June had another engagement in the city, so she was unable to join them. Shirani told me that her yoga teacher was a good naturopath too, and to see her soon, if I wanted to. And to also try acupuncture for the neck and shoulder pains. I agreed to do so.

When I spoke to Nilanthi that night, she sounded very weak and dejected after the bout of dengue fever. She kept dwelling on how serious it was, and how she could have died of it etc. etc. I pacified her, and said that thankfully, she was out of danger now, and to take care and get stronger. But I did not mention anything about all the tests and scans I was undergoing, until I knew what was wrong with me. Nelune sent three hundred and fifty dollars for her hospital bill, as she was anxious about the expenses.

When Nelune called next day, I told her I had a very bad night, as the pain in my side and shoulders was unbearable. I could not even turn around in bed, and it hurt very badly when I sneezed or coughed. She was very sad and concerned, and said that she hoped they would find out what was wrong with me very soon.

A few days later, I had acupuncture at a clinic in Mornington, but it did not help at all. Just lying down on my stomach, while the needles were inserted in my neck and shoulders, was unbearably painful.

I had a biopsy the following week, and it was very sore, as they took tissue sample from the lump in my neck. Nelune warned me that it would be very painful, and to apply an ice-pack on it afterwards. Fortunately, they did not take a sample from the left breast.

The very next day after the biopsy, Amanda's receptionist called, and asked if I could see Amanda in two days time, instead of two weeks. I agreed readily, and when I told Nelune about it, she said she would accompany me to the clinic. And Shirani too wanted to be there to hear the results of the biopsy.

Nelune flew down again on the day of the appointment, and Shirani picked her at the station. When I went into the clinic ahead of Nelune and Shirani, the receptionist asked me, "Which of your sisters is the one from Sydney?" I pointed towards Nelune, and the receptionist just looked at her and nodded.

I noticed that Amanda's attitude had undergone a complete change since our last visit. And she actually smiled at us slightly, before she proceeded. I learnt later that Nelune intervened, and prevailed upon Amanda to bring forward my appointment.

She looked at me and said, "You have got an inflammatory type of cancer, stage four, but you won't be needing surgery. It's gone into your bones, and I would say that you have had cancer for more than two years now. I will have to refer you to an oncologist, who will decide what type of treatment you require. Do you have any preference?" I replied, "It would be good if I see someone in Frankston or Mornington, as it will be more convenient for me." She said, "There's one at the Peninsula Private hospital, and I would like you to see her this very afternoon, if possible. I will call her now, and make an appointment."

While all this was happening, I felt as if I was listening to someone else being diagnosed, as the full implication of what Amanda just said, did not impact on me at all. Shirani and Nelune though, looked very shaken and upset. But I smiled at them as we left her office, and I spoke to the receptionist about the referral etc. Amanda wanted me to do some blood tests immediately, before I saw the oncologist that afternoon.

The three of us sat down outside the clinic, and discussed practical issues, and what needed to be done now. Shirani said, "Nelune and I will try to get Nilanthi down for a few weeks to be with you, when you start treatment." I thanked them profusely for their generosity. Shirani and Ranjith had to leave soon, so Nelune drove me to the pathologist near-by for blood tests.

While we were waiting there, one of the lady's, and her teenage daughter smiled at me in recognition, and she happened to be one of my previous piano students. We had a quick chat, and they were concerned to hear about my health issues.

Nelune told me that when she returned to Sydney a few days ago, she voiced her concern to someone at the cancer council, about Amanda's offhand behaviour. Knowing I was in such severe and constant pain, she did not even prescribe painkillers, and she was too busy to see me for another two weeks. Nelune was very upset over this, and that was why she intervened to bring my appointment forward.

We drove home after the blood tests, then I called Christian, and my close friends, to tell them what the diagnosis was. Christian was subdued, but I told him not to worry, and that I would let him know what the oncologist said. Everyone was very upset about my diagnosis, although I was very positive, and resigned to whatever the future held. They all offered to help in any way they could. From that moment onwards, Christian, Athena, Nelune, Shirani, and all my close friends were there for me every step of the way.

Strangely, I did not feel apprehensive. I believed that whatever God had in store for me, I only had to trust in Him, as my faith dictated. I prayed for strength and guidance now, as I stood on the threshold of this unknown journey - one of pain and uncertainty.

Nelune and I waited a little while in the reception area until the oncologist, Nicole, saw me at Peninsula Private hospital. She came out with a bright smile on her friendly face, and I liked her immediately. Nicole was very attractive, and looked quite young, but she radiated confidence, which made me feel comfortable right from the start. Nelune told me that she knew of another good male oncologist in Frankston, but I said I preferred Nicole, even before I got to know her well.

That first meeting with her was very reassuring. Nicole said I was fortunate because a new drug was on the market, and it had a very good success rate in treating breast cancer. When I told her about my constant unbearable pains, she said, "The *first* thing to do is relieve your pains, and I'm going to prescribe some strong painkillers to help you, especially at nights, so you can get some sleep." Nicole's helpful and caring attitude was such a contrast to Amanda's, I thought.

She said she received all the blood test results too, and once the paperwork was completed, she wanted me to start chemotherapy the following week, after which, it would be every week, for about four months. As she intended using Herceptin, the new drug, she said she had to send some paperwork to Canberra, and hoped to start as soon as that was sorted out.

Nicole asked if I lived on my own, and then I explained about Connie's illness, and that he died the year before. Also, how difficult it was dealing with his dementia-related behaviour, and the added stress of constant conflict with his interfering siblings. She nodded sympathetically, and replied, "There is always some trauma that triggers cancer, and I'm sorry you didn't have mammograms done for so many years, as early detection would have prevented the cancer from spreading to your bones."

Then she asked me to make an appointment with the nurse in the chemotherapy unit sometime that week. She would do the paperwork, and go through all the information I needed to know prior to treatment. It was a fairly long consultation, but she told me I would need to see her again the following week, before treatment commenced. When I spoke to Shirani that night, she told me to see the naturopath soon, before I decided to go ahead with chemotherapy.

I consulted Paula, the naturopath, a day or so later. Paula was a nurse before, and was dead set against invasive treatment, like chemotherapy. After taking down my details, she gave me a few bottles of herbal potions, and charged ninety dollars for them. I told her I would have to ask the oncologist first, before I started taking any of them, even though she assured me they were just herbal remedies. But I did not want to take a chance, as my cancer was advanced and required immediate treatment, not long-term naturopathy.

At the next meeting with Nicole, Elvira and Shirani accompanied me, as Nelune could not make it, due to previous engagements. Shirani asked Nicole about alternative treatment, but she replied, "Nalini needs to start chemotherapy *as soon as possible,* as the cancer is quite advanced, and needs to be treated immediately; scientifically, herbal remedies have not been proved to cure cancer."

This was a difference of opinion, as Shirani believed in naturopathy, and Nicole did not. When I showed Nicole the potions that Paula gave me, she said, "I would rather you *didn't* take any of this while on chemo, because should there be any problems, I wouldn't know what caused it, as I don't know what is in those potions."

I thought that was quite reasonable, and decided not to take alternative treatment, as I somehow had complete faith in Nicole. I took painkillers only at nights, as they contained morphine. And I felt very drowsy during the day, but at least I had some relief from the severe pains.

When I saw Nicole again at the end of November, she apologised, because the paperwork from Canberra was delayed. And she could not start treatment for another two weeks, which meant the first treatment was on Wednesday, 16 December.

Nelune flew down every week to be with me, and she was an incredible source of comfort and strength. Shirani too visited weekly, with plenty of food and healthy juices.

Christian called daily, and visited as often as he could, but I told him not to worry, as I was alright. He worked seven days a week, which was very demanding. Their love and support over-whelmed me. And I thanked God daily for my blessings, and for the generous people around me.

Toula was very upset when I told her, and offered to help in any way she could, and said she would visit me soon. Ninette seemed worried when she knew about it. But she was not herself, and immediately started talking about Luigi, and her problems.

I saw Dr Khelil a few days later, as I needed prescriptions. And when I asked him why he had overlooked the results of the mammogram, and assured me I did not have cancer, he looked sheepish, and mumbled, "You told me you had been doing

gardening, and had sore muscles, that's why I didn't think it was anything serious...."
I lost faith in him, as I could not believe he did not know what carcinoma meant.

When I told Colleen about my forthcoming chemo, she immediately replied, "We are going to take turns to bring you food every week. I will draw up a roster, and you can call me, or any of the staff anytime, if you need anything." Colleen, and the other staff members were very supportive too. I thanked her for her kind offer, but I said I should be able to manage, as my sister was bringing me food, and I would call her if I needed anything.

School closed on Friday, 18 December, but my last day was on Monday, because I was starting chemo on Wednesday, the 16th. They all wished me well, and comforted me, saying they would pray for me.

A few days before I started chemo, Elvira accompanied me to the meeting with Kim, one of the nurses in the infusion unit at Peninsula Private hospital. Kim was very patient, and explained every aspect of what the treatment would be like, and prepared me for hair loss, brittle finger nails, nausea, and diarrhoea. But she also said that chemo did not cause so much discomfort nowadays, and I would have an anti-nausea tablet before they started chemo.

Then she asked if I would like to attend a workshop in mid-February, which the cancer council ran. "Look Good, Feel Good," was a program to help patients to look good, and be positive while undergoing chemo. Elvira said she would accompany me to a venue in Frankston.

I just did not worry about anything even then, as I knew I would somehow overcome this disease. And I did not let any negative aspects disturb me. I believe that because I convinced myself that I would beat this cancer, my brain sent positive vibes to my body, and that was a very important factor in this situation.

Nicole prescribed morphine tablets that I took prior to chemo, and she also wanted me to use morphine patches, as the pain was still very severe. I applied the first patch on 16 December, just before chemo started, and Mary and Elvira drove me to hospital at midday. The friendly nurses were all very pleasant and caring. They smiled brightly, no matter how busy they were.

My friends dropped me and went to the shopping centre, as I told them that Nelune was staying with me until I finished chemo, and I would call them when I was ready to leave. Nelune could stay for a few hours only, and was flying back to Sydney that evening, as she had a medical appointment next morning. Although I told her not to worry, she insisted on being with me for the first treatment.

The infusion centre was light and airy, but very cold, and I shivered constantly although it was quite warm outside. Fortunately, I wore a light cardigan. Ten treatment chairs stood around the room, and the place was already full. Once the nurse finished all the preparations, she gave me an anti-nausea tablet, and an anti-histamine as well.

They served sandwiches and tea, and Nelune walked in just as infusion was about to begin. When the chemo started flowing through my veins, I felt a stinging, burning sensation in my left breast and neck area, where the cancer was located.

This burning sensation continued for about twenty minutes. And when I told the nurse, she assured me that it was nothing to worry about, as it meant the chemo was going through the affected area. Halfway through, they served tea and a biscuit. As I was thirsty, I took a sip of tea, and just a nibble of the biscuit, and then it all exploded!

The nurse just missed giving me the vomit bag, and poor Nelune scrambled around with tissues, as I emptied everything down my chest and chair. It took a while to clean me up, and the nurse could not understand why I was sick, even after the anti-nausea tablet. I was quite dazed, and exhausted at the end of that first treatment, as it took over three hours. Nicole came on her rounds, and spent some time with me, and she spoke to Nelune too. She said the first dose was a very high one, and perhaps that was the reason I threw up, so she would reduce the next dose slightly.

When Elvira and Mary arrived to pick me up, I introduced them to Nelune, and they said they would drop her at the station. Nelune took a taxi to the hospital before, but they insisted on dropping her now, and then drove me home.

Elvira brought me dinner later on, and I rested in the evening. The nurse told me to monitor my temperature daily, as they wanted to know even if it was a little above normal.

So the first thing I did next morning, was take my temperature, and was pleased that it was below thirty seven.

I changed the morphine patch every third day as well, and I had to remember a whole heap of extra things to do now. But all that was nothing, compared to the nightmare, after the first chemo infusion. I was nauseous most of the time, and had loose, bowel motions about eight or nine times daily.

I could not go out anywhere, as my bowels just opened up beyond my control. And when nothing was left in my stomach, I just passed fluid, because I could not eat anything without bringing it up. This was only the first week after chemo.

I kept a vomit bag near me, and wore pads all the time. But I had no idea that the first week was only the beginning of worse things to come. Everyone told me how different chemo was now, and that I would not feel sick and nauseous like in the past, because there was better treatment now. How wrong they were! My diarrhoea and nausea just got worse.

Linda, and her two children, visited me on 21 December, and she brought me a basket of cherries that I could not eat, as I just threw up any food. I survived on dry crackers, and ginger tea, as the sight and smell of food just made me nauseous.

Nelune arrived on 23 December, in time for the next treatment. But when they took blood tests prior to infusion, I was severely dehydrated. So they gave me saline instead, and did not proceed with chemo that week. Nicole prescribed Lomotil, and anti-nausea tablets, to be taken three times daily. But I still threw up, and the diarrhoea continued, in spite of those tablets.

Shirani spent that evening, and next morning with me, and the three of us had a peaceful, happy time together. We went for a long walk before dinner, and enjoyed a beautiful evening. She brought some savoury rice and curry, that I ate hungrily, but a few minutes later, I vomited, and ran to the toilet all evening. The Lomotil did not settle my stomach at all.

Shirani prepared vegetables, and fruit juices, saying I must have some nourishing food. But unfortunately, I could not keep anything down. She went home next afternoon, but I really appreciated the time she spent with me.

Christian and Athena spent Christmas day with Nelune and me, and left late at night. I prepared a simple meal for them, but all I could eat were some dry crackers. That night, I could not keep any of my medication down, and threw up everything.

Nelune left on Boxing Day, and said that she would return in a week's time, when I had the next dose of chemo. Nicole asked me to take panadeine with Lomotil, as she said it would help bind my bowel, but it did not help much at the start.

When I went in with Nelune on 30 December, my stomach settled down slightly. And my bowel motions reduced from seven or eight times a day, to about one or two in the morning. The panadeine, and Lomotil seemed to have helped slightly, as I took eight Lomotil tablets daily. Nelune spent a couple of days more before she left, and Christian and Athena spent New Year's Eve with us too.

Just about three weeks after chemo, the swelling in my neck, armpit, and left breast, reduced considerably. And the sharp, debilitating pain in my rib cage, and shoulders also subsided. Nicole was very pleased, when I told her how the pain and swelling eased so quickly. She said that the new drugs were very effective, but she did not know why I was so sick with diarrhoea and nausea, as other patients tolerated the drugs alright. So I kept on taking Lomotil, and anti-nausea tablets continuously.

She was also concerned that my weight dropped from fifty seven to forty nine kilograms in three weeks. And she urged me to eat as much as possible, because she did not want me to lose any more weight. I tried hard to eat more, but my tongue felt as if it was coated with a chemical substance all the time. And I could not taste any flavours in food except, salt, acid, and sugar. I went off rice and curry completely, because chilli burnt my mouth, which was very tender and sore. So I rinsed my mouth with warm, salt water several times a day to avoid ulcers forming.

By the end of January 2016, I started losing lumps of hair, and because I was prepared for it, I was not too upset or surprised. I was glad I cut my hair short in early December, because it would have been dreadful to have long chunks of hair all over my pillow and bathroom. The nurse gave me "chemo" turbans, that I wore whenever I went out. The nausea and bowel motions eased slightly by the end of January.

I had chicken and rice for dinner, and an apple on 27 January, after several weeks of dry biscuits, ginger tea, and thin soup. Cornelia, Con, and Laura visited me every two weeks or so, and they brought ham, sausages, and processed meats, insisting that I eat all that, because I needed protein. But I just could not even smell them, as waves of nausea overcame me. Shirani continued to bring cooked food for a week at a time, but she stopped bringing juices, as that aggravated the diarrhoea.

Nicole advised me to have a port catheter inserted in my chest, to facilitate infusion. Because the nurses found it very difficult to find suitable veins in my hands, after so many needles.

I booked in at Beleura Hospital, and had the port inserted somewhere in early February. After the sedation wore off, I experienced much pain and soreness around the chest area where the port was. But the pain subsided after a week or so.

The nurses did not use the port for a few weeks though, as the area around was very sore. When they did start using it a couple of weeks later, they said it was much easier. But it was quite painful when the needle went through each time, even though I wore a patch an hour before, to numb the area.

All my friends visited regularly, including Joelle, Celine, and Micheline. Celine went to St Francis's church in the city, and offered special Masses for me for the next twelve months. Del visited a couple of times, and once when Nelune was with me. Nancy brought lunch, and spent an afternoon with me too. Mary and Peter visited a few times. Julie and Paul visited regularly, and so did Linda and Leo. Their kindness and concern over-whelmed me.

All my friends did so much to help me practically, as well as emotionally. Toula visited me at home, and sometimes stayed with me during chemo, but Ninette did not visit at all, as her nervous condition was worse.

Shortly after I started chemo, Ninette was diagnosed with early onset of Alzheimer's, which accounted for her erratic behaviour over the last few months or so. I was extremely sad about it, but I just had to accept it as part of life.

She could speak and think lucidly at times. But more often than not, she could not understand what was being said, and her hearing was worse than ever. My illness, and what was going on in my life, did not concern her at all. Her main anxiety, and fixation was still Luigi, whom she phoned about four or five times a day, and she lived only for those moments.

Whenever I called her now, the first thing she said was, "What's the time now? I have to call Luigi." So I did not call her daily like in the past, but once a week or so, as it was very difficult to converse with her. And she did not call me at all.

Once, when Connie was irritated that I visited Ninette regularly, and cared for her so much, he said, "When I die, you will be okay, because you have Ninette!" It was ironical, that in my time of need, she was no longer there. I really missed her company, and the long talks we had, before her mind started to wander.

I settled into a routine with the weekly chemo now. Elvira, Mary, and Toula, took turns to take me to hospital. Elvira insisted on staying with me for the full three hours or so, as she said she liked to be with me, and hear what Nicole had to say. It was very generous of her, but I told her that it would be best if she picked me up later, but she continued to stay with me.

I convinced Mary to do her shopping, or visit relatives, and pick me up when I called her, which she did. Nelune still flew down to be with me for a couple of days after treatment. And she took good care of me, as she knew exactly what I went through.

After an aggressive series of chemotherapy over two months, I was very relieved when Nicole told me that she would stop chemo, as it was making me so sick. But I would still be on Herceptin (the new drug), and Perjeta, every three weeks, starting in early March. At first, when she told me that chemo would last four months, I was under the impression that would be the end of it. But now she said, "You'll have the other two drugs indefinitely, and we'll take scans every three months, to check your heart, and to see how well the drugs are working to control the cancer."

Chapter 103

Felix and Yasmin visited just before my birthday, and took me out for lunch to a Chinese restaurant in Mount Martha village. I was apprehensive to eat anything, as I dreaded a bout of diarrhoea and nausea. So I had some fried rice, and steamed vegetables, which did not upset my stomach too much. I monitored my foods very carefully, as my stomach was very sensitive, and some foods triggered diarrhoea. Also, any smells, like cleaning sprays with chemicals, fatty foods etc. seemed to bring on nausea. It was like being pregnant, except that I never suffered such severe nausea during pregnancy.

I attended the "Look Good, Feel Good," workshop at Frankston, on 23 February, with Elvira, and Mary joined us too. But Mary did some shopping at the Centre, while Elvira and I spent a couple of hours at the workshop. It was fun, and they served a delicious morning tea, while we tried on wigs and caps, and experimented with make-up.

A few days earlier, Elvira and I went to a wig shop in Tooradin, and I bought two wigs, that looked very natural. Now I was confident to go out wearing a wig, instead of a turban. We picked up Mary afterwards, and then drove to a pastry shop in Mount Eliza Village to have lunch, as they wanted to treat me for my birthday. It was almost forty degrees that day, and we sweltered in the heat, as we walked around the Village. I felt uncomfortable with the wig on, as it was scorching. And I just wanted to take it off, and let the cool air play on my bare head.

When I came home around four o'clock, I noticed that Simba was acting strange. In fact he was very quiet, and hid in corners over the last week or so, but I was too sick to fuss around him. Now when I saw him lying down near the study window, I noticed that the side of his stomach looked bare, with matted fur. I knew then that he must have been in a fight, and was injured. I called the local vet immediately, and said that I could not carry him down to the clinic, as I was too weak after chemo, so could he come over to check him.

I paid a little extra for a house call, but I did not care, as I wanted Simba to be examined without delay. The vet, and a nurse, came in an hour's time with a cat cage. When they put him up on the table, the vet showed me two teeth marks, where he was bitten, and the skin just sagged, as the wounds were ulcerated. It made a sickening, swishing sound, when the vet pulled the skin away. I was so upset to think that he was suffering for a week or more, as the wound was so badly infected. The vet said he needed to have surgery immediately, and they took him to the clinic.

I waited anxiously all evening, and around six thirty, the vet called to say that Simba was doing fine, and they would bring him over soon. He did a good job, as he had cut out all the bruised, sagging skin. Then he stitched up Simba, and shaved the area around. The vet told me that even though Simba could not stretch around, to make sure he did not lick the wound, and pull out the stitches. I said I would keep an eye on him.

It was worse than taking care of a child over the next few days. I fussed over him, and made sure the wounds were clean, and that he did not lick them or pull out the stitches. All my efforts failed though, because a few days later, I noticed that one of the wounds oozed, where Simba had pulled the stitches.

It was another costly visit to the vet to re-stitch the wound. And this time, the vet put a plastic collar around his neck. He mewed disconsolately, and I hated the collar as much as he did. When I came home I removed it, and tied a loose bandage around his stomach, but that did not work. So I sewed a t-shirt, slipped it over his head, and fastened the bottom around his stomach with two ties. That seemed to work, as he could not get at the stitches. And as the vet told me to keep him from licking them for at least another week, I kept a vigilant eye on him.

Laura invited me for lunch on 27 February, as it was her birthday. And I drove that far for the first time in all these months. She told me that we were having lunch at a Chinese restaurant in Keysborough, with Con, Cornelia, and Victor, another friend of theirs. I felt better now, and with my wig on, no one would even guess I was undergoing chemo.

We had a good time, but I ate sparingly, although they kept ordering dish after dish, and insisted that I taste every single one of them. I told them that I just could not eat too much, as I did not want to be sick. Then we drove to Cornelia's place, as they intended selling their home, and buying close to Carrum Downs, or Cranbourne. I offered to help her pack, if she needed extra hands, but Cornelia said they would start packing slowly, and not to worry.

A social worker visited me in hospital in early January, and after assessing my situation, she said I was eligible to get help from the council to clean the house. I was glad of the offer, as the chemo left me very weak, and quite unable to do any strenuous, physical work.

After the first three weeks of chemo, my blood count was so low, that I needed a blood transfusion. The nurses took blood samples before every treatment, and I needed vitamin supplements during the first few months.

I still called Nilanthi often, and although she was much better, she was very depressed and negative. She complained of aches and pains, that were part of dengue fever. My illness seemed to be of secondary importance, as she dwelt on hers constantly. I never told her what I was going through, so she said, "You are better now aren't you? That's good. I could have *died* with dengue fever! Everyone tells me that. I'm still so weak, and my leg is bad." And she went on to enumerate her symptoms.

Nelune and Shirani offered to pay for her ticket, but she said she was unable to come over and be with me, as her health was still very poor, even though it was now more than three months since she was ill. I only needed her companionship, and not to cook, or take care of me. But unfortunately, she was too self-absorbed, and did not make an effort.

I would have been glad if she came even for a few weeks at the start, but now I was used to the weekly treatment. Although my energy levels were at their lowest, I was able to make easy meals, drive short distances, and was as independent as possible.

I even started going to school for a few hours on a Monday afternoon. And I felt better for getting out of the house and being with other people, and teaching music. Nicole was pleased to hear that, and encouraged me to resume a normal life, as much as possible. Christine, one of the teachers from school, visited me at home, and we had a pleasant afternoon.

Christian flew to San Francisco on business, on 11 March, and returned on 18 March. He told me that he wanted to come down, and meet Nicole too. So when Nelune was with me during one chemo treatment, Christian came to the hospital, and I introduced him to Nicole, and the nurses. He was very relieved to hear that I responded well to the treatment, and that the pains had subsided. In spite of his extremely busy work schedule, he called me every day, or sent a text to ask how I was.

Nelune visited almost every week, and when she came for the Easter break on 24 March, we drove down to Woolamai, on Good Friday. Christian and Athena visited later that evening, and we had a good time together. Nelune left on Holy Saturday night, as she had other engagements, so I dropped her at the station next day.

I attended morning Mass on Easter Sunday, and my neighbours, Angela and Elio invited me for afternoon tea. When I went there around two o'clock, their families were there too. I spent a little time chatting to Elio's mother, and the others before I came home.

Linda and Leo visited next day, and Leo helped with some odd jobs. But they did not stay very long, as they were on their way somewhere else with the children. But it was very good of them to visit me.

I dropped in to see Ninette the following day, as Liliana came too, but it was difficult to engage Ninette in conversation now, as she was vague and disoriented. I felt very sad to see her looking like a lost scarecrow, as her weight had plummeted. And there was nothing much left of her, but a skeletal frame smothered in layers of tatty cardigans.

Toula said that she could not get her to change her clothes or wash them, because she would not allow her to put anything in order, or change her clothes. This was all part of her mental state, but it was not easy for Toula, who was her full-time carer now.

I called Ninette one afternoon, and said that I would visit after school, but when I arrived there around three thirty, all the curtains were drawn, and I could hear the television blaring. I knocked and called, and then tried phoning, but her number was busy. Then I called Toula, and she said that most probably she was on the phone to Luigi, so I went home. Ninette called in the night to say she forgot I was visiting.

And that she was already in bed by three o'clock, listening to the radio, and talking with Luigi. That was the last time I visited her after school.

I settled into my usual routine gradually; visiting friends, and going out for tea or lunch regularly. Nicole encouraged me to go out more often, even though I felt like I just wanted to sleep most of the time, as it was an effort to get dressed, or do anything that required physical exertion.

Chris and Peter La Ponder were in Mornington for a brief holiday, and she invited me for lunch in Mornington with their friend, Anne.

I went out with Mary and Elvira on 6 April, to celebrate Elvira's birthday, which was the day before. Then coffee with Toula on Friday, at Bentons Square, and on Saturday, I had lunch at Anne's place, with Chris and Peter. It was lovely to see them again. Anne suggested that it was better to relax at her place, than at a restaurant, so she catered a delicious meal, which we enjoyed.

Con, Cornelia, and Laura came for lunch a few times, although Laura insisted that I did not get too tired cooking for them. But I wanted to make a few curries, as I knew they enjoyed them, and we had some good times. Julie and Paul visited often, and Paul always offered to do odd jobs around the place whenever they came.

A few days later, I had an email from the detective who was in charge of Stacy's case. He wanted to know if I was prepared to be interviewed by a journalist from SBS, who was compiling a documentary on missing persons. She contacted him asking for any information. But he said it was up to me, and I replied that I would give a phone interview.

A day later, Kathy called me, and said she was a freelance journalist, and would very much like to visit me, if I could spare a few hours. She was based in Sydney, but flew to Melbourne, specially to interview me. How could I refuse? We made time to meet at my place a couple of days later, and she was pleased.

Kathy was a pleasant, homely-looking, middle-aged lady, and she wanted a great deal of information. It was quite a long interview, and she was here for about three hours. She said she was compiling six or eight cases, which would go on the SBS website. And she hoped that people who read the articles, would be able to help the police.

It was traumatic talking about Stacy, and going through old reports, photographs etc. but it was soon over. She wanted to interview Christian too, but I asked him earlier, and he did not think it necessary, so I told Kathy I would give any information she required. When we finished, she asked if she could send a photographer to take some photographs of me, and some of the old ones of Stacy. I agreed, and she said he would contact me when he was ready.

I had a scan in February, which showed that my heart was normal, and Nicole was pleased. She said that I would have a scan every three months, as the only down side with Herceptin, was that it could affect the heart muscles. The subsequent scan in May was good too, so I was quite relieved that everything was going well.

Nelune and I went to see a play at Mount Eliza "The Odd Couple" (female version), on Sunday, 24 April. It was very funny, and we had a few good laughs, then I dropped her at the station next day.

Ever since Good Friday, which was a few weeks ago in March, I suffered severe, sharp pains in my upper right arm. I was concerned that it was something sinister, as the pain was unbearable. Once again, I could hardly sleep at nights, as I could not lie down on my right side.

When I mentioned this to Nicole, she sent me for a scan in mid-April. The result, a torn tendon in my upper arm, and nothing cancerous, thank goodness. She prescribed strong painkillers, and asked me to see a physio soon.

As I did not want to end up with a frozen arm, I kept doing exercises that the physio suggested, and hoped it would improve in time. For the life of me, I could not remember what I did to injure it in the first place. And that injury restricted some of my activities now, as it hurt to play the piano too long, or paint. It took more than twelve months to heal, but not completely, as I lost some flexibility in my movements.

Laura, Con, and Cornelia visited on Saturday, 14 May, as they wanted to visit Tyabb Packing house again. We left at ten thirty, as soon as they arrived here, and we had a good time browsing through antiques. But we came back and had lunch, as I prepared rice and a few curries. They left late that evening, but it was a pleasant day.

Nancy visited at the end of May, and had lunch with me. She enjoyed the vegetables, and fish curries. And then we spent a few hours chatting, and walking around in the garden.

Laura invited me on the following Saturday, and Con and Cornelia came too. And we had a good time till late afternoon. I came home around five o'clock, but the others stayed on till night (Laura told me next day).

Damien, the photographer from SBS, arrived on Thursday, 9 June. He removed a few photographs of me, and some of Stacy from old photographs in the album. He was a nice young man, and when he finished, he told me his mother died of cancer only a couple of months ago. His eyes filled with tears, when he related the trauma of her illness, and how long the doctors took to make a correct diagnosis. I sympathised with him, and he wished me well before he left. And he said he would send Kathy the photographs soon.

Liz was retiring on 15 June, and the staff organized a farewell morning tea for her. I was sorry to see her leave, as we became good friends over the years. But she had been teaching close to forty years or more, and said it was time for her to start enjoying life, and "smell the roses."

On the following day, I had another cat scan, and bone scan at Beleura hospital. And they said that Nicole would have the results when I went for treatment the following week.

Shirani and Ranjith flew to Sri Lanka the next day for two weeks, and I hoped they would have a good trip and return safely. But I missed chatting to her, as we spoke almost daily. Shirani was very good at dispensing natural remedies, and advised me on the kind of foods to include in my daily diet, to boost my immune system.

I started seeing a physio in Mornington for five weeks, since 28 April, but I did not get any relief from the pain. When I went for treatment on 22 June, and told Nicole that my arm was still very sore, she suggested that I have a cortisone injection. And she referred me to a doctor there, that very afternoon.

It was very painful though, as the doctor injected right into the torn tendon. But a few days later, I could move my arm freely, and the pain had almost subsided. I was so pleased, that I immediately went out to prune some shrubbery. But when I finished in about an hour's time, my fingers and arm went into spasms, and did not stop trembling for a few minutes.

I thought that I must have over-exerted my arm, so I gave it a rest. But over the next couple of months, my arm felt good. And then, the all too familiar pain crept in once more, though not as severe. Nicole said I would never regain full use of my arm. As most people my age, who had chemotherapy, were prone to torn tendons and ligaments, as the muscles became weak.

I had a recurring dream about Connie on 5 July, that he stood by my bed, and talked to me, but I did not know what he was saying. I cried out in amazement, "You can *talk!* Thank God! *How* did you manage to talk again?" he replied that a doctor helped him to regain his speech. So I asked, "What's the doctor's name? I have to tell Tina about him!" (Tina, my friend, was in the last stages of MND, and unable to speak at that stage). That was the end of my dream, and I could not understand why I kept dreaming that Connie could talk again.

I was happy when Shirani and Ranjith returned on 7 July. She called me a few times when she was at Nilanthi's, but it was good to know she was back. My friends visited me regularly, and on weekends especially, and I was very grateful for their kindness and support whenever they came. I considered myself truly blessed to be surrounded by so many caring friends, who were more like family now. And they all proved the truth of that old adage, "A friend in need, is a friend indeed."

Laura drove me to Con and Cornelia's new house, as it was Cornelia's birthday on 17 July. They sold their place in Keysborough, and bought a smaller house in Cranbourne East. It was about five years old, and the garden too was smaller, and easier to manage. When we arrived, they were still in the process of unpacking and settling down, and had a great deal of work to do in and around the place.

I was pleased to see that they hung about five of my paintings in their new house. The winter scene looked very effective in the dining room, and the High Country scene, decorated a long wall in the corridor. They were very happy with the paintings, so it was worth my effort. My other paintings hung in Cornelia's bedroom, and spare room as well. We had a good afternoon, and I came home around five thirty in the evening, as I had parked at Laura's place, and drove back from there.

I went to George Jenkins Theatre in Frankston, on Saturday, 23 July, to watch a play called "Noises Off," produced by Frankston Theatre Group. It was hilarious, and I laughed throughout the play. I did not see this particular play before, but it was very clever, as it had two on-going plots; a play on stage, and the intrigues going on backstage. The stage kept revolving to show the play, and then the backstage. I ended with a stitch in my stomach when it was over, as I laughed so much.

Karen was living at her in-law's place in Cobram, until they finished building their house in Beechworth. And as she had to work in the city for a few days, she asked if she could stay with me for a week or so. I was happy to oblige, and we had a few nice days together, chatting about our writing experiences, books, cats, and psychic matters. Karen was very interesting, and travelled widely.

Her love of cats made her volunteer to look after homeless cats in an enclosed section in the city of Rome, where she stayed for a few months. Karen related many stories about the cats, as she grew very attached to them. During the few days she spent here, she got up very early in the morning to work out at a local gym. And then spent time writing, as she was completing her second novel.

I gave her a set of spare keys, and the remote control for the main gate, so she was quite free to come and go as she pleased. She left after five days, and said she would visit again. But she was keen to move into their own home soon, as she said she was tired of being "homeless."

Elvira came on 6 August, to practise some songs, as she was holding a charity concert for St Vincent's at Frankston. She asked me to come an hour earlier, and help set up afternoon tea. So I went there at one o'clock, but very soon, her grand-daughters, sister-in-law, and daughter-in-law, not to mention a few friends, were busy helping out in the kitchen.

I rushed there, thinking I was the only one, as she told me that she needed help, and she counted on me. Anyway, I helped as much as I could, and then enjoyed the concert very much. Her grand-daughters, Lauren and Andrea, entertained for half an hour with their singing, and Lauren played the saxophone. Both girls were very talented, especially Lauren, as she played the saxophone expertly. After the show, I congratulated them, and their mother, Anne.

Michael, from Retire invest, wanted to discuss some financial matters with me. I asked Mary if she would accompany me to Dandenong, as I was hesitant to drive there on my own just yet. Mary drove her car, and we went there on Thursday afternoon, 18 August.

She waited in the reception area until Michael finished. And he kept urging me to sell the house, and move to a smaller place as soon as possible. I told him that I was not ready to do that just yet. But he was very insistent, and repeated what he told us a couple of years ago. "You can't *afford* that house in Mt Martha! Sell up, and buy somewhere else!"

I was rather annoyed when I left, as I did not want anyone to pressure me into selling my home. I knew that I would do so, when the time was right. It also irked me to think that he charged $2500 or so annually, for administration costs. I decided to dispense with his services, once I consulted another independent financial advisor.

Mary and I stopped at Karingal for a cup of tea before we came home. And I was surprised to see my previous team leader from the Tax Office, Ian, and his wife, sitting in the same cafe. He smiled and came over and said, "Nalini, you are looking well! How are you?" I wore a wig, so no one could tell I was unwell. I told him that although I was fine now, I was still undergoing treatment for breast cancer. He said, "I'm sorry to hear that, but you look well though, anyway, take care and all the best."

Merian and Mitch visited on Sunday, 21 August, and I made pan rolls for tea, as they enjoyed them very much. It was great to see them, and I could not believe that Mitch was now twenty years old. I knew him since he was eight, and was glad to see what a well-adjusted, polite young man he was.

He always told me that he wanted to be a pilot, ever since I knew him, and now he was almost there. I told him that I was very proud of him, as he stuck to his goal all these years. Merian said she wanted to come over one afternoon, and learn how to make pan rolls, and I told her I would be happy to demonstrate. Just then Christian and Athena dropped in, as I asked Christian to set up the record player for me. They stayed for dinner, and Christian did some odd jobs around. But Mitch and Merian left a little while later, and said they would visit again soon.

Shirani said that the settlement for the townhouse in Casey, went through on 25 August, and invited me there when Suresh moved in. So I drove there in the afternoon, and met Shirani, Ranjith, and Suresh. They brought lunch, and we shared milk rice etc. It was a very nice, compact place, with a little square of lawn at the back, and was just right for Suresh. I hoped he would be happy and settle down there.

I was getting pains, and tightness in my chest for some time, and Nicole was concerned that it may have something to do with the drugs. She asked me to consult a heart specialist whom she recommended, Dr Szto at Beleura hospital.

I saw him on Friday, 26 August, and after he went through my history, he said, "You should have had stents put in when you had the last angiogram done in 2009, after your heart attack." And he wanted me to book in at Peninsula Hospital as soon as possible. So the nurse made an appointment for the following Friday.

Mary drove me to hospital at eight o'clock on Friday, 2 September. And she went shopping, until the nurse called her to say I was ready to go home. I dreaded the thought of staying overnight, because I worried about the cats, and how they would cope without me around. The nurse told me to bring an overnight bag, because if they did insert stents, I could not go home that day.

I asked Shirani to come over and stay the night, as they could feed the cats, and bring them in, if I had to stay overnight. Imagine my relief, when doctor spoke to me after the procedure and said, "I didn't find any major blockages, so I didn't put any stents this time. You can go home in the afternoon, as long as you have someone to stay overnight with you." I replied, "Yes doctor, my sister will stay with me."

Mary picked me up at twelve thirty, and stayed till Shirani and Ranjith arrived at three o'clock. I went to bed immediately, as I was drained. But I woke up in the evening, and we chatted a little while. They relaxed, and had an early night too. And they left at eight o'clock on Saturday morning, as they had bookings that night. Elvira visited in the afternoon, and brought me some dinner as well.

Shirani, Ranjith, and Suresh dropped in again on Sunday, and brought some cooked food to last for a few days. I was very grateful to Shirani for all that she did for me, especially as she was so busy with the restaurant. And yet, she managed to find time to help me.

Christian left for San Francisco on business, on 10 September, and he sent me a text next day to say he arrived safely in New York. I was very relieved, but still worried about him, as it was 11 September, the black day, when terrorists attacked the twin towers in 2001. I prayed there would be no more tragic events on this dreadful anniversary.

Nelune held the Lilac Ball on 10 September as well, and she called to say that they raised a very large amount of money once again. I was very pleased for her, and congratulated her on her marvellous achievements.

I had lunch with Mary, Elvira, and their friends, at Rosebud Hotel, to celebrate one of their friend's birthday. Mary and I went to the Plaza later, and did some shopping, then had coffee before coming home. Mary was upset over some issue with

Elvira, and she complained bitterly. I was sorry that she felt aggrieved, and tried to pacify her, and hoped she would sort out this matter soon.

Christian returned from New York on the following Sunday, the 25th. And I was very very relieved, and happy that he arrived safely, as it was such a long flight. It was good to hear his voice again after some time. I knew he had to travel and live his life, but I could not help worrying, until he arrived home safely.

Shirani invited Elvira, Mary, and me, for lunch to Woolamai, just to say "Thank You" for all their help. Elvira drove us down there on Wednesday, 28 September, and we enjoyed a really delicious lunch. We walked around the gardens later, and looked at the Ashram, before heading back in the afternoon. When Shirani told me that the new medication Suresh was on, was very effective, and that he was improving slowly, I was very pleased, and relieved to hear that.

Del visited next day, and after a relaxed lunch, we spent an interesting afternoon, chatting about our various interests, especially writing, reading, and gardening, among other topics.

I was sad to hear that Christine's mother died after a long illness. She was in her early eighties, but that did not make it any easier for her, as they were very close. Christine was the only daughter, and she had three brothers. She too retired from school a few months ago, after more than forty-five years of teaching, as she wanted to spend time with her mother during her last stages.

I attended the funeral at St Francis Xavier's church at two o'clock on Wednesday, 5 October. Christine was glad to see me, and we chatted briefly before the service began. A couple of staff members from school were present, but I was surprised that more of them did not attend. Christine was disappointed that she did not receive a card or flowers from the staff. But I told her it must have been an oversight, as they were usually prompt in such matters.

Christian flew to Greece on 13 October, to attend a course to gain a higher qualification in TRX training. He sent a text to say he arrived safely, and that the course was hectic. I told him to take care, and looked forward to seeing him soon. Wherever he travelled, he always sent me postcards from overseas, and sometimes they arrived a few days after he returned. But it was so great to hear from him, because these trips were very hectic and tiring for him. But he still found time to contact me via text messages or calls.

Joelle, Celine, and Micheline, visited on Saturday, 15 October, and we enjoyed a pleasant time. They spent a couple of hours chatting and walking in the garden, before they left. It was good to see them again.

I was happy and relieved when Christian returned safely a week later. He called me at five o'clock in the evening, as he said he went straight to bed when he arrived that morning. He was feeling the stress of travelling, and hoped it was the last one for some time. But as he told me, it was important for him to attend those courses, if he wanted to achieve the qualifications he aspired to.

Cornelia, Con, and Laura came for lunch on Saturday, the 22nd, and it was very late when they left in the evening, but we had a good time. Their friend, Victor, bought live crabs at the Victoria market, and they wanted me to make a curry, as they did not taste one before. It was hard work, but he killed the crabs, as I said I could not do that, because Connie always killed them when he bought live crabs. They enjoyed the hot crab curry though, and we had fun, laughing and chatting away all afternoon.

Liz sent a text on 14 November, reminding me to look at the "Super Moon," which came around once in seventy years or so, when it was closest to earth. I looked forward to seeing it that night, but when I went out at ten thirty, it was just overhead, and not very large. I was disappointed, as I expected it to be a spectacular sight, but perhaps I missed seeing it at its brightest.

Laura invited me again on 19 November, and we had a pleasant time, just chatting, and sharing our experiences. It was just the two of us this time, so it was not as noisy and busy without Con and Cornelia, who were away in Queensland for a couple of weeks. I came home around five o'clock, and rested a while.

The next week was very busy; afternoon tea with Christine at Onde's on Tuesday, then Mary and Peter came for lunch, as Peter wanted to do some odd jobs around the place. It was very kind of them to spend time attending to those tasks, and I appreciated their generosity very much.

Nelune arrived on Saturday, 26 November, as we planned to see a play "Allo, 'Allo" at Mt Eliza on Sunday, the last one for the season. Shirani and Ranjith arrived early on Sunday morning, as they wanted to oil the deck, and outdoor benches for me. Shirani brought lunch, and after they finished oiling the deck and benches, we had a delicious meal before they left. And Nelune and I went for the play at one thirty.

It was very funny, and we had a great time laughing all afternoon, and came home around five o'clock. Then we watched a few comedies in the night. I dropped Nelune at the station on Monday morning, before going to school. It was a busy weekend, but I enjoyed it very much.

Felix and Yasmin visited on Tuesday, as they drove from Sydney, and were staying with some other friends near the city. They wanted to take me out for lunch, but then decided to bring "takeaway" rice and curry, from one of the Sri Lankan restaurants in Dandenong. We enjoyed the meal together, and they spent a couple of hours relaxing, before heading back to the city for another engagement. It was really good to have such caring, and sincere friends around me.

Mary's birthday was on Monday, 28 November, but we went out for lunch on Thursday, 1 December, to Rosebud Hotel, where her friends met to celebrate their special occasions. Elvira picked her, and I paid for Mary's lunch, then she decided to come shopping with me to the Plaza. We had cake and coffee there, and spent a couple of hours chatting, and window-shopping, before I dropped her around four o'clock.

Paul and Julie visited on Sunday, 18 December, and they had lunch, before he did some odd jobs around the place. Paul offered to remove the garage door that was rotting at the bottom, and replace it with a new one. I told him I would get the new door delivered, whenever he was free to do that.

Shirani and Ranjith dropped in with Suresh that afternoon, as they wanted to cut the lawns and weed the garden before Christmas. Ron and Monica did not tend the garden since September. Because Ron went in for a few operations to remove cancerous melanomas on his face and arms, but did not recover completely. Monica called me many times in desperation, and told me that he was a changed man, and seemed to have some mental issues as well.

I was sad to hear about Ron's condition, as he was admitted to hospital a few times, and did not want to see Monica at all. She wept, and complained bitterly about how unfairly he treated her, but I just listened, and did not want to take sides.

John recommended Lou, who was distantly related to him, and lived in Frankston. So I engaged him to cut the lawns, but he did not weed or tend the garden like Ron and Monica did, which was a pity. He charged extra, if I wanted him to spray weeds; but I did not have a choice, as I wanted someone reliable. And I felt comfortable, because John recommended him.

Shortly afterwards, Lou went in for an operation, and was unable to resume work for another month at least, so Shirani offered to help out. Suresh did his best, but it was very hard work mowing lawns. It looked a little better than before. And as Lou expected to start work in the New Year, I was happy that the grass would not be too long when he came back.

Toula and I met for a coffee almost every Friday or Tuesday. We spoke about what she endured with Ninette, as it was very stressful for Toula. I stopped visiting Ninette every Tuesday, ever since I started treatment, and I did not call her frequently either. She was vague and disoriented whenever I called her, so it was distressing for me to know she was getting worse.

Toula said she wanted to attend a few workshops organized by Carer Support, so she could gain the required skills, to deal with her mother's dementia. I listened to her, and related my experiences with Connie, as he too suffered from early onset of dementia, which made his behaviour quite unreasonable, and incomprehensible most of the time.

Ninette's weight dropped to about thirty seven kilograms over the last few months, and she neglected to feed the dog, or eat regular meals. Although Toula prepared her meals, she sometimes did not eat. She liked to drink brandy though, and as her sciatica troubled her, she drank more than she should.

A few months later, when I visited her one afternoon, she came up to the car, and said, "Quick, we have to go to Luigi's to help him hang his clothes." She did not give me a choice, so I told her to give me the directions to get there. Of course, she did not know how to get there, except to look out for a "Big, black gate." And I drove round in circles, till I finally called Luigi, and asked him for directions. But he did not even know the name of the street where I had to turn off, to get to his place!

Meanwhile, Ninette had a major panic attack, and kept moaning, "I'm going to get a heart attack! I can't breathe! What are we going to do now? Take me back home! I will die here!"

After a few more wrong turns, I managed to find his unit, and when he saw us he asked Ninette, "Why did you come?" When she replied that she wanted to help him, he just shrugged his shoulders and replied gruffly, "I hung my clothes already." Then in about ten minutes time, she muttered anxiously, "We have to go back home now. I can't wait any longer."

That was the end of that. When I told Toula about that stressful afternoon, she said that it was best not to visit her on my own, because she would repeat the same behaviour.

I invited Mary and Elvira for lunch on 23 December to "Sugo," a nice cafe in Mornington, that my new neighbours owned. Coincidentally, my neighbours on both sides owned cafes on Main Street, in Mornington, so I patronized them regularly. And treating them for lunch, was my way of thanking Mary and Elvira for their kindness in taking me to hospital every three weeks, and for their on-going care and support. The food was delicious, and we enjoyed lunch.

During one of my treatments, when I saw some patients who had finished chemo, giving cards and balloons to the staff, I asked Nicole jokingly, "When can *I* bring balloons and cards to celebrate my last treatment?" The nurse laughed with Nicole when she replied, "You can bring as many balloons and cards as you like Nalini, but you will be here for a long time!"

Then she went on to explain that I would need to be on this treatment for the rest of my life, as the cancer in my bones would always be there. The drugs controlled it from spreading, and as they were working well, Nicole was happy to continue with this treatment.

I was very disappointed, to say the least, but I resigned myself to this routine in my life, which has kept me alive and well so far. At the beginning, when Nicole said I would have four months of chemo, I thought four months was too long to be on chemo, and the other two drugs. But now, it was for the rest of my days.

The side-effects are bearable, and though cramps and spasms can be very painful sometimes, I can tolerate them. And even though I am not as energetic as before, and I tire easily, I can still live a quality life, doing most of the things I did previously, but at a more leisurely pace.

I can never be thankful enough to Nicole, and the dedicated staff at Peninsula Private hospital, as they are the most amazing people I have met. It is now more than two and a half years since I started treatment there, and each time I go for infusion, I cannot help but admire the ongoing care, and commitment of the nursing staff. No matter how busy they are, they have nothing but smiles, and concern for their patients. I am deeply grateful to Nicole, and the wonderful staff, who continue to care for me, and all the other cancer patients with infinite care and patience.

Chapter 104

Christmas Eve was sweltering, and the temperature soared to above forty degrees. I left home early, and arrived at four thirty, in good time for the childrens' Mass at five o'clock. Although I wore a summer dress and the fans whirred overhead, the heat became unbearable when the church started to fill up. I thought I would faint, as I could hardly breathe at times. And I hoped that I would last until Mass was over. I almost rushed outside at the end of service. They served cake and wine outside the church, but I did not want anything except water, and drove home as fast as I could, with the air conditioner on. But it did not cool down that night, and another sizzling day was expected tomorrow.

It was late afternoon when Christian and Athena arrived on Christmas Day. I spent a relaxed morning, listening to some festive music, and trying to stay cool indoors. Athena brought her ukulele that she was learning to play, and spent a couple of hours strumming and singing. She sang beautifully, and accompanied herself, and I enjoyed listening to her. We chatted for a while, and they left before it became too late.

The next few days sped by, and it was time for me to have treatment again on 28 December. Mary dropped in for a little while on the 31st, as Tony and she were attending a dance that night, and she wanted to wish me a Happy New Year. I went for Mass at six o'clock, and then spent a peaceful evening watching a movie, and fireworks on television at midnight.

The neighbourhood was very quiet, as there were no fireworks around. I went to bed at one o'clock after seeing the New Year in.

It was mild and pleasant next day, and I called all my friends and immediate family, to wish them all a very Happy New Year.

Laura and I drove to Tyabb Antique Warehouse on 5 January, and spent the afternoon there. We bought a few knick knacks, and had lunch at the cafe. I treated her, as it was her birthday in a few weeks time. But I instantly regretted having lunch there, because the meals were disappointing, and ridiculously over-priced. I kept telling myself we should not eat at that cafe again, but when it was lunch time, we ended up eating there anyway.

Fr Raj was transferring to another parish in a couple of weeks time, so I went to church on 11 January to wish him farewell. He was sorry to hear about my health issues, and said he would pray for me. I asked him why he was leaving this parish so soon, and he said that his order allowed priests to stay in one parish for three years only, before they were transferred. He accomplished a great deal of work in the church, and most of us were sorry to see him leave.

I went for my annual eye examination next afternoon, and after reading my history, Dr Renehan joked, "You are being poisoned still are you?" I nodded. He asked, "How long are you going to be on this treatment for cancer?" I replied, "Looks like for the term of my natural life." Then we spoke about side-effects, and he told me that my eyes were fine, and no problems, after the cataract operation.

I was relieved to hear him say so, and then I dropped in at Centrelink near-by, to make an appointment with their financial advisor. When I told the officer what my enquiry was about, she said, "You can speak to someone over the phone now, and if you need further help, then you can make an appointment." When the officer connected us, I spoke to the financial advisor over the phone. And after forty minutes or so, my questions were all answered to my satisfaction. I thanked her, and she said I did not need to make an appointment, unless I had further enquiries.

The paint was peeling off on the doors opening to the al fresco area, and I wanted to paint them, but I needed someone to sand them first. Mary and Tony dropped in for tea on Saturday, 14 January, and when I asked Tony if he could sand the doors, he agreed to help me.

Ninette celebrated her 85th birthday on 17 January, and Toula invited Elvira, Melanie, and me, to celebrate the occasion. Toula wanted to have lunch at the RSL in Seaford, but then decided to have it at her place, as Ninette could not handle crowds, and became confused when there were too many people.

When I drove to Toula's that day, Elvira, and Toula's friend, Melanie, were the only ones there. Ninette looked very frail and vague. But I managed to engage her in desultory conversation, mainly about music. And she related the same stories I had heard so many times, but I was happy that she was able to remember them. I did not stay long though, and left in a couple of hours, after she cut her birthday cake.

The last time I visited Ninette at her place, was a few weeks before she was finally admitted into care on 21 August 2017. Her condition deteriorated so rapidly, that it was unsafe for her to be on her own anymore. After sixteen years or more of knowing Ninette, it was the end of that chapter. I grieved deeply, because I loved her very much, and she was very close to me for so long. But she changed completely with the onset of dementia, and was not the same person she was when I first knew her.

I visited her a few times in the home, once with Mary and Elvira, and then with Toula and Liliana, but although she said, "Yes, I remember you, Nalini, my student," she was disoriented, and her mind kept flitting, as she could not converse rationally. It made me so sad to see her wandering around in a daze, and it was pointless to visit her again. Now she barely recognizes anyone, except Toula, and her dog, Fido. And it will not be long before her memory fades altogether.

Nelune flew over to watch the tennis grand finals on Monday, 23 January, and we spent the afternoon together before the match. I made rice and curry for lunch, which we had at Karingal. Then we walked around a couple of hours, before I dropped her at the station, as the tennis match was in the night.

Tony and Mary came on 25 January, and he sanded the door first, then went to Bunnings to change the can of paint I bought. He said that it was the wrong kind, as the paint needed to be water-based, not oil. While we waited, I wrote down Mary's genealogy in the family tree album that she brought. Mary said that would be the best way to help her, as she could not write so many names, because of her sore wrist.

I agreed to write it for her, and I was absolutely amazed when she rolled off names, birthdays, and deaths by memory! Not only did she know all the names, birthdays, and deaths on her side, but she knew details of Tony's parents, uncles, aunts, and cousins too. It was just incredible that she remembered so much. It took more than two hours to write the family tree, and Tony started painting the first coat.

It looked much better already, and I was very grateful for his help. In the evening, I applied a second coat halfway, as I could not reach the top due to my sore arm. Tony and Mary came again on Friday, the day after Australia Day, 26 January, and he finished painting the door. It looked very good, and brightened that whole area.

The days and weeks were busy with visits from friends, scans, treatment etc. I called Christine, Liz, and Helen, as we planned to have lunch on 22 February. Liz's birthday was a week or so earlier, and we thought of celebrating both our birthdays with our good friends. We met at Fratelli's in Frankston, exchanged gifts, and spent an enjoyable time together.

On my sixty-fifth birthday next day, I woke up in the morning, and thanked God for all the wonderful years he gave me. I was alive, and as well as I could be, and survived the onset of breast cancer so far. I do not know what the future holds. But I wake up each day, with a prayer of thanks, and gratitude for God's goodness to me.

After a leisurely morning, reflecting on all the positive aspects in my life, I was ready for Elvira and Mary. They picked me and took me out for lunch to Sugo's in Mornington. And later, we walked along Main Street in the warm sunshine, just enjoying being out on this beautiful summer day.

The years have brought many changes, especially over the last few months. Some of my friends have passed away, or been admitted to nursing homes. Change is the only certain thing in this life, as we know. But as each chapter closes, I cannot help but look back with a touch of nostalgia.

In late September 2017, Cornelia suffered a stroke, while she was at Laura's place one evening. Laura's quick thinking saved her, as the ambulance arrived within ten minutes. Although she spent three months in rehab, and today she is able to walk, and talk almost normally, she will never be the same.

Stacy is missing for twenty four years now. But I still keep hoping I will see him some day soon, as hope is all that sustains me.

Each dawn is a gift that I treasure, and I am determined to live my life to the fullest. I pray I will continue to have strength to face whatever is in store for me, and that is all I can do. My blessings are many; Christian, Athena, my sisters, and my sincere friends. What more can I ask?

To this day, I believe that the most important thing is to have faith in the Almighty. Whoever you conceive a Higher Being to be, you must believe in some Life

Force in our Universe. Without such conviction, there is no way we can deal with the adversities of life, and it is through some Almighty Life Force, that we are able to exist.

Some of us are given a stronger Force than others, and depending on the quantity or measure of that Force, our life spans are dealt out at the time of our birth. This being so, it is only right that we strive to live our lives to the fullest, and attain the highest possible level of fulfilment and perfection, not materially, but spiritually, and emotionally.

Therefore, it is unforgivable, when one human being tries to suppress another, and robs them of their right to be themselves; to reach their full potential as a person, and be the individual that God created, and meant that person to be. To struggle a lifetime to be yourself, and not be beaten into submission, is something no human being should have to endure. No man or woman has the right to deprive another human being's life. These have always been my firm convictions.

I am grateful for the countless blessings and joys I have been showered with in my life. After the maelstrom of years gone by, I am at peace, and am content. I had loving and generous parents in Ammie and Thathie, and I am thankful too for the brief, but joyous years spent with my beloved brother, Nihal, and to have sisters, who were there for me through the most trying times in life, and are still my best friends.

I am blessed with such unique and precious sons, like Stacy and Christian, and a beautiful daughter-in-law, Athena, who is very dear to me. And Janice, our amazing sister-in-law, who has shown nothing but love and concern for me all these years; for my close family members, and every one of my good friends. I cannot name them all here, but they know who they are, and I am deeply grateful to each one.

My life has been full and rewarding, and each moment was filled to the brim. I like to believe that I have not wasted a single moment of my life, which seems to be ebbing away so quickly. And if I had another lifetime, or two, that would be a bonus, so I could complete every single project I have in mind. Since that is impossible, I race against time now, to achieve whatever I can within a limited period. I have learnt that there is no purpose, or time for vain regrets and self-pity. And I like to be occupied continuously, because it helps me maintain my equilibrium.

Keeping busy is my panacea for all modern ailments, such as boredom, and waste of time. I would like to be remembered as someone who tried to be unfailingly kind to all those around me, as I have never hurt or grieved anyone willingly. And if I have failed to achieve this, I regret it very much, as the most important aim in my life is to abide by my faith, and follow the teachings of the Gospel.

Two important sources of wisdom, courage, and precepts to live by, are undoubtedly the teachings of Jesus Christ, and the "Desiderata" (in that order). I have a copy of my first Bible, which I acquired when I was fifteen years old, and a printed copy of the "Desiderata," which hangs on the wall beside my desk.

Each night before I go to sleep, I read a few psalms (especially psalm 23 and 91), and the book of "Wisdom" in my Bible. And when I am at my desk, my eyes often turn to those words that I first read as a very young girl. Here are those gems of wisdom found in old Saint Paul's Church, Baltimore, dated 1692. The words are so powerful and meaningful, even in today's world, that I never fail to be moved each time I read them.

"Go placidly amid the noise and haste and remember what peace there may be in silence. As far as possible, without surrender, be on good terms with all persons.

Speak your truth quietly and clearly and listen to others, even the dull and ignorant; they too have their story. Avoid loud and aggressive persons; they are vexations to the spirit.

If you compare yourself with others, you may become vain and bitter; for always there will be greater and lesser persons than yourself.

Keep interested in your own career, however humble; it is a real possession in the changing fortunes of time.

Exercise caution in your business affairs for the world is full of trickery but let this not blind you to what virtue there is; many persons strive for high ideals and everywhere life is full of heroism.

Be yourself. Especially, do not feign affection. Neither be cynical about love; for in the face of all aridity and disenchantment it is perennial as the grass.

Take kindly the counsel of the years, gracefully surrendering the things of youth.

Nurture strength of spirit to shield you in sudden misfortune but do not distress yourself with imaginings. Many fears are born of fatigue and loneliness. Beyond a wholesome discipline, be gentle with yourself.

You are a child of the Universe, no less than the trees and the stars; you have a right to be here and whether or not it is clear to you, no doubt the universe is unfolding as it should.

Therefore be at peace with God, whatever you conceive Him to be and whatever your labours and aspirations, in the noisy confusion of life, keep peace with your soul. With all its sham, drudgery and broken dreams, it is still a beautiful world. Be careful. Strive to be happy."

Awesome words to live by (as much as possible).

To leave behind an unblemished and loving memory is something we should all aspire to. And at the end of my days, I hope I can truly say, like St Paul the apostle, "I have fought the good fight to the end: I have run the race to the finish."

It is a wonderful life indeed.